Second Edition

THE GROWING CHILD

John F. Travers
Boston College

Scott, Foresman and Company

Glenview, Illinois
Dallas, Texas
Oakland, New Jersey
Palo Alto, California
Tucker, Georgia
London, England

TO MY WIFE
BARBARA

Library of Congress Cataloging in Publication Data

Travers, John F.
The growing child.

Bibliography.
1. Child psychology. I. Title.
BF721.T72 1982 155.4 81-14469
ISBN 0-673-16022-X AACR2

ISBN: 0-673-16022-X

Printed in the United States of America

10 9 8 7 6 5 4 3 2 1

CONTENTS

PREFACE

The preface to the first edition of this book opened with the words, "A person is born, grows, develops, and matures, changing from a child to an adult, and then, gracefully or otherwise, ages." These words briefly sketch the chronology of an individual's life and although they are true, as most generalizations usually are, what is left unsaid guides many of the changes that appear in this second edition.

For example, not all children grow old gracefully. The phenomenon of childhood death can no longer be ignored and is examined here in the light of new perspectives and data. The birth process for all children may not be as simple as our opening sentence implies. Arguments both for and against the use of obstetrical medication rage unabated, with the issue still unresolved. Recent genetic research has provided illuminating insights into the unfolding of human development, both normal and abnormal. The role of single parents has become a significant factor in the lives of many children.

While it is possible to list the many specific changes that appear in this edition, perhaps the simplest means of summarizing them is to state that they *needed* to be made. The research and literature relating to child development has literally exploded in the intervening years. For example, it is no longer possible to discuss infancy as one section of a chapter. The work on infant states, neonatal assessment techniques, and infant cognition now demands separate analysis. Changing family styles and societal expectations have stimulated both research and theorizing about their potential influence on development.

To aid comprehension of this scientifically exciting and personally rewarding discipline, the topical approach still seems most suitable. This is admittedly a personal preference, but one that can be justified given the enormous range of data available to the child development specialist. So that the reader may have a picture of what a child is like at various ages and stages, a new chapter has been added—Chapter Three—"An Overview of Development."

This edition of *The Growing Child* has five parts.

1. "Methods, Theories, and Children," which consists of a discussion of the history and research tools of child development (Chapter One), an explanation of several of the leading theories of child development (Chapter Two), and an overview of development from conception to adolescence (Chapter Three);
2. "The Beginnings," which presents the latest genetic research plus an examination of the prenatal environment and the birth process (Chapter Four), and a careful analysis of infancy (Chapter Five);
3. "Aspects of Development," which discusses physical development with special emphasis on the brain (Chapter Six), cognitive development and individual potential (Chapter Seven), Piaget (Chapter Eight), language development (Chapter Nine), personality development (Chapter Ten), and the search for individuality including sex identity (Chapter Eleven);
4. "Influences on Development," which presents data on the family (Chapter Twelve), the school (Chapter Thirteen), and society (Chapter Fourteen);
5. "The Psychopathology of Childhood," which offers a classification scheme for the many problems facing children and discussion of specific disorders (Chapter Fifteen).

As in the first edition, the integration of human behavior is stressed but with this difference: if indeed we accept the totality of behavior as our starting point, it no longer is feasible to resort to a simple cause and effect explanation of that behavior. For example, a youngster may exhibit the signs of "school phobia" (an irrational desire to avoid school). It is deceptively simple to attribute that behavior to a dislike of a teacher or a subject. Let us assume that the child suffers from enuresis and fears that it might happen in school.

So the problem is not the school; it is within the child. But the problem may also have either physical or psychological origins. We can no longer appeal to simple explanations; consequently Chapter One urges the reader to adopt a biopsychosocial perspective, one that can encompass multicausal explanations of behavior.

This edition continues to employ those study aids that proved so helpful in the first edition. Each chapter opens with *Chapter Highlights,* which quickly present the chapter's contents, major ideas, important research, and significant figures. *Boxed material,* intended to convey vital research or views supplementary to the text information, is found in each chapter. *The Discussion Questions,* presented at the completion of the major sections of each chapter, are intended to help both organization and comprehension. *Summary* sections highlight the features of each chapter. If you experience difficulty with any of the more scientific terms, you will find a *Glossary* at the back of the book.

Finally, we live in an age of objectives, tasks, competencies, and various other labels. If you, as the reader, were to ask me, as the author, what you should gain from reading this text, my answer would be quite simple. I hope that as a result of our mutual effort you achieve a deeper understanding of children and that you look differently at youngsters of all ages because you now appreciate the complexity of their behavior. No author could ask for more.

I am indebted to many people for whatever success this book may enjoy, but three individuals deserve special mention. Christopher Jennison, whose support and encouragement have made possible both editions of this book, has made a transition that few editors can do: he has become a friend. The enthusiastic cooperation and unique talent of Laurie Greenstein have seen both the book and author through many difficult times. And, as always, my indebtedness to my wife, Barbara, to whom this book is dedicated, increases with each year. Wife, mother, child-care expert, and typist, her contributions color every page of this book.

PHOTO ACKNOWLEDGMENTS

Page

6 Charlotte Brooks/Magnum Photos
13 Gary Wolinsky/Stock, Boston
26 Shirley Zeiberg/Taurus Photos
27 James R. Holland/Stock, Boston
34 Sybil Shelton/Peter Arnold, Inc.
52 Arnold/Magnum Photos
55 Mimi Forsyth/Monkmeyer Press Photo Service
56 William MacDonald/Photophile
68 Bob Glasheen/Photophile
103 Sam Sweezy/Stock, Boston
106 Sybil Shelton/Peter Arnold, Inc.
124 George Zimbel/Monkmeyer Press Photo Service
126 Jamie Jaensch
145 Justin Derman
152 Hiroji Kubota/Magnum Photos
160 E. S. Beckwith/Taurus Photos
166 Marc Riboud/Magnum Photos
200 Mimi Forsyth/Monkmeyer Press Photo Service
203 Peter Vandermark/Stock, Boston
214 Barbara Alper/Stock, Boston
220 Wide World Photos
222 Jamie Jaensch
236 Wayne Miller/Magnum Photos
241 Burk Uzzle/Magnum Photos
245 Burt Glinn/Magnum Photos
259 Bob Adelman/Magnum Photos
274 Courtesy Dr. Noam Chomsky

Page

284 Paul Fortin/Stock, Boston
302 Brandeis University, Public Affairs Office
303 Harvard University News Office
319 William Decker/Photophile
330 Olive R. Pierce/Stock, Boston
332 Peter Vandermark/Stock, Boston
341 Shirley Zeiberg/Taurus Photos
347 Harvard University News Office
351 Leonard Freed/Magnum Photos
365 Gerhard E. Gscheidle/Peter Arnold, Inc.
382 Hazel Hankin/Stock, Boston
384 Gary Wolinsky/Stock, Boston
387 Laimute E. Druskis/Taurus Photos
411 Bob Glasheen/Photophile
425 The Granger Collection
427 Mark Dresser/Santa Monica Montessori School
445 Elizabeth Hamlin/Stock, Boston
457 Bruce Davidson/Magnum Photos
475 Owen Franken/Stock, Boston
501 Frank Siteman/Stock, Boston

Production Editor: Laurie Greenstein
Copy Editor: La Donna Wallace
Design and Cartoon Illustrations: Kenny Beck
Photo Research: Jayne Cox
Illustrations: Etc. Graphics
Composition: Graphic Typesetting Service
Cover Photo: The Image Bank West/Jay Fries

PART ONE

METHODS, THEORIES, AND CHILDREN

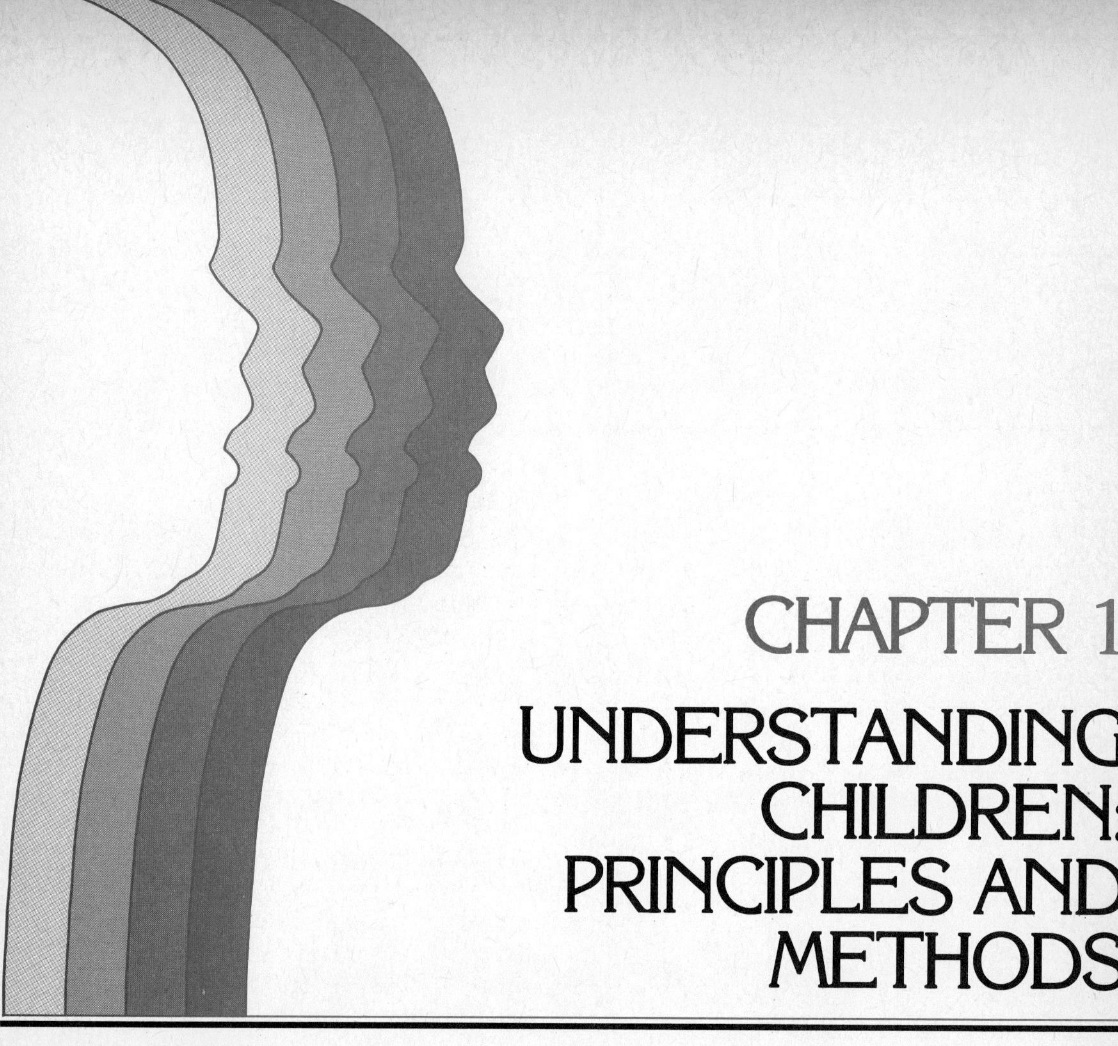

CHAPTER 1

UNDERSTANDING CHILDREN: PRINCIPLES AND METHODS

CHAPTER HIGHLIGHTS

Topics

The Study of Child Development
a. A Biopsychosocial Model
b. Interaction and Integration

Aspects of Development
a. Physical
b. Intellectual
c. Social
d. Emotional
e. Moral
f. Child Development Has a History

The Nature of Behavioral Research
a. Sources of Data
b. The Case Study
c. Longitudinal Growth Studies
d. The Experiment

People

Robert Bremner
George Engel
Arnold Sameroff
Robert Sears
Milton Senn

Special Topics

Great Names in the History of Child Development

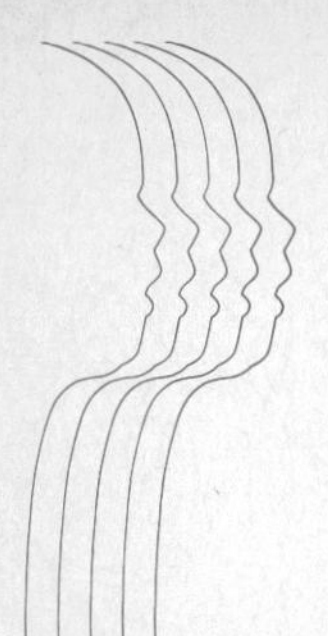

THE STUDY OF CHILD DEVELOPMENT

This is a book about children: their beginnings, their development, and the forces that influence them. To understand children, to comprehend why they do the things they do, requires more than a description of their behavior at each year or even at each month. We must carefully observe developmental trends, study the characteristics and differences of each age, and record the stages through which children pass. But observation alone is insufficient. If we rely solely on these techniques, we will have only an impressive collection of facts, not a genuine understanding of children. Some underlying belief of what a child is must therefore organize these facts. Otherwise we will not understand why children often react unpredictably to tasks that they must master at critical times, or why different children learn skills easily at different ages.

Children grow in ways other than physical. They develop emotional maturity, intellectual acuity, social identity, and moral responsibility. Children learn to live with themselves. Since these various aspects of development are all interrelated, if we are to understand how children manage such total growth, we must view all facets of development and behavior as integrated. Development is not a chronological sequence of ages and stages, but rather an integrated series of personally meaningful events. Although we must at times make generalizations about children, each child remains an individual who differs from every other child in rate of growth, learning capacity, readiness for certain environmental stimuli, and motivation.

But generalize we must, and one safe generalization is that all youngsters manifest certain developmental characteristics that lend themselves to categorization. We know, for example, that all youngsters grow physically, and also mature emotionally, develop intellectually and socially, and gradually learn moral responsibility. At the heart of our study of development is an analysis of each of these aspects of a child's growth. But such a categorization of behavior into different types is merely a convenient device for understanding, and we must never forget that the behavior itself is integrated.

A Biopsychosocial Model

Although we recognize behavioral integration as critical for understanding development, there is nothing superficial about the concept. Integrated behavior implies an acceptance of all developmental aspects—physical, social, psychological, moral, cognitive—as major contributors to growth. To isolate any one contributor is to distort developmental analysis. Quite obviously, any one developmental phase may predominate at any time and under particular circumstances. For example, a five-year-old youngster who fears dogs, whose life is limited by this fear—perhaps because the child is afraid to leave the house—should receive careful examination and treatment of what appears to be an *emotional* disorder. But undoubtedly there are physical consequences (perhaps vomiting if the child is forced to leave the house), social consequences (withdrawal from peers), and cognitive consequences (school refusal may become part of the problem).

It is impossible to escape the integrated nature of behavior, as illustrated in Figure 1.1. Figure 1.1 clearly demonstrates the spreading effect of any developmental change upon all phases of development. Youngsters experiencing social problems—difficulty with friends—usually will simultaneously evidence problems at home and in school. They may lose their appetites. It is impossible to confine the problem to one developmental compartment.

If behavior is integrated, it must also be interactive. Interaction, however, is another term about which it is easy to be glib. For example, although it is true that "development is the result of the interaction of heredity and environment," it is also true that the statement taken alone is almost meaningless. Heredity acts in an incredibly sophisticated, complicated fashion, that is, through gene interaction. Thus genes become the environment for other genes.

Environment, likewise, acts in ways that we are only beginning to comprehend. Thanks to the work of Uri Bronfenbrenner (1978), we now realize that there are many environments acting on the developing child. For example, there is the *microsystem* (family), the *mesosystem* (school), and *macrosystem* (society). To illustrate the interactive nature of these forces, consider the youngster whose father has just lost his job (changes in the macrosystem), which causes the family to move to another location with different friends and schools for the child (changes in the micro- and mesosystems).

Heredity and environment produce their results in a complex, interactive manner. But

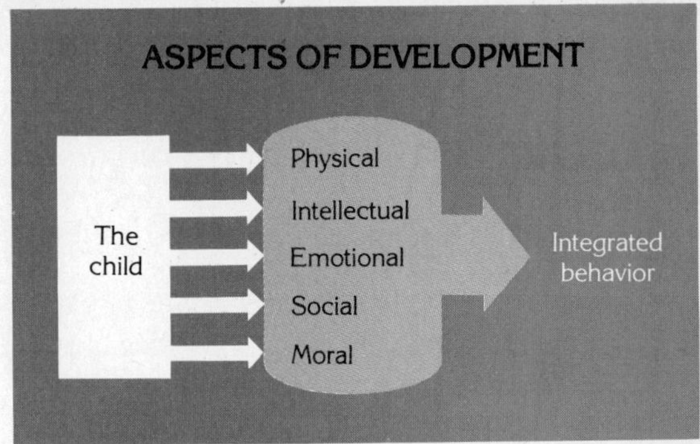

FIGURE 1.1. The Interactive Nature of Development.

to complicate our analysis even further, children themselves are interacting reciprocally with the environment. Remember, youngsters at birth have had nine months of development, which combined with their genetic potential helps to explain their unique form of responding to this new environment. So youngsters help to shape the reactions of those around them; that is, children's responses to those around them have an effect, which causes parents and siblings to respond in a unique fashion. This process never ceases.

Once this powerful usage of interaction is introduced, a simple cause and effect explanation of development becomes unsatisfactory. To facilitate comprehension, a biopsychosocial model of development is urged. Just as there is growing unrest in medicine with the traditional medical model (*these* symptoms mean that *this* agent caused *this* disease), there is also growing dissatisfaction with existing developmental models. For example, George Engel (1977) states that medicine's current crisis derives from adherence to a model of disease no longer adequate. No longer can physicians focus upon biological elements while excluding psychosocial issues. All disease results from disordered somatic processes. Engel (1977, p. 131) states:

> By obliging ourselves to think of patients with diabetes, a "somatic disease," and with

> schizophrenia, a "mental disease," in exactly the same terms, we will see more clearly how inclusion of somatic and psychosocial factors is indispensable for both; or more pointedly, how concentration on the biomedical and exclusion of the psychosocial distorts perspectives and even interferes with patient care.

Consequently, a contemporary medical model must consider the patient, the social context, and health delivery systems. There is no escaping cultural, social, and psychological forces, which, with the individual, constitute a biopsychosocial model.

Sameroff (1976) proposes a similar model that incorporates the biopsychosocial notion but is more suited to developmental analysis. Arguing against a *main-effects* model of development (either heredity or environment is the cause of behavior), Sameroff states that an experience such as a complicated birth does not necessarily produce future disorders. (Obviously, some agents, such as brain damage, are so intrinsic that they alone will be a disorder, but these are *extremes.*)

Sameroff also believes that the usual interactional models, while accepting the mutual influence of both heredity and environment, nevertheless fail to recognize changing constitution and changing environment. The characteristics of both child and environment are constantly changing and these changes are interdependent; that is, as one changes the other changes also. Sameroff (1976, p. 19) summarizes the *transactional* model as follows:

> In order to incorporate these progressive interactions one must move from a static, interactional model to a more dynamic theory of developmental transaction where there is a continual and progressive interplay between the organism and its environment.

Plasticity of both organism and environment is emphasized in a transactional model. A child's behavior is not viewed as static; rather it becomes an active attempt to organize and structure the environment. Sameroff states that the child is in a perpetual state of reorganization; the constants in development are not traits but processes that account for growth by the transactions between organism and environment.

Regardless of the label applied to the model, the intent is identical: to stress the complexity of developmental analysis. There is no simple cause and effect explanation; all forces within the organism are interacting; all relevant external forces are likewise interacting; finally, the internal and external forces are interacting with each other. If you continue to think of development in this manner—that is, employing a biopsychosocial framework—you will appreciate the subtlety and beauty of development, while simultaneously acknowledging the difficulty—but not impossibility—of interpreting developmental data.

ASPECTS OF DEVELOPMENT

Still, analysis requires categorization, so to illustrate the analytic technique, let us briefly examine separate aspects of development. Bodily structure obviously affects all aspects of growth. Learning depends on brain maturation; emotional balance depends on the endocrine system; social maturity depends on body image. For example, imagine how the boy of twelve or thirteen feels when his female classmates suddenly tower over him as the girls are undergoing their adolescent growth spurt. To understand a child's reactions to physical development, anyone working with children needs to know the physical facts.

To help you recognize the importance of body structure, a detailed discussion of genetic facts is initially presented, followed by an assessment of prenatal development. Brain growth is critical in any discussion of human development. Steven Rose (1973), the well-known brain researcher, states:

> Yet the two theses of this book are that for all humans, the quality of being human is that of possessing brains which are capable of interacting in a magnificently adaptable way with the environment, and that the differences in performance and behavior between individual humans reflect differences in their brains. That is, their brains demonstrate at the same time the essential unity of humans and their essential individuality.

Brain development is discussed in many different sections of the text, which not only illustrates its uniqueness as a part of physical development, but also emphasizes the necessity of a truly interactive viewpoint. That is, brain growth influences many aspects of development. The same is true of other physical characteristics. For example, sex differences which make us either male or female are clearly a physical aspect of development, but one that obviously affects social, emotional, and even cognitive growth.

Intellectual Growth

You have undoubtedly heard someone described as "the smartest kid in class" or a "real brain." Developmental psychologists may reach similar conclusions about a child's mental ability, but they do so by examining various measures of achievement. Although, as we will see, there are growing doubts about the precision of such procedures, mental development is a legitimate object of study, and there is a wealth of pertinent information that will enrich our insights into human development.

Animal experiments, for example, have shown that an enriched or stimulating environment produces a brain that has a richer blood supply and a thicker cortex. Another good illustration of the importance of experience is the adverse effect of the absence of stimulation and encouragement at certain times in a child's life (for example, experimenting with speech) on the development of a corresponding mental structure (language).

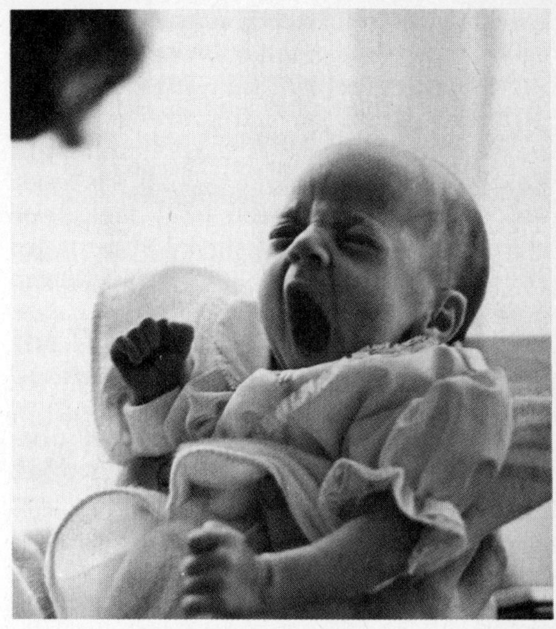

The conclusion is inescapable: a slowdown in the child's mental growth affects many other aspects of development.

Emotional Maturation

Children also grow and develop emotionally, and if their emotional reactions are those of an infant, they cannot adapt to the environment. Children who inhibit normal emotional responses may well become adults who experience severe problems of adjustment. What are "normal emotions"? Emotions are usually healthy expressions of our feelings, and they are normal as long as they damage neither ourselves or others. Essential to the total developmental process are the development and differentiation of the emotions into effective forces toward satisfactory personal adjustment. The effects of emotional responses spread into all phases of life and unless children acquire a certain minimum of emotional stability, life's inevitable shocks may cause frustration, unhappiness, and maladaptive behavior.

The influence of the emotions on development shows how human behavior is integrated. We are all aware of the impact of the emotions on our reactions. An intense emotional experience, for example, produces physical reactions that we are all too aware of: rubbery legs, butterflies in the stomach, and profuse perspiring. Even our motor and intellectual responses change. We find it difficult to exercise normal muscular control over our movements. Concentration on our present activity requires more effort.

Children learn to release emotions in a way that offends no one and to inhibit emotions in a way that is not self-damaging. Only a balanced interaction of all of the developmental forces can result in the gradual emergence of a mature personality. There will, of course, be difficulties; no one goes through life without experiencing emotional upsets. Such difficulties usually occur because of a disruption in one's life. A serious accident, for instance, causes not only physical problems but, because of the integrated nature of human behavior, emotional, mental, and social difficulties also.

Social Interactions

When we chart the progress of children's growth, a discernible set of clues permits us to trace developing reactions to themselves and others. It is fascinating to observe the change as they move beyond the complete self-centeredness of infancy to the development of interactions with others: family, playmates, and society itself. How do children learn to become acceptable members of society? How does this process of socialization occur? Through the results of research in many disciplines, including sociology, anthropology, and psychology, we have come to realize the impact of several forces on the socialization process.

We understand much better, for example, the pressure of social class on a child's development. Does birth into a particular social class mean that children will later show predictable mental, social, and emotional characteristics? We shall devote considerable attention to this and related topics.

Moral Development

For many years most psychologists believed that other aspects of development explained the development of a sense of morality. Recently, however, a realization has been developing that the child's personality includes a separate capacity for moral judgment that deserves more detailed and careful examination. How do children come to distinguish right from wrong, to behave according to society's moral code, and to develop a conscience and values? In other words, how do we explain moral development? Does it result simply from the pressures of society, or from more intricate interactions that require considerable self-evaluation? Several tentative proposals that attempt to explain this phenomenon will guide our efforts.

Child Development Has a History

The issues that face us are far from new. Society and family have long exercised concern about the development of their children. Robert Bremner (1970) quotes a Boston clergyman's advice in 1719 on providing for children. After urging parents not to deprive their children of anything that is good, comfortable, and suitable for them, Benjamin Wadsworth warns:

> Yet by way of caution I might say, let wisdom and prudence sway, more than fond indulgent fancy, in feeding and clothing your children. Too much niceness and delicateness in these things is not good; it tends not to make them healthy in their bodies, nor serviceable in their generation, but rather the contrary.

Many myths, folk tales, and cultural mysticism guided child rearing before it assumed the trappings of the science we know today. Robert Sears (1975) has attempted to trace the roots of child development study and concludes that the stirrings of empathy toward children first appeared in the eighteenth century (as reflected in the Wadsworth quotation). Concern for the mentally ill and delinquent children were followed in the period of the American Civil War by a strong abolition sentiment—a clear humanitarian appeal—that signaled solicitude for children's welfare.

As professions such as education, medicine, and social work grew and prospered, they slowly became intimately involved with the care, health, and schooling of youth. These more professional commitments to children brought with them organizational support, theoretical schools that endeavored to provide insights into the developmental process, and scientific methods designed to discover the data that would provide the energy for both practice and theory.

A growing concern for children and increasing respectability produced several significant themes in the evolution of child development theory and research. Among them are the following (Sears, 1975).

1. *The Testing Movement.* The application of the intelligence test to an American setting by the American psychologist, Lewis Terman, led to the identification of an apparently normal distribution of intellectual ability. A child's capacity, an innate ability, was assumed to be constant, and significantly high correlations between IQ and academic achievement appeared. (We shall discuss current challenges to the concept of intelligence tests in Chapter 7.)

2. *Psychoanalysis.* As Sears notes (1975, p. 36), the infusion of motivational and emotional variables into child development study was a direct outgrowth of Freud's psychoanalytic work. From these beginnings in the early part of the twentieth century, psychoanalysis remained a strong force in child development until the 1960s when cognitive theory—especially the work of the Swiss genetic epistemologist, Jean Piaget—began to attract considerable attention. Sears states that psychoanalysis, while no longer the predominant theory in child development, still retains a powerful place because of its insights into a developing child's personality.

3. *Behaviorism and the Learning Process.* The learning theorists, especially John Watson and Edward Lee Thorndike, mounted a fierce challenge to psychoanalysis and other mentalistic schools. Believing that behavior and development are susceptible to environmental controls, the behaviorists proposed elaborate theories of learning that depended on manipulation of environmental stimuli. Children became what the environment made them. A modern proponent is B. F. Skinner, who has formulated a reinforcement theory that is intended to explain all phases of behavior, including development.

4. *The Longitudinal Growth Studies.* With growing sophistication came the recognition that individual differences in children could not be ignored. Those differences that appeared within the same child over the span of development were particularly intriguing. For example, is it possible to explain the behavior of a child who changes from a mild, passive eight-year-old to a hostile, aggressive teenager? To answer this and similar questions, several longitudinal growth studies were initiated, among them the Berkeley Studies, investigating intellectual and personality development; the Fels Study, analyzing personality development and parental behavior; the Harvard Growth Study, examining intellectual development; and Terman's *Genetic Studies of Genius.*

These themes will appear throughout our work but here they convey the sense of sophistication that was beginning to guide child development research. Sears believes that recent child studies also are marked by definite themes. For example, there is the increasing controversy over environmental versus hereditary determinants of development; which is the more decisive? Regardless of conflict, Sears believes that neither the needs nor the forces that created child development have changed, nor will they. (Sears, 1975, p. 69)

With this brief introduction and a sense of the rich legacy to be found in child development, let us begin our task, using these thoughts to chart our course. Since our topic—a child's life—is so important, we who work

GREAT NAMES IN THE HISTORY OF CHILD DEVELOPMENT

In an engaging and informative essay, Milton Senn (1975) has traced the contributions of some of the major figures in the child development movement. Included are the following.

G. Stanley Hall. Often called the founder of the child development movement in the United States, Hall is best remembered for his belief that a child's growth recapitulates the history of the race, and his introduction of Freud to an American audience. Hall also advocated the use of the questionnaire method to assess the contents of children's minds.

Lawrence K. Frank. Frank was one of the prime movers behind the organizational thrust of child development—societies, institutes, foundations. We have previously mentioned the insights derived from longitudinal growth studies such as the Fels, Berkeley, and the Guidance study. Frank was the inspiration behind each of these, utilizing substantial foundation grants for purposeful research into child development. Many of the principal investigators in these studies credit Frank for not only securing needed funds but also for providing a focus for their research.

John B. Watson. Whether one agreed with Watson's interpretation of behaviorism or not, most historians agree that Watson's influence on child psychology during the 1920s and 1930s was enormous. His forceful presentation of the use of conditioning principles in child development fascinated many and repelled others.

Arnold Gesell. Founder of the Yale Clinic for Child Development, Gesell pioneered the use of creative methods in child development research, such as one-way vision mirrors and motion pictures to record development. His detailed description of growth at various ages enjoyed enormous popularity with the public in the 1930s and 1940s and remained unrivaled until the publication in 1946 of Benjamin Spock's *Common Sense Book of Baby and Child Care.*

There are many other famous individuals associated with child development—Freud, Piaget, Terman—to whom we devote substantial space in the coming chapters. After assessing the contributions of these individuals and those from several related professions, Senn (1975, p. 88) concludes:

> Admittedly, "child development" means different things to different people; to some it has become a slogan, to many a cliche. But the very fact of the existence of a large group of supporters of the concept that it is important and something worth working and fighting for in the laboratories, social fields, and political arena is, perhaps, evidence that we are indeed witnessing a movement.

with children are obliged to be as certain as we can of our facts. Facts do not exist by themselves; if they did, they would be useless. It is when they are used and applied that they achieve significance in helping us to understand a child's behavior and development. But our first responsibility should be to determine which data we can rely on.

THE NATURE OF BEHAVIORAL RESEARCH: STRENGTHS AND WEAKNESSES

For those who work with children the primary goal is clear. The parent, the teacher, the nurse, or the social worker must be able to identify a study as reliable and then interpret the results judiciously. The voluminous literature produced by the study of child development requires extensive and careful reading. A knowledge of the basic tools of the child psychologist is invaluable for our work. The problems of psychology are the same as of other sciences: the search for reliable data, methods, inferences, and theories. In its quest for scientific status, the discipline of child development will receive support to the extent that it maintains a commitment to logical and detailed observation. When used scientifically, its systematized knowledge, its methodology, and its reliance on firm data will yield more satisfactory results than those derived from less well-organized studies.

Yet even the most tightly controlled investigations present difficulties. Scientists have gradually become aware of the alarming limitations of our senses. If you or I were asked to make highly accurate measurements with the most precise instruments available, our results would probably differ, not because of carelessness, but because of a difference in our perceptions. Still, the undeniable orderliness in our perceptions suggests that they have some basis in objective reality. We act on that assumption, and reasonably so, since others presumably see the same colors and hear the same sounds that we do. So we must accept those limitations, which are common to all behavioral sciences, and pursue reliable data objectively and carefully.

The presentation and interpretation of data must be unbiased, clear, and precise. If not, the results will mislead those responsible for children, causing frustrations and dangers. A great deal has been written and theorized, for example, about a child's need for a stimulating environment. Consequently, almost from the time of birth, some infants are surrounded by gadgets that move, make noises, flutter, and compel attention. While levers to press, bars to grasp, and objects to push and pull may be superb playthings for animals, we have no guarantee that they enrich the environment of the human child. A mother who constantly talks to her child may provide experiences more enriching than those that any gadget could provide.

To assess ourselves and others accurately requires knowledge and sensitivity. It now becomes our task to obtain the data that will enable us to make these vital judgments. Before we begin our search, however, it is necessary to pause briefly and discuss the methods by which we secure data in the behavioral sciences.

Sources of Data

Most investigative methods fall into readily discernible patterns. They include techniques such as observation, interviews, and tests of all types (intelligence, personality, aptitude) and may take the form of normative studies (what is characteristic of a youngster at different ages), cross-sectional studies, case studies, longitudinal growth studies, and experiments. Since these techniques can be expanded, abbreviated, or mixed according to the whims of the user, some classification is desirable. The methods most pertinent to child development group themselves into three major categories: clinical and case studies, developmental and growth studies, and, finally, studies involving some experimental design.

In the *case study,* the investigators gather as much information as they can about one child in order to determine the causes of behavior and to make recommendations. Juvenile courts often use this technique when a judge wants to have all possible information about a youth in order to reach a decision.

In contrast to the case study, the *longitudinal growth study* deals with a group of children over a considerable length of time. Changes in characteristics such as intelligence, personality, and achievement are recorded, often from birth through adulthood. Instead of studying just one child, this technique studies many children, making it possible to generalize from its results.

Cross-sectional studies combine greater control of variables with a developmental thrust. Children of different ages are simultaneously studied on one or several aspects of development. For example, to investigate growth changes in problem solving behavior, the researcher would study seven-, eleven-, and fifteen-year-old youngsters.

Probably the most popular technique is the *experiment.* With careful control over the forces that might influence the results, the experiment can be reliable, yielding the same results when it is repeated. If we wanted to discover the effects of watching television on schoolwork, for example, we would first match two groups to make sure that they were as much alike as possible. The most important points of similarity are age, sex, intelligence, grade level, school, home environment, number of brothers and sisters, and school achievement. One group would be allowed to watch two hours of television a night, the other none. After a certain period of time (say two or three months), we would compare the two groups' school achievement. The results would be taken to apply to all youngsters of the kind studied, especially if the study was repeated with another group of youngsters and yielded the same results.

Table 1.1 shows the similarities and differences among the three techniques. Both the longitudinal growth study and the case study method, for example, employ tests, interviews, and observations. And the use of tests and statistics is common to both the experimental technique and longitudinal growth study. All three must state conclusions and recommendations.

To fulfill the requirement that methods of studying children be unbiased, certain criteria must be met.

1. The problem must be stated so clearly that there is no misunderstanding about what is isolated for study or how it is studied.
2. The techniques for gathering data must be appropriate, which is related to the first criterion since a clear statement of the problem may indicate the use of the case-study technique, while another may suggest the use of experimental methods.
3. The data analysis must be careful and objective. There is no excuse for sloppy or prejudiced treatment of the results.
4. The statement of the conclusions, applications, and generalizations should be clear, neither promising too much nor diminishing the significance of the study.

These guidelines are as critical for the behavioral sciences—especially child studies—as they are for the physical and natural sciences. Perhaps more so, since working with children involves the risk of letting one's personal reactions color one's judgments.

The following examples illustrate the three methodological categories that we have summarized.

TABLE 1.1. The Scientific Method and Developmental Studies

Clinical and Case Studies	Longitudinal Growth Studies	Experiments
Use:	**Use:**	**Use:**
1. Detailed analysis of critical incidents in a child's life	1. Developmental tasks (analyzing mastery of critical tasks in a child's life)	1. Matched groups of children
2. Interviews with child, parents, teachers	2. Interviews with child, parents, teachers	2. Various experimental designs
3. Psychological testing (aptitude, intelligence, personality)	3. Observations of child under normal conditions	3. Varied statistical techniques
4. Home and school visits	4. Psychological testing (aptitude, intelligence, personality)	4. Psychological testing (wide variety)
and are composed of:	**and are composed of:**	**and are composed of:**
1. Analysis of the stages of one child's development	1. Repeated studies of the same children for years	1. Hypotheses
2. Search for causes of behavior	2. Comparison of results obtained at different times	2. Careful control of independent and dependent variables
3. Diagnosis	3. Conclusions	3. Objective analysis of results
4. Recommendations and follow-up	4. Generalizations	4. Conclusions, inferences, and generalizations

The Case Study

Case studies are an integral, though frequently overlooked, research tool in child development. Possible reasons for this oversight are their particular suitability for clinical use and their limited applicability. That is, information derived from records, depth interviews, and a wide range of tests shed light upon the development and behavior of *one* child. Although generalization from these conclusions is almost impossible, the insights into the growth and behavior of a child derived from a case study are undoubtedly illuminating.

Consider the tremendous sweep of information provided by the following sources.

1. A detailed presentation of the problem or behavior under analysis usually initiates the progress. Every conceivable dimension of the youngster's behavior is examined ranging from general health to psychiatric disorders.

2. If the child is of school age, pertinent data usually emerge from scrutinizing school records. A child's achievement, peer relationship, and interactions with teachers often furnish telltale clues to the reasons behind certain behavior.

3. An examination of home conditions is essential, including information about the geographic areas, physical characteristics of the home, economic conditions within the home, the nature of the relationship between the parents, between child and parents, number of siblings, birth order, and relationship among siblings.

4. The youngsters themselves are often a fertile source of information. Interviews and tests are normally employed with children.

As you can see, the case study affords rich and detailed information. Nevertheless, use of this method often entails certain difficulties.

Some of the data, for example, may prove unreliable. Can we assume that the observations and conclusions of others are unbiased? And undoubtedly the person with the greatest cause for concern is the individual who must ultimately assess the data and make the recommendations. If, however, the case study meets the criteria for acceptable research, it can be a valuable source of information.

The Longitudinal Growth Study

The technique of studying the same youngsters over a period of years—the longitudinal growth study—has produced some of the best evidence we have about human development. Not only can we determine the pattern of such developmental characteristics as cognition and personality, but we also can observe the rate and nature of such development. This method stands in contrast to another technique known as the *cross-sectional study* in which all the observations are made at one time (or within a few months; the time does not extend for years). The investigators compare the characteristics of different ages by examining *different* children at various ages. A cross-sectional study might, for example, take a group of five-year-olds and a group of nine-year-olds and compare their ability to solve puzzles. A longitudinal study would assess the puzzle-solving ability of certain five-year-olds, and then wait four years to assess how that ability changed in the same group. The disadvantages of spending so much time on one study are obvious. But the longitudinal study allows us to study the same

individuals, thus eliminating possible differences in upbringing, social class, and so on.

It has been the long search for traces of stability in development that has led investigators to use the longitudinal growth study. Although much of childhood behavior disappears by adulthood, there has long been a suspicion that some adult characteristics develop steadily from childhood and remain for life. In his search for such stable characteristics, Benjamin Bloom in his classic work, *Stability and Change in Human Characteristics* (1964), notes that the development of some human characteristics appears visible and obvious, while that of others remains shrouded in obscurity. Are the seeds of aggression planted during the early years? Are there persistent motives that develop early in life and account for many of the person's adult behaviors? Here we see the value of studies that observe individuals over a long period of time. The following are three growth studies in which more than three hundred persons have participated for over thirty years.

1. *The Berkeley Growth Study,* begun in 1928, was designed to study the mental, motor, and physical development of a sample of full-term healthy babies.

2. *The Guidance Study* took youngsters born in 1928 and 1929 and began to study them at twenty-one months of age. The aim was to study physical, mental, and personality development in a normal group, to relate variations at different ages to hereditary and environmental conditions, to scrutinize the combinations of facts that appeared critical, and to assess the value of certain tools of developmental assessment.

3. *The Oakland Growth Study* (1932) of two hundred fifth- and sixth-graders was designed to study many interrelations between developmental changes and behavior. As a result of initial interviews and tests, the investigators tried to discover whether developmental changes affected a child's potentialities.

Studies such as these are arduous, costly, and protracted. What have they shown? One result has been some of the most reliable data that we have about human development. Data from the Berkeley Study, for example, showed that for learning, motivation is more important than small individual variations in intelligence. The study also indicated that a human's capacity for learning remains relatively unimpaired through the years. The Guidance Study provided evidence that the most consistent aspect of personality is a child's behavioral style. Response tendencies such as active or passive proved to be reliable predictors of later behavior. Those characteristics related to the extrovert-introvert continuum were found to be among the most stable. The Oakland Study found that boys with accelerated physical development are not only taller than their peers but also have more favorable self-concepts. The boys who mature earliest also become the most self-controlled adults. But boys who mature later show greater insight and greater adaptibility to new situations.

One of the longitudinal growth studies most often quoted is that of the Fels Research Institute (Kagan and Moss, 1962). The subjects were forty-five girls and forty-four boys, all white, whose personality development was traced from birth through early adulthood. The investigators conducted extensive interviews with both the children and their parents. Among the particular techniques used were:

1. Personality tests given at regular intervals. The child was asked to react to a picture (the Thematic Aperception Test), or to a design such as a Rorschach inkblot. Specially trained persons analyzed responses for clues revealing

personality, including motives, attitudes, and problems.

2. Assessment of mental development by widely accepted tests such as the Newell-Palmer Infant Test and the Stanford-Binet Intelligence Test. The children took these tests at intervals from the ages of six months to seventeen years.

3. Observation of the mother in the home with the child present, and also annual interviews with the mother.

4. Measurement of the intelligence of both the mother and the father, using the Otis IQ test.

5. Regular observation of the child's behavior in the home, in school, and at day camp. The child was also interviewed by workers.

Jerome Kagan and Howard Moss (1962) summarize the obvious advantages of the longitudinal method when they note that it facilitates the discovery of lasting habits and of the developmental periods in which they appear. A second advantage is the possibility of tracing some adult behaviors that have changed their surface characteristics from early childhood responses.

Another tremendous advantage of the longitudinal growth study is the great variety of methods that can be used in investigation. For example, the study of the social environment and its influence on human behavior is a rich source of data. One technique involves studying both parents and children during developmental periods and attempting to discover relationships between adult and child behavior. Still another method is to isolate one aspect of a parent's behavior and watch for its future effects on the child. For example, maternal protection of the child during the first three years predicts school-age passivity more accurately than such protection offered during later years.

Longitudinal growth studies can be a rich source of data. But like any other technique, the longitudinal study is imperfect. The cost, for instance, is almost prohibitive unless the sponsor of the study is an organization of considerable means. The time spent in collecting data means that tangible results, if any, will be forthcoming only after many years of research. Questions always arise about the data-gathering instruments. For example, does the intelligence test actually used really measure intelligence? Will the initial tests used become outdated or invalid before the study is complete? Are the investigators as objective as they should be? Are the subjects interviewed—children or parents—honest with the interviewer, or do they attempt to present the best image possible? Is their motivation unusual enough to make them different from the rest of the general population who may be disinclined to participate but to whom the study's results should apply? Despite the difficulties in using the longitudinal growth study, it still can be an invaluable tool for helping to understand children.

The Experiment

Of all the psychologist's tools, probably none is used more confidently than the experiment. With it the investigator can exercise controls and can thus determine whether or not a certain variable actually influences development. The major identifying characteristic of the experiment is the direct manipulation of experimental treatments. Educators often vary teaching methods, for example, to determine their different effects on student achievement. Or medical researchers may experiment in order to assess the effect of a new drug on patients with a particular illness. The variable (for example, teaching method, drug) that is manipulated or directly controlled by the experimenter is called the *independent variable.* The experimental subjects must respond to some task (a test or another type of performance) selected by the investigator in order to determine the effect of the independent variable. The way in which the subjects respond (test performance, activity after taking a drug) is the *dependent variable.*

The experimental technique should, as realistically as possible, eliminate all disruptive influences. To illustrate the disruptive nature of extraneous influences, imagine that you have just bought a new car and want to find out how many miles it runs on a gallon of gasoline. So you fill the gas tank, drive around until it is about one-quarter full, and then refill the tank to see how many gallons you used. You then divide the number of miles driven by the number of gallons used. But your car had steel-studded snow tires! The results will obviously be distorted. The same conditions apply to scientific endeavors; nonessential phenomena can mask what is sought. For example, early schooling in nursery school or kindergarten is often studied to ascertain its influence on various aspects of development. If elements such as health or home tutoring by parents are not controlled, the true impact of early schooling on development may be missed. This extraneous element that we must eliminate, control, or take into consideration is known scientifically as *error.* Investigators can use any of several techniques to remove error. They may state the problem so precisely that they know exactly what data require the closest scrutiny. They may design the experiment carefully enough to isolate the results from unwarranted contamination. They may use statistical techniques to measure any error that remains.

The classic experiment usually involves two similar groups that are randomly selected and carefully matched. One group, for instance, may be taken on field trips (the independent variable) to various ethnic communities, while the other group remains in school with the traditional curriculum. Both groups are then measured with an attitude scale to determine their reactions (the dependent variable) to those of a different race or religion. Figure 1.2 illustrates the procedure. E represents the experimental group and C represents the control group, which receives no special treatment; X stands for the independent variable; and the subscripts $_b$ and $_a$ respectively refer to times before and after the experiment. There is one inescapable conclusion: without the control of all extraneous elements, the results remain suspect.

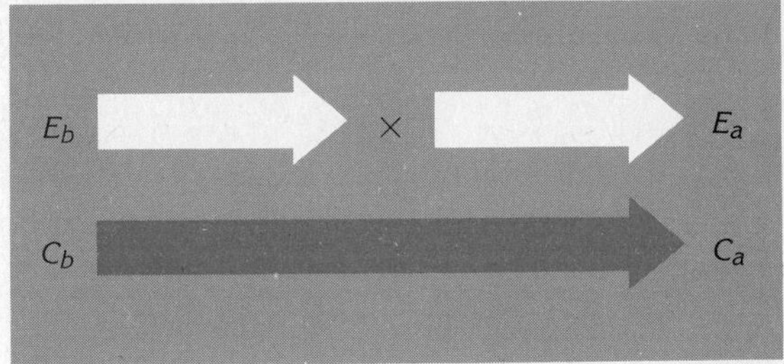

FIGURE 1.2. The Classic Experiment.

Figure 1.3 illustrates some of the many extraneous variables that the investigator must control.

The experiment has occupied a central place in the history of science mainly because the investigator's intervention is of value in determining cause and effect relationships. However, experimentation with human beings must be restricted and, as a result, the behavioral sciences are unlikely to attain the reliability of the physical sciences. This limitation holds especially true for developmental psychology, since we cannot, for example, ruthlessly determine who will use what methods to raise whose children. But most investigators would still agree that the experimental method is really the only sure means for settling disputes about various practices and the only way of establishing a cumulative tradition that lends itself to improvement without the loss of past wisdom.

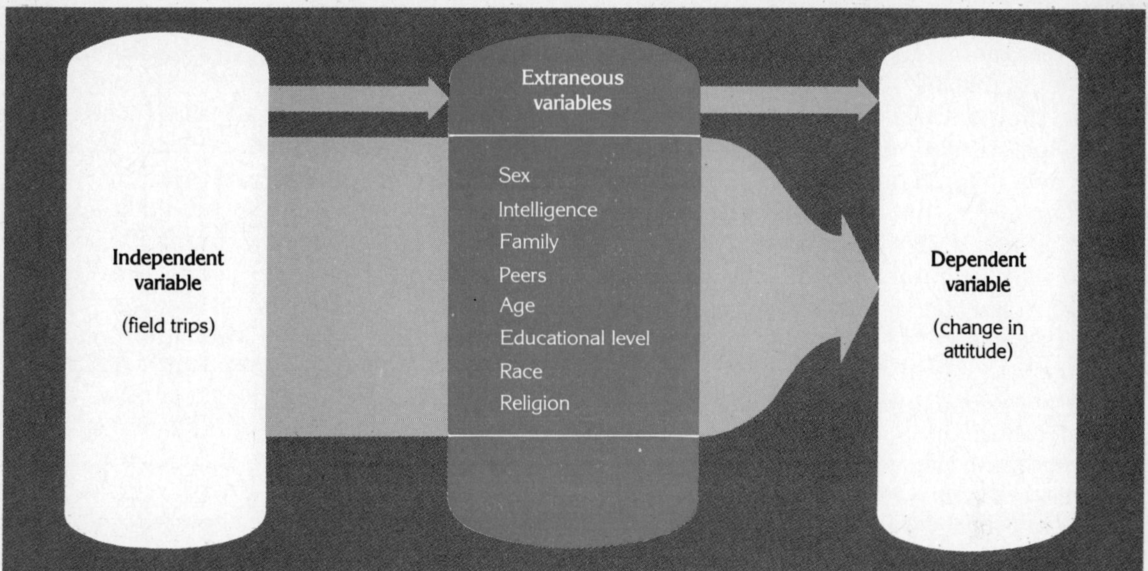

FIGURE 1.3. Isolation and Control of Variables.

A Careful Experiment. In a thoughtful, well-designed, and important study, Wilkinson, Parker, and Stevenson (1979) investigated the effects of schooling on children's memory. The impact of school is currently a controversial topic. Some commentators assert that school has little effect on development, while others maintain that no environment in which youngsters spend fifty percent of their time for many years can avoid influencing development.

The authors began by stating that environmental conditions emphasizing learning, such as schools, hasten the development of memory. They then predicted that memory scores for pictorial stimuli would be higher and the difference between central and incidental memory scores would be greater for schooled than unschooled children.

The children were 331 five-year-olds and 612 six-year-olds who lived either in a deprived section of Lima or in villages in northern Peru. In both areas some of the six-year-olds attended school and others did not. All of the youngsters were from the two main cultural groups of Peru. The authors also attempted to control for social class by including 119 upper-middle-class children who were enrolled in kindergarten and first grade.

The children were required to remember the spatial location of several drawings. A definite design (curves, squares) formed an incidental border around each card. There were two kinds of drawings: one featured common objects (ball, knife, candle); the other, a set of abstract patterns. The authors believed that the youngsters would more easily remember the common objects and distinguish them from the border pattern. They also predicted that differences in memory for the objects and the abstract patterns would diminish with schooling because many school tasks require memory for abstract stimuli.

The authors found that six-year-olds in school performed better than the unschooled six-year-olds in both central and incidental memory tests. Performance was better on the tests for the objects than for the abstract patterns and better for central than for incidental memory. No differences appeared for location or social class.

Wilkinson, Parker, and Stevenson (1979, p. 892) conclude that memory for pictorial stimuli is enhanced by school attendance. They believe that teachers instruct youngsters in improving memory, both directly and indirectly, and children quickly discover personal techniques that aid retention. The authors state that youngsters learn not only the content of the curriculum but also the strategies and skills associated with effective memory. Finally, they warn:

> It is important to keep in mind that all our results and those of other investigators were obtained with pictorial materials. Whether comparable results would be found with less school-like materials remains to be answered in future research. (1979, p. 893)

Note the precise focus of their experimental purpose: do environmental conditions, such as schooling, influence the development of selective memory (central and incidental)? The subjects were carefully selected, and the manipulation of the material to be memorized was carefully outlined to ensure that all subjects received the same treatment. Finally, the results were interpreted with considerable caution: schooling enhances selective memory for pictorial stimuli; whether unschooled children would eventually reach this level remains unclear.

DISCUSSION QUESTIONS

1. What should experimenters consider in order to ensure the reliability and validity of results? Suggest specific kinds of controls that are needed.
2. Why did Wikinson et al. exercise so much caution in their interpretation of the results?
3. If you think that there are weaknesses in this study, what specifically would you criticize and why?
4. We hear much about "intervention" in behavioral science today. What kinds of intervening activities would you suggest that parents employ to improve memory?
5. Which of the research techniques mentioned (case study, longitudinal growth study, cross-sectional study, experiment) is most appropriate for solving the following problems? Why? How should the technique be structured to ensure the reliability of each solution?
   a. A twelve-year-old girl has suddenly begun to have problems with schoolwork, even though her past intelligence test scores indicate that she has high ability.
   b. Does violence on television promote aggression in children who see it?
   c. How does the loss of a father by death or divorce affect the future personality of a growing child?
   d. Are ten-year-olds more able to solve "word problems" in arithmetic than eight-year-olds?
   e. Are lower-class children more likely than middle-class children to become delinquent adolescents?

As the study of child behavior and development becomes more precise in its objectives and more scientific in its methods, valuable information about children will accumulate. But these trends also impose certain obligations on those of us working with children. We must be as certain as possible that the data are reliable and arise from rigorous and objective techniques. This precaution alone, however, is not enough. Work with children must also include the vital quality of understanding or wisdom. We are studying children—not pigeons, not light waves, not the structure of the atom, but children—which demands knowledge, but knowledge tempered with understanding, patience, and even humor. So we will proceed along this course: to search for as many facts as possible, but also to build these facts on a theoretical base that will provide more useful insights into children, their behavior, and their development.

SUMMARY

Each child is a unique, integrated human being who reacts, feels, and thinks differently from every other child.

Yet there is a sameness to human development that enables us, for purposes of analysis, to divide growth into physical, intellectual, emotional, and social categories.

To analyze and comprehend development through the use of reliable, unbiased data, investigators rely most often on such techniques as case studies, longitudinal growth studies, and experiments.

The case study is designed to provide voluminous data on one child. Observation, tests, and interviews are used to compile a history of a particular child in an effort to discover the cause of behavior. While this is an excellent tool for studying one child, it is impossible to generalize from its conclusions.

The longitudinal growth study is a good source of reliable data, since it studies the same children over years. In some of the classic growth studies, the same children were studied for as long as forty years. Growth studies have the disadvantage of being time consuming and extremely expensive.

The experiment is widely used because of the control that an investigator can exercise. By focusing on one problem and controlling as many variables as possible, researchers can usually be confident of their results.

SUGGESTED READINGS

KAGAN, JEROME and HOWARD A. MOSS. *Birth to Maturity: A Study in Psychological Development.* New York: John Wiley & Sons, 1962. An excellent account of the extensive amount of detail and data that are available in a longitudinal growth study.

KERLINGER, FRED. *Foundations of Behavioral Research.* New York: Holt, Rinehart, and Winston, 1973. A careful analysis of the strengths and weaknesses of various research tools.

TURNER, MERLE. *Philosophy and the Science of Behavior.* New York: Appleton-Century-Crofts, 1967. An excellent overview of the relationship between philosophy and science, including the basis of the scientific method.

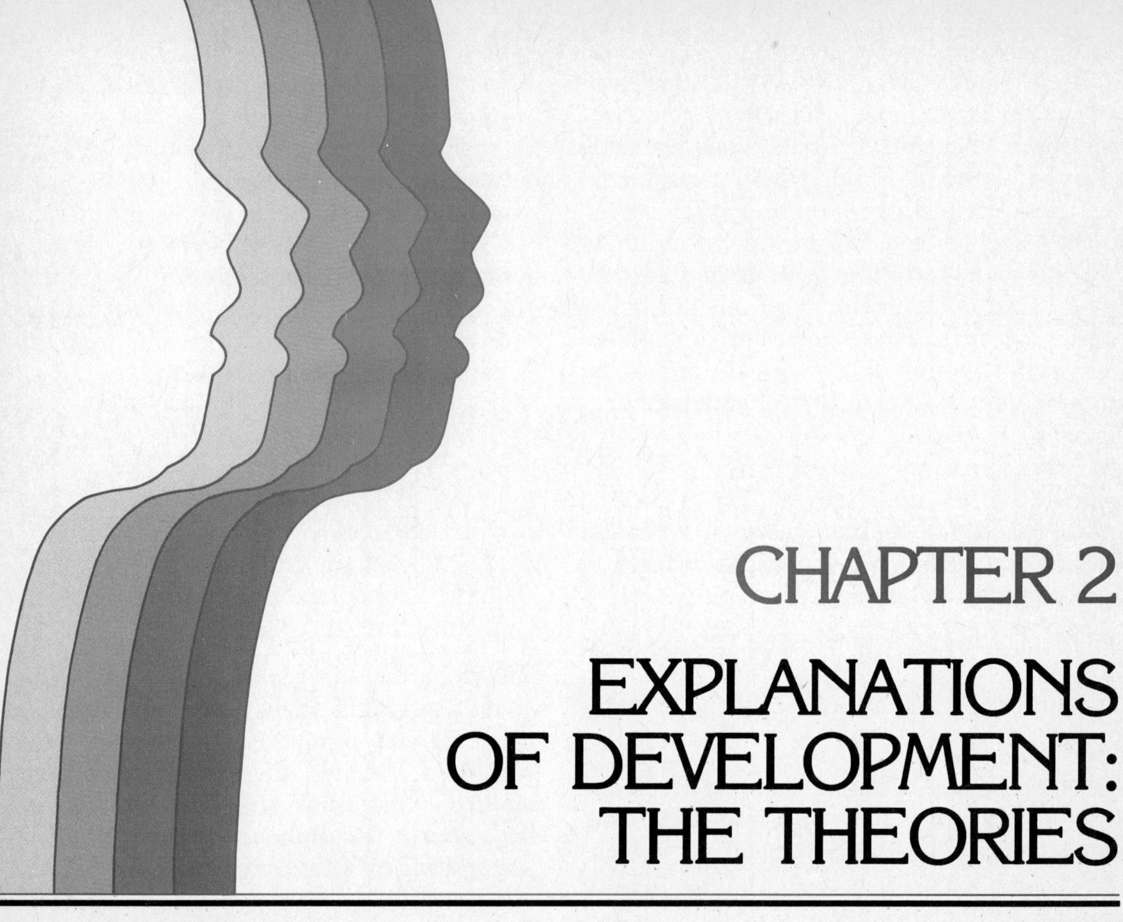

CHAPTER 2

EXPLANATIONS OF DEVELOPMENT: THE THEORIES

CHAPTER HIGHLIGHTS

Topics

Psychoanalytic Theory
a. Sigmund Freud
b. The Structure of Personality
c. The Psychosexual Stages
d. Defense Mechanisms

Behaviorism
a. S-R Theory
b. Pavlov and Skinner
c. Behaviorism and Development

Developmental Task Theory
a. The Theory
b. The Tasks

Self-Realization Theory
a. The Theory
b. Developmental Aspects

People

Sidney Bijou
Charlotte Buhler
Sigmund Freud
Robert Havighurst
Ivan Pavlov
B. F. Skinner

Special Topics

Psychoanalysis: Pro and Con
Pavlov the Man

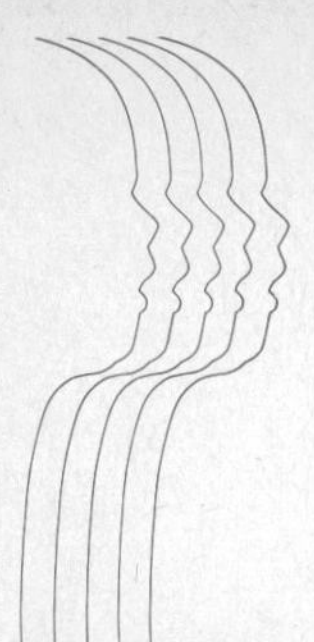

Since there is an incredible amount of data that pertain to child development, emphasis must be on interaction and integration. How can these data best be interpreted meaningfully? What does such interpretation mean for application to children? The primary purpose of this text is to present as much developmental data as possible and to use these data in an effort to understand the total course of children's development.

As we collect these data, our information increases, but our knowledge or wisdom may not. Here we face a dilemma in the study of child development: the available facts are almost overwhelming, but their integration often leaves much to be desired. The sheer accumulation of statistical evidence, while commendable, is insufficient. We need some scheme, or theory, that helps us to discuss the interwoven network of relationships that produces human development.

Whatever your belief about child development, you should recognize that you possess such a belief and you should also recognize how this belief shapes your view of children. Only then can you interpret and apply data effectively. This chapter will be devoted to a consideration of some of the many schools, or theories, that attempt to interpret behavioral data and to explain development.

THEORIES OF DEVELOPMENT: PSYCHOANALYTIC

Theories of development aim to bring order to our knowledge of children. Psychoanalytic thought is a particularly pertinent theory, since it places great emphasis on childhood, both for its own sake and for its importance as an explanation for later, adult behavior. *Sigmund Freud* was one of the pioneers to fight for the acceptance of childhood experiences as a critical element in the developmental process.

To begin our analysis of the mingling of theory and fact in child development, we present a case obtained from one of the leading clinics in a metropolitan area. The wording remains much as it was in the report; the reader is urged to study its interpretation of the child's behavior and its recommendations, both of which are strongly psychoanalytic.

1. *Background Information*

a. Thomas: eight years old
White
Public school
First grade (not promoted)
Sixth of six children

b. Home Conditions
The mother is forty-two years old, separated from her husband, and almost totally blind. Four of the six children live with her in a low-income section

of the city. The oldest son and a married daughter do not reside in the home.

2. *The Problem*

Thomas, bothered by asthma, exhibits frequent temper tantrums and is failing the first grade for the second time.

3. *History*

Thomas is the youngest of six children; his birth was accompanied by marital and family problems. The pregnancy was unplanned and unwanted, and the father left home before the child was born. Thomas was born prematurely, had immediate difficulty with breathing, and was put in a respirator for twenty days before coming home.

Feeding, motor development, and verbal development were all normal, but he manifested considerable separation anxiety; that is, he cried excessively when his mother left him alone. This behavior still occurs at eight years of age, although less frequently. The mother states that he is "fidgety" (cannot remain still) and that he seems to feel inferior because of his small size.

4. *Impressions*

After several interviews with both the boy and his mother, the case worker comments that there is a strong hysterical component in both of them. A definite theme of aggression and violence runs through Thomas's conversation. Teachers report that he exhibits little motivation and bothers other children in the class. He has a very short attention span and shows increasing aggressiveness.

The interviewer reports that the mother is highly nervous, intense, and overly concerned about controls. She seeks constant reassurance and experiences great difficulty with the disciplining of her children. The interviewer states that she seems to be a hysterical personality, while Thomas manifests the developmental deviations that tend toward a neurotic and obsessional personality formation.

5. *Summary*

Thomas seems to have two major developmental problems. First, he has never resolved his Oedipal wish. (The Oedipus complex will be explained in the section that follows.) Second, he is doing very poorly in school. He wants love from and dependence on his mother, yet simultaneously seeks independence and escape from his mother's control. This conflict produces ambivalent feelings toward his mother.

He also displays considerable anger: toward his mother for exercising control and toward his father for his absence. Accompanying the anger is a fear of what might happen if he were to release his feelings. Instead of expressing his anger, he remains passive, especially in school, which is the primary cause of his poor scholastic performance. This reaction resolves his conflict, however, since he can remain with his mother but also strike back at her with his school failure.

Intervention is necessary if Thomas is to be helped. The boy should receive the benefit of a strong male image (teacher or psychologist), who would help him resolve his Oedipal problem. If the problem remains, it will only intensify, with the strong possibility that Thomas will develop a chronic personality disorder.

Here, then, are the case, the interpretation, and the recommendation. It is interesting to note that the report diagnoses the problem as an unresolved Oedipal wish. For an explanation of the theory on which the diagnosis and recommendation are based, let us now turn to the theoretical phase of our discussion.

DISCUSSION QUESTIONS

1. What do you identify as the major problem in this boy's adjustment?
2. Having identified the problem as you see it, what do you identify as the major cause?
3. Do you see any significance in the birth order of the family? (Thomas is the youngest of six.)
4. From this brief description, how would you evaluate the mother's behavior?
5. Now continue your study of psychoanalytic theory and, as you read, consider this question. Do you think that the psychoanalytic technique offers more penetrating insights into behavior than your initial impressions did?

Psychoanalytic Theory

The story of psychoanalysis begins with Sigmund Freud (1856–1939), whose life and influence are now part of psychological history. It seems inevitable that Freud, beginning as a physician and neurologist, should soon have become interested in nervous disorders. After experimenting with several techniques, he turned to *free association*, the "talking-out" method, in which a patient's rambling conversation is analyzed for chance revelations of the nature of the problem. With this tool, Freud began to probe deeply into the human mind. He gradually realized that there are dynamic forces at work of which the individual is almost completely unconscious. From these modest beginnings, Freud formulated a theory of personality that has undergone remarkably little change in the intervening years. To explain the attainment of maturity, Freud suggested that an individual passes through several *psychosexual stages* of development. Although these stages are the main subject of our discussion, let us first consider the nature of personality as Freud saw it.

Fundamental Hypotheses. Charles Brenner (1973) has presented an excellent discussion of the basic, mutually related hypotheses of psychoanalysis. First he postulates the principle of *psychic determinism*, and second the proposition that consciousness is the exception rather than the rule—the tip of an iceberg as opposed to the huge, "submerged" mass of the unconscious mind. Psychic determinism means that in the mind, as in much of the physical world, nothing happens by chance. Every psychological event is somehow *caused* by preceding mental events. If some idea seems unrelated to what went before it, it is only apparently so. There is no discontinuity in mental life. Once we understand this principle, we will never dismiss any psychological quirk as accidental. Every mental event has a cause, although it may often be buried deep in the unconscious, and be difficult to discover. According to psychoanalysis, we do not, for example, make a disastrous slip of the tongue "accidentally"; we actually intend to do so, for some definite purpose. Exactly the same principle holds true for dreams. Although a dream may seem totally bizarre and meaningless, Freud insisted that it carries an intentional message from the unconscious mind.

The principle of psychic determinism is closely linked to the second proposition that unconscious mental activity is frequent and important in our lives. The unconscious nature of much of mental activity accounts for the apparent discontinuity of mental life. That is, an apparently irrelevant idea actually has a causal connection with unconscious mental processes. Since there is no direct method for assessing *the unconscious,* psychoanalysts must infer its existence from dreams or from "talking out," a method that is a source of controversy between psychoanalysts and those who seek more observable data.

The Structure of Personality. Psychoanalytic theorists see personality as consisting of the three systems defined by Freud: the *id,* the *ego,* and the *superego.* The id is the psychic representative of the most primitive instinctual drives; the ego governs the mental functions involved in our realistic interactions with the environment; and the superego comprises our moral precepts and our ideal aspirations. Freud originally assumed that all of the psychic apparatus present at birth consisted of the id, and that the ego and superego, gradually forming out of the id, become sufficiently different to be considered as separate entities.

Following Freud's original hypothesis, we will assume that the id consists of everything psychological that is innate and present at birth, including the instincts. The id acts immediately to relieve tension resulting from states such as hunger, fatigue, and sexual arousal, and tries to restore the organism to a state of rest. Thus, the id functions according to the pleasure principle: there is no question of right or wrong, only that of seizing of pleasure and of avoiding pain. It is interesting and disturbing to speculate about adults who still follow the pleasure principle.

The ego, however, functions according to the reality principle; that is, it works to postpone the discharge of tension until an appropriate outlet is found. The ego carefully examines the environment in order to achieve the maximum possible gratification or discharge for the id. The ego acts to integrate the activities of the id, the superego, and the external world—an unenviable task, since the aims of the three forces often conflict. For the organism to function effectively, the ego must also master the workings of the muscular system, perception, memory, the emotions, and thought. What is particularly significant is that the ego acquires these controls only through the process of growth and development.

TABLE 2.1. The Psychosexual Stages

Stage	Approximate Age	Chief Characteristic
Oral	Birth to one year	Pleasure derived from the mouth
Anal	One to three years	Emphasis on toilet training
Phallic	Three to five years	Awareness of genitals as a source of pleasure
Latency	Five to twelve years	Period of relative sexual calmness; identification with parent of same sex
Genital	Twelve years	Drive toward sexual union

Finally, the superego may be defined as the internal representative of traditional social values and ideals as instilled in the child by his parents and enforced by a system of rewards and punishments. The superego consists of two subsystems: the *ego-ideal* and the *conscience.* The ego-ideal represents what the parents transmit to the child as "good," while the conscience corresponds to what the parents transmit as "bad."

For example, when a youngster whose irrepressible id prompts him to do so steals three cookies, something that his conscience tells him is wrong, his superego ("stealing is bad") punishes him with feelings of fear and guilt, while his ego will try to find a suitable compromise between the two (asking his mother for some cookies). When he does something commendable, he is rewarded by his ego-ideal with feelings of satisfaction and pride. The superego and ego thus serve the purpose of controlling and regulating the impulses whose uncontrolled expression would endanger the stability of home or society.

In the case study that was presented, the id is driving Thomas to express his feelings of aggression, while the superego prods at him by reminding him such behavior is unacceptable. The ego attempts to resolve the problem by suggesting an attitude of passivity, through which the boy can avoid punishment but still strike back at his mother. In the well-adjusted person, however, the three systems usually work together in harmony, producing a mentally healthy individual. And the systems develop, normally or abnormally, as children pass through the stages of development.

The Psychosexual Stages of Development. At the core of the psychoanalytic theory of development is the conflict between instinctive drives and the restraints on these drives. As children grow and develop, they experience a dual maturational process. First, there is the maturation of the ego. As children acquire an acceptable adjustment both to themselves and society, the reality principle begins to function. Second, children pass through a sequence of *psychosexual stages,* in which the source of gratification shifts from the mouth to the anus to the genitals. Accompanying this growth is the emotional impact of milestones such as toilet training and establishing control over sexual behavior. The various events of these stages can be both annoying and satisfying, frustrating and rewarding and, according to psychoanalytic theory, decisive in shaping personality.

Freud theorized that the first three psychosexual stages—oral, anal, and phallic—occur during the first five years of life. A time of sexual latency follows, during which development is more or less stabilized until the beginnings of adolescence, when the fourth or genital stage begins to assert itself. Although it is difficult to specify an exact time for the appearance of each of these stages, the sequence is close to that shown in Table 2.1.

During the *oral stage,* the main source of pleasure is the mouth. Freud (1949) stated that all mental activity centers on the task of immediately satisfying the needs of the oral

zone. He thought that the baby's persistent sucking, independent of any need of nourishment, represented a sexual activity. The pleasure derived from oral incorporation is easily displaced to other modes of incorporation, such as the acquisition of knowledge or possessions. Gullible people are said to be "fixated" at the oral level, since they will "swallow almost anything." (*Fixation* means simply that a person's psychological growth has stopped and remains at a particular level, in this case the oral.) Signs of extreme dependency also indicate fixation at this level, as do such obviously oral needs as heavy smoking and drinking or overeating.

Gradually the infant realizes that the elimination of waste material produces tension reduction and, in turn, it becomes a source of pleasure. When this pleasurable function encounters external regulation in the form of toilet training, the way the infant meets the initial frustration can be highly significant in personality development. Psychologists often trace different adult personality traits to the *anal stage.* A person fixated at this level may become excessively retentive, even miserly, because of restrictive, shame-producing parental methods of toilet training. If the mother is generous in her praise, however, the notion of productivity becomes paramount and may explain the growth of a creative personality.

After the anal period, children grow more and more aware of their sex organs, and this new interest is accompanied by a sexual desire for the parent of the opposite sex. There are several terms used in connection with this period, called the *phallic stage,* so let us pause briefly to define them.

1. *Oedipus complex.* The boy desires his mother sexually and experiences an increased feeling of hostility toward his father. Since he fears that his father will harm him physically, the desire leads to the castration complex.

2. *The castration complex.* This fear centers on the male sex organ; the boy fears that his father will castrate him. He then struggles to suppress desire for his mother and hostility toward his father, thus furthering his psychosexual maturation by identifying more with his father's male image.

3. *Electra complex.* This is the female equivalent of the Oedipus complex. The girl wants her father, but finds the mother in the way. Furthermore, when the girl discovers that she lacks a male sex organ, she blames her mother.

4. *Penis envy.* The girl is disappointed at her lack of a penis and becomes more attracted to her father, who possesses the desired organ.

With the phallic phase, childhood sexuality reaches its peak and then begins to decline. From this time on, the developmental progress of boys and girls differs radically: the boy encounters the Oedipal phase and must resolve the ensuing crisis before he enters *latency;* the girl often resents her mother and becomes more closely attached to her father. But since a girl does not suffer the strong repression that a boy experiences with the castration complex, the Electra complex may remain with her for life. In fact, Hall and Lindzey (1975) believe that differences in the natures of the Oedipal and Electra complexes may account for many of the psychological differences between the sexes.

The first three stages of psychosexual development (oral, anal, and phallic) are referred to as the *pregenital period,* which usually lasts about five years. After latency, the individual's sexual attention is directed toward the biological goal of reproduction. The adolescent is attracted to the opposite sex and this attraction eventually culminates in sexual union. This final phase of development is the *genital stage,* which lasts from the teens well into old age.

Freud noted that since personality represents a changing process, the phenomena he observed must have a logical and sequential explanation. He believed that the causes of emotional disturbance lay in the developmental history of the individual, specifically, in the early stages of psychosexual development. It is interesting, in the light of Freudian theory, to recall the case study with which this section began. Thomas is experiencing difficulty at the age of eight. When we note that his father had left home before he was born, a possible psychoanalytic interpretation would be that Thomas had had no male figure with whom to resolve his Oedipus complex. Perhaps now the study's recommendation that a male figure be found with whom Thomas can identify is more understandable.

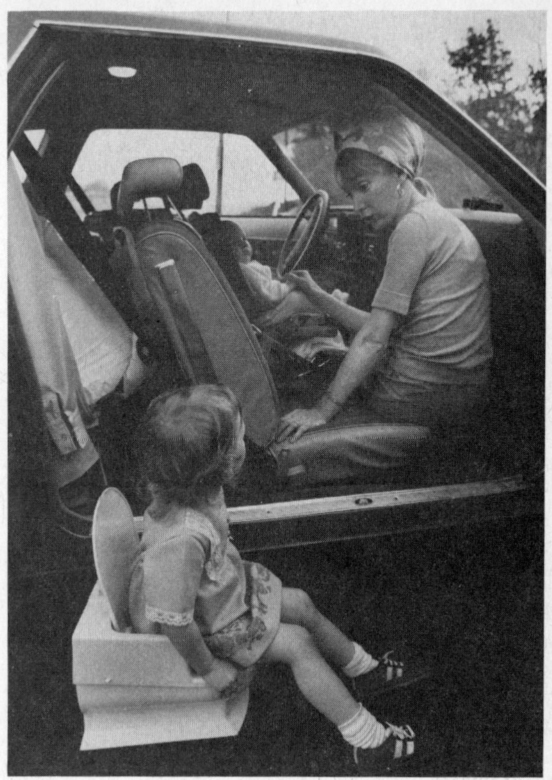

As youngsters pass through these stages of development, problems, frustrations, and conflicts arise in the give and take of daily living. How does a child cope with these situations? All of us, children and adults, may analyze an annoying predicament and come to appropriate conclusions. But not always. Occasionally we adopt very unrealistic attitudes toward a problem, and children are especially susceptible to this tendency. These escape routes, which Freud called *defense mechanisms,* represent our ego's sometimes irrational resolutions of the struggles between the id and the superego. They include the following:

1. *Denial.* Youngsters simply deny that a problem exists by distorting their perception of it. If, for instance, Bill were to take home a failing grade in arithmetic, his superego—not to mention his parents—would begin to chastise him. Denial would be telling himself that since nearly everyone else in the class did poorly, the grade didn't really mean anything.

2. *Repression.* Children simply refuse to think of painful or anxiety-producing memories, burying them in the unconscious. The subject of our case study, for instance, has effectively repressed hostility toward his mother. But even though the hostility is buried, like so many repressed emotions, it has surfaced in another form—poor school performance.

3. *Sublimation.* Youngsters express what may be an inappropriate feeling in a perfectly appropriate manner. For example, early sexual urges may manifest themselves in a tremendous enthusiasm for sports and other vigorous physical activity.

4. *Projection.* Here children attribute anxiety-producing feelings to someone else. For instance, Ruth may have a crush on her male history teacher and, instead of admitting it, may proclaim that her best friend is silly enough to have fallen for him.

5. *Rationalization.* Children can offer what seems to be a perfectly logical reason for their actions. He beat up his brother, for example, because "he had it coming to him—somebody had to straighten him out."

The strong developmental thrust of psychoanalytic thought can be particularly valu-

PSYCHOANALYSIS: PRO-CON

The Freudian explanation of human development has fascinated and repelled, satisfied and infuriated, depressed and stimulated. Whether or not one accepts the theory's basic assumptions, one can have few doubts about two apparent conclusions.

First, Freudian ideas have penetrated nearly every aspect of our lives. Parents cannot read a popular magazine without being warned of the dangerous effects of too rigid or too permissive toilet training methods. It is almost impossible to scan the theater section of a newspaper without being made aware of sexual themes and sexual freedom, which are direct results of Freudian beliefs about the dangers of sexual repression. And terms such as *oral gratification, rationalization,* and *ego* are now nearly household words.

Second, Freud was among the first to alert us to the importance of the early years. There is considerable agreement today that our first years have a lasting impact on our lives. The psychological problems of the adult can often be traced to some conflict at a particular developmental level.

While there are those who agree that a psychoanalytic interpretation of human development is satisfactory, there are many others who vigorously and vehemently reject it as myth. They scoff at those old "ghosts"—the id, ego, and superego—and demand proof of both their existence and the psychoanalytic conclusions that are based on them. Whatever your belief, however, psychoanalysis is a force to be reckoned with in child development.

able in analyzing the causes of a child's behavior. Perhaps we can summarize its developmental value as follows.

1. Freud discovered that there were unconscious rules governing any child's or adult's behavior.
2. There are typical sequences in development.
3. It is possible to trace a child's present behavior to its origins.
4. Therefore, psychoanalysis characterizes psychological phenomena by their position in the developmental sequence.

If we can, indeed, attribute behavior to an earlier developmental level, then we have clarified the meaning of that behavior. For example, crucial situations occur in all of our lives. These may result from events either inside us or outside us. The manner in which someone—child or adult—meets these situations depends on the past. By realizing that certain kinds of behavior are characteristic of a certain developmental level, the analyst can then focus on this level to identify the problem and recommend treatment.

THEORIES OF DEVELOPMENT: BEHAVIORISM

For a good example of a behavioristic interpretation of children's behavior, let us examine a study by Harris, Wolf, and Baer (1964). Although one of the objectives of a nursery school is to foster the social behaviors that enable children to adjust to themselves and others, the means for attainment of this laudable end are shrouded in mystery and controversy. Teachers of some nursery school children with problems have reported success in helping these youngsters by using a combination of practices based on psychoanalytic theory, client-centered therapy, and a vague belief in mental health principles. Although teachers have reported some success with these techniques, it is far from certain just which of the methods was most effective. The only common thread that the authors could discern was that all of the techniques involved adult behaviors of paying attention to the child.

The original problem concerned a three-year-old girl who had regressed to crawling; after three weeks of school, she spent about 80 percent of the time in an off-the-feet position, either crawling or crouching with her face hidden. Her parents reported she always behaved this way when strangers were present. This odd behavior naturally attracted attention, while activities such as standing and walking drew little notice. The teachers drew up a program in which they gave the child *no* attention while she was crawling or crouching, but paid considerable warm attention when she was standing, walking, or running. At first, the child could attract the teachers' attention only if she dragged herself upright by her locker or washbasin. Within a week of the teachers' new pattern of attention, the child acquired a fairly normal pattern of upright behavior.

Next, to determine if the change in the child's behavior was actually *caused* by the corresponding change in the teachers' attention, the procedure was reversed. That is, the teachers again gave considerable attention to crawling and crouching; they used attention to *reinforce* the child's off-the-feet behavior. After two days of this reversal, the little girl again spent 80 percent of the time off her feet. Next, the teachers once more reversed the pattern by reinforcing only upright behavior. Within four days, the child spent about 62 percent of the time on her feet. The pattern is illustrated in Figure 2.1. Once the child began to spend most of the time in an upright position, she became a well-integrated member of the group.

The teachers then attempted to assess the relationship between teacher attention and

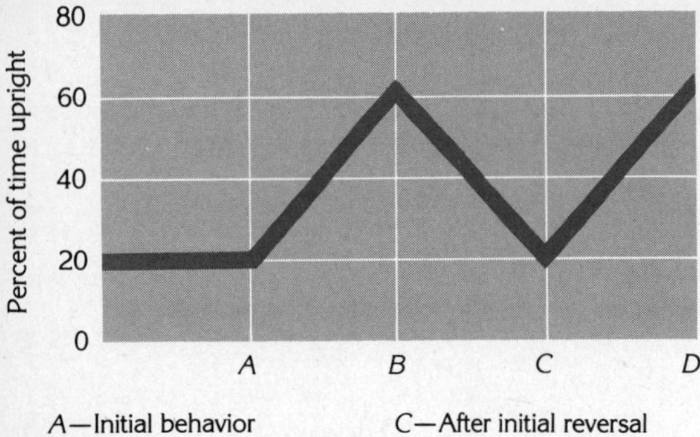

FIGURE 2.1. Effect of Reinforcement on Child Behavior.

other nursery school behavior. The procedures were now established: a child with a behavior problem was selected and a detailed analysis of that behavior was made, including the times when it most often occurred and the consequences of regular teacher guidance. A program of differential teacher attention was then instituted. When the undesirable behavior occurred, the teachers ignored it, but they gave immediate attention to other, desirable behavior. As a result, the child could gain much teacher attention by not engaging in the problem behavior.

Once the problem behavior subsided, the procedure was reversed: the teachers' attention reinforced the problem behavior. When the problem behavior was reestablished, the teachers again reversed the procedure by reinforcing the desirable behavior and ignoring the undesirable. These procedures were eventually applied to two four-year-old boys who cried excessively, to a four-year-old girl and a three-year-old boy who always played alone, and to an exceedingly passive four-year-old boy. Each case had the expected result: teacher attention reinforced and stabilized the behavior to which it was directed.

The authors concluded that for these children, adult attention was a strong *positive reinforcer,* or reward. That is, the child's behavior that was immediately followed by teacher attention increased rapidly and, conversely, declined noticeably when that attention was withdrawn. The authors correctly caution the reader that other forces may also be acting. Some youngsters, for example, may react to adult attention as punishment. In addition, if the desired behavior (the behavior to be reinforced) requires skills that the child does not yet possess, the process may be quite lengthy. But this study is still well suited to our purposes, since it introduces the relationship between reinforcement and the shaping of behavior. By manipulating the environment, the behaviorist ensures that the organism's responses are directed toward desirable goals.

The Theory

In order to explain the twists and turns of development, *stimulus-response* theory (or S-R theory) is primarily concerned with what is done *to* the organism. A stimulus produces a response. Individuals grow and develop as they acquire new responses and integrate them into their response repertoire. According to the *behavioristic* view of development, children are born empty of psychological content into a world of coherently organized content. Children gradually reflect their environment as their responses become less random and more consistent with the stimuli and signals they receive.

S-R theory emphasizes learned behavior; it also stresses that learned behavior is the result of many independent learning experiences. Through learning, behavior is almost infinitely changeable; any combination or sequence of behavior can be learned. Learning is thus the key to understanding child development. Through the experiences of childhood, a person learns adult behavior patterns, values, and anxieties. During growth, some responses are rewarded, some are punished, and some are ignored. Youngsters repeat the responses that are rewarded, suppress the responses that are punished, and simply lose the responses that are ignored. Depending on their consequences, the stimuli associated with these responses become strengthened or weakened. Our response pattern grows and expands, and we gradually acquire the responses that enable us to cope successfully with our environment.

Behaviorism and psychoanalysis yield different interpretations of particular cases, such as that of the little girl who crawled excessively. For example, a behaviorist would say that the attention she received for remaining on her feet was very *rewarding* or *reinforcing.* She continued her new behavior until the teachers ignored it, that is, no longer reinforced it. When the teachers began to reinforce upright behavior once again, she resumed that pattern of responding.

The psychoanalyst would protest that explanation by reinforcement alone does not get back to the roots of behavior but merely treats symptoms. To explain *why* the youngster began crawling, the psychoanalyst would say her behavior regressed to an earlier level. At her age, she may be working out her Electra complex or repressing some unwanted thoughts and retreating to a more secure level.

The data are the same; the interpretations quite different. Since behaviorism has won such wide support, let us examine some of its major principles. The work of *B. F. Skinner* provides an excellent example of the relation of behavioristic thought to child development. But to appreciate Skinner's work, we must distinguish it from the work of I. P. Pavlov in respondent or classical conditioning.

Classical Conditioning. To psychologists, the phrase *classical conditioning* recalls the name of *Ivan Pavlov.* Almost fifty years after his death, the work of this remarkable man is still highly influential. His work is best exemplified in two famous writings: *Conditioned Reflexes* (1927) and *Lectures on Conditioned Reflexes* (1928).

Ivan Petrovich Pavlov (1849–1936) was born in a small town in central Russia, attended a church school, and considered entering the priesthood. But the world of science, particularly the discipline of physiology, had greater lure. His physiological study of digestion in animals led to the discovery of an important psychological phenomenon—*the conditioned reflex.* The anticipation of food caused the flow of saliva in dogs. It flowed at the sight of the food dish or of the attendant, perhaps even at a sound the attendant usually made at feeding time. These are not natural stimuli. Food placed in the mouth of an animal is a natural saliva-producing stimulus. But the sight of a person or the sound of footsteps does not naturally produce salivation. Somehow, the animal "learns" that the dish is a signal that food is coming.

Initially, Pavlov called the dog's salivary response to a signal "psychic secretions." Never enraptured with the study of psychology, he soon designated this response as the *conditioned reflex.* The signal (sight of the attendant or sound of his approach) was termed the *conditioned stimulus.* This phenomenon seemed to represent nervous reaction that was ideally suited for objective experimentation. The search for a substitute for consciousness seemed at an end, since introspection obviously was unnecessary to explain this manifestly superior nervous activity.

Pavlov now turned his attention to the planned establishment of these conditioned reflexes. The hungry dog was placed in the usual situation but with a ticking metronome present. After a certain interval, food (an *unconditioned stimulus*) was placed in the dog's mouth and, naturally, salivation was the result. After several repetitions, saliva began to flow during the interval when the metronome was ticking, before the dog had any food in its mouth. Thus, Pavlov had established a conditioned reflex; the metronome had become a conditioned stimulus.

PAVLOV THE MAN

A well-known biographer of Pavlov, Babkin (1948), has made some interesting comments about the balance between Pavlov's sense of reality and his creative imagination. He notes that artists are often thought to achieve their results through the use of creative imagination, while scientists are thought to attain their goals by observation and analysis. In disagreement with this belief, Babkin suggests that Pavlov had an exceptional scientific imagination. Giving us an insight into Pavlov's methods, he describes how Pavlov would discard an old framework if it could not incorporate a new fact. He would then construct a different framework, one that would accommodate the troublesome fact. And he did not stop there, but would seek more facts to strengthen the new scheme. When he had gathered a certain number of facts, he moved from hypothesis to theory. Finally came a period of relentless theoretical and experimental analysis.

> One must have a general conception of a subject in order to have a framework on which to hang facts, to base something on which one may build, and in order to have a hypothesis for future investigations. In scientific work, such conceptions and hypotheses are indispensible. (Pavlov, 1928, p. 115).

If a conditioned reflex could be established in this way, Pavlov reasoned, *extinction* of the reflex (its elimination) must also be possible. The dog was placed in the usual situation with the metronome ticking and saliva flowing. But, at this point, no food appeared. After several similar pairings of the metronome's clicking and the absence of food, saliva no longer flowed at the ticking. Extinction of the conditioned response had occurred.

Operant Conditioning. B. F. Skinner contends that classical conditioning accounts for only a small portion of learned behavior. To apply its principles to *all* behavior would require that we identify all the stimuli affecting the organism. It is obvious that we cannot do this. Dissatisfied with existing explanations of behavior, Skinner began in 1938 a series of provocative and controversial writings that continues to this day. He has never avoided the challenge of testing his ideas on the practical problems of daily living. Teaching, learning, religion, economics, politics, and psychotherapy have all felt the Skinnerian touch.

Probably the best introduction to his work remains his 1953 text, *Science and Human Behavior.* He begins with the assumption that the methods of science apply to human affairs. Science implies an organized accumulation of information; thus we must use facts and not interpretations. Since behavior is a dynamic and fluid process, it is difficult to analyze, but the problems, if present, are not insoluble. We begin by reporting single events and then search for uniformity among them. We must dispense with attributing behavior to "fictional causes" such as the position of the planets, the nervous system, or the "mind." We should instead concentrate on the variables outside the organism. Behavior, according to Skinner, is a causal chain made up of three links.

ESTABLISHING THE CONDITIONED RESPONSE

Pavlov continued his experiments, steadily refining them. But the process just described captures the essential elements of classical conditioning. Some previously neutral stimulus associated with an unconditioned stimulus gradually acquires the power of eliciting the response by its appearance alone. The sequence appears to be as follows.

1. **US** ----- **UR**

   unconditioned stimulus produces unconditioned response
   (food produces salivation)

2. **CS** -----

   conditioned (neutral) stimulus produces no response
   (metronome alone produces no salivation)

3. **CS + US** ----- **UR**

   conditioned stimulus plus unconditioned stimulus produces unconditioned response
   (metronome plus food produces salivation)

4. **CS** ----- **CR**

   conditioned stimulus produces conditioned response
   (metronome alone produces salivation)

Thus, the CS comes to acquire some of the response-producing potential of the US. Note in particular that the neutral stimulus has been conditioned to the unconditioned stimulus.

1. An operation performed on the organism from without (such as water deprivation).
2. An inner condition (thirst).
3. A resultant behavior (drinking).

If we had accurate information about step 2, we could predict step 3. But since we lack such information, *step 2 is useless in the prediction and control of behavior.* We must begin with step 1.

In *operant conditioning,* for reasons about which we have *no* knowledge, the organism emits a response. No known stimulus elicited it. The organism simply emitted it. If it is a desirable response, it is reinforced, and the probability is thus increased that this class of responses will reappear in similar circumstances. As a result, operant conditioning refers to the conditioning of responses instead of stimuli. The teaching machine is a good example of operant conditioning; youngsters make a response to the machine and are reinforced by the feeling of success. A classic example of operant conditioning in animals is the experimental situation in which a rat's lever-pressing response (at first emitted at random) is reinforced with the presentation of a food pellet immediately after the response. Gradually the response consistently reappears, since the rat has "learned" to associate lever pressing with a reward.

The major concern in operant conditioning is with behavior that affects (*operates* on) the surrounding world, because the consequences of such behavior feed back into the organism and tend to reproduce or inhibit that behavior under similar conditions. Thus we can ensure the probability of response without having to identify the stimulus. We manipulate not a single response, but a class of responses. We designate these responses as *operant behavior* (the organism operates on the environment). Reinforcement depends on the response. Lack of reinforcement produces *operant extinction* (disappearance of the response). Once reinforcement has occurred, we must be careful to state that it does not necessarily *strengthen* the response, since the response has already appeared and nothing will alter it. What changes is the probability of the response's occurrence. Under similar circumstances, the probability that this class of responses will reappear is increased.

In an account of his life Skinner states, in typically operant terms, "I have been powerfully reinforced by many things: food, sex, music, art, and literature—and my scientific results. I have built apparatuses as I have

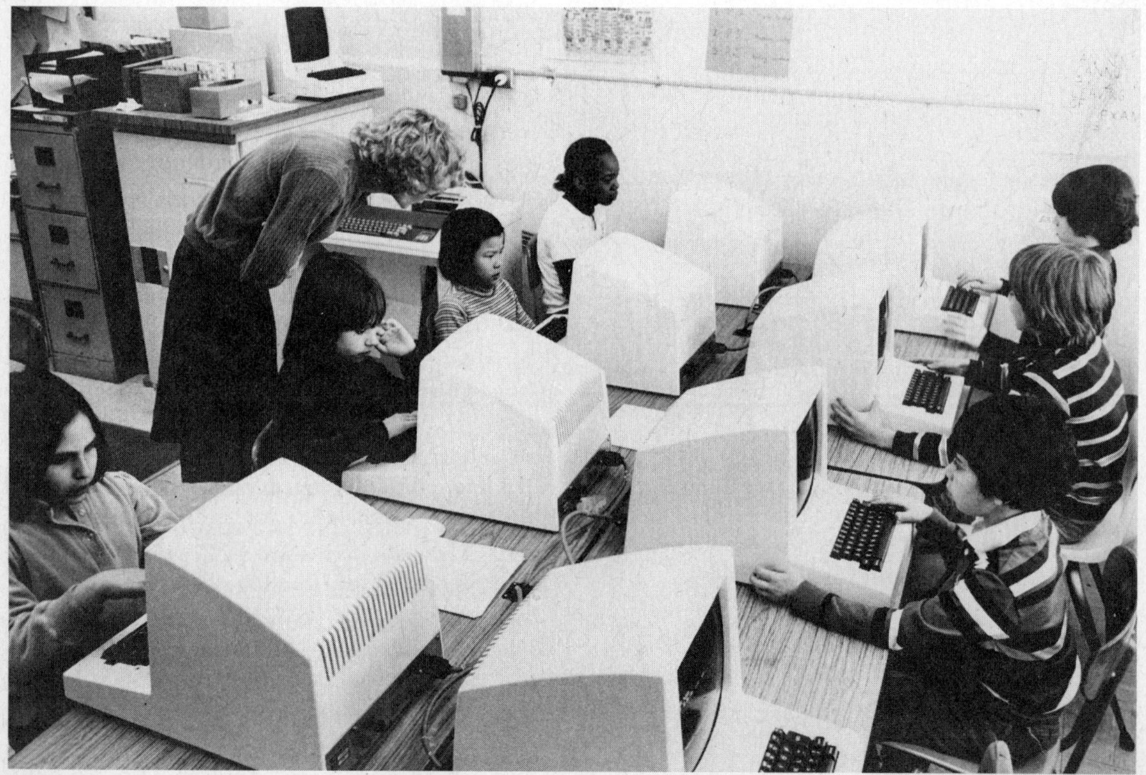

painted pictures or modelled figures in clay. I have conducted experiments as I have played the piano. I have written scientific papers and books as I have written stories and poems. . . . I emphasize positive contingencies." (1967, p. 408)

We must distinguish between operant and respondent behavior (Table 2.2). *Respondent behavior* refers to that governed by Pavlovian classic conditioning which, for Skinner, is comparatively unimportant. Far more significant is operant behavior, since most of our responses fall into this category. Because it is difficult to determine the causes of most of our behavior, we should begin with what we can identify—our responses. By reinforcing favorable responses, we can shape behavior very effectively.

Skinner's system is often also called *instrumental conditioning.* For some reason the organism responds, acting on the environment. This action is *instrumental* in securing reinforcement. The same analysis of behavior holds true for more complex activities such as thinking and problem solving. In thinking, we manipulate the relevant variables and increase the probability of a reinforced response. Problem solving simply represents a situation in which the desired response must be discovered.

TABLE 2.2. Differences Between Respondent and Operant Behavior

Respondent	Operant
Known stimuli	Unknown stimuli
Elicited response	Emitted response
Type S conditioning (the conditioning of stimuli)	Type R conditioning (the conditioning of responses)

Behaviorism and Human Development. What does all this have to do with child development?

We may well ask whether the operant conditioning of animals has any real value for understanding human growth. Behaviorists claim that environmental situations shape the child's responses. Thus, to explain personality development, Albert Bandura and Richard Walters (1963, pp. 23–26) discuss the use of operant conditioning as contrasted with such "stage" theories as psychoanalytic thought. Applying operant principles to social learning, these authors state that stage theory neglects the conditions that produce changes in behavior from one level to another. *Social-learning theorists,* however, predict changes in behavior only as the result of changes in training, or in other relevant biological or environmental variables. This type of explanation helps to account for differences in the social behavior patterns of children from similar sociocultural backgrounds and with similar biological characteristics.

To understand behaviorism as a developmental theory, let us consider the work of Sidney Bijou (1976). In an endeavor to interpret human psychological development from the viewpoint of a natural science, he concentrates on the interaction between the organism and the environment. An interaction is the probability of a given response's occurrence, depending on the stimuli that the environment presents.

Bijou (1976, p. 512) offers the following to illustrate the principles of behavioristic theory of development.

1. *General Formulations*

a. Psychological behavior evolves from the interactions between individual and environment. As the interactions change, development occurs.

b. The child is a unique biological structure possessing the capacity for developing those activities characteristic of the species by continuous interaction with environmental stimuli.

c. The environment is identified as those stimuli interacting with the child. Some stimuli are purely external, some originate within the child, and the child's own behavior is influenced both by preceding stimulation (respondent behavior) and consequent stimulation (operant behavior).

2. *Changes in Respondent and Operant Interactions*

a. Development occurs as both preceding and consequent stimulation change with age, that is, with a maturing biological structure and changing cultural conditions.

3. *Development of Complex Interactions of Respondent and Operant Behavior*

a. Most human behavior at all developmental stages consists of complex interrelationships of respondent and operant behavior occurring in interactional units linked by stimuli with multiple functions. (Bijou, 1976, p. 11)

Bijou (1975, p. 829) argues strongly for a behavioristic interpretation of development as follows:

> The psychoanalytic, the social learning, and the cognitive development theories point up some of the most important behavioral characteristics of the period, but I find them wanting in their attempted explanations because each includes "created" internal, causal structures and processes. There is room, it seems to me, for another model, based on behavioral analysis.
>
> . . . The essential point, and the one that distinguishes it from other behavioral and learning approaches, is that this approach is concerned exclusively with observable accounts of the interactions between stimulus and response functions.

Behaviorism as a developmental theory concerns itself with the changes that take place over months and even years, which holds the key to understanding the developmental sequence. Behaviorists assess such change by analyzing changes in the child's environment, in the child's ability to respond, and in the interaction between the two. Consider, for example, a youngster who has certain response capabilities (walk, talk, and is toilet trained). Now the child's environment is radically changed by school entrance. In school many of the older interactions will change, and many new ones will emerge. Consequently, changes in the way that human behavior interacts with the stimulus environment is a basic concern for the developmental theorist.

Growing children are considered clusters of interrelated responses interacting with stimuli. Some stimuli come from the external environment, some from their own behavior, and some from the biological structure and function. Consequently, children are not only a source of responses, but because part of the stimulus environment is within the body, they are also a source of stimuli. Responses are of two types: respondents, which are controlled by the stimuli that precede them, and operants, which are controlled by the stimuli or reinforcements that follow them. The behaviorist thus explains development by pointing to the constant interaction of stimuli and responses between child and environment.

The behavioristic explanation of human development and behavior stresses the use of scientific methods, the manipulation of relevant variables, the study of observable events, and the critical evaluation of results. Keller and Schoenfeld (1950), in a classic analysis, state that while the capabilities of the human infant are limited to those common to the species, behavior is susceptible to considerable modification. The task of any culture is to make a product acceptable to itself. The culture makes a product desirable by training, that is, by reinforcing approved responses and extinguishing all others. The culture teaches individuals what they may or may not do, what is good and what is bad, what is to be mastered (such as language), what is admired, and what constitutes the ideal personality. Consequently, development takes the direction that culture determines.

Many psychologists, however, have reacted vigorously against such claims for total control by the environment. Stone and Church (1973) state that Skinner paints a coolly rational world without guts, without passions, without illness or grief or jealousy, without responsibility or the need to make decisions and, above all, without free will.

Whether or not we agree with the behaviorist viewpoint, we can easily understand it. Arguing that the only proper explanation of development is based on rigorous experimentation, behaviorists point to what is obvious for them. When we look at a child's environment, what do we see? We see stimuli. When we observe a child's behavior, what do we see? We see responses. Some responses persist and some fade because of what happens after their occurrence. Given these facts, the behaviorists argue that it is logical to explain development by stimuli and responses, instead of by an appeal to vague, mysterious, inner forces.

DISCUSSION QUESTIONS

1. How would you analyze the case of the three-year-old girl with which we began this section? Do you agree with a behavioristic explanation or would you prefer another? Explain your answer thoroughly.
2. Distinguish between operant and respondent conditioning. Suggest some common aspect of human behavior and analyze it according to both respondent and operant principles. Which do you think offers the better explanation? Why?
3. How would you interpret Skinner's dissatisfaction with classical conditioning? What do you see as its failures?
4. Examine Skinner's explanation of behavior as a causal chain of three links. Select some behavior that is occurring now and apply Skinner's chain. Can you analyze it according to these links? Why? Or why not?
5. How can we interpret developmental changes? Be sure to use stimulus-response terms. Does this type of interpretation satisfy you? Why or why not?

THEORIES OF DEVELOPMENT: THE DEVELOPMENTAL TASK CONCEPT

The work of the prolific author and discerning observer of human nature, *Robert Havighurst,* dates back to the 1940s. He defines a *developmental task* as one that arises at a certain period in our lives, the successful achievement of which leads to happiness and success with later tasks, while failure leads to unhappiness, social disapproval, and difficulty with later tasks (1972). The initial words of his text *Developmental Tasks and Education* are a striking example of his disagreement with any theory that proposes an innate interpretation of growth and development: "Living is learning and growing is learning." To understand the process of human development, one must understand learning; human beings learn their way through life.

As an example of the developmental task concept and its usefulness in interpreting behavior, consider a hypothetical case based on Havighurst's (1953) discussion. The average youngster encounters difficulty with some of the developmental tasks that occur at various ages and how she learns to cope with them provides excellent clues to her level of adjustment. Consider Barbara, for example, a friendly but volatile and slightly aggressive girl. She has two older sisters and an elder brother. She is happy at home and close to her parents, but she has difficulty with her friends. At ten, thirteen, and sixteen years of age, she is rated (on a scale of one through ten) on several developmental tasks.

Getting along with age-mates

Age	Average Rating
10	5.5
13	6.4
16	9.5

How would we explain these changes? As Barbara "learns her way through life," she shifts from aggressive attitudes (perhaps fostered by competition with her brother and sisters) to a feeling of more self-acceptance. She is discovering who she is and is undoubtedly acquiring a sense of identity and self-worth.

Achieving emotional independence of parents and other adults

Age	Average Rating
10	4.2
13	5.4
16	8.6

Here we see a different pattern, owing to Barbara's dependence on her parents. Since she lacks satisfactory peer relations, she seeks feelings of security from her parents. Between the ages of ten and thirteen, there is not much change in her emotional dependence. Most youngsters feel emotionally insecure at this time, but Barbara particularly so. She has improved somewhat by the age of sixteen, but she still has yet to achieve the emotional maturity normal to a girl this age.

What can we say about this case? As Barbara encounters the developmental tasks associated with her age, her past learning affects the manner in which she meets each new challenge. Thinking that aggressive behavior is necessary, she complicates relationships with her friends. This behavior then complicates her struggle for mastery over other developmental tasks.

The Theory

Growth and development in a modern technological society require the mastery of a series of tasks. At each level of development children encounter new social demands and expectations. As they meet these challenges, they acquire new philosophical and psychological resources that, combined with environmental stimulation, constitute a series of developmental tasks that are critical to harmonious development. There are three sources of developmental tasks.

1. Tasks that arise from physical maturation: for example, learning to walk, learning to talk, learning to behave acceptably with the opposite sex during adolescence, or adjusting to menopause during middle age.
2. Tasks that have their source in the pressures of society: for example, learning to read or learning the role of a responsible citizen.
3. Tasks that arise from personal sources: for example, those that emerge from the maturing personality and take the form of personal values and aspirations.

The educational importance of the developmental task concept pervades all levels of the school system. There are two reasons for this far-reaching statement. First, it aids in the formulation of more precise and realistic objectives. Second, as Havighurst (1953) states, when the body is ripe, and society requires, and the self is ready to achieve a certain task, the teachable moment has arrived. Thus we can time educational effort better by identifying the tasks that are suitable for a particular level of development.

Once we have recognized the significance of the developmental task concept, we must determine the sequence of these tasks. Havighurst (1953) has suggested six major categories: infancy and early childhood, middle childhood (six to twelve years), adolescence, early adulthood (nineteen to thirty years), middle adulthood (thirty to sixty years), and, rather kindly phrased, later maturity. Table 2.3 presents some typical developmental tasks for each period.

TABLE 2.3. The Developmental Tasks

Infancy and Early Childhood (Birth-Five)	Middle Childhood (Six-Twelve)	Adolescence (Thirteen-Eighteen)
1. Learning to walk	1. Learning physical skills necessary for ordinary games	1. Achieving mature relations with both sexes
2. Learning to take solid foods	2. Building a wholesome attitude toward oneself	2. Achieving a masculine or feminine social role
3. Learning to talk	3. Learning to get along with agemates	3. Accepting one's physique
4. Learning to control the elimination of body wastes	4. Learning an appropriate sex role	4. Achieving emotional independence of adults
5. Learning sex differences and sexual modesty	5. Developing fundamental skills in reading, writing, and calculating	5. Preparing for marriage and family life
6. Acquiring concepts and language to describe social and physical reality	6. Developing concepts necessary for everyday living	6. Preparing for an economic career
7. Readiness for reading	7. Developing conscience, morality, and a scale of values	7. Acquiring values and an ethical system to guide behavior
8. Learning to distinguish right from wrong and developing a conscience	8. Achieving personal independence	8. Desiring and achieving socially responsible behavior
	9. Developing acceptable attitudes toward society	

Early Adulthood (Nineteen-Thirty)	Middle Adulthood (Thirty-Sixty)	Later Maturity (Sixty-one +)
1. Selecting a mate	1. Helping teenage children to become happy and responsible adults	1. Adjusting to decreasing strength and health
2. Learning to live with a partner	2. Achieving adult social and civic responsibility	2. Adjusting to retirement and reduced income
3. Starting a family	3. Satisfactory career achievement	3. Adjusting to death of spouse
4. Rearing children	4. Developing adult leisure time activities	4. Establishing relations with one's own age group
5. Managing a home	5. Relating to one's spouse as a person	5. Meeting social and civic obligations
6. Starting an occupation	6. Accepting the physiological changes of middle age	6. Establishing satisfactory living quarters
7. Assuming civic responsibility	7. Adjusting to aging parents	

Developmental Tasks of Middle Childhood. Let us examine two tasks from the time of middle childhood. According to Havighurst, this period is characterized by three great outward pushes. Children begin to move from parental controls to those of the peer group; there is a physical thrust into the world of games and work; and there is a mental thrust into the world of concepts, problems, and communication. From these three great thrusts of growth emerge the developmental tasks of middle childhood.

1. *Learning physical skills necessary for ordinary games.*

Nature of the task. To learn the physical skills necessary for the games and activities of childhood: throwing, catching, kicking, and swimming.

Biological basis. General bone and muscle growth. During this period large muscle coordination precedes that of the small muscles.

Psychological basis. The peer group rewards skillful performance and often severely punishes failure.

Cultural basis. Boys are expected to master these skills more readily than girls. Poor performance means loss of status for a boy, while it is relatively neutral for a girl's prestige.

Educational implications. The main source of encouragement for developing these skills lies with the peer culture. The school can concentrate on those who have special difficulty.

2. *Developing fundamental skills in reading, writing, and calculating.*

Nature of the task. To perform these tasks well enough to meet the demands of society.

Biological basis. The maturation of the nervous system. For example, most youngsters before the age of six have inadequately coordinated eye muscles, and their gaze may wander down the page instead of making an accurate return sweep to the beginning of the next line.

Psychological basis. By the age of twelve or thirteen most children have acquired the basic linguistic skills sufficient for them to succeed at a normal level of development.

Cultural basis. The minimum level of ability that society requires is undoubtedly higher now than a century ago. Socioeconomic status now depends on a high development of intellectual skills.

Educational implications. The importance of biological maturation for the mastery of these skills indicates that children should not encounter certain of these tasks until they are ready for them.

These are only two of the developmental tasks of middle childhood. If youngsters master these tasks, they will usually experience success with the later tasks they meet. Failure leads to unhappiness, disapproval by society, and difficulty with later tasks.

Again, it is interesting to consider the differences among the theories that we have discussed. Psychoanalytic theory, with its emphasis on psychosexual stage, probes into the manner in which children pass through these stages. If they experience problems, then the source lies in a previous stage. Behaviorism, with its stress on the environment, looks to stimuli and responses for solutions to any problems. According to this view, we should not be concerned with the "inner" child, but should focus instead on tangible S-R events. But Havighurst provides us with yet a third interpretation. As children grow, they find increasing demands made of them, but also new physical and psychological resources available to them. These inner and outer forces determine the series of developmental tasks that they must master to grow and adjust.

Personality is closely related to developmental tasks, since it is the self, reflecting biological and social pressures, that determines any individual's handling of developmental tasks. The personality of the individual is causally related to performance of tasks. The boy with a healthy, friendly attitude toward girls, for example, will obviously be rated more highly on social attitudes. Finally, emotions, rationality, and self-understanding are more closely related to satisfactory performance of tasks than is intelligence. Our emotional life is not separated from any of our endeavors, including the task of achieving intellectual skills.

The developmental task concept has a long and rich tradition. Its acceptance has been partly due to a recognition of critical periods in our lives and partly due to the practical nature of Havighurst's tasks. Havighurst has given teachers, nurses, and parents a clear and excellent guide to some of the obstacles that children must overcome at various ages. There are no inflexible age ranges given for each task; the age span for each period is quite wide and suggests steady progress toward maturity instead of abrupt steps.

Knowing that a youngster of a certain age (say eleven) is encountering one of the tasks of that period (learning an appropriate sex role) helps adults to understand the child's behavior and establish an environment that will help the child to master the task. Another good example is that of acquiring personal independence, an important task for the middle childhood period. Youngsters will test authority during this phase and, if teachers and parents realize that this is a normal, even necessary phase of development, they will react differently than if they see it as a personal challenge. It is, in fact, a learning opportunity. Children challenge authority and seem to be striving for confrontation. Properly handled, they learn that the drive for independence must not affront others for the sheer sake of conflict. But they also should learn that adults will accept growing maturity and will grant a greater degree of independence.

The developmental task concept, then, provides a realistic view of development and also furnishes a useful blueprint of future growth. Thomas (1979) believes that the major flaws in the developmental task concept are its tendency to describe rather than explain and its failure to generate pertinent research. Despite these criticisms, Thomas states that it offers a valuable perspective for understanding children's development. He states (1979, p. 141):

> Despite these limitations, though, the developmental task perspective is useful for interpreting children's behavior. The idea that children are struggling to achieve the goals implied in the tasks makes sense to me.

THEORIES OF DEVELOPMENT: SELF-REALIZATION THEORY

During the 1960s, dissatisfaction with both behaviorism and psychoanalysis led a group of psychologists to articulate a different explanation of human behavior and development. This "third force," called humanistic psychology, pledged itself to a closer scrutiny of normal behavior and the direction of development. One of the movement's leading proponents of a humanistic interpretation of development has been Charlotte Buhler (Buhler, 1959; Buhler and Massarik, 1968; Buhler and Allen, 1972).

Buhler has suggested a different basis for making judgments and decisions about children. Her analysis of life's basic tendencies represents a middle-ground position between an extreme biological emphasis or a radical cultural environmentalism. While physical causes certainly determine maturation and behavior, culture and environment can exercise an influence so strong as to alter an individual's basic tendencies.

The Theory

The core of self-realization theory is the assumption that all children should develop their potential. But basic to this assumption is the inescapable reality that children will become what they think they are capable of becoming. That is, self-perception is critical for success or failure. If they think that they are destined for failure, then they will fail. If they think that they are destined for success, then their chances for success are better.

A recent study by Wallace and Ethel Maw (1970) provides another excellent example of theory in action. The authors studied the relationship between curiosity and high or low self-concepts in fifth-grade boys. Working on the same lines, C. H. Mahone (1960) had found that a person with a poor self-perception is highly motivated to avoid failure and thus sets goals so low that the possibility of failure is almost nil. People high in self-acceptance are willing to take risks in order to prove themselves.

Maw and Maw first determined the curiosity level of the boys and then measured their level of self-esteem. According to the authors' criterion of curiosity for elementary schoolers, curious children react positively to novel elements in the environment (they move toward them to explore), exhibit a need to know more about themselves and their surroundings, seek out new experiences, and persist in examining novel stimuli in order to learn more about them. The boys also rated themselves on their curiosity. To assess the self-concept level, the authors used standardized tests (portions of the California Test of Personality and Children's Personality Questionnaire) and some of their own devising. Finally, boys with special developmental problems were screened out so as not to contaminate the experimental results with the effects of extraneous variables (the disruptive error mentioned in Chapter 1). The authors also cancelled out the effect of intelligence as a cause of self-esteem or curiosity.

The results were as anticipated: differing self-concepts corresponded to different curiosity levels. The high-curiosity boys showed better personal adjustment, a greater sense of personal worth, greater self-reliance, a greater sense of personal freedom, and a lesser tendency to withdraw than the low-curiosity boys. The low-curiosity boys were more prejudiced, had less sense of social responsibility, and were more intolerant than the high-curiosity boys.

The authors note that perhaps boys with low self-concepts lack curiosity because they expect failure and thus tend to shy away from challenging situations. Or perhaps the conditions that produce a low level of curiosity also produce a low self-concept. Still, the two elements seem to be somehow related, and this relationship could well indicate future success or failure, academic and otherwise. (Although our primary intent is to show the practical significance of self-realization theory, we can again see how good experimental studies meet the criteria discussed in Chapter 1.)

According to self-realization theory, there are four basic life tendencies.

1. The tendency toward need satisfaction. (What are children's needs? How can we help youngsters recognize them and select the means to satisfy them?)

2. The tendency toward the upholding of an internal order. (Unless children have feelings of security or an acceptance of themselves and the world that results in a sense of harmony, they will be in turmoil.)

3. The tendency toward adaptation. (How

can children utilize their abilities in a competent, personally satisfying manner?)

4. The tendency toward productivity. (How can children recognize the intrinsic value of their drives and achievement? Life without accomplishment, even for children, is empty.)

For healthy functioning, children must achieve balance and integration of these tendencies. Although any one tendency may be predominant in a single action, exclusive pursuit of one of them will result in psychological illness. All four tendencies, however, usually are working simultaneously. Under unfavorable circumstances, any one of them may turn into its opposite: need frustration, internal disorder, maladaptive behavior, or nonproductivity. We have all seen children who are determined to do just what they want regardless of anyone else, or children who think they are capable of so little that achievement in any activity becomes almost impossible. The essential meaning of Buhler's theory is that children need to assess themselves realistically and within this assessment, to strive to fulfill life's tendencies.

The one system that will adequately incorporate all four tendencies lies in the overall concept of self-realization. Buhler traces the idea of self-realization through Nietzsche, Carl Jung, Karen Horney, Erich Fromm, Kurt Goldstein, Abraham Maslow, Carl Rogers, and others who are searching for some encompassing theory of life's ultimate goal. Self-realization differs from simple drives and needs, since it relates to the entire life span and not just to the moment-to-moment life of the individual. Since the concept implies development and continuity, so one must consider living in the past, present, and future.

Developmental Aspects

Life is lived as a total unit (Buhler, 1959, p. 576). For Buhler, the notion of development incorporates life's basic tendencies and the idea of direction—movement toward a specific goal, the emergence of optimal potential. To achieve this goal requires an identification of the self with the creative process of nature. Self-realization, then, strives toward the fulfillment of life.

Self-realization is a developmental concept, a process of achieving goals and integrating needs and values. Note Buhler's emphasis on process with its clear implication of *becoming*. That is, self-realization does not emerge magically with age; the number of immature adolescents and adults testifies to the insufficiency of time alone to produce self-realization.

The years from birth to two are a time of consolidation of systems; from two to four years, a conscious self begins to appear and children exhibit a unique personality that results from both heredity and environment. The development of a distinct personality continues until about the age of ten or twelve when discernible maturational trends suggest permanent dispositional traits.

For example, these years inevitably cause frustration in youngsters as they struggle with independence needs and parental restraints. How parents treat children and how youngsters react often shape constructive or destructive attitudes that last for life. Youngsters are acquiring personal beliefs and values that, while frequently poorly articulated, nevertheless are intensely meaningful.

The humanistic explanation of development is not one that delineates stages and identifies outstanding characteristics of each stage. Rather it is a view of development that charts the direction of growth, that is, from a self-oriented child to an adult who is fulfilling potential both with regard to self and others.

The Concept of Fulfillment. Fulfillment is subjective, not objective. It is a personal experience, not a measurable accomplishment, a result, not a process. Self-realized people, having discovered their potentialities, can make of themselves what they want. This summary may sound over-idealistic, but surely the examination of the process of development should also discover paths of possible improvement.

Buhler's ideas have practical implications for adults working with children. Whether they know it or not, children have definite ideas about the self. Their self-judgments are, however, often unrealistic. We can help youngsters to select reachable goals, to take activities that produce real worth, and thus to help them accept and realize themselves. And, in learning to accept, to cope, and to share, children learn happiness.

Buhler states that fulfillment for healthy individuals means experiencing happiness. They find self-realization in successful creative accomplishments; they work for, not against, the welfare of others; and they find peace of mind in the resultant order. Such a view of development differs sharply from a theory that emphasizes environmental demands, and relegates our inner strivings to a place of comparative unimportance.

DISCUSSION QUESTIONS

1. Do you feel that a poor self-concept is related to failure and frustration in all aspects of life? Do you know some youngsters who are already showing these signs? How is their schoolwork? Do they have many friends? Are they happy children?
2. In the study by Maw and Maw, why do you think low curiosity is linked to poor self-concept? Give some specific examples in your answer.
3. Using Buhler's four basic life tendencies, give some examples of each. Why must there be a balance among all four? Explain your answer.
4. It is quite easy to talk of self-realization as being the ultimate goal of development. But what can the parent, teacher, or nurse do to guide the youngster toward this goal? Suggest some specific techniques of guidance and encouragement that would help the concerned adult.

The theories of psychoanalysis, behaviorism, developmental tasks, and self-realization exemplify widely differing views of how children develop. These beliefs about development are predicated on equally diverse views of human nature. The behaviorist's mechanistic interpretation of human nature contrasts sharply with the idealistic views of self-realization.

Yet it is unwise to focus solely on the differences among the theories. They all recognize some common, basic developmental facts. The developmental sequence, for example, is the same for all individuals, and each of the theories attempts to explain the aspects of development that it deems important, in order of their appearance. The behaviorist, for instance, would explain a baby's preoccupation with the mouth as representing reinforcement of the behaviors that sustain life, such as digestion and respiration. A psychoanalytic interpretation of the oral stage goes far beyond this explanation and sees far different meanings. Havighurst is much more concerned with the task itself (such as taking food) and then with attempting to identify the source of the task.

TABLE 2.4. Theories of Development: Basic Principles

	Psychoanalytic	Behaviorist	Developmental Tasks	Self-Realization
Major Figures	Freud	Pavlov, Skinner	Havighurst	Buhler
Developmental Explanations	Passage through psychosexual stages	Respondent conditioning, operant conditioning	Mastery of developmental tasks	The basic life tendencies
Essential Features	Id—ego—superego: psychosexual stages	Stimuli, responses	Developmental tasks	Need satisfaction
Source of Problems	Conflict during development leads to fixation, regression, personality problems	Inadequate connection of stimuli with changing response capacity	Failure to master tasks at one period leads to future difficulty	Negative self-concept leads to frustrations
Goal	Sexually mature individual	Socially acceptable behavior by proper conditioning procedures	Adjustment and happiness through success with developmental tasks	Fulfillment of potential

Another example is the continuity of growth. Organisms grow at different rates and in different ways. The human being may continue intellectual growth after physical growth has ceased. Theorists analyze this continuity of growth from different perspectives. Buhler, for example, sees human beings progressing toward self-realization at any age, if the four basic life tendencies are harmonious. Havighurst views growth as divided into six phases. And psychoanalytic theory sees growth as a passage through the various psychosexual stages. Yet implicit in each of these theories is the assumption that growth is continuous. Table 2.4 offers a comparison of the basic principles of each.

Many other similar examples could be given, but the intent is clear: different theorists endeavor to explain the same developmental sequence. The inescapable conclusion is that the different theories merely interpret the same facts differently. If we accept the reality of different views about human nature, the clash of their conclusions is hardly surprising.

SUMMARY

To understand and use data means that we must be able to combine the results of research with a personally compatible, sound theory.

Psychoanalytic theory places great emphasis on the unconscious; psychic determinism; the structure of the personality (id, ego, superego); and passage through the psychosexual stages (oral, anal, phallic, latency, genital). The theory also includes defense mechanisms such as denial, repression, sublimation, projection, and rationalization.

Behaviorism works primarily with two forms of learning: respondent (also called classical or Pavlovian) conditioning, and operant (also called instrumental or Skinnerian) conditioning.

Respondent conditioning emphasizes the use of stimuli, while operant conditioning emphasizes the role of responses.

Havighurst has proposed a series of developmental tasks for different age periods, successful completion of which leads to happiness and success with later tasks. Just the opposite occurs if youngsters are unsuccessful with the tasks.

Self-realization theory stresses children's drive for satisfaction, adequacy, and happiness. Development is seen as the unfolding of personal potential.

SUGGESTED READINGS

BRENNER, CHARLES. *An Elementary Textbook of Psychoanalysis.* New York: International Universities Press, 1973.

BUHLER, CHARLOTTE. "Theoretical Observations About Life's Basic Tendencies," *American Journal of Psychotherapy* 13 (1959), 561–581. A good introduction to Buhler's ideas about the development of potential.

FREUD, SIGMUND. *An Outline of Psychoanalysis.* New York: W. W. Norton, 1949. (First published in German in 1940.)

HAVIGHURST, ROBERT. *Developmental Tasks and Education.* New York: David McKay, 1972.

———. *Human Development and Education.* New York: David McKay, 1953.

HILL, CALVIN. *A Primer of Freudian Psychology.* Cleveland: World, 1954.

SKINNER, B. F. *Science and Human Behavior.* New York: Macmillan, 1953. Of all that has been written by and about Skinner, there is no better source.

THOMAS, R. MURRAY. *Comparing Theories of Child Development.* Belmont, CA: Wadsworth, 1979.

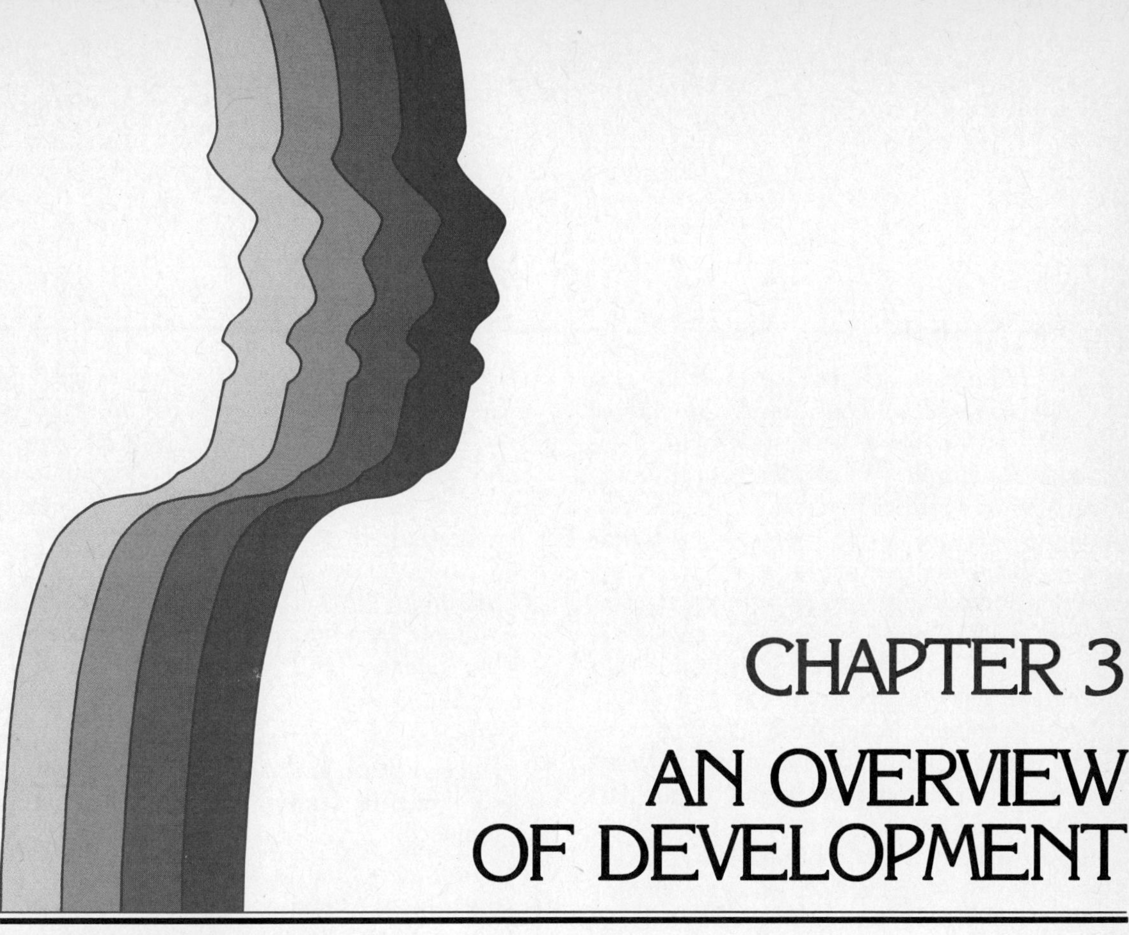

CHAPTER 3

AN OVERVIEW OF DEVELOPMENT

CHAPTER HIGHLIGHTS

Topics

Infancy: Characteristics and Milestones
a. Neonatal Reflexes
b. Visual Adaptation
c. Auditory Development
d. Sleeping
e. Smiling

Early Childhood: Characteristics and Milestones
a. Physical and Motor Development
b. Perceptual Development
c. Cognitive Development

Middle Childhood: Characteristics and Milestones
a. Physical and Motor Development
b. Cognitive Development

Adolescence: Characteristics and Milestones
a. Physical Development
b. Cognitive Development

People

Benjamin Bloom
T. G. R. Bower
T. Berry Brazelton
David Elkind
Eleanor Gibson
Kenneth Keniston
Lewis Lipsitt
Howard Meredith
Steven Rose
J. M. Tanner

Special Topics

Sudden Infant Death Syndrome
Developmental Problems

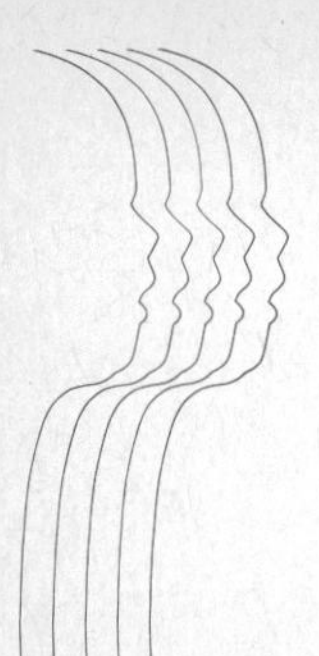

Almost all developmental texts state that development is a "continuous, integrated process." Although a true statement, it is deceptively simple. What does "continuous" mean? As we shall see in the next chapter, psychological continuity may be more myth than reality. Behaviors that appear in the first days following birth such as reaching and imitating quickly disappear only to reappear weeks or months later. It is difficult, if not impossible, to characterize these behaviors as continuous. How "integrated" is behavior? Do cognitive, perceptual, and motor abilities appear, develop, and nicely mesh together? Possibly, but data are so lacking about the mechanism of integration that artificial boundaries—periods, stages, epochs—are imposed on development.

Such descriptive terminology is necessary to categorize the sweep of human development. The restricted scope of current analysis demands that we investigate manageable segments of developmental data. Consequently, while human development refers to an intact organism we must divide that intactness to aid comprehension.

Is there an ideal means of division? Is one procedure better than another? For example, is "stage" (such as Piaget's cognitive stages) more meaningful than division into epochs (infancy, early childhood)? Those who advocate division into stages believe that such analysis permits qualitative investigation. Hooper (1973) states that researchers must distinguish "weaker" uses of stage (those that are essentially descriptive) from the "stronger" uses of stage (those that define stage and attempt to explain progress from stage to stage).

For example, the stronger, explanatory meaning of stage includes three essential characteristics:

1. *hierarchical,* that is, the stages are invariant and later stages can never precede earlier stages; the progression must be A–B–C–D;
2. *integration,* that is, later stages subsume and transform earlier stages into new structural entities (earlier stages are not merely replaced);
3. *structuring,* that is, the clustering or organization of behaviors at a particular level of functioning; the behaviors of any level are not simply lumped together but are inherently interconnected.

Such usage of stage directs developmental investigators to search for cumulative, relatively permanent, sequential, and novel behavior alterations (Hooper, 1973, p. 303). Age is irrelevant; concern is with the order of emerging, conceptually interrelated behavior. Piaget's theory of cognitive development, which appears in Chapter 8, is perhaps the outstanding current example of stage theory.

While stage analysis can be a powerful tool, its major limitation is its restricted application. Piaget's *cognitive* stages, Kohlberg's stages of *moral* development, and the psychoanalytic stages of *psychosexual* development all attempt to explain limited developmental accomplishments. A comprehensive picture of growth demands a more flexible tool such as a description of behavior by age.

Analysis by age or epoch (infancy, early childhood) also has its weaknesses. It is purely descriptive and normative; that is, readers receive a sketch of the normal infant's or ten-year-old's behaviors and characteristics. Deviations are ignored and no causal explanation of behavior and behavioral changes are offered. It is probably better, however, to trace the entire developmental sequence.

Consequently, this chapter will use four developmental periods to portray the growth cycle: infancy, early childhood, middle childhood, and adolescence. The characteristics and milestones of each period will guide analysis. That is, each epoch contains certain outstanding features that demand attention, such as the appearance, use, and disappearance of infant reflexes, or the positive and negative features of sports in middle childhood. Each summary and analysis will conclude with the developmental tasks and common problems of the period.

INFANCY: CHARACTERISTICS AND MILESTONES

Since infancy is now recognized as a critical developmental period, Chapter Five presents a detailed examination of emerging behavior: infant states, assessment techniques, learning, the effects of early experience, and psychomotor, perceptual, and cognitive development. Here, focus will be on the abilities that infants immediately use to adjust to the environment.

Neonatal Reflexes

When a stimulus repeatedly elicits the same response, that behavior is usually designated as a reflex. Popular examples include the eye blink and the knee jerk. As Kessen, Haith, and Salapatek (1970) note, the clarity and regularity of reflex behavior attracted investigators attempting to unravel the chaotic puzzle of neonatal activity. Thus there is an enormous number of reflex studies that classify, describe, and trace the chronology of infant reflexes.

The significance of reflex behavior in an infant's survival also required intense investigation. Caplan (1973) states that all of the activities needed to sustain life function at birth, such as breathing, sucking, swallowing, elimination, hearing, seeing, smelling. Neonatal reflexes serve a definite purpose: the gag reflex enables infants to spit up mucus; the eye blink protects the eyes from excessive light; an antismothering reflex facilitates breathing.

Kessen et al. (1970) warn, however, that studies of reflexes face two limitations: all neonatal behavior is *not* reflexive (some behavior can only be classed as spontaneous activity); there may be variability in the reflex depending on the infant's state. Zelazo (1976) states that although it is unclear why the connection between the unconditioned stimulus and the unconditioned response is not always automatic, it is clear that infants are not at the mercy of stimuli that produce "invariant" reactions.

Kessen et al. (1970) note that the classification of reflexes occasionally resembles list-making, but the more important neonatal reflexes include those that appear in Table 3.1.

The Fate of Neonatal Reflexes. Are neonatal reflexes functional after infancy? Excluding the unchanging reflex, such as the eye blink, does the continued appearance of these early reflexes indicate some pathology? For example, Kessen and his colleagues (1970) state that the Moro reflex differs from the adult startle pattern and its appearance beyond the fifth month suggests neurological damage. These authors believe that while adaptation needs infant reflexive behavior, evidence for any continuity between early reflexes and significant later behavior is lacking.

Others are reluctant to dismiss any connection so quickly. Caplan (1973) states that infant reflexes are not just immediately useful since a baby's brain stores and learns from early reflex experiences thus building for the future. Philip Zelazo (1976) has attempted to demonstrate that neonatal reflexes are gradually incorporated into instrumental behavior. Do infant reflexes merely disappear, later to be replaced by voluntary actions?

Zelazo (1976, p. 88) argues that these reflexes do not disappear but retain their identity within a hierarchy of controlled behavior. Children gradually develop the ability to inhibit and to activate their reflexes. Zelazo believes that the process continues until the reflexes become part of the motor behavior of normal, healthy humans.

Studies have repeatedly shown that the sucking reflex can come under instrumental control (the rate of sucking will accelerate to increase a mobile's movement). We will note in discussing sudden infant death syndrome (SIDS), the danger to infants who cannot adequately use reflexes vital for survival. Zelazo concludes that we may facilitate maturation by providing opportunities to practice these early reflexes, thus lowering the age at which skills such as walking appear and actually aiding them in the development of survival mechanisms (such as pushing away anything blocking breathing).

TABLE 3.1. Neonatal Reflexes

Name of Reflex	How Elicited	Description of Response
Plantar grasp	Pressure applied to bottom of foot	Toes tend to curl
Babinski	Gently stroke sole of foot	Toes spread in an outward and upward manner
Babkin	Press palm of hand while infant lies on back	Mouth opens; eyes close
Rooting	Gently touch cheek of infant with light finger pressure	Head turns toward finger in effort to suck
Sucking	Mouth contacts nipple of breast or bottle	Mouth and tongue used to manipulate (suck) nipple
Moro	Loud noise or sudden dropping of infant	Stretches arms and legs and then hugs self; cries
Grasping	Object or finger is placed in infant's palm	Fingers curl around object
Tonic neck reflex	Place infant flat on back	Infant assumes fencer position: turns head and extends arm and leg in same direction as head
Stepping	Support infant in upright position; soles of feet brush surface	Infant attempts regular progression of steps

SUDDEN INFANT DEATH SYNDROME

Discussion of the survival value of reflexes introduces one of the most perplexing problems facing both parents and researchers—the sudden infant death syndrome (SIDS). Estimates are that 10,000 two- to four-month-old infants die each year from this syndrome. There is little warning, although almost all cases were preceded by mild cold symptoms and usually occurred in late winter or early spring.

While speculation is rampant, no theory has emerged that clearly explains the disease's cause. Several investigators cautiously agree, however, that neurological difficulties seem to be present. Zelazo (1976) states that certain congenitally weak reflexive patterns may jeopardize an infant's survival. For example, blocking a neonate's mouth and nose with a cotton pad should cause infants to twist their heads, cry, and attempt to push it away. Infants quickly learn this technique in their daily life in the crib. If they do not—if their neonatal reflexes are weak—then SIDS may strike.

Lewis Lipsitt (1976) has expanded this view and believes that victims may suffer from a learning disability in which protective reflexes do not become voluntary responses. The ability to alleviate blocked breathing declines rather than improves. The infant simply cannot prepare for survival. Several autopsies suggest a nervous system problem that interferes with normal maturation. Lipsitt notes that obscure difficulties in breathing, reaching, and grasping produced retarded learning in the first two months, a delay that could be fatal.

Other investigators are beginning to report similar results. "Soft signs" of neurological disorders—high pitched crying, excessive eye-crossing and eye-rolling—have been discovered in the case histories of many of the victims. Despite these retrospective signs, the literature clearly describes the SIDS victims as apparently normal after birth.

This appearance of normality poses a danger to researchers: stressing subtle defects as a symptom of SIDS may alarm parents of all children. For example, some investigators believe that apnea (a temporary loss of breathing) is a key element in SIDS. Others disagree, believing that the *absence* of minimal periods of apnea indicates some abnormality.

Experts quarrel; the research is contradictory; the rate of alarm is growing. There is no clinically accurate way of predicting or preventing SIDS. Thus the burden remains with parents: careful observation plus appropriate action.

Visual Development

Research indicates that the visual system develops rapidly during the prenatal months and can function at birth. Infants are alert to a light source held about ten inches from their eyes. They will even follow the light if it moves slowly from side to side. Infants may manifest random eye movements that alarm parents, but they do not persist and are not necessarily a sign of neurological difficulty.

Although some structures within the visual system are not fully formed, the eye is anatomically and physiologically prepared to

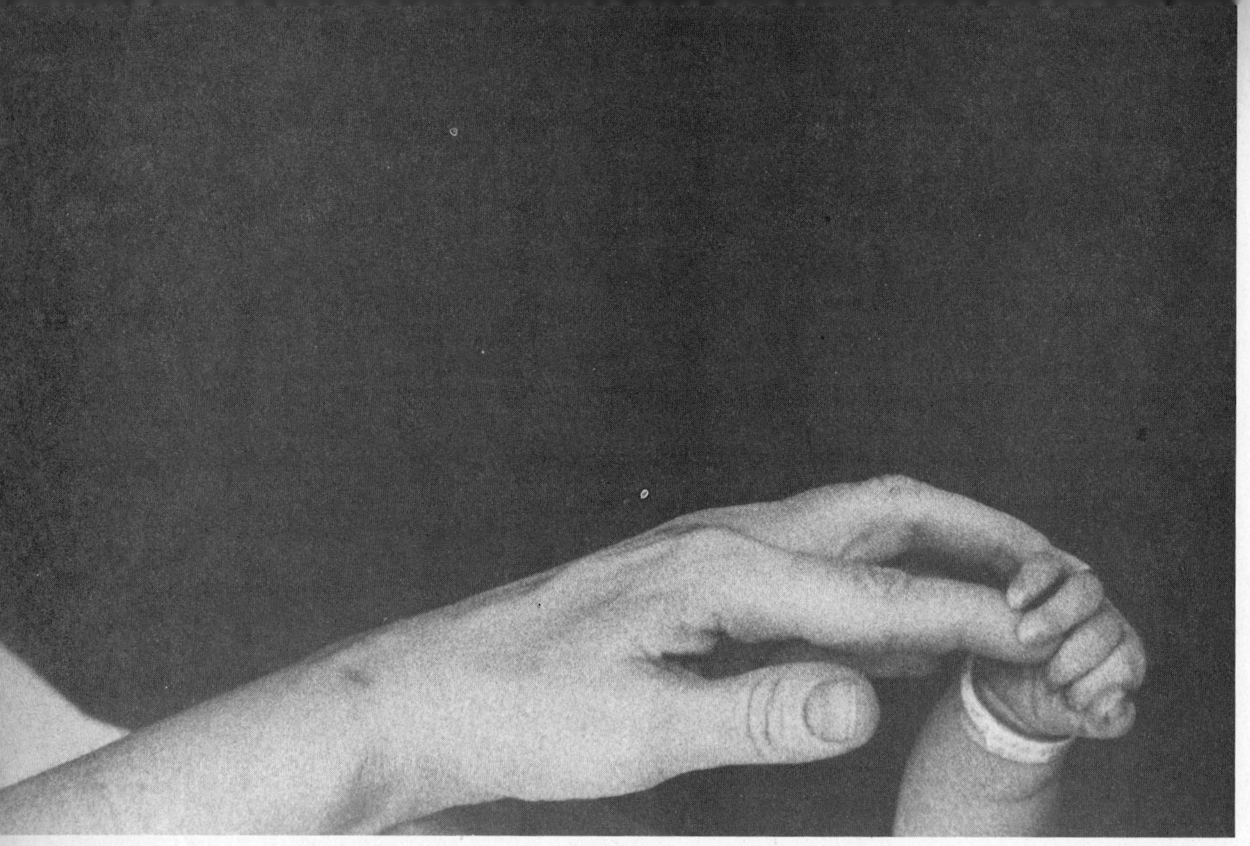

respond to visual stimuli. Caplan (1973) describes the pattern of visual development by noting that humans are born able to see and quickly exhibit a preference for patterns. (Chapter Five presents Fantz's more detailed account of the infant's response to pattern.) They immediately notice a light source and can track it as it moves. During the second to fourth month, most youngsters see the world in color and can focus on objects.

Haith and Campos (1977) summarize recent research on vision as follows:

1. Studies show that variable accommodation (focusing on objects at various distances) appears at about two months;
2. Binocular coordination appears around four months; studies indicate that there may be a critical period for the attainment of stereopsis (three-dimensional vision) since infants born with congenital esotropia have a greater chance of acquiring stereopsis if surgery is performed *before* two years;
3. Infants see color sometime in the two- to four-month period (a major difficulty in establishing an exact time for color recognition has been separating color from brightness; it has only recently been overcome);
4. Individual differences in visual tracking ability exist at birth.

Visual Adaptation. Studying visual development spurs speculation about how growing visual skill helps infants to adjust to their environment. Gibson and Walk (1960) in their famous "visual cliff" experiment reason that infants use visual stimuli to discriminate both depth and distance. The visual cliff is actually a board dividing a large sheet of heavy glass. A checkerboard pattern is attached flush to one half of the bottom of the glass, thus giving the impression of solidity. The investigators then placed a similar sheet under the other half but placed it on the floor thus creating a sense of depth—the visual cliff.

The authors originally tested thirty-six infants whose age was six to fourteen months. Each infant was placed on the center board and the mother called the child from the shallow side and then the cliff side. Twenty-seven of the youngsters moved onto the shallow side toward the mother. When called from the cliff side, only three infants ventured over the depth. The experiment suggests that infants discriminate depth when they begin crawling. Gibson and Walk (1960) conclude that the infants' behavior clearly demonstrates their dependence on vision.

Is the same phenomenon present *before* six months? Campos (1976), discussing the value of heart rate changes in infant studies, has extended the visual cliff experiments. Repeated studies show that cardiac deceleration indicates neonatal attention, while acceleration indicates neonatal fear. Noting that the visual cliff experiments have produced fear in animals as young as one day, Campos and his colleagues directly placed infants of one, two, three, and five months on the cliff fully expecting to find fear responses (cardiac acceleration) even with the prelocomotor infants. They were amazed to discover cardiac deceleration in the two-, three-, and five-month-old infants. The reactions were as follows:

one month—no change in cardiac rate

two months—cardiac deceleration (attention)

three months—cardiac deceleration (attention)

five months—decreasing cardiac deceleration (attention)

nine months—cardiac acceleration (fear)

The pattern is fascinating and raises still unanswered questions. Prelocomotor infants perceive something at two, three, and five months, but is it depth? If they perceive depth, why is there no fear reaction? What explains the developmental shift from attention to fear at about nine months? Does the emergence of memory in the second six months of the first year help to explain the developmental shift? That is, do youngsters recall falling and now relate a previous experience to the present perception of depth?

Although infants demonstrate visual ability at birth and quickly show signs of increasing visual skill, a warning by Kessen et al. makes a timely conclusion: children at three months still make primitive attempts to organize their visual surroundings and to integrate vision with other infant activities.

Auditory Development

Knobloch and Pasamanick (1974), analyzing the critical role of communication in human behavior, believe that normal language development depends partially on the intactness of the hearing mechanism. They state that hearing is a specialized form of tactile sense, making the organism aware of vibrations of distant origin, thus affording contact with the spatially remote. Hearing impairments isolate youngsters from their world, even from themselves. These youngsters are wrapped in an envelope of silence.

As discussed in Chapter 4, evidence clearly indicates that the fetus is capable of hearing by four months and the neonatal auditory apparatus is fully functional at birth. Knobloch and Pasamanick (1974, p. 291) note that hearing includes both the perception of a sound stimulus and its interpretation by complex cortical and subcortical mechanisms. They describe several stages in an infant's development of sensitivity to speech vibrations, a process that involves more than passing sound stimuli through the middle ear. The infant probably first detects vibration frequencies of 100–400 per second, followed by frequencies of 400–2400 vibrations per second, and then those in the 2400–8000 range. An infant is usually sensitive to all frequency ranges.

The authors believe that hearing facilitates social as well as cognitive development. Through sound infants determine the important events in their physical world: some sounds mean people and social contact; others signify the coming of food; still others indicate a change in activity, for example, lowering the shades for sleep. Infants gradually identify these sounds, thus adding to their physical and psychological information about the environment. Not only does the sound of a closing refrigerator door signal food, but the tone of a mother's voice conveys mood and emotion.

By the end of the first year, infants begin to react discriminately to words and by eighteen months they are immersed in a verbal environment. Children who suffer some hearing impairment face difficult problems especially in the mastery of speech. Knobloch and Pasamanick (1974, p. 296) believe that often a child's behavior is the best clue to a hearing problem.

Reese and Lipsitt (1970, p. 53) also afford hearing a key developmental role when they state that sound undoubtedly represents a potent stimulus for building cognitive structures and for learning sets because children need not "focus" their sensory systems before being exposed to the stimulus—it *seeks them out.*

Sleeping

Neonates sleep more than they do anything else, usually about fourteen or fifteen hours per day. Infants exhibit three sleep patterns: light or restless, periodic, and deep. There is little if any activity during deep sleep (about 25 percent of sleep), but neonates are mostly light sleepers with the brain wave patterns associated with dreaming (although infants probably do not dream). Caplan (1973) notes that some internal clock seems to regulate sleep patterns, with most deep sleep spells lasting approximately twenty minutes. At the end of the second week, a consistent and predictable pattern emerges. Neonates sleep in short stretches, about seven or eight per day, but the pattern reverses itself and infants assume an adult's schedule; that is, about 70 percent is deep sleep and the remainder is light or periodic sleep.

Brazelton (1969) and Caplan (1973) trace sleep patterns as follows:

1. During the first month, infants reduce their seven or eight sleep periods to three or four and combine two of them into one lasting about five hours. (If parents are lucky this longer period will occur after a late evening feeding.) Infants are thus establishing a night and day routine.

2. During the third month, sleep patterns are usually regulated with morning and afternoon naps supplementing night stretches ranging from six or seven to ten or eleven hours.

3. Since the last half of the first year (beginning at five or six months) sees the emergence of exciting new abilities, the infant must possess enormous energy. This is demonstrated in changing sleep patterns; the night sleep cycles usually have the infant wide awake at dawn, bursting with excitement and demanding an audience.

4. By eight months, naps are shorter and some infants may require only one in the afternoon. A problem that most infants begin to show at this age is their reluctance to go to bed at night. They now begin to sleep most of the night.

5. At twelve months, napping may be difficult and infants begin to set their schedules; that is, they nap only when tired. There is continued resistance to go to bed at night, but once asleep they usually sleep through the night.

Smiling

Caplan (1973) describes a two-month-old infant as "the smiler." While earlier smiles appear, they lack the social significance of the smile that emerges at six weeks. Caplan believes that babies smile instinctively at faces—real or drawn—and this probably reflects the human tendency to attend to patterns. Infants gradually learn that familiar faces usually mean pleasure, and smiling to *known* faces commences as early as the fifth month. As an agent in developing desirable social relations, smiling is a key element in securing positive environmental reinforcement.

Bower (1977) has attempted to move beyond these general observations and notes that smiling has a history. Smiles of unknown origin appear soon after birth and are usually designated as "false" smiles because they lack the emotional warmth of the true smile. By three weeks the human female voice elicits a brief, real smile. By six weeks the true social smile appears, especially in response to the human face. Bower flatly states that babies smile at a conceptual age of six weeks, regardless of chronological age.

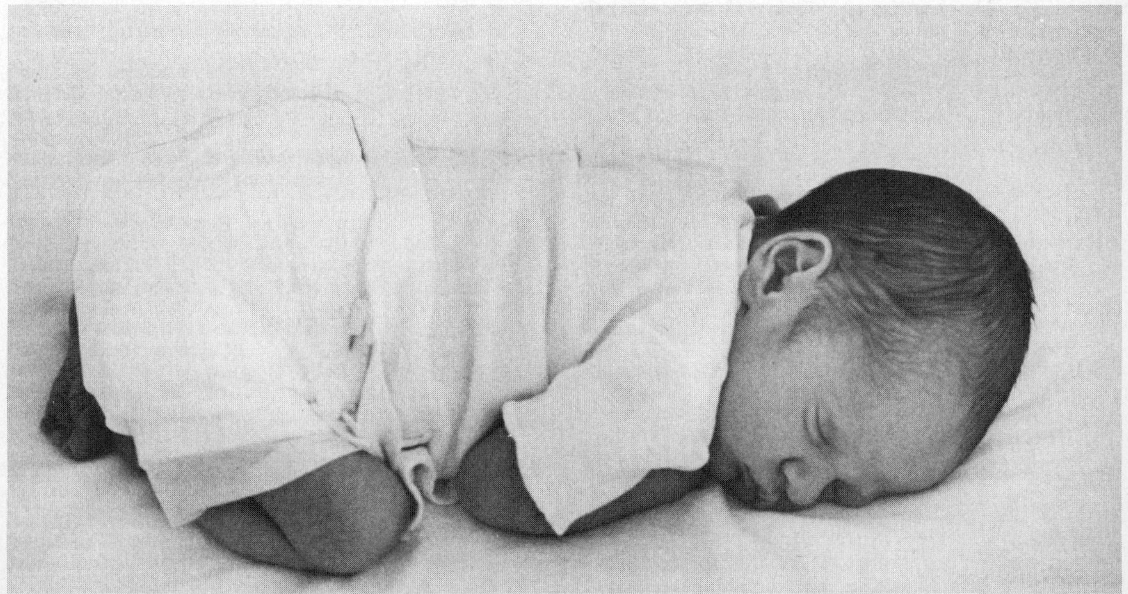

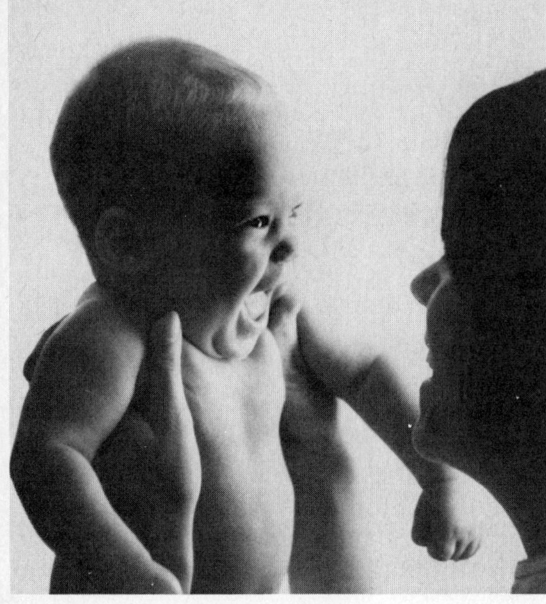

Bower then asks what causes infants to smile. He offers several explanations.

1. Infants smile at human beings around them.
2. Infants smile at any high contrast stimuli, which elicits attention from those around them and causes the infant to link the human face with pleasure.
3. Infants smile at discovering a relationship between their behavior and events in the external world.

Bower concludes his essay by noting that perhaps all of these explanations are correct—that each smile suits a different situation. Bower calls his essay, "The Strange Case of the Smile."

Summary—The Infant

Although we must guard against the seduction of developmental cliches, it would be negligent not to stress the importance of infancy for future development. It is a time of enormous growth and thus also a time of extreme vulnerability. Malnutrition and environmental deprivation can produce long-lasting effects. If you picture the helplessness of the newborn with the relative sophistication of the two-year-old, the results of cognitive, perceptual, and psychomotor growth are unmistakable.

Two-year-olds know who they are and they understand a great deal about their world, especially their relationship to it and their ability to cope with it. If they have encountered love and understanding, they will develop a sense of trust and confidence, and a sense of control. All aspects of growth combine to form a capable, functional individual. Tanner (1978), speaking broadly of growth, states:

> It is like the weaving of a cloth whose design never repeats itself. The underlying threads, each coming from its reel at its own rhythm, interact with one another continuously, in a manner always highly regulated and controlled.

Table 3.2 is intended to help you to recapture a picture of infancy.

Havighurst (1972) believes that there are four developmental tasks of the period.

1. *Learning to Walk.* Most youngsters are ready to walk sometime between nine and fifteen months, since the nerves, bones, and muscles are now ready. Infants become toddlers by pulling themselves up, falling down, receiving support from others, and finally mastering a few tottering steps.

2. *Learning to Take Solid Foods.* During the second year the infant's digestive system is ready to assimilate solid foods, and weaning results in the cessation of sucking. The manner in which this is accomplished affects personality development, since it is an important stride toward independence.

3. *Learning to Talk.* Sounds distinct from crying emerge in the first few months, and by one year most children use single words. The

TABLE 3.2. Some Developmental Characteristics of Infancy

Age (months)	Height (in.)	Weight (lb.)	Language Development	Motor Development
3	24	13–14	cooing	supports head in prone position
6	26	17–18	babbling—single syllable sounds	sits erect when supported
9	28	20–22	repetition of sounds; signals emotions	stands with support
12	29.5	22–24	single words—*mama, dada*	walks when held by hand
18	32	25–26	3–50 words	grasps objects accurately, walks steadily
24	34	27–29	50–250 words, 2–3 word phrases	runs and walks up and down stairs

continuing process is an amazing phenomenon, not only for all that communication implies, but also for the sheer magnitude of the achievement. What language signifies—relationships with things and people, control over the environment, and the abstract side of human nature—testifies to its importance in human development. The verbally troubled child is at a serious disadvantage in society. (Language development is extensively treated in Chapter Nine.)

4. *Learning to Control the Elimination of Body Wastes.* Most parents expect their children to be toilet trained by the end of infancy. Physiologically most youngsters are ready to learn control; socially it is desirable; psychologically it may be traumatic unless parents are careful. If youngsters are punished for a behavior that they find difficult to master, their perception of the environment is affected, which may produce feelings of insecurity. The common sense of most adults results in a combination of firmness and understanding, thus helping youngsters master a key developmental task.

Problems of infancy usually relate to the mastery of these developmental tasks, which represent a combination of psychomotor, cognitive, and personality variables. For example, youngsters exhibiting early physiological difficulties may have a neurological deficit. Youngsters experiencing troubles during toilet training may have, or be developing, personality problems. But the interactional nature of these tasks remains paramount: a neurological deficit may cause personality and cognitive problems, but personality and cognitive difficulties may give the impression of a neurological affliction. Also, in assessing infants' behavior, you must remember that some of these difficulties may simply be a developmental lag (slightly slower growth) that youngsters will gradually overcome.

Clarizio and McCoy (1976, p. 4) perhaps best summarize this need for caution by noting that all children have adjustment difficulties but that having problems is *not* pathological. They state:

> The expanding knowledge of children indicates that "abnormal" behavior among children is plentiful. We now recognize that no child is completely free from emotional difficulties. The prevalence of problems is, in fact, so widespread that some psychologists doubt that these deviations should be regarded as abnormal.

DISCUSSION QUESTIONS

1. SIDS has become a matter of national concern. Can you relate present knowledge of its causes to the work of Lipsitt and Zelazo? Does Zelazo's hypothesis support Lipsitt's views? In what way? How do they differ?
2. How did you interpret the visual cliff experiments? Do you agree with the relationship between depth perception and locomotion? Why? How did you interpret Campos's studies? Is locomotion still a critical element in your answer? How would you explain the developmental shift in cardiac response?
3. Can you link hearing difficulties with behavioral problems? Using the work of Knobloch and Pasamanick, specify the problems that you think could result from the various symptoms they describe.
4. Bower's fascinating account of "the strange case of the smile" raises many questions. Assuming the chronology of the "true" smile is correct, which of the possible explanations do you believe is correct? Why? Is it more realistic to assume a combination of causes? How would you explain an infant's ability to recognize the many different situations that could cause smiling?

EARLY CHILDHOOD: CHARACTERISTICS AND MILESTONES

An interesting pattern appears when we compare the growth characteristics of the early childhood youngsters with those of infants. (An earlier warning bears repetition here: any description of the normal child, whether it is physical, cognitive, or affective, ignores the influence of either enrichment or deprivation, thus masking either temporary or permanent behavioral alterations.) Note the different kinds of acceleration and deceleration in Tables 3.2 and 3.3.

Table 3.2 illustrates a tremendous growth surge during the first two years: an average height gain of about fourteen inches and weight gain of about twenty pounds. Language development apparently proceeds much more slowly. Table 3.3 traces a different pattern: a height gain of ten or twelve inches and a weight gain of seventeen or eighteen pounds. Language development, however, has accelerated sharply, which may reflect the growth spurt of the brain's cerebellum during these years. (Chapter Six offers a detailed discussion of these nervous system changes.)

What is likewise apparent from a comparison of these two tables is the early childhood youngster's increasing ability to cope with the more demanding stimuli that the environment now affords. Speaking, reading, and writing are abstract tasks to match growing cognitive competence, while jumping, throwing, and drawing demonstrate increasing muscular control. A clear picture emerges from these data: the developing child has boundless energy, discernible bodily control, budding mental ability, a tangible sense of self, and a dawning recognition of societal restrictions. It is an almost unequaled time for optimism, joy, and learning.

Physical and Motor Development

As an example of the slowed growth rate, Smart and Smart (1978) note that while dou-

TABLE 3.3. Some Developmental Characteristics of Early Childhood

Age (years)	Height (in.)	Weight (lb.)	Language Development	Motor Development
2½	36	30	Identifies object by use (vocabulary of 450 words)	Can walk on tiptoes; can jump with both feet off floor
3	38	32	Answers questions, brief sentences; may recite television commercials; vocabulary of 900 words	Can stand on one foot; jumps from bottom of stairs; rides tricycle
3½	39	34	Begins to build sentences; confined to concrete objects; vocabulary of 1220 words	Continues to improve 3-year skills; begins to play with others
4	41	36	Names and counts several objects; uses conjunctions; understands prepositions; vocabulary of 1540 words	Walks downstairs, one foot to step; skips on one foot; throws ball overhand
4½	42	38	Mean length of utterance (morphemes) 4.5 words; vocabulary of 1870 words	Hops on one foot; dramatic play; copies squares
5	43	41	Begins to show language mastery; uses words apart from specific situation; vocabulary of 2100 words	Skips, alternating feet; walks straight line; stands for longer periods on one foot
5½	45	45	Asks meanings of words; begins to use more complex sentences of five or six words; vocabulary of 2300 words	Draws recognizable person; continues to develop throwing skill
6	46	48	Good grasp of sense of sentences; uses more complex sentences; vocabulary of 2600 words	Jumps easily; throws ball overhead very well; stands on each foot alternately

bling a boy's height at age two will give an approximation of his adult height, it takes another fourteen or fifteen years to reach that height. Increase in physical size is closely linked to nutrition, and malnourished youngsters in underdeveloped countries usually manifest height and weight retardation. Bloom (1964) has strikingly demonstrated the influence of different environmental conditions on height in Figure 3.1.

In Figure 3.1 the Tudderham and Snyder group probably represent advantageous growth conditions; the Driezen nutritive failure and control groups are ethnically identical youngsters from the same geographic region whose main distinction is adequate nutrition. What is especially startling about the differences between the two extreme groups (abundance and deprivation) is the timing. Trace each height line to age fifteen; note the wide difference between the height figures (160 to 174 centimeters—over five inches). During the early childhood period, however, the difference is much less, suggesting, perhaps, the resiliency of these years and the possibility of reversing damage to the organism.

As Smart and Smart (1978) state, the rate of tissue growth also changes. Fat growth, which accumulated rapidly during the first nine months, slows until the youngster of six has changed from a rotund infant into a slim child. Muscle growth differs sharply from that of fat: a slow beginning followed by a slow increase until puberty. (Remember that these patterns are for most youngsters; there are always exceptions.) The authors comment that by kindergarten or first grade these youngsters more closely resemble children in higher grades than they do their younger brothers and sisters.

Tracing the pattern of motor development, Cratty (1970) employs the following categories.

1. *Running.* While the eighteen-month-old child has a hurried walk, the true run appears between two and three years. By five and six years, youngsters run rapidly (about 11.5 feet per second), employing considerable arm action.

2. *Jumping.* At about eighteen months, youngsters step off a low object with one foot, hesitating slightly before placing it on the ground. At two years, youngsters use what Cratty calls "the two-feet takeoff." Soon they begin to jump over low barriers, and by five years they are skillful jumpers (they can broad jump three feet and hurdle one-foot objects).

3. *Hopping, Skipping, Galloping.* Hopping may be on one foot in place, using alternate feet, or hopping for distance. Sometime from three to four years youngsters can hop from one to three steps on their preferred foot and by five years they can extend hopping to about ten steps. Girls acquire this skill slightly earlier and more successfully than boys. Skillful skipping and galloping appears between six and seven years.

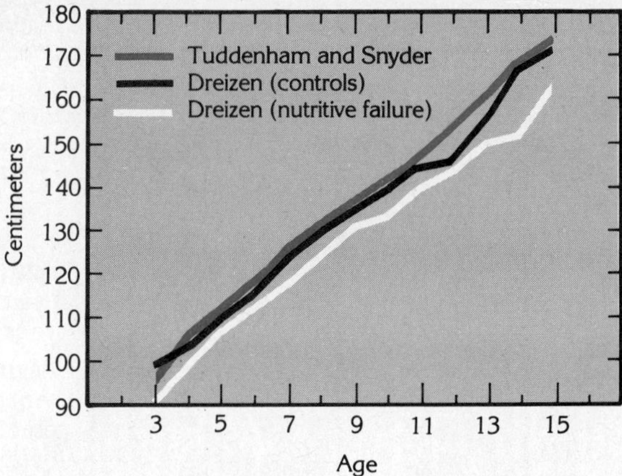

FIGURE 3.1. Height Growth Under Different Environmental Conditions—Males.

From Benjamin S. Bloom, *Stability and Change in Human Characteristics.* New York: John Wiley, 1964.

4. *Balancing.* Balancing, a measure of nervous system integrity, appears quite early. Three-year-olds can walk a reasonably straight line. Five-year-olds can maintain control while standing on one foot with their arms folded. Girls are slightly superior on this task.

The physical picture of the early childhood youngster is one of energy combined with growing motor skill. Smart and Smart (1978) believe that adequate rest and nutrition are critical, and they suggest guidance and the establishment of a routine to avoid problems. For example, to reconcile a rambunctious child to sleep, parents should minimize stimulation by an easily recognized program: washing, tooth brushing, story telling, gentle but firm pressure to sleep. Careful and thoughtful adult care should prevent undue difficulties.

Perceptual Development

Satisfactory explanations of perceptual development remain elusive. While the more diffuse perceptual reactions of infants are detailed in Chapter Five, our concern here is to identify the growing perceptual sophistication of children. Eleanor Gibson (1969, p. 3) defines perception as follows:

> Perception, functionally speaking, is the process by which we obtain first hand information about the world around us. It has a phenomenal aspect, the awareness of events presently occurring in the organism's immediate surroundings. It also has a responsive aspect; it entails discriminative, selective response to the stimuli in the immediate environment. . . . Perception is selective by nature. But the extent of selectivity at birth varies with species. In man, a rather gross selectivity at birth becomes progressively refined with development and experience.

Gibson's definition contains two ideas that are particularly pertinent to child development and that will guide our discussion. First is the phenomenal feature of perception; that is, there is something of *us* in our interpretation of stimuli; our response is not purely objective. Second is Gibson's belief in the progressive refinement of perception, which clearly implies perceptual changes with age.

The real world and the perceived world differ, since we cannot attend to all possible stimuli and therefore we tend to add to or subtract from—that is, distort—those stimuli to which we actually attend. For example, children and adults may see a similar stimulus, perhaps a hole in a gutter, but react quite differently. The child may simply ignore it; the stimulus is essentially meaningless. The adult views the hole and pictures water dripping down the side of a house, possibly causing internal damage to ceilings and walls. The percepts each forms are composed of many previous associations with similar stimuli, which helps to explain the age differences in perception. If previous similar experiences are lacking, children cannot meaningfully organize and interpret stimuli.

With age, individuals see what they expect to see because of experience, learning, and motivation, which help to produce perceptual constancies and enable us to move through our world with feelings of relative certainty. You do not constantly have to examine the flat top and each of the four legs to know that this is a table that will support your books. But these perceptual certainties can cause problems. Look quickly at the following figure and estimate which line is longer, AC or CB.

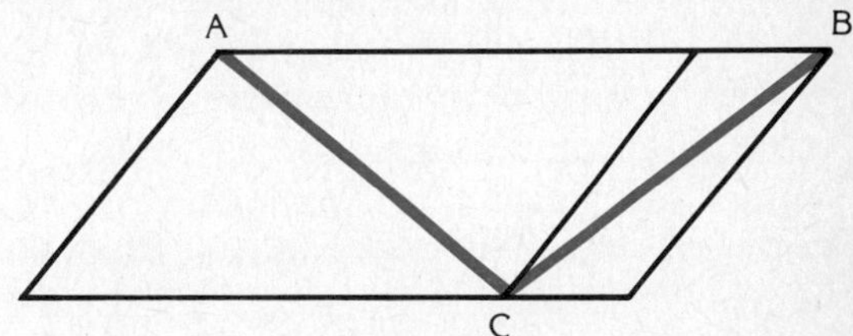

You probably identified AC as the longer line, but if you measure them, CB is definitely longer. Our experience with rectangles causes this confusion; we rarely see them from the top but rather from the side.

Our culture, in the way that it presents various experiences, tends to structure our perception. Consequently our perceptual world is *our* perceptual world and need not be *identical* with that of others. Even with perceptual differences, we see sufficient similarity to agree that a car is a car, a house is a house, or a book is a book, and that children evidence perceptual development.

Perceptual Refinement. Human development dictates changes in perception. As aging occurs, the organization and interpretation of information likewise changes because tasks become more abstract and the ability to master them reflects greater attention, accumulated experiences, additional learning, and different motivation. Gibson (1969) identifies three trends in perceptual development.

1. *Increasing Specificity of Discrimination.* Maturing organisms restrict their reactions to a stimulus; that is, they respond only to the true stimulus or a close approximation. Youngsters show a steady increase in the precision and consistency of their discriminations and they also manifest a constant reduction in the time needed to discriminate.

2. *The Optimization of Attention.* Gibson argues strongly that perception is an active process that changes developmentally. Children of the early childhood age are vigorously active, and their perceptual processes are now more searching than the passive perceptual responses of infancy: their eye movements, for example, no longer fixate on a single spot of an object but follow its contour, seeking distinctive features. They select needed information from complex stimuli, thus demonstrating attention to relevant and disregarding irrelevant stimuli. As Gibson notes, changes in ability to attend to wanted information and ignore the irrelevant occur with age.

3. *Increasing Economy in Information Pickup.* Combining the first two of these developmental trends helps to explain growing perceptual sophistication. Youngsters learn to discriminate an object by focusing on the fewest possible features that distinguish it. If they can isolate some invariant, that is, a feature that remains constant over time, they have drastically improved their perception of an object. They thus increase their ability to process several objects or events simultaneously because they see relationships and can form structures, which facilitates retention and economical recall.

It is difficult to track accurately the path of perceptual development, but it is well worth the effort, because as Gibson (1969, p. 2) states, nature does not turn out an infant with knowledge and strategies ready-made for perceiving the complexities of environmental stimuli. This ability develops with age.

Cognitive Development

Any account of cognitive development must recognize the brain's critical role in mental functioning. Although brain development is a major topic of Chapter 6, its relationship to cognitive growth deserves mention here. Smart and Smart (1978) state that during the early childhood period cortical cells increase in size and complexity, thus facilitating cognitive growth. Myelination, the appearance of a fatty substance around the neuron that aids the passage of nerve impulses, continues and seems to correlate with enhanced behavioral performance.

The brain undergoes a twenty percent increase in size during the early childhood period, from about seventy percent of its adult weight at two years to approximately ninety percent of its adult weight at six years. Figure 3.2 is a quick reminder of important brain parts and comparative size, illustrating the extremely large human cortical area.

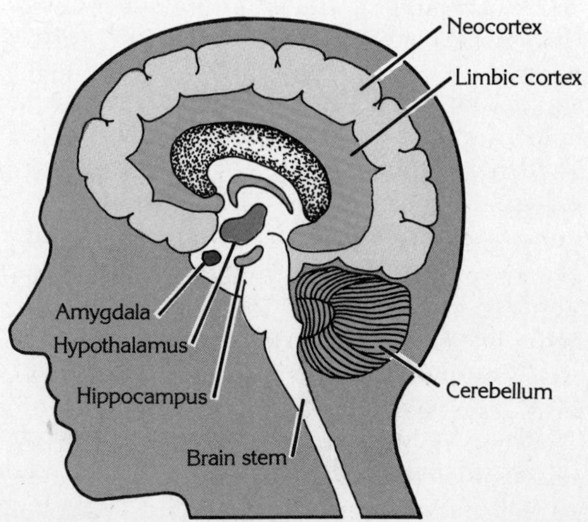

FIGURE 3.2. The Human Brain.

Steven Rose (1973, p. 164) cogently summarizes the relationship between brain growth and cognitive development when he states:

> Between birth and adolescence a series of stages in development clearly occurs in parallel with the final touches to the brain structure itself, its increase in mass, connectivity, and so forth. Obviously one could not match each of these stages against a defined brain structural analog. The process is a gradual one, and a one-for-one matching of structure with behavioral observations is not necessary in order to make the general point that the growth of intellectual capacity in the human matches the anatomical and biochemical development of the brain when viewed ontogenetically, just as the growth of intellectual capacity matches that of brain complexity and, it was argued, neuronal connectivity, phylogenetically as well.

Thought in Early Childhood. When infancy ends children demonstrate the beginnings of representation; that is, they let one thing represent another. During early childhood youngsters acquire a growing ability to think about absent objects, persons, or events; they also use objects and activities in a symbolic manner (Smart and Smart, 1978). Language develops rapidly during these years and swiftly assumes a critical function in the thought process.

If you consider the demands made upon a child this age, you quickly sense a more sophisticated cognitive capacity. Youngsters are straining at the restrictions they encounter but they must comprehend the relationship between adult and child. They rapidly discover what behavior is permissible, which implies that they understand the relationships involved. Simultaneously, they are learning to manipulate their environment; that is, they use their developing mental ability to make demands, to play, and to learn. They inevitably encounter schooling, which ranges from play during the early years to demanding cognitive tasks during the later years of the period.

Perception sharpens, memory expands, and categorization widens to permit youngsters to cope with increasingly complex tasks. Reading is a good example. Mastery of the use of symbols and their translation commences now, and those youngsters who experience difficulty will be at a constant disadvantage in technological societies. These observations suggest that the richness and complexity of the thinking of early childhood youngsters is far greater than originally imagined.

Language in Early Childhood. Although language is treated separately and extensively in Chapter 9, its significant relationship to developing thought in the early childhood period deserves mention. Youngsters soon acquire their native language, a task of such scope and intricacy that its secrets have eluded investigators for centuries. During this period language figuratively "explodes"; that is, children proceed from hesitant beginnings to almost complete mastery by the end of the period (about seven years). All children learn their native language. At about the same age they manifest similar patterns of speech development, whether they live in a ghetto or in some wealthy suburb.

1. At about *three months,* children use intonations similar to those that they hear adults using.
2. At about *one year,* they begin to use recognizable words.
3. At about *four years,* they have mastered most of the incredibly complicated structure of their native tongue.
4. In two or three more years, at about *six or seven years,* they have mastered their language to such an extent that they can speak and understand sentences that they have never used or heard before.

This amazing accomplishment is compressed into a few years, the same years in which a child may have difficulty with subjects such as reading and mathematics. Yet for that same child language mastery comes easily and naturally.

Lenneberg (1967) has constructed an interesting chart that traces the appearance of single words, word combinations, and sentences. Sometime between twelve to eighteen months, children begin to use single words as sentences (holophrases); by two years, they utter two-word sentences; and usually by four years, they produce sentences of several words. The sequence is similar to that in Figure 3.3.

Around ten months children begin to use actual words and can usually follow simple directions; at about one year, or perhaps slightly older, they seem to grasp that words "mean" things, like people or objects. As children grow, it is difficult to specify how extensive their vocabulary may be. Do we mean spoken words only? Or do we include words that children may not use but clearly understand? By whatever criteria we may use, girls seem to surpass boys by about one year of development until the age of eight.

By the age of four, children are well immersed in the linguistic world. And it is a linguistic world. Recall that no two sentences you speak or read are identical, aside from cliches or deliberate emulation. How can this be so? Farb (1973) provides a dramatic illustration of the staggering *quantitative* aspects of language. In our language we primarily use nouns, verbs, adjectives, and adverbs. If English possessed only one thousand nouns (boat, car, dog) and only one thousand verbs (run, shout, throw), the number of possible two-word sentences ("Dog run," etc.) would be 1000^2 or one million. But the same nouns could also be used as objects of the thousand verbs, as in "Man throw ball." So now we have possible three-word sentences of 1000^3 or one billion.

So much for a distressingly limited vocabulary. Almost all languages provide more than one thousand nouns and verbs, and we can also add possible adjectives, adverbs, prepositions, conjunctions, and articles. Think also of four-, eight-, and twenty-word sentences! It has been estimated that it would take ten trillion years to say all the possible English sentences that use only twenty words. Those of us whose heads ache when we have to make

FIGURE 3.3. Milestones in Language Acquisition.
From Eric Lenneberg, *Biological Foundations of Language.* New York: John Wiley, 1967.

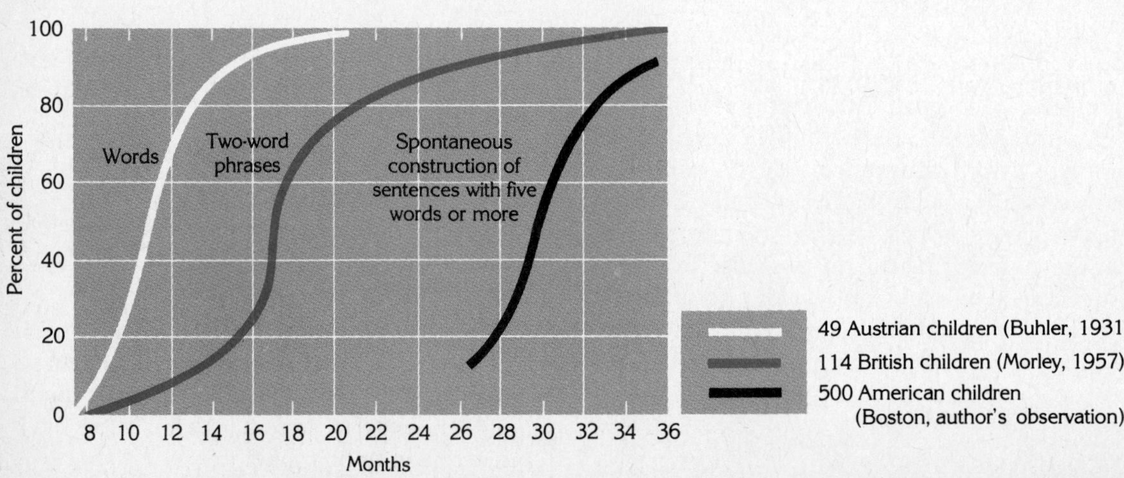

TABLE 3.4. The Acquisition of Language: Sound and Grammar

Sound	Grammar
Prelinguistic (acquiring sound control; after one year can vocalize all sounds)	Passive grammatical control (acquiring rules of grammar)
Period of passive control (distinguishes differences in sounds)	Beginning of grammatical regularity (about two years)
Use of meaningful words (preceded by decreased babbling)	Appearance of definite grammatical system (twenty-four to thirty months)
Sound system approximates that of the adult	Knowledge of basic language structure

change from a dollar bill will need to return to more manageable ideas.

As a result of these and similar studies, it is possible to sketch the observable characteristics of children's mastery of a first language. By the end of the first four years of life, children have mastered the essentials of this distinctively human attribute. For normal children, variations in rates of mastery are minute. In fact, this appears to be such a natural gift of childhood that many children master more than one language during their early years. Table 3.4 (after Ervin-Tripp and Miller, 1963) illustrates the pattern.

The pattern is almost identical for all children. By the end of the first year, children understand some speech, but we know almost nothing about this growth and comprehension. Cooing is gradually followed by consonant-vowel sequences, followed by babbling. During the middle of the second year, the average child begins to use sentences, not sentences that the adult would use, but strings of words that convey meaning.

The relationship of thought to language appears as vocabulary develops and the conceptual system changes. For example, children may use the word "father" to designate all men until they learn to apply it to one man and substitute another term for all men. Youngsters relate words by meanings and grammar instead of by sounds. Each word more rapidly elicits other words, and associations and meanings become richer and more expressive as language and thought constantly supplement each other.

Summary—Early Childhood

The picture of early childhood youngsters that emerges from this overview is one of vigor, energy, and rapid learning. The increasingly formidable tasks that they encounter are matched by their growing intellectual sophistication. Memory, perception, conceptualization, and problem solving behavior show discernible development as youngsters learn to cope with an ever widening social network of individuals and institutions.

Havighurst (1973) identifies four major developmental tasks of the period.

1. *Learning Sex Differences and Sexual Modesty.* These are significant years in the acquisition of a sex identity and the acquisition of an appropriate sex role. Youngsters learn far more about sex than anatomical differences; they learn the meaning of maleness and femaleness as it applies to them. With this basis they can then gradually assume the desirable features of a sex role that their society values. It is a critical task for youngsters, one whose consequences will follow them for life.

2. *Forming Concepts and Learning Language to Describe Social and Physical Reality.* As noted, cognitive growth and language learning dominate this period. Havighurst comments that to further mental development, children must discover regularities and

make generalizations, but such cognitive growth depends on a satisfactory language environment.

3. *Getting Ready to Read.* Youngsters are physically ready to learn by the latter years of the period because of the steady maturation of the nervous system. Manipulating symbols is vital for successful adjustment in an industrial society. Reading reflects the integration of developmental tasks as youngsters mature: society expects five- and six-year-old children to read; youngsters are physically capable of reading; psychologically, they *want* to read.

4. *Learning to Distinguish Right and Wrong and Beginning to Develop a Conscience.* Children of this age must learn to live with restrictions; rules assume a greater role in their lives. Consequently, society, initially represented by their parents and teachers, and perhaps religion, identifies what is good and what is bad. As cognitive development continues and as youngsters assimilate their own developing views of right and wrong, they slowly form a personally enlightened conscience that will guide them throughout life.

During the early years of the period, children's drive toward control of their environment comes into conflict with adult restraints. Consequently problems such as negativism, withdrawal, and difficulty with toilet training frequently occur, and the manner of their resolution strongly shapes a child's self-concept. Herbert (1974, p. 125) comments that the love and affection of the parent for the child during this difficult time (about two to three years of age), and their reactions to impulsive, and what may seem defiant, behavior contribute to the youngster's increasingly sophisticated evolution of a self-image.

During the latter years of the period, children's problems often reflect an uncertainty about their skill to cope with growing environmental demands. If children's responding cognitive capabilities blend with satisfaction of their personality needs, adjustment to parents, school, and society continues harmoniously. Using Erikson's interpretation of initiative, Herbert believes that the major obstacle to adjustment is overly strict discipline, which interferes with spontaneity and reality testing, and leads to feelings of excessive guilt that appear as the more common problems of the period: nightmares, phobias, and anxiety states.

DISCUSSION QUESTIONS

1. Discuss the implications of Figure 3.1. Are youngsters more vulnerable to environmental deficits than adolescents? Using this figure, could you argue for the reversibility of early deprivation? Consider this question carefully; it is critical both politically and economically. To answer thoughtfully, what other variables must you identify?
2. Is there a pattern to perceptual development? How can parents and teachers facilitate the process? Why is it important? Include both general environmental and educational implications in your answer.
3. Do you agree that cognitive development demands more subtle analysis than intelligence tests? Do cognitive style techniques meet this demand? Why? Is there a danger that one may quickly bypass the cognitive and focus instead on the personality components of a child's responses?
4. Consider the language explosion that occurs during the early childhood period. It happens at about the same time to all children of all cultures. What does it mean for a child's relationship to the environment? In your answer, link language to thought.

MIDDLE CHILDHOOD: CHARACTERISTICS AND MILESTONES

Physical growth continues; strength increases; cognitive capacity deepens. But as interesting as are these phenomena, all experiences pale in comparison to that great milestone: school entrance. A new world with new challenges opens. There are different adult authority figures; there is a sudden increase in the number of peers who are contacted daily; there are new and inescapable behavioral restrictions. Adjustment is difficult, but is also a must. Most children adapt quickly and well, and what was initially an overwhelming, perhaps frightening, experience soon becomes something to be enjoyed or at least tolerated. Middle childhood youngsters are well equipped to embark on this novel adventure. Table 3.5 illustrates the major characteristics of the period.

This is a particularly interesting table, one that reflects continuing behavioral integration and complexity. It becomes impossible in middle childhood to differentiate specific developmental changes. For example, language can no longer serve as a measure of development, since extent of vocabulary or use of sentences is now incalculable. Consequently, investigators use other behavioral items to assess growth.

TABLE 3.5. Some Developmental Characteristics of Middle Childhood

Age (years)	Height (in.)		Weight (lb.)		Stanford-Binet Test Items	Motor Development
	girl	boy	girl	boy		
7	48	49	52	53	Child can detect in what way two things are similar: apple, peach	Child has good balance; can hop and jump accurately
8	51	51	60	62	Child can read a paragraph of seven or eight sentences and recall five or six major ideas	Boys and girls show equal grip strength; great interest in physical games
9	52	53	70	70	Child can observe card with two designs and after ten seconds draw the designs' main features	Psychomotor skills such as throwing, jumping, running show marked improvement
10	54	55	74	79	Child can repeat as many as 60 digits	Boys become accurate in throwing and catching a small ball; running continues to improve
11	57	57	85	85	Child can find similarities among three things: rose, potato, tree	Boys can throw a ball about 95 feet; girls can run about 17.5 feet per second
12	60	59	95	95	Child can recognize absurdities: we saw icebergs that had been melted by the Gulf Stream	Boys can run about 18.5 feet per second; dodge ball popular with girls

While there is slow, steady growth in these years, by the end of the period girls may begin to surpass boys physically as they enter their adolescent growth spurt. Observing a mixed group of twelve-year-olds, one is struck by male immaturity and female maturity. These physical differences can have social consequences; that is, girls, aware of their obvious physical maturity, feel ill at ease with their peers and may turn to older groups for companionship.

Middle childhood youngsters are now surrounded by an abstract world: reading, mathematics, decision making, problem solving. Their cognitive growth matches these tasks and they easily discover logical relationships and appreciate the absurdity in an illogical relationship. Learning experiences should match this steady cognitive progression; otherwise excessively abstract tasks during the initial years of middle childhood could produce frustration and failure.

Physical and Motor Development

Smart and Smart (1978, p. 29) state that middle childhood is characterized by slow growth, good health, and work that encourages feelings of adequacy. Physical growth is slow but steady until the end of the period when girls may spurt. The interaction between heredity and environment is apparent in cross-cultural studies of height and weight. For example, in an exhaustive survey, Meredith (1969) gathered physical data on eight-year-olds from many parts of the world.

He notes that the samples are described racially, socioeconomically, and often nutritionally. For the decade studied (1950–1960), differences in the mean standing height were as much as nine inches and differences in mean weight ranged up to twenty-five pounds. Meredith's findings strongly suggest caution in generalizing from these data. Variables such

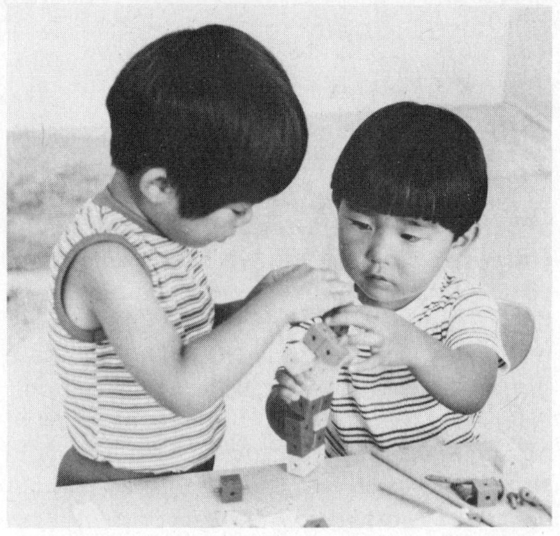

as genetic influence, health conditions, and nutrition cause wide fluctuations in the data. Two middle childhood youngsters may show considerable physical variation and yet both are perfectly normal.

Healthy active children of this age show considerable motor skill. Cratty (1970) states that children from six to twelve years are notably successful in manipulating their environment. Motor skill is obvious. Myelination has progressed steadily; long bone growth proceeds rapidly; both boys and girls exhibit muscular power and coordination.

No discussion of middle childhood physical and motor development is complete without mentioning the role of sports. For many youngsters, perhaps a sizable majority including girls as well as boys, extraordinary status accompanies success in sports. Concomitantly, sports, even at this level, have become highly organized. Since maturation and motor development vary enormously among children, some youngsters are almost instantly banned from participation. Even those sports that are organized to include all youngsters inevitably become self-selecting; that is, no one has to tell youngsters that they are inadequate. They know.

The following diagram illustrates the procedure.

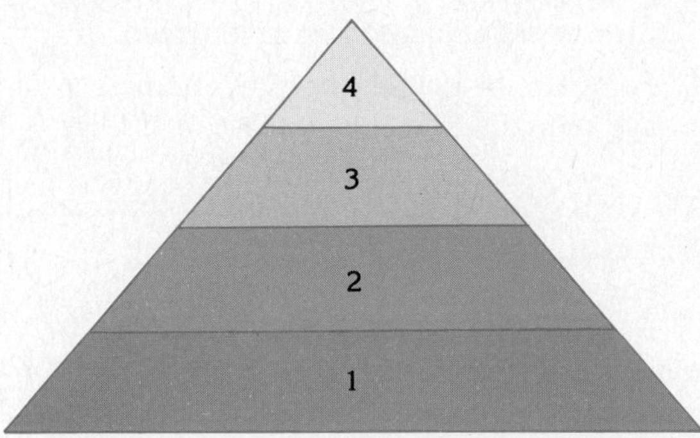

Each sport has its own label for each level. For example, in little league baseball, level one is the "minors," while in youth hockey, it is the "mite" division. Each level of the pyramid represents a decrease in the number of participants; either they are "cut" from the teams or they themselves realize further effort is futile. The damage to self-esteem can be substantial, and those adults around such children should endeavor to cushion the shock of what the youngsters undoubtedly feel is failure, rejection, and shame. It is a difficult time for these children, and while sports can be a healthy, happy experience for most, those concerned with the organization and management of youth activities should give additional thought to wider participation.

Cognitive Development

Tracing responses on intelligence test items indicates the middle childhood youngster's ability to interpret and use the abstract. Although intelligence and intelligence test scores are not our primary concern here, it is interesting to note the high correlations between IQ scores during the middle childhood period and adult intelligence as measured at age seventeen, which range from .77 at the beginning of the period to .93 at the end.

These data indicate that cognitive ability clearly emerges during this period and remains a decisive element in mental performance. Elkind (1971), analyzing mental development during these years, concludes that perception, language, learning, reasoning, and problem solving are extremely significant. Children grow perceptually as they change from focusing on one aspect of an event to exploring systematically the entire field. Elkind believes that as exploration develops, children rearrange and integrate the various elements of the field.

Both perception and cognition are furthered as language is internalized and provides additional organization and direction to thought. Elkind believes that language is a mediating process that aids learning, since labeling a category enables youngsters to include more items in that category. Internalization (both of language and action) also aids reasoning because youngsters no longer are forced to respond overtly to problems—they can think about them, weigh one potential response against another, and select the most plausible. This is a major change in behavior, one that causes Elkind (1971, p. 63) to note that the growth of understanding is always a modification or replacement of previously held notions and is never a simple addition of new information.

A major force in developing cognitive ability is the discernible improvement in memorization ability. Reexamine Figure 3.2 and note the hippocampal area, the seat of memory. This tiny structure, about one inch long, seems to transfer short- to long-term memory. Injury to the hippocampal area affects long-term memory; people cannot retain new information for more than a few hours.

DEVELOPMENTAL PROBLEMS

Today there is a growing tendency to place youngsters with emotional problems in as normal a setting as possible. This has enormous implications for parents, teachers, nurses, recreation workers, and almost all those who work with children. Children bring their problems to the classroom with the hope and expectation that, with help, they will be able to find their own solution.

As an aid for those who work with children, Anthony (1970) has provided a bird's-eye view of behavior disorders by age and sex. Admittedly a quite general overview, it nevertheless provides insight into critical times for the appearance of developmental problems. For a year, Anthony examined terminations from clinics and discovered that the termination rate for boys was almost twice that of girls. For boys, the highest rates were between ten and fourteen years; for girls, it was between fifteen and seventeen years.

Anthony then reports what could be an extremely significant finding: there were two distinct periods of clinic usage for both boys and girls.

1. For boys, there was one peak at about nine years, and another at fourteen.
2. For girls, there was a slight increase at age ten, and marked increase at fifteen.

For both sexes, the rate was much lower at eleven and twelve years.

The number of boys exceeded girls for every problem treated. Anxiety was a commonly reported difficulty for both boys and girls, but depression increased noticeably for adolescent girls. Without dramatizing every difficulty a child might experience, we must be sensitive to these times and provide support and encouragement when needed. These findings should alert us to the increased possibility of problems at ages nine to ten (preadolescence) and fourteen to fifteen (midadolescence).

As the middle childhood youngster faces the multiple challenges of the period, cognitive capacity must also increase to facilitate coping. Storage of information becomes critical as a prerequisite to reasoning and problem solving. The abilities that we have traced in infancy and early childhood—attention, perceptual discrimination, the beginnings of representation—now join to help youngsters *encode* (organize) and store information which they can later retrieve when needed. Middle childhood youngsters demonstrate a notable—even qualitative—difference in their thinking.

Summary—Middle Childhood

With school entrance, youngsters' lives change. They must adjust to peers and pressure, thus furthering unique personality adjustment. Tasks become more abstract, both challenging and aiding intellectual development. Physically, it is usually a good time for youngsters.

Havighurst (1972) identifies three great "outward pushes" of middle childhood.

1. The social thrust out of the home and into the peer group;
2. The physical thrust into the world of games and work;

3. The mental thrust into the world of adult concepts, logic, symbolism, and communication.

These three growth thrusts are responsible for several developmental tasks (some of which we have discussed): learning the physical skills necessary for ordinary games (a task of growing importance for girls); building wholesome attitudes toward oneself; learning to get along with peers; learning an appropriate sex role (what it means to be a boy or girl in a modern society); developing fundamental skills in reading, writing, and calculating; developing concepts necessary for daily living; developing a conscience and sense of morality; achieving personal independence; and developing attitudes toward social groups and institutions. Mastery of these developmental tasks produces children who can cope, reason, and adjust to environmental demands in a personally and socially satisfying manner.

Difficulty with the developmental tasks of the period often causes problems. Herbert (1974) states that middle childhood youngsters are as amenable as they ever will be to learning, direction, and inspiration by others. Problems arise from maladjustment, excessive competition, personal limitations, or conditions that cause failure, inferiority feelings, or poor work habits.

School phobia, that irrational fear of attending school, may affect some children. Whether these are school-related or stem from a child's personality is a question requiring individual analysis. Middle childhood youngsters frequently experience fear and anxiety which peaks at eleven years and which they normally outgrow. If fear is widespread and adversely affects daily functioning, remedial measures may be necessary. Clarizio and McCoy (1976) offer a timely warning here: "All children have adjustment difficulties, but having problems is *not* identical with pathology."

DISCUSSION QUESTIONS

1. Discuss the cognitive implications of Table 3.5. Why is language development missing? What does the progression of intelligence test responses suggest?
2. What are the implications of the height and weight studies? Do they influence your beliefs about the relative impact of heredity and environment? How much can you generalize from these data?
3. Expand on the discussion of sports. Realistically, can changes be made in the organization of youth athletics? If not, what should be the role of parents, coaches, and other interested adults with regard to encouragement, support, and acceptance of failure and success? Do not underestimate the significance of sports in the lives of middle childhood boys and girls.
4. Some investigators believe that the cognitive changes that occur during middle childhood are the most significant qualitative changes in a person's life. Can you give reasons for this belief? What cognitive abilities do you think are most decisive in shaping these changes? Why?

ADOLESCENCE: CHARACTERISTICS AND MILESTONES

Experts have written millions of words about them; investigators have studied, tested, and observed them; philosophers have speculated about them. Yet the words, studies, and speculations retain an air of uncertainty, as if adolescence were a mysterious, magic time that only adolescents can understand. Why? Is it actually adolescence, or our perception of it that causes uncertainty?

Kenneth Keniston (1970), in an insightful analysis of adolescence, states that most modern societies have made adolescence a separate, yet integral part of development with several major themes that dominate growth during this period.

1. Tension between self and society, as a youth struggles for self identity, a struggle that may produce conflict with society.
2. Pervasive ambivalence, a desire for independence coupled with a desire to be effective within society.
3. Wary probe, an interesting expression coined by Keniston to illustrate the adolescent's testing of the adult world (it is often joined with self-probe).
4. Estrangement and omnipotentiality, in which feelings of isolation alternate with feelings of absolute freedom.
5. Youth-specific identities, which are usually temporary roles that inspire intense commitment: hippie, radical, athlete.
6. Youthful countercultures, a grouping with other youths in a deliberate attempt to remain apart from society (Keniston, 1970).

These terms reflect the extension of adolescence as a time of learning to adjust to a complex culture. Such sophisticated knowledge has often been achieved at the cost of social problems. Physical, sexual, and social maturity are at odds with technological innocence, and as the age of puberty has declined (menstruation in North American females now occurs at about twelve and one-half years), personal and social tensions have grown.

Girls begin their adolescent growth spurt about two years earlier than boys and become taller, heavier, about as strong, and a good deal more sexually mature than boys. Maturity of the reproductive system accompanies the growth spurt, which explains the differences in sexual maturity, and which is a striking example of individual differences between sexes and within sex. For example, some girls begin their spurt shortly before eight years of age and others do not begin until after thirteen years. In a recent study (Faust, 1977), the variation in age at onset of the adolescent growth spurt for boys and girls combined was from 7.52 to 15.73 years. This is a stunning example, one that helps to explain the confusion that many adolescents feel. A small, immature twelve-year-old, seeking more physically mature, perhaps more popular peers could easily develop feelings of inadequacy and inferiority.

Cognitive Development

Adolescent thought becomes flexible; it can transcend immediate stimuli (it is not "stimulus bound") and explore possibilities and grapple with contradictions. Memory span lengthens as adolescents master memory techniques and transfer critical information from short-term to long-term storage. Logical reasoning becomes symbolic as the ability to abstract increases the range and application of thinking. This new and powerful cognitive tool qualitatively changes the adolescent's world.

Enhanced cognitive capacity affects adolescents' social and affective lives. Intense self-interest reflects the ability to consider the future; idealism reflects the ability to compare what is with what should be; emotional peer relationships reflect the ability to detect shortcomings in parental behavior. There is no dichotomy among the various aspects of behavior (cognitive, affective, psychomotor); integration is the key to understanding development.

Neimark (1975, p. 587) summarizes adolescent thought as follows:

> . . . the adolescent can devote full time and energy to perfecting developing skills: physical, social, and intellectual. As a formal operational thinker, he (she) is freed from the bonds of personal experience and present time to explore ideas, ideals, roles, beliefs, theories, commitments, and all sorts of possibilities at the level of thought. At the level of thought, the adolescent, aware of the arbitrariness of priorities and institutions, can create more desirable alternatives for himself (herself) and for society.

We may summarize the developmental tasks of the period as follows:

> 1. *Achieving new and more mature relations with age-mates of both sexes.* During these years, boys become men and girls become women. They become members of the adult society working with others and establishing a pattern of sexual behavior. Group approval is probably more important during adolescence than during any other time.
>
> 2. *Achieving a masculine or feminine social role.* Adolescents achieve sexual maturity during this period, but culturally defined sex roles are changing and many girls now wish to combine marriage and career. Contraception and abortion have radically altered many girls' lives, so that achieving an acceptable feminine sexual role is more complicated.
>
> 3. *Accepting one's physique and using the body effectively.* There are extensive physical changes in adolescence, so teenagers need sympathetic advice about early and late maturity to help them accept and understand their physique.
>
> 4. *Achieving emotional independence of parents and other adults.* Adolescents begin the task of freeing themselves from childhood parental dependence. Although most authorities focus upon the physical and sexual aspects of adolescence, a satisfactory relationship with parents dominates much of an adolescent's thinking and some adolescents never fully reconcile dependence and independence. Ask any group of college students what their major problems are, and invariably parental relations is one of the first few mentioned.
>
> 5. *Preparing for marriage and family life.* This task relates to that of achieving a satisfactory sex role; times are changing, roles are changing, but most see marriage as a desirable state. The challenge today is to prepare for its varied nature.
>
> 6. *Preparing for an economic career.* Given the importance of occupations, considerable care and thought is required to prepare for an enjoyable and productive career.
>
> 7. *Acquiring a set of values and an ethical system as a guide to behavior—developing an ideology.*
>
> 8. *Desiring and achieving socially responsible behavior.* Both of these tasks indicate the growing maturity of adolescents, their concern with the abstract, and willingness, even eagerness, to discover personally and socially acceptable values that will permit them to function as mature adults in a complex society. (Travers, 1979)

Aside from deeply disturbed personalities who engage in destructive personal and social behavior, the problems of most adolescents revolve around these developmental tasks. Identity, relations with peers and parents, sexual behavior, future educational or occupational directions, alcohol and drug usage can produce frustration and problem behavior. Neumeyer (1961) classifies the causes of unacceptable behavior as follows:

1. the biological and psychological characteristics of individuals that contribute to delinquency (poor health, mental retardation);
2. the character and behavior facets of personality (attitudes, values, alcoholic and sexual problems);
3. home and family conditions (broken homes, family maladjustments, tension in the home);
4. the influence of peers (types of friends, juvenile gangs, community tolerance of adolescent behavior);
5. media influence;
6. population distribution;
7. lack of personal and societal control.

Problems do not appear instantly, nor are they always antisocial. Children's problems, whether physical, emotional, mental, or social, often have their roots in the early years of childhood. However, there are instances in which the death of a parent, or an accident, or a move to a new home and neighborhood can trigger problem behavior. But even in these situations, there are early warning signs that concerned adults should note and act on immediately.

A parent, a teacher, a counselor, a nurse, or a religious adviser each can use training and good common sense to treat these first symptoms. It is here that the battle may be won, lost, or at least identified. If the problem continues to grow more intense after the attention of concerned adults, then expert help is needed. Anthony (1970) has prepared a list of ages with their associated problems; some of his categories are as follows.

Ages	*Problems*
1. Three to four (preschool and kindergarten)	Phobias, nightmares, speech problems, masturbation, anxiety states
2. Six to eleven (elementary school)	School problems, school phobias, obsessive reactions, tics, depression
3. Twelve to seventeen (junior-senior high school)	Identity diffusion, delinquency, acting-out disorders, schizophrenia

And Wattenberg (1966) speaks of four patterns of behavior that are identifiable quite early.

1. Explosive, unsocialized, aggressive boys from rejecting homes. This is a very difficult group to treat.
2. Boys and girls who manifest a purposeless type of delinquent behavior, usually the children of demanding or vacillating parents. This group responds well to counseling.
3. Boys and girls with weak consciences and good relations with their peers from high-delinquency areas. They tend to "go along with" friends.
4. The "cool-cat" personality, boy or girl, who manipulates others; a rather shadowy group.

Whether categorization is by list or ages, symptoms appear early and alert adults should look for the reasons and act on them.

Adolescence is a time when the potential for problems abounds; changing bodies plus changing societal expectations can be an explosive mixture. Yet it need not be so. Concerned, thoughtful adults who treat adolescents as "nearly equals" can forestall most problems. This view is idealistic, perhaps, but as modern societies see the need for responsible citizens and also see a corresponding loss of talent and its inevitable resulting social diminution, the care, maintenance, and control of adolescents will become a primary concern. There is an old cliche—true as most cliches are—that any society expecting trouble with its adolescents gets it.

DISCUSSION QUESTIONS

1. Comment on Keniston's adolescent themes. Are they realistic? Can you identify others? Are these persistent themes, or do they change with each decade?
2. The physical growth data suggest quite different roles, activities, and interest for males and females. Identify several of these. Do parents, schools, and institutions consider these differences?
3. What specific problems can you associate with each of the developmental tasks? Be specific. Are there problems you are now experiencing that you can trace to unresolved adolescent issues? Why have they lingered? (As an example, most college freshmen and sophomores still feel uncertain about the dependent-independent issue with their parents.)
4. In analyzing adolescent problems, do you prefer to use some scheme such as Havighurst's developmental tasks and identify the problems that might arise from each category, or Anthony's listing of categories that can be applied to adolescence? Why? Which do you think produces most meaningful results? Defend your position.

Data concerning human development have accumulated so rapidly that analysis into aspects of development is almost a necessity. That is, research and theory focuses, usually intensely, on a topic: physical, cognitive, emotional. Consequently, it is helpful to consider occasionally the total path of development from conception onward. This chapter attempts to answer a simple question: what are humans like at various times of development?

Using various developmental epochs—infancy, early childhood, middle childhood, adolescence—it is possible to identify outstanding characteristics that are common to all. For example, infants grow rapidly, quickly display distinctive personalities, and show early signs of cognition. Sometime during middle childhood, all youngsters show greater motor coordination and demonstrate increasing abstract ability; all adolescents experience a discernible growth spurt. But there are also milestones: memory becomes apparent during the last half of the first year; during middle childhood youngsters show a qualitative difference in their thinking (logical thought appears); adolescents become sexually mature.

SUMMARY

Infant growth is usually smooth and swift, but the Sudden Infant Death Syndrome is causing increasing alarm.

Several infant abilities such as smiling, perceptual development, and the dimensions of memory still elude explanation.

There are some discernible trends in perceptual development during the early childhood years.

The use of cognitive style measures, as a technique of assessing intellectual adjustment, yields a rich interpretation of early childhood intelligence.

The language explosion occurs during early childhood, which poses a considerable challenge to language theorists.

Sports occupy a central role in the life of the middle childhood youngsters, with both desirable and undesirable consequences.

A major, qualitative change in thinking appears during middle childhood.

Adolescence, with all its trials, changes, and problems, should also be a time of promise and fulfillment.

SUGGESTED READINGS

BLOOM, BENJAMIN. *Stability and Change in Human Characteristics.* New York: John Wiley, 1964. A classic analysis of some of the great longitudinal growth studies, this text should be required reading for students of human development.

BOWER, T. G. R. *A Primer of Infant Development.* San Francisco: Freeman, 1977. An excellent, readable account of the emergence of infant competencies.

ELKIND, DAVID. *A Sympathetic Understanding of the Child Six to Sixteen.* Boston: Allyn and Bacon, 1971. An interesting, perceptive study of these critical years.

GIBSON, ELEANOR. *Principles of Perceptual Learning and Development.* New York: Appleton, Century-Crofts, 1969. Any study of perceptual development must begin with this comprehensive work.

HAVIGHURST, ROBERT. *Developmental Tasks and Education.* New York: David McKay, 1972. Havighurst's concept of the developmental task provides a needed rationale in any developmental overview.

HERBERT, MARTIN. *Emotional Problems of Development in Children.* New York: Academic Press, 1974. A sound presentation of age-related problems; relates well to a developmental perspective.

LIPSITT, LEWIS. *Developmental Psychobiology.* Hillsdale, New Jersey: Lawrence Erlbaum, 1976. Good review of selected topics of infancy.

SMART, MOLLIE and RUSSELL C. SMART. *Infants: Development and Relationships.* New York: Macmillan, 1978.

———. *Preschool Children: Development and Relationships.* New York: Macmillan, 1978.

———. *School-Age Children: Development and Relationships.* New York: Macmillan, 1978. These three texts provide a thorough, detailed review of the developmental cycle.

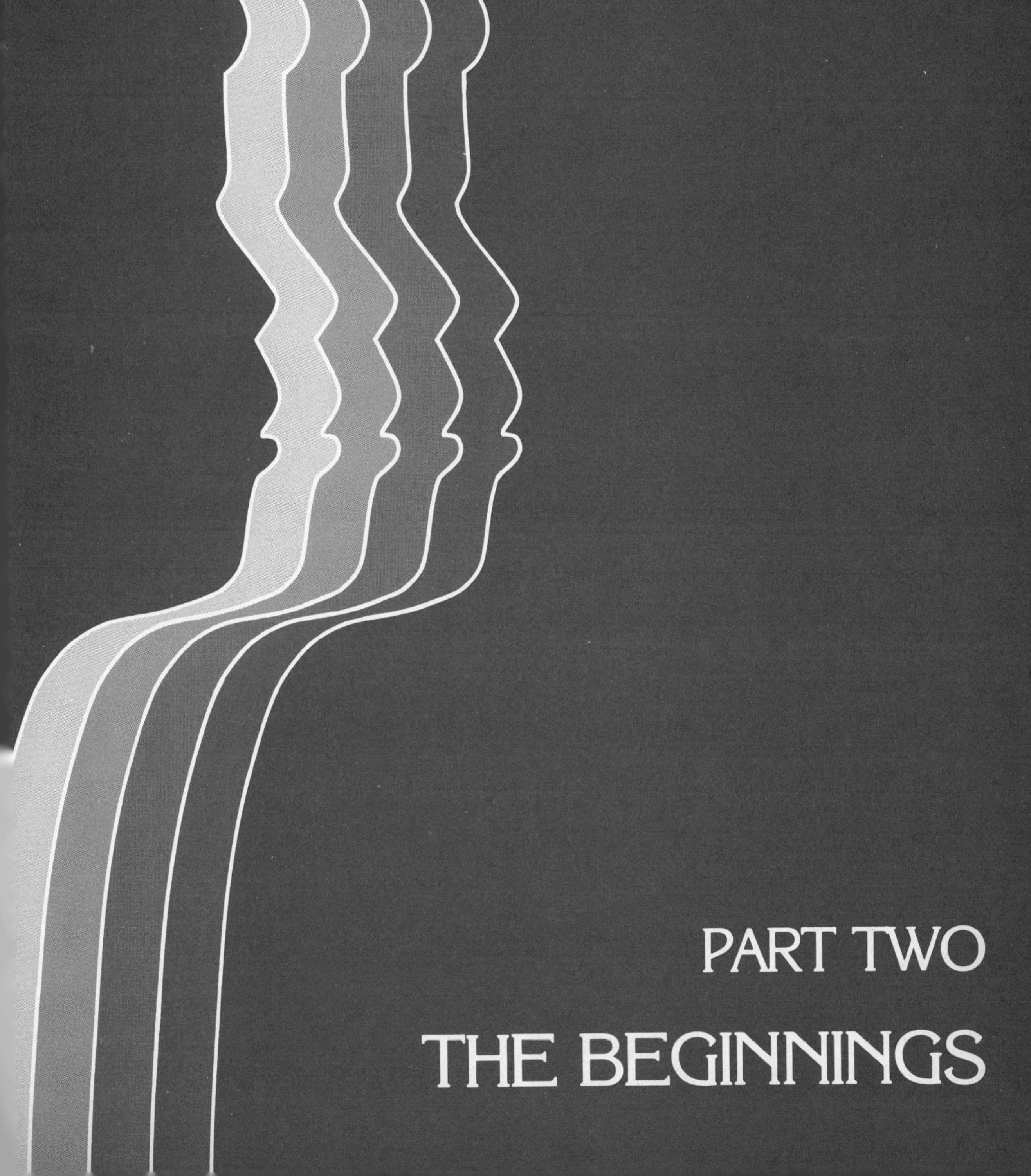

PART TWO
THE BEGINNINGS

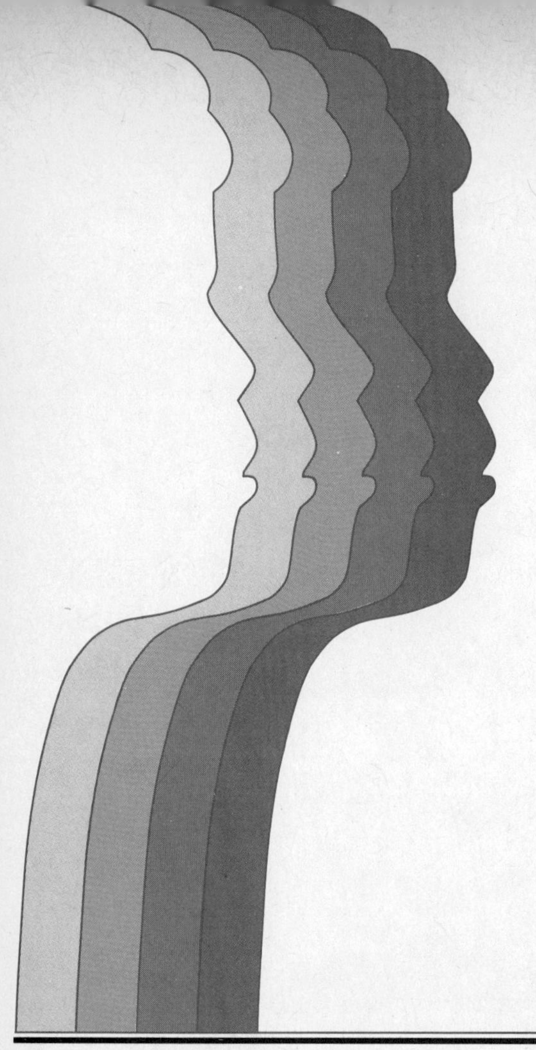

CHAPTER 4
HEREDITY AND THE PRENATAL ENVIRONMENT

CHAPTER HIGHLIGHTS

Topics

The Beginnings of Life
a. A Genetic Glossary
b. Sperm and Egg
c. The Fertilization Process
d. Chromosomes and Genes: The Hereditary Determiners

The Hereditary Process
a. The Principles of Cell Division: Mitosis and Meiosis
b. The Chemical Giant: DNA and the Coding Process

The Transmission of Traits
a. Mendel and Classical Genetics
b. Genetic Grids and the Probability of Traits

The Prenatal World
a. The Periods: Ovum, Embryo and Fetus
b. A Monthly Chronology: The Appearance of Structure and Function
c. The Development of the Senses
d. Pregnancy as a Condition

The Birth Process
a. The Process Itself—Possible Complications
b. Home or Hospital; Natural or Medicated

Contemporary Prenatal Issues
a. The Major Genetic Diseases
b. Amniocentesis—Pros and Cons

People

Leonard Carmichael
David Epel
Fernand Lamaze
Frederick Leboyer
Gregor Mendel
Carl Sagan
J. M. Tanner
James Watson

Special Topics

A Genetic Glossary
The Path of Genetic Research: In vitro.
Research into the Fertilization Process
The Race for the Double Helix
The DNA Alphabet

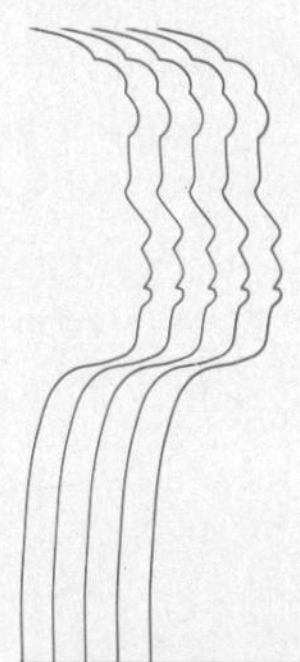

Heredity and environment—probably no other phrase has caused as much mischief in interpreting human behavior as these three words. The first chapter establishes the book's theme—the interaction of heredity and environment—and provides meaning to what has become a glib cliche. Of course behavior results from heredity and environment, but when does the environment begin to exercise its impact? How much do heredity and environment contribute to different traits? If an infant gives evidence of alertness and competence at birth, why is it impossible to predict future cognitive development?

Many genetic facts are well known. Some genes, such as those for blue eyes, are recessive; others, such as those for brown eyes, are dominant. Children of blue-eyed and brown-eyed parents usually have brown eyes (the reasons for the various possibilities appear later in the chapter). But it is imprecise to state that a brown-eyed child inherited brown eyes from the father rather than the blue-eyed mother. The genes, the *potential* for eye color, arc inherited; the actual trait, brown eyes, resulted from the proper interaction with the environment.

If prenatal conditions are sufficiently adverse, *no* development will occur, and the ovum or embryo will perish. This example, while extreme, illustrates the vital environmental contribution to genetic potential and the real meaning of the interaction between heredity and environment. It is not a question of whether heredity or environment is more important; both must contribute. But their contribution to a specific trait may differ; that is, both do not contribute equally to each trait. Heredity, for example, exercises primary control over eye color, while the environment contributes significantly to intelligence.

The environment's influence on genetic potential begins at the moment of fertilization—the union of sperm and egg. When you consider the source of a child's potential—both the male and female contribute half of the genetic material—and the bewildering variety of environmental conditions that children experience, the seemingly infinite patterns of human behavior are better understood. This complicated interaction also helps to explain the nature and extent of genetic malfunctioning. Most infants are born healthy, but hereditary disease occurs frequently; estimates are that about five percent of all live births show some birth defect.

The United States Public Health Service provides the following estimate:

1. Genetic defects cause one-half of all miscarriages;
2. Forty percent of infant mortality is caused by genetic disease;
3. Four-fifths of the mentally retarded show a genetic defect;
4. Each person carries from five to eight recessive genes for genetic defects.

These figures do *not* reflect those diseases thought to have a genetic link if coupled with certain environmental conditions, such as cancer, diabetes, and schizophrenia.

The intent of this chapter is to clarify the process by which heredity and environment immediately begin to interact. The following section addresses the fertilization process: what the sperm and egg contribute and how the process occurs. The next topic examines the prenatal world: what changes appear during each of the nine months and how the intrauterine environment affects development. For example, do the woman's feelings about pregnancy produce any discernible effects? The birth event today raises interesting questions: should birth occur in a hospital or home; what are the advantages and disadvantages of natural childbirth? Is there a relationship among pain, drugs, and birth defects? Finally, as technology progresses, critical issues arise: who needs genetic counseling? Should a woman undergo amniocentesis? If a genetic defect appears, how can individuals reconcile personal beliefs with a recommendation of abortion? The facts are clear; their interpretation and use pose severe challenges. But first, the facts.

THE BEGINNINGS

Human beings, like all living organisms, are composed of cells. Human life begins with the fusion of two specialized cells, the sperm and the egg or ovum. This fertilized ovum contains all of the genetic material that the organism will ever possess. The zygote (the fertilized ovum) immediately begins to divide and tissue differentiation commences. During the initial phase of development following fertilization, it is almost impossible to distinguish the male from the female.

The Sperm. During tissue differentiation, certain cells are destined to become the sperms and eggs. The chief characteristics of the sperm are its tightly packed tip (the acrosome), containing its twenty-three chromosomes, a short neck region, and a tail to propel it in its search for the egg. Sperm are so tiny that estimates are that the number of sperm equal to the world's population could fit in a thimble (Nilsson et al., 1977, p. 27).

Males, at birth, have in their testes the germ cells that will eventually produce sperm. At puberty, a meiotic division occurs that forms the actual sperm (Scheinfeld, 1965, pp. 13–15). Simultaneously the pituitary gland stimulates the hormonal production that results in the secondary sex characteristics: pubic hair, beard, deep voice.

The Egg. The egg is larger than the sperm, about the size of the period at the end of this sentence. Eggs also develop from germ cells, but the process differs for females. The germ cells have already become primal eggs at birth. Estimates are that from one to two million eggs have been formed in the ovaries. Since only one mature egg is required each month for about thirty-five years, the number present far exceeds the need. Nilsson et al. (1977) state that many of these primal eggs succumb

A GENETIC GLOSSARY

Before proceeding, you should know the meaning of the various terms that constantly occur in any discussion of heredity.

Acrosome. area at the tip of the sperm
Allele. alternate forms of a specific gene; there are genes for blue eyes and brown eyes
Autosome. chromosomes other than the sex chromosomes
Chromosome. string-like bodies that carry the genes; they are present in all of the body's cells
DNA. deoxyribonucleic acid, the chemical structure of the gene
Dominance. the tendency of a gene to be expressed in a trait, even when joined with a gene whose expression differs; brown eyes will appear when blue and brown-eyed genes are paired
Fertilization. the union of sperm and egg to form the fertilized ovum or zygote
Gametes. the mature sex cells, either sperms or eggs
Genes. the ultimate hereditary determiners; they are composed of the chemical molecule deoxyribonucleic acid (DNA)
Gene locus. the specific location of a gene on the chromosome
Genotype. the genetic composition of an individual
Heterozygous. the gene pairs for a trait differ; a person who is heterozygous for eye color has a brown-eye and a blue-eye gene
Homozygous. the gene pairs for a trait are similar; the eye color genes are the same
Meiosis. cell division in which each daughter cell receives one-half of the chromosomes of the parent cell. For humans this maintains the number of chromosomes (46) at fertilization
Mitosis. cell division in which each daughter cell receives the same number of chromosomes as the parent cell
Mutation. a change in the structure of a gene
Phenotype. the observable expression of a gene
Recessive. a gene whose trait is not expressed unless paired with another recessive gene; both parents contribute genes for blue eyes
Sex chromosome. those chromosomes that determine sex; in humans they are the twenty-third pair, with an xx combination producing a female, and an xy combination producing a male
Sex-linkage. genes on the sex chromosome that produce traits other than sex
Trisomy. three chromosomes are present rather than the customary pair; Down's syndrome (mongolism) is caused by three chromosomes at the twenty-first pairing
Zygote. the fertilized egg

before puberty. They simply shrivel up and disappear. At puberty the pituitary gland stimulates the hormonal production that produces the female secondary sex characteristics: pubic hair, breasts, wider hips, higher voice.

Although the process of gamete formation seems similar for both males and females, it is far more complicated for females. The interaction between the pituitary and the ovaries occurs in four-week phases—the menstrual cycle. The pituitary gland secretes another hormone that stimulates the ripening of eggs, and after two weeks one egg, which has ripened more than the others, is discharged from the ovary's surface. This process, called ovulation, triggers a chemical reaction that inhibits the ripening of further eggs and simultaneously prepares the uterine lining for a potential fertilized ovum.

If fertilization does not occur, the prepared uterine lining is shed in menstruation. When the menstrual bleeding ceases, the entire process begins again. During each menstrual cycle many of the primal eggs are discarded, so that as a woman approaches the end of her egg-producing phase of life, these last ova have been present for as many as forty years. There is growing speculation today that this lengthy period may explain why the children of older women are more susceptible to genetic defects. The eggs have simply been exposed to environmental hazards such as radiation too long to escape damage.

THE PATH OF GENETIC RESEARCH

As theoretical and technological advances continue, the scope of genetic research has raised questions that cannot be answered by the scientific community alone. For example, the ability to alter the genetic structure of bacteria has necessitated community involvement in decisions about the nature of genetic research within the community. Federal legislation has also demanded conformity to prescribed safeguards.

Now, however, research has raised new ethical issues. In 1973, English scientists devised a method of securing mature eggs after ovulation. Injecting volunteer women with a hormone that caused them to produce more than one mature egg per month, they then intervened surgically by making two small incisions in each woman's side. They inserted a tiny telescope through one incision and an equally tiny suction instrument through the other incision. They were thus able to obtain three or four eggs from some of the women. They then added sperm to these natural eggs, some of which penetrated the egg. Cell division began and lasted for several days before perishing. Greenfeld noted (1973) that the necessary technology was falling into place.

In the summer of 1978, knowledge and technology fused to produce the first "test tube" baby. England's Patrick Steptoe and Robert Edwards successfully followed the established steps with Lesley Brown. Fertility hormones caused the ripening of several eggs, which were located by a laparoscope (tiny telescope). The eggs were removed and one was placed in a dish (in vitro) containing salts, nutrients, and blood serum to which sperm were added for fertilization. After approximately six days of cell division the blastocyst was inserted into the uterus, which was probably the most sensitive step. All went well and a healthy baby girl was born.

Perhaps James Watson, the codiscoverer of DNA, is correct when he states that biologically, it is later than we think.

The Fertilization Process

When the egg is discharged from the ovary's surface, it is enveloped by one of the Fallopian tubes. The diameter of each Fallopian tube is about that of a human hair, but it almost unfailingly ensnares the egg and provides a passageway to the uterus. Figure 4.1 illustrates the relationship among ovary, egg, Fallopian tubes, and the uterus.

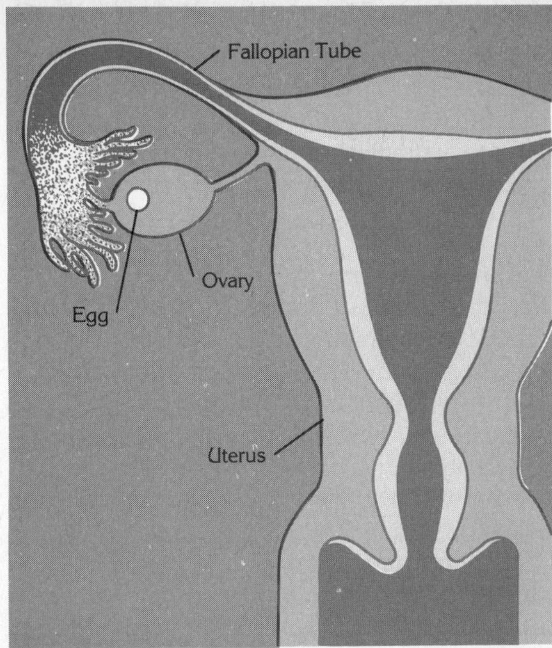

FIGURE 4.1. The Relationship of Ovary, Egg, Fallopian Tube, and Uterus.

If fertilization occurs, it will take place soon after the egg enters the Fallopian tube. Fusion of the two cells is quickly followed by the first cell division, and as the zygote travels toward implantation within the uterus, cell division continues. The cells multiply rapidly and after about seven days reach the uterine wall. The fertilized egg is now called a blastocyst. The journey is pictured in Figure 4.2.

After the sperm and egg unite, the new cell (the potential individual) possesses twenty-three pairs of chromosomes, or forty-six chromosomes, one member of each pair contributed by the father and one by the mother. The fertilized egg at this stage is called the zygote. Figure 4.3 illustrates the basic process.

The forty-six chromosomes that the zygote possesses represent the individual's total biological heritage. By a process of division, each cell in the body will have a replica of all forty-six chromosomes. The significance of the chromosomes is that they carry the genes, the decisive elements of heredity.

FIGURE 4.2. From Ovulation to Implantation.

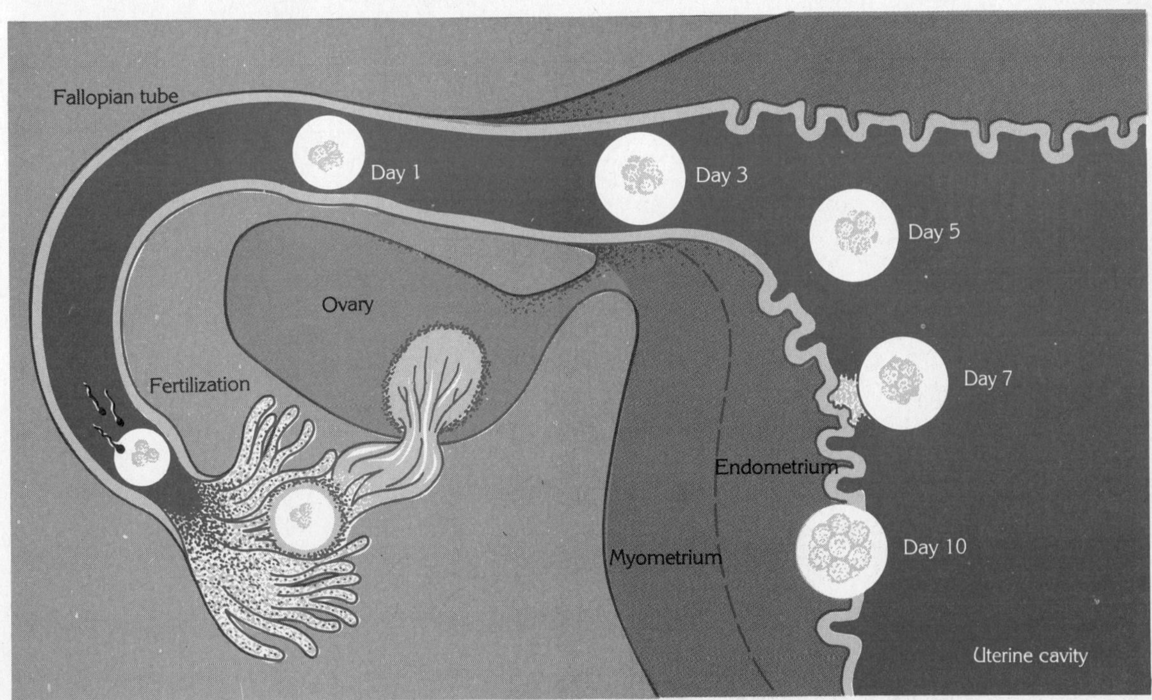

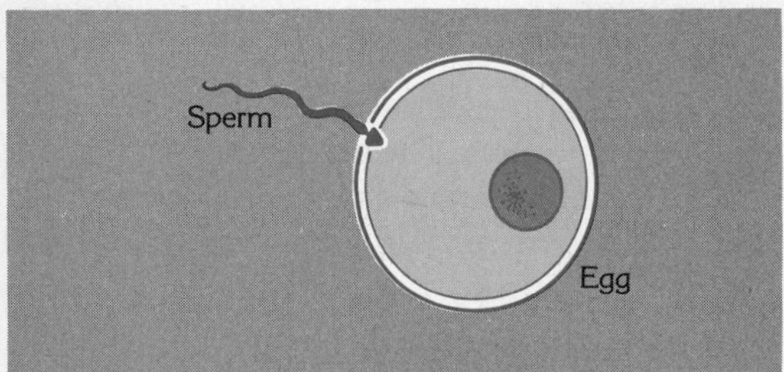

FIGURE 4.3. **Fertilization of the Egg.** The sperm, carrying its twenty-three chromosomes, penetrates the egg, with its twenty-three chromosomes. The nuclei of sperm and egg fuse, resulting in forty-six chromosomes.

The size of the elements involved is almost bewildering. We have commented on the size of the sperm—so small that it can be seen only microscopically. The head of the sperm, which is about one-twelfth of its total length, contains the twenty-three chromosomes.

However radically individuals may change in the course of their lives, their hereditary properties do not change. The zygotal chromosomes are not new products. Under ordinary circumstances, environmental conditions leave the forty-six chromosomes unaltered. (The hesitation expressed by "ordinary circumstances" acknowledges the growing belief that environmental agents such as drugs, viruses, or radiation may cause genetic damage.) Figure 4.4 illustrates the parental role.

Chromosomes and Genes. The fertilized egg, the zygote, thus contains the individual's genetic endowment represented by the forty-six chromosomes in its nucleus. Human chromosomes appear in twenty-three pairs.

Each pair, except the twenty-third, is remarkably alike. The twenty-third pair defines the individual's sex; an XX combination signifies the female, while XY indicates a male. The sperm actually determines sex, since it alone can carry a Y chromosome. Thus there are two kinds of sperm: the X chromosome carrier and the Y chromosome carrier. The Y carrier is smaller than the X, which contains more genetic material. The Y carrier is also lighter and speedier and can reach the egg more quickly. But it is also more vulnerable; if ovulation has not occurred, the Y carrier perishes while the X carrier survives.

Consequently, the male, from conception, is the more fragile of the two sexes. Estimates

FIGURE 4.4. **The Hereditary Process.**

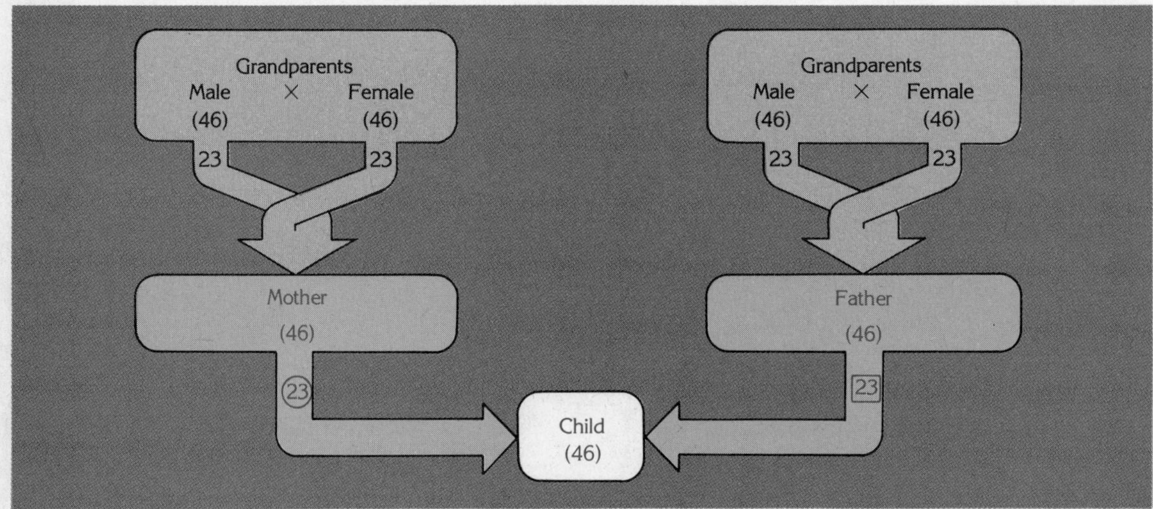

RESEARCH INTO THE FERTILIZATION PROCESS

While studies of the fertilization process leave many questions unanswered, here, as in other phases of developmental research, knowledge accumulates. David Epel states (1977) that the interaction of a sperm and an egg marks a dividing line between life and death. If the interaction is successful, a new life begins; if it fails, two cells die within hours. Fertilization seems to involve three steps: (1) recognition of the egg by the sperm; (2) the regulation permitting only one sperm's entry into the egg; and (3) the activation of the dormant metabolism of the egg so that development can commence.

Using the eggs of marine invertebrates (such as sea urchins), Epel and his associates have shed new light on the mechanism of fertilization. The sperm seems to recognize the egg when it initially contacts the jelly coat surrounding the egg. Chemicals in this jelly coating interact with the acrosome (tip of the sperm) causing it to release digestive enzymes that permit the sperm to penetrate the egg.

Although only one sperm gains entry, many other sperm are attached to the egg's surface. To prevent their entry, a flow of sodium ions into the cell changes its electrical potential, which seems to preclude further penetration. A second, and slower, chemical reaction occurs that adds to the egg's defense against additional sperm entry.

About twenty minutes following penetration, the sperm and egg nuclei fuse and the egg, which until fertilization has been dormant, now becomes active. Cleavage commences and embryonic development begins. What activates the egg remains a mystery; the sperm triggers a genetic program inherent in the egg (Epel, 1977, p. 132).

Fertilization proceeds through these three stages. Epel believes that as knowledge grows about the specific mechanisms at each stage, it will help investigators understand other cellular transformations, such as those that occur in cancer.

are that there are 160 males conceived for every 100 females. However, so many males are spontaneously aborted that only 105 males are born for every 100 females. A similar pattern appears in neonatal life and continues throughout development until women finally outnumber men, reversing the original ratio. Certain conclusions follow:

1. Structurally and functionally, females have an advantage resisting disease.
2. The male is more subject to hereditary disease and defect.
3. Environmental elements expose the male to greater hazards.
4. Females are born with and retain a biological superiority over males (Scheinfeld, 1965, p. 217).

The significance of the chromosomes lies in the material they contain—the genes. Each gene is located at a particular spot on the chromosome, called the gene locus. The genes, whose chemical structure is DNA (deoxyribonucleic acid), account for all inherited characteristics, from hair and eye color to skin shade, even to a tendency toward baldness (Hendin and Marks, 1978, p. 35).

Aside from performing their cellular duties, the genes also reproduce themselves. Each gene constructs an exact duplicate of itself, so that when a cell divides, the chromosomes and genes also divide and each cell retains identical genetic material. As the cells divide, however, they do not remain identical. Specialization appears and different kinds of cells are formed at different locations. The genes, then, are continuously active in directing life's processes according to their prescribed genetic codes. The action of the genes is remarkable not only because of their vastly complicated mechanism, but also because of simpler phenomena. For example, the initial activity of the genes is primarily forming the body's basic materials. Although this activity must continue throughout an individual's lifetime, more specialized functions gradually appear and begin to form a circulatory system, a skeletal system, and a nerve system.

The process continues until a highly complex human being results, but the process of growth and development is similar for all human beings. Every bodily cell possesses a replica of all forty-six chromosomes. The genes that produce eye color are also found in your hair, skin, and blood, which indicates the selective function of the gene once the period of generalization is complete.

DISCUSSION QUESTIONS

1. Be sure you understand the genetic terminology. Can you distinguish between a genotype and a phenotype? How does one become the other?
2. Differentiate the process by which germ cells become sperms and ova. What is the major difference? Why are older women worried about the possibility of giving birth to a genetically defective baby?
3. Once a sperm fertilizes an egg, other sperm are prevented from entering. How does this occur? Describe the process with lower life forms.
4. What determines sex? Do you agree that the male is biologically weaker? Do you think that research supports such a conclusion? Support your answer with current data.

THE HEREDITARY PROCESS

The original cell, the possessor of forty-six chromosomes, begins to divide rapidly after fertilization, until at birth there are billions of cells in the infant. The cells soon begin to specialize; some become muscle, some bone, some skin, some blood, and some nerve cells. These are the somatic or body cells. The process of division in which these cells multiply is called *mitosis* (Figure 4.5). In a mitotic division the number of chromosomes in each cell remains the same.

A second type of cell is also differentiated: the germ or sex cell that ultimately becomes the sperm or egg. These reproductive cells likewise divide by the process of mitosis until the age of puberty. But then a remarkable phenomenon occurs—another type of division called *meiosis*, or reduction division (Figure 4.6). Each sex cell, instead of receiving forty-six chromosomes upon division, now receives twenty-three.

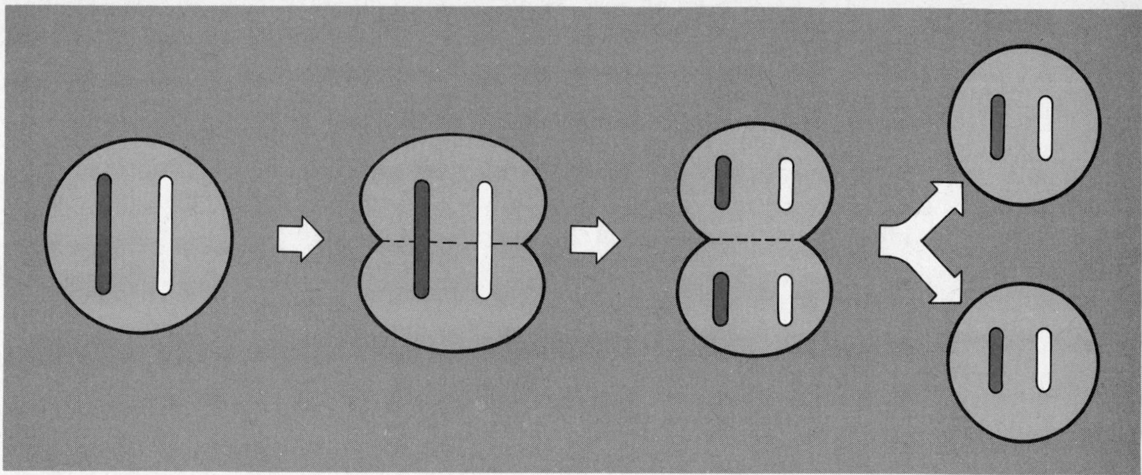

FIGURE 4.5. Mitosis. Only two chromosomes are being used to illustrate the process of cell division in which the number of chromosomes remain the same after the cell divides.

To review, mitosis is basically a division of cells in which each chromosome is duplicated so that each daughter cell receives a replica of each chromosome of the parent cell. Mitotic cell division is of paramount significance in the higher life forms, since it ensures that each daughter cell is genetically alike and therfore compatible with every other cell in the individual's body. What is doubled in mitotic division is the amount of DNA, the chief component of the genes. Meiosis, however, which occurs only in germ cell reproduction, is responsible both for the shuffling of hereditary characteristics received from each parent and for their random appearance in offspring. During the reduction division, the chromosomes separate longitudinally, so that twenty-three go to one cell and twenty-three go to another.

FIGURE 4.6. Meiosis. Again, only two chromosomes are being used, for the sake of simplicity. Here we see cell division occurring in which the number of chromosomes is halved after the cell divides.

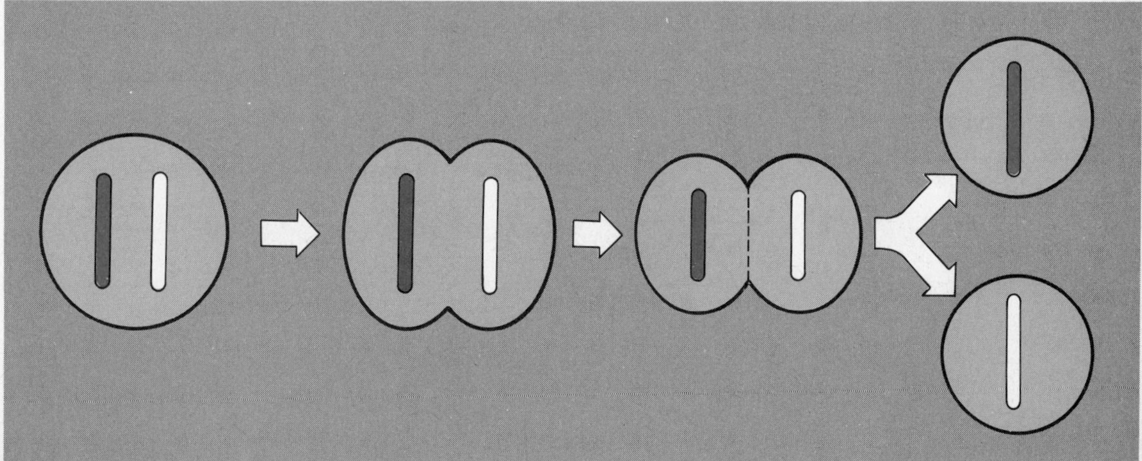

For the male, reduction division begins to occur just before puberty. For the female, the process differs slightly. Since she is required to produce only one mature egg a month, there is no provision for an indefinitely large number of eggs, as there is for sperm. A woman normally sheds only three to four hundred mature ova in her lifetime, while the normal male in a single ejaculation emits two to three hundred million sperm. When a female is born, the initial phases of the reduction division have already occurred, and rudimentary eggs are present. The ovaries at birth contain tiny clusters of all the eggs that will mature in later years. Just before puberty, the final phases of the reduction division occur, and mature eggs are formed. It is as if there were a lengthy waiting period, from birth until about twelve or thirteen years, before the process is finally completed. The twenty-three chromosomes with their hereditary content are thus present at birth but must await the passage of time before biological maturity occurs in the female.

DNA: Structure and Function

Gerald McClearn (1964, p. 434) states that the expression "is inherited" is a convenient simplification of an extremely complex idea. It would be more accurate to say that under certain environmental conditions, through biochemical processes initiated and sustained by the gene products, individuals possessing a certain pair of genes will develop attributes different from those of individuals with different gene pairs.

Each chromosome contains thousands of genes, and each of these thousands of genes has a role in the growth and development of each human being. Furthermore, the chemical key to the life force in humans, animals, and plants is the amazing chemical compound DNA (Figure 4.7), which constitutes about forty percent of the chromosomes and is the molecular basis of the genes. Genes not only perform certain duties within the cell, but also join with other genes to reproduce both themselves and the whole chromosome.

Each gene follows the instructions encoded in its DNA; it sends these instructions, as chemical messages, into the surrounding cell. The cell then produces certain substances or performs certain functions according to instructions. These new products then interact with the genes to form new substances. The process continues to build the millions of cells needed for various bodily structures. Different genes are concerned primarily with different physiological and biochemical processes.

Examining Figure 4.7, note how the strands intertwine. The strands, similar to the sides of a ladder, are connected by chemical rings: adenine (A), guanine (G), cytosine (C), and thymine (T). As Nilsson et al. (1977) note, the letters are not randomly connected; A joins with T, G with C. If a code was written as AGCTTGA, it must appear as:

A G C T T G A
T C G A A C T

Thus one sequence determines the other.

FIGURE 4.7. The DNA Double Helix. (a) The overall structure that gave DNA its famous name. (b) A closer examination reveals that the sides of the spiral are connected by chemicals similar to the rungs of a ladder.

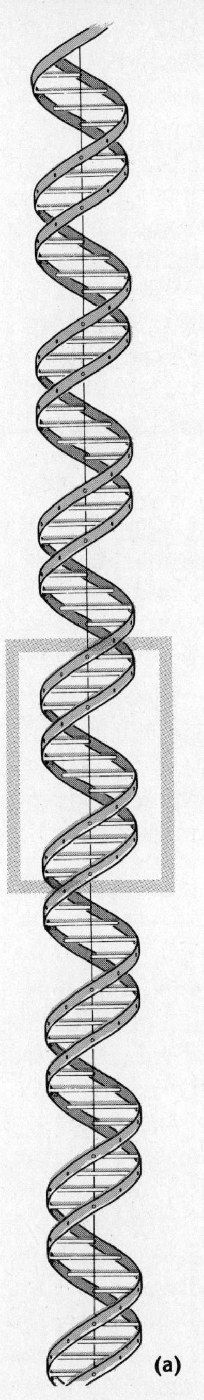

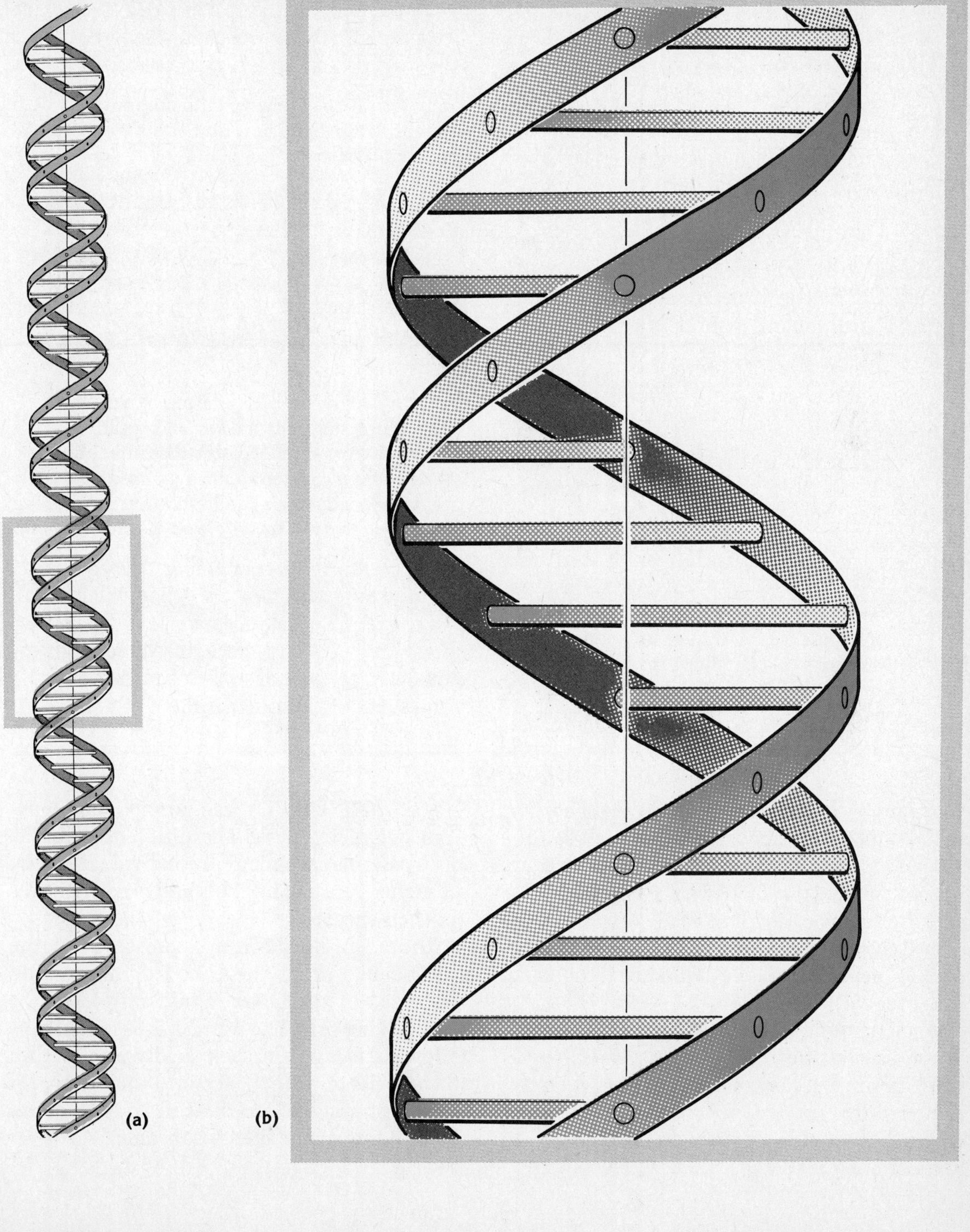

(a)

(b)

THE RACE FOR THE DOUBLE HELIX

The story of the discovery of DNA is as intriguing as it is informative. Dashing out of Cambridge University's Cavendish Laboratory one winter's day in 1953, two young scientists, James Watson, twenty-four, and Francis Crick, thirty-six, ducked into the nearest pub and began to talk excitedly. Asked what the excitement was all about, Crick triumphantly announced, "We have discovered the secret of life!" (*Time*, April 19, 1971). On that day, Watson and Crick had finally determined the exact model of DNA.

For more about this discovery and a look behind the scenes, read James Watson's account of *The Double Helix*. This instructive and entertaining chronology contains such passages as:

> "From the first day in the lab I knew I would not leave Cambridge for a long time. Departing would be idiocy, for I had immediately discovered the fun of talking to Francis Crick. . . . Within a few days after my arrival, we knew what to do: imitate Linus Pauling and beat him at his own game." (Watson, 1968, p. 37)

Another fascinating glimpse into the emotional involvement of scientists in their work is found in Watson's description of a scene with one of his coworkers, Rosalind Franklin. They were arguing about a misinterpretation that Watson felt she had made.

> "Suddenly, Rosy came from behind the lab bench that separated us and began moving toward me. Fearing that in her hot anger she might strike me, I grabbed up the Pauling manuscript and hastily retreated to the open door." (Watson, 1968, p. 106)

But all certainly was not rancor. After engaging in a long and wearying race to be the first to break the code, Watson (1968, p. 138) notes how Pauling accepted defeat graciously. In fact, he describes Pauling's reaction as one of genuine thrill.

A remarkable feature of DNA is its ability to reproduce itself and ensure that each daughter cell receives identical genetic information. During mitosis the DNA splits as readily as a person unzips a jacket. Each single strand grows a new mate, A to T and G to C, until the double helix model is reproduced in each daughter cell.

As Scheinfeld notes (1965, p. 178), the four letter possibilities, A–T, T–A, G–C, C–G, seem to limit genetic variation. But when we consider that each DNA molecule is quite lengthy, involving thousands, perhaps millions of chemical steps, that is, TA, GC, AT, CG, GC, AT, CG, TA, the possible combinations seem limitless. The differences in the DNA patterns account for the individual genetic differences among humans and for differences between species.

An intriguing question is presented by the method by which the encoded information contained in the DNA is transmitted to the surrounding cell. The process is essentially as follows: RNA (ribonucleic acid) forms within the nucleus of the cell, acts as a messenger for DNA, and moves into the cell body to direct the building of the body's substances.

THE DNA ALPHABET

If you examine Figure 4.7 you will notice that the various rungs and sides of the DNA ladder resemble small blocks. These are called *nucleotides* and come in four varieties depending on the AT, GC pairings. Carl Sagan (1977, p. 23) states that the language of heredity is written in an alphabet of only four letters. But the final book is very rich, since the average DNA molecule consists of about *five billion* pairs of nucleotides.

Sagan attempts to estimate the amount of information that our genes contain. Since there are four different kinds of nucleotides, the number of bits of information in a single chromosome is *twenty billion.* To what can we compare twenty billion bits of information? They are the equivalent of about three billion letters, and since the average word contains six letters, each chromosome incorporates information equal to about five hundred million words. At about three hundred words per typical printed page, this translates into the equivalent of about two million pages. The average book consists of about five hundred pages; thus the information in one human chromosome corresponds to that in *four thousand books.* As Sagan states, the rungs on the DNA ladder represent a library of information.

Finally, the author notes that while most organisms on the earth depend on their genetic information, humans have reached beyond this "prewiring" and depend greatly on extragenetic information, that is, ability acquired through learning, and extra somatic information, that is, information stored in books and computers. Sagan's comment about this human uniqueness is pertinent for child development:

> We have made a kind of bargain with nature: our children will be difficult to raise but their capacity for new learning will greatly enhance the chances of survival of the human species.

THE TRANSMISSION OF TRAITS

What color are your eyes? Do your brothers and sisters have the same color eyes? Theirs could be different from yours; the same mother and father who produced a brown-eyed child can also have a youngster with blue eyes. For centuries, guesses, myths, and speculation were used to explain the bewildering and mysterious happenings of heredity. It was not until the end of the nineteenth century that Gregor Mendel offered a scientific explanation. (Note the relatively recent emergence of genetic facts: the transmission of traits by Mendel in the 1860s, the Watson-Crick double helix model of DNA in 1953, the number of human chromosomes in 1956.)

Mendel's Work

Mendel, an Austrian monk who studied plants as a hobby, attempted to cross-breed pure strains of pea plants. He used pure sets of plants, that is, peas that were either round or wrinkled, yellow or green, tall or dwarf. He discovered that the first generation of offspring all had the same trait; after cross-breeding round and unwrinkled peas, the offspring were all round. Did the offspring inherit the trait from only one parent?

Mendel quickly eliminated this explanation since the missing trait (wrinkled) reappeared in the second generation. But the trait that was exclusively expressed in the first generation (roundness) was the majority trait in

TABLE 4.1. Mendel's Round and Wrinkled Peas

I. First Pairing—R × W

	W	W
R	RW	RW
R	RW	RW

II. Second Pairing—RW × RW

	R	W
R	RR	RW
W	RW	WW

the second generation. That is, the ratio of round peas to wrinkled peas consistently remained at 3 to 1 in the second generation. Thus roundness is the dominant trait and wrinkled is the recessive trait. These two genes, round (R) and wrinkled (W), yield four possible peas: RR, WW, RW, WR. RR and WW are pure strains and breed true; RW and WR are heterozygous. A genetic grid based on Mendel's first pairing (round and wrinkled) is shown in Table 4.1. Note how the 3 to 1 ratio appears in the second generation.

Baldwin (1973) uses this model to clarify the genetic terminology. For example, there were two types of each gene in Mendel's research (round or wrinkled, green or yellow).

TABLE 4.2. Your Child's Eye Color

Your or Spouse's Family		Your or Spouse's Eyes
All brown	→	Brown; Small chance of light (grey, green, blue)
Brown or light	→	Brown *or* light
All light	→	Light
You and Spouse		**Child**
Both brown	→	Usually brown; Small chance of light
Both light	→	Light
Brown and light	→	Brown *or* equal chances of light or brown

These are the alleles, the alternate form of a gene pair. Since genes are inherited in pairs, both alleles may be the same as for round peas or blue eyes. Thus, the individual is *homozygous* for the gene. If each parent contributes a different gene, then the individual is *heterozygous* for the genes. One of these genes appears in the trait, for example, round peas or brown eyes. That gene is dominant, the other is recessive.

Baldwin then summarizes Mendel's work as follows:

1. After cross-breeding, all of the first generation showed the trait of one strain and not the other.
2. The trait not expressed in the first generation (f_1) appeared in the second generation (f_2) in the 3 to 1 ratio.
3. Each gene of a pair is equally likely to be passed on to the next generation.

Eye color is a good example of hereditary transmission. Table 4.2 indicates the possibilities of your future children's eye color.

What is the genetic explanation for the presence of different eye colors? There is a gene responsible for blue eyes and another responsible for brown eyes. The "brown-eye" gene is dominant and the "blue-eye" gene is recessive; for example, a child receiving two "brown" genes will have brown eyes; a child receiving two "blue" genes will have blue eyes. Finally, the youngster who receives one of each will have brown eyes, because the gene for brown eyes is dominant. The basic principle is that genes producing dark eye colors (brown, black) dominate over those producing light eye colors (blue, green, gray). If the mother, for instance, has brown eyes, she may carry two brown genes (if her family is mostly brown-eyed) or a brown and a blue (if there are blue-eyed relatives somewhere in the family tree). If the father has blue eyes, he most certainly has two blue genes. The possible results are charted in Table 4.3.

TABLE 4.3. Predicting Eye Color

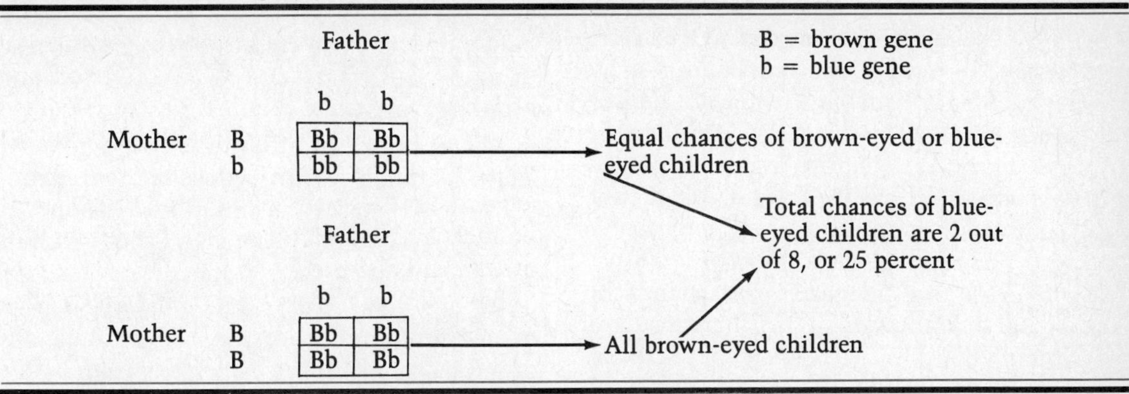

DISCUSSION QUESTIONS

1. Be sure that you understand the difference between mitosis and meiosis. When does meioses occur? Does the process differ for males and females? What is the significance of mitotic divisions? Of meiotic divisions?
2. What does double helix mean? What connects the sides of the "ladder"? How are the chemical rungs arranged? Discuss the possible variations in chemical coding.
3. Use Carl Sagan's work to estimate human genetic information. Explain how the figures are calculated. Why is this genetic information inadequate? How do humans overcome this inadequacy?
4. Explain Mendel's model. If you assume that each parent carries a pure strain of a trait (BB and bb), which traits will appear in the first generation? In the second generation? Fill in both genetic grids and illustrate your answer.

Father—BB Mother—bb

First Generation

Second Generation

THE PRENATAL WORLD

The fertilized egg must pass through the Fallopian tube to reach the uterus, a journey of about seven days to travel five or six inches. Hormones released by the ovary stimulate the muscles of the Fallopian tube wall so that it gently pushes the zygote toward the uterus. During its passage through the Fallopian tube, the zygote receives all of its nourishment from the tube. Figure 4.8 illustrates passage into the uterus and implantation.

After implantation there are three fairly distinct phases of prenatal development: the ovum, the embryo, and the fetus.

The Time of the Ovum

The ovum phase extends through the first two weeks. Since the passage through the Fallopian tube took seven days, the zygote is now one week old and called a blastocyst. During the second week, the blastocyst becomes firmly implanted in the wall of the uterus and from its outer layer of cells begins to develop a primitive placenta, an umbilical cord, and the amniotic sac. The inner cell layer develops into the embryo itself.

FIGURE 4.8. Passage of the Zygote into the Uterus.

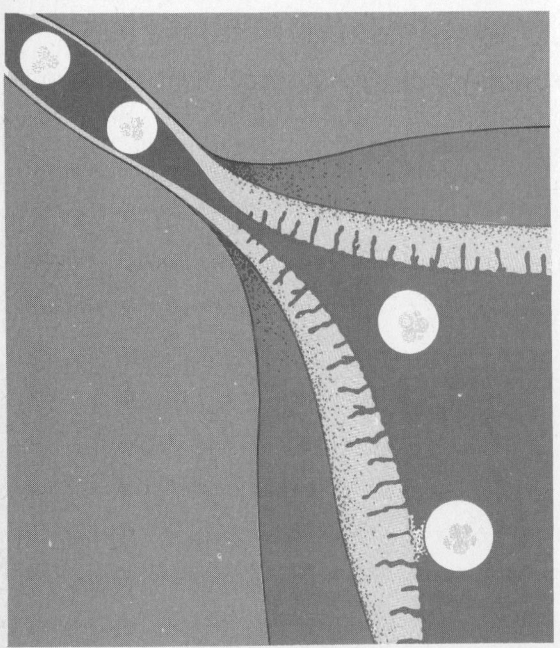

The placenta and the umbilical cord serve a critical function during development. Annis (1978, p. 22) states that the placenta supplies the embryo with all its needs, carries off all its wastes, and protects it from danger. The placenta has two separate sets of blood vessels, one going to and from the baby through the umbilical cord, the other going to and from the mother through the arteries and veins supplying the placenta. Thus the mother nourishes the placenta and the placenta then nourishes the baby. It is an indirect process; materials are exchanged through the permeable walls of the blood vessels. Figure 4.9 illustrates the relationship of the umbilical cord, placenta, and uterine wall.

The Time of the Embryo

When the second week ends, the germinal period, the time of the ovum, is complete. The embryonic period, from the third through the eighth week, sees the development of a recognizable human being. The nervous system develops rapidly, which suggests that the embryo at this time is quite sensitive to any obstructions to its growth. Perhaps the most remarkable change in the embryo is the cellular differentiation. Three distinct layers are being formed: the ectoderm, which will give rise to skin, hair, nails, teeth, and nervous system; the mesoderm, which will give rise to muscles, skeleton, and the circulatory and excretory systems; and the endoderm, which will give rise to lungs, liver, and pancreas.

Usually by the completion of the fourth week, the heart begins to beat—the embryo's

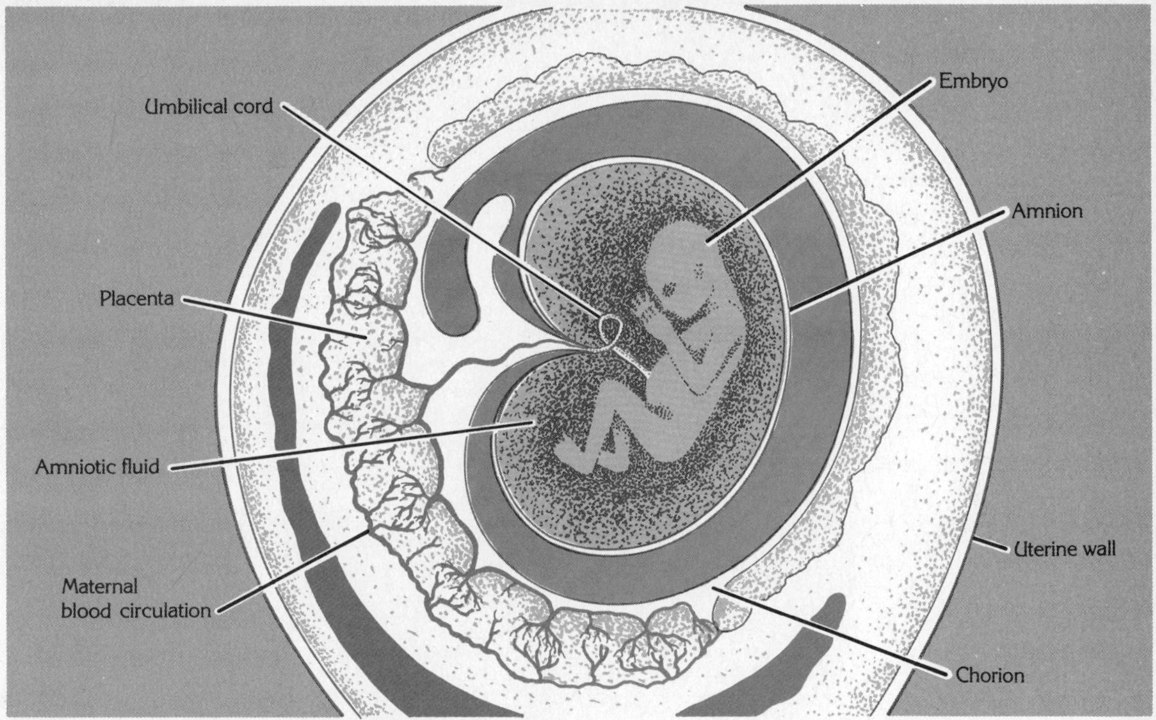

FIGURE 4.9. Umbilical Cord, Placenta, and Uterine Wall.

first movement. The accompanying photographs at the end of this section show that during the fifth week, eyes and ears begin to emerge, bodily buds give clear evidence of becoming arms and legs, and the head area is the largest part of the rapidly growing embryo. During the sixth and seventh weeks, fingers begin to appear on the hands, the outline of toes is seen, and the beginnings of the spinal cord are visible.

After eight weeks, Annis (1978) states, ninety-five percent of the body parts are differentiated and general body movements are detected. The embryonic tissue is particularly sensitive to any foreign agents during differentiation. For example, thalidomide caused its damage when taken during the fourth to sixth weeks of pregnancy; German measles is most dangerous during the first three months of pregnancy.

The embryonic period is an extremely hazardous time for the newly formed organism. J. M. Tanner (1970) estimates that about thirty percent of all embryos are aborted at this time without the mother's knowledge; about ninety percent of all embryos with chromosomal abnormalities are spontaneously aborted.

At the end of this period there is a discernible human being with arms, legs, a beating heart, and a nervous system. It is receiving nourishment and discharging waste through the umbilical cord, which leads to the placenta. The placenta itself never actually joins with the uterus, but exchanges nourishment and waste products through walls of the blood vessels.

The future mother begins to experience some of the noticeable effects of pregnancy—the need to urinate more frequently, morning sickness, and increasing fullness of the breasts.

The Time of the Fetus

The fetal period extends from the beginning of the third month to birth. The sex organs appear during the third month and it is possible to determine the baby's sex. Growth is rapid during the fourth month, and Nilsson et al. state (1977) that to accommodate an increasing oxygen demand, the embryo produces specialized cells: the red blood cells to transport oxygen and white blood cells to combat disease. Annis (1978) notes that the fetus is now active—sucking, turning its head, and pushing with hands and feet—and the mother is acutely aware of the life within her. Figure 4.10 represents the fetus in the fourth month.

FIGURE 4.10. The Fetus—Fourth Month.

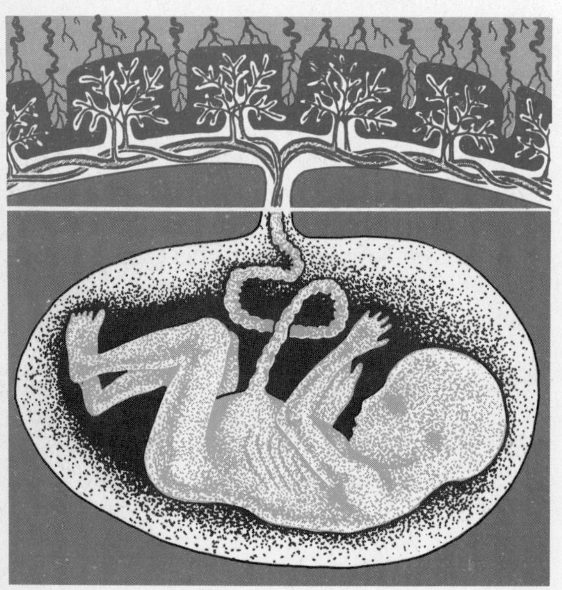

The fetus is able to hear sound, and as Nilsson et al. (1977) state, the silent world of the fetus is a fantasy, unfounded in reality. The fetus hears many environmental sounds—voices, stomach rumblings, the pulsing of the mother's blood. Macfarlane (1977) reports on research in which investigators inserted small microphones through the cervix into the uterus beside the baby's head. Recordings from these microphones demonstrated considerable uterine noise. Macfarlane describes it as a whooshing sound punctuated by the sound of passing air.

By the end of the fifth month the baby is ten to twelve inches long, and weighs about a pound. Annis (1978) notes that the fetus sleeps and wakes as the newborn does, even manifesting a favorite sleep position. Rapid growth continues in the sixth month, another two inches and one pound, but slows during the seventh month. Viability, the ability to survive if born, is attained. During the two final fetal months, organ development prepares the fetus for the shock of leaving the sheltered uterine world. The senses are ready to function (some are already functioning) and the brain at birth is twenty to twenty-five percent of its adult weight. To summarize:

The fetal period extends from about eight weeks after conception until birth. The fetus grows rapidly both in height and weight. By the fourth month, the fetus is one-half its birth size; from the fourth to the fifth month is usually the peak growth period. During this time, the mother begins to feel movement. The fetus now swallows, digests, and secretes urine. Visible sexual differentiation begins, while the nervous system continues to increase in size and complexity. After six months very few new nerve and muscle cells appear. At birth, of course, the nervous system must be fully functioning to ensure automatic breathing.

TABLE 4.4. Prenatal Growth.

Ovum	Embryo	Fetus
Week 1: Movement through tube to uterus Week 2: Forms placenta, umbilical cord, amniotic sac	a. Rapid development of nervous system b. Cellular differentiation Week 4: Heart beats Week 5: Eyes and ears begin to emerge, bodily buds for arms and legs Weeks 6 & 7: Fingers and toes, beginning of spinal cord Week 8: About 95% of body parts differentiated—arms, legs, beating heart, nervous system	Third Month: Sex organs appear Fourth Month: Rapid growth, red blood cells, white blood cells; active, sucking Fifth Month: Hears sound, sleeps, 10–12 inches long, 1 pound Sixth Month: Rapid growth, 12–14 inches, 2 pounds Seventh Month: Growth slows, viability attained Eighth & Ninth Months: Preparation for birth, senses ready to function, brain is 25% of adult weight

Most women begin to experience some discomfort as the time of birth approaches. The extra weight, body changes, and sheer effort of movement all contribute to this unpleasant feeling. During this period of preparation, the major influence on the growing child is its mother. If the mother is healthy, happy, and reasonably cautious, both she and her child will be the beneficiaries. Table 4.4 summarizes the course of prenatal development.

Parents are often concerned about the size of their baby: does "small" indicate some difficulty? Lind (1976) states that small but healthy babies delivered without complication have been small from the first weeks of development. Fetuses taken by hysterotomy (surgical incision of the uterus) from mothers with definite menstrual dates show that as early as ten to twelve weeks there is a wide range of fetal weights.

Thomson and Billewicz (1976) agree, noting that birth weight and gestational age are significant only as they reflect maturity. Size and age are insignificant if the fetus is anatomically and physiologically sound and can cope with birth hazards and an independent postnatal existence. No fetus is mature; tissues and organs attain physiological maturity at different times *after* birth.

Fetal growth curves require cautious interpretation to avoid unwarranted conclusions such as "small is a problem." These curves are based on cross-sectional data. Another reason for such caution relates to fetal age. Most studies use the first day of the last menstrual period as the onset of gestation, which is probably two weeks longer than the true fertilization age. It is almost impossible to determine exact age.

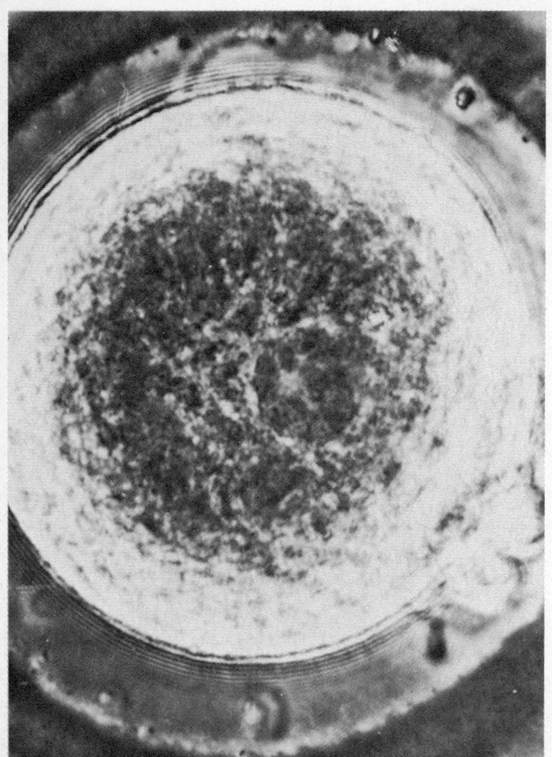

Moment of fertilization

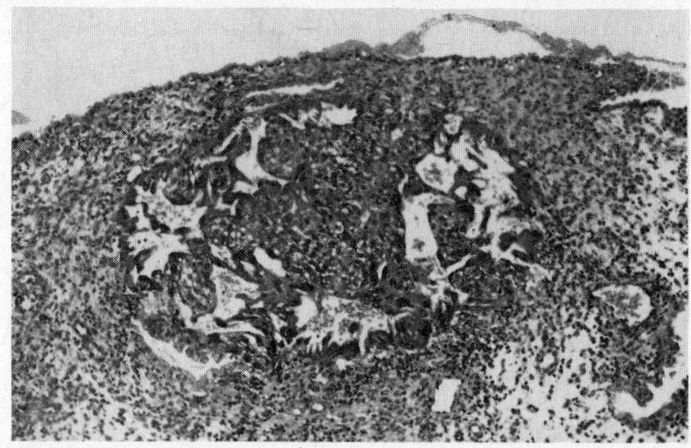

8 days

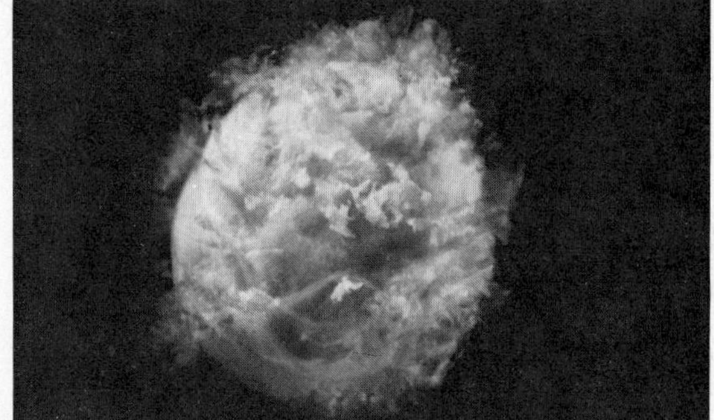

14 days

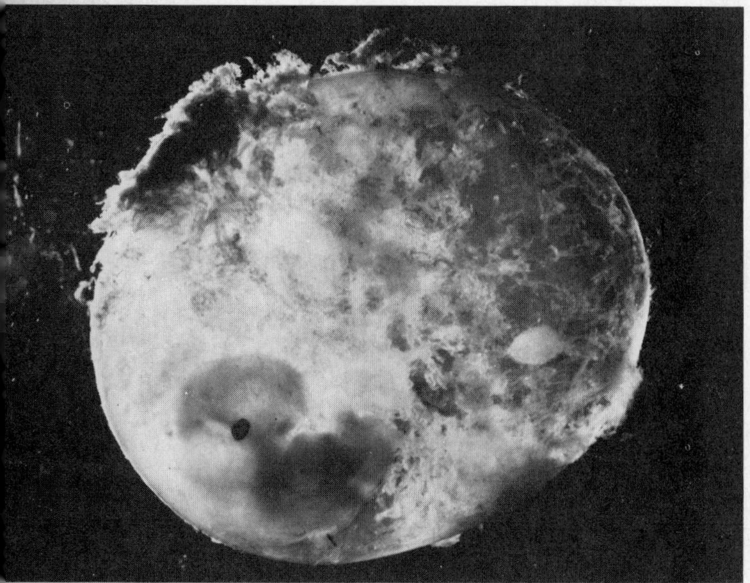

30 days

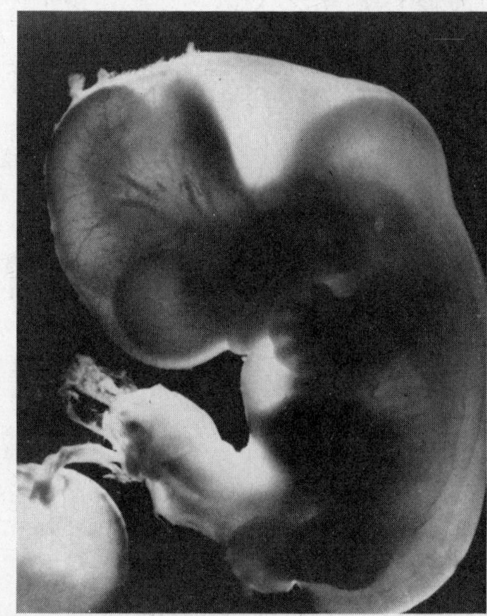

45 days

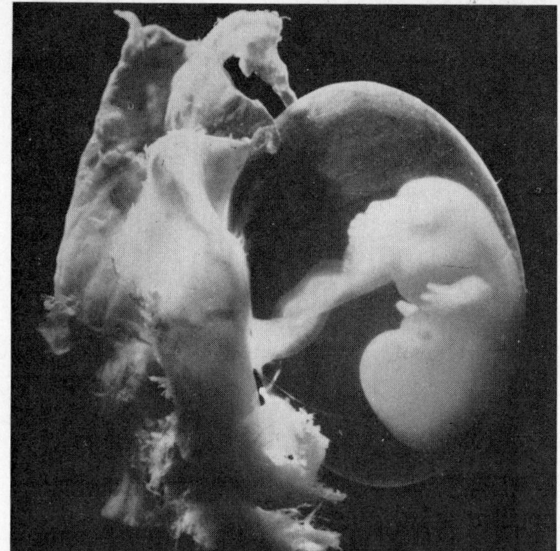

7 weeks

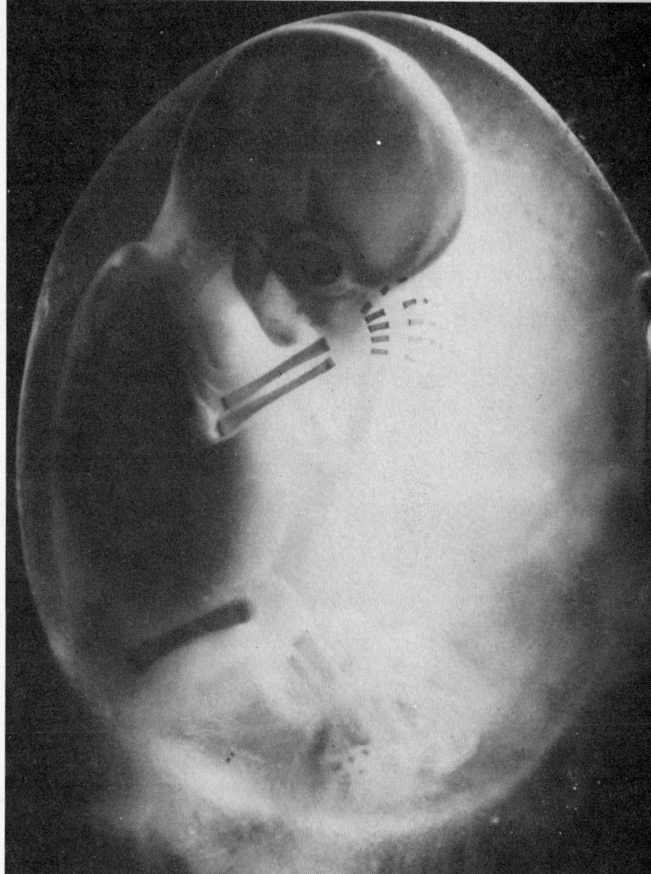

10 weeks

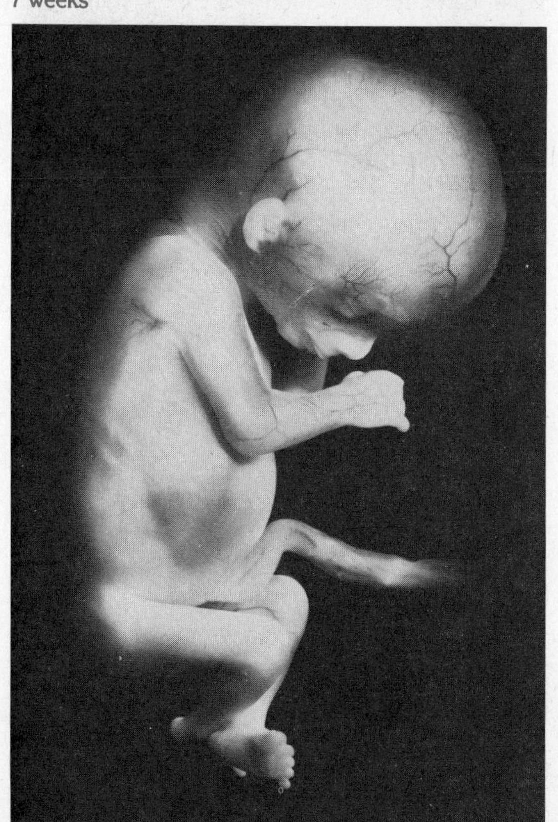

14 weeks

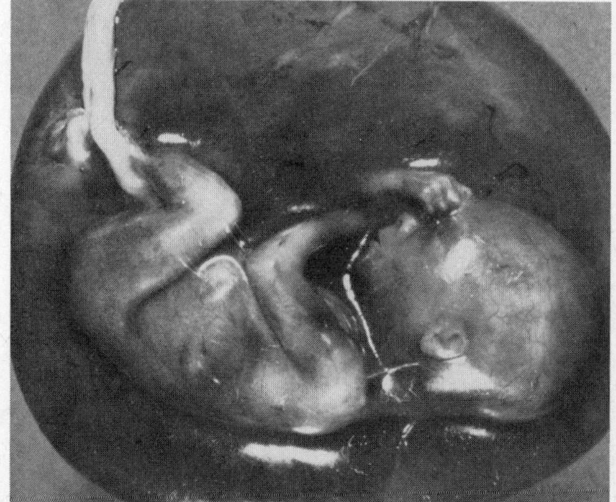

18 weeks

The Development of the Senses

Carmichael (1970) states that historically there has been considerable speculation about the role of the senses before birth. The question today is not one of consciousness before birth, but how and when stimulus control of fetal behavior by the different receptor systems begins before birth and how these capacities develop. Summarizing Carmichael's work, the developmental path is as follows:

1. *Touch.* This sense refers to the reaction to pressure, temperature, and pain, and seems to produce a generalized response. Carmichael states (1970, p. 520) that if a stimulus is applied to a quiescent fetus, there is "one behavior act or reflex set." He concludes that the specialized skin senses are capable of functioning long before birth.

2. *Taste.* Taste buds appear as early as the third fetal month and seem to be more widely distributed in fetal than adult life. Initially, taste buds appear on the tonsils, palate, and parts of the esophagus. In the adult, taste cells are restricted to the tongue. Carmichael believes that although the mechanism for taste is present before birth, the presence of the amniotic fluid limits a true taste response until after birth.

3. *Smell.* Like taste, the neurological basis for smell appears before birth; thus there exists the possibility of response. But since the nasal cavity is filled with amniotic fluid there is little likelihood that the sense of smell functions before birth. Carmichael notes that premature infants, in the last month, can smell substances when air enters the nasal cavity.

4. *Hearing.* As previously noted, most fetuses can hear sound by the fourth month. Carmichael believes that the auditory mechanism is well developed structurally in later fetal life, but since the middle ear is filled with fluid the fetus cannot respond to sounds of normal intensity. Strong auditory stimuli, however, produce a response. Carmichael warns about an overenthusiastic interpretation of the data because it still is impossible to state that such responses are truly auditory and not tactual.

5. *Vision.* There is general agreement that the absence of adequate retinal stimulation eliminates the possibility of true sight during prenatal life. Macfarlane (1977) states that while muscular development enables the fetus to move the eyes while changing body position, little is known about what or how much the fetus sees. By the end of pregnancy the uterus and the mother's abdomen wall may be stretched so thin that some light filters through, exposing the fetus to some light and dark contrast. Carmichael concludes that visual development begins in the second week following fertilization and continues until after birth. At birth, the eye is sufficiently developed to differentiate light and dark.

This summary of fetal life leads to an inevitable conclusion: given adequate conditions, the fetus at birth is equipped to deal effectively with the transition from its sheltered environment to the extrauterine world.

The Prenatal Environment

Since the interaction of heredity and environment is a dominant theme in analyzing human development, it is essential to specify when and how the environment begins to exert its influence. For any growing organism the moment of existence is critical. For example, if the zygote's nourishment is inadequate during its passage through the Fallopian tubes (seven days following fertilization), then its chances of survival are slim. McClearn (1964), a well-known geneticist, states that it is impossible to understand genetic mechanisms without considering the contribution of the environment.

He illustrates the environment's role by rearing drosophila (small flies used in genetic research) in different temperatures. A twelve-degree centigrade difference in temperature drastically reduced the number of eye facets that appeared. McClearn believes that any phenotypic description of gene action is impractical without specifying environmental circumstances. But "environment" needs broad interpretation; "uterine condition" is an insufficient and superficial term. One part of the embryo can become the environment for another; any cell is part of the environment for another cell.

Reviewing the animal literature, Thompson and Grusec (1970) conclude that almost any compound introduced into a pregnant animal affects behavior if the dosage is sufficient. Knowledge of the specific effects of any compound is limited. Even the effects of radiation, known to have grave consequences, depend on its intensity and timing. Prenatal stress *probably* produces later results. Thompson and Grusec conclude that:

1. changes produced by prenatal stress depend on the amount of stress and the age of the fetus when it is encountered;
2. it is doubtful if specific stressors have specific effects;
3. prenatal stress may result from nutritional upset.

These authors believe that studies of prenatal influences depend on animal research for credibility and are less than convincing regarding humans. With few exceptions, the data are mainly correlational and raise questions about any cause and effect relationship. For example, heated controversy now surrounds the use of obstetrical medication. Do advantages offset any potential effect on the newborn child? (For a summary of the literature, see Chapter 5.) One exception would be the thalidomide studies, which discovered that this seemingly safe sedative, taken at about six weeks of pregnancy, produced gross malformation of limbs.

Maternal disease may also cause defects. If the mother should contract rubella (german measles) during the first two or three months of pregnancy it may cause any of several congenital abnormalities, including deafness, muteness, and cardiac problems.

Thus emotions, drugs, and disease become important aspects of the prenatal environment.

Roberts (1976) attempts to specify the conditions affecting fetal growth as follows:

1. the genetic control of the individual fetus's growth; its length of gestation; its structural normality;
2. the quality of the intrauterine environment and the nature of the fetus's interaction with it: Is nutrition adequate? Are other fetuses present? Can the mother retain the fetus until maturity?
3. the mother's external environment; can the mother shield the fetus from environmental adversity?
4. the adequacy of the external environment, which may be determined by the parents' socioeconomic status.

Pregnancy as a Condition

Macfarlane (1977, p. 15) states that there are only two ways to have a baby, vaginally or by cesarean section, but each birth is as uniquely different as the woman herself. Ferreira (1960) administered an attitude questionnaire to women who were thirty-six weeks pregnant. He later observed their babies in the hospital nursery and discovered a significant correlation between the mother's emotions during pregnancy and her baby's behavior. Mothers who were unhappy about their pregnancy and those who feared that they might accidentally harm their babies had "deviant" youngsters who were restless, irritable, or had feeding difficulties, or bowel problems.

Women adjust to pregnancy differently. Since it is a condition that affects the total system, there is an immediate biological difference; some women tire more easily than others and require more sleep and rest. Women differ in their more obvious physical reactions, such as nausea and vomiting; some react better by eating several small servings than two or three large meals. Some women begin their pregnancies with feelings of depression, while others avoid them completely.

Lewis (1971) has attempted to analyze these differences and suggests four categories to explain them. First is the mother's personality, which he believes reflects the woman's personal experience with the mother-child bond. Another major influence on the mother's personality and subsequent attitude toward the child is the woman's relationship with the child's father. Second is the mother's acceptance of pregnancy, which affects her specific attitudes toward the unborn child. Lewis believes that these attitudes emerge from the complex motivation in becoming pregnant (to please a parent, to save a marriage, to prove femininity, or simply to enjoy the entire process).

The third category is the typical psychological reaction to pregnancy. Women usually move from a time of intense self-preoccupation to a gradual recognition of the new person with whom they form a complex relationship. The final category encompasses the mother's expectation of the child. Does she see the child as an independent human being who will forge his or her own way, or as an extension of herself?

The woman, as an individual, thus interprets pregnancy as a crisis and an abnormal state of illness or as a normal occurrence and a state of health. Annis (1978) states that regardless of pregnancy, everyday life continues and most babies are born normal and healthy because their mothers coped with emotional situations without harming themselves or their child. Perhaps Nilsson et al. (1977) offer the best advice when they suggest that the pregnant woman live her usual life but avoid excesses.

DISCUSSION QUESTIONS

1. Where does fertilization occur? How does the zygote achieve implantation? How much time is involved? What happens if fertilization does *not* occur?
2. Define these terms: blastocyst, placenta, umbilical cord, amniotic fluid, embryo. Explain the function of the placenta during prenatal life.
3. What do you think are the major landmarks of the fetal period? When does viability occur? What do you mean by tissue differentiation?
4. Do you think prenatal learning is possible? Consider the development of the senses, the uterine environment, and the mother's role before you answer.
5. Heredity and environment explain development. How can the prenatal environment influence growth? Is there that much individual difference between uterine environments? Be specific in your answer; that is, consider *all* agents that might affect the fetus or embryo and illustrate differences between women in their contact with and reaction to these agents.

THE BIRTH PROCESS

The odyssey that began approximately nine months ago is about to reach its climax—birth. Before this moment arrives, the mother has to make certain decisions. Does she, for example, ask the physician to use an anesthetic, or does she want natural childbirth? Both methods have their advantages and disadvantages. Natural childbirth provides an unforgettable experience for the mother, but it is hard, painful work that some women prefer to avoid. The use of anesthesia prevents much of the birth pain, but the drug may affect the baby adversely, decreasing alertness and activity for days after birth.

The mother usually becomes aware of the beginning of the process of labor by one or more of these signs: (1) the passage of blood from the vagina; (2) the passage of amniotic fluid from the ruptured amniotic sac through the vagina; (3) uterine contractions and accompanying discomfort. The first two clues are sure signs that labor has begun, while occasionally other pains (false labor) may be mistaken for signs of true labor.

Three further stages of labor can also be distinguished: (1) Dilation, in which the neck of the uterus (the cervix) stretches to about four inches in diameter. This is the process responsible for labor pains and may last for twelve or thirteen hours. (2) The expulsion; once the neck or cervix is fully open, the baby passes through the birth canal. This phase lasts about ninety minutes for the first child, and about thirty to forty-five minutes for subsequent children. (3) The afterbirth, in which the placenta and other membranes are discharged.

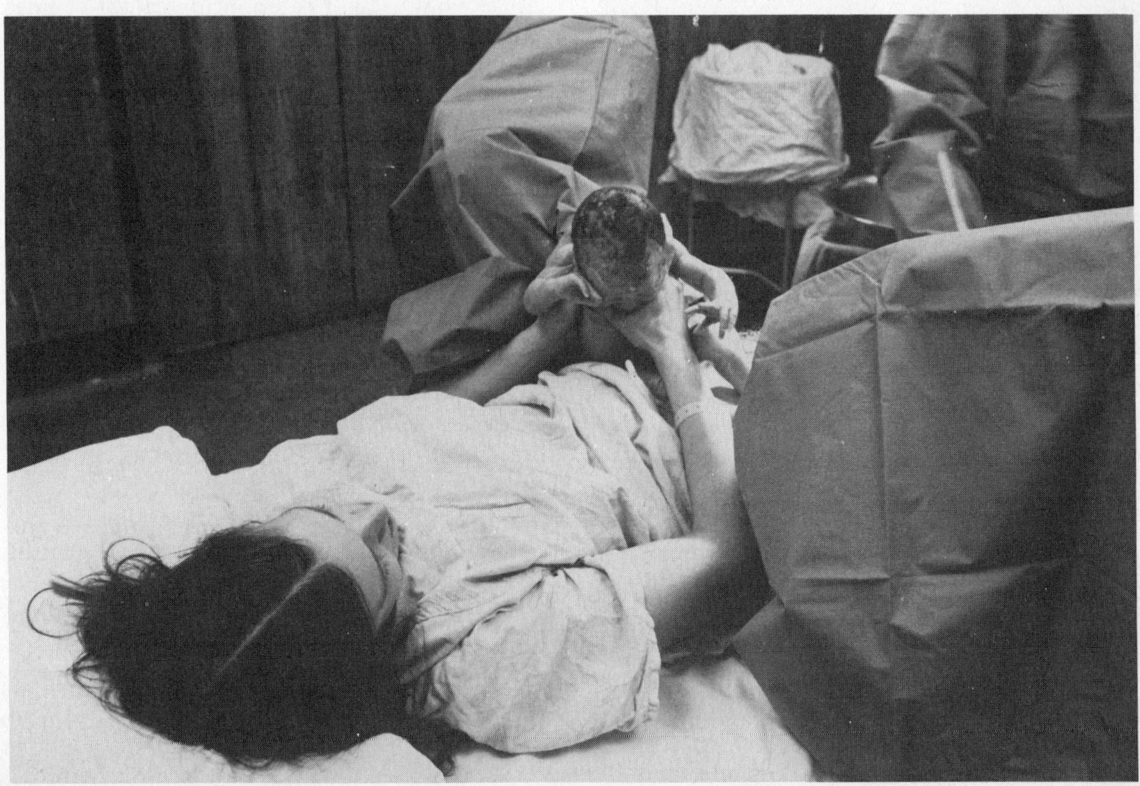

Birth can sometimes be exceptionally difficult, even dangerous. Here are a few of the more common complications.

1. *Breech birth.* About four out of every hundred babies are born feet first, or buttocks first, while one out of a hundred are in a crosswise position (transverse presentation). If the mother's physician has suspected this condition during pregnancy, he or she may be able to facilitate the birth.

2. *High Forceps.* Occasionally, for safety purposes, the physician will withdraw the baby with forceps during the first phase of birth. A forceps delivery presents some danger of rupturing blood vessels or causing brain damage.

3. *Cesarean section.* If for some reason the child cannot come through the birth canal, surgery is performed to deliver the baby through the abdomen. Although now fairly safe, this operation is considered major surgery and is not usually recommended unless necessary.

4. *Prematurity.* About seven out of every hundred births are premature, occurring less than thirty-seven weeks after conception. Fortunately today it is possible to simulate womb conditions so that the correct temperature and humidity, bacteria control, and easily digested food can be provided for the child. Still, prematurity presents real dangers, ranging from mental deficiency to death.

5. *Anoxia (lack of oxygen).* If something during the birth process should cut the flow of oxygen to the fetus, there is the possibility of brain damage or death. Annis (1978, p. 90) states that there is a substantial need for oxygen during birth because pressure on the fetal head can cause some rupturing of the blood vessels in the brain. After the umbilical cord is cut, delay in lung breathing can also produce anoxia. Failure here can cause death or brain damage. Currently, controversy focuses on infants who have experienced anoxia, survived, but show evidence of mental dullness. Is an intellectual impairment permanent?

Sameroff (1977) has reviewed the literature concerning delivery and birth complications and isolated the pertinent studies of anoxia. Investigators assumed that early cerebral oxygen deprivation would cause later intellectual difficulty, so youngsters were studied during infancy, at three years, and finally at seven years. A definite pattern emerged: a few days after birth infants seemed impaired on visual, sensorimotor, and maturational level tests. At three years, studied with perceptual-motor, cognitive, personality, and neurological tests, they showed lower than normal cognitive functioning and an improved performance on the other items. By seven years, significant IQ differences had *disappeared.* Sameroff concludes that anoxia is a poor predictor of later intellectual functioning and that socioeconomic characteristics still remain the best single predictor of future adjustment.

Most babies, however, escape these complications, and sustain little, if any birth difficulty. To aid the newly born child in adjusting to a new environment, Leboyer (1975) believes that we must stop "torturing the innocent." Instead of newborns encountering a cold, bright world that turns infants upside down and slaps them, Leboyer advocates a calmer environment. He suggests extinguishing all lights in the delivery room except a small night light, and making the room silent at the time of birth. Immediately after birth, the child is placed not on a cold metal scale, but on the mother's abdomen, a natural resting place. After several minutes the child is transferred to a basin of warm water. Leboyer claims that this process eases the shock of birth and babies are almost instantly calm and happy.

Birth: Where, When, and How?

Two questions about birth that cause debate ask about birth at home or in the hospital, and the role of pain-relieving drugs. Macfarlane (1977) states that in any discussion of home versus hospital delivery, childbirth in the Netherlands is mentioned. The death rate is lower there than in the United States, but most deliveries are at home. The rationale is that childbirth is natural and needs no interference. A healthy woman spontaneously performs the process in a manner that cannot be improved; only high-risk cases belong in the hospital.

There is no reliable evidence that clearly supports home or hospital births. Macfarlane presents data that suggest home birth decreases postnatal depression, but a hospital delivery lessens the risk of infection and offers instant support for any emergency. Although thinking about childbirth is changing and now reveals concern about medication, an increase in natural childbirth, and the desire for the father's presence at delivery, most American births still occur in hospitals.

The second question involves the mother's tolerance of pain. As Macfarlane (1977) notes, chemical, psychological, and magical attempts to relieve the pain of childbirth are as old as humanity. One increasingly popular method is called psychoprophylaxis, in which, through training, the woman is taught to relax and concentrate on stimuli other than the pain of uterine contractions (Nilsson et al., 1977, p. 114). An example of this is the Lamaze method, based on the work of Dr. Ferrard Lamaze, who believed that if properly trained, women could control their deliveries. Beginning with instruction in the physiology of childbirth, the woman is then taught relaxation techniques to remain calm and special breathing exercises to control the pain of delivery. Although some women who master this method require no medication, most request some form of relief, but usually less than those who have had no training.

The use of drugs during childbirth is the subject of growing concern. Macfarlane states that the epidural block, which prevents the transmission of pain messages from the abdomen and legs and which does not interfere with uterine contractions, is quite popular. The mother remains conscious and aware of delivery. While effective, the drug, nevertheless, enters the mother's bloodstream and through the placenta into the baby's blood. Other drugs, such as demerol, also reach the baby.

Noting that practically all drugs—analgesics, anesthetics, amnesics—pass through the placenta into the fetal blood and tissues, Bowes et al. (1970) studied twenty-three normal youngsters whose mothers had some medication during birth. They conclude that obstetrical medication has a significant effect on early infant sensorimotor functioning, muscular, visual, and neural, which probably disappears at twenty weeks.

Bowes, summarizing the uncertainties surrounding drug use, states:

> The medications used for analgesia and anesthesia, if they do not grossly alter the intrauterine environment, appear to be well tolerated by the fetus; and though there may be transient narcosis, there are probably few long-term untoward effects. It is surprising that the fetus has fared so well, subjected as it is to so many agents. But as physicians and the pharmaceutical industry develop ever more potent and complex ways of altering physiological and pathological states, the fetus is bound to be the inadvertent target of maternal therapy. (1970, p. 23)

CONTEMPORARY PRENATAL ISSUES

As previously noted, each of us carries several faulty genes, but two parents do not usually carry the same defective genes; thus the healthy gene typically dominates any ill effects

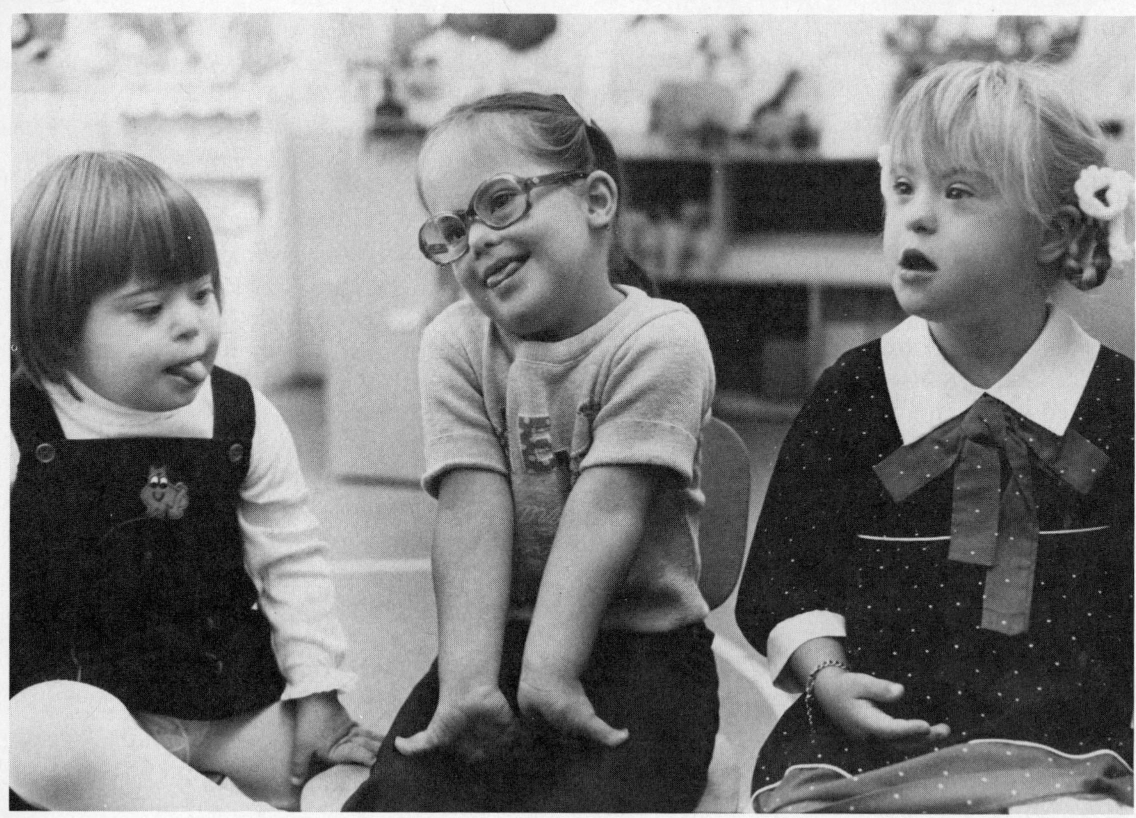

that could arise from the faulty gene. Yet abnormalities and the probability of their occurrence are of concern to all of us. The following are the most common defects.

1. *Down's Syndrome.* Also called mongolism, Down's syndrome is caused by an extra chromosome on the twenty-first pair; the individual has forty-seven chromosomes. This defect was discovered in 1866 by a British doctor, Langdon Down, and produces distinctive facial features, small hands, a large tongue, and possible functional difficulties such as mental retardation, heart defects, and an added risk of leukemia.

The mother's age is closely related to the evidence of Down's syndrome; chances are about 1 in 750 between the ages of 30–35; 1 in 300 between 35–39; 1 in 80 between 40–45; and after 45 years the incidence jumps to 1 chance in 40 births. Under 30 years, the ratio is only 1 in 1500 births (Hendin and Marks, 1978, p. 163). Although the exact cause of Down's syndrome remains a mystery, the answer may lie in the female egg production mechanism, which results in eggs remaining in the ovary for forty or fifty years. Thus they are increasingly subject to the possibility of damage. But Holmes (1978) questions that the female genes alone are responsible. New techniques for staining chromosomes enable investigators to trace the source of the extra twenty-first chromosome. In twenty-three percent of the cases, the male was the source. Another interesting phenomenon has arisen in the 1970s. Statistical trends indicate that ninety percent of all births are to women *under* age thirty-five, who now have fifty to sixty percent of the Down's syndrome children. These new data raise serious questions about causation and whether it can be attributed to male or female, young or old.

Reed (1975) notes that there is no treatment for Down's syndrome other than good medical supervision and special education. These individuals usually are cheerful, perhaps slightly stubborn, with a good sense of mimicry and rhythm. Since the severity of the defect varies, institutionalization of the child is no longer immediately recommended. Some youngsters develop better in the home, especially if the parents believe they can cope successfully.

2. *Other Chromosomal Disorders.* Down's syndrome results from an extra chromosome. If you recall, the twenty-third pair of chromosomes are the sex chromosomes, XX for females, XY for males. Winchester (1977) estimates that one in every 1200 females and one in every 400 males has some disorder in the sex chromosomes. Occasionally a male will possess an XXY pattern rather than the normal XY. This is called Klinefelter's syndrome, and eventually causes small testicles, reduced body hair, and possible infertility. Another pattern that appears in males is XYY, which may cause larger size and increased aggression. Heated controversy and inconclusive results have surrounded the "super male."

Females occasionally possess an XO pattern rather than XX. This is called Turner's syndrome and is characterized by short stature, poorly developed secondary sex features such as breasts, and usually sterility.

3. *Tay Sachs Disease.* This disease strikes hardest at Jews of Eastern European origin and causes death by the age of four or five. At birth the afflicted children appear normal, but development slows by six months and mental and motor deterioration begin. There is no cure, and as Reed notes (1975) the only treatment is the alleviation of symptoms as they appear.

Estimates are that about one in every twenty-five Jews of Eastern European origin carries the defective gene, which is recessive; thus danger arises when two carriers marry. The disease results from a gene failing to produce an enzyme that breaks down fatty materials in the brain and nervous system. The result is that fat accumulates and destroys nerve cells, causing loss of coordination, blindness, and, finally death.

4. *Sickle-Cell Anemia.* This disease, mainly afflicting those of African descent, appeared thousands of years ago in equatorial Africa and increased resistance to malaria (Hendin and Marks, 1978, p. 184). Estimates are that ten percent of the black population in the United States carries the sickle-cell trait. Thus two carriers who marry have a one-in-four chance of producing a child with sickle-cell anemia.

The problem is caused by abnormal hemoglobin. The red blood cells of the victim of sickle-cell anmemia are distorted and pointed; because of their shape they encounter difficulty in passing through the blood vessels. They tend to pile up and clump, producing oxygen starvation accompanied by considerable pain. The body then acts to eliminate these cells, and anemia results.

5. *Cystic Fibrosis.* Reed (1975, p. 75) states that in the population of the United States, cystic fibrosis is the most severe genetic disease of childhood, with about one in twelve hundred children being affected, and one in thirty being carriers. The disease causes a malfunction of the endocrine glands, the glands that secrete tears, sweat, mucus, and saliva. Breathing is difficult because of the thickness of the mucus. The secreted sweat is extremely salty, often producing heat exhaustion. Cystic fibrosis kills more children than any other genetic disease. If diagnosed early and treated properly, these victims today can lead a fairly lengthy life.

There are several aspects of cystic fibrosis that explain its deadliness: its cause remains unknown and carriers cannot be detected although new research offers hope. It is not until a child manifests the breathing and digestive problems characteristic of the disease that identification is possible.

6. *Hemophilia.* The "bleeder's" disease results from a defective gene on the sex chromosome; thus it is a sex-linked disease. The hemophiliac does not bleed faster or harder than others, but cannot form clots to stop the blood flow. Small surface cuts usually are not a problem; it is the bleeding in deeper body areas that causes concern.

The second X of the XX pair prevents the appearance of the disease in females. A carrier mother and normal father have a fifty percent chance that any male child will have hemophilia.

The faulty gene affects the blood plasma, which then lacks the necessary protein for clotting. (There are actually two types of hemophilia, A or B, depending upon the missing protein.) Today it is possible to treat hemophilia by supplying a clotting element, but the process is still expensive. Detection of carriers remains elusive and it is impossible to determine prenatally if the fetus is a hemophiliac.

7. *Phenylketonuria.* PKU results from the body's failure to break down the amino acid phenylalanine, which then accumulates, affects the nervous system, and causes mental retardation. Most states now require infants to be tested at birth; if PKU is present, the infants are placed on a special diet that has been remarkably successful.

But this success has produced future problems. Women treated successfully may give birth to retarded children because of a toxic uterine environment. Thus at the first signs of pregnancy, these women must return to a special diet. As Reed (1975) notes, the "cured" phenylketonuric still carries the faulty genes.

While these are the more common and dramatic genetic diseases, other diseases also have, or are suspected of having, a strong genetic relationship: diabetes, epilepsy, heart disorders, cancer, arthritis, and some mental illnesses.

Amniocentesis

Genetically, some people are "at risk"; that is, they may be susceptible to a genetic disease. Such individuals are urged to visit a genetic counselor who, through a combination of prenatal tests, lab studies, physical examinations, and a review of family histories, may help to prevent some of the difficulties associated with genetic defects.

Today amniocentesis is probably the most widely recommended technique in prenatal diagnosis, a technique that allows a physician to detect a remarkably wide range of genetic disorders. A small amount of amniotic fluid is removed from the uterus during the fifteenth to the seventeenth week after the last menstrual period. In the laboratory, fetal cells are removed from the fluid and reproduced in sufficient numbers to produce cultures. The cells are then examined for incidence of chemical abnormalities (such as Tay Sachs disease), any chromosomal disorders (such as Down's syndrome), or the possibility of any sex-linked defects.

Fuchs (1980, p. 53) summarizes the value of amniocentesis as follows:

> . . . certain inborn errors of metabolism have symptoms that can be alleviated after birth by dietary measures or by the administration of drugs. It is imaginable that such treatment might be applicable to the fetus. Moreover, it is a truism in medicine that the first step in rational treatment is an exact diagnosis, and this is what amniocentesis provides in many cases. The successes of amniocentesis therefore suggest the hope that at some time in the future measures to alter the expression of genes and thereby cure disease might be administered in utero.

Other methods of prenatal diagnosis include ultrasound (using high-frequency sound waves to construct a "picture" of the uterus and fetus), radiography (using X-rays to determine any skeletal abnormalities; best used as a last resort and near the end of pregnancy), and fetoscopy (using an optical rod inserted into the uterus and actually looking at the fetus).

Whatever the technique, the mere availability of these tests poses agonizing questions for many parents. If amniocentesis reveals forty-seven chromosomes, what do parents decide, knowing that they will have a Down's syndrome child? What decision will be reached if a couple "at risk" for hemophilia learn that they will have a male child? The answer to these questions involves a complex and explosive mixture of personal feelings about abortion, religious beliefs, fear, hope, and perhaps conflicting advice from religious and genetic counselors.

DISCUSSION QUESTIONS

1. Summarize the evidence concerning anoxia. What is your reaction to the predictions about future mental performance?
2. Do you have strong feelings about hospital or home birth? Can you justify your position? Do you favor natural childbirth? Why? Do your answers relate to the effects of medication?
3. Be sure you understand the characteristics of the major genetic diseases. For example, what diseases are sex-linked? What does this mean? Since they cannot be detected what does this imply for genetic counseling?
4. Sickle-cell anemia cannot be detected in utero; carriers can be detected. What are the implications of this statement for genetic counseling?
5. Genetic knowledge is increasing the life-span of many individuals suffering from a genetic defect, some of whom marry. Many genetic authorities believe this is a mixed blessing. What do they mean?
6. What are the consequences of amniocentesis for parents? Relate your answer to each of the major genetic defects discussed.

There should not be any glib acceptance of the statement that development results from the interaction of heredity and environment. As you have seen in this chapter, heredity's role can completely determine the extent and quality of an individual's existence, from a decision to abort because of a genetic defect to a decision to provide support for however long it may be needed. And yet the environment in its turn can be equally as supportive or destructive, from a healthy intrauterine environment to the toxic effects supplied by a PKU mother. So environment, also, exerts its influence from the moment of conception.

With this reluctance to accept cliches, the interaction of heredity and environment becomes more meaningful. As the mechanics of the fertilization process, including more detailed knowledge about the nature of egg and sperm, and the mechanics of hereditary transmission become more accessible, recognition of human genetic information becomes staggering. Yet, as Carl Sagan notes, genetic information alone is insufficient; humans need extragenetic, even extrasomatic information.

Tracing the growth pattern during the 280 days of gestation reveals an amazing saga of growing sophistication that culminates in a competent organism capable of adjusting to an alien environment. Some organisms, however, are less competent than others to survive, and an advancing genetic technology raises immediate critical decisions for individuals and perhaps even more excruciating, future decisions for society.

SUMMARY

Not all infants are born healthy; greater genetic knowledge permits a more suitable interaction of heredity and environment that reflects individual needs.

The maturation of sperm and egg cells differs in important respects that may help to explain certain genetic defects.

Although the fertilization process is better understood today, many questions remain unanswered. What limits sperm penetration to one? Why does the fertilized egg suddenly become active?

There are two types of human chromosomes: autosomes and sex chromosomes. The sex chromosome (X) may carry genes for traits other than sex; these are called sex-linked traits.

In a mitotic division the number of chromosomes remains the same; in a meiotic division the number of chromosomes is halved.

Genes are actually DNA molecules, which, because of their intricate chemical coding, contain an awesome amount of information.

Mendel's work, called classical genetics, and studies of DNA, called molecular genetics, explain hereditary transmission.

Prenatal development is usually divided into three phases: the ovum, the embryo, and the fetus.

There is greater recognition today of pregnancy as a condition. The woman's view of herself and her unborn child are important influences on prenatal development.

The birth process itself is currently causing controversy. There are those who argue for home rather than hospital delivery, for natural rather than medicated childbirth.

Advancing technology permits the identification of numerous genetic defects, thus raising serious moral, religious, ethical, and personal questions.

SUGGESTED READINGS

ANNIS, LINDA F. *The Child Before Birth.* Ithaca, New York: Cornell University Press, 1978. A succinct and interesting account of the prenatal months.

HENDIN, DAVID and JOAN MARKS. *The Genetic Connection.* New York: William Morrow and Co., 1978. A fascinating introduction to the latest research in genetic disease. Thorough and well written.

NILSSON, LENNART, MIRJAM FURUHJELM, ALEX INGELMAN-SUNDBERG, and CLAES WIRSEN. *A Child Is Born.* New York: Delacorte Press, 1977. A careful analysis of the prenatal period. One of the most lavishly and beautifully photographed texts available.

REED, ELIZABETH. "Genetic Anomalies in Development," in Frances Horowitz (editor), *Review of Child Development Research,* Volume 4. Chicago: University of Chicago Press, 1975. A good, brief overview of the major genetic diseases.

SAGAN, CARL. *The Dragons of Eden.* New York: Random House, 1977. An intriguing account of the evolution of human intelligence.

SCHEINFELD, AMRAN. *Your Heredity and Environment.* Philadelphia: J. P. Lippincott, 1965. A comprehensive, readable classic that surveys existing genetic knowledge.

WATSON, JAMES. *The Double Helix.* Boston: Atheneum Press, 1968. A personal, captivating account of one of the greatest discoveries in biological history.

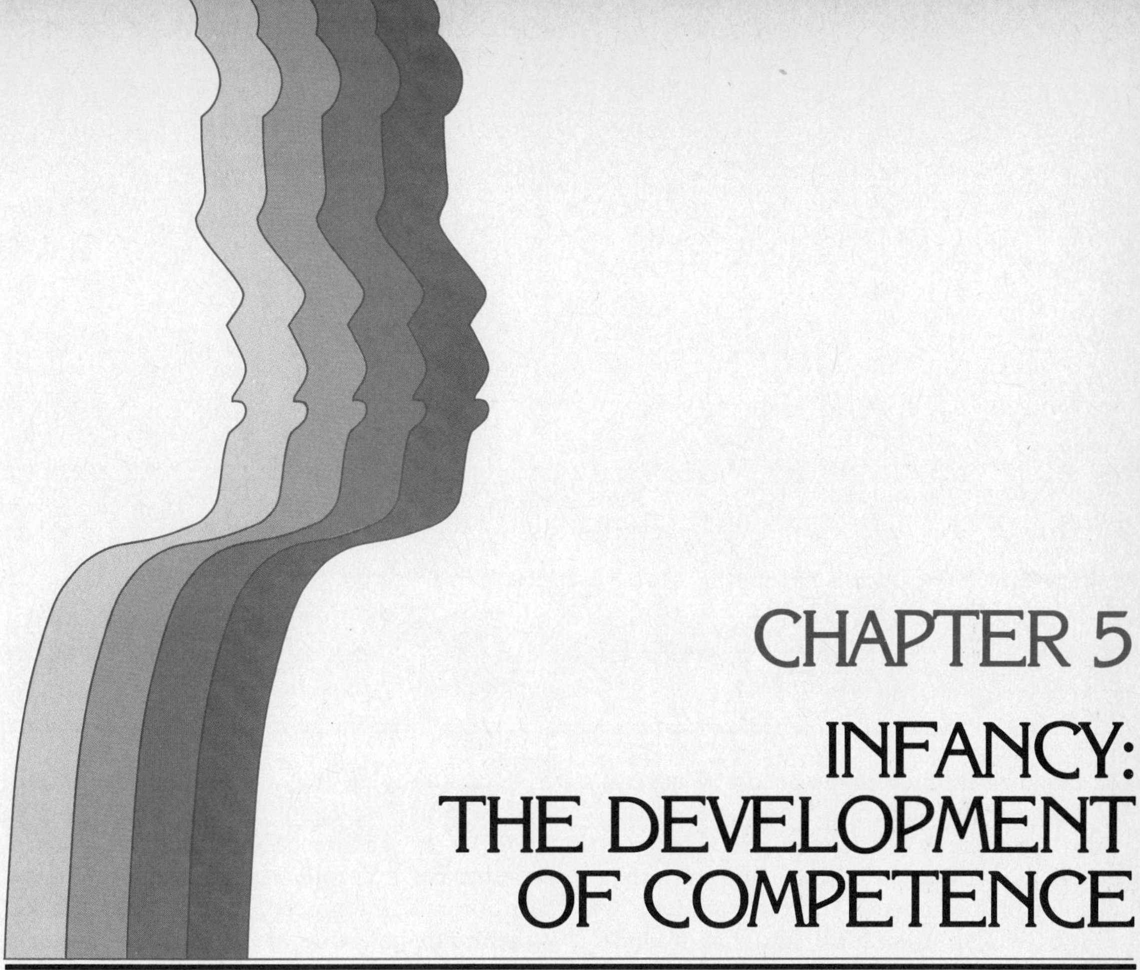

CHAPTER 5

INFANCY: THE DEVELOPMENT OF COMPETENCE

CHAPTER HIGHLIGHTS

Topics

Infant Assessment Techniques
a. States of Infancy
b. Neonatal Assessment: An Overview

Motor Development
a. Head Control
b. Grasping
c. Locomotion: Crawling and Creeping

Perceptual Development
a. Perceptual Trends
b. Relevant Perceptual Dimensions

Cognitive Development
a. Cognitive Trends
b. The Emergence of Memory

Learning and Infant Development
a. Maturation versus Learning
b. Characteristics of Infant Learning

Early Experience and Infancy
a. The Nervous System and Development
b. The Reversibility of Early Experience

People

Virginia Apgar
T. G. R. Bower
T. B. Brazelton
Jerome Bruner
John Eccles
Robert Fantz
Jerome Kagan
Robert McCall
Steven Rose
Harold Skeels

Special Topics

The Brazelton Neonatal Assessment Scale
Medication and Neonatal Assessment
Early Evidence of Perception
Infant Memory
A Special Case of Communication
Imitation
Are the Results of Early Experience Reversible?

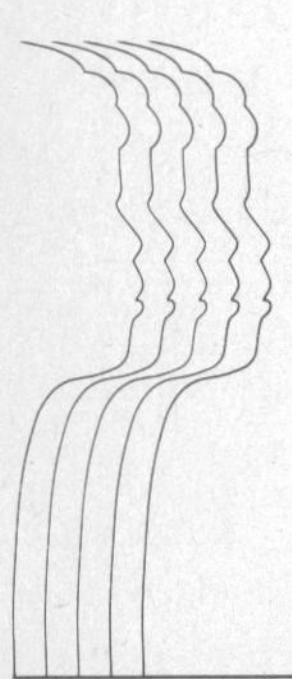

The study of infancy offers a unique appeal. The processes by which a helpless, reflexive neonate becomes a knowing, capable two-year-old demand explanation. The forces that cause an infant to view the environment as either trustful or mistrustful and that produce feelings of autonomy rather than insecurity require detailed scrutiny. The companionship of others, that vital ingredient of humanness culminating in a social being, also thrusts itself upon us as a key developmental element, one compelling analysis. But above all, it is the sheer impact of infant change that attracts.

Bower (1977) states that an infant is literally someone who does not talk. Yet two-year-olds do talk. They also smile, walk, grasp objects, and learn at a phenomenal rate. Lipsitt (1976) comments that these and similar changes are the first and least interesting law of human development—uninteresting because change is obvious, descriptive, and nonexplanatory. Yet this basic law has produced the developmental testing movement and forced investigators to search for the causes of change.

Recent studies of infancy reflect the search for the causes of change. Haith and Campos (1977) note that there is an emerging *theory of infancy.* For example, Piaget's studies of sensorimotor development, recent analyses of attachment behavior, and a growing concern with early neurophysiological development emphasize the study of infants as infants and the use of techniques designed for infancy, not modified versions of adult assessment.

Today there is less doubt of infant competence and greater interest in the transition to more effective functional behavior. Attempts to explain rather than merely describe these transitions show an increasing sophistication and complexity. Theoretical explanation, however, demonstrates a third theme: the tendency to engage in more conceptual endeavors while utilizing technological advances. For example, investigators have used EKG measures to indicate certain emotional behaviors such as fear and separation anxiety.

Macfarlane (1978) illustrates the need for a wide range of investigative tools in his chronicles of an infant's abilities. Beginning with the premise that infants are not passive recipients of stimulation, he states that merely being born human produces unique behaviors. Babies, almost from birth, will scrutinize human faces longer than they look at other objects; patterns seem to attract them. Studies show that two-week-old babies recognize their mothers; infants only a few days old turn their heads toward a sound.

Macfarlane describes studies of infants' sense of smell that again demonstrate complex behavior. Studies have consistently shown that babies can differentiate odors. Observing that a baby turned toward its mother's breast before seeing it, Macfarlane wondered if an infant could possibly recognize the distinctive odor of its mother. To test his theory, he placed against one side of the baby's face pads that the mother had worn inside her bra, and against the other side pads that had not been worn. After one minute he reversed the pads. Five-day-old infants turned their heads toward their mothers' pads more often than toward the unworn pads.

To complicate the experiment, he placed pads worn by someone other than the infants' own mothers next to the infants' cheeks. Among infants two days old there was little difference in response, but infants six days old turned much more toward their own mothers' pads, and among babies ten days old, the distinction was almost complete. To discover whether it was the mother's smell or the breast milk that attracted the infants, Macfarlane had the mothers express milk onto pads and then repeated his experiment. The infants again turned to their own mothers' pads, thus indicating that the milk alone was not the attraction.

Infants exhibit taste differentiation; they feel pain; they imitate. Macfarlane suggests that one conclusion is inescapable: infants, at birth, have the capacity to respond selectively and socially to other humans through a system of mutual attraction that has evolved over millions of years and that ensures survival.

These generalizations, however, should not obscure infant individuality. Brazelton (1969, p. 1) notes that there are as many individual variations in behavioral patterns of newborns as there are infants. Among humans the variety of behaviors that can occur in appearance, feeling, reaction patterns, and movement patterns is bewildering, and can challenge, frustrate, and stimulate the observer.

The search for an explanation of these behavioral changes requires persistence, skill, and tact, qualities that well serve those who work with infants. Burton White (1975) outlines three goals for parents of infants that can also serve as guidelines for those studying the infant period of development and that will appear as chapter themes.

1. Infants should feel loved and cared for.
2. Infants require help in developing specific skills.
3. Infants should be encouraged to become interested in the outside world by stimulation of their curiosity.

To help you understand infants, this chapter will first explore infant assessment techniques: what is an infant's *state* at testing and how will it affect performance? Has the infant functioned normally from birth? What are the most important tests used today? What are their strengths and weaknesses? What effect does obstetrical medication have upon neonatal assessment?

Once the methods for determining an infant's capabilities are analyzed, attention will turn to the various aspects of infant development. The path of motor development—grasping, sitting, creeping, standing, walking—will be traced. Perceptual development, which occurs at a startling rate, is a continuation of a process that was initiated before birth. Vision becomes functional at birth, and the increased information requires integration, causing rapid advances in perceptual development.

As the infant explores the environment and perception widens, cognitive development occurs, gradually enabling the child to utilize an expanding representational system. From a realization that objects exist even when not present (at about nine months), children at the end of infancy (about two years) use one thing to represent another, a clear indication that mental development, although quite limited, is beginning to give them control over the environment.

Growing motor skill, accompanied by perceptual and cognitive development, allows the child to learn at an equally rapid rate. Learning, the process of modifying behavior, depends on the infant's increasing capabilities and ability to employ and interpret multiple and varied stimuli. If development proceeds normally, the environment plays a key role in providing adequate stimulation. If, conversely, youngsters encounter an impoverished environment, notable damage, both physical and psychological, can result. When impoverishment occurs, the question arises whether the damage is permanent.

These are the issues we will consider in this chapter. Understanding the causes of infant development should help us to understand some persistent problems that plague all studies of development:

1. The interaction of physiological and psychological elements.
2. The validity and meaning of stages in development.
3. The relevance of context (the interpretation of emerging behaviors as products of the interaction between the infant and the environment). (Kagan, in Lipsitt, 1976)

We shall return to these developmental questions at the chapter's conclusion.

INFANT ASSESSMENT TECHNIQUES

Understanding infancy necessitates knowledge of an infant's state. Is the infant physically and psychologically able to interact with the environment? Answering this question testifies to the need for accurate assessment techniques, ranging from the newborn's immediate status and neurological well-being to behavioral reactions and personality expression. Chapter Three, "Heredity and the Prenatal Environment," demonstrated that the newborn has had nine months of environmental influence; thus, as Brazelton (1973) notes, the infant's behavior is phenotypic at birth, not genotypic.

States of Infancy

An important element in any type of infant assessment is the baby's state of consciousness (Brazelton, 1973). Brazelton believes that an infant's use of a state of consciousness in regulating both internal and environmental pressures reflects a potential for behavioral organization. Many variables affect an infant's state—hunger, thirst, sleep—and there are various ways of classifying state.

Brazelton (1973) reports that both the pattern of states and movement from state to state are significant indications of an infant's receptivity and ability to respond to stimuli. A state is achieved if an infant remains in it for at least fifteen seconds (Brazelton, 1973, p. 5). There are six states in the Brazelton scheme.

Sleep States

1. Deep sleep: regular breathing, eyes closed, little movement (no eye movement), startle reaction to external stimuli. Any startle reaction is rapidly suppressed and there is very little change from state to state.

2. Light sleep: rapid eye movement under closed lids, low activity level with random movements (movements seem smoother than in the first state), response to stimuli may cause a change of state. Sucking movements may occur.

Awake States

3. Drowsy: eyes are either open or closed, reacts to stimuli with delayed response. State change may occur after stimulation; movements are usually smooth with occasional fussing.

4. Alert: focuses on source of stimulation (an object to be sucked or some attention-provoking stimulus), minimal motor activity.

5. Active: considerable motor activity. Extremities exhibit thrusting movements, difficult to distinguish discrete reactions because of high activity level. Fussing may be present.

6. Crying: intense crying that suppresses the possibility of responding to stimulation.

Infants who exhibit the characteristics of a particular state for at least fifteen seconds are considered to be in that state. Brazelton (1973) believes that state establishes a pattern that reflects an infant's entire behavioral repertoire.

STATES AND DESCRIPTIONS OF INFANTS

Any analysis of infant states raises questions about the means investigators use to describe them. Kagan, Kearsley, and Zelazo (1978) believe that descriptions of infants inevitably reflect what adults want infants to become. For example, Western societies value autonomy; consequently, the development of infants and children is seen as a steady progression from dependency to independence. Eastern societies, however, value intimate interdependence in their adults and see the infant as too independent. Dependency is thus encouraged.

The authors state that the selection of description for children exemplifies the more general problem of categorization. Experience causes humans to group events that share common characteristics and then to label them. But investigators are prone to error if they do not categorize natural phenomena naturally. That is, one cannot describe the behaviors, conditions, or states of infancy by employing adult norms.

Behavioral observations typically are used to describe or explain. Kagan et al. believe that most psychologists describe behavior and compare it to adult standards. Current psychological terminology demonstrates a comparative description: oral as compared to genital, sensorimotor as compared to formal operations. The authors state that greater insights into infancy will emerge if investigators concentrate on the *relations between phenomena* and use these as a basis for categorization.

The warning is timely. As concern grows about the inadequacy of infant assessment, more tests will appear. Based on behaviors or states, they could easily employ the technique of comparative description. The Kagan, Kearsley, and Zelazo discussion of older methods and current trends offers valuable guidelines.

Neonatal Assessment: An Overview

However we characterize a newborn's status, assessment is difficult. St. Clair (1978) states that today's close link between psychology and medicine can obscure the nature and purpose of infant tests. For example, medical tests, which rely on observation and behavioral responses, assess neurological functioning; psychological tests measure behavior, which also reflects neurological functioning. To clarify the purposes of the various tests, Self and Horowitz (1974) suggest three classifications: screening devices such as the Apgar (1953), neurological devices such as the Prechtl and Beintema (1964), and behavioral scales such as the Brazelton (1973).

The Apgar. In 1953 Virginia Apgar proposed a scale to evaluate a newborn's basic life signs. It is administered one minute after birth, and repeated at three-, five-, and ten-minute intervals. Using five life signs—heart rate, respiratory effort, muscle tone, reflex irritability, color—an observer evaluates the infant by a three-point scale.

Considerable care is needed in interpreting the results. Slow stabilization of processes may be temporary but produce low scores. For example, drugs administered to the mother during birth may affect the infant, causing sluggish responses. Note again the importance of an infant's state. Investigators should also avoid predictions of later behavior based on the Apgar. Yet as an immediate assessment of survival, the Apgar has made a notable contribution. Apgar reported that the death rate in her samples was only .13 percent for those newborns scoring ten, but 15 percent for those scoring zero, one, or two. These figures alone testify to the value of the test.

Neurological Assessment. Parmelee and Michaelis (1971) name three purposes of the neurological examination:

1. Identification of an apparent neurological problem to initiate appropriate therapy.
2. Constant monitoring of a neurological problem.
3. Prognosis about some neurological problem.

Each of these purposes requires testing the infant's reflexes, which is critical for neurological evaluation and basic for all infant tests.

St. Clair (1978), tracing the development of neurological assessment techniques, focuses on several recent tests. In 1960 an English version of the work of Andre-Thomas et al. appeared, which summarized fifteen years of research in France and which presented procedures for a highly systematic neurological examination of the neonate. Ranging from norms established by observing normal infants' responses so that investigators could recognize abnormal states, the examination included a family history, pregnancy conditions, birth status, and observation of tone and reflexes. The test was designed for one- to ten-day-old neonates but could be modified for use with older infants. Continued use of the test has produced fairly accurate predictions concerning an infant's future pathological status.

The need for cautiously interpreting neonatal test scores is shown by Yang (1962). Believing that many identified reflexes were of questionable significance, Yang developed a test of twenty-four reflexes and responses that yielded pertinent information about the infant's general status, nerve function, muscular activity, tone, and strength. Examining one hundred newborns on the first and third days following birth, he discovered considerably more adequate states on the third day than the first. Infants who perform poorly immediately after birth require constant reassessment before predictions about future status can be made.

MEDICATION AND NEONATAL ASSESSMENT

Brackbill et al. (1974), discussing the effects of obstetric premedication on neonatal functioning, state that today's improved obstetrical techniques and proliferation of drugs have turned medication into a major obstetric danger. These authors questioned the assumption that the infant quickly eliminates the depressing effects of medication. Hypothesizing that obstetric analgesia affects infants' perceptual and sensorimotor functioning, they studied twenty-five infants born to women who had been given meperidine (commercially known as demerol).

Eleven mothers received no meperidine, while the others received dosages from 50 to 150 mg. The results showed that the infants of mothers who had received no meperidine habituated (inhibited responses to nonmeaningful stimuli) twice as fast as the infants whose mothers had received the drug. Infants whose mothers had no meperidine also performed more efficiently on the Brazelton Neonatal Behavioral Assessment Scale, but there was no difference between the two groups on Apgar scores.

The authors conclude that obstetric premedication not only affects neonatal functioning, but affects it differentially—that is, the most potent effect is on the infant's ability *to stop responding,* followed by the effect on elicited responses and then on spontaneously emitted responses. Consequently, infants whose mothers received meperidine differed from those whose mothers did not in their ability to respond to environmental demands.

Tronick et al. (1977), believing that studies such as Brackbill's ignored the additive effect of medication plus labor and delivery, studied fifty-four healthy neonates whose mothers had uncomplicated pregnancies and deliveries. The infants were divided into three groups: the first consisted of infants whose mothers received no drugs or mild dosages of lidocaine; the mothers of those in the second group received an analgesic; the mothers of those in the third group received an epidural block. The neonates were tested within twelve hours after birth by a neurobehavioral examination, and on days one through five, day seven, and day ten were tested with the Brazelton.

The investigators believe that their study indicated that low levels of medication administered during labor and delivery had little impact on the infants' behavior. The small amounts of medication and the careful selection of the sample to eliminate stress limits generalizations. As the authors note, the results apply to neonates in whom the effects of limited medication were minimized by control of stress variables and who shed any lingering effects of medication by ten days. The results may not apply to a more heterogeneous group.

One conclusion is possible: while the results of the Tronick study are reassuring to those mothers who receive minimal medication, they do not eliminate the need for considerable caution in the use of medication.

In 1964 Prechtl and Beintema published the results of studying fifteen hundred Dutch newborns who had experienced obstetrical complications. For eight years the authors observed the relationships between birth conditions and neurological abnormalities to "obtain more exact knowledge of the developing neurological functions as early as possible and of the relationship of obstetrical complications to neurological abnormalities in later life."

The first part of the examination entails observation of the infant's state, posture, respiration, and color; the second part consists of a neurological assessment of reflexes and responses. While almost anyone can learn to administer the Prechtl and Beintema, St. Clair (1978) cautions that only medically trained persons should interpret the results, make diagnoses, or prescribe treatment. These restrictions limit the test's psychological value and usage, especially when new forms of neurological assessment emphasize more behavioral measures.

Behavioral Assessment. St. Clair (1978) comments that beginning in the 1950s there emerged a growing belief that behavior is closely linked to neurological status. Knobloch and Pasamanick (1974, p. 16), believing that neurological examinations fail to sample behavior adequately because of an infant's immaturity, state:

> All forms of clinical pediatrics, neurology, sociopsychology and psychiatry which are concerned with the developmental welfare of infants and young children must take behavior patterns into account. Behavior patterns are indicators. A developmental assessment is essentially an appraisal of the maturity and integrity of the child's nervous system, with the aid of behavioral stages and information and past and present history.

These authors note that the developmental, neuromotor, and sensory objectives of infant evaluation cannot be divorced; that is, there are no right and wrong behavioral responses; any response is appropriate for some age or level of central nervous system function. The responses that constitute an infant's behavior are matched against the youngster's age, so the behavior may be considered normal, retarded, or advanced. Thus the way was prepared for the acceptance of behavioral scales. St. Clair (1978) states that the Brazelton Neonatal Behavioral Assessment Scale, as a result of Brazelton's own work and collaboration with pediatricians and psychologists, has become one of the most significant tools for infant assessment. While the main emphasis is on behavioral assessment, some neurological items were included.

Brazelton (1973) states that his scale is a means of scoring interactive behavior to evaluate the normal newborn infant. It attempts to measure the infant's available responses to the environment mainly by a behavioral evaluation, although some neurological items are necessary. Lester and Brazelton (1980, p. 182) state:

> The Brazelton scale was developed out of a need to assess the dynamic processes of behavioral organization and development in the neonate. It is a psychological scale for the neonate and views the infant as part of a reciprocal interactive feedback system between infant and caregiver. While the exam includes the assessment of reflex responses, it focuses on the infant's capability to respond to the kinds of stimuli that caregivers present in a fostering situation. . . . The scale was developed to assess the dynamic processes of behavioral organization in the neonate. As infant behavior is viewed in terms of the infant-caregiver interaction system, the exam focuses on the social interactive capacities of the newborn; that is, we attempt to highlight in the neonate those behaviors that are likely to be typical of future interaction.

The Brazelton Neonatal Behavioral Assessment Scale. The Brazelton test includes twenty-six behavioral items, each of which is scored on a nine-point scale. Each of the nine points is a descriptive statement such as: actually resists being held, continuously pushing away, thrashing or stiffening, no startles, body movements delayed, respiratory change, and eye blinks are same in ten trials. The twenty-six behavioral items and their corresponding states are:

1. Response decrement to light (2, 3)
2. Response decrement to rattle (2, 3)
3. Response decrement to bell (2, 3)
4. Response decrement to pinprick (1, 2, 3)
5. Orientation inanimate visual (4)
6. Orientation inanimate auditory (4, 5)
7. Orientation animate visual (4)
8. Orientation animate auditory (4, 5)
9. Orientation animate, visual and auditory) (4)
10. Alertness (4)
11. General tonus (4, 5)
12. Motor maturity (4, 5)
13. Pull-to-sit (3, 5)
14. Cuddliness (4, 5)
15. Defensive movements (4)
16. Consolability (6 to 5, 4, 3, 2)
17. Peak of excitement (6)
18. Rapidity of buildup (1 to 6)
19. Irritability (3, 4, 5)
20. Activity (alert states)
21. Tremulousness (all states)
22. Startle (3, 4, 5, 6)
23. Lability of skin color (1 to 6)
24. Lability of states (all states)
25. Self-quieting activity (all states)
26. Hand-mouth facility (all states)

Als et al. (1977) state that these behavioral items cluster in four behavioral dimensions of newborn organization.

1. *Interactive capacities,* the neonate's ability to attend to and process both simple and complex environmental stimuli.

2. *Motoric capacities,* the infant's ability to maintain adequate tone, to control motor behavior, and to perform integrated motor activities (sucking the thumb).

3. *Organizational capacities relating to state control,* the infant's ability to maintain a calm, alert state in spite of intrusive stimuli.

4. *Organization capacities relating to physiological responses to stress,* the neonate's ability to control physiological systems.

There are twenty elicited responses scored on a four-part scale (no response, 0; low, 1; medium, 2; high, 3). They are:

1. Plantar grasp
2. Hand grasp
3. Ankle clonus
4. Babinski
5. Standing
6. Automatic walking
7. Placing
8. Incurvation
9. Crawling
10. Globella
11. Tonic deviation of head and eyes
12. Nystagmus
13. Tonic neck reflex
14. Moro
15. Rooting (intensity)
16. Sucking (intensity)
17. Passive movements Arms R

18. Passive movements Arms L
19. Passive movements Legs R
20. Passive movements Legs L

The mean score relates to the typical behavior of an average seven-pound, full-term (forty weeks), Caucasian neonate, whose mother had not more than 100 mg. of barbituates and 50 mg. of other sedative drugs prior to delivery, whose Apgar scores were no less than 7 at one, 8 at five, and 8 at fifteen minutes after delivery, who required no special care after delivery, and who experienced an apparently normal prenatal environment. The behavior on the third day provides the expected mean score, and examiners are urged to secure the infant's best performance (Brazelton, 1973, p. 4).

Als et al. (1977) state that five characteristics distinguish the Brazelton scale.

1. It recognizes the neonate as complex, organized, and a seeker of vital stimulation.

2. The Brazelton attempts to elicit the neonate's best performance.

3. The examination attempts to bring the infant through a succession of states: from light sleep to alert, to active, to crying, and back to inactive.

4. Recognition of an infant's states underlies the Brazelton, since a neonate's reactions vary widely depending on the immediate state.

5. This type of infant assessment prevents the use of a single score to label a child; it is the pattern of behavioral clusters that determines whether the infant is "normal" or "at risk."

St. Clair (1978) states that although scoring is cumbersome and standardization data are lacking, the Brazelton scale is one of the most popular medical and psychological tests currently used.

DISCUSSION QUESTIONS

1. Using Kagan's comment about the relevance of context, discuss the possible reasons for the differences in neonatal behavior. Include as many variables as possible in your answer. Do you favor a nature or nurture belief as the cause of behavior?
2. Some investigators call the realization that there is a vital connection between an infant's state and demonstrated behavior a "breakthrough" in the study of infancy. Can you suggest several reasons that help to explain the significance of this discovery?
3. Can you elaborate on St. Clair's statement that the growing relationship between psychology and medicine tends to obscure the purpose of infant tests? Is there any alternative?
4. Do you believe that the results of the Brackbill study diminish the importance of the Apgar Scale? Why? Be sure to note the importance of the purpose of an infant test.
5. Does the Brazelton Neonatal Behavioral Assessment Scale bridge the gap between medical and psychological infant assessment? Justify your answer, that is, explain *why* it does or does not.

MOTOR DEVELOPMENT

The value of neonatal assessment techniques is apparent when one attempts to trace the path of infant development. If any difficulties are suspected, test results can suggest treatment that may help to offset future, more serious, problems. If a youngster appears normal, the sequence of typical growth patterns commences, none of which is more revealing than motor development.

Knobloch and Pasamanick (1974, p. 192) state that maturational status and neuromotor status are intimately related and that any neonatal assessment must recognize the effect of maturation. They warn, nevertheless, that investigators must clearly distinguish between chronological immaturity in motor behavior and symptoms of neuromotor dysfunction, a distinction that depends upon an appraisal of the infant's *behavior.* That is, an infant's reactions to test demands are sensitive indicators of neural functioning. The authors believe that the detection of abnormality depends on knowledge of normal neuromotor development.

Since motor development proceeds in a head to foot direction, the infant's increasing ability to control head movement is a logical beginning in any analysis of motor development.

Head Control

The most obvious initial head movements are from side to side, although the one-month-old infant occasionally lifts the head when in a prone position. The tonic neck reflex (discussed in Chapter Three) is well developed. By two months, infants can hold their heads erect in the midposition, and some can lift their chests slightly when lying on their abdomens. Four-month-old infants can hold their heads steady while sitting and will lift their head and shoulders to a ninety-degree angle when on their abdomens (Marlow, 1973, p. 290).

By six months, most youngsters can balance their heads quite well, a notable accomplishment, since as Knobloch and Pasamanick (1974, p. 145) note, erection of the head against gravity requires coordination and a sustaining strength that newborns lack. Not until twenty to twenty-four weeks can infants maintain their heads in line with their bodies when they are pulled to a sitting position. An infant whose head is still unsteady at twenty-eight weeks may be evidencing an abnormality.

Grasping

There is a distinction between grasping and prehension. Infants are born with a grasping reflex, which means that they will close their hands when either the palms or fingers are stimulated. Prehension is the controlled handling of an object. Marlow (1973, pp. 286–299) traces the sequences as follows:

	Age	*Accomplishment*
1.	One month	Grasps objects placed in hand, but drops it immediately.
2.	Two months	Can briefly hold rattle.
3.	Three months	Carries hand or object to mouth; grasping reflex weakening.
4.	Four months	Begins to use thumb in grasping.
5.	Five months	Uses thumb and forefinger more skillfully.
6.	Six months	Grasps with simultaneous movement of fingers.
7.	Seven months	Grasps toy with one hand.
8.	Eight months	Complete thumb opposition.
9.	Nine, ten, eleven months	Coordinates hand activities (for example, takes objects to mouth accurately); handedness appears.
10.	Twelve months	Holds crayon adaptively and can mark lines.

Note the shift from the grasping reflex to the beginnings of prehension during the fourth month. White and Held's classic study (1966) is an excellent example of developing prehension. Working with babies from birth to six months, they first determined which behaviors ultimately result in eye-hand coordination, that is, learning to reach for and grasp accurately what one sees. They then varied the babies' sensory experiences to discover if this process could be accelerated. The normal behaviors that lead to eye-hand coordination include alertness and visual attention. Newborn infants are usually alert less than three percent of the time, but by six months of age, this time increases to fifty percent. At birth, infants cannot orient themselves to visible targets, but at six months they can use their eyes to follow moving objects at a distance. They also quickly and accurately reach for nearby objects. Thus six-month-old infants have acquired considerable eye-hand competence. White and Held wondered if certain experiences could speed up this process.

Note the clear statement of purpose and the precise guidelines with which the investigators started. Their subjects were sixty-three infants who, because of inadequate family conditions, were born and raised in an institution. After evaluating the medical histories of the babies and their mothers, White and Held included in the study infants who were physically normal and as similar as possible. The next step concerned the independent variable, or the conditions that the experimenters could manipulate. Nurses were instructed to handle infants from one group for an extra twenty minutes each day, from day six through thirty-six. As a result of their special treatment, these infants became significantly more visually acute than the control infants, who received only usual institutional care without much cuddling or contact. A second group was bombarded with sensory enrichment. They received the same extra handling, but they also received, from day thirty-seven through day one hundred and twenty-four, enormous additional stimulation. They were put in a prone position for fifteen minutes after the 6:00 A.M., 10:00 A.M., and 2:00 P.M. feedings, and their crib liners were removed so that they could see all the activity in the ward. Their sheets were changed from white to multicolored, and special mobiles were suspended over their cribs so that they could see beads, rattles, and other objects. The results were fascinating. These infants discovered their hands some two weeks *later* than anticipated. This result is not too surprising, since the control group had nothing much better to do than inspect their own hands. But the infants in the enriched group also exhibited even less visual attention than the controls, ignored the mobile, and cried much more. The authors concluded that sensory enrichment starting at day thirty-seven is useless and perhaps even unpleasant for infants.

The third group had the same initial experiences as the second, but from day thirty-seven to sixty-eight only one modification was made. The prone positioning, multicolored sheets, and gadgets were not used; only two pacifiers were attached to the crib rail. The mobile was introduced at day sixty-eight. Strangely, this group seemed to benefit more from the intervention than any of the others. Hand regard appeared earlier, visual attention improved, and reaching and grasping were markedly superior, all of which suggest that massive sensory stimulation does not have a positive effect on development before about two months of age.

The authors concluded that the age range from one-and-one-half to five months is crucial for early perceptual-motor development. During this period, human infants show a tremendous surge in visual activity and visual development, both of which are very sensitive to changes in the environment. Infants in the first and third groups developed the reaching and grasping sequence in sixty percent of the time required by the control group. Table 5.1 illustrates the various conditions of the study.

Sitting

Marlow (1973) traces the development of sitting as follows:

Age	*Accomplishment*
Three months	Sits with rounded back and knees flexed when supported.
Four months	Sits with adequate support and enjoys being propped up.
Five months	Sits with slight support and when pulled to sitting position back remains straight.
Six months	Briefly sits without support when placed in balanced leaning position.
Seven months	Good trunk control results in periods of independent sitting.
Eight months	Sits alone steadily.
Ten months	Prefers sitting to lying.
Twelve months	Can sit down from standing position.

Knobloch and Pasamanick (1974, p. 201) state that in the initial stages of development, the trunk and legs are passive in sitting, but by ten months, infants have achieved lateral balance without leg support and are now free and able sitters.

Locomotion: Crawling and Creeping

Crawling and creeping are two distinct developmental phases. In crawling, the infant's abdomen touches the floor and the weight of the head and shoulders rests on the elbows. Locomotion is mainly by arm action, while the legs usually drag, although some youngsters push with their legs. These movements appear in most youngsters from seven months.

TABLE 5.1 Conditions of the White-Held Study

	Days		
Group	6–36	37–68	69–124
1	20 minutes extra handling by nurse	No treatment	No treatment
2	20 minutes extra handling by nurse	Prone position after feeding; crib liners removed; multicolored sheets; special mobiles placed over crib	These treatments continued until day 124
3	20 minutes extra handling by nurse	Two pacifiers attached to crib rail	Special mobiles placed over crib

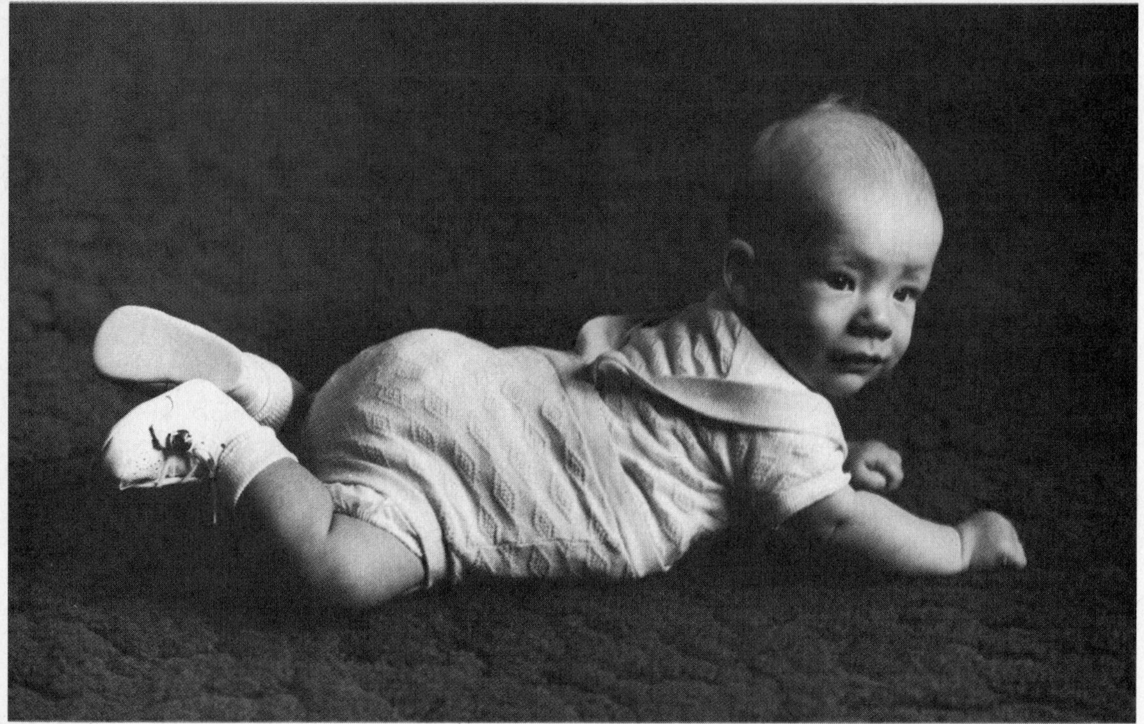

Crawling

Creeping is more advanced than crawling, since movement is on hands and knees and the trunk does not touch the ground. Creeping appears from nine months in most youngsters.

Most descriptions of crawling and creeping are quite uniform; the progression is from propulsion on the abdomen to quick, accurate movements on hands and knees, but the sequence is endlessly varied. Youngsters adopt a bewildering diversity of positions and movements which can only loosely be grouped together.

Standing and Walking

By about seven months, infants when held will support most of their weight on their legs, and if delighted, they will begin to bounce up and down. Shirley's classic study (1938) traced the progression as follows.

Age	*Accomplishment*
Forty-two weeks	Stands holding on to furniture.
Forty-five weeks	Walking when led.
Forty-seven weeks	Pulls to stand by furniture.
Sixty-two weeks	Stands alone.
Sixty-four weeks	Walks alone.

Knobloch and Pasamanick (1974, p. 203) attribute the shift to a dynamic erect position at about forty to forty-two weeks to the incorporation of balance and control into standing. Coordination of arm with leg movements enables infants to pull themselves up and grope toward control of leg movements. The first steps are a propulsive, lunging forward until there gradually emerges a smooth, speedy, and versatile gait. The world is now the infant's to explore. As the authors note, mastery of walking produces rapid and diversified attention shifts. Tremendous energy and mobility, coupled with a growing curiosity, draw infants to search for the boundaries of their world. It is an exciting time for youngsters, but a trying time for parents, since they must draw the line that separates encouraging curiosity and imitation from the possibility of personal injury. The task is not easy; it is, however, a microcosm of all aspects of development: what separates unreasonable restraint from reasonable freedom?

Table 5.2 summarizes milestones in motor development.

TABLE 5.2. Milestones in Motor Development

Age	Head control	Grasping	Sitting	Crawling-creeping	Standing-walking
Three months	Can lift head and chest while prone.	Grasps objects; briefly holds objects; carries objects to mouth.	Sits awkwardly with support.		
Six months	Holds head steady while sitting; balances head.	Develops skillful use of thumb during this period.	Transition from sitting with slight support to brief periods without support.		
Nine months	Infant has established head control.	Coordinates hand activities; handedness begins to appear.	Good trunk control; sits alone steadily.	Crawling movements appear (trunk touches floor); begins about 7 months.	
Twelve months		Handedness pronounced; holds crayon; marks lines.	Can sit from standing position.	Creeping (trunk raised from floor) begins at 9–10 months and continues until steady walking.	Can stand holding onto something; will take steps when held; by 12 months will pull self up.
Fifteen months					Stands alone; begins to walk alone.
Eighteen months					Begins to run.

BLINDNESS AND MOTOR DEVELOPMENT

Knobloch and Pasamanick (1974, p. 307) state that visual perceptions are really visual-motor perceptions and from birth there is a motor aspect to the infant's visual behavior. These authors believe that vision is not an isolated function; that is, developmentally and psychologically, vision is tightly integrated with such sensory activities as touch and kinesthesia. As the eyes move, feeding the infant's information-processing system, additional data are quickly acquired by prehension, manipulation, and locomotion. Knobloch and Pasamanick believe that these dynamic adaptations sketch a pattern: the retina receives impressions; muscles adjust to position, distance, size, and form; the cortex organizes the total experience.

How do serious visual defects or blindness affect motor development? Bower (1977, p. 94) states that development—motor, cognitive, and personality—of visually impaired infants differs from that of sighted babies. Blindness especially affects reaching and independent locomotion, both of which appear much later in development, if at all.

Spatial orientation lags until the muscular system produces the information vital to rudimentary knowledge of the physical world. Since one sense does not compensate for the lack of another, visually impaired infants learn of their surroundings through trial and error, actual movement through space from one spot to another, and using the fingers to trace outlines of objects. It is too easy to underestimate a sightless child's deficiency (Knobloch and Pasamanick, 1974, p. 307).

Commenting on these limitations, Bower presents a particularly interesting description of the typical condition of a sightless baby. Since these infants lack control over incoming auditory stimulation, they eventually become passive to auditory stimuli. Bower wonders if sensorimotor passivity then becomes a generalized personality trait. For those working with sightless infants, the basic problem is sensory supplementation to aid both physical and psychological development.

Creeping

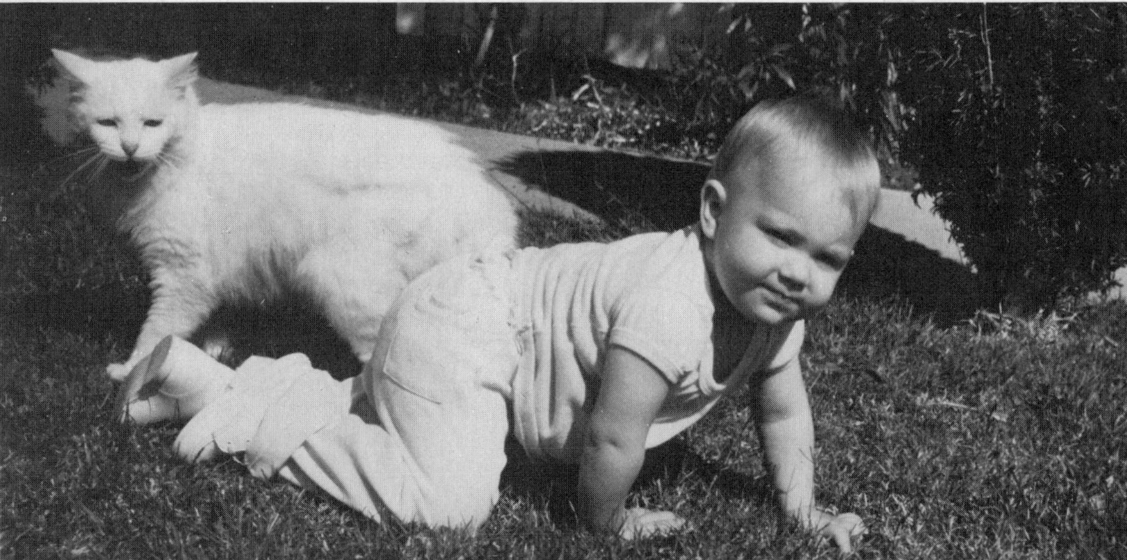

PERCEPTUAL DEVELOPMENT

The statement that human behavior is integrated becomes meaningful and not merely a cliche when we analyze the various aspects of development. Motor development does not proceed in a vacuum; the infant's interaction with the environment immediately becomes a source of knowledge. McCall (1976, p. 117) states that a persistent theme of the first three years is the reduction of perceptual-cognitive uncertainty. Infants acquire information about the world and constantly check the validity of that information; the process defines perception: extracting information from stimulation (Gibson, 1969).

An orderly set of transitions guides the process. McCall describes an infant as a "stimulus-detection device" who attends to objects according to the perceptual information they contain. Seeking information leads to meaning—objects roll, bounce, squeak—thus infants learn what objects are and what they do. During the infancy period youngsters gradually separate themselves from their world and discover what they can do with objects; this is reduction of perceptual-cognitive uncertainty.

Haith and Campos (1977, p. 256) state that current perceptual research also attempts to explain cognitive development and to trace brain maturation. Thus perceptual development is now considered worth studying not only because of its own value but also because perceptual knowledge adds a new dimension to investigations of intellectual and physiological functioning.

Perceptual Trends

Kagan, Kearsley, and Zelazo (1978) believe that infants are born ready to attend to changes in physical stimulation. Repeated experiments have demonstrated that stimuli presented frequently cause a decrease in an infant's attention (habituation). If the stimuli are altered, the infant again attends, thus indicating notice of the difference. Studies have clearly illustrated that contrast, contour, color, and movement catch and hold an infant's attention.

These authors note that infants can detect the similarity between an event and a mentally stored representation of past experience, thus evidencing that they have established a relationship between the immediate perception and stored information.

> The mind is always working on its knowledge, trying to create representations that permit the most efficient recognition of the forms that are functionally equivalent for the child. The mind rushes toward organization and pattern whenever possible; it moves toward prototype. (Kagan, Kearsley, Zelazo, 1978, p. 68)

Haith and Campos note that there is general agreement that before one-and-one-half months, infants process elements of form but are insensitive to visual organization (1978, p. 256). Interesting changes appear at about two months when infants begin to scan the internal features of a form; for example, they concentrate on the eyes of a face. They now become more sensitive to organization; patterns hold their attention. Thus form perception appears initially, followed by pattern perception at about two months.

Kagan, Kearsley, and Zelazo (1978) note that the world usually presents infants with events that differ on many dimensions simultaneously. For example, Brooks and Lewis (1976) in an ingenious study tested infants' responses to midget, adult, and child strangers. While infants' perceptions of the social world have been well studied, the specific characteristics to which they respond have remained unexplored. These investigators studied how forty infants from two to twenty-four months of age responded to four different types of strangers: a male and female child, a female adult, and a female midget. Thus facial configuration and height were varied.

The infants reacted to the children by continuous looking and some smiling, to the midget with considerable attention but no positive response such as smiling or movement toward her, and to the adult by sporadic looking, averting their eyes, frowning, and even crying. Thus the infants used size and facial configuration cues. Brooks and Lewis comment that social responses depend on a complex interaction of past experience, current contextual cues, cognitive capabilities and species-specific predispositions.

Studies such as these help to explain the belief of Kagan, Kearsley, and Zelazo (1978) that a theory of perception and discrepancy must accommodate dynamic changes in knowledge over time. A major problem in tracing perceptual development is the inability of investigators to specify precisely the dimension of classes of patterns. These authors, using visual events, suggest that the following dimensions *might* be relevant.

Linear dimensions with a pattern
Curved dimensions with a pattern
Symmetry of the pattern
Redundancy of individual dimensions
Color
Contour
Vertical/horizontal nature of the pattern
Circular/concentric patterns

Further complicating analysis is an individual's reaction to relations among dimensions. Yet these research problems are presumably the mechanisms that explain perceptual development, because knowledge grows from discrepant events that attract the infant. The infant attempts to assimilate these events into existing mental structures. Kagan and his colleagues term these events "surprises" and believe that infants find surprise first in the physical world, and as they age, in cognitive dimensions. The sensory experiences that an infant encounters are not just mechanically registered and then filed away. The data received by the child merge with past, similar experiences and combine with present physiological and psychological states to produce a particular perception.

Perception depends on both learning and maturation. As Bower (1977) notes, the infant's perceptive system undergoes considerable development following birth, resulting from both greater familiarity with objects and events in the world and from growth. Eleanor Gibson (1969) states that perceptual progress in both humans and animals results from the interaction of learning and maturation.

For example, how do youngsters proceed from a gross reaction to a discriminated response? In Figure 5.1, a gradually more detailed pattern of a face is given. Older subjects often identify it as a face as early as the second figure, while youngsters of even third- and fourth-grade age are unable to identify it until the last line is drawn. Why? What delays the recognition? The older youngsters, because of their experience, added the necessary external details themselves.

FIGURE 5.1. Gradual Differentiation of a Face.

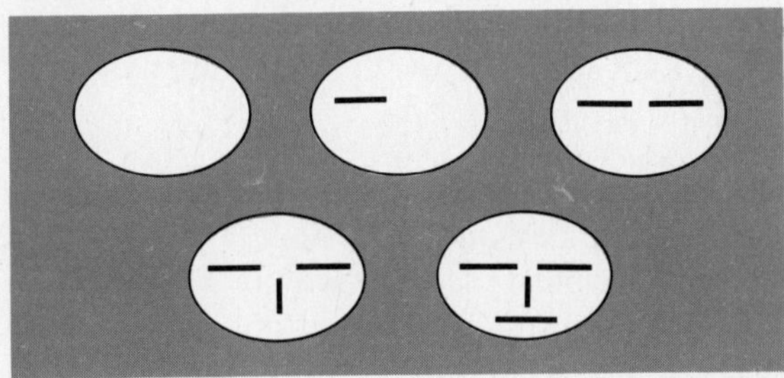

EARLY EVIDENCE OF PERCEPTION

The classic studies of Robert Fantz (1961, 1963) provide dramatic documentation of an infant's perceptual ability. Fantz (1961) states that the best indicator of the visual abilities of helpless infants is the activity of the eyes themselves. Infants who consistently gaze at some forms more than others show perceptual discrimination; that is, there is something in one form that holds their attention.

Using a "looking chamber" in which an infant lies in a crib at the bottom of the chamber and looks at objects placed on the ceiling, Fantz could determine the amount of time that infants fixated on different objects. In his first human experiment (previous work had been done with chimpanzees), Fantz and his colleagues tested thirty infants aged one to fifteen weeks on four pairs of test patterns: horizontal stripes and a bull's eye, a checkerboard and two sizes of plain squares, a cross and a circle, and two identical triangles. The more complex patterns attracted the infants' attention significantly longer than either the checkerboard and squares or the triangle.

The next step involved selective perception to discover if infants preferred facial patterns. They used three flat objects shaped like a head. One had regular features painted in black on a pink background; the second had scrambled features; the third had a solid patch of black at one end. The three forms were shown to forty-nine infants from four days to six months old. Infants of all ages looked longest at the real face. The plain pattern received the least attention.

Fantz next tested pattern perception by using six objects (flat discs six inches in diameter): a face, a bull's eye, newsprint, red disc, yellow disc, white disc. The face attracted the greatest attention, followed by the newsprint, the bull's eye, and then the three plain colored discs (none of which received much attention).

Gibson (1969) states that while these studies do not suggest an instinctive reaction to the human face, they nevertheless indicate that there are definite properties in an infant's visual world. Fantz concludes that an infant's early interest in form and pattern shape developing behavior by focusing attention on stimuli that will have later adaptive significance.

Almost from birth, children react to patterns of stimuli as they perceive them at the moment. Thus learning, maturation, emotions, needs, and values are all intertwined in perception. For example, in one classic study (Bruner and Goodman, 1947) several ten-year-old children from poor homes and a like number from rich homes were asked to estimate the size of some coins. The experimenter first showed the youngsters coins ranging in value from a penny to a half-dollar and then told the youngsters to duplicate the coin sizes by adjusting a knob that projected circles on a screen. The circle on the screen could be made larger or smaller. Interestingly, the poor children greatly overestimated the size of the coins; the value they placed on money apparently affected their perception. The rich youngsters only slightly overestimated the size.

For our purposes it is especially significant that developmental changes occur in the attainment of perceptual acuity. Let us consider some perceptual phenomena that illustrate these developmental changes. Answer the following questions.

1. What do you see?

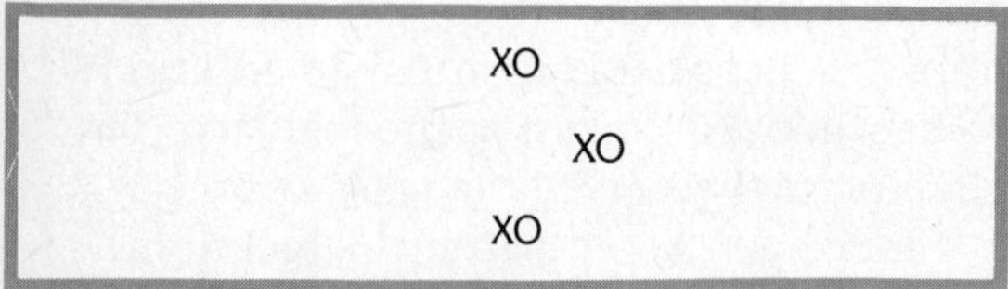

2. Which middle circle is larger?

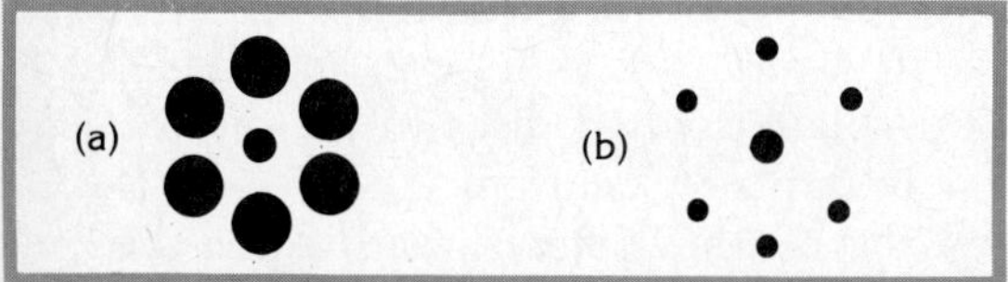

3. What do you see?

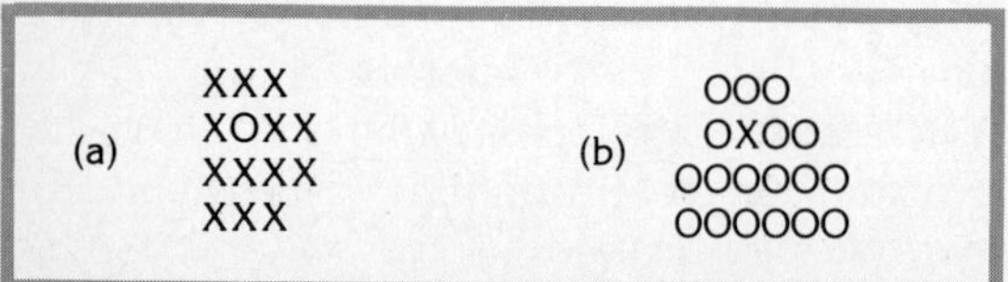

4. Which line is longer?

In examining these illustrations, you probably answered as follows.

1. Three figures of XO. (You grouped them.)

2. You probably identified B as the larger. (Objective measurement reveals that they are identical; the surrounding elements affect your perception of the middle circle.)

3. You probably saw an O in the first illustration and an X in the second. (The difference between the central figure and its surrounding elements is so striking that you focused on the central figure.)

4. Your first reaction was probably line b. (Measurement shows that they are the same length.)

Adult experience enables us to overcome our initial responses with little difficulty. Children are more easily confused, but they gradually develop less susceptibility to such complex stimulus patterns. The task then becomes one of aiding them to acquire perceptual acuity as early as possible, since this is a capacity they possess almost from birth.

According to Reese and Lipsitt (1970), the more we learn about the manner in which an individual gains the ability to identify a complex, unfamiliar stimulus among other similar stimuli, the more knowledge we have about the perceptual process itself. Many of the skills that a child must master in school, such as reading, require accurate discriminations and competence in detecting the unchanging nature of stimulus patterns in spite of possible surface changes.

COGNITIVE DEVELOPMENT

One hardly needs to read a textbook to recognize that there must be staggering differences between the cognitive system of the very young infant and that of the very young child (0–1 versus 18–30 months of age, let us say). These two organisms scarcely seem to belong to the same species, so great are the cognitive as well as physical differences between them. The very young infant is an intellectual zero to the casual observer; he or she seems to have no "mind" at all. While there is now a great deal of research evidence to show that such a judgment does not in fact

> do justice to the babies' capabilities, the intellectual gap between the neonate (newborn) and the two year old child nonetheless remains enormous. (Flavell, 1977, p. 14)

How can we explain the transition that occurs during these two years, a transition in which youngsters move from apparently random sensorimotor activity to an emerging symbolic control of their environment? Although hard data to answer this question remain elusive, there seems to be one constant theme in the research: conflict, or perhaps discord or dissonance.

Whatever the term, the meaning is clear: something in the environment differs from a child's past experience and the existing mental representation or scheme requires change. A subtle distinction must be made here: the new event must not be so discrepant that the youngster ignores it, nor can it be so similar that attention is quickly lost. There must be sufficient familiarity to capture attention and sufficient variety to force cognitive change, thus explaining cognitive development. As learning and maturation proceed, children can react to increasingly abstract stimuli until symbolic interchange characterizes behavior.

While infants show little evidence of abstract, logical reasoning that characterizes adult behavior (the infant reacts as whole, in a manner that suggests an all-or-none response), it is possible to discern the first signs of cognition: infants begin to recognize the same object under different conditions (stimulus equivalence), they begin to explore the environment in the search for novel stimuli, and they gradually learn that an object out of sight still exists.

Object Permanence. Bower (1977) notes that babies obviously do not think of objects as adults do; they identify objects by location or motion. For example, infants shown a moving object that disappears during its trajectory remain unconcerned; babies under five months who are shown multiple mothers are delighted. But at five or six months their reactions change. They will try to track the missing object and are shocked at the multiple mothers. Bower believes that perceptual development is significant at this stage of cognitive growth because infants must recognize objects to detect differences in their characteristics and locations. Most infants acquire object permanence by twelve months, and then slowly acquire the notion of spatial relationships, which continues to develop during the infancy period.

The Emergence of Memory

Kagan, Kearsley, and Zelazo (1978) believe that new behaviors appear near the end of the first year: increased attentiveness, inhibition to a discrepant event, and apprehension.

1. *Increased Attentiveness.* By the end of the first year, infants attend to discrepant events more than at six months. The authors state that if an interesting event is presented to infants from four to thirty-six months old, a U-shaped reaction between age and fixation time appears, with the trough at six or seven months. Showing youngsters drawings of human faces produces marked interest at four months, a decline of attention at six to seven months, and renewed interest during the second year.

2. *Inhibition to a Discrepant Event.* Before seven months infants reach for a novel object after repeated presentation of something familiar. The eleven-month-old infant exhibits an obvious delay before reaching. One-year-olds also show behavioral inhibition when an unfamiliar child appears. Kagan and his colleagues comment on the differences between humans and animals in these circumstances: humans show an absence of excessive fear or aggressive behavior.

3. *Apprehension.* The authors note that apprehension (wariness, inhibition of play, crying) appears in response to a discrepant event. Before seven months there are few signs of apprehension; it slowly increases and peaks from eleven to eighteen months.

Kagan and his colleagues believe that these behaviors appear because infants can now retrieve and retain a schema related to the present event while resolving any discrepancy between the two. When youngsters cannot balance both events, they evidence increased attention, inhibition, and apprehension. During the last half of the first year, changes in the central nervous system enable infants to recall events with minimal cues and to retain that memory longer than they could during the first six months. Thus the growth of memory ability may be one of the central processes of the last half of the first year of life (Kagan, Kearsley, Zelazo, 1978, p. 98).

INFANT MEMORY

Although Kagan and his colleagues have stressed the significance of memory in an infant's cognitive development during the last half of the first year, they hasten to add that stating an infant cannot retrieve a schema until eight months could cause confusion. There seems to be substantial evidence that three-month-olds can retrieve some past events by a process called *reactive memory* rather than regenerative memory, which is retrieval with minimal cues.

Recent studies of infant recognition illustrate reactive memory. Fagan (1977), conducting a series of experiments on visual recognition in four- to six-month-old infants, concluded that youngsters five to six months old exhibit long-term recognition memory (up to two weeks). Yet the memory could be lost in *one minute* if the infants' attention shifted to other stimuli during the retention period. The kind of intervening stimulus and its timing were important determinants of forgetting.

Studying hundreds of twenty-two-week-old infants, Fagan consistently demonstrated that those who failed to recognize which of two face photos they had previously seen had been exposed to highly similar intervening stimuli (other face photos). Stimuli of intermediate similarity (rotated photos) or of low similarity (line drawing) had little adverse effect. Fagan also discovered that infants could recover memory lost due to highly similar stimuli only by additional exposure to the original.

As Fagan notes, loss of recognition seems to be the exception rather than the rule in infant memory, and it is the distraction that is the major interfering element. Consequently, the important issue in studying infant memory is not what is forgotten but what is remembered: what parts of a stimulus are stored, what conditions facilitate storage and what models are most effective for interpreting the data concerning infant memory?

To explain cognitive development, Bruner (1977) returns to the theme with which this section opened: conflict. He states that the important element in cognitive development is conflict between two responses that the infant has acquired independently, thus demanding resolution, usually at a higher level.

Difficulties in Analysis. The problems facing investigators of cognitive development are formidable. Hunt and Uzgiris (1975) identify the dual sources of these problems. They note that assumptions about diverse states, the nature of the changes between these states, and the developmental ordering of the states do not explain the characteristics of the processes and transformations that occur. That is, accurate description of the stages and transformations remains tentative, and definitive explanation remains elusive.

Since most studies of cognitive development (until the late 1960s and 1970s) focused on intelligence testing, it is hardly surprising that today's reports on cognitive development seem diffident. Questions about the nature of intelligence and the predictive validity of infant tests forced researchers into two directions. Some investigators attempted to devise new tests that would not assess all aspects of mental development but concentrate on a particular purpose, such as the Neonatal Behavioral Assessment Scale. Other investigators turned to more theoretical issues and endeavored to formulate tests that would measure such skills as suggested by Piaget for the sensorimotor period (Brooks and Weintraub, 1976).

McCall (1976) presents an interesting rationale for these unsolved problems. He believes that, in spite of powerful contradictory evidence, researchers considered intelligence to be a unitary trait, constant throughout one's life, and dominant in anything cognitive. Infant intelligence tests that did not measure intelligence and could not predict future behavior were blamed for measuring the wrong thing. A new argument then appeared: infants possess intelligence but lack the behavior to express it.

McCall makes the ironic statement that while developmental psychology should study *changes* throughout the lifespan, it has actually searched for developmental *continuity.* Only with the great impetus furnished by Piaget's epigenetic view of intelligence have investigators turned from the search for traditional psychometric data to a quest for a means of describing qualitative transition in infant behavior—cognitive development.

The Role of Language. McCall (1976) believes that the appearance of language serves also to reduce perceptual-cognitive uncertainty by labeling objects. If this linguistic function transfers from inanimate objects to social events, infants gradually acquire more control over their surroundings. The author states that language development proceeds as greater demands are made upon infants, as conflict arises, and as memory emerges.

By the end of infancy (two years) youngsters have acquired a vocabulary of about three hundred words. Considering that they uttered their first word between ten and twelve months, the acquisition of three hundred words seems like a major achievement until we realize that neonates seem to be born with an innate ability to communicate. We can only wonder if the actual appearance of speech is so intimately involved with other cognitive accomplishments that one depends upon the other. As Kagan and his colleagues note, psychology has its share of unexplained regularities, and among the most prominent is the acquisition of language.

A SPECIAL CASE OF COMMUNICATION

In a fascinating account of crying in infants "at risk" (those who exhibit symptoms of, or the potential for, difficulty), Lester and Zeskind (1978) consider crying as a language that represents an adaptive communication system facilitating an infant's chances of survival. The authors attempted to determine what infants try to communicate, how they communicate, and how communication varies because of an infant's status. Infants have different cry patterns for different purposes; thus a cry has definite signaling characteristics that affect the relationship between children and those around them.

The authors describe crying as a motor response to distress followed by sound. While they were primarily interested in analyzing various kinds of crying for clues to their cause, they also note that the cry seems to carry information that affects the infant-caregiver relationship. They report that adults react differently to the cries of high risk and low risk infants; they seem to perceive the cries of low risk infants as primarily unpleasant, while the cries of high risk infants communicate "sickness" and "urgency."

Lester and Zeskind conclude that the cry, as one of the earliest means of communication, is an "imperative signal with powerful eliciting properties." Thus the cry of the high risk infant not only differs acoustically but also is perceived differently, that is, as a signal of the need for special attention. Their final words are particularly pertinent:

> More than a reflex, the cry becomes a window into a sophisticated socio-biological communication system with pathology maintained in proper perspective as we focus on the emerging organization of the infant.

DISCUSSION QUESTIONS

1. What do you think are the most significant aspects of the White and Held study? List them in order of importance. Now extend the ages; that is, project what would be the result of the treatments for six- and nine-month-old infants. Does the hierarchy in your list change? Why?
2. Bower states that passivity becomes a generalized personality characteristic of the sightless. Do you agree? Why? If you disagree, how do you refute his claim that sightless babies are passive receptors of auditory stimuli?
3. Contemporary interpretations of cognitive development stress the detection of stimulus discrepancy. In Fantz's pioneering perceptual studies, how can you reconcile attention to a face with the belief in the attractive qualities of stimulus discrepancy?
4. "Conflict" is a term that appeared frequently in this section. Can you explain its role in cognitive development, beginning with the neonate period and tracing its role throughout infancy? What is the relationship between stimulus discrepancy and cognitive dissonance?

LEARNING AND INFANT DEVELOPMENT

Any analysis of infancy must reckon with the infant's astounding learning capacity. Assuming an intact organism, a newborn child presents a deceptive picture of helplessness. Bower (1977, p. 16) states that parents and scientists ask similar questions: Can the baby see? Can the baby hear? Does the baby know anything? Judging by appearances the answer is yes. The next question is: How does a baby know? Again judging by appearance, the answer seems to be that there is some kind of innate knowledge. Recent data indicate the answer is confounded by the infant's learning ability. From the moment of birth the infant learns rapidly; questions are also raised by the possibility of prenatal learning.

Maturation Versus Learning

In any discussion of learning, especially in the context of infant development, we must separate behavior produced by maturation from behavior produced by learning. It is not always easy to do so. Children may, for example, suddenly find themselves capable of doing something that was beyond them before. We tend to say that they "learned" to do it, but perhaps they were simply physically incapable of doing it previously and are able to do it now because of biological maturation.

Learning is some change that occurs because of contact with the environment. It is the opposite for maturation; changes owing to maturation occur regardless of contact with the environment. The bird will fly without having to learn; children will pull themselves up and stand, walk, and run without having to learn. Consequently, maturation refers to those changes that follow the dictates of heredity. Because I am human, I will crawl, stand, walk, and talk. Development, however, is best explained by an interactionist belief: heredity and environment, maturation and learning. But many would disagree with this interpretation. Behaviorists explain development as the acquisition of learned responses; developmental theorists see learning as a form of maturation. The more logical conclusion seems to be that one influences the other.

Kagan (1968) nicely summarizes the interactionist position when he says that those studying infant development hope to understand the principles of learning and the effect of early learning on later behavior. In Kagan's study, for example, upper-middle-class children had a richer response repertoire at thirteen months than lower-class children did, and they did not tire of their toys as quickly. These children had a more stimulating environment than the lower-class children. Thus differences in behavior, which appear in the first year of life, are related to differences in social class. So learning almost immediately affects the infant as it interacts with the child's maturational pattern. Kagan concludes that educational procedures with lower-class mothers should commence during the first year of the infant's life in order to inform them that children learn from the environment even at this early age.

An Interactionist Interpretation. Most investigators view learning and maturation as interrelated, with one complementing the other. If learning is deficient, then development suffers. If maturation is retarded, learning is severely restricted.

The development of the human being from a dependent, helpless organism to an independent intellectual, problem-solving adult lies in both maturation and learning. Human skills, appreciations, and reasonings in all their variety, as well as human hopes, aspirations, attitudes, and values, are generally recognized as depending largely on learning for their fulfillment. Thus, the learning-maturation interaction helps to explain the extraordinary variations that children manifest in their patterns of development. While learning is limited by capacity, it is equally true that few people ever reach their limits. Innate potential needs environmental stimulation. It seems clear then that the developmental pattern will remain unfulfilled if learning is unsatisfactory.

Behavioral development is the interaction of a biologically ready child with an appropriate environment, but relative contributions of the two conditions differ. Some behavior, such as crawling or walking, appears with little training. Other activities, such as reading or writing, require considerable environmental direction. Thus there is a fluid and dynamic interaction: at one time, maturation is predominant and at another learning is decisive. One complements the other.

Figure 5.2 illustrates the complementary nature of maturation and learning. Note the increasing abstract nature of activities until the role of learning becomes more apparent. Obviously, the use of symbols means that children must have had experiences with various representations of the symbol; that is, they learned their meanings. Such learning, however, can never occur unless children attain the proper developmental level. If they reach the appropriate level of development but do not encounter suitable learning experiences, later learning will be that much more difficult.

FIGURE 5.2. The Dynamic Interaction.

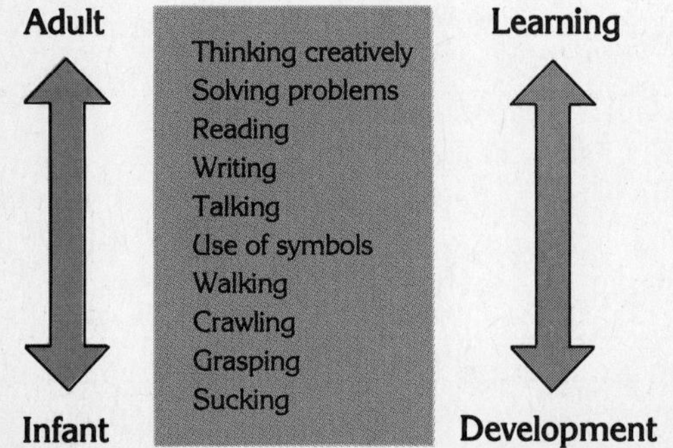

Development seems to be decisive in the "lower" levels of Figure 5.2 (e.g., walking and talking), but early experiences are vital if children are to achieve their potential. Animal experimentation has clearly indicated the need for enriched environmental experiences if blood and nerve supply to the brain is to be as rich as possible. Similar experiments have shown that permanent damage may result if environmental stimuli are deficient. Studies with children have also indicated that a lack of stimulation in the early years retards aspects of development that are thought to occur mainly because of maturation. The conclusion seems inevitable: to fulfill potential, a rewarding interaction between learning and maturation should commence at birth and continue throughout a youngster's lifetime.

Characteristics of Infant Learning

Howe (1975), after commenting that infant learning is far more complex than the simple addition of components, argues forcefully that it is impossible to apportion the contribution of learning and maturation to behavior. For example, sensory receptors influence learning, but they themselves develop independently of learning. The form of the receptor determines the type of energy transmission accepted, and an "effective" environment is one selected by the receptors. So learning—the modification of behavior by environmental contact—has several boundaries; that is, it is limited by the nature of the infant's sense organs.

There are, nevertheless, some dramatic examples of infant learning, such as the classic studies of Papousek (1969). Working with healthy infants as young as three days, he first determined the extent of normal head turning. The investigators sounded a bell behind the infants' heads, which did not elicit any response. Next, they sounded the bell for ten seconds; if the infants turned their heads to the left, they received milk. Nurses then attempted to encourage the other infants to move their heads to the left by touching the left corner of the mouth with the bottle's nipple, or turning the head to the left and placing the nipple in the mouth. Learning occurred when the infants turned toward the sound of the bell five of ten times. With ten trials a day, the average infant required about eighteen days for learning. An interesting feature of the study was that some infants took only seven days to learn while others required over a month.

IMITATION

A major contribution to learning and one which exercises a potent influence on development is imitation. Youngsters imitate and they imitate easily, raising three important questions: *how* do they imitate, *why* do they imitate, *what* do they imitate? Kagan, Kearsley, and Zelazo (1978) state that imitation of an observed act does not appear until the end of the first year. Although some investigators believe that imitation occurs during the first weeks following birth (see Bower, 1977), Kagan and his associates argue that one cannot be certain that the two- or three-week-old baby's imitation is a selective response to an observed action (for example, sticking out the tongue).

Infants duplicate an observed act as a unit, thus indicating that they already possess the needed ability and are not imitating to learn the act. Consequently, the model's action must be within the infant's behavioral repertoire. During the second year, the authors believe that models act as incentives that cue a class of behavior that the infant has previously stored.

Thus, to answer *how* children imitate, they imitate by observation. *What* they imitate is a model displaying behavior that infants have already mastered. Finally, *why* children imitate some acts and not others requires further analysis. Infants primarily wish to prolong the excitement that their actions produce in others. They also want to match the observed behavior to a previously acquired schema and thus convince themselves that they have mastered the act. Once again, we see infants struggling to reduce uncertainty about themselves and their surroundings. The authors state:

> We suggest that acts over which the one- to two-year-old child experiences some uncertainty with respect to overt display are most likely to be imitated. That notion requires the child to possess a schema for the act and a representation of his competence to perform that act, as well as the ability to relate those two representations. He must actively coordinate two schemata, one for the act and one for his competence. (Kagan, Kearsley, Zelazo, 1978, p. 125)

J. S. Watson's (1976) studies of the relationship between early learning and intelligence led him to figuratively throw up his hands in frustration. Noting that reason dictates that higher intelligence should cause faster learning, Watson states that available data simply do not substantiate this conclusion. He warns that conditioning studies may be deceptive, since they view learning as a unitary process rather than as a set of component processes.

Whatever the relationship, it is clear that infants learn. Conditioning experiments, both classical and operant, testify to the possibility of modifying behavior from birth. Howe (1975) notes that classical conditioning experiments have consistently shown that speed of conditioning increases and the number of necessary trials decreases with age. These conclusions must be cautiously interpreted as to the cause of the changes or the relationship between the change and cognitive capacity. As Reese and Lipsitt (1970, p. 94) state:

> The evaluation of these reported age differences in rate of conditioning is that classical conditioning in infants provides little basis for concluding that differences in learning capacities have been demonstrated. Differences due to the effects of variations in motivation, reinforcement, and unconditioned response capacities have not been systematically explored in any of these studies.

Howe (1975) believes that not only do speed and number of necessary trials change with age but the nature of reinforcing events also changes. For example, food reinforces behavior from birth; visual patterns quickly assert their reinforcing qualities; soft tones affect the visual responses of two- to three-month-old infants; by four months novelty demonstrates reinforcing properties. An interesting developmental phenomenon thus emerges: a wider range of events can reinforce the older infant's behavior, but increasing selectivity restricts the variety of events that actually reinforce behavior (Howe, 1975, p. 57).

Infants learn; they learn quickly and they learn well. They may never again learn quite as easily as during the first months, even if they receive proper nutrition and stimulation. Kagan and his associates (1978) note that discrepancy causes mental work; hence an environment containing the necessary discrepant events facilitates cognitive growth. Data concerning the retarded development of youngsters who have suffered deprived environments during infancy are overwhelming. These youngsters are slow to achieve such developmental milestones as stranger anxiety, object constancy, and the comparison of present events with stored schemata. Fulfillment demands a satisfying interaction between genetic potential and environmental stimulation.

EARLY EXPERIENCE AND INFANCY

Do the experiences of infancy produce lasting effects? The possible answers to this deceptively simple question are as important as they are controversial. If the effects are irreversible, then there is little justification in pouring enormous amounts of time and money into efforts to improve children who have suffered serious environmental deficits. If the effects are reversible, then *any* effort is worthwhile, and the sole concern of intervention programs should be the timing and nature of the effort. But as with most human issues, the path to understanding is strewn with obstacles. To help unravel some of the complexities surrounding the question, we shall examine several physiological studies before turning to the psychological evidence.

The Nervous System and Development

The brain at birth is about twenty percent of its adult weight and by age two about eighty percent. These figures are startling since they represent the span of infancy and clearly indicate a time of great growth and potential vulnerability: from birth to two years seems to be a sensitive period for brain development. What happens if youngsters encounter debilitating circumstances? To understand what a sterile environment can do, it is helpful to understand how our central nervous system transmits information.

The basic unit of the brain is the neuron. A human brain contains from 20 to 200 billion neurons, each connecting with as many as a thousand other neurons, thus establishing a gigantic communications network (Teyler, 1978, p. 2). Each neuron contains a cell nucleus and the molecular machinery vital to maintain life. Two types of processes extend from the cell body: there are several dendrites that receive information from other neurons, and one axon that transmits information away from the cell body and which is covered with a myelin sheath (a fatty substance that facilitates passage of the nerve impulse). The synapse is the region of communication between two neurons.

When information arrives at the end of an axon, a chemical substance called a neurotransmitter is released, which alerts the dendrites of the next axon that information is passing. The nerve impulse itself is electrical. Figure 5.3 illustrates the basic structure.

The neurons are not connected in a random manner. A recurring theme in our analysis of perceptual and cognitive development has been the early response of infants to patterns. Supporting these psychological conclusions, John Eccles (1977) states that the neuronal components of the cortex or other regions of the brain are *selectively connected to form organized patterns.*

Two basic principles of neuronal functioning are *divergence* and *convergence.* Divergence is the phenomenon whereby one fiber entering the spinal cord with its message activates many other neurons; conversely, convergence is the arrival of many active neurons on one nerve cell. Eccles emphasizes that everything that happens in the brain has its basis in neuronal activity; consequently, the growth that produces an adult brain is critical. Eccles (1977, p. 185) states that if synaptic growth is required for learning there must be an increase in brain metabolism of a special kind with the manufacture of proteins and other macromolecules. What happens when there is interference with this growth?

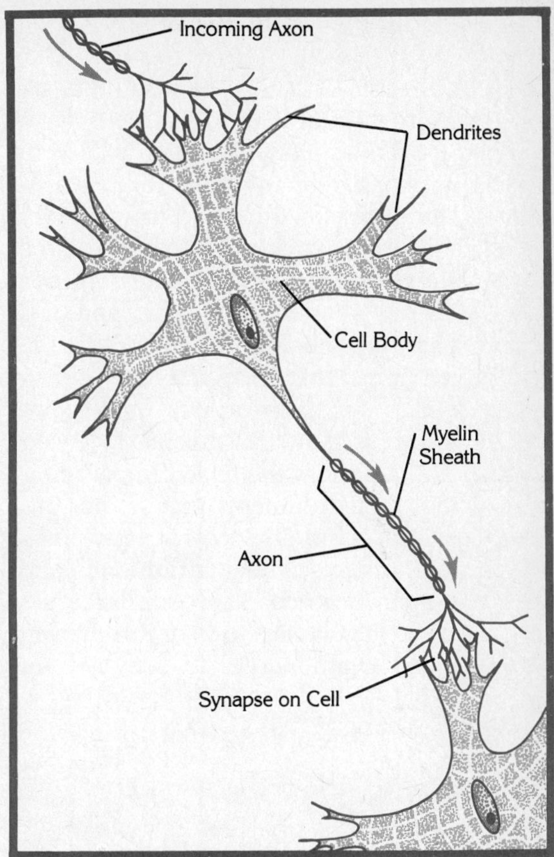

FIGURE 5.3. The Neuron.

Continued studies (Rose, 1973) indicate that food deprivation can cause severe physiological damage. If protein-calorie malnutrition occurs before two years, when eighty percent of adult brain weight is attained, a real possibility exists that permanent mental and motor damage may occur (Cravioto et al., 1969). Researchers have carefully charted the pattern of brain development: between the second and third prenatal months, all adult nerve cells develop; at about five months the glial cells begin to appear, accompanied by growth of the myelin sheath. This second process continues for at least two years following birth.

Since a major part of the brain's growth spurt occurs after birth, anything that interferes during these critical few months can cause serious difficulties. Studies have consistently shown that malnourished rats have significantly smaller brains than their healthy peers. The diminished size seems to reflect fewer connections among the neurons; that is, these animals have fewer (about forty percent less) synapses than normal rats, and thus learning ability is sharply reduced. Figure 5.4 illustrates typical interneuronal networks.

The studies of malnutrition and brain growth of Cravioto et al. (1969), Manocha (1972), and Rose (1973) all stress the added impact of an impoverished environment; that is, not only food deprivation but also lack of stimulation can cause problems. Malnutrition and social deprivation produce remarkably similar results. For example, the classic study of Rosenzweig, Bennett, and Diamond (1972) demonstrated the effects of an impoverished and enriched environment on brain development. Rats that had experienced the enriched environment had thicker and heavier cortexes, better blood supply to the brain, larger brain cells and more glial cells.

FIGURE 5.4. Interneuronal Networks.

The Reversibility of Early Experience

The renowned studies of Rene Spitz (1945) and Wayne Dennis (1960) vividly documented the retarded development of institutionalized children. In each of these studies the youngsters were exposed to particularly sterile environments with disastrous consequences. Lytt Gardner (1972), in the same tradition, reports on the remarkable results of different psychological environments on twins. Boy and girl twins were born to a woman who soon found herself pregnant again, unhappily so. Her husband lost his job and left his wife and children. Until this episode both twins were progressing satisfactorily, with the boy showing a slight superiority in growth. Now, however, the mother directed her hostility about the missing father at the remaining male. Both youngsters were about four months old when suddenly the boy's development slowed noticeably. At one year his height was that of a seven-month-old and his deteriorating condition required hospitalization.

The boy soon recovered with hospital treatment, and before his release the mother and father had reconciled. By two years his development matched his sister's. Gardner terms this phenomenon "deprivation dwarfism" and believes that environmental deprivation and emotional upset have a strong negative effect on development.

The many institutional studies testify to the adverse impact of sterile environments on human development. The results of these studies, both animal and human, establish that psychological as well as physiological events affect brain development. However the critical question remains: Are these negative effects reversible? There can be no definitive answer to this question, because the timing and duration of deprivation varies, as does the damage that any child can tolerate. If deprivation begins at birth and continues for years, permanent damage may well ensue. Yet children are remarkably resilient and can tolerate deprivation, provided it is not too severe and lengthy.

ARE THE RESULTS OF EARLY DEPRIVATION REVERSIBLE?

In a series of carefully prepared articles (Kagan, 1978; Kagan and Klein, 1973), Jerome Kagan has forcefully argued that an infant's early experiences may not cause lasting effects. Reporting on his Guatemalan studies of children reared in small, isolated, subsistance farming villages, he describes infants who spend their first year confined to small, dark, windowless huts, who are not played with, who are rarely spoken to, and who are poorly nourished. When these youngsters are compared to similar American youngsters, they appear retarded. They simply do not manifest the developmental milestones (memory, object permanence) of normal American youngsters.

During the second year, the Guatemalan children leave their huts and play outside where they now encounter much greater stimulation. By four years they play with their peers, and by nine years they share the adult work responsibilities. At this time, these youngsters are still inferior to American children on tests of perception, memory, and reasoning. By *adolescence*, however, the Guatemalan children perform equally as well as their American counterparts; the apparent early cognitive retardation had disappeared.

Kagan (1978) concludes that the fears and joys of the first years seem to be part of nature's script for development and not harbingers of adolescent anxiety or adult retardation. It is a hopeful study implying that if impoverished children score poorly on mental tests, the possibility remains that they may reverse the negative effects, provided that changes occur in their environment.

Other significant studies suggest the same conclusions. The work of Harold Skeels (1966) offers a dramatic and unparalleled insight into the powerful influences of the environment on mental development. His investigation (planned intervention) dates back to 1938 (Skeels et al., 1938) when the authors and several of their associates established a nursery school on the grounds of an orphanage. The school had twenty-one students, ranging in age from eighteen months to five and one-half years. The children were matched with others in the orphanage with respect to sex, age, IQ, and length of stay in the orphanage. The experimental youngsters stayed in the nursery school five hours a day for five days, while the controls remained within the orphanage. The children in the nursery school showed constant IQ gain, while those remaining in the orphanage continued to lose, probably because of the lack of stimulating environment.

The authors (Skeels and Dye, 1939) next reported an amazing result that caused considerable furor. Because of their low IQ and lack of physical progress (they could not stand, walk, or vocalize), two youngsters, one thirteen months old with an IQ of 35, the other sixteen months old with an IQ of 46, were taken from a state orphanage and placed in an institution for the feebleminded. They were placed in a ward with moron girls and women aged eighteen to fifty with mental ages from five to nine years. While visiting the ward about six months later, Skeels noted that the two youngsters seemed much more alert; they were then retested. The younger child's IQ was 77 and the older's was 87. They were tested again at the end of a year, and their IQs were 100 and 88, respectively. When the children were forty and forty-three months of age, their IQs were 95 and 93.

The authors reasoned that the change in environment had produced these astonishing results. Although the youngsters were placed with moron girls and women, this situation was nevertheless much more stimulating than the orphanage. The older women became attached to them and played with them constantly, and the attendants took the children with them to stores and bought them toys, paper, and crayons.

The next phase in this series of investigations entailed the fantastic plan of transferring one- to two-year-old mentally retarded youngsters from the orphanage to an institution for the feebleminded. As Skeels (1966) notes, in light of the experience with the original youngsters, the investigators argued that early transfer to such an institution might prove therapeutic. Thirteen children, all under the age of three, were transferred. A control group of twelve youngsters remained at the orphanage. The results were that every child in the experimental group showed a gain of from seven to fifty-eight IQ points. For the control group, all but one showed a loss of from nine to forty-five points, and ten of the twelve children in the control group lost more than fifteen points. At the experiment's conclusion, the mean IQ of the experimental group was 91.8, while that of the control group had fallen to 60.5.

Skeels (1966) restudied the two groups in the 1960s, about twenty years after the last postexperimental follow-up. He was able to locate all thirteen of the experimental group and eleven of the twelve in the control group (one had died). The author made the decision not to use IQ tests because of the many questions that might arise because of poor reliability of the early childhood tests. He decided instead to relate earlier measures of mental development to adult educational level, occupation, and general social competence. The results shown in Table 5.3 are self-evident.

As Skeels notes, the two groups had maintained their divergent patterns of competency into adulthood. All thirteen persons in the experimental group were self-supporting and none was a ward of any institution. In the control group of twelve children, one had died in adolescence following continued residence in a state institution for the mentally retarded, and four were still wards of institutions, one in a mental hospital and the other three in institutions for the mentally retarded.

Any discussion of the effects of early environments must reckon with Skeel's fascinating tale. In the 1930s, he notes, the prevailing view of intelligence focused on its supposedly fixed and unchanging nature. It was thought to be strictly related to the parents' genetic traits and to be only slightly influenced by the environment. The common belief was that the intelligence of young children could be reliably assessed. The result would be a single, unchangeable figure that would not vary throughout the individual's life. Skeel's painstakingly thorough research seriously shakes this belief. As he concludes, we must constantly be aware that children interact with their environment and do not just passively absorb it.

More precise and pertinent information about constitutional, emotional, and stylistic characteristics of a child are required in order to ensure maximum environmental impact.

While both of these powerful studies generate optimism, we must not be misled by their conclusions. Kagan reasons that children in a natural environment will ultimately fulfill their potential, while Skeel's work showed that a changed environment was necessary. Basic questions remain unanswered. Can we adequately determine the impact of a natural environment? What if youngsters do not receive the benefit of removal from a depressed environment? Finally, we are only beginning to grapple with assessing the severity and duration of deprivation for the individual child. A youngster's constitution and personality are the final determinants of recovery or retardation.

TABLE 5.3. Experimental and Contrast Groups: Occupations of Subjects and Spouses

Case number	Subject's occupation	Spouse's occupation	Female subject's occupation previous to marriage
Experimental group:			
1[a]	Staff sergeant	Dental technician	
2	Housewife	Laborer	Nurses' aide
3	Housewife	Mechanic	Elementary school teacher
4	Nursing instructor	Unemployed	Registered nurse
5	Housewife	Semiskilled laborer	No work history
6	Waitress	Mechanic, semiskilled	Beauty operator
7	Housewife	Flight engineer	Dining room hostess
8	Housewife	Foreman, construction	No work history
9	Domestic service	Unmarried	
10[a]	Real estate sales	Housewife	
11[a]	Vocational counselor	Advertising copy writer[b]	
12	Gift shop sales[c]	Unmarried	
13	Housewife	Pressman-printer	Office-clerical
Contrast group:			
14	Institutional inmate	Unmarried	
15	Dishwasher	Unmarried	
16	Deceased		
17[a]	Dishwasher	Unmarried	
18[a]	Institutional inmate	Unmarried	
19[a]	Composer and typesetter	Housewife	
20[a]	Institutional inmate	Unmarried	
21[a]	Dishwasher	Unmarried	
22[a]	Floater	Divorced	
23	Cafeteria (part-time)	Unmarried	
24[a]	Institutional gardener's assistant	Unmarried	
25[a]	Institutional inmate	Unmarried	

[a]Male.
[b]B.A. degree.
[c]Previously had worked as a licensed practical nurse.

Experimental and Contrast Groups. From H. M. Skeels, "Adult Status of Children with Contrasting Early Life Experiences," *Monographs of the Society for Research in Child Development*, 1966, 31 (Serial #105) Table 5, p. 23.

DISCUSSION QUESTIONS

1. Examine Figure 5.2 carefully and as you follow the behavioral hierarchy, attempt to identify those behaviors that are produced by maturation and by learning. Now for each behavior, attempt to sort out the maturational and then the learning components. Does this help to explain some of the difficulties in analyzing learning?
2. Recent studies have demonstrated that the myelin sheath continues to grow for several years following birth. Combine this evidence with animal studies showing smaller brain growth due to a sterile environment and indicate the possible effect on learning.
3. Can you justify the assumption that an isolated environment produces results similar to the effects of malnutrition? Select human studies that show pronounced retardation. Are you willing to apply the conclusions from the animal studies to children? Specifically state your reasons, either pro or con.
4. The central issue in any discussion of the effects of early experience is the possibility of permanent effects. This is not solely developmental; the education, economic, and political implications are enormous. Elaborate on this statement. Can you compare the Kagan and Skeels studies? Be sure to consider the vital topics of timing and severity of deprivation.

Knowledge about infants has exploded in the last decade. One of the major discoveries was that any assessment of infants' behavior reflected the state of the infant at the time of observation. The concept of state has recast our interpretations of infants' behavior, since a youngster's interaction with the environment depends on existing conditions. Another theme that shades contemporary investigations of infancy is that of interaction. While there has always been a tacit recognition of the interactive nature of development, today it occupies a central position in both research and theory. As Bower (1977) notes, the developmental process is not a passive state, utterly dependent on the environment. Rather, from birth infants attempt to organize their world according to the stimuli they receive. If the environment is barren of challenging stimuli, the results are all too apparent.

Using these basic ideas, Kagan (1976) concludes that there are three major themes in modern developmental psychology:

1. The interaction between biological and psychological elements in development, which means that the maturation of the nervous system sets both constraints and permissiveness on the range of possible behaviors, but which are still inexplicable (Kagan, 1976, p. 433).

2. The increasing tendency to use stages in interpreting development to clarify the structures, processes, and transformations of successive eras.

3. The relevance of context, or as Kagan states, "the power of situational context in infant behavior." Traits are not abstract nor do they exist in a vacuum—they appear, influence, and are influenced by the existing circumstances.

Applied to infancy these themes offer guidelines and potential boundaries for the assimilation, interpretation, and practical utilization for the enormous amounts of data accumulating about infants.

SUMMARY

The "states" of infancy have assumed a major role in any discussion and study of infants.

A range of neonatal assessment techniques permits detailed analysis of neurological and behavioral capabilities.

Neuromotor assessment is a good indicator of the rate and nature of development.

Perceptual and cognitive development seem to have as a primary objective the reduction of uncertainty about the world.

Explanations of cognitive development suggest that cognitive conflict is a major agent in mental growth.

Many phenomena that appear during the last half of the first year, such as object permanence, seem to depend on the infant's emerging memory.

Infants demonstrate a remarkable learning ability, which complicates efforts to separate the products of development from those of learning.

One of the most controversial topics in current developmental psychology is the possibility that early experience produces lasting affects.

SUGGESTED READINGS

BOWER, T. G. R. *A Primer of Infant Development.* San Francisco: Freeman, 1977. An overview of infancy by an author not intimidated by the lacunae in development psychology.

BRAZELTON, T. BERRY. *Neonatal Behavioral Assessment Scale.* London: William Heinemann Medical Books, Ltd. 1973. The manual of Brazelton's scale, with accompanying explanations—clear, precise, revealing.

HOWE, MICHAEL. *Learning in Infants and Young Children.* Stanford: Stanford University Press, 1975. A thorough review of the research and theories surrounding infant learning.

KAGAN, JEROME, RICHARD B. KEARSLEY, PHILIP R. ZELAZO. *Infancy: Its Place in Human Development.* Cambridge: Harvard University Press, 1978. A comprehensive account of infancy by three respected authors.

KNOBLOCH, HILDA and BENJAMIN PASAMANICK. *Gesell and Amatruda's Developmental Diagnosis.* New York: Harper and Row, 1974. An excellent account of development, with special emphasis on identifying and treating developmental problems.

LEWIS, MICHAEL (editor). *The Origins of Intelligence.* New York: Plenum Press, 1976. A pertinent, well written collection of essays about the nature of intelligence and the pitfalls in measuring it.

ROSE, STEVEN. *The Conscious Brain.* New York: Knopf, 1973. A most readable account of the structure and development of the brain.

PART THREE

ASPECTS OF DEVELOPMENT

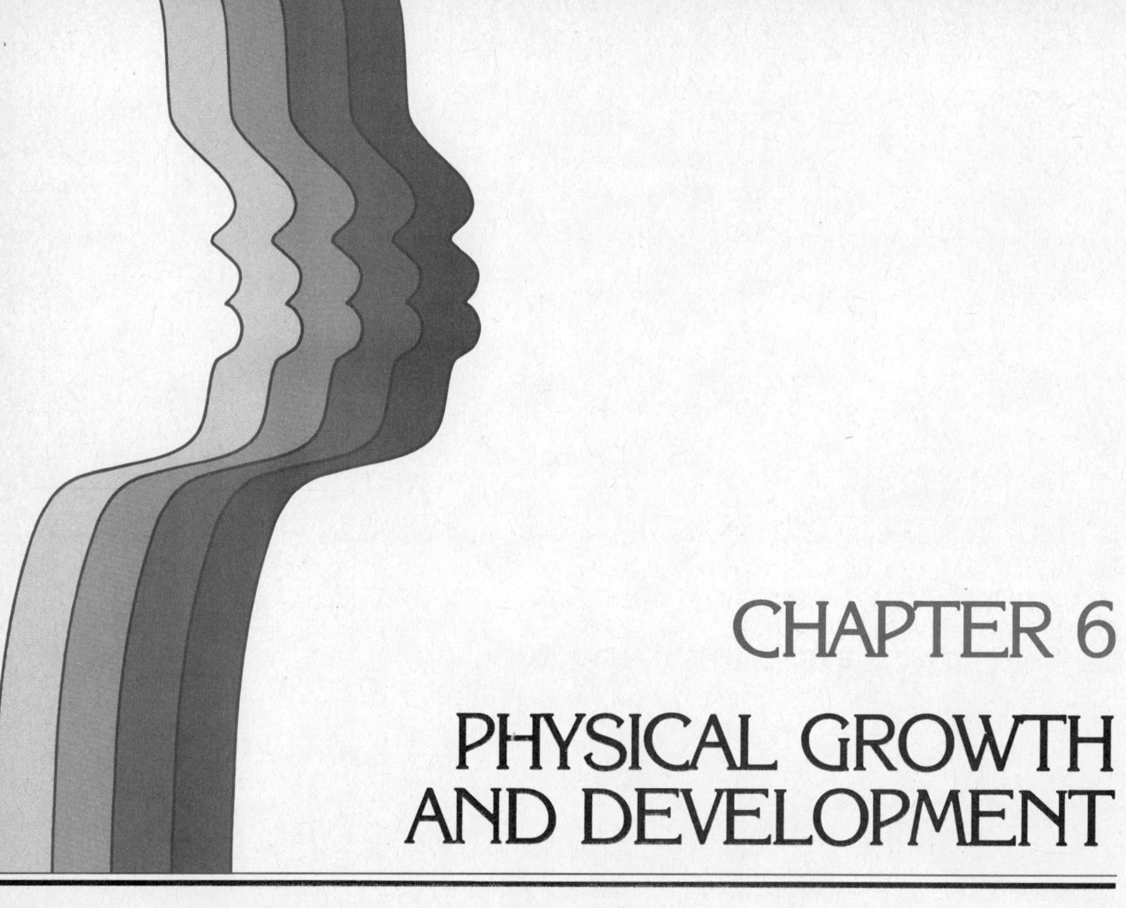

CHAPTER 6

PHYSICAL GROWTH AND DEVELOPMENT

CHAPTER HIGHLIGHTS

Topics

Characteristics of Physical Development
a. The Growth Process
b. Heredity and Environment
c. Nutrition

Characteristics of Brain Development
a. The Brain's Basic Structure
b. The Triune Brain
c. Brain Development
d. Cerebral Lateralization and Development

People

Dirk Bakker
Anthony Buffery
John Eccles
Herman Epstein
Howard Gardner
Marcel Kinsbourne
Robert Knights
Paul MacLean
J. M. Tanner
Timothy Teyler

Special Topics

Physical Development—An Overview
Environmental Deprivation
Malnutrition and Intellectual Performance
Myelination
Left-Handedness
The Minor Hemisphere

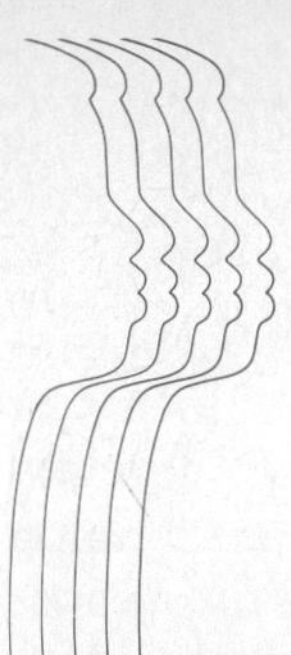

All behavior occurs within a biological structure, and the more we know about that structure the more we understand the resultant behavior. Any physical problems such as disease, accident, or defect may well influence behavior and attempts to explain behavior must deal with the fascinating, yet treacherous, labyrinth of the heredity-environment interaction. Consequently, having investigated the mechanics of heredity, our task now is to examine the apparently more simple and observable physical changes of development. That these changes are "apparently" simple is due to the natural inclination to focus on a child's obvious changes in size, while ignoring more subtle physiological alterations.

For example, what role does the endocrine system play as it releases specific hormones at critical times? Brain growth, which occurs with startling rapidity during the first few years, certainly is a form of physical growth that influences every aspect of a child's life. Even concentrating on obvious size changes, a difficult question arises: what exactly causes these changes? To say that the interaction between heredity and environment causes them is a glib response. How can we interpret the effects of qualitative environmental differences such as enrichment or malnutrition? These differences produce inevitable but elusive results: heredity's potential is enhanced or hindered by environmental circumstances.

All children go through an identical sequence of development: Children crawl before they walk and walk before they run. But children differ in the rate that they achieve these behaviors; some children develop more rapidly than others. This advantage (if it is always that) usually remains constant: smarter children remain smarter; taller children are taller at subsequent ages. And the more skilled, more mature child is usually superior in many other aspects of development. Expectations for such children are higher.

These facts underscore the integrated nature of development. We divide development into neat compartments only for the purpose of analysis; actually various functions depend on each other, and their rates of development are intertwined.

As one illustration of physical development, it is interesting to examine the human growth curve and follow the development of height (Figure 6.1). (Note that ten centimeters equal four inches.) This curve strikingly demonstrates the regularity of growth. With the exception of the two spurts at infancy and adolescence, growth is highly predictable for most boys and girls—given satisfactory conditions.

Most other body measurements follow the pattern of the height curve. Skeletal and muscular measurements are similar, as are those of most of the internal organs (liver, spleen, kidneys). Among some notable exceptions are the brain and reproductive organs, which have major behavioral implications. The hormonal changes associated with adolescence have a direct impact on behavior, and the early development of the brain, which from the fetal period on more closely approximates adult

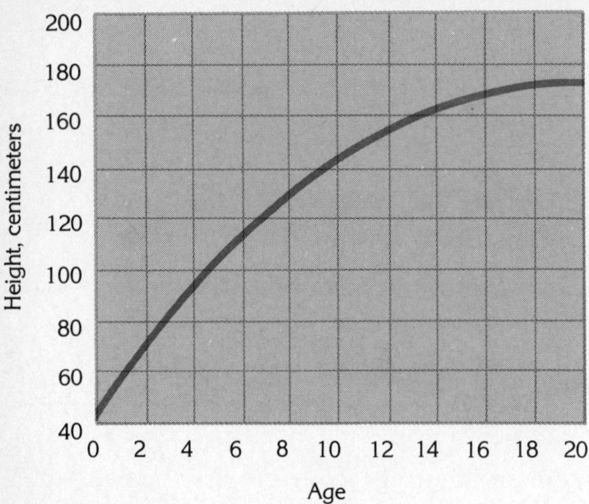

FIGURE 6.1. The Human Growth Curve.

size than other organs, provides the child with the capacity to learn, to adapt, to cope with the environment.

Among the behavioral characteristics accompanying physical growth are the gradual differentiation of behavior from homogeneity to heterogeneity, from mass endeavors to more specialized activities, and from the general to the specific. For example, while infants respond totally (with the entire body) to almost all stimuli (a general reaction), a youngster of eight can skillfully swing a bat at a swiftly moving baseball (a specific reaction). Control of the body and the ages at which motor activities such as crawling, walking, or climbing occur seem to be mainly determined by physical maturation.

The remainder of the chapter will trace the pattern of physical growth, discovering what constitutes normal progress and how development suffers when nutrition is faulty. A major portion of the chapter is devoted to brain development: its changing structure, the concept of the triune brain, and the significance of cerebral lateralization.

Much is known about human physical development, but as Tanner (1973) states, much about the mechanism of growth and maturation still remains obscure.

CHARACTERISTICS OF PHYSICAL DEVELOPMENT

Individuals are born with the heritage of generations, ready to commence the process of development. What does "normal" development entail? Do all children grow and develop similarly? Is it possible to classify the almost infinite changes that we witness as children move through life's journey?

We are concerned here with physical growth and development. Optimum growth requires proper nutrition, temperature, and humidity in order to stimulate internal agents such as the genetic elements, growth hormones, and the processes of differentiation. Tanner (1970) notes that the growth process is self-stabilizing; that is, it is governed by the control system of the genes and fueled by energy absorbed from the environment. If malnutrition or illness deflects children from the normal growth trajectory, but a corrective force (adequate diet or termination of illness) intervenes, the normal course of development will accelerate until the children "catch up"; thereupon growth slows.

Different cells, tissues, and organs grow at different rates. Some tissues never lose the ability to grow (hair, skin, nails). But if growth is out of proportion, the result may be an oddity, a freak. In humans, for example, body length at birth is about four times the length of the face at birth, so the head is relatively large. But the head grows more slowly than the trunk or limbs, so that at age twenty-five body length is about eight times that of face length. Figure 6.2 provides an overview of the first five years of development.

This model is an interesting interpretation of the first five years of life. Knobloch and Pasamanick (1974) state that healthy development depends on the integration of five kinds of behavior:

1. Adaptive, including perception, sensorimotor reactions, and eye-hand coordination.

2. Gross motor behavior, including head balance, sitting, standing, creeping, and walking.

3. Fine motor behavior, including the use of hand and fingers in grasping and manipulating an object.

4. Language behavior, including facial expression, gestures, words, phrases, sentences, and comprehension.

5. Personal-social behavior, including feeding ability, toilet training, self-dependency, and cooperation.

Using and extending the rich and varied work of Arnold Gesell, Yale's famous child psychologist, Knobloch and Pasamanick believe that there are key ages during the first five years of development: four, sixteen, twenty-eight, forty, and fifty-two weeks, and eighteen, twenty-four and thirty-six months. These ages represent integrative periods; that is, the child combines different abilities to produce more organized behavior. The authors (1974, p. 8) summarize these early developmental trends as follows:

1. In the first quarter of the first year, children gain control of oculomotor muscles (these are the muscles that control the movement of the eyeballs).

2. In the second quarter (sixteen to twenty-eight weeks), infants gain control of the muscles that support the head and upper trunk, and those that move arms and hands.

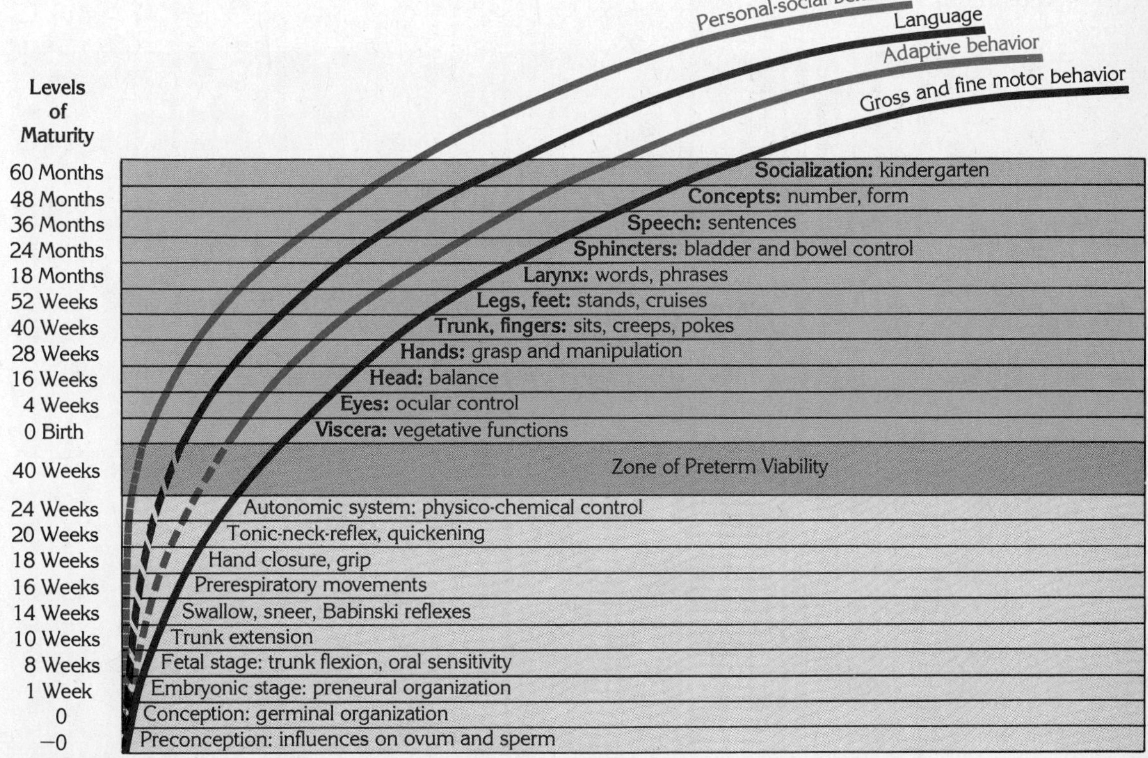

FIGURE 6.2. The Development of Behavior in the Five Major Fields.
Source: Hilda Knobloch and Benjamin Pasamanick, *Gesell and Amatruda's Developmental Diagnosis.* New York: Harper and Row, 1974.

3. In the third quarter (twenty-eight to forty weeks), there is increasing control of trunk and fingers. Children can sit and creep.

4. In the fourth quarter (forty to fifty-two weeks), children control legs and feet, and begin to stand and walk with some support.

5. In the second year, walking and running develop, children achieve bowel and bladder control, begin to speak, and acquire some sense of self-identity.

6. Between the second and third year, children use language as a vehicle for thought.

7. In the fourth year, questioning becomes a way of life, and abstract thinking is apparent. Children should be relatively independent in personal life and home routine.

8. In the fifth year, motor control has matured, language is fairly articulate, and social adjustment is apparent.

The Growth Process

J. M. Tanner (1973), emphasizing that human growth is a "rather regular" process, states that growth in height does not proceed by fits and starts. A good example of such regularity is seen in Tables 6.1 and 6.2, which present height and weight data for both males and females from birth to twenty years.

Examining the growth figures for the fiftieth percentile, note how males begin to surpass females at age fourteen, but particularly note the steady increase in height, which reinforces Tanner's concept of regularity. The same pattern appears for weight, as seen in Table 6.2. It is only gradually that males become larger and more muscular (Tanner, 1973, p. 36).

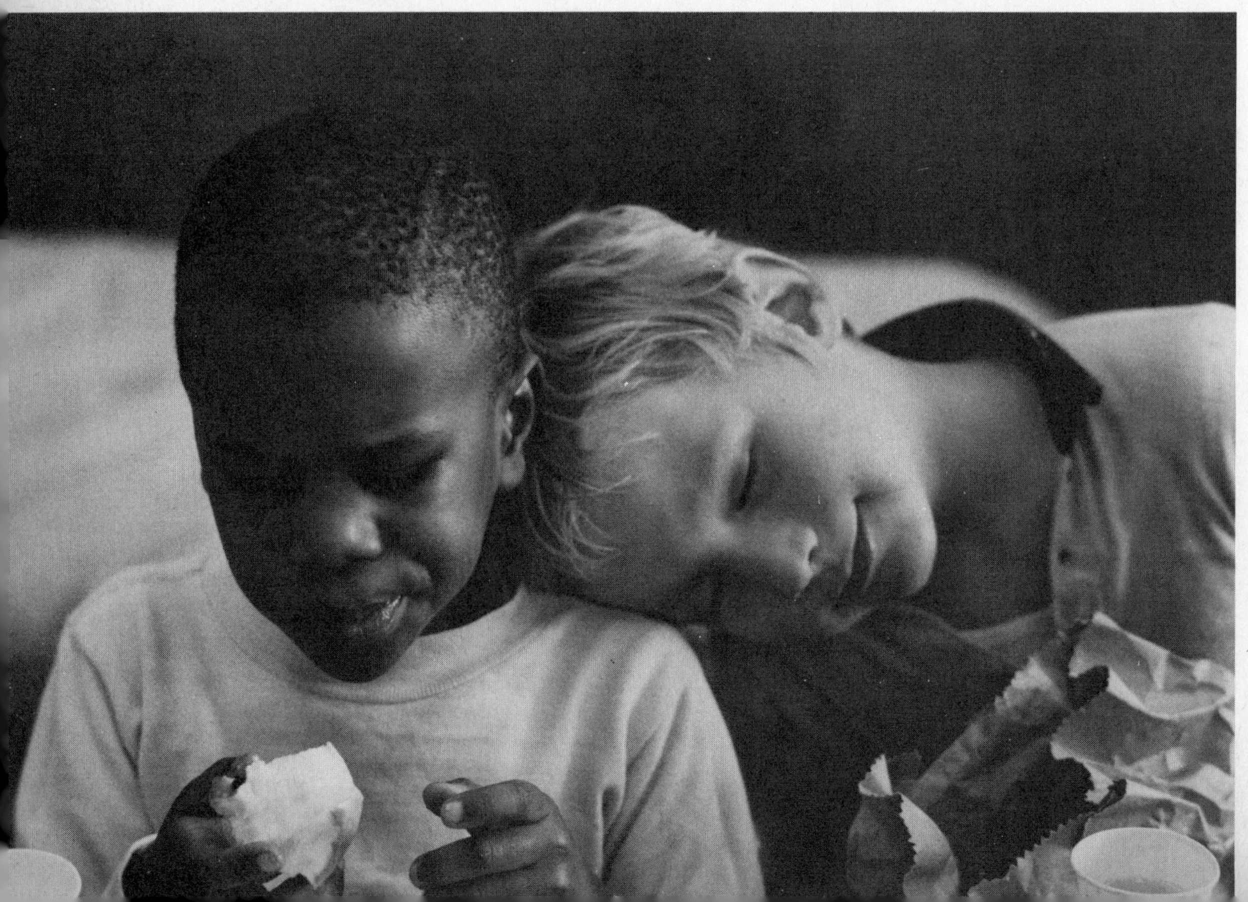

PHYSICAL DEVELOPMENT—AN OVERVIEW

In an excellent overview of physical development, J. M. Tanner (1970) discusses the interaction of heredity and environment to produce the rate and kinds of physical growth. Among the chief contributing forces are:

1. *Hereditary elements.* These elements are of immense importance to the regulation of growth. The genetic growth plan is formulated at conception and functions throughout the entire growth process.
2. *Racial elements.* At birth, blacks surpass whites in skeletal development, which is reflected in the earlier appearance of their teeth. This advancement continues for about two or three years if nutritional and other environmental conditions are favorable.
3. *Nutrition.* Malnutrition delays growth and, if persistent, can cause lasting damage. Children in Stuttgart, Germany, were studied each year from 1911 to 1953. From 1920 to 1940 there was a uniform increase, but in the later years of each war, average height declined as food was curtailed. These children recovered, but chronic malnutrition presents troublesome questions. For example, does chronic malnutrition produce permanent brain damage in the fetus and the one- or two-year-old child?
4. *Disease.* Short-term illnesses cause no permanent retardation of the growth rate, although they may cause some disturbance if the child's diet is consistently inadequate. Major disease usually causes a slowing of growth, followed by a catch-up period if circumstances become more favorable.
5. *Psychological disturbances.* Stress can slow development leading occasionally to deprivation dwarfism. Small children under uncompromising strain such as divorce seem to "turn off" their growth hormone and become almost dwarfed.
6. *Socioeconomic status.* Children from different social classes differ in average body size at all ages. Tanner gives the example of differences in height between British children of the professional and managerial classes and those of laborers. Height differences range from one inch at three years to two inches at adolescence. There is a consistent pattern in all such studies, indicating that children in more favorable circumstances are larger than those growing up under less favorable economic conditions. The difference seems to stem from nutrition, sleep, exercise, and recreation.
7. *Accelerated trends.* There has been a tendency during the past hundred years for children to become progressively larger at all ages. This is especially true in Europe and America.

TABLE 6.1. Observed Percentiles of Recumbent Length (in Centimeters), by Sex and Age: Fels Research Institute, Birth–20 Years

Sex and age	n	Observed percentile						
		5th	10th	25th	50th	75th	90th	95th
Male		**Recumbent length in centimeters**						
Birth	156	45.6	47.1	48.6	49.9	51.5	53.3	54.2
1 month	274	51.1	51.7	53.3	54.8	56.2	57.6	58.4
3 months	438	56.2	57.4	59.2	61.2	63.2	64.8	65.8
6 months	425	63.6	64.4	66.1	67.6	69.4	71.1	72.1
9 months	365	68.2	69.3	70.7	72.4	74.2	75.8	76.8
1 year	374	71.7	72.9	74.5	76.2	77.7	80.1	81.4
1½ years	472	77.4	78.5	80.3	82.3	84.3	86.5	88.2
2 years	425	82.3	83.5	85.6	87.7	89.8	92.2	93.5
2½ years	392	87.2	88.4	90.3	92.3	94.7	97.1	99.1
3 years	364	91.1	92.2	94.1	96.5	98.8	101.4	102.9
3½ years	336	94.3	95.3	97.8	100.5	103.3	105.8	107.6
4 years	319	97.9	99.0	101.2	103.6	106.6	109.0	111.2
4½ years	316	100.8	102.3	104.4	107.4	110.1	112.5	114.4
5 years	302	104.0	105.5	108.0	110.9	113.9	116.7	118.9
5½ years	277	107.1	108.9	111.3	114.2	117.6	120.8	122.4
6 years	266	110.1	111.8	114.4	117.4	120.6	123.4	125.8
6½ years	239	113.6	115.2	117.8	120.6	124.3	127.3	129.3
7 years	265	116.2	118.1	120.4	123.6	127.3	130.0	132.1
7½ years	227	118.5	120.9	123.7	126.7	130.7	133.7	135.3
8 years	242	121.2	123.8	126.2	129.5	133.4	136.4	139.1
8½ years	206	124.5	126.6	129.4	132.6	136.6	139.7	142.0
9 years	159	126.6	129.0	131.7	135.2	139.5	142.8	147.2
9½ years	127	129.2	131.5	134.8	137.7	141.4	145.9	149.6
10 years	147	132.2	134.0	137.4	140.4	145.2	147.8	151.3
10½ years	143	135.1	136.2	140.1	142.8	147.6	150.5	154.6
11 years	139	137.3	138.6	142.0	145.6	150.7	154.2	157.3
11½ years	135	139.2	140.9	145.2	148.7	153.5	158.8	162.4
12 years	148	141.7	143.3	147.2	151.0	156.3	161.7	165.2
12½ years	140	144.2	145.9	150.7	154.5	160.1	165.3	168.2
13 years	143	146.4	148.5	153.7	158.3	163.9	170.4	173.0
13½ years	142	149.0	152.9	157.6	162.5	167.4	174.6	178.0
14 years	146	152.9	154.5	161.7	166.1	171.7	178.5	181.5
14½ years	138	154.7	158.1	165.5	170.0	175.2	180.7	184.1
15 years	134	160.2	163.3	168.4	173.9	177.8	183.1	186.1
15½ years	131	163.0	166.2	170.8	176.4	180.2	184.1	187.3
16 years	126	166.1	169.2	173.3	178.4	181.6	185.5	187.7
16½ years	122	167.2	171.0	174.4	180.0	184.0	187.2	188.8
17 years	132	169.3	172.1	175.2	179.7	183.9	187.5	188.6
17½ years	107	170.0	172.3	175.8	180.6	184.2	188.3	189.1
18 years	124	170.5	172.6	176.2	181.1	184.8	188.7	191.7
20 years	84	169.4	172.3	177.2	182.0	185.0	189.3	191.1

NOTE: n = sample size.

Source: "NCHS Growth Curves, Birth–Eighteen Years, United States," *National Center for Health Statistics*, HEW Publication No. (PHS) 78-1650. Hyattsville, Maryland: U.S. Department of Health, Education, and Welfare, 1977.

TABLE 6.1. Continued

Sex and age	n	Observed percentile						
		5th	10th	25th	50th	75th	90th	95th
Female		**Recumbent length in centimeters**						
Birth	142	44.6	46.1	47.6	49.3	50.5	51.7	52.9
1 month	251	49.8	50.6	52.3	53.8	55.1	56.1	56.7
3 months	426	55.1	56.0	57.7	59.6	61.4	62.9	63.7
6 months	409	61.6	62.5	64.1	65.7	67.6	69.2	70.1
9 months	347	66.3	67.2	68.7	70.6	72.5	73.8	74.8
1 year	335	70.1	71.0	72.6	74.4	76.3	78.3	79.2
1½ years	463	75.6	76.8	78.6	80.8	83.0	84.8	86.1
2 years	410	81.4	82.6	84.4	86.5	88.7	90.8	92.1
2½ years	383	86.2	87.2	88.1	91.4	93.7	95.7	96.7
3 years	357	89.8	90.8	93.1	95.5	98.1	99.9	101.6
3½ years	309	93.0	94.2	96.4	99.1	101.6	104.0	105.8
4 years	319	96.4	98.0	99.9	103.0	105.5	108.3	109.8
4½ years	291	99.4	101.4	103.5	106.2	109.2	111.7	113.0
5 years	291	102.5	104.0	107.0	109.8	112.9	115.4	116.8
5½ years	276	106.0	107.5	110.1	112.8	116.1	119.1	121.2
6 years	263	108.8	110.4	113.4	116.4	119.4	122.4	124.9
6½ years	222	112.0	113.5	116.2	119.6	122.6	126.6	128.2
7 years	247	115.6	116.6	119.3	122.4	125.1	129.1	131.4
7½ years	220	117.6	119.2	122.0	125.4	128.6	132.2	135.0
8 years	228	120.7	122.1	125.0	128.2	131.4	135.5	138.3
8½ years	210	123.4	124.7	127.3	130.9	134.1	137.9	141.5
9 years	153	125.6	127.4	129.5	133.8	136.9	140.5	143.9
9½ years	141	128.6	130.0	132.5	136.3	139.4	143.2	147.4
10 years	140	130.9	132.3	135.2	139.6	142.7	147.9	149.8
10½ years	141	133.6	135.0	138.0	142.5	145.8	151.7	154.9
11 years	131	136.2	137.3	140.7	145.0	149.7	155.4	157.6
11½ years	128	138.7	140.3	143.7	148.7	153.9	158.3	161.4
12 years	135	142.4	143.8	148.0	151.8	157.8	161.0	164.9
12½ years	126	146.2	147.5	151.3	155.2	160.7	165.1	169.2
13 years	126	149.6	151.8	155.1	159.3	163.4	167.7	170.5
13½ years	129	152.6	154.4	157.0	161.4	165.3	170.1	172.9
14 years	120	155.1	157.0	159.1	163.0	167.1	171.0	174.0
14½ years	104	156.1	157.9	159.9	165.1	167.4	172.1	175.7
15 years	114	157.2	158.4	160.8	165.9	168.0	173.0	175.4
15½ years	101	158.0	158.9	161.7	165.8	169.6	174.2	176.5
16 years	108	158.3	159.3	162.5	166.5	169.8	173.9	177.1
16½ years	98	159.2	159.9	162.6	166.4	170.6	174.3	176.5
17 years	117	158.6	159.2	162.6	166.5	171.1	175.4	177.6
17½ years	94	158.9	160.1	163.3	166.6	170.6	175.4	177.0
18 years	101	158.4	159.7	163.0	166.7	170.7	174.6	176.0
20 years	73	158.4	159.8	163.2	167.0	170.8	174.5	175.3

TABLE 6.2. Observed Percentiles of Weight (in Kilograms), by Sex and Age: Fels Research Institute, Birth–20 Years

Sex and age	n	Observed percentile						
		5th	10th	25th	50th	75th	90th	95th
Male		Weight in kilograms						
Birth	300	2.53	2.68	3.06	3.40	3.79	4.12	4.38
1 month	296	3.19	3.50	3.78	4.21	4.66	4.95	5.23
3 months	496	4.38	4.75	5.35	6.01	6.58	7.20	7.42
6 months	458	6.22	6.60	7.17	7.82	8.50	9.07	9.46
9 months	386	7.62	7.98	8.59	9.28	9.92	10.63	10.94
1 year	385	8.38	8.85	9.51	10.10	10.88	11.46	11.98
1½ years	486	9.54	9.88	10.62	11.45	12.32	13.04	13.44
2 years	431	10.33	10.81	11.60	12.57	13.53	14.33	14.79
2½ years	398	11.31	11.74	12.61	13.62	14.62	15.57	16.08
3 years	367	12.20	12.69	13.54	14.61	15.64	16.65	17.35
3½ years	337	13.02	13.46	14.43	15.57	16.82	17.97	18.80
4 years	320	13.66	14.23	15.26	16.55	17.88	19.16	19.82
4½ years	316	14.63	15.21	16.25	17.60	18.83	20.35	21.20
5 years	302	15.37	16.09	17.29	18.70	20.22	21.78	22.77
5½ years	279	16.35	17.11	18.43	19.90	21.71	23.37	24.63
6 years	272	17.56	18.23	19.45	20.84	22.75	24.61	26.17
6½ years	240	18.46	19.20	20.53	22.35	24.04	26.33	28.12
7 years	266	19.33	20.19	21.63	23.54	25.55	28.20	30.09
7½ years	226	20.47	21.40	22.89	25.13	27.28	29.62	32.61
8 years	244	21.40	22.46	24.28	26.30	28.82	32.20	35.45
8½ years	210	22.49	23.57	25.51	28.11	30.95	33.99	36.62
9 years	230	23.54	24.69	26.87	29.31	32.65	35.99	39.37
9½ years	199	24.90	26.26	28.20	30.99	35.02	38.44	42.02
10 years	213	26.09	27.50	29.65	32.96	36.73	40.20	44.35
10½ years	208	27.09	28.71	31.26	34.61	39.46	43.07	46.59
11 years	209	28.74	30.26	32.94	36.90	41.96	48.10	51.18
11½ years	197	29.94	31.48	34.66	38.95	43.97	50.64	54.23
12 years	205	31.21	32.93	36.58	40.37	46.71	53.49	57.68
12½ years	192	32.53	34.80	38.54	43.49	49.40	55.59	61.46
13 years	189	34.61	36.71	40.91	46.74	52.59	60.52	65.54
13½ years	190	36.90	39.33	44.06	49.40	56.82	64.66	70.49
14 years	189	39.27	41.72	47.14	52.93	59.58	66.61	73.54
14½ years	181	42.01	45.54	50.56	56.30	62.85	70.45	78.94
15 years	175	46.15	49.30	54.12	59.87	66.37	72.82	77.25
15½ years	167	50.43	51.89	57.35	62.25	68.64	76.30	80.64
16 years	159	52.28	53.72	59.22	64.93	70.62	78.54	81.75
16½ years	153	54.21	57.07	60.64	66.94	73.95	80.35	83.45
17 years	162	56.02	58.24	62.71	68.30	74.25	79.97	84.30
17½ years	138	55.97	58.55	63.35	69.16	76.16	81.79	89.05
18 years	150	55.87	59.66	64.89	69.85	76.49	84.66	89.49
20 years	90	59.12	60.99	66.12	70.99	78.89	85.99	92.25

NOTE: n = sample size.

Source: "NCHS Growth Curves, Birth–Eighteen Years, United States," *National Center for Health Statistics*, HEW Publication No. (PHS) 78-1650. Hyattsville, Maryland: U.S. Department of Health, Education, and Welfare, 1977.

TABLE 6.2. Continued

Sex and age	*n*	Observed percentile						
		5th	10th	25th	50th	75th	90th	95th
Female				**Weight in kilograms**				
Birth	296	2.22	2.53	2.89	3.25	3.60	3.89	3.98
1 month	281	3.08	3.25	3.62	3.97	4.30	4.49	4.81
3 months	482	4.11	4.45	4.86	5.41	5.93	6.44	6.78
6 months	438	5.81	6.10	6.61	7.20	7.80	8.40	8.74
9 months	365	7.10	7.43	7.89	8.54	9.26	9.79	10.11
1 year	350	7.72	8.14	8.81	9.57	10.23	10.91	11.29
1½ years	474	9.01	9.31	10.02	10.78	11.52	12.25	12.72
2 years	412	9.72	10.23	11.14	11.97	12.79	13.66	14.13
2½ years	391	10.90	11.29	12.12	12.93	13.91	14.84	15.41
3 years	357	11.47	12.08	13.01	13.95	15.10	16.01	16.67
3½ years	310	12.17	12.76	13.70	14.90	16.01	17.04	17.71
4 years	322	13.19	13.69	14.66	15.99	17.34	18.46	19.39
4½ years	293	13.96	14.40	15.42	16.81	18.41	19.67	20.39
5 years	291	14.61	15.26	16.41	17.90	19.54	21.24	21.96
5½ years	278	15.49	16.20	17.42	18.99	20.77	22.48	23.51
6 years	264	16.41	17.19	18.58	20.12	22.28	23.69	25.40
6½ years	222	17.40	18.11	19.55	21.42	23.49	25.52	26.97
7 years	247	18.37	19.26	20.61	22.49	24.81	27.44	28.93
7½ years	221	19.50	20.25	21.72	23.76	26.74	29.13	31.94
8 years	231	20.41	21.27	22.98	25.16	28.09	31.27	33.36
8½ years	216	21.40	22.44	24.15	26.63	29.77	33.79	36.79
9 years	218	22.44	23.43	25.46	27.95	31.81	36.05	39.54
9½ years	221	23.80	24.69	26.79	29.85	34.17	39.07	43.64
10 years	215	24.11	25.76	28.32	31.42	36.59	41.16	45.41
10½ years	214	25.53	26.98	29.61	33.82	39.37	44.84	47.64
11 years	201	27.00	28.45	31.29	35.71	42.30	47.31	49.94
11½ years	199	28.42	29.83	33.26	38.46	45.21	51.61	54.02
12 years	201	30.17	31.84	35.91	41.91	48.15	55.18	59.47
12½ years	185	32.41	34.50	37.49	43.34	52.11	57.37	64.37
13 years	183	33.46	36.29	40.75	46.45	54.08	61.24	64.61
13½ years	184	36.10	39.07	43.62	48.99	55.44	62.79	67.94
14 years	172	39.14	41.15	45.27	50.74	56.59	64.40	69.79
14½ years	152	41.02	42.59	46.59	51.27	58.20	65.40	70.20
15 years	158	43.11	44.16	48.58	52.85	58.37	65.05	71.69
15½ years	141	43.05	45.22	48.87	53.54	59.62	65.94	69.94
16 years	147	43.45	45.23	48.93	53.85	59.06	66.64	70.82
16½ years	134	43.92	46.20	50.07	54.49	60.12	65.92	70.82
17 years	151	44.88	46.36	50.54	55.05	60.45	66.63	71.81
17½ years	118	43.97	46.40	50.12	54.99	61.08	67.73	69.81
18 years	125	45.06	46.82	51.04	55.64	61.37	68.16	72.37
20 years	77	45.92	47.56	52.08	56.49	62.87	69.15	73.15

The males' superior size is reflected in the difference between the sexes in bone and muscle development, and Tanner (1973) states that males also develop larger hearts and lungs (in relation to body size) than females. The shoulders of males widen more than those of females while the hips of females widen more than males. Tanner (1978) believes that the height curve typifies most body measurements (bones, muscles, liver, spleen, kidney), but the brain, reproductive organs, fat deposits, and lymphoid tissues of tonsils, adenoids, and intestines show different curves. There is rapid growth of the reproductive system during adolescence, while brain growth is almost level. Tanner believes that it is useful to identify an age at which growth virtually ceases (while accepting individual variations): in North America and northwest Europe, it is 17.5 years for males and 15.5 years for females.

Sex Differences. During the first two months following fertilization, the gonads appear identical for both sexes. At eight weeks recognizable testes develop in males; at about ten weeks, ovaries appear in females. During the ninth week the testes begin to secrete testosterone, which accelerates the growth of penis and scrotum and which acts on the hypothalamic region of the brain, producing a male hypothalamus.

But there is a critical period in the secretion of testosterone for brain differentiation to occur. In rats it must appear during the first five days following birth, which corresponds to twelve to fourteen post-fertilization weeks in the human (Tanner, 1978, p. 57). Interestingly, both sexes produce the same hormones; that is, both males and females produce the androgens (the male hormones) and the estrogens (the female hormones). Differences in the proportions produced cause the sex differences—males will produce greater amounts of the androgens; females produce greater amounts of the estrogens. Without testosterone (an androgen) a female brain results. As Tanner (1978) states, the "basic sex" is female, because without specific hormonal intervention the fetus will be female.

Other sex differences appear gradually: males have larger forearms than females; females mature more quickly than males; permanent teeth erupt earlier in females than males. Analyzing these sex differences, Tanner makes the interesting statement that girls are physiologically more mature in many organ systems than boys, thus helping to explain the female's greater survival rate both prenatally and perinatally.

Growth Hormone. The endocrine system, which produces the hormones, plays a key role in development. The hormones are discharged directly into the bloodstream and with the nervous system constitute the two great communication systems of the body. Tanner (1978, p. 87) states that the endocrine system is a major force in implementing genetic instructions.

The hormones have precisely defined targets that contain special receptors (protein molecules) which act to capture the appropriate hormone from the bloodstream. There are several hormones that are vital for normal development: thyroxine from the thyroid gland, the androgens from both the testes and the adrenal cortex, estrogens from the ovaries, and the growth hormone (one of many) from the pituitary.

The pituitary, sometimes called the "master" gland, controls the secretions of most of the endocrine glands but is itself controlled by the hypothalamus. So the hypothalamus sends a chemical message (through specialized blood vessels) to the pituitary, which then chemically relays this message to a particular endocrine gland. The growth hormone (GH), released by the pituitary, is essential for normal growth; those who experience a deficiency rarely surpass five feet, although growth is proportional.

GH is released into the bloodstream in spurts; normally children's GH is quite low, but several times in a twenty-four-hour period the GH level rises dramatically for thirty to sixty minutes. It also rises after exercise and after sleep begins. Tanner states that differences between normally large and normally small children are not caused by differences in GH secretion. GH injections (which may be obtained from the pituitaries of deceased individuals) will not transform a normally small youngster into a large child.

Lack of growth hormone, however, creates dwarfism. These youngsters are normal at birth but their developmental rate quickly lags; they can overcome this physical retardation only by injections of GH, which enable them to "catch up" and which must be continued through adolescence. Tanner (1973) believes that the problem lies with the hypothalamus and not the pituitary. He also notes that psychosocial problems may cause a GH deficit resulting in Lytt Gardner's deprivation dwarfism (see Chapter Five), now called "psychosocial short stature."

Heredity and Environment

Physiological data are so intriguing that it is tempting to dismiss the impact of environment or weigh it lightly in considering the causes of behavior. To do so would be highly unfortunate. Bloom (1964) states unequivocally that no theory of psychology, learning, or growth has ever dismissed the environment as unimportant or to be ignored in accounting for development.

Bloom (1964, p. 43–44) gives an example that highlights the relationship between heredity and environment. He notes that Israeli children living in kibbutzim are growing up in an environment different from what their parents experienced as children. Many of the parents knew the hardships of ghettos of eastern and central Europe, while their children in the kibbutz receive a diet as optimal as nutritionists can make it. One result has been that at maturity the children tower over their parents. While the parents grew and developed under physical conditions that were usually deprived, their children have had an environment that stimulated physical growth. The results seem to confirm speculation about the effects of extreme environments.

Usually the correlation between the heights of parents and children is fairly constant, thus indicating the influence of heredity on height. Different results occur when the environmental conditions of one generation differ markedly from the other's. Bloom concludes that it is possible to use height alone to identify the environmental conditions in which both parents and children have been reared. The effect of the environment is greatest in periods of rapid physical development and least in periods of slow development.

Environment: Help or Hindrance. Bloom (1964, p. 187) defines environment as the conditions, forces, and external stimuli that impinge on an individual. These may be physical, social, or intellectual. There is a wide range of environments that extend from the most immediate social circumstances to the more remote, but still potent influences of an entire culture.

A vivid example of the importance of environment can be seen in the growth and development of youngsters born in a Mexican preindustrial community. J. Cravioto and his colleagues (1969) investigated the condition of the children at birth and their subsequent

physical and behavioral progress during the first month of life. They found that progress is stunted when social positions provide a general environment of malnutrition, unsanitary conditions, infection, and poor housing.

The authors state bluntly that their purpose was ecological; they searched for information concerning the physical environment, social conditions, health status, and patterns of childcare. Environmental problems, especially nutritional inadequacies, are not restricted to primitive or underdeveloped countries. Technologically superior countries have also had to analyze the question of nutrition in order to understand more clearly the health and educational performance of their citizens. Whether the issue is between rich, productive countries and underdeveloped regions or between social classes in this or any other country, there is always a parallel between quantity and quality of diet and the rate of growth and adult stature, physical performance, mental ability, and resistance to disease. Since nutrition and income level are highly correlated, children with the greatest nutritional risk are found mainly in the lowest socioeconomic levels. These segments of the population also tend to have poorer housing, higher infection rates, lower levels of educational achievement, primitive patterns of childcare, and a generally disadvantaged way of life.

Impoverished conditions also have a detrimental effect on mental capacity. The physical circumstances associated with such social conditions may directly modify the growth and differentiation of the central nervous system, and indirectly limit the opportunities for profitable experiences. Deprivation may cause several alterations in development if it occurs during a period of rapid growth and differentiation of the nervous system. Thus, not only environmental deprivation, but also its timing is significant for the outcome of the development of the central nervous system.

The Cravioto study also found that at birth the deprived infants' weight was significantly lower than for children born in the United States and Great Britain. The findings were consistent with those for other underdeveloped countries and support the contention that children in technologically underdeveloped communities are of reduced weight and stature at birth.

When growth achievement at birth was related to the mother's biological characteristics, it varied according to the mother's height, weight, and general condition, but not her age. This finding seems to hold true for advanced as well as underdeveloped countries. The authors conclude that larger mothers provide more supportive intrauterine environments with subsequent increased prenatal growth. The authors also discovered that the mother's personal hygiene has direct bearing on the size of the child at birth: the cleaner the mother, the larger the child. The consensus is that the less clean mother is more susceptible to infection, which in turn produces a less adequate nutritional state during pregnancy.

ENVIRONMENTAL DEPRIVATION

Summarizing the extensive data about the effect of environmental deprivation on children, William Thompson and Joan Grusec (1970) reach certain general conclusions.

1. An environment lacking material stimulation or not providing interaction with adults is deficient in learning opportunities.
2. Youngsters from such an environment are frequently retarded intellectually, in motor and language development, and in social skills.
3. This can be especially true of institutionalized youngsters, who lack the fondling, touching, and general feeling of comfort that a mother provides. To phrase it simply, mothers are an almost unending source of stimuli.
4. Youngsters reared in their natural homes are normally exposed to a wide variety of auditory and visual stimuli.

When stimulation is lacking, the entire developmental pattern is adversely affected, and children's reactions to that environment will differ from those of children who experience minimum stimulation. Deprived children rarely learn to react properly to the environment. That is, they may be more easily affected by certain stimuli that should not cause reactions such as nervousness or jumpiness; conversely, they may be sluggish in responding to a dangerous stimulus. Thus the authors' conclusions seem particularly pertinent to the present discussion: a deficient environment retards all of the biological processes involved in development.

Observing the first month of life, the authors again found that growth was significantly associated with maternal height, weight, and general condition, and also with age. The differences attributable to maternal age did not appear at birth, but later there was clear evidence that babies of younger women made significantly greater gains than those of older women.

Two variables that were unrelated to intrauterine growth, family type and family size, were also significantly related to growth during the first month. Children from larger families showed lesser gains than children from smaller families. These findings strongly suggest that growth during that first month of life is closely allied to the biological condition of the mother, a fact which is hardly surprising, since all of the infants were breastfed.

Cravioto and his colleagues conclude that the biological characteristics of the mother vary with her social status, and both her biological condition and her environmental surroundings are inevitably related to fetal and neonatal growth. Thus, the characteristics of the infant at birth are determined partly by environment and partly by heredity.

Several other studies point out the necessity of a harmonious relationship between heredity and environment to ensure normal development. For example, Leonard Carmichael (1926) divided developing tadpoles into two groups before they showed any swimming patterns. The experimental group was anesthetized, while the control group developed normally in water. When the control group manifested swimming movements at about seven days, the experimental group, still drugged, was placed in normal water and within minutes began to swim as well as the control group. This would seem to suggest that the environment has little effect on development. But Fromme (1941) extended the time of anesthesia through thirteen days and found that the swimming pattern was permanently impaired. This classic study supports two conclusions: (1) deprivation for a short period (exact length of time depends on the species) does not cause permanent damage, and if corrected, children automatically accelerate to a normal point of development; (2) if the deprivation is prolonged, however, there may indeed be permanent damage.

Wayne Dennis (1960) studied children in a Teheran orphanage who received little stimulation because of a lack of personnel. Of the youngsters one to two years old, fifty-eight percent could not sit alone. By the age of two years most children from normal homes walk unaided, yet only fifteen percent of the children from this orphanage from ages *three to four* walked alone. In another study (Dennis and Najarian, 1957), infants in an orphanage in Beirut, Lebanon, were compared with infants in an adjacent clinic. The ages and social classes of both groups of children were the same. At the institution there was only one adult for every ten infants. Conditions in the nursery restricted their vision and they were fed with a bottle propped up on a pillow. Using the Cattell Infant Scale, the authors found that the institutionalized children were significantly retarded developmentally compared with youngsters reared at home. Apparently there must be an opportunity for learning as well as simple biological maturation.

The Environment and Children's Health. As knowledge of environmental contamination has grown, there has been a corresponding concern with risk to children's health. Several common environmental agents can adversely affect health, but since individuals react differently to stimuli, including possible noxious environmental elements, it is difficult to state precise effects. Table 6.3 presents some of these agents and their possible effects.

Most adults are aware of the danger of agents such as X-rays and excessive sun, but the harmful effects of others come as a surprise. Note the definite and possible effects of such agents as traffic, vibrations, dust, and urban design. Given the living conditions of many youngsters and the probability of continuing similar circumstances, those sources of potential harm are alarming.

Our discussion has described dangers as "possible" or "potential" mainly because the action of many environmental agents, either independently or through interaction with others, remains unknown. It is possible, however, to identify certain harmful effects during the following periods of development.

1. *Pregnancy.* Since the pregnant woman is experiencing chemical change, the impact of various environmental elements, singly or in combination, may produce such results as spontaneous labor.

2. *The Embryonic Period.* The organism's vulnerability during the first eight weeks has been carefully calculated. Teratogenic agents are particularly devastating during this period, probably causing the majority of the eighty percent of congenital malformation and spontaneous abortions presently classified as of

unknown etiology. Laboratory experiments have shown that a range of chemical agents from antitumor drugs to aspirin *can* (though not all do) cause deviations.

3. *The Fetal Period.* Although less vulnerable than the embryo, the fetus is still subject to adverse influences that can produce retarded growth and postnatal abnormalities.

4. *Infancy.* Following birth, infants are often sensitive to chemicals, and their systems cannot cope with foreign elements.

5. *Lactation.* For some reason mothers may produce an insufficient quantity of milk or even excrete some foreign substance that produces toxic effects in the infant.

6. *Postnatal Functioning.* Research increasingly offers substantial evidence that many developmental processes continue well after birth, for example, maturation of the nervous system. We may therefore anticipate that environmental conditions can continue to produce effects on a developing organism at a time when an infant, child, or adolescent is acutely sensitive to crucial stimuli, either positive or negative.

Our discussion of environmental elements has deliberately emphasized the negative. Children are growing in a time of rising ecological awareness but also in a time of rising ecological danger from lead poisoning, chemical wastes, food additives, and other harmful agents. By emphasizing the dangerous we enhance the nurturant.

Nutrition

> The rate of growth at any age is clearly the outcome of the interaction of genetic and environmental factors. The child inherits possible patterns of growth from his parents. The environment, however, dictates which (if any) of the patterns will become actual. In an environment where nutrition is always adequate, where the parents are caring and where social factors are adequate it is the genes that largely determine differences between members of the population in growth and in adult physique. In an environment that is suboptimal and perhaps changes from time to time, as in the periodic famines characteristic of much of the world, differences between members of the population reflect the social history of the individuals as much as their genetic endowment. (Tanner, 1973, p. 41)

Any discussion of environment must consider nutritional impact, both because of its worldwide repercussions and the substantial data surrounding nutritional deficiency. Malnutrition can have devastating effects. Brozek (1978) states that the results of severe malnutrition are multiple, affecting somatic growth, central nervous system development, metabolism, organ function, and behavior.

The following facts help explain the nuances inherent in analyzing malnutrition.

1. Malnutritional damage is intimately related to the severity and duration of the deficiency and the age of the child when suffering the poor diet.

2. Malnutrition typically appears as one of a cluster of negative influences: low income, poor housing, family problems, apathy, ignorance.

3. There are two basic forms of severe malnutrition: *kwashiorkor,* which involves protein deficiency and produces stunted growth with edema (bloated bellies), and *marasmus,* which implies a general food deficit, especially calories, and produces extreme growth retardation.

4. Authorities distinguish between *clinical malnutrition,* which may be kwashiorkor with edema and moderate loss of weight, nutritional marasmus with either severe weight loss or no weight loss, or marasmic kwashiorkor with edema and severe weight loss, and *subclinical malnutrition,* which is reflected in a generalized growth retardation and decline of soft tissues (Brozek, 1978).

TABLE 6.3. Definite and Possible Health Effects of Environmental Pollutants and (abridged) Exposures

Agent, pollutant, or source	Definite effect	Possible effect
	Housing and household agents	
Heating, cooking, and refrigeration	1. Acute fatalities from carbon monoxide, fires and explosions, and discarded refrigerators	
		2. Increase in diseases of the respiratory infants
Fumes and dust	3. Acute illness from fumes. 4. Aggravation of asthma	
		5. Increase in chronic respiratory disease
Crowding	6. Spread of acute and contribution to chronic disease morbidity and mortality	
Structural factors (including electrical wiring, stoves, and thin walls)	7. Accidental fatality 8. Accidental injury 9. Morbidity and mortality from lack of protection from heat or cold 10. Morbidity and mortality due to fire or explosion	
Paints and solvents	11. Childhood lead-poisoning fatalities, associated mental impairment, and anemia 12. Renal and hepatic toxicity 13. Fatalities	
Household equipment and supplies (including pesticides)	14. Fatalities from fire and injury 15. Morbidity from fire and injury 16. Fatalities from poisoning 17. Morbidity from poisoning	
Toys, beads, and painted objects	18. Mortality and morbidity	
Urban design	19. Increased accident risks	
		20. Contribution to mental illness

Source: "Statistics Needed for Determining the Effects of the Environment on Health," *National Center for Health Statistics*, DHEW Publication No. (HRA) 77-1457. Hyattsville, Maryland: U.S. Department of Health, Education, and Welfare, 1977.

TABLE 6.3. Continued

Agent, pollutant, or source	Definite effect	Possible effect
	Radiation and microwaves	
Natural sunlight	1. Fatalities from acute exposure 2. Morbidity due to "burn" 3. Skin cancer 4. Interaction with drugs in susceptible individuals	5. Increase in malignant melanoma
Diagnostic X-ray	6. Skin cancer and other skin changes	7. Contributing factors to leukemia 8. Alteration in fecundity
Therapeutic radiation	9. Skin cancer 10. Increase in leukemia	11. Increase in other cancers 12. Acceleration of aging 13. Mutagenesis
Industrial uses of radiation and mining of radioactive ores	14. Acute accidental deaths 15. Radiation morbidity 16. Uranium nephritis 17. Lung cancer in cigarette-smoking miners	18. Increase in adjacent community morbidity or mortality
Nuclear power and reprocessing plants		19. Increase in cancer incidence 20. Community disaster 21. Alteration in human genetic material
Microwaves		22. Tissue damage
	Noise and vibrations	
Traffic		1. Progressive hearing loss
Aircraft (including sonic boom)	2. Permanent hearing loss	3. Aggravation or cause of mental illness
Vibrations		4. Articular and muscular disease 5. Adverse effects on nervous system

What Is Malnutrition?

Malnutrition is a condition in which a prolonged lack of one or more nutrients retards physical development or causes specific clinical conditions to appear, such as anemia, goiter, or rickets (Read, 1976, p. 5). Estimates are that two percent of the world's children experience severe malnutrition. Chronic malnutrition results from constant food restriction or vitamin and mineral deficiency. A current United Nations report stated that 400 million people are seriously malnourished, suffering more from insufficient food (calorie deprivation) than vitamin or mineral deficiency (which may, nevertheless, be masked by the food lack).

The pinch of malnutrition is found even in a rich nation like the United States, and Read (1976) states that chronic malnutrition and iron deficiency are surprisingly common. As many as fifty percent of one- to five-year-old American children may have iron deficiency, which produces anemia in as many as thirty percent of this group. These children and any children suffering from prolonged moderate malnutrition are particularly vulnerable to infection.

Although brain development is discussed later in the chapter, its relationship to malnutrition demands comment here. There are two great growth spurts in brain development: the second trimester of pregnancy, which sees the growth of neurons, and from the third trimester to about six postnatal months, which sees the growth of support cells such as the glia. Regional variations in brain development also occur (Read, 1976, p. 12). Severe malnutrition during these periods can cause serious later behavioral effects.

MALNUTRITION AND INTELLECTUAL PERFORMANCE

That severe prolonged malnutrition can cause permanent behavioral impairment seems highly likely. It is difficult, however, to specify the exact results of early deprivation. Does malnutrition produce the damage, or is it so intertwined with other adverse environmental conditions that it becomes impossible to identify cause and effect? Read (1976) believes that severe malnutrition diminishes motivation, arousal, and attention span, thus causing later learning difficulties. Even moderately malnourished children experience some consequences, although to a lesser degree.

Several excellent studies illustrate the problem of analyzing malnutrition's effects. Cravioto and DeLicardie (1970), studying malnourished Mexican children, hypothesized that the results of severe malnutrition on human mental development would vary as a function of age. They studied twenty infants hospitalized for protein-calorie malnutrition and concluded that if severe protein-calorie malnutrition occurs during the first year necessitating hospitalization, mental retardation may result.

Latham and Cobos (1971), reviewing numerous studies of malnutrition, are reluctant to state definitively that malnutrition *causes* mental retardation. They believe that where there is a deficiency of nutrients, there is a corresponding deficiency of intellectual stimulation. So the poor intellectual performance of many malnourished children may be due not to nervous system damage, but to a lack of energy and opportunity to learn.

Lloyd-Still et al. (1974) studied forty-one subjects ages two to twenty-one who had experienced severe malnutrition during the first six months of life. They found differences in intellectual performance only in the two- to five-year-olds, following infant malnutrition. After five years no significant intellectual differences were discovered. The authors cautiously conclude that they did not study individuals who were malnourished after the first six months. They also note that their sample was middle-class, with thirty-four of the youngsters hospitalized because of cystic fibrosis.

What can we conclude from these and similar studies? Malnutrition in infancy can cause later behavioral problems, but more recent and sophisticated research techniques have convincingly demonstrated it is usually difficult, if not impossible, to isolate malnutrition as the most damaging element, in a network of adverse environmental conditions.

Read's conclusions (1976) about the relationship between malnutrition and later behavior offer excellent guidelines.

1. Prolonged severe malnutrition during gestation or early infancy can cause permanent behavioral difficulties.

2. While the effects of moderate malnutrition are even less clearly understood, negative consequences seem inevitable because of reduced attentiveness, curiosity, and activity.

3. National corrective policies are required, even in countries like the United States, to ensure preventive health care and nutritionally adequate food supplies.

DISCUSSION QUESTIONS

1. Do you agree with Tanner's concept of "regularity of growth"? Observers usually think of growth occurring in spurts. Can you reconcile the two? Are there implications for child rearing practices?
2. Explain the statement that the basic sex is female. What is the significance, for both growth and behavior, of the hormonal action that ultimately produces male or female?
3. Trace the action of growth hormone from hypothalamic function to pituitary to growth to behavior. If injections of GH do not transform a normally small child to large, there must be limits to its action. How would you explain that seeming contradiction?
4. How would you explain the results of a deprived environment? Assume that food deprivation, poor housing, and lack of stimulation are all present. Can you isolate causes of particular deficits? Must you employ an interactive model? Are the consequences of deprivation always predictable?
5. Analyzing the effects of malnutrition always presents difficulties. Why? List obstacles to the identification of accurate causes and effects. What are some subtle effects of malnutrition that affect learning and intellectual performance? Whether you agree or not with the possibilities of permanent damage because of malnutrition, be sure to include it in your discussion.
6. Define the following:

   Kwashiorkor

   Marasmus

   Clinical malnutrition

   Subclinical malnutrition

CHARACTERISTICS OF BRAIN DEVELOPMENT

Understanding the development, structure, and function of the brain is vital for understanding human development. Studying brain growth in a chapter on physical development needs little justification; the rationale speaks for itself. But the brain's full significance in cognitive and emotional development has been relatively obscured until recent almost breathtaking discoveries have uncovered its decisive contribution to satisfactory human functioning. For example, recent research has revealed that the myelination process continues well after birth, thus explaining why children have difficulty mastering certain tasks; evidence about surges of brain growth correlate well with theories of cognitive development; brain studies have even forged new links to the world of disturbed minds, such as the suspected connection between schizophrenia and the brain's regulation of dopamine.

Epstein (1978) states that mental development is manifestly linked to and limited by the development of the child's brain. To understand the brain is to understand the guiding genius of human behavior. But as the great neurologist John Eccles (1977) states, this goal may be paradoxical: a brain completely understanding a brain. Eccles believes that the human brain represents an evolutionary development that spans hundreds of millions of years and has attained a highly unique state in its relationship to culture, consciousness, language, and memory. He poetically notes that our brains form the material basis of our experiences and memories, our imagination, and our dreams—the material basis of personal identity, the essential "me."

The Brain—A Survey

The adult human brain weighs about three pounds, which is comparatively large in proportion to body size. One of the heaviest brains ever recorded belonged to the Russian author Ivan Turgenev, but the brain of Anatole France, a French author, weighed only two pounds, four ounces. Size alone is no guarantee of intellectual ability. While the adult brain totals only about two percent of total body weight, it consumes about twenty percent of the body's total oxygen supply. The brain consists of two halves, the cerebral hemispheres, which are connected by a bundle of nerve tissue, the corpus callosum. The outer surface of the cerebral hemispheres is the cortex, which if stretched flat would be about the size of a newspaper page.

Using the diagram initially presented in Chapter Three, let us examine brain structure more carefully.

The cerebral region regulates such critical human functions as vision, hearing, speech, and higher thought processes. The limbic system (amygdala, hippocampus, and hypothalamus) controls the emotions, and the pituitary governs hormonal action. The evolutionary pathway has been from the deep interior areas (brain stem, hypothalamus) to the more recent appearance of the cortical areas. The older portions seem to be more closely linked to the primitive urges of rage, fear, and pleasure. The cerebellum controls the precise muscular movements that enable us to grasp objects accurately and to maintain vital motor coordination. The hippocampus seems to be closely tied to memory; injury here affects the retention of newly acquired information.

Compare Figure 6.3, a side view of the brain, with Figure 6.4, a frontal view. Note particularly in Figure 6.4 how the corpus callosum connects the cerebral hemispheres.

Although the two cerebral hemispheres seem to be identical, they are not; each has a different function. We shall discuss this phenomenon, called cerebral dominance or cerebral lateralization, in greater detail, but for

FIGURE 6.3. The Human Brain—Side View.

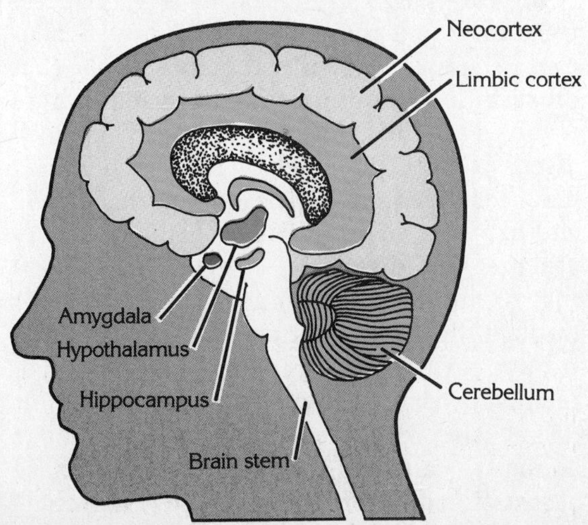

FIGURE 6.4. The Human Brain—Frontal View.

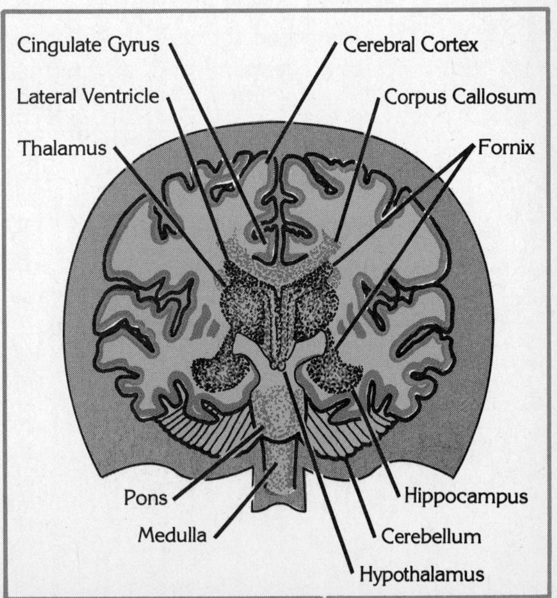

now, remember that the left hemisphere is concerned with language and analytical thought, while the right is involved with the emotions, intuition, and spatial relations. Also remember that each hemisphere controls the opposite side of the body, so that damage to the left cortical area will affect the right side of the body.

If you recall that most people are right-handed, it is obvious that their handedness is controlled by the left hemisphere (the "dominant" hemisphere), which is also the seat of language. Estimates are that only sixty percent of left-handed individuals have their language center in the left hemisphere; the other forty percent have language control located either in the right hemisphere or in both. Hard data about cerebral cooperation in functioning remain elusive, but whatever the explanation about the exact nature of the process, separation of function seems to begin before two years and is completed by about ten years.

The Brain's Basic Structure

The cerebral cortex contains billions of neurons and the processes that connect neurons (Teyler, 1978). The two hemispheres of the cerebral cortex are each typically divided into four lobes: frontal, parietal, temporal, and occipital. To understand the responsibility of the different lobes, you should distinguish among sensory, motor, and associational functions. As Teyler (1978) notes, the sensory and motor areas are just that: regions for bodily sensations (touch, temperature) and regions for the control of muscular contractions. The neurons of the sensory zone receive and process information from the sense organs, while the neurons of the motor zone actually produce muscular movement.

The function of the association areas eludes precise identification. Language, perception, comprehension, and problem solving are all attributed to these regions. Teyler (1978) states that clues to the function of the association areas comes from studies of other species. Rats have tiny association areas; dogs and cats have considerably more. Humans have the largest amount. Since size of the association area increases notably in the species exhibiting cognitive activity, it seems that there is an almost indisputable link between the two. Steven Rose (1973, p. 138) is quite blunt: "functionally, the association areas are quite clearly acting upon information which has already received quite sophisticated processing. . . . But the association areas spread beyond these secondary sensory regions, and these further areas must be integrative, combining data from different sensory modalities, perhaps in a comparative way, relating it to past events."

As Teyler notes (1978), cortical specializations appear in each of the four lobes. The frontal lobe contains the motor areas for all skeletal muscles; the parietal lobe contains the body sense areas; the temporal lobe contains auditory areas; the occipital lobe contains the areas for analyzing information from the eyes. Rose (1973) believes that association areas are found both in the frontal and temporal lobes. Figure 6.5 illustrates various brain areas and their functions.

Information from the senses is not directly transmitted to the appropriate cortical neurons. There are subcortical relay stations that process the incoming information and that are involved in the convergence and divergence discussed in Chapter Five. That is, one area may receive several signals (convergence) while another area may radiate a signal to many other regions (divergence). Teyler (1978) states that as information from the senses passes through these relay stations to designated cortical areas, the signal, although changed, retains its basic configuration. Gunther Stent (1972), the renowned American molecular biologist, calls this process "the selective destruction of information." Rose (1973) char-

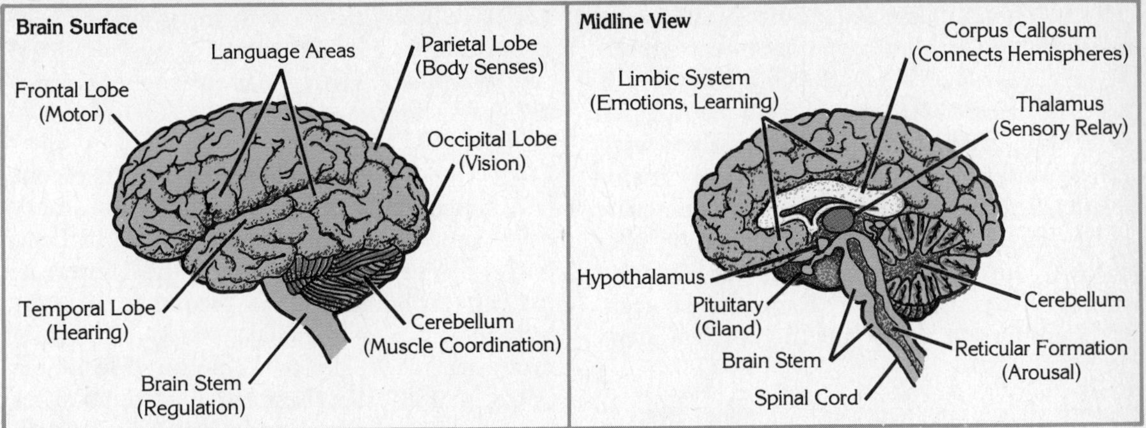

FIGURE 6.5. The Human Brain.

acterizes the notion of selectivity as providing a mechanism whereby information relevant to the organism can be identified and abstracted from the mass of crude data arriving at the senses.

To illustrate the procedure, Teyler (1978) traces the route of a spot of light that reaches the retina. Neural impulses stream from the retina toward the brain. The optic fibers carry the impulses to the thalamus (see Figure 6.5), where they form a pattern. Fibers traveling from the thalamus to the visual cortex retain the original retinal pattern, but the pattern is distorted although all parts are present. For example, in describing the motor cortex, Eccles (1977) states that it is not uniformly spread in proportion to muscle size; muscles controlling the thumb are widely represented, since we use the thumb in so many skilled activities.

John Eccles (1977), a Nobel Prize winner in physiology, has provided some intriguing speculations about the relationship between brain and mind. He postulates three Worlds (1, 2, 3). World 1 is our physical world, including ourselves; World 2 is the subjective realm of perceptions and consciousness, and at its core is the self or ego. Eccles believes that it is in World 2 that we experience our primary reality. Finally, World 3 is the world of civilization and culture, a uniquely human world.

To experience World 3, our cultural world, you must employ World 2, which is ultimately dependent on World 1, the physical world. Eccles gives the example of reading a book. Illumination is necessary (World 1) and then the words form an image on the retina, which initiates neural impulses that finally reach the visual cortex. Decoding commences in the linguistic and liaison areas, which form the neuronal patterns of World 2. These are the sentences that we comprehend and permit us to acquire a "love of literature"—arrival at World 3.

Eccles (1977) concludes by stating that in each of us there is a continuous and intense interaction and flow between the three worlds. So our cognitive experiences depend on outer sensing and perceptions through the sense organs, inner sensing that entails memories and the more subtle experiences that are not immediately dependent on the sense organs, and, finally, the central entity of you as a self.

There are three other structures that demand mention in any discussion of the brain. Examining Figure 6.5, note the location and function of the thalamus, which is a major sensory relay in the brain. Below the thalamus is the appropriately named hypothalamus, which Teyler (1978) specifies as the "brain center." It has connections with many brain areas, especially with the pituitary, and is involved with a wide variety of behaviors (especially maintaining internal conditions and manufacturing hormones). The reticular formation also deserves our attention since it receives the information going to the thalamus and cortex. Its fibers do not go to specific cortical areas but have connections with many brain areas. Experiments indicate that it plays a central role in arousal. Figure 6.6 is an excellent example of its function.

FIGURE 6.6. The Reticular Activating System. Incoming sensory information from touch receptors on the finger is fed into the reticular formation (stippled area). The reticular formation activates the entire cortex by means of a widespread fiber system. The touch information is relayed by the thalamus to the cortical area for tactile information (shaded area located on the lateral surface of the hemisphere).

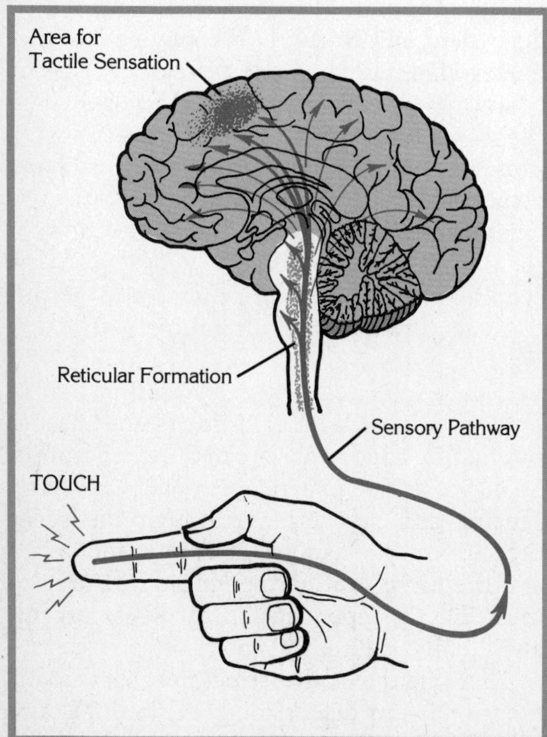

From Timothy Teyler, "The Brain Sciences. An Introduction," *The Seventy-Seventh Yearbook of the National Society for the Study of Education* (Jeanne Chall and Allan Mirsky, editors). Chicago: University of Chicago Press, 1978.

The Triune Brain. There have been recent fascinating attempts to trace the evolutionary development of the human. Paul MacLean (1978) has proposed one of the most interesting, an explanation that theorizes that the human brain has reached its large size while retaining three ancient systems. He states (1978, p. 308) that these three systems differ radically in structure and chemistry and are actually a hierarchy of three brains in one. Consequently we must "look at ourselves and the world through the eyes of three quite different mentalities." Figure 6.7 illustrates MacLean's concept of the triune brain.

If you make two fists and line up your fingers, MacLean (1978) states, you have a model of the human brain. Each fist represents a cerebral hemisphere. Look down at your fists and imagine them covered with gray gloves; this would be similar to the gray matter of the cortex. Your thumbs are at the front of the

FIGURE 6.7. The Triune Brain.

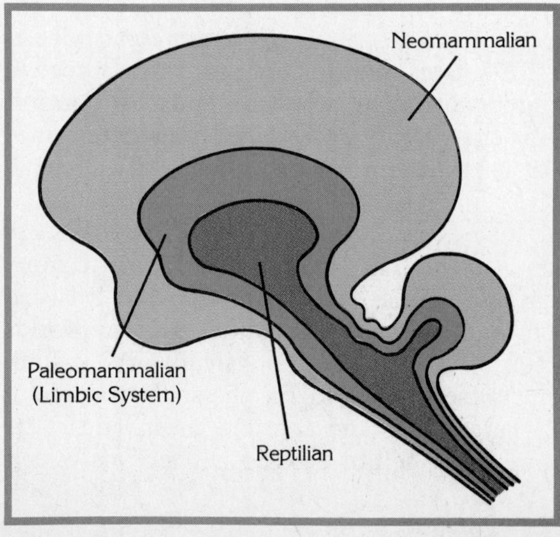

brain; your middle knuckle and the visible part of your finger represent the motor cortex; your auditory cortex would be on the back of your hand below the middle knuckle; the area around your little fingers approximates the visual cortex. These areas would constitute the region of the "new" cortex. Pulling your fists apart exposes the "old" cortex (the limbic area), while opening your fingers will reveal the corresponding reptilian area.

MacLean (1978) states that the forebrain (most of our combined two fists) gives direction to our activities, as the driver of a vehicle. The vehicle itself would be the lower brain stem and the spinal cord, and the problem is that through evolution the brain has acquired *three* drivers: the reptilian (R-complex), the limbic, and the neocortical.

The R-Complex. MacLean believes that the R-complex is importantly involved in aggression, territoriality, ritual behavior, and the establishment of social hierarchies. Carl Sagan (1977), in his brilliant *The Dragons of Eden,* judiciously analyzes the influence of the reptilian brain on our behavior and concludes that while it is unenlightened to ignore its possible existence, the R-complex does not control our behavior. For example, while we cannot deny our ritualistic and hierarchical behavior, it is inconceivable that the reptilian brain could have devised the Bill of Rights of the United States Constitution.

The Limbic System. As noted, the limbic system is identified with strong emotions. The pituitary, amygdala, and hypothalamus are located here, and their role in emotional behavior has been amply demonstrated. Electrical stimulation of the amygdala of placid animals can cause frenzied states of fear or rage. But it is also highly likely that human altruism had its beginnings with the appearance of the limbic system. MacLean (1978) states that clinical findings on patients with psychomotor epilepsy convincingly demonstrate that the limbic system is intimately linked with the experience and expression of emotion.

The Neocortex. We have frequently mentioned that the cortical area seems to be the site of human cognitive functioning. MacLean (1978) states that the neocortex is the mother of invention, father of abstract thought, and promoter of the preservation and procreation of ideas.

Sagan (1977, p. 77) summarizes the functions of the triune brain as follows:

> It seems a useful first approximation to consider the ritualistic and hierarchical aspects of our lives to be influenced strongly by the R-complex and shared with our reptilian forebears; the altruistic, emotional, and religious aspects of our lives to be localized to a significant extent in the limbic system and shared with our nonprimate mammalian forebears (and perhaps the birds); and reason to be a function of the neocortex, shared to some extent with the higher primates and such cetaceans as dolphins and whales. While ritual emotion and reasoning are all significant aspects of human nature, the most nearly unique human characteristic is the ability to associate abstractly and to reason.

Brain Development

A distinguishing feature of the brain is its inability to regenerate neurons; that is, if a neuron dies, it is not replaced. Most of our neurons are formed during the six months following conception. Rose (1973) estimates that as many as twenty thousand neurons are formed each minute. These facts are offered to urge you to think of growth spurts in the brain.

The brain at birth is about twenty to twenty-five percent of its adult size, a dramatic demonstration of rapid prenatal growth.

One indication of brain development is growth of the skull. For example, head circumference grows most rapidly from about fifteen to seventeen postmenstrual weeks, and while there is then a slight deceleration, high growth velocity continues until about thirty-two to thirty-four postmenstrual weeks. Brain weight increases slightly more slowly and peaks at about thirty-two postmenstrual weeks. The relationship of brain weight at various ages to its adult weight follows a definite pattern. At birth, the brain is from twenty to twenty-five percent of its adult weight; at two years it is about seventy-five percent; at five years about ninety percent; and at ten years about ninety-five percent.

Tanner (1978) states that total brain weight is a deceptive figure since different brain parts grow at different rates. At birth the spinal cord, hindbrain, and midbrain are most advanced, followed by the cerebrum. The cerebellum peaks much later.

Cortical Development. Tanner (1978) credits much of our knowledge of cortical development to J. L. Conel who from 1939 to 1967 reported cortical measurements at birth, one month, three months, six months, fifteen months, two years, four years, and six years. It is possible to identify the fetal cortex at eight prenatal weeks (studies indicate that the nervous system begins to function during the second month), and by twenty-six weeks it shows typical adult structure.

Conel identified two developmental gradients that occur during the first two years after birth. The first relates to the brain's functional areas; the second to bodily localizations. For example, the motor areas are the most advanced, followed in descending order by sensory areas, visual areas, and auditory areas. The association areas are the slowest to develop. By two years the sensory area has overtaken the motor regions, and the association areas exhibit noticeable development. These developmental data clearly suggest a close liaison between function and maturation of structure.

Rose (1973), in his analysis of postnatal cortical development, raises a controversial issue regarding the relationship between function and maturation of structure. Noting that the motor and sensory areas show advanced development in the first month, Rose questions whether neurons in these areas can transmit nerve impulses. Although some motor area axons reach the spinal cord, myelination is incomplete and there is little, if any, communication among cortical areas. Rose designates the one-month-old infant as a subcortical organism and sharply disagrees with those who emphasize an infant's perceptual abilities and emerging cognitive competence.

Brain Growth Spurts

Herman Epstein (1978) has offered an attractive theory of growth spurts in brain development—attractive because of its seeming correlation with the stages of cognitive development proposed by such theorists as Piaget. Epstein believes that human brain growth occurs chiefly during certain age intervals: three to ten months, two to four years, six to eight years, ten to thirteen years, and finally, fourteen to seventeen years. The latter two spurts appear slightly earlier for girls and later for boys. The rationale for his belief lies in the meaning of stages of development. If stages exist, why and how do children move to a higher stage if their present stage is stable? Something is needed to explain this movement from stage to stage, and Epstein believes that the explanation is in the changes that occur in the structure containing the mind, that is, in brain expansion.

MYELINATION

A recurrent theme in our discussion of brain development has been that of myelination (sometimes called myelinization). Nerve fibers gradually become enclosed by a fatty layer called the myelin sheath. Although complete comprehension of the myelin sheath's function escapes detection, certain of its activities are now understood. One function is to insulate the nerve fiber, thus minimizing any loss of electric potential. But the chemical composition of the sheath is unusually complex, so that other functions are suspected.

For example, since the axon extends a considerable distance from the cell body, the myelin sheath may help neural communication to remain intact. The sheath also seems to facilitate the passage of the nerve impulse. What seems apparent is that bodily activities remain dormant until the nerves leading to them are myelinated. The optic nerve must be myelinated before babies see (which occurs almost immediately; humans are visual organisms); the nerves leading to the legs are not myelinated until about one year, the time at which normal babies walk. As Tanner (1978) notes, the fibers carrying impulses to cortical areas are myelinated simultaneously with those activating bodily responses, thus myelination occurs as arcs or functional units.

Tracing the timing of myelination is important for a knowledge of developmental competence. It was formerly thought that myelination was completed shortly after birth. Now there is a consensus that myelination of some brain areas continues until adulthood. Tanner (1978) states that the fibers connecting the cerebellum to the cerebral cortex (vital for muscular coordination) begin to myelinate only *after* birth and achieve complete myelination at about four years. Myelination continues in the reticular formation (see Figures 6.5 and 6.6) until well after puberty. Rose (1973) believes that myelination of the association areas may continue throughout adult life and into old age.

Occasionally an adult experiences degeneration of the myelin sheath, resulting in loss of function of the fiber. The most common example of this disease is multiple sclerosis. The nerves that receive sensations are usually affected, so the victim may experience visual difficulty and a strange sense of feeling, among other symptoms. Individuals in the twenty to forty age group are unusually vulnerable, and since the disease is progressive, the outlook for the sufferer has been gloomy. Eccles (1977), however, offers hope when he states that since nerve fibers are not killed, there is the chance of cure if a process is discovered that will restore the myelin sheath.

Aside from the consequences of defective myelination, you should be aware of myelination's critical role in development. Without myelination can there be function? Is the role of myelination development similar for both boys and girls? The answers to these questions carry serious and farreaching implications for both child rearing and education.

Brain and Intelligence. Epstein argues strongly for a link between brain size and intelligence, stating that small brain size in famous individuals (Goethe's brain was 2200 grams) does not destroy his thesis. It is the relationship between brain weight and body weight that is critical. Dobzhansky (1962) agrees, believing that although brain size alone does not determine intelligence, there is no evidence that the two are unrelated. Epstein then uses data from Ernest Hooton's classic study of criminals to forge a connection between head circumference and vocation.

Epstein stresses that there are few studies of the age-relationship of brain growth; autopsy data from three studies surveying human brain weight from birth to eighteen years confirm his conclusions. There are two aspects of brain growth: a relationship between an increase in body and brain weight, and the appearance of the previously mentioned brain growth spurts. Added support for Epstein's thesis comes from recent studies of the association between brain weight and head circumference, which consistently reports that increases in head circumference parallel those for brain weight.

Examining Epstein's beliefs, we may conclude that:

1. There is a definite link between brain size and intelligence.

2. Brain growth occurs in spurts.

3. Head circumference grows by similar spurts.

4. There are sex differences in the timing of the later spurts. (The head growth of girls between ten and twelve years is twice that of boys, while at fifteen years boys show the larger increase.)

5. These physiological data support the claims of the cognitive theorists regarding mental development, a hypothesis that we shall analyze more carefully in Chapter Eight.

Cerebral Lateralization and Development

One of the most popular topics in neurology, psychology, and education is cerebral lateralization. As recognition grows of the brain's key role in human behavior there has been a corresponding interest in hemispheric specialization. Kinsbourne and Hiscock (1978) insist that to avoid confusion there must be a clear distinction between cerebral lateralization and cerebral dominance. For example, lateralization may refer to a theoretical construct or it may refer to a specific behavioral characteristic such as handedness (Kinsbourne and Hiscock, 1978, p. 183). Even using it behaviorally raises problems: how do we characterize a person whose handedness differs from eyedness? Also lateralization is not synonymous with dominance because dominance implies an executive, controlling function that is not inherent in lateralization. While agreement about definition is lacking, there is some consensus that lateralization involves hemispheric specialization.

For example, Kimura (1973) studied hemispheric cognitive processes in normal people by simultaneously presenting listening tasks and visual-perceptual tasks to each hemisphere; through headphones she played a different melody to each ear. In normal righthanders she discovered that the left hemisphere was superior in auditory tasks (words), nonsense syllables, and visually presented letters and words. The right hemisphere was superior at auditory tasks involving melodies and visual tasks such as locating points in two dimensions, matching slanting lines, and depth perception.

Wittrock (1978) summarizes the data by noting that the left cortical hemisphere in about ninety-eight percent of right-handers and in about two-thirds of the left-handers specializes in propositional, analytic-sequential, time-oriented serial organization that is particularly suited to learning and remembering verbal information. The right hemisphere seems to specialize in perceptual organization in which the parts of a whole acquire meaning through their relations with other parts.

Kinsbourne and Hiscock note that solid evidence supports the relationship between the preferred hand and the linguistic cerebral hemisphere. More than ninety-eight percent of right-handers are left-lateralized for language (Kinsbourne and Hiscock, 1978, p. 184). Studies of aphasia—language difficulties following brain injury—convincingly confirm these figures. Kinsbourne and Hiscock (1978) also describe experiments entailing the injection of a barbiturate into the arterial system supplying one side of the brain, which then briefly immobilizes that side of the brain. Left-sided injections impair linguistic functioning in more than ninety-five percent of right-handers. Such safe statements are impossible for left-handers.

LEFT-HANDEDNESS

In a fascinating analysis of left-handedness, Kinsbourne and Hiscock (1978) state that while most left-handers are probably left-lateralized for language, there is a significant proportion who are either right or mixed-lateralized (one-quarter to one-third). This latter group is often referred to as those with "deviant language lateralization," or with "incomplete lateralization."

A persistent issue that has nagged researchers in studies of left-handers has been intelligence. If a substantial proportion of left-handers possess deviant lateralization (and it is impossible to distinguish this characteristic), are left-handers as a group less intelligent than right-handers? Studies show that left-handers are more numerous among the learning disabled, the mentally retarded, and the linguistically disturbed. Yet studies of the general population establish that left-handers are as intelligent as right-handers.

Kinsbourne and Hiscock (1978) believe that these contradictory findings indicate two categories of left-handedness. They classify the first as normal variation; that is, left-handedness runs in some families. Whatever the heredity-environment interaction, the authors believe that these individuals are left-handed for natural reasons. They label their second category "pathological left-handedness"; that is, these individuals are left-handed because of lateralized brain damage. Early left-sided damage (prenatal or perinatal) may produce a shift from right- to left-handedness.

This dual categorization resolves the conflict concerning the equal intelligence of left- and right-handers in the general population but does not explain the overrepresentation of left-handers in a problem population. The authors believe that regardless of the side of language lateralization, left-handers are less completely lateralized than right-handers.

In his intriguing account of the aftermath of brain damage, *The Shattered Mind* (1974), Howard Gardner develops a strikingly similar theme. He states that left-handers belong to one or all of three progressively smaller minorities: (1) those who are predominantly left-handed, thus right-brain dominant in motor activities (about ten percent of the population); (2) left-handers whose language center is primarily in the right hemisphere (about one-half of the first group); (3) left-handers converted to right-handedness in writing but whose language function remains basically in the right hemisphere.

Gardner believes that "all generalizations falter when it comes to left-handed persons" (1974, p. 101). Left-handedness may result from genetic influences, brain damage, or even an abnormal environment. Since left-handers usually have speech more widely spread throughout the brain, they are more vulnerable to speech damage in many places, yet their chances of recovery are better than right-handers.

Development of Cerebral Lateralization. A current complicated question concerns the appearance and development of cerebral lateralization. There are practical as well as theoretical aspects to the issue. For example, does incomplete lateralization cause a cognitive deficit? Does a failure of the cerebral hemispheres to specialize produce learning disabilities? As Kinsbourne and Hiscock (1978) note, the acceptance or rejection of the notion of the development of cerebral lateralization—the "progressive lateralization" hypothesis—determines your view of the relationship between cerebral lateralization and learning disabilities. That is, if the neonate is completely lateralized, then treatment of learning disabilities should be quite different than for a condition of partial lateralization.

Those who believe in the development of cerebral lateralization argue that the neonate is nonlinguistic and that language eventually results from specialization of one of two functionally equal neonatal cerebral hemispheres. Lenneberg (1967) believes that an injury causing aphasia occurring in early childhood seldom leaves permanent damage and that right hemispheric damage produces language problems in children more frequently than in adults. That is, while children have the potential to develop language in both hemispheres, most adults have fully lateralized language in the left hemisphere.

Kinsbourne and Hiscock (1978) question Lenneberg's interpretation and believe that the following recent evidence demonstrates early lateralization.

1. Neonatal cerebral hemispheres differ; that is, the speech region on the left side is usually larger than on the right side. While function need not follow structure, these data contradict the popular belief that both neonatal hemispheres are identical.
2. Measurements of electrical activity show stronger reactions to speech stimuli by the left hemisphere of infants than the right.
3. Most infants display the tonic neck reflex (see Chapter Five) by turning to the right, suggesting greater lateralization of the left hemisphere.
4. Infants as young as three months display hand preference by retaining an object significantly longer in the right hand than the left.

The authors conclude that brain lateralization appears at birth but cautiously note that the degree of hemispheric specialization may increase during childhood.

THE MINOR HEMISPHERE

Our discussion of lateralization has focused on the left, or major hemisphere, almost to the exclusion of the secondary hemisphere. Eccles (1977), analyzing the performance of the minor hemisphere, states that it is tempting to consider it grossly deficient by comparison. But other works (Levy, 1974) suggest many interesting functions of the minor hemisphere, such as spatial construction and nonverbal ideation.

While the major hemisphere is analytical and sequential, its aura of dominance derives from its verbal and ideational abilities. Eccles states that the minor hemisphere deserves its label because of corresponding limitations, but we should recognize its prominence in spatial, pattern, pictorial, and muscle matters. Eccles (1977, p. 221) believes that the two hemispheres are complementary: the minor is coherent and the dominant is detailed. As Eccles notes, the complementarity of the two hemispheres is an attractive hypothesis because each can exercise independent functions but also integrate vital ideational and linguistic functions when necessary.

Whether you incline toward the progressive lateralization hypothesis or an increase in the degree of hemispheric specialization, recent studies clearly suggest change. McBurney and Dunn (1976), while accepting the inconclusive results of studies of developmental patterns of laterality, have documented growth shifts in a longitudinal study of hundreds of children from birth to six and one-half years. They found that at nine months, four years, and six and one-half years, youngsters whose handedness, footedness, and eyedness were not consistently dextral are more likely to be achieving below age level in language tasks and verbal and performance IQs.

Buffery (1976) studied two groups, one of normal children (thirty-two boys and thirty-two girls) from five to nine years of age, and one of normal adults (one hundred males, one hundred females) from eighteen to twenty-five. Each group was studied to detect sex differences in the cerebral lateralization of verbal and spatial function. Data from the child study showed greater lateralization of cerebral functions in the female brain than in the brain of the same age male, especially for verbal abilities. In the adult study, women manifested greater lateralization of hand preference and both verbal and spatial cerebral functioning than men.

Buffery's studies indicate that there may be a sex difference in the development of cerebral functioning, which has implications for the mastery of verbal and spatial skills. That is, achievement may reflect a sex difference in degree of lateralization and not merely a difference in performance level alone. Note in particular one inevitable conclusion of Buffery's work: sex differences in degree of lateralization in adults is similar to that in children, a finding that challenges the progressive lateralization hypothesis.

The lateralization literature is a fruitful field for developmental theorists. The obvious connection between developing structure and function leads to significant and practical implications for developmental expectations by age and sex for such subjects as reading and mathematics. If these differences exist from birth, with the possibility of only slight change, there are clear suggestions for both child rearing and educational practice. If there is a link between either the development of cerebral lateralization or degree of lateralization and learning disabilities, additional research may do much to expel current uncertainty about this important and troublesome subject. There is no escaping the input of cerebral lateralization research on all aspects of development.

DISCUSSION QUESTIONS

1. Do you agree with Eccles about the difficulty of a brain understanding a brain? Why? Must your discussion be bound by physical limitations? Is Eccles's? Could you introduce added nonphysical dimensions?
2. The cerebral hemispheres are asymmetrical. What does that mean structurally and functionally? If expected lateralization does not occur, how could it be a source of difficulties?
3. Data reach the cerebral areas by the "selective destruction of information." Explain this statement. Does it help to clarify a child's ability to adjust to a highly sophisticated environment? Why? Relate the discussion of theories in Chapter Two to evolving physical structures created by selectively destroying information.
4. The concept of the triune brain has attracted considerable attention. Does it help to explain contradictory aspects of behavior? Does it provide a rationale for any psychological theories?
5. Discuss the significance of the myelination process. Can you trace a developmental pattern? Steven Rose's comment that a one-month-old infant is a subcortical organism deserves comment here. Do you agree or disagree? Why?
6. Use your agreement or disagreement with the progressive lateralization hypothesis as a basis for analyzing cerebral lateralization. Include various interpretations of handedness. Can you relate your conclusions to specific aspects of development?

Physical data are voluminous, widely available, and highly significant. Perhaps the best rationale for familiarizing yourself with the details of physical development is to remember that function depends on structure. As a structure begins to change, as we saw with developing sex differences, various bodily activities commence, such as the release of critical hormones, that continue to differentiate the structure and shape function.

We have constantly stressed this relationship and also noted how environmental intervention either facilitates or hinders the interaction. A tangible, and devastating, example is malnutrition. If sufficiently severe, the bodily systems are frustrated, and function ultimately is adversely affected. Suspicion is strong that a sterile environment produces almost as tragic results.

The brain as a physical structure, subject to nature's laws of development, exercises a key role in a child's growth. We are only beginning to understand this enormously complex organ, both its structural formation and functional consequences. For example, the notion of the triune brain suggests that many unexplained behaviors may have a definite physical cause. If Epstein's speculations about spurts in brain growth withstand further examination, their support of cognitive theory promises exciting innovations in child rearing and education. The tantalizing subject of cerebral lateralization also promises much for the future, but hard data still elude our grasp.

The literature and research surrounding physical development reveal that an interdisciplinary approach is furnishing data to challenge both theorists and researchers and to illuminate the entire developmental process.

SUMMARY

There is a regularity to growth that is interrupted only occasionally.

A properly functioning endocrine system is crucial for normal development. Growth hormone is particularly vital in regulating the growth process.

Understanding bodily functioning aids interpretation of the growth process, but environmental conditions constitute one-half of the equation: growth = heredity and environment.

Malnutrition demonstrably alters the developmental pattern, both physical and intellectual. Severe malnutrition may be either kwashiorkor or marasmus, or a combination of both.

There is a developing consensus that the cerebral hemispheres are asymmetrical; that is, they differ in structure as well as function.

Evidence is accumulating about the physiological process that children use in acquiring knowledge—the selective destruction of information.

Brain evolution, as proposed by the theory of the triune brain, offers intriguing conjectures about the appearance of certain behavior that seems incompatible with a child's personality.

Passage of neural impulses depends on the myelination process, which also determines functional abilities.

If continued experimentation verifies spurts in brain development, those cognitive theories that propose similar mental stages will be considerably enhanced.

Cerebral lateralization, while still a relatively obscure topic, provides many insights into child development.

SUGGESTED READINGS

BLOOM, BENJAMIN. *Stability and Change in Human Characteristics.* New York: John Wiley, 1964. This thoughtful book includes one of the clearest analyses yet written of the environment's effects.

ECCLES, JOHN. *The Understanding of the Brain.* New York: McGraw-Hill, 1977. A Nobel Prize winner's account of brain structure and development, with occasional and fascinating flights into fantasy.

"Education and the Brain." *The Seventy-seventh Yearbook of the National Society for the Study of Education* (Jeanne Chall and Allan Mirsky, editors). Chicago: University of Chicago Press, 1978. An outstanding collection of essays about basic brain structure, development, lateralization, problems, and theory.

GARDNER, HOWARD. *The Shattered Mind.* New York: Vantage Books, 1974. In his moving description of a stroke victim's trials, Gardner gives a thorough presentation of brain function.

KNIGHTS, ROBERT and DIRK BAKKER (editors). *The Neuropsychology of Learning Disorders.* Baltimore: University Park Press, 1976. This collection of essays is rapidly becoming a standard reference for those interested in the brain's role in learning disorders.

KNOBLOCH, HILDA and BENJAMIN PASAMANICK. *Gesell and Amatruda's Developmental Diagnosis.* New York: Harper & Row, 1974. This classic text offers a concise overview of development.

TANNER, J. M. *Fetus into Man.* Cambridge, Massachusetts: Harvard University Press, 1978. A renowned English physiologist, Tanner has written a superb account of the human growth process.

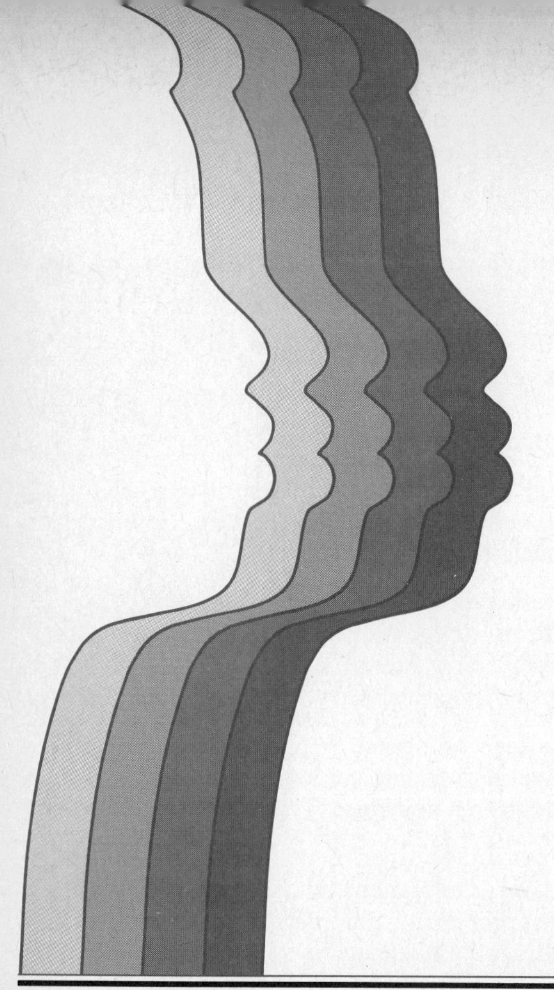

CHAPTER 7
COGNITIVE DEVELOPMENT AND INDIVIDUAL POTENTIAL

CHAPTER HIGHLIGHTS

Topics

The Cognitive Processes
a. Memory
b. Concept Formation
c. Problem Solving

Cognitive Development
a. Patterns of Cognitive Development
b. Heredity and Experience
c. Transitions in Mental Development
d. The Development of Cognitive Style

The Search for Potential
a. Problems of Definition

Intelligence Testing: Facts and Myths
a. Binet
b. Wechsler
c. Multiple Factor Theorists

The Growth of Intelligence
a. Patterns of Intellectual Development
b. Personality and IQ: The Berkeley Growth Study
c. The Meaning of Growth Studies

Influences on Intellectual Growth
a. Heredity and Intellectual Growth
b. Race and Intellectual Growth
c. Socioeconomic Level, Intervention Programs, and Intellectual Growth

People

Alfred Binet
Benjamin Bloom
Jerome Bruner
John Flavell
J. P. Guilford
Rick Heber
Jerome Kagan
Nathan Kogan
Michael Lewis
Robert McCall
Allan Paivio
David Wechsler

Special Topics

The Milwaukee Project

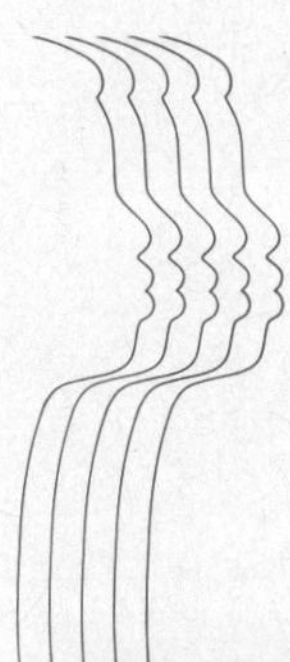

Current explanations of cognitive development and its relationship to intelligence both frustrate and challenge those concerned with the development of a child's mental life. Frustration is caused by the dichotomy between studies of the cognitive that often ignore the basis of cognitive behavior and studies of intelligence that often ignore the qualitative differences in a growing child's mental development. Challenge is presented by traditional studies of intelligence and intelligence testing that offer enriched interpretations of intelligent behavior and cognitive studies that afford insights into fundamental changes in mental development.

Interest in cognitive development has increased with the realization that children think differently than adults and the difference is qualitative as well as quantitative. That is, children are not miniature adults whose thinking process lacks a certain number of experiences. *Children interpret experience according to their level of mental development.* They not only know less, they know it differently; the difference in cognitive ability between adults and children is *both* quantitative and qualitative.

Rohwer, Ammon, and Cramer (1975) address this distinction. They note that the basic assumption of cognitive theory is that human behavior is *not* directly determined by the immediate situation. Interposed between situation and response is cognitive activity—you think and then you act. A second major assumption is that your thought processes are not an accumulation of stimulus-response connections. Cognition intervenes and distinctly colors each of your reactions.

These assumptions are reflected in recent research, and Gelman (1978) has identified several trends in the literature:

1. Adolescent thought processes are now the subject of considerable investigation.

2. The thought processes of the elderly are receiving increasing scrutiny, since the loss of intellectual function is probably as informative as its emergence.

3. Language, reading, and memory are seen as fertile sources of data about cognitive activity.

4. Studies of the relationship between cerebral lateralization and cognitive development have increased noticeably.

5. Cognitive style is viewed as a real source of data about mental activity.

6. The preschooler is recognized as a cognitively competent organism.

Gelman believes that acceptance of the preschooler's competence is probably the most significant trend. While the cognitive capacities of youngsters may be less complex or different from those of adolescents and adults, they nevertheless exist. Gelman's rationale is similar to Kagan's: there is a seductive tendency to make extremely simple value judgments about children's abilities by assuming, for example, that sensorimotor intelligence is not as good as formal operational intelligence or that the preconventional stage of moral development is not as good as the postconventional. Actually, sensorimotor intelligence is entirely appropriate for the one-year-old and is worthy of intense investigation.

Since cognitive development at all ages deserves study, this chapter will examine the nature of key cognitive processes such as memory, concept formation, and problem solving. We have previously discussed attention and perception, and we will discuss insight and creativity in future chapters. We shall examine the development of these processes by age, since formal theorizing demands a lengthy examination of Piaget's stage system, which appears in the following chapter.

There are, however, significant individual differences in the expression of cognitive processes, which introduces the troublesome topic of intelligence. Theories of intelligence, intelligence testing, and intellectual growth studies must be analyzed to comprehend the relationship between cognitive processes and intelligence. Finally, the issue of influences on intellectual growth introduces heated and controversial subjects such as the relationship between race and intelligence, and the success or failure of intervention programs. But first, what are the cognitive processes?

THE COGNITIVE PROCESSES

Rohwer, Ammon, and Cramer (1975) state that when people perceive or think about objects and events, their mental representations are *cognitions*. Cognitions affect a child's—and adult's—behavior; thus the environment and the child's maturation are influential to the extent that they modify cognitive activity. It is almost as if environmental stimuli and inner maturational forces must pass through a cognitive screen before they exercise any influence on behavior.

Bourne, Dominowski, and Loftus (1979) believe that modern cognitive theorists view human beings—actually human minds—as systems that process information. The human information-processing system utilizes *three* sources of information: the environment, memory, and feedback. During processing, information passes through several stages:

1. *Sensory memory,* which means that a child must see, hear, feel, or somehow sense information. Bourne et al. (1979, p. 8) state that although sensory memory is true memory, it is quite primitive; that is, it will record faithfully but decay quickly. The authors believe that, primitive or not, complicated information-processing activities occur; for example, the child manifests both attention and pattern recognition.

2. *Short-term memory,* which means that certain information acquired during the sensory memory phase attains a more lasting state—it is encoded. Bourne et al. (1979, pp. 9–10) state that while there is little agree-

ment about the process of encoding, there is also little argument that it is what we are aware of at any given moment. Its capacity is limited; it retains only those data to which we carefully attend, and information is quickly lost. Memorizing an infrequently used telephone number is a good example. To maintain information and to facilitate its passage to long-term memory requires rehearsal.

3. *Long-term memory,* which means that information is retained, stored, and remembered when needed, although it is not always in our consciousness. Although there are unresolved questions about the permanence of information in long-term memory (once stored there, do we ever forget it?), there is widespread agreement about lengthy duration. Long-term memory may be episodic (recalling events from your personal history), semantic (your knowledge of the world), or procedural (your ability to adapt, to use your knowledge).

The human information-processing system is illustrated in Figure 7.1.

Using information, however, entails more than mere retention; other processes are involved. Concept formation, the construction of categories to classify items, is essential for a child's adjustment to the environment. We tend to group different things that are somehow alike—automobiles, chairs, books—and to understand the relationship among the things we group. We then use concepts to make decisions and to solve problems.

This brief description pictures the human being as an information-processing system, which ultimately determines human behavior. That is, children and adults apply their cognitive processes to information from both the environment and memory and thus they themselves uniquely shape their behavior.

Here, then, is a brief rationale for studying cognitive processes. Accepting the existence and use of environmental stimuli, the first cognitive process requiring our attention is memory.

FIGURE 7.1. A Schematic Representation of the Information-processing System

From Bourne, Dominowski, and Loftus, "Cognitive Processes," © 1979, p. 9. Reprinted by permission of Prentice-Hall, Inc., Englewood Cliffs, New Jersey.

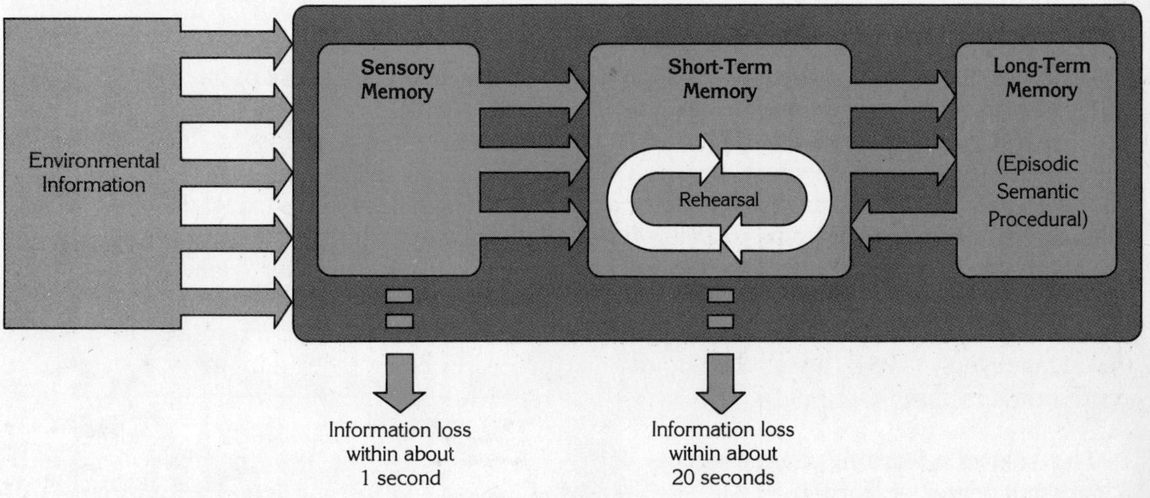

Memory

The recognition that memory, as early as the last half of the first year, exercises a critical function in cognitive development is one of the most important findings in recent studies of infancy. Its role in the child's adjustment to the environment and as a foundation for other cognitive processes compels us to understand its nature and development.

An emergency has arisen and you must call home. What is your telephone number? There has been a robbery in a nearby store. A person with your physical characteristics has been described to the police. Where were you on Thursday evening at eight o'clock? Can you solve this equation: $8x - 7 = 2x + 17$?

These simple questions illustrate the adaptive and cognitive components of memory. There are few people who cannot remember their home telephone numbers; you undoubtedly can recall what you did last Thursday evening. You cannot solve the equation unless you remember that $17 + 7 = 24$, $8 - 2 = 6$, and $24 \div 6 = 4$. Your memory aids in forming concepts, solving problems, and thinking creatively. Picture yourself without memory, a victim of total amnesia. The image is terrifying and helps to explain the popularity of stories and drama about "people without memory."

The Memory Process. Memory has fascinated investigators for centuries. One of the most famous names in memory research is that of Hermann Ebbinhaus, who as early as 1885 gave subjects lists of items to memorize and then tested for recall one day, one week, or one month later. These and similar experiments suggest several facts about memory that Underwood (1964), in a classic essay, summarizes in three categories:

1. The subject's learning ability affects the rate and degree of learning.
2. The meaningfulness of the material affects ease of learning.
3. Similarity or nonsimilarity among items affects rate of learning (similar items tend to confuse subjects).

Underwood then uses these facts to examine some paradoxes that appear in the learning literature. For example, is material that is easy to learn also easy to remember? Surprisingly, no; if the items are equally learned, the rate of forgetting is similar for both. Note that equally learned does *not* mean equal time; if the time for learning is identical for both items, those more easily learned will be better remembered.

Experiments also show that a slow learner, if given time to master a list, will remember as much as a fast learner on later tests. Since forgetting results mainly from interference with previously formed associations, it is quite likely that a bright child could forget more rapidly than a slower youngster. Since brighter individuals process more associations that can cause interference, they may well forget more easily.

The Memory Storage Systems. We have previously identified three forms of memory: sensory, short-term, and long-term. Sensory storage involves the use of one or more of the sense organs; note that Figure 7.1 shows the possibility of almost instant loss of information. Some investigators question the term sensory "memory" and refer instead to sensory register, which implies that we attend to stimuli (they "register") and immediately transfer data to short-term memory.

It is interesting to examine the control processes of short-term memory. *Rehearsal* is repeating information; you remember a telephone number by saying it over and over. *Coding* is storing the information in an easily retrievable form; you put the information in a rhyme or sentence. *Imaging* is placing verbal information into visual images; you put this sentence in a building shaped like an *I* (for image). *Decisions* and *retrieval* strategies reflect the manner in which we organize information; we store by the patterns we impose on data.

Allan Paivio (1971) has made an interesting distinction between visual and verbal storage of information in long-term memory. When individuals form images of stimuli they usually retain these longer than verbally coded material. Both forms of storage occur, however, and Paivio has designated this as the "dual coding" capability of long-term memory.

The basic process is as follows: stimuli are registered in sensory memory and are instantly transferred to short-term memory. If rehearsal commences, information then passes to long-term memory where it remains for an indefinite time. Since children and adults cannot, and indeed should not, store all stimuli that they encounter, short-term memory and rehearsal act as a selective mechanism to eliminate irrelevant data.

Finally the issue of forgetting deserves more attention. It is a normal process, one that we all, either fortunately or unfortunately, experience. What causes you to forget? There are several possible explanations.

1. *Interference.* Previously mentioned in Underwood's discussion, most psychologists readily agree that new learning interferes with earlier learning, but it is not the only cause of forgetting.

2. *Motivation.* Sometimes you forget because you want to forget. Certain experiences have been so unpleasant that to bring them to consciousness causes considerable pain; consequently you actively attempt to repress them.

3. *Extinction and Reorganization.* Experiences seldom used are experiences forgotten. There must be periodic recall to avoid forgetting altogether or to refrain from radically altering the experience when forced to recall it.

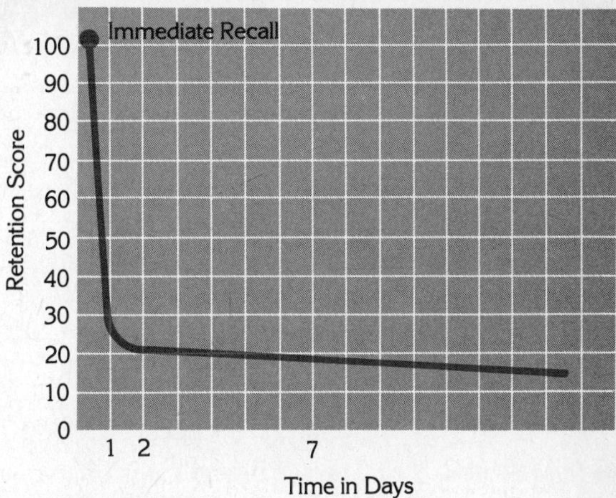

FIGURE 7.2. The Curve of Retention.

4. *Disuse.* Similar to extinction and reorganization, this theory is more extreme because of its either-or nature. For example, you may not have been ice skating for years, but if you attempt it again your former skill begins to return quickly; or you still may be able to recite a poem you learned in elementary school. Yet you may have already forgotten your study of cerebral lateralization. Fading over time, as an explanation of forgetting, raises serious questions. You may quickly forget most of a book, or even a course, but you usually retain something for years. Even after memorizing a list of words, some are retained weeks later, as is seen in Figure 7.2.

Can you recall the genetic defects discussed in Chapter Four? Try it.

Concept Formation

The second major cognitive process that we shall examine is concept formation.

> A concept is an abstraction in the sense that it refers to no particular object, process, state of affairs, or event, but rather to a collection of such concrete entities. Concepts have two fundamental components, a set of defining

> features and a relationship among them. Concepts are learned through experience with real entities. (Bourne, Dominowski, and Loftus, 1979, p. 194)

The authors' definition, which accurately represents current knowledge, is purely descriptive and lacks hard data to support its many assumptions. That is, we can identify those behaviors that indicate concept formation, but we cannot precisely identify the underlying mechanisms that produce concepts.

Concepts are categories to which we apply a label—house, car, boy, girl—and it is by using these labels that children gradually acquire control over their environment. Once concepts are stored in *semantic* memory, they are available for use. For example, once children learn to group concepts, their manipulation of the environment becomes more economical. The youngster who can say to another "shut off the lights," saves time and energy and enhances feelings of competence.

Concept Formation: A Description. Concept formation begins with environmental stimulation; your sense organs register information and a nerve impulse is initiated that the central nervous system will ultimately interpret. Once the process begins, you link the present information with past similar experiences. That is, you retrieve from memory any data that will enrich the present experience. You organize the information so that meaning emerges. The stimulation that originally activated some sense organ is no longer discrete and meaningless. Thanks to the interaction of the cognitive processes, you have imposed organization on and attached meaning to the incoming information.

Your mental activity, however, is restricted to the immediate situation, which is called perception. The process is illustrated in Figure 7.3.

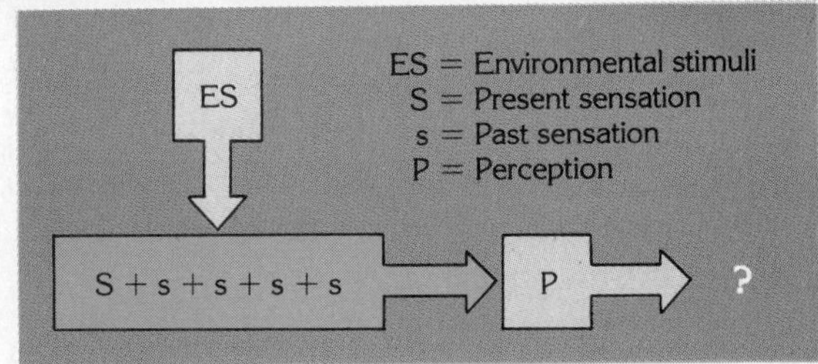

FIGURE 7.3. The Perceptual Process.

You also possess the ability to form mental representation of objects and events not immediately present; you are then using concepts. Forming concepts is a time consuming, challenging task, since the repeated experiences needed to construct categories involve attention, discrimination, and forming relationships. For example, you must experience something the same—a ball—in many guises: different sizes, different colors, different materials, different purposes. But there is a common core in all of these varieties: a ball is round and rolls. Thus, this clustering of constants (rolling and roundness) defines the boundaries of the category into which color, purpose, and material fit. This example, while quite simple, illustrates concept formation. The process appears in Figure 7.4.

Kinds of Concepts. Although the process of concept formation is similar to that described, the manner in which you form the concept permits us to identify different types of concepts. For example, did you group certain

FIGURE 7.4. Concept Formation.

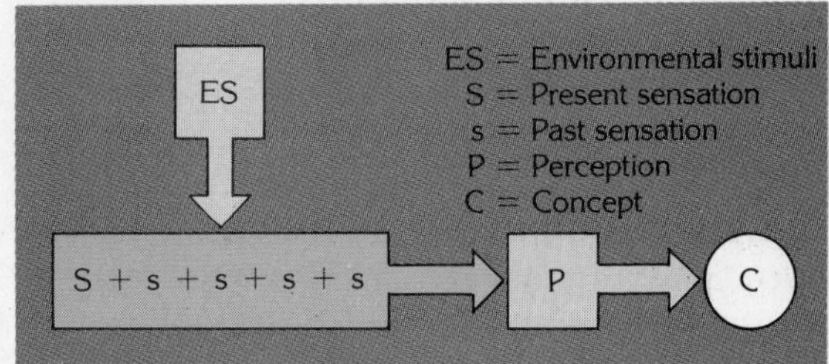

items because of their common characteristics or the relationships among them? Bruner, Goodnow, and Austin (1956) believe that there are three category types that reflect the manner in which the concept's characteristics are grouped: conjunctive, disjunctive, and relational concepts.

1. *Conjunctive Concepts* result from the union of several similar attributes. These attributes emerge from many experiences with balls, oranges, chairs. The category is formed by the conjunction of the attributes.

A ball is round; it rolls, regardless of color.

2. *Disjunctive Concepts* result from attributes any one of which defines the category. A strike in baseball is a good example. The umpire may call a strike; the batter swings and misses; the batter hits a foul ball. Each of these examples is a strike.

3. *Relational Concepts* result from the relationships that exist among defining attributes. The authors use income tax brackets. There are numerous tax brackets, or categories, each of which results from the relationship among income, expenses, and number of dependents. Combining these attributes produces a tax bracket or category.

The authors consider the categorizing process as an "act of invention."

> This hodgepodge of objects is comprised in the category "chairs," that assortment of diverse numbers is all grouped together as "powers of 2," these structures are "houses" but those others are "garages." What is unique about categories of this kind is that once they are mastered they can be used without further learning. We need not learn *de novo* that the stimulus configuration before us is another house. If we have learned to class "house" as a concept, new exemplars can readily be recognized. The category becomes a tool for further use. The learning and utilization of categories represents one of the most elementary and general forms of cognition by which man adjusts to his environment. (Bruner, Goodnow, and Austin, 1956, p. 3)

These authors summarize the significance of categorizing as follows:

1. Categorizing reduces the environment's complexity, since we respond to *groups* and not to individual objects.
2. Categorizing enables us to identify the world's objects, since we place them in classes and label them.
3. Categorizing reduces the need for constant learning, since we have stored an object in a class with a label and can ordinarily retrieve it from memory.
4. Categorizing helps to guide behavior, since we use concepts to interpret and respond to environmental demands.

Concept Formation: Experimental Evidence. Studies of concept formation have a rich tradition in the history of psychology. In 1920 Hull, unhappy with studies of categorization, attempted to discover an effective method of acquiring concepts. Presenting his subjects with a series of 144 Chinese characters taken from a standard Chinese dictionary, he then instructed them to learn the names of the characters. The characters were grouped according to common elements. He found that adequate time was a key factor in discovering the common element in each group.

In the 1950s, Jerome Bruner gave considerable impetus to studies of concept formation by his work with Goodnow and Austin. A typical experiment involved presenting subjects with stimuli of differing characteristics: size, color, number, form. One stimulus represents the desired concept—perhaps a flat, orange square. The subjects form some hypothesis about the concept and then ask the experimenter if a certain stimulus represents the concept. Using the experimenter's answers, subjects then continue until they are reasonably certain they have identified the concept. Bruner and his associates were searching for any systematic strategies that individuals use in forming categories.

Recently the Wisconsin Research and Development Center for Cognitive Learning has reported the results of increasingly sophisticated analyses of concept formation. Studying hundreds of youngsters from four to fifteen years of age, Klausmeier et al. (1974) and Levin and Allen (1976) developed a model of conceptual learning and development (CLD), which reflects the investigators' realization that concept formation represents both external (adequate stimulation) and internal (maturation and learning) conditions. The CLD model contains four progressively more abstract levels of concept attainment:

1. At the *concrete* level individuals distinguish an object that they had previously encountered. Recognizing a flat, orange square requires attention, discrimination, mental representation, and retrieval from storage.

2. At the *identity* level individuals distinguish an object in a different modality than originally encountered (hearing the car start that you initially saw in the driveway). While attention, discrimination, representation, and retrieval are all again involved, generalization emerges as a new cognitive process.

3. At the *classification* level individuals can generalize that two things are somehow alike (an actual car and a toy car are both cars). While this is a major achievement, youngsters at the classificatory level cannot verbalize about *how* they know both are cars.

4. At the *formal* level individuals can define both the name and characteristics of the concept. Youngsters can tell you that both objects are cars, name the characteristics of cars, and provide nonexamples of the categories (a roller skate is not a car). They now think symbolically and use language to further concept formation.

Finally, Eleanor Rosch's work deserves mention. Cohen (1977) states that studies of concept formation have borne little fruit since Bruner's work in the 1950s, until Rosch's studies on the structure of natural concepts, those concepts that we acquire through daily living. Studies of triangles, squares, and Chinese characters have been to little avail. When we acquire natural concepts, we learn more than the characteristics of the concept; we learn the relative importance of the characteristics, and how the concept relates to others we have acquired.

Consequently, Rosch (1975) believes that we represent natural concepts as prototypes, that is, these categories have an internal structure that consists of a core meaning (the prototype) plus a hierarchy of characteristics that define category membership. While appealing, Rosch's conclusions need further testing to verify that all concepts are represented as mental prototypes.

Have you formed a concept of a concept?

Problem Solving

> Attempts to provide a general characterization of the process of problem solving have met, on the whole, with little success, being either too vague, or too incomplete, or both. This is hardly surprising, since the kinds of tasks which come under the heading of problem solving are extremely diverse. (Cohen, 1977, p. 46)

Cohen's comments, while particularly apt, should act as a continuous challenge to investigators to acquire as much data as possible about this cognitive process because problem solving should become a way of life for children. If youngsters are to adjust successfully to their environment, they must learn not to respond instantly to every stimulus they encounter. Called "responding on a one to one basis," such behavior severely curtails thoughtful choice. Children must learn to consider several responses, test them mentally, thus eliminating responses that are obviously incorrect. One or two responses will be more plausible than others, and youngsters can then try these to determine if they will solve the problem. Figure 7.5 illustrates the process, with steps 3 and 4 demonstrating how good problem solvers (4) economically manipulate their environments, compared to poor problem solvers (3).

Problem-Solving—A Descriptive Analysis. Whenever existing behavior fails to achieve a goal, a problem exists. Problems may range from your inability to find the book you thought you left in the car, to complete frustration with an algebra problem. Note the great latitude in what constitutes a problem, from the simple to the highly abstract. There are also tremendous individual differences in children's and adults' abilities. These two variables—the nature of the task and differences in individual abilities—are the pitfalls that have baffled researchers.

Acknowledging these limitations on analysis of the nature of problem-solving behavior, the process seems to be as follows:

1. Youngsters must recognize that a problem exists, which is a troublesome issue when you recall individual variations in experience and ability. What may be an obvious problem to one child, may completely escape another.

2. Youngsters must identify the precise nature of a problem. An arithmetic word problem that requires division cannot be solved by subtraction; certain automotive difficulties require a distributor wrench, and a regular, open-end wrench will not suffice.

FIGURE 7.5. A Problem-Solving Process.

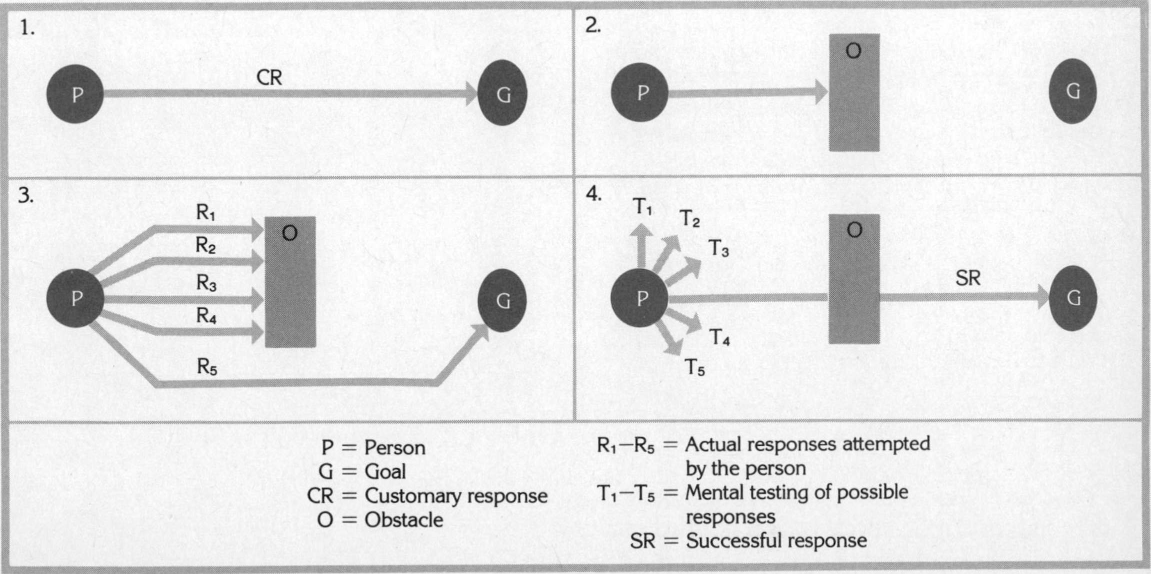

3. Youngsters must learn to generate hypotheses that could possibly solve the problem. For example, in a word problem, children can acquire the ability to think about various combinations of numbers contained in the problem: if I add all the numbers, what do I obtain? if I multiply two sets what does this mean? Here they use environmental clues and also search their memories.

4. Youngsters must learn to act upon the solution that seems best and then check to see if their solution was right or wrong.

A major obstacle that youngsters (and adults) must overcome is mental rigidity, or set. Problem solving demands behavioral change, and humans of all ages tend to resist change. It is much easier to rely upon the familiar than it is to break a habit. Try to solve the problem in Table 7.1, a classic in the psychological literature. To obtain the designated amount of water you may fill or empty any combination of the measures in each problem. For example, in Problem 1, you would fill the twenty-nine quart (or pint or gallon) jar and from it fill the three quart jar three times: 29 − 3 − 3 − 3 = 20.

TABLE 7.1. Luchins's Water Jar Problem

Problem	Given the following empty jars as measures			Obtain the required amount of water
1.	29	3		20
2.	21	127	3	100
3.	14	163	25	99
4.	18	43	10	5
5.	9	42	6	21
6.	20	59	4	31
7.	23	49	3	20
8.	15	39	3	18
9.	28	76	3	25
10.	18	48	4	22
11.	14	36	8	6

You undoubtedly devised a formula as you worked the problem: B − A − 2C. Once you discovered the formula you probably used it for all of the problems, even though Number 9 caused difficulty. Look carefully at Number 9; do you need the formula? Isn't it much simpler to subtract three from 28? Actually Problems 7 through 11 can all be solved by a simple addition or subtraction, yet you probably (and almost all of us) continued to use the formula. Youngsters need encouragement to discover, and use, different techniques.

Problem Solving—A Theoretical Analysis. Speculations about the process just described have produced three major theoretical explanations of problem-solving behavior.

1. *Information Processing.* The chief value of information processing techniques has been the logical presentation of a series of stages through which individuals pass as they attempt to solve problems. The technique which reflects the belief that human beings are information-processing systems proceeds as follows:

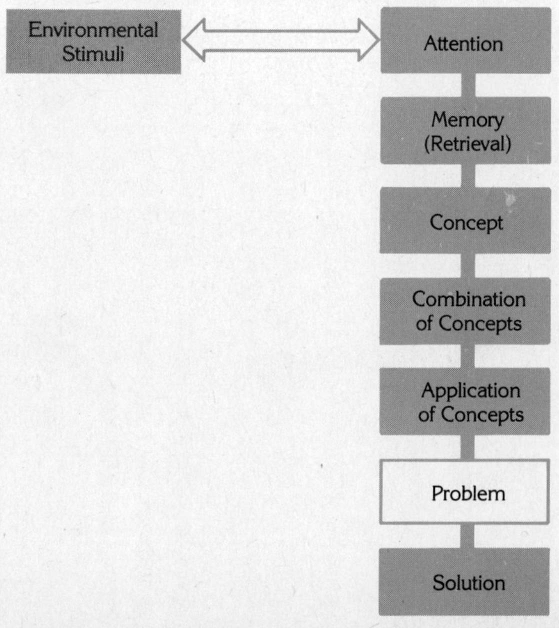

2. *Perceptual or Gestalt.* Perceptual explanations focus mainly on the organization of stimuli; that is, individuals solve problems when they perceive the relationships among the problem's various elements. Children and adults bring to a problem not only individual potential but unique experiences, which helps to explain why they perceive differently and thus also differ in their ability to solve problems. A good example of the perceptual technique in analyzing problem-solving behavior is the water jug problem you just encountered. You developed a set in your perception that interfered with efficient solution of the problem.

3. *Stimulus-Response or Association Theory.* Applying stimulus-response theory to problem-solving behavior forces us to concentrate on explaining why the correct response appeared. If the problem is considered a stimulus, then certain conditions will dictate which response appears: the correct response may have been reinforced in similar, past situations; there may have been frequent past reinforcements of a particular response that could now be appropriate in this problem; previously acquired reinforcement schedules may have generalized to many stimulus situations, one of which resembles the current problem.

These are the major theoretical explanations of problem-solving behavior, each of which possesses serious limitations because of the present inability to control decisive variables, both individual and task.

Can you solve this problem: How much is 20 ÷ ½ + 3? The answer appears at the conclusion of the Discussion Questions.

DISCUSSION QUESTIONS

1. Can you accept an interpretation of yourself as an "information-processing system"? Do the various categories, especially those of memory, describe your cognitive functioning as you are aware of it? Is such an explanation logically appealing?
2. Were you ever conscious of "rehearsing" information? Did you then feel more secure about its retention? Do you deliberately transfer verbal material to a visual form to help you remember? Can you then retrieve it better? In answering these questions, think carefully about your own behavior and attempt to determine if it is an accurate description of how you function when you think, learn, or recall.
3. A zagel is flat, purple, and has three sides. Assume that you want a youngster to acquire this concept; how would you teach it? Link your instruction to current knowledge about concept formation.
4. Be sure that you can distinguish among the various types of concepts. Give examples of each and show how that particular kind of concept is formed.
5. Difficulties in analyzing problem solving behavior are usually traced to two sources: the individual and the task. What does this mean? Give examples of the agents in each category that continue to block accurate analysis.
6. Which of the theoretical explanations of problem solving appeals to you? Why? Justify your answer by relating it both to children and the nature of problems.

Answer: 43

COGNITIVE DEVELOPMENT

The behaviors that we have designated as cognitive processes appear as early as the first days of life (attention) and change throughout our lives, following a discernible developmental pattern. Probably the most comprehensive effort to describe and explain developmental changes has been Piaget's elaborate system, which is the subject of the next chapter. Our purpose here is to present several studies that illustrate the general pattern of cognitive development.

Patterns of Cognitive Development

Bourne, Dominowski, and Loftus (1979) believe that the key question about the development of cognitive processes is not at what age a particular behavior appears, but whether this behavior precedes, follows, or emerges simultaneously with some other behavior. A related issue is our dependence on a child's performance of the behavior, which raises troublesome questions.

If children do not exhibit the behavior, does that mean they lack the competence to perform it, or is it simply due to a lack of suitable environmental stimuli? If children demonstrate the behavior, is it due to the cognitive process we have decided is relevant, or are other forces responsible? For example, if a youngster solves a problem involving geometric designs, we may attribute it to problem-solving ability, when actually the child may have had considerable experience with these lines and angles (perhaps someone in the family is an artist or architect).

Heredity and Experience. There are no clear answers in the maturation-experience controversy. Our previous discussion of genetic programming would suggest that individuals possess an inherent schedule for the rate of cognitive development. The pattern of brain development, mentioned in Chapter Six, would seem to substantiate this belief. Yet there is also substantial evidence demonstrating that varied experiences affect brain development. For example, Rosenzweig, Bennett, and Diamond (1972) have shown that rearing rats in isolated conditions retards brain development: smaller cortical size, less glia cells, and a poorer supply of blood to the brain.

Stevenson et al. (1976) studied the influence of schooling and the environment on cognitive skills in 824 five- and six-year-old youngsters. Some resided in jungle villages; some in slum villages of Lima, Peru. Some of the six-year-olds in both locations attended school. The investigators found that differences between the environmental extremes (jungle and city) caused less than half the children's variability in performance. Age, sex, birth order, and cultural grouping contributed little to differences in performance. Social class influenced performance on *some* verbal tasks. School attendance, however, exercised a strong, positive influence, whether by comparing six-year-olds who had and had not attended school, or by comparing five-year-olds with six-year-olds who did and did not enter school. The researchers cautiously state they could not specify what aspects of school aided children's performance on all memory and cognitive tasks. But as the authors note, although cognitive performance was superior for those who attended school, the effects of schooling on an individual child was highly variable. Again, we see the difficulty and perhaps impossibility of identifying specific causes of cognitive performance.

As Cohen (1977, p. 115) notes:

> Both theoretical and descriptive accounts of the cognitive development of children are controversial. There was disagreement on the nature of the successive stages, on how far the sequence of development is fixed or variable, and especially on the relative influence of maturation, experience and language.

Transitions in Mental Development. McCall, Eichorn, and Hogarty (1977) have reexamined the Berkeley Growth Study in an effort to distinguish significant changes in early mental development. They assumed that developmental change is seen in periods of instability of individual differences and age differences in the behavior itself. (Children in the Berkeley study were tested every month from one to fifteen months, every three months until thirty months, and then every six months until five years.)

The authors state that they discovered both instability in individual differences and discontinuity in developmental function at 2, 8, 13, 21, and 30 to 36 months. They interpret the data to mean that these are major stages in mental development, with the following characteristics:

0 to 2 months. The main aspect of infant mental performance is increased attentiveness to environmental stimuli; infants are essentially passive responders to the environment.

3 to 7 months. Infants begin active exploration and manipulation of the environment by the end of this period.

8 to 13 months. While infants display considerable stability during these months, vocalization appears. The authors believe that infants now begin to separate means from ends, a major accomplishment.

21 to 27 months. Language has emerged as a predominant theme in an infant's life, which facilitates the beginning of symbolic activity.

30+ months. Verbal behavior becomes highly significant in a child's expanding symbolic world.

The Development of Cognitive Style. While McCall and his colleagues focused on traditional intellectual measures, Kagan, Lapidus, and Moore (1978), studying infant antecedents of cognitive functioning, attempted to answer three questions:

1. What is the relation of attentiveness, play, and smiling during infancy to reflection-impulsivity at age ten?
2. What is the relation of these infant variables to IQ and reading ability at age ten?
3. What is the relation between reflection-impulsivity and both reading ability and EMG (electromyographic) levels at age ten?

The subjects were 160 white, firstborn children living near Cambridge, Massachusetts, who were divided into four social class groups based on parental education. The infants were assessed at four, eight, thirteen, and twenty-seven months of age.

The authors discovered no predictive relationships between the dimensions of infant behavior they studied and IQ and reading ability at age ten. They found some relationship between these behaviors and scores on cognitive style tests. For example, there was a relationship between assimilative smiling (smiling when reorganizing a discrepant event) and reflective attitude on the Matching Familiar Figures test, and between slow tempo play and long response times and the Embedded Figure Test. The authors conclude:

> These data, like those from other longitudinal studies, support both those who believe in a slim thread of continuity as well as those who hold that infancy provides a minimal preview of the future. (Kogan, Lapidus, and Moore, 1978, p. 1023)

Kogan (1976), analyzing the cognitive styles of field independence-dependence, reflection-impulsivity, styles of categorization, and styles of conceptualization, has reached the following conclusions about their development.

1. There are significant sex differences in cognitive styles during the preschool years, and these usually favor girls; that is, girls are about six months to one year ahead of boys on many cognitive functions.

2. Preschoolers show remarkable individual diversity in cognitive style.

3. Early cognitive styles are not lost as a child ages, but reemerge in more complex and sophisticated forms over the life span (Kogan, 1976, p. 125).

4. IQ has only a slight relationship to cognitive style.

5. The nature of the task may explain performance differences in youngsters of different ages.

Many investigators believe that analysis of the age differences on cognitive style tests offers the most promising insights into children's cognitive development.

DISCUSSION QUESTIONS

1. Explain the significance of the order in which cognitive processes appear as opposed to age. Why is age variation so widely accepted? Can you relate the order of appearance to the discussion of stages in Chapter Three?
2. The competence vs. performance issue is particularly pertinent in the analysis of cognitive processes. What view do you adopt? That is, if a child does not exhibit a certain behavior, is competence lacking? Select one of the processes—for example, memory—and defend your position.
3. Can you relate your answer to question 2 to a corresponding belief in heredity or environment? For example, if a youngster evidences a memory deficit, to what do you attribute this lack?
4. Does McCall's work suggest any connection to studies of brain development? Include in your answer any beliefs you may have about the advantages or dangers of using physiological data to interpret children's behavior. Do not focus on disease or other abnormalities but on typical developmental information.

THE SEARCH FOR POTENTIAL

While we can speculate about the nature of the cognitive processes, one tantalizing fact remains mysteriously elusive: the cause of individual differences in the expression of cognitive processes. Individuals, both children and adults, differ strongly in their ability to memorize, categorize, and solve problems. To explain these obvious disparities, investigators have usually turned to traditional explanations of intelligence.

Recently this practice has come under vigorous attack. Many think that intelligence as measured by intelligence tests does not represent an individual's potential or capacity, but rather, prior learning. How influential are cultural differences? Are children penalized because of language or a dearth of experience? If they are, then intelligence tests are measuring something other than capacity; they are measuring achievement.

Michael Lewis (1976) believes that there are several basic beliefs about intelligence that deserve consideration.

1. There is a single g (general) factor that underlies all mental activity.
2. The g factor can predict the level of performance in all mental activity.
3. It is easy to measure the g factor.
4. The g factor is innate.
5. Intelligence is not subject to qualitative change.

Note the problem that arises: intelligence is a general, innate element that permeates all mental activity. If a test does not measure this general, innate element, but instead measures learning, then many children unfairly suffer by the contradiction between the *meaning* of intelligence and the *measurement* of intelligence. Properly interpreted, however, intelligence tests are probably the best techniques available to indicate a child's capacity to memorize, form concepts, or solve problems.

The Problem of Definition

A major obstacle to understanding intelligence is that our experience is not with intelligence in the abstract but with intelligent behavior. Some individuals can solve problems rapidly; others master certain kinds of tasks easily; still others are remarkably well adjusted. Each of these examples represents intelligence and explains why there are so many different definitions of intelligence. L. M. Terman (1921) defined it as the ability to carry on abstract thinking. David Wechsler (1944) characterized it as the aggregate or global capacity of the individual to act purposefully, to think rationally, and to deal effectively with his environment. Burt (1955) has defined intelligence as an innate, general cognitive ability. These statements represent the most widely held class of definitions that describe intelligence as a unitary entity.

Other theoretical explanations define intelligence quite differently, however. Researchers view it not as an all inclusive, global concept, but as a cluster of several factors or abilities. J. P. Guilford (1959), for example, states that while some psychologists still view intelligence as a monolith, there is overwhelming evidence to indicate that many elements or factors are involved. Differences within one person's abilities, differing patterns of intellectual growth and decline, the instability of individual IQ scores over years, and the different symptoms of brain damage all suggest that intelligence may be multifaceted.

B. F. Skinner (1953) offers an even more radical analysis. He notes that we can designate almost any characteristic as a dimension of personality, but that this adds little to our knowledge until something beyond mere naming is achieved. We may easily coin the term "intelligence," or even neatly define it, but this alone does little to increase our practical understanding of the concept.

There simply is no universally accepted definition of intelligence. Individuals have intelligence to the extent that they behave intelligently. This statement resembles the definition of intelligence that many psychologists feel is the only one acceptable: intelligence is that quantity that the intelligence test measures. But this is unsatisfactory as well. Before constructing a test, we must make decisions about the nature of what is to be measured. In the instance of intelligence testing, what we want to measure obviously is intelligence. Consequently, items are chosen that are best suited to measure intelligence as we conceive it; and scoring methods are devised that will accurately assess this predetermined quantity.

How can those abilities designated as intelligent be measured? Once data have been secured from tests, can they be utilized to clarify the meaning of intelligence? Basically, common-sense interpretations such as the following have been used in formulating intelligence tests.

1. General information, in which the child or adult is expected to know certain basic facts. (How far is the moon from the earth?)

2. Reasoning problems, in which the individual is expected to see the underlying logic of the problem. (What is the missing number in this series? 2, 4, 6, 10, 12.)

3. Perception of relationships, in which the child is expected to react to more than one element of a situation. (What's wrong with this picture?)

4. Memory, which involves short-term recall. (When I am through, repeat the numbers I have read. 9, 5, 6, 1, 8, 4.)

COGNITIVE PROCESSES AND INTELLIGENCE

The categories most commonly used in formulating intelligence tests—general information, reasoning, perception, and memory—strikingly illustrate the practical, as well as theoretical, aspects of cognition. As you study the various intelligence tests, note how each attempts to assess comprehension or information, which reflect how well a youngster has mastered concepts. Those youngsters who have acquired many attributes for a category will score higher on these tests.

Another example is the perception of relationships. We have traced perceptual development in children and stressed its importance in adapting to the environment. Since intelligence tests pose many problems, those youngsters who perceive the relationships in a situation will undoubtedly score well.

Many other examples are possible: children who have not learned to attend to the important stimuli in their environment and to discriminate significant elements will experience difficulty with test items. All IQ tests sample memory, either directly or indirectly. It thus becomes evident that current intelligence tests depend heavily on the cognitive processes, as does formal schooling. Since intelligence tests sample experiences similar to educational achievement, a youngster who has trouble with any or all of the cognitive processes will encounter school difficulty. Reading is the classic example, since it is so intimately intertwined with attention, perception, memory, and concept formation.

Some investigators rather tersely define intelligence as successful adaptation to the environment. Whether you agree with this definition or not, you can undoubtedly recognize the role of cognitive processes in such adaptation. If someone gives you directions in an emergency during considerable noise, flashing lights, and general confusion, your survival could depend on your *selective* attention. If you fail to remember the directions, you will risk your life and those of others. If you cannot perceive the relationship between what you are told and the route to safety, you could well place yourself in jeopardy.

While these are extreme examples, they vividly emphasize the importance of cognitive processes in all aspects of our lives.

By administering various intelligence tests to large numbers of subjects and analyzing any resulting relationships, investigators have attempted to penetrate the nature of intelligence. But as is apparent from these brief examples, there are several serious problems in any such attempt. For example, are we measuring general intelligence or specific achievement? Do youngsters from different social classes score differently in these tests, and, if they do, does this reflect basic intelligence or merely class differences? Is a youngster nervous when taking a test? Does the person giving the test create a comfortable atmosphere? Is the youngster familiar with test taking ("test wise")?

Let us examine one of the problems more carefully. If the information desired, the problems presented for reasoning, or the material on which judgments are to be made reflect the bias of a certain social class, then some of the test takers are immediately penalized. For example, youngsters who lack certain social class-oriented information or who have not progressed well in school will undoubtedly fare poorly on such tests; consequently, their intelligence will appear "lower" than that of others. Today we would probably resist such a generalization because of the realization that intelligence tests essentially measure learned achievement. Achievement may or may not reflect underlying intelligence, but if lack of environmental opportunity has prevented a youngster from having the opportunity to achieve, tests that largely reflect achievement reveal little about innate intelligence.

Whatever the innateness, generality, or other factors involved in intelligence, children possess the capacity for intelligent behavior, and our task is to provide youngsters with conditions conducive to mental growth and development. In order to provide these conditions, we must know as much as possible about intelligence.

Nancy Bayley (1970) has expertly summarized the dilemma facing those who study the nature of intelligence and its behavioral expression. Commenting that human intelligence is the product of a biological organism and its prenatal and postnatal environments, Bayley (1970, p. 1164) states:

> Children's mental abilities, as measured by records of their performance, whether on intelligence tests, achievement tests, graded series of learned tasks, or other measures of specific abilities, are always end-products of the total prior complex of interactions among these multiple determinants. It is to be expected that there will be differential effectiveness of these various causal factors, between different children, and at different ages, as well as among the different types of ability.

INTELLIGENCE TESTING: FACTS AND MYTHS

The story of Alfred Binet and his search for the meaning and measurement of intelligence is famed in the history of psychology. Binet, who was born on July 8, 1857, and died in Paris on October 18, 1911, was originally trained for law. A time consuming hobby, one that lasted throughout his life, was writing plays for the theaters of Paris. Later, as his interests shifted, he received a doctorate in science from the Sorbonne, where he remained as director of the psychological laboratory. Much of his early work on the intellectual and emotional lives of children was the results of studies of his daughters. He was cofounder, in 1895, of *L'Annee Psychologique,* the journal in which his early studies on intelligence were published.

Binet and Mental Tests

In 1904, Binet was asked by the Parisian Minister of Public Instruction to formulate some techniques for identifying the children most likely to fail in school. The problem was very difficult, since it meant finding some means of separating the normal from the truly retarded, of determining the lazy but bright who were simply poor achievers, and of eliminating the halo effect (assigning an unwarranted high rating to youngsters because they are neat or attractive). Devising such an instrument meant that Binet had to begin with some preconceived notion of intelligence, since it is impossible to fashion the means to measure something unless you know what that something is. In a series of articles published in *L'Annee Psychologique,* Binet therefore outlined his idea of the nature of intelligence. It consisted of three elements.

1. There is *direction* in the mental process; it is directed toward the achievement of a particular goal and to the discovery of adequate means of attaining the goal. In the preparation of a term paper, for example, students select a suitable topic and also the books and journals necessary to complete it.

2. The ability to *adapt* by the use of tentative solutions. Here individuals select and utilize some stimuli and test their relevance as they proceed toward the goal. Before writing the term paper, for example, students may make a field trip to the area they are discussing, or to save time, they may decide to use library resources.

3. The ability to *make judgments* and to criticize solutions. Frequently called "autocriticism" this implies an objective evaluation of solutions. A student may, for example, complete a paper, reread it, decide that one topic included is irrelevant, and eliminate it. This is autocriticism at work. Binet thought that those of low intelligence simply lacked the capacity to make such judgments.

The items in Binet's early test reflected these beliefs. When an item seemed to differentiate between normal and subnormal, he retained it; if no discrimination appeared, he rejected it. Binet defined normality as the ability to do the things that others of the same age usually do. Fortunately for the children of Paris and for all of us, Binet was devoted to his task. The fruits of his and his coworkers endeavors was the publication in 1905 of the Metrical Scale of Intelligence.

Since their publication, Binet's mental age scales have pointed the way for intelligence testing. The success of the Binet scale led a leading American psychologist, Lewis Terman, to adapt it for American usage. Terman's revision, called the Stanford-Binet, first appeared in 1916 and was revised in 1937 and 1960.

Binet's scales were termed mental age scales because each child's results were compared with the average for children of the same age. Thus, estimates of normality, retardation, or acceleration were based on comparisons with the average number of items passed for any particular age. Children passing the same number of tests passed by the average ten-year-old, for example, had the intelligence of a ten-year-old. If these children were actually ten, that intelligence would be normal; if they were younger than ten, they would be above normal; and if they were older than ten, their intelligence would be below normal.

As the reader will quickly notice, here is the basis for the much abused and misused IQ, which dates back to the work of William Stern in 1914. (Although Stern is usually credited with first using the term "intelligence quotient," this is incorrect. Stern referred to the "mental quotient"; the phrase "intelligence quotient" was actually coined by Terman.) Stern's ideas led to a mathematical expression of intelligence. By converting all age levels into months, the formula is as follows.

$$\frac{\text{Mental Age}}{\text{Chronological Age}} \times 100 = \text{IQ}$$

If MA is 10 years (120 months) and CA is 10 years:

$$\frac{120}{120} \times 100 = 100$$

If MA is 10 years and CA is 8 years (96 months):

$$\frac{120}{96} \times 100 = 125$$

If MA is 8 years and CA is 10 years:

$$\frac{96}{120} \times 100 = 80$$

This method of calculating a child's IQ is called the ratio method (the ratio of mental age to chronological age). To eliminate as much unreliability as possible, a new technique (called the deviation method) is used to compute IQ. The deviation method attempts to control the variations that may influence a child's score. Anyone giving the Stanford-Binet can turn to the tables provided in the manual and quickly and more accurately determine the child's IQ. The authors believe that their work provides a basis for interpreting IQ test scores since commonly accepted meanings have been allotted to the various categories (see Table 7.2).

The work of Terman and Merrill has been remarkably faithful to Binet's ideas. As a result of his studies, Binet arrived at some definite conclusions about the nature of intelligence. One such idea was that nearly all of psychology's data relate to intelligence. Another was that intelligence involves the fundamental faculty of judgment (call it common sense, adaptation, or what you will). To judge well, to comprehend well, and to reason well are the essential functions of intelligence.

It is interesting to note the practical nature of Binet's work. He did not become entangled in problems of definition. For Binet, children and adults simply had something that distinguished them from one another and that enabled them to perform well or poorly on any given task. Call it what you will, it existed. How, then, could it be measured? Here the practical side of Binet again manifested itself.

TABLE 7.2. Distribution of the 1937 Standardization Group

IQ	Percent	Classification
160–169	0.03	
150–159	0.2	Very superior
140–149	1.1	
130–139	3.1	Superior
120–129	8.2	
110–119	18.1	High average
100–109	23.5	Normal or average
90–99	23.0	
80–89	14.5	Low average
70–79	5.6	Borderline defective
60–69	2.0	
50–59	0.4	Mentally defective
40–49	0.2	
30–39	0.03	

Source: Lewis M. Terman and Maude A. Merrill, *Stanford-Binet Intelligence Scale.* Boston: Houghton Mifflin Company, 1960, 1972. (Published by the Riverside Publishing Company.)

Age must be a key element, he reasoned, since older children generally do better than younger children on the same task. So one must find tasks that are appropriate for a given age and determine if a youngster does about the same, better, or worse on these tasks than others of his age.

But even if we can measure it on a scale, exactly what meaning are we to give intelligence? Since Binet considered almost all psychological data as intellectual phenomena, to him the fundamental faculty of judgment was critical. All other intellectual faculties were of little importance in comparison with judgment. What was of utmost significance to him in the measurement of intelligence was not that the youngsters made mistakes, but the kind of mistakes that they made. It is the absurd error resulting from a lack of judgment that is so revealing.

Let us continue our study with a theorist in the direct tradition of Binet.

David Wechsler

Dissatisfied with previous attempts to measure adult intelligence, David Wechsler, a clinical psychologist at New York's Bellevue Hospital, left a lasting imprint on the nature and measurement of intelligence. In his hospital work, Wechsler needed some reliable means for identifying the truly subnormal in his examination of criminals, neurotics, and psychotics. The Binet scales, effective through the early teens, simply did not accurately assess adult intelligence. Sympathetic to Binet's view of intelligence, Wechsler likewise considered intelligence a general capacity. He defined intelligence as the aggregate or global capacity of the individual to act purposefully, to think rationally, and to deal effectively with his environment (1958), which closely approximates Binet's reasoning. (Recall, however, that Binet never formally defined intelligence.)

Wechsler made a classic comparison of electricity and intelligence. We do not confuse the nature of electricity with our techniques for measuring it; exactly the same holds true for intelligence. General intelligence, like electricity, is a kind of energy. We do not fully understand its ultimate nature; we understand it by the things it does and enables us to do. Electricity produces heat and magnetic fields in much the same way as intelligence produces associations, understandings, and problem-solving abilities. Consequently, we know intelligence by what it enables us to do.

As we have noted, once a definition of intelligence is formulated, then a researcher can devise tests to meet those criteria. Wechsler first stated that intelligence is a global concept composed of interdependent elements. His next task was to determine the test that best measured the various elements and that jointly gave a comprehensive view of intelligence.

After years of investigation, Wechsler reached the conclusion that intelligence tests measure a quantity that is far from simple. It cannot be expressed in a single figure (a general factor), since it includes more than just a single ability. Intelligence is the ability to utilize the previously mentioned energy in a context that has form, meaning, content, and purpose.

There are three forms of the Wechsler test, designed to measure the intelligence of human beings throughout the life span, beginning at the age of four. These are:

1. *WAIS,* the Wechsler Adult Intelligence Scale, which is a revised form of his first test, originally published in 1939.

2. *WISC-R,* the Wechsler Intelligence Scale for Children-Revised, which first appeared in 1949 and attempts to assess the intelligence of children from five to fifteen.

3. *WPPSI,* the Wechsler Preschool and Primary Scale of Intelligence, which is designed to measure the intelligence of children from four to six and one-half years of age.

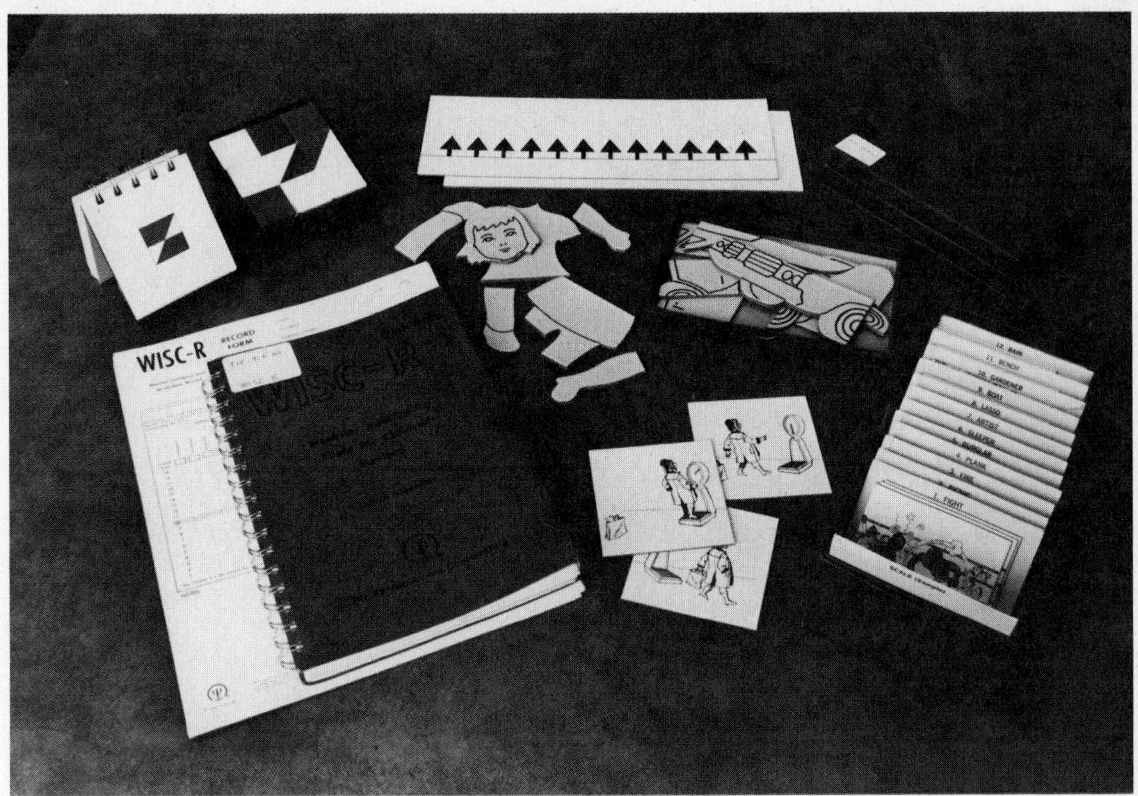

The Wechsler test probably provides a deeper insight into the nature of intelligence than any other current technique. For example, the WAIS consists of eleven subtests, six comprising the verbal scale and five forming the performance scale. Consequently, there are three possible intelligence scores: verbal, performance, and total IQ. Clinicians have found the separation into verbal and performance assessments to be particularly valuable for diagnostic purposes.

Particularly significant in Wechsler's speculation is his firm belief that the definition of general intelligence, far from being merely interesting theorizing, is at the heart of the measurement of intelligence. Does Wechsler believe, then, that intelligence is best summarized by the expression "general intelligence"? Although a firm adherent of intelligence as a general capacity (as his definition shows), he states (1958) that there are other important aspects of intelligence, such as motivation and persistence at a task. For example, individuals achieving precisely the same score in the same intelligence test defy identical classification. One youngster with a Binet IQ of 75 may require institutional care, while another child with the same IQ of 75 may function adequately in the home. Clearly other elements such as adaptation and persistence also become central in assessing intelligence.

THE WISC-R—AN INTELLIGENT TEST

In an intriguing essay, Alan Kaufman (1979) argues that major misunderstandings about intelligence tests have arisen because of the emphasis on IQ and the concept of intelligence, rather than on the child. He then chronicles the limitations of intelligence tests: their failure to adapt to children's qualitative changes in intelligence, the lack of measures to assess diversity in intelligence, the concentration on "left brain" functions.

Kaufman then provides a rationale in defense of intelligence tests: they are the best instruments now available to assess an individual's mental functioning, an extensive literature has grown around them (thus they are known quantities), and they are excellent predictors of school achievement.

The author (1979, p. 11) believes that both limitations and assets suggest that only examiners who are sufficiently knowledgeable should interpret the results. By rearranging the subtests it is possible to interpret the results according to Wechsler, Piaget, or the neuropsychologists. To use the WISC-R intelligently, Kaufman believes that examiners should accept the following premises:

1. The WISC-R subtests measure what a child has learned.
2. The WISC-R subtests are samples of behavior and considerable caution is needed in applying the results to other behaviors.
3. The WISC-R assesses mental functioning under definite experimental conditions, which restricts the examiner's understanding of the child's cognitive processes. That is, objectivity and uniformity in administering the test prevent the examiner from probing more deeply into a youngster's responses.

Intelligent usage of intelligence tests may eliminate much of the needless controversy about the contribution of heredity and environment, and ensure that these tests assume a vital role in the assessment of cognitive processes.

Intelligence: The Two-Factor Theory

Some psychologists have been critical of the claim that intelligence is a general capacity and, instead, focus on differences between specific abilities in the same individual. The first of these theorists, Carl Spearman, tried to reconcile both general and specific capacities. Psychologists have long realized that human abilities manifest a dual character: they are comparatively specific but retain an element of interdependence. This apparent duality has long troubled investigators and produced an unwillingness to accept a definition of intelligence as "general capacity." Is there a tenable middle ground that might offer hope for fruitful research? In this respect Carl Spearman was a transitional figure, recognizing the powerful arguments in favor of a general factor, but also realizing that many specific factors likewise seemed decisive in explaining intelligent behavior. Spearman reasoned that the most logical explanation of the nature of intelligence was that it consisted of both a g factor and an s factor.

Actually psychologists had been assuming a two-factor theory for years. Whenever they tested intelligence, they postulated a general or common factor, which is apparent after examination of tests that reduce scores on definitions, memorization, and problem solving to a single number. The intent of the tests was not to amass multiple separate scores but to measure something that would emerge from the sum of these scores: general intelligence (Wechsler, 1944). When the results of separate tests (arithmetic, problems, information) are combined into a single score, the implication is unavoidable that something joins them, that they are alike in some way. They must share some common characteristic, which is the general factor g, a purely mathematical entity used to explain the correlations among diverse cognitive performances.

In 1927 Spearman wrote what has since become a classic in psychology—*The Abilities of Man*. Here he grappled with one of psychology's nagging problems: the need for an explanation of the correlation between different abilities. The starting point of his inquiry was the curious observation of correlations among apparently different abilities in school children. How does the observed correlation bear on the individual measurements of the correlated abilities? Spearman's answer was that there existed a remarkable phenomenon. Whenever these correlations exist, every individual measurement can be divided into two independent parts that possess momentous properties (Figure 7.6). A general g factor varies from individual to individual, but remains identical for any one individual. The second part is a specific s factor that varies from individual to individual and also varies within any one individual from ability to ability.

Every ability is made up of both these factors, but they are not equally influential in all abilities. The g factor seems to play a greater role in some abilities than in others. Abilities requiring reasoning or the discovery of relationships, for instance, require a higher g factor. And here we see the essence of the whole doctrine: g is the constituent common to all abilities. The magnitude of g tells us nearly

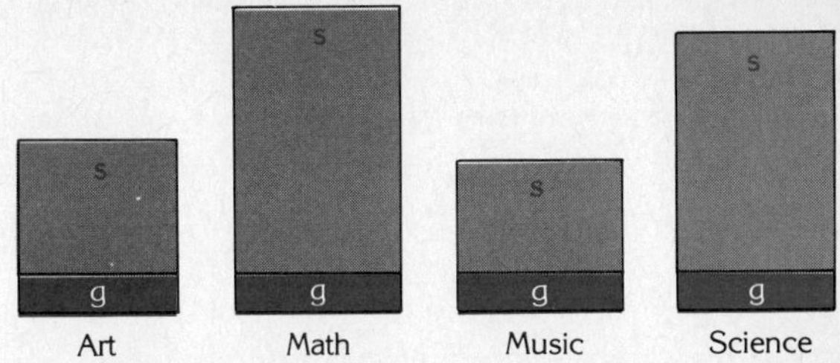

FIGURE 7.6. Variation of s with g Constant.

everything about some abilities and something about nearly all of them. That is, g remains the same throughout all tests, while s varies.

Consequently a person who has a high g should do well in almost all tasks. Intelligence may vary according to motivation, persistence, or personality characteristics. But if a person has low g, then the corresponding specific abilities are necessarily limited; that is, low g puts a ceiling on s. Obviously, since some tasks such as mathematics, science, and languages require considerable g, persons with low g will experience difficulty in those subjects.

Spearman correctly thought that the results of his investigations would produce a psychological revolution. He did not begin with some ill-defined entity (intelligence) and then try to attain a quantitative value. Instead, he started with a quantitative value (g) and then demonstrated what mental entities it really characterized. It proved to be a factor that entered into the measurement of all abilities and that remained constant for any individual in all abilities. Nevertheless, g varies greatly from individual to individual and is an excellent indicator of any person's overall ability.

Multiple Factor Theorists

Some remained dissatisfied with the hypothesis of a general factor or with any theory of general capacity for performance. Those who think that postulating a general intelligence factor does little to explain intelligence usually think that *factor analysis* provides more promising results. You may, for example, have an excellent memory for words and sentences, but have a poor memory for numbers. Or you may have an outstanding memory for numbers, but a miserable memory for anything visual, such as pictures. By using factor analysis, we can reach some conclusions about how much of any single attribute a child may have and use this information as a basis for our work with children. If children are weak in the basic numerical factor, for example, they might well be advised not to pursue a career in science or engineering.

In his discussion of factor analysis, Lee Cronbach (1970) states that it reduces a composite of psychological tests to ordered groups and views intelligence as psychologically independent clusters of aptitudes that can be measured separately. One of the leading exponents of this technique was L. L. Thurstone (1947). He gave his subjects many mental tests, studied the intercorrelations, and conducted multiple-factor analyses. Some of the factors were found so repeatedly in later studies that Thurstone eventually decided that there were seven primary mental abilities: visual space factors (S_1), verbal comprehension (V), number (N), reasoning (R), perceptual speed (P), immediate memory (M), and word fluency (W). Thurstone described each of these abilities as follows.

1. The space factor represents the ability to visualize figures in different positions.

2. The verbal comprehension factor represents the ability to understand the meaning of words and sentences. It is perhaps the most important of the mental abilities for academic achievement.

3. The number factor represents facility in numerical computation.

4. Reasoning combines the processes of both induction and deduction. Induction implies the ability to discover rules and principles, while deduction implies use of rules and principles.

5. Perceptual speed represents the ability to respond quickly to small details.

6. Memory represents the ability to recall letters, words, or numbers.

7. Word fluency represents the ability to produce words as required.

Thurstone also concluded that these primary mental abilities mature at different rates, a fact of considerable significance for education. Likewise interesting for parents and teachers is Cronbach's statement (1970) about one of the major misunderstandings of factor analysis: it has not eliminated the existence of a general ability. The primary mental abilities are correlated, and Thurstone (1947) himself has referred to the primary factors as simply different media for the expression of a general intelligence.

One of the most farreaching excursions into intelligence has been that of J. P. Guilford (1959), who claims that the only serious attempts to achieve a general theory had their roots in factor analysis. But even these attempts have been treated casually because of a persistent belief in Spearman's g factor. Guilford's structure of intellect theory has undergone extensive experimentation since the 1950s. It grew mainly from the application of the multivariate method of multiple factor analysis. The theory's implications have produced many new interpretations of great importance to psychology.

Beginning with his work as a military psychologist in the late 1940s, Guilford discovered evidence for several factors that seemed to represent aspects of spatial ability, reasoning, and memory. In a continuous program of research at the University of Southern California, Guilford and several of his associates conducted investigations into judgment, reasoning, evaluation, and creative thinking. As the number of factors grew, Guilford came to believe that they could be illustrated and their relationships determined by a three dimensional model. This is the famous *structure of intellect* shown in Figure 7.7.

This model classifies three kinds of intellectual abilities.

1. *Operations,* the kinds of thinking that an individual employs. There are five types: cognition (discovery, rediscovery, or recognition), memory (retention), divergent thinking (generating new ideas or new solutions), convergent thinking (searching for the correct answer), and evaluation (was my thinking right or wrong?).

2. *Contents,* the material we use in thinking. There are four types: figural information (concrete materials), symbolic information (letters or numbers), semantic information (meanings of words and sentences), and behavioral information (social relations).

3. *Products,* the results of thinking about content. There are six types: units (nouns such as house or dog), classes (several grouped items with something in common), relations (a connection between two items such as "is the spouse of"), systems (patterns or organizations of items, as in arithmetic problems or outlines), transformations (changes or modifications), and implications (what we should expect from certain information).

FIGURE 7.7. The Structure of Intellect.

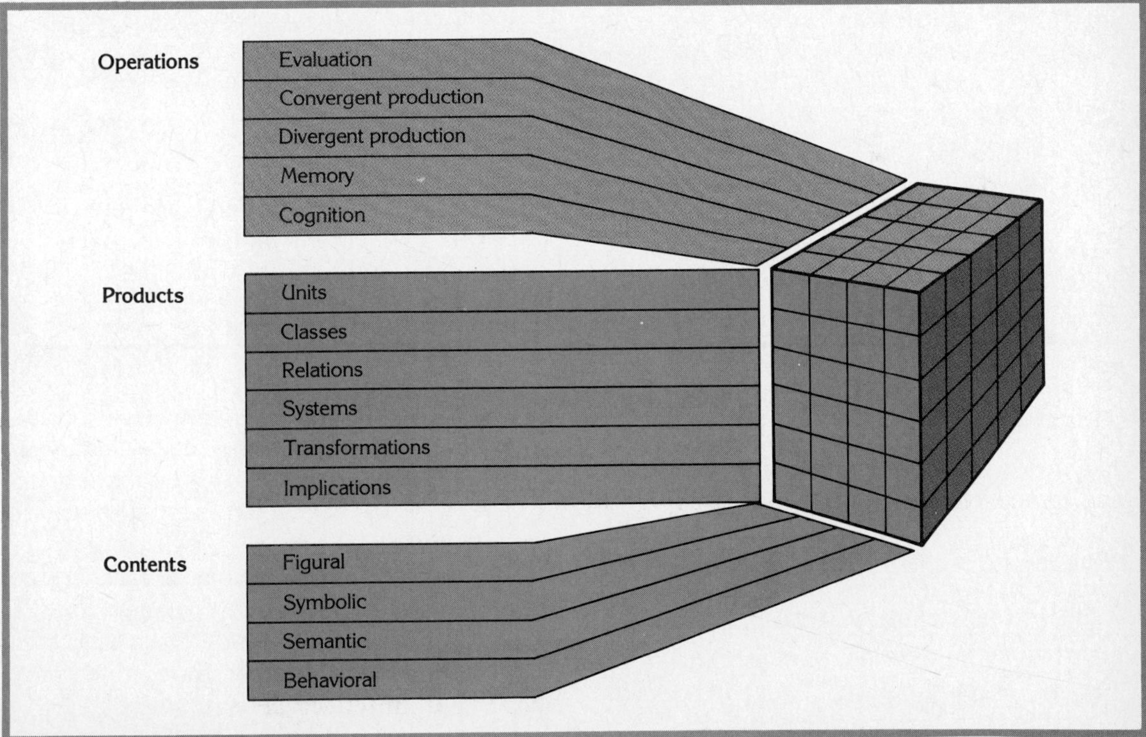

From *The Nature of Human Intelligence* by J. P. Guilford. Copyright 1967 by McGraw-Hill Book Company. Used with permission of McGraw-Hill Book Company.

Since there are five kinds of operations, four kinds of content, and six kinds of products, the result is one hundred and twenty intellectual factors (five × four × six). These comprise intelligence in Guilford's structure of intellect model.

Guilford's intent is to give the concept of intelligence a firm, comprehensive, and systematic theoretical foundation. From the beginning of the era of mental testing, such a theory has been lacking. A firm foundation must be based on detailed observation; the theory itself should include all aspects of intelligence; and the result must be systematic, embracing numerous phenomena within a logically ordered structure. Guilford has made a monumental effort to build such a structure.

DISCUSSION QUESTIONS

1. When Binet was asked to devise his test, what kinds of questions did he have to answer? Separate your answer into categories and list as many specific questions as you can. To help you with your answer, imagine that you have been asked to devise a test for some imaginary process. You will be faced with the same kinds of questions as Binet was.
2. Why do you think that Binet hesitated to define intelligence? If you were asked to define intelligence, would you include the element of good judgment? Why? Give several examples.
3. Compute an IQ for each of the following.

	CA	MA
a.	7 yrs., 6 mos.	9 yrs., 2 mos.
b.	9 yrs., 2 mos.	7 yrs., 6 mos.
c.	8 yrs., 5 mos.	8 yrs., 5 mos.

4. Why would Wechsler be classified with Binet in any discussion of intelligence? Explain the main assumption that both Binet and Wechsler make about intelligence.
5. How would you realistically assess your g and s abilities? Are there certain subjects in which you excel or do poorly? What remains constant?
6. What are the basic differences between "general" theorists and multiple-factor theorists? Which do you think best explains intelligence? Why?

THE GROWTH OF INTELLIGENCE

Evidence strongly suggests that measured intelligence changes during an individual's lifetime. Possible explanations for these differing results are that different tests of intelligence may measure different abilities or that the same tests at different ages may measure something different. While these and other apparent contradictions challenge the concept of a stable IQ, mental tests, properly used, are still the single best indicator of a child's intellectual development.

Patterns of Intellectual Development

Of the various interpretations of intellectual development, let us briefly consider some of Jerome Bruner's ideas (1966). His position is that certain benchmarks must guide any inquiry into intellectual development.

1. Intellectual growth is characterized by increasing independence of response from the immediate external stimulus. The student who prepares for a test without requiring the urging of a parent or teacher is free from the need of an immediate stimulus.

2. Intellectual growth depends on the internalization of events in a storage system that corresponds to the environment. Such a storage system enables the child to go beyond the present situation. A good example is the student who can write an imaginative, "far out" story that has a sprinkling of facts, but much fantasy.

3. Intellectual growth entails an increasing ability to communicate by words or symbols what one has done or will do. The student who can clearly explain a choice to join the ice hockey team instead of the debating society manifests a high level of intellectual development in the use of symbols.

4. Intellectual development depends on a systematic, close interaction between tutor and learner. A growing child needs help and guidance in order to fulfill an innate potential for mastering sophisticated elements in our culture.

5. Language is not only a means of communication, but also an instrument that children can use to order the environment. Language must be considered central to any explanation of cognitive development. A sure sign of mental growth is the child's use of language, particularly as it reflects direction or intent. A child who states a desire and expresses the means to obtain it is not merely reacting to the environment, but is evidencing mastery of it.

6. Intellectual development is marked by an increasing capacity to accommodate several alternatives simultaneously, to attend to several sequences at once, and to allot time and attention appropriately. It is remarkable how a maturing youth can juggle a schedule that includes tennis, debating, dating, work, and study.

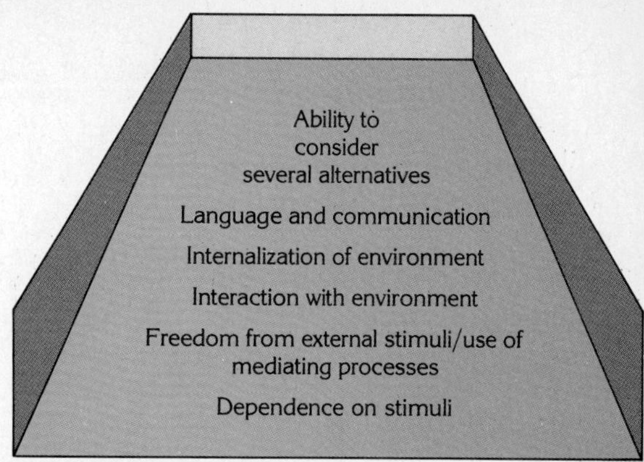

FIGURE 7.8. Intellectual Development: A Suggested Hierarchy.

Figure 7.8 illustrates the pattern.

What do these various benchmarks signify? Developing children are learning to represent their world in a more and more abstract manner.

Infants show little evidence of the abstract, logical reasoning that characterizes the adult's behavior. Infants react as a whole, in a manner that suggests an all-or-none response. Yet it is possible to discern the first signs of cognition: infants begin to recognize the same object under different conditions (stimulus equivalence), and begin to explore the environment in search for novel stimuli.

During the period of early childhood (about two to five years), the great task is the acquisition of language. Children begin to verbalize and thus to bring more order to the environment. During these years, children slowly realize that they are only one among many, to interpret the standards set by family and society, and to establish a sex identity. In identifying the critical tasks of life, some authorities think that as language acquisition absorbs most of children's energy from eighteen months to two years, so the formation of the sex role is vital from two to three years. The importance of these tasks for cognitive development is that children *represent* the world; that is, a concrete object such as a toy or food need not be present for children to know it or talk about it.

From about six to eleven, the time of middle childhood, children's ability to think and reason shows remarkable growth. Their tasks are now based on increasing conceptual capacity; that is, they now can read and write. The thinking process becomes more refined: children handle abstractions more easily, use reasoning to solve problems, transfer solutions to new situations, and commence creative thinking. For example, what is learned in math can be transferred to science. Beyond eleven, children continue to refine and extend these processes.

Personality and IQ: The Berkeley Growth Study

Growth studies enable us to identify changes with age, such as increases in mental ability. In the Berkeley Growth Study (1968), the principal author, Nancy Bayley, examines some of the data that indicate a strong link between personality and IQ. As she notes, the great value of this study is the unusually complete set of longitudinal records, which covers a thirty-six-year span in the life of fifty-four individuals. The subjects were full-term, healthy, hospital born babies of white, English speaking parents.

The author states that the results of this study challenged several current assumptions and theories. The first such challenges appeared in 1933, as a result of studies of mental growth during the first three years of life. The scores did not conform to the widely held belief that IQ remains constant but instead indicated that children's IQs varied over the years. As new and more sophisticated techniques were developed to analyze behavioral data, the author concluded that the cognitive and emotional processes of males and females required separate statistical analysis. Consequently, new clusters of related variables have appeared in the latest studies.

The author compares mental scores and behaviors at midadulthood, adolescence, and infancy (Figure 7.9). The results are fascinating. Twenty-five males adults show a clear pattern of relationship between IQ and personality. For example, impatient men lacking inner controls tend to have low IQs; low IQ scores were also found among those designated as negativistic, self-pitying, moody, and hostile. Higher IQs were correlated with such attributes as being critical, philosophical, perceptive, and introspective. Thus men with high intelligence are best characterized as introspective, thoughtful, and concerned with problems, meanings, and values.

When these figures were examined over a period of years (sixteen, eighteen, twenty-one, and twenty-six years), there seemed to be considerable stability in the correlations between behavioral and mental traits *for men*. The correlations for women, although similar, were much smaller and more unstable. Bayley concludes that we need different hypotheses to interpret male and female patterns of intelligence-personality correlates. Perhaps we can find some answers by tracing the pattern of development of these relationships throughout the individual's history.

The author then analyzes these relationships at adolescence; unfortunately, the correlations reveal little or no pattern or consistency. Bayley reasons that the emotional turmoil of adolescence disrupts the cognitive processes, perhaps even more for girls than for boys.

Next, the same kind of investigation was made using scores from infancy. There appeared to be a consistent pattern of correlations between active, rapid, responsive, calm, positive, happy, and outgoing behavior and IQs over the first eighteen years of life. Boys who

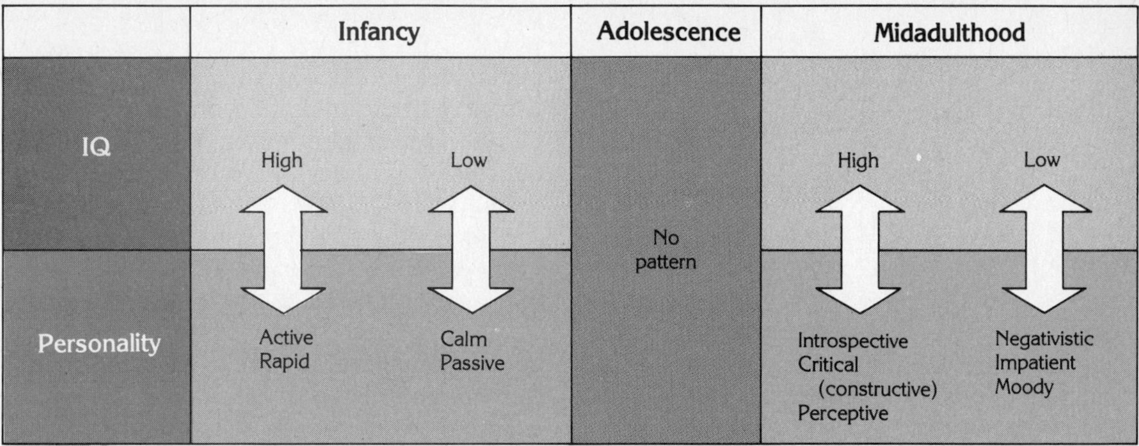

FIGURE 7.9. Relationship Between Male IQ and Personality.

were active and rapid before fifteen months earned high mental ability scores in infancy but lower scores later; if they were active at eighteen to thirty-six months, however, the pattern was reversed. Calm, happy, and positively responding boys earned low IQ scores in infancy but usually had above average IQs at five years and beyond. The patterns of correlation between behaviors in the first three years and verbal scores over the thirty-six-year span were fairly consistent. The verbal scores, which were the most stable, were also most highly correlated with personality variables. Calm, happy, positively responding boys who were active after fifteen months showed high verbal scores, and these scores remained high throughout thirty-six years.

Although we must be cautious in generalizing from a study of only fifty-four individuals, one of Bayley's more interesting conclusions is that during critical periods in the lifetime of any human, emotional turbulence may permanently depress or enhance the abilities of children, especially boys. Teachers and parents should be alert to these situations so that their expectations match the children's abilities. Be it sadness, death in the family, or the emotional lows that we all experience, our ability at these times is more limited and more prone to fall below expectations. Consequently, parents and teachers who are aware of this effect can offer needed support.

The Meaning of Growth Studies

Bloom (1964) has conducted a study of several of the longitudinal studies of intelligence and has reached some interesting conclusions. For example, using the data of the Berkeley Growth Study, he notes that intelligence measured at age one has zero correlation (no relationship at all) with intelligence measured at age seventeen (Figure 7.10). Intelligence measured at age two has a correlation of .41, at age four it is .71, and by age eleven it is .92. (The highest possible correlation is 1.00.) These statistics mean that the younger children are when intelligence is tested, the less reliable the results. Thus, intelligence measured at age one is a poor predictor of intelligence at age seventeen.

Summarizing data from several studies, Bloom concludes that it is possible to describe the development of general intelligence. If measured intelligence at age seventeen is taken as the final achievement, twenty percent is developed by age one, fifty percent by age four, eighty percent by age eight, and

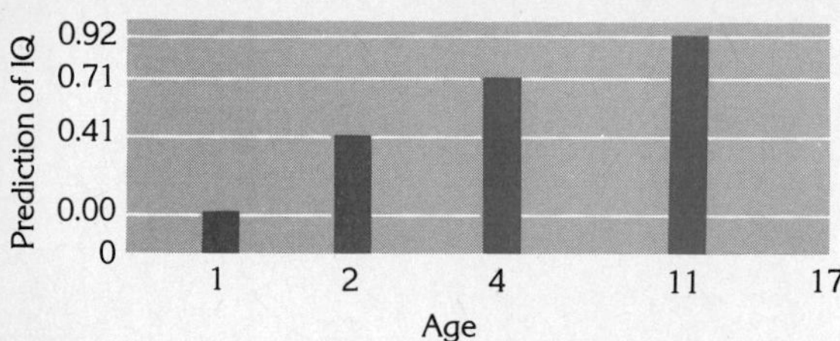

FIGURE 7.10. Correlations Between IQs at Various Ages.

ninety-two percent by age thirteen. With these results, Bloom questions the idea of an absolutely constant IQ. Instead, intelligence appears to be a *developmental* concept, similar to height and weight. These results once again indicate the tremendous importance of enriched early experience for the growing organism.

If at age four, fifty percent of the variance in adult intelligence is present, and as much intelligence develops in the first four years as in the next thirteen, the facts speak for themselves. The early years represent a truly critical period for human intelligence.

In this summary, Bloom states that stability of intelligence is greater over short periods than over longer periods, and that stability also increases with age. Consequently, any decisions about a child's intelligence and the inevitable academic or occupational guidance that accompany such decisions are premature if they are based on an intelligence test score of a very young child.

Brody and Brody (1976, p. 67), after reviewing numerous studies, conclude that:

> On theoretical and on logical grounds it is unattractive to assume that intelligence is constant through the growth period. That is, the structure of intellectual abilities is probably different at different ages. An individual develops new ways of attacking problems and new intellectual strategies as he becomes older. These lead to qualitative changes in intelligence as a function of age.

Further Age Changes in Intelligence

Psychologists long believed that intelligence test scores declined with age, beginning in a person's thirties, possibly even the twenties. Recent research, however, challenges these conclusions. Most of the early studies that indicated declining scores with age were cross-sectional—individuals of different ages were tested at about the same time. But changes may not be caused solely by age; they may also be due to generational differences; that is, those of one generation may have had significant environmental advantages over the other: economic, educational, social, nutritional. A good example is the Depression of the 1930s; many individuals who lived during those difficult days lacked the education available in more recent times.

To avoid these pitfalls, investigators have recently used longitudinal designs, testing the same individuals at different times. These studies report little, if any, decrease in intelligence with age. For example, Schaie and Strother (1968) studied individuals ranging in age from twenty to seventy, *using both techniques*. The cross-sectional data showed definite decreases with age, while the longitudinal method showed no decline.

Eisdorfer and Wilkie (1973) conducted a ten-year longitudinal study of individuals whose age at initial testing was between sixty and seventy-nine. Using the WAIS, they found that over the ten-year period, the average decline for the sixty to sixty-nine group (who would be seventy to seventy-nine at final testing) was four points, while for the seventy to seventy-nine group (who would be eighty to eighty-nine), it was about eight points. While there may be declines in the eighth and ninth decades of life, they are minor. The conclusion now is that there is little decline in intelligence test scores throughout life until advanced age when there is a slight loss. One finding is fascinating. Changes in intelligence test scores in the aged are related to physical changes.

The most dramatic evidence shows that substantial decline in intelligence test scores is a highly accurate prediction of death.

What can you conclude from this discussion? Perhaps Bloom's conclusions offered in his great book, *Stability and Change in Human Characteristics* (1964), present the most pertinent guidelines. There are no hard data about intellectual development. Children gradually manifest an ability to comprehend and use more abstract material as they grow older. (Piaget's work, which we shall examine in Chapter Eight, presents an attractive theoretical explanation of these phenomena.) Bloom believes that intellectual plasticity is greater earlier in life than later, and that IQ is substantially determined by its overlap with the intellectual accomplishment of the early years.

If the IQ scores of youngsters eleven or twelve years of age almost perfectly predict IQ scores at seventeen and eighteen, it strongly suggests that by these earlier years the home and school have worked their influence. Thus early intervention programs are highly desirable not only for their immediate benefit but also for their lifelong consequences.

INFLUENCES ON INTELLECTUAL GROWTH

Since the evidence indicates that intelligence (as measured by intelligence tests) changes, the nature of intelligence seems to be a combination of heredity and environment. Consequently, environmental influences must contribute to fluctuations in expressed intelligence. Nancy Bayley (1970, p. 1186) states that differences in mental abilities have been attributed to many things, some of which may be basically hereditary, and others primarily environmental, with many gradations between these extremes.

Heredity and Intellectual Growth

Brody and Brody (1976) believe that there are three different interpretations of the influence of heredity on intelligence.

1. There is a traditional belief that intelligence is almost a totally inherited capacity. This view, espoused by Arthur Jensen (1969) and others, is closely identified with racial differences. Adherents of this belief assume that heredity may account for as much as eighty percent of intelligence.

2. There are those, such as Christopher Jencks (1972), who believe that heredity may explain as much as forty-five percent of the variance in intelligence test scores.

3. A third group, perhaps best represented by Leon Kamin (1974), believes that there are *no* data indicating that heredity contributes to IQ scores.

Brody and Brody (1976) conclude that there is reasonable evidence testifying to some genetic influence on intelligence test scores. J. McVicker Hunt (1961, p. 362), in an early and compelling statement of an interactionist view, summarizes heredity's role in intellectual development and also presents a strong argument for the recognition of cognition processes:

> It would appear that intelligence should be conceived as intellectual capacities based on central processes hierarchically arranged within the intrinsic portions of the cerebrum. These central processes are approximately analogous to the strategies for information processing and action with which electronic computers are programmed. With such a conception of intellegence, the assumptions that intelligence is fixed and that its development is predetermined by the genes are no longer tenable.

Race and Intellectual Growth

Closely associated with studies of the relationship between heredity and intelligence is the issue of race. Whites score fifteen points higher on intelligence tests than blacks; the question then arises: to what do we attribute the difference? Those who adopt the genetic explanation argue that since heredity contributes to about eighty percent of total intelligence, the difference in scores is clearly attributed to heredity. Environmentalists disagree, noting that most blacks tested came from deprived conditions, which explains the difference.

To help you resolve this dilemma, remember that intelligence is behavior, and behavior results from the interaction of heredity and environment. There is a genetic component in intelligence, but it differs for individuals and not for races. As the Brodys note (1976, p. 168), about fifteen percent of blacks score higher than the mean score of the white sample, so racial characteristics per se are not powerful predictors of intelligence test scores.

Scarr and Wenberg (1978) studied one group of adopted white adolescents and another group of black and interracial children adopted into white homes. Thus the researchers could compare biological and adopted children within the same family, adopted children with their biological and adoptive parents, and identify the origin of differences in children who are reared in similar environments.

The authors state that some of their findings surprised them: there was no evidence of genetic differences in IQ between blacks and whites, while there was strong evidence of genetic differences in IQ among individuals within each race. For example, adopted children derive tremendous benefits from living in an intellectually stimulating environment. The IQs of the black adopted children average 110, which is a fifteen percent increase over the scores of American black children reared by their own parents. The same pattern was true for the white adopted children, and the IQ scores for both adopted groups were almost identical, which raises serious questions about genetically based differences.

Socioeconomic Level, Intervention Programs, and Intellectual Growth

There is general agreement that social class differences influence intelligence test scores. But the mere observation of these differences tells us little about their causes. Children from lower socioeconomic levels may have less genetic ability as well as being from an impoverished area; they may have experienced protein-calorie malnutrition; they may experience a sterile learning environment.

Since it is so difficult to isolate the variables associated with the low SES child, researchers have turned to intervention programs to determine if IQ test scores and school achievement will improve. The rationale is that if intervention programs are ineffective, then perhaps the environment itself is insignficant in shaping intellectual performance. The opposite is also true.

A major national intervention program was Follow Through. Started in the late 1960s as a successor to Head Start, Follow Through was designed to support disadvantaged children in the first years of elementary school. It has involved 79,000 children, 22 different early education programs, and over one-half billion dollars. The evaluation of Follow Through cost 50 million dollars. The results can only be described as inconclusive.

Anderson et al. (1978), members of the evaluation team, state that the test scores of the Follow Through groups were similar to the test scores of other disadvantaged youngsters who were not in Follow Through programs. But House et al. (1978) led a team commissioned by the Ford Foundation to conduct a third-party review of the evaluation. They concluded that the evaluation contained serious methodological problems that weakened its conclusions. All agreed that intervention programs should be designed to meet the different needs of individual students. Perhaps the safest conclusions were drawn by Hodges (1978) when he notes that there were several indisputable benefits derived from Follow Through: parents become much more interested in their children's education; the various programs made schools and homes happier places for the children; excellent models of primary education were developed; a close link was formed between theory and practice.

THE MILWAUKEE PROJECT

One of the most widely publicized intervention programs was initiated by Rick Heber on the basis that four-fifths of the mentally retarded population in the United States manifested no organic difficulty but were mainly poor and members of a minority group. Heber stated that these individuals were victims of "sociocultural mental retardation." He selected as members of his experiment forty black, "high risk" families: the mother had an IQ under 80 (using the WAIS) and had recently given birth. Twenty families were randomly assigned to the experimental group, and twenty to the control. The program began when the children were three months old and terminated when they were six years.

The program had two major features: family intervention and infant intervention. The mothers were given vocational training and help with reading, homemaking, and child rearing skills. The infants were placed in daycare centers for five days a week, twelve months a year. Up to twenty-four months, infants were given perceptual-motor and cognitive-language training; from then until six years they were given more organized instruction in language, reading, and mathematics.

At sixty-six months the experimental group had a mean IQ of 124 compared to the control group's 94. (Better diet and adequate medical treatment, provided to the experimental group, might have influenced the results.) The program seemed to produce its greatest impact from eighteen to twenty-four months, when a twenty-five percent IQ difference appeared between the two groups. The members of the experimental group also demonstrated greater communication with their mothers.

As Heber et al. (1972) note, the ultimate test of the success or failure of his program is how the children perform in school after leaving the program. Continued evaluation of the youngsters seems to indicate a drop in performance as the youngsters age.

DISCUSSION QUESTIONS

1. Select, analyze, and prepare for the class an example of some illustrious individual who has behaved in an extremely intelligent manner. Justify your designation of such behavior as intelligent. Can you relate this intelligent behavior to a theory of intelligence?
2. Of the theories presented in this chapter, which most closely parallel your own understanding of intelligence? Why? Can you defend your position from a philosophical, psychological, and practical viewpoint?
3. What are some of the more important implications of interpreting intelligence as another developmental concept? Is there educational significance in this belief? Is there application to child rearing practice?
4. The link between personality and IQ has been firmly established in this chapter. Are there youngsters of your acquaintance whose behavior has enabled you to assess their IQ fairly accurately? What traits caught your attention? Do you know youngsters whose behavior has misled you? Again, what were their characteristics?
5. Elaborate on the generational differences that could conceivably cause the apparent intellectual decline in old age. Be specific and link your answer to your knowledge of what intelligence tests measure.
6. Comment on the advisability of intervention studies. Be sure to include the heredity/environment aspects of intelligence in your answer, as well as the possibility of sensitive periods influencing results.

Cognitive development implies that change occurs in the cognitive processes: attention, memory, perception, concept formation, problem solving, and creativity. Before it is possible to trace the developmental pathway of these processes, it is necessary to understand their structure. Current research and theory suggest that there are three types of memory, sensory, short-term, and long-term. The manner in which memory processes interact, facts about storage and retrieval, and memory's relationship to the other cognitive processes provide hints to its appearance and development in children.

The nature of concept formation is also vital for understanding the role of cognitive processes in children's lives. The ability to classify and label a group of objects enables children to adjust economically to their environment. Problem solving and creativity, both of which are significant processes for adaptation to a technological society, depend on and utilize previously formed concepts.

Yet examining the structure of these processes is in itself insufficient; it does not explain the obvious differences among individuals in the expression of each and all of the cognitive processes. Psychologists have long turned to the concept of intelligence as an explanation. Fraught with controversy, the notion of intelligence still appeals to many as the cause of individual variation in the appearance, development, and performance of the cognitive processes.

SUMMARY

Memory appears during the first year and plays a key role in the development and function of the other cognitive processes.

Concept formation permits a child to acquire mastery over the environment by grouping objects or events, applying a label to the group or category, and then using the label in environmental interactions.

It is possible to identify different kinds of concepts, and the process of concept formation appears to follow a developmental sequence.

Despite varying theoretical explanations of problem solving, several stages constantly emerge in the process, which enables investigators to propose techniques for improving children's problem-solving abilities.

Tracing the developmental path of the cognitive processes has alerted researchers to the importance of the order in which certain behaviors appear, and the relative insignificance of the age at which they appear.

Traditional explanations of intelligence such as Binet's and Wechsler's, as well as more modern interpretations such as Guilford's structure of intellect model, continue to appeal to investigators.

Intelligence tests continue to be a source of controversy, but there is current widespread agreement that they measure achievement.

Inferring capacity from achievement requires assumptions about the variables that cause "intelligent" behavior and about which little hard data are available.

SUGGESTED READINGS

BLOOM, BENJAMIN. *Stability and Change in Human Characteristics.* New York: John Wiley, 1964. This classic, informative book about all developmental aspects is particularly revealing in its assessment of growing intelligence.

BOURNE, LYLE, JR., ROGER DOMINOWSKI, and ELIZABETH LOFTUS. *Cognitive Processes.* Englewood Cliffs, New Jersey: Prentice-Hall, 1979. An excellent introduction to the cognitive processes literature.

BRODY, ERNEST and NATHAN BRODY. *Intelligence: Nature, Determinants, and Consequences.* New York: Academic Press, 1976. An unusually thorough presentation of all aspects of intellectual development.

BRUNER, JEROME, JACQUELINE GOODNOW, and GEORGE AUSTIN. *A Study of Thinking.* New York: John Wiley, 1956. A seminal work in the study of concept formation.

COHEN, GILLIAN. *The Psychology of Cognition.* New York: Academic Press, 1977. A good, basic introduction to cognitive theory.

FLAVELL, JOHN. *Cognitive Development.* Englewood Cliffs, New Jersey: Prentice-Hall, 1977. A thoughtful analysis of selected cognitive processes.

LEWIS, MICHAEL (editor). *Origins of Intelligence.* New York: Plenum Press, 1976. An interesting collection of essays that focuses on infant intelligence.

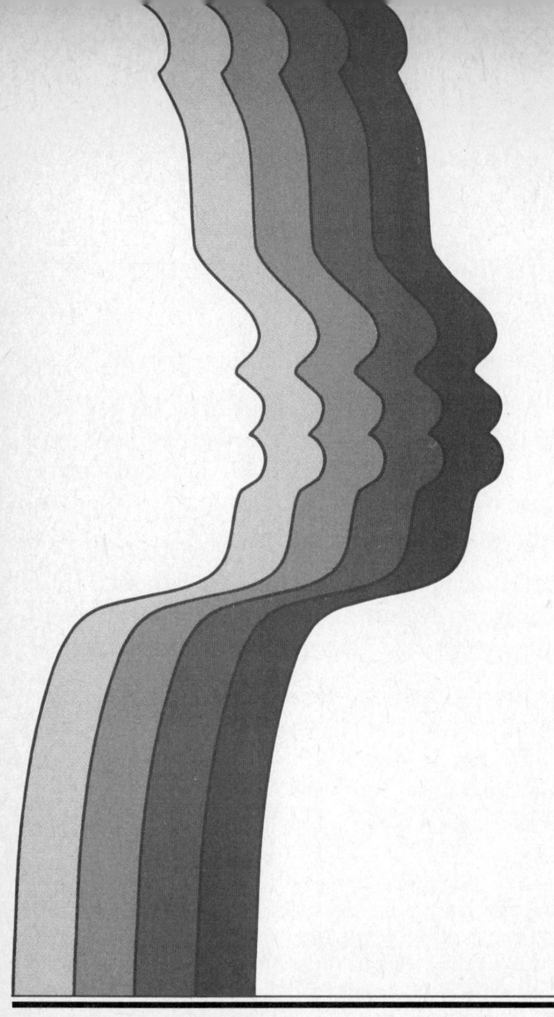

CHAPTER 8
THE IMPACT OF PIAGET

CHAPTER HIGHLIGHTS

Topics

The Man
a. Background Data

The General Theory
a. Two Major Assumptions

Key Concepts
a. The Functional Invariants: Adaptation and Organization
b. Intelligence
c. Content
d. Structure
e. Scheme
f. Operations

The Periods
a. Sensorimotor
b. Preoperational
c. Concrete Operational
d. Formal Operational

Influences on Mental Development
a. Maturation
b. Experience
c. Social Transmission
d. Equilibrium

Piagetian Assessment Technique
a. Construction of the Instrument

People

John Flavell
J. McV. Hunt
Barbel Inhelder
Gary Larsen
Jean Piaget
Ina Uzgiris

Special Topics

Intelligence Equals Biology Plus Experience
Changing Structures—Changing Behavior
Egocentrism
Behavior and Cognitive Level
Challenge and Rebuttal

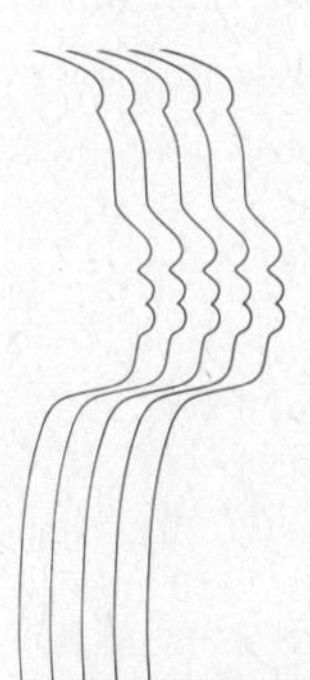

If, as noted in the preceding chapter, children think differently than adults, there must be some basic reason why identical cognitive processes such as memory or concept formation produce different results. Age alone is an inadequate explanation. To solve this puzzling problem, investigators of children's cognitive development have turned to theory and the work of today's leading cognitive theorist, Jean Piaget.

When asked what psychologists have most influenced modern thought, even those with just a smattering of psychological knowledge would probably answer Freud and Piaget. Many other individuals shine in the galaxy of psychological stars, but none glow quite so brilliantly as these two pioneers. The reason for their influence lies in the boldness and creativity of their work. Piaget's studies, in which he described how infants develop a perception of reality and delineated the stages of mental development through which all children progress, have radically changed our thinking about the growth of human intelligence. Since his work is so central to an understanding of cognitive development, we devote an entire chapter to Piaget.

THE MAN

Jean Piaget was born in Neuchatel, Switzerland, on August 9, 1896. Unusually bright, he published scientific papers before he completed secondary school. Also a voracious reader, his interests ranged across philosophy, biology, religion, and sociology. From his readings Piaget speculated that biology could clarify philosophical problems. He also speculated that both external actions and thought processes were logically organized, and he gradually came to believe that thought is basically interiorized action. Consequently, the organization of overt action and inner thinking is essentially similar.

Here we see why Piaget insists on calling himself a genetic epistemologist. An epistemologist is concerned with how we, both children and adults, gain knowledge, while a genetic epistemologist is concerned with

Jean Piaget

changes in the acquisition of knowledge over time. That is, what changes take place in the child's environment? Does more difficult and abstract knowledge, such as mathematics, imply a different kind of interaction and a different kind of child's thinking? Piaget combined his own interest in biology and philosophy to create a *genetic epistemology.*

After receiving his doctorate in 1918, Piaget engaged in several academic activities, including a sojourn in Binet's laboratory at the Sorbonne, where he worked at standardizing tests of reasoning. He became fascinated by the processes by which children derived incorrect answers, especially since the patterns of responses suggested that age differences were involved. In 1921 he became Director of Studies at Geneva's Rousseau Institute, where he continued his studies of children's developing intelligence. He spent hours observing his own three children shooting marbles with their playmates while he discovered their views on ethics and the rules of the game. He questioned schoolchildren about the numbers and groupings of the flowers and beads he gave them. From these investigations flowed a series of articles and books that still are among his best known works. In a sense this is unfortunate, since these studies were his initial gropings toward a formal system and contained two major flaws that Piaget himself mentions. First, the study of verbal behavior alone provided an incomplete picture of intellectual development; second, there was no mental basis (what Piaget later called structures) to explain logical behavior.

In 1923, he accepted an appointment to the faculty at the University of Neuchatel and thereafter divided his time between Geneva and Neuchatel. The years 1925 to 1929 were extremely significant for Piaget's research. It was then that he studied children's reactions to changes in the shape of a substance that remained the same in weight and volume. He also studied the behavior of his own children, which furnished him with data about phenomena such as cognitive adaptation and the relationship between cognitive organization in the sensorimotor period and later periods.

From 1929 to 1939 Piaget studied, taught, and wrote about the history of science and genetic epistemology. He resumed his investigations into the development of number and quantity concepts, which provided insights into the elusive structures of intelligence. From 1940 until his death in 1980, Piaget was caught in a whirlwind of activities: directing the Psychological Institute at Geneva and the International Center of Genetic Epistemology, editing the *Archives de Psychologie,* writing, conducting research, and teaching.

THE GENERAL THEORY

Now that recognition of Piaget has finally come, the multitude of books and articles by and about him can cause considerable confusion. His theory is complex and contains several formidable obstacles. The sheer voluminousness and difficulty of Piaget's own writing causes problems. Another is the temptation to begin discussion with a presentation of Piaget's theory of developmental periods, a practice that is almost certain to produce a superficial knowledge of an extremely complicated system. Still another obstacle is the inclination to consider Piaget as either a psychologist or an educator. He is neither. Instead, as we have stressed, he is a genetic epistemologist. Genetic epistemology is philosophy, but it is experimental philosophy; genetic epistemologists attempt to solve problems of knowledge by studying the developing child. They are concerned with the cognitive structures that provide the basis for intelligence.

Without an understanding of several central concepts it is impossible to comprehend the range, depth, and richness of Piaget's cognitive theory. The ideas that you are about to study are difficult. Familiar terms are often used in a different manner and unless certain subtle distinctions are recognized, the material can become nearly unintelligible. But the extra work will be worth the effort, especially for those who will actually be in continuous contact with children as parents, teachers, nurses, or social workers. The insights that Piaget offers into mental development are richly rewarding.

Two Major Assumptions

There are two major assumptions in Piaget's theory. First is the postulate that mental operations have their source in motor activity. Infants immediately begin to use their reflexes, expanding this usage and slowly developing a network of cognitive structures that culminates in logicomathematical reasoning. Piaget believes that verbal intelligence is based on physical, or sensorimotor, intelligence. It is the use of, and change in, reflex activity that is critical for intellectual activity.

> Concerning its adaptations, it is interesting to note that the reflex, no matter how well endowed with hereditary physiological mechanism, and no matter how stable its automatization, nevertheless needs to be used in order truly to adapt itself, and that it is capable of gradual accommodation to external reality. (Piaget, 1952, p. 29)

Piaget stresses that behavior even as fundamental as the reflex entails the individual utilization of experience. But Piaget is uninterested in the unchanging reflex (the eyeblink or kneejerk); it is the changing reflexes (sucking, for example) that are the basis of mental life. He states (1952, p. 30) that contact with the object modifies the activity of the reflex. For example, sucking varies according to a state of hunger as an infant sucks a nipple or playfully sucks a finger; the sucking reflex has obviously changed in the latter example.

Piaget believes that *states of awareness* accompany a reflex, and that if awareness exists at all, such awareness is from the beginning awareness of meaning (1952, p. 38). Be sure you understand Piaget's interpretation of the beginnings of mental life. Schematically, the observed behavior (sucking, for example) is a unit, composed of two elements, one physical and one mental. It would appear as follows:

Reflex Activity
Accompanying Awareness

Flavell (1963, p. 82) states that actions performed by the subject constitute the substance or raw material of intellectual and perceptual adaptation. The infant's actions are overt: grasping, sucking. Flavell aptly describes the process as the "concept of intelligence-as-action."

Recognizing the awareness that accompanies movement introduces the notion of cognitive structures. If intelligence is a form of biological adaptation (1952, p. 4), then it is essentially an organization whose function it is to structure the universe. But intelligence can only structure the universe in a way that reflects its heredity; that is, heredity determines the manner in which intelligence functions.

Piaget believes that heredity functions in a dual manner, one specific, one general. Heredity's specific action produces the physical child with eyes, ears, nose, and a nervous system; specific biological structures are formed. This is a limited interpretation of heredity, since behavior is restricted to what is possessed anatomically.

Heredity's general role permits children and adults to overcome anatomical restrictions; that is, *we inherit a method of intellectual functioning.* Piaget states (1952, pp. 2–3) that heredity's general role is of primary importance for the development of intelligence because human biological organization thus directs the formation of cognitive structures as the mind contacts reality. These cognitive structures change as children age and encounter increasingly abstract material.

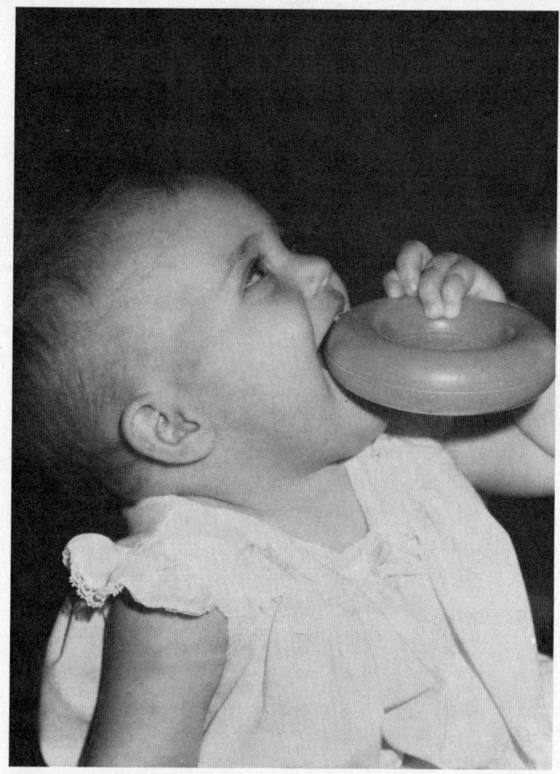

The Four Stages

Children's thinking thus becomes more abstract and leaves a trail that Piaget has traced through four stages of cognitive development:

1. *The sensorimotor period,* which precedes speech, extends from birth to about two years. During this period, children move from reflex activity to primitive mental activity.

2. *The preoperational period,* which begins with speech, extends from about two to seven years. Limited symbolic activity appears during this time.

3. *The concrete operational period,* in which logical thinking about tangible objects appears, extends from about seven to eleven years.

4. *The formal operational period,* during which true logical, abstract thinking appears, commences at about eleven years.

(Note that the ages at which children reach the four stages vary, but the sequence of stages does not vary; that is, every child must pass through the sensorimotor stage before the preoperational, the preoperational before the concrete operational, the concrete operational before the formal operational. There is no omitting a stage. Thus Piaget's theory is called *stage invariant, age variant.*)

To help you understand these assumptions, here is a brief summary of how they relate to the total system.

Piaget cannot escape his training as a biologist. When he was quite young he suddenly saw the problem of knowledge in a new light. For him, problems in philosophy were problems of knowledge, and problems of knowledge were problems of biology. Biologically, acquiring new knowledge is simply the age-old problem of an organism adapting to its environment. Viewed in this manner, the problem of knowledge is susceptible to scientific investigation instead of to mere speculation. Biological structures are stimulated into changes that enable the organism to adjust to its environment. Piaget has taken the biological concept of adaptation and applied it to the study of the developing child. Children receive new stimuli from the environment, adapt them in order to permit their assimilation, and also adapt themselves to accommodate to new demands.

Each change, or adaptation, occurs not in a vacuum, but in a coherent pattern that permits the total organism to adjust in new ways. Such adjustment reflects changes in both the child and environment. Intellectual functioning becomes a special kind of biological activity. While heredity provides the biological structures that determine what you may perceive, this is a specific hereditary contribution (or perhaps limitation). Heredity also acts in a more general manner; you inherit a mode of intellectual functioning. You are, for example, able to reach conclusions about wavelengths that you never see. The manner in which children function intellectually enables them to overcome the specific limitations of sensory and neurological structures.

Piaget's insistence that intelligence is adaptation explains the method by which children can organize more and more complex kinds of adaptation. To say that intelligence is an instance of biological adaptation is thus to say that it is essentially a form of *organization* (Piaget, 1952).

Every organism attempts to organize its processes, both physical and psychological. As you read this page, for example, the muscles and nerves leading to your eyes are working together to enable you to focus and to scan each sentence. Your bloodstream is furnishing nutrients and oxygen to give you the energy to meet the demands of the task. All of these physical structures are working together. But since you may be experiencing some difficulty as you read, you attempt to use other, more familiar ideas in grasping Piaget's system. While reading this text, you may underline important concepts or make marginal notes. Your activities are organized. All of these psychological structures are working together.

These two intellectual characteristics, adaptation and organization, are so important that Piaget calls them *functional invariants*; that is, they are always present in intellectual activity, regardless of age. They are not only at the heart of all intellectual functioning, but also at the heart of all biological functioning. Here is perhaps the ultimate rationale for saying that Piaget's system has strong and pervasive biological roots.

INTELLIGENCE EQUALS BIOLOGY PLUS EXPERIENCE

In all his writings, Piaget has developed a remarkably clear rationale for the biological roots of his system. He states that since the maturation of the nervous and endocrine systems continues until the sixteenth year, mental growth is inseparable from physical growth. Piaget's belief that there is a continuity between biological processes and intelligence is seen in the following schematic representation of his thinking.

1. Verbal intelligence depends on
2. Sensorimotor intelligence, which depends on
3. Habits and associations, which depends on
4. The reflex system, which depends on
5. The anatomical structure.

Child psychology must consequently concern itself with both mental and organic growth. But organically as well as mentally, environmental forces are of increasing importance *after* birth. In its search for influences on development, child psychology cannot limit itself to the study of biological maturation. Experience must also loom large in any such study.

As Piaget states (1952, p. 1):

> A certain continuity exists, therefore, between intelligence and the purely biological processes of morphogenesis and adaptation to the environment.

This is a good example of Piaget's persistent contention that development can only result from the interaction of heredity and environment.

KEY CONCEPTS

You should now understand how cognitive development commences: through the infant's activity an elaborate network of cognitive structures slowly develops, culminating in an ability to engage in highly abstract, propositional thinking. To follow the path of mental development through the cognitive stages, you should first understand several of Piaget's fundamental concepts.

The Functional Invariants: Adaptation and Organization

Piaget believes that all humans, both children and adults, *function* mentally in the same way. This inherited ability enables us to form cognitive structures and then organize these structures to adapt to our environment. We constantly use these intellectual processes—adaptation and organization—in all mental activities. Although we use different environmental stimuli in childhood (toys, for example) than we do as adults (words and symbols, for example), the cognitive method is identical: adaptation and organization. The nature of these processes never varies; hence the term "functional invariants." This concept is so vital to Piaget that each of the functional invariants needs more detailed examination.

Adaptation: Assimilation and Accommodation

Two critical processes to be considered are assimilation and accommodation, both of which make up what Piaget calls adaptation.

They occur in every stage of intellectual development. In new encounters with the environment, children respond as well as they can with their present abilities, but they themselves also change, bettering previous performance. In other words, changes occur within children that enable them to modify their behavior. This is the key to understanding all development.

For example, girls are now interested in a great variety of activities that formerly were thought to be a boy's domain. In learning to play ice hockey, for instance, a girl who is a fine figure skater must learn a different skating pattern—shorter, choppier strides; more and faster stops and starts; and how to react when bumped. But she will initially respond according to her previous experience, using the muscles and physical structures she developed earlier. Gradually, she will change in response to environmental pressures. She will develop new muscles and patterns of responding. She herself changes (accommodation) as a result of adjusting to slightly different tasks (assimilation).

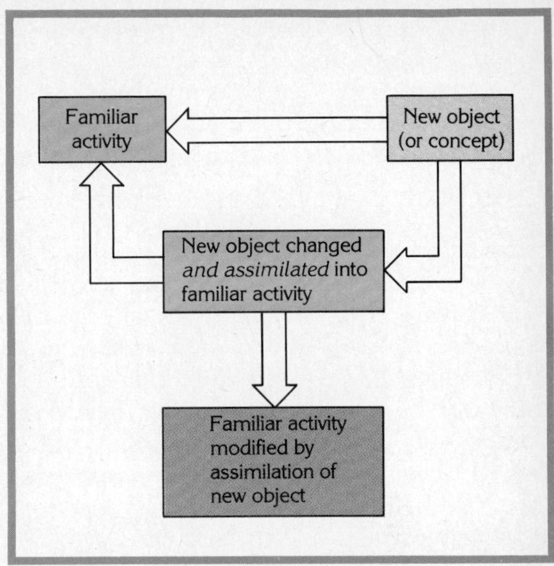

FIGURE 8.1. The Process of Assimilation.

Assimilation. Piaget describes the powers of assimilation (Figure 8.1) as follows: assimilation continues as intellectual structures extend their range of activity. Initially, perception and movement are focused on objects within the field of vision; gradually memory and intelligence provide a mental representation of the object and also project it into future circumstances. The problem is not to locate the first appearance of intelligence, but to understand the mechanism of such intellectual progress (Piaget and Inhelder, 1969). This mechanism, Piaget believes, consists of assimilation, which is comparable to the bodily assimilation of foodstuffs.

Eating is a simple example of assimilation. To take food into our bodies we must change it to fit the structure of our mouths and digestive passages. The mental process is similar: to take ideas into our minds, we modify the ideas to fit our existing cognitive structures, just as we modify food to fit our physical structures. You are now attempting to assimilate Piaget's ideas. How? You are incorporating them in a manner that permits you to understand them—by "making them fit" your cognitive structures (Figure 8.1).

Piaget sees the adaptive interaction between organism and environment as involving the complementary processes of assimilation and accommodation. Assimilation names the process whereby the organism utilizes something from the environment and incorporates it. Cognitive assimilation means a mental reorganization of an object, a restructuring that is consistent with the organism's existing intellectual organization. Every act of intelligence is an interpretation of something in external reality, that is, an assimilation of that something to the individual's present cognitive organization. Although the nature of the material assimilated may differ, the mechanism of assimilation is identical in all cases, both physiologically and psychologically.

For example, youngsters may have a good idea of what an automobile is, based on experience with things that have motors, wheels, and hard tops. But because of industry safety regulations, today's children may see fewer convertibles. What happens when they first see a convertible? Do they place it in a cognitive category with automobiles? Yes, because they take in the motor, wheels, and body, and almost ignore the soft top. They change the input and fit it to the mental structure of automobiles. But the structure changes also, and must now accommodate this new phenomenon of wheels, motor, and body, but a soft top. *That is, we change as we assimilate.*

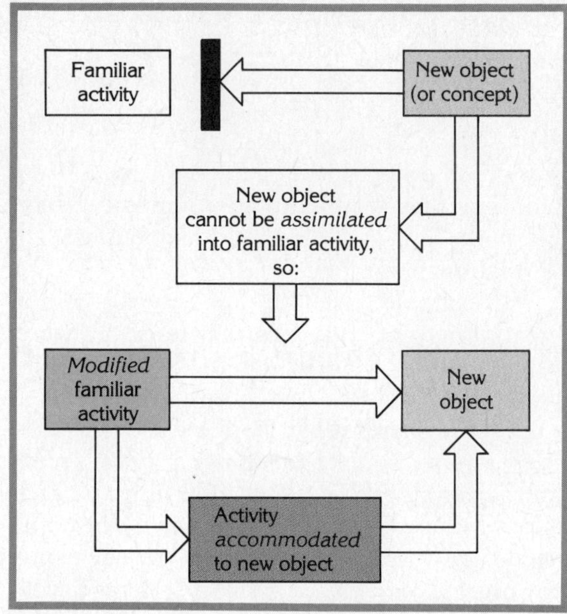

FIGURE 8.2. The Process of Accommodation.

Accommodation. Let us now turn over the coin of adaptation to its reverse side: accommodation (Figure 8.2). Piaget (1967) states that in assimilating objects, action and thought must accommodate to these objects; they must adjust to external variations. He comments further that our activities are modified and enriched when behavior accommodates to the demands of reality. The modification of our internal structures to adjust to reality is called accommodation. We change as the result of environmental pressure. Not only do we somehow change the incoming stimuli to "fit" us, but we ourselves change in order to accept and adjust to these new stimuli. The environment stimulates the organism, not by evoking a fixed response, but by producing changes in the existing, appropriate behavior patterns.

As with assimilation, most illustrations of accommodation begin with a biological example. We do more than merely assimilate food; we also adjust to its intake. Our mouths open; chewing occurs (if necessary) and the digestive process is activated. The food is modified, but it eventually modifies the body that ingests it. We thus accommodate our functioning to the specific contours of the object that we are attempting to assimilate. Accommodation likewise holds true for intellectual functioning. The essence of accommodation lies in our ability to adapt to the demands that the world of objects imposes. We will not grow intellectually unless we adjust intellectual capacities to the shapes that reality imposes.

For example, in our illustration of the convertible, children changed not only the input (how they took in the notion of a convertible) but also the mental structure of automobiles. Now they realized that their structures had to change and expand to include wheels, motor, body, and soft top. Children do not remain static; because of interactions with the environment and through the processes of assimilation and accommodation, they grow and develop. Full adaptation takes place when the organism-environment interaction modifies the organism so that further favorable interactions are encouraged. In our Piagetian example, you not only take in Piaget's ideas but as a result you should modify your knowledge of intelligence and cognitive development. You have changed your cognitive structures.

These complementary processes (assimilation and accommodation) constantly interact and adjust (Figure 8.3) so that the infant's reflexes are slowly transformed by differentiation and coordination into the logical operations of the adult. The mind develops by these processes, building its potential for complex, highly abstract reasoning on its original primitive sensorimotor activities. Although assimilation and accommodation are studied separately, they are actually two aspects of an identical process. There is an assimilation to structure, and an accommodation of structure. Assimilation implies accommodation, but the balance between the two varies. At any given time assimilation may dominate, while at other times accommodation may be the predominant state.

Once accommodation occurs, it changes the underlying structure and thus allows for future assimilations when a similar situation recurs. These additional adaptations need not depend solely on environmental stimulation. Internal reorganization of systems and integration with other systems develop routinely. To summarize, by intellectual functioning, Piaget means the complementary processes of assimilation and accommodation. Changes in the assimilatory structure help to direct new accommodations, and new accommodatory attempts in turn stimulate new structural reorganizations. Both of these intellectual functions are present in every intellectual act, thus ensuring mental progress.

If you understand adaptation, you understand one of the basic ideas in Piaget's system, because *this explains mental development.* Children constantly take in (assimilate) new material; as they do, they change (accommodate). These changes are the observable signs of cognitive development; underlying them is

FIGURE 8.3. The Interactive Nature of Assimilation and Accommodation.

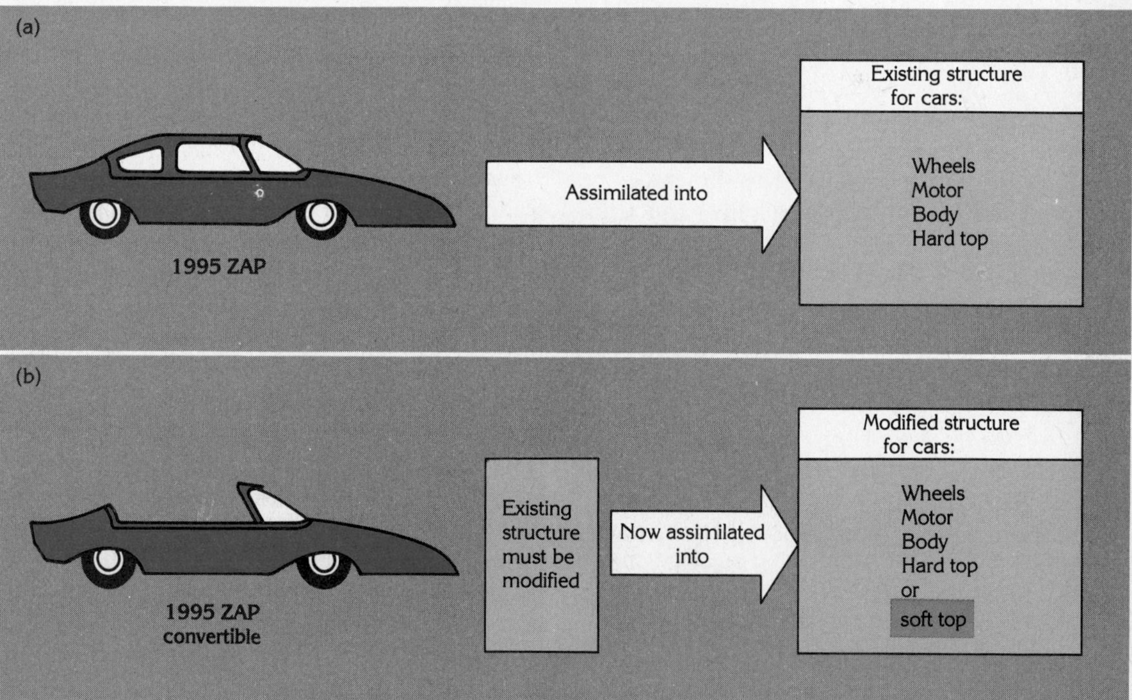

adaptation, which modifies existing structures and forms new cognitive structures. When you were in the fifth grade you could not understand Piaget's work, but now your cognitive structures have changed, cognitive development has occurred, and you can assimilate and accommodate to Piaget's ideas.

Finally, remember that assimilation and accommodation are a single process. There is assimilation to cognitive structures, and accommodation of cognitive structures.

Organization

The second of the functional invariants is organization. Piaget states (1952) that organization and adaptation are two complementary aspects of a single process. A physical example of organization is again a good introduction. All of your physical activities are organized. For example, you may be taking notes on your reading. Your fingers and arms move your pen across the page; your eyes scan each line; you use your fingers and arms to turn both the pages of the text and your notebook. You have organized all of your relevant physical structures to perform a smooth and harmonious activity.

You use exactly the same procedure in organizing your cognitive structures. A mental act is not a wild, random performance. Since cognitive structures are related, there must be harmony or organization among them. (Piaget's ideas are gradually being confirmed by the latest physiological research. Recall from your reading of recent brain research that neurons are *not* randomly connected.)

We use the cognitive structures formed by adaptation in an organized manner to adjust to our environment. Thus the functional invariants—organization and adaptation—are the unchanging properties of mental life.

CHANGING STRUCTURES—CHANGING BEHAVIOR

One of Piaget's famous examples clearly illustrates how cognitive structures affect behavior. If you place five tokens before a five-year-old preoperational child, give the youngster several other tokens, and then ask the child to match them with those on the table, there is little difficulty. The youngster will match them, one to one, and tell you that there is the same number in each row.

• • • • •

• • • • •

But if you now spread the top row, the five-year-old youngster says that there are more in the top row; it is impossible to match them.

•   •   •   •   •

• • • • •

The concrete operational youngster has no difficulty with the task and often thinks that there is a trick involved since both rows still have the same number.

What has happened here? The cognitive structures of the five-year-old are still quite limited, while those of the seven- or eight-year-old child are more flexible, or operational. These youngsters can understand more abstract tasks, and the change in their cognitive structures is reflected in their behavior. As the cognitive structures of preoperational youngsters continue to adapt and organize, using more complex stimuli, the structures change; by seven or eight years children have no difficulty with this and similar tasks.

Intelligence

The next key concept is that of intelligence. Piaget's primary concern is with intelligence, and anything else he discusses is significant only because of its relationship to intelligence. Piaget, the biologist, considers intelligence as a special instance of adaptation. Since life is a continuous interaction between organism and environment, the interaction implies an external coping and an internal organization. Living, then, becomes a continuous creation of more and more complex structures of body and behavior. The structures of the mind are constantly reorganized.

Regardless of one's criteria of intelligence, everyone agrees that it exists before language (Piaget and Inhelder, 1969). This practical intelligence is designed to achieve results rather than state truths. It is used to solve problems of action, such as reaching for an object. Before language is learned, such actions are based on perceptions and movements. We are speaking here not of the conventional interpretation of intelligence as a global capacity, nor the ability to think abstractly. For Piaget, an act of intelligence can be the infant's grasping of an object. He claims (Piaget and Inhelder, 1969) that while pure sensorimotor intelligence exists, one cannot say exactly when it appears. What happens is that a succession of stages appears, each advancing beyond the previous stage, until behavior appears that all psychologists would identify as intelligent.

Content. Piaget has distinguished among the content of intelligence, the function of intelligence, and the structure of intelligence. Flavell (1963) states that when Piaget mentions content, he means raw, uninterpreted behavioral data—what children say or do. Behavioral content is significant as a clue to a child's level of mental functioning (Figure 8.4).

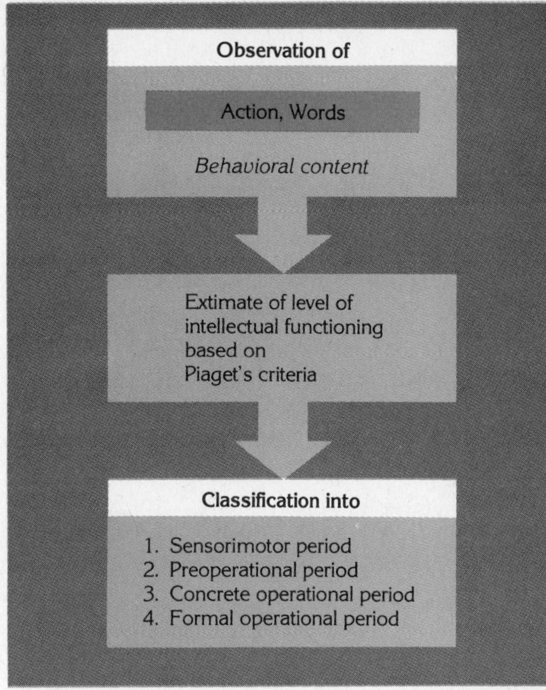

FIGURE 8.4. The Use of Content to Infer Level of Mental Functioning.

Structure. Piaget (1967) believes his studies show how children differ from adults in reasoning abilities. Certain logical-mathematical structures, for example, are not operative at all ages and hence cannot be innate. Also, *structure* is interposed between function and content. Structures change with age (Piaget states that they are not innate), and the identification of these changes has become a major focus of Piaget's work (Figure 8.5). Perhaps the best way to think of structure is to draw a parallel. The physical structure of the eye enables us to see; the physical structure of the ear enables us to hear. The psychological structures of the mind enable us to think and know. Just as the body has physical structures, so the mind has cognitive structures. Piaget states that we inherit a method of intellectual functioning based on our biological organization. In its contacts with the environment, our

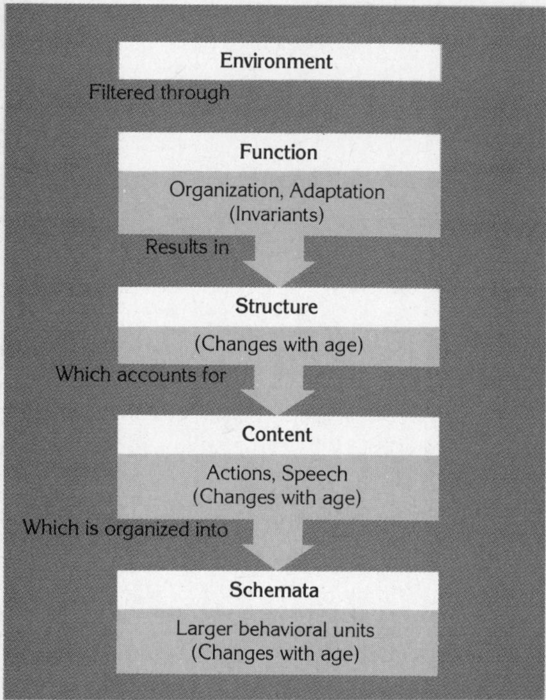

FIGURE 8.5. Structures, created by function, change with age, and may be inferred from content.

mind forms cognitive structures in accordance with our method of intellectual functioning. It is the changes in these structures because of assimilation and accommodation that account for cognitive development.

To summarize function, content, and structure, Flavell offers the following: function is the essence of any organism's cognitive progress; content is the external behavior that informs the observer that functioning is occurring; and structure is the inferred organizational property that explains why this behavior, instead of any other, has emerged.

Scheme. Akin to the idea of structure is the concept of scheme. Scheme is one of the most significant, but also most difficult, of Piaget's ideas. He defines scheme as the structure or organization of actions as they are transferred or generalized by repetition in similar or analogous circumstances (Piaget and Inhelder, 1969). Perhaps a scheme may best be thought of as the inner representation of our activities and experiences.

Some of the reflexes with which we are born, such as yawning or sneezing, are fixed in form. But others, such as grasping or sucking, require stimulation to develop. Each of these reflexes has an underlying mental apparatus. The scheme is named by its activity: the grasping scheme, the sucking scheme. But we must remember that it is this activity and more. Piaget (1952) states that it is highly probable that each reflex is accompanied by a particular state of awareness. Piaget frequently refers to the sucking scheme, a hereditary reflex. But it changes quickly. At first sucking anything that touches its lips, the infant soon displays a variety of sucking behaviors. It may suck in the absence of external stimulation; it soon begins to suck its fingers, for instance. By assimilation and accommodation, the original activity quickly diversifies and development proceeds. Our example, of course, refers to a beginning scheme. As the developing child, adolescent, and adult continue to employ schemes, these become more and more complex and abstract.

The scheme both assimilates information and accommodates to it. It is therefore a mobile, fluid cognitive structure that is created and modified by intellectual functioning. In summary, any intelligent act, whether an infant's grasping an object or an adult's exercising an abstract judgment, is always related to a basic structure. It presupposes a basic organization. This basic structure is the schema—what is generalizable in a given action (Piaget, 1973, p. 114).

Operations. Note how frequently the concept of *operations* appears in Piaget's writings—preoperational, concrete operational, formal operational. For Piaget, an operation is an interiorized reversible action.

> The operative aspect of thought relates to transformations and is thus related to everything that modifies the object, from the moment of the action until the operations. We will call operations the interiorized (or interiorizable), reversible actions (in the sense of being capable of developing in both directions and, consequently, of including the possibility of a reverse action which cancels the result of the first), and coordinated in structures, known as operatory, which present laws of composition characterizing the structure in its totality as a system. (Piaget, 1973, p. 76)

Here is an excellent example of the internal coherence of Piaget's system. Recall his insistence that mental development begins with reflex actions, which are gradually internalized with age and experience. But it is insufficient and inaccurate to state that symbolic competence reflects operations. In Piaget's quotation, reversibility was mentioned; a child must be able to return to a starting point. For example, if 2 + 2 = 4, then *operations* means that a child realizes 4 − 2 = 2.

Piaget flatly states (1964) that to understand the development of knowledge, you must understand the meaning of operation. Knowledge is *not* a copy of reality. To know an object is *not* to look at it or copy it. *To know an object is to act on it.* You modify it; you transform it; eventually you understand the process of the transformation; that is, you learn how to think about things. An operation is never isolated; it is always joined to other operations as part of a cognitive structure. Thus operational structures are the basis of knowledge.

These key concepts explain the mechanism and development of intelligence. Through the functional invariants cognitive structures are formed, coordinated, and changed as increasingly abstract material is assimilated and accommodated. But it is an interactive system, implying activity that leads to operational functioning, climaxing in propositional thinking. Understanding these concepts, you should now be able to trace cognitive development through the four major periods.

DISCUSSION QUESTIONS

1. As you have read, Piaget was dissatisfied with his initial work. Comment on his unhappiness with the use of verbally expressed thought alone. Do you think that verbal behavior is a satisfactory index of intelligence?
2. Be sure that you understand the biological nature of adaptation and organization. Show how Piaget uses these two concepts as the basis of his theory of development.
3. To comprehend the nature of Piaget's system, it is vital to understand the key concepts. Initially, be certain that you can distinguish content, function, and structure.
4. Structures change with age. What are the implications of this statement? Link your answer to your knowledge of content. What does it mean for parents and teachers?
5. What do you mean by the functional invariants? Be sure that you can distinguish between the two types. Is the comparison with biological adaptation valid?
6. Imagine a child of two or three who has a radio in her house, but has never seen television. She has been to the movies, however. Suddenly a television set is brought to the house and turned on. Describe her behavior in detail, employing Piaget's terms *structure, function, content,* and *scheme.*

THE PERIODS

If Piaget's conclusions are accurate, and mounting evidence supports him, there are tangible clues to the normal mental development of children. For parents, warning signals should flash if the infant fails to demonstrate any of the age-level characteristics detected by Piaget. While the timing of their appearance should not cause extreme concern (some youngsters obviously will display these characteristics later than others), the more that parents and teachers know about them, the greater the opportunities for discerning any potential problem.

As we noted earlier, there are four main periods or stages of mental development: sensorimotor, preoperational, concrete operational, and formal operational. Here we see the fruits of Piaget's earlier work: intelligence develops from the continuous transformation of the structures of intellect. The sequence of these periods and their approximate age span is as follows.

1. The sensorimotor (birth to about two years).
2. The preoperational (two to seven years).
3. Concrete operational (seven to eleven years).
4. Formal operational (eleven plus).

A child at each of these periods possesses certain characteristics that enable an observer to identify the child's level of mental development.

Concerning his notion of stages, Piaget (1973, p. 10) states:

> Thus we distinguish successive stages. Let us note that these stages are precisely characterized by their set order of succession. They are not stages which can be given a constant chronological date. On the contrary, the ages can vary from one society to another, as we shall see at the end of this report. But there is a constant order of succession. It is always the same and for the reasons we have just glimpsed; that is, in order to reach a certain stage, previous steps must be taken. The prestructures and previous substructure which make for further advance must be constructed.

The Sensorimotor Period

The sensorimotor period encompasses approximately the first two years of life. Flavell (1963) notes that during this period, the infant moves from a simple reflex level to comparatively coherent organization of sensorimotor actions. This organization is practical; that is, it entails elementary motor and perceptual adjustments instead of any kind of symbolic manipulation of objects. But the sensorimotor schemes developed during this period are the fundamentals that will later develop into the logical, abstract schemes of the adult.

Piaget (1967) states that the period from birth to language acquisition is marked by extraordinary mental development and influences the entire course of mental development. Several developmental changes occur that reflect what Piaget terms the "decentering process" as youngsters overcome the limitations of egocentrism.

Egocentrism describes the initial universe of children; the world centers on them. They see the world only from their point of view, with absolutely no awareness of any other point of view. Very young children lack social orientation; they speak at and not to each other, and two children in conversation will be discussing utterly unrelated topics. Egocentric adults know that there are other viewpoints, but they disregard them; the egocentric child simply is unaware of any other viewpoint.

EGOCENTRISM

The notion of egocentrism often causes considerable confusion since, to a certain extent, we are all egocentric. That is, we have a very human tendency to focus on ourselves even while we realize that there are viewpoints different from our own. Piaget, however, means something quite different by egocentrism. The egocentric child (and this applies to all children) neither knows nor cares about the desires or feelings of others.

Piaget (1954, p. x) summarizes egocentrism as follows:

> Through an apparently paradoxical mechanism whose parallel we have described apropos of the egocentrism of thought of the older child, it is precisely when the subject is most self-centered that he knows himself the least, and it is to the extent that he discovers himself that he places himself in the universe and constructs it by virtue of that fact.

Piaget traces the shortcomings in children's reasoning to egocentrism and to the unconsciousness that it causes (1928). Piaget believes that one of the initial results of egocentrism is that youngsters judge everything from their point of view. Children younger than seven or eight are absolutely assured. When asked how they "know" something, they usually reply "I know!" Facts may be wrong; the children are not. Piaget states (1928) that youngsters overcome this limitation through social intercourse; they begin to experience doubt and feel a growing need to verify their beliefs. Decreasing egocentricity parallels development through the cognitive stages:

1. During the sensorimotor period, the self is the center of reality; consciousness thus begins with an unconscious and integral egocentricity.
2. During the preoperational period, youngsters, while differentiating themselves from their environments, still cannot differentiate between their internal, subjective world and the physical universe. "The moon is following me around." "I'm going to sleep, so it must be night." As Piaget notes (1967), reality is construed with the self as the model.
3. During the concrete operational period, children of seven or eight think before acting; they begin to be liberated from their social and intellectual egocentricity and demonstrate the beginnings of logical thought (Piaget, 1967).
4. During the formal operational period, adolescent intellectual egocentricity is comparable to the infant's: they manifest egocentric assimilation since they believe the world should match their idealistic cognitive structures. Gradually there is a reconciliation between formal thought and reality and adolescents understand that the function of reflection is not to contract but to predict and interpret experience (Piaget, 1967, p. 64).

There are four major accomplishments of the sensorimotor period: object permanence (children realize that there are permanent objects around them; something out of sight is not gone forever); a sense of space (there is a spatial relationship among environmental objects); causality (there is a relationship between actions and their consequences); and, finally, they detect time sequences (one thing comes after another).

Object Permanence. Piaget states (1954) that object permanence is not a given; it is constructed little by little. There are six stages that approximate the infant's cognitive development during the sensorimotor period:

1. In Stages 1 and 2 (those of reflexes and earliest habits), there is no permanence nor spatial organization.
2. In Stage 3 (about four to eight months), the beginnings of permanence are observed when youngsters continue to grasp for something, but there is not yet a continued search for hidden objects.
3. In Stage 4 (about eight to twelve months), youngsters continue to search for hidden objects, but in a random manner.
4. In Stage 5 (about twelve to eighteen months), youngsters will search for the hidden object in the correct spot, but if the location is changed, they are baffled.
5. In Stage 6 (about eighteen months) they have an image of the object and search in various places.

The Spatial Field. Piaget notes (1954) that organization of the spatial field closely parallels that of the development of object permanence. There is a remarkable transition from a practical and egocentric space to a represented space containing the child. Initially there are as many uncoordinated spaces as there are sensory fields (oral spaces, visual spaces), each of which is centered on the child's movements and activities (Piaget, 1967, p. 14). By two years, children have acquired a sense of general space that includes all of the particular spaces; they also recognize the relationship among objects and between the objects and their bodies. Children's sense of space is derived from their actions during these years and is one aspect of a developing sensorimotor intelligence.

Causality. Piaget states (1954) that the notion of causality develops from an initial state in which the universe is a series of temporal settings to a final state in which children recognize a permanent world that obeys physical laws and of which they are one part. The progression is from egocentrism to objective relativism.

Causality thus commences its development with children's actions and egocentrism. For example, when an infant pulls a string attached to a rolling toy, the act of pulling is causally related to the effect of movement. Once this relationship develops, the child will pull the string in an attempt to continue movement in some object in another part of the room; for example, a curtain could be moved by the wind. This "magic causality" is overcome by the end of the second year when children recognize true causal relationships among objects.

Temporal Relations. Piaget believes (1954, p. 362) that time, like space, is constructed little by little and involves the elaboration of a system of relations. Typically, a sense of time begins with the infant's actions and the state of egocentrism, producing a sense that events are ordered by personal action. Since there is no separation between self and world, there is no recognition of a series of events.

At about four months, infants begin to order external events, but only when they are the cause. At about eight months, infants recognize the permanence of objects and exhibit a sense of causality in space; this forces them to arrange events in order, not only by their actions but also by natural sequence. They gradually extend this ability to all objects and events in their perceptual field. Finally, by about two years, this sense of time extends to representation; that is, youngsters use memory to place objects and events in the total chronology of their universe (Piaget, 1954, p. 394). Piaget concludes by noting that this chronology is not necessarily correct but the ability to order time now exists.

As children use growing sensorimotor intelligence, they begin to find order in the universe, they begin to distinguish their own actions as a cause, and they begin to discover events that have their cause elsewhere, either in other objects or in various relationships between objects (Piaget and Inhelder, 1969).

To summarize the characteristics of this period, children, utilizing the basic hereditary structures, expand them by use of the functional invariants, assimilation and accommodation and, by the end of the period, move from purely sensory and motor functioning (hence the name sensorimotor) to a more symbolic kind of activity. These remarkable changes occur within a sequence of six stages; most of Piaget's conclusions about these stages were derived from observation of his own three children. (Jacqueline, Lucienne, and Laurent are becoming as famous in psychological literature as some of Freud's cases or John Watson's Albert.)

> We call it the "sensorimotor period" because the infant lacks the symbolic function; that is, he does not have representations by which he can evoke persons or objects in their absence. In spite of this lack, mental development during the first eighteen months of life is particularly important for it is during this time that the child constructs all the cognitive substructures that will serve as a point of departure for his later perceptive and intellectual development, as well as a certain number of elementary affective reactions that will partly determine his subsequent affectivity. (Piaget and Inhelder, 1969, p. 3)

Stage I. During this stage children do little more than exercise the reflexes with which they were born. Infants possess fairly fixed and predictable reflexes that are developed by exercise and form the points of departure for development of the schemes of assimilation. These inborn reflexes become reflex exercises by means of functional exercise, which gradually becomes a generalizing assimilation (the grasping or sucking scheme). For example, Piaget states (1952) that the sucking reflex is hereditary and functions from birth. The infant will suck anything that touches the lips; then sucking will occur when nothing touches the lips; then the child actively searches for the nipple when the breast is presented. What we see here is the steady development of the coordination of arm, hand, and mouth.

Such behavior must be acquired, since there is no reflex or instinct for thumbsucking. Furthermore, this acquisition is not a random matter. It is incorporated into an existing scheme and extends the scheme by the integration of other sensorimotor elements (Piaget and Inhelder, 1969). Stage I marks the first transformation of the reflexive sensorimotor scheme, a shift from passive responsiveness to stimulation, to active groping. What causes this change from passive responsiveness to active exercising? Piaget's answer is assimilation. The assimilated exercise of functions produces its own inherent satisfaction through reinforcement of the familiar. This stage usually develops during the first month.

> Now this scheme, due to the fact that it lends itself to repetition and to cumulative use, is not limited to functioning under compulsion by a fixed excitement, external or internal, but functions in a way for itself. In other words, the child does not only suck in order to eat but also to elude hunger, to prolong the excitation of the meal, etc., and lastly, he sucks for the sake of sucking. (Piaget, 1952, p. 35)

Stage II. Piaget refers to Stage II (from about the first to the fourth month) as the stage of first habits. These habits are not to be equated with intelligence, however, since they depend on a general sensorimotor scheme and lack any differentiation between means and ends. The end is achieved by a succession of movements, whereas an intellectual act is characterized by a goal that is determined beforehand and by the use of means that are appropriate to the pursuit of that goal.

During Stage II, *primary circular reactions* appear in which infants repeat some act involving their bodies. For example, they continue to suck when nothing is present. They continue to open and close their hands, they continue to pull at a blanket. But there seems to be no external goal, no intent in these actions other than the pleasure of self-exploration.

These are repetitions of a sensorimotor sequence. The first response in a series is always novel to infants; what is significant is the activity that follows the initial response. Flavell (1963) states that because of reproductive or functional assimilation, infants tend to repeat that initial response frequently, thus

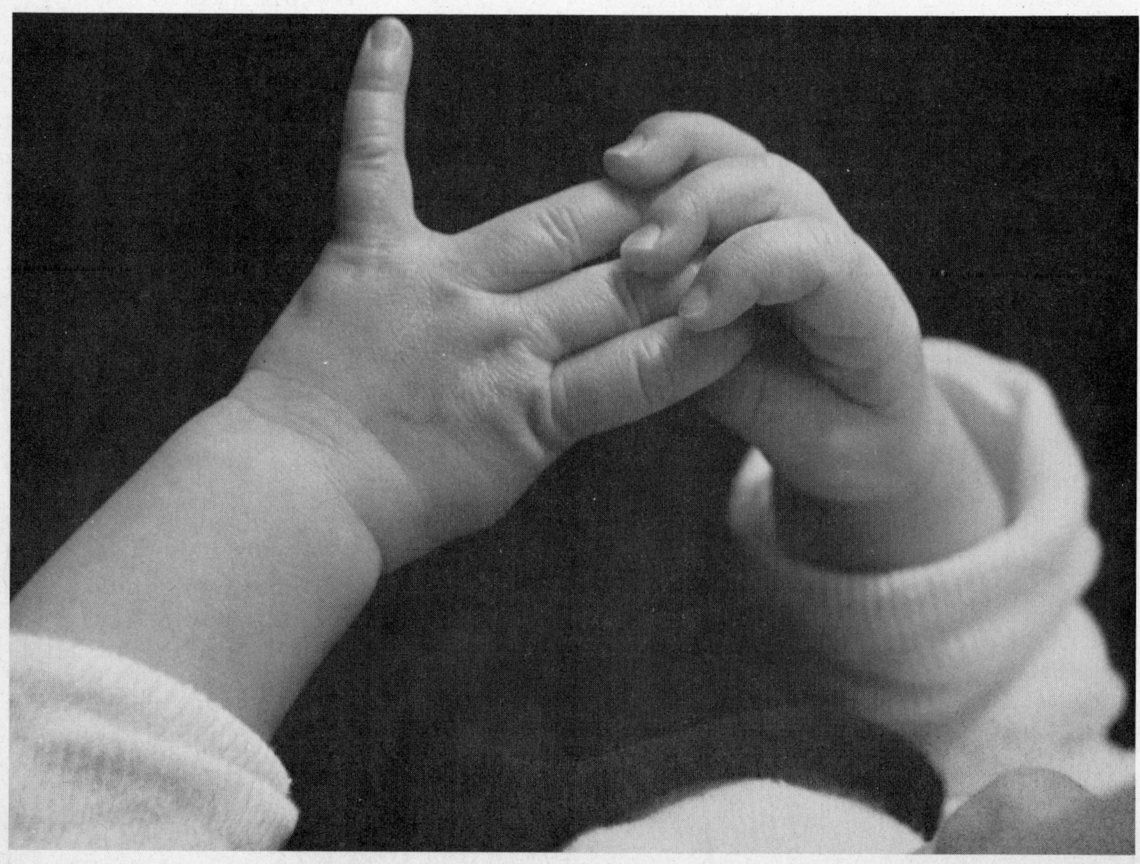

ensuring that the new response is strengthened and firmly incorporated into what is now a new scheme. Flavell also notes that the circular reaction is important because it is necessary for new adaptations that are critical to intellectual development.

> From 0;2(3)* Laurent evidences a circular reaction which will become more definite and which will constitute the beginning of systematic grasping; he scratches and tries to grasp, lets go, stretches and grasps again, etc. . . . But beginning 0;2(7) the behavior becomes marked in the cradle itself. Laurent scratches the sheet which is folded over the blankets, then grasps it and holds it a moment, then lets it go, scratches it again and recommences without interruption. (Piaget, 1952, p. 91)

Stage III. *Secondary circular reactions* appear during this stage, which extends from about the fourth to the eighth month. It is during Stage III that infants direct their activities toward objects and events outside themselves. Secondary circular reactions thus produce results in the environment, and not on the child's own body, as with the primary circular reactions. For example, Piaget's son, Laurent, continued to shake and kick his crib to produce movement and sound. He also discovered that pulling a chain attached to some balls produced an interesting noise; he then repeatedly pursued this activity.

Flavell believes that during this stage children demonstrate four major accomplishments. First, secondary circular reactions develop; they are similar to primary circular reactions, or repetition of chance adaptations. Now, however, the infants are more fascinated with the changes they produce in the environment than they are with their own bodily activities. Second, children manifest motor recognition, a tendency to direct movements in response to some object that customarily causes a secondary circular reaction. For example, when a child sees a doll that she has often grasped and swung, at this stage, she briefly opens and closes her hands with very real effort.

Third, there is the phenomenon of the generalization of secondary circular reactions, or "procedures for making interesting sights last" (Flavell, 1963, p. 101). What happens now is that infants incorporate new objects and events into existing schemes but, as Flavell notes, they act with little, if any, discrimination. Finally, this stage contains the first signs of intentional behavior, or behavior directed toward a definite goal. If behavior is concerned with objects and if intermediary acts are used as means to an end, then the behavior exhibits some intention. Stage III represents a transitional type of intentional behavior; goals appear after means are exercised. That is, the original actions are repetitive and not immediately adaptive. The baby, for example, strikes something accidentally, likes the noise, and repeats the action.

Stage IV. From about eight to twelve months of age, *infants coordinate secondary schemes* to form new kinds of behavior. Now more complete acts of intelligence are evident (Piaget and Inhelder, 1969). The child first decides on a goal (finding an object that is hidden behind a cushion), independent of any concern about means. The means or instrumental acts (moving the cushion) appear later. Piaget (1952) observes that a new act coordinates two or more independent schemata. One scheme becomes the instrument; the other becomes the goal. The infants attempt to move objects to reach the goal, but in Stage IV part of the goal object must be visible behind the obstacle. This limitation vanishes during later stages.

Piaget (1952) refers to the activities of this period as "removing the obstacles." Experimenting with Laurent, Piaget put his watch

* These numbers refer to the year, month, and day of life.

behind a cushion. At about five months, the baby tried to go over and around the cushion to get the watch. It was not until about eight months that Laurent removed the cushion to get the watch. Piaget suggests that such behavior constitutes the first visible acts of intelligence. Behavior is not merely reproduced; the infants desire a goal but have to overcome novel difficulties.

> Now, in order that the two schemata, until then detached, may be coordinated with one another in a single act, the subject must aim to attain an end which is not directly within reach and to put to work, with this intention, the schemata hitherto related to other situations. . . . The intelligent act is thus constituted, which does not limit itself merely to reproducing the interesting results, but to arriving at them due to new combinations. (Piaget, 1952, p. 211)

Stage V. *Tertiary circular reactions* appear from twelve to eighteen months. Recall that with secondary circular reactions, infants are primarily interested in the environmental results of their activity. In the tertiary circular reaction, there is again repetition, but it is repetition with variation. One receives the impression that the infant is exploring an object's possibilities. Piaget thinks that the infant deliberately attempts to provoke new results instead of merely reproducing activities. Thus, tertiary circular reactions indicate an interest in novelty for its own sake. As a result, this continuing interest in novelty produces the curiosity that motivates continuous growth and change in a child's cognitive processes.

Piaget (1953) describes, for example, changes in Laurent's behavior as he progressed from secondary to tertiary circular reactions. At ten months, Laurent discovered the pleasure of "letting things go." (Most of us are all too familiar with the baby's habit of dropping things. Have patience. Now you understand the reasons.) What interested Laurent at ten months was simply the act of letting go. But several months later he suddenly became fascinated with how and where the object fell. He tried to pick it up if he could; he dropped it in front of him, in back of him, to the side. As Piaget notes, the search for novelty lies at the heart of this stage of behavior.

Stage VI. The *invention of new means through mental combinations* characterizes this stage, which appears at about eighteen months. During this stage, the sensorimotor period ends and preoperational thought begins. Thus Stage VI is a transitional period that prepares children to use symbols. Now children can find new means not only by concise groupings, but also by internal combinations that produce sudden comprehension, or insight (Piaget and Inhelder, 1969). Children no longer act blindly, but stop and examine the situation before attempting to solve the problem; they wish to attain a goal but have no habitual schemes that they can use. Now rather than utilizing overt sensorimotor movements to solve the problem, youngsters "invent" a solution by a kind of internal experimentation.

Perhaps we can put it more simply by saying that in Stage VI children develop a basic kind of internal representation. A good example is the behavior of Piaget's daughter Jacqueline. At one year, eight months, she approached a door that she wished to close, but she was carrying some grass in each hand. She put down the grass by the threshold, preparing to close the door. But she stopped and looked at the grass and the door, realizing that if she closed the door, the grass would blow away. She then moved the grass away from the door's movement and then closed it. She had obviously planned and thought carefully about the event before acting.

The End of the Sensorimotor Period. The following table is a summary of the accomplishments of the sensorimotor period.

TABLE 8.1. Outstanding Characteristics of the Sensorimotor Period

The Six Subdivisions of This Period	
Stage 1.	During the first month the child exercises the native reflexes, for example, the sucking reflex. Here is the origin of mental development, for states of awareness accompany the reflex mechanisms.
Stage 2.	Piaget refers to Stage 2 (from 1 to 4 months) as the stage of *primary circular reactions.* Infants repeat some act involving the body, for example, finger sucking. (*Primary* means first, *circular reaction* means repeating the act.)
Stage 3.	From 4 to 8 months *secondary circular reactions* appear; that is, the children repeat acts involving objects outside themselves. For example, infants continue to shake or kick the crib.
Stage 4.	From 8 to 12 months, the child "coordinates secondary schemata." Recall the meaning of schema—behavior plus mental structure. During Stage 4, infants combine several related schemata to achieve some objective. For example, they will remove an obstacle that blocks some desired object.
Stage 5.	From 12 to 18 months, *tertiary circular reactions* appear. Now children repeat acts, but not only for repetition's sake; now they search for novelty. For example, children of this age continually drop things. Piaget interprets such behavior as expressing their uncertainty about what will happen to the object when they release it.
Stage 6.	At about 18 months or 2 years, a primitive type of representation appears. For example, one of Piaget's daughters wished to open a door but had grass in her hands. She put the grass on the floor and then moved it back from the door's movement so that it would not blow away.

The Preoperational Period

Piaget and Inhelder (1969) state that as the sensorimotor period concludes, the function of representation (the ability to represent something by means of a "signifier" such as language) appears. This period extends roughly from two to seven years of age. During this time the child acquires the ability for inner, symbolic manipulations of reality, and the great accomplishments of this period are the use of mental symbols and language. Piaget and Inhelder describe the emergence of what they call the *semiotic,** or symbolic function, as the appearance of behavioral patterns that indicate representational thought. They list five of these preoperational behavior patterns.

1. Deferred imitation, which continues after the disappearance of the model to be imitated.
2. Symbolic play, or the game of pretending.
3. Drawing, which rarely appears before two and one-half years.
4. The mental image, which is a form of internalized imitation.
5. Verbal evocation of an event not occurring at that particular time. A child may point to the door through which the father left and say "dada gone."

* Piaget prefers "semiotic" to "symbolic" because of the distinction that linguists make. Signs (semiotic) have socially shared meanings, while symbols are more private and noncodified, such as dreams or images used in symbolic play.

Imitation. The authors note that the first four of these behavioral patterns are based on imitation. For Piaget, imitation is mainly accommodation, as children attempt to change in order to conform to the environment. When the sensorimotor period ends, children are sufficiently sophisticated for the phenomenon of *deferred imitation* to appear. Piaget cites the example of a child who visited his home one day and while there had a temper tantrum. His daughter Jacqueline, about eighteen months old, watched, absolutely fascinated. Later, after the child had gone, Jacqueline had her own tantrum. Piaget interprets this to mean that Jacqueline had a mental image of the event.

Play. Piaget argues eloquently for recognizing the importance of play in a youngster's life. Obliged to adapt themselves to social and physical worlds that they only slightly understand and appreciate, children must make intellectual adaptations that leave personality needs unmet. For their mental health, they must have some outlet, some technique that will permit them to assimilate reality to self, and not vice versa. Children find this mechanism in play, using the tools characteristic of *symbolic play.*

Drawing. Piaget considers drawing as midway between symbolic play and the mental image. In drawing a person, for example, children go through some interesting and informative stages that demonstrate the increasing use of symbols.

1. Initially they make a head with arms and legs, but usually no body. The importance of the drawing seems to be merely the act of doing it.

BEHAVIOR AND COGNITIVE LEVEL

Gorman (1972) has developed an interesting technique for presenting the kinds of activities that the child is capable of doing at the various stages. Consider, for example, these two youngsters, both at the sensorimotor level. Can you identify the stages?

Child 1 (three months)
Opens and closes his fists.
Fingers his blanket.

Child 2 (four and one-half months)
Grasps at anything near him: his rattle, a cord, the side of the crib.

(Child 1 is manifesting primary circular reactions, while Child 2 is engaging in secondary circular reactions.)

Gorman then asks: What ability has the four-and-one-half-month-old child developed? He then poses two answers.

1. Manual movement and control.
2. Coordination of vision and manual movement.

Obviously the second child shows more advanced development than just manual movement and control. The ability to grasp things demands hand-eye coordination, which is a good example of a scheme—the grasping scheme. Gorman notes that these sensorimotor schemes foreshadow the cognitive coordinations and relationships that will develop years later.

Gorman's format is very interesting and a good supplement to the difficult work of Piaget. He sets problems (as above), asks questions, and gives several possible answers with an explanation of each.

2. There then comes a period of *intellectual realism* where, even if a profile is drawn, it will nevertheless have two eyes.

3. This period is followed by what is called *visual realism,* in which a profile has only one eye, and a pattern appears. Trees, houses, and people are all in correct proportion. This appears at about eight or nine years.

Mental Images. Mental images appear late in this period because of their dependence on internalized imitation. Piaget's studies of the development of mental images between the ages of four and five show that there are two categories of mental images. First, there are *reproductive images,* which are restricted to those sights previously perceived. Second, there are *anticipatory images,* which include movements and transformation. At the preoperational level, the child is limited to reproductive images.

A good illustration of the difference between the two is the previous example of matching tokens. Piaget gave five- and six-year-old children red tokens and asked them to put down the same number of blue tokens. At this age children will put one blue token opposite each red one. But if we change the arrangement and spread out the red tokens, the children are baffled because they now think there are more red tokens than blue. Thus they can reproduce but not anticipate, which reflects the nature of their cognitive structures and the level of cognitive functioning.

Symbolic play.

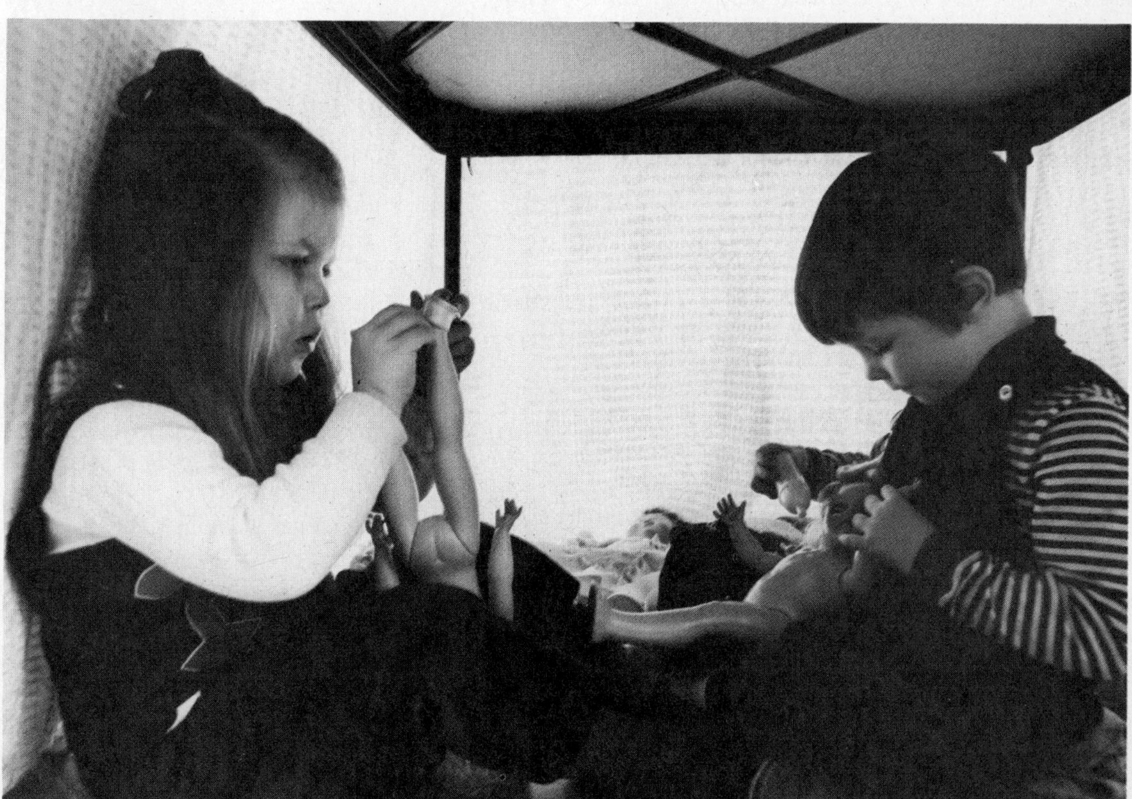

Language. Finally, language appears during this period after children have experienced a phase of spontaneous vocalization, usually between six and ten months; a phase of imitation of sounds at about one year; and one-word sentences at the end of the sensorimotor period. Piaget and Inhelder (1969) note that from the end of the second year the sequence is that of two-word sentences, short complete sentences and, finally, the gradual acquisition of grammatical structures.

In his early writings (1929), Piaget described three fascinating developmental characteristics of preoperational thought.

1. *Realism,* which means that children slowly distinguish, *and accept,* a real world, thus identifying both an external and internal world. Piaget believes that youngsters initially confuse the sign with the thing signified; they confuse internal and external; they confuse thought and matter. The confusion between sign and signifier disappears at about seven years, while the uncertainties about internal and external, thought and matter persist until about nine years.

2. *Animism,* which means that children consider a large number of objects as alive and conscious that adults consider inert. For example, a child who sees a necklace wound up and then released, when asked why it is moving replies that the necklace "wants to unwind." Children overcome these cognitive limitations as they recognize their own personalities; that is, they refuse to accept personality in things. Piaget also believes that, as with egocentrism, comparison with the thoughts of others—social intercourse—slowly conquers animism. Piaget identifies four stages of animism:

a. almost everything is alive and conscious;

b. only those things that move are alive;

c. only those things that manifest spontaneous movements are alive;

d. consciousness is limited to the animal world.

3. *Artificialism,* which consists in attributing human creation to everything. For example, when asked how the moon began, some of Piaget's subjects replied, "because we began to be alive." As egocentrism decreases, youngsters become more objective and they steadily assimilate objective reality to their cognitive structures. Thus they proceed from a purely human or divine explanation to an explanation that is half natural, half artificial: the moon comes from the clouds but the clouds come from people's houses. Finally, at about nine years they realize that human activity has nothing to do with the origin of the moon.

Although we see the steady development of thought during this period, there are still limitations to preoperational thought. Preoperational thought is not "good" thought compared to the conceptual forms into which it develops. As the name "preoperational" implies, this period comes before advanced symbolic operations develop. Piaget (in Ripple and Rockcastle, 1964) says that knowledge is not just a mental image of an object or event. To know an object is to act on it, to modify it, to transform it, and to join objects in a class. The action is also reversible. If two is added to two, the result is four; but if two is taken away from four, the original two returns. The preoperational child lacks the ability to perform such operations on concepts and objects.

There are several reasons for the restricted nature of preoperational thought.

1. *Egocentrism.* In the period of preoperational thought children cannot assume the role of another person or recognize that other viewpoints exist. This differs from sensorimotor egocentrism, which is primarily the

inability to distinguish oneself from the world. For example, preoperational children make little effort to ensure that listeners understand them. Lacking this recognition of other views, they neither justify their reasoning nor see any contradictions in their logic.

2. *Centration.* A striking feature of preoperational thought is the centering of attention on one aspect of an object and the neglecting of any other features. Consequently, reasoning is often distorted. Preoperational youngsters are unable to decenter, to notice features that would give balance to their reasoning. A good example of this is the process of *classification.*

"What things are alike?" When youngsters from three to twelve are asked this question, their answers proceed through three stages. First, the youngest children group figurally, that is, by similarities, differences, and by forming a figure in space with the parts. Second, children of about five or six years group objects nonfigurally; that is, they form the elements into groups with no particular spatial form. At this stage, from about five to six years, the classification seems rational, but Piaget and Inhelder (1969) provide a fascinating example of the limitations of classification at this age. If in a group of twelve flowers, there are six roses, these youngsters can differentiate between the other flowers and the roses. But when asked if there are more flowers or more roses, they are unable to reply because they cannot distinguish the whole without the part (Figure 8.6). This understanding does not appear until the third phase of classification, about the age of eight.

3. *States and Transformations.* Youngsters concentrate on a particular state or succession of states of an object and ignore transformations by which one state is changed into another. Their lack of conservation is a good example of the static nature of preoperational thought.

Conservation means understanding the notion that an object retains certain properties, no matter how its form changes. The most popular illustration is to show a five-year-old two glasses, each half filled with water. The child agrees that each glass contains an equal amount. But if you then pour the water from one of the glasses into a taller, thinner glass, the youngster now says that there is more liquid in the new glass (see Figure 8.7).

Youngsters consider only the static appearance of the liquid and ignore the fundamental transformation. They also do not perceive the reversibility of the transformation.

FIGURE 8.6. Lack of Genuine Classification.

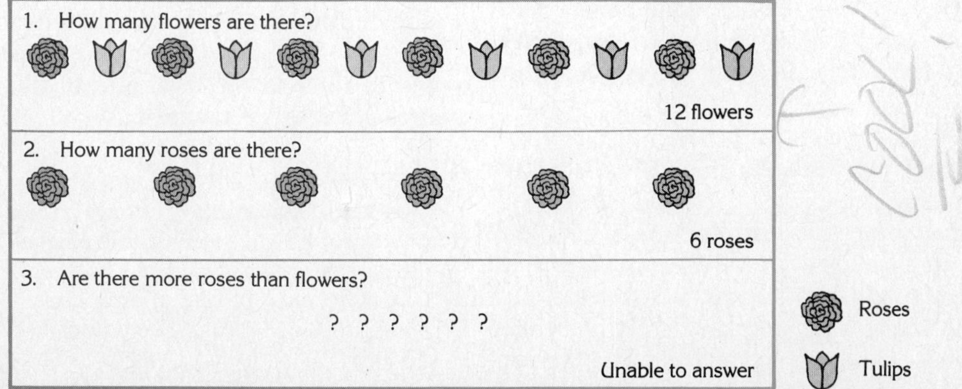

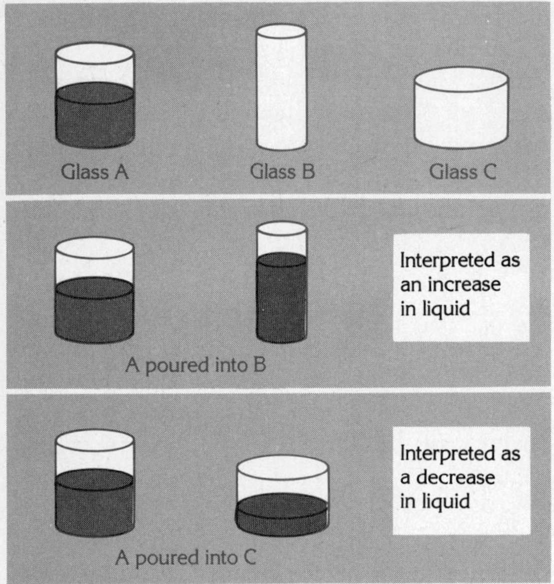

FIGURE 8.7. Lack of Conservation of Liquids.

4. *Irreversibility.* A truly cognitive act is reversible if it can utilize stages of reasoning to solve a problem and then proceed in reverse, tracing its steps back to the original question or premise. The preoperational child's thought is irreversible and entangles the child in a series of contradictions in logic. In the water-level problem, for example, the child believes that the taller, thinner glass contains more water. Youngsters cannot mentally reverse the task (imagine pouring the contents back into the original glass). At the conclusion of the preoperational period, children slowly decenter and learn reversibility as a way of mental life.

Concrete Operations

During the period of concrete operations, children overcome these limitations. They gradually employ logical thought processes with concrete materials; that is, with objects, people, or events that are immediately present to the senses. They decenter attention, concentrating on more than one aspect of a situation and following transformations, realizing that while surface elements may change, the essence remains the same (in the water-level problem, for example). They acquire conservation, and can now reverse their mental processes, realizing that if the water is poured back, the level will be the same.

> About the age of seven, a fundamental turning point is noted in a child's development. He becomes capable of a certain logic; he becomes capable of coordinating operations in the sense of reversibility, in the sense of the total system of which I will soon give one or two examples. This period coincides with the beginning of elementary schooling. Here again I believe that the psychological factor is the decisive one. If this level of the concrete operations came earlier, elementary schooling would begin earlier. (Piaget, 1973, p. 20)

There are still limitations to the child's ability at this time. Children at the level of concrete operations may be able to solve the water-level problem, but they cannot deal effectively with abstract theoretical problems—they are not concrete. Piaget and Inhelder (1969) state that if we compare the levels of preoperation and concrete operations, we witness a transition from subjective centering to a cognitive, social, and moral decentering. In the water-level problem, for example, children no longer concentrate solely on the height of the water in the glass; they also consider the width of the glass. The authors claim that this transition is particularly remarkable because it reproduces and expands at the level of thought what has already occurred at the sensorimotor level.

> This period is that of a logic which is not based on verbal statements but only on like objects themselves, the manipulable objects. This will be a logic of classifications because objects can be collected all together or in classifications; or else it will be a logic of relations because

A conservation task.

> objects can be combined according to their different relations; or else it will be a logic of numbers because objects can be materially counted by manipulating them. This will thus be a logic of classifications, relations, and numbers, and not yet a logic of propositions. (Piaget, 1973, p. 21)

But as Piaget notes, concrete operational children nevertheless demonstrate a true logic since they now can *reverse operations.*

Flavell (1963), in commenting on this period, notes that preoperational children differ from sensorimotor infants because they function on the plane of representation instead of the plane of action. He believes that children at the level of concrete operations differ from preoperational children because the older children (at the level of concrete operations) utilize a coherent and integrated cognitive system in adapting to reality. That is, concrete operational children act as if a rich and integrated assimilatory organization were functioning in equilibrium with a discriminative accommodatory mechanism. The most significant aspect of this level is that children now possess internal representational classifications that have joined to form increasing complex and tightly integrated systems of action. Concrete operational children, for example, can solve the water-level problem; they know the water remains the same.

Concrete operations are the bridge between the schemes of mere action and the logico-mathematical schemes of the adult. But while concrete operations are coordinated into total structures, the structures are still shaky and permit only step by step reasoning. The structures themselves include both classifications and seriations. The essence of these structures, which Piaget designates as groupings, is to constitute progressive logical sequences that involve many combinations of operations. An example of these structures would be seriation, the ability to arrange elements in increasing or decreasing size. The beginnings of seriation are apparent at the sensorimotor level when the child builds a pyramid of blocks whose dimensional differences are clearly seen. At the level of concrete operations, a systematic method of seriation develops that enables the youngster to identify the smallest, and then the next smallest, and so on.

For example, if preoperational children are presented with sticks of progressively greater length that are then rearranged, the children cannot put them in the correct sequence. Or if presented with three sticks, A, B, and C, they can tell you that A is longer than B and C, and that B is longer than C. But if we now remove A, they can tell you that B is longer than C, but not that A is longer than C. They must see A and C together. The child at the level of concrete operations has no difficulty with this problem.

But limitations remain. Piaget states that if the operation is in pure language, the problem becomes more complicated and the concrete operational child cannot solve it. He gives the example (1973, p. 22) of three young girls with different colored hair. The question is who has the darkest hair of the three. Edith is lighter than Suzanne but darker than Lili. Who has the darkest hair? Piaget believes that propositional reasoning is required to realize that it is Suzanne and not Lili, which youngsters do not achieve until about twelve years. While the problem is still seriation, it is a verbal statement.

The child at this level also becomes adept at classification. If you recall our flower problem, the preoperational child had difficulty classifying roses as flowers. In a classic experiment illustrating mastery of classification, Piaget showed a girl about twenty brown wooden beads and two or three white wooden beads. He then asked her to separate the brown from the white beads. Children at both the preoperational and concrete levels can do this. But he asked her, "Are there more brown beads or wooden beads?" The preoperational child answered "brown," while an older child answered correctly.

Another interesting characteristic of this period is the child's acquisition of the *number concept* (Figure 8.8). This is not the same as the ability to count. If five red tokens are more spread out than five blue ones are, preoperational children, although able to count, still think there are more red than blue tokens. Piaget then constructed an ingenious device that enables a child to trace the blue to the red. The preoperational child can actually move the blue token to the corresponding red, but still thinks there are more red tokens! It is with seriation plus classification that the child understands the "oneness of one" that one boy, one girl, one apple, and one orange are all one of something.

When these thought systems of the concrete operational child come into a well organized equilibrium, Piaget refers to them as

FIGURE 8.8. Encouraging Acquisition of Number Concept.

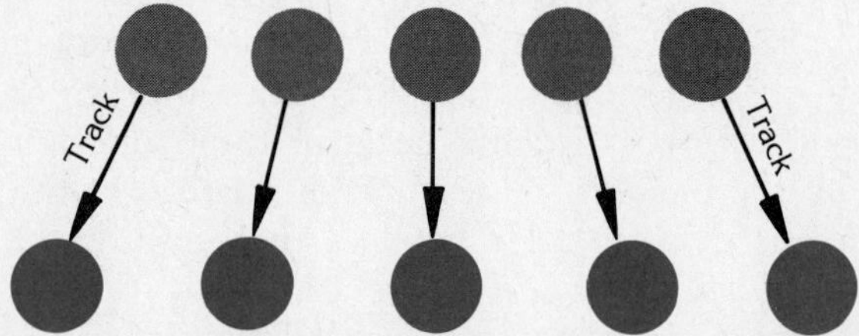

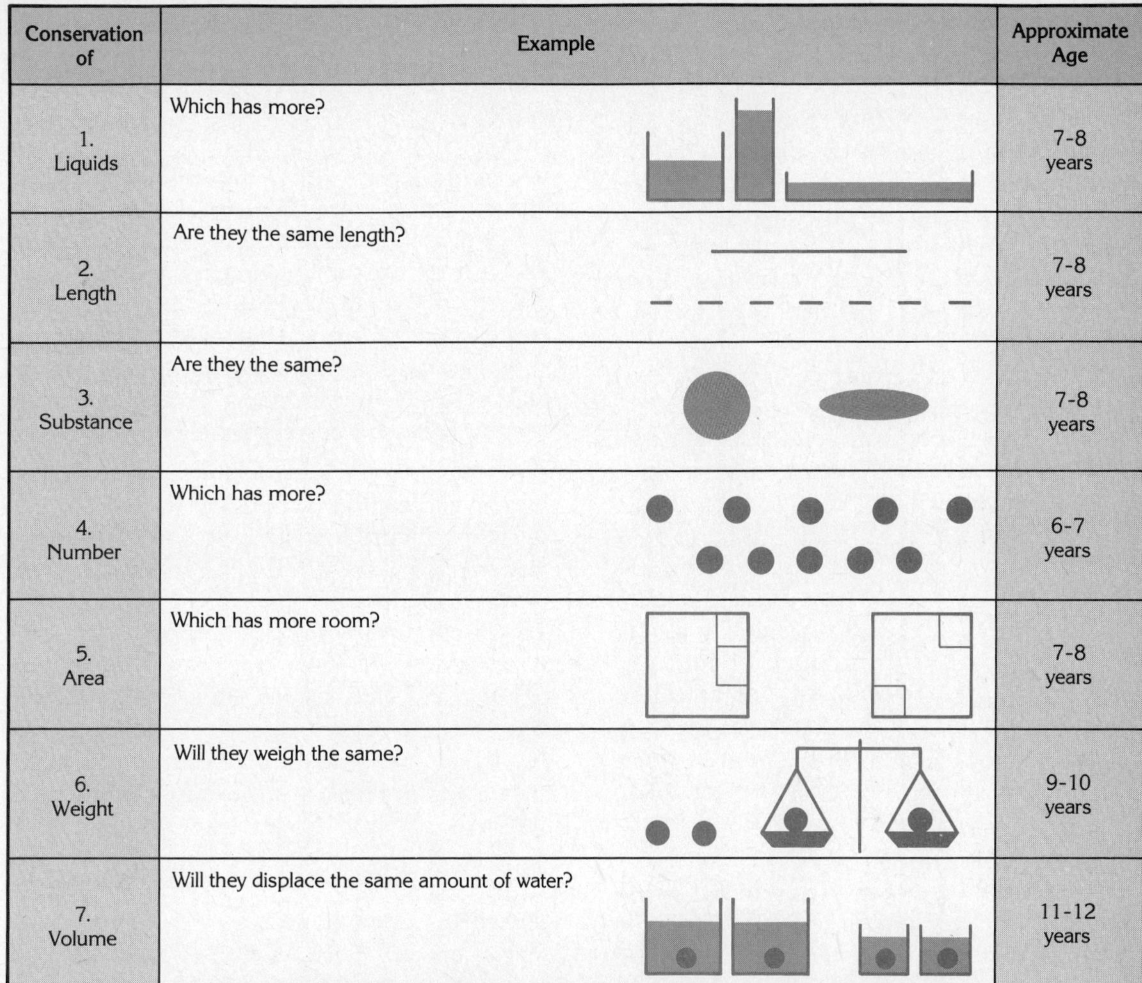

Conservation of	Example	Approximate Age
1. Liquids	Which has more?	7-8 years
2. Length	Are they the same length?	7-8 years
3. Substance	Are they the same?	7-8 years
4. Number	Which has more?	6-7 years
5. Area	Which has more room?	7-8 years
6. Weight	Will they weigh the same?	9-10 years
7. Volume	Will they displace the same amount of water?	11-12 years

FIGURE 8.9. Different Kinds of Conservation Appear at Different Ages.

cognitive operations (Flavell, 1963). The child's tendency to react to a set of different things as similar for some particular reason constructs a class (roses and carnations are both part of the class of flowers). When children reach this phase of cognitive development they are on the threshold of adult thought, or formal operations.

Associated with the accomplishments of this period is the notion of conservation; that is, youngsters realize that the essence of something remains constant although surface features may change. (See Figure 8.9.)

Piaget (1973) believes that youngsters conserve when they use three arguments:

1. *The argument of identity.* For example, think of the water-level problem illustrated in Figure 8.7. The concrete operational child says that since nothing has been removed or added, it is still the "same thing." Piaget states (1973) that by eight years children are amused by the problem, not realizing that a year earlier they probably would have given a different answer.

2. *The argument of reversibility.* Again using the water problem, concrete operational children state that you just have to pour it back and it is the "same thing."

3. *The argument of compensation.* Concrete operational children will say that the water is higher in the taller beaker but it is narrower. That is, these youngsters compensate for the height increase by noting the circumference decrease and realize that it is the "same thing."

> Indeed, if we compare the preoperatory subperiod between two and seven or eight with the subperiod of completion between seven or eight and eleven or twelve, we see the unfolding of a long, integrated process that may be characterized as a transition from subjective centering in all areas to a decentering that is at once cognitive, social, and moral. This process is all the more remarkable in that it reproduces and develops on a large scale at the level of thought what has already taken place on a small scale at the sensorimotor level. (Piaget and Inhelder, 1969, p. 128).

Formal Operations

This period is the peak of intellectual development, and as Piaget and Inhelder (1969) state, it is the time (between eleven and fifteen) when subjects free themselves from the concrete and discover reality within a group of abstract possibilities. Youngsters can now function effectively at the level of hypothesis, utilizing propositions that are unrestricted by any dependence on immediate concrete observations.

The authors argue that although this period signals the establishment of a new group of structures, these are both completions and natural extensions of preceding structures. Until this period of development, logical organization depends on content and not on hypotheses. The great value of the period of formal operations is that individuals can reason correctly about propositions that they do not believe, that is, about the purely hypothetical.

Combinations. The basic achievement of the concrete operational period was reversibility, which permits youngsters to overcome the limitations of the preoperational period. Piaget and Inhelder (1969, p. 136) state that there are two forms of concrete operational reversibility: *inversion* and *reciprocity.* Inversion refers to negation: an inverse operation combined with a corresponding negative operation neutralizes the entire procedure ($+A - A = 0$). For example, in the seesaw experiment, a weight is placed at one end and the problem is then posed: How can you balance it? Inversion simply means taking the weight off; we negate the action by reversing it.

Inversion

Reciprocity means that the original operation combined with its reciprocal results in equivalence. Flavell (1963) refers to reciprocity as a neutralization process; that is, one effect is held constant while a second element is varied. He gives the example of determining the separate effects of metal and length on the flexibility of a rod. Older children utilize the process of reciprocity. They first take two rods of different metals but of the same length. Thus, length is neutralized, while the type of metal is varied. They then reverse the operation and use two rods of a single metal and different lengths. They now have tested both metal and length to determine flexibility.

Another example relates to the seesaw problem. How can the seesaw be balanced? If we place a lighter weight at the farther end, the length compensates for the lesser weight.

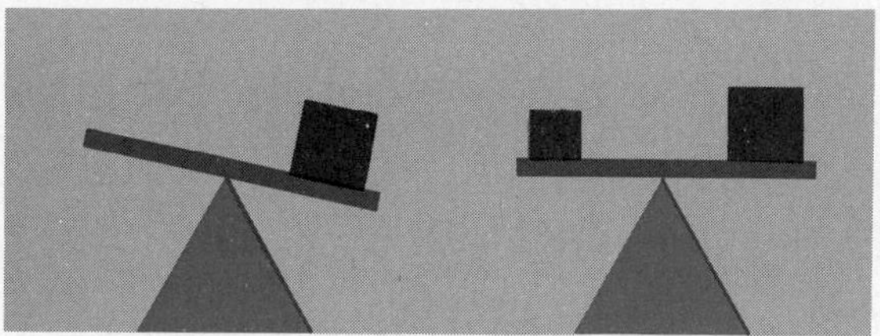

Reciprocity

These two forms of reversibility function separately in the concrete operational child. But Piaget and Inhelder (1969) state that formal operational children's newly acquired independence of content permits them to combine inversions and reciprocities. This new system is a synthesis and not merely a temporary linkage of separate elements. Inversions and reciprocities fuse into an operational whole. Flavell comments that the most significant issue during this period concerns the real versus the possible. Adolescents encounter a problem and attempt to evaluate all the possible relations that could aid in its solution. They then perform experimental and logical tests to determine those that are valid for this particular problem. Which of the possible solutions solves this problem?

> Henceforth every operation will at once be the inverse of another and the reciprocal of a third, which gives four transformations: direct, inverse, reciprocal, and inverse of the reciprocal, the latter also being the correlative (or dual) of the first. (Piaget and Inhelder, 1969, pp. 138–139)

These four transformations constitute the famous INRC group; that is, when adults and adolescents encounter problems, their cognitive structures possess the capability of employing four transformations:

1. I (Identity), a transformation that changes nothing; if you recall your algebra, $a + b = 1(a + b)$.

2. N (Negation), a transformation that changes everything. Piaget gives the example of a light continually flashing when a moving object stops ($P \supset Q$, or light implies stop). Negation means that the light would flash without the object stopping.

3. R (Reciprocal), a transformation that varies the elements. For example, perhaps the light instead of causing the stop, is caused by it ($Q \supset P$). (Note how negation and reciprocal, both forms of reversibility, differ in action.)

4. C (Correlative), a transformation that confirms the reciprocal. To prove that stop causes light, determine if the object ever stops without the light.

Piaget and Inhelder (1969) state that adolescents utilize these four transformations in formal operational thinking as follows:

> *First,* they organize data by concrete operational techniques (classification, seriation).
>
> *Second,* they use the results of concrete operational techniques to form statements or propositions.
>
> *Third,* they combine as many of these propositions as possible (these are hypotheses, and Piaget often refers to this process as hypothetico-deductive thinking).
>
> *Fourth,* they then test to determine which combinations are true (Travers, 1979).

So our journey is complete. Piaget has traced development from the sensorimotor abilities of the infant to the abstract, logical thought processes of the adolescent and the adult. Individuals can now deal with verbal, hypothetical situations, and by assimilation and accommodation, they continue to create and expand cognitive structures. But one critical question remains unanswered: What are the agents that are responsible for movement from one period to another?

DISCUSSION QUESTIONS

1. Give some examples of deferred imitation that you have seen in children. How do you interpret such behavior? What does it indicate to you?
2. All of us have observed children at play. Describe some specific examples that you have seen. Is it possible to give them an interpretation based on Piaget's theories?
3. Flavell mentions that one of the limitations of the preoperational period is centration. What precisely does he mean? How does it apply to a child's behavior? How does it affect his judgment about people, objects, and events?
4. What does it mean to say that a cognitive act is "reversible"? What are the advantages of reversibility? How does irreversibility hinder a youngster?
5. Let us assume that you spread six paperbacks and four hardcover books in front of a youngster. He tells you there are ten books; then he tells you there are six paperbacks. He cannot tell you whether there are more books than paperbacks. Which of Piaget's periods does he represent? Why?
6. Suppose that you ask a child, "Janie, can you count from one to twenty?" The child counts. Now you ask, "Janie, can you add seven and six?" She does so. "Good. Now, how do I get seven again?" If the child answers correctly, what is the period she represents? Why?

INFLUENCES ON MENTAL DEVELOPMENT

In summarizing their presentation of the various periods, Piaget and Inhelder (1969) assert that there are characteristics that hold true for all of the periods, regardless of level.

1. The order of succession is constant, although the age at which children enter the different periods varies from individual to individual.

2. Each period possesses a basic structure that explains the behavioral pattern of that particular period.

3. Each structure emerges from previous structures and prepares for a newer, more complex structure. Piaget (1964) also describes a mechanism for the formation of the periods. Four influences help to explain the passage from one period to another: maturation, experience, social transmission, and equilibration. None of these alone explains development; the interaction of all four is the key.

An underlying agent in mental development is the *maturation* of both the nervous and the endocrine systems. Unless maturation occurs, behavior patterns will be retarded. Maturation alone, however, is inadequate to explain the totality of intellectual development.

We know little about maturation except that it makes possible the emergence of novel behavior. It tells us nothing about the ages at which the different periods appear. While organic maturation is necessary, it does not explain all development. The ages for advancement through the periods in the children of Geneva are not the same ages as in the children in the United States. The youngsters of the Iranian countryside are two years behind the children of the capital, Teheran (Piaget, 1964).

Experience means the experience of actions performed on objects. There are two kinds of experience. First, there is physical experience, which means acting on objects to abstract their properties. To determine which of two objects is heavier, pick them up and lift them. Second, there is a logicomathematical experience, which implies acting on objects but with the intention of learning the result of a coordination of these actions. For example, ten pebbles in a row or circle are still ten pebbles. When children discover this, they know that their actions bring order.

By itself, experience is insufficient to explain all the phenomena of development. Piaget (1964) gives the example of the conservation of substance, which appears at about eight years. No perception or experience can explain the appearance of this aspect of conservation.

By *social transmission* Piaget and Inhelder (1969) mean that children can receive information because they possess the necessary structures. Neither linguistic nor social transmission is effective without complete assimilation by children. That is, to receive information, they must possess structures that enable them to assimilate the information. This is undoubtedly the main reason why Piaget looks with disfavor on attempts to hurry the youngster through the four stages.

Any one of the above three influences or any combination of them is still inadequate to explain mental development. *Equilibration* is a process of self-regulation that is manifested by a succession of satisfactory balances between assimilation and accommodation levels of equilibrium (Piaget, 1964). Some internal mechanism seems to be functioning whenever a child moves from one period to another. The process of reaching equilibrium or self-regulation represents a series of compensations by the individual to external disturbances. Perhaps equilibration is the basic influence on development; it is necessary in order to reconcile maturation, experience, and social transmission. Equilibration by self-regulation is, in fact, the formative process of the structures (Piaget and Inhelder, 1969).

Speculation about the periods and the influences that facilitate mental development leads to the inevitable question: Is it possible to accelerate passage through the periods? Piaget believes that acceleration is certainly possible, but he then asks another question: Is it desirable to encourage acceleration? He reasons that perhaps gradual progress in the assimilation of new concepts is desirable, since ease of learning varies with the developmental level of the child. His answer raises still another vital question: What is the relationship between brain growth and cognitive development?

A PIAGETIAN ASSESSMENT TECHNIQUE

Uzgiris and Hunt, inspired by Piaget's work, have devised an infant assessment technique based on the principle that development is an epigenetic process of evolving new, more complex, hierarchical levels of organization in intellect and motivation (1975, p. 47). Their procedure involved the following steps.

1. Identifying those infant actions that Piaget believed indicated new levels of cognitive organization.
2. Arranging these actions, and the circumstances that evoked them, into schedules.

3. Examining, in their homes, a representative sample of male and female infants to determine the proper selection of appropriate toys and materials.
4. Training a second examiner to ensure interexaminer reliability.
5. Using the resulting instrument to study infant development longitudinally to determine if Piaget's proposed sequential order is indeed accurate.

The first phase of test construction required a list of eliciting situations that Piaget believed would evoke infant actions illustrating a certain level of sensorimotor development. Experiments with forty-two infants convinced the authors that they had successfully identified critical situations.

The second phase entailed the establishment of interexaminer reliability, which had to be separated from the issue of infant consistency (infants' behavior changes from one testing to the next). The authors also revised the situations, attempting more standardization, and abandoned any attempts to quantify their results. Rather than rigidly follow Piaget's six stages of the sensorimotor period, the authors use five age periods: zero to four months, four to eight months, eight to fifteen months, twelve to eighteen months, and eighteen to twenty-four months. These five categories encompassed sixty-three situations (for example, following a slowly moving object, hand-mouth coordination).

The third phase commenced by examining a third group of eighty-four infants to determine interexaminer reliability and intersession stability, both of which remained quite high. The mean percentages of examiner agreement ranged from a low of 93.1 for infants in the four to seven month group to a high of 96.9 for infants in the eighteen to twenty-four month group. The consistency of infant reaction to the same situation in the forty-eight-hour interval was so apparent that the authors questioned the popular belief that infant tests are unreliable (Uzgiris and Hunt, 1975, p. 95).

The authors again revised the instrument, grouping the eliciting situations into six series, or ordinal scales. (An ordinal scale implies a hierarchical relationship between achievements at different levels; each level is intrinsically derived from the preceding level.) These are:

1. *Visual pursuit and the permanence of objects.* The authors believe that development of this category suggests the appearance of representational thought.

2. *Development of means for obtaining desired environmental events.* Here infants combine the use of one behavior (means) with another (the goal).

3. *Development of imitation.* Infants achieve two forms of imitation: vocal and gestural.

4. *The development of operational causality.* By the end of the sensorimotor period infants attempt to find objective causes.

5. *The construction of object relations in space.* Beginning with the recognition that objects differ in their position in space (about two months), older infants (eighteen months) remember the whereabouts of familiar objects and people.

6. *The development of schemes for relating to objects.* Infants initially use objects incidentally (about two months), but later (about eighteen months) they show specific objects and name them.

The authors conclude by noting that while the scales are still tentative, evidence justifies their use. The scales permit comparison of infants but do not depend on any correlation with age; while age standardization could be useful, the tremendous variation in the age at which infants achieve each landmark limit the value of conventional standardization. Consequently, these scales, while still provisional, are a milestone in the quest for assessment techniques to measure infant cognitive development.

CHALLENGE AND REBUTTAL

Piaget does not lack for detractors. Any system so sweeping attracts considerable critical attention, both theoretical and methodological. Theoretically, one either agrees or disagrees with Piaget's assumptions. Methodology, however, invites more subtle attacks. If techniques and instruments can be shown to be faulty, questions can be raised about the truthfulness of the entire theory. For example, Bryant (1974) states, as a result of his work, that children reason earlier than Piaget claims. Dasen (1972), using cross-cultural research, questions the universality of Piaget's stages. Bower (1977), as a result of his research, believes that one-month-old infants show surprise at the failure of an object to reappear.

There are many similar studies, and Larsen (1977) has written a thoughtful critique of the critics. Noting that Piaget's concern is with qualitative aspects of development, not quantitative, he states that critics are primarily conscious of quantitative and isolated characteristics. For example, Brainerd (1973) believes that the major issue for establishing age and sequence of behavioral development is the proper identification of the criteria that indicate whether one has or does not have the concept. Can children explain their reasoning, or do we merely accept their judgment (there is more water in the taller beaker)? Brainerd states that much of the confusion surrounding the conservation literature reflects these two criteria: judgment only or judgment plus explanation. Brainerd argues for judgments only, thus removing language as a criterion.

Larsen (1977) believes that Brainerd's concern for criteria reflects a desire to treat Piagetian concepts as separate, unrelated test items. Thus, cognitive growth becomes the linear accumulation of concepts, which is not Piaget's goal. Piaget is not only concerned with whether a child "has" a concept, but also "how he has it." Larsen also disagrees with those who state that it is impossible to conclude that a child does *not* have a certain cognitive capacity because we cannot positively isolate all pertinent variables. He notes that this argument is an appeal to "peripheral" explanation while ignoring the central fact—the youngster's understanding of conservation.

The arguments pro and con rage unabated, but one conclusion is inescapable: Piaget's role in interpreting cognitive development is paramount, and both attacks on and defenses of his position contribute to the quality of knowledge about cognitive development.

You may have found this chapter extremely difficult. If so, it is only hoped that your struggle to understand it will achieve desirable results. What are these results? You probably will never look at children in quite the same way again. You will evaluate their reactions by intellectual level or by the notion of conservation that they exhibit. Certainly those responsible for children will now examine environmental materials more critically. Are these materials suitable for the intellectual level of the youngster? Do they permit assimilation and encourage accommodatory extension?

And yet there is a sense of disappointment at the conclusion of any discussion of Piaget and his work. So much remains unsaid. To trace the experimental evidence that substantiates and challenges Piaget is a fascinating experience. To diverge, as in the construction of a learning theory, is tempting. Of one thing we can all be certain: the influence of this man and his work is monumental.

SUMMARY

Piaget's system is a theory that traces the mental development of the child from birth through adolescence and adulthood.

The system has deep biological and philosophical roots that reflect Piaget's own experiences and preferences.

Piaget considers himself a genetic epistemologist, that is, an investigator of the changes in the child's acquisition of knowledge over a period of years.

Children's cognitive development reflects the functional invariants of organization and adaptation.

Assimilation (the taking in and modifying of stimuli) and accommodation (changes in the child) are the keys to development.

These processes aid children in passing through the four great mental periods: sensorimotor, preoperational, concrete operational, and formal operational.

Each of these periods has characteristics that indicate the level of mental functioning.

During the sensorimotor period, children's activities center on their physical interactions with the environment.

During the preoperational period, children manifest signs of primitive mental activity, but it is limited by egocentrism, lack of conservation, centration, and irreversibility.

During the period of concrete operations, children demonstrate logical thought processes that are nevertheless restricted to concrete materials.

Finally, during the period of formal operations, adolescents and adults engage in verbal, abstract, and hypothetical reasoning processes that are the culmination of cognitive development.

Passage through these periods is facilitated by maturation, experience, social transmission, and equilibration.

Assessment techniques reflecting Piaget's theory offer bright promise for mental testing.

SUGGESTED READINGS

While the listing of reference after reference has been largely avoided here, those who want to read more about Piaget would probably welcome some guidance. The following readings are offered in that spirit. While in general you should probably read primary sources, the suggested sequence for Piaget is reversed. Since Piaget's ideas are so complex and his writing so difficult, secondary sources on his work are the best introduction.

ALMY, MILLIE, E. CHITTENDEN, and P. MILLER. *Young Children's Thinking.* New York: Teachers College Press, Columbia University, 1966.

BALDWIN, ALFRED. *Theories of Child Development.* New York: John Wiley & Sons, Inc. 1967.

BEARD, RUTH. *An Outline of Piaget's Developmental Psychology for Students and Teachers.* New York: Basic Books, 1969.

FLAVELL, JOHN. *The Developmental Psychology of Jean Piaget.* New York: D. Van Nostrand, Inc., 1963.

GINSBURG, HERBERT, and SYLVIA OPPER. *Piaget's Theory of Intellectual Development: An Introduction.* Englewood Cliffs, N.J.: Prentice-Hall, 1979.

PHILLIPS, JOHN. *The Origins of Intellect: Piaget's Theory.* San Francisco: W. H. Freeman, 1969.

WADSWORTH, BARRY. *Piaget's Theory of Cognitive Development.* New York: David McKay, 1979.

Piaget's writings are so extensive that unless you organize them for reading in correct sequence, it becomes difficult to grasp the logic for his system. His first efforts at presenting his theory include the following.

PIAGET, JEAN. *The Language and Thought of the Child.* New York: Harcourt, Brace, and World, 1926.

———. *Judgment and Reasoning in the Child.* New York: Harcourt, Brace, and World, 1928.

———. *The Child's Conception of the World.* New York: Harcourt, Brace, and World, 1929.

———. *The Child's Conception of Physical Causality.* New York: Harcourt, Brace, and World, 1930.

———. *The Moral Judgment of the Child.* New York: Harcourt, Brace, and World, 1932.

All of these texts are available in paperback, but you should be careful, since these are the initial expressions of a system that is quite complicated. The sheer availability of these books should not blind you to the changes that have occurred since their publication. Later, more representative writings include:

PIAGET, JEAN. *The Child and Reality.* New York: The Viking Press, 1973.

———. *Psychology of Intelligence.* London: Routledge and Kegan Paul, Ltd., 1950.

———. *The Origins of Intelligence in Children.* New York: International Universities Press, 1952.

PIAGET, JEAN, and BARBEL INHELDER. *The Psychology of the Child.* New York: Basic Books, 1969.

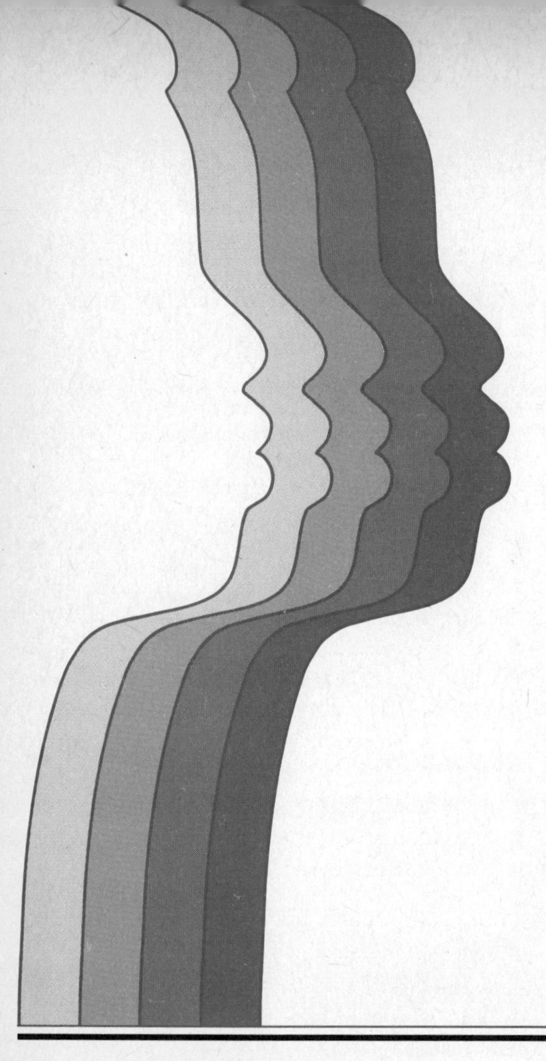

CHAPTER 9

LANGUAGE DEVELOPMENT: ACQUISITION AND PROBLEMS

CHAPTER HIGHLIGHTS

Topics

Language: An Overview
a. The Uses of Sound
b. The Structure of Language
c. The Content, Form, and Use of Language

Language Acquisition: The Theories
a. Biological—Lenneberg
b. Cognitive—Piaget
c. Psycholinguistic—Chomsky
d. Behavioristic—Skinner

The Pattern of Development
a. Phonological Development
b. Syntactic Development
c. Semantic Development

Problems in Language Acquisition
a. Deafness
b. Aphasia
c. Mental Retardation
d. Childhood Psychoses

People

Lois Bloom
Roger Brown
Noam Chomsky
Philip Dale
Jill deVilliers
Peter deVilliers
Peter Farb
Roman Jakobson
Joseph Kess
Margaret Lahey
Eric Lenneberg
William Moulton
Jean Piaget
B. F. Skinner

Special Topics

The Language Game
Defining Language
The Language Context
Language Research
Language in Chimps
A Theory of Phonological Development
Pivot Grammar

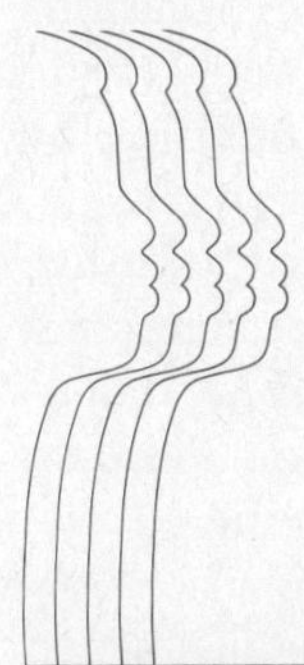

We need to make an immediate distinction among communication, language, and speech. Communication refers to all processes that transmit information, which includes both language and speech as well as computers, the telegraph, and telephone. Language is more restricted and typically refers to verbal or nonverbal communication between organisms. I am communicating with you now by the written word and, as you read, you may turn to a friend and give a thumbs-down gesture, or you may nod in approval. In either instance, you have used nonverbal language to communicate. Bees and dolphins use an involved language to communicate. Speech is even more limited than language; it is the use of the spoken word only, which distinguishes more than anything else what is human.

Recently there has been much discussion about the ability of chimpanzees to communicate by using a nonspoken language. But since it is so common to refer to language as the human use of words, we will continue this usage throughout the chapter. Whenever we refer to other forms of language, we clearly state what is meant. Peter Farb (1973, p.9) expresses this distinction succinctly and precisely.

> Other animals besides man stand upright, have clever fingers and cunning brains, use tools. But man alone possesses the capacity to speak languages of such richness that linguists are still unable to describe them fully. Speech and man first appeared on the planet together, and when one disappears the other will also. Human speech is not merely some improved form of animal communication; it is a different category altogether that separates man, inhabiting the far side of an unabridgeable chasm, from the beast.

Speech is what makes us human. We could rave about its ennobling features almost indefinitely, but these are only surface manifestations. We see its effects and marvel. We point to the Hemingways in awe. These masters of language, these creative geniuses, possess the power to take the ordinary words that we all learn and recombine them into tales that enchant, terrify, or intrigue us. What is the secret of a great writer? Or is it a secret? Could it somehow be locked into the way that they originally learned their mother tongue, some stimulating, enlightening way that kept alive a spark that has been extinguished in the rest of us?

The process of learning a language depends on more than children's ability to imitate or to respond to environmental stimuli. While these are important, other parts of the process seem even more critical. There is evidence, for instance, that children discover quite abstract regularities in the language they hear, analyze them at progressively deeper levels, and reproduce the results of this analysis in personal speech. When they begin to put words together, their sentences immediately reflect some grammatical regularities and yet are quite different from those of the adult.

One other fascinating fact about language, its acquisition, and its expression is that approximately every sentence is unique. Almost without exception, every sentence that you read differs from every other one you have read. We understand sentences not because we have heard them or have read them before, but because we understand the rules of grammatical combination, the syntax of a language. Our knowledge of syntax determines how we construct and understand the almost infinite number of sentences that can be formed from a finite vocabulary.

Dale (1976), commenting on this phenomenon, states that language has an elusive "I can do it but I cannot tell you how" property, which leads to two conclusions:

1. Language is a productive system; that is, using language is a creative act. There is simply no limit to the number of sentences in any language, although the number of words is limited.
2. Most conversational utterances are not perfectly grammatical. Children, listening to the conversation around them, are not presented with perfect models.

Consequently, Dale concludes that children develop language by acquiring a set of patterns, or rules. These rules apply in situations different from those in which they were learned, and it is easy to violate the rules (by forming ungrammatical sentences).

This brief overview charts the path that we shall follow. The initial section presents data that will help you to grasp the meaning of language: what are the basic units, how are they combined, what are some underlying subtleties?

Several elegant theories have been designed to explain language acquisition. Among the most popular, and perhaps perceptive, are those that rely heavily on maturation as the key explanatory element; those that view language as a form of human cognitive development, such as Piaget; those that explain language development as evolving from an innate mechanism, such as Chomsky; and those that see language as rooted in the environment, such as Skinner.

Regardless of the theory, language does develop, and it is possible to trace children's acquisition phonologically, syntactically, and semantically. You may experience your greatest frustrations in this section, because although it is possible to describe significant changes and milestones, explanation remains evasive.

Finally, as with all aspects of human behavior, some children experience problems in language acquisition. The form of these problems and their possible causes pose formidable challenges and are the subject of the final section.

LANGUAGE: AN OVERVIEW

Farb (1978) believes that language allows humans to transcend the limitations imposed by environment and biological evolution by providing a storehouse of information that can be passed from generation to generation. There are several reasons why language can fulfill this role:

1. Humans possess the ability to convey symbolic meanings through language. Farb states that we assign a particular sequence of sounds to an object, and then form associations between sounds and the object. Thanks to the evolving human brain, we rapidly increase the number of these associations, which are distinct cultural symbols; that is, they vary from group to group.

2. The human language is open; thus it is a vehicle both for infinite creativity and for the transmission of information.

3. Displacement is a unique feature of human language, which permits speakers to describe conditions and to communicate data about different times and places. You can tell me something about your parents; you can speculate about the future of computers; you can spin a tale of science fiction.

4. Human language is discrete; that is, each word is composed of an exact and limited number of sounds joined in similarly exact and limited combinations (Farb, 1978, p. 72). These two components, sounds and their combinations, produce a duality of patterning that enables the users of a language to formualte myriad words from a few meaningless sounds.

5. Human language possesses unique perceptual and cognitive characteristics that Farb traces to a large brain with complex neural pathways. Farb concludes that since all other cultural activities stem from language, it is the highest form of "symbolizing."

The Uses of Sound

Perhaps no one has better summarized the relationship between language and communication than William Moulton (1970). He first notes that it is next to impossible for two humans to be together without communicating in some form. Communication is the transmission of information from one person to another. This definition identifies the three elements necessary for communication to occur: a sender, a receiver, and a medium of transmission. In their development, humans have produced one form of communication, language, which far surpasses all other kinds of communication in its flexibility, expressiveness, creativity, efficiency, and sheer elegance.

THE LANGUAGE GAME

Peter Farb in *Word Play* (1973) refers to the language game, which is particularly pertinent to our discussion of the meaning of language. There are certain characteristics of the language game.

1. It has a minimum of two players.
2. Anyone within speaking distance can be forced by social pressure to play.
3. Something must be at stake. This may be tangible, such as receiving a raise from an employer, or intangible, such as making your own beliefs known in a conversation.
4. We all possess a linguistic style that may shift depending on where the game is played and who the players are. For example, we mean the same thing whether we say car, automobile, auto, buggy, jalopy, or wheels. The word chosen reflects subtle social and psychological forces. If I have just bought a new Mercedes, I may refer to it as "the jalopy" to avoid pretentiousness.
5. The language game is structured by rules, and children learn these rules simply by living in a particular speech community.

There are many other subtleties involved in our games with words. For example, "The speaker had to be particularly careful so that he could reflect the appropriate circumstances in his talk." Statements such as this demonstrate the linguistic chauvinism apparent in language. *He* has been generally accepted as the hypothetical person, and *man* and *mankind* used when obviously referring to both sexes.

Musing about the use of the voice as the primary form of communication, Moulton expresses surprise at the source. When we recall that the speech organs are located in the respiratory tract, the phenomenon of sound as the vehicle of communication is all the more remarkable, since the primary function of this area is breathing and eating. The voice may have become the basis of communication because of its versatility. It does not require another human being to be within the range of touch or in our line of vision. Nor does it require the use of the hands to transmit messages, which means that we can be doing almost anything with our hands while we communicate with others.

As we wonder at the uniqueness of language, its ability to carry an infinite number of messages, and its extraordinary creativity (recall that almost all the sentences you hear, say, or write will never be duplicated), one fact begins to emerge. It is the function of language to take the speaker's idea, put it into message form, and transmit the message. The objective is to implant the speaker's original idea in the mind of the receiver.

Moulton constantly marvels at the uniqueness, utility, and creativity of language. Unlike other forms of communication, it permits us to transmit an infinite number of messages. To appreciate this phenomenon, consider some of the other communication techniques that we employ. A stop sign has only one message: stop. A barber's pole tells us that here we can obtain a shave and haircut. Only language can be used for all the messages that the human being wishes to transmit. We can tell someone where to get a haircut, the meaning of the stop sign, where to get something to eat, and how to move from one place to another.

The question that must be asked next is: How is it that humans are able to use language in this manner? As speakers of a language, we carry within us a knowledge of the language, and this knowledge enables us to communicate. How do we acquire this knowledge? We have only external observation from which to infer what happens inside the organism. The manifestations of language are its sound and its meaning, but these alone are not language itself. To comprehend language fully, we must know not only that sound signals meaning, but *how* it signals meaning; that is, we must understand the connection between sound and meaning. This correlation of sound with meaning is the essence of language and, since it occurs within the organism, it defies analysis. But the external features of this correlation permit us to deduce many details of its working.

For example, Hymes (1964), analyzing the components of the relationship among speaker, listener, and topic, has devised the following scheme.

S—*Setting and Scene.* Speech occurs in a definite time and place and in a specific psychological atmosphere: friendly, formal, casual, classroom.

P—*Participants.* The chief participants are the speaker and listener(s).

E—*Ends.* People speak for a purpose—to obtain something, to give information, to interact socially. The goals of speakers and listeners need not be identical—children and parents, opposing lawyers.

A—*Act Sequence.* Speech consists of both form and content; thus *how* something is said is inextricably linked to *what* is said. Speaking to family members at the dinner table is normally much more relaxed (perhaps careless) than speaking to a class.

K—*Key.* Two speech acts may be identical, but the key, or tone, can completely change the message. For example, "Nice going" to a player who has scored the winning touchdown is a friendly, complimentary greeting, quite different from the "Nice going" delivered to a youngster who has just dropped and broken a china cup. Here the message is clearly hostile and sarcastic.

I—*Instrumentalities.* Individuals in different regions may share the same language, but differences in dialect produce different instruments. For example, some southerners may have difficulty understanding the Yankee accent of New England, and many Americans find the English cockney accent almost unintelligible.

N—*Norms.* Certain norms accompany speech. For example, it is customary to whisper in church; interrupting the speaker is considered to be a graceless intrusion. These norms frequently differ from culture to culture.

G—*Genres.* Each speech community constructs categories to classify speech acts: jokes, greetings, condolences.

Hymes's scheme is a thoughtful means of thinking about the general aspects of language and provides a basis for more detailed analysis.

The Structure of Language

Moulton asserts that language is an *abstract structure* connected at two ends with concrete reality. At one end it is connected with sound—the noise made by the speaker. At the other end it is connected with the receiver's experiences. So language is the correlation between these two external ends. Moulton then argues that the most remarkable feature about language is that outside language (that is, at either end, sound or experience), there is no linguistic structure. Inside language, however, all is structure, precise and definite arrangements of linguistic elements. The sound of speech is an uninterrupted stream. But when we understand a spoken language, it seems to consist of specific elements arranged in a specific manner. Moulton (1970, p. 13) uses several illustrations.

Word	Number of Elements
at	two
cat	three
flat	four

To perceive these elements in spoken language, we need not only to hear the physical sounds, but to analyze them, using our knowledge of our own language. The linguist calls these elements *phonemes*—the smallest units of language structure. Standing alone, a vowel phoneme or consonant phoneme usually has no meaning. All of our spoken language derives its meaning from a sequence of phonemes arranged in a particular order.

We can convert the continuum of sound into a sequence of phonemes only if we understand the language of the speaker. It is as if the stream of speech outside of language passes through a filter of phonemes that transforms unintelligible sound into intelligible language. The filter transforms a stream of sound into a sequence of phonemes. And different languages structure sound in different ways. Of course, if we make a mistake in our conversion of sound, the speaker's message is misunderstood. Farb (1973, p. 254) gives a good example of possible misinterpretations. If a girl, while out on a date, says, "I like to bet," but the boy hears it as, "I like to pet," some unexpected kinds of behavior will probably result.

At the other end, language connects with the concrete reality of human experience, which gives it meaning. Moulton states that there are major differences between the concrete realities at either end of language. The number of meaningful units at the experience end is much larger than the number of phonemes. Also, we do not know a great deal about the translation of structured sound into meaningful units. Given the rich experiential background of either child or adult, it is impossible to determine the exact meaning that anyone will give to particular sounds. In summary, the essence of language is the correlation between sound and meaning. Sound passes into language which converts it into meaningful abstract units.

The smallest unit of language to have meaning is the *morpheme.* For example, the word *older* has two morphemes: *old* signifying age, and *er* signifying a comparison. In other words, a morpheme may be an entire word or part of a word. Morphemes are composed of a series of phonemes (the morpheme *if* consists of two phonemes, while *push* consists of three phonemes).

Syntax or grammar represents the combination of morphemes into meaningful sentences. Moulton again offers a fascinating example of the complexity of language. Since syntax occupies a central position in language, he feels it is safe to assume that it possesses two types of structure, one for each end of the language continuum (Figure 9.1).

James Deese (1970) wrestles with the relationship between sound and meaning and notes that the purpose of grammar is to provide a system of rules through which an infinite variety of meanings may be expressed as an infinite variety of meaningful sentences in some language. So grammar is designed only to serve something else: to convert ideas into sentences. The content of language depends on both ideas and sentences, and it exists outside the sentences of the language. But it is the relationship between ideas and sentences that represents the great challenge: the problem of meaning or *semantics.*

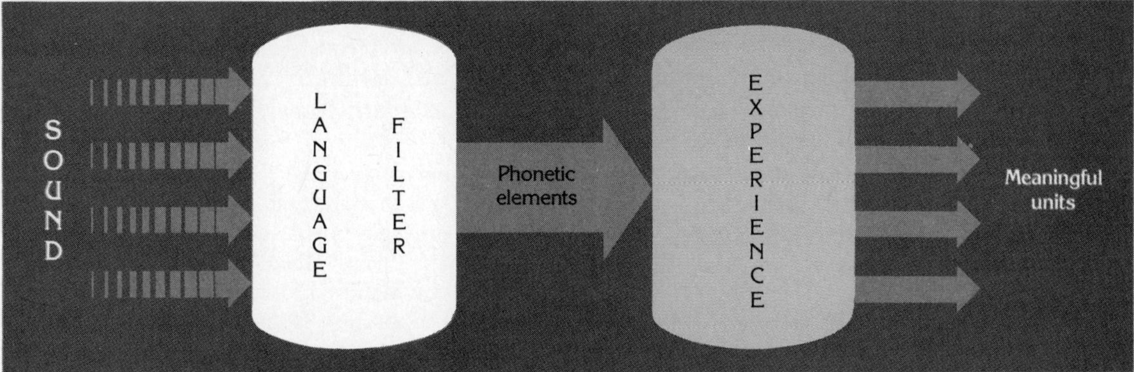

FIGURE 9.1. The Language Continuum.

DEFINING LANGUAGE

Lois Bloom and Margaret Lahey (1978) define language as a code whereby ideas about the world are represented through a conventional system of arbitrary signals for communication. They then elaborate upon the following key terms in their definition.

1. *Language is a code,* which means that language is a way of representing one thing with another. Words and sentences represent objects and events without reproducing them. Language entails *encoding*—combining the code's elements to represent information in a message—and *decoding*—recognizing the code's elements to extract information from a message. The code provides the *form* of the language.
2. *Language represents ideas.* The code (or means of representing information) depends on the speaker's and listener's knowledge of the world. They must know the names of objects and events and the relations between them. Such knowledge provides the *content* of language.
3. *Language is a system.* Sounds form words and words form sentences according to a system of rules. These rules determine which sounds can be combined and which words can be combined. Although the elements of language (sounds and words) are limited, their possible combinations are unlimited, which explains linguistic creativity.
4. *Language is a convention,* which means that words and sentences are used as they are because the members of a particular language community have agreed on the usage. As the authors note (1978, p. 10), language represents shared knowledge.
5. *Language is used for communication.* Not only is language used in social interaction, but it may vary according to the speaker's knowledge of the listener, information and the circumstances surrounding the interchange.

So in addition to learning the code for language *form,* and learning about the world for language *content,* the speaker also must learn how different circumstances determine language *use.*

The Content, Form, and Use of Language

Bloom and Lahey (1978) expand their analysis of the structure of language into three major components: content, form, and use. They believe that the intimate relationship among content or meaning, form or coding, and use or purpose provides a rationale for describing language development and understanding language disorders.

The Content of Language. The topics represented in a message and relationships among them are the language content. The topic refers to particular ideas—the doll, the ball—which then expand into language content by stressing the relationships—*baby's* doll, *throwing* ball. Bloom and Lahey conclude that there are three basic categories of language content: object knowledge, relations between objects, and relations between events. *Semantics,* the content of language, is the linguistic representation of what persons know about the world of objects, events, and relations (Bloom and Lahey, 1978). As youngsters grow, the deeper and richer meanings they derive from their world is a subtle indication of an unfolding cognitive capacity.

The Forms of Language. The authors believe that language form is discernible in the units of sound (phonology), the units of meaning (morphology), and the manner in which units of meaning are combined (syntax). Thus the acquisition of phonology, morphology, and syntax parallel a child's developing speech. Even if this is your initial attempt to understand language, you can recall that a child first utters what appears to be meaningless sounds, then begins to use single words and then, remarkably, begins to use words in a grammatically correct sense (subject-predicate). These are important facts to remember when we specifically trace language development.

The authors warn that while analysis of form is fascinating, it should never be isolated:

> . . . there are levels of formal description and the forms that are used by the language for representing information can be described in alternative ways. However, regardless of the ways in which linguistic form can be described, form in language is the means for connecting sound with meaning and consists of an inventory of linguistic units and the system of rules for their combination.
> (Bloom & Lahey, 1978, p. 19)

The Use of Language. Language usage has two fundamental elements: purpose and context. People speak for a reason, usually to deliver a message that will affect the relationship between speaker and listener. But language is not used in a vacuum; the situation plus the participants shape the nature of the message. The context of language—those conditions surrounding speakers and listeners—affect the form and content of the message. The combination of these elements helps to explain how language "works"; that is, the integration of form, content, and use represents an individual's language competence. A child's competence, or knowledge of language, then guides language performance.

THE LANGUAGE CONTEXT

Peter Farb's book *Word Play* (1973) discusses a phenomenon called the "ecology of language." Our surroundings have a decided impact on our language. For example, while an Eskimo's language provides a great variety of ways to communicate, in reality it is usually determined by the situation or environment. What is said in the igloo is quite different from what is said on the hunt. The Eskimo's language is also restricted by the listener, the role of the speaker in society, and by the presence or absence of an audience.

Similarly, blacks and whites are in close physical contact in many cities, but language has often failed to cross the line between the two communities. Much black language is, in fact, completely foreign to the white. While a white may refer to "common sense," a black will say "mother wit." A black will frequently substitute "it" for "there" in a sentence. "There's no one home" becomes "It's no one home."

Or consider an American visitor to an African tribe. "How many children do you have?" the writer asks the husband and father. "Three," is the reply of the father. Asked the same question, the mother replies, "Five." Why? The man in this community only counts sons, not daughters.

This, of course, raises the whole question of sexism in speech. Women usually employ more prestigious forms of talking in an effort to ensure their status. Occupation and power signal the man's status, but not necessarily the woman's.

These sex differences appear in almost all languages. For example, a woman's voice may be "sexy"; a man's may be effeminate. Males roar, bellow, and growl; women squeal, shriek, and purr. The scientific term, Homo (man) applies to both sexes. The average person is "he." What we can conclude from all this is that language reflects social behavior and that traditional trends, such as linguistic sexism, are difficult to eradicate.

DISCUSSION QUESTIONS

1. Be sure that you understand the distinction between speech and language. List all the forms of communication that could be considered language. Devise a series of gestures or facial expressions for communicating with your classmates. What does this tell you about speech?
2. With your system of gestures (or whatever you devised) what difficulties did you experience in transmitting information? Did your classmates have difficulty in interpretation? What did this experience tell you about the use of language in controlling your environment?
3. Do you agree with Moulton's reaction to sound as the primary mode of communication? Why? Whether you agree or disagree, specify your reasons.
4. If we consider Moulton's statement that language is an abstract structure connected with concrete reality at either end, what can we infer about misunderstanding? What are some apparent sources of difficulty in communication?
5. Be sure you can distinguish between phonemes and morphemes. Give some examples of each.
6. This section presented several perspectives on language: Moulton, Farb, Bloom, and Lahey. Can you integrate the Bloom and Lahey interpretation of form, content, and use, and derive a rationale for understanding how language "works"? Try it. Can you explain it intelligently to your classmates? Can you defend it?

LANGUAGE ACQUISITION: THE THEORIES

Many of the phenomena that we have mentioned so casually are actually amazing accomplishments. For example, imitation does not seem to be the sole explanation of language development, since a child hears so many incorrect utterances. Imitation does not explain the child's seemingly intuitive grasp of syntax, nor the manner by which thoughts are translated into words. How can different surface structures convey an identical meaning?

Attempts to resolve these and similar issues have led to the formulation of four major theories of language development.

1. A *biological,* or *nativist,* explanation focuses on innate language mechanisms that automatically unfold. Language develops similarly under almost any conditions. For example, the language explosion mentioned in Chapter Three seems to be a cross-cultural phenomenon. Eric Lenneberg is probably the most famous of the nativists.

2. A *cognitive* explanation views language as part of the youngster's emerging cognitive abilities. Language is a verbal clue to the complexity and level of a child's cognitive structures. Probably the most famous of the cognitive theorists is Piaget.

3. A *psycholinguistic* interpretation attempts to explain how native speakers can understand and produce sentences that were never spoken or written. Children's mastery of their language depends on an intuitive knowledge of the language rules. Noam Chomsky is probably most widely associated with this theory.

4. A *behavioristic* explanation concentrates on language as a learned skill. Children utter sounds that are reinforced and shaped by the environment, especially parents and teachers, and gradually learn to make distinguishable sounds and to form correct sentences. B. F. Skinner is undoubtedly today's leading behaviorist. A good example of the basic differences between the cognitive and behaviorists' beliefs is seen in Figure 9.2.

FIGURE 9.2. Language Acquisition. A behaviorist *(a)* versus a cognitive *(b)* interpretation.

LANGUAGE RESEARCH

Although our concern here is with theoretical explanation, you should realize the extent and intricacy of current linguistic research. One of the most fascinating is literary detection—the proof of authorship. While language develops in a similar manner for all humans, we all impose our personal idiosyncracies upon our use of language. You can undoubtedly detect differences in this book compared to other texts you are now using.

Computer usage has led to some intriguing results. A. Q. Morton (1979), a classical scholar who is also a computer expert, was struck by the rhythm of certain classical works on a line printer; that is, one or two lines appeared almost separate, then there would be a long burst of lines. Upon analysis, Morton discovered that the same author used techniques that remained constant from book to book. For example, if an author used a pronoun in a distinctive manner in one text, the usage was repeated in all of that author's work. You can see how this is a reliable method to fix authorship.

Morton believes that it is not vocabulary that identifies an author, but style. Particular words seem to be more intimately related to a specific topic than a specific author. It is the choices that confront an author—the language habits—that leave a discernible trace, and these seem to remain constant through the years and from book to book.

Morton gives the example of Jane Austen's "complex style and biting wit." Widely imitated, she left an unfinished novel when she died in 1817. An anonymous author completed it and used many of Austen's literary mannerisms; for example, the use of "and" following commas, semicolons, and colons. But it was the choices (language habits) that betrayed authorship, in this case, Austen's placement of small words. "Such" frequently preceded "a"; "I" frequently followed "and." Both of these usages appeared only rarely in the posthumous novel.

This technique, called *stylometry,* is currently being applied to many famous works, and even has legal application. Forensic stylometry can usually detect the truth or falsity of confessions admitted as court evidence. Did the person in question actually write the confession?

Stylometry is an engrossing and provocative example of language research.

With stylometry as an example of current research, let us examine each of the major theories in more detail.

A Biological Explanation

The rationale for a biological interpretation of language is that if language is a developmental phenomenon, and if it is not wholly dependent on learning, then some inner mechanism must be the explanation. There are linguistic achievements that learning principles alone simply cannot explain. For example, some abnormal children, five or six years of age, have in the course of two years of instruction progressed from no speech whatever to the level of the normal five- or six-year-old.

We must also explain the innovative nature of language. Children do not just imitate those around them. If you listen carefully to the speech of children you may distinguish unique patterns that they have never heard before. Children may well have heard words such as "doll," "man," and "walk," but never the combination "Man walks doll." Such novel utterances testify to the creative aspect of language. If these facts are true, then human beings must be biologically unique in possessing the capacity for creative language. To account for this capacity, let us turn to the work of Eric Lenneberg (1967), who has devoted considerable thought to this subject.

Lenneberg's initial premise is that at a certain time in development, children show an amazing spurt in the ability to name things. It seems to be the peak of a process that begins slowly and continues until, at about eighteen months, children have learned approximately three to fifty words. Suddenly, the process sharply accelerates. There is a rapid increase at twenty-four to thirty months, and at the end of the third year, children have a speaking vocabulary of about a thousand words and probably understand another two or three thousand words. The increase in total vocabulary is an amazing phenomenon to witness. This explosion in vocabulary occurs at about the same age for every normal child in the world.

Lenneberg comments that the specific causal elements and the underlying cerebral mechanisms for the language explosion are still unknown. But as attention is focused on this phenomenon, the direction of research shifts from the external to the internal, from the environment to biology. Lenneberg suggests that imitation, conditioning, and reinforcement are losing their appeal as explanations for language development, while anatomical and physiological agents are receiving more intensive study. As a biological event, language parallels the development of walking and other predominantly innate varieties of neuromotor coordination. Thus it proceeds from genetically determined changes occuring in the maturing child.

Any theory that endeavors to explain language development must account for a subtle form of behavior. In normal children, for example, there is initially nothing to show that such an astounding event is about to occur. When very young infants vocalize they are merely crying or fussing. At about the sixth to eighth week, cooing (sounds that resemble vowels or consonants) appears. Other changes slowly follow: babbling replaces cooing, and primitive phonetic sounds emerge. By the twelfth month, more mature speech sounds are heard, and then the language explosion occurs.

But rapid vocabulary development is only one of the amazing features that we have yet to explain. Youngsters, *without instruction*, are also learning the rules of language, so that by the age of four they have mastered the essentials of adult speech. As Lenneberg notes, the sheer mechanics of speech production demand an unbelievably high order of interpretation and an entire complex of special physiological adaptations. This capacity for language development suggests that development follows a biological schedule, which is activated when a state of "resonance" exists. When children are "excited" in accordance with the environment, the sounds that they have been hearing suddenly assume a new, meaningful pattern. (Lenneberg's discussion of this phase of language development closely approximates an earlier analysis of critical periods.)

LANGUAGE IN CHIMPS

If language results from human biological uniqueness, then humans alone should possess linguistic ability. To test this reasoning, several ingenious animal experiments have been conducted. The chimpanzee research has been both fascinating and informative.

One of the most famous of these experiments concerned Allen and Beatrice Gardner, psychologists at the University of Nevada, and their famous pupil, Washoe. Their basic assumption was that chimps might possess a capacity for language although they lacked the ability to speak it. They decided to teach Washoe, who was then a year old, the American Sign Language (Ameslan), hand signals developed and used by deaf humans. In less than a year, Washoe was combining "words" in crude sentences, and by two years, she had a vocabulary of thirty-four words, or signs. She used a sign to represent a class of things: the sign for *hurt* to indicate scratches, bruises, and strains, for instance. After three years, her vocabulary consisted of eighty-four signs, which doubled at the end of the fourth year, and by the age of six she could use one hundred sixty signs.

Another experiment involved David Premack's chimp, Sarah. Premack used various colored pieces of plastic to represent words. After six years, Sarah had a vocabulary of about one hundred and thirty plastic symbols. She learned to respond to complicated sentences requiring different activities on her part—putting an apple in one place and a banana in another. Sarah, like Washoe, also applied her newly acquired knowledge to situations outside the training context. For example, she was able to apply terms such as *same* or *different* to objects other than the cups and spoons she used in training.

How can we interpret these achievements? Farb (1973), while agreeing with the obvious accomplishments of chimps, disputes that they have achieved language as humans know it. The human child by the age of six has a vocabulary of thousands of words, not the one hundred fifty or one hundred thirty words of the chimp. Chimps give little indication that they understand the principles of grammar that human children have grasped when they begin to string words together. The human child constantly generates novel sentences. While some animals may share a few features of human language, it is based on different principles. People speak because of their vocal apparatus, and no similar animal prototype has yet been found.

The distinctions made among communication, language, and speech at this chapter's opening may help you to interpret these studies. As Roger Brown (1973) notes, Sarah and Washoe are barred from full linguistic participation by their restricted vocal production and aural reception. The chimps' linguistic performance is manual, and not vocal.

DeVilliers and deVilliers (1978) ask the question: can one learn a human language without a linguistic innate ability? The chimps have not demonstrated that they can make the surface structure/deep structure distinction that humans manifest. But as Brown (1973) notes, the human linguistic model is shaky, so while animals may be "out," what use is it if we cannot prove that humans are "in"?

Terrace (1979), analyzing his own and other's data about animal language, raises serious questions about the nature of that language. If chimps can create sentences, then they must employ semantic and syntactic structures. Terrace believes that investigators who reported that animals used simple sentences such as "More drink" had actually recorded instances of both "More drink" and "Drink more." Consequently, Terrace doubts the grammatical relationship between the two. Also, the chimp in Terrace's study (Nim Chimpsky) did *not* increase the mean length of utterances with age as children do, and frequently seemed to respond to the instructor's signs.

Lenneberg (1967) believes that language development parallels motor and cognitive ability. Stance, walking, and general muscular coordination approximate the appearance of certain language characteristics. These schedules—motor, cognitive, and language—seem to follow genetically programmed instructions. They manifest steady, sometimes spectacular, development, level off, and slowly decline.

So language appears at a certain time in our lives and proceeds at a definite pace. Although this development is sensitive to age, and seems to respond to maturational agents, it is quite resistant to adverse environmental events. Language usually develops normally even in apparently restricted environments. Once the process commences, it continues until completion, about twelve or thirteen years of age, when children have mastered the basic linguistic structures. As Kess (1976) notes, if children of the right age are placed in any linguistic community, they will immediately, and with little difficulty, acquire that language. Once the age of puberty passes, the ability to acquire language deteriorates rapidly.

Piaget's Cognitive Explanation

Piaget's interpetation of language development is inextricably linked to the development of cognitive structures. As Flavell (1963) notes, Piaget believes that language is a symptom of existing cognitive structures. In his basic work on language, *The Language and Thought of the Child* (1926), Piaget begins by asking, "What are the needs which a child tends to satisfy when he talks?" That is, what is the function of language for a child? To answer this question, language must be linked to cognitive structures, which means that language function will differ at each of the four cognitive levels.

In a later work (Piaget and Inhelder, 1969), he states that there are significant differences between sensorimotor and verbal behavior.

1. Sensorimotor behavior is active, while verbal behavior can *represent* action.
2. Sensorimotor behavior focuses on immediate time and space, while verbal behavior has no temporal or spatial limitations.
3. Sensorimotor behavior is based on a one-to-one relationship; that is, youngsters react to one thing only; with verbal behavior, children can represent many things simultaneously.

Recording the speech of two six-year-old children, Piaget identified two major speech categories.

A. *Egocentric speech,* which means that children do not care to whom they speak, or whether anyone is listening to them (Piaget, 1926, p. 32). There are three types of egocentric speech:

1. Repetition, which children use for the sheer pleasure of talking and which is devoid of social character.

2. Monologue, in which children talk to themselves as if they were thinking aloud.

3. Collective monologue, in which other children are present but not listening to the speaker.

B. *Socialized speech,* which means that children exchange views with others, criticize one another, ask questions, give answers, and even command and threaten. Piaget estimates that about fifty percent of the six-year-old's speech is egocentric and that what is socialized is purely factual. He also warns that although most children begin to communicate thought between seven and eight years of age, their understanding of each other is still limited.

As Piaget states (1926, p. 139):

> It proves that the effort to understand other people and to communicate one's thoughts objectively does not appear in children before the age of about seven or seven and one half. It is not because the smaller children were romancing that they failed to understand each other in our experiments. In cases where there was no invention the same phenomenon of faulty understanding was observed to take place. On the contrary, it is because he is still egocentric and feels no desire either to communicate with others or to understand them that the child is able to invent as the spirit moves him, and to make so light of the objectivity of his utterances.

Seven or eight years of age sees the slow but steady disappearance of egocentrism, except in verbal thought in which there are traces of egocentrism until about eleven or twelve years of age.

Usage and complexity of language increases dramatically as children pass through the four stages of cognitive development. Piaget insists that this striking growth of verbal ability reflects the development of cognitive structures but is not responsible for advancing symbolic functioning. Table 9.1 illustrates the relationship between cognitive capacity and language.

TABLE 9.1. Piaget—Language and Thought

Period (age in years)	Outstanding Characteristics	Language Equivalent
Sensorimotor (0–2)	1. Egocentrism 2. Organizes reality by sensory and motor abilities	1. Language absent until final months of period
Preoperational (2–7)	1. Increasing symbolic ability 2. Beginnings of representation	1. Egocentric speech 2. Socialized speech
Concrete operations (7–11)	1. Reversibility 2. Conservation 3. Seriation 4. Classification	1. Beginnings of verbal understanding 2. Understanding related to concrete objects
Formal operations (over 11)	1. Development of logico-mathematical structures 2. Hypothetico-deductive reasoning	1. Language freed from the concrete 2. Verbal ability to express the possible

A Psycholinguistic Explanation

During the past few years, transformational grammar has ascended the peak of popularity in linguistic techniques, attempting to explain why the native speaker is able to understand and produce sentences that have never been previously spoken or written. It assumes that language is a system of rules for manipulating linguistic elements to form and understand new sentences. Children's mastery of a language depends on the intuitive knowledge of these rules.

In 1957 Noam Chomsky published a book entitled *Syntactic Structures,* in which he elaborates on our intuitive knowledge of our native language. In brief, Chomsky believes that we are born with an innate capacity to acquire language. This is often referred to as our LAD—*Language Acquisition Device.*

Other important and basic ideas of transformational grammar include the following.

1. All languages possess highly abstract structures and highly specific principles of organization.
2. These structures and principles are innate rather than acquired.
3. They play a central role in how we perceive and produce sentences.
4. They provide the basis for the creative usage of language, which accounts for the novelty of almost all of the sentences we use, hear, and read.

Note the difference between cognitive and psycholinguistic theory: Piaget believes that language develops as cognitive structures emerge, while the psycholinguists believe that speakers have an innate grasp of their native language and intuitively know the correct way to use that language. Farb (1973) believes that children hear relatively few utterances, most of which are grammatically incorrect, and then, using this "scanty and flawed" information, discover the intricacies of native speech—without instruction!

Aitchison (1976) states that psycholinguists are primarily concerned with three questions:

1. Is language innate? This question focuses on the controversy between those who see language as learned and those who insist that humans are linguistically preprogrammed. The psycholinguists thus face the challenge of describing and explaining any innate knowledge.

2. What is the link between language knowledge and language usage? This question focuses on the relationship between children's internal representation of their language and how they actually use that language. Aitchison believes that those who possess language can do three things:

a. They can understand sentences (decode) b. They can produce sentences (encode)	Language Usage
c. They can represent language	Language Knowledge

Psycholinguists must determine if the grammar proposed by linguists reflects a child's innate knowledge of that language.

3. How do children produce and comprehend speech? This question focuses on the distinction between language knowledge and language usage. Psycholinguists wish to discover what happens when a child encodes and decodes.

Kess (1976, p. 6) summarizes the psycholinguistic task when he states:

> The task for the psycholinguist interested in verifying the psychological implications of linguistic models now is to discover to what extent the model accounts not merely for the

language data but also for the possible processes whereby the actual language behavior is acquired and maintained. Much of modern psycholinguistics, like a good deal of modern linguistics, reflects Chomsky's theorizing about the structure of language, and the nature of a theory of language.

Noam Chomsky

Competence and Performance. You must understand the distinction that Chomsky makes between competence and performance to grasp the significance of psycholinguistic theory. Competence refers to the speaker's innate knowledge of a language; performance refers to the speaker's use of that language. Aitchison (1976) believes that one of Chomsky's major assumptions is that anyone who acquires a language learns more than an accumulation of random utterances; they acquire a set of rules for forming speech patterns. It is these rules that enable a person to generate an infinite number of sentences and that explain the creative aspect of language.

Children construct an internalized grammar by gradually recognizing any speech regularities and then making assumptions about the rules that are responsible for these regularities. Aitchison believes that children's assumptions are actually guesses or hypotheses, which become more sophisticated with age. If this is how children function in acquiring language, they must possess an innate hypothesis-making device plus language universals (Aitchison, 1976, p. 92). Thus, like all humans, children function by testing hypotheses based on their innate language knowledge. It then becomes a matter of fitting a particular language to the model. This innate knowledge of language is the language acquisition device (LAD) referred to earlier.

Chomsky has developed a model that employs linguistic evidence to furnish information about perception and learning. After a physical stimulus is filtered through a series of beliefs, strategies, and memory, a person has a percept (S →Filter →PR). Now let us assume that the physical stimulus is a speech signal and that the percept is the representation of what the hearers take the signal to be and the interpretation they assign to it. Under these conditions, the percept becomes the structural description of a linguistic expression that contains phonetic, syntactic, and semantic information. Chomsky then uses three sentences to illustrate the problem of syntactic information.

1. I told John to leave.
2. I expected John to leave.
3. I persuaded John to leave.

While there are similarities here (subject *I*, object *John*, and predicate phrase *to leave*), they are only superficial. The similarities are in the surface structure, whereas there are actually important differences in meaning among them. These functions must exist in the percept, since the receiver of the speech signal intuitively knows them. Since the deep structure is abstract, the concrete surface structure may not reveal it.

As we examine these illustrations more carefully, we see that the percept contains sound and meaning, which are related by grammatical structure. It is the syntax of "John loves Mary" that makes the sentence mean something different from the same sounds in a different order, "Mary loves John." There are two important elements in the syntactic structure. First, the surface structure is directly related to the phonetic form and to the deep structure that underlies the semantic interpretation. Second, the deep structure is represented in the mind and is rarely indicated directly in the physical signal.

As Aitchison (1976) notes, the assumption of a surface and deep structure is an elegant way of accounting for the identical meaning of different sentences, such as the active or passive. For example:

Large brown cows have eaten up the grass

is identical in meaning to

The grass has been eaten up by large brown cows.

Children can detect the identical meaning of the two sentences because of the transformations they can make.

Language gives phonemic structure to sound at one end and semantic structure (meaning) at the other. In the sentence "The man wound up the clock," a continuous stream of sound passes through our language filter, which breaks it into phonetic elements. As we examine the meaningful units that ultimately result, we do more than merely add up the meanings of individual words to understand the whole sentence. That is, the process is not just addition such as, "The + man + wound + up + the + clock." We must also cope with the past tense and other structures in this sentence. Instead, we understand the sentence as, "The man + wound up + the clock."

Thus we have gone far beyond merely treating the sequence of words (surface structure); we have attempted to illustrate how we understand it (deep structure). As one (words) becomes the other (understanding), a set of syntactic transformations makes the change. These syntactic transformations are the rules that guide us to an understanding of the various word combinations. Now we see that the use of language proceeds as follows.

The man wound up the clock (surface structure)
↘ ↙
Syntactic Transformations
↙ ↘
The man wound up the clock (deep structure)

Moulton (1970) notes that the assumption of surface and deep structures, connected by transformations, helps us to comprehend many puzzling aspects of language. For example, he uses the same sentence, but changes the form slightly.

1. The man wound up the clock.
2. The man wound the clock up.

Obviously, these two sentences are different, but just as obviously, they mean the same thing. By utilizing the notion of surface structure and deep structure, we can now state that they are different, but that they are also the same. That is, they possess the same deep structure (meaning) but have different surface structures (sound). It is the recognition that transformations guide us toward meanings that enables us to say that two sentences can be different, but the same.

The innate aspect of language is nicely summarized by Farb (1973) when he states that not every human being can play the piano, do calculus, jump high hurdles, or sail boats —no matter how excellent the instruction. But all children constantly generate completely original sentences. Bright children and stupid children, trained children and untrained children, all learn about the same linguistic system (Farb, 1973, p. 246).

These and similar examples prompt Chomsky to conclude that it is unimaginable that a highly specific, abstract, and tightly organized language comes by accident into the mind of every four-year-old child. Evidence now available supports the view that all human languages share the deep properties of organization and structure. The possession of these linguistic universals seems to be an innate endowment instead of the result of learning. And what is true of language undoubtedly is true of other principles of human knowledge.

Finally, Aitchison (1976, p. 101) summarizes psycholinguistic theory as follows:

> Chomsky considers that children are endowed with an innate hypothesis-making device, which enables them to make increasingly complex theories about the rules which will account for the language they hear going on around them. In making these hypotheses, children arc guided by an inbuilt knowledge of language universals. These provide a "blueprint" for language, so that the child knows in outline what a possible language looks like. . . . In particular, Chomsky assumes that children automatically know that language involves two levels of syntax—a deep and a surface level, linked by 'transformations.'

There are, however, those who disagree violently with Chomsky. Scorning phrases such as "innate mental endowment," "deep structures," or "intrinsic element," they turn to what they consider to be the more tangible and promising data of the environment.

A Behavioristic Explanation

In direct contradiction to Chomsky, the behaviorists believe that all features of language behavior are the result of learning. As mentioned in Chapter Two, B. F. Skinner's basic thesis with respect to all behavior is that we act on the world and change it, and are in turn changed by the consequences of that action (Skinner, 1957). That is, we do something to the environment and, if this behavior is reinforced, the probability is increased that this class of responses will reappear under similar circumstances.

According to behaviorists, the same pattern holds true for language behavior, which is a highly significant portion of human behavior, since we usually act only indirectly on the environment. Instead of crossing a room to close a window, we may simply ask the closest person, "Will you please close the window?" Skinner believes that the ultimate action (the closing of the window) is the result of a complex series of events, including the behavior of the listener.

Verbal Behavior. Skinner believes that verbal behavior is behavior reinforced through the mediation of other persons' needs. Speaking, or responding to speech, is human behavior and thus subject to the rules of an experimental science of behavior. Verbal behavior has many features that cry out for scientific analysis:

1. It is easily observed.
2. There is no shortage of data; children and adults are constantly talking and listening.
3. The facts are substantial and verifiable; there is usually general agreement about what is said.
4. Writing provides verbal behavior that is more convenient and precise than nonverbal data.

Skinner (1957, p. 31) states that children acquire verbal behavior when their relatively unpatterned vocalizations are selectively reinforced and gradually assume forms that produce desirable consequences in the verbal community. *Verbal behavior emerges from children's emitted, raw responses. The vocalizations are not elicited.* Parents and adults simply must wait until an adequate response appears.

Kess (1976, p. 36) summarizes Skinner's beliefs nicely when he states:

> In language, behaviorism implies that a speaker's performance or his responses can be traced back to specific stimulus-response relationships. Thus, a simple behavior theory seeks to determine which of the stimuli present in the environment prompted an utterance and, further, whether it will be reinforced by the behavior of others. Say that a given set of responses, perhaps a half-dozen, is made and that one of these is rewarded and thus reinforced. The state that motivates the speaker has been satisfied, and obviously the response that has been satisfied will be conditioned as being the appropriate one if the same state of affairs arises again. If it does, it is extremely likely, according to this very simple behavioral model, that the same or a similar response will emerge again.

As Kess concludes, Skinner can explain a person's total verbal repertoire by reinforcement and conditioning.

Behavioristic psychology has provided some rigorous experimental designs suitable for all forms of human behavior, including speech. But we must carefully note the assumption on which their principles rest. There obviously is a strong commitment to the belief that animal and human behavior are sufficiently similar so that the methods of behaviorism are mutually applicable. So we now can visualize the great gulf that separates a Chomsky from a Skinner, and how the work of each illustrates the different direction of studies of language and its acquisition.

DISCUSSION QUESTIONS

1. How does Lenneberg use the "language explosion" to explain his maturational view? Can you explain how a child's "state of resonance" furthers language development?
2. Explain Piaget's belief that language emerges from the development of cognitive structures. Do egocentric and socialized speech follow logically from Piaget's cognitive theory? Explain your answer.
3. Chomsky believes that laws of reinforcement are inadequate to explain the generative nature of language. What does he mean? In your answer demonstrate the link between competence and performance, between deep and surface structure.
4. What does Skinner mean by a functional analysis of language? Give specific examples of how Skinner would explain language development. Your answer constitutes what category of verbal behavior? Can you distinguish it from Skinner's other categories?

THE PATTERN OF DEVELOPMENT

All children learn their native language. At about the same age they manifest similar patterns of speech development, whether they live in a ghetto or in a wealthy suburb. Farb (1973, p. 10) has sketched the following general sequence of speech acquisition.

1. At about three months, children use intonations similar to those they hear adults using.
2. At about one year, they begin to use recognizable words.
3. At about four years, they have mastered most of the incredibly complicated structure of their native tongue.
4. In about two or three more years, they have mastered their language to such an extent that they can speak and understand sentences that they have never used or heard before.

As you can readily see, this magnificent accomplishment is compressed into just a few years. What is truly amazing about language achievement is that although children may have difficulty with other tasks during these years (reading and mathematics, for instance), language mastery comes easily and naturally. The mere fact that children are members of a particular species seems to explain this tremendous human attainment. Specific accomplishments are traced in Table 9.2.

TABLE 9.2. Age and Language Development

Language Behavior	Age
cries	from birth
coos	5 to 6 weeks
babbles	4 to 5 months
single words	12 months
two words	18 months
phrases	2 years
short sentences, questions	3 years
conjunctions and prepositions	4 years

As youngsters mature, tracing the pattern of language development becomes increasingly difficult. Table 9.3 presents several language accomplishments.

The path of development is similar for normal children throughout the world; culture has little to do with language emergence and development, but it has everything to do with the specific shape of a language. Children will not speak before a certain time, and once the acquisition process commences, it is difficult to stop. That is, for language development to terminate, some dramatic intervention such

TABLE 9.3. Some Typical Language Accomplishments

Age (years)	Language Accomplishment
6	Vocabulary of about 2600 words Understands use and meaning of complex sentences Uses language as a tool Possesses some reading ability
7	Motor control improves; able to use pencil Can usually print several sentences Begins to tell time Losing tendency to reverse letters *(b, d)*
8	Motor control improving; movements more graceful Able to write as well as print Understands that words may have more than one meaning *(ball)* Uses total sentence to determine meaning
9	Can describe objects in detail Little difficulty in telling time Writes well Uses sentence content to determine word meaning
10	Describes situations by cause and effect Can write fairly lengthy essays Likes mystery and science stories Masters dictionary skills Good sense of grammar

as brain damage or terribly deprived conditions must occur. Around puberty, the ability to acquire language rapidly declines (which you may have noticed when you attempted to learn another language in college).

There is nothing trivial about this accomplishment. Farb (1973) provides an excellent example of the enormity of language acquisition. Every language groups its vocabulary into classes: nouns, verbs, adjectives. If English possessed only 1,000 nouns and 1,000 verbs, the number of possible two-word sentences is 1,000 × 1,000, or one million. But the nouns can be used as both subjects and objects of the verbs, so the number of possible three-word sentences jumps to 1,000 × 1,000 × 1,000, or one billion sentences. And this is with an impoverished vocabulary. Most languages have more than a thousand nouns and a thousand verbs, and possess other word classes such as adverbs, conjunctions, prepositions. One estimate is that it would take ten trillion years to speak all the possible English sentences that use twenty words. These are merely words; we have not mentioned varieties of meaning. When you realize the complexity of the task, it is stunning to think how easily children master language.

Understanding language acquisition requires knowledge of phonological, syntactic, and semantic development.

Phonological Development

At about four months, children make sounds that approximate speech; these increase in frequency until about one year, when they begin to use single words. After children commence using words, babbling is interspersed among the simple words. The precise purpose of babbling remains a mystery; we do not yet understand the relationship between babbling and word appearance. It probably appears initially because of biological maturation (deaf children babble, which would seem to suggest that babbling does not depend on external reinforcement).

DeVilliers and deVilliers (1978) state that late in the babbling period, children use consistent sound patterns to refer to objects and events. These are called "vocables" and seem to indicate that children have discovered that meaning is associated with sound. For example, a lingering *l* may mean that someone is at the door. The authors believe that the use of vocables is a link between babbling and the first intelligible words.

The nature of children's first words suggest that deletions and substitutions may reflect the end of the babbling period when children are acquiring control over articulation. Oller et al. (1976) demonstrated that initial words show similarity to babbled sounds; for example, in their first words children frequently omit the final consonant (*do* for *dog*). During babbling, final consonants are almost always unvoiced; thus there is evidence for some relationship, no matter how tenuous, between babbling and first words.

At about one year, the first words appear. Often called holophrastic speech, it is difficult to analyze. Dale (1976) notes that different criteria identify these words: consistent usage of the word, spontaneity of usage, and evidence of understanding. The child's age at appearance of the first word will vary according to the criterion used. These first words are usually nouns, adjectives, or self-invented words and often contain multiple meanings. "Ball" may mean not only the ball itself, but "Throw the ball to me."

Following these two stages, babbling and first words, Bloom and Lahey (1978) state that during the second year, language learning entails learning words. But they strongly believe that language development is not a compilation of discrete elements:

> babbling → first words → two words → phrases → sentences.

It is a continuum, beginning with the precursors of language, that is, what neonates and infants learn about objects and the relations between objects. The language precursors include the perception and production of sounds, followed by an understanding of the order of words.

These authors believe that one-month-old infants' "tune into" the speech they hear and immediately begin to discriminate distinctive features. Bloom and Lahey also believe that infants are sensitive to the context of the language they hear; that is, they identify the affective nature of speech. So the origins of language appear immediately after birth in infants' gazes and vocal exchanges with those around them. Although these are not specific language behaviors, they are an integral part of the language continuum.

Thus the precursors of language blend with babbling, which then merges into the first words, and is then continuous with the appearance of two words, phrases, and sentences. The period of single words is more than a time of merely accumulating more and more words. Although vocabularies increase, there are notable changes in both the kinds of words used and the way in which they are used between one and two years (Bloom and Lahey, 1978, p. 100). Counting words is a superficial and perhaps even deceptive method of tracing children's language development. (Recall the discussion of the multiple meaning of single words.)

A THEORY OF PHONOLOGICAL DEVELOPMENT

Attempting to explain phonological development, the Russian linguist Roman Jakobson (1968) theorized that babbling is unrelated to adult phonology and that phonological development depends on the mastery of the distinctive features of a language. Children do not imitate an adult's phonemes but form their own system of phonemic contrasts. Dale (1976) states that the contrast between *p* and *b* is similar to the contrast between *t* and *d*, or *s* and *z*. It is the contrast between voiceless and voiced sounds. There are several types of contrasts, which identify all phonemes.

Jakobson believes that these contrasts appear in all languages, that they are universal and develop quite systematically. Although there has been considerable interest in Jakobson's work, some skepticism is apparent about his precise delineation of the development of the contrasts. Although children make the increasingly refined distinctions that Jakobson claims, the order of their appearance may vary. For example, labial-dental contrasts (papa-tata) appear before oral-nasal contrasts (papa-mama).

Nevertheless, it is fascinating speculation based on the universality of contrasts and their systematic development in all languages. Dale (1976), after summarizing many of the questions raised about the theory, concludes that aspects of Jakobson's work are widely used in modern linguistics.

DeVilliers and deVilliers (1978) believe that after two years of age there is some evidence supporting Jakobson's beliefs. For example, once children have organized a distinctive feature contrast, they apply it to all phonemes that are distinguished by that particular contrast.

There seems to be widespread agreement that phonological development proceeds as children discriminate the distinctive features of their language (by contrasts) rather than by learning one speech sound after another. This process applies to all children, regardless of specific languages. While rate of progress may vary with individual children, the process itself seems universal.

Finally, phonological development does not cease at two or three years of age. DeVilliers and deVilliers (1977, p. 46) state that some sounds trouble children for seven or eight years, particularly fricatives. Fricatives are consonants formed by the partial blocking of the flow of air—*t, p, v, f.* In combinations they may cause difficulty, for example, the *th* sound in *their.* Children must also master adult phonological rules, such as the inflectional endings of nouns and verbs. Thus phonological development extends well into the school years, and as children's word usage increases, syntactic questions arise.

Syntactic Development

Kess (1976) believes that at about eighteen months children manifest formal language. Although earlier language may be communicative, it is only from eighteen to twenty-four months that language patterning appears. Two-word utterances with syntactic constructions now appear. Following these two-word sentences, children expand their syntactic rules to include articles, modifiers, and others.

Bloom and Lahey (1978) summarize syntactic development as follows:

1. Successive single-word utterances gradually give way to multiword utterances as children hear speech around them and learn that words are related and express meaning.

2. Relational words (more) become linked with words for objects (candy) to form sentences in a *linear syntactic relationship;* that is, the relational meaning of the two words is determined by the meaning of one word—more.

3. The above processes continue to unfold and gradually become *hierarchical syntactic structures;* that is, children use sentences with verbs—Daddy eat—and thus introduce a larger meaning than that contained in any one word. The relationship of noun to verb is that of subject to predicate. When children construct hierarchical structures they have learned to combine words with a semantic relation between them; the meaning of the words is not dictated by the meaning of one word as in a linear syntactic relationship.

Children's first words indicate both a phonetic similarity to an adult word and continued use of that word in the presence of a specific object or event. The one-word sentence is called a holophrase. Bloom and Lahey (1978) state that just as the single-word period was continuous with the precursors of language in infancy, it is continuous at the other end with the development of grammar. Children begin to use multiple words to refer to the same things that they previously named with single words. These authors believe that rather than learning rules of word combination to express new ideas, children learn to use new word forms (multiple words). Combining words in phrases and sentences strongly suggests that children are learning the structure of their language.

At about two years of age children's vocabularies expand rapidly and simple two-word sentences appear. Although children primarily use nouns and verbs (not adverbs, conjunctions, prepositions), their sentences demonstrate definite syntactic structure. Kess (1976, p. 66) states that although the form classes (nouns, adjectives, verbs) of children's sentences differ from those of adults, the same organizational principles are present. Called telegraphic speech, these initial multiple word utterances (usually two or three words) consist mainly of nouns and verbs. Again, telegraphic speech contains considerably more meaning than superficially appears in the two or three words.

PIVOT GRAMMAR

With the appearance of two-word utterances, Dale (1976) believes that language truly begins, since children are now expressing an unlimited number of ideas with a limited system. Two-word utterances are not random, but reflect two classes of words—pivot and open—that enable children to generate many sentences. Children use many open words but relatively few pivot words. As the name implies, the pivot words serve as pivotal points, that is, the two-word sentences are organized around these words.

De Villiers and deVillers (1978) offer a simplified version of pivot and open words to illustrate the position and frequency of both classes.

Hi doggy	That fell	More soup
Hi Mommy	Doggy fell	More swing
Hi truck	Teddy fell	More milk
Hi dolly	Bottle fell	More jump
Hi horse	He fell	More bottle

You quickly realize that three words appear with considerable frequency—hi, fell, more—each of which appears in a fixed position. The other words are more random and change position. Thus at the two-word stage, there are three types of organization:

pivot + open
open + pivot
open + open

Occasionally children will revert to one-word sentences to express an idea (Milk = Give me a glass of milk).

Pivot grammar was designed to explain how children learn certain words for a definite position and then structure their sentences around them (deVilliers and deVilliers, 1978, p. 71). Although initially widely acclaimed, recent research has raised serious questions about the adequacy of the theory to explain syntactical development

Two basic questions remain unanswered.

1. What is the role of pivot grammar in the acquisition of adult grammar? For example, pivot grammar seems too restrictive. If Mommy and Daddy were both first position pivots, children could not express the sentence: Mommy see daddy.
2. Are there instances that pivot grammar cannot explain? For example, high-frequency words often vary position. Also, the rules restrict the facts. Dale (1976) gives the example of a child saying "Mommy sock," which could either mean the mother's possession of a stocking, or refer to an occasion when the mother put the sock on the child, implying the mother's *action*, and not *possession*.

Bloom and Lahey (1978) summarize the contribution and limitations of pivot grammar when they state that it describes certain distributional facts of child language although pivot grammar is not generative.

With increasing vocabulary, children move from the two-word stage and begin to use noun phrases and expand the verb system (deVilliers and deVilliers, 1978). These authors state that noun phrases have the same grammatical function as single nouns but express much richer meaning: dog = the big dog. Children begin to add inflections; that is, they change the form of a word to indicate a change in use or meaning (loud-louder, have-had). They also begin to build their auxiliary verb system at about four years of age (Daddy go-Daddy has gone).

Dale (1976) states that the two major characteristics of syntactic structure are word order and inflections. During the first stages of language acquisition, word order is paramount. Children combine words without concern for inflections, and it is word order that provides clues as to their level of syntactic development. Once syntactic structure emerges in two-word sentences, inflection soon appears, usually with three-word sentences. The appearance of inflections seems to follow a pattern: first the plural of nouns, then tense and person of verbs, and then possessives.

Dale notes that the overregulation of inflections is one of the most fascinating aspects of language learning. You have probably noticed that children often say:

Daddy com*ed home.*

John breaked the glass.

Children use this form even when they hear correct usage and even *after* they have used correct forms (came, broke). They simply abandon the correct forms (Dale, 1976). The author concludes that since children are pattern learners, they fit all similar words to that pattern.

The progress toward adult grammar can be summarized as follows:

> But we do know that for the child to make progress toward adult grammar, certain structural knowledge seems to be an inescapable prerequisite: an adult grammar has to rely on linguistic categories like parts of speech or constituents like noun and verb phrases, and these structures are mastered early by young children. Furthermore, it seems likely that older children possess the kind of knowledge proposed by transformational grammar, namely the separation of deep structure from surface structure, and an appreciation of interrelationships among sentence types. (DeVilliers and deVilliers, 1978, pp. 119–20)

Semantic Development

Semantic development proceeds much more slowly than either phonological or syntactic development, which is not surprising given the complexity of the semantic system. Kess (1976) believes that there are two main features of semantic development. First, vocabulary constantly expands. Tracing vocabulary development from the Tables in Chapter Three, the pattern is seen in Table 9.4.

TABLE 9.4. The Pattern of Vocabulary Development

Age	Number of Words
2–3 months	cooing
4–6 months	babbling
12 months	3 or 4
18 months	3–50
2 years	50–250
2½ years	250–500
3 years	500–1000
3½ years	1000–1250
4 years	1250–1600
4½ years	1600–1900
5 years	1900–2000
5½ years	2100–2300
6 years	2300+

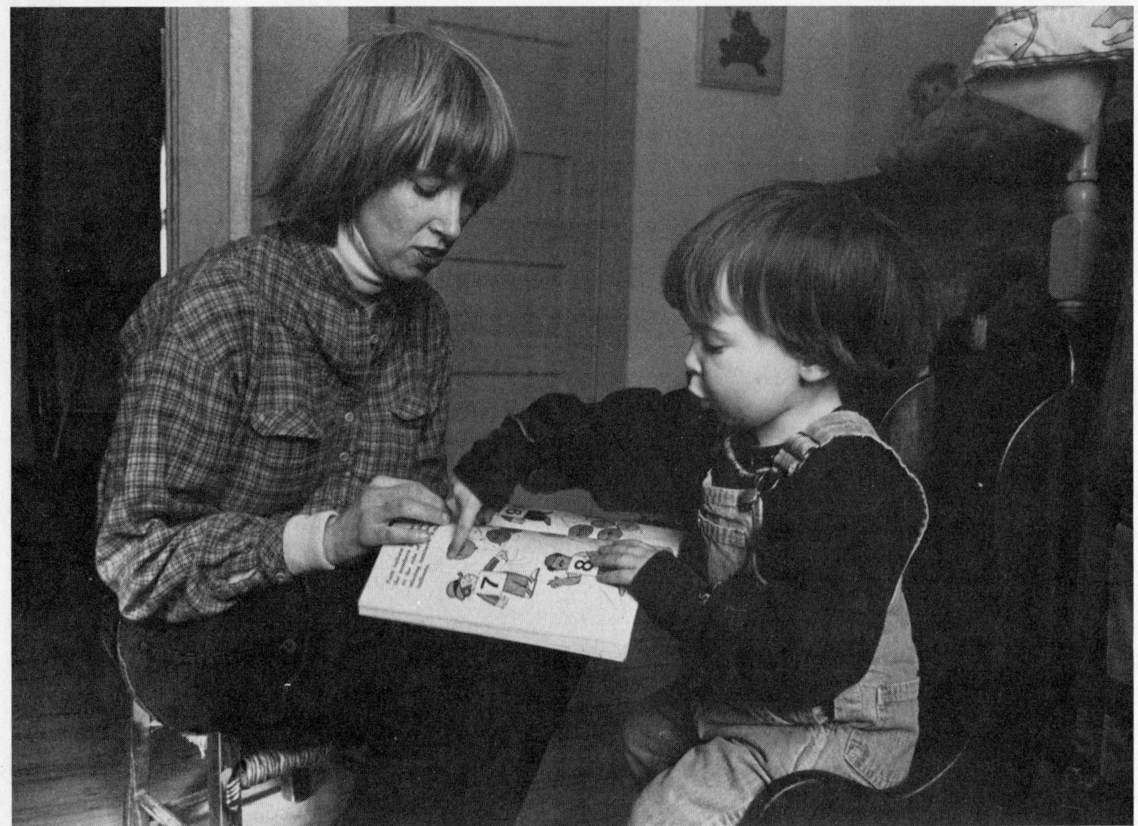

The range for each age indicates the growth for that period. Note that estimates of vocabulary are extremely tentative since youngsters know more words than they articulate; again we see the competency-performance issue.

Second, children constantly reorganize the relationship between words. For example, *Mama* and *Dada* are among the child's first words. Unfortunately, the meaning can be quite different for the father and the child as the disheartened father discovers when his child calls every male "Dada." Such differences extend well into childhood.

Bloom and Lahey (1978) believe that the semantic content of children's first sentences consists primarily of information that expresses relations among objects. Action relations appear most frequently in the early sentences, since children seem to have difficulty encoding states that do not possess action. The authors state that the first action words are quickly generalized; that is, they are used with many different actors, agents, and affected objects (Bloom and Lahey, 1978, p. 134). The authors conclude that action events are the most important category in children's language.

DeVilliers and deVilliers (1978) believe that there are several aspects of semantic development:

1. Children's initial sentences, which express such semantic relations as agent-actor-object, represent the relationships among objects and interactions in the world.
2. At these early stages, children use language to serve different functions (describe, request, deny); that is, these first sentences have a definite pragmatic nature.
3. Meaning involves much more than the association of a sound with an object or event. Children acquire the words for objects and actions, and then learn the relationships among objects and their positions in space and time.

In an analysis of the sequence and types of words that children learn, the authors trace the following patterns.

1. Proper names are acquired initially. We are all familiar with "Mama," "Dada," and names of toys, but note that each word has only one referent. Nelson (1973) believes that children's first words are either referential (naming objects) or expressive (expressing wants or social interactions—bye-bye, need). Referential children are most concerned with labeling, while expressive children use language for social purposes.

2. Common nouns come next, followed by verbs and adjectives. A child's initial use of verbs reflects changes in objects (fill, broke, open) or personal actions (run, throw). Children frequently overextend their use of verbs; for example, a youngster who initially uses "kick" correctly gradually applies it to naming arms or moving an object with any part of the body (de Villiers and deVilliers, 1978). Only by acquiring labels for varied actions do children correctly apply a verb's usage. (Overextensions are frequent; for example, children will often call four-legged animals such as cats and cows "dogs.")

3. Relational words (big, little, short, more) appear quite early but are not used in all their complexity. For example, a child may say "More milk," meaning "Give me more milk," but it is not until much later that a child will use *more* in a relational sense, e.g., "I played more today than yesterday." Correct usage depends on some standard that varies by object, context, or both (deVilliers and deVilliers, 1978). The authors note that children's language is linked to their cognitive knowledge about spatial relations; thus they can measure and compare big and little, tall and short.

4. The deVilliers state that the most complex relational words for children to master are deictic expressions. These expressions definitely identify a specific object, not by naming it, but by relating it to the speaker—here-there, this-that—or by relating an object or event by time—now, yesterday, tomorrow. Children have considerable difficulty mastering these terms, since they must understand the speaker's perspective plus a distance standard that changes with context. The deVilliers give an excellent example of the complexity of deictic terminology: if a speaker is on one side of the street and you are on the other, *this* side of the street for the speaker is *that* side for you.

Dale (1976) believes that semantic development is the least understood aspect of language development, especially since investigators have realized that vocabulary studies tell us little about meaning. That is, when a child speaks a word, it tells us little about the meaning of that word to the child. It also tells us little about the relationships among the words in a child's vocabulary and how they are combined into sentence meanings.

Finally, remember that the pattern of development is not as neatly categorized as presented here. There is necessarily integration among the three categories of language development. Kess (1976, p. 58) summarizes it nicely when he states:

> The acquisition of language involves gradual differentiation in all aspects—phonological, syntactical, or semantic. Children start with very general and undifferentiated categories and then constantly expand and change their classifications. Thus, the child begins with a gross category like the concept of sound and proceeds, by a series of differentiations, to establish and reestablish patterns, each successive stage characterized by a system based on oppositions and functional contrast, but still unlike that of the adult speaker.

DISCUSSION QUESTIONS

1. Trace the path of phonological development. Can you reconcile Jakobson's work with developmental facts? How?
2. Can you explain pivot grammar to your classmates? Does it help to explain syntactic development? Does the work of Bloom and Lahey on hierarchical syntactic structures raise questions about the independent use of pivot grammar?
3. Why do most theorists believe that semantic development proceeds at a slower rate than either phonological or syntactic development? Comment on the inadequacy of studies of vocabulary to explain language development.

PROBLEMS IN LANGUAGE ACQUISITION

With language, as with all other forms of behavior, problems arise for some youngsters. How do children develop problems? The answer to this question is not simple. Recall Chomsky's idea that language emerges mainly because of innate structures that all humans possess. If the capacity is inherited, innate, and within the organism, where do the sources of language disorders lie? Or let us turn to Skinner's work. If it is possible to identify the variables that determine verbal behavior, then those observable features and any resulting disorders should be subject to manipulation by skillful instructors.

While the fundamental pattern of language development is the same for all humans, children differ significantly in the quality of what they acquire. A major difference shown by most studies is that girls surpass boys in all aspects of language development. This superiority includes pertinent signs such as age at onset of talking, size of vocabulary, and length of sentences.

There are interesting parallels between language development and other forms of development. Language is usually thought to be a substitute for other responses. In the early stages of language development, for example, gestures typically accompany linguistic endeavors. Such gestures are actually a primitive form of communication, and as language develops and becomes more precise, the gestures are discarded. However, if children develop an extremely effective gesture language, verbal development may become retarded.

Emotions are another strong influence on language development. Research suggests that delayed or interrupted speech development often cannot be attributed to any specific organic cause. Many children manifest severe emotional shock or some type of psychic trauma that is apparently responsible for their speech failure. Sometimes an adult's criticism is sufficient grounds for a youngster's withdrawal or refusal to speak. When the pressure is withdrawn, it is almost as if a block were removed and language begins to flow smoothly.

Stuttering is often cited as an obvious clue to the relationship between language and the emotions. There are individuals who stutter only in the presence of certain people, and they manifest no difficulty when these disturbing people are not present. Occasionally it is possible to determine whether the emotional condition of children is stable or unstable by analyzing their speech.

There is evidence of another interesting aspect of the relationship between language and the emotions. Children in the initial phases of linguistic behavior speak about objects, events, or people to which they react emotionally. Desires, demands, and threats are a major portion of the speech of the average two-year-old. These overt emotional expressions are gradually submerged as they mature, but it is interesting to speculate on their continued existence. Frequently in times of severe emotional stress our speech is affected. We say things that we never intended to say, and we may omit the most vital parts of our ideas. Sometimes speech is slurred. When we weigh the range of evidence, it is difficult to disprove this interrelationship.

The deVilliers (1978) estimate that five percent of all school children have a language problem. Of these, about eighty-eight percent suffer from articulation difficulties or stuttering. Articulation becomes a problem when a youngster blurs the distinction between phonemes, eventually causing semantic differences. The other twelve percent of language-delayed children seem to have more serious, basic problems.

Some Specific Language Disorders

Lenneberg (1964) states that the differential diagnosis of speech and language disorders poses some serious problems because of ill-defined diagnostic categories, a disturbing trend toward jargon, and a random collection of criteria for establishing classifications. He suggests that diagnosis should proceed by identifying the major causes of speech abnormalities, tracing their developmental history, suggesting symptoms, and indicating treatment.

Bloom and Lahey (1978) have devised a scheme that could resolve many of the difficulties posed by Lenneberg. They state that to acquire a language, children must have:

1. An intact peripheral sensory system.
2. An intact central nervous system.
3. Adequate mental abilities.
4. Emotional stability.
5. Exposure to the language.

Deficits in these categories may produce:

1. Deafness.
2. Aphasia.
3. Mental retardation.
4. Emotional disturbance.

You can readily see how children's language problems emerge from these categories and why intervention must match each child's individual needs.

Several patterns of behavior result from examining each of the sources of language difficulties.

Deafness. Deafness is a major cause of language problems. Usually the antecedents of deafness are clearly evident (German measles, for example) or can be discerned by a study of the family history. Under these circumstances, parents are often forewarned and can take appropriate action. The usual clue to deafness is the child's inability to speak at the average age. The developmental history is especially interesting. The congenitally deaf child has perfectly normal vocal development during the first four to six months. The transition from crying to cooing and babbling occurs as with normal children. It is only after the sixth month that differences appear. One of the more noticeable tendencies is that the normal child vocalizes a wide variety of sounds, while the deaf child repeatedly makes the same sounds.

In cases of simple deafness, children are normal, relate well to others, and present no serious behavior problems. Communication is often in the form of gestures or pantomime. In early childhood, when they want to call attention to themselves or to some objects, they make no effort to employ the vocal apparatus. If they do attempt sound, they will usually also pull or gesture violently at another person to attract attention.

What is immediately recommended for these youngsters is a hearing aid. For deaf children with no other restricting problems, the acquisition of language through the graphic medium (reading and writing) is possible, although some stylistic errors may persist throughout life. Obviously, children who have had hearing until that critical age of three or four have significant advantages over the congenitally deaf person, but both may experience academic difficulties that have no relation to intellectual capacity.

Fry (1966) optimistically notes that deafness alone does not determine the level of language development, but for those with moderately impaired hearing the amount and clarity of speech they hear plus the use they make of their remaining hearing also are important agents in language development. The deVilliers (1978) conclude that properly trained parents and children offer a bright outlook for the moderately deaf infant.

Aphasia. Aphasia, problems with understanding or pronouncing speech, is not clearly defined because of the uncertainty of its causes. The deVilliers (1978) suggest a dual classification.

1. Traumatic aphasia, which follows a brain lesion (if the damage occurs in early childhood and one cerebral hemisphere is undamaged, recovery may be complete).
2. Developmental aphasia (sometimes called dysphasia), which is not a loss, but rather a failure to develop adequate language.

The authors believe that the basic problem in developmental aphasia is not necessarily linguistic, but rather is a general auditory problem. These youngsters may experience difficulty in distinguishing rapid changes in sound.

Mental Retardation. Another major cause of difficulty in language development is mental retardation. Mental retardates are the severely backward who constitute about two or three per thousand in the general population, and not those who suffer from *delayed speech*. The latter is simply a lower than normal vocabulary or the retention of some baby talk beyond three or four years. A good example of delayed speech is Albert Einstein, who did not speak until he was three years old! Lenneberg (1967) states that in seventy-five percent of all cases of mental retardation, the symptoms establish the condition beyond doubt. In other cases, the developmental history is critical. But occasionally the developmental history itself furnishes few clues since early tests are mainly sensorimotor.

Lenneberg further states that language has an individual course of development that is dissimilar, yet dependent on motor maturation. It is independent of the child's acquisition of other knowledge, yet also capable of reflecting this intellectual process. What clouds the picture are the psychological problems that often accompany primary mental retardation. Although mentally retarded children make the same amount or more sound than the normal child, they differ in the age at which vocalization appears. The sequence of crying, cooing, babbling, words, phrases, and sentences is the same as for the normal child, but the final stages may never be attained.

Many severe retardates who fail to master basic academic and social skills can nevertheless acquire speech and language. The total absence of speech and language is seen only in the lower levels of retardation (Lenneberg, 1967). These youngsters have little hope for any improvement in their condition, and parents should avoid taking them from one speech therapist to another in the hope of securing speech improvement. Speech progresses steadily in the mentally retarded, but at a slower pace than in the normal child. Twelve to fourteen seem to be the ages beyond which little advance is made.

Bloom and Lahey (1978) state that the label of mental retardation does not define a language pathology that is restricted to the mentally retarded. The label itself does not furnish specific information about what language deficit needs what type of language interaction. It does suggest considerable care in language instruction to ensure that firm links are made between concepts and words.

Emotional Difficulties. Childhood psychoses, including infantile autism, are usually accompanied by severe language problems. The relationship between psychoses (especially autism) and language difficulty is so close that Wing (1972) states that unless there are both spoken and nonspoken language difficulties, a diagnosis of autism cannot be made. Autistic children do not manifest any single language problem; there is considerable variation in language as well as general behavior. Some characteristics of autistic speech include: shrill intonations, echolalia (echoing sentences they hear), problems with pronoun reversals ("You get hurt," when "I get hurt" is meant), and meaningless sentences. The deVilliers (1978, p. 266) summarize the language difficulties of autistic children by noting:

> The child who is "classically" autistic in the sense that he exhibits all or even most of these symptoms and characteristics is rare indeed. Far more usual is the autistic child who reveals some subset of the symptoms, in particular the social unresponsiveness, and some disruption of language acquisition.

Other less serious problems that arise include lisping, where letter sounds are confused, often because of tongue placement or even a missing tooth; and slurring, where words seem to be carelessly pronounced or even broken off. This is often due to lack of physical development in the tongue muscles, excitement, or even just plain laziness. Parents are usually much more concerned with stuttering. Not too much is known about stuttering; it is fairly common between two and three and appears more frequently in boys than girls. Youngsters become excited and just cannot find the words fast enough to express their ideas. The condition often corrects itself if parents do not become overconcerned and make the child self-conscious about any attempts at speech.

When stuttering has deep emotional roots, the problem becomes more serious. Then it becomes a matter of identifying the cause of the difficulty in order to eliminate it. Starting school, moving to a new neighborhood, or the appearance of a new brother or sister all may trigger stuttering. Support and patience usually alleviate the problem once it has been identified, although the process is gradual and we can expect reversals. It is the chronic stutterer who is otherwise normal and healthy who may require psychiatric help.

As we conclude our work, one fact remains clear: parents and teachers should be aware of the normal pattern of language development so that if the normal signs do not appear, those responsible adults can act swiftly.

Language is an amazingly complex phenomenon, yet youngsters master their language swiftly, and, for the most part, accurately. Analyzing how this happens is both challenging and frustrating. Linguistic theories range from those positing that language is rooted in the body's biological maturation to those positing that the environment determines the path of development.

There are as yet, however, no final answers, and you will be most attracted to the theories and research that most closely approximate your own beliefs. Theoretical uncertainty colors developmental research. While it is possible to trace phonological, syntactic, and semantic development, it is impossible to explain the processes that underlie language growth. Is language inextricably linked to cognitive development? Do youngsters learn their language through imitation?

Another paradox arises when you consider the teaching of English. Small children seem to have this marvelous innate faculty for learning language, and by five or six years, they have extraordinary control over their native language. Their pronunciation, syntax, vocabulary development, and fluency are amazing. It is at this same age of five or six that children enter school and for the next twelve years receive instruction in the language that they have already mastered. Admittedly, some of this instruction goes beyond language as we have been discussing it. Reading and writing, for example, require considerable effort for mastery; certain stylistic skills need instruction as well as practice. But additional instruction should obviously depend on an understanding of language development as it occurs naturally in the human.

Language is a powerful tool for youngsters struggling toward self-realization. It also indicates the level of development; because of the close connection between language and thought, it indicates mental functioning; because of its social characteristics, it indicates adjustment to peers. Our lives revolve around language. Can we do otherwise than to direct our energies to a greater understanding of its nature and development?

SUMMARY

While language in the sense of communication is found among animals, speech is a distinctly human phenomenon.

To produce and understand speech implies that children are able to convert sound into meaning and vice versa.

Language development is best understood by examining phonological, syntactic, and semantic processes.

Several theories have been proposed to explain language development. Among the most prominent are: maturational, cognitive, psycholinguistic, and behavioristic.

Phonological development refers to children's understanding and production of the sounds of their native language.

Syntactic development refers to children's acquisition of the pattern of their native language, that is, the grammar.

Semantic development refers to children's initial understanding of the words of their native language and the slower grasp of the relations among words, phrases, and sentences.

All children follow a similar pattern of language development—crying, cooing, babbling, words, phrases, sentences—of which each aspect is intimately linked to form a continuum of language development

Difficulties in language acquisition may have either serious causes (deafness, mental retardation), or relatively minor sources (temporary physical problem, temporary anxiety).

SUGGESTED READINGS

1. For thoughtful presentations of the process of language development and difficulties in language acquisition, the following are excellent sources:

BLOOM, LOIS and MARGARET LAHEY. *Language Development and Language Disorders.* New York: John Wiley, 1978.

DALE, PHILIP. *Language Development: Structure and Function.* Hinsdale, Illinois: The Dryden Press, 1976.

DEVILLIERS, JILL and PETER DEVILLIERS. *Language Acquisition.* Cambridge: Harvard University Press, 1978.

KESS, JOSEPH. *Psycholinguistics: Introductory Perspectives.* New York: Academic Press, 1976.

2. For theoretical discussions of language acquisition see:

AITCHISON, JEAN. *The Articulate Mammal.* New York: McGraw-Hill, 1976.

LENNEBERG, ERIC. *The Biological Foundations of Language.* New York: John Wiley, 1967

PIAGET, JEAN. *The Language and Thought of the Child.* New York: Harcourt, Brace, 1926.

SKINNER, B. F. *Verbal Behavior.* New York: Appleton-Century-Crofts, 1957.

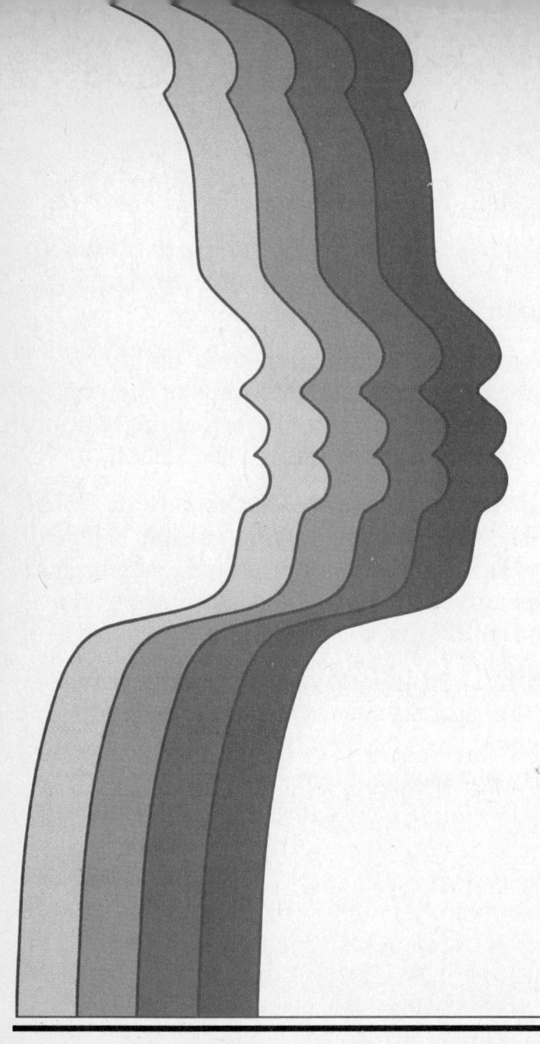

CHAPTER 10

PERSONALITY DEVELOPMENT: THE QUEST FOR IDENTITY

CHAPTER HIGHLIGHTS

Topics

The Theories
a. Trait Theory
b. Social Learning Theory
c. Humanistic Theory
d. Psychosocial Theory

The Course of Personality Development
a. Does Heredity Play a Role?
b. The Roots of Individuality
c. Change and Continuity
d. A Developmental Overview
e. Influences on Personality Development
f. Locus of Control

People

Albert Bandura
Stella Chess
Erik Erikson
Sibylle Escalona
J. R. Guilford
Jerome Kagan
Herbert Lefcourt
Abraham Maslow
Julian Rotter
Alexander Thomas

Special Topics

Peak Experiences
"Good-Me, Bad-Me"
Discipline
Other Important Influences

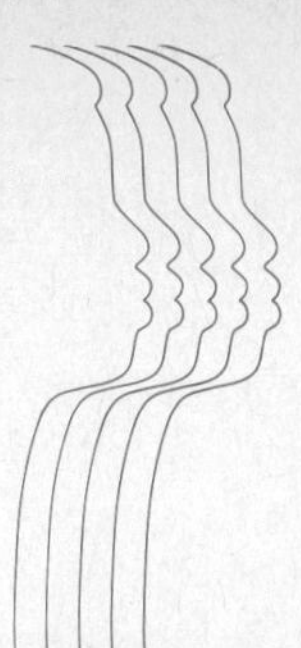

Have you ever asked yourself why some of your friends appeal to you much more than others? The answer undoubtedly lies in the domain of personality, that constellation of characteristics that make individuals what they are. And because you are what you are, certain personalities will appeal to you more than others. Speculations about individual differences in personality cut to the heart of what makes a person a compatible or incompatible companion. How can we account for differences? Are they rooted in the way we assimilate and integrate environmental stimuli? Because of native capacity, because of experiences, and because as individuals we perceive in a unique fashion, do we then put a personal stamp on our behavior?

By "personality" do we mean the characteristics of people who enjoy popularity with their fellow human beings? Or do we mean personality types such as introverts or oral types? Is personality the sum of individual traits, such as friendliness, sociability, and industriousness? Or does it imply something more, some deeper quality that emerges from a child's humanity? These questions indicate the complexity of the term. If we disregard the less sophisticated view of personality as popularity and consider instead other speculations, we see that each definition contains the seeds of a distinct pattern of research.

Your personality is the result of an enormous number of influences, from genetic elements to environmental differences, such as your relations with your parents and even the way in which you learn. Does this mean that personality is simply the sum of these characteristic ways of reacting that develops over a period of years? Or is there something at the heart of all your reactions that accounts for your uniqueness? A belief in the acquisition of traits as the sole explanation for personality dictates a certain kind of research and certain kinds of practice.

Or suppose we believe that what children are during infancy and early childhood indicates the kind of adults they will be. We have then introduced the question of the stability of personality. An investigator concerned with such stability will want to identify certain critical personality characteristics and to follow them throughout a lifetime. Under intensive, long-range scrutiny, the secrets of personality will gradually emerge. We also cannot avoid the problem with which we have wrestled from page one: which is more decisive—heredity or environment? Although we believe an interactionist theory is most productive, there are adherents of either side who deserve our attention.

But do these various possibilities tell us much about why some children adjust easily, proceed smoothly along the path of development, and become desirable companions, wives, husbands, mothers, or fathers? Or do we learn much about the appearance of some forms of maladjustment from these studies? Unfortunately, no. Our studies of personality simply have not achieved this level of sophistication.

Although research does not provide indisputable answers, common sense seems to dictate that personality development should lead to maturity. Mature personalities realistically judge themselves and others; that is, they have a sense of identity. Kilpatrick (1975), in a thoughtful essay, comments that identity does not appear instantly, nor is it ever really completed; rather, it emerges from both childhood identifications and those currently formed. For example, as children grow, they acquire multiple identifications: they identify with parents, teachers, older siblings, heroes, or athletes.

Often these identities may be contradictory. The contradictions are not a problem for children, but are a problem for adolescents, who are experiencing rapid and frequently tumultuous physical, emotional, and cognitive changes. Adolescents must integrate both personal and social change to avoid identity confusion. Kilpatrick believes that only a sense of personal continuity enables individuals to weather this trying process, a sense of continuity that reassures us that a personal, essential being persists.

To maintain that sense of essential self requires the support of the "significant others" in our lives: parents, siblings, teachers, peers, husbands, wives, friends. Kilpatrick maintains that these significant others help us to interpret and relate past, present, and potential experiences to the essential self, thus facilitating a continuity that encourages identity.

The process is similar to Whitehead's (1933) description of the "actual occasion," a happening with a beginning, a middle, and an end. That is, children's (and adults') behavior proceeds from potentiality to actuality. The concept is encouraging because it implies that regardless of circumstances, children have multiple possibilities in expressing their behavior. Thus *children create their personalities.*

Inborn personality characteristics may predispose a child to certain behaviors; the range of environmental stimuli is obviously enormous. Children select and organize from these almost infinite possibilities to form a distinct identity. Selection and organization in personality development is consistent with themes previously discussed in brain development (the cortical neurons are *selectively* connected), and cognitive development (cognitive structures are actually formed and organized). Thus evidence accumulates that personality development parallels that of other forms of human development—it is a creative process.

Personality as a creative process has rekindled interest in theory and research. For example, cross-cultural studies of personality characteristics are flourishing, psychohistory (Erikson's studies of Ghandi and Jefferson) attracts considerable attention, and older analyses (George Kelly and personal construct theory) are being reexamined.

Helson and Mitchell (1978), reviewing personality research and trends, identify several current issues. The study of consciousness, using hypnotism as a technique, promises fruitful results in furthering knowledge of both personality and cognitive control systems. There has been a revival of interest in creativity research. Pervin (1978) states that other current issues include the nature-nurture controversy, aggression, altruism, the relationship between cognition and personality, sex differences, the role of the self, and the connection between theory and research.

Investigators are attempting to formulate a typology in which children and adults manifest different characteristics because of their unique combination of intelligence and creativity. Developmental analyses of personality, both popular (Sheehy's *Passages*) and scientific, are frequently frustrating, but nevertheless attract both theoretical and research interest. Helson and Mitchell (1978) conclude that current personality study is searching for patterns and syntheses, both indications of the creative development of personality.

Tyler (1978) argues forcefully that the patterning of activity is the most individual thing about an individual. Thus a child's or an adult's personality represents wholeness; all of the elements that constitute a child's individuality are interdependent. As you read this chapter, it is important to remember this principle of personality's wholeness or integration, because analysis tends to fragment, causing us to consider personality as a mixture of distinct elements rather than an integrated unit.

With this warning, the chapter will explore several representative personality theories, including experimental, behavioristic, psychoanalytic, and humanistic models. The heart of our work will focus on personality development, beginning with a discussion of the possibility of an inborn disposition, and then moving to an analysis of one of the most troublesome issues facing personality research: the consistency of personality traits. Do the personality characteristics that are identified in infancy and childhood remain throughout a child's life? While common sense dictates that "a personality is a personality," research has been hard put to discover continuity.

Certain dimensions of personality are so outstanding that they demand consideration, so we shall conclude by examining aggression, attachment, and locus of control. Finally, after discussing the research and controversies that swirl around theory and development, we shall examine personality assessment as a source of reliable information about personality.

THE THEORIES

Personality theories are as diverse and controversial as are theories of human nature. For example, the belief that a child's personality represents the thrust of unconscious motives and drives is psychoanalytic theory; the belief that personality results from environmental stimulation is learning theory; the belief that personality is the crowning achievement of human development is humanistic theory; and the view of personality as a constellation of types is trait theory. We shall examine representative interpretations of each theory.

Trait Theory

Trait theory has had an enduring role in personality studies. One of its leading advocates has been J. P. Guilford. Defining trait as a distinguishable, relatively enduring way in which one individual differs from another, Guilford (1959) states that personality is an individual's unique pattern of traits.

By focusing on the child's traits, we can discover personality. We constantly identify youngsters by their traits: Jane is sweet; Liz is pleasant; Johnny is affable; Ellen is considerate. A trait may be as general as an attitude of self-confidence or as specific as a conditioned muscular response. Guilford's analysis of personality affords us a model susceptible to detailed research into specific traits. He suggests that certain classes of traits, or modalities, are not separate parts of a personality: they are aspects of the whole personality. That is, there is a need for the integration of traits. The aspects of personality, then, are intertwined to form a unique individual. (Figure 10.1 shows the seven basic modalities suggested by Guilford.)

1. *Morphology* refers to body structure. There is a long and rich tradition suggesting that a person's body furnishes clues to temperament. Children are extremely conscious of their bodies, whether they are short, tall, fat or thin. More important, they seem to act accordingly. Consider, for instance, the thin, retiring child who cannot compete physically,

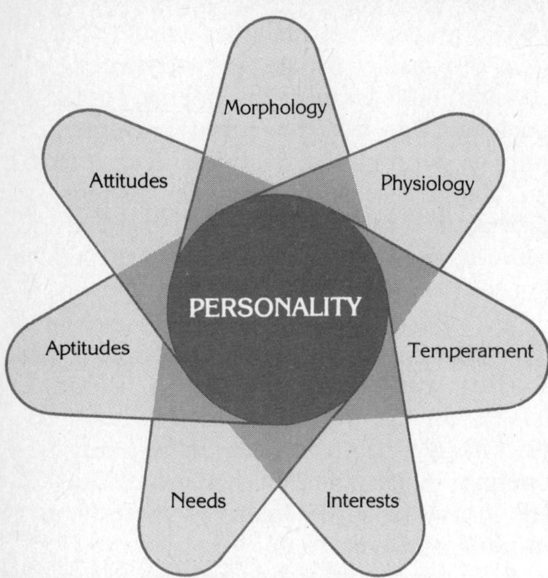

FIGURE 10.1. Modalities of Traits.
From *The Nature of Human Intelligence* by J. P. Guilford. Copyright by McGraw-Hill Book Company. Used with permission of McGraw-Hill Book Company.

or the shy, homely child who tends to withdraw. We characterize such children as shy, quiet, or retiring; that is, we make a personality judgment based on body type: fat and jolly, thin and irritable.

2. *Physiology* refers to such functioning as heart rate, temperature, or glandular secretion. A good example of the effect of this modality is malfunction of the endocrine system, which may produce a hyperactive child. We then tend to characterize the child as impulsive, restless, or nervous, based on a physiological cause.

3. *Interests* are one of three motivational traits (interests, attitudes, and needs) suggested by Guilford. An interest is a generalized behavioral tendency to be attracted to certain activities. We know that children's interests have been almost stereotyped, mirroring environmental pressure: boys played with baseball gloves and girls played with dolls. Although such sexual stereotypes are dissolving, children's interests are still formed according to what they see as attractive and rewarding, and thus they exert a strong influence on personality.

4. *Attitudes* are tendencies to favor or not to favor some social object, event, or activity. Children acquire these attitudes early and easily, as is seen in their attitudes towards race or religion. It is only under considerable pressure, often from peers, that these attitudes change. Once emotions are involved, all of us, children included, resist change.

5. *Needs,* the last of Guilford's motivational traits, are tendencies to acquire certain conditions or statuses to satisfy hunger or thirst or provide recognition or security. Children's needs are as poignant and compelling as those of adults, and if unsatisfied may produce lasting detrimental effects. While adults may direct needs to some activity to achieve satisfaction, children have not yet acquired the necessary maturity to do so. We are all too familiar with the lack of confidence and sense of doubt that permeates the behavior of a child whose need for security has been thwarted.

6. *Aptitudes* are tendencies to perform at a certain level of excellence. Children as well as adults possess aptitudes for perceptual, motor, and intellectual performance. If children have an aptitude for music, this tendency will color the total personality by influencing interests, needs, attitudes, friends, and activities.

7. *Temperament* is a tendency to react in a certain manner, whether cheerfully, happily, or sourly. While Guilford complains that not too much is known about this category, it is usually what we mean by disposition and is often the only dimension used to characterize personality.

Since Guilford proposed his interpretation of personality, trait theory has been severely criticized and hotly defended. One of the chief criticisms is that traits lack consistency; that is, it is impossible to trace continuity of a trait for several years. Block (1977), who has long believed that such studies are methodologically weak, argues that his research, using observational and self-report data from longitudinal studies, yields high correlations (from .4 to .9) for one to ten years.

Zing-Yang Kuo (1977) has proposed the concept of behavior potentials to account for the unique combination of traits that produce *this* personality. In an analysis remarkably similar to Guilford, he states that there are five integrated categories of behavior patterns that form an individual's personality from among myriad possibilities. These are: morphological, biophysical and biochemical, stimulation, previous experiences, and environmental context. Ignoring any of these categories in analyzing personality will produce a distorted portrait of a child or an adult.

Masculinity and femininity, as distinctive personality traits, attract continuing investigations. For example, Hyde and Rosenberg (1976) urge a multidimensional sex role model that provides for diverse ways in which males and females may manifest masculinity or femininity. (Although we may question the precision of these and similar studies, they clearly demonstrate the continuing critical role of traits in personality theory.)

Social Learning Theory

Albert Bandura, a leading figure in the development of social learning theory, has long stressed the potent influence of modeling on personality development. In a well-known statement of social learning theory, *Social Learning and Personality Development* (1963), Bandura and Walters state their thesis that learning occurs through observing others, even if the observer does not repeat the model's behavior and thus does not receive reinforcement.

This statement underlies the authors' belief that all cultures use models to promote the acquisition of desirable behavior. Consequently, children's social-learning history will modify their susceptibility to social influence by either reinforcement or modeling techniques. Thus the authors believe that children do not necessarily do what adults tell them to do, but they will do what they see adults do. Since pictorial models are particularly influential, Bandura and Walters believe that parents and teachers are becoming less potent models compared to high status television models.

In a recent statement, Bandura (1977) notes that observational learning is vital for both development and survival. No society can permit youngsters to discover complex behaviors; modeling is needed. For example, children need to hear linguistic models; they need to observe surgical techniques before becoming physicians. Bandura states that social learning theory regards human nature as an unlimited source of possibilities that both direct and can shape vicarious experience into a variety of forms within biological limits.

The Origins of Behavior. Within these guiding principles, social learning theorists begin to analyze behavior by denying the existence of inborn repertoires of behavior; *behavior must be learned* (Bandura, 1977, p. 16). This is not to deny the biological role; it is to affirm that experience builds behavior on a natural endowment.

Bandura believes that more primitive forms of learning result from the positive and negative effects of behavior, that is, reinforcement. Response consequences have several functions.

1. They impart information. Individuals observe the consequences of their actions and develop hypotheses about which behaviors are appropriate in which settings; these then become a guide for future behavior.

2. They serve as motivators. Previous experiences produce expectations that certain behavior will be rewarded and that certain others avert unpleasant consequences, which encourages some behavior at the expense of others.

3. They serve a reinforcing function, which more precisely means that response consequences regulate previously learned behaviors but are not as efficient in creating new behaviors (that is, there is growing skepticism about automatic reinforcement).

Bandura (1977) believes that learning by reinforcement is exceedingly tedious and laborious and, happily, there is another, more efficient form of learning—observational learning. Bandura describes the four component processes of observational learning as follows.

1. *Attentional Processes.* Bandura (1977, p. 24) states that children cannot learn unless they attend to and perceive accurately the significant features of the modeled behavior. We tend to model those with whom we associate most frequently, those we admire, and those on television who are so obviously admired and rewarded.

2. *Retention Processes.* Children cannot model what they cannot remember. Their increasing abstract ability enables them to represent symbolically—both imaginal and verbal—previously experienced behavior.

3. *Motor Reproduction Processes.* Once symbolic representations are acquired children can convert them into appropriate actions (Bandura, 1977, p. 27). There are difficulties involved here, however. Children may have an "idea" of what to do (the symbolic representation) but simply lack the maturation and physical skills needed to perform the act.

4. *Motivational Processes.* Children are more likely to produce modeled behavior when they have seen that behavior rewarded or when the response results in feelings of satisfaction.

> In any given instance, then, the failure of an observer to match the behavior of a model may result from any of the following: not observing the relevant activities, inadequately coding modeled events for memory representation, failing to retain what was learned, physical inability to perform, or experiencing insufficient incentives. (Bandura, 1977, p. 29)

Three Effects of Observing Models. Bandura and Walters (1963) believe that observing the behavior of models has three effects that may influence the observer's matching responses. The first effect is that of an observer acquiring new responses that the observer must identically reproduce. For the uninitiated, tuning an automobile engine demands just the response that the mechanic makes. The second effect is that of an observer either weakening or strengthening responses that are already present. Watching the mechanic you may realize what you are doing wrong or confirm what you have been doing. The third effect is that of an observer recalling and utilizing past responses. You may suddenly realize, on watching the mechanic, that you were using the wrong tool.

> Imitation plays an important role in the acquisition of deviant, as well as conforming, behavior. New responses may be learned or the characteristics of existing response hierarchies may be changed as a function of observing the behavior of others and its response consequences without the observer's performing any overt responses himself or receiving any direct reinforcement during the acquisition period. (Bandura and Walters, 1963, p. 47)

It is important to understand the authors' intent in this quotation. Modeling is such a powerful tool that all cultures use it to encourage the development of culturally desirable personalities. But deviant as well as desirable behavior may also result. In a classic study, Bandura, Ross, and Ross (1966) examined the influence of live models, filmed human aggression, and filmed cartoon aggression on the aggressive behavior of preschool children. The live models displayed aggression toward an inflated doll. In the film, both human and cartoon models displayed similar behavior. Later all of the children who had observed the aggressive models demonstrated greater aggression and, in a particularly striking statement, the authors note that *film models are as effective as human models in transmitting behavior.*

The authors conclude that today there is more to be gained by studying the effect of social learning variables on personality development than by employing any other technique.

HUMANISTIC THEORY

Attempting to formulate a theory of human personality that avoided the objectivity of behaviorism and the abnormality of psychoanalysis, Abraham Maslow emerged as one of the leaders of "humanistic psychology." The rationale for the system lies in Maslow's belief that, far from being depraved and distorted, the human personality's struggle for growth is a continuous search for health. Growth, as health, entails the satisfaction of a hierarchy of needs. There are five basic needs: physiological, safety, love and belonging, esteem, and self-actualization. Figure 10.2 illustrates the hierarchy of needs.

Physiological needs are extremely powerful and, if they remain unsatisfied, can dominate our lives. The forces of thirst and hunger, and sex cannot be lightly dismissed, but how central are they in the lives of most humans? For children, of course, they can be critical, even in modern societies where scarcity is rare. The youngster who skips breakfast will be a very reluctant scholar by noon.

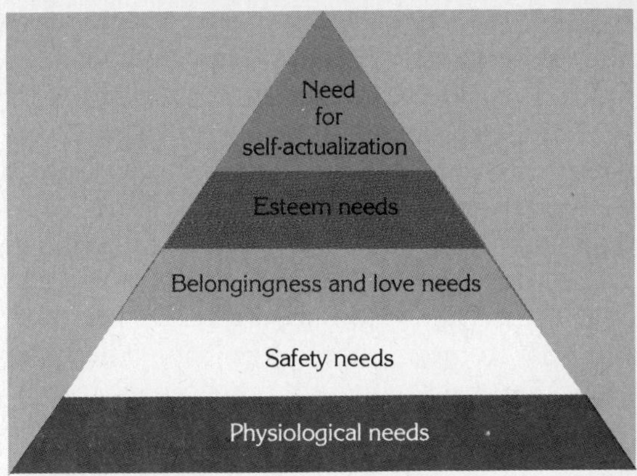

FIGURE 10.2. The Hierarchy of Needs.

Maslow (1970) notes that the physiological needs may serve as channels for other kinds of needs. Children who say that they are hungry, for example, may actually be seeking comfort or dependence. Nevertheless, the physiological needs are the most important of all and, if for some reason they remain unsatisfied, all other needs will fade into the background. But once they are gratified, other higher needs will emerge.

Once the physiological needs are met, a new set of needs appears: the safety needs (security, stability, freedom from fear and anxiety, and the need for structure). Maslow feels that one can best understand these needs by examining the effect on infants and children. Youngsters do not inhibit these needs as adults do; a fearful or anxious youngster shows need in an obvious way. If infants are suddenly dropped, they react vigorously. Youngsters have a powerful need for a safe, stable environment, whether at home, in school, or with peers.

Children also feel threatened by the new and the strange, which implies a great deal for parents, teachers, nurses, and other adults. If not handled properly, these new situations can cause emotional problems that, if unchecked, may well persist into adult life. Why? The safety needs have been challenged and remain unsatisfied. Similarly, children need structure or routine. They need boundaries that they can rely on; youngsters often have a definite sense of security when they are told what they can and what they cannot do. All of us who work with children have seen this phenomenon: children frequently do not want to go somewhere or do something that peers are insisting on. It is comforting to shift the blame by saying, "My mother won't let me," or "My father says no."

If the safety needs are satisfied, the love, affection, and belongingness needs emerge. Children yearn for affectionate relationships with others; they desire an accepted place in the family or the group. Children want to rid themselves of feelings of loneliness, rejection, or friendlessness. Maslow states that we know in a general way the destructive effects on children of moving too often, the overall problem of mobility caused by industrial societies, and the danger of being without roots. Today the frustration of the belongingness and love needs is the most common cause behind cases of maladjustment and even severe pathology.

We should emphasize that this love need is not identical with sex. Sex is only one constituent in the totality of the love, affection, and belongingness needs. Love involves giving as well as receiving, because without the aspect of giving, it would be restricted to the purely physiological level.

We all need self-respect, a sense that we possess some recognizable worth. Maslow believes this particular need has two aspects, (1) the desire for strength, achievement, freedom, and independence, and (2) the desire for recognition. Children who satisfy these needs begin to develop a sense of self-confidence and adequacy. If the needs are frustrated, children develop feelings of inferiority, weakness, and helplessness. The satisfaction of the esteem needs, however, must reflect real achievement and actual competence, not unwarranted self-adulation.

But even if we manage to satisfy all these needs, we still feel restless, even discontented. Maslow thinks that this dissatisfaction is an aspect of human nature that appears when we are not doing all that we feel we could be doing. What we can be, we must be. We all possess the basic desire for self-fulfillment, for actualizing all our potential. This need, of course, will not emerge unless there has been prior satisfaction of the physiological, safety, love, and esteem needs.

Certain conditions act as prerequisites for the basic need satisfactions. Children must have freedom: the freedom to explore, the freedom to question, the freedom to investigate. They must also be able to exercise curiosity in the search for knowledge and truth. However, Maslow does not imply that each need must be one hundred percent satisfied before we progress to the next. Most of us, child or adult, are both partially satisfied and partially dissatisfied in our basic needs. As we become "satisfied with our satisfaction," a new and higher need gradually emerges.

Maslow has realistically added another dimension to his theory. Correctly indicating that most of our knowledge of motivation derives from psychotherapy, he states that we need a theory based on studies of healthy rather than neurotic subjects, a theory that will lead to a greater understanding of the human personality.

Maslow furnishes an excellent conclusion to our brief discussion of humanistic psychology when he states that humans are constantly wanting and their needs require only partial satisfaction before they can turn their attention to other goals; that is, wants are not mutually exclusive. Both children and adults are most often partially satisfied and partially dissatisfied in all their wants. When basic human goals are challenged, or the defenses that protect them are threatened, then the entire realm of psychological fears arises. Here we see the causes of psychopathology, and Maslow believes that a basically thwarted person may actually be defined as sick. These threats to basic goals produce the general emergency reactions of the human. If these basic needs are frustrated in children early and often, it is easy to see how the dissatisfaction creates emotional difficulties in the children that can haunt them for a lifetime.

SELF-ACTUALIZATION—PEAK EXPERIENCES

Maslow's views on the hierarchy of needs are well known, as are his ideas concerning motivation, peak experiences, and self-actualization. As we have seen, self-actualized people have satisfied their basic needs and are now motivated by something higher, something outside themselves.

Some people, but not all, who are "metamotivated" have peak experiences. Maslow feels that peak experiences come from love and sex, from aesthetic moments, from bursts of creativity, from moments of insight and discovery, from moments of fusion with nature. All of us are occasionally capable of these moments.

Those who report peak experiences may be self-actualized or not. Maslow estimates that only a fraction of one percent of the population is self-actualized. These are the people who pursue life's ultimate values and who represent what he calls the "growing tip of mankind." By this he means that humankind advances by this growing tip of pioneers and beginners. The acceptance or rejection of ideas occurs among these people, and it is they who give direction to the whole human race.

Growth toward Self-Actualization. Maslow's study of self-actualization analyzed friends, students, and historical figures. Individuals who seem to be exploiting their talents and fulfilling themselves are the subjects of his studies. Among the most important characteristics of self-actualization are:

1. An accurate perception of reality, that is, the ability to detect honesty and dishonesty in others, and to judge people correctly. Self-actualized people are not afraid of the unknown, rather they see it as a challenge.

2. Acceptance of self and others. The self-actualized have a sense of personal security that frees them from fear and anxiety. These mature, healthy personalities see and accept human nature as it is.

3. Spontaneity. Their behavior is marked by simplicity and naturalness, and lacks artificiality.

4. Autonomy, a relative independence of the physical and social environment. Their healthy sense of privacy enables self-actualized people to withstand life's blows and to maintain a feeling of inner peace, thus providing a continuing sense of stability.

5. Enjoyment. Self-actualized individuals appreciate life. They simply refuse to be bored.

Personality development for Maslow is a search for psychological health, which, he states, not only feels good subjectively but is also correct, true, and real.

Psychosocial Theory

The work of Erik Erikson has been at the center of psychological thought for the past three decades. Born in Frankfurt, Germany, in 1902, his father died soon after Erikson's birth. His talent was quickly recognized, and his stepfather urged him to become a physician, but Erikson was determined to become an artist and left Frankfurt for Vienna. There he came under the influence of the Freudian circle and eventually completed psychoanalytic training with Anna Freud and Aichhorn. Erikson came to Boston in 1933, where he was one of the first child analysts.

He taught at several American universities (Harvard, Yale, Berkeley), but it was his field work with American Indians that caused him to question traditional psychoanalytic theory. Their feeling of a lack of identity—a break with their Indian past coupled with a lack of assimilation into the predominant white culture—caused emotional distress. Erikson's work with World War II veterans reinforced these insights and led him to the concept of identity confusion.

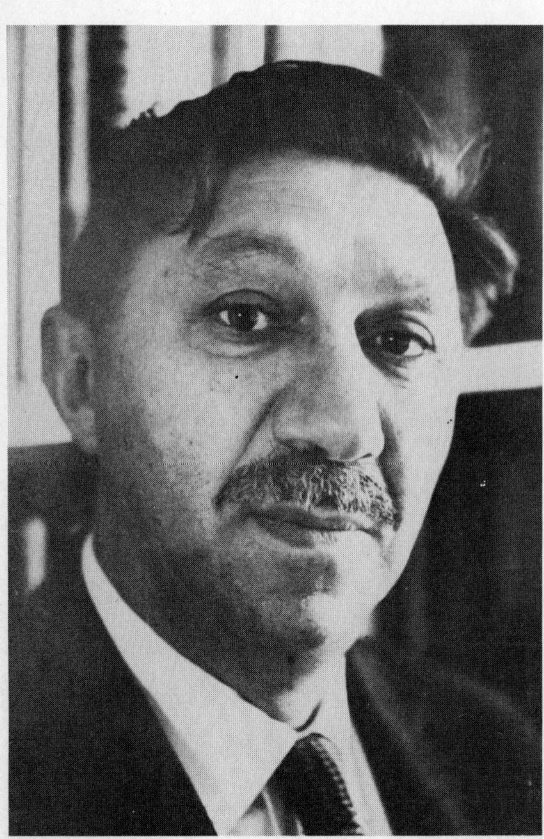

Abraham Maslow

The Emerging Personality. Erikson altered traditional psychoanalytic thinking by positing psychosocial stages of development. Each stage presents critical challenges, which children and adults must overcome to further personality development. Thus there are negative as well as positive features to each of the eight stages. The inner and outer conflicts that children experience, if resolved satisfactorily, produce a more realistic sense of self, that is, a maturing personality.

In perhaps the most famous of his books, *Childhood and Society* (1950), Erikson states that the eight stages of psychosocial development rest on two fundamental assumptions:

1. A child's personality develops through interactions with the environment.
2. Society, by the conditions that it provides, helps to shape the nature of each stage.

As Elkind (1970) notes, a basic theme runs through Erikson's writings: individuals encounter crises that lead to an inner unity and guide future activities. The eight stages and their crises and strengths are as follows.

1. *Trust versus mistrust* (first year). Trust means confidence in others, as well as a fundamental confidence in oneself. The amount of trust derived from infantile experience does not depend so much on quantity of nutrition or demonstrations of love as on the quality of the maternal relationship. A sense of trust can be encouraged by the sensitive care of the baby's needs, together with encouragement of personal trustworthiness. This provides the basis for both being oneself and becoming one who can be trusted. Hope is the chief strength of this stage, by which Erikson means a belief in the ability to succeed.

This stage extends from birth to about one year. During this period, children's needs, while apparently simple, are nevertheless critical. Infants build a sense of trust in the environment through the satisfaction of physical needs such as comfort and contact. Gradually they also develop greater control over their body (e.g., more accurate grasping of objects) and learn to trust their bodies, thus increasing the psychological sense of security. The world becomes a safe and orderly place as children take their first steps toward personal mastery.

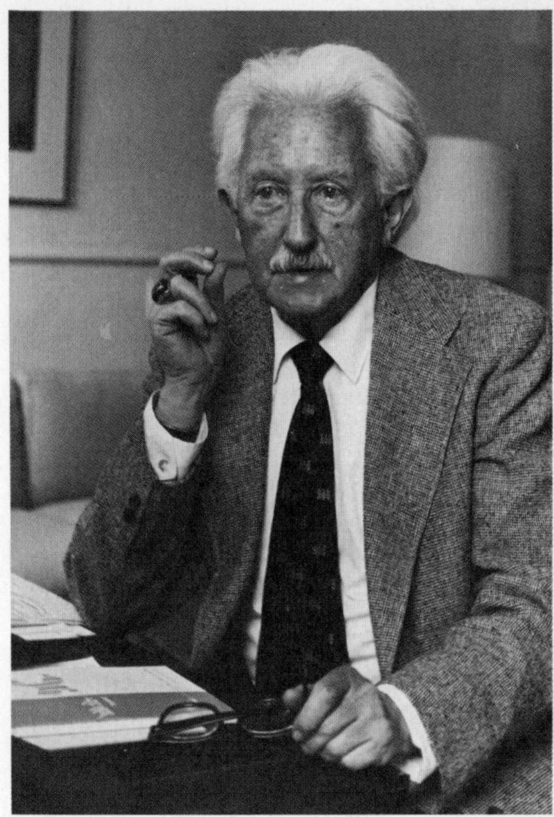

Erik Erikson

2. *Autonomy versus shame, doubt* (2–3 years). For Erikson, the theme of the second stage is that of autonomy versus shame and doubt; it appears while youngsters are undergoing toilet training. As you will note, it parallels Freud's anal period, when personality is shaped by learning a degree of self-control. Erikson claims that this stage is decisive for establishing a proper balance between loving goodwill and hateful self-insistence, between compulsive self-restraint and meek compliance. The objective of this stage is self-control with no loss of self-esteem. If self-control is lost because of parental overcontrol, the result is self-doubt and shame.

If we consider the growing competence of children during this period, we can more easily understand some of the difficulties they experience. They are more and more vocal and parents must exercise increasing control over them. Their growing physical mobility also causes problems; too many restrictions can cause actual physical harm. At the end of Erikson's second stage, children should be relatively self-sufficient, but also willing recipients of parental guidance.

Underlying the sense of autonomy is willpower, by which Erikson means increasing self-control without diminishing self-esteem. Elkind (1970) captures the essence of the stage when he states that children who move through this period with autonomy, buoyantly overcoming shame or doubt, are well equipped to deal with the next set of crises.

3. *Initiative versus guilt* (4–5 years). Erikson's third stage is characterized by a greater freedom of movement, the perfection of lan-

guage, and the expansion of imagination. From these characteristics emerges a sense of initiative that will serve as a basis for realistic ambitions and purposes. The child is now about three years old, and as Erikson notes, the indispensable contribution of the initiative stage to later identity development is that of freeing the child's initiative and sense of purpose for adult tasks that promise fulfillment of human capacities.

An interesting development during Erikson's third stage is the emerging role of conscience. Children now have the ability to cope with the environment, but they are also encountering yes and no reactions from their parents. Consequently they now experience guilt feelings when they know they have done something of which their parents disapprove, or when they even think about doing something their parents frown upon. If parents pose too many restrictions, children could be heavily burdened with a guilt complex. Again, the parents must walk a tightrope at this time, balanced between the negative and the permissive.

The major strength of the stage is a sense of purpose, which motivates children to prepare for future tasks. The feeling of greater bodily control, language mastery, and flights into fantasy produce a sense of excitement, a willingness to seek new challenges.

4. *Industry versus inferiority* (6–11 years). Children now possess a sense of being able to do things well; they want to win recognition by producing things, and they develop a sense of perseverance that enables them to adjust to the requirements of a productive world. But if they constantly experience failure, the result can be a sense of inferiority. As we have indicated, horizons have widened and children now encounter a wide variety of people, tasks, and events. During these years the school becomes a proving ground for children, with success helping them to achieve a sense of industry, and failure plunging them into feelings of inferiority. Some degree of success contributes to both personal adjustment and social acceptance.

If industry entails a concern with knowledge of "how things work," a youngster needs a feeling of personal competence, which will only flourish through the support and encouragement of the "significant others" in the child's environment.

5. *Identity versus identity confusion* (12–18 years). Erikson's fifth stage witnesses the end of childhood and the beginning of adulthood. Youngsters become obsessed with what others think of them; the opinions of their peers play a large part in how they think of themselves. If uncertainty at this time results in identity confusions, a bewildered youth often turns to extremes, such as withdrawal (which may take many forms), running away, or drugs. This is often a troubled time; youngsters faced with the question "Who am I?" may be unable to answer. The challenges are new, the tasks become more difficult, the number of alternatives seems bewildering, and the youth's capacity is taxed. Needless to say, it is a time that requires considerable adult patience and understanding.

The organization of personality so necessary at this stage depends on successfully integrating the experiences of childhood with both native talent and social opportunity. Erikson believes that adolescence need not be a time of storm and stress if a youth, with careful guidance, successfully merges these developmental forces. Fidelity, the search for people and ideas to believe in, is the psychosocial strength of the period; Erikson believes it also helps to explain adolescent idealism.

If youngsters enter adolescence with feelings of mistrust, shame, doubt, guilt, and inferiority, their task of establishing a sense of identity is enormously complicated. Role confusion can result. But Elkind's (1970) view of adolescence offers encouragement: an adolescent's failure to establish a sense of personal identity need not mean perpetual failure. Since life changes, personality may change, and as it does, a person's psychological strength may emerge unshattered.

6. *Intimacy versus isolation* (18–35 years). Although the final three stages extend into adulthood and aging, they deserve our attention for a better understanding of Erikson's interpretation of the life cycle. Here Erikson is referring to a sense of psychosocial intimacy that transcends the sexual. Love, or mature devotion, underlies intimacy and permits us to care about others without fear of losing our own identity. Failure to achieve intimacy with significant others produces feelings of isolation. Erikson phrases this beautifully: "We are what we love."

7. *Generativity versus stagnation* (35–65 years). Middle age brings concern not only about one's immediate family but also about the future of society. It is a more global view that takes us outside ourselves and helps us to avoid excessive self-concern. The psychosocial strength that aids in achieving intimacy is care, a sense of responsibility for the next generation.

8. *Integrity versus despair* (over 65 years). Satisfaction with one's life, satisfaction with pleasure at success, and acceptance of failure, signal a sense of integrity. Strengthened by wisdom, we refuse to despair over missed opportunities.

It is both a popular and positive theory; popular because of its appeal to issues that most of us see as real, positive because of the hope and encouragement that it offers us in meeting life's crises. As Elkind (1970) notes, each phase of growth has its strengths as well as its weaknesses, and we can overcome the failure at one stage by the successes of a later stage; it is a remarkably perceptive analysis of personality. Table 10.1 summarizes the theory.

TABLE 10.1. Erikson's Eight Stages—Crises, Strengths, Influences

Age (years)	Stage	Psychosocial Crisis	Psychosocial Strength	Environmental Influence
1	Infancy	Trust vs. mistrust	Hope	Maternal
2–3	Early childhood	Autonomy vs. shame, doubt	Willpower	Both parents or adult substitutes
4–5	Preschool, nursery	Initiative vs. guilt	Purpose	Parents, family, friends
6–11	Middle childhood	Industry vs. inferiority	Competence	School
12–18	Adolescence	Identity vs. identity confusion	Fidelity	Peers
18–35	Young adulthood	Intimacy vs. isolation	Love	Partners: spouse/lover friends
35–65	Middle age	Generativity vs. stagnation	Care	Family society
over 65	Old age	Ego integrity vs. despair	Wisdom	Mankind

DISCUSSION QUESTIONS

1. Write your own definition of personality. How do people usually interpret personality?
2. Using Guilford's modalities of traits, analyze your own personality. For example, list your interests and what you consider to be your major needs. What skills do you possess? How would you describe your temperament: cheerful, confident, gloomy, negative, optimistic, introverted? Examine the results. Can you now better determine your personality?
3. Erikson's theory enjoys widespread popularity. Many feel that it is particularly insightful. Do Erikson's crises and strengths apply to you now and to earlier stages in your life as you remember them? Give examples.
4. There is little disagreement that observational learning is a powerful force in acquiring behavior. Can you think of any of your behavior that you acquired by observing and imitating? (Relate your answer to the social learning theory principles discussed in the chapter.)
5. Can you say about yourself that you are striving for self-actualization? Why? Relate your reply to Maslow's need hierarchy.
6. Do any of these theories or a combination of them fulfill your expectations of what a "good" personality theory should be? Why? List the pros and cons of each and decide if it is possible to devise a sufficiently encompassing theory.

THE COURSE OF PERSONALITY DEVELOPMENT

Personality results from a complex combination of hereditary and environmental influences. While environmental forces have long been acknowledged to be potent shapers of a youngster's personality, today there is a growing tendency to recognize a genetic thrust, an inborn predisposition. So before we begin to trace the path of personality development, this topic deserves our attention.

One of the most nationally popular pediatricians, T. Berry Brazelton, whose neonatal assessment scale was discussed earlier, has also written several acclaimed books on child care. He states (1969) that normal babies are not all alike, that there are as many individual variations in newborn patterns as there are infants. Infants vary in appearance, feeling, movement patterns, and reaction to stimuli—they are already highly individualistic. Brazelton uses three categories to classify the various types: quiet, active, and average. After repeated observations of newborns, Brazelton believes that distinctions are immediately observable. If the composite classes that he has designated (quiet, active, average) are considered traits, the youngsters, *at birth*, register unique personality dispositions.

Does Heredity Play a Role?

In the 1950s, a team composed of Alexander Thomas, Stella Chess, and the late Herbert Birch, believing that psychology was placing excessive emphasis upon the environment in explaining personality development, turned their attention to constitutional determinants. The authors note that as parents they were struck by the individuality of their children in the days immediately following birth (sleep and hunger patterns, motor activity, intensity of reactions). They also note that as clinicians they could not make a direct connection between environmental influences (parental attitudes and practices) and personality development.

To describe individuality, the authors use the term "temperament," by which Thomas and Chess (1977, p. 9) mean the *how* of behavior, the way that a child behaves. Two children may simultaneously learn to tie their shoes but differ quite noticeably in their intensity during the task or the quickness of their movements. In their remarkably informative study, Thomas, Chess, and Birch (1970) concentrate on what they designate as the source of each person's characteristic temperament. The authors think that, deliberately or not, the emphasis in discussions of personality has been on environmental determinants. While not evoking the old nature-nurture controversy, they suggest that the natural element, which is an integral part of the organism-environment interaction, has been sadly neglected.

They found that many children with severe psychological problems had experienced family conditions identical to those of family members who had no severe problems. Even in those cases where they could clearly identify parental mishandling as the cause of a personality problem, they could not state that this was true for all children. That is, authoritarian treatment might make one youngster anxious and submissive but make another child defiant and antagonistic. The only explanation the researchers could find was that consideration of the child's temperament was ignored. By temperament they mean the individual's unique style of responding to the environment, which, when joined with environmental forces, shapes personality.

To test their hypothesis, the authors designed a longitudinal study, called the New York Longitudinal Study (NYLS), and in 1956 began collecting data on 141 essentially middle-class children. They observed the behavioral reactions of infants, determined their persistence, and attempted to discover how these behavioral traits interacted with specific elements in the infants' environment. The study required information about individual differences in behavioral characteristics during the first months of life, a technique to categorize these differences, and some means for checking these differences at various stages of development. The investigators used a variety of techniques, including regular interviews with the parents beginning when children were two or three months old, and independent investigation by trained observers to verify the parents' descriptions. From the resulting data they found nine characteristics that could be reliably scored as high, medium, or low. These were:

1. The level and extent of motor activity.
2. The rhythmicity, or degree of regularity, of functions such as eating, sleeping, wakefulness, and elimination.
3. The response to a new object or person (approach versus withdrawal).
4. Adaptability of behavior to environmental changes.
5. Sensitivity to stimuli.
6. Intensity of responses.
7. General mood or disposition (e.g., friendly or unfriendly).
8. Degree of distractibility.
9. Attention span and persistence in an activity.

These ratings were used to define the behavioral profile or temperament of the children. Amazingly, the authors found that in a wide variety of population samples they could identify the profile as early as two or three months. Their first hypothesis was thus substantiated: during the first weeks of life, children show individuality in temperament. The investigators found that in most children these original temperamental characteristics persist for years. One of the children, for example, manifested high activity from birth. This behavior persisted through infancy and early childhood, and by the time the boy was seven, his excessive activity in school caused trouble.

In addition, certain characteristics clustered with sufficient frequency to enable the authors to identify three general types of temperament. The first was the type characterized by a positive mood, regularity of bodily functions, low or moderate intensity of reactions, and acceptance of, instead of withdrawal from, new situations. As many as forty percent of the children belonged in this category. The second type was described as the difficult child. Those in the difficult group were usually negative in mood, irregular in bodily functions, intense in reactions, and withdrew from new stimuli. They comprised about ten percent of the sample. The third type was designated as "slow to warm up." They had a low intensity of reaction, and were somewhat negative in mood. They made up fifteen percent of the study. Since only sixty-five percent of the children fit one of these categories, the others had a mixture of traits that defied categorization. The results are shown in Table 10.2.

The authors then expanded their study to include 95 children of Puerto Rican working-class families, 120 handicapped children, and 243 children suffering from the effects of congenital rubella. Thomas and Chess (1977, p. 24) state that although it was possible to identify the nine categories of temperament in all children, predictions of consistent temperamental characteristics remained elusive. They argue that all other psychological phenomena change (values, coping mechanism, intelligence), so it should not be surprising that temperament follows a similar path.

The authors conclude their study by stating:

> Overall we have been impressed by the range and variety of the behavioral repertoire of the young infant. We have seen how this behavior makes it possible for the child to play an active role in his development from birth onward. Any global concept of "personality" becomes untenable as one identifies the many different behaviors in different interactions that each child and adolescent exhibits. All of us play many roles as we go back and forth from one life situation to another. All our roles are

TABLE 10.2. Classification of Temperament

Type of Child	Activity Level	Rhythmicity	Distractibility	Approach Withdrawal
	The proportion of active periods to inactive ones	Regularity of hunger, excretion, sleep, and wakefulness	The degree to which extraneous stimuli alter behavior	The response to a new object or person
"Easy"	Varies	Very regular	Varies	Positive approach
"Slow to warm up"	Low to moderate	Varies	Varies	Initial withdrawal
"Difficult"	Varies	Irregular	Varies	Withdrawal

Source: "The Origin of Personality" by Alexander Thomas, Stella Chess, and Herbert G. Birch.

> interrelated, all are parts of our individuality, and no one can be entitled "the real self" at the expense of others, and endowed with some mystique of personality. (Thomas and Chess, 1977, p. 208)

The Roots of Individuality

In what has become a classic in the search for an understanding of personality, Sibylle Escalona (1968) embarked on a twenty-year study from 1944 to the mid-1960s. She originally studied 128 normal infants, aged four to thirty-two weeks. She identified eight dimensions of infant behavior that reflected both experience and adaptive style. These were:

1. *Activity level,* which refers to the amount and vigor of bodily motion *typically* demonstrated by the infants in a wide variety of situations.
2. *Perceptual sensitivity,* which refers to the degree to which an infant reacts to general sensory stimulation and also to specific sensory stimulation.
3. *Motility,* which refers to neuromuscular actions that lead to displacement in space; that is, the infant demonstrates the capacity to move.
4. *Bodily self-stimulation,* which refers to those movements that deliver direct stimulation to a bodily zone, for example, thumb sucking.
5. *Spontaneous activity,* which refers to self-generated behavior, that is, what infants do when they are awake, alert, and not subject to either bodily discomfort or external stimulation.
6. *Somatic need states* and need gratification, which refer to the infant's response to hunger and fatigue.
7. *Object-related behavior,* which refers to the infant's reactions to objects as distinct from reactions to persons.
8. *Social behavior,* which refers to the infant's responses to people.

She found substantial individual differences among the children on all dimensions. Predictions made about the children's behavior were checked against school records; they were accurate in about two-thirds of the cases, indicating some continuity in personality development. However, troublesome questions persisted: why had some children shown a complete personality reversal, from quiet and passive to lively and resourceful?

TABLE 10.2. (continued)

Adaptability	Attention Span and Persistence	Intensity of Reaction	Threshold of Responsiveness	Quality of Mood
The ease with which a child adapts to changes in his environment	The amount of time devoted to an activity, and the effect of distraction on the activity	The energy of response, regardless of its quality or direction	The intensity of stimulation required to evoke a discernible response	The amount of friendly, pleasant, joyful behavior as contrasted with unpleasant, unfriendly behavior
Very adaptable	High or low	Low or mild	High or low	Positive
Slowly adaptable	High or low	Mild	High or low	Slightly negative
Slowly adaptable	High or low	Intense	High or low	Negative

Hoping to obtain more reliable data, Escalona returned to her original data and selected the sixteen most active (nine boys, seven girls) and sixteen most inactive youngsters (six boys, ten girls) and compared them on the eight dimensions of behavior. She now introduced a new concept, the *stable pattern of experience,* to provide a rationale for describing an infant's behavior and the context of that behavior. The stable pattern of experience (SPE) attempts to determine if an infant's unique behavioral tendencies *make a difference;* that is, does the nature or kind of the interaction between child and environment influence the course of personality development?

For example, Escalona describes two youngsters who differ in perceptual sensitivity; one is particularly responsive, the other relatively indifferent. If the indifferent child is cared for by a mother who provides considerable stimulation (handling), and the responsive child cared for by a mother who avoids direct contact, the subjective experiences of both youngsters would be relatively similar.

Examining each of the thirty-two youngsters on the eight behavioral dimensions, Escalona next derived eight basic stable patterns of experience:

1. frequency of strong bodily arousal;
2. prominence of internal somatic sensations (particularly hunger and fatigue);
3. balance between behavior that responds to internal, somatic causes and behavior that responds to external stimulation;
4. importance of distance receptors (sight and sound);
5. importance of near receptors (touch and passive motion);
6. most prominent modality (vision, sound, touch, passive motion);
7. least prominent modality;
8. frequency of optimal states of animation.

It was then possible for Escalona to evaluate each youngster by behavioral tendency in the light of stable patterns of experience. She called this the "adaptive syndrome." Figure 10.3 illustrates the sequence of Escalona's research.

Escalona believes that this process is an initial step in devising a model for developmental assessment. It is not totally inclusive; for example, to predict accurately she had to introduce the mother-child interactions. As she states (1968, p. 503), success in linking stable patterns of experience to developmental outcome requires a careful scrutiny of infant experiences. Nevertheless SPE reflects real differences in infants' lives.

Note the significance of both distance and near receptors. Yet there are a substantial number of youngsters who vary noticeably. As you would anticipate, age brings change to the stable patterns of experience; for example, the importance of distance receptors increased with age.

Finally, Escalona (1968, p. 517) states:

> In view of the great dispersion of SPE determinants among infants who share one or several patterns of experience, we take this preliminary finding as support for our central hypotheses to the effect that development and adaptation can be anticipated better on the basis of what actually happens to infants than on the basis of organismic or milieu factors, which nonetheless account for these patterns of experience.

It is a perceptive comment suggesting that infants react individually to their environments, the environments (especially mothers) respond, and the most significant aspect of this interaction is the infants' interpretation.

Change and Continuity

Jerome Kagan (1962, 1971) has long been fascinated by the challenge of discovering, or disproving, consistency of personality characteristics. We have all seen children who were

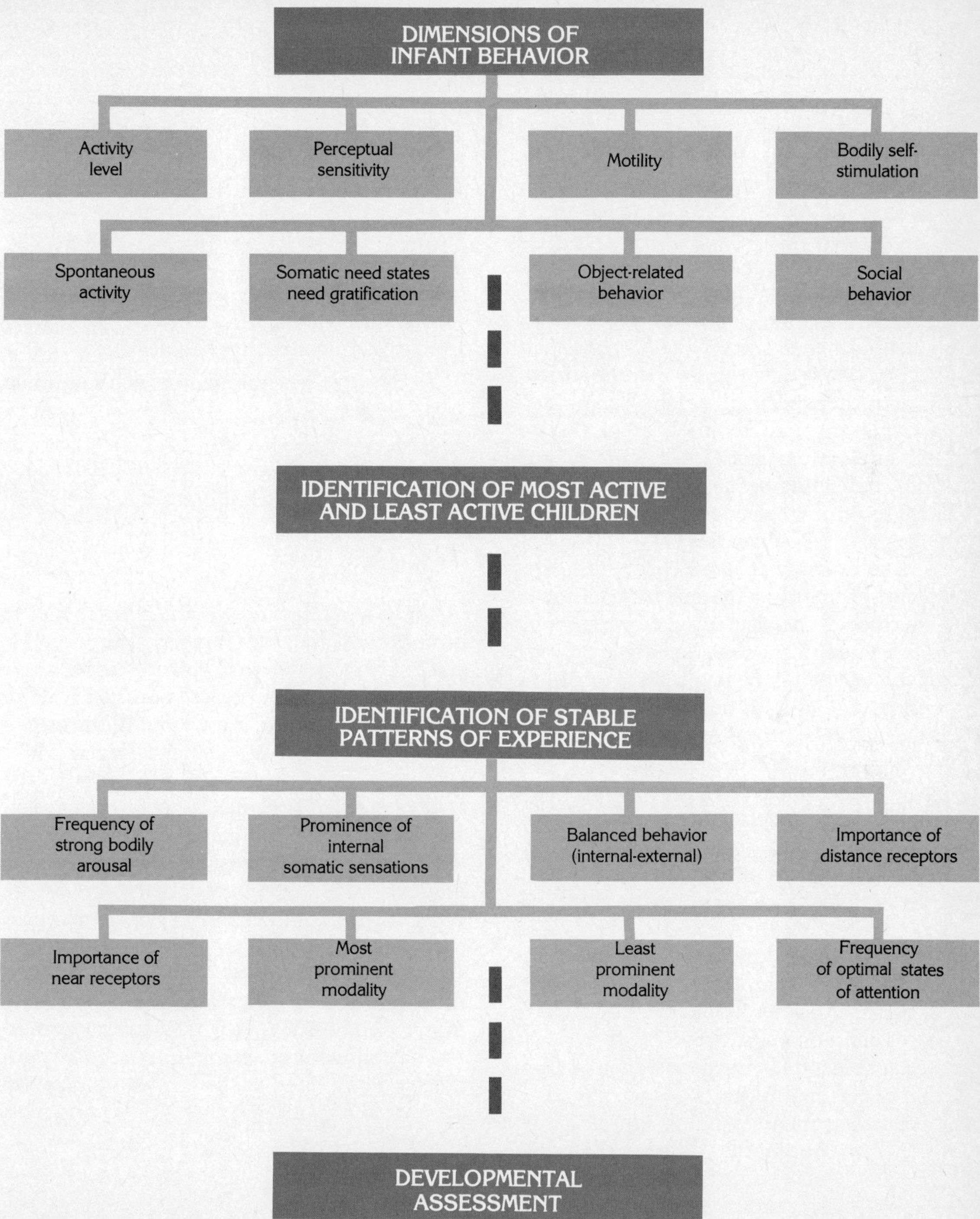

FIGURE 10.3. Identification of Behavioral Dimensions

thoughtful early in life and remained that way, just as we have seen impulsive children become impulsive adolescents. But we have also seen aggressive children gradually lose that aggression. How can we explain this seeming inconsistency? Once a personality characteristic such as withdrawal appears in a child, how stable is it during the individual's lifetime?

From their longitudinal study of personality variables, Jerome Kagan and Howard Moss (1962) concluded that many of a child's behaviors appearing between six and ten years (and a few from three to six) predicted related adult behaviors. Passive withdrawal from stressful situations, dependence on family, impulsive anger, commitment to intellectual mastery, social interaction, anxiety, sex-role identification, and adult sexual behavior were all related to similar behaviors that appeared during the early school years.

It is interesting to note that while these responses evidently remained from childhood to adulthood, the degree of continuity was highly related to sex role. Society approves of passive, dependent behavior in women, but not in men, and both peers and adults communicate this approval or disapproval to the child by a system of rewards and punishments. Once sex-role characteristics are introduced, we more easily understand the persistence of some traits. Our society tolerates, even encourages, aggression in males and discourages it in females. Consequently, we should expect this freedom or inhibition of aggression to become an enduring characteristic and, indeed, it is just that. Kagan and Moss (1962) note that the desire to mold overt behavior to society's definition of sex-appropriate responses is a major reason for the persistence or elimination of personality traits.

Social class membership is another potent influence on the stability of personality characteristics. Thus, knowledge of a child's sex and social class enables us to predict, rather successfully, children's interests, goals, vocational choices, dependence, aggression, sexual and mastery behaviors. But of all the conclusions we can draw from this study, none emerges more clearly than the influence of sex role: if a personality trait persists, it is usually congruent with sex-typed standards.

In a second evaluation, Kagan studied 180 youngsters at four, eight, thirteen, and twenty-seven months. His research had four major objectives:

1. to discern continuities in development;
2. to discover sex differences in attentional processes;
3. to detect the correlates of social class differences;
4. to identify the basis of conceptual tempo (whether a child is reflective or compulsive).

Underlying Kagan's work is a firm belief in *attention* as a key developmental concept. He states (1971, p. 6) that infants under three months need not interact motorically with their environment to learn about it; the investment of attention is sufficient. Kagan (1971, p. 6) then links attentional processes to the development of schemes, which are representations of events that preserve the spatial and temporal arrangements of distinctive elements without being necessarily isomorphic with the event. For example, infants differ in their schemes for faces, and those with poorly articulated schemes will differ in fixation time, smiling, vocalization, and cardiac rate from a child with a well articulated scheme.

The following diagram illustrates Kagan's procedure.

The Theoretical Concept—The Scheme

↓

Developed by—Attentional Processes

↓

Measured by—Fixation Time, Vocalization, Smiling, Cardiac Rate

↓

Leads to Conclusions about—Psychological Continuity, Sexual and Social Class Differences in Attentional Processes, Conceptual Tempo

Kagan found the following measured differences.

Developmental Continuities.

1. *Fixation time* was more stable for girls than boys during the last half of the first year.

2. *Cardiac deceleration* does not always accompany attention; only unexpected events that caused surprise markedly affected heart rate.

3. "*Smiling* serves many different masters during the first three years" (Kagan, 1971, p. 172). Kagan concludes that it is impossible to determine a smile's meaning unless we know the occasion of its appearance.

4. *Vocalization* carries different messages and seems to indicate a diffuse state change without conveying much meaning.

Kagan notes that each of these responses suggested different aspects of attention: vocalization indicated excitement; fixation denoted time needed for assimilation; deceleration signified surprise; smiling demonstrated successful assimilation. All responses displayed moderate stability from eight to thirteen and thirteen to twenty-seven months.

Sex Differences. Obvious sex differences appeared in the vocalization analysis. Vocalizing to an interesting event is more stable for girls than boys and seems to be closely associated with attention. Kagan believes that mothers may cause this difference because their greater reciprocal vocalization with the girls led these youngsters to vocalize more frequently to human faces and states of excitement.

Social Class Differences. Kagan states (1971, p. 181) that meaningful differences emerged during the first year and were unequivocal by twenty-seven months. Kagan notes that while social class itself is not an explanatory construct, it affects child rearing practices, which then affect a child's behavioral and cognitive responses.

Conceptual Tempo. While the link between reflection and impulsivity in infancy and at three years is tenuous, Kagan believes that ten percent of the variance can be predicted during infancy. That is, infant variables account for ten percent of the variance in conceptual tempo at three years.

Finally, Kagan's study, like Escalona's, accentuates infant individuality from birth, but definite continuity between infancy and the later years is difficult to identify.

A Developmental Overview

Studies of temperament, individuality, and consistency enable us to interpret the pattern of personality development more realistically. For example, recognizing the significance of a youngster's interactions permits us to comprehend the personality changes that may occur. The following generalizations seem to apply to most youngsters.

Birth to Eighteen Months. During this period infants learn that the environment provides certain agents who can satisfy their needs.

They also learn to tolerate separation from the mother and the resultant anxiety. It is during this period that children first cry, smile, become wary of strangers, and show a growing awareness of other individuals. Especially important during this period, as during the entire growth period, is the need for regularity in the environment. There should be ample and loving contact between the mother and child, including frequent vocalization, play, and expressions of affection. We have previously spoken of the dismaying results of a lack of such contact among institutionalized children.

Eighteen Months to Three Years. The second major period is marked by startling changes in the youngsters: they are mobile, they communicate, and they must adjust to parental demands. They must now begin to acquire the behavior that will enable them to become members of a family and of a culture. They must reconcile what they think are proper sources of satisfaction for their needs with the restrictions imposed on them by others, especially parents. Poor or incomplete reconciliation of these conflicting demands leaves psychological scars that may remain with children for life.

Three Years to Six Years. Now the father assumes a place of greater importance in the children's lives and youngsters expand their circle of acquaintances. They gradually become aware of the sex role they must play and the behavior deemed acceptable for both age and sex. The psychomotor and cognitive elements of life demand considerable time and attention as they master new tasks, but there also appear those nagging nemeses of guilt and anxiety. How can children adjust their wants to the demands of parents? Or as parents view the problem, how can we save them from injury and help them to adjust without damaging others in any way?

Robert Sears and his colleagues (Sears, Maccoby, and Levin, 1957) state that the use of love-oriented discipline effectively fosters a strong conscience only when the mother has been warm and affectionate during the early years. Guilt, shame, fear, and conscience are not meaningless terms in children's development. Children who have lacked gentle but firm parental guidance will encounter enormous difficulty in accepting the demands of a society that must protect all of its members. Yet if children are given unreasonable restrictions, a hypersensitive conscience will constantly plague them; they will be haunted throughout life by fears, obsessions, and phobias. It is no easy task that we set for parents, but healthy personalities are well worth the effort.

Six to Ten Years. The changes between six and ten years are phenomenal. Physically, intellectually, socially, and emotionally, the variations are legion. Children have established attitudes that may remain with them permanently, such as feelings toward books, learning, school, or almost anything of an intellectual nature. For whatever reason, whether because of personal capacity, lack of success in school, or parental attitude, they may develop a dislike for education; such an attitude will affect future achievement, harmonious adjustment, and even vocational success.

Ten Years to Adolescence. The number of friends now increases considerably, but one or two are usually chosen as constant companions. They exercise a powerful influence on the kinds of activities in which the child engages, whether "hanging out" on street corners or moving from sport to sport with the season. Parents who are unhappy with their youngster's friends should exercise considerable caution in presenting, delicately, a plausible reason for their disapproval.

There are few readers who have not witnessed in their own families how parental disapproval only cemented the bonds of an undesirable friendship more firmly.

Children's friends are often an excellent indication of the state of their relationship with their parents. Children who select companions in direct opposition to parental wishes may well be rebelling against their parents. This is not always so, but if the parent-child relationship has been warm and affectionate, youngsters of this age are usually guided by parental suggestion; if not, it is safe to predict that the teen years for this family will be trying.

Figure 10.4 illustrates the course of personality development.

Influences on Personality Development

Now that you have some insights into the nature of personality and its development, you should consider certain influences that help to mold the developing personality. Having emphasized the possibility of inherent temperamental differences and the nature of a child's interactions with the environment, it seems appropriate to examine several of the more important environmental forces that shape personality.

Personality develops according to what children think they are, that is, according to *self-concept.* Do youngsters think of themselves as strong, honest, loyal, and capable? Or do they think they are weak, afraid, not too bright, and not very capable? These different

FIGURE 10.4. The Course of Personality Development

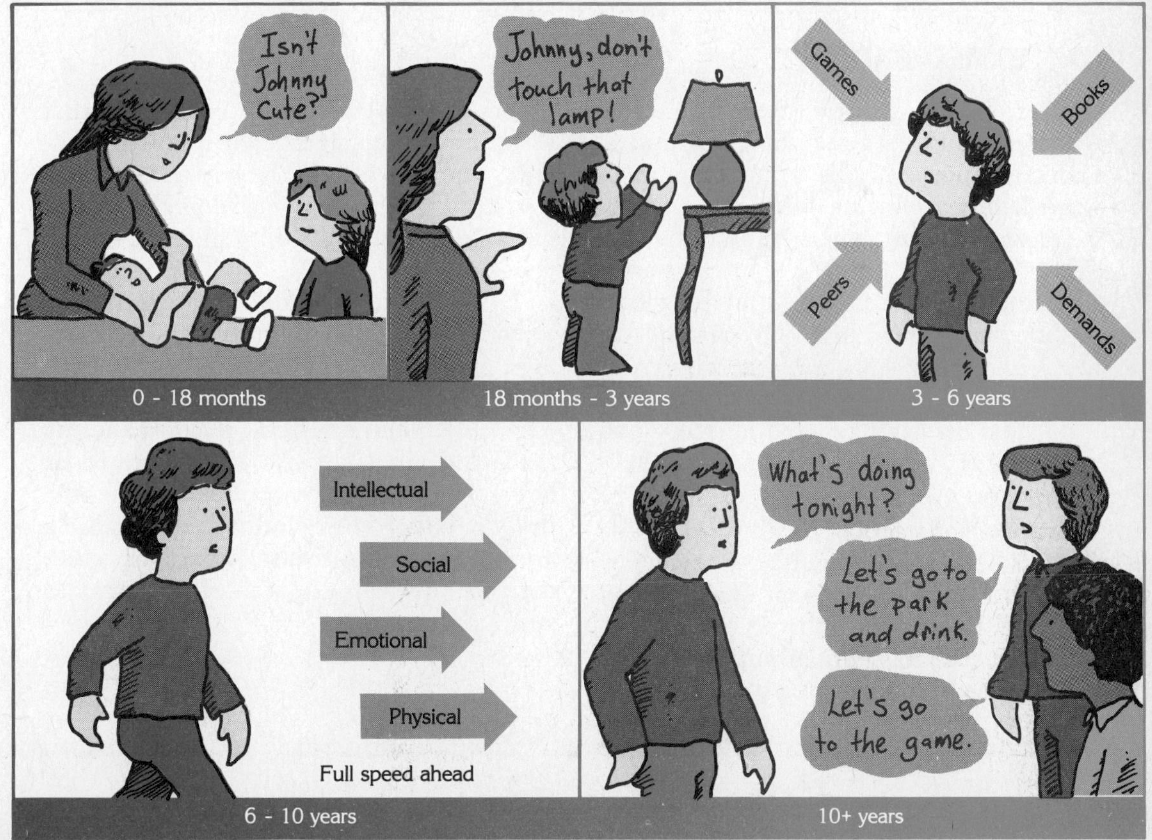

views of self appear in behavior and in the constellation of traits that we call personality. How do children reach these conclusions?

Significant Others. Harry Stack Sullivan, a psychiatrist who has had a powerful impact on American psychology, placed great emphasis on what he termed *significant others* (parents, brothers, sisters, friends, teachers) and their effect on the developing self. His writings about healthy mental development in children and adults contain a wealth of knowledge about personality, by which he meant the relatively enduring pattern of recurrent interpersonal situations that characterize a human life (Sullivan, 1953). Of particular significance for us is Sullivan's insistence on developmental analysis for an understanding of personality.

Sullivan sought the best possible formulations for discovering how children mature and how this development is caused by the influence of significant people. The significant other is any person to whom a child responds, and it is usually significant others who cause feelings of anxiety. The following example is Sullivan's illustration of how significant others transmit anxiety. The infant may be nursing when something happens to make the mother anxious. In some way, the mother's reaction induces anxiety in the infant, who then may release the nipple, cease searching for it, actually reject it, and disrupt the interpersonal situation.

"GOOD ME—BAD ME"

Sullivan has frequently used the terms "good-me" and "bad-me" in his writings. The self-concept begins to appear almost immediately following birth and reflects the reactions of the person "mothering" the child. The "good mother" becomes a source of satisfaction for her child, providing love, comfort, and relief from physical needs. The "bad mother," conversely, betrays rejections and anxiety. These feelings are communicated readily to the child, who then incorporates them into an evolving self-concept.

But the satisfaction of physical needs alone is just not adequate. All evidence points to the need for contact, warmth, and love from the mother so that the "good-me" is encouraged. It is important that these feelings also be transmitted to children by others as they grow older. Then the father assumes a more significant role, strengthening the maleness of the boy and the femininity of the girl, and in so doing, fostering the sense of equality of which we are so conscious today.

The juvenile and adolescent years also provide enormous opportunity for self-development. Here children incorporate the opinions of teachers and peers into the self-concept, either reinforcing or contradicting the self-image that has been fostered at home. The eventual goal of development is the mentally healthy individual who has a predominantly positive self-image, or "good-me," but who, being human, also recognizes personal limitations.

The parental role is crucial in personality development. If children are deprived of kind, loving parents who establish and maintain a warm relationship with them, they suffer a need that will influence them all their lives. There have been a sufficient number of studies of institutionalized children to remove all doubt about the lasting effects of such emotional starvation. Children need a physical and emotional security that demands continual support. We have seen several examples of this need, especially as it affects the self-concept. The mother's reactions begin immediately to influence the child and thus begin immediately to shape personality. The manner in which needs are satisfied tend to form an attitude of trust or mistrust that the children adopt toward the world, thus creating the "good-me" or "bad-me" concept.

Likewise, the example of significant others leaves a lasting impact on such important aspects of development as identification and sex typing. The actions of parents toward one another are not ignored by the child and may actually be one of the decisive elements in shaping personality. Children do more than merely mimic the expressions, acts, and attitudes of others; they tend to observe the models and later reproduce their behavior, often with new twists of their own. (Recall Bandura's discussion of modeling.) The imitation of a parental act may not be immediate; there may be quite a time lag. Here is the significance of modeling. Seeing parents as desirable models, children incorporate such traits in their personalities.

Children also see parents as sources of power: power over them, over brothers and sisters, over home, money, car, and many other objects and activities. Thus by acquiring parental characteristics, they think that they are also acquiring parental power. Children also seem to sense that the more they resemble a parent, the more acceptable they become, and the more likely they will be to receive parental love. Unfortunately, the opposite is also true. A child can easily acquire a negative self-image because of parental attitudes. The "bad-me" is then in ascendancy and the child's self-concept is one of self-doubt, shame, and mistrust.

Discipline. Still, discipline is vital. Read with skepticism those who dwell only on the evil consequences of discipline; there is an equal danger if discipline is lacking. And contrary to so much we hear today, youngsters want a constructive discipline; they want to know the boundaries. We may go so far as to say that proper discipline is an expression of love to a youngster. (Recall Maslow's comments about a child's desire for boundaries.)

Here we are speaking not solely of physical punishment, but of a loving discipline that rewards or withholds reward in a judicious manner, a discipline that is explained to children so that they understand that they have not lost the parents' love. Discipline raises problems, but the parents who refuse to face the difficulties are not fulfilling their parental duties.

Famous studies in the developmental literature support our conclusion about these influences on a child's developing personality. Wesley Becker (1964), after reviewing the literature on the effects of parental discipline, concludes that the results of parental disciplinary practices cannot be interpreted outside the context of the warmth of the parent-child relationship, the prior history of disciplinary practices, the role structure of the family, and the socioeconomic conditions of the family. Thus any generalizations drawn from the research literature must be severely restricted. But some positive methods of child rearing receive support. The significance of warmth and love in aiding the growth of sociable, independent children finds repeated support (Becker, 1964). Parental hostility, especially if extreme, can have a lasting and severe impact. Yet there is no evidence to support the belief that all love techniques are good and all power techniques are bad. What seems to appear clearly in the literature are the desirable and undesirable consequences of the extreme forms of both restrictiveness and permissiveness.

Of one thing we can be sure: the parental role must change during the course of a child's development. The simple yes or no that usually suffices for the four-year-old can become the red flag of challenge for the teenager.

DISCIPLINE

Discipline is undoubtedly one of the most misunderstood notions in child psychology. Throughout our work we have touched on the problem, usually by mentioning the extremes (permissiveness or rigidity) as examples. The parents who refuse to set boundaries for their children, who are afraid to say no, who exercise no supervision over children's activities are actually establishing a potential for future damage.

To children, a parent's no is sometimes the most welcome sound on earth. Under pressure from their peers to do something or go somewhere they actually dislike, it is with an enormous sense of relief that they can say, "My parents won't let me." There is also another important feature of parental discipline. By establishing boundaries, parents give their youngsters something to push against, to test. This can be an important part of development, contributing to the acquisition of responsibility that characterizes the mature personality.

Parents who practice harshness offer the child only the alternatives of "do it or else." How can children develop feelings of warmth and acceptance in such a cold and sterile atmosphere? What does it teach children other than to be harsh in their relations with others? When children do wrong, know that what they did is wrong, and receive no punishment, they soon realize that someone is being dishonest with them. Conversely, when they are excessively punished for some slight offense, they also quickly understand that something is amiss. What is needed is a middle ground: firm and understanding discipline that is provided within an atmosphere of warmth and love.

As children mature, and if the relationship between parents and children has been warm and accepting, parents should explain their reasons for their reactions to a child's requests or behavior. It is a sign of maturity that children understand what the parent is doing and, reluctantly or not, abide by the decision. With added maturity, children become partners in the decision. If, for example, the parents are contemplating a move to a new house, children contribute their ideas to a discussion of neighborhood, friends, school, and even the type of house to be chosen.

During infancy and early childhood, children are loving creatures, warm and responsive. Parents must do everything they can to make themselves happy and comfortable with their children. How? Prenatal programs with the help of professionals such as physicians

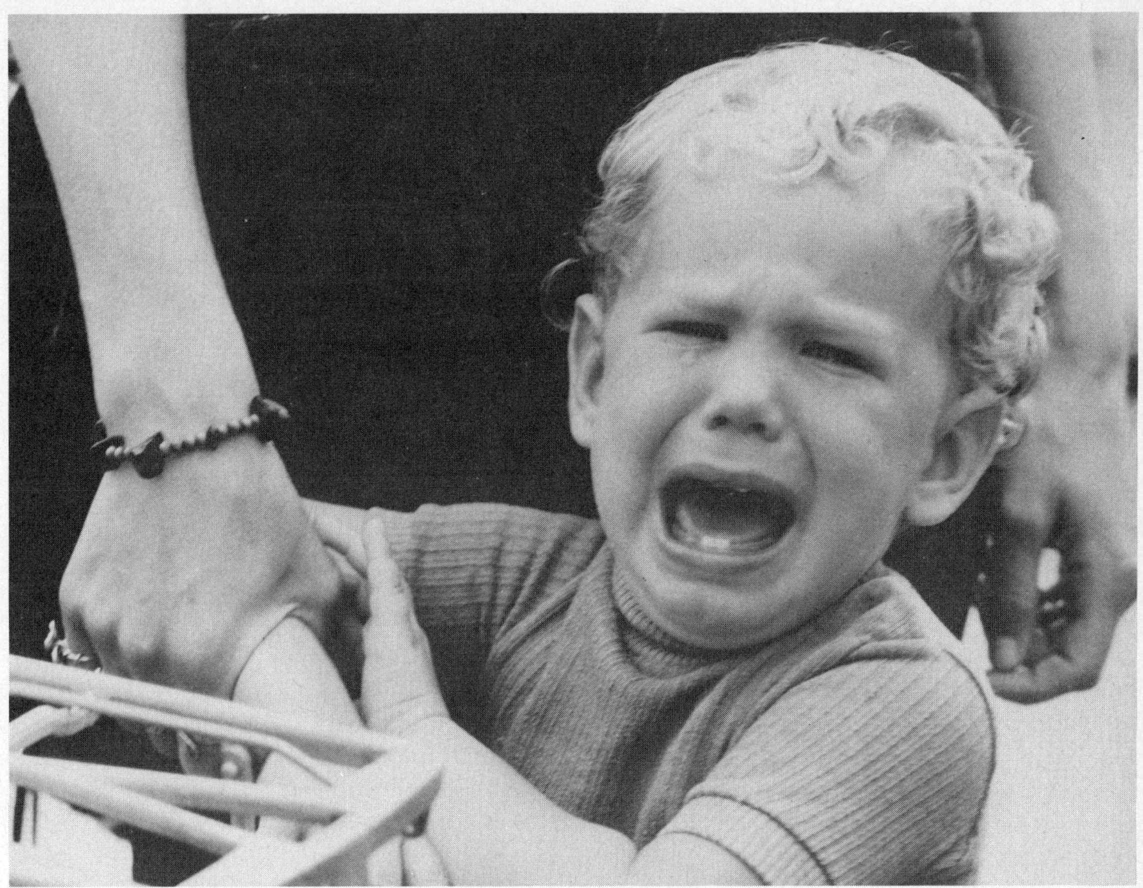

and psychologists are excellent resources. Children as they near two years become more independent, more mobile in explorations; they are also acquiring language. During this period, the parents should be sufficiently restrictive to prevent physical harm, but sensible enough to permit the activity and exploration (including the bumps and disappointments) that will ultimately lead to security and self-confidence—goals not easily achieved.

By the age of three or four, children actively engage in the world of symbols. They understand more of the mysteries of their surroundings, including the relationship between parents, which speaks for itself about a happy home environment. From the age of six on, the impact of peers becomes greater and requires diplomatic handling by parents. Youngsters need friends of their own age, yet we are all aware of the potential hazards of expanding friendships. Parents should discuss such friendships with special care; youngsters often later rebel and leave home because of unreasonable parental demands. It is a rare youngster of these years who will not listen to the reasons of parents and accept their guidance. If this is not the case at six, seven, or eight years of age, then it is a sign of difficulty in the rapport between parent and child.

The role of the school also becomes significant during these years. Youngsters should encounter a happy exciting world of ideas that will help to prepare them for their place in society. If the school does not provide a positive experience, or if the youngster is in constant trouble, the parents should seek the source of the trouble. If the fault lies with the child, parents should accept the responsibility and not blame others. If the school is at fault, the parents are best advised to move their child to another school if possible.

If youngsters have developed well through these formative years, adolescence, in spite of all that is said, will pose few problems. Adolescents are trouble to those parents who make them trouble; the terrible-tempered child of four will be the uncontrollable youth of eighteen, with much more serious consequences. Love, kindness, understanding, and the necessary discipline are the ingredients for a healthy, happy personality.

Locus of Control

Parents, peers, and a child's total environment subtly interact to produce feelings of confidence or uncertainty in a youngster's response toward life's challenges. They face the world with an "I can" or "I can't" attitude. A relatively new concept derived from social learning theory—locus of control—has provided considerable insight into this phenomenon. Did you do well in your last test in this course? You did? Why? Were you lucky? Does the instructor like you? Were you well prepared? Did you study carefully?

If you examine these questions you can discern a pattern: some responses indicate that anything good or valuable that happens to them is caused by chance; others indicate that the person (child or adult) was responsible. Using more refined and sophisticated versions of this basic theme, Julian Rotter (1966, 1975) and E. Jerry Phares (1973) analyzed individuals according to internality or externality. If children believe that they have little control over the consequences of their actions, they are *external*; if they believe that they can control what happens to them, they are *internal*.

If youngsters suppose that success and rewards result from skill and not from luck, they assume that they have control over their own destinies; believing that rewards come from luck and not from skill identifies those who believe in the external control of their lives. Phares states that the internal-external control of reinforcement is a generalized expectancy of children's (or adults') interpretation of the link between their behavior and the consequences of reward and punishment. Developmentally, locus of control soon becomes an enduring personality characteristic. Individuals are typically neither all internal nor all external, but more of one than the other.

Internals seem to act in a careful, calculated manner, rather than in the random "hope for the best" manner of the externals. As a result of his research and that of others, Rotter (1966) states that internals:

1. attend more alertly to their environments;
2. act to improve their immediate environments;
3. emphasize skill, performance, and achievement;
4. make firm decisions and resist influence.

Since internals are characterized as independent, alert, competent, and self-confident, it is difficult to avoid the conclusion that internality is the preferable personality characteristic. Rotter (1975) cautions against such speculation by noting that internals may be cold and rather withdrawn, while externals can just as readily be appealing and socially attractive. He also warns that externality may permit some youngsters to adapt successfully,

OTHER IMPORTANT INFLUENCES

In our discussion of the influences on personality development, we have concentrated mainly on the "most significant" others—the parents. There are, of course, many other important influences. Among them we may include:

1. *Physique and health.* Children's bodies are of constant concern almost as soon as they can compare themselves with others. The husky boy with a rugged physique quickly dominates his peers. The pretty girl with the nice figure is much admired by her peers. There is, also, of course, constant worry: oily hair, lengh of hair, pimples, and sheer physical growth (especially height for boys and breast development for girls) can affect the total personality. What children see as bodily advantages or disadvantages influences the self-concept, resulting in shyness or confidence, popularity or relative isolation, acceptance or rejection.

2. *Intelligence.* Intelligence can be influential in personality development. Success in school leads to a feeling of confidence and a willingness to face new tasks, while failure leads to the opposite: a feeling of shame and inadequacy. But some interesting problems arise, particularly with girls. Bright girls, as they grow older, may fear excelling in school and "beating the boys" because they fear a loss of appeal to boys who perceive them as unfeminine and threatening. We will shortly discuss this in more detail in the section on sex identity.

3. *Teachers.* From the moment children enter school, teachers become significant others in their lives. Teachers become educational parents, acting to encourage change, to support, and to criticize children. The manner in which they do this is extremely important. We mentioned the child's tendency to incorporate the parents' reactions into the developing self-concept, but they also incorporate teachers' reactions. Teachers who make such comments as "How could you be so dumb!" are exercising a decisive negative effect on personality. Perhaps, above all, honesty and moderation are most important in a teacher's reactions to children.

4. *Peers.* As children move from the family activities, acceptance by the peer group becomes exceedingly important. There are many reasons for acceptance or rejection, including some that we have already mentioned: physical appearance, intelligence, and elements such as economic status, experience, and willingness to "go along." The values of the group may clash with those of parents, and a resolution calls for some delicate guidance. But the reaction of peers also affects personality. Acceptance by peers can lead to increased confidence, thus providing a real lift to the self-concept. Rejection can shake youngsters, causing them to question their worth. The nature of the peer group also influences the kind of personality changes that may occur: the likeable, friendly boy may become the tough wise guy; the aggressive, hostile girl may become a more tolerant, friendly daughter.

5. A wide variety of other influences, ranging from family socioeconomic status to a child's position in the family birth order, affect the growing personality. Since these are so important, and since any discussion of them must be extensive, these topics have been allotted a separate chapter early in Part III. They are mentioned here to alert you to their role in personality development.

whereas internality sometimes causes serious problems. For example, youngsters with authoritarian parents realistically assume that they have little control over their actions; youngsters from impoverished environments also realistically recognize that their well-being depends on others. Note that Rotter is not making a value judgment, but simply presenting a practical assessment of how things are. Nevertheless, examining the characteristics of internality and externality makes it clear why internality is favored.

Internals	*Externals*
alert	less attention to environment
competent	erratic performance
resist influence	influenced by status
goal directed	need directed
achievement oriented	influenced by group members
independent	belief in control by others
self-confident	lack confidence in their own ability
perform skillfully	react randomly
react to a predictable world	react to an unpredictable world

Parental behavior seems to be closely correlated with either internality or externality. Lefcourt (1976), summarizing the literature, states that an attentive, responsive, critical, and contingent milieu in which youngsters learn that their actions produce results fosters an internal locus of control.

The less responsive and less opportune circumstances of the poor and deprived (both physically and psychologically) "create a climate of fatalism and helplessness" and produce an external locus of control. Lefcourt concludes that opportunities for contingent responses, either in the home or the larger social environment, is critical for the nature of a child's locus of control.

The parents of internal children are flexible and nonrejecting. They accept their children, use less hostile methods of control, and rapidly establish positive relationships with their youngsters. The parents themselves manifest internality. Externals result from rejecting, authoritarian parental behavior, often accompanied by decidedly inconsistent disciplinary practices.

Table 10.3 summarizes the variables that affect the development of locus of control.

TABLE 10.3. Variables Influencing Locus of Control

Variable	Internal	External
Age	Increases with age	No discernible change
Social class	Upper mobility increases internality	Lower class members exhibit greater externality
Ethnicity	Dominant groups demonstrate greater internality	Greater in minority group members
Intelligence	Inclusive results	Inconclusive
Sex	Males slightly more internal	Females slightly more external

A child or adult's locus of control can change if the individual encounters experiences that meaningfully alter the contingencies between their acts and perceived outcomes (Lefcourt, 1976, p. 126). Lefcourt emphasizes that verbal expressions of causality only suggest the nature of an individual's locus of control and may indeed only be rough approximations of the actual construct. As Lefcourt stresses, locus of control is not a personality trait; it often is a momentary indication of causality.

Change in belief about locus of control is inevitable if conditions change; it is the individual who is trapped in an unchanging environment whose sense of causality remains fixed. We have already mentioned age as an agent of change. Lefcourt describes a study in which student supporters of presidental candidate Eugene McCarthy were administered a locus of control scale after the 1968 Democratic National Convention. The results clearly indicated that the McCarthy followers were significantly more external than the national norms for university students. They manifested more feelings of helplessness; in spite of their efforts, circumstances had conspired against them. Research clearly supports the belief that locus of control is subject to change.

Finally, using James Fenimore Cooper's novel *The Deerslayer* as an example, Lefcourt links the Deerslayer's courage in the face of torture to locus of control. When one believes that hope is possible, that there still exists the opportunity for personal action, then the determination to act seems dramatically evident. Still, Lefcourt's warnings about interpreting locus of control are timely:

1. Locus of control is but one personality variable.
2. People are neither totally internal, nor totally external; the prevalent characteristic merely represents a person's more common expectations about the consequences of actions.
3. Predictions of behavior based on locus of control are usually most accurate when restricted to a specific aspect of an individual's life.
4. Many confounding variables may influence locus of control; that is, sex alone may not be responsible for a person's predominant external locus of control, but age, social class, and race may also be influential.

Tyler (1978, p. 218) summarizes the locus of control concept as follows:

> Generally speaking, internals or origins have a considerable advantage over externals or pawns. They achieve more in schools and in many other situations, they are more resistant to influence, more able to defer gratification. People from less privileged sectors of the population, who in fact do have less control over their destinies than people from more privileged sectors, constantly score in the external direction. But research has also demonstrated that one's orientation can be shifted toward internality by appropriate educational procedures.

DISCUSSION QUESTIONS

1. Do you agree with Thomas and Chess about immediate individuality? How do you explain the thirty-five percent of their initial study who defied classification?
2. Trace the stages in Escalona's research. Give specific examples of how individual stable patterns of experiences, and clusters of them, can shape a child's interaction with the environment.
3. In both of Kagan's studies discussed in this chapter, sex differences and social class differences strongly influenced personality. Give specific examples of how each could affect certain personality characteristics.
4. Who were the significant others in your life? Can you recall how they affected you? Again, be specific and state what personality characteristics reflect their influence.
5. Indicate how parents and teachers would exercise their influence according to social learning theory. Can you discern influences that flow from Maslow's and Erikson's work?
6. Are you aware of any personality changes you may have had? Can you account for their appearance? Assuming that you can identify your infant temperament (from recalling anecdotes about your childhood), has there been consistency in your personality? How can you reconcile change with inherent temperamental tendencies?
7. Is the locus of control concept meaningful for you? Why? How do you characterize yourself—internal or external? Can you add any variables, including prenatal behavior, to your assessment?

Examining the difficulties inherent in any endeavor to formulate a definition of personality, you can better understand its meaning, particularly if you bear in mind that any definition must reflect the definer's view of human nature. You will then have a basis for interpreting any insightful personality theory. Definition also helps to interpret the pattern of personality development, especially as you attempt to penetrate beyond surface behavioral characteristics. Still, the behavioral characteristics are the data with which we work, and they indicate the various stages through which children pass.

Do children manifest consistent patterns in their development? Is this the sort of behavior that we should anticipate from youngsters this age? Or has the behavior become maladaptive? Here, knowledge of the origins of personality is most helpful. Are these characteristics typical of this temperament? Added insights into personality can only help us in our attempt to facilitate children's learning by accommodating techniques and materials to the individual child.

Although investigators have been frustrated in their endeavors to identify consistent personality traits, the search may be aided by a growing recognition that children seem to possess an inherent temperament. If neonates retain certain admittedly general, even vague characteristics for years, it may provide the basis for fruitful research. Until then the quest for the roots of individuality will provide psychological theory and research a formidable challenge.

SUMMARY

While definitions of personality are difficult to formulate, Guilford's judgment that personality is the child's unique pattern of traits seems the most workable.

Regardless of what elements are included in a definition, there should be emphasis on the organization of traits, since this is where uniqueness rests.

The uniqueness of personality and its expression in varied traits is a result of the interaction of heredity and environment.

General characteristics that appear in infancy (activity, intensity of response) seem to persist throughout the lifetime of a remarkably large number of children.

Personality theories, such as social learning, humanistic, and psychosocial, offer useful insights into the nature of personality.

A child's personality is strongly influenced by the "significant others" in the environment.

Significant others, a term coined by Harry Stack Sullivan, refers to those individuals who are extremely important to a child at various stages of development.

There are probably no more significant others than the parents, whom the child observes, models, accepts, rejects, loves and constantly tests.

The work of Escalona and Kagan offers a penetrating view of the origins and path of personality development.

What seems to be as significant as the interaction between infants and significant others is the infants' interpretation of that interaction.

As a characteristic of personality development, locus of control may provide information about a child's behavior under certain circumstances.

SUGGESTED READINGS

BANDURA, ALBERT. *Social Learning Theory.* Englewood Cliffs, New Jersey: Prentice-Hall, 1977. A fine basic analysis of social learning theory and its application.

BLOOM, BENJAMIN. *Stability and Change in Human Characteristics.* New York: John Wiley & Sons, 1964. A thorough assessment of the difficulty in measuring personality stability.

ERIKSON, ERIK. *Identity: Youth and Crisis.* New York: W. W. Norton, 1968. A leading theorist delineates and interprets stages of development.

ESCALONA, SIBYLLE. *The Roots of Individuality.* Chicago: Aldine Publishing Co., 1968. An excellent account of the search for the first signs of individuality.

GUILFORD, J. P. *Personality.* New York: McGraw-Hill, 1959. Thorough and comprehensive, Guilford's work remains a basic source.

HALL, CALVIN and GARDNER LINDZEY. *Theories of Personality.* New York: John Wiley & Sons, 1975. Probably the best summary of the various theories.

KAGAN, JEROME. *Change and Continuity in Infancy.* New York: John Wiley, 1971. A good summary of Kagan's search for continuity in personality characteristics.

KAGAN, JEROME and HOWARD A. MOSS. *Birth to Maturity: A Study in Psychological Development.* New York: John Wiley & Sons, 1962. An invaluable longitudinal study.

LEFCOURT, HERBERT. *Locus of Control: Current Trends in Theory and Research.* Hillsdale, N.J.: Lawrence Erlbaum, 1976. A comprehensive summary of the locus of control research.

MASLOW, ABRAHAM. *Motivation and Personality.* New York: Harper and Row, 1970. Perhaps Maslow's most complete statement about personality, self-actualization, and motivation.

SULLIVAN, HARRY STACK. *The Interpersonal Theory of Personality.* New York: W. W. Norton, 1953. One of Sullivan's basic works, filled with penetrating insights.

THOMAS, ALEXANDER and STELLA CHESS. *Temperament and Development.* New York: Brunner, Mazel, 1977. An articulate account of the renewed interest in inherent personality dispositions.

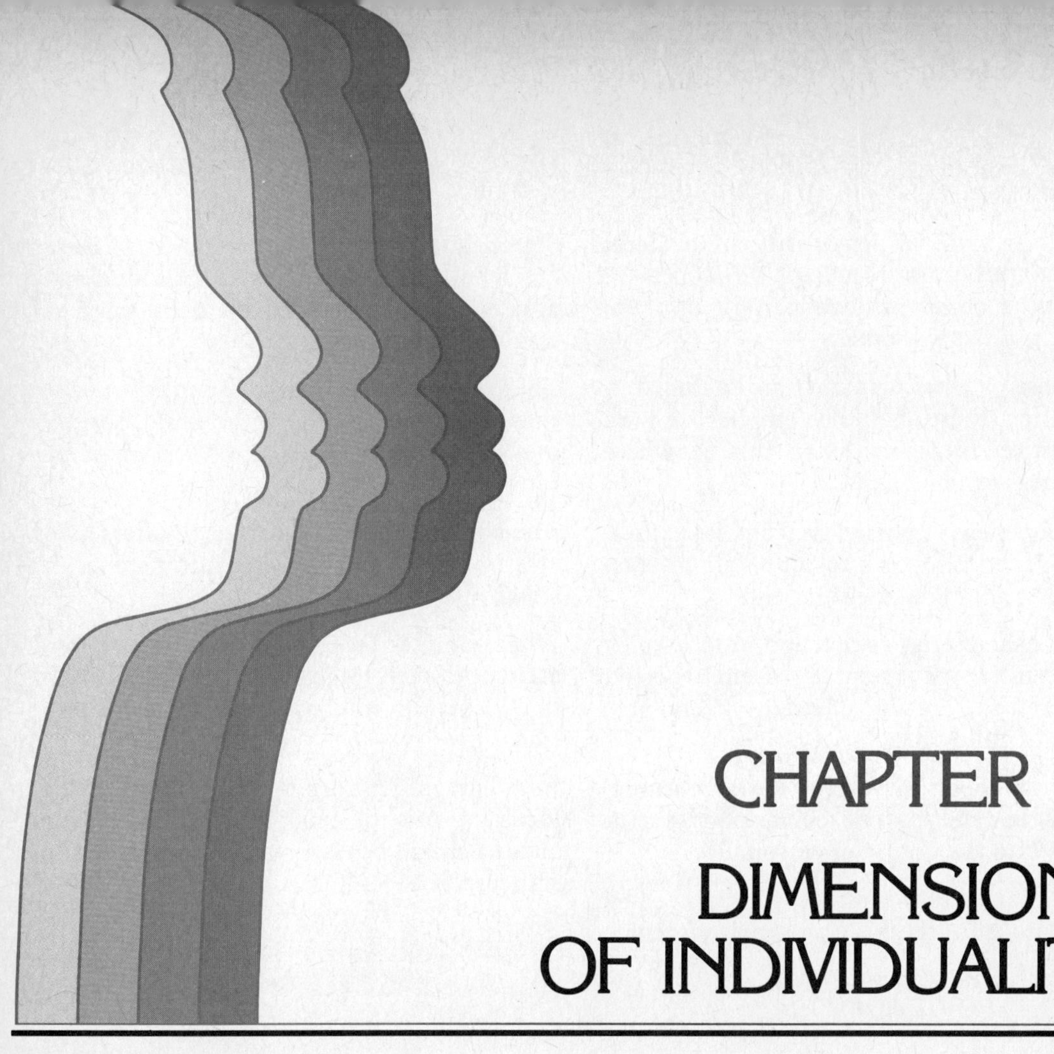

CHAPTER 11
DIMENSIONS OF INDIVIDUALITY

CHAPTER HIGHLIGHTS

Topics

Attachment
a. Bowlby and Attachment
b. Bonding (Klaus and Kennell)

Aggression
a. The Theories (Ethological, Psychoanalytic, Learning)
b. Sex Differences in Aggression
c. A Developmental Overview

Moral Development
a. Learning Theory
b. Cognitive Theory
c. Stages of Moral Development

Sex Identity
a. The Meaning of Gender Identity
b. Theoretical Explanations

People

Mary D. Salter Ainsworth
Leonard Berkowitz
John Bowlby
John Kennell
Marshall Klaus
Lawrence Kohlberg
Konrad Lorenz
John Money
L. Alan Sroufe
Edward Wilson

Special Topics

The Development of Mother-Infant Interaction
Normality
The Sociobiologists
XYY

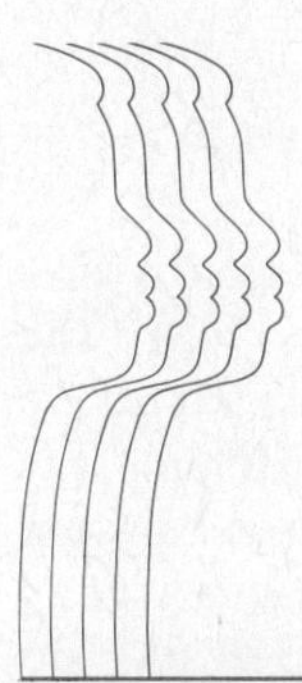

The previous chapter presented a general overview of personality development: the theories, longitudinal studies, and problems of analysis. A central theme that emerged was the search for persistence of personality characteristics and the difficulties in discovering continuity. While "common sense" suggests consistency, evidence fails to uncover it. Whether current research techniques are faulty, or whether continuity is nonexistent remains questionable.

Sroufe (1979) argues persuasively that a belief in the coherence of individual development has been a powerful force in developmental psychology and is now subject to observation. He faults research methodology for focusing on single tests or observations of single tasks and thus missing clues to continuity. He also believes that there are conceptual errors in current research. Since psychological development entails *qualitative* changes (not mere additions), assessments that repeatedly measure the same behavior overlook continuity. Sroufe proposes that investigators should seek qualitative similarities in behavioral patterns, that is, the strategies children use in adapting. Similarities in these strategies through the years may well contain long-sought continuities.

Such research encompasses five features:

1. *Focus on adaptation.* Children interact meaningfully with their environment; they change, and as they do, they change the environment, which then acts on them. It is a continuous, active cycle that reflects Escalona's search for how children feel about their interactions, how they use their environment to satisfy their needs.

2. *Recognition of the person as a coherent whole.* Children may behave differently in different situations, but, as Sroufe notes, *across* situations, their behavior is coherent.

3. *Acceptance of affective behavior.* Children are simultaneously frightened by the unknown, but also attracted by its allure; their fear causes them to seek security. This effect helps to structure behavioral organization.

4. *Focus on individual differences.* While children may differ in their timidity and bravery, they may demonstrate continuity in their ability to maintain organized behavior when challenged and excited. How adults (significant others) help youngsters to master tension is a key element in the type of continuity they exhibit.

5. *Acceptance of developmental reorganization.* Development is not linear nor additive. With new capacities and reorganized behavior, the resulting changes are qualitative, thus transforming not only children but also environments.

Again we note the active role of children in their own development. Sroufe (1979, p. 836) states:

> To understand the coherence of individual adaptation, viewing children as active participants in their own experience is essential. At least by the second half-year, the infant's reaction to events is subjective; it is determined by evaluative processes within the infant, as well as by objective information. Individual infants and children differ in their tendencies to see events as opportunities or threats, in their threshold for threat, in their capacity to maintain organized behavior in the face of arousal (novelty, complexity), and in their ability to derive security from the presence of the caregiver. More generally, children vary in their abilities to draw on personal and environmental resources in the face of a challenge.

The nature of children's interactions with their environment has captured the interest of recent research. It is more than the result of discrete actions; that is, the child does something to the environment and the environment does something to the child. What happens is that they both change and the next interaction is suitably different. Sameroff (1977) has long argued that "interaction" is poor terminology, since it implies a stable child and a stable environment. Both are constantly changing in significant ways; the changes are interdependent and mutually influential. Sameroff urges that "transaction" is a better word to describe the flexible character of both environment and child and far better represents the child's efforts to organize and structure the world. What remains constant are the processes that the child uses, what Sroufe called "similarities in functioning."

Sroufe (1979) states that once constitution and early experience interact to form the beginnings of personality, children are active forces in their own development. He presents a possible model to guide the search for continuity by identifying a series of issues around which development is organized. (Recall Havighurst's developmental task concept.) They form a sequence and each issue helps children to face subsequent issues. Table 11.1 illustrates the various issues.

How children adapt to these issues may provide clues to continuity since the quality of early adaptations will influence the nature of future adaptations. For example, securely attached infants demonstrate different behaviors from those less securely attached, but also exhibit different behavior years later; they are more persistent and enthusiastic when confronted with problem solving tasks at two years, and more curious and exploring at five years. Sroufe concludes that although the consequences of early experience may be obscure, there will be consequences.

This rather lengthy introduction is intended to alert you once again to the problem of continuity. Chapter Eleven will examine attachment, aggression, moral development, and sex identity as dimensions of a child's personality. As you read the theories and follow the research, ask yourself if there is a discernible thread of continuity; are there similar strategies across the ages and situations? Here we may possibly find the clue to consistency.

TABLE 11.1. Issues in Early Development

Phase	Age in months	Issue	Role for caregiver
1	0–3	Physiological regulation	Smooth routines
2	3–6	Management of tension	Sensitive, cooperative interaction
3	6–12	Establishing an effective attachment relationship	Responsive availability
4	12–18	Exploration and mastery	Secure base
5	18–30	Individuation (autonomy)	Firm support
6	30–54	Management of impulses, sex role identification, peer relations	Clear roles and values, flexible self-control

From L. Alan Sroufe. "The Coherence of Individual Development," *American Psychologist*, Volume 34, No. 10, October, 1979, pp. 834–841.

ATTACHMENT

While attachment is a topic that has long fascinated psychologists, the term itself has been a source of controversy. Ainsworth (1973, p. 1) defines attachment as follows:

> An attachment is an affectional tie that one person forms to another specific person, binding them together in space and enduring over time. Attachment is discriminating and specific. One may be attached to more than one person, but one cannot be attached to many people. Attachment implies affect. Although the affects may be complex and may vary from time to time, positive affect predominates, and we usually think of attachment as implying affection and love.

Most investigators find Ainsworth's definition acceptable. Controversy, however, swirls around terminology. Is the more accurate term "attachment," or is "dependency" more suitable? Maccoby and Masters (1970) argue that attachment and dependency both refer to behavior and not to a state of helplessness; it is behavior that maintains a close contact between a child and one or more adults and that elicits supportive behavior from such individuals.

Maccoby and Masters (1970) reason that if children's behavior suggests that they find other people, their presence, and their attention rewarding, then they are exhibiting dependent behavior. They list several behaviors that are generally considered to be dependent.

1. Seeking physical contact.
2. Seeking to be near.
3. Seeking attention.
4. Seeking praise and approval.
5. Resisting separation.

Bowlby (1969) disagrees strenuously with this usage. He states (1969, p. 228) that to be dependent on a mother-figure and to be attached to her are very different things. An infant is dependent on the mother during the first few weeks of life but is not attached to her. A two-year-old child in a daycare center may be attached to the mother but not dependent on her.

Bowlby also makes a value judgment about the term "dependency." Dependency implies an undesirable condition. To call anyone dependent is disparaging; to say that someone is attached is usually regarded as admirable.

If a child carries dependency into adolescence and adulthood, it may indicate pathological behavior.

Perhaps the argument is semantic. While attachment is the preferred term for our work, it nevertheless encompasses the views of Maccoby and Masters.

Segal (1978) asks what explains attachment. Is it something inherent in the mother to which the infant has a biological urge to respond? Is it because the mother is the primary source of reinforcement? Or is it simply because the mother is there? Bowlby's efforts to answer these and similar questions have attracted international attention.

Bowlby and Attachment

Bowlby's basic premise is quite simple. A warm, intimate relationship between an infant and mother is essential to mental health, since a child's need for a mother's presence is as great as the need for food. Attachment has instinctive origins. The continued absence of the mother can generate a sense of loss and feelings of anger. (Bowlby, in his 1969 classic, states quite clearly that a child's principal attachment figure can be someone other than the natural mother.)

Background of the Theory. A series of studies conducted by Bowlby and others, which dates back to the early 1940s, describes a situation in which children of fifteen to thirty months who had good relationships with their mothers were then separated from their mothers. As Bowlby (1969, p. 27) phrases it, "a predictable sequence of behavior" followed: protest, despair, and detachment.

The first phase, *protest,* may begin immediately and persist for about one week. The child's distress is obvious, manifest in loud crying, extreme restlessness, and typical rejection of all adult figures. *Despair* soon follows, which is characterized by behavior that suggests a growing hopelessness: monotonous crying, inactivity, and steady withdrawal. *Detachment* appears when the child shows a renewed interest in his or her surroundings, but it is a distant interest. Bowlby describes the youngster's behavior as remote and apathetic even if the mother visits her child.

The Development of Human Attachment. Sometime during the development of attachment, Bowlby believes, proximity to the mother becomes a primary goal. Table 11.2 presents a chronology of attachment development.

What is the developmental nature of this class of behaviors? In a well-known study, Schaffer and Emerson (1964) observed sixty Scottish infants from five weeks to eighteen months of age. They interviewed the mothers, observed the children in a variety of situations, and evaluated the infants' changing responses to interviewers. During the early weeks (from five to twenty-three weeks), the youngsters evidenced some upset at separation from their mothers, but at about seven months of age when specific attachments emerged, this dependent behavior became much more intense, and it increased during the following three to four months.

The children displayed notable differences in the time of the onset of specific attachments. One youngster manifested a specific attachment as early as twenty-two weeks, while another did not show the same type of dependent behavior until he was one year old. There were also changes in the kinds of situations that produced a disturbance in the

TABLE 11.2. Chronology of Attachment Development

Age	Characteristics	Behavior
4 months	Perceptual discrimination; visual tracking of mother	Smiles and vocalizes more with mother than anyone else; begins to manifest distress at separation
9 months	Separation anxiety, stranger anxiety	Cries when mother leaves; clings at appearance of strangers (mother is primary object)
2–3 years	Intensity and frequency of attachment behavior remains constant; increase in perceptual range changes circumstances that elicit attachment	Notices impending departure thus signaling a better understanding of surrounding world
3–4 years	Growing confidence; tendency to feel secure in a strange place with subordinate attachment figures (relatives)	Begins to accept mothers' temporary absence; plays *with* other children
4–10 years	Less intense attachment behavior but still strong	May hold parent's hand while walking; anything unexpected causes child to turn to parent
Adolescence	Weakening attachment to parents; peers and other adults become important	Becomes attached to groups and group members
Adult	Attachment bond still discernible	In difficulty, adults turn to trusted friends; elderly direct attachment toward younger generation

infants. The youngest children, for example, protested at being left alone or with someone other than the attachment figure, and their objection increased in intensity until eighteen months. Fear of strangers appeared about one month after attachment to a specific person, usually the mother. After the first specific attachment, there was an increase in the number of attachment figures, which occurred fairly rapidly from three months on.

As with most developmental changes, the question may be asked: Is there a sensitive period for the appearance of attachments? Bettye Caldwell (1964) reports that infants placed for adoption at three months showed little upset after placement. But eighty-six percent of the youngsters aged six months or more showed more severe disturbances than the younger children, and the disturbances seemed to become more severe during each month from three to twelve months. These results indicate that the older children (three to twelve months) had formed a much more intense attachment to some attending individual, which supports Bowlby's conclusions.

The Phases of Attachment. Within the chronology just outlined, Bowlby delineates four recognizable developmental phases.

1. *Orientation and signals without discrimination of figure.* Infants display characteristic reactions to people, but their discrimination of others is severely limited. For the normal child, these limitations extend from birth to about eight weeks, during which they are tracking, grasping, smiling, and babbling.

2. *Orientation and signals directed towards one (or more) discriminated figures.* The identical behaviors described in Phase One continue, but now are directed more at the mother-figure. This phase lasts until about six months.

3. *Maintenance of proximity to a discriminated figure by means of locomotion as well as signals.* Discrimination of others continues, and focus on the mother intensifies. With sharpened discrimination, friendliness to everyone diminishes; some figures are selected as subsidiary attachment figures, and strangers gradually evoke alarm. Phase Three appears between six months and persists into the third year.

4. *Formation of a goal connected partnership.* During this phase children not only perceive their mothers as independent objects in time and space (paralleling cognitive development), but they also begin to understand her actions and motives. Consequently, the relationship with the mother becomes more complex and sophisticated and helps to advance children's interpretation of their world.

Analyzing these phases, Bowlby believes that true attachment does not appear until Phase Three.

Finally, the importance of attachment in human lives is dramatically emphasized by Bowlby when he states (1969, p. 350):

> It has been said repeatedly that attachment behavior does not disappear with childhood but persists throughout life. Either old or new figures are selected and proximity and/or communication maintained with them. Whereas outcome of behavior continues much as before, means for achieving it become increasingly diverse.

Recent Research. Ainsworth (1979), who accepts Bowlby's theoretical interpretation of attachment, reviewed current research using the "strange situation technique" to study attachment. Placing children in a strange situation enables investigators to classify behavior according to children's reactions following separation. Ainsworth identified three major types in one-year-old infants:

1. *Group A babies,* who rarely cried during separation and avoided their mothers at reunion. The mothers of these babies seemed to dislike physical contact, or were indifferent to it.

2. *Group B babies,* who were secure and used the mother as a base from which to explore. Separation intensified their attachment behavior; they exhibited considerable distress, ceased their explorations, and, at reunion, sought contact with their mothers.

3. *Group C babies,* who manifested anxiety before separation and who were intensely distressed by any separation. Yet on reunion they displayed ambivalent behavior toward their mothers; they sought contact, but simultaneously seemed to resist it.

Examining the nature of mother-infant interaction, Ainsworth (1979) states that feeling, close bodily contact, and face-to-face interaction seem to be of equal importance in the child's expectations of the mother's behavior. Ainsworth sensibly concludes that a mother who is sensitive to her baby's signals in one context is also sensitive to signals in another context.

The security attained during the early attachment phases seems to have enduring qualities. For example, securely attached infants later have more positive and cooperative relations with family members, are more competent, and have better interactions with their peers. Group A babies later showed more aggressive behavior, while Group C babies were more easily frustrated, less persistent, and less competitive.

THE DEVELOPMENT OF MOTHER-INFANT INTERACTION

Brazelton and Als (1979), in examining children's shaping of their environment, were struck by the power of the dyadic interaction between mother and child, and the importance of *not* analyzing each member of the dyad as an independent actor. Conducting prenatal interviews, the investigators discerned anxiety feelings in the mothers that approached the pathological. Yet after birth, these same women were efficient mothers. The investigators concluded that the "alarm reactions" they had observed were actually an organizational mechanism designed to help women adjust to future varied demands, thus preparing the path for adjustment.

Examining neonatal behavior, the authors believe that in spite of the enormous immediate adjustments that infants must make, there is evidence of cognitive and affective responses. Brazelton and Als state that after employing, almost testing, their reflex behaviors, infants suppress interfering motor activity (as much as possible) to learn about their world. Thus infants immediately begin to control themselves in order to respond appropriately to their environment. So *both* parents and children are learning about themselves and each other.

The authors state (1979, p. 354–355):

> The notion of a feedback system seems to fit our model particularly well, since it presents an adaptive model to stress and change, with a built-in self-regulatory goal. The immature organism with its vulnerability to being overloaded must be in constant homeostatic regulation—the physiological and the psychological. Handling input becomes a major goal for the infant, rather than a demanding and destructive one. Such a system can handle disruption by either negative, stressful or by positive, attractive stimuli; but the organizing aspect of both is seen in the amount of growth of the system.

The authors thus describe a homeostatic circle to which both parents and the child contribute—disruption, progress, reachievement of homeostasis—resulting in four stages of interactive development.

1. Infants achieve homeostatic control; that is, they can both incorporate and exclude external stimuli while maintaining control over differing states (recall Brazelton's six states discussed in Chapter Four).
2. Once control develops, infants can then use social stimuli to prolong states of attention.
3. Using this feedback system, both parents and child extend the infant's ability to incorporate stimuli and then to recover homeostasis.
4. Finally, infant autonomy appears when the mother permits the baby to signal innate actions (reaching for and playing with objects). The authors believe that their model explains flexibility, disruption, and reorganization, thus helping us to understand the reciprocal bond between parent and infant.

Ainsworth (1973), drawing on the attachment literature, has several suggestions for those with responsibility for children.

1. Interaction with a mother-figure, with resulting attachment, is essential for healthy development. Ainsworth stresses that research clearly demonstrates that infants experiencing maternal deprivation (a mother figure) may suffer abnormal development. Sponsored interactions, no matter how sophisticated, usually lack the vitality of a natural attachment.

2. Sensitive periods for attachment seem to exist, but an infant's need is so strong that healthy attachments form after the typical time. For example, adoption studies show that attachment develops for one-year-old infants. Desirable interactions cannot be delayed indefinitely, however.

3. Prolonged separation from the attachment figure produces distress in the child. Once the attachment is formed, separation can cause pathological effects. Ainsworth distinguishes between "major" and "minor" separations. From six months to three years, the attached adults should avoid lengthy separations, even attempting to alleviate the effects of hospitalization. If it is impossible to avoid a major separation, a thoughtful consideration should be given to the child's environment; the home environment should be the first choice, followed by an atmosphere in which the child can receive considerable attention and perhaps form secondary attachments. It is impossible to exaggerate the significance of this conclusion, since research also suggests that even minor separations bother some children.

4. Fostering attachment behavior does not spoil a child. For example, during the first year, babies cry when something is wrong. Maternal responses, encompassing proximity and contact, promote attachment and actually reduce crying by the latter part of the first year.

Bonding

Klaus and Kennell (1976), in their discussion of bonding, analyze its development from the parent-to-infant perspective. The impetus to their investigations came from the puzzling conditions of premature infants who, after heroic measures had been taken to save them, returned battered and bruised to the hospital. A disproportionate number of prematures were among abused infants and those who failed to thrive (see Chapter Fifteen). The most significant difference between these and other babies was their early separation from their mothers.

The authors were intrigued by another condition. Mothers who had successfully delivered and managed full-term infants were anxious and uncertain about their care of a premature. Klaus and Kennell then asked how mothers and fathers become attached to their infants. They concluded that human parenting behavior is derived from a complex interplay of heredity, the infant's reactions to the adult, personal and familial relations, previous pregnancies, cultural expectations, and their own parents' practices with them.

The authors hypothesize that many disorders occur mainly from separation and other unusual conditions immediately following birth. The authors believe that for maternal attachment to develop, the following principles must be recognized.

1. There is a critical period in the initial hours after birth during which mothers and fathers must have close contact with their newborn.
2. There are species-specific parental responses to the infant on first contact.
3. Attachment is structured so that parents become attached to only one infant at a time.
4. To facilitate attachment infants must contribute some signals to the mother.

5. Witnessing a birth causes a strong attachment.
6. Early experiences may have a lasting influence.

Finally, Ainsworth (1979) summarizes both the importance of attachment and the basis for continuity in development when she states:

> It is clear that the nature of an infant's attachment to his or her mother as a one-year-old is related both to earlier interaction with the mother and to various aspects of later development. The implication is that the way in which the infant organizes his or her behavior toward the mother affects the way in which he or she organizes behavior toward other aspects of the environment, both animate and inanimate. This organization provides a core of continuity in development despite changes that come with developmental acquisitions, both cognitive and socioemotional.

DISCUSSION QUESTIONS

1. Do you agree with Sroufe's analysis of continuity in development? Why? Can you give examples of similarities in strategies that you recognize in yourself and others?
2. Explain Sameroff's interpretation of "transaction." Do you consider it a meaningful term? Why? What distinguishes it from interaction?"
3. With whom do you agree concerning the usage of "attachment" or "dependency"? Can you distinguish between the two? How?
4. Why is Bowlby's an instinct theory? Do you agree with his statement that true attachment does not appear until the third of his developmental phases? Why? What do investigators mean when they say that attachment fosters the security to explore?
5. Explain Ainsworth's Group A, B, C babies. What was the basis of classification? Are there any long-term implications?
6. In our work on neonatal assessment, Brazelton's use of state was seen as a major insight into infant behavior. Can you explain how he and Als use state in their delineation of the stages of mother-infant interaction?

AGGRESSION

The second dimension of individuality to be discussed is aggression, which unfortunately cannot be defined as neatly as attachment. If your definition of aggression encompasses all harm, then accidents must be included; but if you consider *intent* to harm, then accidents would be excluded. For our purposes, aggression is behavior directed at an organism or object and causing injury to that object or person. Intent is implied in this definition, since it is difficult, if not impossible, to avoid a person's motives in causing injury. Feshbach (1970) attempts to circumvent the definitional problem by employing two categories of aggression: *unintentional* and *intentional.* Intentional aggression is either instrumental (aggressive behavior designed to secure non-aggressive goals, such as pushing another child to seize a toy), or hostile (designed to hurt another). Recall, however, that intent to harm is the basis of true aggressive behavior.

NORMALITY

Analysis of topics such as dependency and aggression can easily lead to unwarranted conclusions about normality. The well-known British child psychologist C. W. Valentine insists on the use of unselected children for his observations, since there is the danger that if we study only difficult children we become trapped in their problems. For example, there is the tendency to believe that since some neurotic children are dependent, then all children who show signs of dependency are neurotic. Even Freud warned that not all children who show neurotic signs remain neurotic later in life.

Many parents and even teachers become quite worried at indications of dependency or aggression. While current childrearing practices may seem permissive, we are still inclined to expect a child to conform to adult standards. Obviously this is impossible, since children are children and not pocket-sized adults. Only the persistence of these symptoms should alarm parents or teachers. For most youngsters disturbing symptoms are eliminated from about two to six years of age. It is estimated that about five percent of all school-age youngsters manifest serious symptoms and about ten percent show milder degrees of disturbance, leaving about eighty-five percent "normal" children, all of whom have manifested some disturbing symptoms at various ages.

It is the age and the symptoms that are vitally important. More children bite their nails at ten than at five; bed-wetting at eighteen months is natural, but at three or four years, it could indicate some underlying problem. When a youngster of ten behaves like a five-year-old, then there is cause for concern.

Theories of Aggression

There have been several explanations for the appearance of human aggression, ranging from a biological rationale that attributes aggression to maternal deprivation upsetting the brain's pleasure centers, to a strict learning theory analysis. Among the most enduring are the ethological, psychoanalytic, and learning theories.

Ethological Theory. Probably the most popular of the ethological positions is that proposed by Konrad Lorenz in his famous book, *On Aggression.* Lorenz believes that aggression is an innate human characteristic that grows spontaneously until discharged. It is an instinctive drive that simply must have some outlet or it will burst with explosive force when triggered by appropriate stimuli.

In most animals, aggression ceases when the triggering stimuli are removed, but not in humans, as demonstrated by the deadliness of human war. To explain this contradiction, Lorenz turns to "pseudo-speciation," the notion that one's enemies are considered less than human; they have forfeited their rights to be considered human. This, coupled with the social reinforcement that accompanies such behavior, helps to explain human killings.

Lorenz emphasizes the instinctive roots of aggression, but nevertheless recognizes the role of the environment. He states that nothing is totally innate because the genetic program for behavior needs the environment for its expression. Although the genes provide the blueprint and the information for development, human aggression usually responds to certain signals. Lorenz also believes that spontaneous aggression may be channeled into recreational activities such as football, soccer, viewing television. (The conflict between theories is clearly evident here, since learning theorists criticize Lorenz's attempts to inhibit aggression by these techniques. Learning theorists would argue that the violence observed or engaged in may be reinforcing and thus act to *increase* aggressive behavior.)

THE SOCIOBIOLOGISTS

Are human beings innately aggressive? Edward Wilson, the controversial sociobiologist, unequivocably answers yes. With the warning that innateness refers to the probability that a trait will appear under certain environmental conditions (*not* to the certainty that the trait will appear in all environments), Wilson (1979) disagrees sharply with Lorenz's explanation. He argues that research indicates that there is no general instinct for aggressive behavior that is common to most species.

Although humans are "markedly predisposed to aggressiveness," a more subtle explanation is needed than that of inborn drives that inevitably are channelled into violence. Wilson suggests that recent anthropological evidence suggests that aggression is better explained by the interaction of genetic potential and learning. Much of aggression, especially its techniques (military strategy), is learned, but humans are "strongly predisposed to stride into deep, irrational hostility under certain definable conditions" (p. 106).

Thus aggression is neither an animal instinct nor the result of environmental shaping. Humans have a powerful inclination to respond violently to external threats, hoping to overwhelm their source. We tend to solve conflict by aggression. In a time of escalating international violence, Wilson's thoughts (p. 119) about learning the rules of aggression are worth repeating:

> The learning rules of violent aggression are largely obsolete. We are no longer hunter-gatherers who settle disputes with spears, arrows, and stone axes. But to acknowledge the obsolescence of the rules is not to banish them. We can only work our way around them. To let them rest latent and unsummoned, we must consciously undertake those difficult and rarely travelled pathways in psychological development that lead to mastery over and reduction of the profound human tendency to learn violence.

Psychoanalytic Theory. Psychoanalytic explanations of aggression begin with Freud's belief in life and death instincts. The death instinct, which may be directed either internally or externally, is aggression when aimed at others. The life instinct blocks the inward movement toward self-destruction and deflects it outward. Consequently, aggression is an innate drive resulting from the conflict of two fundamental biological processes (Feshbach, 1970). Cofer and Appley (1964, p. 605) summarize this conflict as follows:

> Only in the case of aggression, which Freud attributed to the death instinct, are the manifestations visible. Normally operating internally, and having the goal of death (the individual is said to harbor an unconscious wish to die), the forces of Thanatos are fused with (and/or counterbalanced by) the forces of Eros. Aggression may be (and usually is assumed to be) diverted outward and manifests itself in sadism, destruction, and murder; later it may be turned inward again, as self-aggression sometimes breaks through as in masochism, self-mutilation, self-derogation, or defamation. As we earlier noted, the intensity of the hatred, violence, and destruction of the First World War helped convince Freud of the deep-rooted instinctual origin of aggression and of the need to account for it directly in his motivation theory.

While most contemporary psychoanalytic theorists question the reality of a death instinct, they agree that aggression is an instinctual urge. As Cofer and Appley (1964) note, whether aggression has bodily sources (such as the endocrine system) or simply parallels organic and physiological activities remains an open question. Classical Freudian doctrine interpreted aggression as an innate need to destroy; modern explanations accept frustration and conflict in development as possible sources.

Feshbach (1970) traces the development of aggression and notes that infants express their aggression in two ways:

1. *The rage reaction,* which consists of screaming and violent motor activity.
2. *Oral activity,* which tends to destroy what the infant incorporates; the latter phase of oral development is accompanied by teething and biting, which can have more obvious aggressive consequences.

During the anal stage, youngsters can strike at their parents during toilet training. Gradual control over the sphincter muscles permits them to use bowel movements as an aggressive act, once they learn that adults find feces unpleasant. The aggressive content of such negative behavior is a clear signal of opposition to those adults around them.

Resolution of the Oedipal conflict is an obvious source of aggression, especially for males whose aggression toward the father is an outgrowth of incestuous feelings toward the mother (Feshbach, 1970, p. 16). Modern theorists tend to view the boy's hostility toward his father as a complex mixture of the life instincts, rebellion against the father's authority, and strivings for autonomy.

Contemporary psychoanalytic theorists place greater emphasis on the ego functions as a source of control. Reality testing, information processing, frustration, tolerance, and delay of gratification all assume a more positive role in personality development, and, as Feshbach (1970, p. 199) notes, they determine the amount of frustration children experience and the degree of control they exercise over their aggression.

Learning Theory. In a remarkably persuasive and widely heralded analysis, Dollard et al. published in 1939 the classic *Frustration and Aggression.* Its basic premise was quite simple: aggression always follows frustration. To be more precise, aggression presupposes the existence of frustration, and frustration always causes aggression. In an interesting acknowledgement, the Dollard group recognizes Freud's contribution while simultaneously rejecting any instinctive interpretation of aggression.

Frustrating an individual's present activity produces behavior that is intended to injure another. With this thesis, Dollard and his colleagues attempted to discover what influenced the strength of the tendency toward aggression, what would inhibit the aggression, and whether it is possible to displace and to reduce the aggression. The role of punishment in inhibiting aggression raises serious theoretical problems, because punishment may actually increase aggresion. Punishment thus becomes an added frustration.

Berkowitz (1973) states that the original Frustration-Aggression (F-A) model was both too simple and too sweeping, since it ignored the stimulus properties of the target and also ignored the possibility of a child acquiring aggressive behavior other than by frustration. But Berkowitz argues forcefully that we should not reject the essential validity of the F-A model: frustration *can* lead to aggression. As he states (1973, pp. 102–103):

> Here then are just a few of the conditions that might intervene to affect the relationship between frustration and aggression. Whether a person becomes openly aggressive after being thwarted depends upon such things as his characteristic degree of optimism and trust, the extent to which he has learned to respond constructively to the problem confronting him, his judgement as to how safe it is to attack the available targets or how proper it is to show any aggression in the given situation, his attitude toward the potential targets, the motives he attributes to his frustrater, the degree to which the people around him are also suffering from the frustration inflicted upon him, and his interpretation of his own emotional reaction to the frustration.

These are some of the variables that will affect the nature of the aggression following frustration.

Feshbach (1970) believes that in its emphasis on the motivational antecedents of aggression, the F-A model provided a sturdy bridge between psychoanalytic and learning theory explanations of aggression. Once traditional learning accounts for the initial appearance of aggression—either by trial and error behavior or as prepotent response elicited by such stimuli as frustration—then sophisticated reinforcement contingencies operate either to maintain the aggressive behavior or to inhibit it.

Modeling is another important interpretation of aggression. Bandura (1963) argues against inner forces or passivity in the face of environmental pressures. If the interaction between the child and the controlling conditions explain behavior, then any culture that rewards aggression in its members will produce highly aggressive individuals. Youngsters' aggressive behavior is too often modeled on the aggressive behavior they see around them, especially in the home.

Within the learning theory framework, then, we have seen three distinct views: the F-A model, traditional learning theory dependence on reinforcement, and modeling. The combination of all three greatly extends the range of situations that produce aggression.

Sex Differences in Aggression

Males are more aggressive than females. With regard to human behavior, this simple statement is almost indisputable, but as with most comments about human nature, some qualifiers are needed. *Some* females are more aggressive than *some* males. Reviewing the literature, Lips and Colwill (1978) state that females are not necessarily less aggressive in family conflicts; more women than men abuse children. Yet as Maccoby and Jacklin (1974) state, sex differences in aggression are among the most clearly established findings in the sex-differences literature.

Although the findings may be clear, the cause of these differences remains obscure.

Lips and Colwill (1978) divide the possible antecedents of aggressive behavior into two categories: physiological and learning explanations.

Physiological Theory. Among the most popular, and least documented, explanations of aggression have been the efforts to link aggression and the Y chromosome. Since males and females differ in their chromosomal patterns, the Y chromosome has loomed as an attractive, and easy, explanation of sex differences in aggression. If Y is the reason, then the so-called super male having an additional Y chromosome should be hyperaggressive. Estimates are that one in 550 males has the XYY karyotype, which supposedly is linked with greater body size and more aggressive behavior. Proponents argue that the percentage of such individuals found in mental and penal institutions is greater than their percentage in the normal population.

XYY

Several interesting studies emphasize the physiological roots of violence. Jarvik, Klodin, and Matsuyama (1973) ponder a question that has divided the scientific community for years: Is human aggression an inborn biological urge that eventually erupts into violent behavior, or is it a learned response to environmental conditions?

They then refer to the literature concerning the XYY male. Recall the chromosomal arrangements that determine a male or female: XX = female, XY = male. In the mid-sixties, the discovery was made that certain males—retarded, unusually tall, criminals with a long history of violence—had forty-seven chromosomes, the extra being a Y chromosome (XYY). Several males who had committed especially bizarre crimes were found to have this condition.

There are difficulties associated with these findings. For example, not all XYY males are criminals, nor do all male criminals have the XYY pattern. But the frequency of the XYY arrangement in criminals is fifteen times that in the noncriminal male population. The authors conclude that there is strong presumptive evidence to support an association between the extra Y chromosome and criminal behavior.

While these individuals represent only a small proportion of violent criminals, nevertheless it seems as if the extra Y chromosome predisposes them to aggressive behavior, which suggests a genetic relationship between maleness and violence. As the authors conclude, such research focuses on genetic influences on behavior, yet seeks the solution in the environment.

Lips and Colwill (1978) argue that data from the XXY studies are suspect because of the lack of appropriate control groups. They reason that the Y chromosome alone cannot explain aggression, because aggressive females exist.

The results of these and similar studies reflect a new interest and concern in studies of aggression. For example, long-puzzling statistics are that sixty-three percent of the crimes in America are committed by only five percent of the population and that eighty percent of violent criminals have a long record of such violence. When these figures were coupled with the new physiological evidence, scientists became more receptive to the view that senseless human violence may often be caused by organic brain disorders. Tentative suggestions are being made that repeated violence stems as much from faulty brain functioning as from environmental difficulties.

Another physiological explanation assumes a link between male sex hormones and aggression. When the synthetic hormone *progestin* was given to women to prevent miscarriages, the women gave birth to some youngsters who were extremely "tomboyish," and others who were hermaphrodites. While these results confirm the masculine effects of certain hormones, they provide no strong link to the origin of violence.

Learning Theories. Lips and Colwill (1978) believe that learning theories more successfully explain aggression than do physiological interpretations. The authors believe that male and female aggression is differentially reinforced; thus the "pay-off" is greater for boys than girls. Again we note that the combination of operant conditioning, classical conditioning, and modeling explains many of the sex differences apparent in aggressive behavior.

Mischel (1970) has traced male-female differences chronologically as follows:

1. Observational studies confirm that by three years of age sex differences in aggression are apparent. The author states that aggression has become a key variable in defining masculine and feminine behavior. Boys are more physically aggressive and display more negativisitic behavior.

2. Rating studies also confirm the above findings and show that from five to fourteen years the pattern continues—boys are noisier, more negativistic, and more aggressive.

3. College men rate themselves more directly aggressive than women, particularly after their hostility has been aroused experimentally.

4. Projective tests indicate that adult males express more direct aggression and hostility than females.

A Developmental Overview

The developmental trend seems to be that from the age of two, crying and physical aggression decrease, while verbal aggression increases. The type of aggression changes noticeably for two- to five-year-olds (Feshbach, 1970). The number of undirected temper tantrums slowly decreases during the first three years and shows a sharp decline after four. But the number of retaliatory responses increases with age, especially after three years. The antecedents or provokers of aggression likewise change with age. Discomfort and a desire for attention seem to cause most of the violent outbursts of infancy. For the second and third years, frustration in the learning of motor skills and reactions to authority seem to cause most aggressive displays. Conflicts with peers begin to emerge as a source of difficulty during the third year and increase in intensity thereafter.

An interesting finding of aggression studies concerns the reaction of parents to these outbursts. With the younger child, parents react with physical force or try to divert attention or ignore the outburst. With older children, the more frequent parental responses are scolding, threatening, and ignoring the child (the last is a reaction to the child and not to the behavior). Thus, more authoritarian controls are used with younger children, while verbal controls assume greater importance with older children.

How stable are these aggressive behaviors? There appears to be a high correlation between ratings of aggression for adolescent males and ratings made when they were thirty-three years old. Kagan and Moss (1962), as a result of longitudinal analysis, concluded that aggressive behavior showed greater stability for men than for women. They speculate that the cause may be a complex interaction in which unique personal characteristics find support in the child's culture.

One interesting finding was that aggressive behavior directed toward the mother during the first three years failed to predict future aggression. But aggression directed toward the mother during the years six to fourteen was positively related to adult aggression. Thus, there seems to be a continuity in many aggressive behaviors; aggression manifested during the three-to-six-year span seems to continue into adulthood. This is particularly true for males, while the pattern is more complex for girls. For example, girls make strong efforts to inhibit aggression, often causing internal conflict.

Feshbach (1970, p. 198) concludes that since there are different paths to the development of aggressive behaviors, the study of personality is unable to furnish a composite picture of the aggressive child. Aggression varies with age, sex, and situation. But as times change, so do patterns of behavior. The incidence of female violence is on the increase and, as the stereotype of the female changes, uninhibited behavior becomes more acceptable. For some, both male and female, this leads to a decrease in impulse control and consequently to more violent reactions.

DISCUSSION QUESTIONS

1. Can you define aggression? Does your definition differ from that presented here? Do you think it necessary to include such elements as "intent" and "harm" in your definition? If you exclude them, what happens to your definition; that is, how practical is it?
2. Human killings of humans is difficult to explain. Do you agree with the "pseudo-speciation" theory? Why? If aggression is instinctive, as Lorenz believes, what are the cultural implications for child rearing, education, recreation?
3. Which interpretation of aggression seems most plausible to you, the ethological or the learning theory? Why? Can you offer examples that neither theory can explain? Would psychoanalytic theory help?
4. From the discussion of aggression, does it seem that violence is a part of the male sex-role stereotype? Is it, then, learned? If you agree, reconcile your belief with the growing body of evidence that suggests a physical, even genetic, basis.
5. A two- or three-year-old child will often, in the midst of a temper tantrum, strike his mother as fiercely as possible. What advice would you give the parent? What predictions would you make for the child if this behavior appeared at two? Four? Six? Eight? Explain each of your answers.

MORAL DEVELOPMENT

Moral development today is of growing concern to all those who contemplate their own and their children's futures. The complexities and intricacics of modern technological societies, the assault on traditional values once cherished, and the growing worry that national and international decisions are made with little concern for their moral consequences have produced a receptive climate for speculations about moral development.

While theorists have made determined efforts to exclude value decisions from their work (who is to judge right or wrong?) and to focus their concentration on the processes by which moral decisions are reached, it is difficult to avoid manifesting some commitment. Even the basic theoretical dichotomy used in this section—cognitive or learning—may seem value laden to some readers. Yet the theorizing and research has been remarkably objective and informative.

Hoffman (1970) notes that most moral development research assumes the internalization of socially sanctioned prohibitions and mandates. Thus conformity becomes self-rewarding even when external approval is lacking. Nevertheless, these internalized standards are vulnerable to extreme pressure; notions of right and wrong or good and evil that are transmitted by home, church, and school may not persist unchanged throughout a person's lifetime. As Hoffman notes, how long an internalized standard remains a guide to behavior depends partially on the counter pressures that an individual experiences. Milgram's laboratory studies of the obedience to authority (1963), in which individuals continued to administer electric shock to others even when the subject's supposed reaction was loud screaming, was disconcerting to all who understood its implications. The study evoked memories of the horrors of Nazi Germany, and we saw the laboratory research translated into practice in My Lai. Both situations graphically demonstrated the fragility of internalized standards. Interest in moral development was renewed.

We shall follow Hoffman's classification scheme in this section. Arguing that no one theory has a monopoly on explanation, he states (1970, p. 345) that moral development is a complex, multifaceted phenomenon to which several processes contribute.

Social learning theory seems to provide the best rationale for the beginnings of moral development; that is, through the rewarding and punishing efforts of adults, youngsters learn which behaviors are acceptable and which require inhibition. As Hoffman notes, such behavior reflects external morality; the child's motives are purely hedonistic.

With cognitive development, youngsters gradually shift from external, arbitrary controls to more internal, rational self-control. Thoughtful adults who make sensible demands and a youngster's growing participation in decision making facilitate moral development. Since most interpretations of moral development fall into one of these categories, let us examine each in more detail.

Learning Theory

Children quickly learn what they can or cannot do, and what behaviors bring reward or punishment. Most parents unconsciously use a subtle reinforcement schedule to encourage in their children those behaviors that they (the parents), the parents' peers, and society deem acceptable. But children are also powerfully influenced by observing the adults around them, noting which behaviors are reinforced, which are punished, and which receive no attention. Thus two basic learning models (A and B below) seem to be most effective.

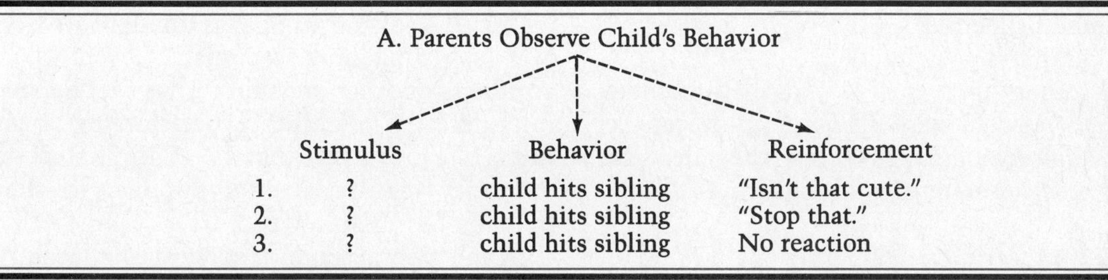

A. Parents Observe Child's Behavior
Stimulus
Behavior
Reinforcement
1. ? child hits sibling "Isn't that cute."
2. ? child hits sibling "Stop that."
3. ? child hits sibling No reaction

Each pattern of reinforcement, particularly if persistent, tends to produce different behavior in a child. The first example will usually produce continuing aggressive behavior, and moral development will undoubtedly follow overt rewards and punishment. In the second example, punishment is used to discourage the behavior, and children quickly learn to suppress aggressive behavior to avoid punishment. In both examples, obviously representing social stereotypes, internalization processes serve to maintain the behavior. The third example, which lacks any immediate environmental response, should produce extinction, provided that similar behavior is *not* rewarded elsewhere.

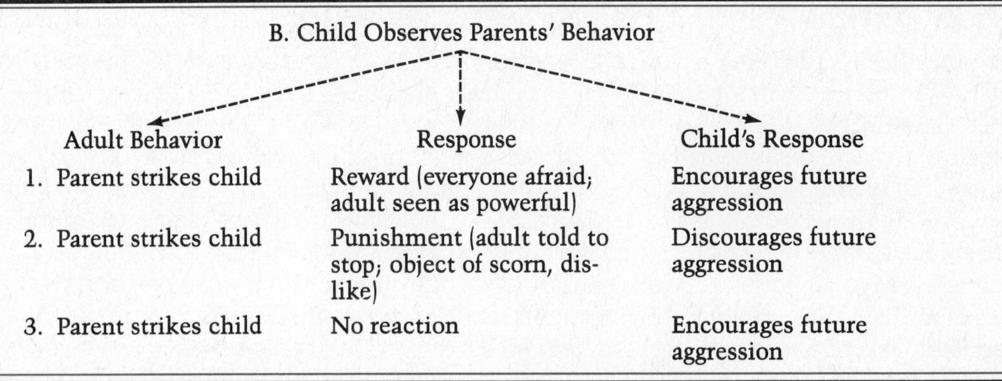

B. Child Observes Parents' Behavior

Adult Behavior	Response	Child's Response
1. Parent strikes child	Reward (everyone afraid; adult seen as powerful)	Encourages future aggression
2. Parent strikes child	Punishment (adult told to stop; object of scorn, dislike)	Discourages future aggression
3. Parent strikes child	No reaction	Encourages future aggression

Here is the classic social learning situation in which a model's behavior receives various kinds of reinforcement. Since observation exercises a strong influence on acquired behavior, moral development will reflect the actions of those around the child. Similar social and cultural backgrounds tend to produce similar levels of moral development, which remain relatively constant during the early years. Social learning theorists would predict changes in behavior, that is, level of moral development, only if there were rather dramatic changes in the behavioral patterns surrounding a child.

If children's socializing agents—the significant others previously described—remain constant, and if these agents employ consistent reinforcement schedules, the effect on moral development may be enduring.

Cognitive Theory

Although learning theory remains an attractive explanation of moral development, probably the most noted interpreter today is Lawrence Kohlberg, a cognitivist. (Kohlberg's work depends on Piaget's cognitive theory, so it would be useful to review Chapter Five now, especially the fundamental Piagetian concepts.) Hoffman (1970, p. [illegible]) summarizes the core of Piaget's views on m[illegible]ality by stating that, for Piaget, a moral act is based on a conscious prior judgment about its rightness or wrongness.

Piaget formulated his ideas on moral development from his observations of children playing games. Watching the children, talking to them, and applying his cognitive theory to their actions, he identified two general stages of moral development.

In the first stage, which emerges at about six years, children believe that the rules of a game are fixed, almost sacred; there is no middle area between absolute right and absolute wrong. It is also a time of immanent justice; that is, wrongdoing is punished by physical accidents or other dreadful things that happen to children. The child's understanding of the rules is egocentric; that is, it is fixated on authority—adults made the rules, so they must be rigidly followed.

In the second stage, at about eleven years of age, youngsters realize that rules emerge from the shared agreement of those who play the game and can be changed by mutual agreement. Youngsters gradually understand that intent becomes an important part of right and wrong; their decreasing egocentrism permits them to see how others view behavior. Peers are a significant component of this transition because in the mutual give-and-take of peer relations, there is not the unquestioning acceptance of an adult view.

Using these Piagetian notions, Kohlberg has formulated a sophisticated scheme of moral development that extends from about four years of age through adulthood. He believes that moral judgment is weighing the claims of others against one's own; thus youngsters must overcome their egocentrism before they can legitimately make moral judgments.

As Piaget believes that cognitive stages form because of children's interactions with their environment, Kohlberg believes that moral stages result from children's active thinking about moral issues and decisions. The moral stages are structures of moral judgment, which may differ from the content of moral judgment (Kohlberg, 1975, p. 671). That is, a person's moral actions may not be at the same level of moral judgment. To put it simply, people may do things they know are wrong.

As Piaget used clinical methods to investigate children's understanding of the rules of the games that they were playing, Kohlberg also employed a modified clinical technique—the moral dilemma—to discover the stages of moral development. One of the most famous is the stealing of a miracle drug to save a dying woman. The druggist is selling the remedy at an outrageous price, which the woman's husband cannot meet. He collects about half the money and asks the druggist to sell it to him more cheaply or allow him to pay the rest later. The druggist refuses. What should the husband do: steal the drug or permit his wife to die rather than break the law?

Kohlberg states that subjects' choices reflect the content of moral judgment, while their reasoning about the choice defines the structure of their judgments. He believes that their reasoning reflects ten universal moral values or issues:

1. punishment
2. property
3. roles and concerns of affection
4. roles and concerns of authority
5. law
6. life
7. liberty
8. distributive justice
9. truth
10. sex

Lawrence Kohlberg

Moral choices entail choosing between two or more of these values when they conflict. In the drug example, property, law, authority, affection, perhaps even sex, are all involved. As a result of analyzing these and similar dilemmas, Kohlberg formulated the three levels and six stages of moral development illustrated in Table 11.3.

TABLE 11.3. Kohlberg's Stages of Moral Development

1. *The Preconventional Level* (4–10 years)	2. *The Conventional Level* (10–13 years)	3. *The Postconventional Level* (13 years and above)
Cultural rules and cultural controls dominate children's behavior, which is primarily designed to win rewards and avoid punishment. There are two stages at this level.	Children at this level wish to meet the expectations of family, groups, and country. Children desire not only to conform to the existing order; they desire to maintain it. There are two stages at this level.	Kohlberg defines this as the principled level when individuals accept notions of right and wrong because of their intrinsic value and not because they reside in some authority. There are two stages at this level.
Stage 1. *Punishment and obedience.*	Stage 3. *The "good boy-nice girl" orientation.*	Stage 5. *The social-contract, legalistic orientation.*
The physical consequences of an act determine whether it is right or wrong. Children value behavior that escapes punishment, not for its moral correctness but strictly for hedonistic purposes.	The approval of others defines good behavior. Being "nice" is important, as is wanting to do the right thing—"he meant well."	Right action is that which has been agreed upon by the entire community. While the legal point of view predominates, the possibility exists of changing laws by consensus and for the sake of social utility. It is a more relativistic interpretation of morality.
Stage 2. *Instrumental-relativist orientation.*	Stage 4. *A law and order orientation.*	Stage 6. *The universal-ethical principle orientation.*
Whatever satisfies a child's needs is right. A sense of fairness exists but is interpreted in a decidedly pragmatic fashion. Kohlberg's famous quote to describe this stage is pertinent here: "You scratch my back and I'll scratch yours."	Children manifest a belief in authority to maintain the social order for its own sake. "One should do one's duty."	An informed conscience defines right. Ethical principles such as justice, equality, and dignity guide a person's actions.

With its dependence on cognitive development, Kohlberg's theory poses the age-old dilemma about knowledge and behavior. As he comments (1975, p. 672), mature moral judgment is a necessary but not sufficient condition for mature moral action. While you cannot follow moral principles that you do not understand, you can understand them and not abide by them. Yet decisions based on an understanding of ethical principles are desirable decisions. Kohlberg (1975, p. 673) states:

> Why are decisions based on universal principles of justice better decisions? Because they are decisions on which all moral men could agree. When decisions are based on conventional moral rules, men will disagree, since they adhere to conflicting systems of rules dependent on cultural and social position. Throughout history men have killed one another in the name of conflicting moral rules and values, most recently in Vietnam and the Middle East. Truly moral or just resolutions of conflicts require principles which are, or can be, universalizable.

Women and Moral Development. In a particularly thoughtful essay, Carol Gilligan (1977) has questioned the role assigned to women by the leading developmental theorists, especially Kohlberg. Gilligan believes the qualities associated with the mature adult—autonomous thinking, clear decision making, and

TABLE 11.4. Gilligan's Levels of Moral Development of Women

Level 1: *Orientation to Individual Survival*	Level 2: *Goodness as Self-Sacrifice*	Level 3: *The Morality of Nonviolence*
Decisions center on the self; concerns are pragmatic; the issue is individual survival. At this level, the self, while the sole object of concern, lacks power.	Recognition of one's responsibilities indicates recognition of social participation; the shift from selfishness to responsibility results in moral judgments based on shared norms and expectations. Societal values assume significance, consensual judgment is critical, and goodness depends on an acceptance by others. The connection between goodness and self-sacrifice fits the classic sexual stereotype.	Since focus on self (level 1) and focus on others (level 2) bring hurt to one or the other, nonviolence now becomes a principle governing all moral action, one that includes both self and others. It is not a new morality but one that recognizes the psychological and moral necessity for an equation of worth between self and others. It is a resolution that encompasses both femininity and adulthood.
First Transition: From Selfishness to Responsibility	*Second Transition: From Goodness to Truth*	
Self-interest is redefined as attachment to others appears. Feelings of self-worth increase, accompanied by the realization that it is possible to do the "right thing."	The woman now begins to examine self-sacrifice in the service of a morality of care (Gilligan, 1977). A moral judgment is slowly emerging as one that involves decisions about selfishness or responsibility with regard to her own needs. Is it possible to be responsible to one's self as well as to others? Since responsibility requires knowledge, the shift is from goodness to truth. Recognition of one's needs is now seen as not selfish; it is honest and fair.	

responsible action—are qualities that have traditionally been associated with "masculinity," rather than "femininity." Kohlberg, for example, places most women at the third stage of his hierarchy because of their desire for approval, their need to be thought "nice." The characteristics that define the "good" woman—gentleness, tact, concern for the feelings of others, display of feelings—all contribute to the low scores for moral development.

Gilligan rationalizes that a woman's sense of powerlessness interferes with her ability to exercise choice and accept responsibility for that choice, which is the essence of the moral decision. As long as women believe that they have no choice, they avoid the corresponding responsibility. But changing concepts of sexuality have altered women's availability of choice. Gilligan believes that women may now begin to make moral judgments independent of their reproductive capacity; no longer limited by a biologically predetermined destiny, women may now experience both the freedom and the responsibility of moral decisions.

Studying women in these and similar situations, Gilligan hypothesizes a different developmental sequence for women. The three levels of Gilligan's model of women's moral development are shown in Table 11.4.

Gilligan's perceptive analysis is not to be taken lightly, especially since Kohlberg's basic work was done with males. Perhaps women see moral problems differently, that is, as a conflict between responsibilities, and their perspective may explain their moral development from concern with survival, to a focus on goodness, to an understanding and acceptance of nonviolence as a resolution of moral conflict.

Hoffman (1979) recognizes women's more humanistic moral values, and attributes this quality to the role of socialization. As stereotypes fade and the differences in the kind of moral instrumental socialization received by girls and boys disappears, the sex difference in morality may also vanish.

DISCUSSION QUESTIONS

1. Once moral standards are internalized, it is difficult to change them, yet it can be done. Given the discussion in this section, provide examples of *how* this could occur.
2. Why is a learning theory model more acceptable to explain moral development in the early years? In your answer, compare basic differences between cognitive and learning theory.
3. Use the Piagetian interpretation of egocentrism to explain changes in moral development. Link your answer to your previous work on Piaget. Now explain how Kohlberg has taken these concepts and elaborated them into a more sophisticated developmental model.
4. Select any one of Kohlberg's ten universal moral values and illustrate *how* developmental changes occur as an individual proceeds through the stages of moral development presented in Table 11.3. Be sure and include theoretical constructs (cognitive structures, stages).
5. Do you agree with Gilligan's account of a different developmental track for women? Does she basically agree with Kohlberg? Does a woman's different rationale for moral decisions explain the sex differences that Gilligan postulates? Do you agree with Hoffman's comments about changes in socialization practices eliminating sex differences?

SEX IDENTITY

The importance of gender in our lives and the acquisition of a personally satisfactory sex role are themes that appear frequently in this text. Sex is such a vital part of development that it is necessary to discuss it in the investigation of every part of human behavior. In any culture, a person's sex reflects not only what he or she does, but also how he or she does it. These sex differences are reflected in personality differences. There is ample evidence to indicate that the traits of attachment, dependency, aggression, and moral development show notable sex differences. As we noted, differences in aggression appear as early as three years, and those differences are actually used to define masculinity and femininity. From these early years, boys are physically more aggressive, display more negative behavior, and are generally more antisocial than girls.

When we turn to the attachment and dependency studies, similar differences appear, although they are not observed as early as

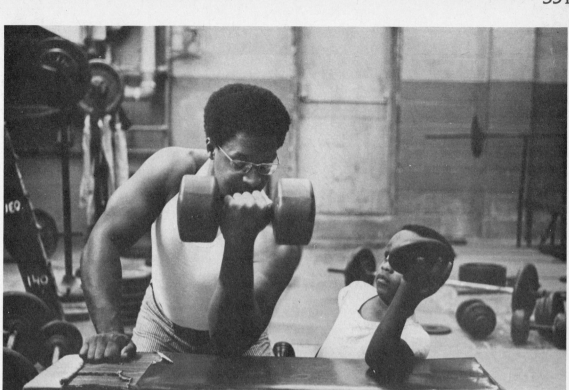

aggression. There is considerable support for the belief that females manifest greater dependency, social passivity, and conformity than males (Kagan and Moss, 1962). Note that these characteristics undoubtedly reflect the expectations of our society. That is, the sex role stereotype encourages belief in the traits that the male or female is expected to possess. Certain sex attributes are *supposed* to appear. Females are expected to suppress aggression and any overt display of sexual urges. Men are expected to be selectively aggressive, that is, only with regard to sex and personal defense; otherwise they are expected to be the masters of their emotions and to suppress any sign of fear or anxiety.

A study by Taylor and Epstein (1967) illustrates the manner in which expectations about sex influence behavior, thus causing us to attribute certain personality characteristics to each sex. In this study, male and female college students were placed in a competitive situation with unseen opponents—in fact, fictitious opponents—described as either male or female. The subjects were caused annoyance, and the aggressiveness of each sex was then measured by having them indicate the strength of an electric shock they would like to administer to their unseen opponent. Both sexes were less aggressive when they believed the opponent to be female. Even when the provocation was strong, both sexes hesitated to use a strong electrical shock on a supposedly female opponent. Another interesting finding was the reactions of females to fictitious male opponents. Contrary to the anticipated reaction that females would remain physically unaggressive, when women faced an unusually aggressive male opponent, they became surprisingly aggressive. Thus apparent sex differences may change as the situation changes. Further, different types of aggression may not be correlated; that is, the level of physical aggression does not necessarily match the level of verbal aggression.

Mischel (1970) concludes that children, early in their lives, categorize themselves as male or female, and that their sex then influences their interpretation of all that they do or encounter. Whether it is called a constitutional determinant or a somatic trait, gender is a potent force in the emergence and expression of almost all other personality traits.

The Meaning of Gender Identity

> Sex identity at first glance appears to be a simple matter of boy/girl. It is, in fact, a most complicated phenomenon. Adult sex identity results from a mixture of genetic, hormonal, cultural, and psychological forces in proportions that are largely unknown. The scientific complexity of sex identity is matched by the emotional reaction it evokes. Sex identity is usually the first question that pops into everyone's mind whenever a new human being enters the world. Moreover, some of our best insights into the nature of sex identity come from studies of homosexuals, transsexuals, and transvestites—sexual minorities that other people often react to with violent emotions. The sex roles that accompany sex identity are equally charged with emotions; few areas of controversy have touched so many nerves as has the topic of sex role liberation. (Kilpatrick, 1976, pp. 61–62)

Kilpatrick, who has written so sensitively about sexual development, emphasizes that gender identity results from a complicated mix of culture and biology. To clarify the meaning of sex identity he cautions that we should make a sharp distinction between sex identity and sex role. He states (1976, p. 69) that *sex identity* is a conviction that one belongs to the sex of birth; a boy or girl, man or woman, is comfortable with his masculinity or her femininity. *Sex role* refers to those characteristics, activities, and opportunities that society has assigned to one sex or the other.

Money and Ehrhardt (1972) state that sex identity results not from a dichotomization of genetics and environment, but from their interaction. The phyletic program—including sex—utilizes both the prenatal and postnatal environment to fulfill its potential. The X or Y chromosome determines sex and the XX or XY combination then passes the program to the undifferentiated gonads (to differentiate testes or ovaries), after which the sex chromosomes normally have no impact upon sexual and psychosexual differentiation (Money and Ehrhardt, 1972, p. 3).

The undifferentiated gonads now pass the program to their own hormonal secretions. Actually, it is the secretions of the testes that are decisive, for without them, the developing child will always be female. These secretions also affect brain organization that will later influence sexual behavior. Thus the gonadal secretions pass the program to two carriers: the genital morphology (male or female), and those elements of the central nervous system that serve the genital morphology.

Genital morphology completes its part of the program by influencing the adults who rear the child as a boy or girl, and also by influencing children once they understand the meaning of their genital organs. The central nervous system completes its part of the program through the formation of behavioral traits. Money and Ehrhardt (1972, p. 4) state that the predominant part of gender-identity differentiation comes through social transmission, which reconfirms the sex assignment. The hormonal changes of puberty further confirm one's sex identity. Figure 11.1 illustrates the process.

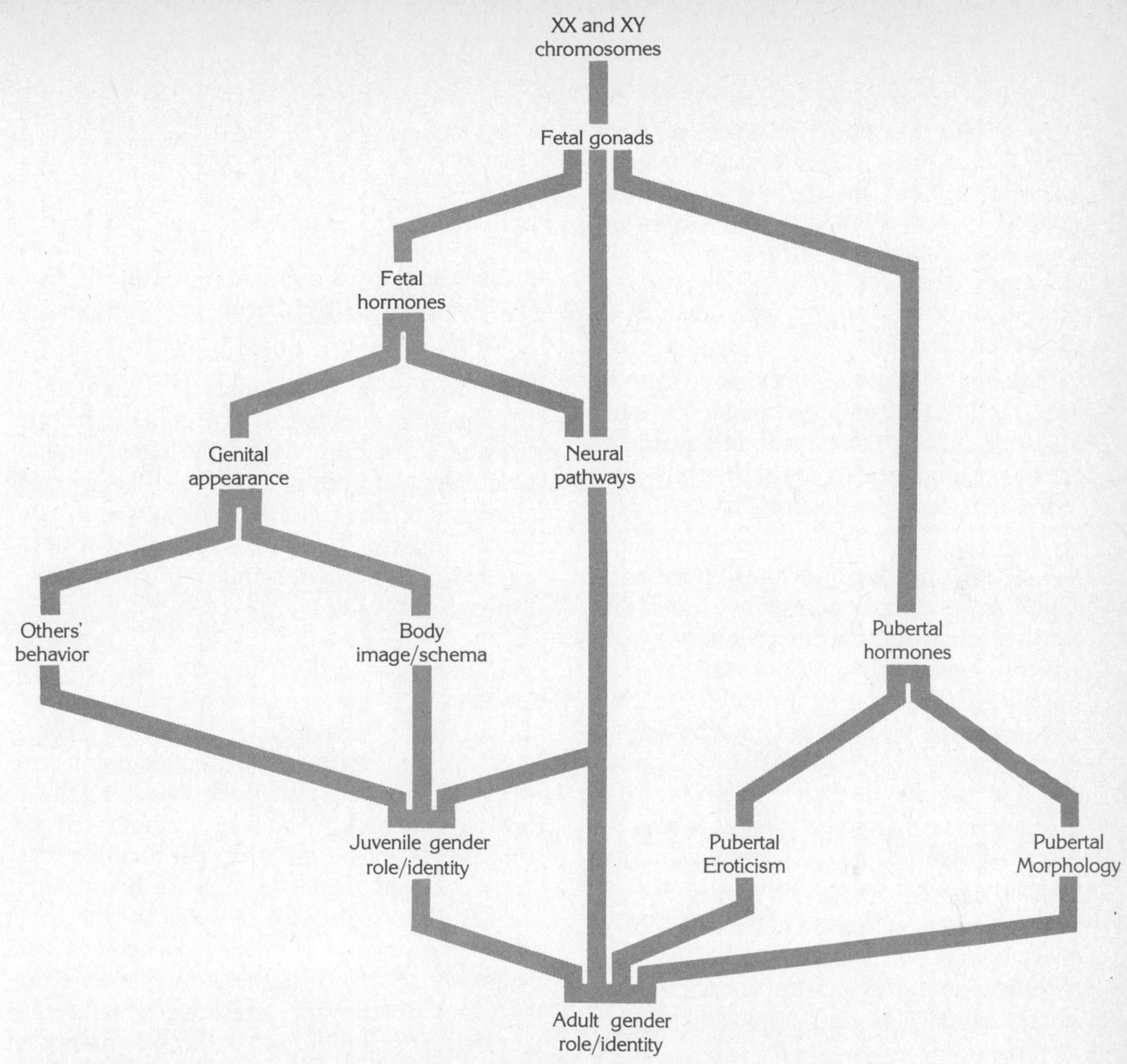

FIGURE 11.1. Sequential and Cumulative Components of Gender Identity Differentiation.
Source: John Money, "Gender Identity Differentiation." Reprinted from *1973 Nebraska Symposium on Motivation* edited by James K. Cole and Richard Dienstbier by permission of University of Nebraska press. Copyright © 1974 by the University of Nebraska Press.

Money (1973) discusses the significance of a critical period in the acquisition of a sex identity by stating that the right age for establishing a sex identity is "not quite from birth onwards," but with bright youngsters it may be as early as six months and with average children from eighteen months onward. The critical period seems to extend from eighteen months to three or four years.

Theoretical Explanations

As with the other dimensions of individuality discussed, various theories have been proposed to explain the development of sex identity. Four are most prominent.

1. *Biological.* Before analyzing the biological interpretation of the acquisition of gender identity, you should be aware of the "variables

of sex." These variables interact to produce the sense of sex that most children develop.

a. *Chromosomal Sex.* We have previously mentioned genetic determinants of sex in discussing Money and Ehrhardt's work and concluded that the XX and XY patterns were mainly responsible for transmitting the genetic program.

b. *Gonadal Sex.* About the sixth week, the genetic program contained in the XY combination causes the developing testes to secrete testosterone; without this step, female anatomy develops.

c. *Hormonal Sex.* Sex differentiation is now under the control of these hormones. The male sex hormones, called the androgens, produce the male reproductive tract and the brain difference previously mentioned. At puberty, they produce the male secondary sex characteristics. The female sex hormones, the estrogens and progesterone, are responsible for the differentiation of the female reproductive system and the mammary glands. Both hormones are intimately involved in the female menstrual cycle.

d. *Reproductive Sex.* Due to the secretion of the male or female hormones, the various sex organs have been organized as male or female.

e. *Nervous System Sex.* When the sex hormones reach the brain (usually at the fetal stage), sexual differentiation of the brain occurs. While the hypothalamus is known to be involved, much remains unknown. Money and Ehrhardt (1972, p. 245) state:

> In the final analysis all of a person's experience and behavior of falling in love and mating belongs to a program in the brain. Some parts of the program may have been phyletically laid down. Some may be the individualized product of prenatal hormonal history, and some the product of individual social history and learning. Whatever its origin, there is no behavior if it is not represented in the functioning of the brain.

f. *Assigned Sex and Rearing.* The environment now treats males as males and females as females, with differing expectations for each.

Those believing in an innate sexuality argue that the inborn maleness or femaleness structures all interactions with the environment. Rosenberg and Sutton-Smith (1972) state that adherents of this position view sexual behavior as pre-formed and all subsequent experiences are superimposed and simply refine predisposed tendencies.

2. *Psychoanalytic.* The psychoanalytic interpretation of sex identity acquisition revolves around the notions of castration anxiety, penis envy, and the resolution of the Oedipal complex. Since we have previously discussed these key psychoanalytic concepts, they will be briefly reviewed here. During the phallic stage, a boy develops sexual feelings for his mother and desires to replace his father in the mother's affection. Since a boy now recognizes the penis as a source of tremendous pleasure, he fears that an angry, powerful father will retaliate by castration. Since castration anxiety is such an overwhelming fear, boys must resolve it, which they do by identifying with their fathers.

For girls, the process leading to sex identity is penis envy. Realizing that she lacks the male organ, the girl is beset with feelings of inferiority, tends to blame her mother, and turns to the father as the primary love object. Gradually she realizes that her desire for the father will remain unfulfilled and also senses that she cannot afford to lose the mother's love. Thus she begins to identify with the mother. With this shift comes resolution of the female equivalent of the Oedipal complex, the Electra complex. Since it is not as intense as the boy's, girls are slower to resolve it, and Freud commented that some females never satisfactorily achieve a complete and unfettered sex identity.

Rosenberg and Sutton-Smith (1972, p. 46) summarize the psychoanalytic explanation of sex identity as follows:

> This, then, in brief, is the basic model of sex role development proposed by the psychoanalytic theory. One gains from it a very real sense of the importance of the physical, erotic, and sensual closeness of children to their parents in this account of the sex role. There is nothing here which is impersonal and unseen like chromosomes and hormones. The analysis in this chapter reveals forms of *passion*, which, though they have played a vast role in human affairs, seldom find their way into accounts of child development.

3. *Social Learning.* Mischel (1966) defines sex-typed behaviors as those that typically elicit different rewards for one sex than the other. The consequences of the different behaviors vary according to sex. The acquisition and performance of sex-typed behaviors follow the same learning principles as all other behavior. The process is as follows:

a. Children learn to distinguish between sex-typed behaviors.
b. They then generalize from early specific learning experiences to new situations.
c. They consistently perform sex-typed behaviors.

As we have seen, observational learning from live and symbolic models initiates the acquisition of sex-typed behaviors. Reinforcement of the observed behavior need not occur for acquisition, since the observer's attention seems to be more significant for the range and accuracy of learning. Mischel (1966) states that the consequences that accrue to the child's initial attempts at sex-typed behavior are crucial. Note that at this stage the child has acquired the behavior; performance is now the issue. Slowly the child learns which sex-typed behaviors are appropriate and bring rewards to one sex or the other.

Mischel (1970) believes that the same causal principles should explain *all* social behavior: cognitive consistency strivings, observational learning, and reinforcement. The combination of these mechanisms cuts across all behavior, and it is doubtful if new laws, new theories, new rules are needed. He states (1970, p. 60):

> Thus sex-typing, in the present view, should be governed by the same fundamental principles that regulate the development and occurrence of other complex forms of social behavior. As these mechanisms become increasingly clear, they should permit us to go beyond the traditional categorization of personality as a set of discrete, unitary dimensions and to elucidate, instead, the causes of socialized behavior regardless of its particular content.

4. *Cognitive-Developmental Theory.* Lawrence Kohlberg (1966), best known for his work on moral development, has also applied cognitive theory to sex identity. Kohlberg's basic theme is that children acquire a sex identity by their cognitive organization of their social world along sex role dimensions (Kohlberg, 1966, p. 83). Sex role concepts and attitudes change because cognitive organization changes. (Kohlberg's reliance on Piaget is again seen; the organization he mentions is the result of the cognitive structures that the child forms at each of the cognitive stages of development.) Thus a young child's thinking about sex differs radically from an adult's—Where do babies come from? Why is a man a man? Kohlberg states that children of two to four years are uncertain of their sexual identity; "boy" and "girl" are simply arbitrary labels. But once sex identity is cognitively stabilized, it tends to remain firm and constant.

Accompanying cognitive development is an awareness of constant gender categories (male-female), the recognition of genital differences, and acceptance of the sexual stereotype. Once cognitive awareness of sex identity is made (stabilization occurs at about seven years), the basic sex role stereotypes cause the appearance of masculine-feminine values in children, usually by eight years of age. Now youngsters tend to identify with same-sex figures.

Kohlberg (1966, p. 165) summarizes the process as follows:

> To a large extent, the foregoing trends follow a regular course of development, which is largely determined by cognitive (rather than physiological-chronological) maturity. These trends are the result of the child's cognitive-developmental organization of a social world in which sex roles are related to body concepts and to basic social functions in relatively universal ways.

The various theories presented in this section all attempt to explain the *development* of a child's sex identity. Money and Ehrhardt (1972) offer a fitting conclusion, perhaps a synthesis of all theories relating to sexual development. They note that the age of establishing conceptual language is also the age of establishing a self-concept, which is by its nature gender differentiated. As a result of their work with hermaphrodites, Money and Ehrhardt state that after eighteen months the child of normal intelligence has considerable difficulty in adjusting to a new, imposed sex role. Why? Youngsters have commenced to stabilize their sex identity.

The Meaning of Sex Role. Regardless of theory, socialization and gender identity are inextricably joined. We began this section by mentioning Kilpatrick's timely warning about confusing sex identity and sex role. Sex role conformity is encouraged early and often: clothes, toys, games, differential patterns of reinforcement. Almost all children respond to these urgings, both direct and subtle. Yet it is more difficult for boys. For both sexes the first figure with which they identify is the mother; the boy must then switch. Society unites with biology to help the youngsters meet sex role expectations (which, as Money and Ehrhardt state, reconfirms the sex assignment and contributes to sex identity).

But it is a time of changing sex roles. Women, as Gilligan emphasized, now have freedom of choice: to continue exclusively the traditional female role of childbearing and caregiving (with all its attendant responsibilities), to pursue a career (with all its attendant responsibilities), or perhaps to combine the two.

Pressure for choosing one role or the other comes from many different sources such as husband, family, friends. For some women, conflict about sex role produces doubt and uncertainty about their femininity.

The modern male is not without sex role conflict. Some, reared traditionally with traditional expectations about male-female relations, face difficult adjustments. Economic pressures may force a wife to work, thus shaking the masculine self-image. Attracted to career women, some men may experience unhappiness at the thought of competing careers plus the added household duties they must assume.

Finally, it is interesting to speculate how much change can alter traditional sex roles. Kilpatrick (1975, p. 187) states:

> Still, sex roles are so closely linked with identity that liberation from one threatens liberation from the other. The question is, What roles are dispensable and what roles are not? How fluid can sexuality get without washing away identity? Perhaps it would be better to rephrase that last question to, How far can we liberate individuals from sex roles without taking away their sense of purpose?

DISCUSSION QUESTIONS

1. Distinguish between sex role and sex identity. Do you consider it a valid distinction? Does the development of one contribute to the development of the other?
2. Trace Money and Ehrhardt's description of gender identity. Given the complex biological scheme they outline, were you surprised at their conclusion concerning social transmission? Why?
3. Three years was mentioned several times with regard to gender identity. Can you accept the belief of a sensitive period for sex identity? Why? If not, how can you explain a youngster's difficulty in adjusting to sex reassignment after three years?
4. Be sure you understand the theoretical explanation of sex identity acquisition. Which do you prefer? Why? Can you reconcile the sensitive period concept with your belief?
5. Discuss the implications of sex role change for today's children. Will early recognition of alternative sex roles help these youngsters to adjust more easily? Can you accept Kilpatrick's warning about overextension of sex roles? Does it coincide or conflict with your views about changing sex roles?

Our quest for insight into individual identity has ended. Throughout these last two chapters we have examined both the global theories of personality and the unique dimensions of individuality. For each, we followed the thread of development, successfully for some, not so for others. The common sense dictate of continuity of personality dimensions remains elusive, but there are sufficient clues to warrant further explanation.

For example, the long-range consequences of attachment were noted, as were the negative aspects of faulty attachment: certain patterns (aggression toward the mother at certain ages) seem to indicate an aggressive developmental sequence. By combining learning and cognitive theory, it is possible to sketch stages of moral development through which humans pass. Much the same holds true for the acquisition of sex identity: a combination of learning and cognitive theory seems to explain the early appearance of a sex identity.

But these are general patterns: the search continues for specific developmental clues that definitely state "if *this* appears at twelve months, then *this* will appear at twelve years." Others argue that the search is doomed to failure because development is change, not continuity. This is true, but it overlooks the possibility that certain changes may be preceded by identifiable clues. The search is well worth the effort.

SUMMARY

Controversy continues to rage over the issue of continuity in development, now focusing on the persistence of similarity of strategies.

Bowlby's interpretation of attachment as instinctive behavior remains the preeminent explanation.

Brazelton and Als stress a powerful theme in current development theory: interaction implies more than an adult doing something to an infant, and the infant then responds. The infant has structured what the adult does; the adult structures what the infant does; the pattern continues in this manner. Perhaps transaction is a better word than interaction.

There is considerable disagreement about a definition of aggression. The issue centers on the intent of the behavior.

The great names of psychological theory are associated with explanations of aggression: Lorenz, Freud, Bandura, Berkowitz.

A learning theory explanation of moral development focuses on selected schedules of reinforcement, coupled with continued observational learning.

The most popular cognitive theory is that of Kohlberg, who relies heavily on Piaget's cognitive developmental theory.

Basing his work on conflict among universal moral issues, Kohlberg reasons that human beings proceed through a series of six sequential stages in their moral development.

Understanding sex identity necessitates distinguishing it from sex role. Although the two are complementary, sex role focuses on cultural expectations and reactions to sex-typed behaviors, while sex identity results from a complex mixture of physiological, psychological, and cultural elements.

SUGGESTED READINGS

BOWLBY, JOHN. *Attachment.* New York: Basic Books, 1969. A basic source, with which every reader should be familiar. Almost all studies of attachment begin with this great reference.

FESHBACH, SEYMOUR. "Aggression," in *Carmichael's Manual of Child Psychology* (Paul Mussen, Editor). New York: John Wiley, 1970. The aggression literature is enormous, and Feshbach's lengthy essay is one of the best surveys of both research and theory.

GILLIGAN, CAROL. "In a Different Voice: Women's Conceptions of Self and Morality," *Harvard Educational Review,* Volume 47, Number 4, November, 1977, 481–517. Although many may find this sensitive essay controversial because of its focus on abortion as the basis of feminine choice, it raises many pertinent questions about women's moral development.

HERSH, RICHARD, DIANA PAOLITTO, and JOSEPH REIMER. *Promoting Moral Growth: From Piaget to Kohlberg.* New York: Longman, 1979. An excellent primer for the reader who is unfamiliar with Kohlberg's work. Especially good in clarifying the Piagetian roots of the system.

KOHLBERG, LAWRENCE. "The Cognitive-Developmental Approach to Moral Education," *Phi Delta Kappan,* 56 (1975), 670–677. An excellent brief account of the theory, its background, link to Piaget, and research.

LIPS, HILARY and COLWILL, NINA LEE. *The Psychology of Sex Differences.* Englewood Cliffs, New Jersey: Prentice-Hall, 1978. An unusually thoughtful, wide-ranging explanation of the development of a variety of male-female differences.

LORENZ, KONRAD. *On Aggression.* New York: Harcourt, Brace, and World, 1966. Lorenz's classic statement on the instinctive nature of aggression, with which every reader should be familiar.

MONEY, JOHN and ANKE EHRHARDT. *Man and Woman, Boy and Girl.* Baltimore: Johns Hopkins University Press, 1972. A fertile source of physiological, psychological, and cultural data about the appearance of sex differences.

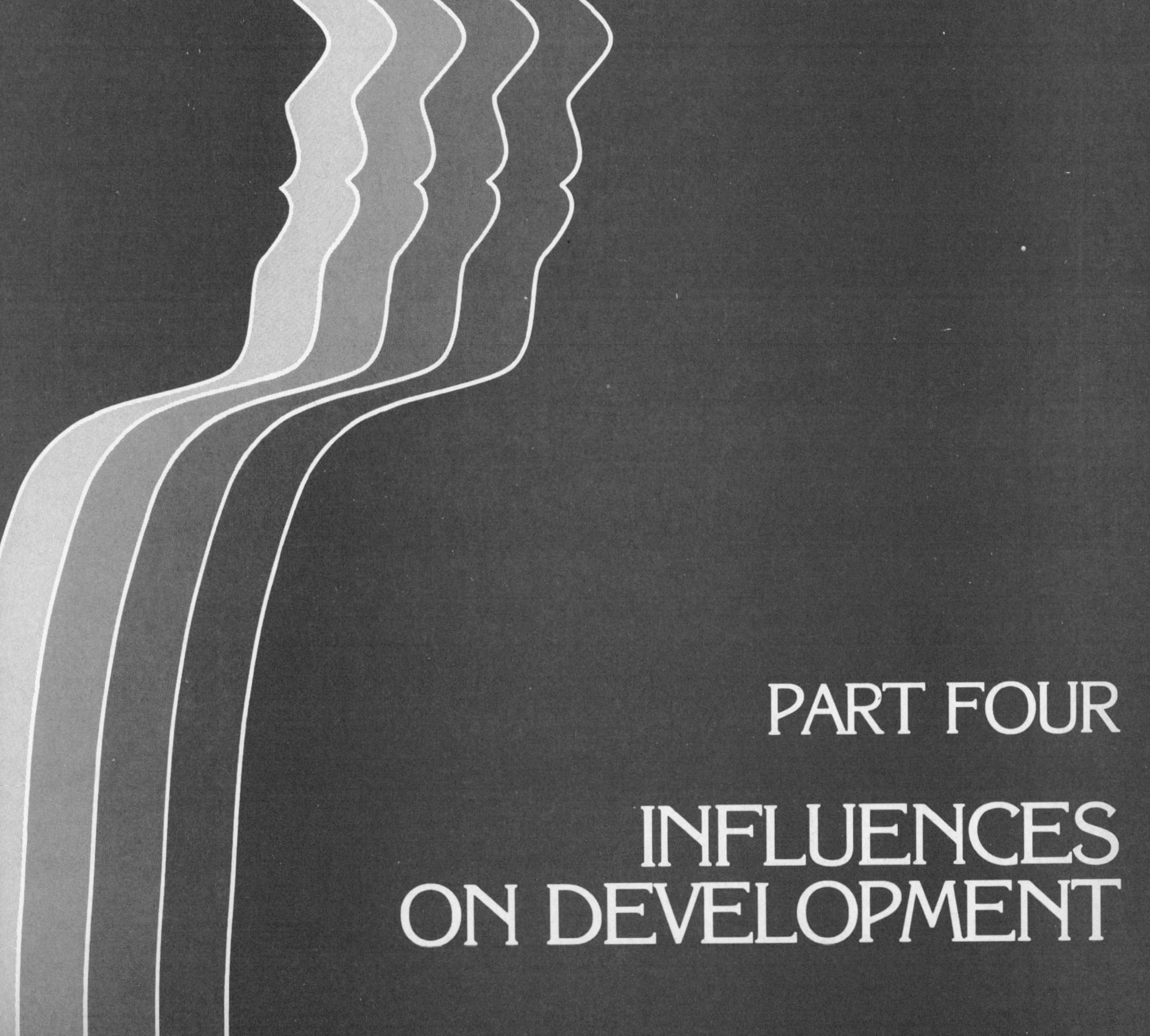

PART FOUR

INFLUENCES ON DEVELOPMENT

CHAPTER 12
THE FAMILY'S INFLUENCE

CHAPTER HIGHLIGHTS

Topics

The Family: A Vivid Example
a. La Vida
b. The Family—An Enduring Institution

The Changing American Family
a. The Family—An Overview
b. What Are the Facts? The Statistical Data
c. Interpretation of Data

Forms of Family Life
a. The Traditional Nuclear Family
b. The Modern Nuclear Family
c. The Extended Family
d. The Androgynous Household
e. Communal Life
f. Single Parent Homes
g. Adoption—Foster Homes
h. Institutional Placement
i. Day Care

Parents, Children, and Developmental Outcomes
a. Recent Findings

A Rationale for the Future

People

Urie Bronfenbrenner
E. Mavis Hetherington
Kenneth Keniston
Christopher Lasch
Oscar Lewis
David Lynn
Salvatore Minuchin
Nathan Talbot

Special Topics

Child Development, Family, and Literature
Worried Parents
In Search of Origins

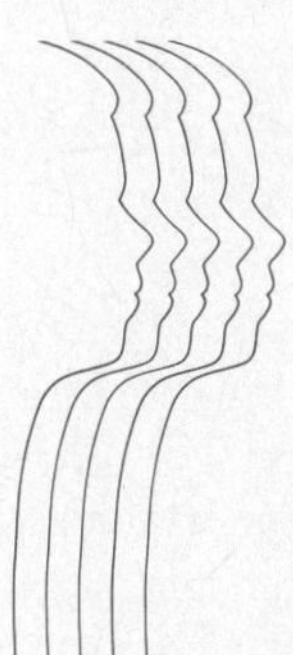

> In all societies, the nuclear family is the initial social matrix within which personality is rooted and nourished. It insures continuity of child care and the primacy of certain relationships above all others. The nuclear family of husband, wife, and children is always a part of a kinship system which in turn is an element of the larger social structure and culture. The family cements the child first to his kin and then to community and society. (Clausen, 1966, p. 1)

Since ninety-eight percent of all American children grow up in families, Clausen's words, somewhat recast to include new, emerging family patterns, summarize the family's impact on a child's development. They signify attachment and personality development, the basics of physical development, continuity of care, and the vital beginnings of the socialization process.

If any institution exercises such vital societal functions, we may well ask why the family has become such a source of controversy. The role of the family in influencing a child's development has come under intensive scrutiny during the past decade, with the result that there has been an outpouring of talks, articles, and books that criticize, tolerate, or support the family concept. Still, believing that love, warmth, attention, happiness, and discipline are the main ingredients for the healthy growth that a child craves, it is difficult to minimize the importance of family life. If these ingredients are amply provided, youngsters are usually assured of a good start on the road to maturity. There is no guarantee that the outcome will be positive, but of this we can be almost certain: without such family support, it is the rare individual who achieves satisfactory and harmonious development.

But a sense of crisis surrounds the family. Divorce rates skyrocket; child abuse is more prevalent (whether by more accurate diagnosis or actual increase is irrelevant); politicians ponder; and presidents call White House conferences. Greer (1979), not knowing whether to worry about the family or worry about those who worry about the family, believes that there are five different viewpoints on the "family crisis."

1. The family is decaying, which threatens not only personal development but also the national community.

2. The family is evolving, which implies that natural changes must occur if families are to continue to exercise their functions in changing societies.

3. The family is basically the same, which attributes any crisis feelings to typical generational gaps.

4. The family is changing but there is no need to worry about it, which suggests that families *must* change to remain intact.

5. Family influence is fading due to a rise in individualism, which is as it should be.

Greer believes that worry about the family has been an historical constant and has always accompanied widespread social unrest. Bronfenbrenner (1970, 1979), a careful student of family life, believes that the American family, as we have known it, is disintegrating. The increase in single-parent families and an increasing number of unmarried teenage mothers raises questions about the quality of care many children are receiving. As yet, there is no national priority for excellent daycare centers, which may reflect a corresponding national indifference to the family. (Although recent research indicates many positive aspects of some daycare programs, these programs are usually private, well financed, and university sponsored. Thus they are not characteristic of all daycare programs. It is an important conclusion, to which we shall return.)

Bronfenbrenner believes that if the family requires support, it must come from the larger society. Conditions have changed, especially with regard to women. We previously mentioned our society's changing attitudes towards the traditional roles of men and women and the corresponding expansion of choices for women. Many more women have entered the work force. Although many women choose their careers or jobs out of a desire for personal fulfillment, most work because of economic necessity. Family financial needs frequently leave little choice. Society must move to accommodate its changed labor force by altering its traditional ways, such as the nine to five day. Many large corporations have recognized this need and have adopted flexible work schedules. As women spend more of their time away from the home, society must develop effective support systems, including responsible and nurturant day care centers.

Our task for this chapter is clear; we will determine the structure of the modern family, trace the changes that have occurred in the last decade, identify the various forms that families have taken, and project, timidly, the course of the future. The theme that unites our work remains constant: the unmistakable influence that the family, whatever its size, form, and characteristics, exercises on a child's development.

First, then, let us attempt to trace the origins of family life and to describe the basic family structure.

THE FAMILY: A VIVID EXAMPLE

Almost everyone pays at least lip service to the notion that the family is a powerful determinant of a child's personality, self-concept, and behavior. But to illustrate this belief logically and coherently is extremely difficult. Rarely do we have the opportunity to study a work on the family that is well written, scrupulous in its methodology, and refreshing in its candor. Such an opportunity is presented, however, in the work of Oscar Lewis, especially *La Vida* (1965). A vivid, dramatic, and moving story of the impact of the family in a poverty setting, *La Vida* brings to life the dynamics of this historically momentous institution. The mother of the family Lewis studied was a woman who had worked as a servant for fifty cents a day and had also been a prostitute. She learned to fight with a razor, scavenged for food, and had been in prison. Most important, however, she gave her children a legacy of toughness, brutality, and animal courage. Need we say more? The impact of this family would be far different from that of a white Protestant, Catholic, or Jewish family, each of which would reflect the emotional, physical, social and intellectual qualities of its particular heredity and environment.

The Rios Family

The Rios family (a fictitious name) of Lewis's study consisted of five households: a mother and two married daughters in Puerto Rico, and a married son and daughter in New York City. Although any family dwelling in a Puerto Rican slum would obviously reflect the culture of poverty, we will reserve our comments concerning societal influence for a later chapter in which we will again use the Rios family as an example. These people manifested a tremendous joy in living, and especially in sex, and they craved excitement and adventure. Not a particularly reflective people, they tended to act instead of think, and they received far more pleasure from spending than saving. Unimpressed with the slow, impersonal tone of justice, they displayed fierce personal loyalities and antagonisms. They were outgoing, fun-loving, and exhibited a great need for companionship. Lewis summarizes it beautifully:

> The Rios family is closer to the expression of an unbridled id than any other people I have studied. They have an almost complete absence of internal conflict and a sense of guilt. They tend to accept themselves as they are, and do not indulge in soul-searching or introspection. (1965, p. xxvi)

He goes on to say that the leading characters in some of his other studies seem mild, repressed, and almost middle class by comparison. For the Rios family, rage, passion, violence, and even bloodshed were not uncommon. Think of some of the characteristics that we have mentioned: the tendency to act instead of think, the need for friends, and the quick surge of passion. These family traits become a way of life. But consider the role of the school in their lives. What kind of curriculum, what kind of instruction would best hold their attention? How could one convert their abundant energy into a passion for knowledge or a desire for self-improvement?

Seemingly characteristic of a poverty culture is a preoccupation with sex. Since it satisfies a variety of needs—for pleasure, money, revenge, love, children, masculinity, or femininity—its function for some is to fill a void caused by the crushing weight of poverty. Unable to afford life's luxuries, they tend to turn to an inherent pleasure that is natural and free from the burdens of society. Lewis states:

> Even family unity, one of the most sacred values in this family-oriented culture, is sometimes threatened by the danger of seduction by stepfathers, the sexual rivalry between sisters, between mothers and daughters, and occasionally even between grandmothers and granddaughters. There is a remarkable openness and frankness about sex, and little effort is made to hide the facts of life from children. Although the children in the Rios family have many problems, they do not suffer from parental secrecy and dishonesty about sex. (1965, p. xxvi)

Male-Female. Interestingly, the women of the Rios family exhibited much greater aggressiveness and violence than the men. They were demanding and assertive. It was the woman who decided when a marriage was finished; who called the police during family battles, and who sued the husband for nonsupport. Lewis makes the telling comment that much of the women's belligerence was directed against men. They degraded them, branding them as inconsiderate, irresponsible, and generally worthless.

If the women drew the children to them and taught them to distrust men, what were the consequences? What influence was there on the children's behavior when the dominant influence in the family was female? Lacking a strong male image, did the boys tend to become more feminine in some of their characteristics? Did the girls follow the pattern established by their mothers? If both male and female continued this tradition, what would it mean for society? Lewis notes that the reluctance of the women to accept the more stereotyped female function created deep tensions and problems for the family. It may have also caused personal problems, since the woman was often torn between the desire to assume the more customary feminine role and the position of authority into which she was thrust. Once men settled into a more passive and dependent behavioral pattern, then what choice did a woman have? Since the pattern was not broken, this role reversal was transmitted from generation to generation.

Perhaps now you can better understand why Lewis's description of this particular family was chosen. It would be difficult to discover a more vibrant account of the influence of family on development. Lewis states that the particular marriage did not explain the role reversal just mentioned. That is, regardless of the type of marriage, it was the man who was far more interested in maintaining a stable family life and who resisted the wife's efforts to separate. The author concludes that the behavior of the Rios family had not changed over four generations, thus suggesting a tenacious cultural pattern.

Influences on Development. Lewis makes some telling remarks about conclusions reached by behavioral scientists when they write about multiproblem families. Stressing lack of order, poor organization, and instability, they frequently overlook the predictability and the obvious patterns in such a family's behavior. Perhaps more striking is the repetitiveness and the firm establishment of behavioral patterns. Often overlooked is the vital role of family unity. Subjected to great cultural pressure and deprivation, their feeling for family gives them something they can cling to, something that offers hope and happiness in the midst of recurring despair.

The Rios family's life was not all negative, in other words. Lewis was impressed by their fortitude, vitality, and coping abilities in circumstances that would be the undoing of many other families. They had their own sense of dignity and morality; they were kind and generous. Their lives were devoted to a search for love. Bound by poverty and influenced by a history of prostitution in the family and the feminine methods of survival, how would one change such a pattern of behavior that has lasted for generations?

Lewis has also made some interesting comments on the effect of prostitution on family life. He notes that prostitution has a different meaning in a community in which about one-third of the families have a history of prostitution and that for the Rios family it had not caused any major changes in the basic fabric of family life. He concludes:

> The data in this book suggest that we have to modify some of our stereotypes about prostitutes. One normally thinks of the role of a mother and the role of a prostitute as being contradictory, if not mutually exclusive. In these life histories, the two roles coexist without too much conflict. Indeed, the relative ease with which the Rios women move back and forth between the role of wife and mother and that of prostitute is remarkable. (1965, p. xxvi)

Lewis has summarized the conditions surrounding the Rios family as those that reflect the nightmare of poverty and social pathology. The life histories of the individual family members reveal a scene of family disruption, violence, brutality, and lack of education and medical attention. Yet within this context, there are positive aspects as well, as we have mentioned. But what is the effect on the two-year-old or the ten-year-old?

What does such a setting have to tell us about physical, social, intellectual, and emotional development? Are these youngsters experiencing "normal" development? Certainly by the standards of this one family, the pattern is one that can be safely predicted. There will be physical problems, probably serious, because of the dearth of medical facilities. Emotional behavior will be uninhibited; no effort is made to hide one's feelings or to teach youngsters to control their emotions. Perhaps this is desirable for them, however, permitting them to tolerate the circumstances of their lives. Social development may be difficult because of the male and female roles; both boys and girls may find it extremely difficult to adjust to the broader spectrum of society and to the narrower confines of marriage. Everything that we have said would also indicate that little value is placed on formal education which, in a society that is becoming ever more technological, bespeaks limited occupational success. In short, there is no escaping the pervasive influence of the family.

The Family—An Enduring Institution

The Rios family is an excellent example of the ability of the family to survive under conditions that would presumably shatter other human relationships. Who would think, for example, that prostitution and marriage could weather unrelieved tensions?

Remember throughout the remainder of our discussion that in spite of widespread despair, changing life-styles, and even governmental assaults (recall the early days of the Russian Communist government), the family, in one form or another, has endured.

The changes that we witness in family life characterize what families have always done: adapt to changing conditions. These changes, then, rather than representing "the breakdown of the fabric of family life," undoubtedly represent a change in the functions of the family. In a perceptive analysis of the functions of a modern family, Farb (1978) has identified four features as especially important.

1. The family provides a structure through which society itself can be populated. The production of children, and their care, should result in actively participating members of that society. While other institutions share in this socialization process, the family makes the initial mark on the child's development, which will affect all other influences.

2. The family provides a means by which society can legitimize offspring, thus affording a means of identifying important relationships among parents, children, and their kin network. The legal consequences of these relationships are obvious. While some believe that legitimacy is no longer of great concern, Farb believes that children of unmarried parents are removed from the mainstream of most of the world's societies.

3. The family is a means of regulating sexual behavior. Although societies vary in their permissiveness toward sexual relations, all societies have norms. Sanctions concerning adultery and premarital sex have changed considerably, but Farb believes that rather than breaking down, the norms are being redefined.

4. The family still exercises an economic function. Modern families, while not producers, are important consumers and are mainly responsible for the economic stability of industrial societies. Primitive societies still view marriage as an economic merger.

These are specific societal functions that the family serves, but what of developmental functions? Farb concludes that the ideal function of the modern family is to provide intimacy, warmth, and affection and to provide an environment in which children are participants in the fulfillment of their potential.

CHILDREN, FAMILY, AND LITERATURE

The importance of family to the developing child is evident in all aspects of our lives. Both physical and mental health, schoolwork, recreation, literature, and theater all reflect familial overtones. In an excellent text, *Children and Books* (1972), Arbuthnot and Sutherland discuss children's needs to love and be loved, and illustrate how this theme runs through children's stories.

They state that it is in the family that children learn their first lessons in the laws of affectionate relationships and that books exemplify these relationships. For example, in *Rainy Day Together* by Ellen Parsons, the main thrust illustrates the love between parents and children. As Arbuthnot and Sutherland note, not only do these family patterns influence the child's feeling of security, but they likewise influence reactions to others and the search for and relationship with a mate.

The status of mother and father within the family provide children with the first sense of male and female roles and strongly affects the acquisition of a satisfactory sex identity. As a child's circle of friends and acquaintances widens, the family provides the means by which true and loyal friendships are made. As the authors state, if children feel loved and know that their own love is accepted, there is a tendency toward friendly relationships outside the family. If the opposite is true, a child's reactions to others is hostile, if not belligerent. This theme appears in a story featuring Gilly, the lonely boy in Julia Cunningham's *Dorp Dead,* who masks his native intelligence because he mistrusts adults, and in one about Ivan, the boy in Paula Fox's *Portrait of Ivan,* who resists any adult overtures as a result of the death of his mother and a complete lack of affection from his father. It is a sensitive theme, one you might like to explore.

The Family Structures. Minuchin (1974) states that the family is a social unit that faces a series of developmental tasks. For example, modern societies require that its members have a relatively high level of education for successful adaptation, so families must provide the support—whether financial or emotional. Society today urges children to leave their families as soon as possible, but parents usually wish to maintain close ties with their children. These are but two of the many pressures that act on today's families.

Any analysis of the changes produced in the American family by a changing society must account for the turmoil and upheaval caused by three major wars: World War II, the Korean War, and the Vietnam conflict. Many family members also were Depression babies, and these two experiences—war and financial problems—have made them conscious of security and wary of the modern products of affluence. The younger generation, sick of war and never having known financial worry, are rebelling against what they see wrong in society. Differences in age, morals, and values all tend to lead to tension and unhappiness. It is easy to write words that encourage love, understanding, and tolerance; it is far more difficult to live them. But what is the alternative? Parents who desire the love and respect of their children are tired of family dissension. Children who desire to have limits and standards imposed on them are searching for emotional security.

We hear frequently of a generation gap. There is and there must be a generation gap. Nothing seems more ridiculous to a child than a parent trying to act like a playmate. But a communication gap is another matter (Figure 12.1); here is the great danger, the gap that separates and finally destroys any vestiges of family cohesion. It is precisely here that families must join and search for solutions. Parents must learn to listen, to recognize and understand the questions and problems that bother

FIGURE 12.1. To Communicate or Not to Communicate. *(a)* Lack of communication between generations. *(b)* Communication between generations.

their children. Physical problems, school problems, peer problems, or emotional problems—children should be urged to bring them home and discuss them. Where possible, parents must not dictate solutions; instead, there should be mutual undertaking in the search for answers. But it is not a one-way street. Children must also attempt to see their parents' point of view, to understand what parents want for them and to respect their judgment.

How can such an ideal situation be brought about? As with everything else, it must begin during those initial critical years. The love, warmth, cooperation and respect that is to be so desperately sought later must commence early. Youngsters must know that they are loved, and during these first months and years this can mainly be communicated physically. Parents must gradually loosen ties and encourage independence, always remembering that freedom carries responsibility. But children crave discipline too; for them, it is a mark of love. We are not implying a harsh unyielding discipline, but the discipline that is protective and plainly speaks of love, affection, and devoted attention.

The manner in which a family manages these developmental tasks has a history. Minuchin (1974) states that a married couple must immediately commence the process of mutual accommodation, from compromise with each other to sharing household tasks. They must adjust to the separation from their original families and make their primary commitment to the new unit. The birth of children marks a new era with shifting demands; that is, the relationship between man and woman changes.

Bronfenbrenner (1979) refers to these changes as ecological transitions; that is, a person's position in the ecological environment, here the family is altered. When a child is born, the father must accommodate to the time the mother gives to the child. Other children are born; they grow and leave the family; grandchildren arrive. Husband and wife are again alone but under different circumstances. These are the family developmental tasks to which Minuchin refers, and, as he notes (1974, p. 18), the family must meet the challenges of both internal and external change while maintaining its continuity. It must also simultaneously encourage the growth of its members while adapting to a changing society—a formidable task.

To understand how families cope with these challenges, Minuchin proposes a family model that includes structure, development, and adaptation. These three components permit us to analyze and rationalize the continued existence of the family in the face of changing societal demands. Remember that change comes from society to family, and it is the family's ability to adapt that forces us to formulate a conceptual model that explains its unique, and persistent, role in all societies.

1. *Family Structure.* Minuchin (1974, p. 51) states that family structure is the invisible set of functional demands that organizes the ways in which family members interact. Two systems of constraints function within the family structures. First is the necessity of a power hierarchy; that is, children and parents have different levels of authority. Second is the mutual expectations of individual family members, expectations that arise from the multiplicity of daily tasks over years. These two systems help to ensure family stability, but they must not become so rigid that a family cannot adapt to inevitable internal and external changes.

2. *Family Development.* Understanding how a family tolerates change and develops through various stages demands a knowledge of the subsystems that occur within a family. Individual family members belong to different subsystems in which they exercise varying degrees of power and in which they learn different skills. For example, a boy has a far different relationship with his father than he does with his younger brother; the power relationship is reversed, and he must learn to adapt to both roles.

There are boundaries between the different subsystems that define who participates, in what they participate, and how they participate. If a family is to function smoothly, the boundaries must be clear. For example, there is a boundary that surrounds the spouse subsystem within which the man and woman must accommodate to each other's needs. Yet the boundary must not be so rigid that the parents become isolated; children must have access to parents, without intruding on spouse interactions. Thus, with children, the spouse system divides to include a parental subsystem. This aids both parents and children, since parents retain needed privacy and children enjoy parental support but are not drawn into parental problems. With additional children, a third subsystem evolves, the sibling subsystem, in which youngsters learn a new set of skills: negotiating, cooperating, competing. They then use these skills with their extrafamilial peers.

3. *Family Adaptation.* All families experience inner pressures from their own development and outer pressures from societal demands. These pressures produce individual transformations within family continuity. Consequently, subsystems change. For example, an oldest daughter goes away to college, and the next oldest assumes many of her duties. Thus there is a shift in the power hierarchy; this daughter now has a different access to the parental subsystem, and relationships within the sibling subsystem have also changed. If the transformations are harmonious, family integrity is ensured; if not, the structure is threatened and the family may well experience difficulties.

Minuchin's model is an excellent tool for analyzing the family and understanding the family's response to changing societal conditions. He concludes that investigators must recognize that families are transformed over time; that is, they adapt and reorganize to maintain their functions. Unless subsystem boundaries are clear and flexible, internal and external pressures can produce dysfunctional patterns of family life.

> According to the suggested model, an effectively functioning family is an open social system in transformation, maintaining links with the extrafamilial, possessing a capacity for development, and having an organizational structure composed of subsystems. The individual, who is himself a subsystem of the family, faces different tasks and acquires different interpersonal skills in the different subsystems. (Minuchin, 1979, p. 255)

DISCUSSION QUESTIONS

1. How do you react to Lewis's assessment of the strengths and weaknesses of the Rios family? Do you agree with the features that he designates as strengths? Do the weaknesses outweigh the strengths? What are the consequences of these forces?
2. What was your reaction to the male-female relationships among the Rioses? Does this add to or detract from family cohesiveness? What does it imply for the acquisition of a sex identity? Relate your answer to circumstances outside of the family.
3. Do you sense a "need for family"? How does family acceptance support you in your endeavors? Does it pose any obstacles?
4. When college students are asked what constitutes their primary concern, the vast majority reply that it is their relationship with their parents. Discuss this in the light of the material that we have just examined.
5. We have, on several occasions, discussed a child's desire for boundaries. Can you relate this desire to Minuchin's family model? How do you interpret this desire in the light of individual transformations and relationships among subsystems?
6. How do you react to the distinction that was made between a communication gap and a generation gap? Need one necessarily imply the other? If so, why? How can parents prevent a communication gap?

THE CHANGING AMERICAN FAMILY

Before we assess the influence of the family on a child's development, we must consider the changing nature of the contemporary family. The woman's role, number of children, the man's place, and the family structure are all changing. Thus, the impact of these changing conditions will surely exercise a different force on development than we have previously seen. These changes may be temporary or permanent, good or bad, and critical or otherwise for a child, but they deserve our attention.

In the Rios family, as in almost all families, a dependence of family members on each other is apparent; this helps to explain the universality of the family. No society has eliminated the family, in spite of attempts such as those of the Soviet Union. Regardless of the society, it is apparent that the family remains an indispensable ingredient. Today throughout the world, a mobile, highly skilled population is challenging the very concept of the family as it has never been challenged before. Separation, change, and rootlessness tear at marriage and introduce different types of strain with which families must cope.

For instance, the typical family does not produce the items that satisfy its needs; they look beyond the family, thus becoming consumers instead of producers. To secure the economic means of acquiring needed goods, mothers, fathers, or both are often separated from their families. In an age of inflation, more and more pressure is being applied to both parents to provide the necessities, which also causes new and different problems. What does the role of the working mother imply for development, for example? As we discussed early in the chapter, either for economic necessity or to fulfill personal needs, many women spend the greater part of a day away from home. If small children are well cared for by other family members or spend the day in a good childcare center and the mothers spend time with their children in the evening, the results can be satisfactory for both mother and child. The crux of this issue seems to be that children need thoughtful, loving care, and that parents are seen as the most stable, reliable figures in a child's life.

The size of the family is also changing. The old line of authority no longer carries the sanctions it once did; therefore, the younger members of the family no longer feel bound, as their parents and grandparents did, to follow traditional beliefs and customs. As family units have become smaller, grandparents and other members of the extended family have become less influential with children. Contact with relatives has decreased because of the modern family's mobility. In addition, divorce, birth control, and abortion are accepted practices for many, practices which are the source of another new and troubling set of problems. Although many people are shrugging off parental or religious restraints, many cannot shake off the psychological burden. They suffer feelings of guilt that may well introduce tensions and discord into the home, affecting both male-female relations and the harmonious development of the children. Note the rapidly increasing divorce rate shown in Figure 12.2.

The increase seen in Figure 12.2 is an international pattern. Comparing the increase in divorce rates for various countries reveals interesting data, shown in Table 12.1.

In eight countries, the increase, represented by the percentage of change, is greater than that in the United States. The rate, based on absolute numbers, is higher for the United States than these other eight countries. While Canada showed the largest percentage change, the figures for the Soviet Union are revealing.

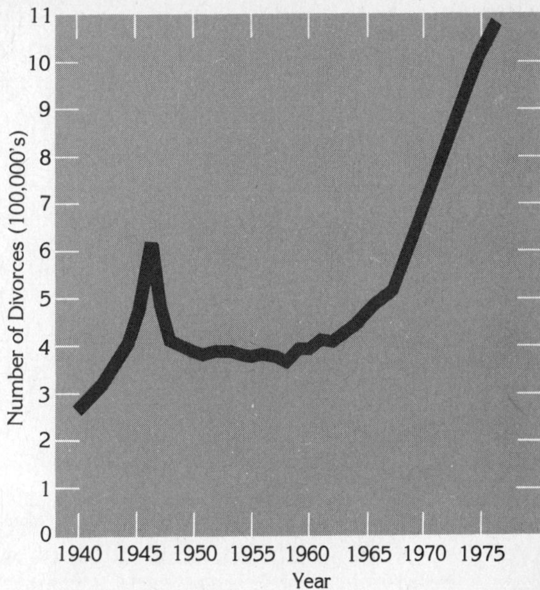

FIGURE 12.2. Number of Divorces: United States, 1940–1976.
Source: U.S. Department of Health, Education, and Welfare. Hyattsville, Maryland: National Center for Health Statistics, 1978.

Russian divorce laws were eased in the early 1960s; the divorce rate doubled from 1963 to 1966 and has declined only slightly since then.

Viewing all these problems, many authorities believe that the family will never again be the same, that it is possibly on the verge of dissolution. Others, however, are more optimistic, viewing the family as essential for the survival of society and recognizing its inherent value as an institution. They agree that we are witnessing the birth of new difficulties for the family, but believe that we can face and overcome them as we have done in the past, employing different techniques. It is doubtful that any society could endure without the family; it is within the family that children initially learn to relate to others, to adjust to themselves, to give as well as to receive. Happily, for most of us, that learning remains with us for life. We need only to examine the many studies that indicate the difficulties that can result when a mother or father is taken from the child at an early age. Or we can refer again to studies of those institutionalized children who received only a minimum of early care to discover how retarded these youngsters are in all phases of development. It is a familiar truism that the family teaches children how to be human and in so doing reflects the unique nature of the surrounding society.

As the demands of society change, the individual members of that society must also change if they wish to do more than just survive. Bettering oneself means gaining the necessary education to secure desirable employment, realizing that improvement often entails physical movement to a different community. We have mentioned this in our discussion of the difficulties inherent in our society, and it becomes more and more clear that the problems of the family are closely entwined with a changing society.

As an example of the changing demands of society on child rearing practices, consider the classic report by Wolfenstein (1951). Analyzing

TABLE 12.1. Divorce Rates per 1,000 Population, with Percent Changes: United States and Selected Foreign Countries, 1960 and 1970 (Countries are listed by magnitude of change. Source of data: United Nations, *Demographic Yearbook*, 1968 and 1974; 1970 for China)

	Divorce rate				Divorce rate		
Country	1970	1960	Percent change	Country	1970	1960	Percent change
Canada	1.36	0.39	+248.7	Denmark	1.93	1.46	+32.2
Dominican Republic	0.92	0.29	+217.2	Belgium	0.66	0.50	+32.0
Scotland	0.88	0.35	+151.4	Bulgaria	1.16	0.90	+28.9
England and Wales	1.18	0.51	+131.4	Japan	0.94	0.74	+27.0
Poland	1.06	0.50	+112.0	Austria	1.40	1.13	+23.9
Soviet Union	2.62	1.3	+101.5	Democratic Republic of Germany[1]	1.61	1.34	+20.1
New Zealand	1.12	0.69	+62.3	France[2]	0.79	0.66	+19.7
Netherlands	0.79	0.49	+61.2	Switzerland	1.02	0.87	+17.2
United States	3.47	2.18	+59.2	Lebanon	0.45	0.43	+4.7
Finland	1.29	0.82	+57.2	China (Taiwan)[2]	0.39	0.44	−11.4
Czechoslovakia	1.74	1.12	+55.4	Guatemala	0.13	0.15	−13.3
Australia	0.98	0.65	+50.8	Yugoslavia	1.01	1.20	−15.8
Germany, Federal Republic of[1]	1.24	0.83	+49.4	Egypt[3]	2.07	[4]2.51	−17.5
Uruguay	1.01	0.68	+48.5	Israel	0.81	1.05	−22.9
Mexico	0.57	0.42	+35.7	Portugal	0.06	0.08	−25.0
Sweden	1.61	1.20	+34.2	Syria	0.57	0.78	−26.9
Hungary	2.22	1.66	+33.7	Turkey	0.28	0.40	−30.0
Norway	0.88	0.66	+33.3	Iran	0.58	1.17	−50.4
Greece	0.40	0.30	+33.3	Romania	0.38	2.01	−81.1

[1]Includes the relevant parts of Berlin
[2]Provisional data.
[3]Data include "revocable divorces" among the Moslem population which approximate legal separations.
[4]Rate listed under United Arab Republic.
Source: U.S. Department of Health, Education, and Welfare, Hyattsville, Maryland: National Center for Health Statistics, 1978.

Infant Care, a publication of the U.S. Labor Department's Children's Bureau, she states that in 1914 American mothers were warned against playing with their children, told to eliminate thumb-sucking, and advised not to be swayed by children's wants, such as their appetites. By 1945, the advice in the same publication had changed radically. Mothers were told to relax with their babies, to enjoy them, and to give them considerable warm attention. Times change and the pressures of society on families and their children likewise change.

In the 1980s there are multiple pressures acting on the family. Television, the schools, peers, "expert" advice, and the commitment of time and money pose particularly pressing problems for parents. There is a growing national concern about the family that may have both positive and negative effects. Governmental intervention may improve the economic conditions of many families but simultaneously erode the family's sense of integrity—another pressure to which the family must adapt.

WORRIED PARENTS

Although family stability has been an historical constant, modern parents are worried and their concern is reflected in a growing number of parent-training programs. Interestingly, the popularity of these programs dramatically illustrates society's influence on the family. For example, if you recall the 1950s, society's expectations for children could be categorized as conformity and success. Consequently, families worked hard, pooled their resources, and sent their sons and daughters to college. Education was the key.

In the 1960s, repelled by war and its treatment of minorities, society moved toward freedom and self-fulfillment. Family solidarity was rocked; children of the affluent scorned conventional work habits and tedious years of education. They feared that families smothered their potential; they wanted to "do their own thing." Individualistic humanism was the key.

The 1970s and early 1980s have seen a retrenchment. Shaken by the unrest of the past two decades, society is seeking stability by restoring ruptured relationships. Harmony is to be the key, even if government has to force it upon us.

In a sophisticated society, how do we achieve harmony? We turn to the experts, in this case, the how-to-parent experts. Their programs range from emphasis on communication between parents and children to resolve conflict (rather than authority and power), to "involvement" with children, to behavior modification, to encouragement. While it is difficult to assess the long-range consequences of these programs, they nevertheless reflect anxiety about familial relationships.

Parents also turn to literature for guidance. Clarke-Stewart (1978) estimates that in the five years preceding her survey, *23 million* popular (Spock, Ginott) childcare books were sold. It is a safe guess that sales since 1978 exceed that number. Most parents read at least one of these books; some read as many as five. Clarke-Stewart notes that these parents are young, worried, and isolated from traditional sources of child care.

Both of these phenomena—parent-training groups and the popular literature—clearly suggest a societal concern to be a "good parent."

What Are the Facts?

Discussion about family life constantly refers to change. To specify what these changes are, and then to interpret their meaning, consider the following:

1. The number of American families has remained relatively constant for the past decade—almost sixty million.
2. Projections to the year 1990 are that this figure will remain about the same.
3. About four-fifths of these families have the basic husband-wife relationship.
4. Families headed by females (no husband present) represent a large group, and demand attention in the formulation of any national family policy. (See Table 12.2.)

TABLE 12.2. Families, by Type and Size: 1950–1990

Year and projection series	Total families (thousands)	Type of family: Husband-wife, husband head		Other male head, no wife present		Female head, no husband present	
		Number (thousands)	Percent	Number (thousands)	Percent	Number (thousands)	Percent
1950	39,303	34,440	87.6	1,184	3.0	3,679	9.4
1955	41,951	36,378	86.7	1,339	3.2	4,234	10.1
1960	45,111	39,329	87.2	1,275	2.8	4,507	10.0
1965	47,956	41,749	87.1	1,181	2.5	5,026	10.5
1970	51,586	44,755	86.8	1,239	2.4	5,591	10.8
1975							
Series A	56,231	47,783	85.0	1,449	2.6	6,901	12.3
Series B	56,219	47,784	85.0	1,449	2.6	6,888	12.3
Series C	56,197	47,785	85.0	1,447	2.6	6,863	12.2
Series K	56,185	47,786	85.1	1,446	2.6	6,851	12.2
1980							
Series A	61,312	51,806	84.5	1,566	2.6	7,858	12.8
Series B	61,234	51,825	84.6	1,561	2.5	7,758	12.7
Series C	61,080	51,864	84.9	1,550	2.5	7,560	12.4
Series K	61,004	51,885	85.1	1,543	2.5	7,463	12.2
1985							
Series A	66,440	55,715	83.9	1,723	2.6	8,942	13.5
Series B	66,255	55,757	84.2	1,713	2.6	8,711	13.1
Series C	65,894	55,845	84.8	1,686	2.6	8,260	12.5
Series K	65,718	55,891	85.0	1,668	2.5	8,040	12.2
1990							
Series A	70,943	59,033	83.2	1,893	2.7	9,983	14.1
Series B	70,606	59,073	83.7	1,877	2.7	9,601	13.6
Series C	69,947	59,163	84.6	1,830	2.6	8,857	12.7
Series K	69,622	59,209	85.0	1,798	2.6	8,495	12.2

Source: U.S. Department of Commerce, Bureau of the Census, 1970 Census of Population, *Current Population* Reports, Series P-20, Nos. 266 and 282, and Series P-25, No. 607.

Note the steady rise in female-headed families from 1950 to 1990. Although the percentage increase seems small, averaging about four percent, the *number* of families headed by females will have grown by about six million. Consequently, the likelihood of governmental intervention increases. Although we shall discuss the meaning of these figures in more detail, a substantial increase in the number of women who head families and who must work suggests the need for a major commitment to daycare programs. The need to ensure quality within programs seems to dictate government intervention in the financial, regulatory and supervisory areas. Figure 12.3 illustrates the changing size of the American family and age of its members.

There are several interesting features to Figure 12.3. The large size of the American family peaked in 1965 at about 3.7 persons, which reflected the "baby boom" of the 1950s. There has been a steady decline since then, and the figure is expected to reach 3.0 persons by 1990. Most of this decline will be in family members under eighteen years, which dramatically illustrates the theoretical issues we discussed in the moral development section. Women, now exercising responsibility for those choices relating to their personal lives, have postponed child-bearing, rejected it, or have opted for abortion. Again we see the intimate link between society and family: a technologically advanced society has made personal choice a woman's responsibility; the nature of these decisions alters not only family life, but also other elements of the society, such as education and the workplace. Figure 12.4 presents additional data about changing family size.

FIGURE 12.3. Average Size of Families, by Age of Members: 1950–1990.
Source: *Social Indicators–1976.* Washington, D.C.: U.S. Department of Commerce, December, 1977.

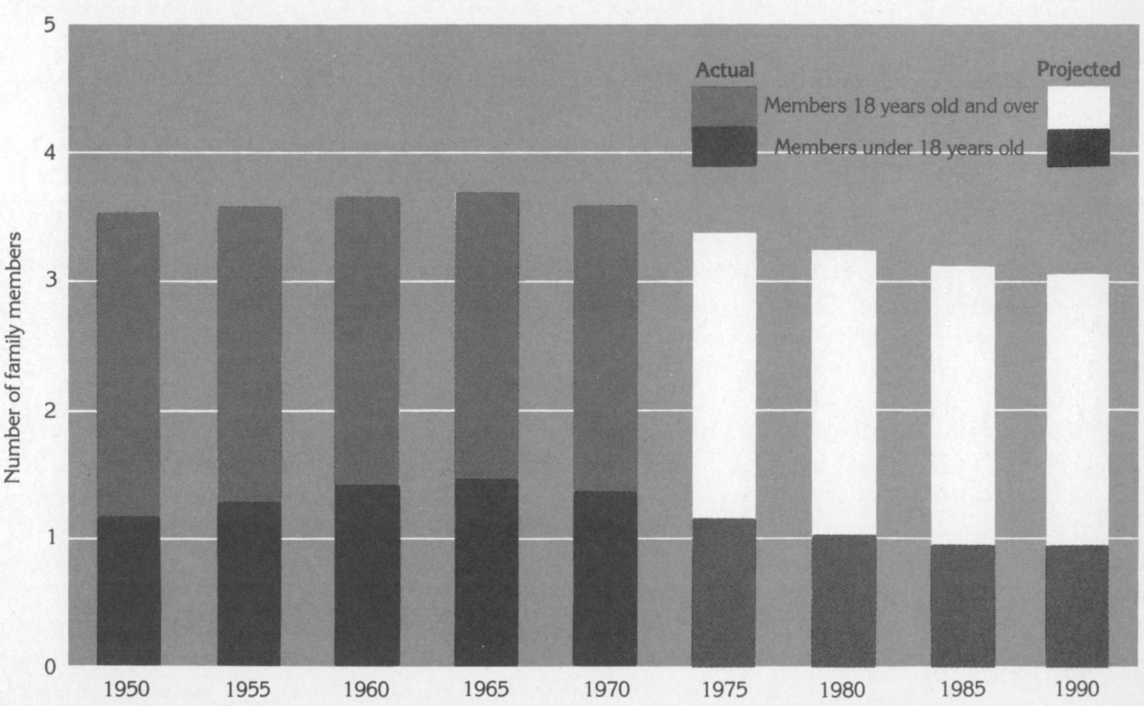

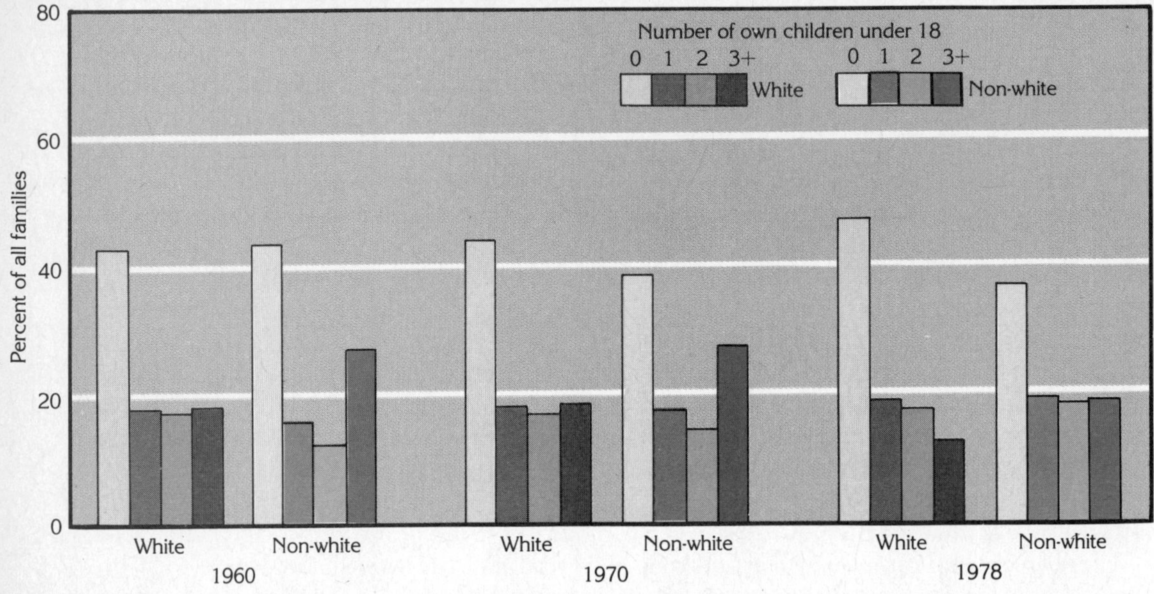

FIGURE 12.4 Families, by Number of Own Children Under 18 Years Old and Race: 1960, 1970, and 1978.

Source: *Social Indicators 111.* Washington, D.C.: U.S. Department of Commerce, December, 1970.

Note the increase in white families with no children and the corresponding slight decline in black families with no children. There is also a decline in the number of white families with three or more children, while the figure for black families is only slightly less after a slight increase in 1970.

A more comprehensive perspective of family life is presented in the pattern of divorces. We have previously seen the numerical increase in the American divorce rate in Figure 12.2. Some additional features—and interesting parallels—are seen in Figure 12.5.

The trend seen in Figure 12.5 represents a 250 percent increase in divorces and annulments. As a consequence of this, there has been an increase in the number of children whose living arrangements changed drastically. For example, Figure 12.6 illustrates the rise in the number of children who are living with their mothers only. There has been a decided increase in the number of families with mothers as the only parent for both blacks and whites, which supports the conclusion that governmental support seems likely, given the need for these women to support their families.

Finally, although a changing picture emerges from these data—marital instability, single-parent families—three out of four individuals state that they are satisfied with their family life. Recent surveys show that as little as three percent of the respondents were dissatisfied with family life. Figure 12.7 illustrates the results of these surveys.

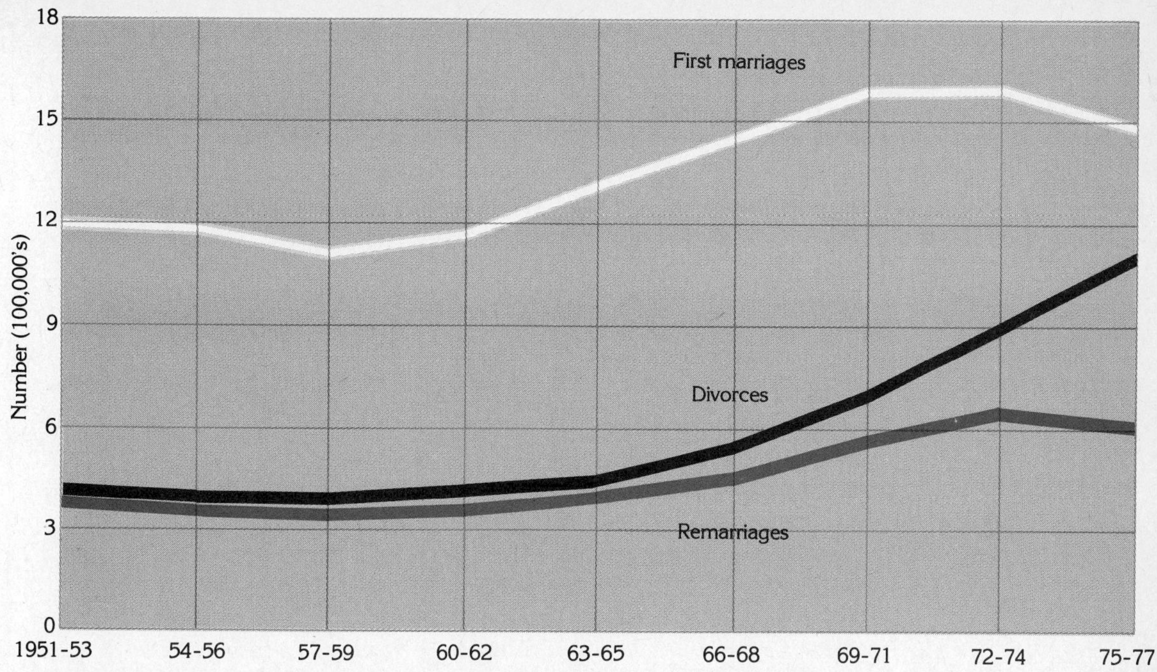

FIGURE 12.5 First Marriages, Divorces, and Remarriages of Women: 1950—1977.
Source: *Social Indicators 111.* Washington, D.C.: U.S. Department of Commerce, December 1980.

An analysis of the results showed the following pattern.

1. There were no significant sex differences in the numbers expressing considerable satisfaction with family life.
2. Individuals who had graduated from high school expressed greater satisfaction with family life than did either the less or more educated groups.
3. There were no significant differences among age groups in satisfaction with family life.

A similar pattern appears in Figure 12.8 when the respondents were asked an even more personal question: How would you evaluate your own marital happiness? Again note the small percentage who reported that they were "not too happy."

The following characteristics were noteworthy.

1. There was an apparent sex difference; women are slightly less likely than men to rate their marriages as "very happy."
2. Individuals with less than four years of high school were less likely than the more educated groups to rate their marriages as "very happy."
3. No age differences were found among the groups.

Thus the statement that the problem with marriage is individuals and not the state of marriage seems to be reinforced by these figures.

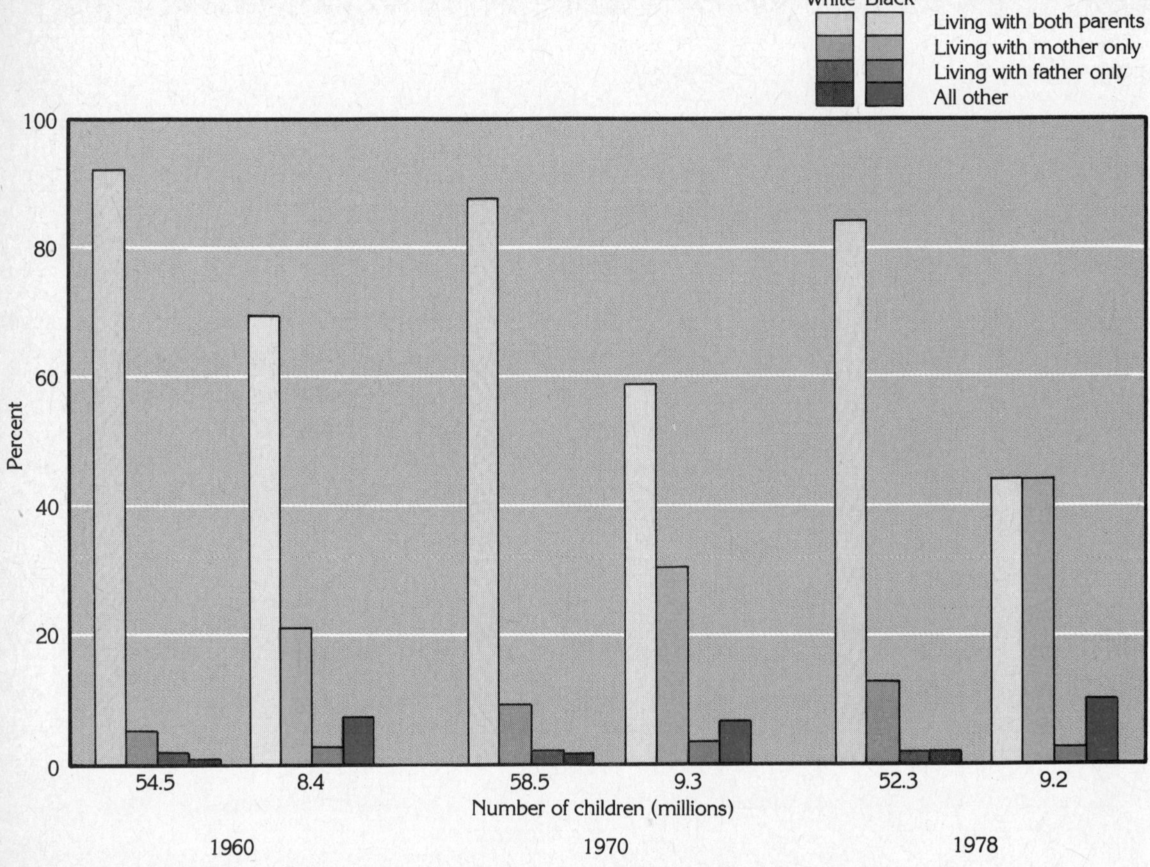

FIGURE 12.6 Children Under 18 Years Old in Families, by Presence of Parents and Race of Children: 1960, 1970, and 1978.

Source: *Social Indicators 111.* Washington, D.C.: U.S. Department of Commerce, 1980.

Interpretation of the Data

Conclusions about marriage, family, and child development demand data. The facts and figures present definite patterns that cannot be ignored. For example, consider the implications of the following facts.

Fact 1. The divorce rate continues to rise, and as it does, the number of involved children also increases. What is not apparent from the sterility of the charts and figures is the impact of divorce on youngsters. Can anyone predict a child's reaction to the tension that must have existed between the mother and father, the trauma of the actual divorce proceedings, and the personal, academic, and peer problems caused by relocation?

Fact 2. A logical consequence of an increasing divorce rate is a corresponding increase in the number of families headed by a single parent. Again, the consequences for a child's development are unclear. Will the tension and instability witnessed in the parent's marriage have some later impact on the child's marriage?

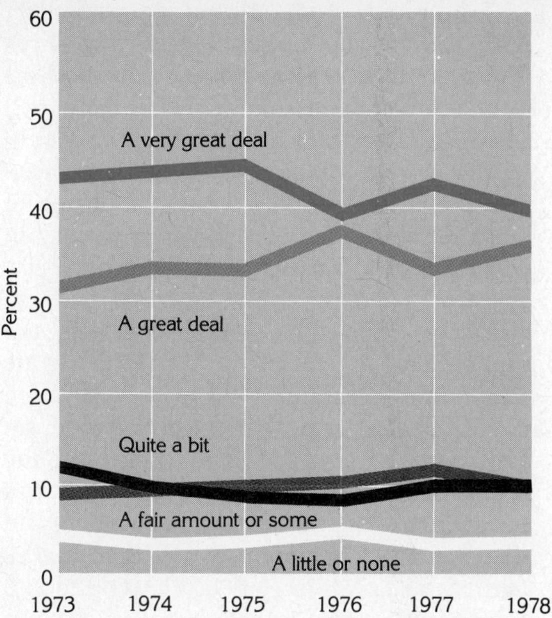

FIGURE 12.7. Satisfaction with Family Life: 1973–1978.

Source: *Social Indicators 111.* Washington, D.C.: U.S. Department of Commerce, December, 1980.

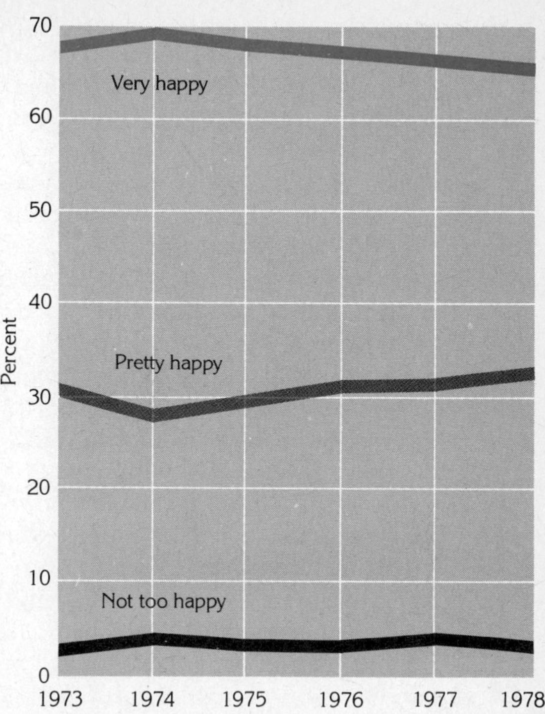

FIGURE 12.8. Marital happiness: 1973–1978.

Source: *Social Indicators 111.* Washington, D.C.: U.S. Department of Commerce, December, 1980.

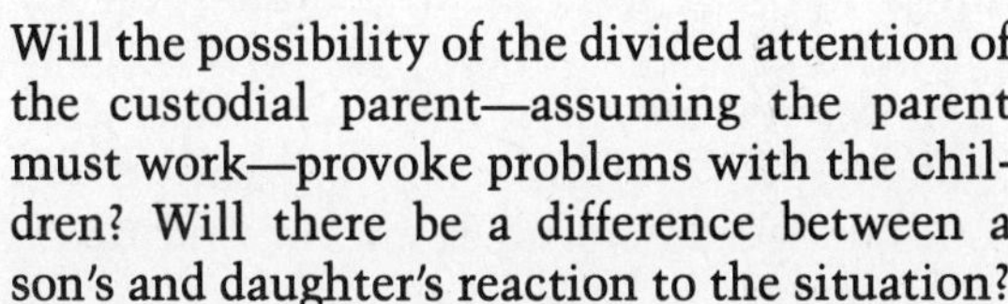
Will the possibility of the divided attention of the custodial parent—assuming the parent must work—provoke problems with the children? Will there be a difference between a son's and daughter's reaction to the situation?

Fact 3. Families have fewer and fewer under-eighteen-year-olds among their members. The inescapable conclusion is that we are becoming an older population. A shift in governmental support programs, changes in the work force, and a shrinking educational base all seem to be natural consequences. What the impact of an older population will be on the overall economy has not yet been fully assessed. For example, the number of Social Security recipients will obviously increase, while the working members needed to supply that financial base will just as obviously decrease.

Fact 4. The remarriage rate following divorce is beginning to decrease. When this fact is linked to the number of children born to divorced couples, what seems to emerge from the combination of facts is that a relatively constant number of single-parent families will become an important aspect of American society. As mentioned previously, these familial patterns seem strongly to suggest some type of governmental intervention.

Fact 5. People are basically satisfied with family life. But what is hidden in these surveys is the kind of family life that satisfies them. As we shall see in the next section, we can identify many forms of family life, including cohabitation, that are far removed from the nuclear family concept. People may be indicating their satisfaction with these different forms of family structure.

Thus, while the data may appear startlingly clear, the implications must be characterized as murky. Westoff (1978), attempting to analyze similar statistical data, argues that we can draw one "fairly certain" conclusion: the present low level of population increase will undoubtedly continue. Even the baby boom following World War II was misinterpreted. The popular view that "everyone married early and had many children" was a misinterpretation. What happened was a movement away from both single status and childless or one-child families. There was a noticeable increase in the number of women having two children, *but the number of families having three or more children played a smaller role in the boom.* The social forces that caused the change in attitude toward marriage and limited child-bearing remain unclear. This kind of change is disturbing demographers because it could reappear at any time (even though it seems unlikely now) and upset projections.

A powerful social force working to maintain the present low child-bearing level is the changed attitude toward children. Many people now see children as a heavy, perhaps unmanageable, drain on financial resources. Westoff (1978, p. 53) states:

> The economic transformation of society has been accompanied by a decline in traditional and religious authority, the diffusion of an ethos of rationality and individualism, the universal education of both sexes, the increasing equality of women, the increasing survival of children, and the emergence of a consumer-oriented culture that is increasingly aimed at maximizing personal gratification. When these changes are combined with the development and diffusion of sophisticated birth control technology, it is hardly surprising that the institution of marriage and family show signs of change.

Westoff believes that these changes, particularly those that relate to the changing status of women, have yet to run their course. Thus every indication is that the birth rate will remain low. Westoff also notes that the declining rate of remarriages following divorce signals a change, possibly a greater degree of cohabitation among all ages. In a society in which men and women have the same incomes, where as many women as men are lawyers, engineers, physicians, and executives, the implications for marriage and fertility are clear. As Westoff states (1978, p. 55) the decline of child-bearing is both a cause and a consequence of the changes in marriage and the family. Having fewer or no children facilitates the economic advancement of women and their equality with men, which then makes marriage and children less attractive and less an automatic social response.

If the birth rate remains below the replacement level, it is interesting to speculate how industrial governments will react. Inducements to bear children must surpass the advantages that are beginning to accrue to the childless: money, status, independence. The initial signs of governmental discomfort are appearing and one can only speculate on any future course of action. We can safely conclude that what we have now is what we will continue to have for the immediate future.

DISCUSSION QUESTIONS

1. Aside from the many factual presentations and analysis of the divorce figures that were presented, to what do you attribute this sharp increase? What are some of the intangibles that have produced this phenomenon?
2. Can you reconcile the divorce figures with the figures on the popular literature on parenting? Does this seem to be a contradiction? Explain your answer.
3. If the growing concern with the breakdown in the family reflects a true societal concern—and it seems to be so—how do you explain the relatively constant, even slightly increasing, number of American families as seen in Figure 12.2? Is there a contradiction, either true or apparent?
4. What specific societal implications do you see in the shrinking number of American families with members under eighteen years? In your answer, indicate the various societal segments that you think will be affected.
5. Numerous conjectures are made concerning the growing number of children living with either their mother or father. What difficulties do you envision, if any, for those children? Be specific. Also indicate any positive aspects of such families.
6. Do you agree with one of Westoff's explanations for the present, and possibly future, low birth rate—that children have become an economic drain. Can you suggest reasons why he may be correct? If you disagree, explain your position.

FORMS OF FAMILY LIFE

One fact emerges with striking clarity from the population projections of marriage and family: modern industrial societies are accepting—if not encouraging—multiple forms of family life. As Westoff comments (1978), the status of women undoubtedly will affect the shape of family life. That is, a continued low birth rate seems probable as more women pursue careers and occupations outside the home. Many women who have not decided against childbearing will postpone that decision and may not feel compelled to have children within the traditional family concept.

Sussman (1976), analyzing various forms of family life, offers some timely warnings about interpreting statistical data. While we can identify family forms that range from the traditional nuclear family to communes, Sussman believes that the data are not completely accurate; they merely represent careful estimates. Also, there is a lack of comparable historical data; that is, we know little about the viability of some of these family forms. What causes problems in interpreting and projecting from the data is the shift in values both in the family and society. For example, the following seem to be producing changing family styles (Sussman, 1976).

1. The acceptance of divorce is increasing. Today there is little social stigma attached to divorce. The individuals involved may be frustrated, angry, bitter, or depressed, but these are

personal feelings. Over thirty states now have some form of no-fault divorce laws which eliminate adversarial processes and which reflect society's position that no guilt should be attached to divorce.

2. As sexuality has become an "open" topic, individuals' sex lives have assumed an importance rivaling their commitment to family.

3. The notion of shared responsibilities in marriage, which is a growing phenomenon (whether contractual or not), will inevitably change family styles and traditional sex roles. For example, males will fulfill greater family responsibilities as females compete in the marketplace.

4. Self-fulfillment has become a significant personal goal, and, consequently, the individual is now regarded as important as the family unit.

5. With emphasis on the individual has come a belief that all family members should achieve a meaningful life; concern should not be focused solely on children.

The statistical data that we have examined, the implications drawn from them, and the shift in values just mentioned have encouraged the societal acceptance of a variety of family forms. Talbot (1976) states that individuals can choose from several options to ensure that no child is left unattended by a committed, concerned, and capable parental person.

The Traditional Nuclear Family

The traditional nuclear family has a married couple living in its own home with unmarried children and with no other relatives. While

this family form represents an adaptation to the industrial society (family mobility to maintain occupational status), it has not been quite so isolated as the literature would suggest. Considerable leisure time is spent visiting relatives and there is frequent contact with kin.

Talbot (1976) comments that the father has usually been the main financial support, while the mother has borne the responsibility of child rearing. Farb (1978) believes that the traditional nuclear family subjects the married pair to considerable pressure. Since kin have little influence on this family, they offer little support, which means that the emotional ties within the family—between man and woman, and parents and children—are intense. As Farb notes, these interactions explain both the intimacy and the fragility of the nuclear family. If the marriage does not fulfill the expectations of the man and woman (love and companionship), they have little incentive to continue the relationship. Consequently, the divorce rate is high in societies where the nuclear family predominates.

Yet the nuclear family has survived. Lasch (1979a) states that the union of love and discipline in mother and father creates a unique environment in which children learn unforgettable lessons. They acquire a tendency to act in certain ways and to recreate these experiences in their later lives. If socialization makes individuals want to do what they must do, then the family is the agency to which society entrusts "this complex and delicate task."

> As the chief agency of socialization, the family reproduces cultural patterns in the individual. It not only imparts ethical norms, providing the child with his first instruction in the prevailing social rules, it profoundly shapes his character, in ways of which he is not even aware. The family instills modes of thought and action that become habitual. Because of its enormous emotional influence, it colors all of a child's subsequent experience (Lasch, 1979a, p. 3).

The Modern Nuclear Family

Talbot identifies this form of family life as married parents and up to two children. The father is the main provider and a weekend companion to the children. During the first months following birth, the mother remains at home and attends closely to the child. After this period, the parents obtain competent childcare services so that the mother can return to work. Recalling the statistics of the preceding section regarding the declining number of children, the status of women, and economic needs, this style of family life will probably be the most prevalent form of the nuclear family.

The Extended Family

The extended family refers to that family style in which members of several generations live in the same household. Farb (1978) believes that an extended family offers several advantages. In more primitive societies which lack organized governmental support, family members can turn to kin in a crisis. Health and financial burdens are spread among more members, thus often preventing the financial desolation of any one member. In those societies lacking the ability to protect the physical safety of their members, the extended family offers greater security. Farb notes that historically the extended family has been more durable than the nuclear family. Individual members may leave and return, but the basic network retains its identity.

Uzoka (1979) raises an interesting question about the distinction between the nuclear and extended family. Adherents of the extended family believe that it wraps the individual in a cloak of love and care, while imposing a system of social duties and responsibilities. It also offers both the fulfillment of material expectations and communal safeguards. After thus defining the nuclear family, Uzoka questions whether the distinctions between the two family life-styles are valid. The use of the telephone may have actually increased contacts among family members. An increasing number of older people are living with their children (for American families, the number has risen above twenty-five percent), and estimates are that of the remainder, seventy-five percent live within thirty minutes of one of their children. Consequently, Uzoka (1979) believes that the assumption of real differences between nuclear and extended families is untenable, and that Western industrialized people manifest the same degree of extended family attitudes and characteristics as nonindustrialized rural people.

With these advantages and with a seeming predisposition toward the extended family, Farb wonders why it is not the prevailing form in all societies. He speculates that those societies that can care for the poor and aged, protect their citizens, and establish a stable economy, have removed the need for an extended family. Also, effective extended families require strong managerial skills, which may not appear in each generation. Finally, as the extended family increases in size with each generation, the economic demands may become overwhelming if societal conditions reverse (inflation, recession, depression). Such reversals usually find some family members breaking away and establishing their own family units.

The Androgynous Household

Androgyny means a combination of both masculine and feminine. In the androgynous household, the man and woman have reached an agreement about duties, both within and without the house, that each will perform. For example, with many mothers working, fathers perform more of the caretaking duties of the children. Men are also assuming household and child rearing tasks unheard of a few years ago: washing dishes, cleaning house, talking to teachers.

Some couples, in an effort to avoid personal problems, sign contracts prior to marriage detailing the tasks each will perform. Talbot (1976) believes that the androgynous arrangement enables couples to care for their own children rather than entrusting them to caretakers. He believes that this form of family life could reinstitute needed strength and stability to the family if parents are sufficiently unselfish to curtail personal ambition for family responsibility.

Communal Living

Rebellion against societal standards, especially during the 1960s, produced a brief resurgence of communal living. The form of communes varies widely: members may be of the same sex or both sexes; there may be rigid rules about all (including personal) aspects of communal life, or the rules may be quite flexible; marriage practices range from no permanent partners to one to several if the members feel that collective living means sharing everything, even themselves.

Farb (1978) uses as an example of communal living the Oneida Community established in 1848 in Central New York state by fifty-eight adults and their children. They completely separated their lives from the larger society, produced their own food, made their own clothes, and devised an excellent educational system. Since they believed that romantic love caused jealousy and selfishness, they practiced group marriage: all adults were "married" to all the members of the opposite sex. The community survived for about thirty years before succumbing for a number of reasons, including the lack of succession of strong leaders, heated attacks by the national society, and the outstanding financial success of their silvermaking venture. (Oneida silverware is still popular today.)

Many of the communes that sprang up during the 1960s were modeled on the Oneida experiment, but few have survived.

A notable exception is a large Tennessee commune known as the Farm. Founded in 1970 by members of the counterculture, the Farm is self-sufficient and supports its 1,500 members from the harvest of its 7,500 acres and from other activities such as book publishing and building construction. The governing body of the Farm has dispatched members to such remote areas as Bangladesh and Haiti and to local communities such as the South Bronx.

Moved by the plight of many residents in the South Bronx, the Farm sent an ambulance unit—called Plenty—whose first step was to restore an abandoned building for their living and work space. They initially established a window-installation company to pay their expenses and last year earned $50,000. With gradual community acceptance, Plenty has also secured private and governmental trusts. Rendering an indispensible service to a region (twenty square miles, 600,000 people) where it was urgently needed, the goal of the commune's members is to move to another medically deprived area, leaving a nucleus of trained local residents to continue its work.

Talbot (1976) suggests that those communes that developed because of the mutual attraction of many people, such as the Farm, survive longer than those settlements that some have used to escape a previous marriage or some other responsibilities. It is too soon to assess the far-reaching developmental effects such environments have on children.

Single-Parent Homes

The statistical analysis of family life previously presented made abundantly clear that the number of children living with one parent is rising rapidly. Talbot (1976) believes that single parents can successfully raise children, but it is a formidable task. The physical well-being of children demands that the parent work, thus raising the issue of adequate substitute care. The emotional well-being of children demands that the single parent carefully compensate for the lack of a male-female balance within the home. Finally, single parents must fulfill their own needs—emotional, social, physical—to function satisfactorily. We can readily sense the meaning of Talbot's description of this "rugged task." Yet, more and more individuals are attempting to find happiness in this form of family life.

Since divorce produces most single-person households, the developmental consequences of the parental split deserve attention. Hetherington (1979), who has conducted several excellent studies of divorce, has analyzed divorce from the child's perspective. Noting that about fifty percent of the children born in the 1970s will spend some time (about six years) in a single-parent family, usually headed by the mother (in ninety percent of the cases), Hetherington argues that divorce is not a single experience in a child's life but a sequence of experiences. Inevitably a child's developmental status undergoes traumatic transformations during the disorganization and disequilibrium of conflict, separation, and divorce. Reorganization and changing family interactions mark the period following these events, and five or six years later most of these children face new adjustments when the single parent remarries.

Hetherington perceptively remarks that while divorce may be the best alternative to a destructive family atmosphere, most children still find parental divorce a painful process. Most children feel anger, fear, guilt, and depression immediately following divorce, feelings which usually last for about one year. It is impossible to chart accurately a child's reaction to divorce; some appear to emerge relatively unscathed, while others suffer severe developmental disruptions. Hetherington believes that each youngster's reaction stems from a unique combination of temperamental variables, previous experience, and developmental status.

Temperamentally, difficult children (such as those described by Thomas, Chess, and Birch, 1970) had the greatest difficulty coping with stress. Complicating life for these children is the tendency for the divorced parent to react more negatively toward them during tense times. Children who have had considerable stress—personal illness, school problems, peer difficulties—also seem to respond more negatively to divorce, which may represent the cumulative impact of stressful situations. Hetherington believes that the developmental status of the child strongly influences the youngster's reactions. For example, younger children with limited cognitive development are more likely to be self-blaming for the tension and loss they perceive. Adolescents, while probably more bitter and angry, can nevertheless assign responsibility and better cope with the consequences.

There are sex differences in the reaction to divorce. Hetherington (1979, p. 853) states that the impact of divorce is greater for boys than girls. The pattern for girls seems to be that they have recovered socially and emotionally within two years of the divorce, although adolescent heterosexual difficulties may appear. Boys of divorced parents show a higher incidence of behavior problems and seem to be much more aggressive in the home. Although many explanations have been proposed—lack of a male model, boys are more naturally aggressive, boys usually are more exposed to parental conflict, boys receive less support than girls—it is probably an individually distinct combination of these causes that explains the sex difference.

Many problems that the single-parent family experiences (especially the ninety percent headed by females) can be directly traced to a lowered economic status. If additional funds for family support are needed (and they usually are) mothers may need an immediate job. Not only does this necessitate substitute care for children, but in a sense, it is a type of double jeopardy, because both parents are suddenly removed. A mother, perhaps bitter, certainly tired and disillusioned, occasionally facing relocation, now must provide added emotional support for children and deal cautiously with boys who seem to be much more antagonistic than girls toward the mother.

Hetherington comments that our present concern with the female single-parent family has caused us to overlook some frequent contributions of the father to family functioning: indirect support of the mother, emotional support, financial support, role model, disciplinarian. For example, Dahl and McCubbin (1976) studied the families of American POW's of the Vietnam war. Fifty-five boys and forty-four girls from five to seventeen years of age had been without their fathers for an average of five years. These children experienced social and personal maladjustments such as withdrawal, antisocial tendencies, and general difficulties adjusting. While such studies are subject to methodological difficulties (determining, for example, whether the father's absence alone produced these results), it is clear that a father's absence can have adverse effects on a child's development.

Earls and Yogman (1979) discuss several animal studies in which the male is the primary caregiver (the stickleback, the marmoset) and conclude that considerable diversity exists between and within species. Societal changes such as we have discussed and growing evidence that the feeding experience is not as critical as once thought lead the authors to conclude that the father-infant relationship closely resembles that of mother and infant. The authors make the interesting comment that recent human studies indicate that immediate contact between the father and infant more positively influences their relationship than does the father's presence during birth. During infancy, the father's physical play with the child parallels the mother's verbal stimulation of the youngster. The authors conclude that the developing father-infant relationship, like almost all other aspects of human development, contains a "plasticity" within which satisfactory adjustments are possible.

David Lynn (1974), in a thoughtful essay on the father's role in development, states that divorce usually separates children and father, although Earls and Yogman (1979) state that in recent contested custody cases, thirty-eight percent of the fathers received custody. Children often feel rejected, angry, and torn by conflicting loyalties to each parent; they may also suffer further discomfort when either or both parents remarry. For some fathers, child support can become a burden that complicates the father-child relationship. Lynn notes that father separation means not only the loss of a father for the child but also the loss of a husband for the mother. That this rupture influences child development is nicely summarized in Lynn's statement (1974, p. 287):

> Considering all the problems the single mother faces, it is not surprising that she sometimes turns to her children to unburden her worries, or that she sometimes vacillates between babying the children one minute and treating them as small adults the next. In short, father-absent children experience not only the lack of a father but also a husbandless mother, with all the additional stress this often implies.

Lamb (1979) argues for a greater consideration of the paternal role in child rearing when he states that the presumption of maternal preeminence developed because mothers traditionally assumed primary responsibility for the child, especially during infancy. From the conclusion that mothers were *most* important, Lamb believes that theorists intuitively inferred that mothers were *exclusively* important. The attachment literature, focusing on mother-infant interactions, buttressed this conclusion.

Using his own work and other surveys of the literature (Parke, 1979), Lamb states that to the surprise of investigators, evidence indicates that fathers can be as competent and responsive as mothers, and infants will attach to *both* parents.

> Equally important, we have been so eager to identify the special or unique contributions of the father—the male adult in the family—that we have lost sight of the fact that he is, along with the mother, a major socializing agent in the child's life. He not only models and teaches sex roles, he also models and teaches other values and mores.
>
> . . . It is likely that the paternal and maternal influences supplement one another to such an extent that it is difficult to identity and quantify the father's unique influence. (Lamb, 1979, pp. 940–941)

Summarizing, then, we can say that single-parent families resulting from divorce usually introduce stress and tension into a child's life. Wallerstein and Kelly (1976), studying thirty-four preschool children, concluded that:

1. In the youngest group (two and one-half to three years), divorce caused fretfulness, cognitive bewilderment, and heightened aggression.

2. In the middle preschool group (three to four years) the youngsters become more unstable, wary, and tearful; aggression increased as their feelings of insecurity about their personal world heightened.

3. In the oldest group (five to six years), anxiety and aggression increased, but the children were able to remove themselves somewhat from any conflict. Many of the youngsters, however, even at this age, expressed sadness about the parental loss.

Love and care help youngsters to overcome these initial shocks, and as the impact of divorce and single-parenting is better understood through research, the likelihood is that youngsters will be further cushioned to absorb the first jolts of separation.

Adoption and Foster Homes

The seventh form of child care suggested by Talbot (1976) is the security provided by good substitute parents. Unfortunately, the foster home atmosphere needs careful scrutiny to avoid a hasty and ill-timed placement that fails to satisfy a child's needs and that may actually aggravate a child's inner turmoil. As society's views toward adoption and foster home placement change—there is a growing recognition that many children are simply unwanted in their natural homes and placement may be better for them—it is increasingly necessary to ensure that youngsters are placed where they are wanted and will be loved.

Keniston (1977) believes that many of our family support systems are ill-advised; he argues that, following institutional placement, foster home placement is most disruptive to a child. Keniston states that foster care costs about twice as much as care in the child's own family, while institutional care costs twice as much as foster care. Yet the federal government has consistently and lavishly funded foster care compared to day care—as much as seventy cents of the child welfare service dollar for foster care as compared to ten cents for daycare. With the gathering momentum for daycare support, the likelihood is for a decreased rate of foster home placement.

Adoption—achieving parenthood through legal and social procedures rather than through the biological process—may be by either relatives or nonrelatives. Slightly more than fifty percent of adopted children are taken by nonrelatives. These children have definite characteristics: most are illegitimate, Caucasian, and under one year of age (Mech, 1973). The goals of adoption are quite clear; adoption provides a family for children who could not otherwise have a home of their own and who will benefit from family life, and provides children to childless parents. Since adoption represents a break with the child's biological roots, most authorities agree that placement should be as early as possible and the children should be told as early as possible that they are adopted; if possible by two or three years, certainly, no later than four years. Mech (1973, p. 476) offers the following guidelines for informing adopted children of their status:

1. A single discussion is insufficient; the adoptive parents should discuss the status frequently, since it is a *developmental* issue and children will interpret it differently at different ages.

2. Adopted children do not fully comprehend their status until adolescence.

3. The adoptive parents should not perceive as threatening any questions about the natural parents.

4. Adopted children view their adoptive parents as "real," particularly if a good parent-child relationship has evolved.

5. Adopted children usually want factual information about their natural parents.

6. Most adopted children, although curious about their natural parents, are reluctant to ask questions about them.

There is a growing interest in placing children with special needs, given the need of the children and the desire of the prospective parents (black market babies are still available). Speaking of these children, Gallagher (1975, p. 11) states:

> The estimated number of children in need of adoption—whether legally free or not—is approximately 100,000. Some of these children remain indefinitely in one foster home; others move from one foster family to another, with each move increasing the likelihood that more changes in placement will be made since the child usually becomes increasingly disturbed and difficult to reach. Further efforts are needed to reduce the number of children who are on such a treadmill of temporary placement or who remain inadvisably in a foster family home or institution.

Institutional Placement

There is general agreement that institutional placement is the most disruptive form of care for children. The older institutional studies such as those by Skeels, Spitz, and Dennis (previously discussed in Chapter Five) testified to the bleakness and desolation of those grim settings. Have conditions changed sufficiently so that we may be more optimistic about the future of children who are placed there?

Talbot (1976) argues that institutional placement remains the choice of last resort and should occur only when the burden of caring for a child could conceivably destroy the family. Then—and only then—should institutional care occur, with the assurance that there is guaranteed personal attention for the youngster by trained personnel at the routine caregiving level. Talbot also pleads that lest the child disappear into limbo for life, there should be constant evaluation of progress in the hope that someday the child will become at least partially self-sufficient.

In one of the most encouraging recent investigations, Tizard and Rees (1975) state that modern institutions bear little resemblance to their ghastly predecessors. The authors studied twenty-six four-and-a-half-year-old children who had been continuously reared in high quality institutions. They were compared with a group of London working-class children living at home. They also studied thirty-nine children either adopted or returned to their natural mothers after spending from two to four years in a residential nursery.

IN SEARCH OF ORIGINS

Adoption practices have not changed much in the last forty years: the natural mother is regarded as a troubled person who has made a critical decision and who needs the protection of permanent secrecy (Sorosky, Baran, and Pannor, 1975). The adoptive parents also require the protection of secrecy for security. Secrecy also aids adopted children in avoiding any conflict about loyalty and furthers the relationship with the adoptive parents. Thus secrecy supposedly benefits everyone. The authors believe, however, that as public disclosure becomes a way of life, an increasing number of adoptees are searching for information about their natural parents and are being thwarted by a wall of silence.

Most of the adopted children who seek their natural parents are female, and they seem to be motivated by a drive to establish generational continuity. Most natural mothers welcome the reunion, as do the fathers. It is often the adoptive parents who feel most threatened. The authors believe that their fears are unwarranted, because the adoptive parents have become the true psychological parents. Actually most adopted children feel closer to their adoptive parents after reunion with the natural parents.

Triseliotis (1973) studied two groups of adoptees, those who wished to meet their natural parents and those who desired only background information. It was during adolescence that most members of both groups began to inquire about their origins. In this and almost all other studies of adoption, a common theme appears; some crisis, such as death of an adoptive parent, serious illness, marriage, or birth of a child, seemed to provide the impetus for the search.

Triseliotis believes that there are three major tasks inherent in the adoption process:

1. The adoptive parents must fully accept their status, while simultaneously accepting the child as their own. Parents must recognize biological reality but combine it with an emotional attachment to the child.
2. The selection process itself should be as comfortable as possible. That is, the agency, although necessarily searching for homes that are warm, loving, and accepting, should also provide helpful preparation for a completely new experience for both adoptive parents and child.
3. The adoptive parents should recognize the child's vulnerability to any feelings of loss or rejection. Almost all studies report that when a sense of belongingness had developed, adoptive children were better able to accept news of their original status and to tolerate future shocks, such as the critical illness or death of one of the adoptive parents.

Finally, Triseliotis (1973, p. 166) states:

> The adoptees' quest for their origins was not a vindictive venture, but an attempt to understand themselves and their situation better. The contribution of the law and of adoption agencies toward such an objective can be of immense value to those who happen to feel in a limbo state. The self-perception of all of us is partly based on what our parents and ancestors have been, going back many generations.

The institutional children were in nurseries that contained fifteen to twenty-five children from one to seven years of age. Each group had its own suite of rooms supplied with books and toys, with both a full-time and assistant nurse. The children also made frequent excursions outside the institution (shopping trips, bus rides, visits). The staffing was good, although many different nurses handled the children. The authors report that the institutional youngsters exhibited no more behavioral problems than the children in their family control group. Bed-wetting, for example, was no greater among the institutional children. Thus the antisocial behavior often linked to these children was probably not due to institutional placement per se, but to poor institutional care or the child's early family experiences.

The authors note one interesting finding: there were *different kinds* of behavioral problems in the institutional group and the family group. The mothers of the family children reported more disciplinary problems, such as difficulty when going to bed, trouble at mealtimes. The institutional staff, however, reported poor peer relations, clinging, and poor concentration as problems.

The nurses stated that they discouraged deep personal attachments with the children, since they felt it was unfair to both nurses and children. Perhaps this explains the different affectionate attachments of the children. While they developed normal bonds with their adoptive parents, they were significantly more friendly and affectionate with strangers than family-reared children.

The concern and care about institutional placement plus relatively encouraging studies such as this offer cautious hope for more positive outcomes for those children receiving this form of care.

Daycare

Daycare is a family and societal issue that demands both theoretical speculation and practical concern. Economic necessity and an era of self-awareness and self-fulfillment have caused many women to be away from the home for lengthy times. This growing phenomenon requires that daycare centers be qualified, responsible settings, and that parental ties be carefully nurtured to avoid any future negative consequences.

Zigler and Heller (1979) state that federal standards are urgently needed to protect children and the national financial investment. The history of such efforts is discouraging; good intentions have foundered on indifference and neglect. Basic requirements of such legislation should specify the minimum training for all personnel, as well as the maximum number of children in a group and the maximum number per caregiver. Such criteria could possibly eliminate some of the conditions uncovered in recent investigations: children tied to chairs, fire hazards, television as *the* caregiver. Interestingly, Zigler and Heller believe that the present kinds of daycare services—babysitting cooperatives, family day care, centers operated by large corporations for their employees, and centers privately operated for profit—are a potential strength, as long as minimum standards are met.

We shall return to society's role in the next chapter, but our concern here is with daycare's effect on children's development. Perhaps the safest conclusion is that it is simply too soon to tell. For example, in a carefully controlled study of Chinese and Caucasian families in the Boston area, Kagan (1978b) established an experimental daycare group, a home control group, and a third group receiving other forms of group care. The children ranged in age from three and one-half to five and one-half months, and remained in the experiment until thirty months. Cognitively, socially, and behaviorally there was little, if any, difference between the family-reared and daycare children.

Belsky and Steinberg (1978, p. 29) state that we know "shockingly little about the impact of day care on children, on their parents, and on the society in which these children and parents live." A partial cause of our ignorance is the limited nature of the present daycare research. The following are the major difficulties:

1. Most research is limited to high quality, usually university sponsored centers. Kagan's study, for example, was in a superb setting, with well-trained personnel, and with an extremely low child to adult ratio. These conditions are simply beyond the reach of a typical center.

2. The studies have been confined to immediate effects; that is, youngsters are tested after several months in a daycare center. It is impossible to state that there are no long-range effects.

3. Samples are not comparable. Youngsters reared at home and those placed in daycare may be quite different. That is, family attitudes and values may have already left their mark.

4. The studies lack ecological validity; that is, they represent what Bronfenbrenner (1979) calls "the science of the strange behavior of children in strange situations with strange adults for the briefest possible period of time." That is, tests under laboratory conditions still tell us little about possible outcomes under different, more natural, conditions.

Finally, if the attachment literature is correct and bonding occurs during the first six months, what are eventual effects when youngsters are placed in daycare centers at three months? For thoughtful, concerned parents who maintain close contact with their youngster in the home, little difficulty is expected. But since it is not an issue to leave to chance, we shall return to this topic in our analysis of society's influence on development.

PARENTS, CHILDREN, AND DEVELOPMENTAL OUTCOMES

The family data suggest an inevitable conclusion: family styles are changing and, as they do, children are exposed to a variety of unique influences. Some live in mother-only households, but a growing number of youngsters find themselves with just the father; some reside in more traditional settings with both mother and father exercising authority, while others live with several adults and multiple lines of authority. *Whatever the circumstances, definite patterns of child rearing behavior emerge.*

Mussen and Eisenberg-Berg (1977, p. 75) testify to the importance of attempting to understand these behaviors when they state:

> Every child-rearing practice and technique of discipline may potentially affect children's behavior: demonstration or modeling (performing behaviors that may be emulated); nurturance (caring for the child with warmth, support, and affection); praise and approval; giving or withholding love or material rewards; explanation and example of rules; lecturing, and giving "lessons," corporal and psychological punishment. All of these, and many others, are used by parents in the process of socialization.

Our concern here is to specify what and how parental behavior shapes development.

Recent Findings

In a careful series of studies, Baumrind (1971, 1973), believing that it is possible to identify clusters of children's behavior, attempted to link child rearing practices to these clusters.

Characterizing the youngsters as competent, withdrawn, or immature, Baumrind and her colleagues then employed four categories of parental behavior as significant: *control* (these parents were willing to exert their influence); *maturity demands* (these parents expected their children to be independent and to perform to high standards); *parent-child communication* (parental behavior in this category ranged from reasoning to subtle manipulation); and *nurturance* (these parents overtly expressed love and sympathy toward their children).

The investigators, after making two home visits, found that competent, happy children had parents who demonstrated considerable control over their children, but who also reasoned with them, while simultaneously offering them warm support. The parents of withdrawn youngsters were demanding and manifested less warmth toward their children than the parents of competent, happy children. Immature children had nurturant parents who exercised little control. (Note that no parent or child exhibits total behavioral consistency, but behavior of a given type occurs with sufficient frequency to permit classification.)

Continuing her work with different parents and children, Baumrind and her colleagues reversed their original procedure: they identified clusters of parental behaviors, which they then linked to children's characteristics. The clusters of parental behavioral behaviors were: *authoritarian* (demanding, controlling); *authoritative* (rational, firm when necessary); *permissive* (few demands, little control).

They found that authoritarian parents had children with little independence and average social responsibility. Authoritative parents had independent, socially responsible youngsters, while the children of permissive parents showed little independence and less social responsibility. Sex difference also appeared: authoritarian parents had angrier and more defiant sons, as did permissive parents. Authoritative parents had more self-reliant daughters, and friendly, cooperative sons.

Consequently, authoritative parental behavior (as defined) seems most effective in producing such child behavior as independence, social responsibility, and maturity.

Emergent Family Styles and Developmental Outcomes. In a major longitudinal study, Eiduson (1978) analyzed fifty single-mother households, fifty social contract couples, fifty living groups (communities), and fifty traditional, nuclear two-parent families. Four years after the study began, all two hundred families remained with the project. The children ranged in age from two and one-half to four years. The parents had essentially middle-class origins, which influenced their child rearing behaviors. For example, although many were products of the counterculture of the 1960s, they reduced drug usage and abandoned food fads with impending parenthood.

The family styles were notably diverse, but mothers were present and intimately involved in child care in almost all of the families. (Single mothers were the most upwardly mobile and closest to the values of the traditional nuclear family.) Given these parental backgrounds, socialization practices among all four family categories was quite similar. Is it possible to link developmental outcomes to these varied family styles? Eiduson (1978) cautiously reaches these conclusions:

1. Physically, the children are similar to others of their age; they are not a particularly sickly group and any problems seem to cross family styles (the only exceptions were the minority who persisted in exotic diets and who were subject to nutritional deficits).

2. Mentally, the children (who were studied on the Bayley Scale of Infant Development at eight months and one year) were similar at

eight months, with those in the traditional and social contract groups scoring slightly higher; these differences disappeared at one year.

3. Emotionally, the youngsters (who were studied on the Strange Situation Test devised by Nancy Ainsworth) showed similar and strong attachments to the mothers.

Eiduson (1978) summarizes the data by noting that few differences appear among the children in the first year, and there are few significant changes in the parental/child unit. As the study continues, it will be interesting to determine if these differing family styles alter children's behavior.

Parental Control. Eleanor Maccoby (1980), in a comprehensive review of parental control literature, has designated several categories of parental behavior.

1. *Consistent enforcement of demands and rules,* which relates to such child behavior as control of aggressive tendencies, less hostility toward parents, high self-esteem, and competence.

2. *High expectations and training to meet them,* which relates to low aggression in boys and girls (low demands seem to produce high aggression, lack of control, and immaturity).

3. *Restrictive parenting* (preventing children from doing what they want), which relates to timidity and lack of persistence in pursuing goals.

4. *Arbitrary power assertion* (authoritarian parenting), which relates to low self-esteem, obedience and lack of independence, poor peer relations (occasionally may relate to hostile, delinquent youngsters if the parents' use of power is accompanied by violence).

5. *Open communication patterns,* which relates to competence, independence, happiness, high self-esteem, and goal orientation.

Maccoby concludes her analysis by mentioning several parental and child characteristics that emphasize our concern with *interaction.* She states that children must exercise some control over their lives, and a responsive parent (one who responds to a child's cues) encourages the appearance of responsible self-control. For example, parents who suggest, rather than just dictate, had more self-directed, independent children with an inner locus of control.

But parental behavior is also influenced by the characteristics of the children. For example, age is (or should be) a potent shaper of parental behavior; a twelve-year-old is not a two-year-old and should be treated accordingly. Birth order seems to affect parental behavior; first borns are the object of unrivaled parental attention and affection, which may be a mixed blessing. Although the sole recipient of parental behavior, they are also expected to achieve well, mature quickly, and behave perfectly—demanding expectations. A potential cause of difficulty is the rapid loss of parental attention when other children appear. Here, using Maccoby's analysis, we see an enriched and insightful interpretation of interaction.

Prosocial Behavior. Mussen and Eisenberg-Berg (1977), concerned about the development of prosocial behavior in children, believe that it is closely correlated with patterns of child rearing behavior. They define prosocial behavior as follows (p. 3):

> Prosocial behavior refers to actions that are intended to aid or benefit another person or group of people without the actor's anticipation of external rewards. Such actions often entail some cost, self-sacrifice, or risk on the part of the actor. A wide variety of behaviors is encompassed by this rubric, including generosity, altruism, sympathy, helping people in distress by giving material or

> psychological assistance, sharing possessions, donating to charity, and participating in activities designed to improve the general welfare by reducing social injustice, inequalities and brutality.

Mussen and Eisenberg-Berg state that:

1. Modeling and identification are the most powerful antecedents of prosocial behavior; thus parents, as both powerful and nurturant models, exercise enormous influence on the appearance of prosocial behavior in their children.

2. Nurturance is an important antecedent, provided it is included within parent-child interactions that include modeling.

3. Reasoning facilitates prosocial behavior, while parents' assertive power retards its appearance.

4. Responsibility and maturity demands also stimulate the acquisition of prosocial tendencies.

The authors conclude (1977, p. 159) that children who will most likely exhibit prosocial behavior are those who are relatively self-confident and active children, advanced in moral reasoning, responsibility, and empathy.

DISCUSSION QUESTIONS

1. Be sure that you can distinguish among the various forms of family life. Define each and indicate its outstanding characteristics.
2. Can the nuclear family survive in a modern, industrialized society? Why? Does your reasoning also apply to the extended family?
3. What is your reaction to the androgynous household? Do you think it will grow in popularity? Why? What is your reaction to couples signing a contract specifying duties and responsibilities?
4. Will there always be some form of communal life? Why? Can you reconcile communal living with the opinion that some form of nuclear family is the basis of society? What causes the disintegration of many communes?
5. What do you think are some of the social consequences of single parent families? Do you see developmental difficulties for boys and girls? Be specific in your answer and attempt to indicate the causes of the problems you suggest.
6. Do you agree with the conclusions about the day care literature? Why? What do you think are the advantages and disadvantages of day care for children? Be specific. Do the same for parents.

A RATIONALE FOR THE FUTURE

Raising children is a sensitive emotional issue, one that most parents view as reflecting their deepest beliefs. They thus opt for a family style most compatible with those beliefs. Featherstone (1979) remarks that familism and child rearing are similar to religious values for many Americans, especially for those who have watched other idols crumble. But what many perceive as family deterioration may well be a constant theme in American life. There has always been a pluralistic quality in American families. We have seen a similar misrepresentation graphically illustrated by an analysis of the "baby boom" following World War II. There have always been working mothers, families headed by women, and sharing of household duties—though not as many nor as widely publicized as today.

But, as Featherstone notes, the family has been, is, and will continue to be the permanent institution for child rearing. Recall the statistic which began the chapter: ninety-eight percent of American children are raised in families.

The changes that we have documented throughout the chapter reflect changes that have occurred in society, and families have always adapted to societal change.

Aside from the developmental consequences of different life styles, if any, there are different currents flowing whose impact is presently difficult to determine. For example, with decreasing family size, the difference between those who raise children and those who do not may assume political significance (Featherstone, 1979). A second fact whose influence is unknown is that today's children are frequently seen as a financial drain rather than an economic resource.

Keniston (1977, p. 3) attempting to separate myth from reality, states:

> American parents today are worried and uncertain about how to bring up their children. They feel unclear about the proper balance between permissiveness and firmness. They fear they are neglecting their children, yet sometimes resent the demands their children make. Americans wonder whether they are doing a good job as parents, yet are unable to define just what a good job is. In droves, they seek expert advice. And many prospective parents wonder whether they ought to have children or not.

Keniston then states that these feelings are neither new nor uniquely American. The intensity with which they are experienced, however, is new and uniquely American.

Two assumptions which Keniston believes shape much of the thinking about the family are that (1) parents alone are responsible for what becomes of their children, and (2) families are autonomous units, relatively free from social pressure. Both of these assumptions have combined to form the myth of family self-sufficiency, which Keniston thinks blinds us to other forces influencing family life. He states that families are not now, nor were they ever, self-sufficient blocks in society. They have always been influenced by powerful social and economic forces over which they have little control.

Today's social forces may ultimately provide the stability that will promote greater cohesiveness in altered life styles. Mothers and fathers, reacting to mobility, impersonal governmental interventions, and the perceived threats of rootlessness, may turn more to each other and their children. As Keniston notes (1977, p. 17) expectations of sharing, sexual compatibility, and temperamental harmony may increase and meld the family closer. These expectations may not assume traditional forms, but one fact should guide our speculations about the family's future: the nature of family life will change as it adapts to shifting social forces.

Any analysis of family life contains two major themes. First is the nature of the family itself, and in the 1980s, the identification of various forms of family living has sharply altered our view of the traditional family. Yet as we have seen throughout our discussion, different family styles have always existed. Population projections and estimates of stability of emerging family styles present a fairly consistent pattern: change will continue, but it will represent a modification of current styles. For example, the number of single mothers will increase, but as governmental support also increases, there will undoubtedly be more and better daycare services, increased after-school programs for the older children, and perhaps greater flexibility in the work schedules of working parents.

The second major theme is the developmental consequences of these changes. Here we find much less certainty, since, as was repeatedly stated, it is simply too soon to make definite statements. While it is relatively easy to state that there should be no attachment difficulties for youngsters who are placed in daycare centers as early as three months of age, this assumption is based on the quality of the original, and continuing, interaction between the mother and child. As we noted, however, the nature of that interaction may be quite different for family reared and daycare children. What will be the lasting effects of a lack of a male model in families headed by women? There may be little, if any, but again, it is too soon to tell.

Society changes, families adapt—perhaps more rapidly than before—and our clear task is to monitor the developmental consequences of these changes.

SUMMARY

The Rios family is an excellent example of a family's adaptation to society.

A family's adaptation to society entails a series of ecological transitions that reflect structure, development, and adjustment.

On examining such statistics as the divorce figures, it is tempting to speculate that family life is deteriorating, but change has always marked family adaptation.

Single-mother families are increasing steadily and must be considered a constant in planning family support programs.

There may be significant political consequences in the declining size of American families; there is no overlooking the economic struggle that may arise between those with and without children.

There is every indication that current low birth rates will continue, thus suggesting that we shall see a continuing modification of existing forms of family life.

There are several identifiable family styles, ranging from the traditional nuclear family to communes, from foster homes to daycare centers.

Families have always reacted to societal change and pressure and will continue to do so, since they cannot exist as independent units.

SUGGESTED READINGS

American Psychologist. Vol. 34, October, 1979. The entire issue is devoted to child development, and is an excellent summary of current theory, practice, and public policy.

KENISTON, KENNETH. *All Our Children.* New York: Harcourt, Brace, Jovanovich, 1977. Summarizing the Carnegie Council Report, Keniston presents a unique analysis of American family life and argues forcefully for greater economic support systems.

LEWIS, OSCAR. *La Vida.* New York: Random House, 1965. A classic description of a deprived family's fight for survival and the styles that the family adopts.

MINUCHIN, SALVADOR. *Families and Family Therapy.* Cambridge, Massachusetts: Harvard University Press, 1974. An excellent presentation of a model to employ in family analysis and suggested techniques for family therapy.

TALBOT, NATHAN. *Raising Children in Modern America.* Boston: Little, Brown, 1976. A wide-ranging report of the Harvard Interfamily Conference on American family life that offers practical suggestions for necessary adaptation.

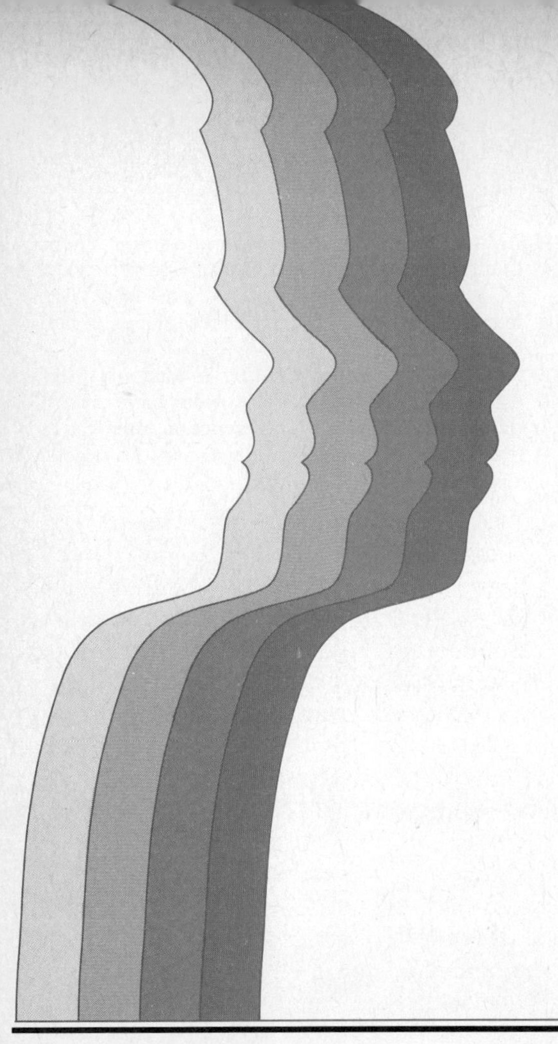

CHAPTER 13
THE SCHOOL'S INFLUENCE

CHAPTER HIGHLIGHTS

Topics

The School's Changing Role
a. Education and American Culture
b. Mainstreaming

School and Society
a. Peer Influence on Development
b. The Influence of the Teacher

Learning and Development
a. Same Clouded Issues
b. The Characteristics of Learning
c. Explanations of Learning: The Theorists

Children and Learning: Theory into Practice
a. Introduction—The Conditioning Studies
b. The Role of Television
c. Readiness

The Montessori Method
a. Thoughts on Development

People

Gordon Bower
Jerome Bruner
R. F. Butts
George Comstock
Lawrence Cremin
Willard Hartup
Ernest Hilgard
Maria Montessori

Special Topics

Peer Relations and Social Deprivation
Reversing Outcomes of Teacher Expectations
Children's Characteristics

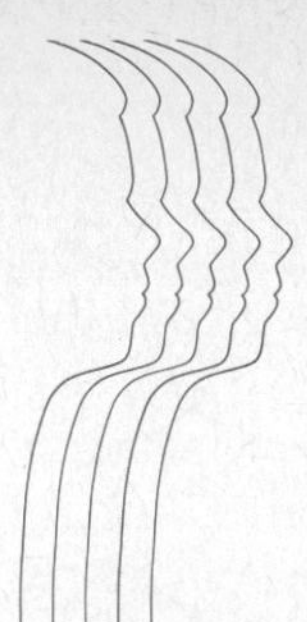

At an early age, youngsters frequently leave the warmth and security of their home and attend some kind of institution for a few hours a day. Here, depending on the prevailing philosophy of the community, they either commence serious, directed study or experience some type of guided play. During the first grade, they begin the serious business of schooling, which will continue until they are at least sixteen and possibly until they are in their thirties. They will acquire the basic language and mathematical skills necessary for independent living in a modern society or they will be doomed to lives of dependence on others or the state. If their academic success is limited, their achievements in life usually will also be limited. Their ability to adjust to others becomes obvious during the school years and usually suggests a permanent behavioral pattern. Their capacity for accepting authority without being either coerced or defiant is also manifested. School begins to exert its influence at a remarkably early age—three, four, five, or six—and seems to exercise a dual function: to strengthen many of the behaviors that children bring to school and also to increase children's ability to respond to rapidly multiplying environmental stimuli.

The school stamps its imprint on the educational product in an unmistakable fashion. But the manner of its stamping is changing radically. As we have seen, daycare centers are expected to increase, which will bring children from their homes perhaps as early as three or four months. The nature of the curriculum is changing as educators respond to challenges to make schooling "relevant." The length of schooling itself continues to increase as academic subjects require more time to encompass added knowledge and as preparation for the professions lengthens because of specialization. Yet the school has historically attempted to achieve certain objectives that have remained remarkably consistent through the years. The school has always concerned itself with the intellectual, social, emotional, physical, moral, and vocational aspects of development. What is seen as desirable social development, for example, may change, but the overall concern for social development itself remains. But the moment we introduce the notion of "desirable" into any discussion of the school's objectives, heated controversy arises. What is desirable? Who is to determine the desirable? We answer these questions according to a personal philosophy and individual beliefs about the nature of the child.

Jacques Barzun's famous statement that education is the dullest of subjects may be unerringly accurate, but education is also the most important of subjects. What other institution assumes the responsibility of teaching academic skills, thinking about a child's emotional adjustment, caring about social responsibilities, recognizing the need for moral standards in human relations, attempting to ensure good health and, finally, looking to the future and trying to help with adult occupational interests? The answer is clear: only the school.

We are a nation committed to the concept of universal education. Figure 13.1 illustrates

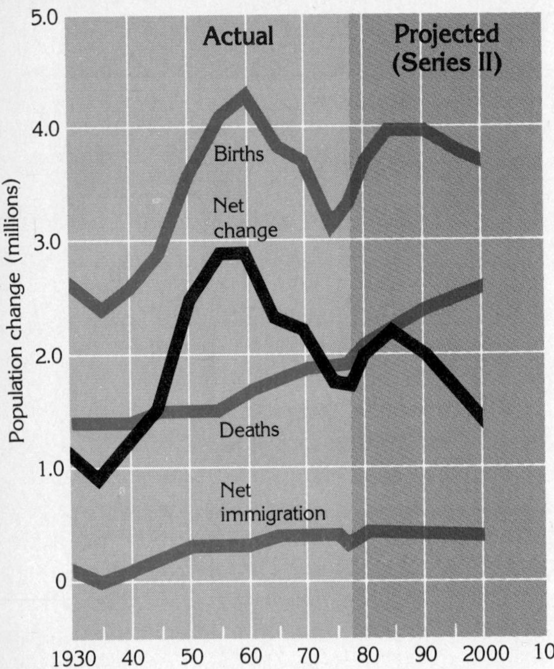

FIGURE 13.1. Components of Population Change, Selected Years: 1930–2000.

Source: *Social Indicators III.* Washington, D.C.: U.S. Department of Commerce, December, 1980.

the changing pattern of the school-age population as it reflects shifting societal conditions. Note how the projected figures predict a growing school population in the 1980s after a slump during the 1970s. This figure is an excellent example of how the forces of family, school, and society are inextricably linked and why they are such a potent influence on human development.

THE SCHOOL'S CHANGING ROLE

That the school is a strong force in development and socialization is so obvious that it needs no repeating. But the school has played several different roles throughout the history of all nations, both ancient and modern. We can return to the days of Athens, Sparta, and Rome and discern very clearly how particular schools shaped children's development in a particular way. We may, however, find it more informative to trace this phenomenon in the American experience.

Many current educational issues had their roots in the tremendous expansion of American power, influence, and economy from World War I to the present. In a nation that had traditionally restricted the role of the federal government in education, would economic conditions foreshadow a change in this policy? What would changes in the role of the family and women mean for early childhood education? Would nursery schools and daycare centers assume greater responsibilities, and if so, what would be their relationship to government, both state and federal? And controversy continues to rage about what should be taught and how it should be taught.

There are those who argue strongly that the traditional curricula of language, math, and grammar are the basics around which schooling should revolve. But they are bitterly opposed by those who argue just as forcefully that the American school has stifled the individual personalities of youngsters, that what is needed is more personal freedom and less emphasis on traditional subject matter. And, of course, there is the giant of issues: equal educational opportunities. An America that grew more socially conscious during the 1950s and 1960s also became aware of the injustice imposed on minorities. Now integrated schools are demanded and opposed, praised and damned.

These are the great unresolved problems that still face us. But we can be sure of one thing: a youngster who attends a traditional classroom will differ socially, intellectually, emotionally, and vocationally from one who attends a progressive school, or an open classroom setting. Butts and Cremin (1953), in their great treatise on American education, summarize the nature of educational controversy by stating that it arises from differences in values and interest. For example, there are several categories that are guaranteed to spark conflict.

1. *Religion.* What should be the role of religion in relation to a public school? The controversy over school prayer today remains as explosive as ever.

2. *Discipline.* Should we stress the "Three Rs," practical subjects, or personal development? What should be the nature of student behavior? To what extent should the state intervene?

3. *Scholarship.* Do we stress the acquisition of knowledge, or do we concern ourselves with the adjustment of children and vocational proficiency?

4. *Vocation.* Should schooling be directed toward occupational preparation so that students can earn a living and be useful to themselves, family, and society?

5. *Individual needs.* How far do we move from emphasis on the group to consideration of the individual? What does this imply for the educational system as it exists today? What does federal legislation concerning handicapped students imply?

6. *Society.* What is the role of society in today's school? Should the school attempt to produce students who will perpetuate society as we know it, or those who will attempt to change it? Do we continue the schools as they are, or do we provide alternate forms of education to effect change and simultaneously encourage changing life-styles? What should be the school's limits regarding noneducational objectives?

These are the questions and issues that face the American school today. There are no firm answers, but there have been unique ways of dealing with past and present problems.

Education and American Culture

In education, as in all matters of public policy, the survival of the democratic way of life depends on reasoned intelligence, a belief in the ultimate value of truth, and a free and open discussion of opposing viewpoints. In its search for the ideal system of education, American society has stamped certain characteristics on its schools. Among these are the following (Butts and Cremin, 1953, pp. 563–610):

1. The concept of centralized authority and decentralized administration, which implies that while ultimate control of the school rests with the state, management has been left to the local community in order to ensure some flexibility. The school can thus respond more quickly to the needs of the community (Figure 13.2).

2. A single-track system open to all. The desire for equal educational opportunity for all led to the formation of a common public system of education from kindergarten through college. This desire also dictated passage of compulsory attendance legislation designed to promote the public welfare by producing good citizens.

FIGURE 13.2. School System Organization.

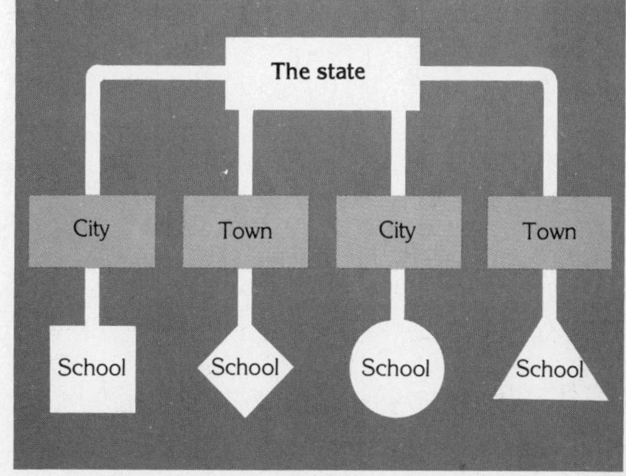

3. A widening role for the educational program. Today's schools are involved in a variety of activities that are far removed from the needs of an agrarian society. Health, vocational preparation, driver training, sex, and drug programs are all legitimate parts of the present curriculum. As the nature of society has changed, so also have the tasks of the school.

4. Humane views of human development in education. No longer is the child considered a sinful individual who needs constant punishment. Now there is a belief that youth is a time of great achievement and that the young can be respected and honored.

In the 1980s we must expand our interpretation of the school's humane attitude toward its students by including the current concern for the handicapped.

Mainstreaming

Mainstreaming is the integration of physically and mentally handicapped children into regular classes. The United States Office of Education states that there are about eight million handicapped children of school age—about twelve percent of the six to nineteen age group. These youngsters, long deprived of normal schooling, now mingle with typical youngsters on the assumption that such integration is beneficial to both groups.

Exceptional children include those who are intellectually exceptional (both gifted and retarded), crippled, learning disabled, emotionally disturbed, deaf or hearing impaired, speech impaired, visually impaired, or multiple handicapped. Figure 13.3 presents a graphic illustration of the population of exceptional children.

If the needs of exceptional children are not too demanding, a combination of regular classwork plus specialized help may afford

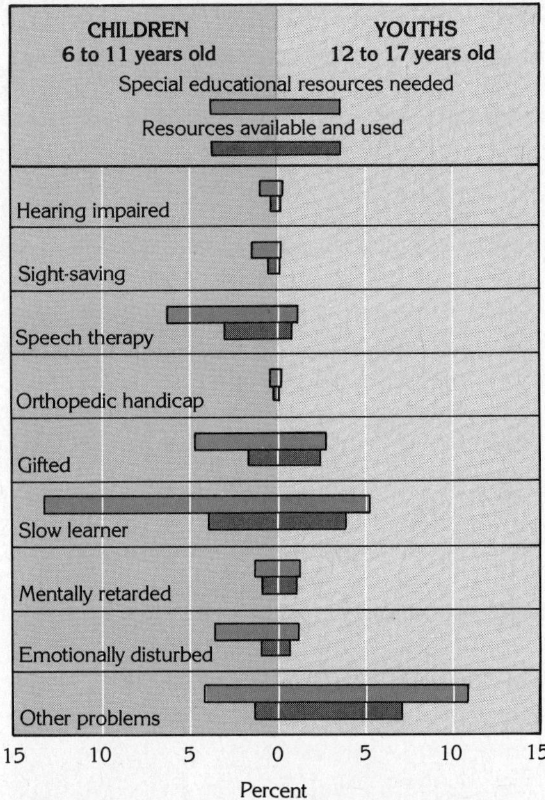

FIGURE 13.3. Population Ages 6 to 11 and 12 to 17 Years Needing and Using Special Educational Resources, by Type of Problem: 1963–1970.

Source: *Social Indicators III.* Washington, D.C.: U.S. Department of Commerce, December, 1980.

these youngsters unique opportunities. The mainstreaming movement became a political force and in 1975 federal legislation was passed, P.L. 94-142, providing appropriate public education for all handicapped children. Praiseworthy as these efforts are, certain cautions urged by Cruickshank and DeYoung (1975) should be heeded if mainstreaming is to succeed: not all exceptional children belong in regular classes; regular classroom teachers and school administrators must thoroughly understand the nature and needs of exceptional children; adequate financial support is critical; and exceptional children must participate in the total educational experience (for example, they should not be left behind on field trips).

Probably the decisive element in determining the success or failure of the mainstreaming movement is teacher attitude. Teachers *idealistically* support the movement, but *practically* are concerned about their ability to cope with special needs students. Teachers not only need reassurance, they need help, such as monitoring of mainstream conditions to ensure that teachers are not overwhelmed by numbers or problems, continued (as needed) in-service programs, and responsive teacher education programs.

For the 1980s, mainstreaming is a societal mandate.

The Gifted. So also is concern for the gifted, that two percent of the population with IQs of 140 or more. Often overlooked, frequently unidentified, and almost always the target of hostility, the gifted have been in—and out—of favor for years. Who are the gifted? The U.S. Office of Education, after extensive research, defines the gifted as follows:

> Gifted and talented children are those, identified by professionally qualified persons, who by virtue of outstanding abilities are capable of high performance. These are children who require differentiated educational programs and/or services beyond those normally provided by the regular school program in order to realize their contribution to self and society.
>
> "High performance" might be manifested in any or a combination of these areas:
>
> 1. General intellectual ability
> 2. Specific academic aptitude
> 3. Creative or productive thinking
> 4. Leadership ability
> 5. Visual and performing arts
> 6. Psychomotor ability

Gifted children are usually in good health, are well adjusted, retain their mental ability as adults, have excellent educational records, and acquire positions of leadership and responsibility. These characteristics, derived from Terman's famous Genetic Studies of Genius (Terman and Oden, 1947), and confirmed by subsequent studies, destroy many of the myths about the gifted: sickly, disturbed, failures, irresponsible.

Since the definition of giftedness has now been vastly widened, educational programs to serve the talented need careful planning. One of these procedures is usually adopted:

1. *Acceleration,* which is an alteration of the typical school program to permit the gifted to complete a certain program in less time or at earlier age (sometimes through early admission, or skipping grades).
2. *Enrichment,* which entails different learning experiences in a regular classroom. Gifted youngsters receive extra readings and assignments, different activities and experiences, and some special tutoring, while remaining with their peers.
3. *Special grouping,* which means that the gifted meet in special segregated classes, removed from their peers.

One of the first two of these options is usually preferred.

It is difficult to predict the educational future of the gifted, since at different times in our history, the nation has provided different answers to the question: Can we be equal and excellent too?

DISCUSSION QUESTIONS

1. Is it possible to specify what the American schools are attempting to achieve today? What type of product is seen as desirable? Be specific in your answer.
2. Do you agree with the premise that the schools influence development? Can you give some concrete examples from your own educational experience.
3. Does society use the school to produce acceptable behavior? How? Does your answer explain the school's role in the turmoil of the last two decades?
4. Do you think that a traditional or an open atmosphere best influences development? Why? Are there various degrees of openness to which you would subscribe? Link your answers to specific characteristics of development.
5. How do you react to the mainstreaming movement? Is it realistic? Can you understand teachers' concern? Can you identify any negative features?

SCHOOL AND SOCIETY

Aside from the critical role of the curriculum (which today's educators are attempting to mold to the individual needs of students), two of the most potent influences on children's development are peers and teachers. Individuals in both categories quickly become "significant others." As youngsters move from home to school, their range of acquaintances increases enormously, and as it does, they are subject to widely different pressures. First, let us consider the influence of peers.

Peer Influence on Development

The appearance of peer groups has been a constant theme in developmental studies of all cultures. Hartup (1976), in analyzing the importance of the age-specific peer group in human socialization, believes that clues to its origin and function lie in the social interaction occurring within the groups. For example, there is more reinforcement for behavior among age-mates than from non-age-mates. Five- and six-year-olds experience little success in their relations with ten- and twelve-year-olds. Thus, same age peers help youngsters to adapt, and Hartup states that signs of difficulty with peers may be a portent of later maladjustment.

Most groups are formed by age and sex. From the early school years to adolescence, sex is the predominant force in group formation, closely followed by age. With maturity, coed activity becomes acceptable, even desirable, and with girls' faster maturation, both age and sex differences begin to diminish. It is clear, then, that group participation is a significant aspect of development at all ages. Campbell (1964, p. 203) states:

> Although the family is rightfully viewed as a prime influence in the child's individuality, his activities in the company of other children contribute to his developing picture of the social world, help to establish his identity, and provide him an opportunity for group experience relevant not only to present functioning but to future social relationships as well.

As children sense the acceptance, rejection, or tolerance by their peers, these reactions become an immediate and significant contribution to a youngster's sense of identity. Peers also influence the formation of attitudes and values. For example, there is general agreement that peers, rather than parents, are the major source of sexual information. Acceptable sex role characteristics are also derived from peers. While society, in general, and parents, in particular, determine the boundaries of an approved sex role, it is peers who give it that special coloring. Much the same is true of aggressive behavior. As Hartup notes, it is impossible for youngsters to learn how to express and control aggression if they deal only with adults, who are much larger and more capable.

PEER RELATIONS AND SOCIAL DEPRIVATION

In one of the most famous studies of social development in the psychological literature, Harlow and Harlow (1962) report the effects of different rearing patterns with rhesus monkeys. Believing that little attention had been given to infant-infant relations, the Harlows commenced a series of studies that deprived the animals of social contact for various lengths of time.

Initially, they removed the infant animals from their mothers and placed them in partial isolation (they could see and hear their peers but could make no physical contact with them). These animals became progressively more disturbed until at about five years, they simply sat, staring into space.

They next separated a group of infants from the mothers and raised them with "surrogate mothers"—a wire form with the feeding bottle's nipple extending from the "breast." Others of this group were raised with a similar form covered with terry cloth. The infants, while showing attachment to the cloth-covered form, nevertheless became sexually and socially aberrant. For example, with only one exception (a female), they never manifested normal mating behavior. Total isolation from birth produced even more devastating effects: constant fear positions, frozen stances, no defense against aggression.

Finally, the investigators stumbled upon unexpected results. Releasing some of their isolated animals into a playroom, they discovered that the monkeys explored the surroundings and each other and eventually displayed normal social behavior. The authors conclude that their experiments indicate that infant-infant interactions may compensate for a lack of, or inadequate, mothering.

The Influence of the Teacher

No analysis of the school's influence on development can ignore the significant relationship of teacher and pupil. Regardless of physical plant, curriculum, and materials, nothing has a more important influence on children in school than the teacher. There are many roles that teachers may select, but in all of them they must furnish the guidance, direction, and encouragement necessary for efficient learning and desirable development. But why do teachers act the way they do in the classroom? Although our task is not to analyze teaching methods, once we accept teachers as decisive forces in a child's life, their behavior becomes highly significant. A domineering, authoritarian teacher may be instrumental in causing

1950 1982

anxiety in one child, but the identical behavior may produce satisfactory learning in another. This question, then, is critical: Why do teachers select the role that they do?

Wallen and Travers (1963) discuss the origin of these roles and group them into six categories:

1. *Patterns derived from teaching traditions.* These teachers teach as they were taught. A most disturbing finding concerning teacher education is that graduates do not teach according to the theories and principles that they learned in college. They rely on the behavior they observed when they were students themselves and on the behavior of their cooperating teacher during the student teaching assignment. Again we can note the powerful force of imitation as a determinant of behavior.

2. *Patterns derived from social learnings in the teacher's background.* Teachers foster the type of behavior that they most value, for example, the behavioral characteristics of a certain class. Teachers' personalities formed before they experience formal teacher training are the main cause of this behavior, and they will then think most highly of those agents that caused them to be what they are. They may also favor pupils who come from the same social class and promote the behaviors that a particular social class most prizes.

3. *Patterns derived from philosophical traditions.* These instructors wish to imitate a Pestalozzi or Socrates in the classroom and are usually graduates of an institution that is strongly committed to a certain philosophy or school of psychology. It is relatively easy to identify a graduate of a school with a strong psychoanalytic orientation. For example, such teachers are primarily concerned with the mental health of their students and are determined to satisfy their needs and remove any potentially damaging frustrations. Most teacher education institutions, however, are so eclectic that it is impossible to identify a single, pervasive philosophy or psychology. Student teachers select what appeals to them, often with unfortunate consequences, since the pattern of behavior that emerges may be inconsistent with the individual's personality or at odds with the community.

4. *Patterns generated by the teachers' needs.* For example, teachers may adopt the lecture method because of personal insecurity. Anxiety in front of others, worry about knowledge of subject matter, or some other personality variable may dictate a certain method. Individuals who engage in a dialogue with students may be most secure in discipline and in technique, but still need the warmth and affection that can come from such an interaction. This explanation probably comes closest to the truth and is the main reason why teachers should develop as much self-awareness as possible so that their classroom behavior will be consistent with their personality.

5. *Patterns generated by school and community conditions.* There is a certain kind of behavior desired in any community, which is reflected in the election of schoolboard members who represent this view. They then establish the policy that leads to suitable pupil behavior and that is to be sought through educational means, that is, in the classroom. Communities exert pressure on their schools and teachers, pressures of which teachers should be aware if they expect to function harmoniously within that system.

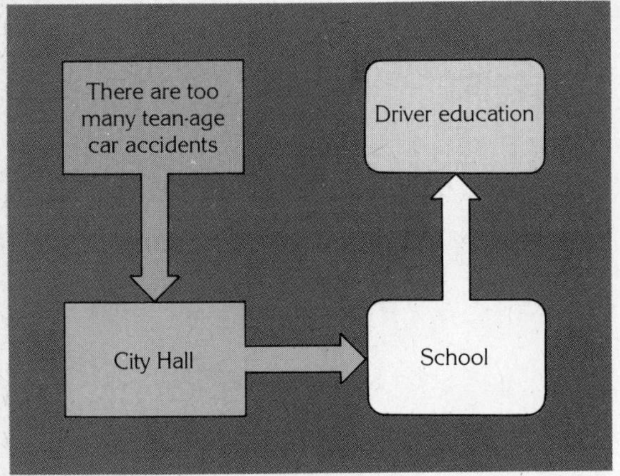

6. *Patterns derived from research on learning.* Here we have the ideal situation: teaching methods based directly on scientific investigations of learning. One should flow both logically and naturally from the other. That this has not resulted seems only to offer further proof of the divergence of views to which students are exposed. If a student likes some conditioning techniques, yet feels that field theory, with its emphasis on perception and wholeness, is also attractive, it becomes difficult to maintain a consistent pattern of behavior. Thus, patterns of teacher behavior and the teaching methods they produce often have little to do with a scientific knowledge of learning.

Teacher Expectations. A vivid example of a teacher's influence on the achievement and behavior of pupils is found in the teacher expectation literature. Since 1968, educators, parents, and much of the general public have been fascinated by the results of a famous study by Robert Rosenthal and Lenore Jacobson, *Pygmalion in the Classroom* (1968). The investigators had elementary school teachers administer a test that supposedly would identify "intellectual bloomers," those who would show an academic spurt during the school year. The instrument actually was a nonverbal IQ test. In the fall, the teachers were told which pupils the test had identified and they were also told that these youngsters would show remarkable progress during the year. There were absolutely no differences between test scores of these youngsters and the control group, yet at year's end, when the pupils were retested on the original instrument, those identified as the intellectual bloomers had scored higher. Are teachers trapped by their self-fulfilling prophesies?

The study generated enormous controversy, largely because of methodological weaknesses and an inability to replicate the original results. Continued experimentation has indicated that while teachers' expectations affect pupils' achievement, it is not a universal phenomenon. Just what is this phenomenon? Brody and Good (1974, p. 32) define teacher expectations as follows:

> By "teacher expectations" we mean inferences that teachers make about the present and future academic achievement and general classroom behavior of their students. Ordinarily, teacher expectations are based in part upon available data concerning students (intelligence and achievement test data, past grades, comments by previous teachers, or knowledge about the student's family) when such data are available. . . . Regardless of the degree to which teachers form expectations on

> the basis of other data, however, their expectations are shaped and changed by contact with students in the classroom (work habits, apparent ability to meet the demands of the curriculum, apparent motivation, willingness to comply to school rules, interest patterns, and so on).

As these authors note, expectations are normal and neither good nor bad in themselves; the critical issue is the accuracy of the expectations, which eventually affects student achievement. The potential of teacher expectations to influence outcome is seen in the kinds of expectations teachers have: whether a student's ability is either changeable or rigid; a student's ability to benefit from instruction; the nature of appropriate material for a particular student.

Brophy and Good (1974) next present a workable model of six stages to demonstrate how such expectations actually function in teacher-student expectations:

1. Teachers, early in the school year, form differential expectations (based on the data previously mentioned) of their students' potential. These expectations may be appropriate or inappropriate, and resist change even when faced with contradictory student behavior.

2. Students are now treated differently because of teacher expectations; such treatment will be appropriate or inappropriate depending on the accuracy of the expectations.

3. Students next react to teachers differently because of the nature of the interaction. (Again, note how a dynamic interpretation of interaction helps to clarify all human relationships.)

4. The student's behavior usually complements and reinforces the teacher's expectations.

5. Gradually, the student's behavior, motivation, and self-concept reflect these expectations.

6. If continued throughout the year, pupil process and product measures are affected. That is, both the student's behavior and achievement tend to match the teacher's expectations.

The teachers' behavior matches the expectations; for example, if they have formed low expectations for certain students, they tend to wait less time for answers, reward inappropriate behavior, criticize more frequently, provide less public feedback, give less attention, and demand less from these students. Here again we have an excellent example of how the nature of a person to person interaction shapes developmental outcomes.

REVERSING OUTCOMES OF TEACHER EXPECTATIONS

Dworkin and Dworkin (1979) provide a practical example of reversing the negative outcomes of inappropriate teacher expectations. They state that the teacher expectation literature has mainly ignored the impact of negative expectations upon a child's behavior. Believing that most teachers will alter their behavior if they realize its explosive potential, they note that the initial step must be to understand the meaning of the expectation research.

1. There is ample negative expectation in almost all classrooms.
2. Teachers who become aware of the implication of these expectations may change their behavior.
3. Encouraging positive expectations as a form of intentional intervention may produce a decided impact on student behavior.
4. It is impossible to change existing negative expectations by mere warning; there must be carryover to teacher behavior.
5. It is often difficult to change negative expectations because teachers almost universally believe that they deal fairly with all children.

The authors then describe a project in which they worked with individual children, their teachers, their parents, and other adults involved with the youngsters. In a meeting with the adults, the authors endeavored to focus on the children's strengths and capabilities rather than dwell on negative expectations. They particularly urged the teachers to avoid negative terms in describing the children and stressed that any school success a child had achieved was undoubtedly due to the teacher. Attempting to change expectations from negative to positive and providing *earned* reinforcement provided heartening results. The youngsters developed greater self-confidence, more realistic appraisals of their performance, and higher achievement levels. Thus, everyone benefited: children, teachers, parents, and school officials, and the project demonstrated the feasibility—even necessity—of formulating practical teaching models directed at changing teachers' expectations.

DISCUSSION QUESTIONS

1. Interest in peer influence is a relatively new phenomenon. Why do you think it has only recently been recognized?
2. Do you think that age and sex are adequate criteria to define group formation? What else would you suggest? Comment on too rigid interpretation of these criteria; that is, are there problems associated with a strict classification by age and sex?
3. The Harlows' studies of mothering deprivation are immensely revealing. Do you support their conclusions? Are they sufficiently exhaustive? They were conducted in 1962; can you apply their conclusions to any social changes of the 1980s?
4. Have any teachers been "significant others" in your life? Why? Describe these teachers. Does your answer have anything to do with the type of atmosphere they created?

LEARNING AND DEVELOPMENT

Schools were designed to organize and facilitate learning, and like a continuous unbroken thread, the influence of learning has been apparent in our discussion of schooling. But it is interwoven so inextricably into the entire spectrum of child and adult behavior that everything we do reflects learning. Learning, a term that we often use so casually, presents several complications in any attempt at analysis. So before we begin to discuss different interpretations of how children learn, it would be well to explore the nature of learning in general. How do we define it? How do we know when it has occurred?

Some Clouded Issues

The basis for any definition of learning is a change in behavior. Any definition must further distinguish between the changes that constitute learning and those that do not. Among the changes that cannot be attributed to learning is maturation, which is learning's chief competitor as a modifier of behavior. In other words, the behavioral changes that occur through regular stages, regardless of practice, are changes caused by developmental maturation. Fatigue also causes some changes in behavior; such temporary losses of efficiency do not represent learning. Drugs are another example; behavior may change when an individual is drugged but returns to normal; performance also returns to previous levels with no intervening training. A change has occurred, but we cannot say that learning has taken place.

A learning theorist must also answer certain other questions. Ernest Hilgard and Gordon Bower (1975) consider the following questions central to any learning theory.

1. What are the limits of learning? The limits of learning depend upon the capacity of the individual learner and individual differences among learners of the same species. Does capacity change with age?

2. What is the role of practice in learning? Obviously, continued performance of an activity leads to improvement, but what precisely do we know about practice? Is it repetition

that causes progress, or the conditions under which practice occurs, or is some type of reinforcement produced by the practice? Can repetition be harmful as well as helpful?

3. How important are desires and incentives, rewards, and punishments? There is little doubt that rewards and punishments can alter performance, but how do they affect the individual? That is, how do they act on the nervous system? What happens to the punished response after suppression? Is it lost to the child's response repertoire, or is it merely submerged until a more appropriate occasion for its appearance arises? Are rewards and punishments equal and opposite in their impact on the organism?

4. What is the role of understanding and insight? We are all familiar with instances in which learning is easier if we understand the purpose of our task. Yet there are other tasks, such as hitting a golf ball, in which we are told that it is better "not to think." Which is true, or should we even try to make a distinction? If the distinction is valid, does this imply that learning differs from task to task?

5. Does learning one thing help you to learn another? This question raises the vital issue of transfer of learning. Does transfer occur, and, if so, how much and under what conditions? It seems quite clear that transfer is the pivotal question of all instruction, whether at home or at school. If transfer is a figment of some psychologist's imagination, how can we justify any instruction under any circumstances?

6. Is it possible to explain memory and forgetting? The tricks of memory are legion: we forget what we supposedly wish to remember; we are plagued by memories that we desperately desire to forget. These are the usual phenomena. But if I ask you to multiply 9 by 7, you may immediately reply 56 (oops, 63). What chemical or electrical mysteries are at work within our nervous system that usually enable us to recall instantly?

With these questions in mind, how then can we define learning? Any definition must incorporate the notion of behavioral change. But, in itself, this is unsatisfactory. Consider what you are doing right now. You are reading this book and perhaps you are learning something. But how can anyone tell? There is undoubtedly no observable change in your behavior, yet you are probably learning. So we are forced to judge your learning by your performance. It is important, however, to remember that learning may occur before performance is changed. With these warnings, we may define learning as a process that results in modification of behavior. This modification of behavior must be due to learning and not to other agents such as maturation, drugs, or fatigue. The outcomes of the learning process are called learning products. But our definition also recognizes the unique and dynamic form of organization that each of us brings to our experiences, which is the reason that we also refer to learning as a process.

The Characteristics of Learning

The acceptance of learning as both process and product is important. If you believe that learning is a product, then you see children as mere mechanical models who respond almost automatically to environmental stimuli. Thus, we can only know learning from its results; that is, we restrict our analysis solely to discernible modifications of behavior. If, however, you believe that individuals alter stimuli in some unique manner, and that this produces responses that differ from those of other individuals, then learning is seen as a process. This view is far less mechanical. The model is that of a restless, inquiring organism that selects some stimuli over others and uses them in accordance with its own singular pattern of experiences in the attainment of personal goals.

We can use the following example to analyze the process of learning. A father is fortunate enough to be able to obtain tickets to an outstanding professional football game. His son, age eleven, is engrossed in the world of sports. But he has also been experiencing difficulty in school, particularly in mathematics, learning how to do percentages. The father promises his son that if his math work improves, they will go to the game. Now, let us look at the learning sequence (Figure 13.4).

1. There must be a motivated individual, because there simply will be no learning if motivation is lacking. Faced with challenges, frustrations, and stimulation, unmotivated individuals will react not by generating new patterns of behavior, but with previously learned responses, that is, by relying on old habits, or they do not react at all. In our example, the father, in cooperating with the school, is encouraging the youngster by supplying him with a strong motive to display new behavior. The problem is to furnish youngsters with real and vital goals that they themselves wish to attain.

2. Assuming that individuals are motivated, we must suppose that they are encountering some obstacle blocking progress to a goal, represented in our model by the white figure numbered 2. Without some block, no new behavior is required. Individuals simply repeat past behavior that was successful in similar situations. Only when they cannot attain a goal by customary responses must they learn new pathways. The nature of the obstacle is crucial; it must be sufficiently frustrating to challenge, but not so frustrating as to discourage. In our example, the new math work is the obstacle. The youngster's past

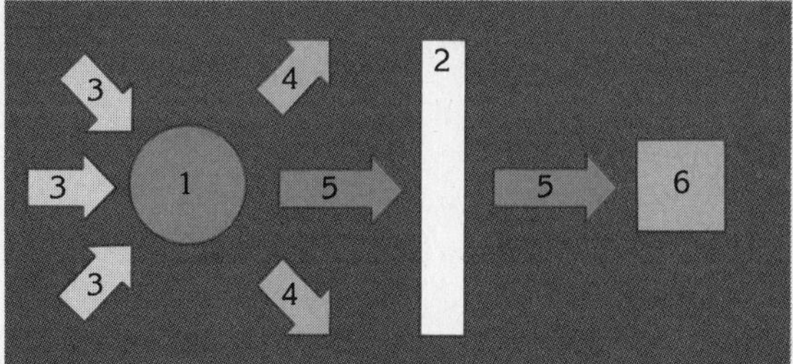

FIGURE 13.4. The Characteristics of Learning.

learning is no longer sufficient, and he must acquire new behaviors. In this case, the obstacle is challenging but not defeating for most eleven-year-olds.

3. Environmental stimuli must be present. If individuals are to overcome the obstacle, they must be able to capitalize on clues that will help them solve problems. The notion of environmental stimuli is significant for both readiness and motivation. To prod youngsters, to encourage them in their search, the stimuli must be suitable for the developmental level. In our example, this implies that the youngster must understand the material. It must be presented in an interesting manner, with both support and constructive criticism offered to the youngster when needed.

4. The individuals now perceive their fields. Depending on background, present state of motivation, and the environmental stimuli, they respond according to how they perceive the relationship between self and the goal. Here children frequently need help to distinguish the important stimuli, to see how they relate to each other and the goal, and to learn not to be distracted by irrelevant stimuli. In our example, the boy is motivated, challenged, and provided with stimuli. Now, to achieve his goal, he must perceive new relationships and learn new steps, such as when to divide and when to multiply. Consequently, he is looking at his problem in a new way, trying to join the old pieces with the new in a novel pattern that will bring him success.

5. Individuals decide on the route that they will take to the goal; that is, they choose a response pattern. It is a purposeful choice, based on perception of stimuli and their relationship to the goal. If they are successful, their behavior is reinforced and the response pattern becomes a part of the behavioral repertoire. If the response is unsuccessful, they must reexamine the stimuli, search for new clues, and select a new and different road to the goal. The importance of the obstacle is again evident. If it is sufficiently challenging, but not overwhelming, the learner will conduct a new search; this in itself is a learning experience. We all encounter failure throughout life, but how we react to it is critical. Youngsters should learn not to be defeated by failure, yet such defeat will happen if all they realize is failure. In our example, the boy wants to go to the game, so he decides what he must do. He reexamines the series of steps that preceded the new work, seeks the advice of his teacher, examines other books and examples, works on some sample problems, and decides that he is ready to be tested. If he succeeds, the response pattern will be established. If he does not, he must search for the mistakes, determine where he went wrong, and try again. The manner of meeting failure is thus as important as the achievement of success.

6. A goal is selected. Because of particular needs and background of experiences, youngsters pick definite goals, hoping that achievement will bring happiness, success, or whatever urged them toward it initially. The role of parents and teachers in helping youngsters to choose appropriate and attainable goals is almost self-explanatory. Many youngsters choose unreachable goals because they expect to fail. Consequently, if they are unable to attain these unrealistic goals, no one will blame them; there is no humiliation attached to their failure. The task of helping youngsters to select suitable personal and social goals is both difficult and sensitive, yet cannot be abandoned. In our example, the goal—mastery of percentages—was realistic. Achieving such a goal enables the youngster to experience success and to proceed confidently to new tasks with an enhanced self-concept. The learning sequence is essentially the same when we meet any challenging new task. From motivation through goal acquisition, if any of the steps produces failure, learning either suffers or is lost.

Explanations of Learning: The Theorists

Consider the following passage. "The boy carefully studied the pages in front of him. The subject, the tangled web of causes of the American Civil War, was difficult. He read the text; he checked the maps; he followed class discussions with attention. When the class was examined he did quite well, and in the follow-up session, he showed a genuine comprehension of the problem." How would you explain the learning that occurred?

Your answer probably falls into one of two general categories. You either tended toward a stimulus-response-reinforcement explanation, or you emphasized insight, perception of relationship, and comprehension. Thus, you are predominantly either a behaviorist or a cognitivist. You may say that you actually believe in both; nevertheless, most of us depend primarily on one of them without totally rejecting the other. This is extremely important (and very practical) since it affects everything you do with children. You will use techniques that are suited to your belief.

There are two major theories of learning: those that depend on stimulus-response explanations and those that prefer to look inside humans for explanations. The S-R theorists see children's cognitive ideas as either nonexistent or relatively unimportant. Their responses are determined by patterns of stimuli or schedules of reinforcement. Cognitive theorists, on the other hand, see children's

TABLE 13.1. Great Names in Learning Theory

Associationism (also called behaviorism, S-R theory, conditioning)		Cognitive theory (also called field theory, Gestalt theory, perceptual theory, phenomenology)	
Name	**Concern**	**Name**	**Concern**
Greek philosophers (Aristotle)	Principles of association (similarity, contrast, contiguity)	Classical Gestalt school (Wertheimer, Koffka, Kohler)	Insight
English philosophers (Locke, Berkely, Hume)	Association of ideas	Kurt Lewin	Life space
Alexander Bain	Turned to S-R	Jerome Bruner	Perception, concept formation, education
Edward Thorndike	Theory called Connectionism	Arthur Combs, Donald Snygg	Phenomenology
John Watson	Theory called Behaviorism		
Ivan Pavlov	Classical Conditioning		
Edwin Guthrie	Contiguous Conditioning		
B. F. Skinner	Instrumental Conditioning		

behavior as too complicated to explain in behavioristic terms. They believe that children can solve problems and express themselves creatively through insightful behavior. Youngsters do not respond in an absolutely predetermined manner; instead, they respond to the pressures of the environment in a unique manner.

Neither explanation is altogether satisfactory, yet both have made significant contributions to our knowledge of learning. Table 13.1 offers a historical chronology of some of the major figures and movements identified with each of the two schools.

CHILDREN AND LEARNING: THEORY INTO PRACTICE

Several developmental changes in children's learning follow the classical conditioning model. Since we are concerned with the sequence of the changes in learning that accompany age, an unavoidable and intriguing question is: Does learning occur before birth? One of the few studies that attempted to answer this question is that of David Spelt (1948). He secured the cooperation of a group of women who were at least seven months pregnant and attempted to establish a classical conditioning pattern in the unborn babies. As the first step, Spelt determined that a vibrator placed on the abdomen of the mother-to-be produced no movement in the fetus. With another group he discovered that a loud noise (an oak clapper striking a wooden box) actually produced fetal movement. Then, with a third group, Spelt tried his conditioning technique: the Conditioned Stimulus (vibrator) was presented for five seconds, followed by the loud noise (Unconditioned Stimulus).

After presentation of fifteen to twenty pairings of the CS-US (vibrator and loud noise), the fetuses showed movement in response to the vibrator alone, to which they had not reacted before. In a particularly interesting result, one of the subjects left the experiment after conditioning (fetal movement in response to the vibrator) had been established, but returned eighteen days later. The CS (vibrator) was still effective. Although this experiment is fascinating in its implications, considerable caution is necessary in its interpretation. Was the fetus responding to the noise, or was it responding to the mother's response to the noise? In either case, however, the results suggest prenatal conditioning.

Another example of early learning is seen in the work of the American psychologist, John B. Watson, whose experiments on classical conditioning with little Albert showed how easily children acquire fear. Each time the boy touched a rat, which he did not fear, a loud noise was produced to startle him. Gradually his noise induced fear spread to all furry objects.

Similar results have been obtained in studies that use the techniques of instrumental conditioning. Perhaps the most famous of these were conducted by Papousek (1967). Working with youngsters from birth to eight months of age, he studied conditioning, extinction, reconditioning, and discrimination learning procedures. Head-turning was the desired behavior, and milk was used as the reinforcer. The conditioning procedure was as follows: the CS (a bell) was sounded for ten seconds, and the infant was reinforced with milk if it responded with a left head-turn during the ten-second interval. If the head-turn did not occur during the ten seconds, the experimenter tried to induce it by rubbing the infant's cheek. If this was also unsuccessful, the experimenter gently turned the infant's head in the required direction. Reinforcement was given each time the head moved to the left (either emitted, elicited, or forced).

Each experimental session consisted of ten trials: five consecutive responses in one session were taken to indicate conditioned head-turning. The author studied three age groups: newborns, three-month-old infants, and five-month-old infants. All three groups demonstrated conditioning within twenty-eight days. The results seemed to demonstrate that instrumental learning occurs during the first weeks of life. The newborn infants, however, were slower to condition than both of the older

FIGURE 13.5. Albert Is Conditioned To Fear All Furry Objects. *(a)* Albert is frightened as he pats rat. *(b)* Albert jumps away from rat. *(c)* If this happens often, Albert becomes frightened of all furry objects, even a fur coat.

groups. Papousek stresses the high correlation between age and the ease of conditioning.

Studies of instrumental conditioning lead Reese and Lipsitt (1970) to conclude that the human infant is, from birth, an active, adaptive organism as well as a reflexively reacting organism. The infant's reactions to reinforcement contingencies show that instrumental learning is highly significant in the child's adaptive interactions with the environment.

Speculations and assumptions afford some unusual practical implications. The term "readiness," for example, suggests the relationship between development and learning. Youngsters are ready to learn at certain key moments in development (critical periods). If the environment then furnishes appropriate opportunities, they learn rapidly and become ready and eager to take the next step in the developmental sequence. If, however, the environmental stimuli do not "match" the developmental period, both development and learning suffer. Motivation also plays an important role in connecting development and learning. The unmotivated child misses many experiences that provide opportunities for learning and developmental progress. "No motivation, no learning" was never truer than in development. Worse yet, the information gained in carefully controlled studies suggest that if either learning or development suffers, both are damaged, perhaps permanently.

Our consideration of schools and learning raises the controversial issue of television as a competitor of the schools and as a potent influence on development.

The Role of Television

We live in a visual age. From the time that children are born, they are subjected to almost unceasing images demanding attention. Public acceptance of television is now so widespread that estimates are that almost one hundred percent of American households possess at least one television set. While television usage has increased dramatically, use of written materials (newspapers, magazines) has remained level. The implications are enormous. Exposed to exciting visual stimuli from birth, children come to school and enter an environment that values the written word. The challenge is instant and immense.

The following statistics illustrate the dilemma. (You may have seen slightly different figures; almost all such data are estimates.)

> The television set in an average household is on an average of 6 hours a day.
>
> The average viewer watches about 28 hours of television per week.
>
> By the age of 65, an average viewer has seen 9 years of television.
>
> By age 18, a student has watched 15,000 hours of television.
>
> By age 18, a student has attended school 11,000 hours.
>
> By age 15, a youngster has seen about 13,000 killings on television.

Studies have shown that people will refuse large sums of money to go without television for specific periods of time. The 1972 report of the Surgeon General concluded quite clearly that television influences development and that there was a causal relationship between televised violence and antisocial behavior. Since then, television programs have become *more* violent and *more* sexual.

How does television exercise its influence? One view is by the nature of its programming. Comstock et al. (1978) state that program preferences appear early and are good indications of what is viewed throughout the child's lifetime:

1. Preschool children prefer cartoons, situation comedies, and noncartoon children shows.

2. By the first two grades, comedies are the preferred shows, a tendency that persists until adolescence.
3. By the end of elementary school, children find action-adventure shows attractive.
4. By the mid-teens, adult shows are preferred.

The viewing of violent programs definitely increases with age, which raises the question of whether such viewing increases the possibility of aggressive behavior among young people. If you recall Bandura's work on modeling and imitation, it is difficult to dismiss the link between filmed aggression and actual violent behavior. Comstock and his colleagues (1978), after an exhaustive review of the evidence, conclude that exposure to violence increases the likelihood of subsequent aggression. There is every indication, also, that carefully prepared material can increase *prosocial* behavior.

The speculations about television's impact on development are endless, and the studies almost equally so. What can we conclude about this technological force in our midst? Children *like* watching television. This simple statement should be a guide for all analysis. If youngsters like watching it, they will continue to do so. Consequently, one suggestion is for more careful monitoring of children's viewing habits by parents. Since not all parents will accept this responsibility, organizations such as Action for Children's Television (formed by a Boston group concerned about the content and commercials on children's programs) need support and encouragement to disseminate their views.

The core of the problem, however, is not solely in the nature of programs; it is in the nature of viewing. Optimal development requires an interaction with the environment. For growing children, the interaction should be physical as well as mental and emotional. Exploring the environment physically—touching, throwing, tracing, bumping, pushing—is a vital part of the necessary experiences of the early years. Recall Piaget's designation of this time—the Sensorimotor Period. Animal studies dramatically indicate how physical interaction with the environment alters the brain and nervous system.

Passivity is not the norm; activity remains the goal. Describing the two-year-old child as an enormously energetic, dynamic organism, Winn (1977, p. 18) states:

> In the life of a small child the television experience is an unmistakable return to the passive mode of functioning. It is quite unlike any other form of play. And thus since parental anxiety is often a finely-tuned indicator that something is amiss in the child's life, parents' widespread anxiety about the passivity of their children's television experience may carry survival value for the child.

Readiness

When parents choose toys for their children, or teachers select curricula for their students, they have the notion of readiness in mind. Readiness reflects many characteristics, including biological equipment, ideas, skills, habits, attitudes, and values.

As we trace development, we see some themes constantly recurring. Even though readiness has not been explicitly mentioned until now, our work has been replete with its implications. In our discussion of motor learning, we mentioned muscular development: when children cannot manipulate a thin pencil, we give them a fat crayon. Or recall Piaget's work. Early in the concrete operational period, children cannot cope with problems demanding highly abstract thought. In neither instance are they *ready*. In the first, they lack physical coordination; in the second, they lack certain cognitive abilities. Readiness is thus the result of development interacting with learning. The question that should concern parents and teachers is: What is the youngster ready for—third-grade reading, fifth-grade arithmetic, or sixth-grade social studies? The aim is to develop a sequence of environmental experiences that will enhance development and encourage further learning. We cannot afford the luxury of assuming that since Jane is six and a half years old, she must be reading at a first-grade level. If there has been a deficit in the child's past experiences, anything so symbolic may well leave her thoroughly confused. On the other hand, because of enriched experiences, she may profit from reading at a higher level.

A particular readiness condition does not remain steady without changing. Frequently, interpretations of behavior have assumed the contrary, with the result that there has been a tendency to wait for the clear appearance of a particular state, such as reading readiness. This interpretation ignores the value of new stimuli for creating a state of readiness, for allowing students to make mistakes, and for discovering the source of their errors. The policy of postponement—of waiting for the appearance of definite clues to readiness—may needlessly handicap the child's ability to master a task. Perhaps the best attack on this policy has been articulated by Jerome Bruner, who stunned the educational world with his challenging proposal. He believes that at any age a child can be taught anything in some intellectually honest way. His position is open, however, to misinterpretations, and unfortunately, some have occurred.

Can Anything Be Taught to Anyone? To avoid misinterpreting Bruner's famous statement (1960) that any subject can be taught effectively, in some intellectually honest form, to any child at any state of development, we must grasp three basic ideas: the intellectual development of children, the act of learning, and the use of a spiral curriculum.

At each stage of development, children have their own unique perceptions and interpretations of the environment. Therefore, in order to teach children some subject, one must organize it in a way appropriate to the level of development. According to Bruner, the job is one of translation. That is, the discipline must be presented in a form appropriate to children's thought patterns. Later, the first learning can be expanded and transformed into a powerful tool for exploring, discovering, problem solving, and creating. To acquire concepts, children need help in moving from dependence on the tangible, concrete things in the environment to the use of adequate modes of thought. This transition requires more than giving a purely logical explanation, which is completely foreign to their way of thinking. In essence, the fundamentals of the subject are treated like building blocks; the concrete facts support the more advanced, abstract notions at the frontiers of knowledge.

Perhaps nothing that Bruner, long a respected figure in American psychology, has said or done has provided more controversy than his views on readiness in *The Process of Education.*

> We begin with the hypothesis that any subject can be taught effectively in some intellectually honest form to any child at any state of development. It is a bold hypothesis and an essential one in thinking about the nature of a curriculum. No evidence exists to contradict it; considerable evidence is being amassed that supports it. (Bruner, 1960, p. 33)

To link this basic hypothesis to actual curriculum construction, Bruner introduced the notion of the spiral curriculum (Figure 13.6). He believes that if we respect the thinking process of children, if we are courteous enough to translate the material into a form they can work with, and if we are challenging enough to motivate them to advance, then we can introduce children at an early age to the ideas and styles of the educated adult. Bruner then asks some crucial questions. Is some primary school subject worth knowing to an adult? Does having learned it as a child make the person a better adult? When the answers to these questions are negative, or even ambiguous, then the material is simply cluttering up the curriculum.

The spiral curriculum treats the same topic with increasing sophistication that matches the increasing maturity of children. They progress from simple facts about the war (dates, opponents, immediate outcome) to abstract political and economic considerations, as they are ready for them. Lest you feel uneasy at what appears to be a policy of postponement (wait for a certain level of mental development before offering more advanced material), Bruner hastens to add that this is far from his intent. Children's intellectual development follows no neat and simple pattern. It is remarkably responsive to environmental stimuli. Instruction, then, need not be the slave of development; it may well lead development by challenging children to further their own progress. Any complex idea can be restated in simpler terms, so concrete instances enable seven-year-olds to understand that a problem exists. Later they will translate this problem into more abstract terms with which they can grapple mentally. Thus they are examining the basic ideas of a subject repeatedly, but in a different form. This process is the essence of the spiral curriculum.

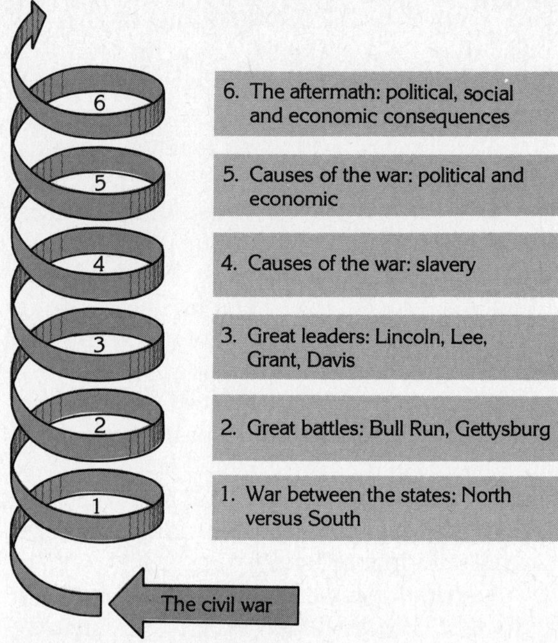

FIGURE 13.6. The Spiral Curriculum.

Bruner and his associates have also reached the conclusion that by the age of two, children have invented the rules of grammar and that at birth, they possess the capacity for the intelligent use of hands, eyes, and tools. Gradually, the conviction has grown that infants actually invent strategies to explain what they perceive and, as early as the first month of life, they possess complex hypotheses about the world. These speculations by a noted psychologist may herald a new and vastly different concept of readiness.

DISCUSSION QUESTIONS

1. How would you answer the questions about learning posed by Hilgard and Bower? Examine your answer. Are you an associationist or a cognitivist? Why?
2. Describe something that you have recently learned. Now analyze it according to the characteristics of learning. Be sure to specify how each characteristic applies to your description. Were all the characteristics present?
3. Are you afraid of anything? Using Watson's experiment with little Albert, can you explain how your fear may have developed? How do generalizations cause the fear to spread?
4. Do you see television as a positive or negative force in development? Are our fears, so frequently expressed, exaggerated? Why? What would be your recommendations to improve both the nature and conditions of children's viewing? Can you be age specific?
5. Do you agree with Bruner's famous statement on readiness? Why? How could it easily be misinterpreted? Does it help you to understand the meaning of readiness? Do you think that readiness can be linked to the notion of sensitive periods? Why?

THE MONTESSORI METHOD

Any discussion of child development that divorces itself from practical implications is remarkably limited. Since the theme of this text is that children strive unceasingly for self-realization, speculation alone is insufficient; there must be a link between theory and practice. How can responsible adults aid children in the search for self? Nowhere is the interaction between learning and development better illustrated than in the techniques devised by Maria Montessori. Here we have a happy blend of theory and practice that is experiencing a rebirth throughout the world today.

The popularity of the Montessori method is reflected in a rapidly increasing number of Montessori schools. But with their spiraling popularity has come renewed criticism. When the Montessori method first attempted to establish a foothold in the United States during the first two decades of this century, it fought a furious but losing battle with such towering figures as John Dewey and William Kilpatrick. It was subsequently relegated to the files of forgotten educational theories. Now it is sustaining renewed attacks by those who question its effect on personality or who protest its structured environment, which is almost directly opposed to a more open classroom atmosphere. How, then, can we explain its rebirth? Undoubtedly, the explanation lies in today's concern with a child's early years and the realization that young children are capable of so much more than we previously thought. Consequently, the Montessori method, with all its suggestions for formalized education for the very young, has considerable contemporary appeal.

CHILDREN'S CHARACTERISTICS

What were some of the capacities of young children that Maria Montessori had apparently uncovered? Among them are the following.

1. Amazing mental concentration, during which children become so engrossed in a task that they are oblivious to everything around them. Here we see the vital role of spontaneous interest.
2. Love of repetition, in which children continue to repeat something and which seems to be an essential feature of their manner of working, undoubtedly representing some psychological need.
3. Love of order. Children seem to enjoy putting things in their proper places. Otherwise it would be impossible to grant them the necessary freedom of movement.
4. Freedom of choice. Children seem to want some degree of personal selection, which is essential for them as they mature and move toward more complete independence.
5. A preference for work over play. Children prefer work over play if the work is a result of spontaneous choice.
6. No need for external rewards and punishments. Children definitely show that rewards and punishments are relatively meaningless to them and are unnecessary once they have learned how to work and how to direct their energies into desirable outlets.
7. Love of silence. Children seek occasional quiet times.
8. A sense of personal dignity. Children need to avoid derision and humiliation or they will be wounded and oppressed to an extent that adults cannot imagine.
9. An explosion into writing. Montessori found that several children, four or five years of age, learned to write with no instruction. They "burst spontaneously into writing."
10. The discovery of reading, when youngsters learn that written words are a means of communication. Interestingly, Montessori found that learning to write came several months before reading.
11. Spontaneous self-discipline. This is particularly significant, since the original purpose of the Montessori experiment was to reduce disorderly conduct. As time passed and the children became absorbed in their new surroundings, spontaneous and extraordinary self-discipline appeared.

Thoughts on Development

Montessori believed that developing children pass through different epochs of uniform growth that alternate with periods of transition. This belief applied to both physical and mental development and suggested that children possess different types of minds at different periods. These periods differ so sharply that Montessori referred to them as a series of new births. Montessori described three major periods of development:

1. The first stage: birth to six years (transition).

Maria Montessori

a. The absorbent mind: birth to three years (unconscious).
b. The absorbent mind: three to six years (conscious).
2. The second stage: six to twelve years (uniform growth).
3. The third stage: twelve to eighteen years (transition)
a. Puberty: twelve to fifteen years.
b. Adolescence: fifteen to eighteen years.

After eighteen years, there are no more transformations, but simply a continuing process of aging.

The First Stage. Stressing the importance of the first stage of development, Montessori (1967) has commented that the greatness of the human personality begins at the hour of birth. The child's mind during this period differs sharply from that of the adult. In the first substage (birth to three years) the mind absorbs impressions from the environment, but does so in an unknowing manner. Hence it is given the title "the absorbent mind, unconscious phase." This period witnesses the beginnings of intelligence.

Montessori notes that the first two years of life open new horizons, since here we see the laws of psychic construction in full operation. She makes the intriguing statement that during this period the adult cannot exert any direct influence on the child's mind. This helps to explain why most children enter a Montessori school at about three years of age. They are thought to be more susceptible to adult influence during the second substage of the first period.

The second substage is similar to the first, but now children begin to become susceptible to adult influences and the personality undergoes great change. Children move from an unconscious to a conscious state through motor activity. Montessori stated that children fashion human intelligence with their hands; so during the first three years, children create their faculties, and during the next three years they develop them.

The school day in a Montessori school was designed to match the developmental level of the child. Some of the initial exercises include:

1. Arranging the seats.
2. Learning to lace shoes, to button hooks.
3. Arranging rods in order of size.

The work with the rods is the most useful, since it forces children to fix attention on a definite activity, comparing, selecting, and thus exercising intelligence.

The Second Stage. The second developmental epoch (six to twelve years) is a period of great stability; that is, growth continues in much the same manner as earlier, developing the same kind of mind and manifesting the same kind of psychological characteristics. It is a time of growth with little transformation; Montessori has noted that it is a period of growth unaccompanied by other change. Children are calm and happy. For typical children, it is a time of good health and growing strength, and an ideal time for considerable mental work. Mind and body are ripe for proper environmental stimulation. Some typical exercises at this time would include:

1. Free drawing and use of watercolors.
2. Creative writing.
3. Continued arithmetic work with the rods.*

The Third Stage. The period of adolescence (twelve to eighteen years) is a time of great transformation, both physical and mental. Here we begin to see new psychological characteristics: doubt, hesitation, violent emotions, and discouragement. What is now developing is a socially conscious individual with increased sensitivity to social life. Physical health is less robust than it has been previously. It can be a difficult time because of rapid development and the changes that result.

During the first substage, children undergo noticeable changes that produce considerable agitation. But it is also a time for much optimism because of the enthusiasms, energy, and creativity displayed by youngsters of this age.

*The rods used in Montessori schools are numbered according to length (1 is short, 10 is long). The children are taught to put the shorter pieces together to form tens. For instance, a number 2 rod and a number 8 rod would equal the length of a number 10 rod. These exercises are repeated, and slowly the child acquires the technical language: 2 plus 8 equals 10. When children can write, they learn the written names of the numbers and the words *plus* and *equals.* They then proceed to taking a number 2 rod away from a number 10 rod, leaving a number 8 rod. Subtraction has thus commenced.

In the second substage, Montessori refers to the "newly born." Children become aware of themselves as members of society; they feel the need for dignity and respect and are quick to detect any criticism, direct or implied. Education for this age group should relate to practical activities so that they become truly acquainted with society.

A youngster reaches this level by what Montessori calls the "prepared environment." A prepared environment consists of much more than tables and chairs. It would include:

1. Necessary materials that aid both practical and intellectual development.
2. Sensorial materials, such as rods to teach lengths, cubes to teach size, and bells to teach musical pitch.
3. Materials for the acquisition of cultural geography, history, art, and arithmetic.
4. Materials and techniques necessary for the development of the child's religious life.

Montessori maintained that a prepared environment was necessary mainly because adults could not always provide an ideal environment for a child. But you may ask: Why not allow children to develop naturally, as unimpeded as possible? The answer lies in both children and the environment. Most children do not possess ideal surroundings and, since children love order, they receive tremendous satisfaction from perceiving order in their environment. It helps them to develop the concept of a stable world.

As children grow older, they also find satisfaction in discovering order in more abstract materials, not only the sensory. The prepared paths to culture are mainly the materials that lead to mastery of arithmetic, geography, grammar, and history. These subjects flow naturally from the early use of sensory materials and, again, help the older youngsters to discern order in these more abstract phases of the environment.

The Conditions of Growth. Speaking of these periods of development, Montessori (1967) has commented that the first period of development is the most important. Any obstacle to development during this period may have lasting effects. Youngsters of this age are endowed with greater creative energies that are extremely fragile. These energies are the product of an unconscious mind that must become conscious by work and experience. We must always recall that the child's mind is different from that of the adult and that it cannot be reached by verbal instruction during the first months. (Recall Piaget's similar conclusions.)

To facilitate such early development, Montessori directed her attention to the conditions of growth. Since our ability to categorize is one of the outstanding features of the human species, Montessori, by the use of sensorial materials, attempted to help children to form abstractions more readily and accurately. The materials, such as red rods to teach the idea of length, were designed to aid children to focus on a particular quality—length, width, height, or weight. There are two preconditions for the process of abstraction: first, concrete examples must be perfectly clear; second, children must have achieved a certain mental maturity. The process of abstraction is particularly individual; all we can do is to help youngsters by providing suitably helpful materials. The idea or the abstract notion that we wish children to attain must be inherent in these materials. Children working with the concrete are able to act on it and finally determine the general principle involved. Thus there is an interdependence between the purely intellectual and the purely material that is characteristic of all humans, especially children.

A Montessori school

The Sensitive Periods. Perhaps the best known of Montessori's ideas is that of sensitive periods, another expression of the concept of critical periods. (Recall Scott's work in preceding chapters.) Montessori considered a sensitive period to be a time of special sensitivity in the development of the individual. During each of these periods, children manifest special capacities that encourage them to develop physical and psychological prowess by the acquisition of appropriate functions. One of the earliest and most vital of these periods is concerned with the attainment of language. To understand more graphically what language implies, picture yourself trying to learn German, Russian, or Swahili. Most of the readers of this book are relatively young, yet you will still have difficulty, usually to the extent that you will always be a foreigner in that tongue.

But human infants, unskilled and untutored, learn to speak their native tongue fluently and almost grammatically correct. How? This is the great secret and, as we have seen, some of our leading theorists have devoted large parts of their lives to solving the riddle. The secret persists, however, and all we can say with certitude is that at a certain time of life, humans have a definite aptitude for language acquisition.

If we link this phenomenon to the concept of sensitive periods, it explains the difficulty that an adult has in mastering a new language. The sensitive period for language attainment is over, never to reappear. The sensitive period for language attainment in children is present before the child actually begins to speak. Since this is such an exceedingly intricate and complex task, the sensitive period for language lasts longer than any other.

Montessori (1967) stated that language development does not appear slowly and smoothly, but just the opposite. It is a truly explosive happening that occurs, not produced by external stimulation, but spontaneously. All children, at a particular period in life, burst forth with a number of words, all perfectly pronounced. Within three months, they easily use varied forms of nouns, suffixes, prefixes, and verbs. This occurs at the end of the second year for the average child. But the process does not terminate at the end of two years. Complex sentences, tense, mood, and clauses are also conquered. Beyond the age of two and a half, a new period of language development appears that lasts until age five or six. During this time, children extend their vocabularies and perfect their grammar.

Montessori has designated several sensitive periods (for language, order, small objects, good manners, social development, moral development, and rational thinking). If we accept Montessori's thinking and link it with our previous work on critical periods, one fact emerges clearly: once a sensitive or critical period has passed, the optimum time for learning is lost. This is not to say that experiences critical to that period will never be learned, but the learning will be much more difficult than if it had occurred at the optimum time.

The school, as a great force in the socialization process, captures youngsters for a considerable period of time at a sensitive moment in development. As such it is in a unique position to influence the direction of that development, which it does in responding to society's dictates. That is, societal conditions largely determine the kinds of schools that a community sponsors.

Within the confines of the school, peers and teachers become specific shapers of development, both serving different, but vital, roles. Youngsters in modern societies must also reckon with another powerful force, one that frequently frustrates the school's objectives: television. Its effect—both prosocial and antisocial—is one that generates considerable heat and little light.

Finally, as stated frequently in this section, family, school, and society are all agents of the socialization process, which is clearly evident in recent events. As society encourages women's self-fulfillment, more women work; children require care; preschool programs (daycare, nursery) flourish. But as they do, an encouraging trend is apparent: these new programs are more specifically designed to meet the needs of children, not only of parents. They are becoming more responsive by becoming more age-specific and more aware of developmental data.

SUMMARY

A changing school population has dictated significant alternatives in the American educational system.

Mainstreaming is a concept whose humane intent is laudatory, but whose attainment presents difficult, but surmountable, challenges.

Peer influence on development is now reckoned as one of the major forces affecting children.

Teachers occupy the sensitive position of "significant others" in children's development; as such they possess unique opportunities to further healthy growth.

There are various interpretations of learning, but learning itself is marked by certain notable characteristics.

Television, with its tremendous visual appeal, is one of the school's great competitors for children's time and attention. The consequences of extensive viewing remain a controversial issue.

Readiness, which is essentially a developmental concept, determines the academic success or failure of children and thus should be analyzed carefully so that material matches motivation.

The Montessori method is an excellent example of translating developmental theory into educational practice.

SUGGESTED READINGS

BRUNER, JEROME. *The Process of Education.* Cambridge, Massachusetts: Harvard University Press, 1960. A fascinating and challenging book, offering enjoyable reading. It is brief and simply written.

BUTTS, R. R. and LAWRENCE CREMIN. *A History of Education in American Cultures.* New York: Holt, Rinehart, and Winston, 1953. An excellent, comprehensive review of the history of American education.

COMSTOCK, GEORGE et al. *Television and Human Behavior.* New York: Columbia University Press, 1978. A wide-ranging study of television's impact presenting an excellent analysis of its prosocial and antisocial aspects.

HILGARD, ERNEST and GORDON BOWER. *Theories of Learning.* Englewood Cliffs, N.J.: Prentice-Hall, 1975. A classic in its field, this text is an excellent overview of the entire subject of learning theory.

MONTESSORI, MARIA. *The Montessori Method.* New York: Schocken Books, 1964. A good reference that combines theory and practice.

CHAPTER 14
SOCIETY'S INFLUENCE

CHAPTER HIGHLIGHTS

Topics

Does Society Really Influence?
a. The Rios Family
b. Two Worlds of Childhood
c. A Preindustrial Community
d. Culture and Neonatal Development

A Changing Society
a. Social Indicators—Facts and Figures
b. The Achieving Society

The Socialization Process
a. A Descriptive Analysis
b. Developmental Changes
c. Influences on Socialization
d. Principles of Socialization

Social Class Differences
a. A Descriptive Analysis
b. Specific Class Differences
c. Like It Is in the Alley
d. Children of Affluence

Children and Society
a. Children and the Courts
b. Child Abuse

People

T. Berry Brazelton
Urie Bronfenbrenner
James Coleman
Robert Coles
C. Henry Kempe
Ruth S. Kempe
Oscar Lewis
David McClelland
J. Paul Scott

Special Topics

Life Expectancy—A Matter of 50 Doublings?
Children's Literature and Socialization
The Child Killers

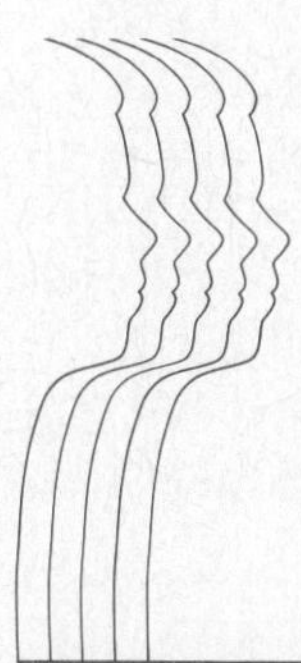

We are all products of some society; some of us accept its traditional ideas and values and live comfortably within their limits, making no strenuous efforts to modify or destroy them. Others, for whatever reasons, react against the old ways and search for means to restructure the rules and regulations of society. It is not our purpose here to analyze these forces and search for their roots in the individual, in the family, or in the society. Our intent is simple: to demonstrate that society exerts an enormous influence on development and that an individual's manner of responding to that society does much to shape the direction of development.

Leiderman, Tulkin, and Rosenfeld (1977, p. 1), examining cultural influences in infant development, state:

> The human environment is inescapably social. From the moment of birth, human infants are dependent on others for biological survival. Psychologically, their cognitive, social, and emotional development is also predicated on human interaction. Adult independence and self-sufficiency are achieved gradually through years of contact and interaction with others. Thus, despite the sometimes heroic efforts of children to resist the pressures of family and society, the process of acculturation continues generation after generation. This process, commonly termed socialization by behavioral scientists, is actually a form of adaptation, since for those who become acceptably socialized there are physical, economic, and psychological rewards and benefits; for those who do not, there can be ostracism, exile, imprisonment, institutionalization, or even death.

This powerful statement succinctly summarizes the enormous influence that any society exerts on its developing members. If a society is to survive, children must become mature, responsible adults; to ensure successful completion of this task, a society establishes certain institutions through which most, if not all, children must pass. We have seen the socializing influence of both family and school, and while there is variety within each, there are decided limitations on the expression of variations. Society determines these limits, and as the above quote implies, those who resist socializing influences inevitably experience difficulties in adapting. The pattern, then, is clear: while individual differences may be tolerated, even encouraged, by a society, there are boundaries; those who push beyond them and refuse to conform to societal expectations are somehow punished by that society. As Leiderman and his colleagues indicate, that punishment may range from mild social isolation to confinement or even death.

Since different times and different conditions demand different methods to ensure the production of mature citizens, a society will afford status to different procedures. For example, our society is now concerned about the duration of schooling. Since schooling has been a valued method of preparing for constructive citizenship, the vast majority of young people feel compelled to obtain some degree of formal education. As economic opportunities for educated youth lag behind the numbers seeking positions commensurate with their schooling, society has subtly shifted status to occupations not requiring higher education.

Coleman (1974), reflecting these views, argues that today's youth need two types of experiences: those that guarantee the acquisition of adequate personal skills, and those that provide opportunities for responsibilities affecting other persons. The specific objectives of both categories are as follows:

1. *Personal Skills*

a. Those cognitive and noncognitive skills necessary for economic independence and occupational opportunities.

b. The skills necessary for the effective management of one's own affairs. Coleman believes that modern youth have had little opportunity for self-management and thus suffer shock upon leaving the sheltered educational environment and facing the responsibility of personal decision.

c. The skills necessary to be consumers not only of material goods, but also of the cultural riches of civilization.

d. The capability to engage in intense, concentrated involvement in an activity. Here Coleman is arguing for the development of inner motivation, that internal drive that focuses attention and provides meaning to life.

2. *Responsibilities for Others*

a. The experience of interacting with those differing in social class, subculture, and age.

b. The experience of having others dependent on one's actions. This has become an increasing concern in our society; youngsters mature without having cared for babies or children, helped the ill, or served in any caring capacity.

c. The involvement in interdependent activities directed toward collective goals. Youth can enhance personal growth by working with others, sometimes guiding, sometimes following. In today's society, youth are usually told what to do and seldom experience the consequences of their own decisions.

By combining these two categories, and designing activities that urge youngsters toward these objectives, it should be possible to encourage positive participation in society, while simultaneously aiding youth to establish a sense of identity and to further self-esteem.

Coleman's discussion is a good example of societal expectations of its youth and suggested means for fulfilling these expectations. But as we continue to analyze society's influence throughout this chapter, it is well to remember that society, or "the environment," consists of many different parts. For simplicity, our study of the human socialization process has included the family, school, and society. Bronfenbrenner (1979) has divided a child's ecological environment into the following systems.

1. *The Microsystem* refers to the immediate setting. The complex interrelationships of the microsystems are most strikingly seen in the home and classroom.

2. *The Mesosystem* refers to the interrelationship between settings in which the child actually participates. The link that exists *between* home and school is a good example.

3. *The Exosystem* refers to settings in which the child is not present. For example, parental employment strongly affects a child's development.

4. *The Macrosystem* refers to the organizational blueprint of a particular society. For example, a society's economy at any moment is a potent influence on development.

Finally, as youngsters move throughout these systems, abrupt changes occur, which Bronfenbrenner calls *ecological transitions* and which are extremely significant for development. For example, the birth of a baby, entering school, employment, and marriage drastically alter the relationships within and across the various systems.

Bronfenbrenner's model enables us to examine, more critically than previously, the forces that shape development—the ecology of human development. It also highlights the interactive theme of our work. Forces do not act upon children in an isolated manner; they interact one with another to produce their effects. Children also shape the forces that surround them. Consequently, unique individuals, responding uniquely to the interactive forces surrounding them, produce unique patterns of development.

To assess the significance of society in a child's development, we must first demonstrate that society is the potent force that we believe. A return visit to the Rios family should remove any lingering doubts. And as a chart for the remainder of the chapter, we will again present some pertinent facts about our society and then examine what is known as the socialization process; that is, how humans assume the veneer of civilization that enables them to interact as social beings with other social beings. Closely allied to this concept is the impact of social class on development, an impact that is all too real and often too permanent.

Certain aspects of our society such as peer influence and television demand separate scrutiny as powerful socializing agents, as does the strange and tragic phenomenon of child abuse. Finally, we shall address the question of public policy toward children.

But before we discuss these topics, we must first demonstrate that society does indeed influence development.

DOES SOCIETY REALLY INFLUENCE?

Before we begin any detailed analysis of the societal role, it would be well to illustrate that society truly influences development and that there are many who feel that society, or the state, should intervene even more directly during those critical years. These are two quite different issues, since one, society's influence, comes naturally. The mere existence of a society means that the needs, values, beliefs, and security of the total community will have some effect on the individual's development. The other, direct societal control, means that the state intervenes to specify who will become parents, how the child will develop, and what the child will become. Currently, there is heated controversy between those who believe in the need for state supervised early childhood education and those who feel that it should remain a parental function. But before we begin our analysis of these issues, however, let us examine how different societies influence development. Another visit to the colorful Rios family is a good beginning.

A Return Visit to the Rios Family

The Rios family exemplifies the culture of poverty. Lewis (1965) states that throughout recorded history, there have always been two opposing views of the poor. Some consider them to be superior beings who are virtuous, honest, upright, and happy. Others see them as evil, violent, sordid, and criminal. It requires little imagination to recognize both these beliefs in today's controversy concerning the poor. Lewis observes that the confusion results from the failure to distinguish between poverty per se and the culture of poverty; there is a tendency to focus on the individual instead of the group. The author feels that to understand poverty we should think of it as a subculture, with its own structure and rationale, which then becomes a way of life passed down from generation to generation. Consequently, the culture of poverty is not only a matter of economic deprivation, but also a positive concept that provides some rewards without which the poor could hardly exist.

The culture of poverty flourishes in societies having the following characteristics.

1. A cash economy, wage labor, and production for profit.

2. A persistently high rate of unemployment, especially for the unskilled.

3. Low wages.

4. The failure to provide social, political, and economic organization for the low income group.

5. A bilateral kinship system where descent is traced through both males and females.

6. A dominant class whose values reflect both the accumulation of wealth and property and upward mobility and who blame poverty on personal inadequacy or inferiority (Lewis, 1965, pp. xliii–xliv).

In such a society there evolves a culture of poverty that is both an adjustment and a reaction to the loser's position. Otherwise, how could anyone trapped in the horrors of the slum face the dawn of each new day? The lifestyle of a member of the culture of poverty usually represents an attempt to solve problems that remain either insoluble or ignored by society's institutions.

Lewis makes the cogent observation that the culture of poverty is not merely an adaptation to the standards of the total society. As a way of life, it tends to perpetuate itself. For example, in *La Vida,* Lewis describes the behavioral patterns of four generations of the Rios family. By the time slum children are six or seven, they have absorbed the basic values and attitudes of their subculture and thus remain totally ill equipped to seize any advantages that might be available to them. (This conclusion should not surprise us; all of our comments about sensitive periods and the effects of the early years substantiate Lewis's observations.) In a changing society, fewer opportunities beckon to the members of such a subculture. These are the people at the bottom rung of the social ladder. Any geographical shift is likely only to worsen their status. So rural workers with no property who migrate to the cities in search of the better life speedily develop a new form of the culture of poverty.

Lewis (1965, pp. xlv–lvii) concludes his analysis identifying certain additional characteristics of the culture of poverty.

1. *The lack of any effective participation and integration of the poor in the major institutions of society.* The reasons for such a lack of participation are fairly simple to isolate, if not remedy. Low wages and persistent unemployment cause low income, little or no property, and a constant need for cash. All of these combine to work against any effective participation in the institutions that facilitate upward mobility. A need for money means that children will leave school early, and thus will lack the skills that society values in its managerial class. They usually do not join a union, and consequently lack the power of this force behind them. They are seldom members of a political party and hence have no avenue toward this part of the power structure.

As a result, society effectively bars the poor from upward movement and they begin to manifest certain other, fairly common traits: mistrust of society's powerful institutions, hatred of the police (whom they consider their oppressors), and even a dislike of their church, which they frequently feel is only one more of society's arms designated to crush them. Consequently, they become an extremely volatile sector of society that usually is more than willing to join in attacks on the status quo.

2. *A lack of community organization.* Lewis goes so far as to state that most primitive people have achieved a higher level of sociocultural organization than modern slum residents. However, children develop a feeling of camaraderie, a sense of "we'll take care of ourselves" that effectively bars any outsiders from participating. A slum population similar in ethnic, racial, linguistic, and familial traits often produces an approximation of a local, relatively independent, community.

3. *A lack of real childhood for the children of poverty.* Children mature rapidly under these conditions and become acquainted at an early age with sex. Many are members of single-mother families.

Two Worlds of Childhood

In one of the most famous analyses of society's influence on development, Bronfenbrenner (1970) has contrasted the Soviet Union and the United States. Asking the question, "How shall we judge the worth of a society?" Bronfenbrenner suggests that along with birth rates, crime rates, and the gross national product, we should examine, in each society, the concern of one generation for another.

In the Soviet society, the following practices seem to be significant.

1. Russian infants receive considerably more physical contact than American youngsters. Breast feeding is customary, and holding, hugging, and kissing occurs more frequently than with American infants. Yet Russian adults restrict infant mobility much more than American adults, presumably to protect the children.

2. Russian adults have little hesitation in assuming parental roles; this applies to strangers, as well as relatives. Bronfenbrenner gives the example of a mother placing her infant in the lap of a stranger, who graciously receives the child. Adolescents exhibit the same behavior, so in a society where most adults are ready to assume some responsibility for children, youngsters have little difficulty in adjusting to nurseries or other forms of child care.

3. Accompanying adult affection is adult expectation of obedience and self-discipline. Children are expected not only to obey adults and parents but also to respect them. Obedience leads to self-discipline, and self-discipline leads to an independence that is reconciled to the laws of living in Soviet society. If

disobedience necessitates punishment, Soviet authorities recommend the withdrawal of affection, a common Russian technique.

4. Children's collectives are a common feature of Russian society, and while they care for a minority of Russian children (Bronfenbrenner estimates that ten percent of Soviet youngsters under two years of age are enrolled in public nurseries), they are an important part of the Russian system. These children quickly learn the experience of collective living, which at this age emphasizes the training of sensorimotor functioning and the development of self-reliance.

5. Children enter a school at seven years and immediately encounter an emphasis on *vospitanie*, or character education, a term used for the encouragement of Communist morality. As Bronfenbrenner notes, each classroom is a unit of the Communist youth organization, each youngster is raised "in the collective, by the collective, and for the collective."

6. Finally, women are an extremely important aspect in a Russian youngster's life. There is a larger number of women in the population (about 20,000,000 more), most teachers are female, and women achieve more "status" positions than those in many other countries. These facts, coupled with the affectionate, yet constricting, mother-child relationship tend to support the conclusion that Soviet youngsters are more dependent and conforming than American children. (They also tend to be less aggressive, rebellious, and antiadult than their American counterparts.)

In analyzing the world of the American child, Bronfenbrenner discusses the issues that have occupied us since page one: a child's biological potential, attachment, dependency, peers, schools, television. He is particularly concerned about the fragmentation of America's life and its impact upon children, especially the phenomenon of segregation by age. He believes that if the trend continues, there will be increased alienation, indifference, and violence in youngsters from all social classes.

Bronfenbrenner (1970, p. 170) concludes his comparison by stating:

> If the Russians have gone too far in subjecting the child and his peer group to conformity to a single set of values imposed by the adult society, perhaps we have reached the point of diminishing returns in allowing excessive autonomy and in failing to utilize the constructive potential of the peer group in developing social responsibility and consideration for others. . . . What is called for is greater involvement of parents and other adults, in the lives of children, and conversely—a greater involvement of children in responsibility on behalf of their own family, community, and society at large.

A Preindustrial Community

Cravioto et al. (1969) have studied the growth and development of all children born during one year in a rural preindustrial community in the hot semihumid zone of Mexico. They concentrated on the conditions of the children at birth and on their physical and behavioral progress during the first month of life. The research orientation was purely ecological; thus, they derived as much information as possible about the physical environment, social conditions, health status, and patterns of child rearing. To maintain consistency, which often is difficult in an ecological study, they chose nutrition as their focus. Study after study has shown that because of the intimate association between nutritional status and income level, children with the greatest nutritional risk cluster mainly in the lowest social and economic levels.

This segment of any population differs from the remainder of the people not only in nutritional risk, but also in poor housing, higher infection, lower educational achievement, greater attachment to more primitive child-bearing practices, and in general, circumstances less conducive to the development of potential. Perhaps most serious of all, the results of these environmental conditions may pass from one generation to another and become a facsimile of hereditary processes.

The main occupation of the villagers was agriculture, with a relatively small amount of people scattered throughout other pursuits as laborers, masons, carpenters, shopkeepers, or teachers. The group also included one architect, one engineer, and two doctors who served the village and surrounding communities.

Cravioto et al. note that the village was in a slow state of transition from its strict dependence on agriculture of thirty years ago. Consequently, transportation had improved and there had been a greater interaction between the people of the village and adjacent centers. Nevertheless, we can conclude from the above data that the village remained primarily preindustrial.

The authors state that given these data, the opportunities for physical or mental growth were inevitably associated with social status and the variables attached to it. But to say that social status alone was responsible for the developmental outcomes masks many of the interactions. For example, the undeniable link between depressed social status and undesirable developmental outcomes needs more than a statement that one causes the other. Analysis should seek those other influences that affect physical, sexual, emotional, and mental outcomes.

Malnutrition, for example, is associated with many social variables that are themselves capable of producing developmental difficulties. Illiteracy, low income, retarded learning, poor housing, and crowded living conditions can all be found in environments that are characterized by childhood malnutrition. Malnutrition, plus these other variables that produce poor development, causes considerable frustration in estimating the precise source of any developmental deficit.

As a result of their investigations, the authors determined that the best way to understand these complicated interactions was to take the mother as the ecological focus. The condition of the child at birth, and gains after birth, seem to be significantly related to the biological condition of the mother. Since the physiological state of the mother varies according to her social status, both of these conditions (mother's health and environmental aspects) are linked to fetal and neonatal growth. The authors (1969, p. 60) stress that the social elements act directly on the infant, but are indirectly associated with growth and development because of their influence on the mother's biological fitness. Taller and heavier women produced taller and heavier babies, and this fact was significantly related to higher incomes, better housing, and smaller families. These women were cleaner and more careful of their personal hygiene; thus, they themselves were healthier and in turn provided a healthier atmosphere for the children they were carrying.

Smaller children were more representative of the lower economic levels and were subjected to far more negative environmental forces. Women from these social strata produced smaller babies at a low birth weight who grew slowly during the first month of life. That is, the environmental conditions that influenced the mother as a child affected her own child.

Culture and Neonatal Development

Lester and Brazelton (1980) state that most cultures select and preserve adaptive behaviors that are appropriate for the goals of that culture. Recognizing the individual differences that are present at birth, the authors believe that the infant is both a shaper of and shaped by cultural expectations. Working with African neonates, they observed the effects of the mothers' expectations of their youngsters. Because of poor nutrition, the youngsters were initially depleted and dehydrated, but the mothers expected that their children would respond well to vigorous handling. They simply ignored their limp behavior and treated them as if they were healthily responsive. The authors state that after hydration and feedings, *the babies became rapidly responsive.* They summarized their personal reactions as follows:

> We began to wonder whether the potential for this kind of motor and responsive development was communicated in some way to the mother who then acted upon and facilitated the infant's organization, and if her experience with other babies in the culture led her to expect recovery so that she handled him accordingly. This was our first experience with maternal expectations not set by the neonate himself, and we were impressed that previous culture experience of the mothers could have overridden the mother's personal experience with her baby and shape her reactions to him in such a significant and effective way. (1980, p. 82)

In a study of Indian youngsters from the highlands of Southern Mexico, the authors report different neonatal responses, but which again reflected cultural expectations. The youngsters experienced prenatal subclinical malnutrition, infection, and mild hypoxia (oxygen deficiency), all of which contribute to quiet, passive, although alert, newborn behavior. The caretaking practices are passive, thus helping the infants to adapt to difficult environmental conditions. The youngsters are not sickly, but simply small.

The mother's delivery is natural, without drugs. There is considerable and constant emotional support. From birth, the infant's needs are anticipated, so there is no pattern of frustration and gratification, which would lead to self-activity and independence. Rather, the authors describe an interplay between quiet nonmotoric infants and a relatively passive environment that ultimately produces quiet, imitative children who display the conforming adult behavior needed for viability in a difficult environment. The authors conclude:

> Culture then becomes a way of broadening our perspective on underlying processes of development and provides a matrix within which we can learn about and understand the adaptive capacities and strategies of infants. It is another window that enlarges our vista upon the range and variability of forms of adaptation and enables us to expand our basic principles and understanding of the processes of organization and development. Culture and biology are as inseparable as heredity and environment: each is the expression of the other, and together they extend the potential of human experience. (1980, p. 169)

After examining these illustrations of both primitive and industrial societies, it is difficult to ignore the potential of society's influence upon development. Perhaps, however, you will conclude that the products of both of these systems are more alike than they are different, since almost all youngsters experience physical deficits and academic retardation, and acquire a personal toughness and craftiness that enables them to survive against different but often overwhelming odds. Regardless of your conclusions, there can be little doubt about society's impact.

DISCUSSION QUESTIONS

1. Do you agree with the concerns of Coleman and others who believe that our society has misguided development by removing from children any responsibility for the care of others? If you agree, what specifically would you suggest? Should there be programs in the schools, in the home, or in various community agencies? Who would staff them? How would you pay for them?
2. Can you suggest other examples that illustrate Bronfenbrenner's system analysis of developmental influences? Explain the significance for development of the relationships within and between systems. Have you experienced ecological transitions that you remember? How important were they in your life? Did they affect your development?
3. What does Lewis mean by his statement that the poverty of culture contributes to the culture of poverty? What does this imply for children, family, school, opportunities, and future?
4. Were you convinced of society's influence on development by the examples presented? How realistic is it to assume that different societies produce different developmental outcomes? What does your answer suggest about the interaction of heredity and environment?
5. From your classwork and text reading, if you were to specify age differences between a Russian and American youngster from birth, what would be some of these differences? For example, would three-year-olds differ cognitively, socially, morally, emotionally?
6. Comment on Brazelton's work and the striking results that cultural expectations produce. Is this characteristic of all societies? What are some expectations for American infants and what are the results of these expectations?

A CHANGING SOCIETY

There seems little doubt that society, acting upon a child's unique potential, exercises a decided influence upon development. As societies change, then, we may anticipate changes in the developmental pattern. For example, the statistical data in the family chapter concerning the increase in female heads-of-families strongly suggest the need for a national daycare policy. Consequently, youngsters placed in these programs at an early age may well exhibit different characteristics, such as less fear of strangers, better adaptation to strange locations, or greater imitability.

Before we can draw conclusions, however, we must identify the features of our society. Therefore, we shall follow the same procedure as in the family chapter.

What Are the Facts?

Ethnic and Racial Diversity. There has been a strong belief that much of the vitality and creativity that has marked American society is due to the rich cultural traditions brought here by our immigrant population. The ethnic and racial diversity they have contributed has altered society in ways that could not help but shape the developmental path of American children. For example, mere exposure to cultural differences alerts youngsters to their existence. The great wave of Italian immigrants reached this country during the first forty years of this century; the number of German immigrants increased sharply following World War II. Recently there has been an influx of individuals of Spanish origin.

Changing population patterns inevitably produce social changes. Neighborhoods change; local economies change to meet the demands of a new group; churches feel the change and must meet the demands of different congregations; support systems must help the new population until they become established; and schools must move to meet new needs, such as language and reading difficulties. Particularly interesting is the changing occupational distribution of the new immigrants. During the first two decades of the twentieth century, the great majority of the new immigrants were laborers and only about one percent were professional workers. In 1970, only about twelve percent of the immigrants were laborers, and nearly thirty percent were professional or technical workers.

Although the characteristics of an immigrant population may change, persistent problems plague any such group. Prejudice and discrimination follow these groups and raise many of the issues that American blacks have fought to overcome. For example, almost all societies tend to judge individuals by the color of their skin and relegate those of other races to lower occupational levels than their skills may warrant. Many still interpret language difficulty as a sign of mental retardation. This becomes a trial for children and may haunt them throughout their lives. Careless labeling categorizes a child, and not only is it difficult to cast off the label, but a child may begin to exhibit the behavioral characteristics of the category, those of the slow learner, learning disabled, or mildly mentally retarded.

An immigrant population, while encountering both hope and frustration in their dreams and desires for a new and better life, themselves leave an indelible mark on society. Our society has been, is, and probably will continue to be, marked by change due to immigration.

Public Institutions. The confidence that Americans feel in their leaders raises some troublesome questions. Figure 14.1 illustrates the respondents' attitudes toward leaders of various institutions.

It is a revealing chart. Those representing medicine and science seemed to retain the highest favor among the people, while those representing television, the federal government, and labor instilled "hardly any confidence." Public confidence both in the executive and legislative branches of government slumped sharply in 1974 and has remained low.

Note the fluctuating pattern representing public reaction to education. As favorable public opinion increased, the atmosphere within

FIGURE 14.1. Confidence in Leaders of Specified Institutions: 1973–1980.

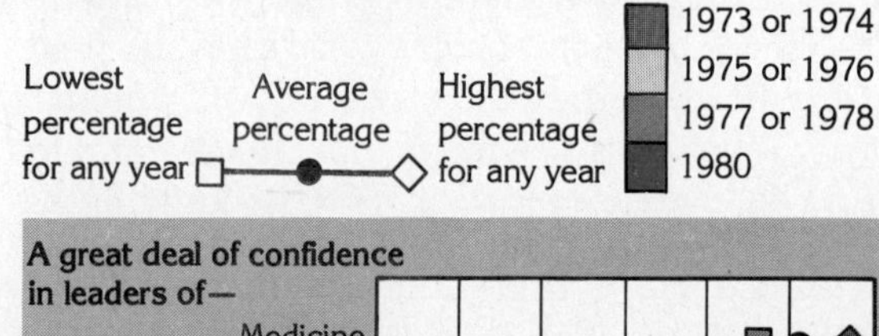

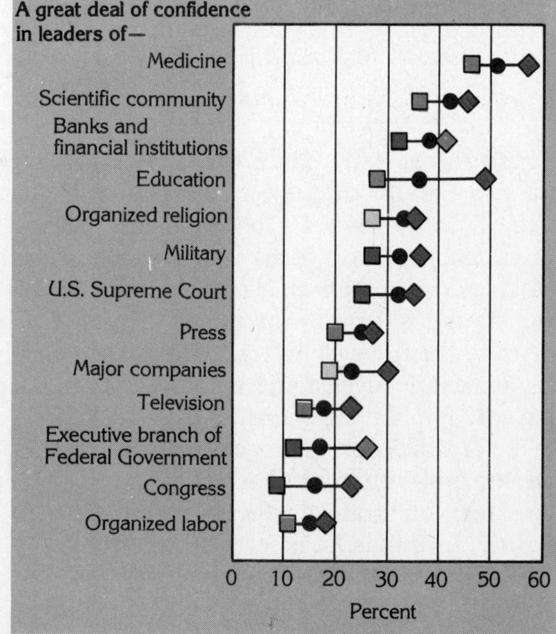

Source: *Social Indicators*, III. Washington, D.C., U.S. Department of Commerce, December, 1980.

the school was changing. For example, recent Gallup polls show a leveling of public concern about school discipline; Gallup believes that 1976 may represent a turning point in the public's attitude toward the schools (Travers, 1979). This changed attitude accompanied an educational shift toward more traditional values and stricter codes of conduct in the schools.

The banks have maintained public confidence through economically difficult days, while simultaneously the major American corporations have lost public confidence and organized labor has shown a precipitous decline. That these social indicators have developmental consequences is seen in the shifting educational values. As the educational atmosphere changes, youngsters at the earliest levels will experience changed expectations. Whether these are behavioral, which seems likely, or curricular, which seems certain, youngsters will differ from their counterparts of a decade ago when they leave school.

Life Expectancy and Mortality. Figures 14.2 and 14.3 illustrate perhaps the most dramatic impact of society on development: life and death.

These figures speak for themselves. The remarkable increase in life expectancy leaps out at the reader. What is even more remarkable is the added statistic that if a female reaches sixty-five years, she has an excellent chance of living to eighty-five; if a male reaches sixty-five, he has an excellent chance of living until eighty. As the birth rate dips and life expectancy increases, our society will become steadily older. Better living conditions, nutrition, and medicine have produced tangible developmental results. What is fas-

FIGURE 14.2. Life Expectancy at Birth, by Race and Sex: 1900–1977.

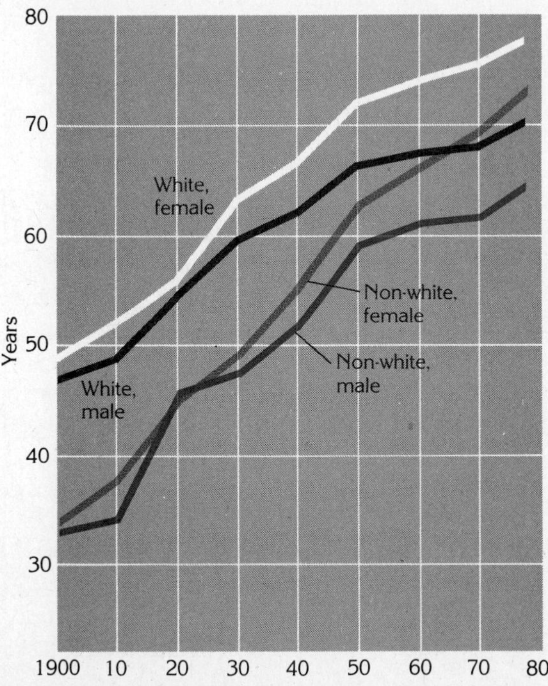

Source: *Social Indicators,* III. Washington, D.C., U.S. Department of Commerce, December, 1980.

FIGURE 14.3. Infant Mortality Rates, by Race: 1960–1977.

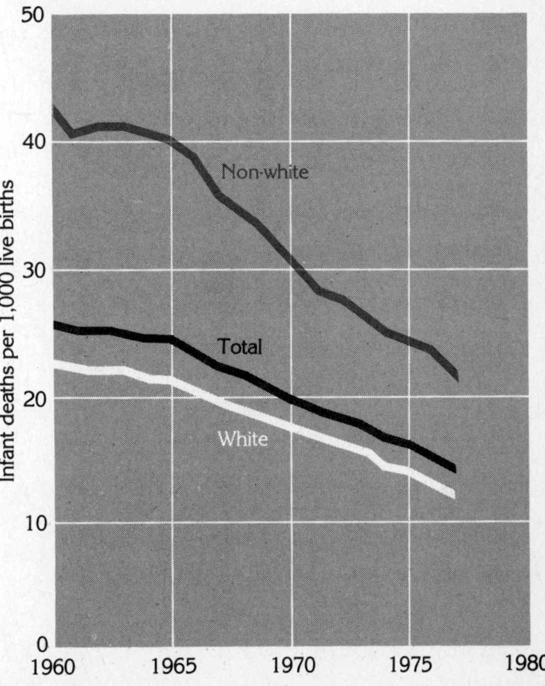

Source: *Social Indicators,* III., Washington, D.C., U.S. Department of Commerce, December, 1980.

cinating is that life expectancy still has not surpassed the traditional "four score and ten"; what has happened is that fewer die at earlier ages, as shown in Figure 14.3. Perhaps we can offer no more vivid evidence than these two figures that society influences development.

LIFE EXPECTANCY—A MATTER OF FIFTY DOUBLINGS?

Leonard Hayflick (1980), in a fascinating account of the aging process, states that while life expectation has changed, people still live the proverbial "four score and ten" years. Scientific advances have permitted more people to reach their life potential. What causes increased vulnerability as individuals age? With the exception of nerve cells and some muscle cells, the vast network of human cells have experienced a cycle of death and replacement. Replacement cells, however, do not maintain the age of the organism. *Aging refers not to individual cells, but to cell lineages.*

Hayflick and his colleagues discovered that normal human cells divide many times, slowly stop dividing, and eventually perish. Hayflick believes that aging is an innate property of cells. His experimental technique was fairly simple. Subjecting embryonic lung tissue to digestive enzymes, he was able to separate the tissue into millions of individual cells. The cells were then placed in a bottle containing a nutrient solution and kept at body temperature. They began to divide, and after about one week the surface of the culture was covered by a layer one cell thick. To facilitate cell division, the cells were then removed from the initial container and distributed among two other culture bottles containing fresh nutrient. By the time these two containers were filled, the cells had doubled in number. The ability of Hayflick's culture to divide was limited to fifty population doublings.

Thinking that experimental error might have caused this effect, the investigator mixed female cells that were ten population doublings old with male cells that were forty population doublings old. After twenty additional population doublings, the investigators found only female cells present. The researchers next froze cells taken from a human embryo and found that the cells had a remarkable memory: if they froze at the twentieth population doubling, upon thawing, the cells completed thirty more doublings. One human cell strain was frozen for thirteen years and still retained this memory upon thawing.

Thus, normal human cells have a limited capacity to divide. It is possible, however, to produce "immortal" cells by treating them with the cancer causing monkey virus SV40. One human cell line (called Hela) has been in culture and dividing continuously since 1952. These abnormal cells cause tumors when injected into laboratory animals.

Studies done with older human cells (taken at autopsy from adults aged twenty to eighty-seven) showed that the cells doubled from fourteen to twenty-nine times—always significantly lower than the fifty population doublings of embryonic tissue. If there is, indeed, a "death clock" ticking inside us, the author suggests that its normal timing may eventually be found in the relationship between the life span of the species and the capacity of its cells to divide.

Occupational Patterns. Table 14.1 illustrates changing occupational patterns that have clear developmental outcomes. For example, the number of female workers has increased from approximately twenty million to well over thirty-eight million during this period. Consequently, the number of employed mothers has also increased dramatically. Not only have the numbers changed, but the pattern of occupations has also changed. There have been significant increases in the number of professional-technical, clerical-sales and service positions, with corresponding declines among farmers and laborers. While the pattern holds true for both males and females, there has been a much greater shift from household work to clerical and sales jobs for women.

What are some developmental consequences of these societal changes? Again, as more women work, the need for substitute child care assumes pressing urgency. Our analysis of both family and society point

TABLE 14.1. Occupational Distribution of Employed Workers, by Sex and Race: 1958, 1968, and 1978

		Occupational distribution (percent)								
Year, sex, and race	Number employed (thousands)	Total	Profes-sional and technical workers	Managerial and adminis-trative workers	Sales workers	Clerical workers	Crafts workers	Other blue-collar workers	Service workers	Farm workers
1958										
Total	63,036	100.0	11.0	10.8	6.3	14.5	13.4	23.6	11.9	8.5
Male	42,423	100.0	10.4	13.6	5.7	6.9	19.4	27.4	6.4	10.4
Female	20,613	100.0	12.3	5.0	7.6	30.1	1.1	16.0	23.2	4.7
White	56,614	100.0	11.8	11.7	6.9	15.4	14.3	22.3	9.5	8.0
Black and other races	6,422	100.0	4.1	2.4	1.2	6.1	5.9	34.8	33.0	12.5
1968										
Total	75,920	100.0	13.6	10.2	6.1	16.9	13.2	23.1	12.4	4.6
Male	48,114	100.0	13.4	13.6	5.7	7.1	20.2	27.2	6.9	6.0
Female	27,807	100.0	13.9	4.5	6.9	33.8	1.1	15.8	21.8	2.1
White	67,751	100.0	14.3	11.1	6.6	17.5	13.8	21.7	10.4	4.5
Black and other races	8,169	100.0	7.8	2.8	1.9	11.8	8.0	34.4	28.3	4.9
1978										
Total	94,373	100.0	15.1	10.7	6.3	17.9	13.1	20.3	13.6	3.0
Male	55,491	100.0	14.7	14.0	5.9	6.2	21.1	25.3	8.7	4.1
Female	38,881	100.0	15.6	6.1	6.9	34.6	1.8	13.0	20.7	1.3
White	83,836	100.0	15.5	11.4	6.7	18.0	13.7	19.2	12.3	3.0
Black and other races	10,537	100.0	11.7	4.8	2.8	16.9	8.8	28.4	24.1	2.4

Source: U.S. Department of Labor, *1978 Employment and Training Report of the President,* tables A-15 and A-16, and *1979 Employment and Training Report of the President,* tables A-16 and A-17.

directly to this need, which is not likely to diminish, given the changing status of women. The combination of achievement, money, and personal satisfaction provided by a career is a powerful motivator that most women will find appealing.

There are other, more subtle implications in Figure 14.4. For example, the movement of women into higher occupational levels will also act to maintain a low, perhaps not even constant, birth rate. The impact on education is obvious. Also, given these statistical facts, will immigration quotas change? If we examine the educational implications more closely, the rise in service workers will influence schools, especially the curriculum. As more youngsters choose service careers, vocational programs will undoubtedly expand, and college preparatory programs, perhaps reflecting substantial increases in college tuition, may well decline. The cognitive, emotional, and social consequences of these changes are yet to be documented, but we can be certain that there will indeed be developmental outcomes.

The major contribution of married women to family income poses several questions. Whether from economic necessity or a need for self-fulfillment, once a married woman is committed to work, that commitment is usually long lasting. Before reentering the work force she has undoubtedly made provisions for child care; if subsequent problems arise—illness, separation or divorce—she has that much greater need for her earned income. These figures lend considerable support to the developmental conclusions we have reached throughout our analysis of family, school, and society.

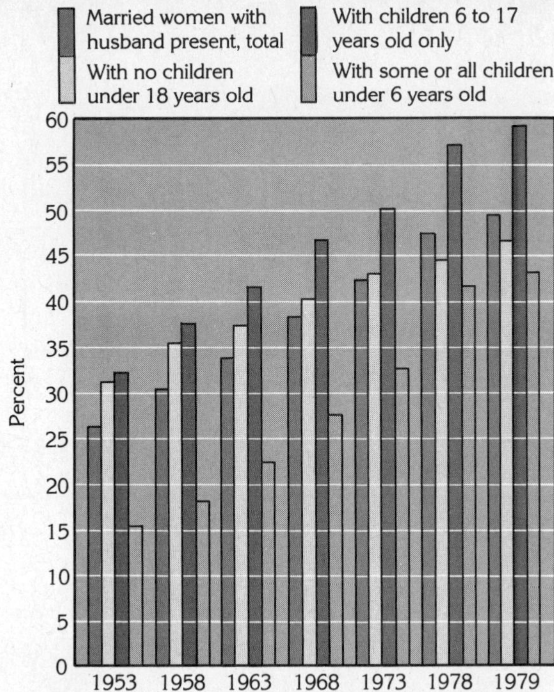

FIGURE 14.4. Married Women, Husband Present, in Labor Force, by Presence and Age of Children, Selected Years: 1953–1979.

Source: *Social Indicators*, III. Washington, D.C., U.S. Department of Commerce, December, 1980.

The Achieving Society

A constant theme throughout this discussion has been that of change, of movement toward the better life, which indicates emphasis on achievement. Regardless of any clamor concerning nonworkers and governmental support, most individuals are motivated to achieve and they likewise encourage their children to achieve. In a society where achievement is promoted and rewarded, its influence on individual development and societal conditions is tangible.

If achievement is indeed a critical aspect of development, and if it is possible to identify the level of a child's need for achievement, it may mean that adults should use certain teaching techniques for children with low achievement needs and other techniques for those with high achievement needs.

This is precisely what David McClelland (1969) has attempted to do: identify the level

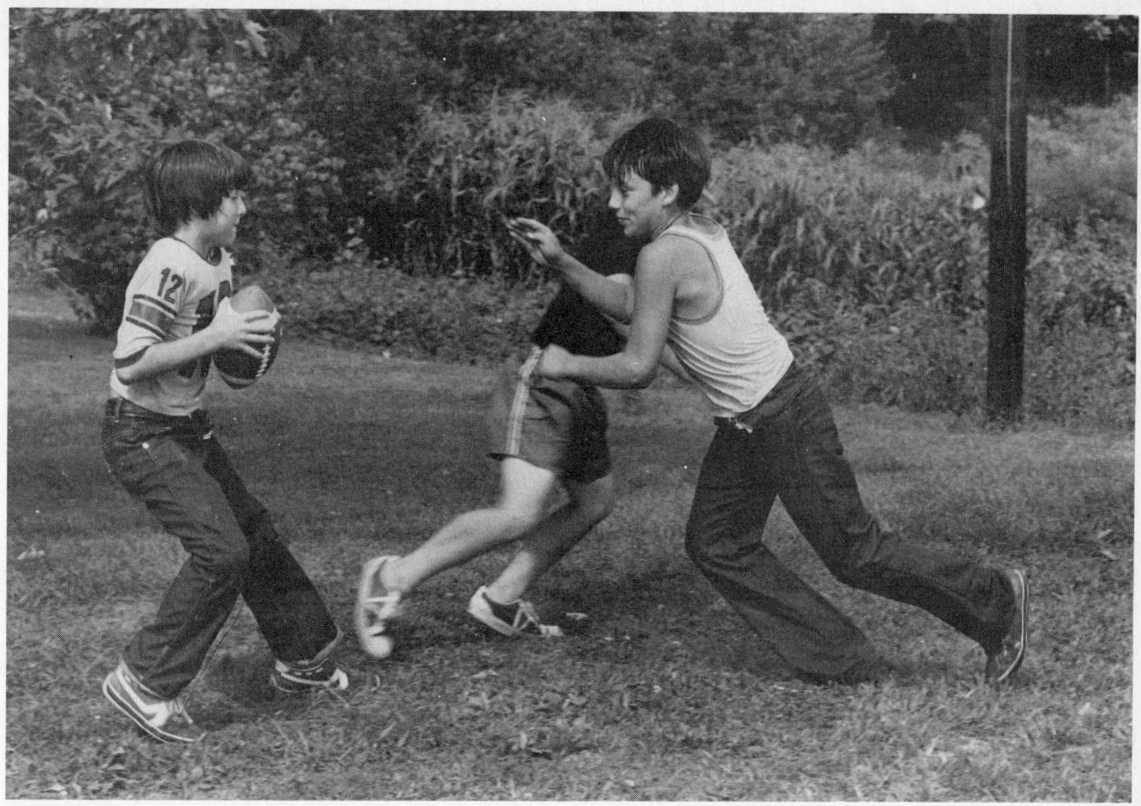

of need achievement and then apply the results for practical purposes. For example, children with high need for achievement (nAch) play differently than those with a lower level. They choose tasks in which they have a good chance of success, but do not reduce the odds so that there is no challenge to the game. Children with low nAch show no concern about the probability of success. They either ensure defeat or select some task that is actually no challenge at all. Knowing this, the adult can help youngsters make realistic assessments of the probability of their success with tasks that are suited to their abilities.

It is interesting that parents with a high achievement need do not automatically transmit it to their children. McClelland mentions a Japanese study that showed that the higher a mother's need for achievement, the lower the child's. Children whose families encourage independence seem to develop a high need for achievement. In another of McClelland's studies, small boys were blindfolded and asked to arrange irregular blocks with their left hands. The investigators, however, were more interested in the parents' behavior than the boys'. The parents of high-nAch boys consistently felt that their boys would build higher piles and gave a general kind of encouragement instead of giving specific orders. But the fathers of the low-nAch boys tended to give more specific orders.

Level of aspiration studies have also been done with children in order to determine if a willingness to take risks is associated with strength of achievement motives. Children tossed a ring at a peg, choosing whatever distance they wished to stand from the peg. The results showed that children strong in achievement motive took more shots from an intermediate distance than children weak in achievement motive did; they thus had a realistic chance of success, but the task still remained a challenge. Youngsters who stood too close or too far away had an instant excuse for failure, thus revealing their low need for achievement.

The anxious children tend to set their aspirations very high or very low, since anxiety is greatest when the task is of intermediate difficulty. Both of these unrealistic choices are protective, since they minimize the arousal of anxiety about failure. When the level chosen is too high, there is no shame of failure, because children then attempt the impossible. When the level of aspiration is too low, there is no anxiety about failure, because the probability of failure is remote.

McClelland next turned his attention to the societies that seemed to have achieved more than other nations and to the prediction of economic trends. McClelland claims that there is nothing mysterious about his work. He believes that the level of achievement imagery serves as a good indicator of an entire people's desire to progress. Men and women with high nAch will manifest economic advancement in spite of social structure or economic system.

But how can this be predicted? McClelland and his associates collected second to fourth grade readers from around the world and studied those published in 1925 and 1950. They randomly chose twenty-one stories from each country's readers and scored them much like the TAT (Thematic Apperception Test). Some of McClelland's results are shown in the following examples.

If the story's themes emphasized the pleasure of accomplishing a task, McClelland interpreted this as need for achievement (Figure 14.5).

If the theme dramatized the pleasure and value of working together, McClelland interpreted this as the affiliation need (Figure 14.6).

If the theme demonstrated leadership, McClelland viewed this as a need for power (Figure 14.7).

The results were amazing. In twenty-two nontropical countries from which 1925 readers had been collected, there was a 0.53 correlation between the nAch score and the rate of economic growth during the next twenty years. The 1950 books were excellent predictors of even a brief span of time: 1952–1958. Twenty countries scored above average in nAch, and thirteen of them grew very rapidly. Of nineteen low scores, only five grew rapidly. Thus three out of four losers were accurately identified. McClelland interpreted these results to mean that regardless of war and depression, the economic growth of most countries followed the level of its people's achievement need.

The achievement needs of countries such as France, Germany, and Russia were all low in 1925, but by the 1950s had risen sharply. England and Sweden showed a reverse trend. For the United States, nAch rose from 1830 until 1890, and then declined rapidly, until the 1950 level was about the same as that for 1850. McClelland feels that these results are substantiated by the nAch curve, which is almost identical with the number of patents issued by the U.S. Patent Office for one hundred and forty years. The peak of nAch seems to precede an economic peak by about fifty years. Communist countries such as Russia and Poland are now very high in nAch, and the achievment need of China is rising. In 1926 America was low in power motivation, but high in affiliation and achievement. By 1950, the power motive had moved up sharply, the affiliation motive was down, and nAch had slipped. McClelland speculates that nAch may have declined even further during the last twenty years.

FIGURE 14.5. Achievement Need.

FIGURE 14.6. Affiliation Need.

FIGURE 14.7. Power Need.

What does this mean for the improvement of any society, with the resultant impact on the development of its children? For a clue, let us turn to McClelland's work in India, where he attempted to train individuals in achievement motivation. His main goal was to make his trainees conscious of the images and activities associated with achievement. Initially, they took the TAT, *Thematic Apperception Test* (a personality test), and scored their own stories. They then rewrote the TAT stories until they scored much higher. This was done so that they could form a network of images that represented the motive; thus, they were shaping their own fantasies.

Next, they played a business game in which they set attainable goals and engaged in problem-solving activities. What were the results? The Indian business people who took the nAch training course started four times as many businesses, invested twice as much in new capital, and created more than twice as many new jobs as the control groups who received no training. All of this occurred within two years after the training courses, each of which lasted only ten days.

If there are consistent results when McClelland's work is applied to other nations, it may be helpful for combating poverty in underdeveloped nations. While there may be strong arguments that raising the standard of living does not necessarily improve all phases of development, it does, nevertheless, provide conditions favorable for the improvement of all aspects of development. Our goal and society's goal should be to better the condition of both children and adults. By understanding and utilizing the ideas of theorists such as McClelland, we may be able to improve society's influence on its children by providing better physical, intellectual emotional, and moral conditions for development.

DISCUSSION QUESTIONS

1. Population experts claim that one of the techniques a nation uses to offset a low fertility rate that may not reach the replacement level (births balancing deaths) is to increase immigrant quotas. What specific societal repercussions would follow such a decision? Expand on the discussion presented in this chapter.
2. When there is a decline in a people's confidence in their leaders, the impact is felt throughout a society. What are some specific developmental outcomes? Use psychological, educational, political, and financial categories to shape your answer.
3. The economic charts show a steady rise in family income but there are frequent references to the problems of the "children of affluence." What are some of these problems? Are they age related?
4. Alienation is a concern for any society. Do you think that it is a condition that will grow in intensity? Why? Will the next generation react similarly? Why? How will this affect children *now?*
5. How would you assess McClelland's work? Is it a realistic view of human motivation? Can you accept his societal conclusions drawn from his studies of children's readers? Why?

THE SOCIALIZATION PROCESS

We now face the difficult question of how children acquire characteristics necessary to function as social beings. If society influences development, then it must establish certain codes of conduct that are almost categories of behavior. Children, through the agencies of society (family, school, church, and organizations), gradually assume those behavioral traits that others have also acquired and that permit meaningful interactions with peers and adults. Thus the socialization process is the training or molding by which an individual is made a member of a particular society, that is, how an infant becomes a child and the child an adult. Continuity is provided, since the socializing process is directed by members of the same society, and thus traditions, customs, skills, and morals are passed from one generation to another. Socialization implies child rearing in its broadest interpretation: all the people around the child, not just the parents, participate in all those ways that change the infant into a member of a particular society.

A Descriptive Analysis

Farb (1978) summarizes the socialization process quite simply: humans must learn to be human. As children develop they interact with their environment, parents, siblings, peers, and individuals from all aspects of society, thus acquiring adaptive behavior. But socialization is not just "stamped in"; as we have repeatedly stressed, the adaptive process is as much a result of the child's uniqueness as it is society's shaping. Children react to societal influence in highly personal ways which preserve their singular personalities. Born with distinct temperaments, youngsters interact individually with their socializing agents, thus producing both the creativity needed to advance society and the conformity needed to maintain societal stability.

Although we usually relate socialization to childhood and adolescence, there are those who argue that the socialization process continues beyond adolescence, extending until death. If socialization represents adjustment, it is an adjustment to changing demands. We all leave school, find employment, usually marry, have children, have grandchildren, retire, and ultimately die. New roles appear with each change; thus, socialization as adjustment implies an ongoing process.

Developmental Changes. Since our concern is childhood, let us attempt to trace the early pattern, using the work of J. P. Scott (1968). Noting that social behavior is limited in the neonate, Scott believes that its most overt form is care soliciting, especially in the form of crying. The initial major signal that social behavior is present is the appearance of the social smile, which we have previously placed at six weeks. From six weeks until about eight or nine months, the infant is friendly and easy to approach. During this period attachments are formed, and by its end, stranger anxiety appears. Scott (1968, p. 38) designates this time as *the period of primary socialization.*

It is important to note that although the true social smile appears at six weeks, its precursors—the constant interaction between children and those surrounding them—have led to its emergence. As infants endeavor to organize these processes, they demonstrate certain overt behaviors at various times that enable us to link a tentative chronological age to the behavior. These are undoubtedly the culmination of the organization of underlying processes. Smiling seems to be one of these tangible events.

Once infants attain the period of primary socialization, the following periods all contribute to the socialization process. *The acquisition of mobility* enables a child to maintain contact with the mother; *the emotional tension of separation* signals attachment; *verbal communication* furthers the learning of desirable behaviors and attitudes. If humans need to learn to be human, then Scott's work vividly demonstrates the importance of the early years.

Long interested in critical or sensitive periods, Scott (1968, 1972) describes a situation in which he and his wife kept a newborn lamb in their house for ten days. The animal became quite attached to them, following them like Mary's little lamb. After ten days she was placed with other sheep but remained unresponsive to them, and three years later still remained aloof from the flock. The lamb had apparently become attached to humans during the critical period that would usually result in attachment to the flock.

This is a perfect example of a critical period: a brief duration during which little effort is required to produce a major and lasting effect. Following much the same procedure, Scott later repeated the experiment with a puppy. Since dogs are more immature at birth than lambs, the dog was kept with humans for nine weeks instead of ten days. The results were negative; the dog developed normally and there was no evidence of a critical period. He then compared dogs that had some human contact with those that had none. The results were dramatic: dogs reared without human contact seemed to become wild. The experiment was expanded; some newborn puppies had human contact at various times before returning to a "dog" environment. If the puppies were removed from the mother and other dogs during the first five weeks of life and exposed to humans, they developed normally; if they were not removed and exposed to humans until fourteen weeks, they became wild animals requiring confinement. So dogs manifested a critical period for establishing satisfactory contacts with humans, from about three to twelve weeks of age.

Scott states that critical periods always occur during times of rapid change or growth. The organism, animal or human, organizes its behavior, which quickly becomes stable. But once organized, the human being or animal resists reorganization of its behavior. Scott suggests that extending this reasoning implies that any period in life when a major new relationship is being formed is critical for determining the nature of that relationship. Since the early years are crowded with such developing relationships, any upset in these emerging associations is a disturbing emotional experience. As Scott states: (1968, p. 88)

> The results of early experience in the social environment are difficult to separate from those of later experience. The nature of an experience in early infancy may have relatively little effect in itself but nevertheless lead to a series of consequences whose effects are exerted over many years.

Rutter (1979), asking whether certain experiences must occur in the early years for normal social development to proceed, reaches much the same conclusion as Scott. Rutter interprets the work of Tizard and Rees with institutionalized children (discussed in Chapter Twelve) to mean that if key relationships are not formed during these early years, then later difficulties may appear. If you recall, the institutionalized youngsters in Tizard's study who were adopted formed close attachments to the adopting parents but many of them demonstrated exaggerated friendliness to strangers. They also showed the same kinds of problems as those who remained in the institutions. Rutter questions the possibility of normal social development if early bonding is lacking. He believes that the evidence clearly suggests a sensitive period for optimal early socialization.

Thus children learn to be human through the process of socialization, and their initial contacts in the process are those surrounding them. These first months are a time of rapid organization of processes and a time of major new relationships. Thus, Scott's criteria are not only present, but massively intensified. The social, cognitive, emotional, and physical aspects of socialization immediately exert their influence. As the socialization process continues from infancy, verbal elements assume significance in childhood, while peers are a dominant force in adolescence.

Finally, Scott (1972) emphasizes the interactive nature of socialization when he states that human biological nature prepares children for a wide range of complex social relationships. The result should be the ideal human being, one who develops diversified social relationships suited to individual needs and abilities, residing in the ideal human society that is based on these relationships.

Influence on Socialization

Reese and Lipsitt (1970) state that socialization is a class name for all the appropriate behaviors that children learn concerning other people, either directly or indirectly. To evaluate a youngster's socialization on any type of scale, we must know the accepted standards of behavior within that culture, the child's sex, the chronological, mental, and physical age, and the social class. For example, different societies accept different behavior; only by examination of the society can we discover just what behaviors are encouraged. We also know that there are sex role stereotypes that are extremely potent in the acquisition of approved behavior. A good illustration of this is the once prevalent disdain in America of men who cry. Another example is age; certain behaviors that are tolerated or even encouraged at five years are frowned on at ten as completely unacceptable.

Well-socialized children are above average in the major aspects of social behavior according to their culture. It is clear, then, that no absolute definition of socialization is possible. Yet there are certain characteristics that exert a discernible influence on the socialization process. These include the following.

1. *Intelligence.* Once children reach a stable level of mental functioning, IQ is extremely significant in mastery of socialization techniques. Reese and Lipsitt reach the sound conclusion that low intelligence is associated with socialization problems only because modern society is so complex that it requires a minimum level of intelligence to cope with everyday tasks.

2. *Body build.* Studies have convincingly demonstrated that mesomorphic (muscular) and ectomorphic (thin) boys and girls receive better acceptance by others, from the age of four on, than do endomorphic (fat) boys and girls. Reese and Lipsitt, in commenting on the social expectations for each of these types, doubt that the constitutional type automatically dictates personality (a fat person is always jolly), but they feel that body build may mediate temperament, since we all behave as we are expected to behave. If mesomorphs—well built, muscular, and aggressive—are expected to be leaders and to excel in almost everything, this may occur because they learn to play the expected role.

3. *Time of sexual maturation.* The individual who matures early enjoys distinct social advantages. Since dating usually begins around the ninth grade, the tall, mature girl and the short, immature boy both may experience difficulty. The girl, embarrassed by her obvious physical superiority, may seek the company of older boys, which then entails a different concept of the sex role, ranging from sexual relations to early marriage. Both of these results may cause psychological problems for the girl. Nevertheless, at about this time the mature girl will be searching for something more than that offered by immature boys, who may still be running around in baseball hats and chewing bubble gum. For the mature boy, things are quite different. The road to maturity is much easier simply because

he does not have to expend great effort to master the physical skills, and everything proceeds more smoothly.

4. *Activity level.* Reese and Lipsitt state that with a stimulating environment, a high level of activity seems to be an asset in socialization. Energetic youngsters will encounter and use more aspects of their environment, meet more people, and do more things than less energetic counterparts.

5. *Bodily contact.* Children who enjoy bodily contact or hugging from their first days will in the future accept such attention more warmly and with less resistance than children who lack contact. They will undoubtedly be more open to warmth, which will encourage them in their relationships with other human beings.

Principles of Socialization

Certain common principles seem to emerge from the many analyses of socialization.

1. A minimal amount of physical stimulation is necessary for the normal maturation of the senses. For example, those who have been blind from birth, both animal and human, have difficulty with the simplest of discriminations upon recovery of their sight. This principle has not only a biological interpretation but also a social meaning. That is, since the behavior that we designate as human is primarily learned behavior, normal adult human behavior appears only through stimulation by other human beings.

2. A lengthy separation from the mother or from a secure home produces serious emotional and intellectual retardation, difficulty in relating to others, a short attention span, retarded speech, and severely adverse physical development. This is especially true if the separation occurs from the age of three months up to about five years, particularly in the three- to thirty-month age span. And the more isolated and deprived the child, the greater the impact on all of his abilities. Bowlby has gone so far as to state that severe maternal deprivation in cases of prolonged hospitalization or institutionalization results in retardation of all phases of development, and the symptoms of physical and mental illness frequently appear. The great danger is that such damage may be permanent.

3. The more the socializing agencies (home, school, church, peers) work together, the better the resulting socialization; the more conflicts, the slower the process and the more uncertain the outcome.

4. There are cross-cultural similarities in socialization. Certain common reactions are to be anticipated simply because we are all human beings. For example, all humans are helpless at birth and thus suffer feelings of dependence. Sibling rivalry is seen in all cultures. And sex differences emerge because of biological determination.

5. Parents tend to raise their children in the same manner that they were raised, which is an old and familiar pattern. Regardless of the latest literature and child rearing practices, most parents, especially mothers, feel that they know best. Thus, in their interactions with their children, they are either in accord with or against their personal experiences as children.

6. In their child rearing practices, parents create a certain emotional atmosphere. This affects development more than any other technique (such as reward, punishment, permissiveness, or restriction). Depending on which emotional tone the parents use, identical techniques employed by different parents have entirely different meanings for the children.

7. It is difficult, if not impossible, to assess the effects of punishment. The question of punishment is a recurring theme in the psychological literature. While it may suppress

CHILDREN'S LITERATURE AND SOCIALIZATION

From the perspective of the cultural influence on children, it is interesting to return to children's literature and examine some children's stories of various times. In their excellent text, Arbuthnot and Sutherland (1972) point out that although books are written for children, the editor decides on the manuscript, the reviewer makes judgments, teachers and librarians exhibit the books and guide children in their reading, and it is usually a parent or other adult who buys the children's book.

Why do adults make the choices that they do? Helson (1973) believes that the reader who follows Alice through Wonderland or Dorothy to the Land of Oz ordinarily does not realize that such fantasies express hidden longings of the time and society in which they were written. The main characters in these stories differ from one historical period to another, and the story actually holds a mirror to the existing culture. Helson states that these children's stories reflect the social pressures of the time, problems of sex role and identity, and the changing role of the artist.

An excellent example is *The Wizard of Oz.* When it was first published in 1900, the economy had suffered reverses, there was general dissatisfaction with the existing institutions, and a genuine conflict between religion and science appeared. In this context, the male is cast in about as negative a role as for any time in history, which seems to indicate the pessimism with which leaders of the time were viewed. The Wizard is a false friend, a pure fraud. Dorothy is sent to kill the Wicked Witch, but the Wizard secretly hopes that the Witch will win.

Helson compiled a list of the best fantasies for eight- to twelve-year-old children in three periods: the Victorian period (mid-nineteenth century), 1880 to World War I (turn of the century), and 1930 to 1970 (the contemporary period). The difference in themes is amazing: social values in the stories changed from conformity to the influence of mass culture between 1900 and 1970; from anxiety and conflict to alienation and identity problems during the same period.

Helson offers a fine instance of this when she states that today's authors are writing stories that revolve around male *and* female, young *and* old. Thus, characters are more complex, combining masculine, feminine, and age roles. She uses Alan Garner's *Owl Service* to illustrate this conclusion. Here the attraction of an adolescent boy and girl turns temporarily to hate when they relive similar circumstances that ruined the boy's parents. But through these experiences, both boy and girl widen their perspectives and avert disaster.

From the Victorian period to the 1970s, we see stories illustrating less constraint about relations with the opposite sex; independence, achievement, self-discipline, and imitation are less important; faith in authority and religion has declined; and artists and intellectuals are more alienated from the main current of society. As Helson concludes, changes in the characters of fantasy appear to relate to a new picture of the child reader as well as to a new social climate.

the immediate behavior, and while it occasionally may be the lesser of two evils, no one is certain of its consequences. As a guideline for child rearing, perhaps the best and only advice is to be cautious. Punishment may take many forms, from the withholding of a piece of candy to the more brutal slap across the face. Properly handled, punishment by withholding a reward may be more beneficial, both immediately and later, than more strongly aversive actions.

Finally, Clausen and Williams (1963) state that children develop within a social matrix, which influences what they learn and how they feel about it. Each culture and each group to which children belong possess expectations and relationships that influence their behavior. Thus it is only by becoming a participant in that society that children become fully human and acquire a sense of self.

DISCUSSION QUESTIONS

1. How do you react to the statement that "children learn to be human"? What kinds of learning are involved? What are the stimuli, or the sources, of this learning? Is the process age related? Link your answer to your understanding of the socialization process.
2. Do you agree with Scott's identification of the period of "primary socialization"? How do precursors act to structure this achievement? How does communication extend the process? Discuss positive and negative future effects of these early experiences.
3. Sensitive, or critical, periods is a controversial topic. Do you agree with Scott's analysis of times of rapid organization? Why? Can you have social relationships within that definition? Give some examples.
4. Recalling our discussion of the family's influence on development, can you use Scott's experiments and theorizing to argue for or against the social decisions that will soon become public policy? Weigh your answer carefully; consider the pros and cons of the studies about family, daycare, adoption, and early experience.
5. Can you demonstrate specifically how the various principles of socialization actually function? Give both positive and negative examples.

SOCIAL CLASS DIFFERENCES

The phenomenon of social class is so important that it demands special consideration in our discussion of the socialization process. It came as a distinct and unpleasant surprise to most Americans in the 1940s to discover that they lived in communities that could be fairly rigidly defined according to social class. Studies of suburbia, such as those by Warner and Lunt (1941) and Lynd (1937), clearly demonstrated that each community had definite social classes to which each individual belonged. People could be classed together if they ate or drank together socially, visited each other's homes, and married into each other's families.

What has this to do with the development of children? If we answered "Everything," we would be quite close to the truth. Study after study has reported that social class influences social, intellectual, moral, emotional, and even physical development. For example, consistent differences in average intelligence test scores have been reported between groups from different socioeconomic levels. Leona Tyler (1978) goes so far as to state that the relationship of measured intelligence to socioeconomic level is one of the best documented findings in the history of intelligence testing.

Working with children is a sensitive and demanding task that requires flexibility on the part of the adult. Not that you should be flexible about your principles or the beliefs about children to which you are deeply committed, but you should be able to adapt your methods of working with children. Children are different, and some of the behavioral differences represent distinctions among social classes.

There are obvious developmental considerations to our discussion. Children, as they grow and develop, initially see the world through the eyes of the family. How often do children react to others because of what a brother or sister or parent said? Their world is colored by the tint the family gives to it. Family members label certain things, events, and people as significant or not, and children quickly acquire these labels. And family members label things as important or unimportant partially or totally because of their social class.

As youngsters grow older and form their own values, opinions, and beliefs through contact with the environment, the family becomes less important as a molder of opinion. Now children usually do one of two things: they continue to accept those ideas that have been with them since infancy or they rebel against them. But rebel or accept, it is mainly social class, filtered by family and friends, to which children react.

All of us, author, reader, or child, display social class characteristics, and in our own contacts with youngsters, we must be cognizant of these characteristics so that we may employ the techniques that are best suited for the kind of youngster with whom we are working.

A Descriptive Analysis

Every society is stratified, and as society's complexity increases, so also does the number of social classes. Many variables contribute to a person's social class—wealth, age, sex, ability, and skin color—and each society uniquely combines these to make its assessment of an individual's social standing. For example, financial status is critical in the United States, while family position is paramount in England and Japan.

Farb (1978) summarizes the American position when he states that in the United States, higher status accrues to those who are white, Protestant, rich, white collar workers, and married. What is remarkable about these assessments is that almost all members of a particular society agree about high and low class occupations. Industrialized societies seem to have evolved remarkably similar occupational evaluations.

Any analysis of social class suggests that children are not born with the same "life chances" because of the social class of their parents. Health, education, proneness to delinquency, and even survival itself are linked to social class. For example, Tulkin (1977, p. 577), while arguing that present definitions of social class membership are faulty, addresses health variables and child development as follows:

> Whatever one's definition of social class or socio-economic status, it is clear that within many societies, there are relatively widespread differences in diet, eating patterns, family size and spacing, breast versus bottle feeding practices, use and access to health care, and physical demands on parental time and energy that can vary from one class to another.

> . . . In England and America, for example, significant differences in infant mortality and morbidity across social classes have been demonstrated, usually with lower rates in the upper classes. Lower-class infants generally stand a higher risk of low birth weight, congenital malformations, pulmonary disease, or poor pre- and postnatal nutrition or protein deprivation, and many other health problems that might interfere with normal development and optimal performance.

Specific Class Differences. Hess (1970) has analyzed social class differences in children's behavior and concludes that:

1. Lower SES level parents are less concerned with and exercise less control over their children's activities outside the home during the later childhood years.

2. Lower-class children adopt sex-typed behaviors earlier than middle-class children.

3. Middle- and upper-class children manifest significantly higher educational achievement than lower-class youngsters.

4. Considerable language differences appear between the classes: middle- and upper-class youngsters communicate more meaningfully and explicitly than lower-class children.

5. Differences in IQ test scores clearly and consistently favor middle- and upper-class children.

In a fascinating study of the effects of the Great Depression upon youngsters from different social classes, Elder (1974) found both age and class differences. The subjects of the study were born in 1920–1922, so they were old enough to comprehend the economic ravages their parents were experiencing. Boys from middle-class families hardest hit by the Depression became the adult males who were committed to their work, persisted at a particular job, and were remarkably family centered. The girls became women who were deeply committed to the traditional female sex roles. Boys from lower-class families exhibited less positive characteristics as adult males: they showed greater psychological disturbance and had the highest percentage of heavy drinkers in any of the groups studies.

Using data from another longitudinal study, Elder then analyzed youngsters born in 1928–1929, who had felt the Depression in their early childhood. Both working-class and middle-class boys achieved poorly, were less likely to complete college, and seemed to have lingering psychological problems. The results of the Great Depression study clearly suggest specific age differences in the effects.

Like It Is in the Alley

In an essay that is as graphic as it is depressing, Robert Coles (1968) relates the kind of life a nine-year-old boy from the ghetto lives. Peter is black, originally from Alabama, and now dwells in the ghetto section of a large northeastern city. The boy's father died when Peter was six; the boy has never been examined by a physician. The apartment where he lives has three rooms for six people.

The influences on Peter are staggering. For example, he and his friends wash cars for a group of older boys. The cars are stolen. The older boys take bets, sell stolen liquor, and push pills. They engage in a wide range of drug peddling and have connections with a group of prostitutes.

Peter's account of a typical day is devastating. His mother wakes him early and they have a good breakfast—if the welfare check has come. Then he goes to school with a friend who "knows everything," whose brother is high on drugs, and who is making payments to the police. Peter has been bitten by ever-present rats. Coles describes the rats as large, confident, and unafraid; they seem to feel that the garbage is theirs, the land is theirs, the building is theirs, the human flesh is theirs. Peter usually causes considerable trouble in school, since he has decided that school

"wasn't made for me." He seems to delight in letting the authors know about slogans that spoke of freedom, democracy, and equality. He shrewdly observes that the teachers are growing afraid of their pupils and that control is breaking down. For this boy and those like him, school is a total loss. After school, he stays in the alley until six o'clock, then eats and watches television until about ten or eleven.

Coles states that Peter trusts no white, neither teacher, policeman, storekeeper, welfare worker, or Coles himself. At the age of nine, he has learned to be very careful, wary, guarded, doubtful, and calculating. Peter is tough and he knows how "to get along." He must be tough, and he must know how to get along if he is to survive. It is as simple as that.

The Invulnerable Child. Perhaps Peter will become one of a select minority of children who do not break or bend regardless of circumstances. Only recently have investigators turned their attention to the youngsters who retain their normality, achieve well, and seem destined for success in spite of devastating conditions. Segal (1978) traces a profile of these children.

1. They are socially skillful and relate well to both peers and adults, and are obviously popular.

2. Not only do others think well of them, but they think well of themselves; that is, they possess a good self-concept.

3. They are reflective children, unlike many other youngsters from disadvantaged circumstances who tend to be impulsive.

4. These youngsters manifest inner motivation; they are driven to do well. Frequently they come from families who share and encourage their aspirations.

5. Invulnerable children almost all have identified with someone who is an inspiration to them; often it is the parent who strives to keep the family together, the one who makes the sacrifice so that other family members may have more.

While these efforts at understanding invulnerable children are encouraging, they will become even more valuable when they move from description, such as the above profile, to discovery of causes. Thus far, the most striking single feature that researchers have identified in these children is their *competence.* But what produced their competence still remains elusive.

Children of Affluence

Robert Coles (1977) has continued his chronology of the children of crisis by examining "the privileged ones." The children of affluence live well; their homes, even if a townhouse in the city, are "removed" from the city. Their position derives from money, social class, and political lineage. Cars are everywhere; activities, especially golf, are a way of life; there are often second or third homes near water or mountains; private education extends from nursery school to country day school to elite high schools to the best colleges and possibly graduate education.

But most significantly, these children live with *choice;* they have so much that they begin early in life to make personal decisions about clothes, bikes, games, or activities. Similarly, they see parental authority and choice exercised not only at home but also in the world. As Coles notes (1977, p. 28), theirs is a world of excitement and achievement, but also disaster, tragedy, and failure.

Coles uses a particularly apt word, "entitlement," to describe what affluent American families transmit to their children: an emotional expression to describe the prerogative of money and power. He traces the early ages (two and three years) during which children discover what belongs to whom—special nursery schools, friends' homes that resemble their own, a multitude of toys, swimming pools, boats, horses. By five or six years, they have a very realistic idea of their economic worth; it is a recognition, usually not of specific dollars, but of present and future affluence.

Still, as Coles comments, these children are not always as confident as they appear. They are haunted by their demons: failure to measure up, loss of good standing, anxiety, and loneliness. They are faced with that one great issue that all of Coles's children of crisis, and all children face: coming to terms with the one and only chance—life (Coles, 1977, p. 548).

Can we compare the lives of children from two environments? Can we project developmental outcomes? Should we even attempt to do so?

DISCUSSION QUESTIONS

1. How would you evaluate the impact of social class on development? From your own experience, is it as powerful as has been suggested? Has your social class either helped or hindered in your development?
2. In a contemporary, industrialized society, is it realistic to speak of difference in "life's chance"? Governmental support programs, universal education, and nondiscriminating legislation would seem to have eliminated these critical class differences of yesteryear. Do you agree with the statement? Why?
3. What determines class membership? Think carefully about your answer and compare it with some of the variables discussed here. Which of the elements that identify class are most important? Why? Class members who are familiar with other countries should determine whether the same criteria apply to those nations.
4. Why would an economic catastrophe such as the Great Depression affect individuals differentially? That is, why would age and class determine the future effects of financial difficulty? Can you relate Elder's work to Bronfenbrenner's system analysis of development?
5. Give specific examples of how children from different social classes—from the alley to affluence—see their opportunity of seizing that one great chance. Be sure to include invulnerable children as well as the disturbed affluent.

CHILDREN AND SOCIETY

With regard to children, ours is a strange society. We pride ourselves on our love and concern for children, yet our Supreme Court, the final appellate court in a "nation of laws and not of men," has refused to overturn a state court ruling that teachers may strike their pupils. We agonize over individual stories of abandoned children, yet remain relatively unconcerned about the implications of child placement (foster homes, institutions). We contribute generously to appeals to battle childhood disease but remain almost totally ignorant about conditions that can cause psychological disturbance.

Perhaps this is an unfair indictment; we are describing the current state of national knowledge about child development. Those who read textbooks and those who write them remain a small, select group on the national scene. Still, it is encouraging to note a growing recognition of, and a willingness to face, subtle and sophisticated issues that have been cloaked throughout the recorded history of childhood.

Since we are a nation of laws, we can best follow these changes by examining recent court decisions.

Children and the Courts

Rodham (1973) notes that legal definitions of "children" are hard to find. Those under eighteen or twenty-one are described as either infants or minors, terms which completely ignore well documented age changes and needs. Early American courts followed English common law and regarded children as chattels of the family or wards of the state, with few legal rights. Older children possess a few additional rights, such as the right to drive or to leave school at a certain age. In recent years the Supreme Court has more frequently ruled that society must recognize particular rights of children, among which are the right to procedural protection in juvenile courts, the right of freedom of expression, including the right to refuse to salute the flag if it violates religious beliefs, and the right to express philosophical beliefs by wearing a black armband to protest the Vietnam war.

These protections sharply delineate the basic dilemma facing the courts: an acceptance of the belief that a child's well-being is best enhanced by parental, not state, dominance, and yet a willingness to act in place of parents, if necessary for the health or welfare of the child. The family is thus subject to the benevolent intrusion of the state in extreme cases.

The gradual recognition of childhood as a unique phase of development, helped considerably by developmental research, has focused attention on the rights of children. In recent decisions affording legal protection to children as individuals, the courts have extended adult rights to children, and they have created legally enforceable recognition of children's special needs and interests.

The Supreme Court and Children's Rights. Rodham (1973) states that most child questions that reach the U.S. Supreme Court involve education, child welfare, and juvenile court procedures. As Rodham notes, whether we agree with a particular court decision or not, we must admire the Court's willingness to attempt to separate parental dominion from state prerogatives. Among its more important decisions have been:

1. *Brown* v. *Board of Education (1954)*, the famous school desegregation case in which the Court held that the constitutional rights of black children were violated by segregated education.

2. *In re Gault (1967),* in which the Court held that children in juvenile court were constitutionally entitled to procedural due process guarantees.

3. *Ware* v. *Estes (1971),* in which the Court refused to reverse a lower court's decision that upheld the right of school systems to use corporal punishment for discipline.

4. *Wisconsin* v. *Yoder (1972),* in which the Court held that Amish parents, because of their religious beliefs, had the right to refuse to send their children to the local high school. Particularly interesting in this case is the dissenting opinion written by Justice Douglas. Arguing that it was not the parents' interests that were at issue, but those of the children, Douglas buttressed his opinion by appeals to Piaget, Kohlberg, Gesell, and other developmental theorists.

The state's difficulty is to determine when and under what circumstances the state's prerogative should supersede parental dominion. It is a difficult decision, particularly in light of the state's appalling record in caring for the children once they are removed from their families. Yet it has been a great service in tragic instances of physical abuse.

Child Abuse

Characterizing ourselves as a nation concerned with the optimal development of children causes both reluctance and difficulty in discussing the phenomenon of child abuse. As Kempe and Kempe (1978) state, work on child abuse was not discussed in the last century, although its evidence was visible everywhere. It is only as our sensitivity to children's needs sharpened, accompanied by a willingness to admit that such conditions existed, that the issue invited investigation.

Starr (1979) states that child abuse has always been with us but it has only been a matter of public awareness for the past quarter-century. It still remains an elusive subject that defies precise definition, because as Starr notes, there are many forms of abuse: physical, emotional, and sexual. While physical and sexual abuses that leave evidence are easy to detect and describe (if they are reported), other forms of abuse that emotionally wound youngsters are perhaps never detected.

Professionals believe that abusive behavior involves direct harm (physical, sexual, deliberate malnutrition), intent to harm (which is difficult if not impossible to detect), and intent to harm even if injury does not result. In 1974, Congress passed the Federal Child Abuse Prevention and Treatment Act, P.L. 93-247. This act defines child abuse as

> the physical or mental injury, sexual abuse, negligent treatment, or maltreatment of a child under the age of 18 by a person who is responsible for the child's welfare under circumstances which indicate that the child's health or welfare is harmed or threatened thereby, as determined in accordance with regulations prescribed by the Secretary.

Even with this legal definition, you can see how difficult it is to detect, report, and prove child abuse.

Another troublesome issue is that of incidence. Figures show tremendous variability, and the actual data are undoubtedly only the tip of the iceberg. The figure we have represents only reported cases, and estimates suggest that the extent of the problem may be staggering. Starr (1979) reports a random survey of households where 3.5 percent of the parents admitted that during the past year they had acted toward their children in a way calculated to injure. Projecting from these figures, Starr estimates that each year from 1.4 to 1.9 million children are subjected to violence severe enough to cause injury. He concludes that this is probably an underestimate since the survey included only voluntary admission by intact families, and the children were all over three years old and less subject to abuse than younger children. It should be apparent that child abuse is not a trivial problem restricted to obviously pathological parents. It is a national, deadly disease with an estimated mortality rate of from five to twenty-seven percent.

Nature of the Problem. Although child abuse has a lengthy history, it was not until the 1920s that Dr. John Caffey, studying bone fractures and other physical injuries, suggested that parents might have caused the injuries. The skepticism that greeted his conclusions prevented him from officially reporting his findings until the late 1940s. In 1961 C. Henry Kempe and his associates startled the annual meeting of the American Academy of Pediatrics by their dramatic description of the "battered child syndrome."

Kempe and Kempe (1978) state that four categories of adult behavior are classified as abusive:

1. *Physical violence,* which means harmful physical actions directed against the child resulting in head injuries, broken bones, abdominal injuries, or poisoning.
2. *Neglect,* which may be difficult to determine and which may include malnutrition, lack of medical care, and lack of vital protection.
3. *Sexual exploitation,* which includes such actions as incest, molestation, and rape.
4. *Emotional abuse,* which is extremely difficult to prove but nevertheless may cause lasting psychological trauma.

Examining these categories, Kempe and Kempe point out several misconceptions:

1. Abusive parents are incurably abnormal, psychotic, criminal, or retarded.
2. Abusive parents are invariably disadvantaged.
3. Child abuse is rare in our society.

One positive conclusion that these researchers report is that although child abuse is a problem, it is not hopeless. They estimate that, with help, four out of five abusive parents will stop physically injuring their children.

Characteristics of Abused Children. While there is no definitive list of characteristics, the following are found in many abused children.

General	*Physical Abuse*
Unduly afraid of parents	Unexplained and untreated injuries
Frequently exhibit bruises, welts, cuts	Strange reasons for injury
Injuries inadequately treated	Behavior problems

General	*Neglect*
Exhibit behavioral extremes	Often hungry
Fear physical contact	Exhibit signs of malnutrition
Exhibit sudden changes in behavior	Irritable
Frequently truant or absent	Need medical attention
Unusually tired	

It is important to remember a theme that has continued throughout our work: children shape their parents as much as parents shape their children. If a child's acts or looks irritate a parent predisposed to violence, then the results of the parent-child interaction may be preordained. Kempe and Kempe (1978) state that the earliest evidence of trouble is the FTT (Failure to Thrive) infant, which they believe may be the first symptomatic behavior of the abused or neglected children; it is the beginning phase of their way to cope with experiences not faced by most youngsters.

The authors believe that these children, growing up in a hostile environment, feel that to survive they must totally submit to their parents' wishes. They often exhibit continual staring, and a passive acceptance of whatever happens bordering on stoicism. It is only later in a permissive setting that the pent up fury explodes. They slowly develop complete distrust of others, which often translates into school problems with any kind of communicative task.

Characteristics of Abusive Parents. The pattern of characteristics is not rigidly defined. Some parents are negativistic and aggressive; others alternate between compliance and aggression. The following parental characteristics are frequently found:

They themselves were abused.

They are "loners."

They refuse to recognize the seriousness of the child's condition.

They resist diagnostic studies.

They delay medical care for the child.

They believe in harsh punishment.

They have unreasonable expectations for the child.

They lack control and are often immature and dependent.

They feel personally incompetent.

Kempe and Kempe (1978, p. 12) refer to a cycle of abuse. The most consistent feature of the histories of abusive families is the repetition, from one generation to the next, of a pattern of abuse, neglect, and parental loss or deprivation. In each generation we find, in one form or another, a distortion of the relationship between parents and children that deprives the children of the consistent nurturing of body and mind that would enable them to develop fully.

The authors then suggest four categories that encompass parental abuse.

1. The parents have a background of abuse and neglect.
2. Parents perceive the child as disappointing or unlovable.
3. Stress and crisis are usually associated with abusive behavior.
4. No "lifeline" exists; that is, there is no communication with helpful sources in times of crisis.

THE CHILD KILLERS

Kaplan and Reich (1976) report that at least one New York City child, usually one to four years old, is murdered each week, and the number is steadily increasing. In their study of all victims in one year, boys outnumbered girls by fifteen percent, and of victims over ten years of age, two boys were murdered for every girl. Fifty-two percent of their survey were under one year, and another twenty-six percent were from one to five years.

Most of the families of the murdered children lived in poverty and almost all were known to the city's welfare agency. Two-thirds of the murdered children were illegitimate. In nine-tenths of the cases the victims had been either abused or neglected before the killing. Over two-thirds of the killers were either parents or lovers, and the *most frequently accused assailants were the mothers,* who usually acted alone, or occasionally with the help of a lover. The biological father was the killer in only ten percent of the cases. The older the victim, the less frequently was the murderer a parent, but parents killed babies eighty-three percent of the time, preschoolers fifty-three percent of the time, schoolchildren under ten years thirty percent of the time, and over ten years seventeen percent of the time. Except for children under two years, assailants and victims were usually of the same sex. In eighty-one percent of the cases in which information on the assailants was available, they showed prehomicidal deviant behavior, alcoholism, narcotics usage, and criminal involvement.

The victim's families showed a characteristic pattern: the biological parents were less frequently present; there were more children under three years, and there were significantly more teenage mothers. As the authors note, the murder of a child is the final chapter in the youngster's history of maltreatment.

Prevention of Child Abuse. The grim tale of "The Child Killers" emphasizes the need to predict, prevent, and possibly intervene where necessary. The means to accomplish these three goals are currently inadequate and great effort is being given to their improvement. Since the abused grow up abusive, early detection must be high on the list of research priorities. Prevention often implies intervention, and it is here that recent progress has occurred. Figure 14.8 illustrates the use of community resources.

Teachers, physicians, police, and welfare workers all should be involved in informational reporting and interaction procedures. The task is difficult. People are reluctant to become involved, there are no clear lines of authority and responsibility, and procedures after involvement are vague. Kempe and Kempe state (1978, p. 118):

> Aside from the constant shortage of time and the maze of red tape, nothing is more frustrating to child-protector workers than the primitive nature of the services aimed at prevention. Always to be there after the event is clearly not good enough. Many workers are now beginning to get personally involved with maternity hospitals and in early child care so that they can help when abuse is likely but has not yet occurred.

Of one fact we can be certain: attempts to prevent and eliminate child abuse will continue to strengthen and attract support from all segments of the national community.

FIGURE 14.8. Community Resources and Child Abuse.

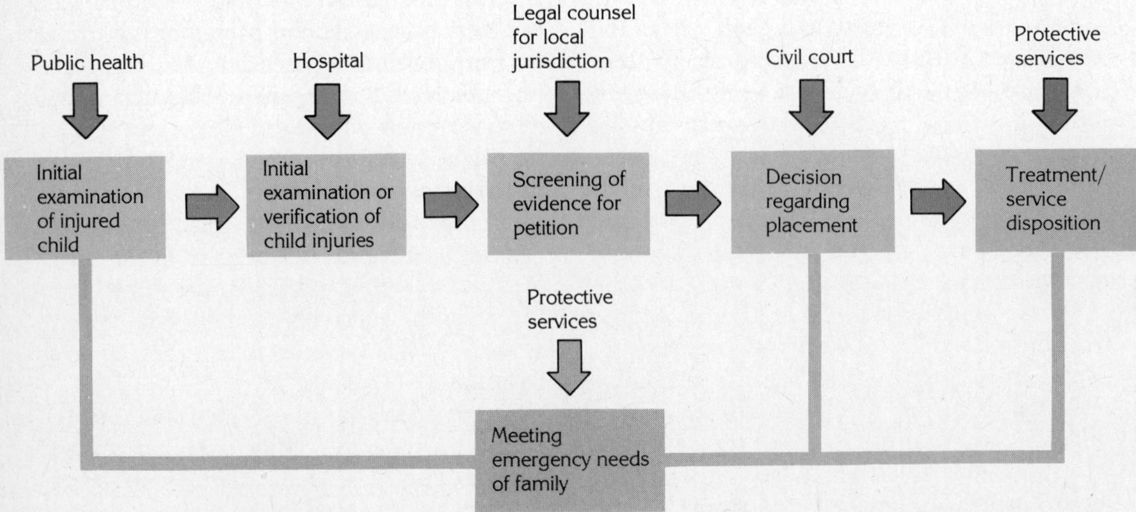

Source: *Child Abuse Intervention.* Washington, D.C.: Law Enforcement Assistance Administration, U.S. Department of Justice, 1976.

DISCUSSION QUESTIONS

1. Can you explain, or attempt to explain, some of the legal contradictions about children that were mentioned? How do we reconcile these contradictions with our image of ourselves as a nation devoted to children?
2. Can you suggest reasons why child abuse has become such a prominent issue? It has always been here; what caused this change? In your answer, consider legal, social, and psychological reasons.
3. Why is it difficult to state precisely the characteristics of abused children and abusive parents? If we could identify such individuals, prediction and prevention might be possible. What would you suggest to facilitate the process? Is your solution possible?
4. The shattering details surrounding child murders raises several penetrating questions. Could these individuals be identified earlier? If so, why are they not so identified? In cases where a child's murderer is suspected to be a parent, *but not proven,* what should be done with any remaining children?

Our initial question concerned the influence of society upon children's development. There seems to be overwhelming evidence that development does indeed reflect such influence, and in many ways not previously suspected. Any society sustaining rapid change, as most industrial societies are, will either encourage or inflict change on its youthful citizens. As it does, the nature of the socialization process for that society also changes. In our society, the ultimate effects of daycare have yet to be shown.

One of the great determiners of development, social class, remains as powerful and as decisive as it ever has been. The two examples highlighted in this chapter—the alley and affluence—can hardly avoid producing different outcomes. And in a society determined to eradicate as much as possible the benefits and disadvantages of class difference, the great struggle against child abuse has taken shape, a struggle that probably cannot be completely won but, thanks to growing indignation, will no longer be completely lost.

SUMMARY

Cross-cultural studies of widely divergent societies testify to the potent influence of society and development.

Rapid changes in modern societies will have inevitable consequences for child development.

The process of learning to become human is called socialization and is susceptible to many forces: family, school, peers. Any interruption or deviation in the process can alter the adult outcomes.

Animal experimentation suggests that there are sensitive periods in the socialization process, periods during which desirable environmental stimulation is required to facilitate positive development.

Social class still, even in enlightened, modern societies, exerts a tremendous impact on all aspects of development: physical, emotional, cognitive, and social.

In a world plagued by concern about the differences between the "haves and have nots," it is difficult for the children of affluence to understand the children of poverty; theirs are different worlds, different concerns.

Child abuse is a developmental phenomenon too long hidden, too frequently ignored, and too often fatal.

The statistics of child abuse testify to its prevalence and its ability to warp a child's development. Rudimentary efforts at prediction, prevention, and intervention have commenced and will continue to gather momentum.

SUGGESTED READINGS

BRONFENBRENNER, URIE. *The Ecology of Human Development.* Cambridge, Mass.: Harvard University Press, 1979. Bronfenbrenner's monumental work is an excellent source for understanding society's influence.

COLEMAN, JAMES (editor). *Youth: Transition to Adulthood.* Chicago: University of Chicago Press, 1974. This valuable book, focusing upon adolescent change, is a fine chronicle of modern society changing.

COLES, ROBERT. *The Privileged Ones.* Boston: Little, Brown, 1977. All of Coles's *Children of Crisis* are a valuable, and even necessary, source of information about children from different regions and classes.

KEMPE, RUTH S. and C. HENRY KEMPE. *Child Abuse.* Cambridge, Mass.: Harvard University Press, 1978. A superb summary of the recent research and literature about child abuse.

LEWIS, OSCAR. *La Vida.* New York: Random House, 1965. This exciting book dramatically illustrates society's role in development.

SCOTT, J. PAUL. *Early Experience and the Organization of Behavior.* Belmont, California: Brooks/Cole, 1968. Scott's experiments furnished the theoretical basis of the critical period hypothesis and here he turns his attention to the socialization process.

PART FIVE
PROBLEMS OF DEVELOPMENT

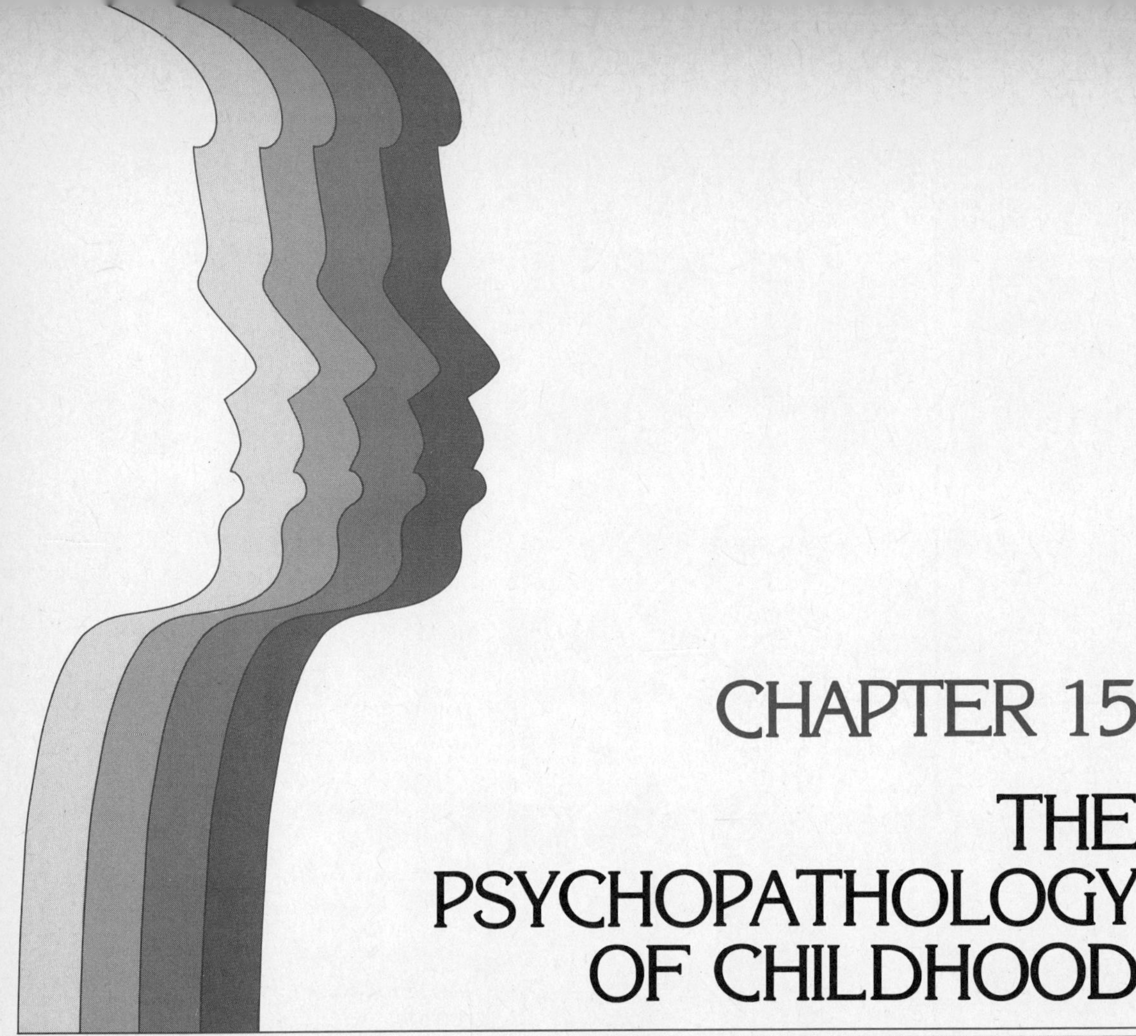

CHAPTER 15 THE PSYCHOPATHOLOGY OF CHILDHOOD

CHAPTER HIGHLIGHTS

Topics

Introduction
a. A Classification Scheme

Clinical Psychiatric Syndromes
a. The Emotional Disorders (fears, phobias, anxieties, depression, obsessions, hypochondriasis)
b. The Conduct Disorders (aggression, hostility, delinquency, drug usage, infantile autism, childhood schizophrenia)

Intellectual Elements
a. Classification
b. Etiology

Biological Elements
a. Gender
b. Genetics
c. Physical Illness (failure-to-thrive, asthma, sleep disorders, enuresis, encopresis, anorexia)

Psychosocial Elements
a. Discipline
b. Death
c. The Schools
d. Stress

Learning Disorders
a. Development and Learning Disorders
b. The Meaning of Underachievement

People		**Special Topics**
Hilda Bruch	M. Hassibi	The Makings of a Criminal
Stella Chess	Peter Knapp	Can Delinquency Be Prevented?
Leon Eisenberg	Melvin Levine	Children and Death
Sheldon and Eleanor Glueck	Michael Rutter	

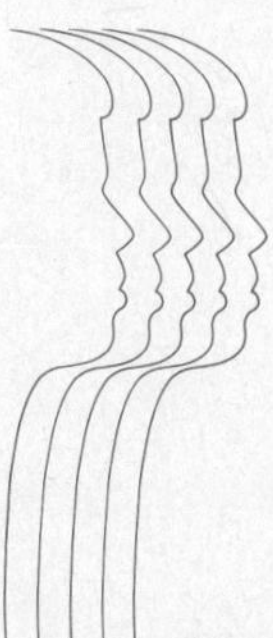

Most children develop normally, that is, with a minimum of difficulties. Even those who experience some emotional and behavioral problems usually do *not* suffer from serious psychiatric illness. Their problems are minor deviations from the typical developmental sequence; they are typically transient and leave no lasting scars. Their roots may be traced to many sources—the child, family, school, society—and again dramatically illustrate the importance of an interactive analysis of development. The scheme initially advocated in Chapter One, the biopsychosocial model, is particularly applicable to an investigation of childhood disorders.

It is deceptively simple to classify a child's problem along a single dimension: a disturbed personality, parental separation, school. But a youngster's behavior represents the interaction of many causal points. Eisenberg (1979) argues forcefully against simplistic explanations. He states:

> Given the amalgam of strange and persistent disease conditions assigned to them, psychiatrists have attempted to use what theory they have to order the phenomena they observe. The ambitious efforts of the 1930's and 1940's to confer psychodynamic specificity on "psychosomatic" diseases was a brave effort but one that failed, in part because psychiatrists as keepers of the psychological flame shunned biology. Given the power of the biological paradigm in modern medicine, "psychosomatic" has been reserved for that borderland in which orthodox therapies are unsuccessful and psychosocial aspects of management are unavoidable.
>
> Yet, *all* disease is psychosomatic; the experience of illness is a social construct not fully determined by the biology of disease. Moreover, the distribution of disease in populations reveals both host factors and social factors as determinants, even when the immediate cause (a bacterium or a toxin) can be identified. The efficacy of treatment, even the highly "specific" treatments, depends upon the social context of medical care.

Eisenberg's argument is clear: there is no avoiding the biological, psychological, and social consequences of disease, either physical, emotional, or behavioral. For example, it is possible to classify many of the disorders to be discussed in this chapter as *mental*, or *emotional*. To do so is a disservice to the youth experiencing the problem. There may well be a physical cause behind an apparent emotional problem such as anxiety; any physical difficulty, such as asthma, can have definite, even serious emotional consequences. The etiology of maladjustment thus appears as follows:

1. Emotional Antecedents (fear, stress) →
   Physical Illness (nausea) →
   Consequences (Maladjustment)
2. Physical Antecedents (asthma, diabetes) →
   Emotional Illness (fear, anxiety, conduct disorders) →
   Consequences (maladjustment)
3. Treatment of Consequences

In each example, the interaction of physical and emotional forces has produced undesirable consequences. Chess and Hassibi (1978) summarize the interactive viewpoint when they state that disturbances and deviations of children's development are seen as interdependent, interactional phenomena, with the child acting as a developing biopsychological organism within a social environment. No one external or internal agent directly determines a child's personality; rather, the cumulative effects of a lasting undesirable environment and suboptimal biological endowment will inevitably influence a child's emerging personality.

Another warning to avoid attributing behavior to a single cause is the source of the child's referral. That is, the child rarely initiates the therapeutic process; it is usually a parent or teacher who expresses concern about the youngster's behavior. Frequently, the source of the referral—perhaps family or school—may also be the source of the problem. Rutter (1975) states that it is vital to understand the dynamics of the referral.

Chess and Hassibi (1978) demonstrate the issue of causation, single or multiple, and the difficulty of analysis in their discussion of genesis and etiology. Their presentation ranges from emotional antecedents such as stress to constitutional and genetic antecedents (including temperament) to prenatal, perinatal, and postnatal conditions, to sex (male-female differences in various deviations), to family and social causes. While attempting to categorize the many causes of problem behavior, the authors' discussion of each reflect their basic interactive interpretation. For example, in their commentary on schizophrenia, they note the genetic thread of the disease but also comment on the similarity of environmentally induced forms of the illness.

Maternal infections contracted during pregnancy can cause congenital defects; anoxia during the birth process is linked to future neuropsychiatric disorders. These prenatal and perinatal sources of future behavioral disorders reflect the organism's interactions with a particular familial or sociocultural environment. They also may produce different effects depending on the infant's or fetus's constitution. We have previously seen that the results of anoxia, over a period of approximately seven years, may be retardation in one youngster but may disappear in another.

These examples seem simple, but on further examination the complexity of analysis becomes apparent. Other causal categories pose more immediate complicated and frustrating challenges. For example, why are certain emotional and conduct disorders found much more frequently in males? As the authors conclude, the cause of the preponderance is a matter of conjecture.

The growing realization and acceptance of the interactive nature of the causes of childhood problems has raised another equally controversial issue—classification.

A CLASSIFICATION SCHEME

> Ideally, the diagnostic classification of childhood and adolescent psychiatric disorders should indicate the nature of the individual's pathology; the severity; the etiological agent or agents, if known; and the prognosis, if known. (Chess and Hassibi, 1978, p. 201)

Classification is especially critical in diagnosing and treating childhood psychiatric disorders. Once the problem is diagnosed, it is possible to collect the known pertinent data, the successful management strategies, and the success ratio of various techniques. Classification also permits comparison among different groups and provides a useful guide both for research and for practical purposes such as health insurance. Unfortunately, in spite of a clear and critical need, diagnostic nomenclature and categorization are far from settled.

However, as Chess and Hassibi (1978) note, while no classification scheme or diagnostic term will be forever complete and accurate, they are vital in identifying the nature of deviant behavior sufficiently clearly to aid those working with troubled children to obtain clear and useful clues to treatment.

Michael Rutter (1975) suggests that before commencing a psychiatric assessment, several items require attention. These include the following.

1. *Children are developing organisms.* Any diagnosis must consider the youngster's developmental level, since one of the major criteria in judging the abnormality of a child's behavior is its age-appropriateness. Since children behave differently at different ages, it is important to know what behavior is typical of the various ages. Youngsters are vulnerable to different stresses at different ages. At some ages they may be particularly susceptible to an interruption of *physical* development whose consequences are both physical and psychological (anorexia nervosa in adolescents, for example). At an earlier age, interference with *psychological* development may have physical and psychological consequences (separation from the mother during the first months of life, for example).

2. *Epidemiological Considerations.* Since any information concerning the nature and dimensions of the problem will facilitate evaluation, studies that examine the distribution of the problem in the general population are usually helpful. Rutter (1975) notes that these studies show that from five to fifteen percent of children suffer from sufficiently severe disorders to handicap them in daily living. While the precise number may vary, it is clear that except for a minority of cases, these disorders are not *qualitatively* different from normality. They represent *quantitative* differences and may be better identified as developmental deviations. Lesser versions of the same problems appear in many children not identified as troubled.

3. *The abnormality and severity of the handicap.* Several criteria are employed in assessing abnormality, the first of which is the age and sex appropriateness of the behavior. For example, certain behavior is normal at one age and not another; bedwetting is common until four or five years, but uncommon by ten years. Persistence of a problem is another criterion; a reluctance to leave home and attend school is normal in the early years, but abnormal in the later grades. Other criteria that cluster and indicate a problem are the extent of the disturbance and the intensity of the symptoms under different circumstances.

The severity of a problem is judged by four criteria. *First* is the degree of personal suffering that the child experiences; *second* is the social restriction involved (does it prevent the child from doing what is desired?); *third* is any interference with development that appears (for example, does dependency on the parents become so intense that the youngster finds it impossible to formulate normal peer relationships?); and *finally,* is there an effect on others? (has the child's behavior become so maladaptive that interpersonal relationships deteriorate?).

Having presented these criteria to determine that a psychiatric assessment is needed, Rutter next turns to diagnosis—determining the nature of the disorder—and here faces the issue of classification. He urges that we avoid the medical model that applies one diagnostic term to describe all aspects of the disorder. For example, the patient's blood vessels display an excessive amount of cholesterol; the identification of the problem labels the cause and suggests prognosis and treatment. While considerable information is conveyed in this model, it hides the considerable complexity of the disease. *Why* is excessive cholesterol present? Is it due purely to diet, or could there be a genetic tendency at work? If diet is the cause, are there family or social elements that are bothering the patient and perhaps causing needless food consumption?

Most psychiatric problems are too intricate to be explained by one cause and can only respond to a search for multiple causes. Rutter uses the term "minimal brain damage" to illustrate how a diagnosis can be misleading, even dangerous. There are several, not one, brain damage syndromes, and the form they take is often indistinguishable from the behavior of children without brain damage. Further, brain damage does not directly lead to psychiatric disorder, although it may increase a child's vulnerability to such disorders through interaction with many psychosocial influences.

In accordance with the World Health Organization's suggestions concerning the classification of psychiatric disorders, Rutter proposes the following multiaxial scheme, which encompasses symptom description, developmental data, biological concomitants, and pertinent environmental data. (Note the use of the adjective "associated" in two of the axes, indicating that while they may be causative, the link remains tenuous.) There are five axes.

1. *Clinical psychiatric syndromes,* including emotional disorders, conduct disorders, hyperkinesis, infantile autism, schizophrenia, and other disorders such as enuresis (bedwetting), encopresis (soiling) and tics.

2. *Intellectual level,* in which the expression of intelligence is associated with behavioral disorders, especially those relating to mental retardation.

3. *Associated or etiological biological elements,* which include sex differences, temperament, physical illness, and brain disorders.

4. *Associated or etiological psychosocial elements,* with particular references to unique family, school, and societal conditions.

5. *Learning disorders,* a deceptively simple label that includes problems ranging from a lack of maturation to reading retardation to neurodevelopmental lag.

The multiaxial classification scheme, which is receiving widespread acceptance, is the model this chapter will follow. First, then, is consideration of the clinical psychiatric syndromes.

CLINICAL PSYCHIATRIC SYNDROMES

Two cautions should always accompany the analysis of children's problems. First is the warning that not all problems are psychiatric disorders. As mentioned earlier, many youngsters experience transient difficulties that differ somewhat from normal development. For example, many children exhibit temper tantrums. Careful examination usually reveals that the behavior does not differ significantly from that of other youngsters either in abnormality or severity; that is, the behavior often occurs in youngsters of this age and, most importantly, does not persist. Here the behavior is not a cause for concern. Second is the warning that the antecedent-behavior-maladaptive consequences chain is inextricably linked. Pinkerton (1974) states that it is the success or failure of individuals to adapt to the environment with their basic equipment that determines the clinical pattern.

Pinkerton then varies the elements in the equation, thus producing different outcomes. For example, if a youngster of low intelligence must interact with a father who stresses academic achievement, the result will be not only educational failure but concomitant behavioral problems. Or if a youngster of six or seven years who still occasionally wets his bed must interact with a tense, demanding mother while beginning school, the result will be increasing stress, perhaps accompanied by school refusal. It is tempting to continue specifying antecedents and speculating about maladjustment in light of environmental conditions, but these warnings should suffice.

The first of the clinical psychiatric syndromes is emotional disorders; recall, however, as Rutter (1975) notes, that childhood emotional disorders are not synonymous with adult neuroses. Adult neuroses are diagnosed more frequently in women than in men, while occurrences of childhood emotional disorders seem to be equally divided between boys and girls. Most youngsters who have experienced emotional difficulties do not become neurotic adults; the outlook for emotional disorders is quite good.

The Emotional Disorders

Childhood disorders involve states such as fears, phobias, anxiety, depression, obsessive-compulsive behavior, hypochondriasis, and hysteria in which the label identifies the condition: a youngster has a depressive disorder, or is in a phobic state, or is consistently obsessive. Chess and Hassibi (1978) state that although all aspects of a child's functioning are affected, there is no lasting intellectual deterioration, no primary mood disturbance, and the total personality remains intact. These disorders result from each child's unique style of activity and reactivity, which is in continuous interaction with the environment.

Fears, Phobias, Anxiety. These emotional problems can occur at any age, but are most common during early childhood and at puberty. For example, fear of dogs and cats is usually seen at two or three years, fear of the dark appears during the fourth year, and an impressive array of social and sexual fears occur during adolescence. Herbert (1974, p. 249) states:

> An analysis of children's fears at various age levels suggests that certain types of situations tend to evoke more worries at one particular phase of development than another. For example, the fears of three-year-olds are more often reality fears; as children get older, a majority of fears tend to be vague anxieties rather than focused fears of realistic danger. In deciding whether a child's fearfulness amounts to an out-of-the-ordinary emotional problem, it is obviously necessary to be familiar with the normal fears that children experience while growing up. A large number of fears are "outgrown" in the way that the child outgrows many childish toys, games, and interests.

Jersild and his colleagues (1935), in their classic investigation of four hundred children, studied twenty-five boys and twenty-five girls ranging in age from five to twelve years. Only *nineteen* of these children denied that they had ever experienced fear. Fear of the mysterious, giants, corpses, and witches were most

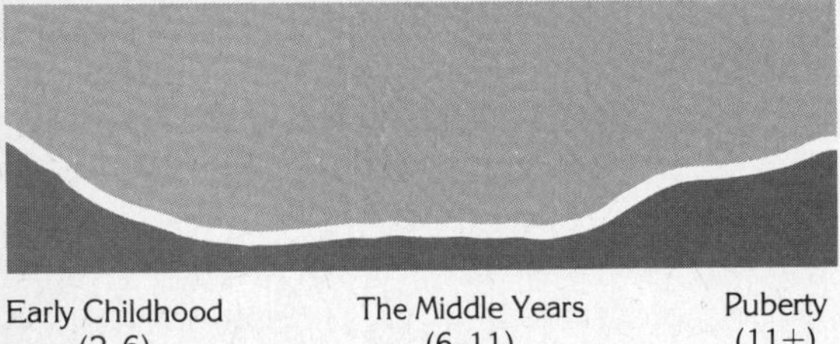

FIGURE 15.1. The Appearance of Fears.

common, followed by fear of animals, strangers, and being alone. Next were fears of bodily injury and nightmares. While the fears of the five- and six-year-olds differed from the older youngsters, the frequency of fears rose sharply for both age groups. Figure 15.1 illustrates the pattern.

Rutter (1975) believes that fear may focus on one object, person, or situation, or it may generalize widely. Childhood fears usually arise from some personal experience or from observation. A youngster who has been bitten by a dog may be terrified by the sight of any dog; youngsters who are insecure in their relations with parents may be fearful in most situations; children who have watched parents or siblings exhibit fear in a specific situation (crowded elevators, flying) may develop similar fears.

Anxiety lacks the specific focus of fear. Chess and Hassibi (1978, p. 241) define anxiety as an unpleasant sensation that is usually experienced as feelings of apprehension and general irritability accompanied by restlessness, fatigue, and such somatic components as headaches, a "funny feeling" in the stomach, and a heaviness in the chest. Both constitutional and environmental conditions seem to be present in anxiety. Treatment usually entails adult reassurance, a mild tranquilizer, and environmental manipulation. If acute anxiety persists, individual psychotherapy is recommended.

When fears and anxieties become so overwhelming that they dominate a child's feelings and behavior for lengthy periods, the term *phobic reaction* is used (Chess and Hassibi, 1978, p. 245). Children who develop such a fear of animals that they refuse to leave the house, older children who develop a morbid fear of dying, and the special case of school refusal are all examples of phobias.

School phobia is a particularly interesting example of this disorder, which usually appears at one of two times. The first occasion may be at the time of school entrance when children fear new situations and are reluctant to separate from the mother. These youngsters develop somatic symptoms before departing for school that are almost immediately relieved when the mother allows them to stay at home. With older children who have not previously demonstrated this phenomenon, refusal is typically linked to an examination, fear of a teacher, or difficulty with peers.

The symptoms are early morning stomach problems, headaches, and nausea. They may cry and cling to the mother, begging to stay home. Most authorities recommend a quick return to school. For younger children the outlook is good, while the prognosis for older youngsters is less optimistic.

Rutter (1975) has used school refusal to illustrate the necessity of identifying the various syndromes that appear because of different psychological mechanisms. Stating that school phobia is an important cause of psychiatric referral, he notes that there may be several reasons for its appearance: the parents may keep the youngster at home to babysit a sibling; the child may be truant; the refusal may arise from an emotional disorder, which in itself may reflect different causes.

Rutter states that the initial issue is determining if the child is at home when not at school. If the youngster is wandering the streets or is at a movie, the problem seems to be truancy and is usually associated with other delinquent acts. If the youngster is at home with the parents' knowledge, then the parents are keeping the child at home, or it is a case of school refusal. If it is the latter, then an emotional disorder is present, which may stem from different causes. The youngster may fear school, worry about separation from the parents, or manifest general social withdrawal.

Rutter then asks what the child is like when not at school. If normal and cheerful, then eliminate social withdrawal. Is school refusal linked to the school's curriculum? If it occurs on days when math is taught (or some other specific school activity), then the problem seems to be rooted in the school's activities. Is it linked to any particular condition in the home? For example, did it begin when the mother started to work?

Once the source is identified, the next question is why. Is the problem rooted in the child; that is, has the youngster always been anxious and fearful? With regard to the school, have any conditions (teachers, classes) changed? As for the home, are the parents conveying their anxieties about the child, work, or illness to the child?

Depression. Chess and Hassibi (1978, p. 139) state that depression is a pathological state, which like sadness, can be linked to environmental conditions, but, unlike sadness, is distinguished by the severity of the behavior. Depression is characterized by a depressed mood, psychomotor retardation, and difficulty in thinking. Other symptoms, such as fatigue, lack of enthusiasm, and numerous somatic complaints, may also be present.

Childhood depression is a controversial issue. Some authorities deny that it can appear in youngsters with the same symptoms that affect adults; others, lacking solid evidence and acknowledging children's inability to

express their subjective feelings, nevertheless believe that children suffer from depression. Rutter (1975) states that children undoubtedly suffer from depression but the manifestations are less clear. The feelings are not as acute as in adults, the depression seems to be more specifically linked to the contributing condition, and the feelings are more transient.

Cytryn and McKuen (1974) have identified three levels of childhood depression:

1. Depressive themes are present in dreams, fantasies, and responses to items in projective tests. These themes include preoccupation with death, personal injury, and rejection.

2. Feelings of unhappiness, worthlessness, and helplessness are expressed verbally.

3. Behavioral signs such as disturbed sleep, loss of appetite accompanied by weight loss, and psychomotor retardation appear. Conversely, delinquency can also result from feelings of depression.

A genetic tendency, coupled with contributing environmental conditions, causes depression. Depression seems to run in families, with a specific stimulus, such as the severing of an attachment, acting as the immediate precipitant.

For example, Cytryn and McKuen (1974) studied all the children and grandchildren of adult patients at the National Institute of Mental Health. The children were four to fifteen years of age and received a psychiatric examination that would uncover depressive symptoms. One psychiatrist conducted the interview, while two others observed through a one-way mirror. None of the psychiatrists knew the child's background or were specifically directed to look for symptoms of depression. Twenty-five evaluations were completed, and more than half of the youngsters were rated as overtly depressed. This is but one of the many studies indicating that there are genetic elements in depression.

These authors believe that there are three forms of childhood depression:

1. *A chronic depressive reaction of childhood,* which characterizes children who have experienced separation from loved ones or who have an emotionally disturbed mother.

2. *Acute depressive reaction,* which marks a child's response to a great personal loss.

3. *Marked depressive reaction,* which is distinguished by serious behavior problems.

Finally, any discussion of childhood depression should contain one warning: not all low spots in a child's mood are signs of depression.

Other Emotional Disorders. The third subdivision of emotional disorders consists of behavior that assumes many different forms. *Obsessive-compulsive* behavior is relatively rare in children, although adults suffering from this problem often date the beginning to the middle childhood years. Chess and Hassibi (1978, p. 250) describe obsessions as undesirable ideas, fears, or doubts that intrude on a child's consciousness without reasonable provocation. Compulsions are repetitive, stereotyped acts that the child uses to avoid imaginary threats. The obsessive-compulsive personality structure is rigid, self-righteous, excessively orderly, and perfectionistic.

The largest number of these children come from middle-class white families, with males outnumbering females. Symptoms include persistent questioning, frequent hand-washing, and ritualistic behavior, any one of which the child may use to cope with excessive anxiety. Treatment is usually lengthy; about fifty percent of the children show complete recovery and twenty percent demonstrate some improvement. The remaining thirty percent show increasing symptoms, and some of these become adult schizophrenics.

Hysterical conversion reactions are disorders whose physical symptoms arise from a psychological base—they are converted. Acute anxiety, for example, may be expressed by loss of speech (elective mutism) or some other form: blindness, paralysis, or inability to swallow. Rock (1971), reporting on ten cases of conversion reactions, referred to the Walter Reed Hospital, listed the following clinical symptoms: coma, flexion contracture at right knee, stiffness of leg and limping, seizures, aphoria (loss of voice), scoliosis with obvious deformity, loss of vision, hearing loss (total and partial).

Conversion reactions are most common in the middle childhood years. The problem responds well to treatment, but the long-range consequences of an obvious vulnerability to stress and anxiety remain uncertain. Rutter (1975) offers a timely warning in analyzing conversion reactions. While symptoms that appear with dramatic suddenness suggest a conversion reaction, there is always the possibility of organic disease.

Hypochondriasis is an exaggerated physical complaint: headaches, backaches, stomach problems. These are the chronic complainers who are the subject of so many jokes. Again, however, it is a learned method of coping with the environment in which the child by means of the headache or stomach ache avoids stress (going to school) and also accumulates rewards for the sickness (stays at home, watches television, has the mother's attention).

Hypochondriasis is similar to conversion reaction, but is not as severe and is typically linked to specific, relatively mild environmental stresses. Treatment is usually twofold: a thorough medical examination to ensure that the child is physically sound, followed by discussion to determine the source of the difficulty. Prognosis is good.

Conduct Disorders

> Conduct disorders are those in which the chief characteristic is abnormal behavior which gives rise to social disapproval. The category includes some types of legally defined delinquency, but it also includes non-delinquent disorders of conduct as shown by lying, fighting, bullying and destructive behavior. The mere fact that a child has transgressed the law does not, of course, mean that he has a conduct disorder. It is also necessary for the behavior to be abnormal in its sociocultural context and for there to be social impairment. (Rutter, 1975, p. 29)

The above quotation aptly delineates the parameters of conduct disorders. Many youth, deliberately or otherwise, break the law, but their offenses are comparatively minor and merely passing acts; these obviously are *not* conduct disorders. There are, however, youth who commit serious law violations; these obviously *are* conduct disorders. As Rutter notes, other instances (such as persistent bullying and fighting) are not law violations, but are conduct disorders.

Children with conduct disorders frequently have an accompanying emotional disorder, but it is the severity of the behavior that initially signals difficulty. Conduct disorders seem to fit a chronological hierarchy, which, while not age-specific, presents a logical sequence. The pattern is as follows:

Impulsive, unpredictable temperament
Often described as "difficult" babies
Generalized aggressive pattern appears
Lying
Fighting, bullying
Defiance of teachers

} *Predelinquent*

Stealing Educational difficulties Truancy Arson Problems with sex, alcohol, and drugs	} *Delinquent*

These are not finely discriminated categories. For example, predelinquents steal, have reading problems, and are truant. Delinquents lie, fight, and defy teachers. But the path is clear, from minor to serious conduct disorders that eventually involve the police and the courts. Since we have previously discussed temperamental characteristics and the development of aggression and hostility, the appearance of delinquent behavior will be our concern here.

Delinquency: An Overview. One misconception that we should dispel immediately is that delinquency is solely an American or a French or a British problem. It is no exaggeration to say that today juvenile delinquency exists on both a national and an international scale. Probably every reader of this text knows someone who has run afoul of the law or who has committed an act that would have resulted in some legal sanction if caught. Whether it be America, England, France, Japan, or Kenya, some delinquent subculture is present. The nature of the delinquency may vary, but the problem exists everywhere.

For example, youthful crime is on the rise in America probably as a direct result of the growing drug culture. As we have seen, youngsters are often forced into crime to feed a habit. How else can a relatively unskilled youth acquire the necessary fifty, sixty, or one hundred dollars a day for drug purchases? In more primitive societies, any rebellion against the customs of the older generation may be termed delinquent behavior. Obviously the nature of the deviant behavior differs in both societies, but in each example, a youth is in some sort of legal difficulty because of behavior.

The term "youthful crime" itself is a misnomer. Anyone who has been beaten, robbed, or raped by a juvenile will find it difficult to accept the terms, "youthful offenders, juvenile crime, or crimes of youngsters" with any degree of equanimity. One of the disturbing elements of juvenile crime is its tendency toward increasing violence. The rate of delinquency is also increasing more rapidly than the teenage population, and certain kinds of delinquency are more apparent than others. It should be expected that the type of delinquency will change as society changes, but because we are affluent, technologically advanced, and a mobile population, must we expect such a staggering increase in juvenile crime? It is alarming to contemplate that at least one of every five male adolescents will become a delinquent. And males have no exclusive right to crime; female delinquency is increasing at a rapid rate. Girls are manifesting a surprising increase in violations of the narcotics laws, even surpassing those for their male counterparts.

The increase in juvenile delinquency is related to changes in the structure of society such as our growing mobility, which disrupts both cultural patterns and family ties. We might also include the expanding population, the chaos of the large cities, and the seeming inability of the federal government to comprehend the extent of the social problems plaguing America. There is also an unknown amount of "hidden delinquency" in more affluent areas. The rate of crime nevertheless appears disproportionately high in low-income sections. The great number of juvenile offenders seems to come from deteriorated neighborhoods that are next to industrial regions and close to the centers of large cities. These sections of the city are subject to rapid population change, economic difficulties, and social disorganization. Here delinquency is frequently an approved way of life, and youngsters are formally taught the techniques of criminal behavior.

The formal structure of the youthful gang is amazing. For example, there may be both an elementary school and a junior high school in the school district where one particular gang is especially active. When gang members are inevitably arrested and sent to reform school, the gang's effectiveness is rarely hindered, since the members have trained some of the elementary school youth to fill any unexpected vacancies. Fifth-grade boys are often taken out with the gang and taught how to steal cars by shorting the ignition (starting a car without a key).

A girl may have a different kind of indoctrination. She accompanies gang members while they go from door to door in their housing project, taking orders for shirts, ties, skirts, blouses, and sweaters. Then they go to the city department stores and steal the desired merchandise. On returning to the project, they sell the goods at an enormous discount, say a thirty-dollar sweater for ten dollars. When apprehended, they feel that they have done nothing wrong; the stores can afford it, and they are helping their people.

THE MAKING OF A CRIMINAL

How does a youngster become entrapped in a life of delinquency and crime? Peter Maas (1968) has written a book called *The Valachi Papers*, an insider's account of organized crime in the United States. While it is itself fascinating, what is pertinent for us is Valachi's own story of how he was drawn into the criminal network.

Here are Valachi's memories of the road that led to delinquency and crime. He recalls that his was "the poorest family on earth . . . three rooms, no hot water, no bath, only a toilet out in the hall." This was for a family of eight. Valachi was constantly truant from school, and when he was eleven he hit a teacher in the eye with a rock. He was then sent to a disciplinary school, returned to the public schools, and left school to work after completing only the sixth grade.

It was then that he started to steal, because his father kept his money for the family. By the time he was eighteen, Valachi's petty thefts had earned him membership in a burglary gang. At nineteen he was arrested and sent to the notorious Sing Sing prison. Released, rearrested, and returned to Sing Sing, Valachi made his first contact with members of the crime syndicate.

The road Valachi travelled is clear—poor, needing money, truant, petty theft, making the contacts that lead to organized crime, acceptance into the syndicate and, finally, murder. Most cases are not so clear, but the pattern is identical. Organized crime is an almost irresistible lure to a susceptible youth.

Many delinquents come from economically impoverished or broken homes. Although many delinquents come from affluent homes with concerned parents, which presents a great obstacle in searching for crime causation, nevertheless, the problem arises more frequently among the deprived. These are the families whose children are exposed to delinquent practices early in life, whose parents are so concerned with, and perhaps defeated by, their own problems that they are unable to provide their youngsters with the care and guidance they need. Youngsters from such an environment suffer enormous frustration in life and yearn for some of the material signs of success. So they turn to crime to satisfy these needs and to the gang as the vehicle that eliminates some of the frustrations. The gang furnishes the know-how that is required to obtain the clothes and the flashy car, and it also furnishes an emotionally satisfying climate for the youngster who has probably suffered as much from emotional deprivation as from economic deprivation.

Healy and Bronner, in their classic research (1936), reported that ninety-one percent of the delinquents in their studies gave clear evidence of disorientation and extreme emotional disturbance. They felt rejected, deprived, insecure, and unloved. Only thirteen percent of the nondelinquent subjects in the control group manifested similar inner stresses. As Healy and Bronner noted, to the onlooker, delinquency merely signifies misconduct, while for the offender it is a response to inner drives and outer stimuli. Delinquency is only a small part of the person's life activities, and its level of significance represents a response to inner or outer pressures. It is one form of self-expression. The label that we apply to the delinquent act (larceny, truancy, breaking and entering) describes behavior that is in no way related to what the delinquent is expressing by this behavior. We need labels, but we must remember that the label reveals nothing about the determinants of that behavior.

Differences between Delinquents and Nondelinquents. The question may well be asked whether delinquents actually differ from nondelinquents. Glueck and Glueck (1950) suggest a dynamic pattern of delinquency that is neither exclusively biological nor sociological. They found the delinquents in their studies differed from the nondelinquents in the following ways:

1. Physically they were mostly mesomorphic (solid and muscular).
2. Temperamentally they were restlessly energetic, impulsive, extroverted, aggressive, destructive, and often sadistic.
3. In attitude they were hostile, defiant, resentful, suspicious, stubborn, adventurous, and nonsubmissive to authority.
4. Psychologically they were more interested in the concrete instead of the abstract and were less methodical in their attempts to solve problems.
5. Socioculturally they were more often reared in homes that offered little understanding, affection, stability, or moral fiber.

The Gluecks interpret these findings to mean that while any one of these pressures may account for the individual's delinquency, usually a high probability of delinquency depends on the interplay of them all. In the stimulating but culturally inconsistent milieu of underprivileged areas, those with delinquent tendencies express their impulses and selfish desires with little thought of self-control.

CAN DELINQUENCY BE PREVENTED?

In 1942, a program was devised at Aberdovey, Wales that was designed to prepare young merchant seamen for the dangerous duties of maritime service. They were exposed to situations of actual physical danger and given a chance to prove themselves. The survival rate among these young men soared and after World War II, the basic idea of this program began to spread around the world. Called Outward Bound, there are now twenty-eight schools functioning on five continents. In the United States, more than two hundred and fifty secondary schools and colleges are using some of the Outward Bound features.

What is the core of this program? Instead of telling youngsters that they are better than they think, a series of challenges are presented whereby youngsters can actually prove their worth to themselves. This is accomplished through severe physical obstacles that call on all of a youngster's skill, courage, and ingenuity. All programs stress:

1. Physical conditioning (running, hiking, swimming).
2. Technical training (use of tools, equipment, map reading).
3. Safety training.
4. Team training (rescue techniques, fire fighting).

Kelly and Baer (1971) emphasize that the programs are also proving quite successful in the prevention and treatment of juvenile delinquency. For example, in their study of sixty delinquents who participated in Outward Bound, only twenty percent had any further difficulty with the law, while in a control group of sixty other delinquents, forty-two percent experienced further difficulty. The authors feel that these programs can be a major weapon in the battle to prevent delinquency and recidivism (repeated delinquent acts).

Drug Usage. As mentioned previously, the spiraling rate of delinquency is undoubtedly linked to the proliferating drug culture. Experimenting with drugs is a way of life in certain subcultures. Once hooked, the need to maintain a steady supply at a dazzling cost frequently turns teenagers to crime: robbery, breaking and entering, car theft, arson for hire—the list is almost endless. Of current concern is the early age at which children first encounter drugs—during the elementary school years—making the onset of delinquent behavior earlier and earlier.

Any discussion of drug usage necessitates knowledge of the various drugs, especially for those who work with susceptible youngsters. Parents, counselors, and teachers quickly lose youngsters if they classify LSD and marijuana as narcotics. Table 15.1 provides a comprehensive list of drugs, their popular names, their source, classification, effects, and method of administration.

TABLE 15.1. Drug Classification

Name	Slang name	Chemical or trade name	Source	Classification	Medical use	How taken
Heroin	H., horse, scat, junk, smack, scag, stuff, harry	Diacetylmorphine	Semisynthetic (from morphine)	Narcotic	Pain relief	Injected or sniffed
Morphine	White stuff, M.	Morphine sulphate	Natural (from opium)	Narcotic	Pain relief	Swallowed or injected
Codeine	Schoolboy	Methylmorphine	Natural (from opium), semi-synthetic (from morphine)	Narcotic	Ease pain and coughing	Swallowed
Methadone	Dolly	Dolophine Amidone	Synthetic	Narcotic	Pain relief	Swallowed or injected
Cocaine	Corrine, gold dust, coke, bernice, flake, star dust, snow	Methylester of benzoylecgonine	Natural (from coca, *not* cacao)	Stimulant, local anesthetic	Local anesthesia	Sniffed, injected, or swallowed
Marijuana	Pot, grass, hashish, tea, gage, reefers	Cannabis sativa	Natural	Relaxant, euphoriant, in high doses hallucinogen	Experimental	Smoked, swallowed, or sniffed
Barbiturates	Barbs, blue devils, candy, yellow jackets, phennies, peanuts, blue heavens	Phenobarbital nembutal, seconal, amytal	Synthetic	Sedative-hypnotic	Sedation, relieve high blood pressure, epilepsy, hyperthyroidism	Swallowed or injected
Amphetamines	Bennies, dexies, speed, wakeups, lid proppers, hearts, pep pills	Benzedrine, dexedrine, desoxyn, methamphetamine, methedrine	Synthetic	Sympathomimetic	Relieve mild depression, control appetite and narcolepsy	Swallowed or injected
LSD	Acid, sugar, big D, cubes, trips	d-lysergic acid diethylamide	Semi-synthetic (from ergot alkaloids)	Hallucinogen	Experimental study of mental function, alcoholism	Swallowed
DMT	AMT, businessman's high	Dimethyltriptamine	Synthetic	Hallucinogen	None	Injected
Mescaline	Mesc.	3,4,5-trimethoxyphenethylamine	Natural (from peyote)	Hallucinogen	None	Swallowed
Psilocybin		3 (2-dimethylamino) ethylindol-4-oldihydrogen phosphate	Natural (from psilocybe)	Hallucinogen	None	Swallowed

Source: U.S. Public Health Service, *Resource Book For Drug Abuse Education* (Washington, D.C.: U.S. Government Printing Office, 1970), pp. 34, 35.

TABLE 15.1 Continued

Usual dose	Duration of effect	Effects sought	Long-term symptoms	Physical dependence potential	Mental dependence potential	Organic damage potential
Varies	4 hours	Euphoria, prevent withdrawal discomfort	Addiction, constipation, loss of appetite	Yes	Yes	No
15 milligrams	6 hours	Euphoria, prevent withdrawal discomfort	Addiction, constipation, loss of appetite	Yes	Yes	No
30 milligrams	4 hours	Euphoria, prevent withdrawal discomfort	Addiction, constipation, loss of appetite	Yes	Yes	No
10 milligrams	4 to 6 hours	Prevent withdrawal discomfort	Addiction, constipation, loss of appetite	Yes	Yes	No
Varies	Varies, short	Excitation, talkativeness	Depression, convulsions	No	Yes	Yes?
1 to 2 cigarettes	4 hours	Relaxation, increased euphoria, perceptions, sociability	Usually none	No	Yes?	No
50 to 100 milligrams	4 hours	Anxiety reduction, euphoria	Addiction with severe withdrawal symptoms, possible convulsions, toxic psychosis	Yes	Yes	Yes
2.5 to 5 milligrams	4 hours	Alertness, activeness	Loss of appetite, delusions, hallucinations, toxic psychosis	No?	Yes	Yes?
100 to 500 micrograms	10 hours	Insightful experiences, exhilaration, distortion of senses	May intensify existing psychosis, panic reactions	No	No?	No?
1 to 3 milligrams	Less than 1 hour	Insightful experiences, exhilaration, distortion of senses	?	No	No?	No?
350 micrograms	12 hours	Insightful experiences, exhilaration, distortion of senses	?	No	No?	No?
25 milligrams	6 to 8 hours	Insightful experiences, exhilaration, distortion of senses	?	No	No?	No?

Marijuana. Now let us examine some specific drugs and their effects, beginning with marijuana. Marijuana, one of the most popular drugs now in use, comes from a hemp plant, cannabis. It has many popular names, as we see in our chart: pot, grass, weed, Mary Jane. The drug is usually rolled and smoked as a cigarette or in a pipe. The cigarette form is frequently called a joint, a stick, or a reefer. Its sweet odor is quite easily recognized.

Although the drug is widely used, it is not well understood, and authorities clash violently over its effects on the user. During the 1960s, there was a phenomenal increase in its use, and arrests for marijuana more than doubled. It has become so troublesome that some authorities are now arguing that the lesser of the evils would be to legalize its use. Others, arguing that the extent of its ill effects is still unknown, believe that the laws should be retained, if not made harsher.

One of the reasons for disagreement is that medical science is still uncertain as to how the drug works in the body. When marijuana is smoked, it enters the bloodstream quickly and acts on the brain and the nervous system. But there is still no definite answer to the question of how the drug produces its effects. So the impact of long-term or heavy marijuana use remains a cloudy issue. The immediate effects, however, are readily apparent: rapid heartbeat, lowering of the body temperature, and reddening of the eyes.

The effect on the emotions varies enormously, depending on the amount, strength of the drug used, and the "atmosphere." One fact has been clearly established: the drug's effect is felt quickly, usually about fifteen minutes after inhaling. Its effects can then remain for about two to four hours, and may range from feelings of depression to excitement. Perception is often influenced, and users may experience a distortion of time and space, feeling it difficult to make decisions. They usually discover that their reflexes have slowed. Here we see a potentially dangerous result if users then find it necessary to drive.

The National Institute of Mental Health recently reported the results of a study that showed that one marijuana cigarette can make the user feel excited or silly. After four cigarettes, the user's perception becomes noticeably distorted; some users report that their senses are drastically sharpened. After ten cigarettes or a similar dose, visual hallucinations appear, and there are mood changes that reflect great joy and then extreme anxiety. Depression, panic, and fear are all reported.

Marijuana is not a narcotic and hence does not produce the physical dependence of drugs such as heroin. About the only almost complete agreement that one can discern among the "experts" is that we need more knowledge of the physical, personal, and social consequences of marijuana before we can reach any definite conclusions. Still, the physical risks cannot be discounted. A lasting impression may be made on a youth's personality, especially when we realize that children are experimenting with drugs at an age in which they are undergoing considerable change. Adjustment during these years is sufficiently difficult without complicating it with the use of drugs.

Way Up—Way Down. Some of the most commonly used drugs are the amphetamines (uppers) and the barbiturates (downers) because they are supposedly "harmless." These drugs are frequently used by students as they struggle through their school year. The amphetamines are a stimulant used to combat fatigue and drowsiness. Obviously they are relied on during periods when students are "catching up" for exams, term papers, or projects, and feel they cannot afford the time to sleep. The barbiturates have just the opposite effect: they act to relax the central nervous system.

The amphetamines stimulate the central nervous system and are sometimes used as diet pills to curb the appetite. The most frequently used stimulants are Benzedrine, Dexedrine, and Methedrine. They are also called bennies, pep pills, and speed. They increase the heart rate, raise the blood pressure, produce palpitations, and can also cause sweating, headaches, diarrhea, and pallor. The amphetamines account for about twenty percent of all prescribed mood-affecting drugs. When they are advised by a physician, they are employed to reduce fatigue, to increase alertness, or to lose weight. Even with the most careful supervision, however, their use can be followed by depression, or "crashing." It has been estimated that the drug industry manufactures enough of these pills each year to provide every American with twenty-five doses. Users range from housewives to truck drivers, from airline pilots to students.

Again, these drugs do not cause the physical dependence of the narcotics. It often happens that the user's body develops a tolerance for them, and ever larger doses are needed to achieve the desired effect. Perhaps the most serious concern relates to the state that they produce; stimulants may drive people to attempt feats of which they are incapable. Physical endurance is surpassed, and there may be lasting physiological damage. Also, heavy doses may lead to hallucinations, and speeding (injecting the drug directly into the vein instead of taking it in pill form) may even cause death.

The sedatives designed to "take the edge off" are best represented by the barbiturates (Nembutal, Seconal, Amytal, and Butisol), also called boobs and goof balls. Of all prescriptions written for mood-affecting drugs, one out of every four is for a barbiturate. The sedatives have a variety of legitimate uses: to relax a person before surgery, to treat high blood pressure, and to ease emotional problems, insomnia, and epilepsy. They depress the nervous system, slow down the heart rate, and lower blood pressure. Heavy doses cause drowsiness and sleep. When taken excessively, however, they may be fatal. These drugs slow reflexes and distort perception, and they should never be used before driving. The barbiturates are also physically addictive. Some authorities consider barbiturate addiction more difficult to cure than narcotic dependency. Withdrawal is so severe that it often must be undergone in a hospital, and the body may take several months to return to normal. If not treated properly, sudden withdrawal can sometimes be fatal.

LSD. LSD *(d-lysergic acid diethylamide)* is one of the most powerful drugs now in use. A single ounce of LSD will provide three hundred thousand average doses. A hallucinogen, LSD can provoke strange and bizarre mental reactions in the user and cause weird perceptual distortions. Concern is growing that the use of LSD can produce chromosomal damage. With such warnings, how can anyone justify its use? The answers are familiar and as ancient as the taking of drugs itself: to help me know myself, to see more deeply and vividly into the secrets of nature, to achieve certain mystical experiences. Yet the results of LSD usage can be so dangerous that the drug is illegal in the United States.

If the user is lucky, the effects of an average dose of LSD will leave in about eight to ten hours. But many cases have been reported in which the user again feels the effects in flashbacks occurring days, weeks, or even months after the initial dose. It is usually taken in the form of a sugar cube or capsule; occasionally it may be incorporated into another substance, such as a cookie. Pulse and heart rate increase, blood pressure rises, the individual usually begins to shake and to perspire, and may become nauseous. Equilibrium is frequently lost as perception becomes wildly distorted.

There are also garish psychological effects. Colors become almost overwhelming in their brilliance; walls seem to move, closing in and then receding; strange patterns appear; and sense impressions merge into each other—for example, users think that they can taste cold. One of the most devastating effects is that opposite emotions are experienced simultaneously; that is, people may feel both relaxed and tense. To put it both bluntly and simply, there is no safe prediction of a good or a bad trip. The dangers of LSD have been fairly well documented and include the following.

1. *Panic.* Since there is no way of stopping the drug's action, users may become tremendously fearful and feel that they are losing sanity.

2. *Paranoia.* Users become more and more suspicious, feeling that someone or something is trying to harm them. This effect can last as long as seventy-two hours after other effects of the drug have left.

3. *Recurrence.* We have previously mentioned this phenomenon and indicated that it is one of the more terrifying aspects of LSD. Weeks and months after people have ceased using the drug, they may be going about daily activities and suddenly experience some of the same feelings they had when using the drug. There is nothing better calculated to make people feel that they are going mad than these bolts from the blue.

4. *Accidental death.* Since perceptions can be so wildly distorted, there is constant danger of physical harm. For example, feeling that they can fly like a bird or walk on water, they may attempt to do so.

The hazards that result from the use of LSD are almost unlimited. The worry, depression, distortions of reality, and panic that can accompany a trip may cause lasting mental damage, especially in young users. We have mentioned possible harm to the chromosomes, which manifest unusual breaks and naturally may transmit any flaws to children. It is indeed foolhardy for anyone, especially a young person who is still developing mentally and physically, to experiment with this unpredictable mood changer.

Narcotics. Narcotics include opium and opium derivatives such as heroin, morphine, and codeine. They have great medical value as painkillers but, as used by addicts, heroin is probably the most popular. These narcotics, as contrasted with the other drugs we have discussed, are physically addictive. When users are "hooked," the body requires ever larger doses of the drug. As tolerance builds, more and more of the drug is required to surpass this point and to achieve the desired result.

There are clear signs of heroin addiction. When users stop, they suffer chills, shakes, diarrhea, nausea, and cramps. One of the more recent findings about withdrawal is that heroin addiction may be of much longer duration than originally suspected. And there is also the psychological dependence that occurs. It is much simpler to escape the harsh realities of life with a dose of heroin than to face life's challenges.

Once the tension is relieved and fear seems to disappear, it becomes easier to take that next injection. Anyone who has had to take large amounts of some painkiller knows that tremendous feeling of relief once the drug starts to work. For example, morphine or its synthetic form, Demerol, makes patients forget pain, which rides away on a cloud of euphoria. There is a feeling that all is well, accompanied by a sense of relaxation and calm. It is almost as if one can float above troubles. Heroin also kills appetite, and many addicts are so badly malnourished that they require special nutritional treatment. For the addicted individual, withdrawal symptoms begin to appear about eighteen hours after the last dose.

Those who are especially susceptible to heroin addiction are the youth of the slums, who are trying to escape the ugly reality of their daily living. Still, the addicts are not confined to urban areas. Anyone who has been forced to depend on painkillers for some lengthy period, because of an illness or accident, is a potential addict. Those who have easy access to drugs, such as doctors, nurses, and druggists, are also vulnerable. Although availability is the easy explanation, there is usually a more complicated cause; those readily tempted seem to be suffering from emotional difficulties not terribly different from those of the addict.

The first step toward heroin addiction may begin as early as the elementary school years. A child is usually enticed into sniffing heroin, which then moves very quickly through the nasal membranes into the bloodstream. The next step is injection into the fleshy parts of the body, but not directly into the veins. Users soon begin to build a tolerance for this amount, however, which leads to the next step: direct injection into the veins, which gives almost immediate pleasure. For a few hours, everything becomes tranquil and reality recedes into a blurred background. As users return to reality, worry sets in about the source of the next "fix." This soon becomes an obsession as the need builds to three or four injections a day. When the need becomes this great (possibly one hundred dollars a day) life is dedicated solely to obtaining the needed money. All other activities are discarded, and the user frequently turns to crime.

Once addicted, life becomes an inescapable hell. Where will the next fix come from? What can I use for money? When hooked, maintaining the supply becomes the main goal in life. Education, work, and family suffer as the addict concentrates on the means for satisfying the need. Imagine the task of obtaining fifty or even one hundred dollars every day. Education suffering, work suffering, and family suffering, where will the money come from? There is only one logical next step: steal it. The tremendous rise in crime rate is certainly partially due to addicts' insatiable need to keep their supply at a necessary minimum. Once hooked, addicts are at the mercy of suppliers.

Addicts are sick. They require expert treatment for both physical addiction and withdrawal ills, and then need special help to prevent a return to the drug. This is unquestionably the most difficult part of the therapy, because life has revolved around obtaining the drug and the release it offered. There is no simple solution to this phase of the problem. One experimental technique is to provide addicts with a drug such as methadone when their craving is almost unmanageable. Supposedly this currently controversial drug acts in place of the narcotic, without its damaging effects.

Authorities trying to convey an accurate meaning of drug abuse have devised the term "drug dependence," an expression that seems to suggest both a physical and psychological sense of dependence. This state of psychic or physical dependence, or both, arises after administration of a drug on a particular or continuous basis. Simply phrased, users cannot do without the drug.

Recent Trends. Any society that urges its citizens to avoid even minimal discomfort encourages drug usage. Do you have a headache? Try aspirin. Are you anxious? Try valium. As Ray notes (1978), if you weren't paying attention in the mid-sixties and seventies, don't bother to look for the drug scene—it's gone. That is, it is gone as a phenomenon because drugs now have become part of our society.

This change has been accompanied by the rise and fall in popularity of particular drugs. LSD, one of the "in" drugs of the sixties, declined in use with the advent of the seventies. Marijuana usage, while still increasing, has nevertheless slowed. Today, two of the most popular drugs are cocaine and PCP (phencyclidine piperidine hydrochloride).

Wealthy young people have found cocaine especially attractive in the seventies and the beginning of the eighties. Cocaine is particularly potent in arousing the central nervous system; it acts as a stimulant and the user immediately feels good—an effect that quickly passes. While heavy and prolonged use can have serious consequences (loss of appetite, paranoia), this does not seem to characterize current patterns of cocaine use. Nevertheless, almost ten million Americans have used cocaine recreationally, which elevates it to a drug of concern.

PCP, frequently referred to as "angel dust," is one of the most lethal drugs now in popular use. It seems to have become the hallucinogen of the late seventies and early eighties. PCP first was accepted in the streets during the late sixties but reactions were so bad that its popularity quickly declined. It is difficult to explain its reemergence.

Many misconceptions surround PCP. While usually classified as one of the major hallucinogens, its chemical structure is quite different. It was never intended to be an animal tranquilizer; it is an effective analgesic-anesthetic for animals; most PCP now on the street has been illegally manufactured and has not been stolen from veterinary sources. It is relatively easy to manufacture, which is one of its dangers. Users report feelings of dying and some experts believe that taking PCP can be a disguised death wish.

The link between serious conduct disorders (such as the law violations of the delinquent) and the drug culture is clear. Not that this is the sole cause of the problem, because it is clear that some antisocial behavior is caused by a psychiatric disorder, some is caused by family discord, and some is learned behavior.

Hyperkinesis. Although restlessness and overactivity are characteristic of many children with psychiatric problems, some youngsters (primarily boys) manifest a degree of overactivity that is a problem in itself. These are hyperkinetic youngsters. Chess and Hassibi (1978, p. 334) note that while hyperkinesis and minimal brain dysfunction (MBD) are often used synonymously, the preferred label is minimal brain dysfunction, although there is *no* direct evidence of brain damage in these children. (Recall Rutter's warning about such usage.) Chess and Hassibi stress that the clinical picture of MBD is not directly connected to central nervous system damage. Rather, the hypothesis is that central nervous system impairment causes a distorted interaction with the environment.

The extreme overactivity usually appears by three or four years; it is accompanied by a short attention span so that the child is constantly moving from one activity to another. Educational problems, especially with reading, quickly result and aggravate the condition. Relations with others—parents, peers, and teachers—deteriorate, further intensifying the problem.

It is clearly impossible to designate any single cause of the disorder. Chess and Hassibi (1978) state that there seems to be a higher than usual rate of abnormal prenatal conditions and difficult births among these children. Neurological examinations show signs of deficits in sensorimotor coordination (clumsiness, difficulty with buttons, and tying shoe laces). There are some signs of abnormal brain wave patterns in many hyperkinetic children, and they evidence difficulty with the spatial-motor tasks of such tests as the Wechsler Intelligence Scale for Children.

These youngsters usually require special educational programs (for themselves and their parents), perhaps psychotherapy, and occasionally, drug treatment. Drugs that act as stimulants for adults have been found to have a calming effect on hyperkinetic youngsters, but the treatment is still controversial because of lack of knowledge of precisely how these drugs work on these children. Tranquilizers may help certain of these youngsters. The prognosis for hyperkinetic children is not good because the social consequences of the disorder extend into adolescence.

Infantile Autism. This is a severe and rare disorder that appears before thirty months of age, and was first described by Leo Kanner in 1944. Among the characteristics of the autistic child are the following:

1. A profound withdrawal of contact from other people.
2. Severe language problems.
3. Obsessive preservation of the status quo.
4. Skill in fine motor movements.
5. An inability to deal with people.
6. A good cognitive potential as opposed to poor intellectual performance.

The problem appears more frequently in boys, and most of these youngsters require special education. The prognosis is poor. Autistic children who possess normal intelligence may complete basic school and secure employment; they rarely marry. Controversy rages around the issue of causation. Suran and Rizzo (1979, p. 382) probably best summarize the current status:

> Our review of environmental and biological theories of the causation of early infantile autism suggests that the once popular notion regarding parental mishandling as the primary causative factor in autism is on the wane. By contrast, convincing evidence is accumulating that autism is the result of central nervous system impairments resulting from prenatal and perinatal damage. The nature of such impairments is far from clear, but the progress made thus far has been exciting, and investigators from many disciplines ranging from psychiatry and neurology through experimental psychology are beginning to fit together pieces in an important developmental puzzle.

Childhood Schizophrenia. This severe disorder, slightly more common than infantile autism, is described by Suran and Rizzo (1979) as a severe disorder of childhood characterized by some combination of extreme interpersonal isolation, noncommunicative use of speech, repetitive body movements, self-injurious behavior, regression in behavior, abnormal responses to light or sound, problems in feeding and sleeping, abnormal fears or lack of fears, and delusional behavior. Many of these characteristics apply to infantile autism, but the age of onset differs: autism appears before thirty months, while childhood schizophrenia appears mainly from four to seven years. Current research seems to point to neurological difficulties, genetic elements, or both as the chief causes, although environmental agents are not discounted.

Rimland (1964) distinguishes infantile autism from childhood schizophrenia by detailing characteristics of both disorders. Among his distinctions are the following:

1. *Onset and Cause.* Signs of autism are present from birth, whereas schizophrenic children commence normal development.

2. *Health and Appearance.* Autistic children are usually quite healthy, while schizophrenic children manifest poor health from birth.

3. *Electroencephalography.* Autistic children have normal EEGs; schizophrenic youngsters manifest abnormal patterns.

4. *Physical Responsiveness.* Schizophrenic children mold themselves into adults, while autistic babies stiffen their bodies away from adults.

5. *Autistic Aloneness.* Autistic youngsters are withdrawn and indifferent; schizophrenic children respond to adults.

6. *Motor Performance.* Autistic children show greater motor coordination than schizophrenics.

7. *Family History.* Families of autistic children show high intelligence, emotional stability, low divorce rate, and significantly low rates of mental illness.

Rimland's other categories were mentioned in the initial description of childhood schizophrenia. While schizophrenia usually is a lifelong problem, the outlook is a little brighter than for autism. Estimates are that about two-thirds of schizophrenic children will make some adjustment to society—from marginal (in the home) to acceptable (some community involvement).

DISCUSSION QUESTIONS

1. Explain the etiology of maladjustment using the antecedents-consequences diagram. Fill in with specific disorders, for example, fear or asthma.
2. If you were judging the abnormality and severity of a problem, what criteria would you use? Give specific examples, and emphasize age and sex appropriateness.
3. Use specific examples to illustrate when you would identify a fear or anxiety as a problem. Explain the criteria discussed earlier.
4. Is it possible to trace the chronology of delinquency? Do you "lean" to any specific cause of delinquent behavior? From your knowledge of the youth culture today, would you agree that drugs are a main cause of much violent behavior? If your answer disagrees with that of your classmates, attempt to discover the reasons.
5. While relatively rare, infantile autism and childhood schizophrenia are dramatic behavior disorders that attract considerable attention. How would you distinguish them?

INTELLECTUAL ELEMENTS

While mental retardation is such a unique handicap that many of these youngsters require special education, some do not and thus become the responsibility of parents, teachers, and counselors. For all of these children, it is safe to state that as the intellectual level drops, the prevalence of psychiatric disorders rises. Retarded youngsters are limited in their ability to learn, they are usually socially immature, and some carry additional physical and emotional disabilities.

Classification

The most widely accepted definition of mental deficiency is that proposed by the American Association on Mental Deficiency:

> Mental retardation refers to significantly subaverage general intellectual functioning existing concurrently with deficits in adaptive behavior and manifested during the developmental periods.

This definition clearly transcends a purely cognitive interpretation, and stresses the entire spectrum of adaptive behavior. Estimates are that about three percent of the population is mentally retarded. Table 15.2 presents the estimated number of retardates by category.

Note the label on each category, which is intended to signify IQ range, characteristics, and prognosis. The description of each category is as follows.

1. The profound mentally retarded represent about 1.5 percent of the retarded population. Infant mortality is high; survivors require total care.

2. The severe mentally retarded encompass about 3.5 percent of this population. They are usually institutionalized and require constant supervision. They usually have the potential of acquiring language and self-care skills after intensive training.

3. The moderate mentally retarded are about 6 percent of the retarded. Many are in institutions, but some can remain at home and help with household chores.

4. The mild mentally retarded constitute about 89 percent of the retarded and can usually adjust to society, provided they receive help with more abstract complicated tasks. Interestingly, only about 1 percent of this group are institutionalized, and then not for low intelligence but for conduct disorders. They may be found in the special classes of the public schools, but the majority are in regular classes (especially at the elementary level) and are classified as slow learners.

Table 15.3 summarizes the potential for adaptation of each category.

TABLE 15.2. Estimated Distribution of Retarded Persons in the United States by Age and Degree of Retardation

Degree of retardation	All ages		Age by years	
	Number	Percent	Under 20	20 and Over
Total	6,000,000	100.0	2,455,000	3,545,000
Mild (IQ 52–69)	5,340,000	89.0	2,136,000	3,204,000
Moderate (IQ 36–51)	360,000	6.0	154,000	206,000
Severe (IQ 20–35)	210,000	3.5	105,000	105,000
Profound (IQ 0–20)	90,000	1.5	52,900	37,100

Source: *The Problem of Mental Retardation.* U.S. Department of Health, Education and Welfare, Office for Handicapped Individuals. Washington, D.C.: U.S. Government Printing Office, 1975.

TABLE 15.3. Adaptive Behavior Classification for the Retarded

Mild	Development slow. Children capable of being educated ("educable") within limits. Adults, with training, can work in competitive employment. Able to live independent lives.
Moderate	Slow in their development, but able to learn to care for themselves. Children capable of being trained ("trainable"). Adults need to work and live in sheltered environment.
Severe	Motor development, speech, and language are retarded. Not completely dependent. Often, but not always, physically handicapped.
Profound	Need constant care or supervision for survival. Gross impairment in physical coordination and sensory development. Often physically handicapped.

Source: *The Problem of Mental Retardation.* U.S. Department of Health, Education, and Welfare, Office for Handicapped Individuals. Washington, D.C.: U.S. Government Printing Office, 1975.

Etiology

Knobloch and Pasamanick (1974) state that deviant development demands analysis to determine if the problem is deeply entrenched or transient, generalized or delimited, ameliorable or ineducable. These authors believe that many children escape early detection because observers fail to make critical distinctions among disabilities, thus causing them to diagnose retardation when another cause is responsible, such as undetected organic disease, or failing to recognize retardation because it is masked by an accompanying emotional disorder.

If you examine Table 15.4 carefully you will discover developmental characteristics that shield the condition from an observer, especially for the mildly mentally retarded. Note the comment in the first block for mild mentally retarded, "often not distinguished from normal until later age." Thus the degree of the child's slowness is not apparent until abstract material is encountered and it becomes clear that the youngster is not experiencing a temporary learning difficulty.

Smith (1977, p. 258) summarizes some of the characteristics of retarded children as follows:

> Some behavioral components likely to be found in the more severely mentally deficient children include perseveration with a lack of change in responsiveness, dependency on routine, stimulus-bound and therefore, easily distractible, fear, lack of spontaneity, and diminished ability to maintain a chain of thought, and, therefore, poor judgment. Such children are liable to manifest repetitive physical activities that are disturbing to other people, such as oral preoccupation, rocking, head-banging, hyperactivity, and temper tantrums. Neurological functioning is also frequently altered, as evidenced by such signs as hypertonicity, hypotonicity, ataxia, altered reflexes, poor coordination, and a variety of minor and major types of seizures.

While there is no direct connection between the level of retardation and its cause, there is a tendency to divide these children into two categories:

1. Those with mild (and perhaps some moderate) mental retardation who do not demonstrate severe organic pathology. These may be the children of mentally dull parents, or come from deprived socioeconomic conditions.

2. Those with severe retardation who usually manifest some central nervous system damage.

Focusing upon the second group, the severely mentally retarded, Smith (1977) offers the following subcategorization based on the apparent age of onset of the problem.

TABLE 15.4. Developmental Characteristics of Mentally Retarded Persons

Degrees of mental retardation	Preschool age (0–5) Maturation and development	School age (6–20) Training and education	Adult (21 and over) Social and vocational adequacy
Mild	Can develop social and communication skills; minimal retardation in sensorimotor areas; often not distinguished from normal until later age.	Can learn academic skills up to approximately sixth-grade level by late teens. Can be guided toward social conformity. "Educable."	Can usually achieve social and vocational skills adequate to minimum self-support but may need guidance and assistance when under unusual social or economic stress.
Moderate	Can talk or learn to communicate; poor social awareness; fair motor development; profits from training in self-help; can be managed with moderate supervision.	Can profit from training in social and occupational skills; unlikely to progress beyond second-grade level in academic subjects; may learn to travel alone in familiar places.	May achieve self-maintenance in unskilled or semiskilled work under sheltered conditions; needs supervision and guidance when under mild social or economic stress.
Severe	Poor motor development; speech is minimal; generally unable to profit from training in self-help; little or no communication skills.	Can talk or learn to communicate; can be trained in elemental health habits; profits from systematic habit training.	May contribute partially to self-maintenance under complete supervision; can develop self-protection skills to a minimal useful level in controlled environment.
Profound	Gross retardation; minimal capacity for functioning in sensorimotor areas; needs nursing care.	Some motor development present; may respond to minimal or limited training in self-help.	Some motor and speech development; may achieve very limited self-care; needs nursing care.

Source: *The Problem of Mental Retardation.* U.S. Department of Health, Education, and Welfare, Office for Handicapped Individuals. Washington, D.C.: U.S. Government Printing Office, 1975.

Category I: Prenatal Problem in Morphogenesis of the Brain. Smith believes that this category encompasses the largest number of severely retarded and represents those with a primary defect in brain morphogenesis, such as microcephaly, hydrocephalos, or neural tube defects.

Category II: Perinatal Insult to the Brain. Defects during the birth process include perinatal hypoxia, hypoglycemia, and intracerebral hemorrhage. Smith cautions investigators not to leap at perinatal problems as the primary cause of mental deficiency; these children may manifest difficulty with neonatal adaptation because of Category I problems.

Category III: Postnatal Onset of Problem in Brain Function. These youngsters resemble normal newborns but gradually evidence deterioration in development. Their condition may result from postnatal infection (meningitis, lead poisoning, enzyme difficulties).

Category IV: Undecided Age of Onset of the Problem in Brain Function. These youngsters give no evidence of a prenatal problem in brain morphogenesis nor do they have any history of brain insult in the perinatal period. They merely show delayed development with no apparent cause. This is the second largest group.

Chess and Hassibi (1978) have grouped the causes of mental retardation as follows:

1. *Genetic factors,* which include both chromosomal abnormalities (Down's Syndrome) and genetic defects (PKU).

2. *Prenatal factors,* which include a range of causative agents ranging from maternal malnutrition and stress and toxemia of pregnancy to specific viral infections.

3. *Perinatal and neonatal factors,* which include oxygen deficit, deformities of the birth canal, and uncommon fetal position.

4. *Postnatal factors,* which include brain damage, endocrine problems, poisoning, and physical accidents.

While mental retardation obviously affects cognitive functioning (learning, attention, memory, problem solving), the retarded child is increasingly vulnerable to personality disorders. Emotional growth is usually far below normal, socialization suffers, and tolerance for anxiety and frustration is low. As Chess and Hassibi (1978, p. 295) conclude, various studies have shown a higher incidence of psychiatric disorders among the mentally retarded.

BIOLOGICAL ELEMENTS

Certain physical problems often cause psychiatric disorders, but they probably just as often are *caused* by psychiatric disorders, or at least aggravated by such disorders.

Gender

Even such fundamental physical characteristics as sex differences deserve consideration in any analysis of the role of biological functioning in children's problems. It is a well established finding that psychiatric disorders are much more frequently diagnosed in boys than girls. Whether this is because of a greater constitutional vulnerability to stress, or a male's native temperament, or because of some cultural difference is unknown, but the data clearly indicate a strong sex difference in the frequency of psychiatric disorders.

Genetics

Although genetics may be a component of a psychiatric problem, Rutter (1975, p. 136) states that only relatively rare disorders constitute a single disease that is inherited as such (PKU, Down's Syndrome). Even schizophrenia, whose hereditary significance is apparent, results from an interaction between the genetic influence and environmental conditions. Rutter (1975, p. 136) summarizes the issue as follows:

> As already noted, genetic factors are very influential in the development of many temperamental attributes. But their effect is not to predestine a child to the inevitable development of any particular kind of behavior. Rather there is an ongoing interaction with environmental influences which results in the eventual individual personality traits.

It is the child's unique genetic pattern, interacting with a particular environment, that produces a unique personality. As Rutter notes, we cannot expect children whose genes dispose them toward introversion to become outgoing, ebullient extroverts.

Physical Illness

Chronic physical illness is associated with higher rates of emotional, behavioral, and educational problems. While the disorder is usually not the direct result of the disease, it undoubtedly results from a cluster of difficulties that all children encounter. For example, forced inactivity can cause a diminished self-concept, with the resulting negative influence on behavior.

Among the diseases that subtly wcavc in and out of the antecedents-behavior-consequences framework are the following.

1. *Failure-to-Thrive.* FTT is a label applied to children whose weight remains below the third percentile for age. This problem accounts for approximately one to three percent of pediatric hospital admissions; its incidence in the nonhospitalized population is uncertain. There is a decided split between those who believe that FTT is primarily caused by a detectable organic disease, and those who believe that its cause is far more mysterious. For example, some authorities attribute eighty-five percent of all FTT cases to a chronic disease; for others the estimate is between ten and twenty percent.

Where the cause is discovered to be organic, the gastrointestinal tract is frequently the source; these youngsters often have a history of vomiting. For nonorganic FTT, a medical explanation eludes detection; these youngsters often exhibit unusual social behavior such as avoidance of any close physical contacts. The basic early studies attributed the cause to maternal inadequacy, but today's work stresses an interactional etiology in which infants contribute to their own nurturant patterns.

The prognosis for nonorganic FTT youngsters is not good. Physically they may show a weight increase, but estimates are that more than fifty percent will experience serious educational problems, especially with verbal skills, and behavioral disorders.

2. *Asthma.* Chess and Hassibi (1978, p. 237) define asthma as an episodic bout of breathing difficulty caused by overactivity of the parasympathetic system involving the bronchial tubes. It affects about two percent of the population; boys are the more common sufferers. For some youngsters, psychological conditions can elicit attacks, while others manifest a psychological reaction to the disease. Knapp (1977) states that both experimental and clinical evidence suggests that psychological factors have the potential and actual capacity to influence pulmonary function in asthma, both adversely and beneficially.

Knapp (1977), calling asthma a "physiologically treacherous disease," raises a strong warning about the use of steroids such as cortisone in medical treatment. Although these drugs are immediately beneficial, the long-range consequences are distressing; they can cause osteoporosis, ulcers, cataracts, hypertension. Thus in cases of severe asthmatic impairment, psychotherapy must be in close conjunction with medical treatments. Behavior modification, hypnosis, drugs, group therapy, and family therapy have all been attempted, with limited success, to reduce the extent of physical impairment and also to alleviate psychological consequences.

3. *Sleep Disorders.* Most children establish a sleeping rhythm between three and six months that provides a period of uninterrupted sleep during the night. Sleep disorders take many forms:

a. Sleepwalking

b. Sleeptalking

c. Pavor Nocturnus or Night Terrors (child wakes terrified, breathing heavily, perspiring, perhaps screaming)

d. Narcolepsy (sudden episodes of sleepiness)

e. Developmental, transitory difficulty (bad dreams)

Sleep disorders usually arise from parental handling, a definite environmental cause, or some rare deep-seated emotional disorder. Levine, Brooks, and Shonkoff (1980) state that this is a difficult problem for both parents and pediatricians, but the parents should initially offer as much support as possible during the night, deal directly with any reality distortions the child may have, and attempt to establish a regular schedule. Prognosis is good, but progress is slow.

4. *Enuresis.* Chess and Hassibi (1978, p. 234) define enuresis as the involuntary incontinence of urine after the age of four. By six or seven years, eighty percent of all children have achieved bladder control; among the remaining twenty percent, boys outnumber girls. Behavioral problems are associated with enuresis; for example, aggression is common, perhaps an indication of poor impulse control. Conversely, some studies have shown enuresis to be linked to shyness. Again, a familiar pattern appears: in some youngsters, when bladder control is established, psychiatric disorders disappear; in others the underlying psychiatric disorder precedes the bladder problem and remains after bladder control is established.

There may be sex differences in the appearance of enuresis, that is, in boys it may be due to a maturational lag, while in girls it may suggest an emotional disorder. Evidence does not point to any clear cluster of causes; different circumstances cause the problem in different children. Treatment usually involves retraining (limit liquids and awaken the child every few hours; use of "bell and pad"—the first drop of urine on the pad activates a buzzer, awakening the child), and chemotherapy (use of stimulant drugs to interfere with dry sleep). Psychotherapy has not proven very successful. Prognosis is good.

5. *Encopresis.* Uncontrolled defecation is much more rare than enuresis—about one child in sixty-five—and is a problem that begins at about four years and peaks at six or seven years. It is about five times more common in boys than girls. Levine (1979) defines encopresis as the regular passage of stools in inappropriate sites by children beyond four years of age. Traditionally, encopresis is divided into two types: *primary,* mainly linked to environmental circumstances such as faulty training—forty percent; and *secondary,* a child for some reason loses previously acquired control—sixty percent.

Rutter (1975) distinguishes three forms: those youngsters who simply fail to gain bowel control (frequently associated with enuresis), those who retain matter because of difficulty or pain connected with bowel movement (here there is secondary overflow causing the soiling), and those who acquire bowel control but lose it because of some psychiatric disorder (here soiling is not accompanied by wetting; the movements are normal but deposited in unsuitable places).

Levine, Brooks, and Shonkoff (1980), after discussing organic causes of the problem, analyze environmental circumstance that may be causative. Some children develop an irrational fear of the toilet (they fear being flushed down, falling off the toilet seat, or some may be similar to the youngster who feared toilets because of the "fish monsters that bite your rear end whenever you sit down"). School age youngsters can develop encopresis because of school toilets; wild stories about lavatory activities, toilet seats without doors, and sheer ignorance all contribute to the problem.

These authors believe that youngsters need both information, respect, and ongoing support. Intervention strategies must be structured for the child, because encopresis, due to feelings of humiliation and self-debasement, can cause serious psychiatric disorders. Levine (1979) estimates that about half the cases respond immediately to treatment, with age as the great healer. Remission is common with encopresis.

6. *Anorexia Nervosa.* Bruch (1978) states that a disease that selectively strikes the young, rich, and beautiful is rare, but today it has appeared in affluent societies. Severe starvation leading to devastating weight loss causes the victim to resemble the inmates of concentration camps. Over ninety percent of its victims are teenage girls whose irrational pursuit of thinness can cause a cessation of menstruation when weight loss reaches 10–20 percent.

Three classes of symptoms are present: behavioral (refusal by food restriction to maintain normal weight), physical (the weight loss itself), and psychological (usually a distorted body image accompanied by an intense fear of obesity). There is no known medical cause.

Bruch (1978, p. ix) states:

> There is now broad agreement that anorexia nervosa is a distinct illness with an outstanding feature: relentless pursuit of excessive thinness. . . . It is also recognized that anorexia nervosa is an incorrect name for this illness, but it is generally accepted and probably will continue to be used. Anorexia means lack of appetite. Though food intake is sharply curtailed, this is not because of poor appetite or lagging interest in food.

Prevalence of the problem is difficult to establish, although estimates are now as high as one in two to three hundred teenage girls; there is general agreement that the disease is increasing. Treatment includes the resumption of an adequate diet, drugs (especially if depression is involved), and psychotherapy, perhaps including family therapy. Prognosis is mixed: estimates are that from thirty to fifty percent recover completely, about thirty percent manifest intermediate recovery (marked by periodic crises), and the remainder never fully recover.

These are only the more prominent of the biological elements that could fit our antecedent-behavior-consequence framework. Brain disorders (cerebral palsy, epilepsy), sexual problems, obesity, allergies, and physical handicaps all deserve study within a development framework, testing the severity, appropriateness of the behavior associated with the difficulty, and causes of the appearance of the disorder.

DISCUSSION QUESTIONS

1. Are the categories of mental retardation that were presented workable for identification and treatment? If not, what would you suggest?
2. If you accept the premise that some youngsters mask their characteristics—that is, they are not obviously overt—and will appear in regular classrooms, what does this imply for the "mainstreaming" movement?
3. Select any one physical problem discussed here or one of your own choosing and place it in the antecedent-behavior-consequence framework. What does this tell you about identification, cause, severity, appropriateness, treatment, and outcome? Is the problem you raise "self-feeding," that is, is it a problem with psychiatric origins whose expression intensifies the cause?
4. Encopresis is an excellent example of the "self-feeding" problem. Identify possible causes, suggest an intervention strategy, and predict outcome. Now justify your prediction in light of the data you presented. Indicate clearly how the physical and psychological aspects interact to prolong, even intensify, the disorders.

PSYCHOSOCIAL ELEMENTS

In Chapter Twelve we traced the dramatic changes that have occurred in family styles and also stressed the vitality that families bring to any society. The changes that we traced will undoubtedly remain since they reflect societal change. There is a classic list of family conditions that are associated with psychiatric disorders: broken homes, institutional upbringing, death, abuse, separation, and family discord, all of which have been discussed. However, as Rutter (1975, p. 138) states, it is insufficient to identify these negative conditions; we must attempt to understand the psychological mechanisms that are active.

Discipline

An important mechanism that Rutter mentions is the relationship between child rearing and discipline. Other than the safe statement that excessively harsh or excessively lax discipline produces negative effects, there is little that can be positively said about the middle range of disciplinary practices. Only two aspects of discipline seem noteworthy: frequency of punishment and consistency of discipline. Constant punishment and inconsistent measures appear to produce later hostility and aggression. With the goal of helping a youngster acquire personal internal controls, discipline can be positive, especially if parents explain the reason behind the action.

Death

Although we have previously discussed the consequences of separation, the impact of parental death deserves special consideration. The risk of psychiatric disorder following a parent's death seems greatest at three or four years of age, especially if it is the same-sex parent. Probably there are additional aspects of death that contribute to later disorders: illness preceding the death, the surviving parent's grief, any concomitant family disruption (having to stay with relatives), social and economic difficulties that may follow, and problems adjusting to parental remarriage. Older children usually display grief patterns similar to adults.

The Schools

Just as youngsters can develop psychiatric disorders by their interaction with family members, so can the community itself contribute to psychiatric disorders. We have already discussed "life in the alley" and the propensity for delinquency associated with particular geographic areas. Housing, social status, and migration (moving to new neighborhoods means breaking old ties and forming new friends), but especially schools are all critical social elements in personality adjustment. As Levine, Brooks, and Shonkoff (1980, p. vii) state:

> In addition, we now have evidence, after a period of denigration, of the effectiveness of schools. Rutter has shown that certain kinds of schools are more effective in dealing with children with behavior and learning problems than others.

Clearly an institution in which youngsters spend so much time must have as much influence on their personal development as on their academic development. Segal (1978) speaks sensitively of the school's impact on a child's self-image; it is in the school that children realistically begin to assess capacity and competence. It is one thing to speak generally of the school's influence on child development; it is quite another to specify exactly what school activities influence what behavior.

Rutter and his colleagues have examined certain aspects of the school (resources, teacher punctuality, actual time spent teaching, mix of pupil ability) and attempted to link them to such student behaviors as achievement, delinquency, and disruptive behavior. Among their findings was that schools with a high rate of

CHILDREN AND DEATH

A grim, but significant, aspect of child development has finally emerged—children and their concept of death. It is a difficult topic, both emotionally and cognitively; emotionally, since no one enjoys discussing the meaning of death with children; cognitively, since children think differently about their own death than that of others. For example, level of cognitive development seems to be critical to understanding the full meaning of the term (finality, irreversibility), yet realization of one's approaching death seems to advance comprehension beyond the level of cognitive development.

As people live longer, children are experiencing the deaths of close loved ones and so are made more aware of the entire process: illness, hospitalization, wakes, funerals. As the effects of diseases such as cancer touch children, they must face the prospect of their own finiteness. Death is a fact that children need help in understanding, but the best method of aiding youngsters remains in doubt. Certain guidelines may help.

1. Age itself is not a true indicator of exactly what a child can grasp; most authorities agree that children do not acquire a true understanding of death until nine or ten years.
2. The level of cognitive development is a better indicator: children's understanding of death increases as they progress from preoperational, animistic thinking to concrete operational thinking with its decreasing egocentrism. It is during this time that they realize that everyone dies.
3. No sex differences in the acquisition of the concept have been found.
4. Religion seems to color how a child feels about death.
5. Adult evasion of, and substitution for, the truth frighten and confuse children.
6. Sadness is often accompanied by other emotions: grief, anger, fear, and loneliness.
7. Although children's ability to mourn is limited, they should be given the opportunity for their own emotional release and for expressing their love for the person that they have lost.
8. Adults discussing the meaning of death with children should consider their level of cognitive development, emotional stability, and religious beliefs.

Attempts to incorporate death into the school curriculum have met with limited success, so parents must continue to carry the responsibility. To guide them, parents should try to teach children that death is a natural part of life, that once death occurs people and animals no longer experience pain and suffering, that it helps to talk about people that they have loved and who have died.

teacher and pupil turnover had the most problems, and that pupils seem to do better when there is a reasonable distribution of all ability levels. These and other findings led to the conclusion that schools make a difference.

Stress

As we move from enumerating the psychosocial elements that influence children's development and that can also cause disorders, it becomes more apparent that these familial and societal elements and their interactions with each other and with the child can create stress of various intensity. Chess and Hassibi (1978, p. 217) state that an adjustment reaction denotes a combination of the stress response and compensatory adaptive mechanisms that characterize the behavior of an individual who experiences disruptive life events, usually of an unpleasant nature. It is important to remember that a child's cognitive level determines the perception of stress, and the nature of the youngster's response (intensity, duration) reflects the level of behavioral organization.

The body clearly signals stress—increased pulse rate, elevated blood pressure, muscular tension—that eventually produces listlessness accompanied by feelings of helplessness. Among the stress danger signals are the following:

- prolonged unhappiness
- explosive anger as a reaction to minor provocation
- long-lasting anxiety
- insomnia
- inability to relax
- upsets of the cardiovascular, digestive, and respiratory systems
- alcohol and/or drug usage

Stress and Illness. Recent research on stress will better help us to understand the potential impact of stress upon a youngster's development. The relationship among life events, stress, and the onset of illness (both physical and psychiatric) has become a carefully studied, well documented finding. Scientists now believe that stress can be a component of any disease, not only those designated as psychosomatic. An etiological (medical) model would trace disease onset as follows:

1. The presence of stressful environmental conditions.
2. The child's (or adult's) perception that these conditions are stressful.
3. The ability, or lack of ability, to cope with or adapt to these conditions.
4. Genetic predisposition to disease.
5. The presence of a disease agent.

Including stress in the etiological model helps to explain why some children are more prone to disease than others. Life events that require adaptive response are viewed differently by individual children; for example, because of constitutional and environmental differences children perceive school differently; they react to separation differently; they respond to peers differently.

Since some people, again both children and adults, develop physical disease, psychiatric disorder, or both after stress, but others do not, Rabkin and Struening (1976) urge that other agents deserve consideration: characteristics of the stressful situation, individual biological and psychological attributes, and the characteristics of the child's support system. What is particularly interesting in this cluster of characteristics is the child's perception of stressful events. It is this perception, shaped by internal elements such as intelligence, morale, past experiences, personality, and locus of control, combined with external agents such as family, neighborhood, and school, that differentiates a stress from a stimulus and determines the nature of the stress reaction and the coping mechanism utilized.

Children and Stress. Children's reactions to stresss are varied: aggression, withdrawal, morbid fantasies, loss of interest in their surroundings. Each child reacts individually; merely identifying the cause of stress will not predict the behavioral outcome. For example, school difficulty may cause school phobia in one youngster and conduct disorder *in school* in another.

Pinkerton (1974) traces children's stress to three sources: home, school, and neighborhood. These are subdivided as follows.

1. *Home-based Stress*
   a. Socioeconomic adversity, such as overcrowding, abuse, drunkenness, limited play facilities.
   b. Anomalies of family structure, such as divided authority in an extended family.
   c. Disruption of family group, from causes such as death, desertion, divorce, separation.
   d. Prolonged parental absence, for reasons such as hospitalization, military service.
   e. Substitute parents, such as step, adoptive, and foster parents.
2. *School-based Stress*
   a. Learning, such as academic difficulties.
   b. Social, such as problems with peers.
   c. Reflection of home problems, such as tensions associated with the marital problems of parents.
3. *Neighborhood Stress*
   a. Geographic conditions, such as a move to a new neighborhood, vandalism, gangs.

Helping youngsters cope with stress primarily entails providing support. Some specific suggestions for parents, counselors, and teachers would include the following:

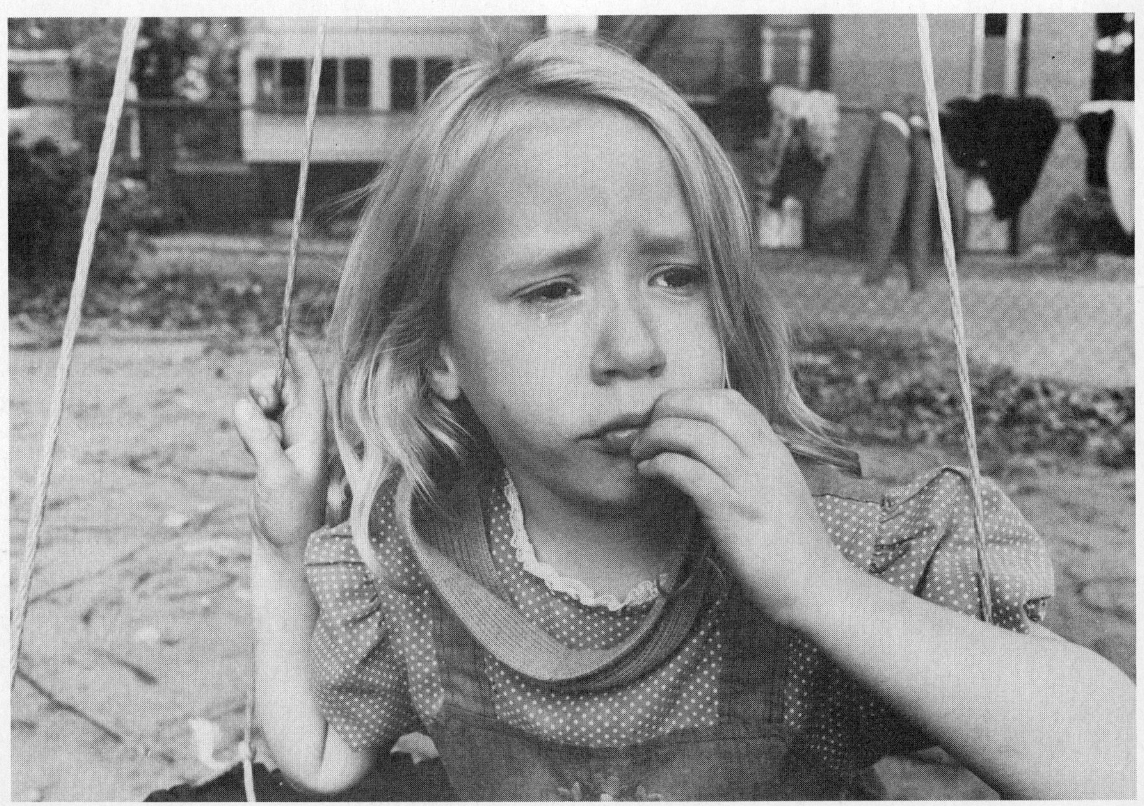

1. Aid youngsters in identifying the root of the problem; for example, reading may be the cause of considerable educational difficulty.

2. Suggest remedial procedures, both personal and academic. Locate a source of remedial instruction for problem readers, and also encourage youngsters to express their feelings, while simultaneously informing them that they are not alone in their problem.

3. If the problem is school-related, such as reading, ensure that children receive deserved reward and praise for other school activities.

4. If possible, help the youngsters to maintain a positive outlook by support, encouragement, and a belief that they can overcome their problem.

LEARNING DISORDERS

> In circles where public policy is formulated, the disorders of learning frequently are referred to as the *high incidence-low severity* handicaps of children. Such deficiencies are said to affect from 4 to 20% of school-age children with a boy-girl ratio of between 6 and 8 to 1. The notion of *high incidence-low severity* handicaps can be useful in differentiating this population from those children who endure multiple or major handicapping conditions, including mental retardation, blindness, and severe learning impairment. These latter are subsumed under the *high severity-low incidence* handicapping conditions (Levine, Brooks, Shonkoff, 1980, p. 4).

Learning disorders are probably the most common of the problems that plague children. Parents and teachers are usually involved immediately, but frequently psychiatric help is needed because of accompanying emotional or behavioral difficulties. Learning disorders provide a graphic illustration of the antecedents-behavior-consequences framework: children with learning problems often have behavior difficulties that arise from the source of the learning disorder; personality problems may mask a learning disorder and be identified as the source of behavior difficulties; an emotional problem may cause learning disorders. (Rutter's warning about the factors needed in making a psychiatric assessment are particularly pertinent here.) But wherever particular learning disorders "fit" in our framework, they usually are thought to be developmental variations, deviations, or delays.

Development and Learning Disorders

Levine, Brooks, and Shonkoff (1980) have attempted to link developmental characteristics and milestones with clinical dysfunctions in children who evidence learning problems. They employ the following categories.

1. *Selective Attention and Activity*

Youngsters labeled "hyperactive" or "minimal brain dysfunction" are increasingly identified as having attention difficulties. Unless youngsters can focus on meaningful stimuli, they will encounter adjustment problems from birth. As we have seen, infants can discriminate detail and detect differences between the familiar and the discrepant, thus facilitating cognitive development. During the preschool years attention becomes more efficient, preparing the child for more formal schooling. It is during these years that attentional problems become apparent. As the authors state (1980, p. 50), much of early academic success depends upon the capacity to select and sustain a focus.

Attention deficits are associated with academic, social, and behavioral problems, especially for boys. Some of the signs of an attention deficit are: easy distractibility, impulsivity, task impersistence, insatiability (never satisfied), impaired and poor reinforceability (rewards and punishments are meaningless for these children).

2. *Visual-Spatial and Gestalt Processing*
Some youngsters have difficulty with spatial relations, which affects their performance in activities ranging from catching a ball to reading. The authors note (1980, p. 61) that the nearly instantaneous or Gestalt appreciation of configuration, pattern, or shape is critical for comprehending the physical world. Although visual processing is the primary modality used to apprehend configuration, both proprioceptive and kinesthetic sources function as well. Early signs of this problem are difficult to detect and usually are not recognized until formal reading begins.

3. *Temporal-Sequential Organization and Segmental Processing*
It is difficult to learn something unless you place it in the right order. Words, numbers, and the steps in a task (learning to tie shoes) involve order. Most of a child's daily routine employs sequential organization and with maturity and education comes greater demands to cope sequentially. Storage and retrieval of information is a particular problem for these youngsters, as is following directions. "Open your book to page 20, do the first three problems, and then check the answers on page 132." Since an attention deficit may be involved, help in focusing upon steps, accompanied by reinforcement, is helpful.

4. *Perceptive Language Function*
Some youngsters have difficulty in interpreting auditory stimuli and in obtaining meaning from words and sentences. The strong link between language development and academic success poses obstacles for these children that unless quickly overcome can cause educational failure.

5. *Expressive Language Function*
Competent spoken language depends on a number of factors, including the capacity to retrieve relevant words from memory, arrange these words in phrases or sentences that conform to linguistic rules, develop ideas in a meaningful sequence or narrative, and plan and execute the highly complex motor act of speech (Levine, Brooks, and Shonkoff, 1980, p. 77). Acquiring these abilities also carries with it the potential for difficulty: poor articulation, lack of ability to convey symbolic meaning, stuttering.

6. *Memory*

7. *Voluntary Motor Function*

8. *Developmental Facilitation* (including intelligence, cognitive strategies, and social adjustment).

These categories were discussed at length previously and the possibility of associated disorders was mentioned.

Underachievement

Academic achievement is tied tightly to these categories, especially in such subjects as reading, writing, spelling, arithmetic, and general knowledge acquisition. But caution is needed in interpreting a youngster's performance and designating it as a problem or disorder. Again, Michael Rutter (1975) offers sensible suggestions. Originally, learning problems and underachievement meant that youngsters were not "working up to potential," a statement based on the belief that IQ scores represented a youngster's innate capacity. As we have demonstrated, IQ is not a pure measure of potential; it is a test of current performance. An IQ score is an acceptable predictor of *attainment*, and if a youngster's academic performance is far below IQ, then an academic alert has been sounded.

Youngsters rarely perform at the expected level, but if their performances vary markedly from the predicted level or from the norms for age, then there is cause for concern. For example, there is no perfect correlation between performance and mental age. A ten-year-old with a mental age of thirteen who has a reading age of twelve is at the correct level. Highly intelligent children attain slightly below mental level; slow youngsters usually attain a level slightly above that of their mental age.

Finally, if learning is obviously below level, is it because of a general backwardness, is it only in certain subjects, or is it a loss of previously acquired skills? Answering these questions may involve a series of assessments: a developmental health history, a general physical examination, a neurological examination, and finally, determination of appropriate intervention.

DISCUSSION QUESTIONS

1. The literature on discipline, in spite of its quantity, is far from conclusive. Given the interactive nature of our discussion, can you speculate why hard data are lacking? Now include the two aspects of discipline about which there seems to be consensus. How can you explain such agreement, given the general conclusions of discipline studies?
2. If you had to discuss death with a four-year-old child, how would you proceed? What would you take into consideration other than age? What examples would you use? Follow the same procedures for a six-year-old and an eight-year-old.
3. Give some specific examples of events that you think children would find stressful. List them in order of stress intensity. (You probably placed parental death near the top of your list. If you were the one to discuss death with the six-year-old child of the preceding question, how would you attempt to keep stress manageable for the child? Use the characteristics of the situation, the child, and any support system in your answer.
4. If you were speaking to a group of parents and you wished to calm their fears about the relationship of achievement to potential in their children, how would you proceed? Give a specific example.

Most children develop normally, and most children manifest problems in their development. There is nothing contradictory in this statement. The youngster is rare who does not experience at least some minor developmental deviance in the course of growth, most of which are transitory and leave no lingering effects. As we have seen, however, some disorders are more serious and the prognosis is doubtful.

As you conclude your reading of this chapter, remember three basic ideas:

1. It is almost impossible to employ a medical model in analyzing psychiatric disorders, since cause and effect do not seem to be in a one-to-one linear relationship. A reading problem may apparently cause school conduct disorders, but the reading problem itself may be the product of an underlying emotional disorder.

2. The roots of any problem may be in the child, the family, the school, and the social environment, or in some complex mixture of some or all of these.

3. Following the classification scheme presented in the initial part of the chapter will give you a means of placing and interpreting various disorders.

SUMMARY

One of the major difficulties in analyzing the psychopathology of childhood is a method of classifying syndromes.

The classification scheme utilized in this chapter employed five multiaxial categories.

Clinical psychiatric syndromes provided a means for grouping and discussing some of the more common childhood problems such as fears, phobias, anxieties, delinquency, infantile autism, and childhood schizophrenia.

Labeling, developmental characteristics, and intervention strategies are common problems in discussing mental retardation. Mainstreaming raises issues about *which* youngsters can benefit from regular classroom instruction.

Discussion of biological elements reinforces the importance of the antecedent-behavior-consequence framework. For example, physical illness can be an antecedent or consequence of a psychiatric disorder, or both.

Stress is now recognized as an important part of a child's life. Coupled with other psychosocial elements—home, family, school—it can exercise a strong influence on a child's development.

Recent research has clarified much of the uncertainty around learning disorders, especially the increasing tendency to analyze a specific disorder within a developmental framework.

SUGGESTED READINGS

The literature relating to childhood disorders is voluminous and highly specialized. The following references are among the best *general* reviews of the field.

CHESS, STELLA and M. HASSIBI. *Principles and Practice in Child Psychiatry.* New York: Plenum Press, 1978. An excellent review of current research and practice that examines the various problems by a traditional format.

LEVINE, MELVIN, ROBERT BROOKS, and JACK SHONKOFF. *A Pediatric Approach to Learning Disorders.* New York: John Wiley, 1980. Although focusing on learning disorders, this comprehensive text ranges widely and presents pertinent data about a variety of problems.

PINKERTON, PHILIP. *Childhood Disorder.* New York: Columbia University Press, 1974. A good, brief overview of the field.

Psychosomatics in Childhood and Adolescence. Conference Report, Harvard Medical School, 1979. Fine analysis of multiple child and adolescent problems with a strong psychiatric perspective.

RUTTER, MICHAEL. *Helping Troubled Children.* New York: Plenum Press, 1975. A superb text—thorough, sophisticated, yet so clearly written that all can benefit from it.

GLOSSARY

Accommodation. The modification of our mental structures as the result of assimilating, taking in, stimuli from the environment. For example, we assimilate food, but our body then changes; it accommodates. Similarly, we assimilate stimuli that change our cognitive structures; that is, they accommodate to the new stimuli. It is the second aspect of adaptation; for the other, see assimilation. Assimilation and accommodation are called functional invariants; that is, they explain how we function mentally.

Adolescence. A term used to describe the time between puberty and maturity, from about twelve to twenty-two years.

Adaptation. A term referring to an organism's ability to adjust to the environment. A key notion in Piaget's theory; he uses it to explain our biological adjustment. Intelligence thus becomes one form of biological adaptation. See also assimilation and accommodation.

Aggression. Behavior intended to cause injury or harm to some other person, animal, or object.

Alcoholism. A term used to describe a condition in which an individual drinks excessively and habitually.

Amniocentesis. A process in which the physician withdraws small amounts of amniotic fluid that is then analyzed for any chromosomal abnormality in the fetus.

Amphetamines. A class of drugs used to stimulate the central nervous system. Benzedrine, dexedrine, and methedrine are the most popular.

Anal stage. The second of the psychosexual stages of development during which elimination is the chief source of pleasure.

Androgyny. A term that implies a combination of both masculine and feminine.

Anorexia nervosa. A condition in which deliberate avoidance of food causes devastating weight loss.

Anoxia. A term referring to lack of oxygen. If oxygen is insufficient during the birth there is the possibility of brain damage or death.

Apgar. A scale that permits observers to evaluate a newborn's basic life signs.

Aphasia. Problems with understanding and/or pronouncing speech.

Assimilation. The incorporation of environmental stimuli into existing mental structures. For example, as we take food into our physical structures, so also we take stimuli into our cognitive structures, thus facilitating development. It is one aspect of adaptation; for the other see accommodation. Assimilation and accommodation are called functional invariants; that is, they explain how we function mentally. See also adaptation.

Associationism. That school of psychology concerned with the connection between elements. In philosophy, the connection was between ideas; in modern psychology, the emphasis is on the connection between stimuli and responses.

Attachment. Affectional tie that binds one person to another, usually infants and mothers.

Autism. A term used to describe severe mental, language, and social problems that appear before thirty months.

Autonomy. The acquisition of independence. Erikson describes it as the development of self-control with no loss of self-esteem. Autonomy versus shame or doubt is Erikson's second stage of personality development.

Babbling. Repetition of sounds that approximate speech; early phase of speech development.

Barbiturates. A class of drugs used as sedatives. They depress the central nervous system and induce relaxation and drowsiness. The most popular are nembutal, seconal, and amytal.

Behaviorism. A term expressing the belief that any analysis of behavior should concentrate on observable stimulus and response.

Biopsychosocial. A term used to indicate an integrated analysis of behavior, combining physical, psychological, social, moral, and cognitive elements.

*All definitions reflect use in this text but also are consistent with standard dictionaries and dictionaries of psychology.

Birth order. The rank or position of a child in the family; first child, second child, third child, oldest, youngest, middle child.

Blastocyst. A term referring to the fertilized ovum immediately preceding the period of the embryo.

Breech birth. Baby born feet or buttocks first instead of head first.

Caesarean section. Baby is delivered through the abdomen by surgery.

Case studies. Collection of all pertinent information about one person.

Castration complex. A psychoanalytic term referring to a boy's fear that his father knows he loves the mother and will punish him by cutting off his sex organ.

Centration. Piaget's term, which describes the preoperational child's tendency to focus on one aspect of an object and to neglect any other feature.

Cerebral lateralization. Specialization of the cerebral hemispheres; for example, a right-handed person is usually left-lateralized for language.

Chromosome. Found in the nucleus of the cell, the chromosomes are the carriers of heredity, the genes.

Classical conditioning. A term referring to the procedure whereby a neutral stimulus (a bell) repeatedly paired with a natural stimulus (food) eventually acquires the ability to produce a response (flow of saliva). Also called Pavlovian conditioning, S*S*R conditioning, Type S. conditioning.

Clinical psychiatric syndromes. A label designed to include emotional disorders, hyperkinesis, infantile autism, schizophrenia, enuresis, encopresis.

Cloning. A term referring to the possibility of reproducing identical humans by removing the nucleus from any cell in a person's body and implanting it in an egg that has had its nucleus removed.

Coleman report. Massive survey conducted by James Coleman that showed student achievement is closely linked with self-concept and feelings of control over the environment.

Communication. Transmission of information from one organism to another. It does not require speech; therefore, animals also possess this ability.

Concept. The process of knowing by grouping things into classes because of common elements—ball, orange, cat, dog.

Concrete operations. The third of Piaget's four stages of cognitive development that describes a child's ability to think logically, but only with concrete materials (objects or events present to his senses). The period extends approximately from seven to eleven years.

Conditioned reflex. A term referring to a response that is learned to a formerly neutral stimulus. Also called conditional response. See also conditioning.

Conditioning. A term referring to the basic behavioristic explanation of learning. See also classical conditioning and operant conditioning.

Conduct disorders. Behavior, often abnormal, that causes social disapproval.

Connectionism. A psychological theory made famous by Edward Lee Thorndike. What is connected is a stimulus to a response. This connection occurs at the synaptic junction. Also called the synaptic theory of learning.

Conservation. Piaget's term to describe a child's ability to realize that an object retains certain essential properties no matter how its form may change.

Content. A term used by Piaget to mean raw, uninterpreted behavioral data. What we do, what we say, with no attempt at explanation.

Control group. Subjects who are selected for their similarity to members of an experimental group. The control group does not experience the independent variables. The two groups are compared after the experiment to see if any differences resulted. Also see experimental group.

Creativity. The production of novel responses in any endeavor: literature, art, architecture.

Critical period. A time of development during which the organism is highly sensitive to particular stimuli. Also called sensitive period.

Cross-sectional study. A technique that investigators use to study many children at different ages. Investigators, for example, would study fifth- and ninth-grade children and compare differences. (Opposed to the longitudinal growth study in which the *same* children are studied for many years.)

Cystic fibrosis. A genetic disease that causes breathing difficulties because of an extremely thick mucous. Cystic fibrosis kills more children than any other genetic disease.

Deep structure. Our understanding of words, sentences, paragraphs.

Defense mechanism. A term, usually psychoanalytic, that refers to an individual's tendency to avoid feelings of guilt, shame, or anxiety. See also denial, repression, projection, rationalization.

Deferred imitation. Imitating someone or something after the disappearance of the model. A term often used by Piaget to describe one phase of the preoperational period.

Denial. A psychoanalytic term referring to a tendency to distort reality and avoid anxiety by simply denying that a problem exists.

Deoxyribonucleic acid (DNA). The molecular basis of the genes; contains the chemical codes that issue the instructions that result in life's functions.

Dependency. The tendency to find rewarding the presence and attention of other people.

Dependent variable. Changes in a subject(s), a result of experimental manipulation (use of independent variables). Also see independent variables.

Depression. A state in which the child is sad, withdrawn, and apathetic.

Deprivation dwarfism. Children who are emotionally deprived may actually be physically stunted.

Developmental task. A term referring to the tasks that arise at certain times in our lives, successful completion of which leads to happiness and future success, while failure leads to unhappiness and later difficulty. Associated with Robert Havighurst.

Displacement. A psychoanalytic term referring to the transfer of feelings from one object to another.

Distributed practice. The spacing of practice periods over several learning sessions. Opposed to massed practice.

Dominant gene. A gene that produces a certain result in the presence of a recessive gene for the same trait. If an embryo receives a dominant gene for brown eyes and a recessive gene for blue eyes, the child's eyes will be brown.

Down's Syndrome. Also called mongolism, Down's syndrome is caused by an extra chromosome on the twenty-first pair. Usually accompanied by distinctive physical features and mental retardation.

Drug dependence. A term used to describe a person's dependence, physical and psychological, on a particular drug for the person's well-being.

Ectoderm. A term referring to the outer layer of the developing embryo; from it skin, hair, teeth, nails, and nervous system will arise.

Ectomorph. A term used to describe the thin, angular individual.

Ego. A psychoanalytic term referring to that segment of personality whose function it is to establish realistic interactions with the environment.

Egocentric. Focus on self to the exclusion of others. Used by Piaget to explain the child's inability to recognize that other people and other views exist.

Ego integrity. Erikson's term to describe the person who has taken care of people and things throughout a lifetime and has adapted to the triumphs and disappointments common to us all. Ego integrity versus despair is Erikson's eighth and final stage of personality development.

Electra complex. A psychoananalytic term referring to a girl's sexual desire for her father, which occurs during the phallic stage of development.

Elicited response. A response that is linked to a definite stimulus.

Embryo. A term referring to the developing organism from about two to eight weeks.

Emitted response. A response that appears with no apparent link to any definite stimulus.

Encopresis. Uncontrolled defecation.

Endocrine glands. The glands that pass their secretions directly into the bloodstream.

Endoderm. A term referring to the innermost of the three embryonic layers, from which lungs, liver, and pancreas will develop.

Endomorph. A term used to describe the heavy, possibly fat individual.

Enuresis. Involuntary incontinence of urine after the age of four.

Experiment. A technique that investigators use to study one or more persons in which some stimuli (variables) are controlled and some are changed. The results of these changes are then recorded and interpreted.

Experimental group. Children (or adults) who receive the independent variable. After the experiment, the control and experimental groups are compared for any differences. Also see control group.

Extended family. A family consisting of husband, wife, children, and any or all of the following: grandparents, aunts, uncles, siblings of parents, cousins.

Extinction. Loss of a response because of a lack of reinforcement.

Eye-hand coordination. The ability to reach for and grasp accurately what the eye sees.

Failure-to-thrive. Children whose weight remains below the third percentile for age.

Fetus. A term referring to the developing organism from about eight weeks to birth.

Fixation. A psychoanalytic term referring to a child's inability to pass through psychosexual stages. The child, or adult, remains psychologically at one stage; for example, in anal fixation, development is arrested or fixed at the anal stage.

Formal operations. The fourth and final of Piaget's four stages of cognitive development. From about the age of eleven or twelve the youngster shows all the characteristics of adult thinking—abstract and hypothetical.

Free association. The talking-out method devised by Freud, in which a person says whatever comes to mind. These sayings then become the data for psychoanalytic study.

Freud, Sigmund. Founder of psychoanalysis. Born in Czechoslovakia, long-time resident of Vienna. Freud was a trained physician, specializing in neurology. He became interested in nervous disorders, studied hypnosis, and gradually developed the "talking-out" method so frequently associated with psychoanalysis. Using this free-association method, Freud discovered the importance of our unconscious lives.

Function. A term used by Piaget to refer to the nature of intelligent behavior. We function intellectually by assimilation and accommodation.

Functional invariants. A term referring to the two phases of intellectual functioning: organization and adaptation.

G (general factor). A general ability that is characteristic of all intellectual functioning. Proposed by Carl Spearman.

Gamete. A term referring to the sex cells.

Gene. The basic element of heredity, found in the chromosomes.

Generative grammar. The set of rules that explains the correlation between the sound and meaning of words; it permits the speaker to form and understand an indefinite number of sentences.

Generativity. Erikson's term for the concern about establishing and guiding the next generation. Generativity versus stagnation (self-absorption) is Erikson's seventh stage of personality development.

Genetic epistemology. A term that Piaget uses to describe his work. Refers to the study of the developmental changes that occur in a child's search for knowledge.

Genital stage. The last of the psychosexual stages of development during which interest focuses on the opposite sex as a source of sexual satisfaction.

Gestalt psychology. The school of psychology concerned with experience as wholes. To analyze into parts is to lose something of the whole. Emphasis on perception, figure-ground relations, and dynamic fields.

GH. Growth hormone, which is secreted by the pituitary gland and which is vital for normal growth.

Hallucinogen. A term used to describe a drug that induces hallucinations, a radically distorted impression of reality.

Hemophilia. A genetic disease that interferes with the blood's clotting process. Often called the "bleeder's" disease.

Hermaphrodites. Those born with both male and female sexual features (organs, glands, and secondary sexual characteristics).

Holophrase. Single words used as sentences.

Homeostasis. The tendency of any organism to maintain a state of equilibrium, to reduce tension.

Hyperkinesis. A term used to describe the excessively active child who is unusually restless, excitable, and impulsive.

Hypochondriasis. A condition marked by exaggerated physical complaints.

Hysterical conversion reactions. Acute physical reactions, such as loss of speech or paralysis, to an underlying psychological problem.

Id. A psychoanalytic term referring to the segment of personality that is the psychic source of our instinctual drives.

Identity. The ability to answer the question "Who am I?" Identity versus identity confusion is Erikson's fifth stage of personality development.

Imitation. Learning by observation. More complex than formerly thought. A child will observe someone or something and incorporate what is witnessed into behavior.

Imprinting. Specific behavior released by appropriate stimuli during sensitive periods of development.

Independent variable. The variable that the experimenter uses (manipulates) for the purpose of observing its effect on the subject. Also see dependent variable.

Industry. A sense of being able to do things well, joined with a desire to win recognition by producing things. Industry versus inferiority represents Erikson's fourth stage of personality development.

Initiative. Freedom of movement; the tendency to use the imagination to propose new ideas. For Erikson, initiative versus guilt is the third stage of personality development.

Insight. Sudden solution of a problem. Gestalt psychologists claim that it is due to the perception of relationships within a field.

Intelligence. A disputed term that usually refers to a child's or adult's ability to adapt to circumstances or to the environment.

Intelligence quotient. A measure of ability or brightness compared to others of the same age. Obtained by dividing mental age by chronological age and dividing by 100 ($MA/CA \times 100 = IQ$).

Intelligence test. A series of tasks usually graded in difficulty, designed to measure a child's or adult's adaptation or adjustment. It is often claimed that these tests measure an individual's capacity, but this is hotly disputed today.

Intimacy. The capacity to affiliate with others, to form partnerships. It may be found in sexual relationships, friendship, or joint inspiration. Intimacy versus isolation is Erikson's sixth stage of personality development.

In vitro. A term used to refer to the "test tube" babies, so called because fertilization may occur in a glass dish.

Jensenism. Refers to Arthur Jensen's belief that intelligence is primarily due to genetic factors.

Juvenile delinquent. A youth, usually under the age of eighteen (in some states, twenty-one), who manifests antisocial or criminal behavior or both.

Language. Use of symbols to communicate with another. In humans, the symbols are usually verbal, and the term language is often used synonymously with speech.

LAD. Language acquisition device, which is Chomsky's explanation of the innate ability of humans to acquire language.

Latency. A psychosexual term referring to the time between the phallic and genital periods of psychosexual development during which sexual interest and activity is relatively dormant.

Learning. A process that results in the modification of behavior.

Locus of control. An expression coined by Julian Rotter to explain whether people believe they have control over the environment or are doomed to be buffetted by environmental forces.

Longitudinal growth study. A technique that investigators use to study the same individuals over many years. (Opposed to the cross-sectional study in which many different children at different ages are studied.)

LSD. Lysergic acid diethylamide. This drug is an hallucinogen and causes strange perceptual disorders and bizarre mental images.

Marijuana. A drug, usually smoked, that produces feelings of relaxation. It is classified as a relaxant and considerable controversy surrounds its use.

Massed practice. Learning material with little or no rest between practical sessions. Opposed to distributed practice.

Masturbation. The self-stimulation or excitation of the sex organs to produce feelings of sexual pleasure, even orgasm.

Maturation. A developmental process that produces behavioral change because of heredity. Changes occur because the organism is a member of a particular species (people walk; fish swim). The environment exercises some influence on the form of the behavior.

Meiosis. Division of the sex cells in which the number of chromosomes is halved. Each half receives twenty-three chromosomes. Contrast to mitosis.

Menstruation. The monthly vaginal discharge of blood and dead cells from the uterus of the mature female.

Mesoderm. A term referring to the middle of the three embryonic layers from which muscles, bone, and the circulatory and excretory systems will develop.

Mesomorph. A term used to describe the well-built, muscular individual.

Mitosis. Division of the somatic cells in which the number of chromosomes remains the same; each half receives forty-six chromosomes. Contrast to meiosis.

Modalities. Classes of traits.

Modeling. Models (human, television, movies, theater) become the source of behavior. A child observes someone or something, acquires symbolic representation of the event, and subsequently shows behavior similar to the previously witnessed event.

Montessori method. Those techniques devised by Maria Montessori to facilitate the interaction between learning and development.

Morpheme. The smallest unit of language having meaning. *Younger* has two morphemes: *young* signifying age, and *er* signifying comparison.

Motivation. The study of those elements that arouse, sustain, and direct behavior toward some goal.

Motor learning. Skill learning involving muscular coordination. Often referred to as psychomotor learning.

Multiple factor. A belief that intelligence is composed of relatively independent factors. Adherents include Thurstone and Guilford.

Mutation. A genetic mistake; the chemical arrangement within the DNA molecule is altered, thus producing strange, usually undesirable, characteristics.

Myelination. The process by which nerve fibers become enclosed by the myelin sheath; essential for organ function.

Narcotic. A term used to describe a drug that dulls the senses; usually refers to opium and opium derivatives such as heroin, morphine, and codeine.

Need achievement (nAch). All humans possess a need to achieve, to accomplish something; varies from individual to individual.

Negative reinforcement. Withdrawal of an unpleasant stimulus.

Neonate. A term referring to the newborn infant.

Normative studies. Those studies investigating characteristics of youngsters at various ages.

Nuclear family. A family consisting of husband, wife, and children.

Object constancy. Piaget's term for a child's developing ability to realize that an object exists even when it is no longer within the field of vision.

Oedipus complex. A psychoanalytic term referring to a boy's sexual desire for his mother. It occurs during the phallic stage of development and is usually resolved by identification with the father. (While the term may refer to both sexes, often Electra complex is used to signify the girl's desire for her father.)

Open classroom. An educational environment in which pupils initiate activity, participate according to their ability, and have considerable freedom.

Operant behavior. Behavior not caused (elicited) by an identifiable stimulus.

Operant conditioning. The procedure whereby the probability of a desirable response recurring is increased by reinforcement. Also called instrumental conditioning, Type R conditioning.

Oral stage. The first of the psychosexual stages of development during which the mouth is the chief source of pleasure.

Ovum. 1. Female sex cell, or egg (plural ova). 2. Also refers to the immediate time after conception, about one to two weeks.

Peak experience. Those moments of insight, discovery, and joy that only infrequently occur in our lives.

Penis envy. A psychoanalytic term referring to a girl's desire for a penis.

Perception. The process of knowing something by combining immediate experience with past experiences.

Personality. A child's or adult's unique pattern of traits.

Phallic stage. The third of the psychosexual stages of development, during which the sexual organs become a source of pleasure.

Phenylketonuria (PKU). An inherited condition causing chemical disorders that can produce brain damage and mental retardation unless detected immediately.

Phoneme. The smallest unit of sound (vowel, consonant). It has no meaning in itself.

Placenta. The organ through which the embryo and fetus receive food from the mother and dispose of waste. It is formed from the outer layer of cells of the blastocyst.

Positive reinforcement. Presenting something pleasant (a reward) after a desired response has occurred so as to increase the probability that the response will recur.

Pragnanz. A Gestalt law of organization that refers to the tendency to have as good a perceptual field as possible, to impose order, to eliminate disorganization.

Prematurity. A term referring to birth before the thirty-seventh week of pregnancy.

Preoperational period. The second of Piaget's four stages of cognitive development. It extends approximately from two to seven years. During this period the child masters the use of mental symbols and language.

Primary circular reaction. Piaget's term to describe an infant's tendency to repeat some activity involving the body. For example, sucking the thumb, opening and closing the hands.

Primary reinforcement. The stimuli that satisfy basic physiological needs, such as food and water.

Proactive inhibition. Present learning interferes with future learning. Opposed to retroactive inhibition.

Programmed instruction. Material used for self-instruction. Each step in the learning sequence is sufficiently small so as to eliminate error and provide each response with reinforcement.

Projection. A psychoanalytic term referring to the tendency to attribute one's own fears or anxieties to another.

Psychoanalysis. A system that explains human behavior mainly as a reaction to unconscious forces and the manner in which the human expresses these reactions.

Psycholinguistics. An attempt to understand speech by examining the characteristics of those who speak. The assumption is that the human possesses some innate structure that accounts for the varied use of language. Often referred to as the study of the relationship between language and thought.

Psychosexual stages. A psychoanalytic term for stages of development through which all children pass. So named because of the sexual interpretation given to each stage (oral, anal, phallic, latency, genital).

Puberty. The time of sexual maturity when the individual becomes capable of sexual reproduction.

Pubescence. The onset of puberty.

Pygmalion effect. Children become what we expect them to become. In education, the expression is usually associated with the work of Robert Rosenthal.

Rationalization. A psychoanalytic term that refers to the tendency to remove the emotional aspects of behavior and attribute that behavior to purely rational or logical reasons.

Readiness. A period during which the child is highly receptive to particular environmental stimuli.

Recessive gene. A gene that will not produce its characteristics in the presence of a dominant gene. A blue-eyed gene is recessive to a brown-eyed gene. When paired with another recessive gene, its characteristics can become apparent.

Reflex. A relatively stereotyped class of behavior. When a stimulus repeatedly elicits the same response, the resulting behavior is called a reflex.

Reinforcement. Increasing the probability that a response will recur under similar conditions.

Reminiscence. Recall of past events with no practice.

Repression. A psychoanalytic term referring to the tendency to banish from consciousness any idea, impulse, or experience that could lead to anxiety, shame, or guilt.

Respondent behavior. A term referring to behavior produced by a known stimulus.

Retroactive inhibition. Present learning interferes with recall of past learning. Opposed to proactive inhibition.

Reversibility. Piaget's term to describe a child's ability to reverse thinking. For example, if 2 + 2 = 4, then 4 − 2 = 2.

Ribonucleic acid (RNA). The medium by which the instructions encoded in DNA are transmitted to the surrounding cells.

Rote learning. Memorization involving little comprehension. Learning the alphabet, or a list of nonsense syllables.

Schedule of reinforcement. A program that determines when an organism will be reinforced. There are continuous schedules (every response is reinforced), or intermittent schedules (reinforcement follows certain responses by time between responses or number of responses).

Schema (scheme). A term used by Piaget to describe an individual's action and its underlying mental structure (the grasping schema, the sucking schema). Plural—schemata.

School phobia. Dramatic behavior used to avoid school; may include tantrums, crying, vomiting.

Secondary circular reactions. Piaget's term to describe an infant's tendency to repeat some activity with objects *not* involving the body, for example, repeated kicking of the crib.

Secondary reinforcers. A stimulus that acquires reinforcing power because of its association with primary reinforcers.

Self-actualization. A fulfillment of potential.

Self-concept. The image of self that each person possesses. Some children and adults consistently underestimate themselves; some are wildly extravagant in their opinion of self; others are realistic in their self-appraisal.

Semantics. The study of the meaning of words.

Sensorimotor. The first of Piaget's four stages of cognitive development. It lasts approximately from birth to two years. It is called sensorimotor because the child develops mentally during these two years mainly by sensory and motor activity.

Seriation. Piaget's term to describe a child's ability to arrange things in increasing or decreasing size, to put them in order.

Sex identity. The realization that a child acquires that he is a boy or she is a girl. It is not only physical; it is also psychological. That is, the child understands masculinity or femininity.

Sex role. Those characteristics, activities, and opportunities that society assigns to each sex.

Sickle-cell anemia. A genetic disease predominant among blacks, causing a clumping of blood cells that produces oxygen starvation.

SIDS. Sudden Infant Death Syndrome, which can strike two- to four-month-old infants.

Significant others. A term used by Harry Stack Sullivan to refer to those people who are particularly important to us, such as parents and teachers.

Social class. An expression used to designate how people are grouped. Usually an individual is assigned to a particular level of society because of economic conditions or family.

Socialization. The process whereby a child acquires the behaviors acceptable to a particular society.

Spiral curriculum. A curriculum that is designed to present a subject with increasing abstractness to match the increasing maturity of the child. From initial presentation in a tangible, concrete manner, the subject is presented in gradually increasing symbolic form.

Split-brain. Severing of the corpus callosum so that the cerebral hemispheres are divided. Results in two brains in one organism.

Stage invariant. Everyone passes through the same stages in the same sequence but not necessarily at the same age. Piaget's theory is stage invariant.

Stanford-Binet Intelligence Scale. Terman's Revision of Binet's work, first published in America in 1916, then revised in 1937 and 1960.

Structure. A term used by Piaget to explain our mind's organization. As our body functions through physical structures, so our mind functions through cognitive structures. To see, we use the physical structure of the eye; to think, we use the cognitive structure of the mind.

Structure of intellect. A model designed by J. P. Guilford to illustrate the many intellectual factors.

Summerhill. English school founded by A. S. Neill in 1921 whose basic principle is freedom for the child.

Surface structure. The appearance of words, sentences, paragraphs; the way we say them or read them.

Superego. A psychoanalytic term referring to that segment of personality that governs our moral lives. It approximates the term conscience.

Symbolic play. The game of pretending. Often used by Piaget to describe a phase of preoperational development.

Syntactic transformations. The method by which we relate deep structure to surface structure. They are rules that enable us to understand the surface structure of various word combinations.

Syntax. The grammar of a language.

Tay Sachs. A genetic disease predominant among those of Eastern European Jewish origin. It affects the nervous system, causing an early death.

Telegraphic speech. Two or three words used as a sentence.

Tertiary circular reactions. Piaget's term to describe an infant's tendency to repeat activities but with the intention of producing novelty in the actions, for example, dropping things.

Trait. Any distinguishable, enduring way in which one individual differs from another.

Transfer. The process whereby learning one thing helps you to learn another.

Transformational grammar. A theoretical model prepared to explain the infinite capacity of the human to generate new sentences. Also called generative grammar.

Trial-and-error learning. The acquisition of stimulus-response connections entailing little comprehension.

Triune brain. A concept of the brain proposing that the developing brain has evolved and retained three basic systems: reptilian, limbic, and neocortical.

Trophoblast. The outer layer of the fertilized ovum, designed to protect the developing embryo.

Trust. Used in Erikson's sense—faith or confidence in one's self and in others. Trust versus mistrust is Erikson's first stage in personality development.

WAIS. Wechsler Adult Intelligence Scale.

WISC. Wechsler Intelligence Scale for Children.

WPPSI. Wechsler Preschool and Primary Scale of Intelligence.

Zygote. The fertilized cell, formed by the union of sperm and egg.

BIBLIOGRAPHY

Ainsworth, Mary D. Salter. "The Development of Infant-Mother Attachment," in *Review of Child Development Research.* Edited by Bettye Caldwell and Henry Ricciuti. Chicago: University of Chicago Press, 1973.

———. "Infant-Mother Attachment," *American Psychologist,* 34 (October 1979), 932–937.

Aitchison, Jean. *The Articulate Mammal.* New York: McGraw-Hill, 1976.

Almy, Millie, E. Chittenden, and P. Miller. *Young Children's Thinking.* New York: Columbia Teachers College Press, 1966.

Als, Heidelise, Edward Tronick, Barry Lester, and T. Berry Brazelton. "Specific Neonatal Measures: The Brazelton Neonatal Assessment Scale," in *A Handbook On Infancy.* Edited by J. Osofsky. New York: John Wiley, 1977.

Anderson, Richard, Robert St. Pierre, Elizabeth Proper, and Linda Stebbins. "Pardon Us, But What Was the Question Again? A Response to the Critique of the Follow Through Evaluation," *Harvard Educational Review,* Vol. 48, No. 2, May, 1978, 161–185.

Andre, Thomas, Y. Chesni, and Dargassies Saint-Anne. *The Neurological Examination of the Infant.* London: William Heinemann, Ltd., 1960.

Annis, Linda F. *The Child Before Birth.* Ithaca, New York: Cornell University Press, 1978.

Anthony, E. David. "Behavior Disorders of Childhood," in *Carmichael's Manual of Child Psychology.* Edited by Paul Mussen. New York: John Wiley & Sons, 1970.

Apgar, Virginia. "A Proposal for a New Method of Evaluation of the Newborn Infant," *Current Researches in Anesthesia and Analgesia,* 32 (1953), 260–267.

Arbuthnot, May, and Zena Sutherland. *Children and Books.* Glenview, Illinois: Scott, Foresman, 1972.

Atkinson, Richard, and Richard Shiffrin. "The Control of Short-Term Memory," *Scientific American,* August, 1971.

Babkin, B. R. *Pavlov.* Chicago: University of Chicago Press, 1949.

Baldwin, Alfred L. *Theories of Child Development.* New York: John Wiley & Sons, 1967.

Baldwin, Roger. *Genetics.* New York: John Wiley & Sons, 1973.

Bandura, Albert, *Social Learning Theory.* Englewood Cliffs, New Jersey: Prentice-Hall, 1977.

Bandura, Albert, Dorothea Ross, and Sheila Ross. "Imitation of Film-Mediated Aggressive Models," *Journal of Abnormal and Social Psychology,* 66 (1963), 3–11.

Bandura, Albert and Richard Walters. *Social Learning and Personality Development.* New York: Holt, Rinehart and Winston, 1963.

Bannister, D. B., and J. M. Mair. *Re-evaluation of Personal Constructs.* New York: Academic Press, 1968.

Baumrind, D. "Current Patterns of Parental Authority," *Developmental Psychology Monographs,* 4 (1971), 99–103.

———. "The Development of Instrumental Competence Through Socialization," in *Minnesota Symposia on Child Psychology,* Vol. 7. Edited by A. Pick. Minneapolis: University of Minnesota Press, 1973.

Bayley, Nancy. "Development of Mental Abilities," in *Manual of Child Psychology.* Edited by Paul Mussen. New York: John Wiley, 1970.

———. "Behavioral Correlates of Growth: Birth to Thirty-Six Years," *American Psychologist,* 23 (1968), 1–17.

Beard, Ruth. *An Outline of Piaget's Developmental Psychology for Students and Teachers.* New York: Basic Books, 1969.

Beck, Robert. *Motivation: Theories and Principles.* Englewood Cliffs, New Jersey: Prentice-Hall, 1978.

Becker, Wesley. "Consequences of Different Kinds of Parental Discipline," in *Review of Child Development Research,* Vol. 1. Edited by Martin Hoffman and Lois Hoffman. New York: Russell Sage Foundation, 1964.

Belsky, Jay, and Lawrence Steinberg. "The Effects of Day Care: A Critical Review," *Child Development,* 49 (December, 1978), 930–949.

Berkowitz, Leonard. "Control of Aggression," in *Review of Child Development Research.* Edited by Bettye Caldwell and Henry Ricciuti. Chicago: University of Chicago Press, 1973.

Bernstein, Emmanuel. "What Does a Summerhill Old School Tie Look Like?" *Psychology Today,* 2 (October, 1968), 37–41, 70.

Bijou, Sidney. *Child Development: The Basic Stage of Early Childhood.* Englewood Cliffs, New Jersey: Prentice-Hall, 1976.

———. "Development in the Pre-School Years: A Functional Analysis," *American Psychologist,* Vol. 30, No. 8 (August, 1975), 829–837.

Binet, Alfred, and Theodore Simon. "The Development of Intelligence in Children," *L'Annee Psychologique* (1905), 163–191.

Block, J. "Advancing the Psychology of Personality," in *Personality at the Crossroads.* Edited by D. Magnussen. Hillsdale, New Jersey: Lawrence Erlbaum, 1977.

Bloom, Benjamin. *Stability and Change in Human Characteristics.* New York: John Wiley & Sons, 1964.

Bloom, Lois, and Margaret Lahey. *Language Development and Language Disorders.* New York: John Wiley & Sons, 1978.

Bourne, Lyle, Jr., Roger Dominowski, and Elizabeth Loftus. *Cognitive Processes.* Englewood Cliffs, New Jersey: Prentice-Hall, 1979.

Bower, T.G.R. *A Primer of Infant Development.* San Francisco: Freeman, 1977.

Bowes, Watson, Yvonne Brackhill, Esher Conway, and Alfred Steinschneider. "The Effects of Obstetrical Medication on Fetus and Infant," *Monographs of the Society for Research in Child Development,* Vol. 35, No. 4 (1970).

Bowlby, John. *Attachment.* New York: Basic Books, 1969.

Brackbill, Y., J. Kane, R. L. Manniello, and D. Abramson. "Obstetric Premedication and Infant Outcome," *American Journal of Obstetrics and Gynecology* (February, 1974), 377–385.

Brainerd, Charles. "Judgments and Explanations as Criteria for the Presence of Cognitive Structures," *Psychological Bulletin,* 79 (1973), 172–179.

Brazelton, T. Berry. *Infants and Mothers.* New York: Delacorte Press, 1969.

———. *Neonatal Behavioral Assessment Scale.* London: William Heinemann Medical Books, Ltd., 1973.

Brazelton, T. Berry, and Heidelise Als. "Four Early Stages in the Development of Mother-Infant Interaction," *The Psychoanalytic Study of the Child,* 34 (1979), 349–369.

Bremner, Robert. *Children and Youth in America: A Documentary History* (3 volumes). Cambridge, Massachusetts: Harvard University Press, 1970, 1971.

Brenner, Charles. *An Elementary Textbook of Psychoanalysis* (Revised edition). New York: International Universities Press, 1973.

Brody, Ernest, and Nathan Brody. *Intelligence: Nature, Determinants, and Consequences.* New York: Academic Press, 1976.

Bronfenbrenner, Uri. *The Ecology of Human Development.* Cambridge, Massachusetts: Harvard University Press, 1979.

———. "Toward an Experimental Ecology of Human Development," *American Psychologist,* 32 (November, 1977), 513–531.

———. *Two Worlds of Childhood: U.S. and U.S.S.R.* New York: Russell Sage Foundation, 1970.

Brooks, Jeanne, and Michael Lewis. "Midget, Adult, and Child: Infants' Responses to Strangers," *Child Development,* 47 (1976), 323–332.

Brooks, Jeanne, and Marsha Weintraub. "A History of Infant Intelligence Testing," in *Origins of Intelligence.* Edited by Michael Lewis. New York: Plenum Press, 1976.

Brophy, Jere, and Thomas Good. *Teacher-Student Relationships.* New York: Holt, Rinehart and Winston, 1974.

Brown, Roger. *A First Language.* Cambridge, Massachusetts: Harvard University Press, 1973.

Brozek, Josef. "Nutrition, Malnutrition, and Behavior," in *Annual Review of Psychology.* Edited by Mark Rosenzweig and Lyman Porter. Palo Alto, California: Annual Reviews, Inc., 1978.

Bruch, Hilda. *The Golden Cage.* Cambridge, Massachusetts: Harvard University Press, 1978.

Bruner, Jerome. *The Process of Education.* Cambridge, Massachusetts: Harvard University Press, 1960.

———. *Toward a Theory of Instruction.* New York: Norton, 1966.

Bruner, Jerome and Cecile Goodman. "Value and Need as Organizing Factors in Perception," *Journal of Abnormal and Social Psychology,* 42 (1947), 33–44.

Bruner, Jerome, Jacqueline Goodnow, and George Austin. *A Study of Thinking.* New York: John Wiley, 1956.

Bryant, P. *Perception and Understanding in Young Children: An Experimental Approach.* New York: Basic Books, 1974.

Buffery, Anthony. "Sex Differences in the Neuropsychological Development of Verbal and Spatial Skills," in *The Neuropsychology of Learning Disorders.* Edited by Robert Knights and Dirk Bakker. Baltimore: University Park Press, 1976.

Buhler, Charlotte. "Theoretical Observations About Life's Basic Tendencies," *American Journal of Psychotherapy,* Vol. 13 (1959), 561–581.

———. "Humanistic Psychology as an Educational Program," *American Psychology,* Vol. 24 (1969), 736–742.

Burt, Cyril. "The Evidence for the Concept of Intelligence," *British Journal of Educational Psychology,* Vol. 25 (1955), 158–177.

Butts, R. F., and Lawrence Cremin. *A History of Education in American Culture.* New York: Holt, Rinehart and Winston, 1953.

Caldwell, Bettye. "The Effects of Infant Care," in *Review of Child Development Research,* Vol. I. Edited by Martin Hoffman and Lois Hoffman. New York: Russell Sage Foundation, 1964.

Campbell, John. "Peer Relations in Childhood," in *Review of Child Development Research,* Vol. 1. Edited by Martin and Lois Hoffman. New York: Russell Sage, 1964.

Campos, Joseph. "Heart Rate: A Sensitive Tool for the Study of Emotional Development in the Infant," in *Developmental Psychobiology.* Edited by Lewis Lipsitt. New York: Lawrence Erlbaum, 1976.

Caplan, Frank. *The First Twelve Months of Life.* New York: Grosset and Dunlap, 1973.

Carmichael, Leonard. "Onset and Early Development of Behavior," in *Manual of Child Psychology.* Edited by Paul Mussen. New York: John Wiley & Sons, 1970.

Chess, Stella, and M. Hassibi. *Principles and Practices in Child Psychiatry.* New York: Plenum Press, 1978.

Chomsky, Noam. *Syntactic Structures.* The Hague: Mouton, 1957.

Clarizio, Harvey, and George McCoy. *Behavior Disorders in Children.* New York: Harper & Row, 1976.

Clarke-Stewart, K. Alison. "Popular Primer for Parents," *American Psychologist,* Vol. 33 (April, 1978), 359–369.

Clausen, John. "Family Structure, Socialization, and Personality," in *Review of Child Development Research,* Volume II. Edited by Martin Hoffman and Lois Hoffman. New York: Russell Sage Foundation, 1966.

Clausen, John, and Judith Williams. "Sociological Correlates of Child Behavior," *Sixty-second Yearbook of the National Society for the Study of Education,* Part I. Chicago: University of Chicago Press, 1963.

Cofer, Charles, and Mortimer Appley. *Motivation: Theory and Research.* New York: John Wiley, 1964.

Cohen, Gillian. *The Psychology of Cognition.* New York: Academic Press, 1977.

Coleman, James. *Youth: Transition to Adulthood.* Chicago: University of Chicago Press, 1974.

Coles, Robert, *The Privileged Ones.* Boston: Little, Brown, 1977.

———. "Like It Is in the Alley," *Daedalus,* Vol. 97 (Fall, 1968), 1315–1330.

Comstock, George, Steven Chaffee, Nathan Katzman, Maxwell McCombs, and Donald Roberts. *Television and Human Behavior.* New York: Columbia University Press, 1978.

Cratty, Bryant. *Perceptual and Motor Development in Infants and Children.* New York: Macmillan, 1970.

Cravioto, J., H. G. Bisch, E. DeLicardie, L. Rosales, and L. Vaga. "The Ecology of Growth and Development in a Mexican Preindustrial Community. Report I. Method and Findings from Birth to One Month of Age," *Monographs of the Society for Research in Child Development,* Vol. 34, No. 5 (August, 1969).

Cravioto, J., and E. DeLicardie. "Mental Performance in School-Age Children," *American Journal of Disabled Children,* Vol. 120 (November, 1970), 404–411.

Cronbach, Lee. *Essentials of Psychological Testing.* New York: Harcourt, 1970.

Cruickshank, William, and Henry De Young, "Educational Practices with Exceptional Children," in *Education of Exceptional Children and Youth.* Edited by William Cruickshank and G. Orville Johnson. Englewood Cliffs, New Jersey: Prentice-Hall, 1975.

Cytryn, L., and D. H. McKuen. "Factors Influencing the Changing Clinical Expression of the Depressive Process in Children," *American Journal of Psychiatry,* Vol. 131 (1974), 879–881.

Dahl, Barbara, and H. McCubbin. "Prolonged Family Separation in the Military: A Longitudinal Study," *Families in the Military System.* Beverly Hills, California: Sage Publications, 1976.

Dale, Philip. *Language Development: Structure and Function.* Hinsdale, Illinois: The Dryden Press, 1976.

Dasen, Pierre. "Cross-cultural Piagetian Research: A Summary," *Journal of Cross-Cultural Psychology,* Vol. 3 (1972), 23–29.

Deese, James. *Psycholinguistics.* Boston: Allyn and Bacon, 1970.

Dennis, Wayne. "Causes of Retardation Among Institutional Children: Iran," *Journal of Genetic Psychology,* Vol. 96 (1960), 47–59.

Dennis, W., and Perghrouhi Najarian. "Infant Development Under Environmental Handicaps," *Psychological Monographs,* Vol. 71 (1957), 60–61.

DeVilliers, Jill, and Peter deVilliers. *Language Acquisition.* Cambridge: Harvard University Press, 1978.

Dollard, J., L. Doob, N. Miller, O. Mowrer, and R. Sears. *Frustrations and Aggression.* New Haven: Yale University Press, 1939.

Dworkin, Nancy, and Yehoash Dworkin. "The Legacy of 'Pygmalion in the Classroom,'" *Phi Delta Kappan,* Vol. 60 (June, 1979), 712–715.

Earls, Felton, and Michael Yogman. "The Father-Infant Relationship," in *Modern Perspectives in the Psychiatry of Infancy.* Edited by James Howells. New York: Brunner/Mazel, 1979.

Eccles, John. *The Understanding of the Brain.* New York: McGraw-Hill, 1977.

Eiduson, B. "Child Development in Emergent Family Styles," *Children Today* (March–April, 1978), 56–62.

Eisdorfer, C., and F. Wilkie. "Intellectual Changes with Advancing Age," in *Intellectual Functioning in Adults.* Edited by L. Jarvik, C. Eisdorfer, and J. Blum. New York: Springer, 1973.

Eisenberg, Leon. "Perspectives on Psychosomatics as a Concept," in *Psychosomatics in Children and Adolescents.* Unpublished manuscript, 1979.

Elder, Glen. *Children of the Great Depression.* Chicago: University of Chicago Press, 1974.

Elkind, David. *A Sympathetic Understanding of the Child Six to Sixteen.* Boston: Allyn and Bacon, 1971.

———. "Erik Erikson's Eight Ages of Man," *New York Times Magazine* (April 5, 1970).

Engel, George. "The Need for a New Medical Model: A Challenge for Biomedicine," *Science,* 196 (April, 1977), 129–135.

Epel, David. "The Program of Fertilization," *Scientific American,* Vol. 237 (November, 1977), 129–138.

Epstein, Herman. "Growth Spurts During Brain Development," *The Seventy-seventh Yearbook of the National Society for the Study of Education.* Edited by Jesse Child and Allan Minsky. Chicago: University of Chicago Press, 1978.

Erikson, Erik. *Identity: Youth and Crisis.* New York: W. W. Norton, 1968.

———. *Childhood and Society.* New York: W. W. Norton, 1950.

Ervin-Tripp, Susan, and Nick Miller. "Language Development," *The Sixty-second Yearbook of the National Society for the Study of Education.* Chicago: University of Chicago Press, 1963.

Escalona, Sibylle. *The Roots of Individuality.* Chicago: Aldine Publishing Co., 1968.

Fagan, Joseph F., III. "Infant Recognition Memory: Studies in Forgetting," *Child Development,* Vol. 48, No. 1 (1977), 68–78.

Fantz, Robert. "Pattern Vision in Newborn Infants," *Science,* Vol. 140 (1963), 296–297.

———. "The Origin of Form Perception," *Scientific American,* Vol. 204 (1961), 66–72.

Farb, Peter. *Humankind.* Boston: Houghton-Mifflin, 1978.

———. *Word Play.* New York: Knopf, 1973.

Faust, Margaret S. "Somatic Development of Adolescent Girls," *Monographs of the Society for Research in Child Development*, Vol. 14, No. 169 (1977).

Featherstone, Joseph. "Family Matters," *Harvard Educational Review*, Vol. 49 (February, 1979), 20–52.

Ferreira, A. J. "The Pregnant Mother's Emotional Attitude and Its Reflection Upon the Newborn," *American Journal of Orthopsychiatry*, Vol. 30 (1960), 553–561.

Feshbach, Seymour. "Aggression," in *Carmichael's Manual of Child Psychology*. Edited by Paul Mussen. New York: John Wiley & Sons, 1970.

Flavell, John. *Cognitive Development*. Englewood Cliffs, New Jersey: Prentice-Hall, 1977.

———. *The Developmental Psychology of Jean Piaget*. New York: D. Van Nostrand, Inc., 1963.

Freud, Sigmund. *An Outline of Psychoanalysis*. New York: W. W. Norton, 1949.

Fromme, A. "An Experimental Study of the Factors of Maturation and Practice in the Behavioral Development of the Embryo of the Frog, Rara Pipiens," *Genetic Psychology Monographs*, Vol. 24 (1941), 219–256.

Fry, D. B. "The Development of the Phonological System in the Normal and the Deaf Child," in *The Genesis of Language*. Edited by F. Smith and G. A. Miller. Cambridge, Massachusetts: M.I.T. Press, 1966.

Fuchs, Fritz. "Genetic Amniocentesis," *Scientific American*, Vol. 242, No. 6 (June, 1980), 47–63.

Gallagher, Ursula. "What's Happening in Adoption?" *Children Today*, Vol. 32 (November-December, 1975), 11–13, 36–38.

Gardner, Howard. *The Shattered Mind*. New York: Vantage Books, 1974.

Gardner, Lytt. "Deprivation Dwarfism," *Scientific American*, Vol. 227 (July, 1972), 76–82.

Gelman, Rachel. "Cognitive Development," in *Annual Review of Psychology*. Edited by Mark Rosenzweig and Lyman Porter. Palo Alto, California: Annual Reviews, Inc., 1978.

Gibson, Eleanor. *Principles of Perceptual Learning and Development*. New York: Appleton, Century-Crofts, 1969.

Gibson, Eleanor, and Richard Walk. "The Visual Cliff," *Scientific American*, Vol. 202 (April, 1960), 64–71.

Gilligan, Carol. "In a Different Voice: Women's Conception of Self and of Morality," *Harvard Educational Review*, Vol. 47 (November, 1977), 481–517.

Ginsburg, Herbert, and Sylvia Opper. *Piaget's Theory of Intellectual Development: An Introduction*. Englewood Cliffs, New Jersey: Prentice-Hall, 1979.

Glueck, Sheldon, and Eleanor Glueck. *Unraveling Juvenile Delinquency*. New York: The Commonwealth Fund, 1950.

Gorman, Richard. *Discovering Piaget: A Guide for Teachers*. Columbus, Ohio: Charles Merrill, 1972.

Greenfeld, Josh. "Advances in Genetics that Can Change Your Life," *Today's Health* (December, 1973).

Greer, Colin. "Once Again the Family Question," *New York Times* (October 14, 1979).

Guilford, J. P. *Personality*. New York: McGraw-Hill, 1959.

———. *The Nature of Human Intelligence*. New York: McGraw-Hill, 1967.

Haith, Marshall, and Joseph Campos. "Human Infancy," in *Annual Review of Psychology*. Edited by Mark Rosenzweig and Lyman Porter. Palo Alto, California: Annual Reviews, 1977.

Hall, Calvin, and Gardner Lindzey. *Theories of Personality*. New York: John Wiley & Sons, 1975.

Harlow, Harry, and Margaret Harlow. "Social Deprivation in Monkeys," *Scientific American* (November, 1962).

Hartup, Willard. "Cross-Age Versus Same-Age Peer Interaction: Ethological and Cross-Cultured Perspectives," in *Children as Teachers*. Edited by Vernon Allen. New York: Academic Press, 1976.

Havighurst, Robert. *Developmental Tasks and Education*. New York: David McKay, 1972.

———. *Human Development and Education*. New York: David McKay, 1953.

Harris, Florence, Montrose Wolf, and Donald Baer. "Effects of Adult Social Reinforcements on Child Behavior," *Journal of Nursery Education*, Vol. 20 (1964), 8–9.

Hayflick, Leonard. "The Cell Biology of Human Aging," *Scientific American*, Vol. 242 (January, 1980), 58–65.

Healy, William, and August Bronner. *New Light on Delinquency and Its Treatment.* New Haven: Yale University Press, 1936.

Heber, Rick. "Rehabilitation of Families at Risk for Mental Retardation," *A Progress Report on the Milwaukee Project*, University of Wisconsin at Madison (December, 1972).

Helson, Ravenna. "Through the Pages of Children's Books," *Psychology Today*, Vol. 7 (November, 1973), 107–117.

Helson, Ravenna, and Valory Mitchell. "Personality," in *Annual Review of Psychology.* Edited by Mark Rosenzweig and Lyman Porter. Palo Alto, California: Annual Reviews, 1978.

Hendin, David, and Joan Marks. *The Genetic Connection.* New York: William Morrow, 1978.

Herbert, Martin. *Emotional Problems of Development in Children.* New York: Academic Press, 1974.

Hersh, Richard, Diana Paolitto, and Joseph Reimer. *Promoting Moral Growth: From Piaget to Kohlberg.* New York: Longman, 1979.

Hess, Robert. "Social Class and Ethnic Influences on Socialization," in *Carmichael's Manual of Child Psychology.* Edited by Paul Mussen. New York: John Wiley & Sons, 1970.

Hetherington, E. Mavis. "Divorce: A Child's Perspective," *American Psychologist*, Vol. 34 (October, 1979), 851–856.

Hilgard, Ernest, and Gordon Bower. *Theories of Learning.* Englewood Cliffs, New Jersey: Prentice-Hall, 1975.

Hodges, Walter. "The Worth of the Follow-Through Experience," *Harvard Educational Review*, Vol. 48, No. 2 (May, 1978), 186–192.

Hoffman, Martin. "Moral Development," in *Carmichael's Manual of Child Psychology.* Edited by Paul Mussen. New York: John Wiley & Sons, 1970.

———. "Development of Moral Thought, Feeling and Behavior," *American Psychologist*, Vol. 34, No. 10 (October, 1979), 958–966.

Holmes, Lewis. "How Fathers Can Cause the Down's Syndrome," *Human Nature*, Vol. 10 (October, 1978), 70–72.

Hooper, Frank. "Cognitive Assessment across the Life-Span: Methodological Implications of the Organismic Approach," in *Life Span Developmental Psychology.* Edited by John R. Nesselroads and Hayne W. Reese. New York: Academic Press, 1973.

House, Ernest, Gene Glass, Leslie McLean, and Decker Walker. "No Simple Answer: Critique of the Follow-Through Evaluation," *Harvard Educational Review*, Vol. 48, No. 2 (May, 1978), 128–160.

Howe, Michael. *Learning in Infants and Young Children.* Stanford: Stanford University Press, 1975.

Howell, James (editor). *Modern Perspectives in the Psychiatry of Infancy.* New York: Brunner/Mazel, 1979.

Hull, Clark. "Quantitative Aspects of the Evolution of Concepts," *Psychological Monographs*, Vol. 28, No. 123 (1920), 1–86.

Hunt, J. McVicker. *Intelligence and Experience.* New York: Ronald, 1961.

Hunt, J. M., and Ina Uzgiris. *Assessment in Infancy.* Urbana, Illinois: University of Illinois Press, 1975.

Hyde, J. S., and B. G. Rosenberg. *Half the Human Experience.* Lexington, Massachusetts: D. C. Heath, 1976.

Hymes, Dell. *Language in Culture and Society.* New York: Harper and Row, 1964.

Jakobson, Roman. *Child Language, Aphasia, and Phonological Universals.* The Hague: Mouton, 1968.

Jarvick, Lissy, Victor Klodin, and Steven Matsuyama. "Human Aggression and the Extra Y Chromosome: Fact or Fantasy?" *American Psychologist*, Vol. 28 (August, 1973), 674–682.

Jencks, Christopher. *Inequality: A Reassessment of the Effects of Family and Schooling in America.* New York: Basic Books, 1972.

Jensen, Arthur. "How Much Can We Boost I.Q. and Scholastic Achievement?" *Harvard Educational Review*, Vol. 39, No. 1 (1969), 1–123.

Jersild, Arthur, and F. B. Holmes. "Children's Fears," *Child Development Monographs*, No. 20. New York: Teachers College, Columbia University, 1935.

Kagan, Jerome. *Change and Continuity in Infancy.* New York: John Wiley & Sons, 1971.

———. "Three Themes in Developmental Psychology," in *Developmental Psychobiology.* Edited by Lewis Lipsitt. New Jersey: Lawrence Erlbaum, 1976.

———. "The Baby's Elastic Mind," *Human Nature,* Vol. 1, No. 1 (January, 1978a), 66–73.

———. "The Effects of Infant Day Care on Psychological Development," in *The Growth of the Child.* Edited by Jerome Kagan. New York: W. W. Norton, 1978b.

Kagan, Jerome, and Howard Moss. *Birth to Maturity: A Study in Psychological Development.* New York: John Wiley & Sons, 1962.

Kagan, Jerome, Richard Kearsley, Phillip C. Zelazo. *Infancy: Its Place in Human Development.* Cambridge: Harvard University Press, 1978.

Kagan, Jerome, and Richard Klein. "Cross-Cultural Perspectives on Early Development," *American Psychologist,* Vol. 28 (November, 1973), 947–961.

Kagan, Jerome, Deborah Lapidus, and Michael Moore. "Infant Antecedents of Cognitive Functioning: A Longitudinal Study," *Child Development,* Vol. 49 (1978), 1005–1023.

Kamin, Leon. *The Science and Politics of I.Q.* Hillsdale, New Jersey: Lawrence Erlbaum, 1974.

Kanner, Leo. "Early Infantile Autism," *Journal of Pediatrics,* Vol. 25 (1944), 211–217.

Kaplan, David, and Robert Reich. "The Murdered Child and His Killers," *American Journal of Psychiatry* (July, 1976).

Kaufman, Alan. *Intelligent Testing with the WISC-R.* New York: John Wiley & Sons, 1979.

Kelly, Francis, and Daniel Baer. "Physical Challenge as a Treatment for Delinquency," *Crime and Delinquency,* Vol. 17 (October, 1971), 437–444.

Kelly, George. *A Theory of Personality.* New York: W. W. Norton, 1963.

Kempe, Ruth S., and C. Henry Kempe. *Child Abuse.* Cambridge: Harvard University Press, 1978.

Keniston, Kenneth. *Youth and Dissent.* New York: Harcourt, Brace, Jovanovich, 1970.

———. *All Our Children.* New York: Harcourt, Brace, Jovanovich, 1977.

Kerlinger, Fred. *Foundations of Behavioral Research.* New York: Holt, Rinehart, and Winston, 1973.

Kess, Joseph. *Psycholinguistics: Introductory Perspectives.* New York: Academic Press, 1976.

Kessen, William, Marshall Haith, and Philip Salapatek. "Infancy," in *Carmichael's Manual of Child Psychology.* Edited by Paul Mussen. New York: John Wiley & Sons, 1970.

Kimura, Doreen. "The Asymmetry of the Human Brain," *Scientific American,* Vol. 228 (March, 1973), 70–78.

Kinsbourne, Marcel, and Merrill Hiscock. "Cerebral Lateralization and Cognitive Development," *The Seventy-seventh Yearbook of the National Society for the Study of Education.* Edited by Jeanne Chall and Allan Mirsky. Chicago: University of Chicago Press, 1978.

Klaus, Marshall, and John Kennell. *Mother-Infant Bonding.* St. Louis: The C. V. Mosby Co., 1976.

Kilpatrick, William. *Identity and Intimacy.* New York: Delta, 1975.

———. "Boy, Girl, or Person?" in *The First Six Years.* Edited by John F. Travers. Stamford, Connecticut: Greylock, 1976.

Klausmeier, Herbert, Elizabeth Ghatala, and Dorothy Frayer. *Conceptual Learning and Development.* New York: Academic Press, 1974.

Knapp, Peter. "Psychotherapeutic Management of Bronchial Asthma," in *Psychosomatic Medicine: Its Clinical Applications.* Edited by E. D. Wittkower and H. Warnes. New York: Harper and Row, 1977.

Knights, Robert, and Dirk Bakker (editors). *The Neuropsychology of Learning Disorders.* Baltimore: University Park Press, 1976.

Knobloch, Hilda, and Benjamin Pasamanick. *Gesell and Amatruda's Developmental Diagnosis.* New York: Harper and Row, 1974.

Kogan, Nathan. *Cognitive Styles in Infancy and Early Childhood.* Hillsdale, New Jersey: Lawrence Erlbaum, 1976.

Kohlberg, Lawrence. "The Cognitive-Developmental Approach to Moral Education," *Phi Delta Kappan,* Vol. 56 (1975), 670–677.

———. "A Cognitive-Developmental Analysis of Children's Sex-Role Concepts and Attitudes," in *The Development of Sex Differences.* Edited by Eleanor Maccoby. Stanford, California: Stanford University Press, 1966.

Kuo, Zing-Yang. *The Dynamics of Behavior Development: An Epigenetic View.* New York: Random House, 1967.

Lamb, Michael. "Paternal Influences and the Father's Role," *American Psychologist,* Vol. 34 (October, 1979), 938–943.

Larsen, Gary. "Methodology in Developmental Psychology: An Examination of Research on Piagetian Theory," *Child Development,* Vol. 48 (December, 1977), 1160–1166.

Lasch, Christopher. *Haven in a Heartless World.* New York: Basic Books, 1979a.

———. *The Culture of Narcissism.* New York: W. W. Norton, 1979b.

Latham, M. C., and F. Cobos. "The Effects of Malnutrition on Intellectual Development and Learning," *American Journal of Public Health,* Vol. 61 (July, 1971), 1307–1324.

Leboyer, Frederick. *Birth without Violence.* New York: Knopf, 1975.

Lefcourt, Herbert. *Locus of Control: Current Trends in Theory and Research.* Hillsdale, New Jersey: Lawrence Erlbaum, 1976.

Leiderman, P. Herbert, Steven Tulkin, and Anne Rosenfeld (editors). *Culture and Infancy.* New York: Academic Press, 1977.

Lenneberg, Eric. *Biological Foundations of Language.* New York: John Wiley & Sons, 1967.

Lester, Barry, and T. Berry Brazelton. "Cross-Cultural Assessment of Neonatal Behavior," in *Cultural Perspectives on Child Development.* Edited by H. Stevenson and D. Wagner. San Francisco: W. H. Freeman and Co., 1980.

Lester, Barry, and P. Zeskind. "The Organization of Crying in the Infant at Risk," in *The High Risk Newborn.* Edited by T. Field. New York: Spectrum Publications, 1978.

Levin, Joel, and Vernon Allen (editors). *Cognitive Learning in Children.* New York: Academic Press, 1976.

Levine, Melvin. "Encopresis," in *Psychosomatics in Children and Adolescents.* (Unpublished manuscript, 1979.)

Levine, Melvin, Robert Brooks, and Jack Shonkoff. *A Pediatric Approach to Learning Disorders.* New York: John Wiley & Sons, 1980.

Lewis, Melvin. *Clinical Aspects of Child Development.* Philadelphia: Lea & Febiger, 1971.

Lewis, Michael (editor). *The Origins of Intelligence.* New York: Plenum Press, 1976.

Lewis, Michael, and S. Lee-Painter. "An Interactional Approach to the Mother-Infant Dyad," in *The Effect of the Infant on Its Caregiver.* Edited by Michael Lewis and L. A. Rosenbloom. New York: John Wiley & Sons, 1974.

Lewis, Oscar. *La Vida.* New York: Random House, 1965.

Lind, T. "Techniques for Assessing Fetal Development," in *Biology of Human Fetal Growth.* Edited by D. F. Roberts and A. M. Thomson. New York: John Wiley & Sons, 1976.

Lips, Hilary, and Nina Lee Colwill. *Psychology of Sex Differences.* Englewood Cliffs, New Jersey: Prentice-Hall, 1978.

Lipsitt, Lewis (editor). *Developmental Psychobiology.* Hillsdale, New Jersey: Lawrence Erlbaum, 1976.

———. "Developmental Psychobiology Comes of Age," in *Developmental Psychobiology.* Hillsdale, New Jersey: Lawrence Erlbaum, 1976.

Lloyd-Still, John, Irving Hurwitz, Peter Wolff, and Harry Schwachman. "Intellectual Development after Severe Malnutrition in Infancy," *Pediatrics,* Vol. 54 (September, 1974), 306–311.

Lorenz, Konrad. *On Aggression.* New York: Harcourt, Brace, and World, 1966.

Lynd, R. S. *Middletown in Transition.* New York: Harcourt, Brace, and World, 1937.

Lynn, David. *The Father: His Role in Child Development.* Monterey, California: Brooks/Cole Publishing, 1974.

Maccoby, Eleanor, *Social Development.* New York: Harcourt, Brace, Jovanovich, 1980.

Maccoby, Eleanor, (editor). *The Development of Sex Differences.* Stanford, California: Stanford University Press, 1966.

Maccoby, Eleanor, and Carol Jacklin. *The Psychology of Sex Differences.* Stanford, California: Stanford University Press, 1974.

Maccoby, Eleanor, and John Masters. "Attachment and Dependency," in *Carmichael's Manual of Child Psychology.* Edited by Paul Mussen. New York: John Wiley & Sons, 1970.

Macfarlane, Aidan. *The Psychology of Childbirth.* Cambridge: Harvard University Press, 1977.

———. "What a Baby Knows," *Human Nature,* Vol. 1, No. 2 (February, 1977), 74–81.

MacLean, Paul. "A Mind of Three Minds: Educating the Triune Brain," *The Seventy-seventh Yearbook of the National Society for the Study of Education.* Edited by Jeanne Chall and Allan Minsky. Chicago: University of Chicago Press, 1978.

Mahone, C. H. "Fear of Failure and Unrealistic Vocational Aspirations," *Abnormal and Social Psychology,* Vol. 60 (1960), 253–261.

Manocha, Sohan. *Malnutrition and Retarded Human Development.* Springfield, Illinois: Charles C Thomas, 1972.

Marlow, Dorothy. *Textbook of Pediatric Nursing.* Philadelphia: Saunders, 1973.

Maslow, Abraham. *Motivation and Personality.* New York: Harper and Row, 1970.

Maw, Wallace, and Ethel Maw. "Self-concepts of High and Low Curiosity Boys," *Child Development,* Vol. 1 (1970), 123–129.

McBurney, Annetta, and Henry Dunn. "Handedness, Footedness, Eyedness: A Prospective Study with Special Reference to the Development of Speech and Language Skills," in *Neuropsychology of Learning Disorders.* Edited by Robert Knights and Dirk Bakker. Baltimore: University Park Press, 1976.

McCall, Robert. "Toward an Epigenetic Connection of Mental Development in the First Three Years of Life," in *Origins of Intelligence.* Edited by Michael Lewis. New York: Plenum Press, 1976.

McCall, Robert, Dorothy Eichorn, and Pamela Hogarty. "Transitions in Early Mental Development," *Monographs of the Society for Research in Child Development,* Vol. 3, No. 42 (1977).

McClearn, Gerald. "Genetics and Behavior Development," in *Review of Child Development Research,* Vol. 1. Edited by Martin and Lois Hoffman. New York: Russell Sage Foundation, 1964.

McClelland, David, and D. G. Winter. *Motivating Economic Achievement.* New York: Free Press, 1969.

Mech, Edmund. "Adoption: A Policy Perspective," in *Review of Child Development Research.* Edited by Bettye Caldwell and Henry Ricciuti. Chicago: University of Chicago Press, 1973.

Meredith, Howard. "Body Size of Contemporary Groups of Eight-Year-Old Children Studied in Different Parts of the World," *Monographs of the Society for Research in Child Development,* Vol. 34, No. 125 (1969), Table 4, 19.

Milgram, Stanley. "Behavioral Study of Obedience," *Journal of Personality and Social Psychology,* Vol. 67 (1963), 371–378.

Minuchin, Salvador. *Families and Family Therapy.* Cambridge: Harvard University Press, 1974.

Mischel, Walter. "Sex-Typing and Socialization," in *Carmichael's Manual of Child Psychology.* Edited by Paul Mussen. New York: John Wiley & Sons, 1970.

———. "A Social Learning View of Sex Differences in Behavior," in *The Development of Sex Differences.* Edited by Eleanor Maccoby. Stanford, California: Stanford University Press, 1966.

Money, John. "Gender Identity Differentiation," Nebraska Symposium on Motivation, 1973. Edited by James Cole and Richard Dienstbier. Lincoln, Nebraska: University of Nebraska Press, 1973.

Money, John, and Anke Ehrhardt. *Man and Woman, Boy and Girl.* Baltimore: Johns Hopkins University Press, 1972.

Montessori, Maria. *The Montessori Method.* New York: Schocken Books, 1964.

———. *The Absorbent Mind.* New York: Dell, 1967.

Morton, A. Q. *Literary Detection: How to Prove Authorship and Fraud in Literature and Documents.* New York: Charles Scribner's Sons, 1979.

Moulton, William. "The Study of Language and Human Communication," in *The Sixty-ninth Yearbook of the National Society for the Study of Education.* Edited by Albert Marckwardt. Chicago: University of Chicago Press, 1970.

Mussen, Paul, and Nancy Eisenberg-Berg. *Roots of Caring, Sharing, and Helping.* San Francisco, California: Freeman, 1977.

National Center for Health Statistics. "Growth Curves, Birth-Eighteen Years, United States," *Department of Health, Education, and Welfare Publication No. (PH) 78-1650.* Hyattsville, Maryland: U.S. Department of Health, Education, and Welfare, 1977.

Neill, A. S. *Summerhill.* New York: Hart, 1960.

Neimark, Edith. "Intellectual Development During Adolescence," in *Review of Child Development Research.* Edited by Frances Horowitz and E. Mavis Hetherington. Chicago: University of Chicago Press, 1975.

Nelson, K. "Structure and Strategy in Learning to Talk," *Monographs of the Society for Research in Child Development,* Vol. 38, No. 149, 1973.

Neumeyer, Martin. *Juvenile Delinquency in Modern Society.* New York: D. Van Nostrand, 1961.

Nilsson, Lennart, Mirjam Furuhjelm, Alex Ingelman-Sundberg, and Claes Wirsen. *A Child Is Born.* New York: Delacorte Press, 1977.

Oller, D. K., L. A. Wieman, W. J. Doyle, and C. Ross. "Infant Babbling and Speech," *Journal of Child Language,* Vol. 1 (1976), 133–138.

Osofsky, J. (editor). *Handbook on Infancy.* New York: John Wiley & Sons, 1977.

Paivio, Allan. *Imagery and Verbal Processes.* New York: Holt, Rinehart and Winston, 1971.

Parke, Ross. "Perspectives on Father-infant Interactions," in *Handbook of Infant Development.* Edited by J. D. Osofsky. New York: John Wiley & Sons, 1979.

Papousek, H. "Conditioning During Early Postnatal Development," in *Behavior in Infancy and Early Childhood.* Edited by Y. Brackbill and G. G. Thompson. New York: Free Press, 1967.

———. "Individual Variability in Learned Responses in Human Infants," in *Brain and Early Behavior.* Edited by R. J. Robinson. New York: Academic Press, 1969.

Parmelee, Arthur, and R. Michaelis. "Neurological Examination of the Newborn," in *Exceptional Infant.* Vol. II. Edited by J. Hellmuth. New York: Brunner/Mazel, 1971.

Pavlov, Ivan. *Conditioned Reflexes.* London: Oxford University Press, 1927.

———. *Lectures on Conditioned Reflexes.* London: Oxford University Press, 1928.

Pervin, Lawrence. *Current Controversies and Issues in Personality.* New York: John Wiley & Sons, 1978.

Phares, E. Jerry. *Locus of Control: A Personality Determinant of Behavior.* Morristown, New Jersey: General Learning Press, 1973.

Phillips, John. *The Origins of Intellect: Piaget's Theory.* San Francisco: W. H. Freeman, 1979.

Piaget, Jean. *The Language and Thought of the Child.* New York: Harcourt, Brace, and World, 1926.

———. *Judgment and Reasoning in the Child.* New York: Harcourt, Brace, and World, 1928.

———. *The Child's Conception of the World.* New York: Harcourt, Brace, and World, 1929.

———. *The Child's Conception of Physical Causality.* New York: Harcourt, Brace, and World, 1930.

———. *The Moral Judgment of the Child.* New York: Harcourt, Brace, and World, 1932.

———. *The Origins of Intelligence in Children.* New York: International Universities Press, 1952.

———. *The Construction of Reality in the Child.* New York: Basic Books, 1954.

———. *Psychology and Intelligence.* London: Routledge and Kegan Paul, Ltd., 1950.

———. "Development and Learning," in *Piaget Rediscovered.* Edited by Richard Ripple and Verna Rockcastle. Washington, D.C.: U.S. Office of Education, National Science Foundation, 1964.

———. *Six Psychological Studies.* New York: Random House, 1967.

———. *Biology and Knowledge.* Chicago: University of Chicago Press, 1971.

———. *The Child and Reality.* New York: The Viking Press, 1973.

Piaget, Jean, and Barbel Inhelder. *The Psychology of the Child.* New York: Basic Books, 1969.

Pinkerton, Philip. *Childhood Disorders.* New York: Columbia University Press, 1974.

Prechtl, H., and D. Beintema. *The Neurological Examination of the Full-Term Newborn Infant.* London: William Heinemann, Ltd., 1964.

Rabkin, Judith, and Elen Strening. "Life Events, Stress, and Illness," *Science,* Vol. 194, No. 3 (December, 1976), 1013–1020.

Ray, Oakley. *Drugs, Society, and Human Behavior,* St. Louis: C. V. Mosby, 1978.

Read, M. S., and D. Felson. *Malnutrition, Learning and Behavior.* Bethesda, Maryland: U.S. Department of Health, Education, and Welfare, 1976.

Reed, Elizabeth. "Genetic Anomalies in Development," in *Review of Child Development Research,* Vol. 4. Edited by Francis Horowitz. Chicago: University of Chicago Press, 1975.

Reese, Hayne, and Lewis Lipsitt. *Experimental Child Psychology.* New York: Academic Press, 1970.

Rimland, B. *Infantile Autism.* New York: Appleton-Century-Crofts, 1964.

Roberts, D. F. "Environment and the Fetus," in *The Biology of Human Fetal Growth.* Edited by D. F. Roberts and A. M. Thomson. New York: John Wiley & Sons, 1976.

Rock, N. K. "Conversion Reactions in Childhood: A Clinical Study on Childhood Neurosis," *Journal of the American Academy of Child Psychiatry,* Vol. 10 (1971), 65–93.

Rodham, Hillary. "Children Under the Law," *Harvard Educational Review,* Vol. 43 (November, 1973), 487–514.

Rohwer, William, Paul Ammon, and Phoebe Cramer. *Understanding Intellectual Development.* Hinsdale, Illinois: Dryden Press, 1975.

Rosch, Eleanor. "Cognitive Reference Points," *Cognitive Psychology,* Vol. 7 (1975), 532–547.

Rose, Steven. *The Conscious Brain.* New York: Knopf, 1973.

Rosenberg, B. G., and Brian Sutton-Smith. *Sex and Identity.* New York: Holt, Rinehart, and Winston, 1972.

Rosenthal, Robert, and Lenore Jacobson. *Pygmalion in the Classroom.* New York: Holt, Rinehart and Winston, 1968.

Rosenzweig, Mark, Edward Bennett, and Marion Diamond. "Brain Changes in Response to Experience," *Scientific American,* Vol. 10 (February, 1972), 22–29.

Rotter, Julian. "Generalized Expectancies for Internal Versus External Control of Reinforcement," *Psychological Monographs,* Vol. 80, No. 609 (1966).

———. "Some Problems and Misconceptions Related to the Construct of Internal versus External Control of Reinforcement," *Journal of Consulting and Clinical Psychology,* Vol. 43 (1975), 56–67.

Rutter, Michael. "Maternal Deprivation, 1972–1978; New Findings, New Concepts, New Approaches," *Child Development,* Vol. 50, No. 2 (June, 1979), 283–305.

———. *Helping Troubled Children.* New York: Plenum Press, 1975.

Sagan, Carl. *The Dragons of Eden.* New York: Random House, 1977.

Sameroff, Arnold. "Early Influences on Development: Fact or Fancy?" in *Annual Progress in Child Psychiatry and Child Development.* Edited by Stella Chase and Alexander Thomas. New York: Brunner/Mazel, 1977.

Scarr, Sandra, and Richard Wienberg. "Attitudes, Interest, and I.Q.," *Human Nature,* Vol. 1 (April, 1978), 29–36.

Schaffer, J. R., and P. Emerson. "The Development of Social Attainments in Infancy," *Monographs of Society for Research in Child Development,* Vol. 29, No. 3 (1964).

Schaie, K. W., and C. R. Strother. "A Cross Sequential Study of Age Change in Cognitive Behavior," *Psychology Bulletin,* Vol. 70 (1968), 671–680.

Scheinfeld, Amran. *Your Heredity and Environment.* Philadelphia: J. P. Lippincott, 1965.

Scott, J. Paul. *Early Experience and the Organization of Behavior.* Belmont, California: Brooks/Cole, 1968.

———. *Animal Behavior.* Chicago: University of Chicago Press, 1972.

Sears, Robert. "Your Ancients Revisited: A History of Child Development Research," in *Review of Child Development Research.* Edited by E. Mavis Hetherington. Chicago: University of Chicago Press, 1975.

Sears, Robert, Eleanor Maccoby, and H. Levin. *Patterns of Child Rearing.* Evanston, Illinois: Row, Peterson, 1952.

Segal, Julius. *A Child's Journey.* New York: McGraw-Hill, 1978.

Senn, Milton, "Insights on the Child Development Movement in the United States," *Monographs of the Society for Research in Child Development,* Vol. 40, Serial No. 161 (1975).

Shirley, M. M. "The First Two Years: A Study of Twenty-five Babies and Locomotor Development," *Institute of Child Welfare Monographs,* Vol. I, Serial No. 6. Minneapolis: University of Minnesota Press, 1933.

Skeels, Harold. "Adult Status of Children with Contrasting Early Life Experience," *Monographs of the Society for Research in Child Development,* Vol. 31, No. 3 (1966).

Skeels, Harold, and H. B. Dye. "A Study of the Effects of Differential Stimulation on Mentally Retarded Children," *Proceedings of the American Association of Mental Defectives,* Vol. 44 (1939), 114–136.

Skinner, B. F. *The Behavior of Organisms.* New York: Macmillan, 1938.

———. *Science and Human Behavior.* New York: Macmillan, 1953.

———. *Verbal Behavior.* New York: Appleton-Century-Crofts, 1957.

Smart, Mollie S., and Russell C. Smart. *Infants: Development and Relationships.* New York: Macmillan, 1978.

———. *Preschool Children: Development and Relationships.* New York: Macmillan, 1978.

———. *School-Age Children: Development and Relationships.* New York: Macmillan, 1978.

Smith, David. *Introduction to Clinical Pediatrics.* Philadelphia: W. B. Saunders, 1977.

Sorosky, A. D., A. Baran, and R. Pannor. "Identity Conflicts in Adoptees," *American Journal of Ortho Psychiatry,* Vol. 45 (1975), 18–27.

Southgate, D. A. T., and E. Hey. "Chemical and Biochemical Development of the Human Fetus," *The Biology of Human Fetal Growth.* Edited by D. F. Roberts and A. M. Thomson. New York: John Wiley & Sons, 1976.

Spearman, Charles. *The Abilities of Man.* New York: Macmillan, 1927.

Spelt, David. "The Conditioning of the Human Fetus in Utero," *Journal of Experimental Psychology,* Vol. 38 (1948), 338–346.

Spitz, Rene. "Hospitalism," in *The Psychoanalytic Study of the Child.* Edited by O. Fenichel. New York: International Universities Press, 1945.

Sroufe, L. Alan. "The Coherence of Individual Development," *American Psychologist,* Vol. 34, No. 10 (October, 1979), 845–851.

"Statistics Needed for Determining the Effects of the Environment on Health," *National Center for Health Statistics,* D.H.E.W. Publication No. (HRA) 77-1457. Hyattsville, Maryland: U.S. Department of Health, Education, and Welfare, 1977.

Starr, Raymond H. "Child Abuse," *American Psychologist,* Vol. 34 (October, 1979), 872–878.

St. Clair, Karen. "Neonatal Assessment Procedures," *Child Development,* Vol. 49, No. 2 (June, 1978), 280–292.

Stent, Gunther. "Cellular Communication," *Scientific American* (September, 1972), 52–79.

Stevenson, H., and D. Wagner. *Cultural Perspectives on Child Development.* San Francisco: W. H. Freeman and Co., 1980.

Stevenson, Harold, Timothy Parker, Alex Wilkinson, Beatrice Bonneavauz, and Max Gonzalez. "School, Environment, and Cognitive Development: A Cross-Cultural Study," *Monographs of the Society for Research in Child Development,* Vol. 43, No. 3 (1976).

Stone, L. Joseph, and Joseph Church. *Childhood and Adolescence.* 4th edition. New York: Random House, 1979.

Sullivan, Harry Stack. *The Interpersonal Theory of Personality.* New York: W. W. Norton, 1953.

Suran, Bernard, and Joseph Rizzo. *Special Children: An Integrative Approval.* Illinois: Scott, Foresman, 1979.

Sussman, Marvin. "What Every School Principal Should Know About Families," *The National Elementary Principal,* Vol. 55 (July–August, 1976), 32–44.

Talbot, Nathan. *Raising Children in Modern America.* Boston: Little, Brown, 1976.

Tanner, J. M. "Growing Up," *Scientific American,* Vol. 229 (September, 1973), 34–43.

———. *Growth at Adolescence.* 2nd edition. Oxford: Blackwell Scientific Publications, 1962.

———. "Physical Growth," in *Carmichael's Manual of Child Psychology* (3rd ed.). Edited by Paul Mussen. New York: John Wiley & Sons, 1970.

———. *Fetus into Man.* Cambridge: Harvard University Press, 1978.

Taylor, S. P., and S. Epstein. "Aggression as a Function of the Interaction of the Sex of the Aggressor and the Sex of the Victim," *Journal of Personality*, Vol. 35 (1967), 474–480.

Terman, L. M., "In Symposium: Intelligence and Its Measurement," *Journal of Educational Psychology*, Vol. 12 (1921), 127–133.

Terman, L. M., and M. Ogden. *The Gifted Child Grows Up*. Stanford: Stanford University Press, 1947.

———. *The Gifted Group at Mid-Life*. Stanford: Stanford University Press, 1959.

Terman, L. M. et al. *Genetic Studies of Genius: Vol. I. Mental and Physical Traits of a Thousand Gifted Children*. Stanford: Stanford University Press, 1925.

Terman, Lewis, and Maude Merrill. *Stanford-Binet Intelligence Scale: Manual for the Third Revision, Form L-M*. Boston: Houghton-Mifflin, 1960.

Terrace, H. S. "How Nim Chimpsky Changed My Mind," *Psychology Today*, Vol. 13 (1979), 65–76.

Teyler, Timothy. "The Brain Sciences: An Introduction," *Seventy-seventh Yearbook of the National Society for the Study of Education*. Edited by Jeanne Chall and Allan Mirsky. Chicago: University of Chicago Press, 1978.

Thomas, Alexander, and Stella Chess. *Temperament and Development*. New York: Brunner/Mazel, 1977.

Thomas, Alexander, Stella Chess, and Herbert Birch. "The Origin of Personality," *Scientific American*, Vol. 223 (August, 1970), 102–109.

Thomas, R. Murray. *Comparing Theories of Child Development*. Belmont, California: Wadsworth, 1979.

Thompson, William, and Joan Grusec. "Studies of Early Experience," in *Manual of Child Psychology*. Edited by Paul Mussen. New York: John Wiley & Sons, 1970.

Thomson, A. M., and W. Z. Billewicz. "The Concept of the 'Light for Dates' Infant," in *The Biology of Human Fetal Growth*. Edited by D. F. Roberts and A. M. Thomson. New York: John Wiley & Sons, 1976.

Thurstone, L. L. *Multiple-Factor Analysis: A Development and Expansion of the Vectors of the Mind*. Chicago: University of Chicago Press, 1947.

———. *The Differential Growth of Mental Abilities*. Chapel Hill, North Carolina: University of North Carolina, 1955.

Tizard, Barbara, and Judith Rees. "The Effect of Early Institutional Rearing on the Behavior Problems and Affectional Relations of Four-Year-Old Children," *Journal of Child Psychology and Psychiatry*, Vol. 16 (1975), 61–73.

Travers, John F. *Educational Psychology*. New York: Harper & Row, 1979.

Triseliotis, John. *In Search of Origins*. Boston: Beacon Press, 1973.

Tronick, Edward, Susan Wise, Heidelise Als, Lauren Adamson, John Scanlon, and T. Berry Brazelton. "Regional Obstetric Anesthesia and Newborn Behavior: Effects over the First Ten Days of Life," *Pediatrics*, Vol. 58 (1977), 94–100.

Tulkin, Steven. "Dimensions of Multicultural Research in Infancy and Early Childhood," in *Culture and Infancy*. Edited by P. Herbert Leiderman, Steven Tulkin, and Anne Rosenfeld. New York: Academic Press, 1977.

Turner, Merle, *Philosophy and the Science of Behavior*. New York: Appleton-Century-Crofts, 1967.

Tyler, Leona. *Individuality*. San Francisco: Jossey-Bass, 1978.

Underwood, Benton. "Forgetting," *Scientific American* (March, 1964), 91–99.

Uzgiris, Ina, and J. M. Hunt. *Ordinal Scales of Psychological Development*. Urbana, Illinois: University of Illinois Press, 1975.

Uzoka, Azubike. "The Myth of the Nuclear Family: Historical Background and Clinical Implications," *American Psychologist*, Vol. 34 (November, 1979), 1095–1106.

Wadsworth, Barry. *Piaget's Theory of Cognitive Development*. New York: David McKay, 1979.

Wallen, Norman, and Robert Travers. "Analysis and Investigation of Teaching Methods," in *Handbook of Research on Teaching*. Edited by N. L. Gage. Chicago, Illinois: Rand McNally, 1963.

Wallerstein, J. S., and J. B. Kelly. "The Effects of Parental Divorce: Experiences of the Preschool Child," *Journal of Child Psychiatry*, Vol. 14 (1975), 600–616.

Warner, A. Lloyd, and P. S. Lunt. *The Social Life of the Modern Community*. New Haven: Yale University Press, 1941.

Watson, James. *The Double Helix*. Boston: Atheneum Press, 1968.

Watson, John S. "Early Learning and Intelligence," in *Origins of Intelligence*. Edited by Michael Lewis. New York: Plenum Press, 1976.

Wattenberg, William. "Review of Trends," *The Sixty-fifth Yearbook of the National Society for the Study of Education*. Chicago: University of Chicago Press, 1966.

Wechsler, David. *The Measurement of Adult Intelligence*. Baltimore: Williams and Wilkins, 1944.

———. *The Wechsler Adult Intelligence Scale Manual*. New York: Psychological Corporation, 1955.

———. *The Measurement and Appraisal of Adult Intelligence* (4th ed.). Baltimore: Williams and Wilkins, 1958.

Westoff, Charles. "Marriage and Fertility in the Developed Countries," *Scientific American*, Vol. 239 (December, 1978), 51–57.

White, Burton. *The First Three Years of Life*. Englewood Cliffs, New Jersey: Prentice-Hall, 1975.

White, Burton, and Richard Held. "Plasticity of Sensorimotor Development in the Human Infant," in *The Causes of Behavior*. Edited by Judy Rosenblith and Wesley Allensmith. Boston: Allyn & Bacon, 1966.

White, R. K., and R. Lippit. *Autocracy and Democracy: An Experimental Inquiry*. New York: Harper and Row, 1960.

Whitehead, Alfred N. *Adventures of Ideas*. New York: Macmillan, 1933.

Wilkinson, Alex, Timothy Parker, and Harold Stevenson. "Influence of School and Environment on Selected Memory," *Child Development*, Vol. 50, No. 3 (September, 1979), 890–893.

Wilson, Edward. *On Human Nature*. Cambridge: Harvard University Press, 1979.

Winchester, A. M. *Heredity: An Introduction to Genetics*. New York: Barnes and Noble, 1977.

Wing, L. "What Is an Autistic Child?" *Communication*, Vol. 6 (1972), 5–10.

Winn, Marie. *The Plug-In Drug*. New York: Viking Press, 1977.

Wittrock, M. C. "Education and the Cognitive Processes of the Brain," in *Education and the Brain. The Seventy-seventh Yearbook of the National Society for the Study of Education*. Edited by Jeanne Chall and Allan Mirsky. Chicago: University of Chicago Press, 1978.

Yang, D. "Neurologic Status of Newborn Infants on the First and Third Day of Life," *Neurology*, Vol. 12 (1962), 72–77.

Zelazo, Philip. "From Reflexive to Instrumental Behavior," in *Developmental Psychobiology*. Edited by Lewis Lipsitt. New York: Lawrence Erlbaum, 1976.

Zigler, Edward, and Kirby Heller. "On Day Care Standards," *Newsletter, Society for Research in Child Development* (Winter, 1979).

INDEX

HOW TO PLAN YOUR *Successful* RETIREMENT

LOOKING AHEAD ■ Expanded and Updated

An AARP Book
published by
American Association of Retired Persons, Washington, D.C.
Scott, Foresman and Company, Lifelong Learning Division,
Glenview, Illinois

AARP Books is an educational and public service project of the American Association of Retired Persons, which, with a membership of more than 26 million, is the largest association of persons fifty and over in the world today. Founded in 1958, AARP provides older Americans with a wide range of membership programs and services, including legislative representation at both federal and state levels. For further information about additional association activities, write to AARP, 1909 K Street, N.W., Washington, DC 20049.

Credits

Page 12: Theodore Berland, *Fitness for Life: Exercises for People Over 50.* Washington, D.C.: AARP; Glenview, Ill.: Scott, Foresman & Co., 1986 (An AARP Book), pp.80, 88.

Page 26: Daniel Goleman, "Meaningful Activities and Temperament Key in Satisfaction with Life." *New York Times*, December 23, 1986.

Page 29: *Older Americans and the Peace Corps.* Washington, D.C.: U.S. Peace Corps, p.10.

Page 37: Rosalind Massow, *Travel Easy: The Practical Guide for People Over 50.* Washington, D.C.: AARP; Glenview, Ill.: Scott, Foresman & Co., 1985 (An AARP Book), p.11.

Page 50: "Are You Ready to Remarry?" from "A solo needs rehearsing" by Jean L. McCoy from *Dynamic Years*, January-February 1985. Reprinted by permission of the author.

Page 51: Quotation by Dr. Michael Metz from "To rekindle the marital fire" by Nancy Badgwell from *Dynamic Years*, September-October 1985. Michael E. Metz, Program in Human Sexuality, University of Minnesota, reprinted by permission.

Page 54: Eda LeShan, *The Wonderful Crisis of Middle Age.* New York: David McKay Co., Inc., 1974.

Page 57–58: *Think of Your Future: Preretirement Planning Workbook.* Washington, D.C.: AARP; Glenview, Ill.: Scott, Foresman & Co., 1986 (An AARP Book), p.15.

Page 71: "A little store with 100,000 workers" by Joseph Fenwick from *Dynamic Years*, November-December 1984. Reprinted by permission of the author.

Page 72: Excerpt from "From empty nest to cast of thousands" by Sylvia Jeter Cooke, from *Dynamic Years*, July-August 1984. Reprinted by permission of the author.

Page 87: *Making Wise Decisions for Long Term Care.* Washington, D.C.: American Association of Retired Persons, 1986, pp. 3, 6–7.

Illustrations: Hal Grossman

Library of Congress Cataloging-in-Publication Data

How to plan your successful retirement.

Rev. ed. of: Looking ahead. c1985.
Includes index.
1. Retirement—United States. I. American Association of Retired Persons. II. Title: Looking ahead.
HQ1064.U5L65 1988 646.7'9 87-19465
ISBN 0-673-24889-5

5678910-WEB-95949392919089

Contents

Chapter 1

Why Plan for Retirement?

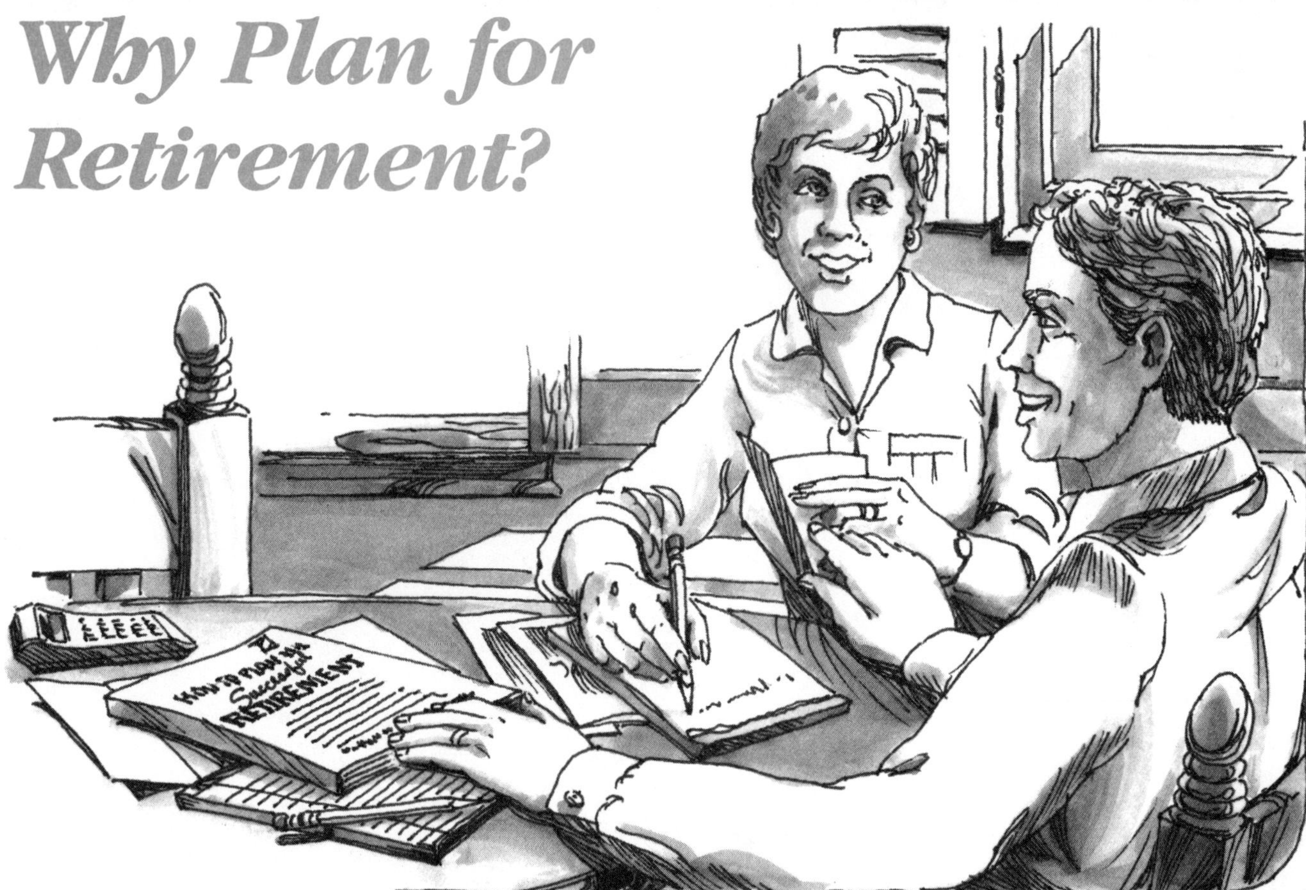

Retirement today can be the most enjoyable and productive time of your life—a time of fresh opportunities, expanded interests, new friendships, and deeper understanding of yourself—if you plan for it. You have more options than ever before for designing and achieving a retirement lifestyle that's right for you.

Today the word *retirement* has many definitions. It can mean a traditional, full retirement. It can mean a phased retirement—a gradual withdrawal from the work force. Or it can mean cyclical retirement—retirement from one job to another full- or part-time job, even a completely new career, several times during a person's work life. Some people have one retirement, others have many, and still others have none.

What picture does the word *retirement* conjure up in your mind? Being absorbed in volunteer work? Having more time for family, friends, or an interesting hobby? Working part-time? Starting your own business? Most likely, your retirement will consist of a mix of these and other pursuits that have personal meaning to you.

Retirement is a unique experience for each person—an experience that must be fashioned by you, for you. Only you have your unique combination of life experiences, personality, hopes, and expectations. Only you can determine, according to your circumstances and preferences, what your retirement goals are and how best to achieve them.

Planning: The Key to Success

The key to creating and experiencing a satisfying retirement is planning—preparing yourself psychologically, physically, and financially. Such planning will give you a sense of control, raise your expectations, and turn you toward the future with enthusiasm.

Retirees today are generally better educated, healthier, and more politically astute than their predecessors. But they also face a greater task than those who preceded them. Retirement planning is becoming increasingly complex, reflecting the growing complexity of the world we live in. The combination of early retirement, longer life expectancy, and rapidly changing economic conditions requires you to plan, both psychologically and financially, for a retirement that could span twenty, thirty, or more years of your life. Over the course of those many years, your personal definition of retirement is likely to change one or more times. How will you know what kind of world it will be in even ten years, much less thirty?

Let's look at one important area, financial planning. Among other things, astute financial planning requires careful management of all your resources; the development of investment strategies to meet different goals before and after retirement; management of health, life, and other insurance; knowledge of Social Security and pension laws and benefits and how they interact; and an understanding of the financial ramifications now and later of taking early, normal (age sixty-five), or late retirement.

Financial security means accumulating the financial resources to support yourself for two, perhaps three, decades. It means having ways to counteract fluctuating inflation and changing tax laws. It means having a strategy for dealing with the possibility of serious chronic health problems in later life. It means, for many, having a strategy for dealing with emergencies such as the need to provide financial support to an elderly parent. And it means realizing the growing importance of work as one strategy for achieving a financially secure retirement.

Studies show that those who enjoy their retirement most fully have laid careful plans, well in advance, regarding not only finances but also how they will maintain their health in retirement, how they will use their time, and where they will live.

This last point is of particular concern today with the current rush of early retirement incentive packages that often seem too financially beneficial to refuse. These packages threaten to leave many persons prematurely cut off from work, frequently with no real preparation or understanding of the trade-offs involved now and several years down the line. For a variety of reasons (discussed in chapter 5), many may find that the decision to retire is not easily reversible. People need time to explore the many options available to them rather than rush into early retirement. Only with such planning can a person make genuine choices based on well thought out short- and long-term goals.

A Period of Adjustment

Your attitude toward work has a significant bearing on how well you will adjust to retirement. If work has always seemed humdrum and unexciting, you may welcome retirement as a refreshing change of direction. On the other hand, if work has given you satisfaction, recognition, companionship, and other rewards, you may miss these benefits.

Before you retire, begin to seek new activities—perhaps a part-time job or volunteer work—that will replace the benefits currently provided by work. Doing so will help you make a smooth transition into retirement.

Before you start to make any decisions about your retirement lifestyle, ask yourself some questions: Who am I? What activities do I enjoy most? What talents do I want to develop further? After you outline your needs, likes, and dislikes, discuss your future with others—your spouse, if married; other relatives; close friends; retirees you know; and any technical experts whose advice you need, for example, a lawyer or financial planner. Then investigate all the options open to you.

As you begin to make decisions about investments, housing, interests, and the like, remember that you are free to change your mind. Be flexible, and don't make the mistake of feeling locked into a decision you made some time earlier.

No matter what choices you make, think of the early stages of retirement as a period of adjustment. Adjustments aren't something new to you. You've been making them all your life—as you went through school, raised your children, switched jobs, moved from one place to another, or lost loved ones. Change is simply a natural part of living. The key is not to resist change but to accept it and actively participate in it.

Retirement provides you with the opportunity and the time to grow in new and exciting directions. In fact, free time is one of retirement's greatest gifts. Yet many retirees feel guilty because they no longer are required to "do something useful." When you become responsible for structuring your own time, it is up to you to discover uses for that time that are varied, meaningful, and enjoyable.

Another great delight of a successful retirement is friendship. It is likely that your circle of friends will change considerably when you leave your job. But, at the same time, retirement provides the opportunity to rekindle old friendships and develop new ones. As with discovering new free-time pursuits, it's best to begin discovering new friends outside of work before you retire.

Along with pursuing personal interests and other plans for retirement, there are three indispensable qualities you should bring to your retirement years: your *curiosity*, your *interest in others*, and your *joy in living*. With these valuable qualities, you'll find yourself open to an array of new experiences, satisfactions, and adventures. As a physician said of her retirement, "In some ways it feels like being young again, but without the uncertainties and stresses."

Start Planning Now

Ideally, retirement planning is a continuation of your lifelong planning that focuses on a particular, and important, phase of life. But whether you're thirty years, five years, or only one year away from your expected retirement date, *now* is the time to take charge of planning for that retirement.

You can do a great deal to ensure that you live your retirement—however you define it—with comfort, security, purpose, and joy. Planning for your retirement can be an exhilarating experience as you start shaping the future to your liking.

This book will help you on your way by providing basic information and by raising important issues for you to think about in areas such as health and fitness, changing roles and relationships, meaningful use of time, working in retirement, housing and lifestyle, and legal readiness.

Once you define your lifestyle goals and set priorities among them, you will need to analyze your current and future financial situation and your estate planning goals to

determine whether or not you can afford the retirement lifestyle you want. This book will help you analyze retirement income and expenses and explore ways to enhance your income now so that you can enjoy a secure and rewarding retirement later.

Finally, this book lists resources (people, organizations, and publications) that can provide more in-depth assistance as you develop and test your retirement plans.

Start your retirement planning by doing Positive Action 1 on page 8. It will help you identify where you are now in the

Life Expectancy

If your age today is—	You can expect, on average, to live—	
	Men	**Women**
40	34.3 more years	40.1 more years
45	29.9	35.5
50	25.6	30.9
55	21.5	26.6
60	17.9	22.5
65	14.6	18.6

Source: U.S. Bureau of the Census, 1987.

planning process and point out some key actions you may need to take as part of your retirement planning.

Planning: A Step-by-Step Process

Retirement planning is not a one-time event. It's an ongoing process of identifying wants and needs, developing plans to fulfill those wants and needs, acting on your plans, and continually reviewing and revising those plans as necessary. Retirement planning professionals recommend the following major steps:

1. Start assembling needed background information regarding the important aspects of retirement: health, use of free time, personal adjustments, housing, finances, and legal matters.
2. Talk things over with the people close to you, those who will be affected by your decisions. Invite them to participate in your plans and explorations. Let them support and encourage your efforts.
3. Obtain trusted advice. Retired friends can contribute excellent first-hand knowledge. Seek professional guidance on complex matters such as housing, legal issues, pension benefits, and financial and estate planning.
4. Set definite but realistic goals for retirement income, activities, health, and housing. They will keep you focused and provide powerful incentives for action.
5. Put your retirement plans in writing, including your list of needed actions. Specify deadlines. You will find that your planning must proceed in stages, each stage providing the foundation for others. For example, a savings program can give you the means for later investments; educational courses may lead to a part-time job or a new hobby; and vacation travel may be used to inspect possible retirement locations.
6. Retire before you retire. Test out some of your plans. Try out a new hobby; see if you like it and if you can afford it in retirement. Meet new people not associated with your work. Volunteer one or two hours a week. Identify and start using community resources now.
7. Review and update your plans at least once a year or when a change in your work or family situation makes adjustment desirable.

Positive Action 1

Twenty Questions: Are You Ready to Retire?

Retirement has many facets. Think about each of the questions listed below and circle the answer that seems appropriate for you. The more answers you have in the Yes column, the more ready you are for retirement.

1. Do you discuss retirement freely with your spouse or companion, family, and friends?	Yes	No
2. Have you identified your social support system of family, friends, and acquaintances outside of work?	Yes	No
3. Have you considered meaningful retirement roles that will provide the rewards you now receive from your work role?	Yes	No
4. Do you know the community, state, and federal resources available to you in retirement?	Yes	No
5. Do you engage in meaningful civic, educational, and leisure pursuits?	Yes	No
6. If married, have you considered the consequences of losing your spouse?	Yes	No
7. Do you have regular medical checkups and follow your doctor's advice?	Yes	No
8. Do you exercise regularly consistent with your physical condition, age, and gender?	Yes	No
9. Do you have a sensible diet that helps you maintain the proper weight?	Yes	No
10. Have you investigated your options regarding health insurance and health care in retirement?	Yes	No
11. Do you have a psychologist, religious adviser, or other professional to whom you can turn for guidance or counseling, if needed?	Yes	No
12. Have you determined whether your current housing and community will support your chosen retirement lifestyle now and later?	Yes	No
13. Do you have a lawyer you trust?	Yes	No
14. Do you have other professional advisers that you trust—financial planner, insurance agent, real estate broker, banker, etc.?	Yes	No
15. Do you have an up-to-date will, and, if married, does your spouse also have one?	Yes	No
16. Do you know your current net worth?	Yes	No
17. Do you have a current workable budget?	Yes	No
18. Do you have tentative retirement budgets for both early and late retirement?	Yes	No
19. Do you know the amounts of your financial resources—savings, pension, Social Security, etc.?	Yes	No
20. Do you have retirement income-producing possibilities lined up?	Yes	No

Getting in Shape for Your Future

George E. is fifty-nine, but his friends tell him he looks years younger. At his wife's urging, George had a physical examination last year, his first one since he took early retirement four years ago. The exam revealed not only that George was overweight, having gained twenty-five pounds since retiring, but also that he suffered from borderline high blood pressure and had a very high blood cholesterol level. George and his doctor agreed that his sedentary lifestyle in retirement was a major factor contributing to these problems.

With his doctor's guidance and that of other health care professionals she recommended, George began a daily walking program, found ways to make activity part of his daily routine, and started changing his eating habits. Finally, at a stress-management clinic offered by the health maintenance organization (HMO) he and his wife belonged to, George learned how to identify and reduce the tension and stress in his life.

Since George embarked on his program, he has lost weight and has gotten his blood pressure and cholesterol level under control. He looks and feels better, and he says he has a lot more energy and enthusiasm to devote to enjoying his retirement years. George's only regret is that he didn't start getting in shape sooner, before he retired.

As with George, the quality of your retirement years will, to a large degree, depend on your level of health and fitness. Your health could improve in retirement. According to the President's Council on Physical Fitness and Sports, "Much of the physical decline attributed to aging is actually the result of inactivity, poor diet, and boredom. Many of the problems commonly attributed to 'growing old' can be minimized, halted, even reversed, through changes in lifestyle."

No matter how sedentary your life has been, no matter what unhealthful habits you may have developed over the years, you can begin today to improve your health and with it the quality of your life, now and in retirement.

The first step is to accept responsibility for your health and to adopt a wellness approach to dealing with it. Doing so will motivate you to begin finding ways to make health and fitness an integral part of daily life.

In recent years, increased awareness of the importance of actively maintaining good health throughout every stage of life has resulted in a proliferation of health and fitness products and services. Yet, a good health and fitness program needn't be complicated, inconvenient, or expensive. This chapter describes straightforward strategies that you can use to promote and maintain good health. Specifically, it discusses how you can do the following:

- Develop an appropriate exercise program.
- Modify your eating habits.
- Recognize and reduce the stress in your life.
- Recognize normal and abnormal physical changes and determine what to do about them.
- Identify and begin using community health and fitness resources.

Your strategies for good health now and in retirement should also include the wise use of our nation's health care system and services. With the high cost of health care today, it is crucial for people to see themselves not only as patients but also as intelligent consumers of health care services and products. This chapter provides information to help you do the following:

- Evaluate your health insurance options for your retirement years.
- Evaluate both traditional and alternative forms of health care now available.
- Communicate effectively with your health care providers.
- Save money on health care without sacrificing quality.

You are in charge of your health just as you are in charge of your finances. It is important for you to become a well-informed, assertive consumer of health care services and products. The choices you make today will exert a strong influence on the quality of your retirement years. Take the time now to learn about your health care rights and options.

Your Lifestyle and Your Health

With increasing age, certain biological changes appear inevitable. For example, lung capacity becomes lower, blood vessels narrow, and the lens of the eye tends to become opaque. Yet, much of the damage our bodies suffer over time is self-inflicted, the result of certain choices we make about how we want to live. Examples are smoking; lack of exercise; poor nutrition; abuse of alcohol and other drugs, including medications; and too much stress.

Since these situations represent our choices, there is, obviously, much we can do ourselves to improve and maintain our health. Before making major changes such as starting an exercise program or going on a new diet, consult your doctor. With his or her help, you can take that all-important first step. And your doctor can help you overcome any setbacks that may occur on the way to better health. The rewards are well worth the effort.

Some Pointers About Exercise

Why exercise? Regular, vigorous, and appropriate exercise will do these things:

- Increase strength and endurance.
- Improve functioning of lungs, heart, and blood vessels. (Active people, research shows, have fewer heart attacks than sedentary people.)
- Increase flexibility of the joints (which can help retard the development of arthritis).
- Relieve mental fatigue, stress, and boredom. (Exercise can have a calming effect, serving as a natural tranquilizer.)
- Aid weight loss and control. (Exercise does not increase your appetite; it can actually help control it and your weight. If you consumed an excess 100 calories a day, you could burn that amount by taking a brisk mile-and-a-half walk. If you don't exercise, that same 100 extra calories a day could add up to ten pounds a year. Studies indicate that the majority of overweight people not only eat too much but also are inactive.)

Proper exercise can also provide more energy for daily activities; improve posture, balance, and coordination; help us sleep, look, and feel better; and further a versatile, independent lifestyle now and in later years.

In spite of this impressive list of benefits, a survey of Americans age fifty and older by the President's Council on Physical Fitness and Sports found that "a majority of men and women past fifty don't exercise at all [though] nearly three-fourths of them say they are getting all the exercise they need."

How to Get Started

Your first step *must* be a visit to your doctor. He or she can help you assess your current fitness level, establish short- and long-term fitness goals, and develop a program for achieving those goals. Your doctor may also refer you to a fitness expert or program in your community.

The *American Journal of Cardiology* recommends that all adults over forty have a complete physical examination before starting an exercise program. This also holds true for an adult of any age who has been inactive; is overweight; has hypertension, back, or joint problems; or has a family history of heart disease.

What Kind of Exercise Is Best?

Not all exercise programs condition you in the same way. Specific body changes occur only with certain kinds of exercise and under certain conditions. For example, isometrics and calisthenics can improve strength, flexibility, and muscle tone, but they won't increase heart and lung capacity.

Aerobic exercises are rhythmic, continuous, and vigorous. They stimulate the heart, blood vessels, and lungs. Particularly recommended are brisk walking, swimming, cycling, rope skipping, aerobic dancing, light jogging, and cross-country skiing. Many popular sports such as tennis, golf, and bowling don't meet aerobic criteria because they involve long pauses or start-and-stop actions.

If exercise is to be truly beneficial to your circulatory system, it must meet certain standards. If all of the following descriptions do not apply to a particular exercise, little conditioning will occur.

- *Gradual and progressive.* Begin slowly and build up gradually, perhaps over several months. For the novice, experts recommend periods of exertion followed by periods of rest. Don't strain your body too suddenly. By building up gradually, you challenge your cardiovascular system to handle increased physical demands more efficiently.
- *Of some duration.* Gradually build up to exercising at least twenty to thirty minutes exclusive of warm-up and cool-down periods.
- *Frequent.* Three times weekly, preferably on alternate days, is recommended. Exercising only on weekends isn't enough and could be dangerous. Supplement your aerobic exercise with other physical activities on alternate days, for example, walking, dancing, yoga, or gardening. Keep moving.
- *Intense.* The best exercise elevates the pulse rate, makes you breathe deeply, and causes you to perspire. The "overload" principle states that exercise must be strenuous enough to use 60 to 75 percent of your maximum heart rate.

Danger signs that tell you to stop immediately include tightness or pain in the chest, lightheadedness, trembling, pounding in the head, severe breathlessness, loss of muscle control, or nausea. If symptoms persist, see your doctor.

- *Ongoing.* Gains from exercise are lost quickly. If you become bored, switch to a new exercise program. Try exercising to music or with friends to increase your motivation and enjoyment.
- *Appropriate.* Choose a program tailored to you. Don't force yourself into the water if you hate to swim. In choosing an exercise program, ask yourself, Is it appropriate given my age, gender, condition, and fitness goals? Is it fun? convenient? Can it become part of my routine?
- *Includes a warm-up and a cool-down period.* Five- to ten-minute periods before and after strenuous exercise are essential to allow the body to prepare for and then recover from exercise. Mild stretching exercises may be used, as may an Exercycle® or a slow version of the main exercise such as walking, jogging, or swimming.

How to Find a Program

If you're not a self-starter, look into fitness programs in your community. Hospitals, clinics, community centers, or the YMCA or YWCA may offer low-cost or free exercise programs staffed by specialists who can tailor a program to your needs. Check with local high schools and colleges to see if they have facilities (pools, gyms, weight rooms) that the public can use during certain hours. They may also offer fitness programs geared toward specific goals or conditions, such as aquatic exercise classes for people with arthritis. (See For Further Reading, page 126, for more information on assessing your fitness level and developing an appropriate exercise program.)

A Few Words of Encouragement

A common mistake people make in the early weeks of a new exercise program is to expect startling results right away. Experts stress that at least six weeks are needed for you to notice a real difference. So stick with it and you will eventually reap the rewards you seek.

Positive Action 2

Beginning Exercises

Rear Leg Raise. Feet together, stand behind your chair, facing it. Grasp the back. Lift your left leg back, and raise it as high as you can. Try to keep your knee straight. Slowly lower your leg back down to the floor. Do the same with your right leg. Repeat five times to help firm your buttocks, strengthen the lower back, and limber your hips and legs.

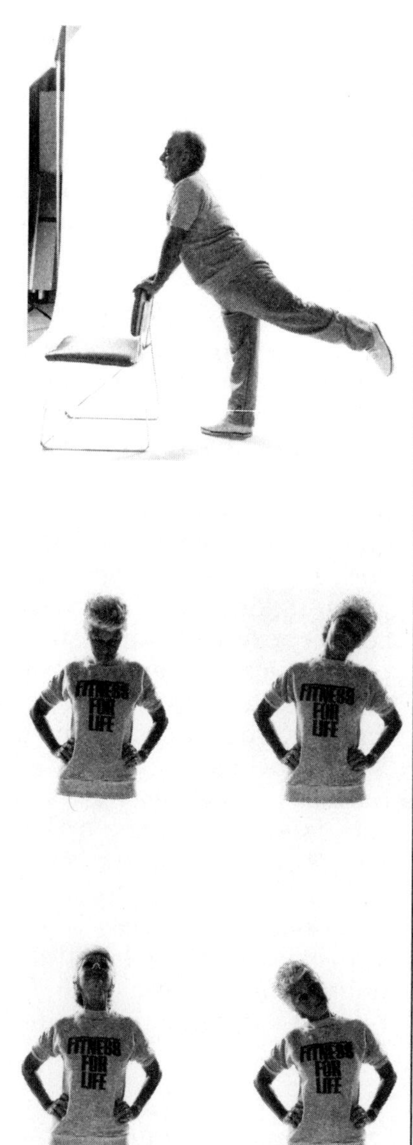

Head Roll. Standing, with legs spread and hands on hips, slowly roll your head around in a circle through its entire range of motion. Begin by gently dropping your head forward, to your chest; then rotate it to the left shoulder, then to your back, then to the right shoulder, then forward. Close your eyes, and try to relax your shoulders as you revolve your head five times clockwise and five times counter-clockwise to limber those tight neck muscles and joints. After doing this daily for a week, increase to ten revolutions in each direction.

Don't Just Sit There

If the very word *exercise* makes you feel like taking a nap, think, instead, in terms of *activity*. Our bodies are designed for lifelong physical activity. So don't just sit there—keep moving. Find ways to combine physical activity with socializing (for example, join a folk dancing group) or with a favorite hobby or interest (for example, gardening). And don't pass up any opportunity to bend, move, or stretch. Take the stairs instead of the elevator or escalator, get off the bus or subway one or two stops early and walk, walk to the store with a backpack or cart for carrying groceries, and so on.

Some Pointers on Nutrition

News about food seems to bombard us on all sides: claims extolling a new "miracle" diet, headlines about the cancer-causing agents in some foods, tidings about the benefits of fiber. Which claims are true, and which are false? Probably no other health topic is so full of fallacies or so subject to fads.

Just what foods are needed for fitness? The U.S. Department of Agriculture recommends that we include in our daily diet foods from the following four groups:

- *Milk*—milk, cheese, yogurt, and other dairy products (two or more servings daily).
- *Meat*—poultry, fish, seafood, eggs, meat, and protein alternatives such as dried beans, peas, nuts, peanut butter, and tofu (two or more servings daily).

- *Grain*—whole-grain breads and cereals, pasta, and rice (four or more servings daily).
- *Fruit and Vegetable*—fruits, green and yellow vegetables (four or more servings daily).

Experts also recommend that we drink six to ten glasses of water each day to aid digestion and elimination.

Many Americans don't eat well-balanced diets. Why? Perhaps they live alone and dislike cooking for themselves, perhaps they're too busy, or perhaps they snack on the "empty" calories of sugar products or consume too much alcohol. Foods eaten between meals are usually equated with poor nutrition practices, but snacking can be good for us, as long as the snacks we choose are nutritious.

Food and nutrition labels, found on most food containers, can help you get the best food value for your money and plan nutritionally balanced meals. Included on most labels are listings of ingredients in descending order of amount; percentages of the U.S. Recommended Daily Allowance (RDA) for seven major vitamins and minerals per serving; the number of calories per serving; and the number of grams of protein, fat, carbohydrate, and salt per serving.

Food additives, of which there are nearly 3,000, range from such staples as salt and sugar to other substances that keep food from spoiling, enhance flavor, or add color. Some are potentially hazardous. For example, nitrites add color and flavor to many cured meats (hot dogs, bacon, and so on) and prevent the formation of deadly botulism toxins, but under laboratory conditions, they have been shown to cause cancer in rats. The government has reduced the amount of nitrites that can be added to meats and continues to monitor use of the substance.

Let's take a look at some other nutritional matters currently before the public eye:

- ***Fast foods and convenience foods.*** Neither group is necessarily lacking in essential nutrients if chosen and used sensibly. Frozen foods can be equal in nutritional value to fresh foods, which will rapidly lose nutrients if they are overcooked, stored at the wrong temperature, or kept too long. Be sure to supplement convenience foods with fresh fruits and vegetables.

- ***Health foods.*** The U.S. Agricultural Research Service reports, "There is no scientific evidence that plants grown with only organic fertilizers, or meat from animals raised on only organically fertilized feed, have greater nutritive value than our regular food produced by the usual agricultural methods."

- ***Vegetarian diets.*** Many vegetarian diets can supply the nutrients of more conventional diets that include meat, fish, and poultry as long as the vegetarian's protein intake is sufficient and he or she eats a variety of foods. Nutrition experts recommend that Vitamin B_{12} be added to a purely vegetarian diet.

- ***Fiber.*** It's generally agreed that fiber, or "roughage," in the diet can help regularize bowel function, prevent hemorrhoids, and lower cholesterol levels. Recent evidence also indicates that fiber reduces the risk of heart disease and certain forms of cancer. To ensure enough fiber in the diet, eat whole-grain breads and cereals and fresh fruits and vegetables daily.

- ***Vitamin and mineral supplements.*** Most vitamins that occur naturally in foods are abundant

Desirable Weights

Weight in pounds according to frame, ages 25–59

Women*

Height Feet	Height Inches	Small frame	Medium frame	Large frame
4	10	102–111	109–121	118–131
4	11	103–113	111–123	120–134
5	0	104–115	113–126	122–137
5	1	106–118	115–129	125–140
5	2	108–121	118–132	128–143
5	3	111–124	121–135	131–147
5	4	114–127	124–138	134–151
5	5	117–130	127–141	137–155
5	6	120–133	130–144	140–159
5	7	123–136	133–147	143–163
5	8	126–139	136–150	146–167
5	9	129–142	139–153	149–170
5	10	132–145	142–156	152–173
5	11	135–148	145–159	155–176
6	0	138–151	148–162	158–179

MEN**

Height Feet	Height Inches	Small frame	Medium frame	Large frame
5	2	128–134	131–141	138–150
5	3	130–136	133–143	140–153
5	4	132–138	135–145	142–156
5	5	134–140	137–148	144–160
5	6	136–142	139–151	146–164
5	7	138–145	142–154	149–168
5	8	140–148	145–157	152–172
5	9	142–151	148–160	155–176
5	10	144–154	151–163	158–180
5	11	146–157	154–166	161–184
6	0	149–160	157–170	164–188
6	1	152–164	160–174	168–192
6	2	155–168	164–178	172–197
6	3	158–172	167–182	176–202
6	4	162–176	171–187	181–207

*In 1-inch-heel shoes and 3 pounds of indoor clothing.

**In 1-inch-heel shoes and 5 pounds of indoor clothing.

Prepared by the Metropolitan Life Insurance Co. from 1979 Build Study, Society of Actuaries and Association of Life Insurance Medical Directors of America, 1980.

Released by the Metropolitan Life Insurance Co., 1983.

in a well-balanced diet, so there's usually no reason to take vitamin supplements, unless they are prescribed by your doctor. Some vitamins (A and D) are stored in the body, and excessive doses may have toxic effects.

■ *Calcium deficiency.* Osteoporosis is a reduction in bone mass caused by calcium deficiency. It most often afflicts postmenopausal women, though the condition starts years earlier. The condition is exacerbated by smoking, alcohol, poor diet, and inactivity. Osteoporosis typically has no symptoms. It cannot be cured, but it can be treated and the rate of bone loss slowed, usually through diet, vitamin supplements, and exercise to build bone mass and strengthen the muscles supporting the bones. The recommended amount of calcium for older adults is 1,500 milligrams a day, the equivalent of six glasses of milk. Calcium can also be obtained by eating low-fat yogurt, cheese, sardines, salmon canned with bones, and dark green, leafy vegetables.

■ *Salt, sugar, and caffeine.* Intake of these substances should be decreased by people of all ages. Salt is a factor in hypertension and cardiovascular disorders. Sugar promotes tooth decay, precipitates diabetes, and contributes to weight problems. Caffeine can induce an irregular heartbeat and a jittery feeling. Check nutrition labels for amounts of salt and sugar.

The National Research Council has indicated that 1,100–3,300 milligrams of sodium a day is a "safe and adequate" amount for an adult. (One teaspoon of salt contains about 2,000 milligrams of sodium.)

Sugar may be listed on food labels as sucrose, dextrose, glucose, fructose, corn syrup, or corn sweetener.

Besides tea and coffee, caffeine can be found in cocoa, chocolate products, colas, and some other soft drinks.

■ *Cholesterol.* Concern about high cholesterol and its link to heart disease has led many people to reduce the proportion of saturated fat (found in butter, eggs, and red meat) in their diets. In fact, cholesterol levels have declined in recent years for some segments of the population.

There are actually two kinds of cholesterol: high-density lipoproteins (HDLs) and low-density lipoproteins (LDLs). A relatively high ratio of HDLs is believed to be a protective factor against coronary heart disease, while high levels of LDLs can increase the risk. Heredity, exercise, and other factors influence the way each person's body uses and stores these two kinds of cholesterol. Middle-aged people should have their cholesterol levels tested regularly.

Dieting—Separating Fact from Fiction

Our calorie needs usually decrease with age. Between ages twenty-three and fifty, the average man requires 2,700 calories per day; between ages fifty-one and seventy, this decreases to 2,400. For the average woman aged twenty-three to fifty, the caloric requirement is 2,000; it drops to 1,800 for women between ages fifty-one and seventy.

As we grow older, a slower metabolism rate coupled with less exercise and activity will typically result in weight gain unless eating and exercise habits are changed. Thus, the ultimate goal of your diet may be to change permanently what and how much you eat. Begin by examining your current eating habits. Keep a record of what you eat, how much you eat, when you eat, and what you're doing when you decide to eat. This information will help you find out why you eat as you do and then modify your eating patterns.

How can you find a sensible diet? If you are twenty or more pounds overweight, consult your doctor and ask for a diet regimen. Self-help groups such as Weight Watchers can provide strong motivation and have helped many men and women achieve permanent weight loss. Remember that the safest, surest weight loss is slow and steady—one or two pounds a week.

Amid all the fad diets, the most sensible method of dieting is to eat a variety of nutritious foods while cutting down on

Test Your Nutrition IQ

Test your nutrition knowledge by checking the ten statements below. If you score eight correct or better, consider yourself well informed about food and nutrition subjects.

	True	False
1. Fresh foods are almost always more nutritious than frozen ones.	☐	☐
2. As we get older, our calorie needs decrease.	☐	☐
3. Most of us should take vitamins to supplement our diets.	☐	☐
4. Fast foods and convenience foods are, as a rule, nutritionally deficient.	☐	☐
5. Fiber in the diet can help regularize bowel function.	☐	☐
6. The high-protein diet is an excellent method of losing weight.	☐	☐
7. Organically fertilized produce is superior nutritionally to synthetically fertilized produce.	☐	☐
8. Snacks can be nutritionally beneficial.	☐	☐
9. The person intent on permanent weight loss should concentrate on modifying his or her eating patterns.	☐	☐
10. Vegetarian diets can't supply enough of the body's protein needs.	☐	☐

Answers: 1.F; 2.T; 3.F; 4.F; 5.T; 6.F; 7.F; 8.T; 9.T; 10.F.

quantities, reducing intake of sweets and alcohol, and exercising appropriately for your age, gender, and general condition.

Rules for Safe Drug Use

- Buy over-the-counter drugs in tamper-proof containers, and, if possible, buy tablets rather than capsules.
- Keep drugs in the original container and store in a cool, dry place (some drugs require refrigeration).
- Don't take drugs prescribed for someone else.
- Follow the directions on the label.
- If you suffer any adverse side effects or drug reactions, inform your doctor immediately.
- Continue taking a drug as long as it's prescribed, but stop using it when no longer necessary.
- Ask your doctor whether the drug reacts adversely with alcohol or any medication you're taking. Let the doctor know what allergies you have.
- Throw out old medicines. Some medicines lose potency; others can be harmful if kept too long.
- Don't take medicines in the dark; read the label first.
- Don't carry pills in pillboxes for very long; they can lose their effectiveness.
- When traveling, take an ample supply of a medicine in the original container.
- Refer all questions about drugs to your doctor or pharmacist.

Wise Use of Drugs

Appropriate use of alcohol and medication and the elimination of smoking will contribute substantially to your healthful lifestyle.

Alcohol

According to the National Clearinghouse on Alcohol Information, an estimated 10.6 million Americans suffer from alcoholism. Alcohol taken in excess over a period of time can damage the liver, brain, and heart. Malnutrition is often a by-product, since alcohol contains no nutrients and the alcoholic often skimps on food. A recovered alcoholic should steer clear of alcohol for the rest of his or her life.

For nonalcoholics, research indicates that moderate drinking (one or two drinks a day) may aid digestion, relieve stress, and stimulate the coronary arteries. As people grow older, however, their bodies change the way they metabolize alcohol. Thus, the same amount of alcohol that was manageable at a younger age may pose a problem later on.

People who are dieting should know that alcohol contains quite a few "empty" calories. And those taking medications should check with their doctor to see if alcohol may interfere with the therapeutic action of any drugs they are taking.

For free information on all aspects of alcohol use and alcoholism, write to the National Clearinghouse on Alcohol Information, 1776 East Jefferson Street, Rockville, MD 20852.

Smoking

According to the surgeon general of the United States, "cigarette smoking remains the largest cause of premature death" in the nation. Cigarette smoking contributes to deaths from heart disease and lung cancer. It is also linked to increased risk of cancer of the mouth, pharynx, larynx, esophagus, and bladder, as well as with emphysema and chronic bronchitis.

Smoking can be both psychologically and physically addicting. It is often a way to handle stress, anxiety, and boredom. Those who would like to try quitting will find encouragement in the Public Health Service pamphlet *Clearing the Air—A Guide to Quitting Smoking*. It says that your body begins to heal itself twelve hours after your last cigarette. (For a free copy of this pamphlet, see the ordering information on page 126.)

For information on local programs and support groups such as Smokenders, contact a hospital or the local chapter of the American Cancer Society, the American Heart Association, or the American Lung Association. If you belong to an HMO, see if it sponsors clinics on how to stop smoking.

Medications

Prescription and over-the-counter drugs are big business in the United States. Many of us prefer to look for quick, easy remedies for what ails us rather than seek out alternative treatments. And many of us simply take too many drugs. The most frequently misused legal drugs are tranquilizers, sedatives, amphetamines, laxatives, and vitamins.

Prescription (Rx) drugs—drugs obtained from a pharmacist with a doctor's prescription—are usually more expensive, more powerful, and more capable of producing side effects than drugs bought without a prescription.

Over-the-counter (OTC) drugs—drugs bought without prescription—include many kinds of sleeping pills, cough medicines, laxatives, aspirin, and aspirin substitutes. Although usually safe if taken as directed, all OTC drugs have potential risks. For example, aspirin can lead to stomach irritation if too many tablets or capsules are consumed.

In spite of advertising claims, research has shown OTC sleeping pills to be ineffective in combating insomnia. These pills may actually interfere with natural sleep and dream patterns, so a person may wind up feeling more fatigued.

Laxatives are greatly overused. According to the Food and Drug Administration (FDA), laxatives, when used repeatedly, can impair normal bowel function and, ironically, lead to chronic constipation.

As we grow older, our bodies tend to metabolize drugs more slowly, requiring changes in dosages. The National Council on Patient Information and Education suggests that you periodically review your medications with your doctor, including not only your prescription and over-the-counter drugs but also any other drug you may occasionally take. Drugs can work at cross-purposes or duplicate their therapeutic effects. Ask these questions about each medication prescribed:

- What is its generic name?
- What good does it do?
- How should it be taken, and for how long?
- What food, drink, other medication, or activities should be avoided while taking the medication?
- What are the possible side effects?
- What should be done if side effects occur?
- Is there any literature about the medication?
- What alternative treatments are available? Diet? Exercise? Therapy?

Stress and Your Health

Stress is the response to any demand made upon the mind or body. More specifically, stress is the effect of the wear and tear of daily living. It may be constant, as with a job; moderate, as with a mild upset in plans; or severe, as with a major life change such as the death of a loved one, divorce, or loss of a job. Stress can also result from a positive life experience such as writing a bestseller, winning a contest, or going on a vacation.

Acute, short-term stress causes a basic "fight or flight" response in everyone—the pulse rate quickens, blood pressure rises, we perspire, and the hormone adrenaline is released. These reactions are normal. But chronic and unrelieved stress can also produce more insidious body responses: inability to concentrate, irritability, fatigue, loss of appetite, chronic anxiety, or depression.

Stress can interfere with job performance and interpersonal relationships and may lead to a variety of illnesses from headaches to ulcers and hypertension—even cancer, heart attack, and stroke.

Certain people deal with stress better than others; some individuals seem to thrive on it. Every person needs to find his or her most comfortable stress level and learn how to alleviate stress that goes beyond that point.

What's the Best Way to Cope with Stress?

Experts recommend the following:

- *Recognize stress.* It's all right to admit you feel stressed.
- *Identify the cause of the stress.* Withdraw for a while each day to talk to yourself about the day's stress-producing problems. Identify those situations that regularly cause an unacceptable level of stress and take action to change them. Decide what you want out of the situation, set realistic goals, and then act to achieve those goals. Indecision is one of the worst stress producers.
- *Rest and relax.* Mental and physical fatigue make even small problems appear worse than they are. Set aside time each day to genuinely relax. Relaxation is the fine art of becoming sensitive to and re-

sponding to your needs for peace and self-awareness. Many mind-relaxing techniques exist. Find those that work best for you. They include biofeedback, meditation, music, yoga, hypnosis, progressive body relaxation, and T'ai Chi Ch'uan, an ancient Chinese form of gentle body movement.

- *Seek advice.* Sharing problems with others, individually or in a group, can help you find new ways of coping. Seek guidance from a person with whom you can talk honestly: a trusted friend, family member, religious adviser, or lay counselor. If, however, you feel that your stress symptoms warrant medical attention, don't delay in getting professional help.

- *Decide whether what's causing the stress is worth it.* Are you driving yourself to achieve an impossible goal? Stop and examine that goal. Is it really worth all the worry?
- *Avoid self-medication and potentially abusive substances.* Caffeine, nicotine, alcohol, medicines, and excessive food only appear to relieve the symptoms of stress. And they don't deal with the problem.
- *Laugh more.* Find something to laugh about at least once a day. Laughter is a proven stress reducer. It helps put things in perspective.

Health Concerns of the Middle Years

Be on the lookout, during the middle years, for certain health conditions that go hand in hand with getting older. The good news is that many of these conditions aren't serious if they are caught and treated in time.

Sight

After age forty, the eyes don't function as well for near vision because the eye lens becomes less able to focus. This condition, called *presbyopia*, can easily be corrected with reading glasses or bifocals.

Cataracts, a cloudiness in the eye lens that interferes with vision, may develop quickly or over a number of years. Usual signs are hazy vision, double vision, or difficulty seeing at night. Special eyeglasses may help initially, but surgery is needed when the lens becomes opaque. Once cataract surgery involved a lengthy and painful recuperation period, but today, with the advent of new techniques for lens removal, the patient can be fitted with cataract eyeglasses, contact lenses, or lens implants and resume most normal activities soon after surgery.

Glaucoma, loss of vision associated with increased pressure on the eye due to fluid buildup in the eye, can lead to blindness if left untreated. When detected and treated promptly, however, it needn't cause serious vision loss. Because glaucoma is usually painless, tests to detect the condition are essential. Vision that is lost cannot be restored. Glaucoma can be controlled by eye drops, pills, laser treatments, or surgery.

For diagnosis and treatment of these and other eye conditions before they become advanced, visit your ophthalmologist (eye specialist) regularly.

Hearing

An estimated 16 million people in the U.S. are hearing impaired. Of these, approximately 60 percent are fifty-five years of age or older. Poor hearing can lead to isolation and be a safety hazard.

Look for these signs of gradual hearing loss: Do you ask people to repeat what they say? Do you turn up the volume of the radio or TV? Do you withdraw from conversation at social functions? If any or all of these signs are present, visit an otologist (a specialist in the diagnosis and treatment of hearing problems). Even if you aren't experiencing a hearing loss, a hearing checkup once every two years is recommended.

Don't buy a hearing aid until you have consulted with a doctor who specializes in hearing problems. Hearing-aid dealers usually are not qualified to diagnose. If you buy a hearing aid, ask for a thirty-day trial period. Hearing aids take getting used to and often need adjustment.

Dental Care

In the middle years, gums may begin to recede, exposing more tooth surface to possible decay. The following practices help counteract decay: using a fluoride mouthwash if fluoride is not in your drinking water supply; brushing your teeth at least twice a day; using dental floss once a day, preferably before bedtime; and limiting foods with high sugar content.

Periodontal, or gum, disease is easy to control if detected early. *Pyorrhea*, the most common form, starts with inflamed gums and occasional bleeding. Gums then begin to recede, and roots are exposed. Eventually, teeth loosen and are lost. To help prevent pyorrhea, use dental floss daily and have hardened plaque (tartar) removed by your dental hygienist or dentist every four to six months. If periodontal disease becomes advanced, surgery may be needed.

Foot Care

To stay active in the middle years and beyond, your feet must be kept in good condition. Aching feet can bring on fatigue and leg and back pain and generally make us feel miserable. But foot problems are frequently ignored until they become unbearable.

Corns, calluses, plantar warts, excessive sweating, and itching may all be signs of foot problems. Foot problems can also be symptoms of disease. Arthritis, diabetes, kidney disease, and heart trouble are sometimes indicated first through the condition of the feet. Signs to look for include dry skin, brittle nails, numbness, and discoloration.

To keep your feet in good condition, walk as much as possible; bathe and powder them daily; buy shoes that fit properly and provide necessary support; and, if you notice any unusual signs, see a podiatrist (a doctor who specializes in treatment of foot disorders).

The Major Diseases—What You Should Know

The following diseases are not necessarily caused by growing older; however, they do account for most of the deaths and disabilities of the forty-to-sixty-four age group.

Cardiovascular Disease

According to the National Center for Health Statistics, although deaths from coronary artery disease and stroke have declined, cardiovascular disease remains a major health problem.

Coronary artery disease, the most common form of heart disease, results from blockage of arteries supplying blood to the heart muscle. Symptoms, including shortness of breath, pain, weakness, and fatigue, don't usually occur until the disease is advanced. To guard against premature heart disease, control these risk factors:

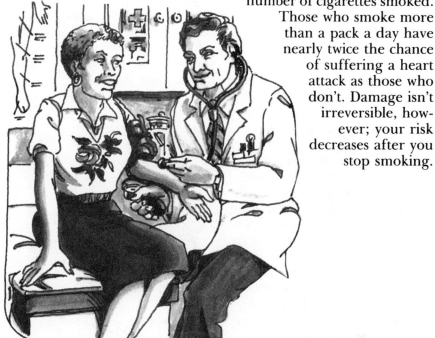

- *High blood pressure (hypertension).* This condition is easy to diagnose but often goes undetected. Check your blood pressure regularly. You can do this yourself, at home.
- *Overweight.* Significantly overweight men of middle age have three times more risk of fatal heart attack than their thinner counterparts.
- *Cigarette smoking.* Heart attack risk relates directly to the number of cigarettes smoked. Those who smoke more than a pack a day have nearly twice the chance of suffering a heart attack as those who don't. Damage isn't irreversible, however; your risk decreases after you stop smoking.

- *Lack of exercise.* Inactive people have been shown to have a higher risk of fatal heart attack than those who exercise. Research shows that exercise lowers low-density lipoprotein cholesterol, the substance in blood that clogs arteries.
- *High blood cholesterol level.* If your cholesterol level is not within normal range, your doctor will likely prescribe a diet lower in calories, saturated fat, and cholesterol.

Stroke, or cardiovascular accident, results from lack of oxygen to or hemorrhage of the brain, which can result in paralysis, and, in some cases, death. Stroke is associated with many of the same risk factors as coronary artery disease.

Cancer

An abnormal growth of cells that invades and destroys normal body cells, cancer can spread quickly and be fatal if not detected early. The hopeful side of cancer is that, because of early detection methods, many forms of the disease can be arrested before they spread.

Pain is not usually present when cancer starts, so regular physical checkups are a must. The American Cancer Society lists these danger signals: change in bowel or bladder habits, a sore that does not heal, unusual bleeding or discharge, a thickening or lump in the breast or elsewhere, indigestion or difficulty in swallowing, obvious change in a wart or mole, and nagging cough or hoarseness. If any of these danger signs persists for two weeks, see your doctor immediately.

No cure for cancer has yet been found, but surgery, radiotherapy, chemotherapy, and other methods of treatment may arrest the disease or slow its advance.

Diabetes

At least 90 percent of those people with the disease have Type II, non-insulin-dependent, diabetes. Type II diabetes occurs when the body's insulin is not used effectively to change glucose into the energy the body needs to function properly.

Type II diabetes usually occurs in adults over forty who are overweight. Symptoms may include excessive thirst and hunger; rapid weight loss; frequent urination; tingling or numbness in the legs, feet, or fingers; fatigue; drowsiness; skin infections; and blurred vision.

Type II diabetes, however, is often present with none of these symptoms. Therefore, have your doctor periodically check your urine and blood, especially if you are overweight, inactive, or have a family history of the disease. Type II diabetes cannot be cured, but it can usually be controlled through diet and exercise. Sometimes, injections or oral medication is also needed.

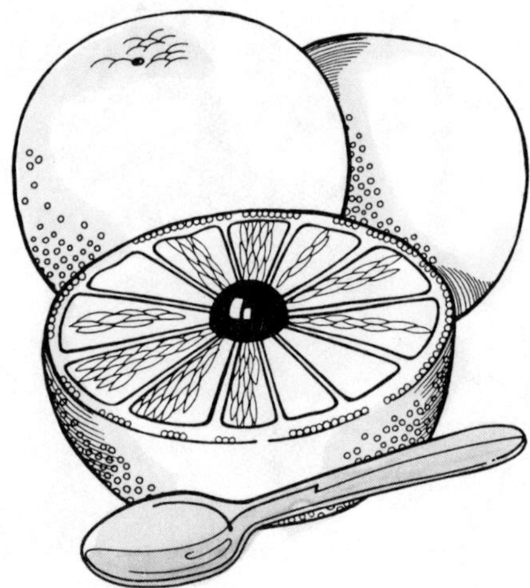

Arthritis

The term *arthritis* literally means "inflammation of the joint." It refers not to one disease but to scores of different chronic conditions. Arthritis attacks joints, causing pain throughout the body. But not all aches and pains indicate the disease. Thus, it's essential to get proper medical diagnosis. The most common forms of arthritis are rheumatoid arthritis and osteoarthritis.

Rheumatoid Arthritis

Mild or severe, it tends to recur. It can strike suddenly and cause disability, yet no two cases are alike. Symptoms include fatigue, muscle stiffness, and swelling in one or more joints. Aching and stiffness are usually worse in the morning and improve as the day goes on. Although causes and cures aren't known, medication, rest, heat, exercise, and surgery can help control and relieve the pain.

Osteoarthritis

Most of us get a "touch" of this form of arthritis as we get older. Although the disease is chronic, it seldom cripples, and pain is usually moderate. As we age, normal wear and tear on joints causes cartilage (a substance that lines the outside of bones) to fray and, in time, wear away partially or completely, so joints become irritated. Symptoms are pain in and around joints, inability to move a joint comfortably, and muscle weakness. Treatment is generally the same as for rheumatoid arthritis.

You and the Health Care System

Between 1975 and 1985 national health care costs rose 217 percent, according to the Health Care Financing Administration. While the rate of increase began to slow in the early 1980s, it still remains at almost twice the general rate of inflation. Today, one dollar in ten of the U.S. gross national product is spent on health care. It's big business. Being a well-informed, assertive consumer is crucial to your individual well-being, as well as that of others in the nation.

It is important that you begin to take charge of your health and use health services wisely by doing the following:

- Find doctors who have appropriate training and with whom you feel comfortable.
- Learn about new forms of medical care.
- Learn when not to see a doctor and how often to have various examinations, immunizations, and tests performed.
- Periodically review with your doctor all drugs and medications you are using.
- Make sure you have sufficient information when surgery or another form of nonroutine treatment is recommended.

Health Insurance in Retirement

Often health insurance terminates when a person reaches age sixty-five or retires. Planning for your retirement requires that you determine how your future health care needs will be met, what it will cost you, and what impact the cost will have on your tentative retirement budget.

Medicare

Medicare is a federally administered health insurance program for eligible people age sixty-five and older. People who are under sixty-five and disabled may also be eligible for Medicare. Anyone with sufficient quarters of creditable earnings under Social Security becomes eligible for Medicare upon reaching his or her sixty-fifth birthday, even if that person continues to work. Upon reaching age sixty-five, spouses and widows of covered workers and divorced spouses of covered workers—if they were married at least ten years—are also eligible for Medicare. Spouses must apply separately for coverage.

Medicare is a two-part program. Part A provides hospital benefits and is available without charge to anyone who is automatically eligible for it. People who are not automatically eligible may enroll by paying a monthly premium for this coverage.

Part B is optional medical insurance. Those who sign up for it must pay a monthly premium. Part B helps pay for doctors' services, not only those of your regular physician but also those you might need in a hospital, such as the services of an anesthesiologist. Part B also helps pay for medical supplies, outpatient hospital care, physical therapy, and diagnostic tests, among other things.

It is advisable to enroll in Medicare at least three months before your sixty-fifth birthday. To enroll, visit your local Social Security office; bring along your birth certificate or other proof of age.

Supplemental Health Insurance

Medicare, which was never intended to serve as a comprehensive medical insurance program, on average, covers about 40 percent of health care costs. The remaining costs are typically borne by one or more of the following:

- Your former employer's group plan if you can and do elect to carry it over into retirement.
- A private health insurance carrier, assuming that you obtain supplemental health insurance.
- An HMO (health maintenance organization) that you enroll in that provides services to Medicare beneficiaries.
- You, out of your own pocket.
- Medicaid—assistance for those in low-income brackets who are eligible.

If you are under sixty-five and still working, see if your employer's group health plan can be continued after you retire. Find out what and who (you, your spouse, your children) it will cover and what it will cost. Determine how its benefits mesh with your Medicare coverage. Your employer's plan may well serve as an adequate supplement to Medicare.

If you have an individual health insurance policy, find out if it is guaranteed renewable and to what age. Also find out what benefits it provides once you reach age sixty-five. It may be an appropriate supplement to Medicare.

(For help in understanding Medicare coverage and in evaluating supplemental health insurance options, see For Further Reading on page 126.)

Choosing Your Health Care Providers

Chief among your health care providers is, of course, your personal physician. Your team of health care professionals will also consist of your dentist, your vision care specialist, and perhaps a nurse practitioner or physician's assistant, a physical therapist, a fitness specialist, a podiatrist, or a nutritionist, depending on your needs at different times.

It is important to have a good doctor, someone you feel comfortable with and trust, who knows your medical history. If you are moving in retirement, you will need to get recommendations for new health care providers, possibly from your current doctor if he or she knows people in the area you are moving to. Also ask friends and family already living in the area or call the nearest medical school or the local medical society.

In evaluating potential physicians, you will want to obtain basic information about fees, payment schedules, office location and hours, hospital affiliation, other professionals employed, how emergencies are handled, and who substitutes for the doctor in his or her absence. Also find out if the doctor accepts Medicare assignment. This means that he or she agrees to charge only the price allowed by Medicare for covered services or supplies (you are then responsible for 20 percent of that allowable charge). If the doctor does not accept assignment, you will be responsible for paying the entire amount of the bill and will be reimbursed by Medicare for the amount that it will cover—80 percent of the *allowable* charge.

Once you make a tentative choice as to physician, visit the office. Determine if you feel comfortable with the person and if he or she explains matters to your satisfaction and gives you the time and atten-

Suggested Frequencies for Preventive Medical Services

Examination or Test	Suggested Frequency
Complete physical examination	Determine in consultation with your physician.
Blood pressure screening	At every office visit—or at least annually
Glaucoma test	Every two years after age fifty-five; annually for patients with family history of glaucoma
Breast examination	Annually by physician; monthly self-examination
Pelvic examination	Annually for women
Pap test	Annually
Rectal examination	Annually for women (with pelvic examination); every two years for men
Prostate examination	Every two years
Dental examination	Annually—or on complaint for patients with their own teeth; every two years for patients with dentures
Dental cleaning	Every four to six months for patients with own teeth

tion you need. Is the office well organized? run efficiently? Are schedules kept, within reason?

Communicating with Your Health Care Providers

In visiting your doctor or another health care professional, be prepared. Provide as much detailed information as you can about your symptoms, your medical history, and any medications you are taking. Feel free to write down questions you want answers to. And persist until you feel you understand the answers. Ask about alternative treatments; side effects of medications; and costs of tests, treatments, medicines, and so on. Remember that if you are uncomfortable with your doctor's recommendations regarding surgery, another nonroutine procedure, or the treatment of a chronic condition, you are free to seek another opinion. Medicare and most private health insurance carriers now pay for second opinions regarding surgery.

The Physical Examination

How often you have a complete physical examination should be determined by both you and your doctor based on your medical history and present condition. A new doctor will need to obtain baseline data on you for later comparisons. Perhaps of greater importance than a complete physical examination is periodic testing for certain conditions (see the chart on page 22 for suggested frequencies for various examinations and treatments).

Health Care Options

Depending on your personal circumstances and what is available in your area, one or more of the following health care options may be useful to you. Before using any of them, however, determine what their services and costs are and whether they are covered by your health insurance.

■ *HMOs.* Group practice HMOs (health maintenance organizations) are prepaid group health care plans that provide physician, hospital, and other health care services for a monthly or quarterly fee. The HMO uses one or more centrally located offices with physicians and other health care professionals either on salary or under contract. Certain hospitals are designated for use by people who enroll in the HMO. Many HMOs have their own X-ray department, laboratory, and pharmacy and may also offer health education services such as classes in stress management and how to quit smoking. Medicare covers participation of Medicare beneficiaries in licensed or approved health maintenance organizations.

■ *IPAs.* Independent practice associations are a fairly new kind of HMO. An IPA contracts with doctors in private practice to also see plan members. You may be able to enroll in an IPA and keep your current doctor if he or she participates in the plan. As with group practice HMOs, certain hospitals are designated for use by plan participants.

■ *PPOs.* Preferred provider organizations are health plans in which contractual arrangements have been made between an employer, insurance company, or similar group and certain physicians and hospitals to provide health care to the group's members for prenegotiated fees. Enrollment is not required. PPOs are usually available only to people who are still working.

■ *Same-day surgery centers.* These centers, which can be free-standing or part of a hospital, perform carefully selected surgical procedures on an outpatient basis.

■ *Emergicenters.* Also called urgicenters and walk-in medical offices, emergicenters usually provide care for injuries, acute illnesses, and other emergencies that are not life-threatening and that require little or no follow-up. They may also provide immunizations and physical examinations.

■ *Home health care.* Depending on where you live, home health care services could include nursing care, physical therapy, occupational therapy, speech therapy, and housekeeping assistance. Some of the cost of these services may be covered by Medicare.

Some Tips for Keeping Health Care Costs Down Without Sacrificing Quality

The following measures should prove beneficial:

- Take care of yourself. Listen to your body. Recognize early warning signs and follow up on them promptly.
- Examine all doctor and hospital bills thoroughly. Be sure you understand everything on them. Learn what your rights of appeal are.
- Comparison shop for doctor and hospital fees and services. If you think you are being overcharged, find out what other doctors and hospitals in your area charge for the same thing.
- Comparison shop for medications. Compare brand-name prescription drugs and their generic counterparts. Also compare prices for nonprescription medications and supplies.
- Obtain a second opinion for nonemergency surgery and other nonroutine procedures.
- Take advantage of free community clinics, health fairs, emergicenters, and same-day surgery centers when appropriate. If there's a medical or dental school in your area, see if it provides low-cost treatment. Also avail yourself of free procedures offered by your employer or a community agency or group, for example, blood pressure, diabetes, and colorectal cancer testing. Do certain procedures at home, such as taking your blood pressure and examining your breasts.
- Analyze your health insurance policies to see if you are underinsured, are overinsured, or have overlapping coverage.
- Consider signing up with a health maintenance organization (HMO).
- Read everything before you sign it, especially financial and "informed consent" documents.
- Ask if tests can be done on an outpatient basis.
- If it is not an emergency, avoid weekend admissions to a hospital.
- Go home as soon as you are able. Check into home health care if you think you will need it.
- Check out of the hospital before the next day's billing period begins.
- Keep track, or ask a friend or relative to keep track, of services and treatments.
- Keep all receipts for medical expenses, including transportation to and from doctors' offices and hospitals, medications, eyeglasses, orthopedic shoes, and so on, for insurance and income tax purposes; you may qualify for the medical expense deduction.
- Comparison shop for eyeglasses (you are entitled by law to a copy of your prescription), . dentures, and hearing aids.
- Know your rights and benefits under Medicare, and Medicaid if eligible. Keep up-to-date on changes in these programs.

The cost of health care in the United States continues its dramatic rise, though at a slower rate. The rate of increase in 1980 was 15.6 percent, compared with 8.9 percent in 1985. In addition to personal health care costs, the figures in the chart include costs for research, construction of medical facilities, government public health activities, and administration .

Health Care Costs in Total Dollars and per Capita

Year	Total	Per capita
1960	$26.9 Billion	$146 per person
1965	$41.9 Billion	$176 per person
1970	$75.0 Billion	$304 per person
1975	$132.7 Billion	$521 per person
1980	$248.1 Billion	$934 per person
1985	$425.0 Billion	$1,721 per person

Health Care Financing Administration, U.S. Department of Health and Human Services, updated 1987.

The Time in Your Life

Susan R., a lawyer with the state government and a recently divorced mother of three grown children, had always lived by the clock and her "to do" lists. Even so, there never seemed to be enough time for what needed to be done. Suddenly, upon retiring, Susan found herself at loose ends, unable to cope with the endless days with nothing to do. By eight o'clock each morning, she was up, dressed, and ready to go—but where?

"After nearly two months of pretending to enjoy not having plans and commitments and responsibilities, I accepted some truths about myself and developed a plan that works for me," said Susan. "Mondays, Wednesdays, and Fridays I work halfdays providing legal services for the elderly. On Tuesdays, I volunteer at a children's daycare center. Because my children and grandchildren live in another state, I don't get to see much of them. This way I can stay in touch with younger people.

"Thursday is strictly my day. I sleep in—for me, that means ten o'clock at the latest. Right now I'm taking a yoga class and a watercolor class at the community center. I may go for a swim at the local high school's pool or have lunch with a friend, then get my hair done or go shopping—whatever strikes my fancy."

Susan also pointed out the importance of single people making some specific plans for their weekends, for example, dinner and a movie with a friend or a concert.

"I like my life now," continued Susan, "but it took a lot of time and effort to get to the point where I can honestly say that." And she added, "I won't hesitate to make changes if I think I should."

Too often, people approach retirement without at least a tentative plan for reallocating the time in their life. Many people actually resist the idea of planning, preferring instead to entertain vague pipe dreams about sleeping in, fishing, golfing, or traveling. These activities are all well and good, but even the most avid golfer can't spend one-fourth to one-third of his or her life on the golf course. And with early retirement and longer life expectancy, that's just what your retirement can be—fully one-third of your life.

Thorough retirement planning involves identifying your needs and desires and then finding activities that help you achieve them. This is especially important if most of your key needs have been met through work.

Which of the following needs are most important to you? How are you currently meeting those needs? How can you meet them once you retire?

- Commitment, involvement.
- Recognition.
- Friendship.
- Structure to daily living.
- Personal or intellectual growth.
- Self-esteem.
- Creativity, productivity.
- Development of new skills.
- Adventure, fun.
- Relaxation, recreation.
- Health and fitness.
- Service to others.

In his book, *Growing Old, Staying Young,* Christopher Hallowell states: "The key to successful aging is involvement. People who age the best tend to be involved in various interests; they are involved with people; they are curious and they are flexible."

In his studies of the life satisfaction of retirees, Dr. Daniel Ogilvie, a psychologist at Rutgers University, found that "a powerful factor in satisfaction is how much time a person can spend doing those things that he does best, enjoys the most, and finds most meaningful."

Researchers have also found that how people spend their free time can make a real difference in their health. It's commonly agreed that being in good health will make you more satisfied with your life. But "being more satisfied with life, and so being in positive moods more often, seems to be good for your health," says psychologist Ed Diener, of the University of Illinois.

The information and ideas in this chapter will help you begin now to do the following:

- Identify your key needs and desires.
- Identify possible activities that will help you achieve those needs and desires.
- Obtain further information on these activities through literature, people, and organizations.
- Get started "testing the waters," that is, trying out these activities before you retire, for several reasons: (1) to see if you really like them, (2) to find out how much each activity will cost and then figure that cost in your tentative retirement budget, and (3) to aid your transition to retirement by having some structure, commitment, and companionship to replace what you will be losing when you stop working.

Free-Time Guidelines

To help you begin, here is advice from successful retirees:

- Consider variety, since few people can engage in even the most absorbing activity all day, every day.
- Plan some activities you can do alone and some to do with other people. Everyone needs private time, but social contact is vital too.
- Commit yourself to an activity. Experts say it helps to involve others, not only because company adds zest to what you're doing but also because you'll be embarrassed to quit if you've "dragged" friends along.
- Make sure that some of your activities are demanding enough so that they're not too

Time and Money

This chapter deals with ways you can make your free time in retirement rewarding and meaningful. But a warning is in order: Inflation, the enemy of fixed incomes, may eat away at your retirement budget, forcing you to seek full-time, or more likely, part-time employment. Chapter 7 will help you estimate your financial needs in both early and later retirement. Chapter 5 provides information on how to fit work into your life at any age so that it enhances your retirement years as well as contributes to your long-term financial security.

easily mastered and provide the challenge of increasing levels of difficulty.

- Consider activities that offer you the sense of contribution to others that is vital to a feeling of self-worth.
- Don't overextend yourself. In spite of all our exhortations to keep active, consider quality rather than quantity as your main criterion for choosing activities.
- Consider the possibility of some physical slowdown in later years. Again, a variety of activities—some physical and some creative or intellectual—is the key.

So much for the pep talk. Below is a questionnaire to start you thinking about what you want to do. Answer it before you read on.

What Do You Want to Do?

The following self-assessment items will help you choose your retirement activities. You may want to check more than one alternative on some items and fill in additional ones.

1. Do you like to do things alone or with other people?

   ☐ alone ☐ with others

2. Are you a self-starter, or do you need a push?

   ☐ self-starter ☐ need a push

3. Do you prefer playing for fun or playing to win?

   ☐ for fun ☐ to win

4. Do you prefer competitive sports or programmed exercise?

   ☐ sports ☐ exercise

5. Do you want to satisfy yourself or become a recognized expert?

   ☐ satisfy self ☐ become expert

6. Do you read for pleasure or to learn "how to do it"?

   ☐ pleasure ☐ how to do it

7. Do you want to do something for fun or to make money?

   ☐ for fun ☐ to make money

8. Would you rather work with people, ideas, or things?

   ☐ people ☐ ideas ☐ things

9. My favorite job-related activities are

   ☐ writing ☐ organizing

   ☐ training ☐ working with my hands

   ☐ ______________________

10. My favorite spare-time activities are

    ☐ reading ☐ sports ☐ hobbies

    ☐ theater ☐ ______________

11. I've enjoyed participating in

    ☐ politics ☐ social clubs

    ☐ community service ☐ choir

    ☐ ______________________

12. I've always wanted to

    ☐ write ☐ play an instrument

    ☐ paint ☐ run for office

    ☐ ______________________

13. My special skills are

    ☐ teaching ☐ listening ☐ singing

    ☐ accounting ☐ ______________

Time for Others Is Time Well Spent

"No one is useless in this world who lightens the burdens of another." This quotation of Charles Dickens sums up the essentials of the case for volunteering in terms especially appropriate for retirees, who report that among the greatest threats to their happiness is a sense of loss of identity, a lack of self-worth—a feeling of uselessness.

Those who begin volunteering on a regular basis before they retire, however, find the transition to retirement much easier because volunteering helps them maintain a sense of accomplishment and involvement with the world. As postretirement volunteers, they go right on putting their skills and talents to good use.

And consider the other advantages of volunteering. You'll meet new people and expand your social network, enhance your identity by taking on a new role, and begin to structure your time to fight that tendency to drift that comes with idleness. You may also be able to acquire new skills and gain experience that will be useful in obtaining paid employment in the future. This may be especially true for women reentering the work force or entering for the first time in later life.

How to Choose a Volunteer Activity

In choosing a volunteer activity, select something you firmly believe in—something to which you are committed. Convince yourself that you can indeed make a difference in this world. But don't overextend yourself. Devote your energy to one, maybe two, causes instead of parceling yourself out in little bits to every organization that calls. Otherwise, you'll find yourself missing that feeling of a job well done because you won't have had time to do it.

How do you find the organization or cause that warrants your devotion? Approach your search with all the care you'd give to finding a paid job. After all, this is a job you're seeking—an important one.

Thus, some serious self-evaluation is in order, a little like the exercise on page 27, but with volunteering in mind. Start by writing a brief description of yourself, listing your present and past occupations, your interests, and your talents. Then ask yourself the following questions, designed to reveal preferences that might point to a volunteer position.

1. Can you work well by yourself, or do you function better with a group?
2. Do you like children, and do you know how to relate to them? tutor them? play constructively with them?
3. Do you prefer being with adults? Can you work well with people younger or older than yourself? with the very old?
4. Can you work well with persons with physical or mental impairments?
5. Are you good at clerical work, or do you prefer more creative endeavors?
6. Do you prefer to work in the background, or do you want to be seen and heard?
7. Do you prefer to be in the same place, or are you willing to go to different sites?

8. Are you able and willing to extend yourself physically?
9. Is public acknowledgment of your efforts important to you?
10. What interests you most? The troubles of people in your own age group? Teenage conflicts? Child abuse? Abuse of the elderly? The drug problem? Homeless people? Women's rights? Some other aspect of life in your community?

Think of what you have to offer to each interest you identify. Are you a patient teacher? a good listener? a born salesperson? a talented carpenter? Every ability or gift has a volunteer application. Now that you have some idea of the direction in which your inclinations lie, you must find the cause, project, or organization whose needs match your talents and interests. A good place to start looking for openings is at your local voluntary service bureau or volunteer clearinghouse. Look it up in your phone book under any of a variety of names beginning with *Volunteer* or *Voluntary*, or try looking under United Way, Community Chest, Council of Social Agencies, and so on. You can also ask about volunteering at your city hall, your chamber of commerce, or a religious center.

The American Association of Retired Persons has a computerized Volunteer Talent Bank to match the interests and skills of potential volunteers with AARP programs and programs of other national organizations. The service is available to anyone age fifty and over; membership in AARP is not required. To obtain a registration form, write to the address listed on page 30.

Make an Honest Commitment

When you think you've found the place for yourself, be honest with yourself and the organization about how much time you're willing to put in. It also helps—and this was part of the point of your self-evaluation above—if you can be fairly specific about what you want to do. "I'll be happy to do anything," although meant sincerely, is rarely the case in the long run, and voluntary agencies know it. People differ in what they enjoy doing, and it's to the agency's advantage to find the right job for you.

Be realistic in your preferences. You're unlikely to be running the show in the first

Narrowing the Space Between People

Peace Corps photo by Linda Bartlett.

Mary Le Baron, at the age of sixty-one, became a Peace Corps volunteer in Honduras. Mary, who completed her master's degree in international education at the age of fifty-eight, had reared nine children. She was looking for a change—something that would narrow the space between peoples. In Honduras, she is a teacher/counselor/friend to sixty-nine girls living in a group center, helping them become successful, productive adults. Mary lectures in Spanish on nutrition, cooking, gardening techniques, sewing, and crafts. She also teaches English. Her goal is to help these young women go into business for themselves. And she is instilling in them a sense of voluntarism, having them work with the malnourished babies at the local maternity hospital. Mary lives in a three-bedroom home with a family of three and shares with them "a common bond in feeling that family is the most important element in life and that love and affection are natural and necessary." Mary believes that she has learned to be "happier with a small success" and to value herself more as a person than before she joined the Peace Corps.

Voluntary Action Resources

Write or call the following organizations for more information:

ACTION, 806 Connecticut Avenue, N.W., Washington, DC 20525. Or call toll-free 800-424-8580. Administers VISTA, RSVP, Foster Grandparents Program, and Senior Companion Program.

AARP Volunteer Talent Bank, AARP, 1909 K Street, N.W., Washington, DC 20049. Matches volunteers with AARP programs and programs of other national voluntary organizations.

Volunteer: The National Center, 1111 N. 19th Street, Arlington, VA 22209. 703-276-0542. A clearinghouse for information on volunteer programs throughout the country.

National Park Service, Office of Information, U.S. Department of the Interior, PO Box 37127, Washington, DC 20013-7127. Contact the park you're interested in or write for a brochure on volunteering in national parks.

National School Volunteer Program, 701 N. Fairfax Street, Alexandria, VA 22314. 800-992-NSVP. Information on how to start or join a school volunteer program.

SCORE/ACE (Service Corps of Retired Executives/Active Corps of Executives), 1129 20th Street, N.W., Suite 410, Washington, DC 20036. 800-368-5855. Information on how to use your skills to help new and struggling businesses.

Peace Corps, The Peace Corps, Washington, DC 20526. 800-424-8580, extension 93. Recruits older Americans with skills to share.

Veterans Administration. Maintains a large volunteer program in its various locations. Contact the Office of Voluntary Service in the VA center near you.

VITA (Volunteers in Technical Assistance), 1815 North Lynn Street, Suite 200, Arlington, VA 22209. 703-276-1800. Provides volunteers to help in developing countries.

Literacy Volunteers of America, 5795 Widewaters Parkway, Syracuse, NY 13214. Or call toll-free Contact Literacy Center at 800-228-8813. Helps adults learn to read.

two months, and there's no point in expecting to—especially if you're working for one of the larger service organizations.

Where to Volunteer

What follows is a brief list of volunteer possibilities—a complete list would look like the Manhattan Yellow Pages! It's just to start you thinking creatively about your options.

■ *Education.* This is one of the most fruitful fields for retired persons because schools, public schools in particular, are often in need of people to take some of the burden off hardpressed teachers and administrators. According to the National School Volunteer Program, about 4.3 million adults of all ages are participating in some 3,000 school volunteer projects today. What can you do? You can grade papers, design bulletin boards, monitor the lunchroom or playground, help in the school office or library, be a crossing guard, assist in dramatics programs, tell stories, and much, much more. See your local school board or go right to the school principal.

Literary Volunteers of America (see the box on this page for the address) is a nationwide organization that is training volunteers to teach adults to read. A number of the teachers have joined the projects through employer volunteer programs—a good way to begin volunteering before you retire.

■ *Culture.* Museums, art centers, theater groups, opera and ballet companies, and orchestras all need help to get started and keep going. Needed services range from fund-raising to typing subscribers' lists, from making posters to acting as a guide or an usher. One man specialized in tracking down hard-to-find props for his local repertory theater.

■ *Hospitals and other health services.* Hospitals need volunteers to act as receptionists, nurse's aides, gift shop attendants, file clerks, or friendly visitors to patients who want someone to talk with. Most hospitals have a director of volunteers who will be glad to explain their volunteer program and get you started.

There are, of course, many health-related jobs to be done outside the hospital, and your local chapter of the Red Cross is a good place to find them. Everyone thinks of the Red Cross in connection with rescue work during disasters, but the organization provides other much-needed services. These include first aid, water safety, and baby care instruction. Red Cross volunteers also serve in rehabilitation centers and nursing homes.

And don't forget the critical area of mental health. Your local mental health association can tell you where you can help. For example, you could work on a telephone hot line, talking to people in trouble and steering them to those who can help them.

■ *Politics and civic affairs.* Working for good government can take many forms. You can serve the party of your choice, getting involved in the excitement (and hard work) of a local, state, or national campaign. You can even run for office. Surprisingly, a number of low-level positions sometimes go unfilled for want of someone to run for them! Or, if you're not sure where you stand politically, you can join a nonpartisan group such as the League of Women Voters.

Civic affairs is an umbrella label for the work of any number of organizations ranging from the chamber of commerce and service organizations to committees focusing on specific environmental, consumer, or political concerns. For example, if you like children, consider the Boy Scouts of America, the Girl Scouts of the USA, or the Big Brothers/Big Sisters of America.

■ *Services to the aging.* You may find it fulfilling to help older people by performing such needed services as visiting nursing homes, providing transportation, delivering meals to shut-ins, and telephoning persons who live alone to be sure they are all right.

Moreover, fighting for the rights of the aged is a cause retirees, in particular, can readily endorse. There may be a local senior activist group in your community, or you can join a national organization with local affiliates, such as the American Association of Retired Persons (AARP).

■ *Government programs.* The federal government sponsors a number of volunteer programs, some especially geared toward older volunteers. The ACTION agency administers VISTA (Volunteers in Service to America), RSVP (Retired Senior Volunteer Program), the Foster Grandparents Program, and the Senior Companions Program. Volunteers in these programs may receive a small stipend. The National Park Service has volunteer openings, as does the Veterans Administration. Volunteers for SCORE/ACE (Service Corps of Retired Executives/Active Corps of Executives) use their skills to help people starting their own businesses. To contact these groups, see the box on page 30.

■ *International opportunities.* The Peace Corps is very interested in recruiting older Americans willing to share their skills and experience. VITA (Volunteers in Technical Assistance) is a private, nonprofit organization that provides technical assistance to people and groups in more than 100 developing countries. To contact these groups, see the box on page 30.

■ *Do-it-yourself service.* You may prefer to think up your own way of serving the cause of your choice. Often, individuals come up with remarkably creative ideas when they perceive an unfilled need. For example, the retired owner of a kitchen and bathroom fixture business designs safe kitchens and bathrooms for elderly people, free of charge. A retired personnel officer realized her community needed a counseling service for women trying to enter or reenter the job market, so she set up such a service on her own.

Volunteer now, before you retire. You may be surprised at the number and diversity of employed persons who are volunteering these days. So start now, even if you can only give one or two hours a week. Soon you will have acquired the volunteering habit.

Helping People Start Their Own Business

Since 1975, William E. Kidd, Jr., has been volunteering his time and expertise—through the Baltimore chapter of SCORE (Service Corps of Retired Executives)—to help people trying to start their own small businesses.

After retiring in 1973 as merchandising manager of a company in New York, Bill Kidd and his wife moved back to Baltimore. Bill devoted the first two years of his retirement to remodeling the family home and playing golf. Once the house was finished, he found himself with lots of time on his hands. An article on SCORE in the local paper gave him the opportunity he was looking for to do something useful and interesting.

Today, Bill is district representative for Maryland, overseeing the state's five SCORE chapters.

His former profession gave him a thorough background in advertising, marketing, and publicity that he has been able to put to good use both in promoting SCORE and in helping new entrepreneurs. Bill also speaks on advertising and marketing at SCORE's monthly workshop on How to Start and Manage Your Own Business. In addition, he has developed a series of commercials promoting SCORE's services.

According to Bill, when someone contacts SCORE for help, the person is asked to fill out a Request for Counseling form. Based on that information, the client is matched with a counselor or possibly a team of counselors who will work with the client as long as he or she wants them to, without charge.

Talking about his twelve years with SCORE, Bill says, "The bottom line is, I have a good reason for getting out of bed in the morning. It's meaningful, satisfying work, and I enjoy it."

The Time to Learn Is Any Time

A fifty-year-old New Jersey salesman—a high-school dropout—enrolled in college full-time, earned a bachelor's and a master's degree in German, and now teaches at the college that took a chance on him.

A fifty-five-year-old housewife went to school to become a practical nurse after working as a hospital volunteer for several years.

A sixty-three-year-old Ft. Lauderdale grandmother earned her pilot's license, the fulfillment of a lifelong dream.

The three cases above are but a tiny sampling of the adventures in the world of learning awaiting midlife and older adults these days. The examples only hint at the variety of motivations at work, the myriad directions the search for knowledge is taking, and the richness of opportunity available for learning new skills, exploring new interests, or pursuing a never-completed diploma or degree.

The thousands of older adults who sign up for courses and become experts on everything from collecting antiques to the Franco-Prussian War don't believe that they lose their ability to learn as they grow older. And they're right. Research has shown that healthy people can continue to learn up to and beyond their nineties. In fact, studies have indicated that using the mind preserves it.

Many people find that social contact is a bonus that comes with participating in educational programs. For some retirees, cut off from their business acquaintances, meeting people with similar interests is the main attraction of returning to the classroom.

The reason adults study, the subjects they choose, and the sites of their educational efforts are almost as numerous as the students themselves. Where do you fit into the educational picture?

We urge you to investigate the possibilities mentioned below and others that may occur to you. Embracing the concept of lifelong learning will immeasurably enrich your pre- and postretirement years.

■ *High-school diploma.* If you want to complete your high-school education, contact your board of education or a local public high school for information. Both can also provide information on how you can earn a diploma by taking the General Educational Development (GED) examinations and on special courses to help you prepare for the tests.

■ *Community colleges.* Community colleges usually emphasize technical and vocational training and offer two-year programs leading to an associate of arts degree. They also frequently offer special degree and nondegree programs for adults, with classes held at convenient day and evening hours and often at convenient off-campus locations. Contact the college's admissions office for more information.

■ *Four-year colleges and universities.* If your goal is to attend regular college classes, don't be concerned about sitting there with all those kids. Many older adults are doing it; you'll be surprised at how well you'll get along.

A number of colleges offer reduced tuition to older adults in regular undergraduate and graduate programs. You can either take classes for credit or audit them, that is, attend without being required to take tests or submit assignments.

You may be able to use the knowledge you've acquired over a lifetime to earn college credit through the College Level Examination Program (CLEP). Check first to see if the college or university you plan to attend accepts CLEP credits.

For more information on undergraduate and graduate programs, contact the school's admissions office.

■ *Adult continuing education.* Credit and noncredit courses are being offered in high schools, community centers, college and university extension centers, community colleges, religious centers, and museums all over the country. Adult continuing education has become big business.

Through these offerings, you can earn an undergraduate degree, sharpen old skills, learn new skills, or simply pursue a favorite subject. For example, you could take shorthand and typing courses to get a secretarial position, a real estate course to prepare you to obtain a license, or marketing and accounting classes in case you plan to start your own business. Or you could pursue a hobby such as woodworking or pottery, learn to play a musical instrument, take a course in how to stop procrastinating, or learn how to make home or car repairs.

For more information, contact the institution's continuing education office.

■ *Correspondence courses.* Correspondence courses are offered by colleges, universities, and private organizations on a variety of topics to help you earn credit toward a high-school diploma or a college degree, to help prepare you for a new career, or simply for your enjoyment. Some institutions may offer televised courses in conjunction with their correspondence courses. For more information on correspondence courses, see the listings for the National University Continuing Education Association and the National Home Study Council in the box on this page.

■ *Vacation schools.* One way to find out if you want to go back to the campus is to take one of the noncredit week-long summer "vacation college" courses being offered by several institutions. One such program is Elderhostel, which offers liberal arts and science courses to people age sixty and over. (A younger spouse or companion

Education Resources

For more information, write to the following organizations:

College Level Examination Program, CN 6600, Princeton, NJ 08541-6600. 215-750-8420. Write for free brochures: *CLEP Colleges* and *Moving Ahead with CLEP.*

Elderhostel, 80 Boylston Street, Suite 400, Boston MA 02116. Will send catalog describing their low-cost, short-term academic programs held in colleges and universities in fifty states, Canada, and abroad.

Institute of Lifetime Learning, AARP, 1909 K Street, N.W., Washington, DC 20049. Provides activities kits for mini-courses on a variety of topics.

National University Continuing Education Association, One Dupont Circle, N.W., Suite 420, Washington, DC 20036. 202-659-3130. For a list of member universities that offer independent study programs through extension services, send $8.95 plus $1.75 for postage and handling to Peterson's Guides, PO Box 2123, Princeton, NJ 08543-2123. Or call 800-225-0261.

National Home Study Council, 1601 18th Street, N.W., Washington, DC 20009. 202-234-5100. Provides a free *Directory of Accredited Home Study Schools.*

can also participate.) Courses, which are normally one week long, cover a broad spectrum of subjects from literature to marine biology. Classes are supplemented with field trips and social events. To obtain more information, write to the address listed in the box on page 34.

■ *Self-study.* You may be one of those people who don't go in for organized programs. If so, you'll find plenty of intellectual stimulation in libraries and museums. You can embark on an individualized study program in anything from the Victorian novel to ornithology. Of course, to enjoy reading, you don't need a programmed study plan; one of the greatest joys of being retired is finally having the time to read all the books you've been stockpiling over the years.

There are other, slightly more directed, ways to learn on your own. In recent years, several university systems have begun individualized courses that allow students to study on their own, at their own pace, with guidance from faculty advisers.

■ *Other options.* People are also acquiring some rather specialized skills before and after retirement. Witness the Ft. Lauderdale flying grandmother mentioned earlier. If you want to become a pilot, a trail guide, a deep-sea diver—whatever—don't let your age discourage you from investigating. Check the Yellow Pages and find out how to get started in your community.

A new idea in adult education is the "swap meet," a gathering where retirees teach one another. For example, a person who is an expert weaver will exchange lessons with another who is fluent in Spanish. Or consider organizing an informal discussion group to meet regularly to talk about a subject of mutual interest. To find other interested people, post signs on bulletin boards, run announcements in community newspapers, or ask friends if they know someone already involved in the topic of interest.

Having a Wonderful Time

Time is definitely on your side when it comes to travel in retirement. You now have the flexibility for travel you've never had before. You can choose your seasons, and you can move at a more leisurely pace while you take advantage of special package deals and group charters aimed at those with time to spend.

Today, travelers can choose from a variety of tours, modes of travel, and places to stay. And the cost can be remarkably flexible too—if you plan your trip carefully. Below is just a sampling of some of the ways people are finding to get away these days.

■ *Home exchanges.* Trading homes with someone is a great way to really get the feel of a place and save on hotel, restaurant, and, often, auto rental expenses. Veteran house exchangers don't worry much about the care their house is receiving, but for your peace of mind, you can agree on mutual deposits against damage.

To arrange an exchange, you can register with organizations that maintain exchange lists; advertise in a newspaper or magazine or use a directory to set up your own swap directly; or work privately through social, business, or professional organizations.

■ *Cruises.* A luxury cruise can be the ultimate way to relax. Although cruises range in duration from a three-day "cruise to nowhere" to a round-the-world

voyage, most last from seven to eighteen days. Even though cruises can be expensive, remember that all your living expenses are included in the fare.

Today many cruises highlight a certain theme: fitness and sports, Big Band music, murder mysteries, or brushing up on everything from bridge to the stock market.

- *Theme tours.* If you prefer to pursue a favorite subject on dry land, you can find a group tour that follows in the footsteps of a famous person, samples gourmet food and drink in the various regions of France, or observes the archaeological wonders of Greece. Ask your travel agent or contact the relevant group or club about a particular theme tour you are interested in.

- *Farm and ranch holidays.* How about taking your vacation on a working farm or ranch? You can get involved in the daily chores or just sit back and enjoy the scenery and clean air. You can also participate in easy to strenuous trail rides. You need not be an expert rider for most rides; just be able to stay on a gentle horse.
- *Travel by recreation vehicle (RV).* Is mechanical horsepower more to your taste? RVs have become extremely popular with midlife and older travelers because they offer independence, flexibility, and usually cost savings. Buying an RV can be a substantial investment; a wise way to find out if you like this mode of travel is to rent one for your first trip or two.
- *Travel by bus or train.* If you'd rather leave the driving to someone else, look into special train and bus passes that allow unlimited travel for specified lengths of time. Overseas there are Eurailpass and BritRail Pass, among others. Here, Greyhound (Ameripass) bus line offers similar deals. Such passes are only economical if you'll be traveling long and far enough to make them worthwhile. The overseas passes must be purchased in the U.S. before you go. If seeing the U.S. by train interests you, call Amtrak (800-USA-RAIL) for information on discounts.

Do Your Homework

Planning is the key to a successful trip. Decide first what interests you, what you can afford, and what level of comfort you require. Then see a travel agent, whose advice and services are usually free. But don't stop with an agent. Write to appropriate organizations and tourist offices (most countries have offices in New York City); ask friends and friends of friends; read books and articles (the *Reader's Guide to Periodical Literature* lists magazine articles about particular destinations and modes of travel).

Before you sign up for anything, study the fine print. With tours and airfare packages, be certain you understand all the terms. You might even call the Better Business Bureau or your local consumer office to see if the tour operator has an established reputation.

You can enhance your enjoyment of future retirement trips by attending travelogs, studying the art and culture of countries you'd like to visit, or acquiring hobbies (photography or a foreign language, for example) that can be furthered by travel. Then, as soon as you have the flexibility to go the way you want to go, you'll be prepared to get the most from your travels.

Travel Tips

Most of the following advice from seasoned travelers is along the money-saving line:

- Use public transportation. You'll save money and get to know the territory better.
- Investigate less-expensive tourist homes, guest houses, bed-and-breakfast accommodations, and no-frills budget motels. Most foreign and many domestic cities have tourist bureaus—often located in airports or railroad stations—to help you find accommodations to suit your budget.
- Use toll-free 800 numbers when making hotel reservations in the U.S. You can usually obtain these numbers from telephone information.
- When traveling overseas, use credit cards infrequently. They may place you at an exchange-rate risk because the rate is figured the day your bill is processed, not the day you used the card.
- Single persons should investigate "shared accommodations" arrangements on tours and cruises to avoid the considerable single supplement charged by an industry that is based on double occupancy.
- There are numerous airfare deals available today. Be sure to ask your travel agent or the airlines about the best terms for you.
- "Tip packs" of foreign coins can be bought here for immediate needs on reaching your destination.
- Travel light. Pack everything you think you'll need; then remove half of it. There'll inevitably be times when you'll

have to carry your own bags. And you may want to do some shopping on the trip.

- Carry copies of prescriptions, extra pairs of glasses, and a medical information sheet if you need special care of any kind. You may wish to join an organization that provides names of approved English-speaking doctors overseas.
- Finally, get in shape before you go. Start walking!

What About Travel for the Single Older Person?

You can have your choice of group and escorted tours, or you might want to travel alone. If you are considering a trip alone, ask yourself the following questions. They should help you decide whether it's a good idea for you.

1. Are you gregarious? Can you talk to strangers easily?
2. When you encounter problems, can you assert yourself?
3. Are you a self-starter? Can you plan your days?
4. Do you have a good sense of humor?
5. Can you read a city map? Do you have a good sense of direction?
6. Can you afford to stay at a first-class hotel? (They usually have their own dining room, should you choose to stay in for dinner.)
7. Can you go into a hotel bar alone, sit down, and order a drink without pain and suffering?
8. Are you flexible?
9. Do you enjoy your own company?
10. Can you get to the train or plane on time?
11. Can you limit your luggage to what you yourself can carry?
12. Are you in good physical health?
13. Can you handle solitude?

Travel Resources

For more information on some of the travel opportunities mentioned on these pages, contact the following organizations:

House Exchanges
Vacation Exchange Club, 12006 111th Avenue, Youngtown, AZ 85363. 602-972-2186.

Land and Water Travel
BritRail Pass, c/o BritRail Travel International, Inc., 630 Third Avenue, New York, NY 10017. 212-599-5400.

Eurailpass, c/o French National Railroad, 610 Fifth Avenue, New York, NY 10020. 212-582-2110.

AARP Travel Service, 5855 Green Valley Circle, Culver City, CA 90230. 800-227-7737. Domestic and foreign escorted tours for AARP members.

Bed and Breakfast/Country Inns
The Globe—Pequot Press, Old Chester Road, Box Q, Chester, CT 06412. 800-243-0495. Publishes listings of bed-and-breakfast homes and country inns for various regions in the United States and for certain foreign countries.

Single Travel
Gramercy Singleworld, 444 Madison Avenue, New York, NY 10022. 800-223-6490. Organizes singles groups of all adult ages and arranges shared accommodations.

The Great Outdoors
National Park Service, Office of Information, U.S. Department of the Interior, PO Box 37127, Washington, DC 20013-7127. Obtain information about Golden Age (62+) and Golden Eagle (under 62) passes and about the national parks.

Farm and Ranch Vacations, Inc., 36 E. 57th Street, New York, NY 10022. 212-355-6334. Publishes *Farm, Ranch, and Country Vacations; Adventure Travel North America;* and *Adventure Travel Abroad.*

Woodall's Campground Directories, Woodall Publishing Company, Lake Bluff, IL 60044. 800-323-9076. Annually publishes the *National Directory,* $12.95; *Eastern Directory,* $8.95; *Western Directory,* $8.95. Also check bookstores and local RV dealers.

Medical Assistance Overseas
Intermedic, Inc., 777 Third Avenue, New York, NY 10017. 212-486-8900. Members receive a listing of English-speaking doctors in foreign countries.

Guides
For more travel information, see the Fodor, Fielding, Frommer, and Mobil travel guides, all of which should be available in local bookstores.

Perfect Pastimes

Experienced retirees say that it's great to have a hobby in retirement but that you must not count on it to provide full-time satisfaction. You should be able to spend as much or as little time on your hobby as your other interests allow, keeping in mind that too much of even a good thing will probably make its charms fade fast.

Now we hasten to add that there are always exceptions. People have been known to become so passionately involved, in, say, beekeeping, that all else ceases to interest them. But we tend to feel that this is no longer a hobby; it's an occupation.

The word *hobby,* for us, encompasses not only craftlike activities but also collecting of all kinds, dramatics and music, writing—in fact just about any pursuit that offers you the following:

- Relaxation and absorption.
- Satisfaction in doing and accomplishing.
- Involvement in productive or simply pleasurable activities.
- Expansion of your knowledge and skills.

Thus, the list that follows is far from complete and is only provided to start you thinking about what might interest you. Your next step is to follow up on your ideas. Get a good hobby book or ask about a class at your community center, "Y," or adult continuing education center.

Arts and Crafts

This category deserves a chapter of its own. In fact, there are dozens of crafts books that you may want to consult. Here are just a few of the more popular activities in this category:

- *Mosaic art.* Creating designs using tiny pieces of glass, pebbles, tiles, or seeds is an ancient art that is once again thriving.
- *Pottery and ceramics.* Creating something from the raw earth, experimenting with shape and color, is enormously satisfying; consequently, pottery making is one of the fastest-growing crafts.
- *Jewelry making.* Using your imagination to create works of art out of a variety of raw materials is an ancient art form.
- *Woodworking.* Here's a craft choice that has income potential, since skilled woodworkers, carpenters, and furniture restorers are much in demand.
- *Sewing, knitting, crocheting, and weaving.* As pastimes, these handicrafts have the virtue of being readily started and stopped as time permits, and the products make greatly appreciated gifts.
- *Drawing, painting, and sculpting.* Look into these arts even if you think you have no talent. Sign up for lessons. You may be surprised at the results. You'll acquire an increased sensitivity to shape and composition and possibly discover a rewarding pursuit to enrich your life.
- *Music.* Learn to play an instrument; collect or make folk instruments; attend concerts; add to your record and tape collections; join a chorus or orchestra, or form your own. Music is an ideal interest because it lends itself to both

solitary and social enjoyment.

- *Theater.* Don't just attend the theater—join it! Participating in amateur theater groups is a great way to meet people, and you don't have to act. There are dozens of jobs to be done, from props to publicity.
- *Writing.* The old saying that we all have at least one novel in us may or may not be true, but how about a short story? a journal? a family history for your grandchildren? Even if you're never published, putting your observations and feelings on paper will help you gain a fresh perspective on yourself and your world.

Nature

This category encompasses a variety of interests from bird-watching to fossil hunting to astronomy. A perennial (and economical) favorite is gardening, whether you're farming the back forty or raising some herbs on your windowsill. People who love to grow things never quite get over the thrill of the season's first zinnia or red tomato. Gardening can be good exercise too.

Collecting

What do you treasure? Porcelain-faced dolls? Victorian washstands? Stamps? Whatever it is you value, you can be sure that someone, somewhere, has a collection. What about cup and saucer sets, thimbles, teddy bears, or paperweights? Collecting is a flexible pastime; you can pick up an item here and there for fun, or you can make a lifework of researching, enlarging, cataloging, and maintaining your collection. A few suggestions for would-be collectors follow:

1. *Collect only what you love.* Your collection may well increase in value, but if you love what you're collecting, the monetary return or lack of it will be a secondary consideration.
2. *Collect only what you can take care of and have room to store.* You may love antique cars, but your neighbors may object to your backyard parking lot!
3. *Collect only what you can afford.* Only you know what a particular collectible is worth to you. But just the same, it's wise to do the necessary research. When you're facing the auctioneer or shopkeeper, you'll feel secure in the knowledge that you won't be overcharged.

Libraries, bookstores, and local and national collectors' clubs can provide you with information about how to get started and how to evaluate and sell your collections.

Reading and Library Activities

Retirement is a great time to catch up on all the reading you've been meaning to do. In addition to books, your local library may provide an assortment of other materials and services:

- Special events such as book discussions, film forums, lectures, and poetry readings.
- Specialized newspapers and magazines.
- Records; audiotapes of music, speeches, and books; and instructional videotapes and feature films.

Sports

There has been a burgeoning of opportunities for older Americans to pursue sports and fitness activities through

organized programs. If you are age fifty or older and are interested in competitive or recreational sports, contact the National Senior Sports Association (317 Cameron Street, Alexandria, VA 22314, or call 703-549-6711). The association sponsors golf, tennis, and bowling tournaments at major resorts worldwide at economical rates through group purchasing power.

Social Clubs and Special Interest Organizations

Participating in clubs can provide you with the opportunity to socialize and to pursue a special subject of yours with people who share your enthusiasm and interest.

Television

According to the 1986 *Nielsen Report on Television,* women fifty-five and over watched television the most of any other age group—forty-two hours a week; men fifty-five and over came in second—with thirty-eight hours. Television offers many entertaining, interesting, and educational programs. But it can be an addictive activity, especially for homebound or otherwise isolated persons. People of all ages should guard against substituting too much television for more worthwhile and challenging activities.

Pets

People can gain a great deal from animal companionship. Pets can provide acceptance, amusement, attention, unconditional love, and a sense of purpose and commitment. The emotional and physical therapeutic effects of pets have been scientifically proven. Pets can also help break the ice when a person moves into a new area. Take your dog for a walk; you're sure to have at least one or two people strike up a conversation about it.

Contemplation

Midlife is an appropriate time to spend some time reviewing our lives. Doing so can be good for both physical and psychological health. Quiet time alone can help alleviate stress and put problems in perspective. And it gives us a chance to identify our many accomplishments over a lifetime and pat ourselves on the back from time to time.

Socializing

Unless you have the instincts of a hermit, you're going to want and need to spend some of your retirement time with other people. We're not suggesting a constant social whirl. As we just mentioned, everyone needs some time alone—time to think and reflect. But the company of others is one of the best ways to keep yourself both interested and interesting.

In retirement, you might have to work a little harder

than before at having a social life because, for many people, work is the chief source of friends and acquaintances. Of course, a few of these job-related friendships may endure, but once the common interest of work is removed, contacts with people from the workplace tend to diminish.

So, it may be necessary to cultivate social contacts outside of work, and the time to start is now, before you retire.

How do you go about it? Your attitude is crucial. You must be friendly to make friends. Look for interesting people at the local church bazaar, at the community center, or on the golf course. Seek out activities that will put you in contact with others. Take courses; do volunteer work; join clubs.

When you've met people you think you'd like to know better, invite them to your home. You have to extend invitations to receive them. Of course, not everyone you seek out in this way will become a close friend, but you're bound to form some new associations to enjoy in retirement.

We'll talk more about building and reinforcing your support system of family, friends, acquaintances, and organizations in the next chapter, "Midlife Roles and Relationships."

Positive Action 3

The Postretirement Time in Your Life

Start thinking creatively right now about what you'll be doing with those years of opportunity. Then make specific plans to explore specific activities that appeal to you.

The circle above visually represents the free time you probably will have in retirement. Aside from sleeping and eating, that amounts to ninety-eight hours a week. How do you want to fill those hours? Consider hobbies, religious activities, sports, exercise, community service, family, clubs, learning, travel, earning money, and quiet time.

Sleeping and eating	**70 hours/week**
______________________	__________
______________________	__________
______________________	__________
______________________	__________
______________________	__________
______________________	__________
______________________	__________
______________________	__________
______________________	__________
______________________	__________
TOTAL:	**168 hours/week**

Now think about what you can do today to test out some of your ideas about how to spend your free time.

Midlife Roles and Relationships

When Robert P. decided to retire from his position as an investment counselor with a firm based in New York City, he and his wife, Lucy, agreed it was time for a big change. They wanted to start a new life in a different part of the country. Robert and his wife realized that they would miss their grown daughter and her family, who lived in New Jersey. Robert, in particular, enjoyed taking his two teenage grandsons to ball games during the summer. But both Robert and Lucy wanted to get away from the big-city hassle, the big-city expense, and the harsh northern winters. Robert wanted to move someplace where he could play tennis outdoors nearly year-round. And Lucy had long dreamed of tending a huge garden and rows upon rows of flower beds—something she had to give up when Robert was transferred to New York City many years ago.

The key factor, however, in determining just where they would relocate was Lucy's parents. They lived in a retirement community in Arizona. Both were now in poor health, and Lucy wanted to be near them and to help them out. So Robert and Lucy packed up and headed for the Southwest.

After two years in Arizona, their new retirement lifestyle was definitely agreeing with Lucy. She enjoyed being a gardener again. In fact, she even got a part-time job making flower arrangements for a local florist. And she received deep satisfaction from being a caring daughter to her parents at this time in their lives.

Robert, on the other hand, was not happy with the way things were going. He missed the excitement and challenge of his job. He missed the time he had spent with his grandsons. He even missed being chairman of a small investment club he started among friends and neighbors back home.

Robert also sensed that he was beginning to resent the emotional and social demands his in-laws were making on Lucy and him. Even the tennis had lost its appeal when Robert realized that he was redirecting his competitiveness and his frustrations into his tennis matches.

Lucy's constant puttering in the garden also put him on edge. He felt left out. Yard work had never appealed to him. He'd just as soon pave the lawn and paint it green.

Robert's one real pleasure in retirement came from teaching a course on investing for retirees at the community center. As an instructor, he felt challenged, stimulated, respected, and useful.

What went wrong? How could the problem have been prevented? Before answering these questions, let's look at some of the more significant role changes that can occur at midlife. Some of these changes may be voluntary and eagerly awaited; others may be forced upon us by circumstances. When these changes occur, we can choose to resist them, to ignore them and hope that they'll go away, or to accept them and see the opportunity for growth and learning inherent in them. Philosophers and psychologists, alike, never tire of telling us that it's not what happens to us but what we think and do about what happens that determines our ultimate success.

For example, take the "empty nest syndrome." You're middle-aged parents. You watch your last child leave home. You wonder what you'll do with your time and your life now. Depending on your attitude, you can view the situation as a major loss and brood about it periodically. Or you and your spouse can pat yourselves on the back for a job well done and then shift your focus from your roles as parents to renewing and revitalizing your roles as husband and wife.

Other changes that commonly occur in midlife include these:

- Taking on the rewarding and vitally important role of grandparent.
- Adjusting your relationship with your aging parents, perhaps even taking partial responsibility for their welfare. (And often, it's in midlife that we first experience the death of a loved one, usually a parent.)
- Becoming a single person again, at least temporarily, as a result of divorce or the death of a spouse.
- Experiencing burnout in your career or plateauing (reaching your highest job level). Many midlife people use these experiences constructively to make major career moves or to shift priorities from career to family, friends, and nonwork interests. (Due to the economic transition taking place in this country, many midlife people are also finding themselves in the role of dislocated older worker, presumably "too old to hire but too young to retire." See chapter 5 for more on this subject.)

These and other changes can happen to people in midlife. In addition, as we saw in the case of Robert P., retirement, and especially relocating in retirement, brings its own set of adjustments that must be dealt with. The key prerequisites to successfully meeting these midlife "course corrections" are (1) a willingness to change and grow and (2) advance planning.

Your Midlife Review

In contemplation of retirement, it is essential to take the time to identify the various roles you play and to determine which of these roles give you the greatest satisfaction and why. If, in doing this analysis, you discover that your identity through your work has provided the greatest rewards, you can give careful consideration to what you will replace your work role with when you retire. You will need to find something that affords you the same kinds of satisfaction that work now provides. The same is true for any other roles that will disappear or change significantly when you retire or relocate.

At any point in your life, you are playing many roles. Retirement provides the time, freedom, and flexibility to vary these roles according to your interests, resources, and state of health. But new roles are not assumed automatically. They must be learned. That takes time and planning. It's wise to recognize that these changes are coming and begin adjusting to them *before* you retire.

Your Support Systems

Another way of identifying and analyzing our relationships in preparation for retirement is to examine our support systems. Researchers have found a strong link between the strength of our social support systems and our health and life satisfaction in retirement. Yet, in a mobile, career-oriented culture like ours, we frequently make major life decisions based on status and financial needs without considering the consequences to our relationships. While we are striving to get ahead, we tend to take our support systems for granted. Then we arrive at middle age, and whether our career goals have been achieved or not, we begin to sense a need to reassess our priorities and to establish a healthier balance between work and family and friends.

Before retirement, it is important to examine your support system of colleagues, friends, family, neighbors, clubs, community, and religious groups. Each one provides you with something that contributes to your psychological and emotional health—recognition, companionship, a sense of being needed. When retirement comes, particularly if you plan to move, which of your support systems will disappear? Can you do without them? Can you replace them? How? For example, in retirement, you won't be able to depend on your job for a circle of friends and acquaintances. You will have to make an effort to find new friends, preferably before you retire. Determine now which of your support systems are crucial to your psychological and emotional well-being and decide how you are going to enhance them or replace them in retirement.

Positive Action 4

Who Are You? Who Would You Like to Be?

You are unique. No one else has your assortment of experiences, memories, characteristics, hopes, and expectations. Get to know yourself. On a separate sheet of paper, write the numbers 1 through 20 down the left-hand side. Now write twenty answers to the question, Who am I? in terms of the roles you play. Consider your roles connected with work, family, and friends as well as social, civic, religious, and special interest activities (for example, supervisor, co-worker, father, husband, bowler, election judge, choir member, gardener).

Now ask yourself:

1. Which roles are most important to me (really)? Why? What satisfactions do I receive from them (love, status, fun, involvement—see the list on page 26 in chapter 3 for more possibilities)?
2. Which roles will change when I retire? How?
3. Which roles will disappear entirely when I retire? How can I obtain the satisfactions received from those roles in retirement?
4. What new roles do I want to take on in retirement? What can I do now to begin establishing myself in those roles?
5. What current roles do I want to expand in retirement? How?

Think about who you are and who you want to be in the years ahead and begin taking steps now to reach your goals.

Friendships

In retirement, it may take more effort to make and keep friends. You'll have to search for common interests. The more activities you participate in with other people of similar interests, the more likely it is that you'll make friends.

If you are thinking of relocating to a new area when you retire, experienced retirees suggest that you select a location where you know you will find people with backgrounds and interests similar to yours. If you do, it'll be easier to meet people.

Of course, don't limit your friendships to people your own age. A good way to maintain a youthful attitude and enthusiasm is to mix with younger adults and with children of all ages.

The best way to cultivate friendships with younger adults is to actively pursue your own interests and meet people who share them in classes, clubs, organizations, and various activities.

If you don't have grandchildren or other young relatives living near you, perhaps you can cultivate friendships with children in your neighborhood, at the religious center you are affiliated with, or through an intergenerational volunteer program. Everyone will benefit—you, the children, their parents, and society as a whole.

Had Robert and Lucy P. analyzed their roles, relationships, and support systems more carefully before relocating, they could have anticipated some of the problems that eventually surfaced and adjusted their retirement plans to eliminate or at least minimize them. Begin your analysis of the roles, relationships, and support systems in your life by trying Positive Action 4 on this page.

Marriage in the Middle Years

What typically happens to the institution of marriage during the middle years? A statistical look at the current scene shows that the divorce rate for midlife people and for other age groups continues to increase, but at a slower rate. In 1965, among people forty-five to fifty-four who had ever been married, only 3.5 percent of the men and 4.5 percent of the women were divorced. In 1982, the percentages were men, 8.6 percent; women, 11.1 percent. In 1986, the percentages were men, 9.2; women, 12.7.

Despite divorce, middle-agers hold on to a faith in marriage itself. A second marriage may be, as Samuel Johnson said, "the triumph of hope over experience." In 1980, of all the women forty-five to fifty-four who had ever been divorced, 48 percent remarried. Of all the men in that age group who had ever been divorced, 63 percent remarried.

These statistics on remarriage are as impressive and important as the divorce figures because they show that the old institution is here to stay. People just can't do without it. They have to have intimacy and companionship on the kind of durable, continuing basis that marriage provides best.

Intimacy is more than sex. It is the sharing of real feelings with another human being. It means that you care very deeply if some other person lives and thrives.

So what we're talking about is not merely sex and most particularly not superficial glamor but basic imperatives of nature that no one can ignore.

You may—or may not—be married to the right partner. Regardless of what you do, marriage is going to go on. It's a good point to remember if you're considering ending your present marriage. Despite all the new "open" options—open marriages, open extralegal living arrangements—in all likelihood, you're going to wind up married anyway.

The real marital problem of the late twentieth century is as old as marriage itself—how do a man and a woman provide each other with the enduring intimacy and companionship they both need? It somehow seems harder today than ever.

Dr. E. James Lieberman, a Washington, D.C., psychiatrist and noted marriage counselor, says "a failure of intimacy" is our biggest problem. "I think that's what psychotherapy now is all about—a structured introduction to intimacy."

Lieberman views marriage as a kind of seesaw. On a playground seesaw, two partners maintain a relationship while each moves in a separate direction. The basic relationship is preserved because the seesaw is solidly balanced. In marriage, the crucial balance is "trust—trusting each other," Lieberman says.

With women as well as men holding jobs involving constant encounters with the opposite sex, trust these days takes on new dimensions. It is trust that permits both spouses to have friendships outside marriage. They *should* have freedom to have friendly relationships with persons other than spouses, Lieberman says. The marriage partner denied such freedom feels "in chains." That's not healthy. The psychiatrist says that, in a marriage, there has to be "enough balance—enough trust—to have outside relationships."

He adds that "venturing outside marriage is a risk. It means the discovery that there can be intimacy, excitement, confirmation [of one's beauty, professional capabilities, etc.] with someone besides the marriage partner." But discovery alone doesn't upset seesaws. Nor does an occasional innocuous luncheon, an exchange of ideas, or an uncomplicated friendship. In fact—if they don't go too far—cross-sex friendships can be very constructive. Lieberman suggests, "Not all growth can occur just between two people. Some growth requires other important relationships."

You may have "some loving or sexual feeling which you only *think* about or *talk* about with a sexually attractive person—but which you don't pursue because it carries the risk of upsetting the [marriage] balance." That's okay. Chalk it up to growth.

An affair is different—and very risky—Lieberman says: "The marriage partner who has an affair takes a bigger risk. He or she risks hopping off the seesaw—and having the whole thing collapse. The person who betrays may cause needless pain and feel guilt—which he or she can't absolve by saying "the affair helps me grow."

There is nonsexual betrayal too. "If one has a friendship outside the marriage, it is a betrayal to reveal to the friend—male or female—matters that are sacrosanct within the marriage," says the counselor.

"Intimacy means uniqueness, a private exchange of feelings. One does not have it if one treats all friends the same. On the other hand, there is a need for openness—the willingness to let things happen. The need, again, is for a balance. The important thing is that spouses trust each other to keep the balance."

To avoid upsetting the marital seesaw, experts say the individual spouse must grow—grow up enough to assume responsibility for his or her own feelings and actions. Then the relationship will more or less take care of itself.

Dr. Murray Bowen, Georgetown University psychiatrist and family therapist, thinks the key to many marital problems lies in a process he calls "differentiation of self." That involves learning to distinguish between "feeling," on the one hand, and thinking and assuming responsibility for one's own actions, on the other. It means you can't blame somebody else for what you do.

"If people could work on themselves," says Bowen, "that's the one magic turning point to it."

Essentially you focus on yourself, instead of blaming your emotional states and reactions on your partner.

"You focus on becoming a more responsible person—on controlling yourself and permitting others to be themselves, rather than blaming them or trying to change them."

Bowen believes that even small steps in this direction eventually result in a different marital lifestyle. Here's how he says it works: When one spouse begins to assume responsibility as an individual, the other may at first feel insecure and threatened by the change. But if the maturing partner states a position calmly—without attacking the other—and continues to show warmth and affection, the reacting spouse will adjust and begin to take similar steps toward individuality. Change and growth breed more change and growth, Bowen suggests.

Tips for a Happier Marriage and a Successful Retirement

Relationships are never static—they get better or worse. The changes that retirement brings can strain a relationship. Here are some tips that can ease your approach to retirement and make for a happier marriage.

- Plan your retirement together. Be mutually supportive. Reaffirm your mutual love and respect.
- Plan and oversee your finances as a team. Establish goals, select advisers, determine the disposition of assets, and draw up separate wills—together.
- Encourage the development of mutual and individual friendships *before* you retire.
- Develop new activities and routines. But be flexible and open to spontaneous suggestions (for a picnic, a weekend trip, and so on).
- Respect each other's privacy. Each of you should have private space and time for whatever you want to do.
- Renegotiate your marriage arrangements. Exchange and share roles.
- Keep up your appearance. Feel free to dress casually but be neat and well groomed.
- Communicate. Make time to talk. Listen carefully. Be sure you understand what the other person is saying.
- Recommit yourselves to the success of your relationship during this important phase of life.

Many experts on marriage stress the need for each spouse to take the responsibility for personal problems, the need for a separate sense of identity—and the need for growth. The last is most important, says the Reverend John L. Thomas, a Jesuit sociologist. As he puts it, "What have you got to give to a relationship if you haven't grown?"

It's Her Turn Now

As women continue to enter and reenter the work force, more and more families are having to plan for not one but two retirements. Because a wife is typically several years younger than her husband and may begin and peak in her career later than he does, the two retirements often take place at different times. These circumstances may call for both major and minor role adjustments between husband and wife.

Take the case of Bill and June M. At fifty-eight, Bill, an executive with an electronics firm that was taken over in a merger, decided to accept a very generous early retirement package from the new owners. For the last few years, he'd felt burned out and discontented in his job. The offer provided a great opportunity to get out gracefully. Bill figured that he and June could sell the house and move into their vacation home in Florida, where he looked forward to golfing, sailing, and fishing.

Much to Bill's chagrin, June received his plans for their retirement with something less than enthusiasm. When their youngest child was in high school, June took a secretarial job with the local office of a national public relations firm. Her drive, enthusiasm, and ability soon won her a position as a junior account executive. And she loves it—the people, the work, the challenge, the travel, and the excitement.

June believes that the next few years are important to her career—not only will she become vested in the firm's pension plan but also she expects to be promoted to senior account executive. June let Bill know that she wasn't ready for retirement.

Once Bill realized that she meant what she said, he and June began serious discussions about their future. And they eventually came to an understanding. Bill agreed that they would stay put long enough for June to become vested and take a shot at a senior position. In the meantime, June would discreetly investigate possibilities for PR work in Florida, including the feasibility of starting her own business. She would begin making appropriate contacts now. After he retired, Bill would take over more of the household responsibilities and would also begin fixing up their home for when it came time to sell it.

Contrary to the prevalent stereotype, many middle-aged men are demonstrating flexibility and fair-mindedness in adjusting to their wife's midlife career aspirations.

Couples who have been through such experiences point out that the keys to a successful transition for husbands and wives are (1) ongoing communication and (2) respect for each other's rights and feelings. Major life decisions should not come as a surprise to either party. Let the other person know what you're thinking. Share your long-range goals with each other. Then both of you can plan ahead for the changes that will be necessary when the wife goes to work or continues working after her husband retires.

Experts advise that the people who are at risk in a situation like this are those husbands and wives who have never seen themselves as distinct individuals in their marriage. Sometimes, such a man feels lonely and adrift when his wife goes to work because he has become so dependent on her to meet his needs and plan his social life and free-time activities.

The situation calls for a period of adjustment. And it may take some time for that adjustment to come about. But once it does, the husband will see the opportunity in the situation: to do the things he really likes to do, to have more interesting topics to discuss with his wife when they're together, to develop friendships on his own rather than relying on her to arrange their social life, and to be relieved of some of the financial pressure now that she is bringing home a paycheck and building up her own retirement fund.

Single Living

Nearly half of all older Americans (age sixty-five and over) are either divorced or widowed or have never been married. Single persons preparing for a secure, independent, and rewarding retirement may face some problems, challenges, and situations that are quite different from those faced by couples preparing for retirement. But whether you live as a single person for most of your adult life or for only a certain phase of it, you are part of a generation of older single adults who have more options and resources available to them for achieving a satisfying retirement lifestyle than any previous generation.

Always Single

Most people who have never married have, over the years, developed a satisfying lifestyle, with varied activities and a network of friends. Although always-single persons may miss sharing some experiences with others, being alone does not mean being lonely. And they know from experience that they are capable of dealing with life situations either alone or with the help of family and friends.

As with couples, always-single adults would be well served by taking stock of their roles, relationships, and activities. Of particular importance to a retired single person is the support system of friends and family members. It is likely that these people will be crucial to your health and happiness in retirement. Take time now to reinforce and strengthen relationships with those special people in your life who know you well and have always been there for you.

If you are thinking about moving to a new location, investigate the new community thoroughly for clubs, organizations, and recreation centers that welcome and serve single people. Also find out whether you will be able to actively pursue your special interests and hobbies in the community. Doing so will provide the opportunity to meet people who share your interests and enthusiasm.

Divorced

Currently, 5.8 percent of men forty-five and over and 7.6 percent of women forty-five and over are divorced. Divorce in midlife, after many years of marriage, can be a painful and complicated matter, affecting almost every aspect of a person's life.

Finances

At midlife, a couple's financial worth is probably at its peak. Dividing property and other assets can be at best a trying experience, one with the potential for creating a great deal of acrimony. Divorced women often find that their standard of living drops dramatically after the divorce.

Family

What happens to the divorcing couple will have an effect on other family members, possibly provoking anxiety, anger, fear, and other negative feelings among children and aging parents.

Identity

A suddenly single person often finds that his or her social identity and family role are markedly changed. Friendships based on being part of a couple must be reassessed and re-established on another basis. Many such friendships disappear entirely. And perhaps for the first time, a newly single person finds he or she has lots of free time alone and may be at loose ends for a while. Those people who have made the effort to develop individual identities within their marriage rather than being totally dependent on their spouse will have an easier time making the transition to their new status because they will already have in place at least a partial network of friends, organizations, and activities.

Future Prospects

Women who divorce in midlife have fewer prospects for remarriage than men, since there are more midlife and older women than men. Men frequently marry women seven or eight years younger than themselves, while relationships between older women and younger men are still relatively rare.

After dealing with the emotional trauma of the divorce, newly single persons need to reassess their identities, their

support systems, and their activities and then accept the challenge of building a new life for themselves.

Support groups for separated and divorced persons can provide emotional support and valuable practical advice to newly single persons. To locate a support group, check with your local library or social services agency, ask your religious adviser or physician, or look in the telephone directory for listings and your newspaper for meeting announcements. You can obtain information about support groups from the National Self-Help Clearinghouse, 33 W. 42nd Street, Room 1222, New York, NY 10036.

Widowed

Planning for the death of a spouse should begin in midlife. For women, the chance of becoming widowed is far greater than for men. Fifty-one percent of women sixty-five and over are widows; only 14 percent of men in that age group are widowers. Women are widowed at an average age of fifty-six and face twenty or more years of being single, a state for which many of them are not prepared either financially or emotionally.

Planning for the death of a spouse should involve candid discussions about the financial and emotional resources that each partner would need in adjusting to life alone. Each partner should have a will, be acquainted with various advisers (lawyer, banker, financial planner), and know the whereabouts of valuables, securities, and important documents.

One cannot, of course, prepare to any great extent for the emotional shock and grief following the death of a loved one. But those who have made the effort over the years to develop a network of family and especially friends will find them a valuable source of comfort and assistance as they adjust to their new status.

Newly widowed men find loneliness a major problem because many of them have depended solely on their wives for close friendship and emotional support. After the wife's death, the widower has no one close to turn to. This may help explain why 52 percent of widowers remarry within eighteen months of the spouse's death, according to AARP's Widowed Persons Service. And this may reflect, in some cases, an attempt to escape from the problems of the now-single life and the work of coming to terms with themselves as individuals. Both these issues should be dealt with before contemplating marriage (see "Are You Ready to Remarry?" on page 50).

Various religious and service groups offer counseling and assistance to newly widowed persons. AARP sponsors the Widowed Persons Service (WPS). WPS volunteers, who themselves have been widowed, offer support to newly widowed persons through nearly 200 WPS programs nationwide. For information on a program in your community, write to the Widowed Persons Service, AARP, 1909 K Street, N.W., Washington, DC 20049.

Getting Back in Circulation

An older adult, single for the first time in many years, may well wonder how to "get back in circulation." You may feel some uncertainty and apprehension about what's appropriate and expected when it comes to dating and intimacy. Midlife adults "who've been through it" advise the newly single person to date on his or her own terms and not to worry about "what's in." Don't feel you have to do anything you're not comfortable with just because someone else expects it.

If you are newly single, you are reentering the "dating game" at a time when health and other concerns are causing the pendulum to swing back to a more conservative and cautious approach to dating and sexual intimacy among people of all ages. People are taking more time to get to know each other before "hopping into bed." So if you last dated in a less permissive time, you're not as out of touch as you may have thought.

OK. You're ready to meet other midlife single people. But how? You could go to singles' bars, clubs, dances, and parties; advertise in singles' publications; or sign up with a dating service, some of which have members make videotapes for prospective dates to review. All of these activities have worked for people, but they're not the answer for everyone.

More likely, your first step will be to find some new *friends*, both men and women, who don't know you as part of a couple and who share your interests and enthusiasm. Engage in various activities that you truly enjoy and meet people through them. You will then have a basis for establishing a friendship and possibly a more intimate relationship in time. Review the suggestions for the meaningful use of time in chapter 3. Get out; get involved. You will have worthwhile experiences and grow into a more interesting person who attracts other interesting people to you.

Remarriage in Midlife

Remarrying in midlife can provide the marriage partners with companionship, affection, and mutual security at a time in life when they are especially needed and their importance truly appreciated. But the following matters should not be overlooked: sex, money, and each other's children from previous marriages.

Sex can be an important aspect of a mid- or late-life marriage. Before you marry or remarry later in life, you and your prospective mate should discuss your expectations about sex. By talking this matter over beforehand, you may save yourselves possible embarrassment and disappointment after marriage.

Another problem some older persons may have to deal with in contemplation of remarriage is adult children who have difficulty accepting their parent's new relationship. The source of the problem may be a misplaced sense of loyalty to the other parent or the idea that older people should not be sex-

Are You Ready to Remarry?

1. Have you been widowed or divorced at least two years?
2. Have you built a successful and full life for yourself alone?
3. Are you happy with your life?
4. Have you known your potential spouse at least six months, and do you feel you know each other well?
5. Are you both willing to give up your present homes and make a new home together?
6. Will your joint incomes support you in the style to which you are both accustomed?
7. Are you both well-adjusted people?
8. Have you agreed on your hopes and dreams for the future and on a basic "life plan" for your years together?
9. Do your children, close friends, and families support your decision to marry?
10. Can you talk comfortably together about your previous mates without making comparisons?

If you answered no to even one question, try to resolve the issue before going ahead.

ually active. Often, however, these concerns may mask the real concern over assets and inheritance.

As unromantic as it is, there's a business side to marriage that should be addressed before the marriage takes place. Remarriage in midlife can be a very complex matter, involving, as we've mentioned, children from previous marriages but also one or more homes, investments and securities, and a large amount of personal property.

The prospective couple need to determine, beforehand, which assets will be placed in separate estates and which ones will be combined. The next step is to have the respective lawyers draw up a prenuptial agreement spelling out exactly who owns what going into the marriage. Such an agreement will eliminate questions about ownership and inheritance later on.

Lawyers who regularly draw up prenuptial agreements advise that the discussions preceding the formal agreement provide a valuable opportunity to raise important issues and to learn more about your future spouse's attitudes, values, and lifestyle. (See page 124 of chapter 8 for a list of items that should be included in a prenuptial agreement.)

Sex in the Middle Years

In midlife, many couples find it useful to take a new look at their sexual relationship. It's also a good time to reassess individual attitudes toward sex and to determine to what extent those attitudes are influenced by cultural stereotypes about the sexuality of mature adults. Fortunately, we are seeing major changes in the way society views midlife and older persons. Indications of these changes can be found in the movies, on television, and in magazine advertisements. Hollywood and Madison Avenue have discovered the attractive, sensual middle-aged man and woman.

According to Michael E. Metz, Ph.D., of the University of Minnesota's Program in Human Sexuality, "nothing helps enhance the vibrancy of a relationship as much as talking about one's sexual interests, feelings, desires, and ideas. Research consistently suggests that the ability to discuss these things, and to creatively decide how to sexually please each other at this time, are indispensable to sexual satisfaction."

Sexuality is an important part of our lives and our identities. Male, female, married or single—if you're healthy, you can enjoy sex all your life. In the middle years, men and women have an opportunity to grow in their relationship with each other. For this growth to occur, partners need to take the time to understand each other's thoughts and feelings about sexuality and about physical changes that typically occur as we grow older. Middle age can make some people vulnerable to rejection and to despair, which can result in a less-than-satisfying sex life. As author Eda LeShan has noted, a satisfying sex life demands "a happy connection between brains and genitals." Discuss your needs. Listen to each other. Try to empathize. Intimacy involves being genuinely moved by another's pain, fears, and pleasures. Through mutual support and renewed commitment to each other, couples can revitalize their relationship and enrich their sex life.

The Physiology of Midlife Sex

We slow down, it's true. We change. But the changes are gradual, and the body accommodates. The four stages of the sex act are excitement; plateau; orgasm; and postcoital relaxation, sometimes called resolution.

In the middle years, the excitement stage is shorter, less intense. But the plateau phase may be longer—bonus pleasure time. Orgasm is satisfying. Resolution may be comparatively short.

It takes longer to stimulate an older woman. But it all works out, since older men take longer to achieve an erection. Older men have longer refractory periods—there's a longer intermission between erections.

But love has pleasure deeper than orgasms. There need be no refractory time between caresses, comforting embraces, affectionate gazes, and moments of genuine caring. Sex researchers have found that for women of all ages, the key to satisfaction with a sexual relationship is how the partner behaves after the sex act. By caressing her and talking to her, he conveys the message that he cares for her as a person, which is important to the long-term success of the relationship.

According to Washington, D.C., psychiatrist E. James Lieberman, "Sex in the middle years is important in a different way than it is in youth.

"In the twenties," he says, "sexual excitement is created by physical stimuli. As time passes, these must be supported by an emotional component. Emotional intensity must compensate for the flagging biological component."

The popular notion is that the hottest bodies are the youngest and strongest. It may be true "in terms of certain kinds of heat," Lieberman says. But "in terms of lasting warmth," what counts is whether there is "a deepening emotional relationship."

The name of the sex game now is intimacy—the sharing of real feelings with another person.

About Men

Sex is a driving force in how a man views himself. Many men fear impotence as they grow older. When a middle-aged man partially, temporarily, or prematurely loses his ability to perform, his masculine identity may reel. As noted sex researcher William Masters put it, "I don't suppose the man who is impotent thinks about it more than fifty to one hundred times a day."

Impotence is *not* a natural part of the aging process. According to Dr. Robert Butler, noted gerontologist, impotence indicates "physical disease or disability and/or psychological problems that often can be successfully resolved with diagnosis and treatment." Until recently, an estimated 10 percent of all cases of impotence were considered to have a physiological basis; the vast majority were thought to stem from psychological problems. But now improved diagnostic techniques indicate that physiological impotence may be more prevalent, requiring medical intervention.

About Women

At midlife, many women become concerned about how menopause will affect them and their sexual relationships. Menopause is a decrease in the hormone level of the ovaries. It ends chances of having babies. It is normal. There are two common symptoms: hot flushes and the end of menstruation.

Many women feel little distress. Others suffer a long list of symptoms. Much depends on the health and emotional makeup of the particular woman. Symptoms may last a few months, or many years. To help, medicines and, if necessary, counseling are available.

Much concern has been expressed lately over estrogen replacement therapy for postmenopausal women to slow down the rate of bone loss and treat vaginal dryness and other estrogen-related problems. The concern centers on research demonstrating a link between uterine cancer and long-term estrogen use. While the matter is not resolved yet, research with various dosage levels and with estrogen combined with other hormones is making it possible for more women to take estrogen under the guidance of a physician.

Caught in the Middle

Middle age has been called the time of life when you're caught in the middle—caught between obligations to parents and responsibilities to children.

On one side, you get to know more than you may want to know about the generation gap. Your son tells you that your values are all wrong. He criticizes your "work ethic." But the criticism doesn't prevent him from allowing you to pay for the car he drives, the tennis racket he swings, and the Adidas shoes he wears.

The middle-ager pays bills, bills, bills. College costs soar. Many children reach the supposedly magical age of twenty-one—and still they are financially dependent. Parents, as they continue to pay bills, are asked to understand the agonies of the unemployed off-

spring who's "getting my head together." (Is he really searching for direction and his inner self? Or is he just too lazy to find a job?)

The young put a lot of pressure on parents—just at a time when parents may be wrestling with their own midlife crisis.

On the other side, an aging parent requires attention. You visit often. You telephone regularly. You send clippings, magazines, books, and family snapshots. But no matter how much you do, you sometimes wonder if you shouldn't be doing more.

What do you do? You have been told repeatedly that middle age is *your* time to live. Experts say you have a right to your life—and the time to live it is now. To your elderly parents, you will surely give respect, attention, and reassurances of love. But there is a difference between giving and overgiving, which doctors say is unhealthy.

Similarly, in your relations with your children, there is a balance between caring and overcaring. Caring is constructive.

Experts advise that you get rid of your guilt feelings. They cause trouble. They make you wonder if you've been a good parent.

One emotion that causes difficulties in parent-child relationships is anger. Your son decides to leave college during his senior year. Your daughter brings home a "friend" and takes his suitcase to her bedroom. The different attitudes, morals, even music—suddenly it's all too much.

You get angry. It's normal. Psychiatrists say you're entitled to your angry feelings. And it's okay to tell your nearly grown child you're angry. Often, it's easier to express feelings of love once the anger is out. There is one caveat: don't criticize a child's character or personality. Such criticism creates hostility. And too much anger can damage the relationship.

A mother of eight, unhappy at the alienation of her oldest son, a nineteen-year-old on drugs, recently confided, "I am not sure if there is a right—or a wrong—way to bring up children. But I know one thing: I deeply regret that we let anger go on to the point where it became the pattern of feelings and expressions between our son and us."

Suppose you are in an undeclared war with a teenager. It is not too late to turn things around so that you have a friendly relationship.

Authorities agree you may accomplish a lot simply by listening. You may not agree with what you hear. If your children reject your ideas, try to remember that you probably rejected your parents' ideas too. It may take all the maturity you can muster to listen. But it's crucial. You communicate respect when you listen to a teenager's fears and problems.

Understand as much as you can. Accept as much as you can. Through understanding and acceptance comes intimacy—the capacity to empathize with another's feelings. Young people, like adults, need intimacy. It leads to something hard to define but nonetheless real—communication. And that's the beginning of a friendly relationship.

You try to know—and nurture—your child. But there are limits beyond which it is unwise to go, experts say. Dr. Robert Butler, for instance, thinks it's a mistake to support grown children.

He says, "Parents who are now forty-five and over had children in an era when children were the center of the universe. . . .

"Many of these children are now spoiled, and parents have a hard time letting go. They're supporting that twenty-five-year-old rascal on a farm in Pennsylvania, when in my judgment they should have stopped long ago and started living a little. I'm amazed at the people who feel terribly responsible—and dreadfully depressed—because they regard themselves as failures as parents."

Guilt grips us when we deal with aging parents too. We shouldn't let it.

Growing numbers of midlife persons are taking partial or full responsibility for an elderly parent—not simply providing financial support but social and emotional support as well. Many situations concerning aging parents are summed up by author Eda LeShan: The parents "unconsciously want their middle-aged children to make them feel healthy and young again," she says. That makes them demanding—they make claims. They want "attention, constant reassurances of love."

"We . . . resent many of their claims on us," LeShan says, "and yet—making everything only more heartbreaking—there is great love and caring on both sides. We find ourselves caught in an agonizing web of human feelings and frailties, and we are profoundly frustrated by our helplessness. The most common and typical comment I've heard . . . has been 'I love them but I can't save them from old age and dying—and so I feel like a monster.'"

We owe aging parents tenderness, strength, and nurturing. We also owe it to them to help them maintain their independence and a sense of usefulness as long as possible. But experts say we do not owe them the sacrifice of our own lives.

It may be comforting when you're trying to work out problems for an aging parent to know you have company. In 1986, there were 29.2 million Americans over sixty-five and 45.1 million forty-five- to sixty-four-year-olds.

Many middle-agers feel guilty because they think they should ask parents to live with them—but they don't want to because of personality clashes. There's no need for guilt. Experts say there are many legitimate reasons for not wanting parents to live with you. A personality clash is one of them. National surveys show that the majority of American adults—young and old alike—think it's a bad idea for elderly parents and their children to live together. (If you are considering such an arrangement, try Positive Action 5 on this page.)

Planning works best. If possible, discuss with your parent how he or she would like things handled in the event of illness. What living arrangement would he or she prefer? Discuss expectations, finances, and insurance before a crisis occurs. Identify family, friends, and local organizations that can support you or share the responsibilities.

For specific advice on solving various problems, consult your local social services agency or the state or area Agency on Aging. They can tell you what services and facilities are available in your community. (Some of the more common housing options and community services geared toward elderly persons are described on pages 86–87 in chapter 6.)

Remember, you owe it to yourself to balance your needs and desires against those of others. If you have difficulty resolving a conflict between your needs and those of your elderly parents, seek counseling through your religious adviser, a counselor, or a family services agency in your community.

Caregiving: Helping An Aging Loved One by Jo Horne (Washington, D.C.: AARP; Glenview, Ill.: Scott, Foresman & Co., 1985) is a helpful guide for children of aging parents.

Positive Action 5

Living Together Again

For economic, health, or other reasons, it may one day seem sensible for you to consider having an elderly parent (or an adult child) move in with you. The questions below will help you consider various aspects of the situation before making a decision.

1. What is my current relationship with my elderly parent (adult child)?
2. Can my parent and I discuss a variety of subjects without becoming embarrassed or angry?
3. Who will have to give up what (for example, a bedroom) if my parent moves in with me?
4. Would everyone have some privacy?
5. Could we adjust to each other's way of life?
6. Will my parent be dependent on me for a social life?
7. Would I be "in control"?
8. Could we work out a way to share expenses?
9. Could we establish clear and fair "ground rules" regarding such matters as selecting TV programs, shopping, and preparing meals?
10. Could I avoid overprotecting my parent and vice versa? Could we relate to each other as adults?

Work in Retirement

At forty-eight, Larry S., a New York advertising executive, quits his lucrative, high-pressure job; moves with his wife and two teenaged children to a small town in Maine; and opens a convenience store.

After several years in retirement, Sara H., a sixty-seven-year-old former accountant, takes a part-time bookkeeping job with a home health care agency to supplement her retirement income.

A foreman at a truck assembly plant in the Midwest, Ken C. felt secure in his job even with production rollbacks. But a slumping economy prompted the owners to close the outdated, unprofitable plant. With no comparable jobs available in the area, Ken, at age fifty-two, enters the growing ranks of the displaced worker. He decides to undergo career testing and counseling before selecting a new line of work.

Margaret W., a fifty-five-year-old grandmother, served as a hospital volunteer for many years. When her husband died, she decided to become a professional nurse. It was something she always wanted to do and, besides, now she needed the money. Margaret received the required training and credentialing—graduating first in her class—and got her first paying job. Today, she teaches a course in practical nursing at the school she attended.

When Jack A., a plant electrician, reached fifty-seven, he jumped at the chance to take early retirement. He couldn't wait to get away from the time clock and the pressures and frustrations connected with his job. But after a couple months of having "all the time in the world" and nothing to do, Jack felt bored, restless, and out of touch. Knowing that he possessed a specialized body of knowledge and a knack for explaining it to others, he decided to market his skills to the local school district. Jack is now teaching an adult education course on home electrical repairs.

Today, many midlife people are looking for new ways to integrate work into a balanced and satisfying lifestyle. This generation of midlife workers is changing the way society perceives both older workers and older persons. As a member of this generation, you have the opportunity to help carve out new and exciting roles for yourself and other mature Americans.

As discussed in chapter 1, the definition of retirement is changing dramatically. "Retirement" once meant a slower pace, lots of leisure time, and withdrawal from life's mainstream. Today, retirement means opportunity—the opportunity to redesign your life, to rearrange your life to suit your current goals. Work is one aspect of their lives that many midlife and older people are choosing, for various reasons, to keep in some form rather than eliminate from their lives.

Let's look at some of the major factors that are causing people to reassess the role of work in their future.

A Period of Transition

The American economy is going through a transition period. Major shifts—called workquakes by some experts—are expected to hit the economy repeatedly over the next decade. These workquakes, in turn, are caused by the interaction of certain demographic, social, and economic forces unique in our history. For example:

- We are living longer lives—lives of health and vigor, not just added years.
- As a nation, Americans are aging. The Baby Bust generation is coming of age. There will be a 25 percent reduction in the number of sixteen- to twenty-four-year-olds between 1985 and 1995. This is predicted to result in severe labor shortages in many entry-level and technical jobs. The Baby Boom generation is reaching maturity. This is likely to cause a glut of middle-aged workers competing for promotions at middle management and higher levels.
- Unpredictable economic realities such as fluctuating inflation and changing government policies on Social Security, Medicare, and pensions are causing individuals to take greater responsibility for their long-term financial security.
- New technology is altering the nature of work. Much work today and tomorrow will be, at least to some extent, indifferent to age, thus enabling more people to extend their work lives. New technology will also affect the growth and location of employment and the relationship between work life and personal life.
- The number of working women will continue to increase. Because many women are in lower-paying positions and often do not qualify for retirement benefits, work in some form will play a significant role in their long-term financial planning.
- Stiff regional and international competition has already led to cutbacks in the labor force, plant closings, and growing numbers of displaced workers. And it is causing significant changes in the way American business is operating, with serious ramifications for workers of all ages. (See page 58.)

Depending on individual circumstances, this news is either good or bad. Certain of these factors will enable some workers who want to do so to extend their work life. On the other hand, certain of these factors will require some workers to extend their work life or modify it whether they want to or not. For growing numbers of people, work in some form will be a necessity throughout most of their adult life.

You may need to work in retirement to make ends meet. Or you may want to work because of the various psychological benefits that work can provide—status, structure to daily living, recognition, companionship, a sense of belonging, and usefulness. Whatever your reasons for extending or modifying your worklife in your middle or later years, the work you choose should support and enhance the other aspects of your life—your health, your relationships, your personal interests, and growth. Before you can find the right job for yourself, you need to know what you want out of life in general. Then you can begin to think creatively about how work will contribute to a satisfying and rewarding lifestyle during this important phase of your life.

The previous chapters in this book helped you define your lifestyle goals. This chapter will provide you with information and insights you can use in adapting to changes in the workplace and the economy and in finding satisfying work now or later on.

Challenges Facing the Older Worker

In addition to being healthy, active, well educated, and politically astute, older workers today have more to offer a potential employer. In fact, older workers excel in many of the qualities most highly valued by employers. Take a moment to review the list of qualities below. Awareness of these characteristics will boost your self-confidence and help you deal effectively with any negative stereotypes you may encounter as you conduct your midlife job hunt.

- *Stability.* Older workers stay on the job longer than younger workers. Employees ages fifty to sixty average fifteen years with the same company.
- *Productivity.* Research shows that older workers are as productive as younger workers in most jobs.
- *Reliability.* Older workers are rarely absent or tardy. Their attendance records are equal to or better than those of most other age groups.
- *Maturity.* Older workers bring years of experience and seasoned judgment to a job.
- *Good basic literacy skills.* Generally, older workers excel in basic math, spelling, writing, and problem-solving.
- *Conscientiousness.* Older workers give a full day's work for a full day's pay. They take pride in the quality of their work. And they are safety conscious. Research shows that job-related accidents are few among older employees.
- *Loyalty.* Older workers identify with the organization and feel a strong sense of responsibility to contribute to it.
- *Interpersonal skills.* Older workers have highly developed "people" skills. They know, through experience, how to cooperate, collaborate, and negotiate to get the job done.
- *Decision making and leadership.* Studies show that older managers are capable decision makers. The age of candidates for top-level positions has steadily increased over the last fifteen years.
- *Learning and memory.* Research shows that age-related declines in memory are slight and have little effect on job performance. People who use their learning skills throughout life maintain their ability to learn well into their later years.

Those are the *facts* about older workers. But what about the *perceptions* of older workers held by business and industry? An AARP survey of a random sample of 400 companies studied the attitudes that company executives have toward older employees. The executives rated older workers *higher* on the following characteristics:

- Good attendance and punctuality.
- Commitment to quality.
- Loyalty and dedication to the company.
- A great deal of practical, not just theoretical, knowledge.

- Solid experience in job and/ or industry.
- Solid, reliable performance record.
- Reliability in a crisis.
- Ability to get along with co-workers.
- Emotional stability.

The same executives rated older workers *lower* on these characteristics:

- Physical agility.
- Desire to get ahead.
- Good educational background.
- Ability to learn new skills quickly.
- Comfortable with new technology.

The perceptions of executives, whether right or wrong, have important implications for older workers who want to stay on the job. Since the early 1980s, the U.S. business climate has been characterized by a resurgence of competitiveness. This new business climate is being shaped by increased global competition. Companies are stripping themselves of redundant functions and layers of management so that they can respond more quickly to changing markets and economic conditions. And they are streamlining operations by introducing the latest technologies.

These changes are leading to new expectations of employees. Flexibility is replacing loyalty as the most desirable employee characteristic. Older workers who want to compete in the workplace must find ways to address the negative perceptions of their willingness to acquire new skills and adapt to new technologies.

Lifelong Learning

Experts predict that there will be an increasing mismatch between skills and jobs if government, business, and the workers themselves don't collectively and individually take preventive measures. The key to turning the situation around is education and training. The old progression from learning to earning to retirement no longer applies. Learning is becoming a lifelong process, vital to our work lives.

Changing our attitudes about the role of education, training, and retraining is one part of the answer. We must also begin to redefine ourselves—to get away from identifying ourselves with a particular job title. We need to see ourselves in a broader context, as workers possessing a configuration of attributes and skills that can be adapted to meet our own changing work needs and the changing needs of business and industry.

Good adult education courses today are designed with the needs and assets of the adult learner in mind. They are practical. They are experiential and interactive—you learn by doing and by sharing your experiences and know-how with others in the class, not merely by listening and reading. To compete effectively in the job market, seek out training opportunities offered by your employer and by educational institutions in your community.

Barriers and Deterrents to a Longer Work Life

For more than forty years, the policies of government and private industry have encouraged midlife people to leave the work force. These policies have been very successful. According to the General Accounting Office, the usual retirement age is now sixty-one for men. Major deterrents to a longer work life include these:

- Early retirement programs that are often too financially beneficial to refuse. (Unfortunately, they can leave many people prematurely cut off from work, without adequate financial and psychological preparation for what lies ahead.)
- Social Security earnings limitations (see page 59).
- Potential taxes on Social Security benefits for those with incomes above certain levels.
- Blatant and insidious forms of age discrimination in hiring, training, promotion, and retention. (As older workers become more informed about their rights, the number of age discrimination cases con-

tinues to increase. In 1981, the Equal Employment Opportunity Commission [EEOC] reported that 12,710 charges containing allegations of age discrimination had been filed in their offices. In 1986, EEOC reported 26,549 such cases—an increase of more than 100 percent in just six years.)

For more information on age discrimination and legal remedies that may be available to you, contact the nearest EEOC district office (see the listing on page 69 for a toll-free phone number). Also, see page 127 for ordering information for a free AARP booklet about your rights under the Age Discrimination in Employment Act (ADEA).

Recent actions indicate that government, if not industry, is reversing itself on the issue of a longer work life. Signs to this effect include the following:

- The 1986 amendments to the Age Discrimination in Employment Act, which remove the age-seventy limit for all employees forty and over who are protected by the law. The amendments make mandatory retirement at any age illegal for most private- and public-sector employees beginning January 1, 1987.
- The Ninety-ninth Congress also voted to require pension plans to accrue for workers age sixty-five and over, beginning for most plans in 1988, thus removing a major deterrent to work for many older workers.
- While Social Security earnings limitations are still a deterrent to work for many older persons, the 1983 amendments to the Social Security Act do promote a longer work life. They provide that the normal age for receiving retirement benefits will gradually rise from sixty-five to sixty-seven after the turn of the century. The credit for each year you delay collecting Social Security benefits past the normal retirement age is being increased gradually from 3 percent today to 8 percent in the year 2008.

At the same time, business and industry continue to encourage workers in their fifties to retire. This push for early retirement for workers with many productive years ahead of them indicates a growing need for career planning as part of retirement planning programs.

Does It Pay to Work in Retirement?

If you are already retired, or will be retiring soon, and are thinking about working in retirement, you have some financial realities to consider.

Changes in Social Security Benefits

If you work after beginning to receive Social Security benefits, you will lose some or all of your benefits if your income from work exceeds a certain annual exempt amount. For 1987, persons between ages sixty-two and sixty-four may earn $6,000 without losing benefits. People between sixty-five and sixty-nine may earn $8,160 without losing benefits. There is no earnings limit for people seventy and older.

If you earn more than the applicable exempt amount, you will lose one dollar in benefits for every two dollars earned above the limit. Your nonwork income such as insurance, pensions, interest, and dividends is not included in the calculation of earned income. In 1990, the

Women and Work

Women are expected to continue entering the labor force in increasing numbers. For a variety of reasons, some of which are listed below, work will play a significant role in the financial security of many women for most of their adult life.

- The personal income of women is far below that of men in the same age group. Women typically earn between 60 and 66 percent of what men earn.
- The jobs most frequently held by women are less likely to offer pension plans than the jobs held by men.
- Time out of the work force to rear children or care for elderly parents adds up to years lost by women when calculating their Social Security, pension, and other retirement benefits.
- Women who have been full-time homemakers and who are married to workers covered by pension plans often lose that protection if widowed or divorced.
- Only 20 percent of older women receive pension benefits other than Social Security either on their own work record or that of their husband.

rule changes: If you are sixty-five to sixty-nine, you will lose one dollar in benefits for every three dollars earned above the exempt amount.

Once you have started receiving Social Security benefits, if your income exceeds a certain amount, you may have to pay federal income taxes on a portion of your benefits. The current threshold amounts are $25,000 for individuals and $32,000 for couples filing joint returns. Ask your local Social Security office for the particulars, including how income is figured for this purpose.

Finally, if you continue to work once you have started receiving Social Security benefits, you will have to continue paying Social Security taxes on your earnings, as will your employer.

Potential Expenses

To find out your net income from work in retirement, you will have to scrutinize both the potential income and the potential expenses involved. From your expected income, subtract the cost of clothing, transportation, meals, and so on; income taxes; Social Security taxes; and any loss in Social Security benefits. Then balance your net income against the psychological benefits of working before you decide whether to work and how many hours to work in retirement. The worksheet on this page will help you sort out the financial issues involved in your decision to work.

Positive Action 6

Does It Pay to Work in Retirement?

A. Annual Social Security benefits*

at age 62: $ ______________

at age 63: $ ______________

at age 64: $ ______________

at age 65: $ ______________

B. How much can I earn from work each year before I start to lose some of my Social Security benefits? See the earnings limitations for 1987 listed on page 59 or call your local Social Security office. These figures are recalculated each year in the fall.

Earnings limitation: $ ______________

C. If I earn $ ______________, I will lose $______________ of my Social Security benefits.

D. Plus, I will pay $ ______________ in Social Security taxes.

E. That will leave me with $ ______________.

F. If my earnings from all sources push me into the bracket where my Social Security benefits will be subject to income taxes, how much more do I stand to lose?

Additional income loss: $ ______________

Does it pay to work?

* If you are age fifty-nine or older, your district Social Security office will estimate your monthly Social Security benefits if you provide the amount of your last year's earnings. Ask your local office for the name and number of someone to contact at your district Social Security office.

Accepting the Challenge

Older workers today are pioneers, building new roles for themselves and for those who will follow. They are educating business, government, and society at large about their abilities and their right to participate fully in the mainstream of life.

As an older worker, you can begin to accept that challenge and to enhance your own life by doing the following:

- Rethinking the role of work in your life today and in the future.

- Advocating for greater work options for yourself and for other people who are trying to integrate work into their lives in a more balanced and satisfying way.

- Taking advantage of every opportunity offered by your employer, your community, or any other source to update your skills and knowledge.

Your Work Options

Now or sometime in the future, you may want to change your work situation to get ahead financially, to find more challenge and fulfillment, or to achieve a better balance between work and the other important areas of your life. Essentially, you have three options, each with a number of variations:

1. Go to work for yourself, full-time or part-time, in the same field or in a new line of work.
2. Switch to a new full-time career that involves working for someone else.
3. Switch to one of the part-time work options that involve working for someone else.

Let's look at some of the issues involved in each of these choices.

A New Career—Working for Yourself or Someone Else

Many workers take early retirement to begin new careers. For them, retirement is just another career stage. People in other circumstances are also making the move to new careers. For example:

- The full-time homemaker who wants to parlay years of volunteer experience into paid employment.
- The burned-out or plateaued worker seeking new challenge and commitment.
- The displaced worker and the worker who believes that his or her job is threatened by technical obsolescence, mergers, takeovers, or competition.

The person contemplating a new career is well advised to go slowly and lay solid groundwork before taking the plunge. A thorough self-assessment is the first order of business. Ask yourself these questions: What can I do? What do I want to do? What do I want out of life at this point? How will this career change help me achieve my life goals? What preparation and training will I need? What will it cost, and how long will it take? How can I get some hands-on experience before quitting my current job? Who can I talk to who's already doing what I want to do? What are the long-term prospects for the field locally and worldwide? How vulnerable is the field to technological obsolescence and competition? What community and other resources are available to me?

Should you decide to seek professional counseling as to your skills and aptitudes for a new career, caution is in order. The field of career counseling is not subject to regulation. In addition, the plethora of titles and similar fields is often confusing. Also be wary of implied promises of jobs and job leads.

If you want the guidance of a career counselor to supplement your own self-assessment, know exactly what you want that person to do for you. You are looking for help in identifying your goals, assessing your skills and aptitudes, and thinking creatively about how your skills and aptitudes can be packaged to help you achieve your life and career goals.

For-profit career counseling firms may charge considerable fees for testing and counseling. It's worth your while to see if similar testing is available through local colleges, universities, state employment services, senior centers, or community or religious organizations. You might also ask your college placement office if it provides such services for alumni.

If you decide to go ahead with your plans for a new career, give yourself plenty of time. And remember that change of any kind involves loss before it leads to new gains. At midlife, you will be giving up a work role that you are competent in, one in which you have attained a certain identity and status. You will be taking on a new work role for which you do not have an established track record. You will have to prove yourself all over again. Your self-confidence may be shaken for a while until you get some experience and some successes under your belt. But you did it before, and you can do it again.

If your new career involves starting your own business, give even more thought to what it will take to succeed and whether you're willing to commit the necessary time, effort, and resources.

The basic ingredients for a successful business are these:

- A good idea. What do you have to offer? Is your product or service really needed?
- A good location—if you are starting a retail business.
- Good management skills. Can you keep accurate records, control costs, manage cash flow, market and distribute your product, and deal effectively with people?
- Money. How will you finance your new business? Should you finance it out of your reserves? For how long? What will you live on while you are building the business?
- A practical, well thought out business plan. You will need a detailed plan for the first three years of business, projecting sales (of products or services) and just how you will achieve those sales. You will also need a cash flow projection that forecasts expected income and expenses for each of those three years. Can you develop a realistic budget, analyze variances to it, and make adjustments on an ongoing basis?

Also take a hard look at your personal attributes. Many people, though creative and hardworking, are not cut out to head up their own business.

- Are you in good health, energetic, and hardworking? Can you put in twelve- to fifteen-hour days, including weekends, and forgo vacations for the first few years?
- Are you able to make good decisions quickly and stick to them?
- Are you willing to take responsibility for everything, including mistakes?
- Are you a risk taker?
- Are you calm, poised, and clearheaded in a crisis?
- Can you be objective about yourself, the business, and other people? Do you know your own limitations and how to compensate for them?
- Do you know when it's time to invest some money in professional advice and services?
- Can you work alone? Are you comfortable depending on yourself for success?
- Are you detail-oriented in addition to being able to see the big picture?
- Once you make it to the top, will the thrill be gone? Will complacency set in? Entrepreneurs cannot rest on their laurels. To remain competitive, a business must be in a constant state of change, requiring your ongoing attention.
- Do you have the support of those close to you—family and friends? Are you willing to let the people affected by your decision to start your own business participate in your plans?

Thorough research and preparation are crucial to your success. Begin by reading everything you can about the prospective business. Then talk to knowledgeable people who are

Resources for Entrepreneurs

SCORE (Service Corps of Retired Executives). Provides expert guidance and information to would-be entrepreneurs through a nationwide system of local chapters. Check your telephone directory or contact the national office: SCORE, 1129 20th Street, N.W., Suite 410, Washington, DC 20036. The toll-free number is 800-368-5855.

Small Business Administration (SBA), Office of Public Information, 1441 L Street, N.W., Washington, DC 20416. Provides free information on home-based businesses, franchising, and other business opportunities. Has loan programs and training programs. Call toll-free to be referred to the nearest district office: 800-368-5855.

International Franchise Association, 1350 New York Avenue, N.W., Suite 900, Washington, DC 20005. Write for a list of publications on franchising.

Chamber of commerce. Contact your local chamber of commerce for information on the local business climate.

Community colleges. Contact local colleges for career testing and counseling and for adult education courses on starting your own business, bookkeeping, marketing, and so on.

Reader's Guide to Periodical Literature and *The New York Times Index*. List recent articles on a wide variety of business-related topics.

Internal Revenue Service. The nearest office can provide publications on how small businesses are set up and taxed and on how to maintain accurate records for tax purposes.

doing what you think you want to do; observe their operations. (Find these people through friends and acquaintances, a local SCORE chapter [see page 62], the chamber of commerce, professional or trade associations, or the Yellow Pages.) Take courses to obtain necessary business skills. Many community colleges offer business courses through their adult education programs.

People usually succeed in a business in which they've had some experience. If the business you want to start represents a complete career change for you, moonlight for someone else to obtain valuable first-hand experience and to confirm for yourself that it's what you really want to do. Before starting to moonlight, however, consider these important factors:

- Your current employer's policy on moonlighting.
- The tax implications of the additional income.
- The physical, mental, and emotional strain on you and perhaps those close to you. (What changes will they be required to make to accommodate your plans? How do they feel about it? Try to get these people to "buy into" your plans; it'll make things easier for you and them in the long run.)

Once you decide to go into business for yourself, obtain expert professional advice. Its cost will be a worthwhile investment in your future. A tax accountant, a lawyer, and other professionals can save you time, effort, and legal hassles. They can help you analyze the business and draw up a business plan—even help you implement it. They can see that you comply with zoning and tax regulations, obtain appropriate insurance coverage, and comply with a variety of regulations if you plan to employ other people. If you will be working out of your home, they can help you sort through the regulations affecting home-based businesses of various kinds. (See "Resources for Entrepreneurs" on page 62 for a list of key resources for people starting their own businesses.)

Popular choices for self-employment include consulting, turning hobbies into businesses, selling of all kinds, franchising, and home-based businesses such as repair work, catering, accounting, and data and word processing. Each of these options has its own set of requirements and pitfalls to avoid. Books and articles have been written on each option. A good place to start researching your area of interest is your local library or bookstore.

Flexible Work Options

A survey of retirees found that one-third of them would prefer to be working. Surveys of older workers indicate that at least half of them would like to continue working past age sixty-five. One of the major deterrents to a person's extending his or her work life is the lack of part-time and flexible work options that would permit a better balance between work and other activities. But there are signs that business is becoming more receptive to these work options. Reasons for this change in attitude include the following:

- New technology, which makes some of these options more feasible and cost-effective.
- The desire to retain good workers who don't want to work full-time.
- A growing awareness of the demand for these options among workers.
- The desire to streamline the work force and supplement it with part-time workers during business upswings and peak periods.

Consider the work options described below. None of them is widespread yet. Workers who are interested in these options can help raise the level of awareness about them among their co-workers, supervisors, and employers.

Part-Time Employment

Part-time work permits greater flexibility in handling family responsibilities, physical limitations, and leisure activities. Some businesses rehire their retirees on a part-time basis, either directly or through job banks or employment agencies. Rehired workers help with problem situations, train new employees, and work during peak periods. If you are interested in working part-time after retiring and believe your job would lend itself to part-time work, begin discussing the possibility with your employer well in advance of your retirement date. Also contact small and medium-sized businesses in your area; they are more likely than large firms to hire part-time workers.

There's a negative side to part-time employment, which you should be aware of. For example, many union contracts and pension regulations restrict the hiring of part-time workers and the rehiring of retirees. Frequently, part-time workers receive a lower hourly rate than their full-time counterparts. They typically receive few fringe benefits, but there are exceptions. Some temporary agencies, for example, provide benefits such as health insurance and paid vacations and holidays to workers who have been on their roster for a defined length of time.

The benefits provided to part-time workers are usually related to the number of hours worked per week. The most frequently provided benefits, in order, are paid holidays, paid vacations, medical benefits for the worker, and medical benefits for the worker's dependents. The least frequently provided benefit is disability insurance.

Job Sharing

Job sharing, a form of part-time work, entails two workers splitting the hours, responsibilities, and benefits of one full-time job. Many employers, leery of extra costs and supervisory hassles, need to be apprised of the many benefits of job sharing: the worker's ability to maintain higher job performance over the fewer number of hours worked; less turnover; year-round job coverage; retention of valued employees who don't want to work full-time; reduced training costs; and the skills, experience, and ideas of two people for almost the price of one.

Temporary Work Through an Employment Agency

As mentioned, you may be able to obtain certain benefits by working through a temporary agency. Temporary work is also an excellent way to obtain training, update work skills, and preview different work environments.

Flexible Programs

A flexible program requires all workers to be on the job during specific core hours each day. Workers can arrange the rest of the work time to suit their personal needs and preferences—for example, to attend day classes or to care for a family member. Such programs often enable younger women and older workers to stay on the job because they allow these people to handle family obligations more easily.

"Flexiplace" Programs

Flexiplace programs enable people to work partly or entirely at home, frequently using computers to communicate with the office or plant (*telecommuting*). New technology is making this option more feasible for a growing number of jobs. Some jobs that are already being done via telecommuting include data and word processing, programming, production planning, inventory control, and marketing. Working at home can save money on work clothes, lunches, transportation, and parking. It can also reduce the stress of commuting to work. On the other hand, typical problems with flexiplace programs include lack of needed supervision, isolation, and, in some cases, lower pay and fewer benefits.

Because women form a large part of the home-based work force, women's groups are concerned not only about the lower pay and fewer benefits but also about fewer opportunities for training and advancement. Many also feel that women who are telecommuting may wind up doing two jobs at the same time: caring for family members and their paid work.

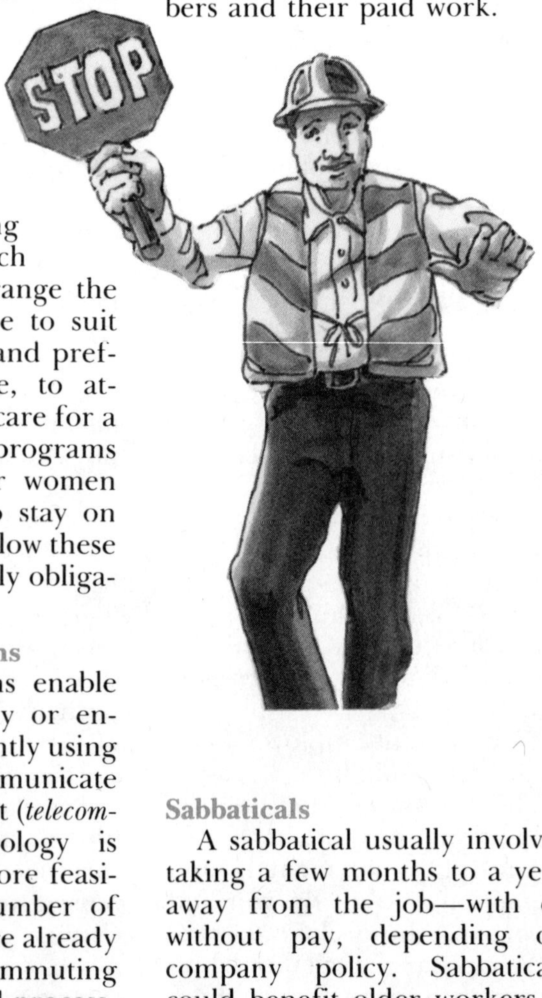

Sabbaticals

A sabbatical usually involves taking a few months to a year away from the job—with or without pay, depending on company policy. Sabbaticals could benefit older workers if they use the time to update their job skills and learn new skills, develop personal interests and volunteer activities in preparation for retirement, or obtain training and experience for a new career. Periodic sabbaticals could also decrease the possibility of burnout by giving long-term workers a welcome change of pace.

Phased Retirement

Going from full-time work to full-time retirement in the course of one day can be traumatic. Phased retirement programs offer a solution by gradually reducing a person's work hours over the course of a year or two. For example, one firm allows employees to work four days a week for one year, then three days a week for the second year, before taking full retirement. Program participants continue to receive full benefits. However, reduced earnings during the last two years of employment may cause a decrease in pension benefits.

Rehearsal for Retirement

Like phased retirement, rehearsal for retirement involves a reduction in work hours. But rehearsal for retirement also offers a trial retirement period of several months, after which the employee can choose to make the retirement permanent or return to work. Drawbacks to rehearsal retirement include the loss of pay and, perhaps, benefits during the trial period and problems for the company in finding a qualified temporary replacement for the worker.

Job Redesign

Organizations can redesign work tasks to reduce physical strain. Such changes can include introducing new technology, improving lighting and acoustics, permitting individually controlled assembly-line speeds, and other innovations to alleviate stress and strain and improve productivity. Job redesign can enable some older workers to extend their work life and can benefit younger workers as well.

Volunteer Work

Depending on your personal circumstances, volunteer work may be worth considering. Through well-chosen volunteer work, you can obtain valuable experience and develop skills and contacts that can lead to paid employment. It can also give you a firsthand look at various work environments.

More and more employers are giving serious consideration to volunteer experience when hiring for a position. In selecting volunteer work, identify the marketable skills you will be able to develop—for example, organizing, planning, fundraising, recruiting, lobbying, event planning, and promotion. Keep detailed records of your volunteer activities, including job descriptions, hours worked, levels of responsibility, accomplishments, and performance evaluations. Employment experts recommend that you include this information in the main section of your resume, rather than under a separate heading such as Personal Interests or Volunteer Activities.

Women who are planning to enter or reenter the work force should think about whether volunteer work might provide greater opportunities to gain relevant experience and skills than taking an entry-level job for pay.

Bartering

Another work-related option, bartering refers to trading your goods or services for those of someone else. It could mean giving your neighbor some homemade bread in exchange for waxing your car. Or it could mean exchanging landscaping services for car repair services. To facilitate these exchanges, nonprofit and for-profit bartering services have been set up in many communities.

A typical nonprofit bartering service keeps a list of its members' goods and services that are currently up for swap. It arranges one-to-one exchanges between people. In contrast, for-profit bartering services may charge a fairly high fee to join and take a percentage on every purchase. They do not match people up; rather, they issue credit cards or checks for members to use in making purchases. At the end of each month, members receive a statement listing checks written and received. Most members of for-profit groups are business owners who look on bartering as a way to obtain needed goods and services without making cash outlays.

The Internal Revenue Service looks closely for barter income. It can examine a barter service's books. So while you may not need to report the homemade bread, a more substantial exchange, such as landscaping for car repair, will have to be reported. Your tax consultant can give you specific advice on what's taxable and how values are figured.

Local barter services are listed in the Yellow Pages under headings such as Barter Exchanges, Social Service Organizations, or Trade Clearing Exchanges. Also check your local library or bookstore for publications on the fine art of bartering.

Conducting a Midlife Job Search

Perhaps it's been many years since you last had to sell yourself to a prospective employer. Where do you start? Finding the job you want and then getting hired requires diverse skills and knowledge. You must know—really know—what you have to offer; be able to match your abilities to the employer's needs; be able to package your product, that is, yourself, attractively and effectively; know how to reach the person who can hire you; and then be able to convince that person that you're the best choice for the job.

The steps outlined below will help you develop your own job search. For more detailed information on a particular aspect of a job search, such as interviewing or resume writing, consult the publications listed on page 127 or other resources available through your local library, bookstore, adult education center, state employment service, senior center, community college, or college placement service.

Your Self-Assessment

Self-assessment is the crucial first step and should not be skipped or glossed over on the assumption that you already know yourself and what you want. An honest midlife assessment can provide valuable information that will facilitate your search and increase your chances of success. A thorough self-assessment will include an analysis of the following areas:

Special Interests

A special interest is something you are naturally drawn to—something that you are willing to devote time, energy, and perhaps money to learning and pursuing. You probably think of your special interests as hobbies or leisure activities. Special interests are acquired through school, clubs and organizations, hobbies, sports, workshops, books, jobs, travel, volunteer work, other people, leisure-time activities, and contemplation. Some experts believe that your interests are better indicators of the kind of work you should be doing than your experience, skills, or education.

Work Values

Values are deeply rooted beliefs about what is good and what is important. They serve as our guides in making choices and as standards for judging ourselves and others. One person may value power, wealth, and creativity. Another person may value security, inner peace, and service. Values exert a strong influence on the fit between a person's personal life and work life. To achieve maximum job satisfaction, our work must reflect our deeply rooted values, or at least not conflict with them.

Work Environment

The kind of organization you work in; its size; its methods of communication and administration; its physical facilities; and its use of time, space, and equipment make up your work environment. People—supervisors, co-workers, staff, clients, and customers—are perhaps the most important aspect of the work environment for most of us. What work environment do you need to do your best work? To find out, identify those aspects of previous work environments that you want to avoid in your next job, anything from "no windows in office" to "dishonest supervisor." Once you know what you don't want, you can use those negative characteristics to develop a list of the positive characteristics you want on your next job. Use this list to evaluate potential work environments as you conduct your job search.

Earnings Requirements

What financial compensation do you need from your next job? By knowing how much money you need, you can (1) quickly eliminate job options that don't meet your requirements and (2) discuss and negotiate salary and benefits during a job interview. The forms on pages 92–94 in chapter 7 will help you estimate your income requirements now and in the future.

Skills

If asked, most of us can claim perhaps a half-dozen skills for ourselves. Yet some experts say that each of us actually possesses hundreds of skills. While skills are often developed through formal education and job training, many of our top skills are learned over the course of a lifetime through personal interests and hobbies, volunteer work, reading, sports, family responsibilities, self-study, and social activities.

There are three kinds of skills:

1. Action skills. What can you *do?* (I can drive a bus.)
2. Personal skills. What *are* you? (I am flexible.)
3. Work/leisure skills. What do you *know?* (I know basic bookkeeping principles and procedures.)

Your action skills can be readily transferred from one job to another without additional training. They are particularly important if you want to change careers.

Your personal skills determine how you get along with people and how you cope with circumstances and situations. They are your personality characteristics.

Work/leisure skills are the skills needed to perform a particular task. They are specific to a job and are usually mentioned in the job description.

Spend some time identifying and analyzing your skills. Knowing the true extent of your skills will open up a great number of job possibilities for you.

Depending on your specific work goal, you may want to arm yourself with a list of new accomplishments to include on your resume and to discuss during interviews. Update your skills. Learn how to operate a new piece of equipment. Learn about the new technology in your field. Take some classes. These efforts to enhance your skills will convey to a prospective employer that you are serious about the job and your work future.

Selecting Tentative Job Possibilities

Based on the information and insights gained in your self-assessment, you are now ready to identify a half-dozen or more job possibilities that call for your unique combination of skills, values, interests, and preferences. You can identify these jobs through library research and career counseling (see page 61) and by talking to people—friends, family, co-workers, and persons who are using the skills you want to use in your next job.

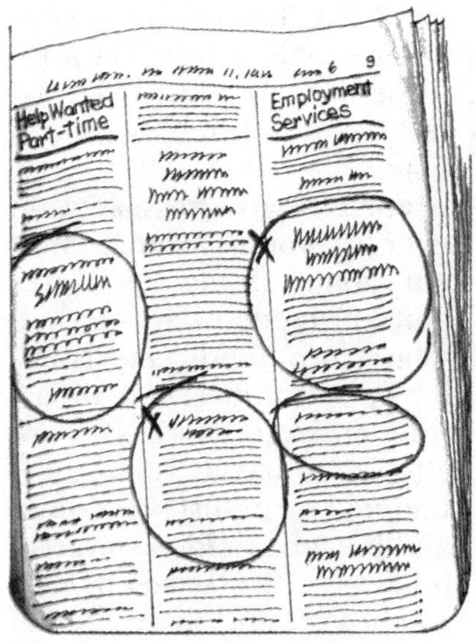

Gathering Information

The next step is to narrow down the number of job possibilities to your top two or three choices. To do this, you will need to do some research:

- *Read.* Most libraries have large collections of job-hunting materials, references, catalogs, directories, and information on economic and business trends.
- *Observe* workers and work environments, perhaps in the role of customer or client.
- *Talk to people*—people who are doing what you think you want to do and people who know about the organization or industry you are interested in. The best way to identify these people is through your library research and through your networks. Most people will be glad to talk to you for twenty to thirty minutes if you clearly and honestly state that you're not looking for a job, just information. Prepare three or four pertinent questions, things you couldn't find answers to in your library research. When the interview is over, ask for the names of other people to contact for information. Within a day or two, send a brief thank-you note.

  For each job possibility on your list, you will want to find out about duties, skills required, credentials needed, salary, promotion and training opportunities, major frustrations, major rewards, what a typical workday is like, how the field or industry is doing, and how the field or industry is likely to be affected by new technology and international competition.

Developing Your Networks and Support Groups

Networking is the process of utilizing the people you know to obtain job information and to meet other people who can help in your job search. As an older person, you probably belong to a variety of networks and can list scores of people you know through those networks. But don't limit yourself to the people you already know. The key to success is to continually expand your networks by having one person refer you or introduce you to other people.

Through different networks, you can obtain information about counseling and testing, training opportunities, skill development, contacts, referrals, job openings, resource materials, and practical advice. Kinds of networks include the following:

- State, county, and city government networks such as state employment services, volunteer action centers, the U.S. Civil Service Commission, and public libraries.
- Educational networks such as adult education programs, community colleges, vocational schools, and colleges and universities.
- Community and affiliation networks such as religious and civic organizations, professional and trade associations, and social and special interest clubs.
- Personal networks such as friends, relatives, friends of friends, and casual contacts (the grocer, the barber, the dry cleaner).
- Support groups ranging from structured organizations with formal programs, such as Forty Plus clubs, to small, informal groups of people who meet regularly to share experiences, leads, and contacts and to provide moral support.

To locate a support group near you, check with commu-

Special Employment Resources for Women Job Seekers

Catalyst, 250 Park Avenue South, New York, NY 10003. 212-777-8900. This national research and advisory organization helps corporations foster the career and leadership development of women. Write for a list of career counseling centers and a list of publications.

Displaced Homemakers Network, 1411 K Street, N.W., Suite 930, Washington, DC 20005. 202-628-6767. This organization serves as a clearinghouse for information on displaced homemakers. Contact the national office for referral to a local affiliate.

nity college placement offices, alumni associations, adult education centers, senior centers, state employment offices, and religious and fraternal organizations. If none exists, why not start one yourself?

Targeting the Specific Job You Want

Through your self-assessment and research, you've narrowed down your job possibilities to the top two or three choices. Now it's time to begin targeting those organizations that have positions like the one you want. You can identify those organizations using the same resources and research techniques you used in gathering information about your preliminary list of job possibilities. Explore both the traditional and hidden job markets. The traditional job market includes positions offered through newspaper classified ads, personnel departments, and employment agencies. But, according to many people, it's the hidden job market where the majority of non-entry level jobs are—by some estimates up to 80 percent of them. Tap positions found in this hidden market through business sections of newspapers; the local chamber of commerce; professional journals and trade news-

Employment Resources for the Older Job Seeker

Forty Plus Clubs. Located in a number of major cities, these nonprofit, self-help support groups assist unemployed professional, supervisory, and management personnel over age forty in finding employment. Check your local telephone directory for a club in your area.

Association of Part-Time Professionals, Flow General Building, 7655 Old Springhouse Road, McLean, VA 22102. 202-734-7975. A nonprofit membership organization, the association promotes part-time employment opportunities. Write for a brochure of services and a list of publications.

Equal Employment Opportunity Commission, 2401 E Street, N.W., Washington, DC 20507. The commission provides information and assistance regarding the rights of older workers under the Age Discrimination in Employment Act (ADEA). Call 800-USA-EEOC for recorded information and referral to the nearest district office.

Job Training Partnership Act. The act provides job training and some employment referrals to economically disadvantaged persons, displaced workers, and others who face significant employment barriers. Contact the governor's office for referral to the agency or department overseeing the program in your state.

Senior Community Service Employment Program (SCSEP). SCSEP trains economically disadvantaged persons age fifty-five and older and helps place them in permanent, unsubsidized jobs. The program has offices at more than 110 sites in thirty-three states and Puerto Rico. For more information, contact SCSEP, American Association of Retired Persons, 1909 K Street, N.W., Washington, DC 20049, or call 202-662-4800.

Senior Environmental Employment Program (SEE). This program taps the talents and experience of unemployed older workers to help meet the mandates of the Environmental Protection Agency (EPA). Program enrollees serve EPA in various technical areas, including hydrology, chemistry, engineering, and technical writing as well as provide administrative and clerical support. For more information, contact SEE, American Association of Retired Persons, 1909 K Street, N.W., Washington, DC 20049, or call 202-662-4800.

U.S. Civil Service Commission Federal Job Information Center. (Check your telephone directory for a local number.)

Also find out if job search assistance in your area is provided by employment agencies that specialize in placing older workers, senior centers, religious organizations, state employment services, community colleges, women's centers, local AARP chapters, and professional and trade associations.

papers; membership associations; religious, service, and community organizations; and word of mouth among your network of friends and acquaintances.

Once you've targeted the companies that have the job you want, stay abreast of developments in them. Make some contacts inside each organization. Find out about job turnover, company expansion plans, and new product lines—anything that may signal the creation of new positions.

You might consider taking a temporary job with the organization. If you're out of work, having a job of any kind will boost your self-confidence. Temporary jobs often lead to permanent jobs. As a temporary worker, you can show what you can do, make contacts, and check out the organization to make sure you want to work there permanently. You will be in a good position to hear about full-time job openings too.

Marketing Yourself

Marketing yourself means communicating your skills, experience, and know-how in a way that clearly conveys to a potential employer that you are the best person to help that individual solve his or her problems and achieve his or her goals. In marketing yourself, you use three modes of communication: written, verbal (what you say), and nonverbal (how you look and what you do).

Your written materials consist of your resume(s), cover letter(s), thank-you notes, and the manner in which you fill out job application forms. Besides knowing how to prepare these materials, you should know how and when to use them to your greatest advantage. Each one says something about you. The message should be positive, clear, and consistent. For specific suggestions on preparing your written materials, consult one of the books listed on page 127 or other resources available through your local library or bookstore. As you proceed in your job search, evaluate your written materials from time to time to assure yourself that they are working for you, not against you.

Preparing for the Job Interview

The purpose of your written materials is to get you a job interview. The interview process may involve one interview or a whole series of interviews with different people before a decision is reached. A good deal is riding on the first interview. You can prepare for it through (1) research and (2) practice.

Through your self-assessment (pages 61–62) and your research (pages 62–63), you will gather insights and information about yourself, the job, the organization, and the field that will be useful to you during a job interview. Knowing about the company's history and growth, products and services, position in the market place, and the like will help you ask pertinent questions and respond intelligently to the interviewer's questions.

Practice will improve your interview skills. Ask family, friends, or members of your job support group to help you prepare for an interview by asking you tough interview questions and critiquing your responses. Such practice will provide you with experience and confidence. Your local library or bookstore should have

A Former Systems Analyst, He Now Runs . . .
A little store with 100,000 workers

© Phil Schermeister

Stepping inside Frank and Helynn Carrier's little shop in San Jose, California, is like stepping into a friendly country store at the turn of the century—with a twist.

Familiar display cases of polished wood and glass proudly exhibit assorted merchandise, and an antique brass cash register stands ready to pop up the next sale. But here the similarity ends. The customer sees no keg of nails on the floor, no pickle barrel by the front door; instead, there is a puzzling variety of frames, extractors, and specialized clothing. The shelves hold no big glass canisters of lemon drops or horehound but rather jars of golden honey in neat rows.

What the Carriers own is a beekeeping-supplies store. And to listen to the bearded proprietor advise a fledgling apiarist, one would think he'd been in the business all his life. ("I wouldn't wear a felt hat. Bees tend to sting materials of animal origin much more quickly than vegetable materials like cotton or straw.") But actually, the former aerospace systems analyst opened his shop just a few years ago. While he'd been a hobbyist for more than twenty-five years, it one day occurred to him that bees could be the basis for a prospering business. What prompted him to look into the possibility was his lackluster aerospace career; although it paid well, he was bored with it. "I dreaded going to work each day," he confesses, "because it was sure to be the same as the day before."

Things got worse when he fell victim to the industry's early-1970s crunch. Frank was laid off, and Helynn was forced to shelve her interest in genealogy for an uninspiring secretarial job.

After three unemployed years, Frank went back into aerospace—but when that position, too, fell under the ax in just ten months, he decided a major career change was in order. "My beard was graying, and I realized there were lots of younger men who could be hired for less money." He pondered his future with considerable self-doubt.

Then Helynn made the all-important suggestion: "You've always enjoyed your bees so much. Why not try something with them?" The idea intrigued Frank, and he offered to teach beekeeping at a community college. Not only was the first class successful, but the students eagerly sought his assistance in setting up their own hobby.

Next, Frank wrote to his major supplier in Illinois and asked to be the company's Western representative. The supplier agreed. "We had no preplanned idea where the business would go," Helynn admits. "We made no cost analysis, no consumer surveys." The enterprise simply grew until it became obvious they should open a store.

Volume doubled in the second year and has since increased to 2,500 customers. Besides providing financial security, the beekeeping-supplies business has both drawn the Carriers closer together and given each the freedom to explore new interests. Frank wrote and Helynn helped edit two books—*Begin to Keep Bees* and *Keeping Bees: A Handbook for the Hobbyist Beekeeper*. Helynn also supplied the photos (after a free-lancer was frightened off when a bee flew up his nose), and her newly acquired skill earned her an award for macrophotography last year from the Western Apicultural Society.

Schoolchildren on field trips often troop into the store to touch the unusual items and gaze at the sample glass-covered beehive. Outdoors, they cautiously approach the well-spring of the little shop. There, in hives neatly lining a garden wall, are about 100,000 bees that may well be the most productive employees in the fabled Silicon Valley.

More important, they enable the Carriers to sleep better at night. If there's one thing these business owners will *never* have to worry about, it's shoplifting.

—*Joseph Fenwick*

publications about job interviews with lists of typical and tough interview questions.

The Job Interview

Before you say anything, your appearance and your body language are communicating information about you to the interviewer. What you wear; how you look; how you shake hands, walk, and sit; and how you make eye contact and listen will influence the interviewer's opinion. Don't underestimate the importance of appearances. Especially for older persons, having an attractive, professional, contemporary (though not faddish) appearance will help dispel negative stereotypes. Don't try to affect the style of a much younger person, but look smart, stylish, and up-to-date.

The interviewer's objective is to obtain answers to five basic questions: (1) Why do you want to work here? (2) What can you do for me? (3) Have you done this kind of work before? (4) Will you fit in here? (5) How much will hiring you cost me? Typically, these questions are not asked directly but underlie other questions and comments.

Listen carefully to the interviewer. And attempt to see the interview from his or her perspective. It will help you answer the questions clearly and concisely and to your best advantage. Don't criticize former employers, co-workers, or supervisors. Don't volunteer any negative information about yourself. Speak with confidence about your experience, skills, and work goals.

Negotiating Salary

Your research should tell you whether the salary range for a particular job is acceptable to you. But be realistic in assessing your earning capacity, especially if you are a displaced worker or are trying to switch to a new field. Look at the long-range prospects for the job. And assess the total compensation package. Benefits such as health insurance, sick leave, paid holidays, and pension plan could at least partially offset a cut in take-home pay.

Try to avoid discussing salary expectations until you have received a firm job offer. Don't specify a figure on your resume or cover letter. Write *negotiable* on the job application form. If you are asked your salary requirements in the first interview, say that salary is negotiable or that you expect to receive the going rate for the job. Indicate that you would like to know more about the job before discussing salary. If you must state a salary, mention a salary range based on your research of the job. If your range is in the ballpark and you get a job offer, you can make a case for receiving a salary near the top of the range given your skills and experience.

From empty nest to cast of thousands

Mary Gaffney recalls with pride the day she finally decided to do something about the empty-nest syndrome.

For years, the Mobile, Alabama, homemaker had followed the same uninspired routine to keep busy, devoting herself to a variety of activities that filled the long hours of the day but did little to enrich or add much excitement to her life.

Gaffney dropped her weekly bridge game, cut down on community work, and confronted the question of what she *really* wanted to do. Her instincts led her to become part of a little theater group, an idea that had always appealed to her.

The varied experience she gained there led to the next step—a job with a local children's television show, where she was put to work doing everything from making costumes to performing with a hand puppet. The television contacts eventually led to some work as a movie extra—and ultimately to her first real break.

Close Encounters of the Third Kind was filming in Alabama, and Gaffney decided to see if provincial fame was to be her only destiny. She contacted the production staff, offered her services, and to her surprise was hired instantly. She eventually became a casting assistant.

"The rest is hectic history," she says. Today Gaffney's a successful free-lance motion picture casting director whose credits include (besides *Close Encounters*) *Norma Rae* and *Breaking Away*. And you watched the Continental army she "recruited" defeat the British in CBS's highly rated eight-hour miniseries, George Washington.

—Sylvia Jeter Cooke

Chapter 6

Housing Choices

A few years before Fred W. planned to retire, he and his wife, Ann, decided it was time to assess their current housing situation and discuss where they should live in retirement.

After their children left home, Fred and Ann realized that their house had become "too big" in several ways. First, the cost of maintenance and property taxes would take a big bite out of their retirement income. Second, they had long planned to travel, but that would mean leaving their house and yard untended for months at a time. Third, their home was now their largest asset. Over time, the value had risen, while the mortgage balance had been reduced. Could the cash value in their home—their equity—be used? How much income could it produce if they sold their home and invested the proceeds?

Fred and Ann narrowed their choices to these possible courses:

- Remain in the same home.
- Remain in the same home but convert part of the house to an apartment and rent out the apartment.
- Sell their present home and rent or buy a smaller home of some kind.
- Rent out their present home and rent or buy a smaller home of some kind.

After examining the alternatives, Fred and Ann chose the one that was best for them. Because of their interest in travel, they sold their home and bought a condominium apartment in the same community. They invested money left over from the sale of their house to add to their retirement income. This plan gave them the kind of life they wanted. At home, they were among old friends and familiar surroundings. They were accustomed to the climate and enjoyed the change of seasons. When they felt the urge to leave on one of their extended trips, they simply turned the key in their apartment lock and took off.

Like Fred and Ann, most people decide to stay put in retirement; they choose to re-

main in the same home (80 percent) or, at least, in the same area (15 percent). Only 5 percent move to a new location either in retirement or in preparation for retirement.

Staying put or moving to different housing or a different area should be an active decision based on careful analysis, first of your current housing, neighborhood, and community and then of nearby housing alternatives or entirely new locations and the housing options available in them.

Your retirement housing and location should come as close as possible to satisfying four basic human needs:

- Health—a climate and housing suited to your physical condition.
- Economic security—enough money to afford your chosen lifestyle.
- Identity—a position or voice in the community.
- Friendship—a place where you already have friends or an opportunity to make new friends.

In addition, you will want to choose retirement housing that supports and enhances your chosen retirement lifestyle. And because early retirement and longer life expectancy often result in retirements lasting twenty, thirty, or more years, you will want your housing to be appropriate for both your early and later retirement years.

As you grow older, you may pass through three stages of functioning: active participation, slowdown, and dependency. In the middle years, you are still in the active stage; you're still working and able to care for yourself and your home. In the slowdown stage, you may no longer be working full-time, but you can still take care of yourself. At this stage, you may want to be close to public transportation and shopping facilities. The dependent stage covers that time when you might need regular medical care. Medical facilities should be nearby. Your home should be on one level in case you are in a wheelchair or need a walking aid. Most people think only of their current stage when selecting housing, but thinking ahead to the slowdown and the dependent stages of life is important as you make plans.

If you are married, it is important to choose a retirement home and area that suits both you and your spouse. Yet, your planning together should take into consideration the likelihood that one of you (usually the wife) will survive the other and may need to make new housing arrangements for the later years of life.

Finally, if, like most people, your housing is your biggest asset, it will figure prominently in helping you achieve your financial and estate planning goals. Decisions you make about housing today will have a major impact on both your financial resources and your range of options later in your retirement.

Chapters 1 through 5 of this book have helped you identify a tentative retirement lifestyle. In thinking about health and fitness, the roles you want to develop in retirement, meaningful use of time, and whether work of some kind will play a part in your retirement, you have begun to fit together many of the building blocks of your retirement lifestyle. You have already asked yourself these questions to define your lifestyle:

- How do I want to spend my time?
- What is important to me?
- How important to me are my current friends in everyday living? in times of stress?
- How might my lifestyle change if my spouse or companion is no longer with me?
- How important is entertaining—having friends and family visit?
- Will I want to go back to school or get a part-time job after I retire?
- Do I want to be where I am already known, or do I want to make a fresh start somewhere else?

- How much privacy, space, and security do I need to be comfortable?

Perhaps, like Fred and Ann, you plan to travel a good deal in retirement. It's likely, however, that you will be spending more time, not less, in your retirement home—all the more reason that the home be comfortable, secure, pleasant, and easy to maintain, as well as affordable—in both early and later retirement.

Retirees are not a homogeneous group of people. As with every other age group, they differ greatly as to background, lifestyle, education, needs, preferences, and expectations. Thus, the answer to the question, What retirement housing is best? is, It depends. Today, there are more housing options than ever before. Your task is to consider carefully each viable option in terms of your short- and long-term goals, keeping in mind the financial ramifications of each decision you make.

This chapter will help you do the following:

- Assess current and potential housing and locations based on your chosen retirement lifestyle, affordability, and your financial and estate planning goals.
- Consider ways to adapt current housing to suit your retirement lifestyle.
- Review ways to tap the equity in your home while still living there and to take advantage of government programs geared toward older homeowners.
- Evaluate the pros and cons of selling or renting your present home if you decide to move in retirement.
- Consider additional housing options suitable for some elderly and single retirees.

Assessing Your Present Home, Neighborhood, and Community

Take an objective look at your present home. Does it suit you today? Will it suit you in early retirement? in later retirement? Is the home energy efficient? Is it safe? Is the physical layout convenient? Will you be able to maintain the house and yard? pay the upkeep, taxes, and insurance? Or will fluctuating inflation and reduced income make your current home unaffordable at some point in your retirement?

Also take an objective look at the ability of your neighborhood and community to meet your current and future needs. Do most of your friends and family still live nearby? How important is your family in day-to-day living and in times of crisis? Are you satisfied with the cultural and recreational facilities available? What services does your community provide for older persons? Could you get a part-time job or go back to school if you wanted to? Do you have special health needs that can be met best where you are now or in a new area?

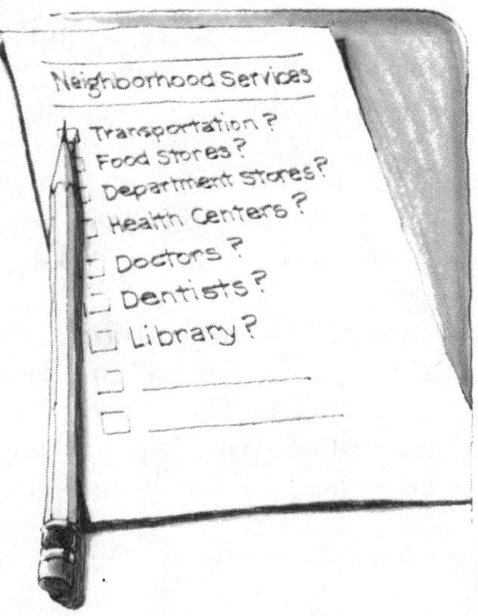

A good way to start your analysis of current housing, neighborhood, and community is to develop a list of reasons for staying (for example, the house is paid for, my best friend lives across the street) and a list of reasons for moving (the neighborhood isn't safe anymore, there's no public transportation nearby). The checklist on page 76 will help you identify things to look for in your analysis. Review it to determine which items are important to you. Add other items to the list.

If you are married or are planning to live with someone in retirement, it's a good idea for each of you to draw up your own lists—separately and honestly—and then compare them. Doing so will reveal each person's expectations and will highlight areas of difference that should be investigated, discussed, and negotiated.

If, after listing and evaluating the pros and cons of your current living situation, you are still on the fence about what to do, take another look at the financial implications of moving. Is your mortgage paid off or nearly so? Can you find comparable housing at the same or less cost? How do you feel about financing a new home in retirement? Would you prefer to have more of your monthly retirement income free to use for nonhousing needs? How does the money tied up in your housing figure into your long-range estate planning goals?

Neighborhood and Community Checklist

This checklist will help you make a thorough assessment of your current neighborhood and community and new locations you are considering.

Check the appropriate box as to whether each of the following is available:

Yes	No	
☐	☐	Affordable housing
☐	☐	Affordable utilities (heat, air conditioning, electricity, water)
☐	☐	Conveniently located shopping facilities (bank, hairdresser, dry cleaner, deli, and so on)
☐	☐	Adult education
☐	☐	Health care providers/hospitals/other medical services
☐	☐	Recreation (golf, tennis, swimming, and so on)
☐	☐	Clubs and social and other organizations of interest
☐	☐	Entertainment (movies, theater, opera, and so on)
☐	☐	Restaurants and fast-food places
☐	☐	Spectator sports (baseball, football, and so on)
☐	☐	Public transportation
☐	☐	Religious organization of interest
☐	☐	Compatible, pleasant, considerate neighbors
☐	☐	Adequate police and fire protection
☐	☐	Area essentially pollution-free (dust, soot, smoke, and so on)
☐	☐	Adequate garbage and trash removal

Yes	No	
☐	☐	Acceptable traffic pattern (not noisy, congested, or unsafe)
☐	☐	Adequate parking for self and guests
☐	☐	Good landscaping (attractive and to prevent erosion)
☐	☐	Reliable, drinkable water supply (good water pressure)
☐	☐	Acceptable climate year-round (What are the extremes of heat and cold? For how many days a year?)
☐	☐	Acceptance of pets (and enough space for them)
☐	☐	Acceptable population density (What are the growth projections for the area?)
☐	☐	Employment opportunities (appropriate part-time or full-time jobs)
☐	☐	Friends nearby
☐	☐	Family nearby (if not, convenient transportation available, for example, buses, trains, airport)

Other:

____

____

____

Finally, don't minimize the importance of your subjective feelings about your housing. They will likely play an important part in your decision making whether you realize it or not.

Modifications to Current Housing

If you want to stay in your present home but think that it will be too expensive to maintain on your retirement income, consider these options:

- Shut off rooms or entire floors to save on heat, air-conditioning, and upkeep costs.
- Consider renting rooms, if zoning laws permit and you feel you can forgo a certain amount of space and privacy.
- Turn part of the house into a rental apartment. Again, check zoning laws and weigh both the financial and psychological trade-offs—for example, the cost of remodeling versus expected income and tax deductions. How will renting part of your house affect any tax breaks you may be entitled to if you decide to sell the house some day (see the discussions about tax breaks on page 83)?

- Set up your own business in your home. Check zoning laws, other restrictions, and the tax ramifications before proceeding.
- Investigate home equity conversion plans and property tax relief programs that may be available to you (see page 78).

If you decide to stay in your present home, perhaps investing some time and money now in repairing and remodeling will make it more suitable, more comfortable, safer, and more manageable for your retirement years.

Thoroughly evaluate the major systems in your house (wiring, heating, plumbing) as well as items such as roofing, siding, and major appliances (include your car[s] in this evaluation because they're big-ticket items too). List each major system or item. Then ask yourself, How old is it now? How long will it probably last? Will it need to be repaired or replaced? What will it probably cost? When is the best time for me to repair or replace it and incur the expense?

Also consider the value and cost of adding safety features and doing remodeling that will make for more carefree, independent living in your later years. Check into local programs that help older homeowners maintain their homes. (AARP's free booklet *The Do-Able, Renewable Home: Making Your Home Fit Your Needs* lists a variety of minor and major modifications that will make your home safer and more livable. See page 126 for ordering information.)

A thorough evaluation of your current housing will include an assessment of its energy efficiency. Local utilities usually provide home energy audits at no cost or for a small fee. Take advantage of this service if you haven't already. According to the National Association of Home Builders, "Energy use in a typical new home can be cut by up to 50 percent by taking actions for which the owners would recoup their costs in six years." Many of these same actions can trim energy costs in older homes too. Energy-conserving actions range from installing a heat pump and storm windows to stopping drips from faucets and drawing the drapes at night.

Using the Equity in Your Home

Equity is the difference between what you owe on your house and its appraised value. If, for example, the appraised value of the house you bought ten years ago for $50,000 is now $125,000 and you owe $40,000 on it, your equity is $85,000.

Home equity conversion makes it possible for homeowners to increase their monthly cash resources by drawing on the equity in their home while continuing to live in it. It is important to remember, however, that home equity plans may not be available in all communities nor be in the best interests of all older homeowners. For example, one of the big risks with one kind of home equity conversion, the reverse mortgage, is that the homeowner will live longer than the term of the loan and will have to sell the house to repay the loan. Investigate and compare these plans carefully and obtain the advice of a lawyer or other appropriate professional.

Home Equity Conversion Loan Plans

Home equity conversion loan plans include reverse mortgages, adjustable rate reverse mortgages, and shared appreciation reverse mortgages. The loan is paid to the homeowner in monthly payments, with the amount determined by the amount of home equity borrowed against, the interest rate, and the length of the loan. The loan is repaid at a scheduled time or, under some arrangements, when the homeowner dies or sells the home. A variation on the reverse mortgage is a line of credit that the homeowner has access to based on the equity in the home. The amount used does not have to be repaid until the homeowner dies or sells the home.

Deferred Loan Plans

Deferred-payment loans differ from reverse mortgages in that the loan(s) are usually for some specific purpose such as payment of the real estate taxes, home repairs, or remodeling. Such loans are usually made by a public or private nonprofit organization. They typically carry a low interest rate. The loan is secured by a lien that must be satisfied to clear title for sale of the property.

Home Equity Conversion Sale Plans

In a sale/leaseback arrangement, the owner sells the property, often at slightly below the market rate, to an investor. The owner retains the right to live in the house for life as a renter. The investor pays the owner in monthly installments over an agreed-upon period and also covers the obligations of home ownership such as insurance, taxes, and repairs. Frequently, a deferred-payment annuity is purchased by the investor to provide the former owner with continued monthly income once the house has been paid off by the investor.

State Home Equity Conversion Plans

Currently, Connecticut and Rhode Island have state-sponsored reverse mortgage programs for older residents. Other states are considering such programs. Check with your state department of aging to see what is available in your state.

Homeowner Equity Accounts

Homeowner equity accounts are, in effect, a second mortgage in the form of a revolving line of credit. They are offered by brokerage houses, finance companies, and banks. These institutions will provide a line of credit up to 80 percent of the unmortgaged value of a home. The homeowner draws on the line of credit if and when he or she chooses by using a credit card or checks provided by the lender. Currently, most homeowner equity accounts have a variable interest rate, plus an origination fee and an annual service fee. Typically, there is no ceiling on how much the interest rate can rise from month to month or over the life of the loan.

In evaluating this option, experts advise that you calculate the long-term costs, limit your credit line to what you know you will need and use, keep track of the changes in the interest rate, and set and stick to an appropriate repayment schedule. Also, understand that the lender places a lien on your home at the time of the transaction.

Other Considerations

Depending on your circumstances, there may be other options for either saving money on your home or obtaining funds to meet specific needs. Consider these:

- Refinancing your house via a regular second mortgage.
- Obtaining an FHA Title I loan for emergency or other home repairs.
- Selling a portion of the lot your house sits on for development.
- Investigating state and local property tax relief programs for older persons, including homestead exemptions and circuit breaker, property tax deferral, and property tax freeze programs. *Homestead exemptions* exempt a certain amount of the assessed value of one's property from taxation. These are typically granted before the property tax bill is tallied. *Circuit breaker programs* are available in some states to both renters and homeowners and provide rebates to those whose income levels entitle them to relief from property tax or rental rates. *Property tax deferral programs* lend the homeowner money to pay property taxes and require repayment of the principal and interest at the time of the sale of the property or the owner's death. These programs usually place a lien on the home. *Property tax freeze programs* eliminate yearly increases in property taxes for older persons.

For information on programs provided by your state, write your state department of revenue. (AARP provides a series of brochures describing the state property tax relief programs in most states. The brochures explain who is eligible and how to apply. See page 126 for ordering information.)

CAUTION

In entering into an equity conversion plan or in taking out a home equity loan, caution is advisable. The only thing you have to lose is your home! Obtain sound legal and financial advice before proceeding.

AARP provides help with specific questions about equity conversion through its Home Equity Information Center. Write to the center care of AARP, 1909 K Street, N.W., Washington, DC 20049. Or contact the National Center for Home Equity Conversion, 110 East Main Street, Room 605, Madison, WI 53703. ■

Assessing Other Housing Options

In thinking about their retirement housing options, many preretirees think in terms of a smaller home requiring less maintenance and day-to-day care. If you are considering a move to smaller quarters, ask yourself these questions:

- Will my furniture and furnishings fit in the new house, or will I have to purchase new items? What will it cost?
- Will I have storage and display space for my lifetime of mementos and other items, or will I have to part with them? Can I?
- Will my spouse and/or roommate and I each have enough work space for favorite hobbies and interests and enough privacy? Will each of us have an area or room to call our own?
- Is the home small enough not to be a burden but large enough to comfortably accommodate long-term house guests (for example, grandchildren)?
- Will my pet(s) have enough room in the house and yard?

Many of the most popular retirement housing options available today are described below. Other options that may be suitable for some elderly or single retirees are described on pages 86–87.

Single-Family Homes

Single-family units include the familiar homestead in the general community or in a retirement community, a vacation or second home that eventually becomes a retirement home, a manufactured (mobile) home, or even a houseboat or recreational vehicle (RV).

New Home

When buying or building a new home, you probably will be concerned about getting a new mortgage. In shopping for a mortgage loan, decide in advance whether you want a fixed rate loan (the interest and monthly payments remain constant) or an adjustable rate loan (the interest and monthly payments can fluctuate). Find out what, if any, protections are built into an adjustable rate loan to protect you from a sharp upward swing in interest rates. Shop for a mortgage loan before you go house hunting. Find out how much of a loan you can obtain based on your down payment and income. Then you'll save time by shopping for a home in your price range.

To obtain a mortgage, income must be high enough to support monthly payments. Once retired, older persons sometimes have difficulty obtaining a mortgage.

Some financial advisers suggest that you try to get the largest possible mortgage on the property and not worry about paying it off before you retire. They believe that good housing is likely to continue to be a sound investment. You may, however, prefer the peace of mind of paying for your new home with cash from the sale of your current home or of obtaining a shorter-term mortgage with higher monthly payments.

The discussion on pages 83–84 will raise issues for you to consider in deciding which housing alternative is best for you. In addition, be sure to get expert legal, financial, and tax advice and to work out the financial implications of each course of action using paper, pencil, and calculator. Don't guess.

Vacation and Second Homes

Vacation homes that become full-time homes upon retirement are a popular option for some people. Reselling a second home can be difficult, however, and unless you've given a vacation home a thorough trial as a year-round residence, you can't be sure that you'll really want to live there permanently.

If you are planning to invest in a bit of land on which to build a second home, think the idea through carefully. Buying land can be risky and complicated. Many preretirees have been hooked into buying worthless land, either site unseen or after a brief trip to the area.

Manufactured, or Mobile, Homes

Manufactured homes offer an economical, low-maintenance housing alternative. Since 1976, federal construction standards require that units be stronger, safer, more energy-efficient, and better built than formerly.

Today, purchasers have a wide choice of sizes, floor plans, and furnishings—up to three bedrooms and two baths, plus options such as porches, patios, and carports.

In 1985, the average price (without land) for a single-width manufactured home was $17,800; for a multiwidth, it was $30,100. In 1986, the average price nationwide for a conventional single-family home was $111,700.

To purchase a manufactured home, you can get Federal Housing Authority (FHA)-insured loan with a low down payment or a Veterans Administration (VA)-guaranteed loan, which requires no down payment. Also look into a conventional real estate loan from a bank or credit union. In most cases (90 percent), however, dealers of manufactured homes arrange financing through chattel loans, which operate like car loans and typically have higher interest rates and shorter repayment periods. Since loan rates vary, shop around for the best deal. Before buying, ask about any warranties that come with the home.

About 60 percent of all manufactured homes are placed on individually owned sites, which allows the home to appreciate in value. Before buying a site, check local zoning laws and environmental restrictions. If you decide to move into a mobile home park, find out if there is an entrance fee, what the monthly rental fee is (fees range from $50 to $300), what is included in the rental fee (lot, utility hookups, recreational facilities, and so on), how often and how much the fee has increased over the years, and what the park's regulations and restrictions are concerning pets, guests, remodeling, and the like.

Be aware that manufactured housing may be more difficult to resell and may depreciate in value or appreciate more slowly than more conventional dwellings.

Multiple-Unit Housing

Multiple-unit housing includes duplexes, condominiums, cooperatives, rental apartments, and facilities available in retirement communities and continuing care retirement communities.

Duplexes

Consider buying a duplex, or two-family dwelling. You could live in one unit and rent the other for additional retirement income and certain tax deductions. But first, ask people who already do this about the financial aspects and other pros and cons of such an arrangement.

Condominiums and Cooperative Housing

If you want to live in a smaller place but prefer to own rather than rent, you might consider condominiums or cooperatives, which offer freedom from many outdoor maintenance chores. Units can be garden apartments, town houses, or high-rise apartments, either in new buildings or old buildings that have been converted.

The major difference between condominiums and cooperatives is the manner of ownership. With condominiums, each unit is owned individually, but there is joint ownership of common areas such as halls, lawns, and pools. Owners of cooperatives possess stock in a nonprofit corporation that owns all units and all common areas. A stockholder in a cooperative has the right to occupy a certain unit and has access to all communal property.

Each form of ownership is taxed differently. With cooperatives, the organization is responsible for all taxes. In a condominium, each owner is responsible for the taxes on a particular unit and a proportionate share of the common property. Further, mortgage obligations are held differently. Condo owners pay mortgages separately, while in a co-op, the organization is responsible for financing the entire project. In both cases, mortgage interest and real estate taxes are deductible. Finally, the owner of a co-op has one vote in the corporation, while a condo owner votes on a proportional basis, usually based on the size of his or her unit.

Generally, it is easier to sell a condominium than a cooperative because a condominium unit is clearly defined, and a lender can determine the value—and risk—of any loan. With a co-op, shares rather than real property are for sale.

When considering a particular condominium or a cooperative, watch for escalator clauses concerning the monthly maintenance fees, refund arrangements, restrictions on your personal life and rights, and restrictions regarding selling or bequeathing the property. Before signing any contract, have a lawyer review it.

If you are a tenant in a building that may be converted into a condominium, you will need to know your legal rights and obligations. State and local laws vary widely, but many give tenants the right of first refusal. And in some states, older persons are given certain protections, such as being able to retain their unit on a rental basis. Conversion can be a complex and emotional matter; tenants should organize and retain a lawyer or get other expert opinion to protect their rights.

Rental Apartments

Renting in retirement offers several advantages. You usually won't have to worry about maintenance, inside or outside.

And you have more freedom to take off for a period of time without worrying about leaving the apartment empty. But there are disadvantages too. If you are accustomed to a house and a yard, you may find an apartment too confining. Before signing a lease, read it carefully, and find out about the likelihood of rent increases, the possibility of condo conversion, the building security system, fire prevention, and escape facilities. Visit the prospective apartment at night and on weekends. Are the neighbors loud? Is the parking adequate? Is the area safe? Is there public transportation? shopping? open space? recreation? Also learn about any local rent control ordinances.

Retirement Communities

Retirement communities differ greatly as to type and cost of housing available and services and activities provided. A retirement community may be an entire subdivision of a town or one high-rise apartment building.

Most retirement communities provide a variety of recreational and social activities—among them golf, tennis, swimming, card games, cookouts, exercise classes, crafts, bingo, and dancing. And most communities require the resident to pay a monthly fee for maintenance and repair. Often, additional fees are charged for meals, if provided, and specific activities.

Weigh the pros and cons of a retirement community as you see them. One person considering a particular retirement community will be impressed by the many stimulating people and activities; the good social and recreational facilities; the carefree living free from yard work, snow shoveling, and major repairs; the many safety features of the dwellings; and what seems to be a good financial investment.

Another person looking at the very same community will be impressed, too, by the crowded conditions, high costs, seemingly endless regulations and restrictions, distance from an urban center, segregation from life's mainstream, and depressing atmosphere.

Investigate the community thoroughly. Talk to the staff, the managers, the residents and their families, and local businesses. Ask yourself, Will the retirement community suit my lifestyle, my temperament, and my pocketbook?

Life-Care, or Continuing-Care, Retirement Communities

Life-care retirement communities are frequently sponsored by nonprofit religious or fraternal organizations. Others are commercial enterprises.

Housing in a life-care community may be houses or cottages, apartments, or furnished rooms, plus an affiliated nursing home. Life-care communities typically provide more personal care than other retirement communities and offer various levels of medical care for life. Residents usually live independently in their own units until they need help in daily living or require nursing or medical care.

Entrance fees for life-care facilities may range from $20,000 to $300,000, with most facilities also charging monthly fees of from $650 to $2,500, which may increase over time. Unless one is wealthy, it may be hard to raise this amount of money. Many homeowners do so by selling their house and using the proceeds for the entrance fee. The entrance, or endowment, fee is essentially an insurance policy. It guarantees shelter and services, including health care services, for as long as the resident lives in the community.

Because many life-care communities have long waiting lists, an interested person should apply as soon as possible. But first, investigate the place thoroughly. Visit it often. Talk to staff and residents and their families. Check the buildings and the grounds for upkeep and safety features. Also check on the facility's financial stability and the reputation of the management. Be sure you understand the financial and legal arrangements before signing any papers. Have the documents checked by your lawyer. Find out about trial periods, refund arrangements, entrance fees and requirements, your rights and restrictions as a resident, services and activities provided, the ability of the facility to adapt to your changing needs, and the extent to which the residents have a say in how the facility is operated.

The American Association of Homes for the Aging publishes an annual *Directory of Members,* which provides state listings of life-care communities. Its cost to members and retirees is six dollars; to others, twelve dollars. Write to the association at 1129 20th Street, N.W., Washington, DC 20036. Also see the listing for the *National Continuing Care Directory* on page 127.

Should You Sell or Rent Out Your Present Home?

If your retirement housing-lifestyle analysis convinces you that you should move, it will pay to take your time and evaluate the short- and long-term financial ramifications of each of several alternatives. If you move, your basic options are these:

- Sell your present home and buy another home of equal or greater value.
- Sell your present home and buy a more appropriate retirement home. Pay cash and invest any money that's left from the sale of your present home.
- Sell your present home and buy a more appropriate retirement home. Finance the purchase of the new home. Use some of the money from the sale of your home for the down payment and invest the rest.
- Sell your present home, rent a more appropriate house or apartment, and invest the cash from the sale.
- Rent your present home to others and buy a more appropriate retirement home.
- Rent your present home to others and rent a more appropriate retirement home.

Let's look at some of the key issues involved in determining which option is the best one for you, both psychologically and financially.

Consider the Tax Breaks

If you decide to sell your family home outright, be aware of two important tax matters. You can sell your home without being taxed on the profit from the sale if you buy or build and occupy a new house within two years before or after the sale of your old house, and if the price you pay to buy or build your new house is at least as much as you were paid for the old one. If you are a homeowner age fifty-five or older, you may be eligible for another tax break. If you have used your home as your principal residence for three of the five years preceding the sale, you have the once-in-a-lifetime right to declare tax-free up to $125,000 of appreciation gained on the house. If you reinvest the proceeds in another house and postpone payment of taxes, you can claim this exclusion at a later date.

There are many intricacies to this tax break. For example, if you marry someone who has already used the privilege, you can't. Check with a qualified tax consultant for the details.

Some Pros and Cons of Selling versus Renting Out Your Present Home

To size up the advantages and disadvantages of selling versus renting, follow these steps and fill out the form on this page:

1. Determine how much it costs you to live in your present home. Add up the mortgage payments, if any; property taxes; insurance; utility bills;

Positive Action 8

Selling versus Renting Out Your Present Home: What Are the Numbers?

Present Home

Mortgage payment ________ × 12 = $ ____________

Property taxes ____________

Property insurance ____________

Maintenance and repairs ____________

Electricity ____________ × 12 = ____________

Gas or fuel oil ____________ × 12 = ____________

Other Costs ____________ ____________

Total Carrying Costs $ ____________

If You Rent It Out

INCOME
Monthly rental

$ ____________ × 11 = $ ____________

(Use eleven months to allow for tenant changes.)

EXPENSES
Mortgage payments $ ____________

Property taxes ____________

Maintenance and repairs ____________

Liability insurance ____________

Management fee or collection expenses ____________

Other Costs ____________ ____________

Total Costs $ ____________

If You Sell

Estimated selling price $ ____________

Commission ____________

Miscellaneous costs ____________

Mortgage ____________

Potential taxes ____________

Other Costs ____________ ____________

Total Costs $ ____________

Net Benefit (Selling price minus costs) $ ____________

and maintenance and repair costs.

2. Estimate the price you might get for your house if you sell it. At this point, a good guess will do, based on prices that similar houses have been bringing in the neighborhood.

3. Estimate how much rental income your home might bring in if you rent it out. Again, this can be based on rents being charged for similar homes in your area, or ask a real estate broker for an estimate. In figuring your return, however, consider that the property may be vacant at times during a change of tenants; and, as owner, you will still be responsible for taxes, mortgage payments, insurance, maintenance, and management costs.

If you consider renting out your home, remember that your cash profit, if any, may benefit from certain tax considerations such as depreciation and costs of repairs. Also, in some cases, it pays to rent out property even though you lose cash each month. The profit here comes from tax advantages plus the rising value of the house.

Remember, however, that if you convert your home to rental property, you may not be able to take full advantage of the tax breaks described under the heading "Consider the Tax Breaks," on page 83, if you decide to sell it at a later time.

4. If you hope to buy or build a new home, estimate the cost of the down payment, the closing costs, monthly mortgage payments, real estate taxes, any special assessments, maintenance and repairs, insurance, utilities, trash removal, decorating, furnishing, and landscaping. If you buy into a condo, co-op, or retirement community, figure in any monthly fees. If you are interested in a particular housing development, you can get figures from the developer or the manager.

5. Estimate what it would cost you to live in an apartment or a smaller rented house. You can get rent quotations from real estate brokers or apartment managers.

These calculations should help you compare the financial advantages and disadvantages of the basic courses open to you. Your figures might show that becoming a landlord instead of selling your home will be your most profitable course. But this, too, has its pros and cons. On the favorable side, you will continue your investment in property that may gain in value (and keep any sentimental attachment to it). You will be able to deduct management fees, depreciation, property taxes, and other costs on your income tax. But you will also pay taxes on additional income, if any. On the risk side, if you buy another house to live in, you may find yourself carrying two mortgages. There may be times when the old house isn't rented. And the neighborhood and value of the house might decline. Furthermore, do you really want to become a landlord, or would you feel that it interfered too much with your other retirement plans?

If you decide to relocate to a new area, renting out your current home and renting a home in the new area for a year or two might be the safest and surest method of trying out the new location without making a large financial commitment that would be difficult to get out of should you decide to move back home or somewhere else.

No single decision is best for all people. In reaching the right choice for you, ask yourself, Which option (a) is most suitable to my retirement lifestyle, (b) am I most comfortable with, (c) is the best deal for me financially, and (d) fits best with my long-term estate planning goals?

Relocating to a New Area

Selecting a new location will require even more time, effort, careful research, and discussion than assessing your current housing and nearby alternatives to it. Your goal is to find an area that will provide you with the lifestyle and environment you want at a price you can afford, now and later.

Again, the best way to get started is to ask yourself some key questions:

- What will I gain and lose by moving?
- What environment do I think would appeal most to me? Why?

- What kind of housing do I think would be most appropriate for me in that new environment?

The items on the Neighborhood and Community Checklist (page 76) can be employed to evaluate potential retirement areas and the housing options available in each one.

Let's look at several key issues that people often do not research well enough before making their decision to relocate.

Your Support System

In chapter 4, "Midlife Roles and Relationships," you identified your social support system of family, friends, acquaintances, and community organizations. You also identified those roles that you want to develop in retirement. Will you be able to follow through on those plans in a new area? For example, perhaps you want to develop your role as grandparent in retirement but for various reasons you have decided not to relocate near your grown children. How can you express the nurturing role of grandparent in your new area? Before moving, see what kinds of intergenerational volunteer programs exist in your new location. Will they fill the bill for you? And will your retirement housing accommodate long-term house guests such as your grandchildren? Does the new area offer activities that you would enjoy sharing with your grandchildren when they visit (for example, a zoo, movie theaters, a local baseball team, a fishing hole)?

If you have lived in one place for many years, your identity is tightly interwoven with that community. You are known to people. You have a place there.

Are you able to leave that security and establish a new identity on new terms with new people if you relocate?

On the other hand, your close family and friends may have already moved away, your present neighborhood may be changing for the worse, or the climate may be bad for your health, and you are looking forward to making a fresh start somewhere else.

If you don't know anyone in the area you are considering for your retirement home, experts and retirees recommend that you look for some people who are similar to you in background and interest. This will make it easier for you to meet people and develop new friends.

The Costs of Living

If you're looking for an area with lower living costs, you'll need to do some research beyond comparing real estate prices. Be sure to check out the costs of items such as food, gasoline, car repairs, utilities, and any hobbies or interests you plan to pursue in retirement. Find out whether the state or community provides relief programs on things such as income and property taxes. (See ordering information on page 126 for AARP's *Your Retirement State Tax Guide.*) Does the community make additional discounts for items such as public transportation, adult education classes, and movies?

Subscribe to a newspaper in the town or city you are thinking of moving to. It's a good way to obtain information on taxes, business activities, employment opportunities, and prices for everything from pizza to real estate. Look for items that might give you a feel for the community: social activities, crime rate, major events, recreation, and entertainment. Also ask your local librarian for help in finding out if prices in the new location are rising faster than in the nation as a whole.

High-Quality Health Care

Many younger retirees overlook the need to plan ahead for the long-term health care that may be needed as they grow older. Find out what's available now and what's in the planning stages. Obtain information on the local hospital(s), such as the accreditation status, the percentage of medical staff that is board certified, and the hospital's bed occupancy rate (a rate below 70 percent may indicate financial problems that in turn may result in lower standards of care). Ask your family physician for help in assessing the new location's ability to meet your future health care needs.

Climate

If you're looking for a location with a better climate, it's a good idea to know for sure just what you can expect in your target area year-round. Every part of the country has both agreeable and disagreeable weather at times. Research the climate and living conditions thoroughly by visiting the area long enough to experience the whole range of weather—or better yet, by making a trial run at living there.

Myths abound about the relative health-giving qualities of various climates. The Southwest, southern California, Florida, and the Gulf Coast have been touted as places for the relief of arthritis, respiratory ailments, and heart disease. Yet all of these areas experience wide climatic variations within their boundaries. So before you decide to move for health reasons, check with your doctor and do some extensive research.

Other Considerations

As indicated on the checklist on page 76, you will also want to evaluate the potential retirement locations for affordable recreational, educational, and entertainment opportunities. Is the radio and television reception good in the area? What about the local public transportation and bus, train, and airport facilities? Verify that various consumer services are also provided at affordable prices, for example, groceries, shoe repair, and dry cleaning. Find out about both the current and the projected crime rate in the area and the quality of police and fire protection. What kinds of emergency medical services does the area support? What are the long-term growth projections for the area, and what do they mean to you personally and financially?

Finally, how does the area make you feel? Good? Healthy? Energized? Peaceful? Relaxed? Do the style and pace of living appeal to you? If so, the area could contribute significantly to your long-term health and happiness in retirement.

More Housing Options for Single or Elderly Retirees

At some point, it may be necessary for you to help an older relative find appropriate housing—or to find it for yourself. If so, the information provided below will prove useful in selecting the most suitable option.

The key factors to consider in evaluating these options are (a) the ability of the person to stay as independent as possible for as long as possible, (b) the nearness of family and friends, and (c) the availability of good medical care and other necessary services.

Staying at Home

Depending on individual circumstances, support options that may enable people to remain in their own homes include the following:

- *Renting out rooms or an apartment.* This can be done to generate income or in exchange for needed services such as shopping, cooking, yard work, and transportation.
- *Equity conversion and property tax relief programs* (see the discussion on pages 77–78).
- *Homemaking services.* These can include light housekeeping, laundry, food shopping, meal preparation, and personal care.
- *Nutrition programs.* These can offer home-delivered meals and nutrition sites, which provide meals at a central location.
- *Telephone reassurance programs, friendly visiting programs, and emergency response programs.*
- *Home maintenance and repair programs.* Chores and repairs are done by volunteers who frequently are retired plumbers, electricians, carpenters, and so on.

- *Home adaptation programs.* Minor and major modifications can help compensate for diminishing strength, eyesight, hearing, mobility, and dexterity. (On page 126 see the ordering information for AARP's free booklet *The Do-Able, Renewable Home.*)
- *Home health care services.* These may involve regular home visits by a nurse, therapist, nutritionist, or other health care provider.

- *Homesharing.* The older person shares the entire home with one or more people who are not related (check the zoning laws).
- *Federal programs.* The Department of Housing and Urban Development (HUD) provides some assistance to low- and moderate-income older homeowners and renters. Contact your HUD regional or field office for current information about these programs.

New Housing Arrangements

One way to be near your elderly relative, while preserving the person's independence, is to build an *accessory apartment.* An accessory apartment is an independent living unit added on to or carved out of a single-family house. Zoning regulations generally are strict regarding such apartments, but in some communities the restrictions are being relaxed.

Another possibility is *ECHO housing.* The acronym stands for Elder Cottage Housing Opportunity. ECHO is a small, free-standing, energy-efficient, barrier-free housing unit that is installed adjacent to an existing single-family home. ECHO units provide comfortable, efficient housing for older relatives, and their proximity to the main house encourages day-to-day support that benefits both households. When no longer needed, the ECHO unit can be easily removed.

Completely equipped and installed, the estimated cost of an ECHO unit is about $18,000. In some areas, nonprofit organizations buy and then rent these units to those who need them. ECHO housing is subject to strict zoning laws.

Having an elderly relative under the same roof may create tension, but help can be obtained from various state and local organizations. Thousands of *senior centers* across the country provide a wide variety of recreational, legal, financial, educational, and counseling services. And there are a growing number of *adult day-care centers* in the United States. These facilities provide more comprehensive programs than do senior centers, including health assessment and care, social activities, and, often, at least one meal during the day. *Respite centers* care for elderly persons when their families go on vacation or when they need some assistance while recuperating after a hospital stay.

Perhaps your elderly relative could participate in *shared housing* by having someone move into his or her home or by moving into someone else's home. About seventy-five nonprofit agencies nationwide match homeowners with home-seekers. Before making such a move, the individuals involved should honestly discuss their needs, preferences, and expectations. Here, too, zoning laws must be checked. For more information on this housing option, write to the National Shared Housing Resource Center, 6344 Greene Street, Philadelphia, PA 19144.

Supportive Housing

Board and care homes are usually privately operated facilities that provide a room, meals, and some personal care services such as help with bathing, dressing, and taking medication. No health care is provided.

Congregate housing facilities traditionally have been operated by government agencies or nonprofit groups but now are operated increasingly by for-profit sponsors. They provide room, meals in a central dining room, transportation, and social and recreational programs. The services of health and social welfare professionals, housekeepers, and personal assistants may be available.

Life-care, or continuing-care, retirement communities offer lifetime housing and a range of health care, social, and other services. They emphasize independent living in apartments, rooms, or individual cottages for as long as possible. Frequently, substantial one-time entry payments are required in addition to monthly charges. Nursing facilities typically are provided also. (See the discussion on page 82.)

Nursing home care is for people who are chronically ill or are recovering from an acute illness and who need extended care but not hospitalization. Level of care ranges from twenty-four-hour skilled nursing care to custodial care for people who need assistance with personal care but who don't need health care services.

To find out which of these options are available in your area, contact your city or county social services agency or your Area Agency on Aging. *Homesharing and Other Lifestyle Options* by Jo Horne with Leo Baldwin (Washington, D.C.: AARP; Glenview, Ill.: Scott, Foresman & Co., 1987) is an excellent book on this topic. AARP also publishes a number of helpful booklets describing these and other housing options for older Americans in greater depth. (See pages 126–127 for titles and ordering information.)

Charting Your Financial Future

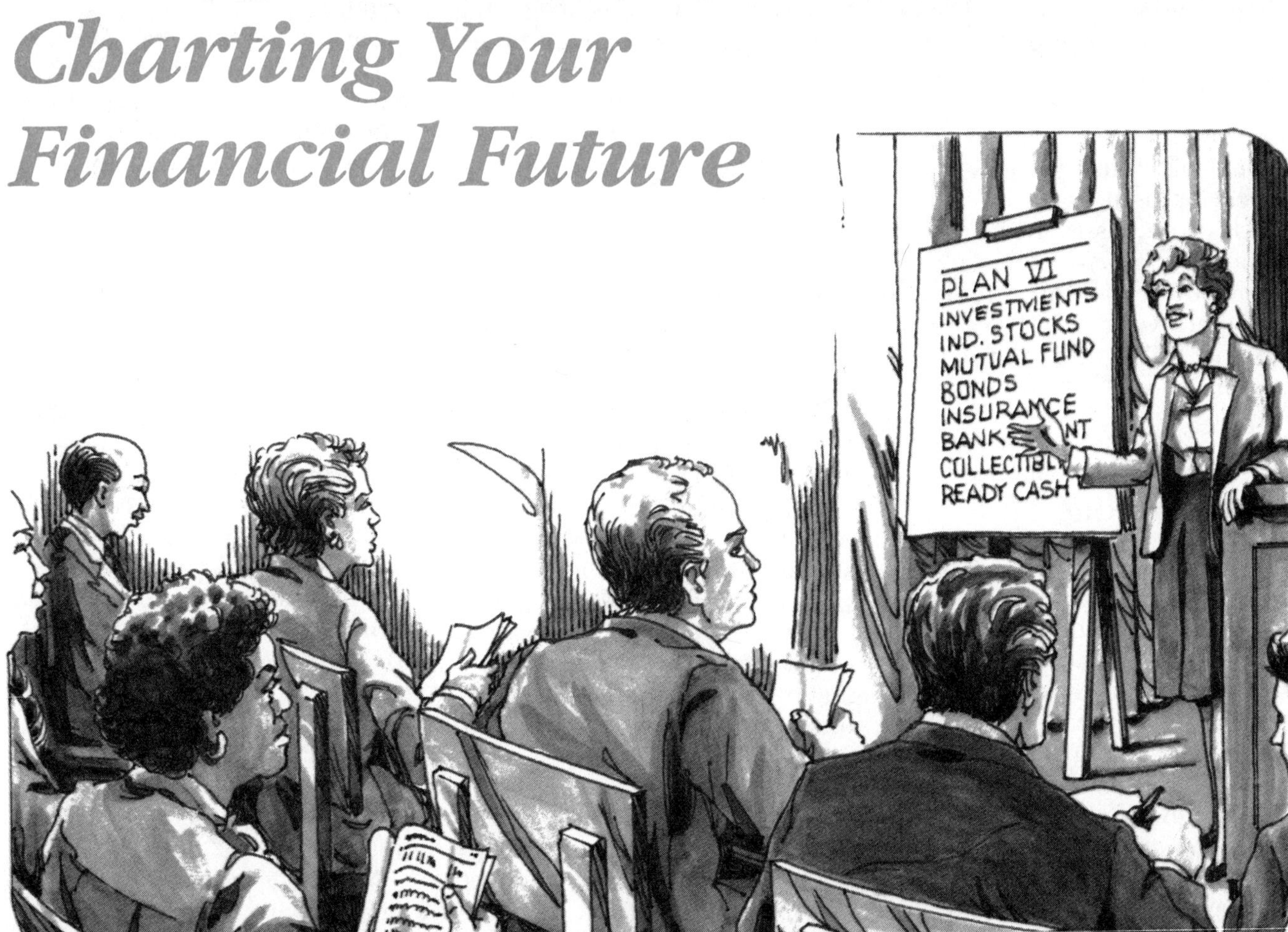

Who hasn't daydreamed about suddenly coming into a large sum of money that assures future financial security—winning a huge lottery, inheriting $500,000 from a distant relative, owning common stocks that soar in value?

Such daydreams are fun, but rarely do they come true. In real life, most of us have to work hard for our money. And when regular paychecks cease, we must plan to rely upon our own resources—savings, investments, property, pensions—to provide the financial security we need.

More than money is involved, of course. A basic purpose and goal for people in their middle years should be independence—freedom to continue to lead a comfortable and rewarding life. To achieve such a goal requires careful planning based upon the realities of one's own financial situation. It's much like charting a course for an interesting trip. You need to know (1) where you are now, (2) where you want to go, and (3) your best route for getting there.

Like any journey, this one must be accomplished one step at a time toward definite objectives. Along the way, you may have some pleasant surprises and, perhaps more important, learn how to avoid some unpleasant ones.

Count Your Blessings (and Other Assets)

Do you know how much you are really worth? Bankers and money managers call it *net worth* and consider it a key to sound financial planning. As a first step in mapping your course toward financial security, you should set up a complete, accurate listing of your resources. When you know what you own and subtract from that what you owe, you'll have computed your net worth.

Phil and Mary J. worked out their net worth statement together. They believed that if they both understood their net worth, they would be more effective in managing their money.

When Phil and Mary completed their computations, they were pleasantly surprised by their total worth—particularly by the value of their pension rights and their home.

They could see also that some of their assets were "lazy"—they couldn't be expected to grow or to offer much protection against inflation. Their new car and their household furnishings were fast losing value. Their savings account and U.S. savings bonds, totaling $9,500, provided a fair but not fully adequate cushion for emergencies. The less said about the loan to Phil's brother, the better—it probably never would be repaid.

After Phil and Mary determined their net worth, it was clear to them that they would have to spend less on current living and invest more in assets that could be expected to produce income for their future. A bright spot in their financial picture was their home. It was in a good neighborhood, and it could be expected to continue to increase in value. Meanwhile the mortgage was decreasing rapidly.

"At least, we know where we stand," said Phil. "From now on, before we buy anything we don't really need, we'll ask ourselves, 'How much would that amount of money earn in interest or dividends?'"

To launch your financial planning, insert your own tentative figures on the Net Worth Statement on page 90. Tips for filling it out follow. Later, you'll want to make more accurate entries.

Figuring Your Net Worth

Calculating your net worth the first time isn't easy. But once you have established a pattern, it becomes fairly simple to update this guide for management of your resources. Each year's updating will measure your financial progress.

Some financial managers regard 10 percent growth in net worth per year a feasible goal, particularly in the middle years, when the expenses of family rearing are dwindling, home mortgages are shrinking, and income is likely to be at its peak.

So take a pencil in hand—one with an eraser. Mistakes made with a pencil are easier to erase.

1. Be honest with yourself. Your assets are worth what you can sell them for, not what you originally paid for them.

2. Stocks and bonds should be valued at the market price as of the date of your calculation.

3. Your pension rights, if vested, and/or your share in a profit-sharing plan are part of your net worth. Your employer can give you an estimate of their present value.

4. Don't forget the cash and other conversion values of your insurance. Your insurance company will supply the figures.

5. Your home or other real property is worth no more than it would bring on the market, minus sales costs. You can approximate the worth of your house by the current prices of similar homes in your neighborhood. Or you can ask a real estate agent. But remember, an agent may place the value high enough to permit bargaining.

6. In general, household goods are worth far less than you paid for them new or what they would cost to replace. Unless you have rare antiques or art objects, your furnishings are worth only what they would bring on the secondhand market.

7. You can make your net worth statement as simple or as detailed as you wish. It should be complete enough to show you how you stand now so that you can measure your financial progress in the future.

Positive Action 9

Net Worth Statement

For year:	19____	19____	19____
Assets (what I/we own)			
Cash on hand	$________	$________	$________
Bank accounts (checking and savings)	________	________	________
Credit union account	________	________	________
Savings and loan accounts	________	________	________
Other savings accounts	________	________	________
House, market value	________	________	________
Other real estate, value	________	________	________
Household furnishings, value	________	________	________
Automobile(s), blue book value	________	________	________
Life insurance, cash value	________	________	________
Stocks and bonds, today's value	________	________	________
IRA plans	________	________	________
U.S. Savings Bonds	________	________	________
Money owed me/us	________	________	________
Other assets/investments:__________	________	________	________
Personal property	________	________	________
Total assets	$________	$________	$________
Liabilities (what I/we owe)			
Mortgages, balance due	$________	$________	$________
Other loans (bank, credit union)	________	________	________
Installment debts, balance due	________	________	________
Credit cards, balance due	________	________	________
Charge accounts, owed	________	________	________
Other debts, total owed	________	________	________
Insurance premiums due	________	________	________
Taxes owed	________	________	________
Other current bills	________	________	________
Total liabilities	$________	$________	$________
Net Worth (Assets minus liabilities)	$________	$________	$________

Setting Retirement Goals

Phil and Mary J. realized that a second step in their financial planning must be to estimate retirement expenses. They wanted to know what they could do *now* to improve their chances of having enough retirement income, since they feared inflation's impact on fixed resources.

Phil and Mary first figured out their current annual expenses. Next, they estimated what their annual costs would be in retirement. They figured that some of their current expenses would shrink or disappear in the future.

Phil's commuting and lunch expenses would be eliminated, as would outlays associated with a working wardrobe. In fact, eliminating work-related expenses would decrease their outgo by about 30 percent.

Moreover, there would be other savings they could count on by the time they retired. Their mortgage would be paid off and their children educated. Their life insurance could be converted to paid-up policies, so there would be no more premiums. Also, once they retired, their income taxes would be much lower, they would no longer have to pay Social Security taxes, and they would be receiving Social Security benefits.

Phil and Mary based their budget on spendable income they now had, exclusive of taxes, and they used a form similar to the one provided for your figures on pages 92–94. As you set *your* retirement goals, you, too, should budget based on your current expenses.

Your Budget and the Bite of Inflation

After you complete your estimates, one big unknown factor will remain—inflation, the enemy of retirees, many of whom are living on fixed incomes. It's impossible to know what the inflation rate will be for any future year, but it is a fact that inflation does compound. For example, a 7 percent price rise adds $1,050 to a $15,000-a-year budget, making the next year's budget $16,050. The following year that budget must be increased by another 7 percent (assuming that rate of inflation continues), and so on. After 10 years of 7 percent inflation, you'll need about $29,500 to buy what $15,000 will buy today.

However, the true bite of inflation may be considerably less. For example, most mortgage payments for people in midlife remain constant. This factor alone can cut your true inflation rate by almost one-third of the Consumer Price Index (which measures cost-of-living increases). Changes in lifestyle brought about by retirement—no commuting ex-

Using Credit Wisely

Prudent management of your current cash situation can have a considerable effect on your future comfort and security. Every dollar spent today is a dollar that won't be available tomorrow. Every dollar saved or invested today can generate more for future use.

The proper use of credit—your ability to borrow—can be an important tool in your financial planning. For example, you may need funds for any number of purposes: a vacation, a down payment on a car, or your youngest child's college tuition. You don't want to cash in certain investments prematurely to obtain the needed funds. So you may borrow, temporarily, until a better time arrives to cash in other resources.

With your banker's or financial planner's guidance, use credit constructively to enhance your lifestyle and comfort without saddling yourself with unwieldy repayment obligations.

Remember, imprudently used, your borrowing ability can damage your otherwise nicely crafted retirement plans. The use of credit can add from 12 percent to 30 percent to the cost of an item.

penses, for instance—can also soften the blow.

Further, cost-of-living increases in Social Security and in some pensions add income to retirement budgets. And, as prices increase, so do available yields on such investments as certificates of deposit.

Read the instructions on this page for preparing a current budget and for estimating retirement budgets for your early and later retirement years.

The Inflation Impact table on this page will help you project what inflation will do to your retirement budget. It is important to plan now, while you are still drawing paychecks, to build defenses against inflation.

Positive Action 10

Preparing Your Current and Retirement Budgets

The backbone of your financial plan is your annual budget. The budget worksheets on the next two pages can help you determine whether your retirement goals are financially attainable. Below are instructions for the worksheets on pages 93–94.

A. Expenses

1. Estimate your current expenses item by item and post in column B on page 93.
2. Estimate your expenses for the first year in retirement using today's dollars and post in column C on page 93. Remember, some expenses will decrease when you stop working.
3. Determine the number of years until you plan to retire.
4. In the table that follows, find the inflation factor that corresponds to the number of years until you retire. (EXAMPLE: If you plan to retire in three years, the inflation factor is 1.225.)
5. Multiply your "Annual Expenses in Today's Dollars" in column C by the inflation factor and post the figure on the line "Annual Expenses" (Inflation Adjusted) on page 93. (EXAMPLE: First-year retirement expenses of $12,000 × 1.225 = $14,700. If you retire in three years, you will need $14,700 to cover expenses that would cost you $12,000 figured in today's dollars.)
6. Use the same steps to plot your expenses and inflation at some future time (for example, five years).

B. Income

1. Post your current income from each source in column B on page 94.
2. Estimate your income from each source for your first year in retirement and post in column C on page 94. Remember, income from some sources may increase over the years at various rates; income from other sources may lessen or disappear entirely.
3. Choose some point further into your retirement (for example, five years) and post income estimates for that time.

C. The Bottom Line

1. Transfer your "Annual Expenses" for each year estimated from the bottom line on page 93 to the appropriate line at the bottom of page 94.
2. Subtract "Annual Expenses" from "Annual Income" to discover your "Annual Surplus," or gap, for a particular year.
3. How are you doing?

Inflation Impact

(Compounded at 7% per year)

End of Year	Inflation Factor	End of Year	Inflation Factor
1	1.0700	16	2.9543
2	1.1449	17	3.1611
3	1.2250	18	3.3823
4	1.3107	19	3.6191
5	1.4024	20	3.8724
6	1.5005	21	4.1434
7	1.6055	22	4.4334
8	1.7178	23	4.7437
9	1.8380	24	5.0757
10	1.9666	25	5.4310
11	2.1042	26	5.8112
12	2.2514	27	6.2179
13	2.4117	28	6.6532
14	2.5805	29	7.1189
15	2.7611	30	7.6172

Positive Action 10

(continued)

Budget Expenses

A. Expenses (self and spouse)	B. Now	C. First year in retirement*	D. ____ year in retirement*	E. Survivor #1	F. Survivor #2
	19____	19____	19____		
Pension, IRA, or Keogh plan contribution	$____	$____	$____	$____	$____
Rent or mortgage	____	____	____	____	____
Food	____	____	____	____	____
Clothing	____	____	____	____	____
Amusement	____	____	____	____	____
Medical	____	____	____	____	____
Transportation	____	____	____	____	____
Telephone	____	____	____	____	____
Electricity, fuel, water, etc.	____	____	____	____	____
Home maintenance ...	____	____	____	____	____
Appliances and furniture...........	____	____	____	____	____
Working expenses.....	____	____	____	____	____
Personal items	____	____	____	____	____
Insurance: *life, health, auto, home*	____	____	____	____	____
Education	____	____	____	____	____
Taxes: *income, other*....	____	____	____	____	____
Gifts	____	____	____	____	____
Other items	____	____	____	____	____
____	____	____	____	____	____
____	____	____	____	____	____
Annual Expenses in Today's Dollars	$____	$____	$____	$____	$____
× Inflation Factor	×NA	×____	×____	×____	×____
Annual Expenses (Inflation Adjusted) ...		$____	$____	$____	$____

* Use an inflation factor of 7% for each year beyond that used in the "Now" column; use the Inflation Factor table on page 92. (Remember that some costs will stop or decrease in retirement.)

Positive Action 10

(continued)

Budget Income

A. Income (self and spouse)	B. Now 19____	C. First year in retirement* 19____	D. ____ year in retirement* 19____	E. Survivor #1	F. Survivor #2
Salary/Wages	$____	$____	$____	$____	$____
Social Security	____	____	____	____	____
Other gov't. income	____	____	____	____	____
Pension plan	____	____	____	____	____
Profit-sharing plan	____	____	____	____	____
Deferred comp.	____	____	____	____	____
Other employee income	____	____	____	____	____
Gov't. securities	____	____	____	____	____
Corporate securities	____	____	____	____	____
Savings plans	____	____	____	____	____
Other investments	____	____	____	____	____
IRA	____	____	____	____	____
Keogh plan	____	____	____	____	____
Annuities	____	____	____	____	____
Life ins. cash value	____	____	____	____	____
Sale of business	____	____	____	____	____
Sale of other assets (property, collectibles, etc.)	____	____	____	____	____
Other ____	____	____	____	____	____
____	____	____	____	____	____
____	____	____	____	____	____
____	____	____	____	____	____
The Bottom Line Annual Income	$____	$____	$____	$____	$____
minus **Annual Expenses** (from page 93)	$____	$____	$____	$____	$____
equals **Annual Surplus,** or **gap**	$____	$____	$____	$____	$____

Where Will the Money Come From?

Workers who have pension plans tend to assume that their pension and Social Security benefits will provide all the retirement income they will need. This blithe assumption can lead to bitter disappointment and sometimes to actual hardship.

Many retirees discover belatedly that their pension income is far less than what they had anticipated. In some cases, expected pensions do not materialize at all for a variety of reasons including insufficient funding of the plan, business failure of the employing company, or loss of a job before pension rights become vested—that is, when some pension income becomes guaranteed at retirement age. Many people are not participants in any pension plan. They may be relying on Social Security to be the mainstay of their retirement income. Yet, Social Security was never intended to be the chief source of retirement income; rather, its purpose is to supplement other sources.

Nevertheless, many people see Social Security and pension benefits as the basic elements of their retirement income. Count yourself fortunate if you will be eligible for high-level benefits from both sources. Before you do any counting, however, determine for yourself as accurately as possible what you can expect from each one. Your need for additional sources of income may then become apparent.

The major sources of retirement income are described below. Which ones can you count on? Which ones will be temporary, and which will be permanent? Which will be stable, and which will fluctuate in value? Which will survive the death of a spouse, and which will not? Don't guess about these matters. Get accurate information and estimates from your pension plan administrator; your district Social Security office; and a stockbroker, financial planner, or other financial professional.

Sources of Income for Individuals Age 65 and Older:

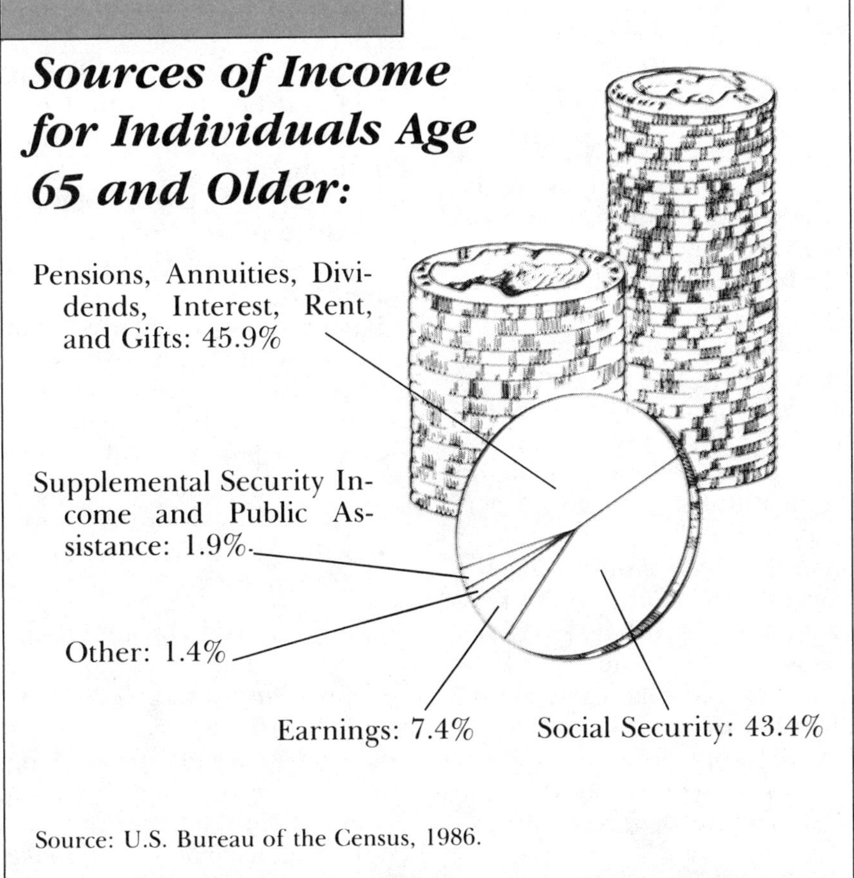

Source: U.S. Bureau of the Census, 1986.

Employer Pension and Profit-sharing Plans

If you are participating in an employer pension or profit-sharing plan, it is to your advantage to understand it thoroughly and to estimate accurately what your benefits will be. You can then judge what supplementary retirement income you will need. If you have any questions about the provisions of the plan, ask your employer's pension plan administrator.

A key point in any pension plan is vesting rights. When do you get "locked in" to the plan? When can you be assured of some pension benefits when you reach retirement age? You will find answers to these questions in your plan's eligibility rules, which prescribe how long you must work for the company and what age you must be before you can retire with full pension benefits.

Vesting formulas are either "all at once" or phased in. Prior to 1989, for example, an employer could choose an "all at once" formula that would give an eligible employee 100 percent vesting after ten years but nothing at all if the employee worked less than ten years. A phased-in formula could last for upward of fifteen years. Under the 1986 Tax Reform Act, new vesting formulas will begin in 1989. The "all at once" formula will give workers 100 percent vesting after five years of service. The phased-in formula will give an employee 20 percent vesting after three years, then 20 percent per year thereafter, until the employee is fully vested after seven years. Employers could choose to use shorter vesting formulas but not longer ones.

The Employee Retirement Security Act (ERISA) requires your employer to keep you informed about your status with respect to a pension, any profit-sharing plan, and any other employer-sponsored retirement plan. Ask the plan administrator for a summary plan description and a copy of the official plan document. Also ask your employer to calculate what your pension will be at early retirement age, at age sixty-five, and at age seventy. Obtain answers to these and other essential questions:

- Is the plan insured? By whom? For what?
- What is your pension as of today?
- What are your payout options (for example, lump sum versus annuity)?
- Are your benefits guaranteed for life?
- Will your benefits be reduced if you receive Social Security benefits? By how much?
- What benefit options for survivors are available if you die before retirement? after retirement?
- How will these options affect your monthly benefit?
- Do you have an option for early retirement? When must you apply for benefits?
- Can your employer change or discontinue the plan?

Lump Sum versus Annuity

Choosing between taking the money in one lump sum versus receiving an annuity payout may be the biggest decision you have to make regarding your retirement income. Get expert advice about the pros and cons of each option. You may also have the choice of several annuity plans. Some terminate on the death of the employed person; some pay a smaller amount per month to the worker but continue making payments to the surviving spouse after the worker's death. If you take early retirement before reaching age fifty-five and opt for a lump-sum pension payment, under the 1986 Tax Reform Act, you will have to pay a 10 percent penalty tax.

About Early Retirement

The tax implications of various payout options make up only one of several important matters to consider before deciding whether to take early retirement. Find out the answers to these questions:

- Exactly what is the early retirement package worth, including cash payments, pension benefits, health and life insurance, and any other incentives?
- How do these benefits compare with what you would receive if you were to retire later? Would working one, two, or three more years significantly increase your pension benefits?
- Are you financially ready to retire? For example, are the house and car(s) paid for, or nearly so? Can you meet ongoing expenses and maintain a cash reserve for emergencies without a steady paycheck?
- If you will need another job, will you be able to find one where you plan to live after retiring?
- Do you feel psychologically ready to retire? What are you going to do with the extra time you will have? Do you have at least a tentative plan for your life after work?
- If you do not accept the early retirement offer, what are the chances that you will be laid off or reassigned? (See page 59 regarding your rights under the Age Discrimination in Employment Act.)

The financial considerations alone are of great importance to your long-term well-being. Get help from an accountant or financial planner in working through the numbers for each option. Then factor in the psychological variables and make the best decision for you.

Do-It-Yourself Pensions

Basically, there are three kinds of do-it-yourself retirement plans: individual retirement accounts (IRAs), Keogh plans, and 401(k) plans. If you have income from work, you may be eligible for an IRA. And if your employer offers a 401(k) plan, you may be able to take advantage of that as well as an IRA. If you are self-employed full- or part-time, you are eligible for a Keogh plan (actually known as the self-employed person's plan) as well as an IRA plan.

Under the 1986 Tax Reform Act, the deductibility of IRA investments is limited. You are entitled to the full allowable deduction for your IRA if you are *not* covered by another retirement plan at work. Even if you are covered by another retirement plan at work, you may still be entitled to a full IRA deduction if your adjusted gross income is less than $25,000 (for single filers) or less than $40,000 (for married couples filing jointly). If your adjusted gross income is between $25,000 and $35,000 (single) or between $40,000 and $50,000 (joint), you are entitled to a *partial* deduction for your IRA investment. If your adjusted gross income exceeds $35,000 (single) or $50,000 (joint), you are not entitled to any deduction for your IRA investment.

With Keogh and 401(k) plans, the amount you invest each year reduces the amount of your income that is subject to taxation. In all three plans—IRA, Keogh, and 401(k)—all the money invested earns on a tax-deferred basis until the money is withdrawn.

Check current tax laws to determine the amount that can be invested in each of these plans annually and the penalties for withdrawing the money before reaching age 59½. IRA and Keogh withdrawals must begin before age 70½.

With IRAs and Keoghs, you can choose your own investment vehicles within the scope of those allowed by law. Banks, savings and loan associations, mutual funds, stock brokerage firms, and insurance companies offer a wide variety of investment opportunities for IRA and Keogh plans.

With the 401(k) plan, the employer chooses the investment vehicle, and you may have a choice of two or three different modes for your own contributions. Many employers will also supplement the worker's contribution with an added sum—perhaps forty cents or fifty cents for each dollar the worker contributes. In the 401(k) plan, however, the worker's taxable income for the year is reduced by the amount he or she contributes to the 401(k) plan. That, in turn, might affect the worker's pension benefits with the company, since pension benefits are often based on earnings during the final years of work. In other words, by reducing your earnings through a 401(k) plan, you might also be cutting your pension benefits. Determine what the effects would be in your case.

The 1986 Tax Reform Act sets lower limits as to the amount that can be put into a 401(k) plan each year. For 1987, the maximum a worker can defer is $7,000. That amount will be indexed for inflation beginning in 1988. Contributions made to other plans can also restrict the amount a worker can defer through a 401(k) plan. Check with your tax adviser for details.

Social Security

Social Security is a basic source of income for many people. For planning purposes, it is important to know whether you qualify for Social Security benefits and to have a reasonably accurate estimate of what your

benefits will be. To obtain a statement of the earnings credited to your Social Security number, ask your nearest Social Security office for the postcard "Request for Statement of Earnings." You may also ask for the pamphlet *Estimating Your Social Security Retirement Check.* If you are age fifty-nine or older, your district Social Security office will figure your monthly Social Security benefit. Ask your local Social Security office who to contact to obtain this estimate and what information you will need to provide. You will want to plug this estimated figure into your tentative retirement budget on page 94.

If you are, or have been, self-employed, you should have made your Social Security payments along with your income tax payments. For you, as well as for the salaried employee, it is a wise precaution to verify the present status of your Social Security account.

You can begin receiving Social Security benefits at age sixty-two, but you will receive a lesser monthly amount than if you retire at age sixty-five. This reduction (currently 20 percent) is permanent. And future increases in benefits will be based on this reduced amount.

If you continue to work after starting to receive Social Security benefits, you will lose some or all of your benefits if your income from work exceeds a certain annual amount. (Your nonwork income from interest, dividends, and so on, does not cause a reduction in benefits.) If you are between ages sixty-two and sixty-four, you can earn up to $6,000 in 1987 without losing any Social Security benefits. If you are between ages sixty-five and sixty-nine, you can earn up to $8,160. If you are age seventy or older, you can earn all you want to from work without losing any benefits. These annual exempt amounts are refigured each year based on increases in average wages nationwide. If you earn more than the exempt amount from work, you will lose one dollar in benefits for every two dollars earned above the limit. In 1990, if you are between sixty-five and sixty-nine, you will lose one dollar in benefits for every *three* dollars above the limit.

A portion of an individual's Social Security benefit is considered taxable income if his or her adjusted gross income plus nontaxable interest income and half of the Social Security benefits exceeds $25,000 for an individual or $32,000 for a couple filing jointly.

Besides the Medicare program (see page 21 in chapter 2), Social Security provides disability, survivors', and minor children's benefits. Supplemental Security Income (SSI) is available for those whose total retirement income does not meet a minimum standard.

Work in Retirement

As you develop your retirement budget, you may find that you'll need to or want to work in retirement. Such employment may range from a new full-time career to part-time or temporary work. Consider now what you would like to do, where you can do it, and whether any training or education is required. Various work options and issues relevant to extending your work life are discussed in chapter 5.

Before deciding to work, recognize that there may be expenses and other financial deterrents associated with continued employment. As just pointed out, for example, provisions in the Social Security program can affect your decision to work and the number of hours you will be able to work without losing benefits. Positive Action 6, "Does It Pay to Work in Retirement?" on page 60 in chapter 5, will help you sort out the financial ramifications of the decision to work after beginning to receive Social Security benefits.

Annuities for Assured Income

Annuities, often described as life insurance contracts in reverse, are contracts between a financial firm, such as a life insurance company, and an individual. The individual pays a sum of cash to the firm, which contracts to make monthly payments to the individual for the rest of his or her life. There are many kinds of annuities, including those that pay benefits to the surviving spouse after the death of the original annuitant.

While traditional fixed annuities usually do not grow or yield high returns to provide a hedge against inflation, their chief advantages are (1) you are freed of the job of money management; (2) you can never outlive your capital; (3) while making it easier to save for old age, annuities also make it difficult to use any of your savings beforehand; and (4) annuities draw interest during your working years, but you pay no income tax on that interest until you collect it—at a time when your tax bracket may be lower.

It pays to shop around among insurance companies selling annuities because rates vary, but typically a man of sixty-five who buys a straight life annuity gets about nine dollars a month for life for each one thousand dollars of annuity. A woman of the same age would receive less per each one thousand dollars because of the longer life expectancy for females. Only if the annuity is pension-related must payouts be equal.

You may wish to consider one of the new variable annuities that allow you to invest in a wide variety of securities. While such an annuity offers the potential for a higher return and a possible inflation hedge, it also subjects you to more risk. Learn the level of this risk before you invest.

Life Insurance

Life insurance policies are among the important papers one tends to file away and forget, except to pay the premiums when billed for them. You should have reviewed your insurance program periodically, of course, but in any case, it is important that you take a hard look at these policies during your middle years, when you are establishing future financial goals.

You probably purchased your life insurance policy or policies at an earlier stage in life for a primary purpose—to provide economic protection for your family if anything happened to you. Then the children were young, and the high costs of education loomed ahead. And there was that hefty mortgage on your house to think about.

But now the high costs of education have been met, or largely so. An end to mortgage payments may be in sight. If you have been prudent and fortunate, you have financial resources in addition to Social Security benefits and a possible pension. So what can life insurance do for you now?

The answer is, a great deal, depending upon a number of factors and possibilities you should explore. Life insurance can protect your dependents against any financial hardship they might suffer if you were to die prematurely. Life insurance can also provide liquid assets to settle an estate. The need for life insurance often diminishes after the children grow up and leave home. But each person's situation is different. Before determining your insurance needs, you need a clear picture of your current coverage and possible options.

First of all, you need to know what insurance you have—and where your policies are kept. You should be able to answer such elementary questions as the face value of your policies; the designation of beneficiaries; and cash, loan, and other conversion values, if any. Many people don't know the answers to these easy questions. And there are more difficult ones.

What kinds of insurance do you have? If you have forgotten or never knew, you may have to read your life insurance policy several times and then consult an agent to determine exactly what you have and what it can do for you. Basically, there are only four kinds of individual policies: *term, whole life, endowment, and universal life.* Most life insurance policies are variations of the first two, with perhaps an annuity feature added.

Term insurance is purchased for a limited number of years and has to be renewed periodically at a higher premium rate based on age. However, some companies offer term policies that run to age sixty-five and beyond. The price of term insurance can be deceptive. It starts out very low, but if you keep the insurance for many years (which you may need to do), you will pay more for it than for alternative policies.

Further, a term policy may be *convertible*; that is, you may be able to exchange it for permanent insurance, which initially costs more but which builds up cash values. A term policy in itself accumulates little or no cash value.

Group term insurance may be paid for in whole or in part by the company you work for. This is a valuable fringe benefit of some kinds of employment. (Group insurance also may be purchased through other groups and organizations.) Group insurance is normally convertible; you can keep the policy when you leave the company by converting it to an individual policy and paying for it yourself, usually at a higher rate.

Many companies now continue group term insurance for a former employee after retirement. The face value may drop drastically at sixty-five, however, and drop more as the retiree ages. It is wise to check whether this is so, and to what age and for how much the policyholder will continue to be insured. Another important thing to know about *any* policy is whether it contains a disability provision—a waiver of premium, and sometimes payment of monthly income, if the policyholder becomes permanently disabled.

Whole life policies (also known as straight life) are those that insure for the life of the policyholder and at death pay the face value to the beneficiary. (The face value is the amount stated on the face of the policy that will be paid in case of death or at the maturity of the contract. It does not include amounts payable under accidental death or other special provisions.) Whole life policies are offered on the "level premium" plan, which means that the premium stays the same even though the policyholder grows older. Whole life policies usually accumulate a cash and loan value after a specified number of years.

An **endowment** policy (also called retirement income insurance) enables a person to accumulate cash, which will be paid according to various options he or she may select at a date named in the policy (the *maturity* date). If you have an endowment policy, or one with certain endowment features, you will receive a definite sum of money or income at some future date. Meanwhile, your dependents have insurance protection. It is a relatively expensive way to buy protection and to save for the future.

Universal life (also known as flexible premium life) is a modern version of whole life that combines term insurance and a tax-deferred investment component. You can adjust premium payments and the death benefit periodically, if needed, within limits. The investment rate quoted is a gross rate, before expenses and deductions. With interest rates lower today, universal life will perform no better than a high-quality whole life policy, but it does offer convenience and flexibility not available through whole life insurance.

Conversion Options

Depending on the kind of insurance you have, you should consider what it can do for you now.

Among your options are those of retaining all your life insurance; dropping some; or, as part of your estate and tax planning, buying more. You may even be able to have insurance but stop paying for it. This is possible when the cash value of your present policy is great enough to pay for extended term insurance, which will provide the original amount of insurance for a limited period of time. Another option is buying reduced paid-up insurance with your policy's cash value—the amount received when you "cash in" your policy. This will cover you with a lesser amount of insurance for as long as you live.

The chart on this page illustrates how these options—often referred to as nonforfeiture values—can work. Bear in mind that the value will differ from policy to policy. You can check the values in your own policies by looking for the chart in each policy entitled "Nonforfeiture Values."

As an example, let's assume that a life insurance policy for $10,000 was taken out in the mid-1950s. After the policy had been in force for twenty-five years, the owner could cash it in for $2,740, and coverage would cease. Or the owner could borrow that amount against the policy and continue keeping the policy in force by paying the premiums regularly.

Another option would be to convert the policy to reduced paid-up life insurance worth $5,590. The owner could stop paying premiums altogether and be insured for that $5,590 for life.

A third option would be to convert the policy to extended term coverage. The owner could stop paying premiums and would remain covered for the full original $10,000, but only for a limited length of time—in this case 29.9 years—after which the coverage would cease altogether.

Whether you decide to keep what insurance you have, convert your insurance, or buy more, you should be certain that the beneficiary or beneficiaries—those to whom the money will be paid on your death—are the persons you want to leave the proceeds to. It is important to review your beneficiaries periodically, especially when there is a change in your family and life situation. And when you're reviewing your policies, check into the estate tax implications of ownership of a life insurance policy.

You may decide you need much less or no life insurance as you approach retirement. In this case, you can take the cash value of your whole life policy and invest the money in other ways to produce income. You can receive the cash in a lump sum or in payments at regular intervals, while the money not yet paid to you continues to earn interest.

Your insurance policies may also have a loan value. Borrowing upon one's life insurance is not so dire or difficult as it may seem. Some people do it routinely when they purchase a new automobile—they like the very low rate for such a loan, and the insurance company will send a monthly reminder to pay it back. One danger is that it is easy not to pay back, for you cannot be forced to do so. As long as you pay the premiums and the interest on the loan, your insurance will remain in effect, and the amount will be deducted from the face amount payable to the beneficiary upon the policyholder's death.

Finally, the savings feature of life insurance policies, although secondary to the primary purpose of providing death benefits, is worth consideration. Those who find it easy to backslide on a savings program rarely neglect to pay an insurance premium when billed. And, although the interest yield is modest compared with other forms of savings, insurance savings with a reputable company are safe and certain.

Should people approaching retirement change their life insurance? For some the answer is no; for some, yes. Life insurance holdings and needs differ for almost everyone depending upon circumstances and financial goals. But for all the answer is, Take a look. Know what your options are.

Assets

"Real" property, land and buildings, has long been regarded as a sound investment and a defense against inflation. With proper selection—and good luck—it still is. Many people in their fifties have established the larger portion of their nest egg through the buying and selling of houses.

One drawback is that profitable ownership of real estate depends upon personal management and maintenance. A further drawback is that some real estate investments lack liquidity, and it may be difficult to turn your investment into cash quickly without risking a loss.

Conversion Values per $1,000 of Face Value

Age of Policy	Cash or Loan Value	Reduced Paid-up Value	Extended Term Coverage
20 years	$209	$471	30.5 years
25 years	274	559	29.9 years
30 years	343	637	28.5 years

Home

Owning the house you live in is usually a sound investment. Most well-located residences increase in value. Your equity in your home (your home's cash value less your mortgage) may represent a large portion of your net worth—money that, if invested in other ways, could substantially supplement your retirement income. However, selling the old homestead to move into a smaller house or apartment requires the most careful consideration. Also, in most instances there are dollars-and-cents reasons to hold on to your residence until you are fifty-five.

> ## *Rule of 72*
>
> How long would it take to **double** your money at various interest rates? To find out, simply divide 72 by the interest rate:
>
> **For a 6% interest rate:**
> **6)72 = 12 years to double your money**
>
> At 6% interest, $1,000 becomes:
> $2,000 in 12 years
> 4,000 in 24 years
> 8,000 in 36 years
>
> How long would it take various inflation rates to **halve** the **purchasing power** of your money? To find out, divide 72 by the inflation rate:
>
> **For an 8% inflation rate:**
> **8)72 = 9 years to halve the purchasing power of your money**
>
> At 8% inflation, $10,000 becomes **worth**:
> $5,000 in 9 years
> 2,500 in 18 years
> 1,250 in 27 years

Before age fifty-five, if you sell your house at a profit, you must pay income taxes on that profit. However, you can postpone the payment of that tax if you reinvest the proceeds of the sale in another house of equal or greater value. You must do this within twenty-four months of the sale of the original house. Eventually, if you sell your house and do not buy another (if you rent an apartment, for example), the tax will become payable.

If you sell your house after either you or your spouse has reached fifty-five, you have two choices: (1) you can roll over the proceeds as indicated in the foregoing paragraph and delay the payment of tax, or (2) you can elect to declare tax-free up to $125,000 worth of profit. (Profits in excess of $125,000 will be taxable.)

Excluding up to $125,000 worth of profit is a once-in-a-lifetime right. If you do it once, you can't do it again. Thus careful planning is called for, and the advice of your tax counselor is necessary if a large profit is involved.

You can supplement your retirement income by tapping the equity in your home while continuing to live there. The basic equity conversion options available to you are described on pages 77–78 in chapter 6.

Land

Undeveloped land is often a risky investment because there is only one way to make money—through future appreciation of its value. Financing the purchase of undeveloped land is often difficult and usually expensive; also, taxes must be paid on the land even though it produces no income.

Beware of hard-sell inducements to invest in land developments, even if you plan to build a second home or a retirement home and live there. Most such small lots cannot be expected to increase in value as much or as soon as salespeople imply. To start, you must pay their commission and high promotion costs. Later, if you wish to sell such land, you may find it difficult to attract a buyer. This form of investing has been rife with fraudulent dealings, shattered dreams, and lost bankrolls. Utmost caution is advised.

Nonproductive Items

Nonproductive assets can include furniture and furnishings, appliances, silver, crystal, tools, and collectibles of all kinds—coins, stamps, dolls, and so on. By selling these items, you can generate cash that can be invested to create additional retirement income. Have antiques, jewelry, furs, and collections appraised by a professional before selling them. Those items you cannot sell can be donated to your favorite charity, and you may be able to claim a deduction on your income taxes.

Investments

A wisely chosen and carefully managed investment program may mean the difference between living a comfortable, secure retirement and just getting by.

There are two ways to put your money to work: lending and buying.

The Debt (Money) Market

When you lend money, you receive a legal promise that it will be repaid at a specific time in the future, and you receive a fee, or interest, for the use of your money. For example, if you lend money to the U.S. government, you may receive a

U.S. savings bond, a Treasury bill, or some other government security in exchange. Other forms of investing in the debt, or money, market include passbook savings accounts, interest-bearing checking accounts, certificates of deposit, corporate bonds, money market mutual funds, annuities, and mortgage pools.

The Equity Market

The other way to put your money to work is by buying something. You expect (hope) that, at some point in the future, you will be able to sell whatever it is for more than you paid for it, thus reaping a profit. In some cases, the thing you bought may also generate income while you own it, such as the dividends from stocks or the rent on a house. There is no guarantee of profit, however. In fact, you may actually take a loss on the item. Thus, investing in the equity market is considered to be a riskier venture than lending money in the debt, or money, market. Forms of investing in the equity market include common and preferred stocks, mutual funds, real estate, commodities, metals, gems, and collectibles.

A Look at Some Investment Options

Once you have a substantial cash reserve, investment in securities—bonds, stocks, and mutual funds—can be a rewarding way to build income. But remember, unwise investing can lead to financial distress, so proceed with caution.

Bonds are IOUs. The issuer of the bond promises to pay you a specified amount, on a certain date, usually at a fixed interest rate. Although bonds do not have the growth potential of stocks, they are less risky, since they are a legal promise to pay, assuming the issuer can do so. Bonds are bought and sold on the open market, however, and their market value can fluctuate. If you need cash quickly, you may have to sell at a loss.

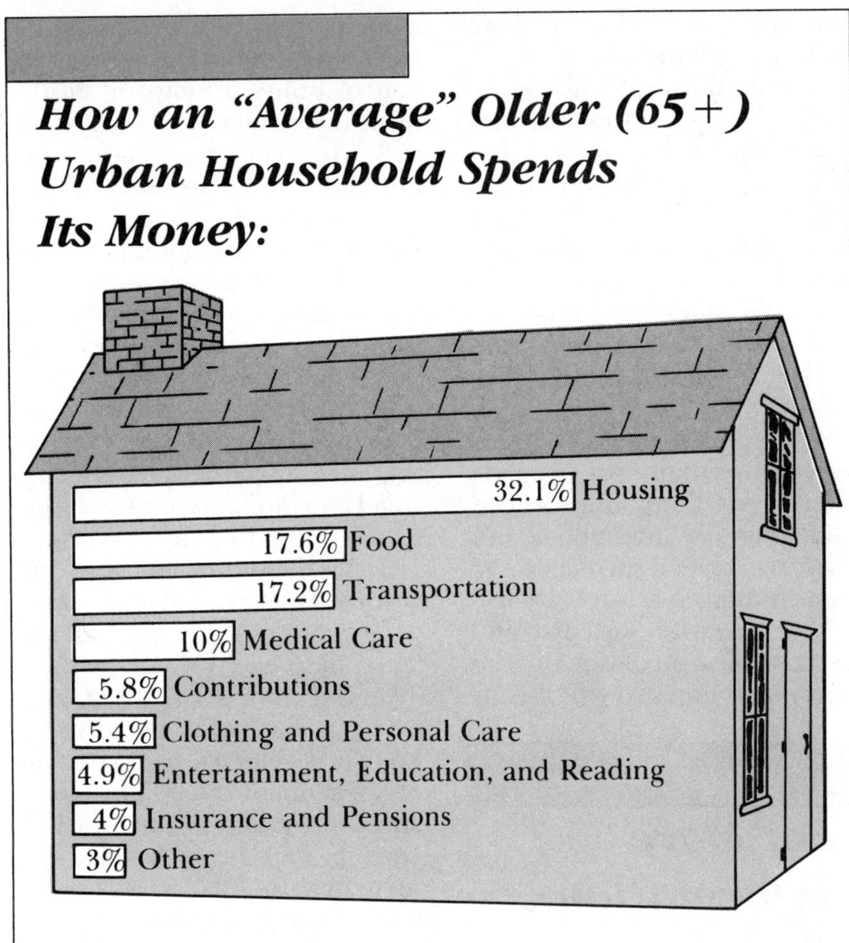

Source: Bureau of Labor Statistics, U.S. Department of Labor, 1986.

Among the types of bonds you might consider are corporate, government, and municipal.

Corporate bonds are issued by companies, usually in multiples of $1,000, and generally pay interest semiannually. Bonds are rated from AAA (the highest) to C (the lowest) according to the judgment of special bond-rating services as to the financial backing of the bond. In general, the higher the rating, the lower the yield you may expect and the lower the risk.

U.S. government bonds, apart from savings bonds, are bought and sold on the open market. The longer-term government IOUs are called *bonds;* intermediate-term, *notes;* and short-term, *bills.*

Municipal bonds are IOUs from towns, cities, counties, and states. They usually give less return but generally are exempt from federal taxes, so they attract people in high tax brackets. As a result of the 1986 Tax Reform Act, a number of taxable municipal bonds will be issued. Check the tax consequences before investing.

Common stocks are shares of ownership in a company. When you own stock, you are entitled to share in the part of the company's profits that it pays out in dividends. In addition, if the company performs well, the value of your stock may increase so that you can sell it at a profit.

Preferred stocks, like common stocks, represent part ownership in a company, but they carry fixed dividends, which must be paid before holders of common stocks are paid their dividends. Thus, preferred stocks are more secure than common stocks and in this regard are more like bonds.

Which securities you select is most important, of course. There are no guaranteed guidelines for investment, but here are several principles to keep in mind:

1. Define your objectives and invest with a purpose. Do you want maximum growth of your principal, or do you want a high yield in dividends? Are you planning a long- or short-term investment?

2. Your objectives should be tailored to your present and future needs. Investors in their middle years may look for common stocks that appear to have a good chance of appreciating in value even though present yields are low. However, someone nearing retirement may decide to shift to investments that have a record of producing steady income, even though the growth potential may be less.

3. You should plan your investments as part of your total program and not put all of your nest egg in one basket. There is always risk in stocks, even in the solid performers known as "blue chips." You can offset some of the risk by a balanced program, putting part of your money in such fixed-return investments as preferred stocks or high-grade bonds.

4. Handle your investments through established, reliable securities firms. Don't buy wildcat stocks from fast-talking salespeople, and don't be pushed into buying any security hurriedly.

Mutual funds are one answer to the question of what to buy. A mutual fund operates through the services of professional money managers. These managers receive a fee to invest the money of many small investors, who purchase (and may sell) shares in the fund. A mutual fund can provide a diversified investment—in effect, can put eggs in many baskets—and good managers may avoid some of the risks to which an inexperienced small investor is especially vulnerable. While the majority of mutual funds specialize in common stocks, today many funds also specialize in other investment vehicles, such as corporate bonds, municipal bonds, options, and commodities.

One popular type of mutual fund is the *money market mutual fund*, which invests in such instruments as government bonds, certificates of deposit, and corporate bonds. Many investors prefer them to certificates of deposit because they can be cashed in at any time without penalty. Unlike certificates of deposit, though, these funds are not insured, and the interest earned will fluctuate.

Since 1982, banks and savings and loan associations have been allowed to compete with the money market mutual funds by offering federally insured money market deposit accounts. Interest rates on these accounts vary from one financial institution to another.

It is important to ascertain a mutual fund's investment objective; for example, some funds strive for income, while others work for a balance between growth and income. You should also look at the length of time the fund has been in operation and at the amount of its total assets.

In addition, you must decide whether you want a load or no-load mutual fund. A load fund charges you a fee at the outset as well as an annual service charge. No-loads have no initial fee, but, like load funds, charge an annual service fee.

To choose a mutual fund wisely requires considerable study. Although you will want to study the past performance of a fund, you should keep in mind that past performance is no guarantee of future success. To help you in your search, studies and ratings of funds are made each year by financial publications and investment services such as Moody's Inves-

For More Information...

About pensions:
Pension Rights Center, 1346 Connecticut Avenue, N.W., Washington, DC 20036. 202-296-3778.

About Social Security:
Call your local Social Security office or write to Social Security Administration, 6401 Security Boulevard, Baltimore, MD 21235.

About life insurance:
American Council of Life Insurance and Health Insurance Association of America, 1850 K Street, N.W., Washington, DC 20006. 800-423-8000.

About investing:
American Association of Individual Investors, 612 N. Michigan Avenue, Chicago, IL 60611. 312-380-0170.

Principal ($10,000) Plus Interest (compounded quarterly)

	Potential Interest Rate				
Years	5%	8%	9%	10%	12%
1	$10,509	$10,824	$10,930	$11,038	$11,255
2	11,045	11,716	11,948	12,184	12,667
3	11,608	12,682	13,060	13,448	14,257
4	12,199	13,727	14,276	14,845	16,047
5	12,820	14,859	15,605	16,386	18,061
6	13,473	16,084	17,057	18,087	20,327
7	14,160	17,410	18,645	19,964	22,879
8	14,881	18,845	20,381	22,037	25,750
9	15,639	20,398	22,278	24,325	28,982
10	16,436	22,080	24,351	26,850	32,620
11	17,274	23,900	26,618	29,638	36,714
12	18,154	25,870	29,096	32,714	41,322
13	19,078	28,003	31,804	36,111	46,508
14	20,050	30,311	34,765	39,859	52,346
15	21,072	32,810	38,001	43,997	58,916
16	22,145	35,515	41,538	48,565	66,310
17	23,273	38,442	45,405	53,607	74,633
18	24,459	41,611	49,631	59,172	84,000
19	26,352	45,041	54,251	65,315	94,542
20	27,694	48,754	59,301	72,095	106,409

The power of compound interest (interest paid on the principal) and on accumulated interest can make your money grow steadily. This chart shows how an initial investment will grow over the years at various interest rates, compounded quarterly. Interest rates and methods of compounding vary from one institution to another. Figures in the chart are rounded off and do not take into account the effect of income taxes on the investment.

tors Service, Inc., 99 Church Street, New York, NY 10004; The Investment Company Institute, 1775 K Street, N.W., Washington, DC 20006; and No-Load Mutual Fund Association, Inc., Valley Forge, PA 19481.

As you near retirement, reevaluate your investment strategies and objectives. You will probably choose a more conservative approach because you have less time to recover from investment mistakes. Evaluate how each current or potential investment meets your new objectives. Also consider the tax consequences of each investment. Income from investments can be taxed several different ways: at ordinary tax rates, as tax-deferred income, as tax-sheltered income (which is hard to come by these days), or as tax-exempt income. An investment that promises a tax-exempt return of a certain percent annually may actually be a better deal than a fully taxable investment that returns a greater percent annually. To know what you are really making on an investment, you have to determine how much of those earnings will go to taxes.

And remember, your net return on an investment (your after-tax return) must at least equal the inflation rate; otherwise, you are losing ground. Keep up-to-date on changes in tax laws that may affect your investments. Also investigate the following aspects of each current and potential investment:

- *Yield.* What yield, or return, can you expect on each investment? What assurance is there that the promised yield will continue for the foreseeable future? How will the yield be affected by commissions, service charges, and other fees in addition to taxes?
- *Safety.* How safe is your principal? What fluctuations in value might occur? What can cause those fluctuations? Are they in your control?
- *Liquidity.* How quickly can you cash in your investment should the need arise? Would you suffer a loss or penalty if you did so?
- *Guarantees and insurance.* To what extent, if any, are your yield and principal guaranteed? Is either of them federally insured? Who is making the guarantee? Where will you be if the guarantee is not honored?
- *Term.* If the investment plan runs for a stated length of time, is that term in line with your future needs? Are you staggering maturities so that you will have cash available for other investments that might come along?
- *Inflation hedge.* To what extent will the value of your investment keep up with inflation?

To make the best investment decisions possible, invest some time in doing your own research and some time and money in obtaining trusted professional advice.

Retirement Expenses—Where the Money Will Go

Developing a tentative retirement budget involves estimating your expenses both for routine items such as taxes and for big-ticket items such as a grand tour of Europe or a child's college education. The major expense categories are housing, including mortgage, taxes, upkeep, and utilities; food, clothing, and personal items; federal, state, and local taxes; life, health, automobile, and homeowner's insurance; transportation; hobbies and special interests; gifts and contributions; and potential dependent care. Here are some things to keep in mind when estimating expenses for your retirement budget:

- *Housing.* Identify any remodeling or repair work that is needed to make your home suitable for retirement. Estimate the cost and determine the best time for you to incur each expense.

- *Food, clothing, and personal items.* People of all ages can take advantage of these simple cost-cutting strategies: discount coupons, generic brand products, special sales, seasonal savings, and buying in bulk.

- *Health care and insurance.* On average, Medicare covers about 40 percent of health care costs. Can your employer's plan be carried over into retirement? Investigate the cost and coverage of supplemental health insurance and health maintenance organizations (HMOs) now. (See the discussion of these options on pages 21–22, in chapter 2.)

- *Life, homeowner's, and automobile insurance.* You may be able to decrease or eliminate life insurance depending on personal circumstances. But, to protect your assets, continue to carry (and possibly increase) your homeowner's and automobile insurance. Review your homeowner's insurance policy. Does the value of your home and furnishings exceed the amount of coverage you have? Does your policy pay the "current market value" or the "full replacement cost"?
- *Transportation.* If you are a two-car family, can you eliminate one car in retirement? If so, you will save in a number of ways: the monthly car payment, gas, insurance, repair, and maintenance. Can some of your transportation needs be met by public transportation?
- *Hobbies and special interests.* Try out new hobbies and activities before you retire to see if you really enjoy them and what they will cost. Get estimates for trips you would like to take. Plug these figures into your retirement budget. You may find that you will have to establish priorities among these activities or find additional sources of income to pay for them.
- *Dependent care.* About one retiree in five provides some financial support for an elderly relative, usually a parent. For your own financial security, plan now for this possibility. What are your options if such a need arises in your family? Is everyone properly insured? Who can share the financial burden with you? Would insurance for long-term care be a worthwhile investment in your financial security and peace of mind? What will it cost you?

The Dollar Diet

Is there too much month left at the end of your money? Do you wonder where your money goes? Find out by putting yourself on the dollar diet.

1. Carry a pencil and a notebook with you at all times.
2. Every time you spend money for any purpose, write the purchase and the amount spent in your notebook.
3. Do this for two or three months.

After that time, you will reap these benefits:

1. Know where every penny of your money is going.
2. Develop the habit of reconsidering each potential purchase.
3. Be able to reduce many of these expenditures.

Don't wait until retirement to put yourself on the dollar diet; start today.

Do You Need a Financial Planner?

Given the growing complexity of financial planning and the high stakes involved—your long-term financial security—would it be a wise investment of time and money to obtain the services of a financial planner?

Some experts say that to benefit from the services of a financial planner, a person's income should be at least $25,000. Others say a $50,000 income is the threshold level, beyond which the financial benefits will exceed the costs. Since each person's situation is unique, only you can decide whether the benefits of professional services will be worth the cost. And that cost will vary considerably depending on what the financial planner does for you and how he or she charges for services.

A financial planner charges for services in one of three ways: (1) a flat fee or hourly rate, (2) commissions only, or (3) a combination of 1 and 2. Fee-only (or hourly rate) financial planners are thought to be the least biased in their recommendations regarding purchases of insurance and stocks and bonds.

The best way to find a good financial planner is by word of mouth. Ask friends, business associates, and professionals you deal with for recommendations. Then interview several financial planners to compare their manner, methods, and fees before making your decision. Some key questions to ask them are these:

- What are your areas of expertise? What kinds of clients are you looking for? Are there areas you avoid or refer to other professionals?
- What is your professional background? What did you do before becoming a financial planner? (Having been a lawyer or stockbroker does not necessarily qualify the person as a financial planner.)
- What are your credentials and professional affiliations? (The most common designations are Certified Financial Planner [CFP], Chartered Financial Consultant [ChFC], and listing in the Registry of Financial Planning Practitioners. See the box for information on contacting people with these designations.)
- Are you registered with the federal Securities and Exchange Commission (SEC) or with a state agency?
- How do you keep up-to-date on the latest financial developments?
- What is your fee structure? How do you get paid for your services?
- What will I get for my money—a comprehensive financial plan? help in implementing it? recommendations for improving my financial situation? the pros and cons of each option? periodic review? coordination with other professionals?
- Are you willing to work with my current attorney, accountant, banker, and other professional advisers?
- What about follow-up and monitoring of the plan? (The financial planner should want to review your plan with you at least annually and after any major change in your situation or the tax laws.)
- What information do I need to provide you? How long will it take to develop the initial plan?
- Whom will I be dealing with on a regular basis? (Ask this if the planner is with a large firm.)

Information Sources

The two organizations listed below can provide you with the names, addresses, and phone numbers of certified financial planners in your area.

International Association for Financial Planning (IAFP). Two Concourse Parkway, Suite 800, Atlanta, GA 30328. 404-396-1605. Provides the names of members who qualify—through rigorous experience, education, and testing—for the IAFP's Registry of Financial Planning Practitioners. Also provides the free booklet *Building a Capital Base,* which gives an overview of financial planning and a glossary of terms.

Institute of Certified Financial Planners (ICFP). 2 Denver Highlands, 10065 E. Harvard Avenue, Suite 320, Denver, CO 80231. 303-751-7600. Provides a free list of CFPs in your area.

Should You Invade Your Capital?

Such various sources of income during retirement as stocks, bonds, and real estate have already been discussed. The income that you can derive from these sources, including interest on your savings and dividends on your stocks, can play an important role in your overall financial security during retirement.

But the question arises, Should the capital itself be invaded? When, if at all, should a retiree cash in some investments and use the money to live on? This is a deeply personal matter for which there is no rule of thumb. Some retirees spend too much of their capital too soon, to their great regret. Others leave their capital untouched, when in fact they could easily afford to dip into it and allow themselves more comforts and luxuries.

The extent to which you might, or should, dip into your capital will depend on many factors, such as how much you may want to leave family members and friends in gifts or inheritances, how well you are protected by insurance against medical and other catastrophes, how capably you cope with inflation, and how your more speculative investments fare.

It is not necessarily wrong to dip into capital, provided you do it prudently. To help you determine how much "dipping" might be wise for you, look at the following table, which shows how long a given nest egg will last if it is periodically reduced by withdrawals from the principal of the fund.

Let's say that Phil and Mary have accumulated a savings fund of $30,000. It earns 7 percent interest per year, compounded quarterly. Thus, their income from this fund is about $2,200 per year, or $183 per month. They have been using this income to supplement their pension and Social Security payments.

They'd like to increase their spendable income and are thinking about dipping into this savings fund. As the table shows, they can withdraw $348 per month for ten years, $232 per month for twenty years, or $199 per month for thirty years—at the end of which time the total nest egg will be gone.

You can use the table to determine how much dipping you can allow yourself from a similar nest egg.

Dipping into Your Nest Egg

Starting with a lump sum of	you can withdraw this much each month for the stated number of years, reducing the nest egg to zero					OR, you can withdraw this much each month and always have the original nest egg intact.
	10 yrs.	**15 yrs.**	**20 yrs.**	**25 yrs.**	**30 yrs.**	
$ 10,000	$ 116	$ 89	$ 77	$ 70	$ 66	$ 59
15,000	174	134	116	106	99	88
20,000	232	179	155	141	133	118
25,000	290	224	193	176	166	142
30,000	348	269	232	212	199	179
40,000	464	359	310	282	266	237
50,000	580	448	386	352	332	285
60,000	696	538	464	424	398	360
80,000	928	718	620	564	532	467
100,000	1,160	896	772	704	668	585

(Based on an interest rate of 7% per year, compounded quarterly.)

Chapter 8

Legal Readiness for Retirement and Estate Planning

For nine years, Fred and Margaret W. mailed a fifty-dollar check each month for installments on a "retirement ranchette" they were buying in the Southwest. But their dream fell through after Fred's retirement when they left their Philadelphia home and visited the site for the first time. The "adjacent" town proved to be twenty-five miles away from their plot, accessible only via a neglected dirt road. They learned that many lots had been abandoned after the owners had spent large amounts of money drilling for water that wasn't there. Even if Fred and Margaret had been lucky enough to find water, building a home would have involved astronomical costs, since workers would have to commute fifty miles each day from town. Margaret and Fred are still living in Philadelphia, with little hope of unloading their property or recovering the money they invested in it.

Al H. and Pete Z. had long been friends and golfing partners, so when they retired, they thought it was a good idea to go into business together—some small enterprise that each one could run half-time so neither would be too tied down. Since they were such good friends, they saw no need for any written agreement between them. They settled on a village sporting goods store, and for a while things went well. Then Al discovered that Pete was lazy, taking more than his share of days off, while Pete found Al to be a penny-pinching nitpicker. Finally, Al declared he wasn't going to let his retirement be ruined by a no-good partner and offered to sell out, but Pete refused to buy. The partners wound up suing each other, and the business went down the drain.

Claire W., a widow with two grown children, married Charlie A., a widower who also had an adult daughter and son. Claire and Charlie put all their property in joint tenancy "to beat probate" and promised each other that the survivor would leave the estate in equal shares to both sets of children. But an automobile crash killed

Charlie instantly. Claire lived for a few more days. During the brief time that she outlived her husband, Claire became sole owner of their joint property. Because she died without a will, the whole estate passed by law to her children. Not only have Charlie's children stopped speaking to Claire's, but they have also started a lawsuit seeking a share of their father's estate.

Do you know which of your plans for retirement have legal implications? Which ones may affect the size, safety, management, and distribution of your estate? Any of the actions listed below could, for example, play a part in your legal readiness for retirement and estate planning:

- Making or revising a will.
- Buying or selling a home.
- Tapping the equity in your home while continuing to live there.
- Leasing a house or apartment or signing a contract for retirement housing.
- Investing in real estate.
- Putting your property in joint ownership.
- Making substantial gifts to children, other relatives, friends, or organizations.
- Setting up a trust fund or other estate-planning device.
- Entering into a late or second marriage or terminating an existing one.
- Establishing a new business or selling an existing one.
- Planning a joint venture or partnership.
- Handling the affairs of an ill or incompetent person.
- Lending or borrowing a large sum of money.
- Moving to another state.
- Choosing between a lump-sum or an annuity payout of a retirement or profit-sharing plan.

Some Important Legal Considerations

As you near retirement, mistakes in any one of the areas noted below can become quite serious. Obtain trusted professional advice before engaging in any of the following undertakings:

Buying or Selling a Home

A contract or agreement you make for buying or selling probably involves more time, money, and potential legal hazards than any other deal you ordinarily make.

Buying a Home

In buying housing, whether a new home, a condominium, or a cooperative, you usually go through the following steps:

1. An offer to buy, to be valid, will be put in writing and signed by you. The seller accepts your offer by signing the agreement. Commonly, a deposit, or binder is required of the buyer, and this deposit may be forfeited if the buyer backs out of the transaction.

When buying housing, you should have an attorney to protect your interests, and the best

time to hire one is before you make the written offer, which becomes a sales contract or part of one. That sales agreement should cover such important points as a legal description of the property, the amount of the deposit and the conditions under which it will be returned if the deal falls through, the purchase price, the way the title is to be transferred, the fees and taxes to be paid and who will pay them, and the arrangements for settlement.

2. In arranging financing for the house, you may be helped by the real estate company or developer, who may also handle the details of the title search and insurance. However, neither the agent nor the developer represents your interests to see that you get the best deal; that's up to you. You should understand thoroughly the terms of any proposed mortgage, since a seemingly small difference in the terms can add up to a good deal of money before it's paid off. Does it have a fixed interest rate, or can it be escalated under some conditions? Are you penalized if you pay off the loan before it is due? What insurance are you required to carry to protect the mortgage holder, and does the insurance fully protect you as well?

3. When you take title to your home, you want the title to be as secure as possible. Both you and the mortgage holder have a stake in the title search and the title insurance policy. The title company will check the records for any conditions that might threaten your ownership, and if the title is insurable, the company will issue title insurance. The policy will describe the property and what interest you have in it. It will also list any defects, liens, easements, unpaid taxes, or other encumbrances on the property. Keep in mind that title insurance protects the named insured. The lender (mortgagee) will want to have his or her interest in the property protected, as will you as the owner. Thus, the best kind of title insurance policy is an owner's policy, which protects both the mortgagee and the owner.

4. A property buyer sometimes is required to put money in escrow while various procedures are under way to close the transaction. That is, the buyer's money and the seller's deed may be placed in the custody of a third party, usually a bank or title company, under an agreement setting forth the conditions that must be fulfilled before the money can be paid and final settlement made. It's best to have your lawyer check that the terms of the agreement fully protect your interests.

Special Kinds of Housing

If you are thinking of buying into special kinds of housing—such as a condominium, cooperative apartment, or life-care residence—or if you sign a contract for space and amenities in a manufactured home court, you should have a clear understanding of what you are getting, what the total cost will be, and what rules and restrictions you will be legally bound to observe.

Caution: A lawyer can interpret the fine points in many of these housing contracts, which may have been carefully worded to protect the housing organization rather than the individual resident. It's wise to pay a fee for legal advice rather than sink your savings into retirement housing that could tie you into an unhappy situation or leave you without sufficient funds. (See the discussion on page 81 in chapter 6.)

Selling Your Home

If you decide to sell your present home to achieve your retirement goals, a key rule is, Take your time. You have a large investment at stake. Take the time to avoid mistakes and to realize the maximum return. Also, as in buying property, selling it involves a number of legal angles, documents, agreements, and tax liabilities with which you should become familiar.

As a first step, you probably will want to select a licensed real estate professional to help you sell your house.

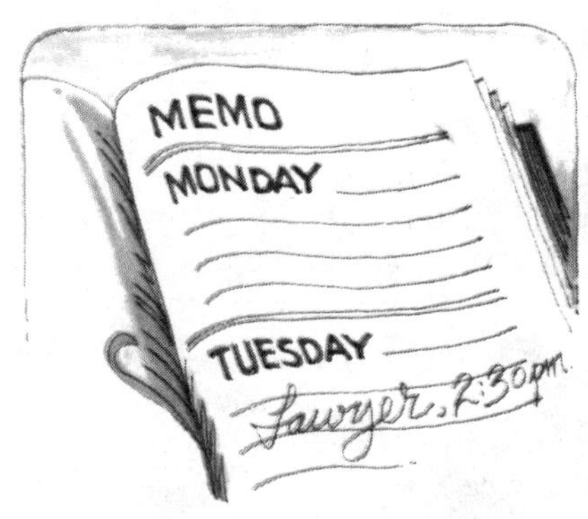

You definitely need a lawyer if you decide to sell your house yourself. As a seller, you have certain legal obligations and financial liabilities. For example, if you misrepresented certain features of your house, even unwittingly, the buyer may be able to cancel the deal and possibly sue for damages. Also, there will be an agreement of sale under which you, as the seller, bind yourself to perform certain actions, such as delivering a clear title to the property. The agreement should spell out conditions under which the sale will proceed or may be canceled.

Some do-it-yourself sellers believe that standard printed sales contracts, with blanks to fill in dates and property descriptions, are sufficient for their purposes. Such documents, when signed, can become binding legal contracts. However, very few property sales are "standard." For your own protection, you probably should have a contract specially drawn to suit your needs.

A clause describing in detail the property involved and a clause making the contract contingent on the buyer's obtaining a loan should be included in any contract.

At the settlement, your attorney can conduct the closing and review all papers associated with the sale. One rule: Do not sign any documents until they have been examined by your lawyer.

Check fees for legal work beforehand. Do not hire an attorney for a percentage of the sale.

Tapping the Equity in Your Home

Also obtain legal counsel before entering into any one of the home equity conversion programs now available. A brief description of these programs is provided on pages 77–78 in chapter 6.

Setting Up Your Own Business

If, like many preretirees, you dream of setting up your own small business when you retire, be sure you have advice from a lawyer who is thoroughly conversant with the laws pertaining to small businesses. A maze of ordinances, zoning restrictions, licensing requirements, permits, and taxes apply to business—and these vary from state to state and county to county. You want your enterprise to be legal, and you don't want to make an error that could jeopardize your business.

You can get free advice and counseling on small businesses from several government agencies, such as the federal government's Small Business Administration (see the listing on page 62 in chapter 5). Most states have commerce divisions or economic development agencies that offer advice at no cost to you. These offices may also offer free literature. They cannot, of course, advise you on purely local regulations.

Small business enterprises frequently start as partnerships—perhaps because this seems to reduce the insecurity of going it alone in a new venture. Also, there may be a desire to team up with a relative or a close friend for mutual benefit. However, a partnership is a tricky form of business relationship and should be considered with eyes wide open and a lawyer's counsel in framing a detailed partnership agreement. In a partnership, for example, you may be liable for 100 percent of the debts of the partnership, not just your share. In case of an argument over an important business decision, whose opinion prevails? Or what happens if the business is crippled by lack of cooperation between the partners?

A partnership can be a satisfying business structure if it is carefully planned with all legal angles covered—including provision for dissolution of the partnership.

More information about starting your own business can be found on pages 61–63 in chapter 5.

Knowing Your Pension Rights

In 1974, Congress passed the Employee Retirement Income Security Act (ERISA). To secure your pension benefits, ERISA does the following:

- Requires your employer to provide a summary of pension plan provisions and benefits. The report must be written in easy-to-understand language.
- Establishes an insurance program that will provide a certain level of pension benefits to eligible retirees in the event the employer goes out of business or the pension fund is otherwise terminated.
- Sets rules for the management and investment of pension funds.
- Establishes several vesting formulas guaranteeing that all covered workers will be at least partially vested after ten years and fully vested after

fifteen years. Under the 1986 Tax Reform Act, new vesting formulas will go into effect in 1989. (See page 96 for more information.)

In addition, the Retirement Equity Act of 1984 offers ways for women to protect themselves against losing their own or their husband's pension benefits. The law lowers the age at which pension plans begin counting service for vesting purposes from twenty-two to eighteen. It authorizes courts to treat a spouse's pension as an asset of the marriage that can be divided as part of a divorce settlement. And the law makes survivors' benefits automatic. The worker must obtain the spouse's written, notarized permission to remove the spouse as a pension beneficiary.

If you have questions about your pension benefits, contact the company's pension plan administrator. (For more information about pensions, see pages 95–96 in chapter 7.)

Using a Power of Attorney

A power of attorney is a legal device that may be useful in a number of situations, but the limitations and liabilities of such an instrument should be understood before you grant or accept such a responsibility. A power of attorney is a document by which the principal—the signer—designates another person, not necessarily a lawyer, to act on his or her behalf.

If you give a general power of attorney to a relative or friend, that person becomes your "attorney-in-fact" and can sign checks on your bank account, buy or sell property or securities for you, negotiate contracts on your behalf, and so on. Obviously, before you grant such power to anyone, you must be certain that the individual is absolutely trustworthy and has good judgment. A power of attorney should probably be drafted by a lawyer.

More suitable than a general power of attorney in many situations is a limited, or special, power of attorney, which limits the agent to certain specific actions on your behalf, such as receipt of money due you and payment of current bills with checks drawn on your account.

A power of attorney is useful, for example, if you wish to travel extensively and need someone to handle your routine affairs while you are away from home. It also can offer you freedom from stress if you find it difficult to handle business and financial matters and wish to put them in the hands of a financial manager or bank. Single persons may find a power of attorney a valuable tool in the event of extended disability.

A power of attorney usually terminates when the person who gave the power becomes legally incompetent or dies. In some states, however, it is possible to create a "durable" power of attorney, which will continue in force or begin to take effect if the giver of the power becomes incompetent.

Caring for an Ill or Incompetent Person

If you have a parent, other relative, or friend who is no longer competent to handle his or her affairs because of illness or injury, you may petition the court to appoint you or some other member of the family as the person legally responsible for the financial and/or personal needs of that person. Depending on the state and on the circumstances, you might be named the *conservator* or the *guardian*, legal terms that are similar in meaning though somewhat different legally. But before you assume such responsibilities, you should thoroughly familiarize yourself with the duties and obligations that accompany the situation.

Making a Living Will

Through the vehicle of a living will, an individual provides instructions as to the terms and conditions under which medical treatment is to be given or withheld in the event of a terminal illness or accident.

Living wills have been developed in response to advances in medical technology that many believe may infringe on a person's right to die with dignity. A living will is a separate entity from a regular will and does not involve distribution of property.

Currently, thirty-five states and the District of Columbia recognize living wills as legally binding documents. Consult your lawyer about whether your state recognizes living wills as legally binding and about the specifics of the living will declaration in your state.

To obtain formats for living wills and information on requirements, write to Concern for Dying, Inc., 250 West 57th Street, New York, NY 10107.

Protecting Your Consumer Rights

In recent years, Congress has passed a number of laws designed to protect consumers. In addition, various federal regulatory agencies have rules and regulations that offer consumer protection in certain circumstances. Following is a brief recap of some of the essential features of these laws and rules:

- **The Truth in Lending Law** requires lenders and others who extend credit to quote all financing costs in terms of the annual percentage rate (APR). This is true for almost all common financing transactions. Prior to the law, interest costs were quoted in a variety of ways, so it was difficult to compare them. When you shop for a loan, be sure the rates are being quoted in terms of the APR if you want to keep borrowing costs as low as possible.

  The Truth in Lending Law also offers protection to parties signing loan papers. In some cases, borrowers now have the right to cancel a contract. In other words, if you sign the papers and then want to back out, you can do so if you act within three days.
- **The Fair Credit Reporting Act** gives you the right to examine your credit history at your local credit bureau. If you find that there is erroneous or misleading information in your file, the law sets forth the steps you can take to correct these mistakes. A review of your credit file every two or three years is wise. Errors may sneak in, and a credit file with "bad marks" on it can weaken your credit record.
- **The Equal Credit Opportunity Law** provides that credit shall not be denied individuals on the basis of gender and also allows both spouses to establish individual credit histories in their own names.

  If you feel that you have been unjustifiably denied credit, you can demand a written explanation for the refusal. The company denying the credit must respond within thirty days.
- **The Fair Credit Billing Law** allows you to be free of a creditor's demands for payment if you have a valid objection to your bill. The law prescribes certain steps to take if you believe there is an error. Any firms that bill you for credit accounts (credit card companies, department stores, and so on) are required to provide you with copies of the law from time to time.
- **The Mail Order Merchandising Rule** of the Federal Trade Commission (FTC) states that the seller must furnish the goods you ordered within thirty days of receiving your order unless the advertisement specifies a longer waiting period. If you don't receive your goods in the specified time, you can demand a refund, which the seller must then mail to you within seven working days. If you paid by credit card, the seller must credit your account within one billing cycle. This mail-order rule does not apply to all orders. Exceptions include film developing and plants and items ordered COD or by telephone.
- **The Cooling Off Rule** of the Federal Trade Commission gives you three days to change your mind about most goods or services bought from door-to-door salespeople. Some exceptions include purchases under twenty-five dollars; purchases of real estate, insurance, or securities; purchases of home repairs if you waive your right to cancel; and purchases of home repair or maintenance services that you initiate.

Your rights are set forth in these laws and rules, but it's up to you to pursue them. The law shows you the right road, but you have to walk down it. Also keep in mind that successful assertion of your rights often hinges on prompt action. To obtain more information on any of these laws or rules, contact the Federal Trade Commission, Office of the Secretary, 6th Street and Pennsylvania Avenue, N.W., Washington, DC 20580. 202-523-3598.

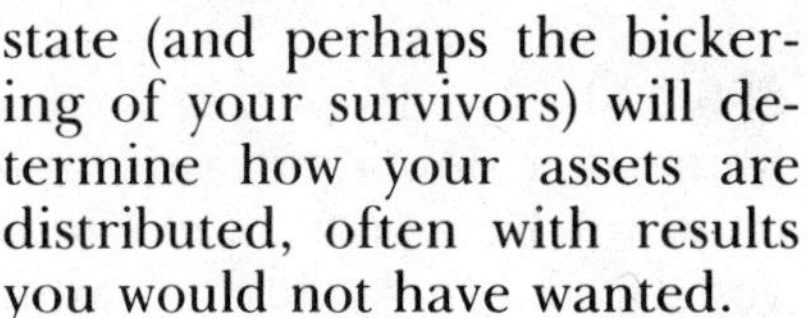

Estate Planning—What It Can Do for You

You can accumulate a great deal in the course of a forty- to fifty-year working career: a home, some investments, insurance, a pension, and personal effects.

You'll want to be certain that you can pass along your wealth—however great or small—to the persons you have selected. You'll want it to pass directly, quickly, and with a minimum of bother or expense.

This is what estate planning is all about. It is a combination of financial and legal steps that will assure your welfare and peace of mind and also that of your heirs.

Estate planning is of concern to everyone—married or single, male or female, wealthy or of modest means. Certain steps *must* be taken, particularly with regard to your heirs and survivors, lest the law dictate that your wealth pass in a way you may not have wanted.

The middle years become a critical time in which to accomplish the necessary estate planning. The end of your working career, the amount of your ultimate wealth, and the needs of your family come into clearer focus.

What Is an Estate?

Your estate is the sum total of all that you own plus all that is owed to you, minus all that you owe. It is sometimes called your net worth (see page 90 in chapter 7). Upon your death, your estate becomes a legal entity in its own right—the estate of John (Jane) Doe. The estate then consists of all the assets and debts you had while alive.

A Two-pronged Estate Plan

A firm grasp of your current financial situation is the foundation for any sensible estate plan. You must know what you have now if you want to be able to define your goals and create a program to meet them.

Two essential elements of estate planning are (1) *arranging your assets* so that they can be distributed with maximum ease and minimum cost and (2) *setting forth binding instructions* so that your assets are distributed and your other wishes are carried out as you desire. You will probably need professional assistance in carrying out both of these steps.

If there are no binding instructions, the laws of your state (and perhaps the bickering of your survivors) will determine how your assets are distributed, often with results you would not have wanted.

Ignoring the need to create an estate plan now heightens the risk of family squabbles, loved ones being left uncared for, and possibly heavy and unnecessary expenses for your survivors.

Defining Your Estate

What are your resources for accomplishing your estate-planning goals? There is no room for playing guessing games. Accurate estimates must be made of your current estate, and, as closely as you can, you must project what your estate will be in the future. The worksheet on page 90 in chapter 7 will help you with this task. It may take you some time to complete it, but the effort is crucial to your long-term well-being.

As you estimate various assets, take into account *liquidity*, that is, how readily you can convert an asset into cash. This may affect value. For example, perhaps your house should bring $90,000, but the market in your area is slow and you must sell in a hurry. So you take

$80,000. In this case, your home is a nonliquid asset and may not be worth as much as you think. In evaluating your assets, base their value on how much cash you could realistically generate at any given time. Savings accounts and stocks are relatively liquid. Real estate and family business interests can be quite nonliquid.

Estate-planning Devices

There are a number of devices for managing and distributing your estate.

Gifts

You can give some or all of your estate away as an outright gift while you are still alive. Proper use of tax-exempt gifts can reduce the size of your estate and thus minimize estate taxes. You can give up to $10,000 a year to any person or organization you wish without having to pay federal gift taxes. If married, you and your spouse can make joint gifts of up to $20,000 per recipient per year. If your gifts exceed the tax-exempt allowance, the excess will be considered a taxable transfer and may be subject to tax (see the discussion of how an estate is taxed on pages 122–123). Married couples can make unlimited gifts to each other without having to pay federal gift taxes. However, they may have to pay state gift taxes.

Single persons may find tax-exempt gifting a particularly useful strategy for avoiding taxes on their estates, since they cannot take advantage of the marital deduction to reduce their tax obligations (see page 122).

Trusts

You can transfer your wealth by trust, either during your life or on your death. A trust is an arrangement whereby an individual places all or part of his or her wealth, including property, in the hands of a trustee (lawyer, bank, or trusted relative or friend) with instructions as to how that wealth is to be managed and distributed. The trustee must account periodically to those designated as having an interest in the trust.

A trust may be entered into while the person is living (living trust), or it may be arranged to take effect after the person's death (testamentary trust). A trust may be revocable (cancelable) or irrevocable (not cancelable). Testamentary trusts are often used for management of funds for minor or incompetent heirs. Living trusts are one way for individuals to free themselves of the day-to-day management of their own investments. The laws of trusts and their tax consequences are complex; proceed only with proper counsel. The 1986 Tax Reform Act specifies major changes in one popular estate-planning tool—the Clifford trust. A Clifford trust is an irrevocable trust that is generally set up for a specific purpose, such as to pay for a child's education. At the end of a ten-year period, the trust assets are returned to the creator of the trust to be included in his or her gross estate. The 1986 Tax Reform Act severely limits the tax benefits formerly available through Clifford trusts. Check with your lawyer or tax accountant regarding these changes.

Property Ownership

You can pass part of your estate along through joint ownership, which may involve tax liabilities. There are four kinds of joint ownership:

Community property. In community property states (Arizona, California, Idaho, Louisiana, Nevada, New Mexico, Texas, and Washington) anything acquired by the efforts of either husband or wife during marriage generally belongs equally to both.

Joint tenancy with right of survivorship. Two or more persons hold property jointly; each owns the whole property and not a fractional part. If one person dies, his or her interest ordinarily passes to the other joint tenants without need of probate. It generally cannot be passed along by will as long as there is a surviving owner. Under certain circumstances, a surviving wife's interest may be included in her deceased husband's estate for federal tax purposes.

Tenancy by the entirety. This form of joint ownership is limited primarily to spouses and sometimes is further restricted to real estate. As in joint tenancy, each spouse owns the whole property. Upon the death of one spouse, the other automatically becomes the sole owner. It is not recognized in some states.

Tenancy in common. Each person owns an undivided fractional part of the property. Unlike joint tenancies, a surviving wife's interest in a tenancy in common is never included in her deceased husband's estate for federal estate tax. The husband's interest passes to his heirs through the probate process.

There is no best way to establish property ownership. The

choice depends on your own situation. The proper way to determine the correct form of ownership for you is to discuss the matter with your attorney, giving consideration to your overall financial and estate programs. In general, you should remember that when you put any property into part ownership with another person, you lose some degree of legal control over it.

Life Insurance

You can transfer some wealth through life insurance, either outright in a lump sum or in partial payments over a set period of time. The role of life insurance in your estate planning hinges on the needs of your survivors. If other sources of income will provide the necessary protection for loved ones, you may not need to carry much life insurance. (See the discussion of life insurance on pages 99–101 in chapter 7.) You may, however, want to carry enough life insurance to pay the expenses involved in settling your estate. And remember, life insurance policies owned by you will be included in your estate for income tax purposes. Ask your advisers about the appropriate kind of policy and amount of coverage and about ways to minimize or eliminate taxes on the proceeds from your life insurance.

A Will

The final way for you to distribute your wealth is through a will. This important estate-planning device is discussed in the following section.

An individual might use one or a combination of the devices described above to manage and distribute an estate. Your attorney can help you decide which are right for you after determining the extent of your estate, your goals, and your intentions.

Your Will—The Foundation of Your Estate Plan

For your instructions about the distribution of your estate to be legally binding, they must be set forth in proper legal fashion. The device most frequently used for this purpose is a will.

A properly constructed will can do much more than simply indicate who gets what. It can also provide for various methods of management of funds; help minimize taxes; name guardians for children and conservators for the elderly; and provide incentives for survivors, such as a special gift upon graduation from college.

It is wise for each spouse to have a will because each may have property that he or she would like to dispose of separately. Furthermore, if a wife inherits her husband's estate but does not have a will of her own, on her death, the estate may not be distributed as she would have desired.

The Cost of a Will

Consider the development of your estate plan as an investment. You're investing in peace of mind and future financial security for your survivors. The return on your money can be well worth the expenditure. In the normal probate proceedings, there will be legal fees for the preparation of the documents, the time involved in court proceedings and related matters, and the time involved in advising the executor. There will be court expenses. There may be accounting fees, custodial fees, and trustee fees. The amount of these costs will depend on your prior understanding with your lawyer, the size and nature of your estate, and your agreement with the executor.

Your lawyer should be able to give you a reasonably close estimate of all these costs at the very outset of your planning.

Can these costs be avoided? In recent years, there has been talk of avoiding probate. This can be dangerously misleading, prompting some people to fail to draw up a will or make other estate-planning provisions. They then risk the possible chaos of intestacy. Probate might be avoided with some large estates through trusts or gifting programs. While some of the costs of the probate procedure can be avoided, legal costs of preparing the more complicated documents will still be incurred. Whether or not any net savings are realized depends on the expertise of the attorneys and tax counselors involved.

Naturally, you want to keep your costs to a minimum. But you don't want to be penny-wise and pound-foolish. Only your lawyer should determine the best course for you, costs considered. In most cases, the best course is a simple will.

Before You See Your Lawyer

There are a number of things you can do before you sit down with your lawyer:

- If married, confer frankly with your spouse. Your lawyer's office is no place to bicker over who should get the grand piano.
- Prepare a thorough financial analysis of your estate and include an estimate of how you think it will change in the years ahead. (You've done most of this work already on page 90 in chapter 7.) You'll also want to note how each of your assets is owned—by you, by your spouse, or jointly.
- Write down all your wishes about distribution of your estate.
- Choose your executor. This is a very important task. The job of the executor can be rigorous and time-consuming. Commonly, one spouse will name the other as executor. It may also be feasible and prudent to name a coexecutor, such as a bank or a lawyer. They are more skilled handling such matters and can offer a greater measure of security to the overall plan.
- Make a date with your lawyer and don't let anything distract you from keeping that appointment. You never know when it might be too late.

Once you have had your will completed, don't forget about it. Review it periodically and if any of the following situations arise:

- You marry, divorce, or separate, or your spouse dies.
- Any beneficiaries die.
- You wish to add new beneficiaries.
- You change your mind about any of the beneficiaries. (In some states, if you fail to mention an heir, that person may still be entitled to a share of your estate.)
- Your executor dies or moves away.
- You move to a new state. (You need to establish legal residence in your new state and verify that your will conforms to the laws of that state.)
- There are any changes in federal or state laws that could affect your will.
- There has been an increase or decrease in your assets that would affect the amounts you wish to distribute to certain individuals. (Some people avoid this problem by making bequests as percentages of the total estate.)

Facts About Wills

Here is a step-by-step look at the creation and operation of a will and some other important information pertaining to wills:

1. There is an initial interview between client and lawyer. In certain situations, other advisers—accountant, banker, and/or insurance agent—may also be called in.
2. The will is prepared by the lawyer, setting forth the client's wishes and instructions. The will also names an executor, or personal representative, who is responsible for carrying out its provisions. The duties of an executor can be extensive. You can choose to have the executor serve without bond, which will save your estate some expense. (A bond insures the beneficiaries against loss due to improper administration of the estate.) Either the will or, at some later time, the executor may designate a lawyer to represent the estate after the death of the testator (the maker of the will).

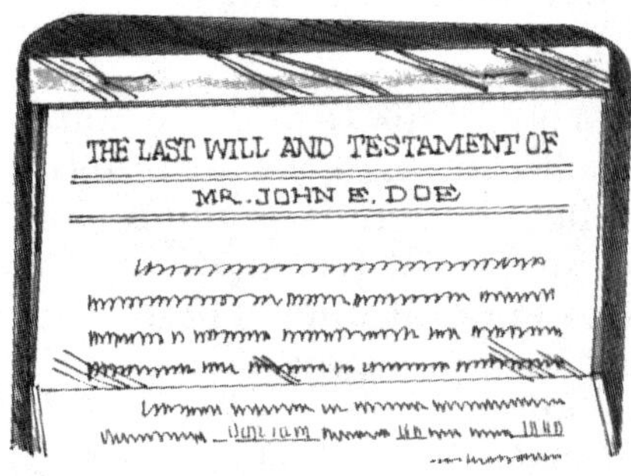

3. The completed will should then be reviewed by the lawyer, the client, and the other advisers.
4. The will is executed, that is, signed by the testator in the presence of witnesses. The number of witnesses is set by state law. They generally should not be designated beneficiaries of the estate.
5. The original of the will may be kept by the lawyer; however, you do not have to give the lawyer the original or even a copy if you don't want to. The original of the will should, however, be kept in a safe place, and another person should know where it is. You should keep a copy. Because some states require that safe-deposit boxes be sealed upon the death of the renter, it may be unwise to keep the original of the will in a safe-deposit box.
6. After the will has been created, it should be reviewed periodically and amended as necessary.

7. Upon the death of the testator (now called the decedent), the will is presented to the proper state court, usually known as the probate court. Except for jointly owned property passing to the survivor, life insurance proceeds payable to a named beneficiary, U.S. savings bonds with designated beneficiaries, and certain trusts, all the real and personal property of the deceased is subject to probate. It is the job of the probate court to "prove" that the will is, in fact, the valid will of the decedent.

   All beneficiaries are notified of the proceedings. A person who believes that the will is not valid may contest the proceedings. If a contest is successful and the will is invalidated, the decedent's estate is then distributed in accordance with a prior will, if one exists, or under the state's intestacy laws. A properly drawn and executed will is the best assurance against such a contest. A do-it-yourself will might be more successfully contested. In rare cases, and only in some states, a holographic (handwritten) will or a nuncupative (spoken) will may be valid. But relying on these devices is risking invalidation of your will.
8. Assets may be frozen until the probate process is completed, which can take a year or more. During the probate procedure, the court may grant the survivors an allowance to be drawn from the estate's assets.
9. Once the will has been proven, the executor must satisfy the court that all outstanding bills and taxes have been paid before distributing property to heirs and carrying out other instructions. The executor must satisfy the court that such duties have been properly discharged.
10. If you die intestate (without a will), the court will appoint an administrator to manage the estate. The administrator will distribute assets, pay bills, and name guardians for children, for example. The court may require the administrator to be bonded. If so, the cost of the bonding and the administrator's fees will be charged against the estate—and can run as high as 10 percent of the estate's value.

Where to Go for Advice

You must do a certain portion of your estate planning on your own. Only you (and your spouse, if married) can determine your estate-planning goals. Once you identify your goals, you'll need some advice about the best way to attain them.

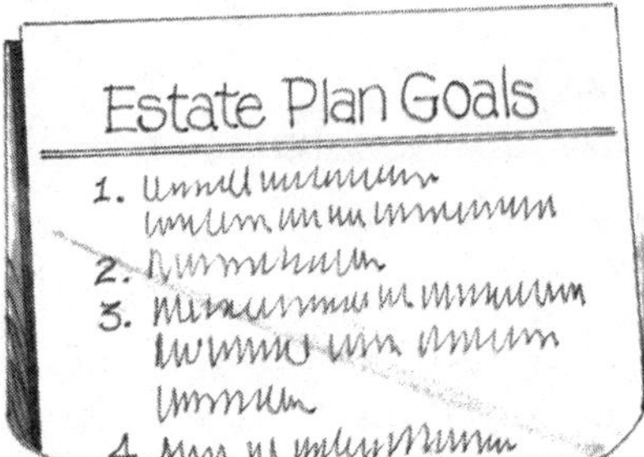

Professionals Who Can Help

A lawyer, a tax accountant, a banker, an insurance agent, and a financial planner can each be a part of your estate-planning team.

Wills, trusts, and gifting programs are among the devices for passing along assets to survivors. In preparing the necessary documents, there's a job for each member of your team. The most important person is your lawyer. He or she can help you determine which devices to use and then prepare them and see that they are properly signed and witnessed. In addition, real estate transactions can be fraught with legal and financial liabilities that require consultation with your lawyer.

Unless your lawyer is a tax expert, you might need a tax accountant to help you minimize estate tax liabilities. Confer with your accountant before retirement to learn the specifics about tax breaks in retirement. If you plan to work after you begin receiving Social Security benefits, your accountant can help you figure out how working will affect your after-tax income. A tax accountant can also explain the advantages of tax-deferral retirement plans such as Keogh plans, individual retirement accounts (IRAs), and 401(k) plans. You may also want to have your accountant explain the tax breaks available to people when they sell their home, especially if the owner is age fifty-five or older.

A banker's advice can be useful in considering your overall plan and should be sought specifically when it comes to trust arrangements and to the appropriateness of certain kinds of savings plans and investments.

Your insurance agents should be consulted about the effect of life insurance on your estate and the appropriateness of your homeowner's and automobile coverage.

A financial planner can advise on all aspects of your estate—taxes, investments, trusts, and so on—thus enabling you to deal with one person. He or she, in turn, consults with other professionals as needed. With a complete picture of your estate, the financial planner can recommend how best to preserve and enhance it. For suggestions on selecting a financial planner, see page 107 in chapter 7.

Cost of Professional Advice

Accountants usually charge on a per-hour basis; in some cases, they may charge a set fee for services, such as preparing a standard income tax return. Always determine the fee structure in advance.

Insurance agents don't charge for their counsel. A good agent should be willing to talk with you for a reasonable time with the understanding that you'll want to do some comparison shopping. Remember that insurance agents generally earn commissions from the company with whom they place a policy, and, thus, their recommendations may not be totally unbiased.

Cultivate a rapport with a banker, who also charges nothing for counsel. Obviously, to do this, you should be a customer of the bank, but that requires only that you open an account. If you contemplate a trust arrangement, confer with your banker about charges for such a service.

Financial planners may charge anywhere from $500 to $5,000 for a master financial plan. Some planners will advise on specific topics for $50 to $150 an hour. While some financial planners charge a set fee for their work, others earn commissions on the stocks, bonds, mutual funds, and insurance they sell in connection with the financial plan they develop for you.

For information on what a lawyer charges, see the discussion that follows. In choosing any of your advisers, it is wise to seek personal recommendations from others in similar situations who have used their services.

Why Consult a Lawyer?

Consulting lawyers is much like consulting doctors. Lawyers are highly trained professionals. They have access to a vast reservoir of legal information, know how the law works, and have, no doubt, dealt with many situations similar to yours. Lawyers can guide you through not only the general legal thicket but also the specific laws of your city and state. They can diagnose your case and suggest the soundest course of action.

Remember, the best and most economical service lawyers can provide is preventive advice and legal counsel that helps you avoid costly and distressing legal pitfalls. Many people put off talking to a lawyer until they are in serious legal or financial trouble: they have unwisely signed a contract without understanding the fine print, they have entered into an agreement that threatens financial loss, they have incurred heavy tax liabilities that could have been avoided, or they are being sued because of a misunderstanding about transfer of property. These people usually discover that their attempts to practice do-it-yourself law have multiplied both their problems and the legal fees they must pay to get them resolved.

How Much Does a Lawyer Charge?

Lawyers' fees are usually determined by the amount of time they spend on a case, the difficulty of the job, and the client's ability to pay. Many charge by the hour, which includes time spent talking to you, looking up the law, preparing legal documents, writing letters, and contacting or negotiating with other individuals.

Some attorneys simplify matters by setting a flat fee for such standard services as drawing up a will, preparing a simple contract, or handling a real estate transaction. In addition to hourly or percentage charges, lawyers also bill for actual out-of-pocket expenses incurred in handling your problem. These expenses might include long-distance phone calls, certain court costs and filing fees, travel expenses, and costs for acquiring nonlegal information (property appraisals, private investigation, and the like). You can request that these expenses be itemized on your bill.

Because time is a key element in legal fees, wasting a lawyer's time can be costly.

Have the relevant facts and figures organized and in hand when you visit your lawyer's office; it's a good idea to ask what information you need to bring when you call to make your appointment.

You should definitely ask how much your lawyer will charge in your particular case and how payment is to be made. He or she will welcome the opportunity to reach an early understanding with you on fees, since this reduces the possibility of confusion and ill feeling. You should also be candid about your ability to pay, as this is often a factor in an attorney's scale of fees. If a lawyer's fees are prohibitively high, look elsewhere for one with lower charges.

Trusting Your Lawyer

An attorney cannot achieve the best results for you unless you state all the pertinent facts in your case as accurately as possible. Remember that the client-lawyer relationship is recognized by the law as confidential and privileged. Any confidential statement made to your lawyer—as to your doctor or clergyperson—is not subject to disclosure in court and cannot be used against you.

From a practical standpoint, you owe it to yourself to be truthful with your lawyer, since his or her judgment and actions on your behalf must be guided by what you say. Concealment of facts that may be embarrassing or seem unimportant might well impair the effectiveness of your lawyer's efforts.

It may happen that you will not be satisfied with the results your lawyer produces for you. It is possible that your cause may just not have been a winning one and that you are too close to the situation to analyze it impartially. However, if, after careful consideration, you feel that your lawyer has not fulfilled his or her professional obligations to you, you might consider asking a local consumer group or bar association about grievance procedures.

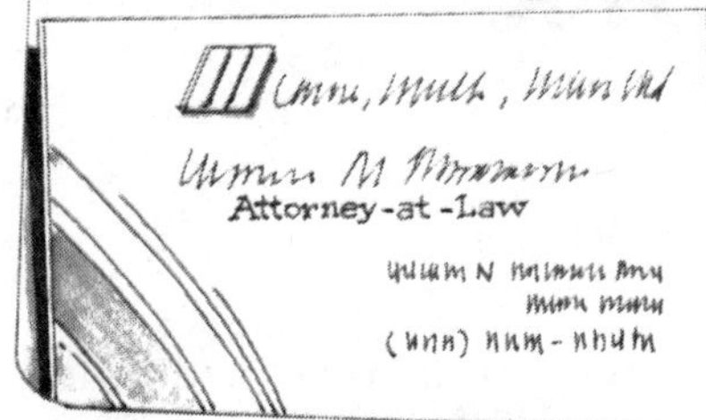

Choosing the Right Lawyer

Just as it is best to have a physician on call before you become seriously ill, it's good legal insurance to have access to a reliable attorney before you find yourself confronted with a legal problem.

There are many kinds of lawyers—corporation, tax, divorce, and criminal lawyers, to name a few. Unless you have a specialized problem, you will probably want a general practitioner, one who handles a wide assortment of legal work for clients. Also, you'll want someone you can respect as a person and who will understand your problems, identify with your interests, and respect your pocketbook. How do you find such a lawyer?

- Seek recommendations from friends, relatives, and coworkers. Lawyers may now advertise their services. But the ads generally contain little useful information, so you should still seek personal recommendations before engaging the services of a lawyer.
- Call your local bar association and ask for recommendations from their lawyer referral service. After an initial conference with the recommended lawyer, which usually doesn't cost very much, you can either continue with him or her or seek help elsewhere.
- Contact your banker, accountant, insurance agent, or employer, any of whom may be able to recommend a reliable lawyer.
- Check legal directories, usually available at your local library. The *Martindale-Hubbell Directory* gives listings of lawyers and will show how your prospective lawyer is rated.

Alternatives to Lawyers

If you don't think you can afford a lawyer, consider the following alternatives:

- Many communities have legal aid societies, which provide attorneys for persons who can't afford standard fees.
- Local law schools may maintain legal clinics, where students, under proper supervision, serve the public.
- In some larger communities, groups of lawyers maintain legal clinics, where "no frills" services are offered at "no frills" prices.
- The federal government's Legal Services Corporation funds offices to serve low-income clients.

Not all cases require a lawyer. When small amounts of money are in dispute, the local small claims court provides a forum for resolving the matter without legal representation. Disputes with local businesses may be resolved by using the arbitration procedures of the Better Business Bureau or a local consumer protection group. Various city, state, and federal agencies are responsible for protecting citizens' rights in a variety of areas such as fair labor practices, public health, housing, commerce, and trade. They may be able to help you with a grievance in one of these areas.

If you are receiving assistance from a public agency, it may be able to provide you with legal services. Or your local area Agency on Aging may be able to refer you to an appropriate organization.

Estate Taxes—How They Work

The Economic Recovery Tax Act of 1981 gradually phased out estate taxes for all but a very small percentage of the population. However, you should know that the following tax liabilities are possible:

- The federal government levies a unified estate and gift tax on certain transfers of wealth between individuals other than spouses.
- Some states also levy an estate tax.
- Some states levy an inheritance tax, payable by the recipient of the inheritance.
- If you receive a cash inheritance, the amount received is not subject to federal income taxes. If you invest your inheritance, income from the investment is taxable, as is profit from the sale of the investment.
- If you receive property as an inheritance (such as stocks or a building) and you sell the inheritance, the gain realized can be taxable. And any earnings generated by that inheritance can be taxable as income.

Federal Taxes

Stipulations of the 1986 Tax Reform Act may have an impact on your estate. Any wills, trusts, or other forms of estate planning that were completed before the changes went into effect should be reviewed and adjusted where appropriate.

Below is a very simplified version of how federal estate and gift taxes work.

Taxable Transfers

The federal unified estate and gift tax is levied on so-called taxable transfers—money or property that one has passed along, either in the form of trusts and gifts while alive or through estate distribution after death.

Gifts

As discussed on page 116, you can make gifts of up to $10,000 per person per year to as many persons or organizations as you wish without having to pay federal gift taxes. If spouses join in making gifts, the annual tax-exempt limit per recipient is $20,000.

If you make gifts in excess of the tax-exempt allowances, the excess will be considered as a taxable transfer and may be subject to tax.

Gross Estate

An estate is valued as of the time of death or, under certain circumstances, six months after death or at the close of probate. The gross estate generally consists of all that the individual owned plus all that was owed to him or her. This can include a home, investments, proceeds of life insurance policies owned by the decedent, personal property, money due under pension and profit-sharing plans, and any business interests. Jointly owned property may be included in the gross estate under certain conditions.

Adjusted Gross Estate

From the gross estate are subtracted the debts of the decedent as well as funeral and burial costs, charitable bequests, and the costs of administering the estate. The remainder is known as the adjusted gross estate.

Marital Deduction

The amount of the adjusted gross estate can be further reduced by the marital deduction, which is that portion of the estate that is left, in proper legal fashion, to the surviving spouse. Prior to 1982, there were limits to the maximum allowable marital deduction. But for deaths occurring since that year, the limits have been removed. *This change is not automatic; you may have to change your will to benefit from it.* Remember, though, that if the surviving spouse dies without having remarried, no marital deduction will be allowed on this "second estate."

Taxable Estate

The marital deduction is subtracted from the adjusted gross estate. The result is the taxable estate. (By separate calculation, the taxable estate will also include any taxable gifts made in excess of the gifting allowances.)

Tax Calculation

Two steps are used in calculating the amount of tax actually due: (1) The tax is figured. (2) From this amount is subtracted the unified tax credit. The difference between the would-be tax and the credit is what is owed to the federal government. Beginning in 1987, a taxable estate of as much as $600,000 is exempt from federal taxes.

Is Your Estate Taxable?

You may be thinking, The estate tax affects only relatively large estates, so why worry? There are three reasons: (1) You don't know if your estate would be currently taxable until you do the basic evaluation. (2) Although you may find that your estate is not large enough now to be taxed, it may grow to a taxable status via inflation, newly acquired assets, increased income, or receipt of a windfall. (3) You must consider the "second estate," that of your spouse, if you are married. Sound estate tax planning requires that you focus on both possible taxes—husband's and wife's. Your advisers can help you work out alternatives to minimize, or totally eliminate, taxes on the combined estates.

Special Considerations of Estate Planning

Estate planning isn't all wills, trusts, and taxes. A number of other special considerations fall within the overall concept of estate planning.

Facing the Death of a Spouse

Women generally outlive men. The odds are that most married women will eventually become widows. Psychological and financial planning now can make it easier to cope with widowhood.

Frequently, widows are faced with the need to manage a fairly large sum of money but are not always prepared for the task. For example, statistics indicate that the average widow spends her husband's life insurance proceeds in about two years. There are several reasons for this:

- The average amount of life insurance carried is equal to only about two years of income. Still, prudent management of the insurance proceeds can stretch the income out over a longer period.
- Many widows lack financial experience. In many families, the wife may be in charge of the day-to-day budget, but the husband often assumes full responsibility for the family investments.
- Many widows are victims of unscrupulous con artists who prey on their grief and confusion.

The best protection for the new widow, or widower, is to take a very conservative position in financial matters for at least a year or two, until she or he has had a chance to recover from the loss of the spouse. During that period, it might be wise to opt for federally insured savings plans.

Getting Married

A second marriage can bring with it a great deal of property and concerns on the part of children from previous marriages about the disposition of that property. A prenuptial agreement can spell out who will get what and when. In preparing such an agreement, each party should be repre-

sented by an attorney. Some items to address in a prenuptial agreement include earnings from employment; assets such as savings accounts and annuities; pension funds; insurance; real estate; automobiles; furniture and furnishings; checking accounts; debts; credit cards; promises to children and others concerning financial support for education, weddings, and other life events; obligations to a former spouse; financial and other obligations to elderly parents; and the provisions of separate wills. It is a good idea to select a date (say, two or three years into the marriage) to review the agreement and make any adjustments.

Caring for an Elderly Relative

A major portion of your overall estate planning is geared to assuring your comfort and security while you are alive—not just distributing your estate upon your death. That comfort and security can be severely disrupted by the *unanticipated* need to care for an elderly parent. If you can anticipate this possibility, you can develop strategies that will minimize any disruptions to your own life. If you have brothers or sisters who could share the responsibility, discuss the matter with them and your parents now, before a crisis occurs. One part of your strategy should be to make sure that your parents have a sound health insurance program in conjunction with Medicare. You may also want to look into long-term care insurance.

Selling a Business

The money you expect to get from the sale of your business or practice may be an important factor in your estate planning.

The transfer of a business or professional practice—whether to partners, children, or strangers—must be timed very carefully. There is a peak period during which you should begin to make your move. Your object is to get the best possible selling price *and* retain the maximum amount of income for as long as you remain involved. To formulate your plans most efficiently, you will need the help of your banker, your lawyer, your accountant, and your insurance agent. As with all the other planning concerns, the time to get some advice is *now*.

Preparing Your Children

Your estate plan can have an effect on your children's lives and on their subsequent estate plans as well. How much do you want to provide for them now or in the future? How much can you afford to provide without cutting into your own pleasure, comfort, and security? You should answer these questions in your own heart and mind and then communicate your thinking to your children.

Children who anticipate an inheritance that never materializes or who do not expect one that, in fact, does materialize might shape their lives differently if they knew just what to expect.

To the extent that you can help shape your children's lives for the better, the subject of your estate deserves frank discussion with them.

Summing Up: The Exhilarating Adventure of Middle Age

Middle-agers are realistic. They know they won't climb mountains as rapidly or as easily as they once did. They accept the physical signs of aging as inevitable.

But they are a healthy generation. They exercise. They bike. They watch their diets. They seek help from psychologists and psychiatrists if they need it.

Beyond that, they have acquired assets that offset physical losses. Over the years, they have picked up some useful tools for coping with problems.

Middle-agers have strength, maturity, and wisdom—the payoffs for a lot of living. They know people. They know how the world works. They cut quickly through irrelevancies and make sound decisions from habit.

They have a sensitized awareness of time. They can identify what's unimportant. Knowing that life is not limitless enhances the ability to make good judgments.

They know it's human to regret past mistakes. But they know, too, there isn't time to wallow in vain regrets.

Their intelligence is a formidable ally. Intelligence isn't like the body—it can improve with age. But it must be exercised. The more the brain is used, the more work it will do.

Many middle-agers are going back to school—and are doing very well. Their experience and judgment have happy effects on their learning capabilities. They enjoy the process of learning. They are not anxious about the material rewards of education. They revel in what has been called "the sacred present."

Middle-agers have the creativity to become what they want to be. Few may match the accomplishments of Benjamin Franklin, who invented bifocals when he was seventy-eight, or of Grandma Moses, who launched her painting career at the same age. But they don't have to. It's not the size of the accomplishment that counts. To be creative, one need only cook a soup the best way he or she can—simply for the sake of doing as good a job as possible.

If you are a middle-ager, you may feel a need to pause and catch your breath. Well, no wonder.

Your whole generation has gone through a marathon of radical changes. You've been catapulted from car running boards to space shuttles. You've traveled the worrisome financial distance between deep recession and soaring inflation. You've been confused runners in an uncertain race between old values and new lifestyles.

But you've survived. That entitles you to some kind of reward—and you have it. Yours is the first generation of middle-agers to be able to create whole second lives for yourselves after fifty. You have the option of being independent and of molding a productive, useful, and enjoyable life.

To exercise that option, you have to be willing to grow. You have to go on a voyage of self-discovery. You have to be introspective. You must take a creative approach to your life and your problems. And you must use your mind.

There are endless pleasures in finding your own purpose and creating your special life. So be creative. Use your intellect lavishly. Tackle new challenges. You are off on the exhilarating adventure of middle age.

For Further Reading

Most of the publications listed under the heading "Books" can be found in your local bookstore or library.

AARP Books

Price and ordering information for books listed under the heading "AARP Books" can be found on the card insert following the index. AARP books are copublished by the American Association of Retired Persons, Washington, D.C., and Scott, Foresman and Company, Glenview, Illinois.

Free AARP Publications

One free copy of publications listed under "Free AARP Publications" can be obtained by writing to AARP Fulfillment, 1909 K Street, N.W., Washington, DC 20049. Specify the title and item number. Allow four to six weeks for delivery.

Government Booklets

To order publications listed under "Government Booklets," write to Consumer Information Center, P.O. Box 100, Pueblo, CO 81002. Specify the title and item number. If you order two or more free booklets, include $1.00 for handling and shipping. Make your check payable to Superintendent of Documents.

Why Plan for Retirement?

Books

Comfort Zones: A Practical Guide for Retirement Planning. Elwood N. Chapman. Los Altos, Calif.: Crisp Publications, Inc., 1987. $13.95.

AARP Books

Life After Work: Planning It, Living It, Loving It. Allan Fromme, Ph.D. 1984.

Getting in Shape for Your Future

Books

How a Man Ages—Growing Older: What to Expect and What You Can Do About It. Curtis Pesmen and the editors of *Esquire* magazine. New York: Ballantine Books, 1984. $7.95.

How a Woman Ages—Growing Older: What to Expect and What You Can Do About It. Robin Marantz Henig and the editors of *Esquire* magazine. New York: Ballantine Books, 1985. $7.95.

AARP Books

Fitness for Life: Exercises for People Over 50. Theodore Berland. 1986.

Medical and Health Guide for People Over Fifty. The Dartmouth Institute for Better Health. 1986.

Walking for the Health of It: The Easy and Effective Exercise for People Over 50. Jeannie Ralston. 1986.

A Woman's Guide to Good Health After 50. Marie Feltin, M.D. 1987.

Free AARP Publications

Information on Medicare and Health Insurance for Older People. C38.

More Health for Your Dollar: An Older Person's Guide to HMOs. D1195.

Pep Up Your Life: A Fitness Book for Seniors. D549.

The Prudent Patient: How to Get the Most for Your Health Care Dollar. D12031.

Government Booklets

Clearing the Air: A Guide to Quitting Smoking. 548R. Free.

Guide to Health Insurance for People with Medicare. 411 R. Free.

Nutrition and Your Health: Dietary Guidelines for Americans. 519R. Free.

Osteoporosis, Calcium, and Estrogens. 556R. Free.

The Time in Your Life

Books

How to Get Control of Your Time and Your Life. Alan Lakein. New York: Signet/New American Library, 1984. $2.95.

Volunteer! The Comprehensive Guide to Voluntary Service in the U.S. and Abroad. Marjorie Adoff Cohen. Yarmouth, Maine: Intercultural Press, updated annually. $5.50.

AARP Books

On the Road in an RV. Richard Dunlop. 1987.

Travel Easy: The Practical Guide for People Over 50. Rosalind Massow. 1985.

Midlife Roles and Relationships

Books

The Grandparents' Catalog: An Idea Book for Family Sharing. Charles S. Slaybaugh, ed. New York: Doubleday & Co., 1986. $12.95.

Love and Sex After Forty. Robert N. Butler, M.D., and Myrna I. Lewis. New York: Harper & Row, Pubs., 1986. $15.45.

Pathfinders. Gail Sheehy. New York: Bantam Books, 1985. $4.95. Survey of 60,000 men and women to identify true pathfinders—people who came through an adult crisis in a creative or expanding way.

AARP Books

Alone—Not Lonely: Independent Living for Women Over 50. Jane Seskin, 1985.

Caregiving: Helping an Aging Loved One. Jo Horne. 1985.

Survival Handbook for Widows (and for relatives and friends who want to understand). Ruth J. Loewinsohn. 1984.

Work in Retirement

Books

The Damn Good Resume Guide. Yana Parker. Berkeley, Calif.: Ten Speed Press, 1983. $4.95.

Finding a Job. Nathan H. Azrin and Victoria B. Besalel. Berkeley, Calif.: Ten Speed Press, 1983. $6.95.

What Color Is Your Parachute? Richard N. Bolles. Berkeley, Calif.: Ten Speed Press, revised annually. $8.95. (Contains "The New Quick Job-Hunting Map.")

One on One: Win the Interview, Win the Job. Theodore T. Pettus. New York: Random House, 1981. $12.95.

You Can Negotiate Anything. Herb Cohen. Secaucus, N.J.: Citadel Press, 1983.

Wishcraft: How to Get What You Really Want. Barbara Sher with Annie Gottlieb. New York: Ballantine Books, 1983. $5.95.

Free AARP Publications

The Age Discrimination in Employment Act Protects Your Rights. 1985. D12386.

Working Options: How to Plan Your Job Search, Your Work Life. D12403.

Government Booklets

Financial Management: How to Make a Go of Your Business. 143R. $2.50.

Opportunities in Franchising. 173R. $1.00.

Starting and Managing a Business from Your Home. 146R. $1.75.

Tomorrow's Jobs. 106R. $1.25.

Housing Choices

Books

All America's Real Estate Book: Everyone's Guide to Buying, Selling, Renting, and Investing. Carolyn Janik and Ruth Rejnis. New York: Viking Press, 1986. $12.95.

Places Rated Almanac: Your Guide to Finding the Best Places to Live in America. Richard Boyer and David Savageau. Chicago: Rand McNally, 1984. $14.95.

AARP Books

National Continuing Care Directory. American Association of Homes for the Aging. 1988. Comprehensive information on retirement communities offering prepaid medical plans for long-term care (also called life care).

Planning Your Retirement Housing. Michael Sumichrast, Ronald G. Shafer, Marika Sumichrast. 1984.

Free AARP Publications

The Doable, Renewable Home. D12470.

Home Equity Conversion Fact Sheet. D1159.

Housing Choices for Older Homeowners. D12026.

Housing Options for Older Americans. D12063.

State Tax Relief Brochure. (Be sure to indicate which state you are interested in.)

Your Home, Your Choice. D12143. Help in making decisions about living arrangement alternatives.

Government Booklets

Buying Lots from Developers. 128R. $2.50.

How to Buy a Manufactured (Mobile) Home. 418R. Fifty cents.

The Mortgage Money Guide. 129R. $1.00.

Turning Home Equity into Income for Older Americans. 130R. $1.25.

Charting Your Financial Future

Books

The Complete & Easy Guide to Social Security & Medicare. Faustin F. Jehle. Los Altos, Calif.: Crisp Publications, Inc., 1987. $9.95.

The Dow Jones–Irwin Guide to Retirement Planning. Ray Vicker. Homewood, Ill.: Dow Jones–Irwin, 1985. $19.95.

AARP Books

Policy Wise: The Practical Guide to Insurance Decisions for Older Consumers. Nancy Chasen. 1983.

Free AARP Publications

Your Retirement Income Tax Guide. C175. Revised annually.

Your Retirement State Tax Guide. C182.

Government Booklets

What Every Investor Should Know. 141R. $1.25.

A Woman's Guide to Social Security. 512R. Free.

Your Social Security. 513R. Free.

Legal Readiness for Retirement and Estate Planning

Books

The Price Waterhouse Guide to the New Tax Law. New York: Bantam Books, 1986. $3.95.

AARP Books

Essential Guide to Wills, Estates, Trusts, and Death Taxes. Alex J. Soled. 1988.

Your Vital Papers Logbook. 1985.

Government Booklets

Consumer's Resource Handbook. Lists contacts to assist with consumer problems or complaints. 560R. Free.

Index

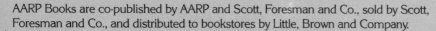